ADJUDICATION

Appeal
Only 6 percent of convicted defendants win a significant victory

New trial granted

Acquitted

Trial
Juries convict 2 out of 3 times

Evidence
Suppression motions are rarely granted

Conviction

Sentencing
7 million persons in prison, on probation, or on parole

Arraignment
A plea is entered

Charge dismissed

Plea bargain
90 to 95 percent of felony defendants admit their guilt

Preliminary hearing
Cases are rarely dismissed

Grand jury jurisdictions only

Refusal to indict

Grand jury
Indicts the defendants the prosecutor wants indicted

W9-ADJ-001

AMERICA'S COURTS

AND THE CRIMINAL JUSTICE SYSTEM

ELEVENTH EDITION

AMERICA'S COURTS

AND THE CRIMINAL JUSTICE SYSTEM

David W. Neubauer, Ph.D.
UNIVERSITY OF NEW ORLEANS

Henry F. Fradella, J.D., Ph.D.
CALIFORNIA STATE UNIVERSITY, LONG BEACH

WADSWORTH
CENGAGE Learning·

Australia · Brazil · Japan · Korea · Mexico · Singapore · Spain · United Kingdom · United States

WADSWORTH
CENGAGE Learning·

America's Courts: And the Criminal Justice System, Eleventh Edition
David W. Neubauer and Henry F. Fradella

Editor in Chief: Linda Ganster

Senior Acquisitions Editor:
Carolyn Henderson-Meier

Developmental Editor: Shelley Murphy,
Julie Martinez

Assistant Editor: Casey Lozier

Media Editor: Ting Jian Yap

Brand Manager: Melissa Larmon

Market Development Manager:
Michelle Williams

Senior Content Project Manager:
Christy A. Frame

Senior Art Director: Maria Epes

Senior Manufacturing Planner: Judy Inouye

Rights Acquisitions Specialist:
Tom McDonough

Production and Composition Service:
MPS Limited

Photo and Text Researcher: PreMedia Global

Copy Editor: Debbie Stone

Text Designer: Lisa Delgado

Cover Designer: Riezebos Holzbaur/
Brieanna Hattey

Cover Image: Downtown Fort Worth :
© Jeremy Woodhouse/The Image Bank/
Getty Images

For product information and technology assistance, contact us at
Cengage Learning Customer & Sales Support, 1-800-354-9706

For permission to use material from this text or product,
submit all requests online at **www.cengage.com/permissions**
Further permissions questions can be e-mailed to
permissionrequest@cengage.com

Library of Congress Control Number: 2012937192

Student Edition:

ISBN-13: 978-1-285-06194-8

ISBN-10: 1-285-06194-2

Loose-leaf Edition:

ISBN-13: 978-1-285-06223-5

ISBN-10: 1-285-06223-X

Wadsworth
20 Davis Drive
Belmont, CA 94002-3098
USA

Cengage Learning is a leading provider of customized learning solutions with office locations around the globe, including Singapore, the United Kingdom, Australia, Mexico, Brazil, and Japan. Locate your local office at **www.cengage.com/global.**

Cengage Learning products are represented in Canada by Nelson Education, Ltd.

To learn more about Wadsworth, visit **www.cengage.com/wadsworth**

Purchase any of our products at your local college store or at our preferred online store **www.cengagebrain.com.**

Printed in the United States of America
2 3 4 5 6 7 16 15 14 13

From David
To Jeff, Kristen, and Amy

From Hank
To the great mentors I have had, for
their friendship and guidance:

Henry F. Dressel, Esq.
Dr. Robert L.K. Richardson,
The Honorable Stephen M. McNamee,
Dr. John R. Hepburn,
Dr. Ronald E. Vogel, and
Dr. M. Sue Stanley

DAVID WILLIAM NEUBAUER was born in Chicago. He grew up in Aurora, Illinois, graduating from West Aurora High School in 1962. After receiving a B.A. in political science from Augustana College in Rock Island in 1966, graduating *cum laude* and being elected to Phi Beta Kappa, he began graduate work at the University of Illinois, receiving a Ph.D. in 1971.

Neubauer has previously taught at the University of Florida and Washington University in St. Louis. He is now professor emeritus at the University of New Orleans, where he chaired the political science department from 1982 to 1986.

Neubauer served as a consultant to the Federal Judicial Center on two court management projects, and he worked with the American Judicature Society as principal investigator on a project (funded by the National Institute of Justice) concerning court delay reduction. Over the years he has served on review panels for the National Institute of Justice, the Bureau of Justice Statistics, the National Science Foundation, the National Institute of Mental Health, and the National Center for State Courts. He also served as a consultant to the Metropolitan Crime Commission of New Orleans.

Neubauer is the co-author of *Judicial Process: Law, Courts, and Politics in the United States*, Sixth Edition (2013), co-author of *Battle Supreme: The Confirmation of Chief Justice John Roberts and the Future of the Supreme Court* (2006), and editor of *Debating Crime: Rhetoric and Reality* (2001). All are published by Wadsworth.

HENRY F. FRADELLA was born in New York, NY and grew up in that city and its Monmouth Country, NJ suburbs. After graduating with highest honors from the Searing School in Manhattan in 1986, Fradella earned a B.A. in psychology in 1990 from Clark University, graduating *summa cum laude* and as a member of Phi Beta Kappa. Fradella then earned a masters in Forensic Science and a law degree in 1993 from The George Washington University, and a Ph.D. in interdisciplinary justice studies from Arizona State University in 1997.

Prior to becoming a full-time academic, Fradella worked as an autopsy technician in the Office of the Chief Medical Examiner of Washington, D.C.; practiced law; and worked in the federal courts as a judicial law clerk. He began his career in academia as an assistant professor at The College of New Jersey. After having earned tenure and promotion to the rank of associate and then full professor over 10 years, Fradella resigned from TCNJ in 2007 to become a professor in, and chair of, the Department of Criminal Justice at California State University, Long Beach.

Fradella is the author of over 70 articles, reviews, and scholarly commentaries; three sole-authored books; and five additional books written with co-authors. Four of these six books were published by Wadsworth. Dr. Fradella has guest edited two volumes of the *Journal of Contemporary Criminal Justice*, and served three terms as the legal literature editor for West's *Criminal Law Bulletin*.

CHAPTER 1
Courts, Crime, and Controversy 2

PART I
THE LEGAL SYSTEM

CHAPTER 2
Law and Crime 26

CHAPTER 3
Federal Courts 54

CHAPTER 4
State Courts 88

PART II
LEGAL ACTORS

CHAPTER 5
The Dynamics of Courthouse Justice 120

CHAPTER 6
Prosecutors 146

CHAPTER 7
Defense Attorneys 172

CHAPTER 8
Judges 196

CHAPTER 9
Defendants and Victims 220

PART III
PROCESSING THE ACCUSED

CHAPTER 10
From Arrest and Bail through Arraignment 244

CHAPTER 11
Disclosing and Suppressing Evidence 274

CHAPTER 12
Negotiated Justice and the Plea of Guilty 306

CHAPTER 13
Trials and Juries 330

PART IV
SENTENCING THE CONVICTED

CHAPTER 14
Sentencing Options 368

CHAPTER 15
Sentencing Decisions 400

PART V
APPELLATE AND JUVENILE COURTS

CHAPTER 16
Appellate and *Habeas Corpus* Review 434

CHAPTER 17
Juvenile Courts 468

Preface   xxii

CHAPTER 1

Courts, Crime, and Controversy   2

Courts and Crime   5

Courts and the Criminal Justice System   6
An Interdependent Criminal Justice System   7
A Fragmented Criminal Justice Nonsystem   7
Tensions and Conflicts   8

An Overview of U.S. Courts   8

Identifying the Actors in the Courthouse   10
Prosecutors   11
Defense Attorneys   11
Judges   11
Defendants and Victims   11

Following the Steps of the Process   11
Crime   12
Arrest   12
Initial Appearance   12
Bail   12
Grand Jury   13
Preliminary Hearing   13
Arraignment   13
Discovery   13
Pretrial Motions   13
Plea Negotiations   13
Trial   14
Sentencing   14
Appeal   14

Law on the Books   14

CASE CLOSE-UP: *BROWN v. MISSISSIPPI*   16

Law in Action   17

Courts and Controversy   18
Crime Control Model   19
Due Process Model   19
Shifting the Balance   20

Media Depictions and Distortions of Criminal Courts   20

COURTS, CONTROVERSY, & REDUCING CRIME:
IS IT TIME TO END THE WAR ON DRUGS?   21

COURTS, LAW, & MEDIA:
THE CASEY ANTHONY TRIAL   22

Conclusion   23
Chapter Review   23
Critical Thinking Questions   24
Key Terms   24
Web Resources   25
For Further Reading   25

PART I • THE LEGAL SYSTEM

CHAPTER 2

Law and Crime   26

The Basis of Law   29

The Common Law Heritage   30
Judge-Made Law   30
Precedent   30
Multiple Sources of Law   32
Constitutions   32
Statutes   32
Administrative Regulations   32
Judge-Made Law   33

The Adversary System   33
Safeguards   33
Presumptions and Inferences   34
Burdens of Proof   34

COURTS, LAW, & MEDIA:
CHICAGO (2002)   36

The Rights of the Accused   36
Due Process   37
Bill of Rights   38

Civil Law Overview   39
Types of Civil Disputes   40
Civil Remedies   40
Using Civil Remedies to Fight Crime   41

COURTS, CONTROVERSY, & REDUCING CRIME:
SHOULD ASSET FORFEITURE BE LIMITED?   42

Law in Controversy: The Incivility of Civil Justice   42
Civil Liability of Criminal Justice Officials   43

Criminal Law Overview   43
Elements of a Crime   44
Actus Reus: The Guilty Act   45
Mens Rea: Criminal Intent   45
Union of Act and Intent   46
Attendant Circumstances   46
Results   46

Defining Crimes   46
Criminal Defenses   46
  Defenses that Negate *Mens Rea*   48
  Defenses of Justification   48
  Procedural Defenses   48
  Insanity   48

CASE CLOSE-UP: *UNITED STATES v. LOUGHNER*   49

Delinquency   50

Effects of Criminal Law on the Courts   50
  Criminal Law and Inconsistencies   50
  Criminal Law and Plea Bargaining   50
  Criminal Law and Sentencing   50
Conclusion   51
Chapter Review   51
Critical Thinking Questions   52
Key Terms   52
Web Resources   53
For Further Reading   53

CHAPTER 3
Federal Courts   54
Basic Principles of Court Organization   57
  Dual Court System   57
  Jurisdiction   57
    Geographical Jurisdiction and Venue   57
    Subject Matter Jurisdiction   59
    Personal Jurisdiction   59
    Hierarchical Jurisdiction   60

COURTS, CONTROVERSY, & THE ADMINISTRATION OF JUSTICE: SHOULD THE DOUBLE JEOPARDY CLAUSE PROHIBIT PARALLEL STATE AND FEDERAL PROSECUTIONS?   60

Differentiating Trial and Appellate Courts   61
History of the Federal Courts   61
  The Constitutional Convention   61
  The Judiciary Act of 1789   62
  1789–1891   62
  Court of Appeals Act of 1891   63
  Federal Courts Today   63
U.S. Magistrate Judges   65
  Caseload of U.S. Magistrate Judges   65
U.S. District Courts   65
  Caseload of U.S. District Courts   66
  Diversity Jurisdiction   66

Federal Questions   67
  The Constitutionalization of Criminal Procedure   68
  Discrimination Laws and Civil Rights Cases   68
  Prisoner Petitions   69
  Discrimination and Civil Rights Caseload in the Federal Courts   69
U.S. Courts of Appeals   70
  Caseload of U.S. Courts of Appeals   72
U.S. Supreme Court   72
  Granting Cert: The Rule of Four   72
  Caseload of U.S. Supreme Court   73
  Circuit Justices   73
Specialized Federal Courts   73
  Military Justice   75
  Enemy Combatants   75

COURTS, LAW, & MEDIA: *THE RESPONSE* (2010)   76

Foreign Intelligence Surveillance Court   77

CASE CLOSE-UP: WAS ZACARIAS MOUSSAOUI THE 20TH HIJACKER?   77

Federal Judicial Administration   79
  Chief Justice   79
  Judicial Conference of the United States   81
  Administrative Office of the U.S. Courts   81
  Federal Judicial Center   82
  Judicial Councils   82
  U.S. Sentencing Commission   82
Caseloads in the Federal Courts   82
  Increase the Number of Federal Judges?   82
  Reduce Federal Jurisdiction?   83
Consequences of Federal Involvement in the Criminal Justice System   83
  Forum for Symbolic Politics   84
  Federal Dollars   84
Conclusion   84
Chapter Review   85
Critical Thinking Questions   86
Key Terms   87
Web Resources   87
For Further Reading   87

CHAPTER 4
State Courts   88
History of State Courts   91

Colonial Courts 91
Early American Courts 91
Courts in a Modernizing Society 92

Trial Courts of Limited Jurisdiction: Lower Courts 92
Cases in the Lower Courts 93
Nonfelony Criminal Cases 93
Traffic Offenses 93
Small Claims Civil Cases 94
Justice of the Peace Courts 94

COURTS, CONTROVERSY, & REDUCING CRIME: SHOULD DUI AND DISTRACTED DRIVING PROSECUTIONS BE INCREASED? 95

Lower Caseloads 97
Lack of Resources 97
Familiarity 97
Reforming JP Courts 98
Municipal Courts 99
Assembly-Line Justice and the Courtroom Work Group 99
Sentencing in the Lower Courts 100
Problems of the Lower Courts 100
Inadequate Financing 101
Inadequate Facilities 101
Lax Court Procedures 101
Unbalanced Caseloads 101
Community Justice 101
Alternative Dispute Resolution (ADR) 102
Community Courts 102

Trial Courts of General Jurisdiction: Major Trial Courts 102

COURTS, LAW, & MEDIA: AMERICAN GANGSTER (2007) 104

Intermediate Courts of Appeals 105

State High Courts of Last Resort 106

Court Unification 107
Key Components 107
Simplified Court Structure 107
Centralized Administration 107
Centralized Rule Making 107
Centralized Judicial Budgeting 108
Statewide Financing 110
Analysis 110

Problem-Solving Courts 110

CASE CLOSE-UP: EWING v. CALIFORNIA AND THREE STRIKES LAWS 111

Drug Courts 112
The Effectiveness of Drug Courts 112
Juvenile Drug Courts 113
Domestic Violence Courts 113
Mental Health Courts 114

Technology Shapes the Courtrooms of the Future 115

Consequences of Court Organization 115
Decentralization and Choice of Courts 116
Local Control and Local Corruption 116
Uneven Court Financing 116

Conclusion 117

Chapter Review 117

Critical Thinking Questions 118

Key Terms 118

Web Resources 119

For Further Reading 119

PART II · LEGAL ACTORS

CHAPTER 5

The Dynamics of Courthouse Justice 120

The Courthouse and the People Who Work There 123
The Courthouse 123
The Courtroom 124
Behind the Scenes 126

Courthouse Security and Changing Technologies 128

COURTS, LAW, & MEDIA: LAW & ORDER 129

Dynamics of Courthouse Justice 130

Assembly-Line Justice 130
Strengths of the Explanation 131
Weaknesses of the Explanation 131

Discretion 132

The Courtroom Work Group 133
Mutual Interdependence 133
Shared Decision Making 134
Socialization 134
Normal Crimes 134

COURTS, CONTROVERSY, & GENDER EQUITY: IS GENDER BIAS A SIGNIFICANT PROBLEM IN THE COURTS? 135

Rewards and Sanctions   136
Variability in Courtroom Work Groups   136

The Problem of Delay   136
Consequences of Delay   137
Assessing the Costs of Delay   139

**Law on the Books Approach to
Court Delay   139**
Speedy-Trial Laws   140
Limits of Speedy-Trial Laws   140

Law in Action Approach to Court Delay   140

CASE CLOSE-UP: *BARKER v. WINGO*
AND THE RIGHT TO A SPEEDY TRIAL   141

Case Scheduling   142
Efforts at Coordination   142
Variability in Courtroom Work Groups Revisited   142

Legal Ethics   142

Conclusion   143

Chapter Review   144

Critical Thinking Questions   144

Key Terms   145

Web Resources   145

For Further Reading   145

CHAPTER 6

Prosecutors   146

Role of the Prosecutor   150
Broad Discretion   150
Charging Decisions   150

CASE CLOSE-UP: *CONNICK v. THOMPSON* AND
PROSECUTORIAL MISCONDUCT   152

Decentralization   154

Prosecution in Federal Courts   155
Solicitor General   155
Criminal Division of the Justice Department   155
U.S. Attorneys   156

Prosecution in State Courts   156
State Attorney General   156
Chief Prosecutor   157
Local Prosecutor   158

The Prosecutor's Office at Work   159
Assistant District Attorneys   159
Learning the Job   159
Promotions and Office Structure   160
Supervision   161
Attempts at Greater Supervision   161

Prosecutorial Ethics   162
Prosecutorial Immunity   162
Ethical Duties of Prosecutors   163

COURTS, LAW, & MEDIA: *NANCY GRACE*   164

**Prosecutors and Courtroom
Work Groups   164**
Conflicting Goals and Contrasting Work Groups   165
Political Styles and Contrasting Work Groups   165

The Expanding Domain of the Prosecutor   166
Improving Police–Prosecutor Relationships   166
Community Prosecution   167

**COURTS, CONTROVERSY, & GENDER
EQUITY:** ARE SEXUAL ASSAULTS AGAINST
WOMEN UNDERPROSECUTED?   168

Conclusion   169

Chapter Review   170

Critical Thinking Questions   170

Key Terms   171

Web Resources   171

For Further Reading   171

CHAPTER 7

Defense Attorneys   172

The Right to Counsel   175
Nonfelony Criminal Prosecutions   175
Stages of the Criminal Process   175

CASE CLOSE-UP: *GIDEON v. WAINWRIGHT*
AND THE RIGHT TO COUNSEL   177

Ineffective Assistance of Counsel   179
Self-Representation   179

**Defense Attorneys and Courtroom
Work Groups   180**
Rewards and Sanctions   181
Variations in Cooperation   182
An Assessment   182

The Criminal Bar   183
Diversity and Stratification of the Legal Profession   183
Environment of Practice   183

Providing Indigents with Attorneys   184
Assigned Counsel   185
Contract Systems   185

**COURTS, CONTROVERSY, & ECONOMIC
INEQUALITY:** ARE WE SPENDING TOO LITTLE OR
TOO MUCH ON INDIGENT DEFENSE?   186

Public Defender 187
Assessing the Merits of Public Defenders 187

Lawyers and Clients 188
Lawyers' Views on Their Clients 189
Defendants' Views on Their Lawyers 189

Defense Attorney Ethics 190

COURTS, LAW, & MEDIA: *BOSTON LEGAL*
(ABC TELEVISION, 2004–2008) 192

Conclusion 193

Chapter Review 193

Critical Thinking Questions 194

Key Terms 194

Web Resources 194

For Further Reading 195

CHAPTER 8

Judges 196

The Position of Judge 199
Powers of the Judge 199
Benefits of the Job 199
Frustrations of the Job 200

COURTS, LAW, & MEDIA: *JUDGE JUDY*:
JUSTICE WITH AN ATTITUDE OR JUST
PLAIN NONSENSE? 201

Judges within the Courtroom Work Group 202

Varying Roads to a Judgeship 203
Executive Appointments 203
Election of Judges 205
Merit Selection 206

Consequences of Judicial Selection 207
Which System Is Best? 207
Similarities in Judges' Backgrounds 208
Diversity and the Judiciary 208

Judging the Judges 209
Judicial Independence 209

CASE CLOSE-UP: *CHISOM v. ROEMER*
AND DIVERSITY ON THE BENCH 210

**COURTS, CONTROVERSY, & THE
ADMINISTRATION OF JUSTICE:** IS JUDICIAL
INDEPENDENCE BEING UNDERMINED? 211

Judicial Misconduct 212
State Judicial Conduct Commissions 212
Federal Conduct and Disability Act 213

Judicial Ethics 216

Conclusion 217

Chapter Review 218

Critical Thinking Questions 218

Key Terms 219

Web Resources 219

For Further Reading 219

CHAPTER 9

Defendants and Victims 220

Characteristics of Defendants 223
Overwhelmingly Male 223

**COURTS, CONTROVERSY, & RACIAL
DISCRIMINATION:** CAN LATINOS GET
EQUAL JUSTICE UNDER THE LAW? 224

Mostly Underclass 224
Racial Minorities Overrepresented 225

Defendants in Court 226
Pro se Defendants 226
Social Media Trap Defendants 227

**Courts through the Eyes of Victims
and Witnesses 228**
Frustrations in Coping with the Process 228
Travails of Testifying 228
Surprising Support for the System 229

**Victims and Witnesses through the
Eyes of the Court 229**
Lack of Cooperation 229
Witness Intimidation 231

Characteristics of Victims 231
Prior Relationships between Defendants and Victims 231
Domestic Violence 232
Domestic Violence and the Police 232
Domestic Violence in the Courts 232

CASE CLOSE-UP: *THURMAN v. TORRINGTON*
AND DOMESTIC VIOLENCE ARRESTS 233

Aiding Victims and Witnesses 234
Victim/Witness Assistance Programs 235
Victim Compensation Programs 236
Victims' Bill of Rights 237
Victim Impact Statements 237
Constitutionality of Victim Impact Evidence 238
Victim Impact Evidence and Restorative Justice 238
Effects of Victim Impact Statements on Sentences 238

COURTS, LAW, & MEDIA: *LAW & ORDER: SPECIAL VICTIMS UNIT* (NBC, 1999–PRESENT) 239

Aiding or Manipulating Victims 240
The Victims' Rights Movement 240
Differing Goals 240
Do Victims Benefit? 241

Conclusion 241

Chapter Review 242

Critical Thinking Questions 242

Key Terms 243

Web Resources 243

For Further Reading 243

PART III • PROCESSING THE ACCUSED

CHAPTER 10

From Arrest and Bail through Arraignment 244

Crime 247
Measuring Crime 247

Arrest 248
Quality of Arrests 251

Initial Appearance 251

CASE CLOSE-UP: *COUNTY OF RIVERSIDE v. MCLAUGHLIN* AND A PROMPT HEARING BEFORE A MAGISTRATE 252

Charging 253
Law on the Books: Prosecutorial Control 253
Law in Action: Police Influence 253
Courts and Controversy: Charging Decisions 253

COURTS, CONTROVERSY, & ECONOMIC INEQUALITY: ARE WHITE-COLLAR CRIMINALS UNDERPROSECUTED? 254

Bail 254
Law on the Books: The Monetary Bail System 254
Bail Procedures 255
Forms of Bail 256
Preventive Detention 256
Law in Action: The Context of Bail Setting 256
Bail Agents and Bounty Hunters 257
Effects of the Bail System 258
Jail Conditions 258
Race and Ethnicity 258

Failure to Appear 259
Case Disposition 259

Preliminary Hearing 259
Law on the Books: Weighing Probable Cause 260
Law in Action: Variations in Using the Preliminary Hearing 260

Grand Jury 261
Law on the Books: Shield and Sword 262
Law in Action: Prosecutorial Domination 263
Courts and Controversy: Reform the Grand Jury? 263

Arraignment 265

Law in Action Perspective: Case Attrition 265

Why Attrition Occurs 266
Legal Judgments 266
Policy Priorities 267
Personal Standards of Justice 267

The Criminal Justice Wedding Cake 267
Celebrated Cases 267
Serious Felonies 268
Lesser Felonies 269
The Lower Depths 269

COURTS, LAW, & MEDIA: CRIME ON THE NIGHTLY NEWS 269

Conclusion 270

Chapter Review 271

Critical Thinking Questions 272

Key Terms 273

Web Resources 273

For Further Reading 273

CHAPTER 11

Disclosing and Suppressing Evidence 274

Discovery 277
Law on the Books: Rules Requiring Disclosure 277
Discovery of Exculpatory Evidence 278
Discovery of Impeachment Evidence 278
Law in Action: Informal Prosecutorial Disclosure 279
Law and Controversy: Requiring Reciprocal Disclosure 281

Suppressing Evidence 282
The Exclusionary Rule 282
Fruit of the Poisonous Tree 282

Interrogations and Confessions 283
The Voluntariness Standard 283
The Birth of *Miranda* Warnings 284
Interrogations and the Sixth Amendment 284

CASE CLOSE-UP: *MIRANDA v. ARIZONA* AND POLICE INTERROGATIONS 285

Interrogations and the Fourteenth Amendment 286
Applying the Law of Interrogation 286

Search and Seizure 289

Search Warrants 289
  Applying for Search Warrants 289
  Issuing Search Warrants 290
  The Requirement of Particularity 290
  Executing Search Warrants 290
Warrant Exceptions 291
Electronic Surveillance 291
  Eavesdropping and Consent Surveillance 293
  Electronically Stored Information 294
  Video Surveillance 294
Intelligence Surveillance 294
Applying the Fourth Amendment 295

The Exclusionary Rule and the Courtroom Work Group 295

Pretrial Motions 295
Defense Attorney as Prime Mover 295

COURTS, LAW, & MEDIA: *MINORITY REPORT* (2002) 299

The Defensive Posture of the Prosecutor 300
Trial Judges as Decision Makers 300
Police Testimony 300

Law and Controversy: Costs of the Exclusionary Rule 301

COURTS, CONTROVERSY, & REDUCING CRIME: SHOULD THE EXCLUSIONARY RULE BE ABOLISHED? 302

Conclusion 302
Chapter Review 303
Critical Thinking Questions 304
Key Terms 305
Web Resources 305
For Further Reading 305

CHAPTER 12

Negotiated Justice and the Plea of Guilty 306

Law on the Books: Types of Plea Agreements 309

Charge Bargaining 309
Count Bargaining 310
Sentence Bargaining 311

Law in Action: Bargaining and Caseloads 311
Law in Action: Bargaining and Discretion 311

Presumption of Factual Guilt 312
Costs and Risks of Trial 312
What to Do with the Guilty 312

Bargaining and the Courtroom Work Group 313

Prosecutors 313
Defendants 314
Defense Attorneys 314
Judges 315

Dynamics of Bargaining 315

Decision-Making Norms 316
Why Cases Go to Trial 316
Jury Trial Penalty 317

COURTS, LAW, & MEDIA: *AMERICAN VIOLET* (2008) 317

Copping a Plea 318

Questioning the Defendant 320
  Waiver of Rights 320
  Allocution 320
  Competency 322
No Contest and *Alford Pleas* 322
Acceptance and Withdrawal of Pleas 322

CASE CLOSE-UP: *SANTOBELLO v. NEW YORK* AND HONORING A PLEA AGREEMENT 323

Effective Assistance of Counsel during Plea Bargaining 324

Law in Controversy: Abolishing Plea Bargaining 324

COURTS, CONTROVERSY, & THE ADMINISTRATION OF JUSTICE: WHO BENEFITS FROM PLEA BARGAINING? 325

Are the Changes Implemented? 326
Is Discretion Eliminated or Just Moved Elsewhere? 326
Do Offsetting Changes Occur? 326

Conclusion 327
Chapter Review 327
Critical Thinking Questions 328
Key Terms 328
Web Resources 328
For Further Reading 329

CHAPTER 13

Trials and Juries 330

History of Trial by Jury   333
English Roots   333
Colonial Developments   333

Law on the Books: The Constitution and Trial by Jury   334
Jury Size   335
Unanimity   337

Law on the Books: Selecting a Fair and Unbiased Jury   338
Master Jury List   338
Summoning the Venire   339
Venire Eligibility   339
Voir Dire   339
The Accuracy of Voir Dire   340
Excusing Jurors through Voir Dire   341
Serving on a Jury   341

CASE CLOSE-UP: *PEOPLE v. GARCIA (CAL.APP.2000)*: SHOULD *BATSON* EXTEND TO SEXUAL ORIENTATION?   342

Law in Action: Choosing a Jury Biased in Your Favor   343
Educating Jurors   343
Jury Consultants   343

Presumptions and the Burden of Proof   344
Starting Presumptions   344
Burdens of Proof   344

Overview of Basic Evidence   345
Differentiating Direct and Circumstantial Evidence   345
Types of Evidence   345
Basic Rules of Evidence   345

Special Rules of Evidence Governing Expert Witnesses   346
Determining Reliability   347

Forensic Scientific Evidence in the Age of *Daubert*   347
The CSI Effect   348

Objections to the Admission of Evidence   350

COURTS, LAW, & MEDIA: *CSI: CRIME SCENE INVESTIGATION (CBS, 2000–PRESENT)*   351

COURTS, CONTROVERSY, & THE ADMINISTRATION OF JUSTICE: *SHOULD FINGERPRINT EVIDENCE BE ADMISSIBLE?*   352

Challenging Forensic Evidence   352

Steps in the Trial Process   353
Opening Statements   353
Prosecution's Case-in-Chief   353
Motion for Judgment of Acquittal   353

Defense's Case-in-Chief   355
The Defendant as Witness   355
Renewed Motion for Judgment of Acquittal   356
Rebuttal   356
Closing Arguments   356
Jury Instructions   356
Jury Deliberations   357
Are Juries Biased?   357
The Verdict   358
Postverdict Motions   359

Law in Action: Trials as Balancing Wheels   359
Popular Standards of Justice   359
Uncertainty   359

Prejudicial Pretrial Publicity   360
Limited Gag Order   360
Change of Venue   361
Sequestering the Jury   361

Media in the Courtroom   361
Changing Views on Cameras in the Courtroom   361
Current Broadcasting Rules   362
Technology beyond "Cameras"   362

Conclusion   363

Chapter Review   364

Critical Thinking Questions   366

Key Terms   366

Web Resources   367

For Further Reading   367

PART IV • SENTENCING THE CONVICTED

CHAPTER 14

Sentencing Options   368

Why Do We Sentence?   371
Retribution   371
Deterrence   372
Rehabilitation   373
Incapacitation   374
Restoration   375
Competing Sentencing Philosophies   375

Who Should Decide the Sentence?   376
Legislative Sentencing Responsibility   376
Judicial Sentencing Responsibility   376
Executive Sentencing Responsibility   377

What Sentence Should Be Imposed? 377

Imprisonment 378
  Overcrowding 379
  Conditions of Confinement Lawsuits 379
  High Costs 380
Probation 382
Fines 383
Restitution 383
Intermediate Sanctions 384
  Community Service 384
  Intensive-Supervision Probation 385
  Home Detention with Electronic Monitoring 385

COURTS, LAW, & MEDIA: INTERMEDIATE SANCTIONS AND LINDSAY LOHAN 386

  GPS Monitoring 387
  Boot Camp and Shock Incarceration 387

The Death Penalty 387
  Eighth Amendment Standards 388
  Method of Decision Making 388
  Method of Execution 389
Death-Qualified Juries 391

COURTS, CONTROVERSY, & JUDICIAL ADMINISTRATION: SHOULD A MORATORIUM ON THE DEATH PENALTY BE IMPOSED? 392

Narrowing Death-Eligible Cases 393
  Crime Limitations 393
  Developmental Limitations 393
Lengthy Appeals 393

CASE CLOSE-UP: *ROPER v. SIMMONS*: SHOULD JUVENILES BE SENTENCED TO DEATH? 394

Cost Concerns 395

Conclusion 396

Chapter Review 396

Critical Thinking Questions 397

Key Terms 398

Web Resources 398

For Further Reading 398

CHAPTER 15

Sentencing Decisions 400

The Courtroom Work Group and Sentencing Decisions 403
  Probation Officers 403
  Prosecutors 405
  Defense Attorneys 405

COURTS, LAW, & MEDIA: USING MITIGATION VIDEOS AT SENTENCING 406

Judges 406

Normal Penalties and Sentencing Decisions 408
  Seriousness of the Offense 409
  Prior Record 409
  Aggravating or Mitigating Circumstances 409
  Law in Controversy: Uncertainty and Public Opinion 410

Differences in Sentencing Outcomes 410
  Imbalance versus Discrimination 411
  Sentencing Disparities 411
    The Geography of Justice 411
    Judges' Backgrounds and Attitudes 411
  Discrimination in Noncapital Sentencing 413
    Economic Status 413
    Sex 414
    Race 415
    Interaction Effects 416
  Discrimination and Capital Punishment 416
    Offender–Victim Dyad 417
    Evidence of Discrimination since *Gregg* 417
    Evidence of No Discrimination since *Gregg* 418
    McCleskey v. Kemp Rejects Social Science Evidence 418

Changing Sentencing Structures 418
  Law in Controversy: Reducing Judicial Discretion 419
  Law on the Books: Variations of Determinate Sentencing Return 418

Structured Sentencing Schemes 419
  Presumptive Sentencing in the States 419
  State Sentencing Guidelines 421
    The Continuum of Voluntary to Required Use 422
    The Constitutionality of State Sentencing Guidelines 422
  Federal Sentencing Guidelines 423

CASE CLOSE-UP: *KIMBROUGH v. UNITED STATES* AND FEDERAL SENTENCING GUIDELINES IN CRACK COCAINE CASES 424

Law in Action: Diverse Impacts 425

Increasing the Severity of the Penalty 426

COURTS, CONTROVERSY, & REDUCING CRIME: ARE "THREE STRIKES AND YOU'RE OUT" LAWS FAIR? 426

Law on the Books: Mandatory Minimum Sentences 427
Law in Action: Nullification by Discretion 428
Law in Controversy: Negative Side Effects 430

Conclusion 430

Chapter Review 431

Critical Thinking Questions   432

Key Terms   432

Web Resources   433

For Further Reading   433

PART V • APPELLATE AND JUVENILE COURTS

CHAPTER 16

Appellate and *Habeas Corpus* Review   434

Nature of the Appellate Process   437

The Purposes of Appeal   437

Limitations on the Right to Appellate Review   437

Appellate Standards of Review   439

Appellate Court Procedures   441

Notice of Appeal   441

Appellate Court Record   442

Appellate Briefs   442

Oral Argument   443

Written Opinion   443

Disposition   444

Reversible vs. Harmless Error   444

Rising Caseloads and Expedited Appeals   444

Criminal Appeals   445

Law on the Books: Expanded Opportunity to Appeal Criminal Convictions   445

Law in Action: Defendants Rarely Win on Appeal   445

COURTS, LAW, & MEDIA: THE AMANDA KNOX CASE   447

CASE CLOSE-UP: *HOUSE v. BELL* AND FEDERAL COURT SCRUTINY OF STATE DEATH ROW INMATES   448

Postconviction Review   448

How Postconviction Remedies Differ from Appeals   449

COURTS, CONTROVERSY, & THE ADMINISTRATION OF JUSTICE: SHOULD FEDERAL COURTHOUSE DOORS BE CLOSED TO STATE PRISONERS?   450

Judicial Expansion and Contractions of *Habeas* Access for State Prisoners   451

Congress Greatly Restricts Federal *Habeas* Access   451

Habeas Corpus Relief for Federal Prisoners   451

Wrongful Convictions   453

How Many Wrongful Convictions Are There?   453

Why Do Wrongful Convictions Occur?   454

Mistaken Eyewitness Identifications   454

Improper Forensic Evidence   455

False Confessions   455

Unreliable Informants   456

Tunnel Vision and Misconduct by Justice Professionals   456

Inadequate Defense Representation   457

Reducing Wrongful Convictions   458

State Courts of Last Resort   458

Law on the Books: State High Courts and Discretionary Dockets   458

Law in Action: State High Courts as Policy Makers   459

Law in Controversy: State High Courts and Death Penalty Cases   459

The U.S. Supreme Court and Criminal Justice Policy   460

The Warren Court (1953–1969)   460

The Burger Court (1969–1986)   461

The Rehnquist Court (1986–2005)   461

The Roberts Court (2005–)   462

The Supreme Court in Broad Perspective   463

Conclusion   463

Chapter Review   464

Critical Thinking Questions   465

Key Terms   465

Web Resources   466

For Further Reading   466

CHAPTER 17

Juvenile Courts   468

Juvenile Courts 100 Years Ago   471

Industrialization, Cities, and Crime   471

The Child Savers and the Progressive Movement   471

Parens Patriae   472

How Juvenile Courts Differ from Adult Courts   472

Emphasis on Helping the Child   472

Informal Proceedings   472

Proceedings Based on Civil Law   473

Secret Proceedings   473

Absence of Jury Trials   473

The Organization of Juvenile Courts 473
Juvenile Court as a Separate Court 474
Juvenile Court as Part of Family Court 474
Juvenile Court as a Unit of Trial Court 474
Law in Action: The Impact of Structure 474

Juvenile Court Jurisdiction: Subject Matter 474
Juvenile Delinquency 475
Status Offenses 475
Children in Need of Supervision 475
Law in Action: One-Pot Jurisdiction 475

Juvenile Court Jurisdiction: Age 476
Age Limits for Original Jurisdiction over Delinquency Matters 476
Age Limits beyond Original Jurisdiction 476

Transfer to Adult Court 478
Types of Transfers 478
Judicial Waivers 478
Prosecutorial Waivers 479
Statutory/Legislative Waivers 489
Automatic Waivers 489
Corrective Mechanisms 479
Use of Waivers 479

COURTS, CONTROVERSY, & REDUCING CRIME:
SHOULD JUVENILES BE TRIED AS ADULTS? 482

Due Process in Juvenile Courts 483
Key Court Decisions 483

CASE CLOSE-UP: *IN RE GAULT* AND DUE PROCESS
IN JUVENILE COURTS 484
Important Congressional Acts 485

Courtroom Work Group 486
Judges 486
Hearing Officers 487
Prosecutors 487
Defense Attorneys 487
Probation Officers 488

Steps of the Juvenile Court Process 488
Delinquency (Crime) 488
Summons (Arrest) 490
Intake (Initial Hearing) 490
Detention Hearing 490
Petition 491
Conference 491
Evidence: Gathering and Suppressing 491
Plea Bargaining 492
Adjudicatory Hearing 494
Disposition 492

COURTS, LAW, & MEDIA:
DOG POUND (2010) 494
Appeal 495

The Future of Juvenile Courts 495
Crime Control Model: More Adult Penalties 495
Due Process Model: More Youth Crime Prevention 496

Conclusion 496
Chapter Review 497
Critical Thinking Questions 497
Key Terms 498
Web Resources 498
For Further Reading 498

Appendix A: Criminal Court Landmarks 501
Appendix B: Overview of the Constitution of the United States of America 506
Appendix C: Constitution of the United States 510
Appendix D: Legal Reasoning 522
Glossary 533
References 551
Case Index 589
Index 595

CASE CLOSE-UP

Chapter 1   *Brown v. Mississippi*   16
Chapter 2   *United States v. Laughner*   49
Chapter 3   Was Zacarias Moussaoui the 20th Hijacker?   77
Chapter 4   *Ewing v. California* and Three Strikes Laws   111
Chapter 5   *Barker v. Wingo* and the Right to a Speedy Trial   141
Chapter 6   *Connick v. Thompson* and Prosecutorial Misconduct   152
Chapter 7   *Gideon v. Wainwright* and the Right to Counsel   177
Chapter 8   *Chisom v. Roemer* and Diversity on the Bench   210
Chapter 9   *Thurman v. Torrington* and Domestic Violence Arrests   233
Chapter 10   *County of Riverside v. McLaughlin* and a Prompt Hearing before a Magistrate   252
Chapter 11   *Miranda v. Arizona* and Police Interrogations   285
Chapter 12   *Santobello v. New York* and Honoring a Plea Agreement   323
Chapter 13   *People v. Garcia*: Should Batson Extend to Sexual Orientation?   342
Chapter 14   *Roper v. Simmons*: Should Juveniles Be Sentenced to Death?   394
Chapter 15   *Kimbrough v. United States* and Federal Sentencing Guidelines in Crack Cocaine Cases   424
Chapter 16   *House v. Bell* and Federal Court Scrutiny of State Death Row Inmates   448
Chapter 17   *In re Gault* and Due Process in Juvenile Courts   484

COURTS AND CONTROVERSY

Chapter 1   Is It Time to End the War on Drugs?   21
Chapter 2   Should Asset Forfeiture Be Limited?   42
Chapter 3   Should the Double Jeopardy Clause Prohibit Parallel State and Federal Prosecutions?   60
Chapter 4   Should DUI and Distracted Driving Prosecutions Be Increased?   95
Chapter 5   Is Gender Bias a Significant Problem in the Courts?   135

Chapter 6   Are Sexual Assaults against Women Underprosecuted?   168
Chapter 7   Are We Spending Too Little or Too Much on Indigent Defense?   186
Chapter 8   Is Judicial Independence Being Undermined?   211
Chapter 9   Can Latinos Get Equal Justice Under the Law?   224
Chapter 10   Are White-Collar Criminals Undeprosecuted?   254
Chapter 11   Should the Exclusionary Rule Be Abolished?   302
Chapter 12   Who Benefits from Plea Bargaining?   325
Chapter 13   Should Fingerprint Evidence Be Admissible?   352
Chapter 14   Should a Moratorium on the Death Penalty Be Imposed?   392
Chapter 15   Are "Three Strikes and You're Out" Laws Fair?   426
Chapter 16   Should Federal Courthouse Doors Be Closed to State Prisoners?   450
Chapter 17   Should Juveniles Be Tried as Adults?   482

COURTS, LAW, AND MEDIA

Chapter 1   The Casey Anthony Trial   22
Chapter 2   *Chicago* (2002)   36
Chapter 3   *The Response* (2010)   76
Chapter 4   *American Gangster* (2007)   104
Chapter 5   *Law & Order*   129
Chapter 6   Nancy Grace   164
Chapter 7   *Boston Legal* (ABC Television, 2004—2008)   192
Chapter 8   *Judge Judy*: Justice with an Attitude or Just Plain Nonsense?   201
Chapter 9   *Law & Order: Special Victims Unit* (NBC, 1999–Present)   239
Chapter 10   Crime on the Nightly News   269
Chapter 11   *Minority Report* (2002)   299
Chapter 12   *American Violet* (2008)   317
Chapter 13   *CSI: Crime Scene Investigation* (CBS, 2000–present)   351
Chapter 14   Intermediate Sanctions and Lindsay Lohan   386
Chapter 15   Using Mitigation Videos at Sentencing   406
Chapter 16   The Amanda Knox Case   447
Chapter 17   *Dog Pound* (2010)   495

America's Courts and the Criminal Justice System, Eleventh Edition, examines the history, traditions, and philosophy underlying our system of justice as it is played out in the criminal court. In a complex, sometimes contradictory, and often fragmented process, defendants are declared innocent or found guilty, and the guilty are fined, placed on probation, or sentenced to a period of incarceration. This book is about the defendants caught up in the process: the three-time losers, the scared young first offenders, and the business executives who are before the court to answer an indictment. But most of all, this book focuses on the prosecutors, judges, defense attorneys, and jurors who are involved in the daily decisions about guilt or innocence, probation or prison.

The impact of these decisions on crime and criminals is the subject of widespread controversy. Concern over how the courts handle criminal cases has been a staple of American political rhetoric for decades. The nature of this public debate, as well as solutions proposed to correct the problems, are integral parts of this book. To be sure, the past few decades have witnessed significant deep-seated changes and readjustments in the criminal justice system—given all the public posturing, one would hardly expect less.

This book is written for undergraduate courses that deal with America's criminal courts. Such courses (or parts of courses) are taught in various departments: criminal justice, criminology, administration of justice, political science, sociology, psychology, and social welfare. This book highlights not only the pivotal role of the criminal courts within the criminal justice system but also the courts' importance and impact on society as a whole.

America's Courts and the Criminal Justice System, Eleventh Edition, focuses on the dynamics of the courthouse. Thus, it differs from casebooks, which use appellate court decisions to highlight the history, structure, and philosophy of courts. Although these are important matters, casebooks often project a rather sterile image of courthouse justice and omit what courts do in practice, how they do it, and, most important, why they do it.

This book's emphasis on the dynamics of courthouse justice grows out of our own research. During our professional careers, we have spent considerable time in state and federal courts in all parts of the nation. One of us worked in a federal courthouse; the other has conducted years of field research, interviewing numerous judges, jurors, prosecutors, defense attorneys, probation officers, jailers, police officers, and defendants. We have observed these officials in action and discussed with them their problems and their views of possible solutions. By the luck of the draw, one of us has also served on juries in state and federal court, while the other has appeared in court as both a lawyer and as an expert witness. Throughout this book, we have tried to convey to the reader the sense of being in the courthouse.

Central Themes

Law on the Books

The starting point of this text is to provide readers with a working knowledge of the major structures and basic legal concepts that underlie the criminal courts. In deciding guilt or innocence and determining the appropriate punishment, the courts apply the criminal law through a complicated process termed "criminal procedure." The structure of the courts, the nature of the criminal law they apply, and the procedures followed all have important consequences for how the courts dispense justice.

But to understand the legal system, one needs to know more than the formal rules. Also necessary is an understanding of the assumptions underlying these rules, the history of how they evolved, and the goals they seek to achieve. A discussion of the assumptions, history, and goals makes clear that America's criminal justice process is not monolithic but consists of a number of separate and sometimes competing units. It also points out conflicts over the goals the criminal courts are expected to achieve.

Law in Action

Many books leave the false impression that an understanding of the formal law and major structures of the court is all that one needs to know about the criminal courts. This kind of analysis provides only a limited view of how the courts administer justice.

The law is not self-executing. It is a dynamic process of applying abstract rules to concrete situations.

In making decisions about charges to be filed, the amount of bail to be required, and the sentence a convicted person will receive, judges, prosecutors, and defense attorneys must make choices for which the formal law provides few precise guidelines. Thus, the second theme of this book is law in action, which emphasizes the dynamics of the criminal court process.

An examination of law in action reveals a gap between how the law is supposed to operate and how it is actually applied. For example, the law in theory suggests that the guilt of defendants should be decided by a jury trial. In practice, however, trials are rare. Most defendants plead guilty without a trial. Asking why there is a gap between the law on the books and the law in action is a big step toward understanding the dynamics of courthouse justice.

Law in Controversy

No treatment of the criminal courts would be complete without a discussion of the problems they are confronting. Are the courts too slow? Are judges too soft in sentencing? Does the criminal court process discriminate against the poor? These are just a few of the questions about the operations of the criminal courts that this book will consider. In turn, many organizations, groups, and individuals have probed the problems facing the criminal courts and proposed reforms. The third theme of this book is to discuss and analyze the controversies surrounding courthouse justice and to analyze the reforms that have been suggested for what ails the courts. Not everyone agrees on the types of changes needed. Some argue that certain reforms will produce greater difficulties without solving the original problems. This book examines competing perspectives on the changes and reforms that are being proposed.

Key Features

Case Close-Up

Each chapter highlights an important court decision that has affected our nation's criminal justice system. Some, like *Miranda* and *Gideon*, are familiar names.

Others are less well known. But each highlights the dynamic nature of courts in the United States.

Courts and Controversy

These boxed features provide multiple perspectives on the topics discussed in the chapter. To better focus on the wide-ranging debate surrounding the criminal courts in the United States, these controversies have been given an expanded subhead. Thus, throughout the book, these features will discuss controversies centering on judicial administration, crime reduction, gender equity, racial discrimination, and economic inequality.

Courts, Law, and Media

In the Tenth Edition, we added a new feature entitled "Law and Popular Culture." This feature highlighted movie and television portrayals (and distortions) of the justice system to focus on the contrasting caricatures offered by fictional treatment. In the Eleventh Edition, we have retained this pedagogical feature, but have broadened it to encompass news coverage. Accordingly, we have retitled the feature to reflect this broader coverage of media. To help students think critically about their media-formed misconceptions about the courts system, each chapter of this book focuses on a media depiction of one of the chapter's primary themes.

New to this Edition

Writing the Eleventh Edition was gratifying and stimulating. It was gratifying to learn from peer-reviewers that numerous colleagues in the professoriate and their students have found previous editions of the book useful. It was stimulating because it involved closely examining recent changes in both scholarship and public dialogue. The Eleventh Edition offers a current perspective on a continually evolving subject: the criminal court process.

In this edition, the chapter structure has been modified in response to reviewer feedback. Specifically, we have reduced the overall chapter count by two chapters to produce a 17-chapter book which aligns more easily with the average-length semester. This was accomplished by integrating the material on bail into Chapter 10 (on pretrial criminal court processes)—a wonderfully natural fit—and by integrating the material on the lower courts into Chapter 4 (on state courts). We are especially pleased with this latter change because it moves coverage of lower courts including traffic offenses, justices of the peace and municipal courts—the kinds of issues students often find among the most engaging and relevant—forward in the book, which we hope will help you better capture their interest early on.

We have added several new topics in the Eleventh Edition. We examine several of the ways that the ever-increasing role of technology plays in our lives has affected the courts, ranging from electronic monitoring of offenders to social media in the courtroom. We highlight advances (and corresponding questions and concerns) regarding forensic evidence in criminal cases. And, the courts' role in reducing wrongful convictions has been highlighted throughout the book. Finally, we have made every effort to report the most up-to-date statistics available and to cite current empirical research throughout the Eleventh Edition.

Chapter-by-Chapter Changes

Chapter 1—This introductory chapter takes a look at several different public perceptions of the criminal courts on which this text will focus. In the Tenth Edition, Chapter 1 introduced readers to the three main pedagogical features used in the book. To streamline Chapter 1 and make it more directly relevant to students, the overview of that material has been removed from the chapter and has been placed in this Preface. In its place, three substantive pedagogical features now appear in Chapter 1. The former chapter opener on *House v. Bell* has been replaced with the media frenzy surrounding the Casey Anthony case. The Casey Anthony case has been integrated throughout the chapter to illustrate several of the chapter's main points. A new flowchart of the steps in the criminal justice process has been added. New material on media depictions and distortion of criminal courts has been added.

Chapter 2—Chapter 2 contains expanded coverage of basic legal issues ranging from presumptions and inferences to the complexities of the different burdens of proof. The Second Amendment

implications of *McDonald v. City of Chicago* (2010) are now integrated. The summary of the criminal defenses has been expanded and new examples are provided, including a new Case Close-Up on Jared Loughner. The coverage of civil justice now includes a discussion of both media depictions of civil court disputes and the incivility that commonly accompanies routine civil litigation.

Chapter 3—This chapter now includes the most up-to-date information and statistics on the federal judiciary and its caseload (including coverage of federal question jurisdiction, diversity jurisdiction, discrimination and civil rights cases, and prisoner petitions). A new chapter opener has been added concerning Oscar Ramiro Ortega-Hernandez, the so-called White House shooter. The discussion of prisoner cases has been streamlined. A new "Courts and Controversy" feature on double jeopardy has been added. Recent changes in the processing of enemy combatant cases have been integrated, including coverage of *Rasul v. Bush* (2004) and a new Courts, Law, & Media feature on *The Response*. Additional examples of military justice cases have been added.

Chapter 4—This chapter has undergone as significant transformation to include information on the lower courts (which had previously been addressed in a separate chapter at the end of the book in earlier additions). The issue of driver distraction has been added to the "Courts and Controversy" feature on driving under the influence. This chapter now includes the most up-to-date information and statistics on the state judiciary and its various caseloads. In this chapter, we have again expanded coverage of specialized courts, especially drug courts and mental health courts, and have integrated the recent evaluation research on these problem solving courts. The "Courts, Law, & Media" feature has been updated to the hard-hitting movie *American Gangster* to illustrate how the war on drugs continues to affect state court caseloads.

Chapter 5—In this chapter on the courthouse and the individuals who work there, we have included the latest research on court delay and information on the professionalization of court administration. A diagram of a typical courtroom setup is now included. We have expanded our coverage of courthouse security, changing technologies in the courtroom, and legal ethics.

Chapter 6—Prosecutors are the focus of this chapter. We include an expanded discussion of the Duke lacrosse-player rape prosecutions, focusing on the ethical failures of the prosecutor and his manipulation of media coverage of the case. This is accomplished, in part, by including specific provisions of the American Bar Association's Model Rules of Professional Conduct relevant to prosecutors. The new "Case Close-Up" highlights the recent Supreme Court decision in *Connick v. Thompson* (2011). Table 6.3 has been redesigned to including more data, all of which have been updated with the latest statistics. The chapter now differentiates between absolute immunity and qualified immunity for prosecutors. A new "Courts, Law, & Media" box focuses on Nancy Grace.

Chapter 7—The chapter on the defense attorney now includes expanded and up-to-date coverage on defenders' caseloads and of case law concerning the right to counsel, self-representation, and ineffective assistance of counsel—including *Padilla v. Kentucky* (2010), *Maples v. Thomas* (2012) *Lafler v. Copper* (2012), and *Missouri v. Frye* (2012). We have expanded our coverage of legal ethics to include specific provisions of the ABA's Model Rules of Professional Conduct relevant to defense counsel.

Chapter 8—The chapter on judges examines the diminished role of the ABA in federal judicial appointments, discusses the growing controversy over judicial elections, analyzes recent social scientific literature on the quality of judges and judicial decision-making, and adds both updated and expanded information concerning judicial diversity issues. The chapter also includes a discussion of the Breyer Commission Report (2006) and the 2008 Judicial Conference Rules for Judicial-Conduct and Judicial-Disability Proceedings. Table 8.2 has been updated to present the most up-to-date data. The section on diversity and the judiciary has been updated to reflect the most recent data on both federal and state court judges. Exhibit 8.1 on errant state court judges has been expanded to several cases of judicial abuses, including the "kids-for-cash" sentencing controversy in Pennsylvania. Exhibit

8.2 has been similarly updated to include recent disciplinary action against federal judges.

Chapter 9—The most current research on both victim and perpetrator demographic characteristics is presented in this revised chapter, with updated data on sex, age, and race/ethnicity. An updated feature on "Courts, Controversy, and Racial Discrimination" explores how the growing population of Hispanics in the United States continues to reshape the U.S. justice system. Three new sections have been added on *pro se* defendants, social media and defendants, and victim impact statements. The chapter's coverage of the proposed Victims' Rights Amendment has been streamlined significantly. A new "Case Close-Up" highlights civil liability for police who fail for respond appropriately to domestic violence incidents.

Chapter 10—This chapter on the processing of criminal cases explores the most current research on the pretrial processing of criminal felony cases. It includes a new chapter opener on Pfc. Bradley Manning's alleged involvement in the WikiLeaks case. It also offers an expanded discussion of methodological issues involved with measuring crime; a new Table 10.1 comparing Type I and Type II UCR offenses; a new Table 10.2 on clearance rates; a new Figure 10.1 on criminal arrests; an updated Figure 10.2 illustrating case attrition; and up-to-date information on recent high-profile white-collar criminal prosecutions. The most significant change to this chapter is the integration of significantly streamlined material on bail that was formerly covered in a separate chapter.

Chapter 11—This chapter includes substantial new content, including a more in-depth analysis of the rules for disclosing exculpatory or impeachment evidence; expanded coverage of the exclusionary rule and the "fruit of the poisonous tree" doctrine; a more detailed exploration of the search warrant process, including information on affidavits, warrant particularity, and limitations on the execution of search warrants; and coverage of key U.S. Supreme Court decisions concerning search and seizure, especially in the area of warrantless searches and exceptions to the exclusionary rule (including a new Table 11.1 summarizing the major doctrines with supporting case law). The section on "Interrogations and Confessions" has been reorganized and expanded to present Fifth, Sixth, and Fourteenth Amendment implications. The section on the Fourth Amendment now includes information on "stop and frisk" procedures, protective sweeps, and exigent circumstances. A new section on electronic surveillance has been added, which includes coverage of Title III, the Stored Communications Act, and the Foreign Intelligence Surveillance Act. Numerous new case citations are presented, including the key developments stemming from *Arizona v. Gant* (2009), *Berghuis v. Thompkins* (2010), *Florida v. Powell* (2010), *J.D.B. v. North Carolina* (2011), *Maryland v. Shatzer* (2010), and *United States v. Jones* (2012).

Chapter 12—The most up-to-date research on plea bargaining is integrated into this chapter, including a new Figure 12.1 showing trial rates for typical felonies. The chapter contains expanded coverage of Rule 11 hearings concerning waiver of rights, allocution, and competency when guilty pleas are entered. A new section on no contest pleas and Alford pleas has been added. The cases of. *Iowa v. Tovar* (2004), *Lafler v. Copper* (2012) and *Missouri v. Frye* (2012) have been integrated into the chapter.

Chapter 13—This chapter has been significantly overhauled since the Tenth Edition to include expanded coverage *Daubert*, the so-called CSI effect, and the use and misuse of forensic science in the courtroom, focusing on its roles contributing to wrongful convictions and in exonerating the wrongfully convicted. A new "Courts and Controversy" feature explores whether fingerprint evidence should be admissible in criminal trials, focusing on *United States v. Llera Plaza* (2002). Information about former Illinois Governor Rod Blagojevich's trial now opens the chapter. A new "Case Close-Up" on extending *Batson* is presented. And the chapter ends with a new section on media in the courtroom, covering not only cameras in the courtroom, but also the use of social media. Numerous cases have been integrated into the chapter, including *Hollingsworth v. Perry* (2010).

Chapter 14—The chapter on sentencing options contains expanded coverage of the philosophical justifications for punishment, including a new section on restorative justice. California's efforts at prison realignment has been integrated into the chapter. Figure 14.1 has been updated to show the full range of adults under correctional supervision in the United States using the most up-to-date data. The Key Developments feature concerning imprisonment has been expanded to include landmark cases in correctional law and the rights of prisoners. The coverage of intermediate sanctions has been expanded to include home detention with electronic monitoring and GPS monitoring. A new "Courts, Law, & Media" feature further explores intermediate sanctions by examining Lindsay Lohan's criminal troubles. Death penalty data and case law have been updated and are now presented in several new tables and figures.

Chapter 15—This chapter presents the latest developments concerning state and federal sentencing, including changes in the interpretation of sentencing guidelines. Also included are the latest studies examining both legal and extralegal factors affecting sentencing, including a new Figure 15.1 showing prisoners in custody per 100,000 population. A new table (Table 15.1) presents data on the types of sentences imposed by conviction offense. Coverage of structured sentencing scheme has been expanded to differentiate presumptive sentencing from different forms of sentencing guidelines, including a new table (Table 15.2) comparing and contrasting the key characteristics of different sentencing schemes. *Pepper v. United States* (2011) and *Tapia v. United States* (2011) are now integrated into the chapter's coverage of case law relevant to sentencing. A new "Courts, Law, & Media" feature examines whether custom-made documentary movies should be used to present mitigation evidence at sentencing hearings.

Chapter 16—This chapter has been significantly updated to offer a much more in-depth study of the role of appellate and *habeas corpus* courts in addressing wrongful convictions. The number and leading causes of wrongful convictions is explored in detail. A new "Courts, Law, & Media" feature examines the Amanda Knox case by comparing the Italian appeals system to that used in the United States. A revised Figure 16.2 presents the most current data on the distribution of criminal appeals in the federal appellate courts. The chapter presents expanded coverage of *habeas*-type relief for both state and federal prisoners, including a new Key Developments feature on leading *habeas* case law and legislation.

Chapter 17—This chapter looks at new citations and updated statistics on juvenile crime and transferring juveniles to adult court. A new section has been added to the chapter exploring the various types of juvenile transfers. Several new tables, figures, and exhibits have been added to illustrate the workload of the juvenile courts and the evolving nature of limitations placed on the exercise of juvenile court jurisdiction. A new "Courts, Law, & Media" feature examines juvenile incarceration as depicted in the film *Dog Pound*.

Pedagogical Innovations

This edition contains an array of pedagogical aids to facilitate student learning. These include:

- Chapter learning objectives open each chapter and are revisited in the Chapter Review to facilitate student mastery of chapter concepts. The learning objectives are also linked to the text's supplements (test bank and website quizzes) to further advance learning.

- End-of-chapter critical thinking questions provide students with an opportunity to practice their skills in the chapter's key area.

- An end-of-chapter list of key terms with page references serves as a helpful study tool.

- Suggestions for further reading are offered so students can explore chapter concepts further.

- Numerous exhibits and figures amplify text coverage for easier understanding by students.

Supplements

An extensive package of supplemental aids is available for instructor and student use with this edition of *America's Courts and the Criminal Justice System*. Supplements are available to qualified adopters. Please consult your local sales representative for details.

For the Instructor

- **Instructor's Resource Manual with Test Bank.** Revised by Valerie Bell of Loras College, the manual includes learning objectives, key terms, a detailed chapter outline, a chapter summary, discussion topics, student activities, and a test bank. Each chapter's test bank contains questions in multiple-choice, true–false, fill-in-the-blank, and essay formats, with a full answer key. The test bank is coded to the learning objectives that appear in the main text and includes the page numbers in the main text where the answers can be found. Finally, each question in the test bank has been carefully reviewed by experienced criminal justice instructors for quality, accuracy, and content coverage. Our Instructor Approved seal, which appears on the front cover, is our assurance that you are working with an assessment and grading resource of the highest caliber.

- **Lesson Plans.** Revised by Robert Fog of Bakersfield University, the lesson plans bring accessible, masterful suggestions to every lesson. This supplement includes a sample syllabus, learning objectives, lecture notes, discussion topics, in-class activities, a detailed lecture outline, assignments, media tools, and "What if …" scenarios. Current events and real-life examples in the form of articles, websites and video links are incorporated into the class discussion topics, activities, and assignments. The lecture outlines are correlated with PowerPoint® slides for ease of classroom use. Lesson plans are available on the PowerLecture resource and the instructor website.

- **PowerLecture with ExamView and JoinIn.** This one-stop digital library and presentation tool includes preassembled Microsoft® PowerPoint® lecture slides—created by Marcy Hehnly, Chattahoochee Technical College—linked to the learning objectives for each chapter. Also included are an electronic copy of the *Instructor's Resource Manual with Test bank*, the Student Study Guide, ExamView computerized testing, and more. Based on the learning objectives outlined at the beginning of each chapter, the enhanced **PowerLecture** lets you bring together text-specific lecture outlines and art from this text, along with new video clips, animations, and learning modules from the web or your own materials—culminating in a powerful, personalized, media-enhanced presentation. The **PowerLecture** DVD integrates

ExamView®, a computerized test bank available for PC and Macintosh computers software for customizing tests of up to 250 items that can be delivered in print or online. With ExamView you can create, deliver, and customize tests and study guides (both print and online) in minutes. You can easily edit and import your own questions and graphics, change test layouts, and reorganize questions. And using ExamView's complete word-processing capabilities, you can enter an unlimited number of new questions or edit existing questions.

- **The Wadsworth Criminal Justice Video Library.** This contains many exciting new videos—many great ways to enrich your lectures and spark discussion of the material in this text. Your Cengage Learning representative will be happy to provide details on our video policy by adoption size. The library includes these selections and many others.

  - *ABC® Videos.* feature short, high-interest clips from current news events as well as historic raw footage going back 40 years. Perfect for discussion starters or to enrich your lectures and spark interest in the material in the text, these brief videos provide students with a new lens through which to view the past and present, one that will greatly enhance their knowledge and understanding of significant events and open up to them new dimensions in learning. Clips are drawn from such programs as *World News Tonight, Good Morning America, This Week, PrimeTime Live, 20/20, and Nightline,* as well as numerous ABC News specials and material from the Associated Press Television News and British Movietone News collections.

  - *Cengage Learning's "Introduction Criminal Justice Video Series"* features videos supplied by the BBC Motion Gallery. These short, high-interest clips from CBS and BBC news programs—everything from nightly news broadcasts and specials to CBS News Special Reports, *CBS Sunday Morning, 60 Minutes,* and more—are perfect classroom discussion starters. Designed to enrich your lectures and spark interest in the material in the text, these brief videos provide students with a new lens through which to view the past and present, one that will greatly enhance

their knowledge and understanding of significant events and open up to them new dimensions in learning. Clips are drawn from the BBC Motion Gallery

- **Criminal Justice Media Library.** Cengage Learning's Criminal Justice Media Library includes nearly 300 media assets on the topics you cover in your courses. Available to stream from any web-enabled computer, the Criminal Justice Media Library's assets include such valuable resources as: Career Profile Videos featuring interviews with criminal justice professionals from a range of roles and locations, simulations that allow students to step into various roles and practice their decision-making skills, video clips on current topics from ABC and other sources, animations that illustrate key concepts, interactive learning modules that help students check their knowledge of important topics, and Reality Check exercises that compare expectations and preconceived notions against the real-life thoughts and experiences of criminal justice professionals. All of the video assets include assessment questions that can be delivered straight to your gradebook, and the Media Library can be uploaded and customized within many popular Learning Management Systems. Please contact your Cengage Learning representative for ordering and pricing information.

- **WebTutor™ on Blackboard® and WebCT®.** Jump-start your course with customizable, rich, text-specific content within your Course Management System. Whether you want to Web-enable your class or put an entire course online, WebTutor delivers. WebTutor offers a wide array of resources, including media assets, a test bank, practice quizzes linked to chapter learning objectives, and additional study aids. Visit www.cengage.com/webtutor to learn more.

For the Student

- **CourseMate.** Cengage Learning's Criminal Justice CourseMate brings course concepts to life with interactive learning, study, and exam preparation tools that support the printed textbook. CourseMate includes an integrated eBook, quizzes mapped to chapter learning objectives, flashcards, videos, and more, and EngagementTracker, a first-of-its-kind tool that monitors student engagement in the course. The accompanying instructor website offers access to password-protected resources such as an electronic version of the *Instructor's Resource Manual* and PowerPoint® slides.

- **Careers in Criminal Justice Website.** Can be bundled with this text at no additional charge. Featuring plenty of self-exploration and profiling activities, the interactive Careers in Criminal Justice website helps students investigate and focus on the criminal justice career choices that are right for them. Includes interest assessment, video testimonials from career professionals, resume and interview tips, and links for reference.

- **CLeBook.** Cengage Learning's Criminal Justice ebooks allow students to access our textbooks in an easy-to-use online format. Highlight, take notes, bookmark, search your text, and, for most texts, link directly into multimedia. In short, CLeBooks combine the best features of paper books and ebooks in one package.

Acknowledgments

Writing the Eleventh Edition was made easier by the assistance and encouragement of people who deserve special recognition. First and foremost, we would like to thank the Wadsworth criminal justice team, especially Carolyn Henderson Meier (senior acquisitions editor) and Shelley Murphy (senior developmental editor). We are particularly grateful to Julie Martinez, our lead development editor, who provided a fresh perspective on the new edition and guidance whenever we needed it. Julie, you are truly outstanding at what you do and we are indebted to you for your consistently first-rate work.

We are also grateful to the gifted production team who turned raw manuscript into a polished book and dispensed good cheer along the way, especially Virginette Acacio, Casey Lozier, Christy Frame, and Lindsay Schmonsees at MPS.

As always, David's wife and children deserve a special note of thanks for their love and support. He dedicates the book to his children, in response to their bemusement at the idea that Daddy was busy writing a book.

Hank thanks David for asking him to become a co-author on this most influential of books. Dave, I was honored when you selected me to assist with this project and I continue to enjoy working with you immensely. Hank's partner Kyle also deserves special thanks for being supportive and putting up with his long hours of work on the book even when it meant feeling neglected.

David W. Neubauer   **Henry F. Fradella**
Slidell, Louisiana   **Irvine, California**

Reviewers of America's Courts and the Criminal Justice System

Special thanks are due to the reviewers of this and all previous editions.

James Alfini
American Judicature Society

Ruben Auger-Marchand
Indiana University; Purdue University

E. Stan Barnhill
University of Nevada–Reno

Barbara Belbot
University of Houston–Downtown

Larry Berkson
American Judicature Society

Patricia A. Binfa
Westwood College

Anita Blowers
University of North Carolina–Charlotte

Paula M. Broussard
University of Southwestern Louisiana

Mark S. Brown
University of South Carolina

Frank Butler
Temple University

Elizabeth Callahan
Lincoln University

Kathleen Cameron-Hahn
Arizona State University

Reynolds N. Cate
St. Mary's University

Bill Clements
Norwich University

Glenn S. Coffey
University of North Florida

George Cole
University of Connecticut

Beverly Blair Cook
University of Wisconsin–Milwaukee

Cathy Cowling
Campbell University

Mark Dantzker
Loyola University of Chicago

Erika Davis-Frenzel
Indiana University of Pennsylvania

Chris DeLay
University of Louisiana–Lafayette

Max Dery
California State University–Fullerton

Scott Donaldson
Tarrant County College

Thornton Douglas
University of Illinois–Chicago

Eugene J. Evans, Jr.
Camden County College

Mary Ann Farkas
Marquette University

Roy Flemming
Wayne State University

David O. Friedrichs
University of Scranton

James A. Gazell
San Diego State University

Marc Gertz
Florida State University

Gary S. Green
Minot State University

Pamela L. Griset
University of Central Florida

Joseph Hanrahan
Westfield State University

Peter Haynes
Arizona State University

Michael Hazlett
Western Illinois State University

Edward Heck
University of New Orleans

Ellen Hockstedler
University of Wisconsin–Milwaukee

Lou Holscher
Arizona State University

N. Gary Holten
University of Central Florida

Vincent R. Jones, Esq.
Governors State University

Kimberly Keller
University of Texas–San Antonio

Rodney Kingsnorth
California State University–Sacramento

Karl Kunkel
Southwest Missouri State University

Jim Love
Lamar University

Patricia Loveless
University of Delaware

David O. Lukoff
University of Delaware–Newcastle

James Maddex
Georgia State University

Stephen Meinhold
University of North Carolina–Wilmington

Larry Myers
Sam Houston State University

Elizabeth Pelz
University of Houston–Downtown

Richard Perry
San Jose State University

Eric Rise
University of Delaware

Linda Robyn
Northern Arizona University

John Paul Ryan
American Judicature Society

Joseph Sanborn
Glassboro State College

Jefferey M. Sellers
University of Southern California

William F. "Wic" Southern, Jr.
Carteret Community College

Jose Texidor
Penn State University

David O. Thysens
Saint Martin's College

Frederick Van Dusen
Palm Beach Community College

Donald Walker
Kent State University

Russell Wheeler
Federal Judicial Center

Paul Wice
Drew University

Sheryl Williams
Jersey City State College

Nancy Wolfe
University of South Carolina

Courts, Crime, and Controversy

Casey Anthony sits in court during sentencing at the Orange County Courthouse in Orlando, Florida. Although Anthony was acquitted of murdering her two-year-old daughter Caylee, she was convicted of lying to the police and sentenced to four years prison. However, because she received credit for the time she served awaiting trial and for good behavior while in pretrial detention, she was released shortly after sentencing. ■

POOL New/ REUTERS

Chapter Outline

COURTS AND CRIME

COURTS AND THE CRIMINAL JUSTICE SYSTEM
An Interdependent Criminal Justice System
A Fragmented Criminal Justice Nonsystem
Tensions and Conflicts

AN OVERVIEW OF U.S. COURTS

IDENTIFYING THE ACTORS IN THE COURTHOUSE
Prosecutors
Defense Attorneys
Judges
Defendants and Victims

FOLLOWING THE STEPS OF THE PROCESS
Crime
Arrest
Initial Appearance
Bail
Grand Jury
Preliminary Hearing
Arraignment

Discovery
Pretrial Motions
Plea Negotiations
Trial
Sentencing
Appeal

CASE CLOSE-UP: *Brown v. Mississippi*

LAW ON THE BOOKS

LAW IN ACTION

COURTS AND CONTROVERSY
Crime Control Model
Due Process Model
Shifting the Balance

Courts, Controversy, & Reducing Crime
Is It Time to End the War on Drugs?

MEDIA DEPICTIONS AND DISTORTIONS OF CRIMINAL COURTS

Courts, Law, & Media
The Casey Anthony Trial

Courts, Crime, and Controversy • Courts, Crime, and Contr
nd Controversy • Courts, Crime, and Controversy • Courts,

Learning Objectives

After reading this chapter, you should be able to:

LO1 Describe how the courts are related to the other components of the criminal justice system.

LO2 Discuss the major types of courts found in the United States.

LO3 Identify the most important actors in the courthouse.

LO4 List the steps in a typical felony prosecution.

LO5 Explain how a law in action perspective complements a law on the books approach to studying the criminal courts.

LO6 Distinguish between the crime control model of criminal justice and the due process model of criminal justice.

Even though her two-year old daughter Caylee was missing, Casey Anthony partied, got a tattoo, and otherwise lived her life by making up a series of stories to explain Caylee's whereabouts. After Caylee's body was discovered close to the Anthony home, Casey was charged and tried for her daughter's murder. Although a significant amount of circumstantial evidence suggested that Casey was guilty, no forensic evidence tied her directly to Caylee's death—a factor that may have led to her acquittal. The not-guilty verdict sparked great public outrage that a "baby killer" had gone free. But jurors interviewed after the conclusion of the nearly two-month-long case said the prosecution had not proven how Caylee died and whether Casey was involved in her daughter's death.

Casey Anthony's case highlights a common disconnect between the way a case is perceived by those evaluating the evidence presented in a court of law and the ways in which a case is perceived in the court of public opinion. In a courtroom, defendants are presumed innocent until proven guilty beyond a reasonable doubt. In contrast, reporters, media pundits, and their audiences are not constrained by formal presumptions or the rules of evidence. This disparity often causes people to misperceive the criminal judicial process as unfair. This book seeks to correct the most common misperceptions about the role of the courts in the U.S. criminal justice system.

and Controversy • Courts, Crime, and Controversy • Courts, Crime, and C
y • Courts, Crime, and Controversys • Courts, Crime, and Controversy • C

Is Casey Anthony truly innocent of any criminal wrongdoing in the death of her daughter, or did jurors unjustly acquit her because of a lack of forensic evidence they expected, but which did not exist? We may never know the answers to such questions, but research suggests that "changes in popular culture brought about by rapid scientific and technological advances and widespread dissemination of information about them" has "heightened juror expectations and demands for scientific evidence in almost every respect" (Shelton, Kim, & Barak, 2009, p. 2). Some scholars and practitioners call this phenomenon the *CSI effect*, even though forensic science on television appears to be only one factor in an overall social trend that embraces technology while discounting logical inference (see Chapter 13).

There can be no doubt that changes in popular culture affect America's legal institutions. Indeed, jurors expect sophisticated forensic evidence in even the most mundane cases (Shelton, 2008). But the widespread use of forensic evidence to convict guilty defendants at trial and exonerate the innocent on appeal is just one example of the dynamic nature of the legal system in the United States. Although courts and law have a long history that provides stability, this does not mean that courts and law are static institutions. On the contrary, changes in society end up in courthouses in a variety of ways. At times, specific events are the catalyst for change. In the aftermath of the terrorist attacks of September 11, 2001, for example, courts wrestled with questions about the scope of electronic eavesdropping and whether alleged terrorists can be held indefinitely in military prisons without trials. At other times, courts have been forced to adapt to changes in other branches of government. Legislatures across the nation, for example, have launched wars on drugs that have flooded the courts with a growing number of cases even as the incidence of other crimes decreases. Likewise, changes in public opinion affect how justice is administered. Concerned about crime rates that are too high, the public has demanded that judges get tough with criminals.

Courts are independent from the other branches of government, but this does not mean that they are divorced from the society they serve. Rather, societal issues impact the kinds of cases brought to court and how they are handled. For example, concerns about gender equity prompted examination of how courts handle domestic violence and why district attorneys decline to prosecute many sexual assault cases. How courts adapt to social changes is important. And while change in society is inevitable, it is also unsettling. Simply stated, change produces controversy. A good deal of this book examines the controversy surrounding courts and crime.

COURTS AND CRIME

In July 2008, Cindy Anthony reported to police that she had not seen her two-year-old granddaughter, Caylee, for more than a month, even though the toddler lived with her, her husband George, and their daughter, Casey (Caylee's mother). Cindy also reported that she had smelled a foul odor, consistent with that of a dead body, in her daughter Casey's car.

Yet, during the period of time Caylee was missing, Casey Anthony was photographed scantily clad and grinding on the dance floor of local clubs. She also got a tattoo reading *"bella vita"* ("beautiful life" in Italian). The police and the general public had a hard time understanding how Casey could engage in such conduct while her daughter was missing. When the remains of Caylee's body were eventually found in a wooded area near her family's home in December 2008, Casey Anthony was charged with murdering her daughter.

The death of Caylee Anthony provides a poignant example that crime has been a pressing national concern for decades. Newspapers headline major drug busts. Local television news broadcasts graphic footage of the latest murder scene. Not to be outdone, the national media offer tantalizing details on the latest sensational crime or prominent criminal. Meanwhile, official government statistics document that levels of crime are high (but declining), and unofficial pollsters report that Americans believe crime rates are too high. These concerns prompt governmental response. Candidates for public office promise that, if elected, they will get tough on criminals. Government officials, in turn, announce bold new programs to eradicate street crime, reduce violence, and end the scourge of drugs. In some areas, most notably in New York City and San Diego, such crime control efforts significantly reduced crime (Corman & Mocan, 2005; Jacobson, 2005). Such efforts, however, have been less effective in other areas of the United States, where street crime remains a volatile, persistent, and intractable issue.

A good deal of the political rhetoric about crime focuses on the criminal courts. Prosecutors are viewed as being too ready to engage in plea bargaining. Judges are accused of imposing unduly lenient sentences. Appellate courts are blamed for allowing obviously guilty defendants to go free on technicalities. Meanwhile, the police complain that Supreme Court decisions handcuff the fight against crime. Victims of crime become frustrated by lengthy trial delays. Witnesses protest wasted trips to the courthouse. Judges and defense attorneys—much more so than police chiefs and prison wardens—are blamed for high crime rates.

The purpose of this chapter is to build on public perceptions of the criminal courts by focusing on a few basic topics. We begin by discussing where the courts fit in the criminal justice system. Next, attention shifts to the three activities that set the stage for the rest of the book:

- The organization of the U.S. courts system
- Identifying the actors in the courthouse
- Following the steps of the process

As we will see below, the judicial process is complicated, so throughout this book we will examine the courts from three complementary perspectives:

- Law on the books
- Law in action
- Courts and controversy

The "law on the books" perspective helps us understand the legal foundations of our nation's criminal justice system. The "law in action" perspective helps us understand how discretionary decisions are made within the context of the formal law. Finally, the "courts and controversy" perspective helps us think about policy choices, priorities, potential reforms to the system, and what directions such reforms should take.

COURTS AND THE CRIMINAL JUSTICE SYSTEM

The Orange County, Florida, Sherriff's department took the lead in investigating the disappearance of Caylee Anthony. But the detectives had little to go on besides the inconsistencies in the statements of Casey Anthony, who offered a series of suspicious explanation's for her daughter's whereabouts. She even told detectives a made-up story about how Caylee had been kidnapped by a fictitious nanny. Casey claimed she had spent more than month looking for her daughter in the wake of the alleged kidnapping, but had been too afraid to notify the police, allegedly fearing what might be done to her daughter if she told authorities. The major break came when a meter reader called police about a suspicious object found in a forested area near the Anthony residence. The police at first dismissed the tip but months later went back to the spot and eventually found Caylee Anthony's badly decomposed body. In the months that followed, numerous local, state, and federal law enforcement agencies became involved in the investigation.

The diverse groups of people and agencies involved in the arrest, prosecution, and conviction of Casey Anthony provide an insight into the size and complexity of the criminal justice system in the United States. Fighting crime is a major societal activity. Every year, local, state, and federal governments spend approximately $228 billion on the criminal and civil justice system in the United States (Bureau of Justice Statistics, 2011). These tax dollars support an enormous assortment of criminal justice agencies, which in turn employ a large (and growing) number of employees; approximately 2.5 million people earn their living working in the criminal justice system. These government officials are quite busy: Every year, the police make more than 13 million arrests, not including traffic violations. And every day, correctional personnel supervise approximately 7.3 million people. Yet as large as these figures are, they still underestimate societal activity directed against crime. A substantial number of persons are employed in the private sector in positions either directly (defense attorneys and bail agents) or indirectly (locksmiths and private security) related to dealing with crime (Hakim, Rengert, & Shachmurove, 1996; Ribovich & Martino, 2007).

The numerous public agencies involved in implementing public policy concerning crime are referred to as the criminal justice system. Figure 1.1 depicts the criminal justice system as consisting of three overlapping circles: Police are responsible for apprehending criminals; the courts are responsible for deciding whether those arrested are legally guilty and, if so, determining the sentence;

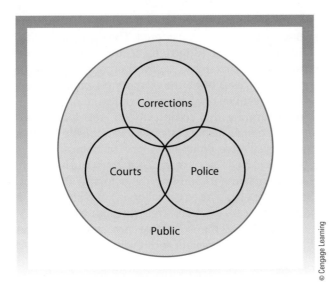

© Cengage Learning

Figure 1.1 ■ The Overlapping Circles of the Criminal Justice System

corrections is responsible for carrying out the penalty imposed on those found guilty.

The major components of the criminal justice system do not make up a smoothly functioning and internally consistent organization. Rather, the criminal justice system is both interdependent and fragmented.

An Interdependent Criminal Justice System

Viewing the various components of criminal justice as a system highlights the fact that these different agencies are interdependent and interrelated. Police, courts, and corrections are separate government institutions with different goals, histories, and operating procedures. Though separate, they are also tied together because they must interact with one another. The courts play a pivotal role within the criminal justice system because many formal actions pertaining to suspects, defendants, and convicts involve the courts. Only the judiciary can hold a suspect in jail prior to trial, find a defendant guilty, and sentence the guilty person to prison. Alternatively, of course, the courts may release the suspect awaiting trial, find the suspect not guilty, or decide to grant probation.

The decisions that courts make have important consequences for other components of the criminal justice system. Judges' bail policies, for example, immediately affect what happens to a person arrested by the police; likewise, corrections personnel are affected because the bail policies of the judges affect the size of the local jail population. If the decisions made by the courts have important consequences for police and prisons, the reverse is equally true: The operations of law enforcement and corrections have a major impact on the judiciary. The more felons the police arrest, the greater the workload of the prosecutors; and the more overcrowded the prisons, the more difficult it is for judges to sentence the guilty.

A Fragmented Criminal Justice Nonsystem

The system approach to criminal justice dominates contemporary thinking about criminal justice. But not everyone is convinced of the utility of this conceptualization. Some people point to a nonsystem of criminal justice. Although the work of the police, courts, and corrections must, by necessity, overlap, this does not mean that their activities are coordinated or coherent. From the perspective of the nonsystem, what is most salient is the fragmentation of criminal justice. Fragmentation characterizes each component of the criminal justice system. The police component consists of nearly 18,000 law enforcement agencies, with varying traditions of cooperation or antagonism. Likewise, the corrections component includes more than 1,820 state and federal correctional facilities, to say nothing of the thousands of local jails. But corrections also encompasses probation, parole, drug treatment, halfway houses, and the like.

The same fragmentation holds true for the courts. In many ways, talking about courts is misleading, because the activities associated with "the court" encompass a wide variety of actors. Many people who work in the courthouse—judges, prosecutors, public defenders, clerks, court reporters, bailiffs—are employed by separate government agencies. Others who work in the courthouse are private citizens, but their actions directly affect what happens in this governmental institution; defense attorneys and bail agents are prime examples. Still others are ordinary citizens who find themselves in the courthouse either because they are compelled to be there (defendants and jurors) or because their activities are essential to the disposition of cases (victims and witnesses).

The fragmentation within the three components of the nonsystem of criminal justice is compounded by the decentralization of government. American government is based on the principle of federalism, which distributes governmental power between national (usually referred to as federal) and state governments. In turn, state governments create local units of government, such as counties and cities. Each of these levels of government has its own array of police, courts, and corrections. This decentralization adds tremendously to the complexity of the American criminal justice system. For example, depending on the nature of the law allegedly violated, several different prosecutors may bring charges against a defendant, including the following: city attorney (local), district attorney (county), attorney general (state), U.S. attorney (U.S. district court), and U.S. attorney general (national).

Tensions and Conflicts

Criminal justice is best viewed as both a system and a nonsystem. Both interdependence and fragmentation characterize the interrelationships among the agencies involved in apprehending, convicting, and punishing wrongdoers. In turn, these structural arrangements produce tensions and conflicts within each component. For example, the prosecutor may loudly condemn the actions of a judge, or a defense attorney may condemn the jury for an unjust verdict.

Tensions and conflicts also occur among the components of criminal justice. The interrelationships among police, courts, and corrections are often marked by tension and conflict because the work of each component is evaluated by others: The police make arrests, yet the decision to charge is made by the prosecutor; the judge and jury rate the prosecutor's efforts.

Tensions and conflicts also result from multiple and conflicting goals concerning criminal justice. Government officials bring to their work different perspectives on the common task of processing persons accused of breaking the law. Tensions and conflicts among police, courts, and corrections, therefore, are not necessarily undesirable; because they arise from competing goals, they provide important checks

on other organizations, guaranteeing that multiple perspectives will be considered. The same holds true within the courts. Judges, prosecutors, and defense attorneys, for example, share the common task of processing cases but at the same time exhibit different perspectives on the proper outcome of the case. Understanding this complexity, in *America's Courts and the Criminal Justice System* we examine the nation's judiciary in five complementary sections. Part I is about the basic organization of our court system; Part II concerns identifying the actors in the courthouse; Part III focuses on following the steps of the judicial process after an arrest through trial; Part IV examines how the convicted are sentenced; and Part V looks at appellate and juvenile courts.

AN OVERVIEW OF THE U.S. COURTS

Because Caylee Anthony's murder occurred in Orange County, Florida, the courts in that county heard the case. If Casey Anthony had been convicted of murder, her appeals would have been heard in the Florida appellate courts. And if the jury had found her guilty and imposed the death penalty, Casey Anthony would likely have had the opportunity to challenge her conviction in the federal courts as well. Clearly, the Casey Anthony trial was atypical because it had so much publicity; ordinary felony cases rarely involve more than one court and one appeal. Nonetheless, it begins to illustrate the complexity of the court system in the United States.

By rough count, 17,000 courthouses are operating in the United States. Some are imposing turn-of-the-century buildings noted for their elaborate architecture. Others are faceless modern structures marked by a lack of architectural inspiration. A few courts, you might be surprised to learn, are in the front of a funeral parlor or the back of a garage, where justices of the peace preside in rural areas. Buildings aside, courts are governmental organizations created to hear specific types of cases. Figure 1.2 offers a preliminary overview of different types of courts in the United States.

One distinction is between federal and state courts. The term *dual court system* refers to separate state and federal courts (rarely do cases move from one system to the other). Another important difference between courts relates to function. Most

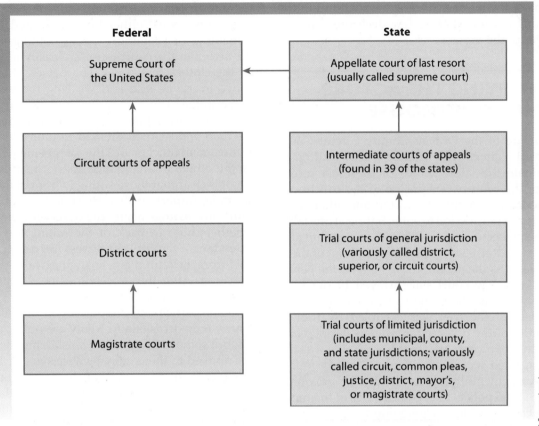

© Cengage Learning

Figure 1.2 ■ Overview of Court Structure in the United States

courts are trial courts. As the name implies, this is where trials are held, jurors sworn, and witnesses questioned. Trial courts are noisy places resembling school corridors between classes. Amid the noisy crowd you will find lawyers, judges, police officers, defendants, victims, and witnesses walking through the building during working hours.

Trial courts, in turn, are divided between major and lower. Lower courts initially process felony cases (set bail, for example) but cannot find the defendant innocent or guilty and therefore cannot sentence. Their primary activity involves processing the millions of minor offenses such as public drunkenness, petty theft, and disorderly conduct. Major trial courts, on the other hand, are responsible for the final phases of felony prosecutions. In these courts, defendants charged with crimes such as murder, robbery, burglary, and drug dealing enter a plea of guilty (or occasionally go to trial), and the guilty are sentenced.

Other courts (fewer in number) are appeals courts that review decisions made by trial courts (usually only the major trial courts). Appeals courts review decisions made elsewhere, but no trials are held, no jurors employed, and no witnesses heard. Rather, appellate courts are places where lawyers argue whether the previous decision correctly or incorrectly followed the law. In many ways, appellate courts are like a monastery, where scholars pore over old books and occasionally engage in polite debates. Given the growing volume of cases, the federal government and most states have created two levels of appellate courts: intermediate courts, which must hear all cases, and supreme courts, which pick and choose the cases they hear.

Although the U.S. Supreme Court stands atop the organizational ladder, it hears only a handful of the cases filed each year (often fewer than 85 per year). Thus, its importance is measured not in terms of the number of cases decided but in the wide-ranging impact these few decisions have on all stages of the process.

IDENTIFYING THE ACTORS IN THE COURTHOUSE

The outside of the Orange County Circuit Court resembled a circus with satellite trucks waiting to disseminate the latest details of the most recent crime of the century. The inside of the courtroom was packed with as many reporters and others who had received permission to enter. Sitting at one table were the prosecutors; at another, the defendant and her defense attorneys. Immediately in front of these two tables was the judge, sitting high on the bench with several key court staff arrayed below him. On one side was the witness chair, which during the course of the trial was occupied by friends and family of the deceased as well as various law enforcement officers. And on the other side was the jury box, filled with local citizens. The jury found Casey Anthony guilty of four misdemeanor counts of lying to the police, but acquitted her of the more serious charges of first-degree murder, aggravated manslaughter, and aggravated child abuse. All of these persons in the *Casey* case are important. For this reason, Part II of this book focuses on the actors in the courthouse.

Enter a trial courtroom, and you will observe numerous people either busily engaged in doing something or seemingly doing nothing. Some of the actors in the courthouse are easily identifiable by the clothes they wear. The person sitting high above everyone else and wearing the black robe is the judge. The person in handcuffs arrayed in a bright orange jumpsuit is the defendant. And the men and women dressed in uniforms are law enforcement officers. But the roles being performed by the others in attendance are not readily apparent. It is clear that those sitting in front of the railing are more important than those in back of it. Until court proceedings begin, the observer is never sure whether those in back of the railing are victims, defendants, family, witnesses, reporters, potential jurors, or retired citizens whose hobby is court watching. After the proceedings begin, their roles become more apparent.

Some participants are present on a regular basis; others, only occasionally. Many are public employees, but some are private citizens. Using the categories applied to the criminal justice system, Table 1.1 provides a chart of many of the actors one would expect to see in a courthouse on any given day. Some of the titles vary from place to place. Similarly, the participants vary depending on the type of case. In a murder case, for example, a scientist from the crime lab may be presenting evidence, but in a child sexual abuse case, the actors will more likely include a

TABLE 1.1 ■ ACTORS IN THE COURTHOUSE

	Justice Professionals			Members of the Public	
Police	Lawyers	Court Support Staff	Corrections Officials	Regular Participants	Irregular Participants
Federal	Prosecutors	Clerks of court	Probation officers	Bail agents	Defendants
State	Public defenders	Court reporters	Jail employees	Reporters	Victims
Sheriff	Private defense attorneys	Pretrial services personnel	Prison employees	Social services personnel	Witnesses
Local	Judges	Bailiffs	Drug rehabilitation program personnel	Select expert witnesses	Jurors
Special districts	Law clerks	Court administrators			Victim advocates
Private security		Victim-/witness-assistance program personnel			
		Rape crisis center			

© Cengage Learning

social worker or psychiatrist. A brief overview of the main actors will help set the stage.

Prosecutors

The organization of prosecutors in the United States is as fragmented as the courts in which they appear. Limiting ourselves here only to state courts and state prosecutions, in most states you find one prosecutorial office for the lower courts (typically the city attorney), another for the major trial court (typically called the district attorney or the state's attorney), and yet another at the state level (almost uniformly called the attorney general).

Regardless of the level, prosecutors are the most influential of the courthouse actors. Their offices decide which cases to prosecute, which cases to plea-bargain, and which cases to try. They may also be influential in matters such as setting bail and choosing the sentence.

Defense Attorneys

The U.S. Constitution guarantees defendants the right to counsel. But for most defendants, this abstract "right" collides with economic reality. Many defendants cannot afford to hire a lawyer, so the government must provide one at government expense, either a court-appointed lawyer or a public defender. Only a handful of defendants hire a private lawyer.

Our notions of defense attorneys have been shaped by fictional characters on television and in movies who are always able to show that their clients are innocent. Reality is strikingly different. Often defense attorneys urge their clients to plead guilty based on the assessment that a jury will find the defendant guilty beyond a reasonable doubt. Even when cases are tried, defense attorneys only occasionally are able to secure a not-guilty verdict for their clients.

Judges

Judges in state courts are by and large elected by the voters. Federal judges, on the other hand, are nominated by the president of the United States and confirmed by the U.S. Senate. Judges are the ultimate authority figures in the courthouse because only judges can set bail, only judges can

instruct jurors about the meaning of the law, and only judges can impose sentences. Exercising this authority, though, is limited by the reality of high caseloads. The quickest way to dispose of cases is by a plea of guilty. Thus, judges must be responsive to prosecutors and defense attorneys if they are to achieve their principal goal of disposing of cases.

Defendants and Victims

Defendants are, by and large, young, poor, uneducated males. A large percentage stand accused of property crimes (theft and burglary) or low-level drug offenses. They are hardly the clever and sophisticated criminals portrayed in fiction. African-Americans and Latinos comprise a disproportionately large percentage of felony defendants, a fact that has placed race and ethnicity at the forefront of the politics of justice (Walker, Spohn, & DeLone 2007).

The victims of crime are playing an increasingly important role in the criminal courts. Once banished to a bit part of testifying, they are increasingly demanding major roles in setting bail, agreeing to pleas of guilty, imposing sentences, and granting release from prison. Groups such as Mothers Against Drunk Driving (MADD) and the National Organization for Victim Assistance (NOVA) have become a potent political force.

FOLLOWING THE STEPS OF THE PROCESS

In several important ways, Casey Anthony's case is atypical. First, she was charged with murder. Contrary to their omnipresence in the media, murder and nonnegligent homicide cases account for less than 1/10 of 1 percent of all criminal arrests (Bureau of Justice Statistics, 2011). Second, Casey Anthony was charged with capital murder, meaning that if she had been convicted, she could have been sentenced to death. In contrast, very few homicides are death-penalty-eligible. Third, Casey Anthony's case went to trial, rather than being resolved via the plea-bargaining process like 90 to 95 percent of all felony cases. And, finally, Casey Anthony was acquitted, while the overall conviction rate at trial for felonies is upward of 90 percent.

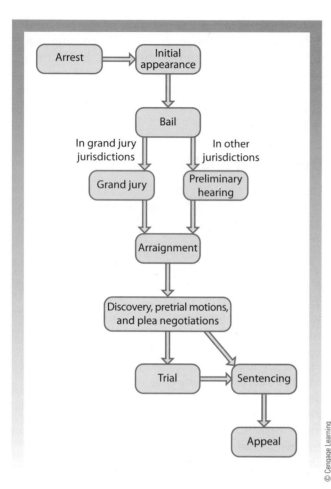

© Cengage Learning

Figure 1.3 ■ Flowchart of the Steps in the Criminal Judicial Process

Both Figure 1.3 and the "Law on the Books vs. Law in Action" feature on page 15 present an overview of the stages a felony case passes through from arrest to appeal. The specifics of criminal procedure vary from state to state, and federal requirements differ from state mandates. Rest assured that the remainder of the text will complicate this oversimplification. But for now, we focus on a defendant charged with a noncapital state felony.

Crime

The amount of crime in the United States is difficult to quantify precisely, but compared to other industrialized nations it is high. Although the media focus on crimes of violence, the overwhelming majority of crimes involve burglary and theft. In fact, people report about 1.25 million violent crimes and 9.1 million property crimes to the police each year. However, many crimes are never reported and, therefore, never make the official statistics.

Legally, crimes fall into three categories: **felonies** (in most states punishable by 1 year or more in prison); **misdemeanors** (typically punishable by up to a 1-year sentence in a local jail); and violations (subject to fine or a short jail term). Felonies are filed in major trial courts, whereas misdemeanors and violations are typically heard in the lower courts.

Arrest

Every year the police make more than 11 million arrests for nontraffic offenses. Most are for minor crimes, but nearly 1.86 million involve serious crimes, such as murder, rape, assault, robbery, burglary, and theft. The police are able to make an arrest in only one out of five crimes known to them. As a result, only a fraction of the nation's major crimes ever reach the courts.

Initial Appearance

An arrested person must be brought before a judge without unnecessary delay. For felony defendants, the initial appearance is largely a formality because no plea may be entered. Instead, defendants are told what crime they are alleged to have committed and perfunctorily advised of their rights, and a date for the preliminary hearing is set. For misdemeanor defendants, the initial appearance is typically the defendant's only courtroom encounter; three out of four plead guilty and are sentenced immediately.

Bail

The most important event that occurs during the initial appearance is the setting of bail. Because a defendant is considered innocent until proven guilty, the vast majority of defendants have the right to post bail. But this legal right is tied to the defendant's economic status. Many defendants are too poor to scrounge up the cash to pay the bail agent's fee; thus, they must remain in jail awaiting trial. The overriding reality, however, is that U.S. jails are overflowing. As a result, pretrial detention is limited largely to defendants who are alleged to have committed serious crimes; judges set a very high bail because they do not want these defendants wandering the streets before trial. For defendants charged with less serious crimes, judges and prosecutors may want to keep them in jail while awaiting trial, but the citizens are often unwilling to invest the tens of millions of dollars needed to build more jails.

Grand Jury

The grand jury is designed as a check on unwarranted prosecutions. Grand juries are required in all federal felony prosecutions, but only about half the states use them. In grand jury proceedings, a prosecutor must convince a simple majority of the grand jurors that a crime was committed and that there is probable cause that the defendant committed crime. Probable cause is not a particularly high or exacting standard of proof. All that needs to be shown to meet this burden of proof is a "fair probability" that the defendant committed the crime.

If the grand jury finds probable cause to hold the defendant for trial, it returns an indictment (also called a "true bill") charging the defendant with a crime. On rare occasions, grand juries refuse to indict (such refusal is called a "no bill" or a "no true bill"). Legal theory aside, grand juries are dominated by the prosecutor, and they obligingly indict whomever the prosecutor wants indicted.

Preliminary Hearing

Like grand jury proceedings, preliminary hearings provide a check against unwarranted prosecutions. During a preliminary hearing, the prosecutor must prove to a judge (rather than to a grand jury) that a crime was committed and that there is probable cause to believe that the defendant committed the crime. Given the low burden of proof, most of the time a judge finds that probable cause is present and orders the defendant held for further proceedings. In most courthouses, few cases are dismissed at the preliminary hearing for lack of probable cause.

Arraignment

Although the two terms are often used interchangeably, an arraignment differs from the initial appearance. During arraignment, the defendant is given a copy of the formal charges, advised of his or her rights (usually more extensively than at the initial appearance), and for the first time is called upon to enter a plea. Not surprisingly, most defendants plead not guilty, but a few admit their guilt then and there and enter a plea of guilty. Overall, little of importance happens during arraignment.

Discovery

The term *discovery* refers to the exchange of information prior to trial. In some states, but not all, the prosecutor is required to turn over a copy of the police reports to the defense prior to trial. In general, however, the defense is required to provide the prosecutor with little if any information. The formal law aside, many prosecutors voluntarily give defense attorneys they trust extensive information prior to trial, anticipating that the defense attorney will persuade the defendant to enter a plea of guilty.

Pretrial Motions

Motions are simply requests for a judge to make a decision. Many motions are made during trial, but a few may be made beforehand. The most significant pretrial motions relate to how the police gathered evidence. Defense attorneys file motions to suppress evidence—that is, to prevent its being used during trial. Motions to suppress physical evidence contend that the police conducted an illegal search and seizure (*Mapp v. Ohio*, 1961). Motions to suppress a confession contend that the police violated the suspect's constitutional rights during questioning (*Miranda v. Arizona*, 1966).

Plea Negotiations

Most findings of guilt result not from a verdict at trial but from a voluntary plea by the defendant. Ninety percent of all felony convictions are the product of negotiations between the prosecutor and the defense attorney (and sometimes the judge as well). Although the public thinks of plea bargaining as negotiating a lenient sentence, the reality is that each courthouse has an informal understanding of what a case is worth. Thus, plea bargaining is governed by informal understandings of what sentence is appropriate for a given type of defendant.

Trial

Trial by jury is one of the most fundamental rights granted to those accused of violating criminal law. A defendant can be tried either by a judge sitting alone (called a "bench trial") or by a jury. A jury trial typically begins with the selection of 12 jurors. Each side makes opening statements, indicating what they think the evidence in the case will show. Because the prosecutor has the burden of proving the defendant guilty beyond a reasonable doubt, he or she is the first to call witnesses. After the prosecution has completed its case, the defense has the opportunity to call its own witnesses. When all the evidence has been introduced, each side makes a closing argument to the jury, and the judge then instructs the jury about the law. The jurors retire to deliberate in secret. Though the details of trial procedure vary from state to state, one factor is constant: The defendant's chances for an acquittal are not good.

Sentencing

Most of the steps of the criminal process are concerned with determining innocence or guilt. In upwards of 90 percent of criminal cases, criminal trials end with convictions. At that point, the members of the courtroom work group strive to help a judge determine what sentence to impose. Indeed, defendants themselves are often more concerned about how many years they will have to spend in prison than about the question of guilt.

The principal decision the judge must make is whether to impose a prison sentence or place the defendant on probation. Fines are rarely used in felony cases. The death penalty is hotly debated but in actuality is limited to only some first-degree murder cases. Prison overcrowding is the dominant reality of contemporary sentencing; roughly 1.7 million inmates are incarcerated in state and federal prisons. Only recently has attention begun to focus on the fact that the political rhetoric of "lock them up and throw away the key" has resulted in severe prison overcrowding, causing policy makers to consider a range of intermediate sanctions that provide alternatives to incarceration.

Appeal

Virtually all defendants found guilty during trial contest their fate, filing an appeal with a higher court in the hope that they will receive a new trial. Contrary to public perceptions, defendants are rarely successful on appeal; fewer than 1 in 10 appellants achieve a victory in the appellate courts, and of those who do, most are reconvicted in a subsequent trial. Moreover, appeals are filed in only a small proportion of all guilty verdicts; defendants who plead guilty rarely appeal.

Appellate court opinions affect future cases because the courts decide policy matters that shape the operation of the entire criminal justice system. The "Case Close-Up" on *Brown v. Mississippi* (1936) illustrates this point.

LAW ON THE BOOKS

The structure of the courts, the legal duties of the main actors, and the steps in the criminal process are all basic to understanding how the courts dispense criminal justice. These elements constitute *law on the books*—the legal and structural components of the judiciary. In essence, the starting point in understanding the legal system is knowing the formal rules.

Law on the books is found in constitutions, laws enacted by legislative bodies, regulations issued by administrative agencies, and cases decided by courts. Little doubt exists that decisions by the U.S. Supreme Court have far-reaching ramifications. To highlight the importance of court decisions, each chapter's Case Close-Up provides an in-depth look at some of the court decisions that have shaped our nation's criminal justice system, such the one below.

These three points exemplify "law on the books." But one need not be an expert in law and justice to know that these terse statements of the law do not account for the way that confessions are obtained by police and used in courts of law, especially when issues like racism, sexism, and homophobia come into play. Such factors can only be accounted for by a "law in action approach" to the study of criminal courts and the people who participate in their operation.

LAW ON THE BOOKS VS. LAW IN ACTION
STEPS IN THE CRIMINAL JUSTICE PROCESS

	LAW ON THE BOOKS	LAW IN ACTION
Crime	Any violation of the criminal law.	People report about 1.25 million violent crimes and 9.1 million property crimes to the police each year.
Arrest	The physical taking into custody of a suspected law violator.	Every year, the police make more than 11 million arrests for nontraffic offenses. Most are for minor crimes, but nearly 1.86 million involve serious crimes.
Initial appearance	The accused is told of the charges, bail is set, and a date for the preliminary hearing is set.	Occurs soon after arrest, which means the judge and lawyers know little about the case.
Bail	Money or property is pledged as a form of guarantee that a released defendant will appear at trial.	Bail is tied to a variety of factors, including some that seemingly have little to do with the case. But whether someone is released on bail has a significant effect on the rest of the case.
Charging decision	Formal criminal charges against the defendant, stating what criminal law was violated.	Between arrest and appearance at the major trial court, half of cases are dropped.
Preliminary hearing or grand jury	Judicial proceedings to determine whether probable cause exists to make the accused stand trial on felony charges.	Cases are rarely dismissed at this stage.
Arraignment	The defendant is informed of the pending charges and is required to enter a plea.	Most defendants plead not guilty at this stage and then later change their pleas as part of a plea bargain.
Discovery	Formal and informal exchange of information before trial.	Prosecutors turn over evidence of guilt in hopes of obtaining a plea of guilty.
Pretrial motions	Defense may seek to have evidence suppressed because it was collected in a way that violates the Constitution.	Suppression motions are rarely granted but are at the heart of a major debate.
Plea negotiations	The defendant pleads guilty with the expectation of receiving some benefit.	About 90 to 95 percent of felony defendants plead guilty.
Trial	A fact-finding process using the adversarial method before a judge or a jury.	Most likely only in serious cases; defendant is likely to be convicted.
Sentencing	Punishment imposed on a defendant found guilty of violating the criminal law.	Seven million persons in prison, on probation, or on parole.
Appeal	Review of the lower-court decision by a higher court.	The overwhelming majority of criminal cases are affirmed on appeal.

CASE CLOSE-UP

BROWN v. MISSISSIPPI

In April 1934, Ed Brown, Henry Shields, and Yank Ellington were indicted for murdering Raymond Stewart. Around 1:00 p.m. on March 30, 1934, Deputy Sheriff Dial discovered the body of Raymond Stewart. Later that evening, Dial and some colleagues went to the home of Yank Ellington and requested Ellington to accompany them to the house of the deceased. Ellington was a poor, uneducated black man who complied with the deputy's request. Once they arrived at Stewart's home, a number of white men accused Ellington of having killed Stewart. When Ellington denied doing so, the group seized him and—with Deputy Dial's participation—hanged him by a rope to the limb of a tree. They let him down before he died, only to hang him again. After they let him down a second time, Ellington still maintained his innocence. So, the group tied him to a tree and whipped him, demanding that he confess. He continued to maintain his innocence. He was finally released and returned home in intense pain.

A day or two later, Deputy Dial, accompanied by another deputy, returned to Ellington's home and arrested him. While en route to the jail in a neighboring county, the two men again severely whipped Ellington, declaring that the whipping would continue until he confessed. To stop his torture, Ellington agreed to confess to whatever statement the deputy dictated. He then did so and was put in jail.

Two other black men, Ed Brown and Henry Shields, were also arrested and taken to the same jail. Deputy Dial, again accompanied by a number of white men (one of whom was also an officer and one of whom was the jailer), came to the jail. They made Brown and Shields strip and then beat their bare backs with a leather strap with buckles on it. As had been done with Ellington, the men made it clear that the beatings would continue unless and until Brown and Shields confessed with all of the details demanded of them. The whippings continued until Brown and Shields adjusted their confessions to match the specific details demanded by their torturers.

After what was later described as a "solemn farce" of a hearing at which the three men's "free and voluntary confessions" were admitted into evidence, the men were tried and convicted of Stewart's death based on their confessions and then sentenced to death.

The three men's cases were appealed to the U.S. Supreme Court, which wrote:

[T]he trial court was fully advised by the undisputed evidence of the way in which the confessions had been procured. The trial court knew that there was no other evidence upon which conviction and sentence could be based. Yet it proceeded to permit conviction and to pronounce sentence. The conviction and sentence were void for want of the essential elements of due process, and the proceeding thus vitiated could be challenged in any appropriate manner. It was challenged before the Supreme Court of the State by the express invocation of the Fourteenth Amendment. That court entertained the challenge, considered the federal question thus presented, but declined to enforce [the defendants'] constitutional right. The court thus denied a federal right fully established and specially set up and claimed, and the judgment must be reversed. (*Brown v. Mississippi*, 1936, p. 287).

Sadly, such brutal tactics were frequently used against criminal suspects prior to the decision in *Brown v. Mississippi*. In fact, the Wickersham Commission, a federal commission set up to investigate police conduct in the early 1930s, used the term *the third degree* to describe police tactics at the time (Penney, 1998, pp. 336–337). They defined the term as "the inflicting of pain, physical or mental, to extract confessions or statements" (Wickersham Commission, 1931, p. 19).

The Commission documented the use of a litany of sadistic practices, including beating with fists, blackjacks, rubber hoses, and telephone books; the use of hot lights;

Continued on next page

Continued from previous page

confinement in airless and fetid rooms; and hanging from windows. The Commission was also concerned with psychologically abusive tactics, such as incommunicado detention, prolonged relay questioning, stripping the suspect of clothing, and the deprivation of sleep and food (Penney, 1998, p. 336).

The Wickersham Commission's report facilitated widespread change in policing in the United States. Not only did the report set in motion many efforts to stop police corruption and brutality (see Skolnick & Fife, 1993), but also it affected the decision making of the U.S. Supreme Court. The Court began citing the Wickersham Commission's report on police brutality in obtaining confessions as evidence that confessions were often involuntary and/or unreliable.

In reversing the defendants' convictions in *Brown v. Mississippi*, the Supreme Court ruled that confessions beaten out of suspects were clearly inadmissible because they were involuntary. The Court did so using the Fourteenth Amendment's guarantee of "due process of law."

As a result, several bedrock principles of contemporary criminal procedure are attributable to the landmark decision in *Brown v. Mississippi*. Specifically:

1. An involuntary statement is considered to be inherently untrustworthy or unreliable, and convictions based on unreliable evidence violate due process.
2. Coercive police practices are a violation of "fundamental fairness," an essential element of due process. Therefore, a confession coerced by the police violates due process, even if that confession is otherwise reliable.
3. Free choice is an essential aspect of due process, and an involuntary confession cannot be the product of a person's free and rational choice.

Finally, note that *Brown v. Mississippi* marked the beginning of the Supreme Court's review of how police obtain confessions and when those confessions may be used as evidence in a court of law—a process that continues today (Chapter 11).

LAW IN ACTION

Law on the books only partially explains how a criminal case unfolds. Although the formal law was certainly important, it cannot totally explain why the jury voted to acquit Casey Anthony. Indeed, technology and media may both have played a role in the case outcome. Nor can law on the books explain why different judges looking at the same facts and reading the same law can reach opposite conclusions.

In many ways, law on the books represents an idealized view of law—one that stresses an abstract set of rules that is so theoretical that it fails to incorporate real people. On the one hand, law on the books provides only an imperfect road map of the day-to-day realities of the courthouse. The concept of law in action, on the other hand, focuses on the human factors governing the actual application of the law. This view stresses the mutual interdependence of courtroom actors and the ways in which

they devote considerable time to processing criminal cases from intake through plea bargaining and determining the appropriate sentence to impose on defendants who are found guilty. Table 1.2 presents a few differences between law on the books and law in action; many others are explored throughout this book.

The law in action perspective also stresses the importance of discretion. At virtually every step of the process a choice has to be made about whether to move the case to the next step or to stop it now. These decisions are made by the legal actors—police, prosecutors, and judges, for example. They are also made by ordinary citizens, whether in their role as victims, witnesses, or jurors.

A wide gap exists between legal theory (law on the books) and how that law is applied (law in action). Although some people find this gap shocking, actually it is not; after all, few, if any, human institutions ever live up to the high ideals set out for them. If you spend five minutes observing a stop sign on a well-traveled street, you will find

TABLE 1.2 ▪ EXAMPLES OF THE DIFFERENCE BETWEEN LAW ON THE BOOKS AND LAW IN ACTION

Law on the Books	Law in Action
The U.S. Constitution guarantees the right to a speedy trial.	The major trial courts of many counties are so backlogged that the median time between arrest and trial varies between 6 and 12 months (see Chapter 10).
The U.S. Constitution guarantees the right to a trial by jury in all criminal prosecutions in which the defendant faces imprisonment for more than 6 months.	Trials occur in fewer than 10% of all criminal cases. The remaining 90% of cases are disposed of through the plea-bargaining process (see Chapter 12).
Every defendant convicted at trial has the right to one appeal.	The overwhelming number of criminal cases are not appealed; of those that are appealed, more than 90% of convictions will be affirmed (see Chapter 16).

© Cengage Learning

that not all cars come to a complete stop, and some do not slow down much at all. Yet at the same time, the stop sign (the law on the books in this example) clearly does affect the behavior of drivers (law in action). The criminal process is filled with numerous detours. At each stage officials decide to advance the defendant's case to the next step, reroute it, or terminate it. The result is that many cases that enter the criminal court process are eliminated during the early stages.

A law in action perspective helps us understand the dynamics of courthouse justice. High caseloads are the reality in courthouses across the nation. As a result, judges are under pressure to move cases lest a backlog develop. Similarly, in most cases the formal rules found in law on the books fail to provide answers to all the questions that arise in a case. As a result, prosecutors must make discretionary choices about matters such as what sentencing recommendation to make to the judge. Finally, cooperation, rather than conflict during trial, often characterizes the behavior of courthouse actors. As a result, defense attorneys often find that negotiating a plea of guilty, rather than going to trial, is in the best interest of their client.

COURTS AND CONTROVERSY

The trial of Casey Anthony illustrates some of the controversies surrounding courts and crime in the United States. The verdict sparked great public outrage that a "baby killer" had gone free. But many experts explained the verdict as a result of lack

of evidence. The prosecution's case rested largely on the circumstantial evidence of Casey Anthony's delay in reporting her daughter missing and partying until being taken into custody. Notably, there was no forensic evidence—such as DNA or fingerprints—directly linking Casey Anthony to Caylee's death.

At the heart of the public's concern about crime has been a debate over the actions and inactions of the criminal courts. What the courts do (and do not do) and how they do it occupies center stage in the nation's continuing focus on crime. Numerous reforms have been suggested, but no agreement has been reached as to what types of change are in order. Throughout this book, the "Courts and Controversy" boxes, such as the one on page 23, highlight many issues being debated by the courts today.

In the public dialogue on the issues facing the criminal courts, conservatives square off against liberals, and hard-liners against those said to be soft on crime. This sort of terminology is not very helpful. Such phrases as "soft on crime" attract our attention to questions about the goals of the criminal courts, but they are not useful for systematic inquiry because they are ambiguous and emotional (Neubauer, 2001).

More constructive in understanding the controversy over the criminal courts are the crime control and due process models developed by Herbert Packer (1968). In an unemotional way, these two models highlight competing values concerning the proper role of the criminal courts. The conservative crime control model proposes to reduce crime by increasing the penalties on criminals. The liberal due

TABLE 1.3 ■ COMPETING VALUES IN THE CRIMINAL JUSTICE SYSTEM

	Crime Control Model	Due Process Model
Key goal	Repression of criminal conduct.	Respect for and protection of individual rights.
Focus	Apprehend, convict, and punish offenders.	Protect the innocent/wrongfully accused; limit governmental power.
Values	Expeditious processing of offenders to achieve justice for victims and society as a whole.	Dignity and autonomy of both the accused and the system are to be preserved.
Mood	Certainty; focuses on factual guilt. Assumes someone arrested and charged is probably guilty. Relies on informal, nonadjudicative fact finding—primarily by police and prosecutors.	Skepticism; focuses on legal guilt. Assumes that someone is innocent until proven guilty beyond a reasonable doubt. Relies on formal, adjudicative, adversarial fact-finding processes.
Goal of courts	Assembly-line justice: Process cases quickly and efficiently to promote finality of convictions.	Obstacle court justice: Presents numerous obstacles to prevent errors and wrongful convictions by ensuring careful consideration of each case.
Attitude toward defendants' rights	Technicalities permit the guilty to go free.	Technicalities prevent abuses of governmental authority to foster freedom in a constitutional democracy.
Sentencing	Punishment deters crime and incapacitates offenders.	Rehabilitation prevents crime.

© Cengage Learning

process model advocates social programs aimed primarily at reducing crime by reducing poverty. Table 1.3 summarizes the two views.

Crime Control Model

The most important value in the **crime control model** is the repression of criminal conduct. Unless crime is controlled, the rights of law-abiding citizens will not be protected and the security of society will be diminished. Conservatives see crime as the product of a breakdown of individual responsibility and self-control. To reinforce social values of discipline and self-control, and to achieve the goal of repressing crime, the courts must process defendants efficiently. They should rapidly remove defendants against whom inadequate evidence exists and quickly determine guilt according to evidence. The crime control model holds that informal fact finding—initially by the police and later by the prosecutor—not only is the best way to determine whether the defendant is in fact guilty but also is sufficiently foolproof to prevent the innocent from being falsely convicted. The crime control model, therefore, stresses the necessity of

speed and finality in the courts to achieve the priority of crime suppression.

According to the crime control model, the courts have hindered effective law enforcement and therefore have produced inadequate protection of society. Advocates of this model are concerned that criminals "beat the system" and "get off easy." In their view, the cure is to eliminate legal loopholes by curtailing the exclusionary rule, abolishing the insanity defense, allowing for preventive detention of dangerous offenders, and increasing the certainty of punishment.

Due Process Model

In contrast, the **due process model** emphasizes protecting the rights of the individual. Its advocates are concerned about lawbreaking; they see the need to protect the public from predatory criminals. At the same time, however, they believe that granting too much leeway to law enforcement officials will only result in the loss of freedom and civil liberties for all Americans. This alternative diagnosis stresses different causes of crime. Liberals see crime not as a product of individual moral failure, but as the result of social influences (Currie, 1985).

In particular, unemployment, racial discrimination, and government policies that work to the disadvantage of the poor are the root causes of crime; only by changing the social environment will crime be reduced (Currie, 1989).

Although adherents of the due process model do not downgrade the need for controlling crime, they believe that single-minded pursuit of such a goal threatens individual rights and poses the threat of a tyrannical government. Thus, the key function of the courts is not the speed and finality projected in the crime control model, but an insistence on careful consideration of each case. The dominant image is one of the courts as an obstacle course. The due process model stresses the possibility of error in the informal fact-finding process and therefore insists on formal fact finding to protect against mistakes made by the police and prosecutors.

Proponents of the due process model believe that the courts' priority should be to protect the rights of the individual. Any resulting decrease in the efficiency of the courts is the price we must pay in a democracy based on individual liberties. The due process model emphasizes the need to reform people through rehabilitation. Community-based sentencing alternatives are considered preferable to the extensive use of prison sentences. Advocates of this approach are concerned that the court system is fundamentally unfair to poor and minority defendants; they therefore support leading court decisions protecting the rights of those accused of crimes.

Shifting the Balance

The U.S. justice system strives to control crime while simultaneously honoring the constitutional rights of the accused. At different stages in our nation's history, we have clearly focused more on the underlying values of one model over the other. Consider that in the first half of the twentieth century, increased urbanization, immigration, and industrialization contributed to an increase in criminal activity. The increase in crime combined with the fears of people from different backgrounds and cultures led to increases in police power, with a focus on "law and order" crime control.

In the 1950s and 1960s, social consciousness began to focus on social equality and equal justice under the law. Part of this new consciousness brought to light abuses of police power. Led by Chief Justice Earl Warren, a former public defender, the U.S. Supreme Court began to "constitutionalize" criminal procedure, with a focus on due process and individual rights and liberties. Since the 1970s, though, and continuing through today, "wars" on crime, drugs, and terrorism have contributed to a renewed emphasis on crime control (see the "Courts, Controversy, & Reducing Crime" feature below). Thus, the pendulum can swing. The law, however (especially constitutional law), helps to provide a certain level of stability even as society places changing levels of value on crime control and due process. Still, as controversies like the war on drugs illustrate, reasonable people can differ as to the proper scope of the law in crime control efforts.

MEDIA DEPICTIONS AND DISTORTIONS OF CRIMINAL COURTS

Most people in the United States learn about the ways in which criminal cases are processed through the courts from the media (Surette, 2010). Sometimes this media coverage takes the form of intensive news coverage, just as it did in Casey Anthony's case. Other times this media coverage comes from dramatized or even completely fictionalized portrayals of criminal trials on television and in the movies. From the perspective of *America's Courts and the Criminal Justice System*, the extensive media attention to law has major advantages. Media coverage of real trials and portrayals of fictitious ones provide dramatic illustrations that the outcome is influenced by the law (law on the books), the actions of people (law in action), and the disagreements that result (law in controversy). The same can be said for police drug busts, prosecutors' decisions to seek the death penalty, defense attorneys cross-examining witnesses, and judges' decisions to admit evidence. But there are disadvantages as well. In trying to dramatize occasionally dull legal proceedings, the media coverage can distort reality (Surette, 2010). This is especially a concern when jurors expect to be dazzled with forensic scientific evidence, as they see on television. Media coverage can provide caricatures, not pictures, of courts and the criminal justice system. Thus, at times, a principal task of a book on courts and the criminal justice system is to encourage readers to "unlearn" what they think they know.

COURTS, CONTROVERSY, & REDUCING CRIME

IS IT TIME TO END THE WAR ON DRUGS?

The association of drugs with social problems begins to explain why the war on drugs enjoys considerable public support. There is no doubt that drug addiction produces untold human suffering in the United States. And there is little doubt that drugs are also associated with crime; indeed, two out of three people arrested by the police show evidence of recent use of illegal drugs (crack, methamphetamines, and marijuana, for example) and/or legal drugs (primarily alcohol).

Public support for the war on drugs is also fueled by its link to controlling marginal groups. Historians suggest that medical or scientific knowledge about the harm of drugs has never played a significant role in formulating U.S. drug policy. Rather, U.S. policy has been driven by the desire to control groups considered to be threats to the existing social order. Thus, the Harrison Narcotics Act of 1914 targeted opium (used by Chinese in California), marijuana (smoked by Mexican-Americans in the Southwest), and cocaine (allegedly being used by African-Americans in the South).

One reason that the war on drugs is difficult to wage is because the focus of the debate is always changing. The administration of George W. Bush made marijuana the major focus of its antidrug efforts partly, it said, because pot is a "gateway" drug—kids try it and then move on to more serious drugs. To law enforcement officials around the nation, though, *meth* (methamphetamine) is America's most dangerous drug (Jefferson, 2005). More recently oxycodone has emerged as a major drug problem. Indeed inappropriately used prescription pain medications like oxycodone kill 15,000 people a year in the United States according to the Centers for Disease Control and Prevention (Gupta, 2011).

After four decades of presidents waging various wars on drugs, these efforts are being pushed out of the public limelight by the "war on terror." Even though the war on drugs is less visible today, arrests and convictions for drugs continue to be one of the main reasons for the swelling prison population.

There appears to be a growing disquiet with the war on drugs. Some criminal justice officials guardedly express reservations about the war on drugs (Lacey, 2011). On the record, an organization called Law Enforcement Against Prohibition (2012) favors ending the war on drugs.

Some scholars have argued that it is time to rethink the war on drugs. In *Drug War Politics: The Price of Denial*, Eva Bertram and her colleagues (1996) argue that despite spending billions of dollars on reducing the supply of drugs and punitive approaches to those who use illegal drugs, the war on drugs is a failure. Failure, however, only convinces the advocates of the war on drugs that greater efforts need to be made.

It is not just the failure to reduce drug supply (or demand) that concerns critics, but also the social impact of these efforts. Some critics, for example, blame U.S. drug policy for destroying inner-city communities by swelling prison populations with the unemployable minority poor (Currie, 1993), while others point out that the race-neutral language of the law merely hides racial meanings (Provine, 2007).

The disagreement over continuing the war on drugs reflects the differences between the crime control and due process models of criminal justice. Three points—focusing on causes, equality, and punishment—are at issue.

- The crime control model begins with the judgment that drug abuse is caused by a breakdown of individual responsibility. The due process model views substance abuse as a disease that needs to be treated.

- According to the crime control model, the solution is punishment. Arrest and conviction will serve as a lesson to the violator and will also deter others. The due process model replies that filling the prisons is costly and ineffective. It is therefore more effective and also less costly to emphasize rehabilitation programs.

- The due process model is very concerned that current drug policies fall unequally on racial minorities. The crime control model counters with seemingly banal indifference: "You do the crime, you serve the time."

Where do you stand on this issue? Why?

The task of thinking critically about how the media both portray and distort the justice system is to focus on the contrasting caricatures offered by fictional treatments. Depending on the dramatic needs of the movie or TV show, the police may be portrayed as diligent or brutal, prosecutors pictured as crusaders of justice or preventers of justice determined to convict the suspect who is easiest to try, judges presented as insightful masters of the system or politically motivated hacks, defense attorneys projected as crusaders for their clients' interests or corrupters of the justice system, and prison guards presented as understanding human beings or brutal sociopaths.

To highlight the importance of media depictions of criminal justice, each chapter of this book focuses on some news, movie, or television depiction of some aspect of the criminal courts, like the one below on the Casey Anthony case.

THE CASEY ANTHONY TRIAL

COURTS, LAW, & MEDIA

In July 2008, Cindy Anthony reported to police in that she had not seen her two-year-old granddaughter, Caylee, for more than month, even though the toddler lived with her, her husband George, and their daughter, Casey (Caylee's mother). Cindy also reported that she had smelled a foul odor, consistent with that of a dead body, in her daughter Casey's car.

Casey Anthony offered a series of suspicious explanations for her daughter's whereabouts. She even told detectives a made-up story about how Caylee had been kidnapped by a fictitious nanny. Casey claimed she had spent more than month looking for her daughter in the wake of the alleged kidnapping, but had been too afraid to notify the police, allegedly fearing what may be done to her daughter if she had told authorities. Yet, during the period of time Caylee was missing, Casey Anthony was photographed scantily clad, grinding on the dance floor of local clubs. She also got a tattoo reading "bella vita" ("beautiful life" in Italian) while Caylee was missing. The police and the general public had a hard time understanding how Casey could engage in such conduct while her daughter was missing. The remains of Caylee's body were eventually found in a wooded area near her family's home in December 2008. Casey Anthony was charged and tried for her daughter's murder.

During a 6-week trial in the summer of 2011, the prosecution argued that Casey Anthony killed her daughter because she wanted her freedom from the responsibilities of caring for a child she never really wanted. The state asserted that that Casey Anthony used chloroform to render her daughter unconscious and then suffocated Caylee by placing duct tape on her mouth and nose. The prosecution further alleged that Casey wrapped Caylee in a Winnie the Pooh blanket and black trash bags, keeping the body in the car's trunk until the odor was too strong and then dumping it in the woods. In contrast, the defense team argued that Caylee had accidentally drowned in the family pool and Casey tried to cover up the accidental death fearing that she would spend the rest of her life in jail for child neglect. After 11 hours of deliberation, the jury convicted Casey Anthony of four misdemeanor counts of lying to police, but acquitted her of first-degree murder, aggravated manslaughter, and aggravated child abuse.

1. Do you think Casey Anthony's behavior is consistent with that of a parent concerned with the whereabouts of a missing child? If so, why? If not, do you think that her behavior is evidence of her guilt in Caylee's death? Explain your reasoning.

2. According to a study conducted by Shelton et al. (2009), 58.3% of prospective jurors expect to see some kind of scientific evidence in every criminal case; 42.1% expect to see DNA evidence in every criminal case; and 56.5% expect to see fingerprint evidence in every criminal case. Expectations for forensic scientific evidence are even higher in murder/attempted murder cases, with 83.3% expecting some kind of forensic evidence, 84.5% expecting fingerprint evidence, and 74.6% expecting DNA evidence. Do you think that the lack of forensic scientific evidence affected the jurors in the Casey Anthony case? Do you expect prosecutors to present forensic scientific evidence in homicide cases? Why or why not?

CONCLUSION

"Why did the defendant do it" is the dominant question the public asks in a murder case, particularly one as bizarre as the death of Caylee Anthony. Alas, trials do not always provide an answer to the question of why, especially when the defendant fails to take the stand in her or his own defense (Turley, 2012). When a defendant, on the advice of counsel, decides not to explain their side of the story, the public often looks to science to answer why. Indeed the prosecution in the Casey Anthony trial introduced over 400 pieces of evidence, but neither the jury nor the public (for seemingly very different reasons) found the truth amid the scientific evidence. In essence, the plot line in the Casey Anthony trial is centuries old. What is new is the public expectation that scientific evidence will provide the answers, but the public seems to have an insatiable appetite for more. And the modern media is able to provide its attentive audience with even more information, always on the lookout for the next trial of the century, even if the question of why the defendant may have committed the crime remains unanswerable.

Ours is a law-drenched age. Voters and elected officials alike see the solution to pressing social problems in terms of passing a law. It seems we are not serious about an issue unless we have a law regulating it, and we are not really serious unless we have criminal laws. But laws are not self-enforcing. Some people delude themselves by thinking that passing a law solves the problem. This is not necessarily so. Indeed, if the problem persists, frustration sets in. Thus, legislatures mandate that drivers purchase automobile insurance, but accident victims become frustrated when they discover the other party has no insurance.

Similarly, judges require defendants to pay restitution, but crime victims discover that impoverished defendants (particularly those in prison) have no ability to pay. In the same vein, conservatives call for preventive detention, but jailers have no jail cells available.

Although most people know something about the law, they also "know" much that is contrary to fact. Some of these public understandings and misunderstandings about law are the product of education. High-school-level American government and history textbooks, for example, offer a simplified, formal picture of law and the courts, lawyers, and trials. Americans also learn about the legal system by going to the movies, watching television, and reading fiction. At times, people who rely on these sources are badly misled. Entertainment programs misrepresent the nature and amount of crime in the United States. Because murder makes a much better show than embezzlement or burglary, entertainment media rarely show street crime other than drug offenses.

Television also offers a number of false or doubtful propositions. It tells us, for example, that criminals are white males between the ages of 20 and 50, that bad guys are usually businesspeople or professional criminals, and that crime is almost always unsuccessful in the end. Television and film also often misrepresent the roles of the actors in the legal system. For example, with few exceptions, police are in constant action, chasing crooks in cars, running after them on foot, and capturing them only after exchanging gunfire. In addition, entertainment media distort important issues of civil liberties. As soon as we know who did it and that the guilty crook has been apprehended, the case is solved, with no need for the prosecutor to prove the defendant guilty. These understandings and misunderstandings form the backdrop for this book.

Chapter Review

LO1 **1.** Describe how the courts are related to the other components of the criminal justice system.

Law enforcement, courts, and corrections are separate sets of organizations, but they are also interdependent. The courts process cases after suspects are arrested, and corrections handles defendants who are found guilty by the courts.

LO2 **2.** Discuss the major types of courts found in the United States.

In the United States, separate systems of federal courts and state courts exist. Within each system one or two levels of trial courts and one or two levels of appellate courts hear cases.

LO3 **3.** Identify the most important actors in the courthouse.

Judges, prosecutors, and defense attorneys are the most important actors in the courthouse. Defendants and victims are also important because they are the source of cases for the courts.

LO4 **4.** List the steps in a typical felony prosecution.

A typical felony prosecution begins with an arrest, followed by an initial appearance, the setting of bail, and either grand jury proceedings or a preliminary hearing. If a case survives these hurdles, it proceeds to a formal arraignment, after which decisions about evidence discovery, pretrial motions, and plea negotiations may occur. Cases that

are not resolved by plea bargain go to trial. Those convicted at trial are then sentenced and have the right to file an appeal.

LO5 **5.** Explain how a law in action perspective complements a law on the books approach to studying the criminal courts.

The law on the books approach to studying the criminal courts stresses the importance of examining the formal law and how courts interpret that law. The law in action approach is complementary because it stresses the importance of discretion throughout a criminal prosecution.

LO6 **6.** Distinguish between the crime control model of criminal justice and the due process model of criminal justice.

The crime control model emphasizes the need to repress crime and efficiently process the large number of guilty defendants. The due process model of criminal justice emphasizes the importance of protecting the rights of citizens and providing careful consideration for each case.

Critical Thinking Questions

1. On a sheet of paper, apply the general overview of court structure in the United States (Figure 1.2) to your local community.

2. On a sheet of paper, apply the list of actors in the courthouse (Table 1.1) to your local community. If you live in a rural area, how does your list differ from that of someone who lives in a larger community? If you live in a large metropolitan area, how does your list differ from that of someone living in a more rural area?

3. What private, nongovernmental organizations are important to the criminal justice system of your community?

4. Use newspapers, radio, and criminal justice discussion lists or chat groups to monitor discussions concerning the criminal justice system. Do citizens make distinctions among police, courts, and corrections, or do they lump everything under the general rubric of the criminal justice system?

Key Terms

crime control model 19

criminal justice system 6

CSI effect 5

due process model 19

felonies 12

misdemeanors 12

Web Resources

Go to the *America's Courts and the Criminal Justice System* companion website at
http://www.cengage.com/criminaljustice/neubauer,
where you will find more resources to help you study.
Resources include web exercises, quizzing, and flash cards.

For Further Reading

Bogira, Steve. *Courtroom 302*. New York: Vintage, 2005.

Dixon, Jo, Aaron Kupchik, and Joachim Savelsberg (Eds.). *Criminal Courts*. Surrey, United Kingdom, 2006.

Dombrink, John, and Daniel Hillyard. *Sin No More: From Abortion to Stem Cells, Understanding Crime, Law, and Morality in America*. New York: NYU Press, 2008.

Ferdico, John, Henry F. Fradella, and Christopher Totten. *Criminal Procedure for the Criminal Justice Professional*. 11th ed. Belmont, CA: Wadsworth, 2012.

Fox, Richard, Robert Van Sickel, and Thomas Steiger. *Tabloid Justice: Criminal Justice in an Age of Media Frenzy*. 2nd ed. Boulder, CO: Lynne Rienner, 2007.

Garland, David. *The Culture of Control: Crime and Social Order in Contemporary Society*. Chicago: University of Chicago Press, 2002.

Gardner, Thomas, and Terry Anderson. *Criminal Law*. 10th ed. Belmont, CA: Wadsworth, 2009.

Kappeler, Victor, and Gary Potter. *The Mythology of Crime and Justice*. 4th ed. Prospect Heights, IL: Waveland Press, 2004.

Marion, Nancy. *A Primer in the Politics of Criminal Justice*. 2nd ed. Monsey, NY: Criminal Justice Press, 2007.

Neubauer, David. *Debating Crime: Rhetoric and Reality*. Belmont, CA: Wadsworth, 2001.

Neubauer, David, and Stephen Meinhold. *Judicial Process: Law, Courts, and Politics in the United States*. 5th ed. Belmont, CA: Wadsworth, 2010.

Owen, Stephen S., Henry F. Fradella, Tod W. Burke, & Jerry Joplin, 2011. *The Foundations of Criminal Justice*. New York, NY: Oxford University Press.

Shelton, Donald E., Young S. Kim, and Gregg Barak. 2009. "An Indirect-Effects Model of Mediated Adjudication: The CSI Myth, the Tech Effect, and Metropolitan Jurors' Expectations for Scientific Evidence." *Vanderbilt Journal of Entertainment and Technology Law*, 12(1), 1-43.

Unnever, James, Francis Cullen, and Bonnie Fisher. "'A Liberal Is Someone Who Has Not Been Mugged': Criminal Victimization and Political Beliefs." *Justice Quarterly* 24: 309–334, 2007.

2 Law and Crime

This 2011 file photo provided by the Pima County Sheriff's Office shows **Jared Lee Loughner**, the man charged with multiple counts of murder and attempted murder for a shooting rampage in Tucson, Arizona. Loughner was taken into custody shortly after the shooting and hospitalized as mental health professionals attempted to restore his competency to stand trial through the forced administration of anti-psychotic drugs. ■

POOL New/ REUTERS

THE BASIS OF LAW

THE COMMON LAW HERITAGE
Judge-Made Law
Precedent
Multiple Sources of Law

THE ADVERSARY SYSTEM
Safeguards
Presumptions and Inferences
Burdens of Proof

Courts, Law, & Media
Chicago (2002)

THE RIGHTS OF THE ACCUSED
Due Process
Bill of Rights

CIVIL LAW OVERVIEW
Types of Civil Disputes
Civil Remedies
Using Civil Remedies to Fight Crime

Courts, Controversy, & Reducing Crime
Should Asset Forfeiture Be Limited?

Law in Controversy: The Incivility of Civil Justice
Civil Liability of Criminal Justice Officials

CRIMINAL LAW OVERVIEW
Elements of a Crime
Defining Crimes
Criminal Defenses

CASE CLOSE-UP: *United States v. Loughner*

Delinquency

EFFECTS OF CRIMINAL LAW ON THE COURTS
Criminal Law and Inconsistencies
Criminal Law and Plea Bargaining
Criminal Law and Sentencing

Law and Crime • Law and Crime • Law and Crime • Law
Crime • Law and Crime • Law and Crime • Law and Crime

Learning Objectives

After reading this chapter, you should be able to:

LO1 List the four key elements defining law.

LO2 Identify the three key characteristics of common law.

LO3 Explain the importance of the adversary system.

LO4 Name the four amendments of the Bill of Rights that deal specifically with criminal procedure.

LO5 List five major areas of civil law.

LO6 Identify the major elements of a crime.

LO7 Identify some of the most important legal defenses in American law.

LO8 Discuss the effects of the criminal law on courts.

On January 8, 2011, Jared Loughner opened fire at a Safeway grocery store, killing six people—including a federal judge, and injuring 13 others, including a member of Congress. At first, the nation responded with rage over the incident, with some blaming access to guns and others pointing the finger at the inflammatory tone of political rhetoric in the United States that may have contributed to Loughner targeting Democratic U.S. Representative Gabrielle Giffords. But as the weeks went by, a much more nuanced and arguably disturbing image emerged of a seemingly ordinary boy who had slowly descended into the depths of a serious psychotic illness.

Loughner had dropped out of high school before his senior year. He began to self-medicate using alcohol and marijuana. He began to speak in random jumbles of words. He grew paranoid that the government was trying to control him. His ability to function deteriorated so badly that he was unable to maintain his jobs working in a sandwich shop and at a local animal shelter. And his bizarre behavior at a local community college led faculty and fellow students to fear him. Indeed, according to some news reports from interviews with former classmates, Loughner even made comments about terrorism and laughed about killing babies. His frequent classroom and library disruptions led Pima Community College to suspend Loughner until such time as mental health professionals documented that he was not a danger to himself or to others. But by that point, Loughner's mental function had declined significantly. He lived each day in a paranoid and delusional world that was a product of schizophrenia. Just before the shootings, friends noticed that he had significantly changed from the person they once knew.

After the Tucson-based shooting, Loughner was taken into custody. He was subsequently declared incompetent to stand trial. But after more than a year of forced administration of antipsychotic medications, Loughner was found competent to stand trial and he entered a plea of guilty. In doing so, he avoided a possible death sentence if he had been convicted at trial. That conviction would have turned on whether Loughner was legally insane. Insanity is a rare, complex, and controversial criminal defense that raises issues about criminal law, defenses, and the propriety of punishment that will be explored in more detail in this chapter.

This chapter begins by providing a working definition of law, then examines our common law heritage, including the adversary system and the rights of the accused. Next, the discussion shifts from procedure to substance. After looking at differences between civil law and criminal law, we will concentrate on the elements of a crime and legal defenses. The chapter concludes with a discussion of the consequences of criminal law for the criminal court process.

THE BASIS OF LAW

The basis of law can be summarized in two words: human conflict. A controversy over how much money is owed, a quarrel between husband and wife, a collision at an intersection, and the theft of a television set are a few examples of the great number of disputes that arise and threaten to disrupt the normal activities of society. Business and everyday activities depend on mechanisms for mediating inevitable human conflicts. Without such mechanisms, individual parties might seek private, violent means of settlement. The legendary feud between the Hatfields and the McCoys illustrates the disruptiveness of blood feuds motivated by revenge—not only in the lives of the individual parties directly involved but also in the larger society.

Law is an everyday word, but as Professor Lawrence Friedman (1984, p. 2) suggests, "It is a word of many meanings, as slippery as glass, as elusive as a soap bubble." Although there are various approaches to defining the term, most scholars define **law** as a body of rules enacted by public officials in a legitimate manner and backed by the force of the state (Neubauer & Meinhold, 2013). This definition can

be broken into four phrases, and each has important implications for how we think about law.

The first element—law is a body of rules—is self-evident. What is not immediately obvious, however, is the fact that these rules and regulations are found in a variety of sources, such as statutes, constitutions, court decisions, and administrative regulations.

The second element—law is enacted by public officials—is of critical importance. All organizations of any size or complexity have rules and regulations that govern their members. But these private rules are not law under our definition unless they are recognized by public officials—judges, legislators, and executives in particular.

The third element—law is enacted in a legitimate manner—means that it must be agreed upon ahead of time how the rules will be changed. Thus, legislatures have methods for passing new laws, bureaucrats have procedures for applying those laws, and judges follow a well-known process in interpreting those laws.

The final element—law is backed by the force of the state—says that these rules and regulations would be largely meaningless without sanctions. Thus, what differentiates law from other societal rules is that law has teeth to it—namely, the consequences of legal sanctions. As Daniel Oran's *Law Dictionary for Nonlawyers* (2000) puts it, law is "that which must be obeyed." In most instances, though, it is not necessary to apply legal sanctions, because the threat is enough to keep most people abiding by the law most of the time.

It is also important to stress what this working definition of law omits—namely, any mention of justice. In a representative democracy, public perceptions of law embody fundamental notions of justice, fairness, and decency. It is the potential linking of law and justice (in the form of unjust laws) that also makes law so difficult to define. But law and morality do not necessarily equate. Our working definition of law deliberately excludes any reference to justice because there is no precise legal or scientific meaning for that term. Furthermore, people use the term *justice* to support particular political and social goals. In the public arena, it is a catchall term used in several different ways (see Owen, Fradella, Burke, & Joplin, 2012). As discussed in Chapter 1, backers of the crime control model see justice differently than do supporters of the due process model.

THE COMMON LAW HERITAGE

The legal systems of the United States and other English-speaking nations that were once British colonies (including Australia, New Zealand, and Canada) trace their origins to England and its so-called **common law**. The common law first appeared in medieval England after the Norman conquest in 1066. The new rulers gradually introduced central government administration, including the establishment of courts of law. Initially, the bulk of the law was local and was administered in local courts. A distinct body of national law began to develop during the reign of Henry II (1154–1189), who was successful in expanding the jurisdiction of the royal courts. The king's courts applied the common customs of the entire realm rather than the parochial traditions of a particular village. Thus, the term *common law* meant "general law" as opposed to "special law"; it was the law common to the entire land.

Common law is used in many English-speaking nations, including England, Australia, New Zealand, Canada, and the United States. Because the common law of England forms the basis of law in all U.S. states other than Louisiana (which derives its civil law from the Napoleonic Code and the Continental legal heritage; the state's criminal law, however, derives from the common law), U.S. law is sometimes referred to as **Anglo-American law**.

During the development of the common law legal system, a distinctive way of interpreting the law gradually emerged. Three key characteristics of this common law heritage stand out: The law was judge-made, based on precedent, and found in multiple sources.

Judge-Made Law

One key characteristic of the common law is that it was predominantly **judge-made law** (rather than legislatively enacted). Until the late 19th century, no important body of statutory law existed in either England or the United States. Rather, judges organized social relationships through law. In the field of civil law, for example, the common law courts developed the rights and obligations of citizens in such important areas as property, contracts, and torts. Even today, American law in these areas is predominantly judge-made.

Similarly, in the field of criminal law, by the 1600s the English common law courts had defined felonies such as murder, arson, robbery, larceny, and rape. Moreover, the legal defenses of insanity and self-defense had also entered the common law. These English criminal law concepts were transplanted to America by the colonists. After the Revolution, common law crimes considered applicable to local conditions were retained. Although legislative bodies, not the courts, now define crimes, contemporary statutory definitions often reflect their common law heritage.

Precedent

A second key characteristic of the common law is the use of **precedent**, often referred to as *stare decisis* ("let the decision stand"). The doctrine of precedent requires a judge to decide a case by applying the rule of law found in previous cases, provided the facts in the current case are similar to the facts in the previous cases. By following previous court decisions, the legal system promotes the twin goals of fairness and consistency. Exhibit 2.1 gives an example of the precedent-based citation system used in American law. For insight into the legal reasoning processes that judges use when applying precedent, see Appendix D.

The common law's reliance on precedent reflects a cautious approach to problem solving. Rather than writing a decision attempting to solve the entire range of a given legal problem, common law courts decide only as much of the case as is necessary to resolve the individual dispute. Broad rules and policy directives emerge only through the accumulation of court decisions over time. Unfortunately, many Americans make the mistake of translating the common law heritage, particularly the doctrine of precedent, into a static view of the courts and the law. The entire history of Anglo-American law emphasizes the importance of common law courts' shaping old law to new demands. In the words of Justice Oliver Wendell Holmes (1920, p. 187): "It is revolting to have no better reason for a rule of law than that it was so laid down in the times of Henry IV. It is still more revolting if the grounds upon which it was laid down have vanished long since, and the rule simply persists from blind imitation of the past."

Exhibit 2.1 HOW TO READ LEGAL CITATIONS

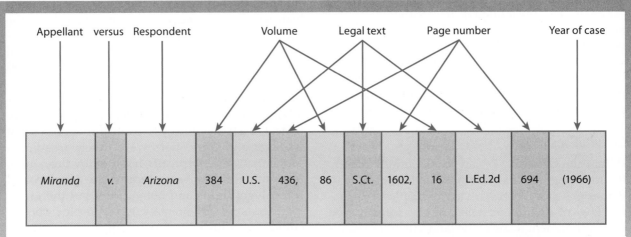

When first confronted with legal citations, students are often bewildered by the array of numbers. But with a few basics in mind, these citations need not be confusing; they are efficient aids in finding court decisions.

The full citation for *Miranda* is as follows: *Miranda v. Arizona*, 384 U.S. 436, 86 S.Ct. 1602, 16 L.Ed.2d 694 (1966). The lead name in the case usually refers to the party who lost in the lower court and is seeking to overturn that decision. That party is called the "appellant." The second name refers to the party (or parties) who won at the lower level (in this instance, the state of Arizona). The second party is called the "appellee," or more simply, the "respondent." Miranda is the appellant who is seeking to overturn his conviction. The state of Arizona is named as the respondent because criminal prosecutions are brought in the name of the state.

After the names of the parties come three sets of references. All decisions of the U.S. Supreme Court are reported in the *Supreme Court Reports*, which is published by the U.S. Government Printing Office. It is the official reporting system and is abbreviated U.S. In addition, decisions of the Supreme Court are reported in two private reporting systems: the *Supreme Court Reporter*, which is abbreviated S.Ct., and in *Lawyers Supreme Court Reports, Lawyers Edition*, which is abbreviated L.Ed.2d. The numbers preceding the abbreviation for the volume refer to the volume number. Thus, *Miranda* can be found in volume 384 of the *Supreme Court Reports*. The number after the abbreviation refers to the page number. Thus, the *Miranda* decision in volume 384 begins on page 436; in volume 86 of the *Supreme Court Reporter*, it is on page 1602. A library usually carries only one of the reporting systems, so the multiple references make it easy to locate the given case, no matter which of the three reporting systems is available. The final number in parentheses is the year of the case.

Decisions of other appellate courts at both the federal and state levels are reported in a similar manner in other volumes.

One way courts achieve flexibility is in adapting old rights to new problems. Another is the ability of courts to distinguish between precedents. Recall that the doctrine of precedent involves previous cases with a similar set of facts. Courts sometimes state that the present facts differ from those on which previous decisions were based and reach a different ruling. Finally, judges will occasionally (but very reluctantly) overturn a previous decision by stating that the previous court opinion was wrong. However, the common law is committed to gradual change to maintain stability; it is often said that the law and the courts are conservative institutions.

Multiple Sources of Law

The third key characteristic of the common law is that it is found in multiple sources (a concept sometimes expressed as "uncodified"). In deciding the legal meaning of a given crime (murder, for example), it is not sufficient to look only at the legislative act. One must also know how the courts have interpreted the statute. Depending on the issue, the applicable rules of law may be found in constitutions, statutes, administrative regulations, or court decisions.

Constitutions

Within the hierarchy of law, constitutions occupy the top rung. A **constitution** is the first document that establishes the underlying principles and general laws of a nation or state. The U.S. Constitution is the fundamental law of the land. All other laws—federal, state, and local—are secondary. Similarly, each state has a constitution that is the "supreme law of the state." State courts may use the state constitution to invalidate the actions of legislators, governors, or administrators.

Constitutions define the powers that each branch of government may exercise. For example, Article III of the U.S. Constitution creates the federal judiciary (see Chapter 3). Constitutions also limit governmental power. Some limitations take the form of prohibitions. Thus, Article I, Section 9, states, "The privilege of the Writ of *Habeas Corpus* shall not be suspended." Other limitations take the form of specific rights granted to citizens. The clearest example is the first 10 amendments to the U.S. Constitution, known collectively as the Bill of Rights. For example, the First Amendment begins, "Congress shall make no law respecting an establishment of religion, or prohibiting the free exercise thereof." State constitutions also contain bills of rights, many of which are modeled after their national counterpart.

Constitutions also specify how government officials will be selected. The U.S. Constitution provides that federal judges shall be nominated by the president, confirmed by the Senate, and serve during "good behavior." Similarly, state constitutions specify that state judges will be selected by election, appointment, or merit (see Chapter 8).

Statutes

The second rung of law consists of **statutes**. Laws enacted by federal and state legislatures are usually referred to as "statutory law." A statutory law enacted by a local unit of government is commonly called a **municipal ordinance**.

Until the latter part of the 19th century, American legislatures played a secondary role in the formulation of law. It was not until the 20th century that state legislatures became the principal source of law (Friedman, 1984). A fundamental reason for the growing importance of legislatively enacted statutes was that rapidly industrializing society was faced with new types of problems. Questions of how to protect the interests of workers and consumers were much broader in scope than those typically handled by the courts. The common law took decades to develop and refine legal rights and obligations, but the growing needs of an increasingly complex society could not afford the luxury of such a lengthy time frame. Legislators could enact rules of law that were not only much broader in scope than those adopted by judges but also were more precise and detailed. Thus, a great deal of law today is statutory.

Administrative Regulations

The third rung of American law consists of **administrative regulations**. Legislative bodies delegate rule-making authority to a host of governmental bureaucracies called by various names, such as agencies, boards, bureaus, commissions, and departments. All levels of government—federal, state, and local—authorize administrative agencies to issue specific rules and regulations consistent with the general principles specified in a statute or municipal ordinance. The Internal Revenue Service, by rule, decides what constitutes a legitimate deduction. State boards, by rule, set standards for nursing homes. Local zoning boards, by rule, decide where restaurants may be built.

Administrative regulations are the newest, fastest growing, and least understood source of law. The rules and regulations promulgated by government agencies are extensive. The federal bureaucracy alone issues thousands of pages of new rules and policy statements each year. These extensive regulations promulgated by government agencies must often be interpreted by courts.

Judge-Made Law

Court decisions remain an important source of law. According to the common law tradition, courts do not make law, they merely find it. But this myth, convenient as it was for earlier generations, cannot mask the fact that courts do make law. This tradition, though, suggests a basic difference between legislative and judicial bodies. Legislative bodies are free to pass laws boldly and openly. Moreover, their prescription of the rules is general and all-encompassing. Courts make law more timidly, on a piece-by-piece basis, and operate much more narrowly.

Although American law today is primarily statutory and administrative, vestiges of judge-made law persist. The law governing personal injury remains principally judge-made, as do procedural matters such as rules of evidence. The major influence of case law (another term for court decisions), however, is seen in interpreting the law of other sources. The Constitution is a remarkably short document—some 4,300 words—and it is full of generalizations such as "due process of law," "equal protection of the laws," and "unreasonable searches and seizures." The Founders left later generations to flesh out the operating details of government. Supreme Court decisions have been primarily responsible for adapting constitutional provisions to changing circumstances. Through an extensive body of case law, the Court has applied specific meaning to these vague phrases. (See Appendix D for more information on judge-made law.)

Judge-made case law is vital in determining the meaning of other sources of law as well. Statutes, for example, address the future in general and flexible language. The interpretations that courts provide can either expand or contract the statute's meaning. No lawyer is comfortable with his or her interpretation of an alleged violation of the criminal law without first checking to see how the courts have interpreted it.

THE ADVERSARY SYSTEM

Law is both substantive and procedural. **Substantive law** creates legal obligations. Tort, contract, and domestic relations are examples of substantive civil law. Murder, robbery, and burglary are examples of substantive criminal law. **Procedural law**, on the other hand, establishes the methods of enforcing these legal obligations. Trials are the best-known aspect of American procedural law, but trials do not exist alone. Before trial there must be orderly ways to start, conduct, and end lawsuits. An important aspect of procedural law centers on the roles lawyers and judges play in the legal process.

In many nations, criminal investigations are conducted by a single government official whose function is to establish a unified version of what happened, seeking out facts that show the defendant's guilt as well as those that indicate his or her innocence. The Anglo-American legal system rejects such an approach. Its guiding premise is that a battle between two opposing parties will uncover more of the truth than would a single official, no matter how industrious and well-meaning. Under the **adversary system**, the burden is on the prosecutor to prove the defendant guilty beyond a reasonable doubt, and the defense attorney is responsible for arguing for the client's innocence and asserting legal protections. The judge serves as a neutral arbitrator who stands above the fight as a disinterested party, ensuring that each side battles within the established rules. Finally, the decision is entrusted to the jury (although, in some instances, a judge alone may decide).

Safeguards

The guiding assumption of the adversary system is that two parties, approaching the facts from entirely different perspectives, will uncover more of the truth than would a single investigator, no matter how industrious and objective. Through cross-examination, each side has the opportunity to probe for possible biases in witnesses and to test what witnesses actually know, not what they think they know. The right to cross-examination is protected by the Sixth Amendment: "In all criminal prosecutions, the accused shall enjoy the right . . . to be confronted with witnesses against him."

By putting power in the hands of several different parties, the adversary system creates another type of safeguard. Each actor is granted limited powers, and each has limited powers to counteract the others. If the judge is biased or unfair, the jury has the ability to disregard the judge and reach a fair verdict; if the judge believes the jury has acted improperly, he or she may set aside the jury's verdict and order a new trial. This diffusion of powers in the adversary system incorporates a series of checks and balances aimed at curbing political misuse of the criminal courts.

In diffusing power, the adversary system provides a third safeguard: It charges a specific actor—the defense attorney—with asserting the rights of the accused. Defense attorneys search out potential violations of the rights of the accused. They function as perpetual challengers in the criminal court process and are ready at every juncture to confront the government by insisting that the proper procedures be followed.

Presumptions and Inferences

All trials are governed by both rules of procedure and rules of evidence. One of the foundations of evidence law is that the trier-of-fact must have an evidentiary starting place at the outset of a trial. In a criminal trial, that starting place usually involves two presumptions. A **presumption** is a conclusion or deduction that the law requires the trier-of-fact to make in the absence of evidence to the contrary. In contrast, **inferences** are permissive; they are conclusions or deductions the trier-of-fact may reasonably make based on the facts that have been established by the evidence, but the trier-of-fact is not required to do so.

The two presumptions with which criminal trials start are the presumption of sanity and the presumption of innocence. The **presumption of sanity** requires that all defendants be presumed sane unless sufficient evidence of their insanity is proven, usually by clear and convincing evidence (see the Case Close-Up on Jared Loughner later in this chapter). Recall from the discussion of the Casey Anthony case in Chapter 1 that the **presumption of innocence** requires the trier-of-fact to accept that the defendant is innocent unless the prosecution meets its burden to prove that the defendant is guilty beyond a reasonable doubt—a level of proof explored in greater detail in the next section.

Burdens of Proof

The concept of the "burden of proof" actually encompasses two separate burdens: the burden of production and the burden of persuasion.

If a party has the **burden of production** (often referred to as the burden of going forward), he or she must produce evidence to put facts in issue. The **burden of persuasion**, more commonly called the "burden of proof," is the obligation of a party to prove a fact to a certain level, either beyond a reasonable doubt, by a preponderance of the evidence, or by clear and convincing evidence. The various levels of proof used in evaluating whether the burden of persuasion has been met are depicted in Table 2.1. The burden of persuasion comes into play after all the evidence is produced, when it is time for the judge to decide the ultimate issue in a bench trial or time to instruct the jury. The prosecution always bears the burden in persuading the trier-of-fact that the defendant committed each and every element of all crimes charged. In some circumstances, however, the defendant in a criminal trial bears the burden of persuasion to prove a certain defense, such as insanity. When the defendant bears the burden of persuasion to prove a defense, it is called an **affirmative defense**.

At the low end of the scale, there is no proof. Just above that, there is what the law calls "mere suspicion"—a hunch or an intuition. Although intuitively knowing something is undoubtedly a skill that serves law enforcement officers well, mere suspicion is insufficient proof of any fact in a court of law.

The next level up from mere suspicion is **reasonable, articulable suspicion**. This differs from mere suspicion only slightly, but in an important way. Instead of just having a hunch or an intuitive feeling, a person can articulate the reasons why he or she is suspicious. Moreover, the explanations offered as the bases for the suspicion are objectively reasonable—clearly understandable to another person who hears the explanations. This level of proof is necessary for law enforcement personnel to conduct a "stop and frisk." These brief, limited, investigative detentions are also known as "Terry stops" as a result of the U.S. Supreme Court's landmark decision in *Terry v. Ohio* (1968).

The next highest level of proof is called **probable cause**. Defining probable cause is no easy task. It is differentiated from reasonable, articulable suspicion by the existence of facts—independently verifiable factual information that supports the

TABLE 2.1 ▪ LEVELS OF PROOF

No Proof	Mere Suspicion	Articulable Reasonable Suspicion	Probable Cause	Preponderance of the Evidence	Clear and Convincing Evidence	Beyond a Reasonable Doubt	Beyond All Doubt
	A "hunch" serves law enforcement officers well, but is insufficient proof in any stage in the judicial process.	Standard established in *Terry v. Ohio* for a "stop and frisk"—a limited investigative detention.	Necessary to arrest a person, conduct a search, or seize evidence.	Plaintiff's burden in most civil cases; burden for establishing "knowing, intelligent, and voluntary" waivers of most constitutional rights; burden for establishing exceptions to the exclusionary rule.	Plaintiff's burden in some civil cases; defendant's burden for proving insanity; government's burden to civilly commit a dangerous person.	Prosecution's burden to prove each element of a criminal offense	Proof to an absolute certainty is not required in any phase of the judicial process in the United States.

SOURCE: John Ferdico, Henry F. Fradella, and Christopher Totten. *Criminal Procedure for the Criminal Justice Professional.* 11th ed. Belmont, CA: Wadsworth, 2012.

conclusion that there is a "fair probability" that a crime occurred or that a particular person was involved in a crime.

In most civil cases, the standard of proof is a **preponderance of the evidence**—commonly understood as proof that something is more likely than not. Thus, if the plaintiff is able to show that the probability is more than 50 percent that the defendant did what is claimed, the judgment will be for the plaintiff. It is also the standard of proof used to establish the validity of waivers of constitutional rights, as well as the burden for proving that exceptions to the exclusionary rule apply (see Chapter 11).

Clear and convincing evidence is a higher level of proof than the preponderance of the evidence standard, yet it falls short of proof beyond a reasonable doubt. It is the standard of proof in some civil cases. It is also the level of proof to which a defendant in some criminal cases must establish an affirmative defense such as insanity. If there is clear and convincing evidence, the trier-of-fact should be reasonably satisfied as to the existence of the fact, yet they may have some doubts.

One of the most fundamental protections recognized in the American criminal justice process is the presumption of innocence. The state has the burden of proving all the elements of the crime(s) charged **beyond a reasonable doubt**; defendants are not required to prove themselves innocent. If the prosecution fails to meet this burden of proof on any element of a crime, the defendant must be acquitted (*In re Winship*, 1970). A specific definition for the "beyond a reasonable doubt" standard has not been adopted by the U.S. Supreme Court, leading to some confusion among jurists and jurors alike. In fact, jury instructions explaining reasonable doubt are often the basis for appeal. It is sufficient to say that proof beyond a reasonable doubt requires that the guilt of the defendant be established to a reasonable, but not absolute or mathematical, certainty. Probability of guilt is not enough. In other words, to satisfy the standard of "beyond a reasonable doubt," the jury must be satisfied that the charges against the defendant are almost certainly true. A challenged definition of beyond a reasonable doubt that was upheld by the U.S. Supreme Court reads as follows: "A reasonable doubt is an actual and substantial doubt arising from the evidence, from the facts or circumstances shown by the evidence, or from the lack of evidence" (*Victor v. Nebraska*, 1994, p. 18). Keep in mind that reasonable doubt is an inherently qualitative concept; it cannot be quantified, and any attempt to do so for a jury is likely to result in reversible error (see Chapter 13).

COURTS, LAW, & MEDIA

CHICAGO (2002)

In an effort to remake the image of his client Roxy Hart (played by Renee Zellweger), lawyer Billy Flynn (played by Richard Gere) holds a press conference. He starts by calling on Mary Sunshine, an obviously friendly reporter who poses a predictably softball question: "Do you have any advice for young girls seeking to avoid a life of jazz and drink?" "Absolutely," Flynn responds. "Mrs. Hart feels it was the tragic combination of liquor and jazz which led to the downfall." And then he launches into a song called the "Press Conference Rag," intended to influence how his client's story gets told.

The film *Chicago* (2002), based on the musical of the same name, is set during the Roaring Twenties, when jazz, illegal liquor, sin, and the city of Chicago seemed synonymous. What is somewhat unusual is that it focuses on women killing men, a topic not typically portrayed in works of fiction. What is not unusual, however, is how lawyers try to manipulate the press to influence judges and juries. From the nation's beginning, defendants have hired lawyers to improve their public standing, hoping that it will translate into favorable treatment by the criminal justice system.

The fictional, media-savvy Billy Flynn uses the press in an effort to complete an extreme makeover of his client Roxy Hart, who suffered from very serious image problems. (She murdered her lover and then tried to have her husband take the fall.) Real-life celebrity lawyers, such as Mark Geragos, use similar strategies for clients such as Michael Jackson and Scott Peterson, who also need extreme makeovers of their public images. The late pop star Michael Jackson was charged with sexually molesting several young boys and then paying their families in a cover-up. Scott Peterson was accused of murdering his pregnant wife and unborn child and then concocting an elaborate cover-up story.

Formal press conferences and informal news leaks played key roles during the prosecutions of Peterson and Jackson. In an earlier era, lawyers often preferred to keep their clients and their legal woes out of the public eye. But today many lawyers seem to delight in calling public attention to their clients and their legal peccadilloes. Not surprisingly, high-profile lawyers are accused of playing to the cameras (and reporters) both inside and outside the courtroom. Indeed, an assistant

THE RIGHTS OF THE ACCUSED

Procedural law in the United States places a heavy emphasis on protecting the individual rights of each citizen. A key feature of a democracy is the insistence that the prevention and control of crime be accomplished within the framework of law. The criminal process embodies some of society's most severe sanctions: detention before trial, confinement in prison after conviction, and, in certain limited situations, execution of the offender. Because the powers of the criminal courts are so great, there is concern that those powers might be abused or misapplied.

Restrictions on the use and application of government power take the form of rights granted to the accused. One of the most fundamental protections is the right to remain silent. Another is the right to a trial by jury. These protections exist not to free the guilty but to protect the innocent (see Table 2.2). Basing the criminal justice process on the necessity of protecting individual liberties (of the innocent and guilty alike) obviously reduces he effectiveness of that process in fighting crime. To ensure that innocent persons are not found guilty, Anglo-American criminal law pays the price of freeing some of the guilty.

The primary justification for providing constitutional safeguards for those caught in the net of the criminal process is to ensure that innocent persons are not harassed or wrongly convicted. The American legal system is premised on a distrust of human fact finding. The possibility of wrongly convicting an innocent person arises when honest mistakes are made by honorable people. But it also arises when dishonorable officials use the criminal district attorney suggested, "It looks like Geragos is trying to manipulate the media and the jury and he's been pretty good at it" (CBS News, 2004). At times, though, such complaints are little more than sour grapes; after all, police and prosecutors regularly use the media to project a negative image of defendants.

Trials are an obvious source of interest for journalists because they represent the classic "whodunit." Thus, it is not surprising that the press follow some trials closely. Most trials are too mundane to evoke much public interest, but the legal woes of Peterson and Jackson proved to be major news events that often displaced other news. What has changed over time is the advent of cable news channels, which provide extensive coverage of celebrity trials. The challenge for the media is how to cover those trials when a legal team is trying to manipulate the press. In turn, the growth of electronic media has made the reporters as much of the story as the lawyers (and their clients). The O.J. Simpson trial, for example, made legal reporter Greta Van Susteren a household name in the same way the Peterson and Jackson trials contributed to Nancy Grace's rise to fame.

It is unclear whether efforts by celebrity lawyers ultimately matter to either the jury or the rest of the public. Peterson was convicted of murder and sentenced to death. Jackson, on the other hand, was acquitted (although Geragos

had left the Jackson defense team before the trial). One thing is clear, though—the media appear more than willing to continue to cover these trials and the actions of the celebrity attorneys. Whether that is good for the legal system or for justice is a question that remains unanswered. As we will discuss in Chapter 13, prejudicial pretrial publicity is a major concern in high-profile cases.

In a highly dramatic fashion, the movie *Chicago* illustrates the tension between law on the books and law in action. Law on the books projects the rules of law as abstract and absolute. Law in action, on the other hand, stresses real people and the subjectivity of facts. From arrest to sentencing, prosecutors, defense attorneys, judges, jurors, and probation officers are required to interpret what facts are most relevant and what conclusions to draw from those facts. That there may be disagreements in these assessments produces another theme of this book—law in controversy.

1. What do you think? Do the media have an obligation to ignore events concocted by lawyers simply to put a favorable spin on their clients' situations?
2. How could you study whether television coverage of these trials has an influence on the trial or the verdict?
3. In what ways do modern celebrity attorneys resemble the fictional Billy Flynn in *Chicago*?

justice process for less-than-honorable ends. In countries without built-in checks, the criminal justice process provides a quick and easy way for government officials to dispose of their enemies. For example, a common ploy in a totalitarian government is to charge persons with the ill-defined crime of being an "enemy of the state." The possibility of political misuse of the criminal justice process by a tyrannical government or tyrannical officials is a major concern in the Anglo-American heritage.

Another reason that democracies respect the rights of those accused or suspected of violating the criminal law is the need to maintain the respect and support of the community. Democratic governments derive their powers from the consent of the governed. Such support is undermined if power is applied arbitrarily. Law enforcement practices that

are brutal or overzealous are likely to produce fear and cynicism among the people—lawbreakers and law abiders alike. Such practices undermine the legitimacy that law enforcement officials must have in order to enforce the law in a democracy.

Due Process

The principal legal doctrine for limiting the arbitrariness of officials is due process. Due process of law is mentioned twice in the Constitution:

- "No person shall . . . be deprived of life, liberty or property without due process of law." (Fifth Amendment)
- "No state shall deprive any person of life, liberty or property without due process of law." (Fourteenth Amendment)

TABLE 2.2 ▪ PROVISIONS OF THE U.S. CONSTITUTION DEALING WITH CRIMINAL PROCEDURE

	Constitutional Language
Crime	Article I Section 9.3: No bill of attainder may be passed by the legislature. Article I Section 10.1: No state may pass any bill of attainder. Article I Section 9.3: The legislature may not pass an ex post facto law. Article I Section 10.1: No state may pass an ex post facto law.
Arrest	Amendment IV: Right against unreasonable search and seizures applies to arrest.
Initial appearance	Amendment VI: Right to know charges.
Bail	Amendment VIII: Right against excessive bail.
Preliminary hearing	Amendment VI: Right to assistance of counsel.
Charging	None
Grand jury	Amendment V: Right to a grand jury for a capital or otherwise infamous crime.
Arraignment	Amendment VI: Right to know charges.
Evidence	Amendment IV: Right against unreasonable search and seizures. Amendment V: Right against self-incrimination.
Plea bargaining	None
Trial	Amendment V: Right not to be tried twice for the same crime. Amendment VI: Right to a speedy trial; right to an impartial jury; right to a public trial; right to be confronted by witnesses against oneself; right to a jury from state or district where crime shall have been committed; right to obtain witnesses in one's favor; right to conduct cross-examination; right to speak at trial.
Sentencing	Amendment VIII: Right against excessive fines; right against cruel and unusual punishment. Amendment XIII: Right against involuntary servitude.
Appeal	Article I Section 9.2: Privilege of the writ of habeas corpus shall not be suspended.

The concept of **due process of law** has a broad and somewhat elastic meaning, with definitions varying in detail from situation to situation. The core of the idea of due process is fundamental fairness insofar as a person should always be given notice of any charges brought against him or her, that a person should be provided a real chance to present his or her side in a legal dispute, and that no law or government procedure should be arbitrary or capricious. The specific requirements of due process vary somewhat, depending on the Supreme Court's latest interpretations of the Bill of Rights.

Bill of Rights

The major obstacle to the ratification of the Constitution was the absence of specific protections for individual rights. Several of the most prominent leaders of the American Revolution opposed the adoption of the Constitution, fearing that the proposed national government posed as great a threat to the rights of the average American as had the king of England. Therefore, shortly after the adoption of the Constitution, 10 amendments, collectively known as the **Bill of Rights**, were adopted. Many of these protections—particularly the Fourth, Fifth, Sixth, and Eighth Amendments—deal specifically with criminal procedure.

Originally, the protections of the Bill of Rights restricted only the national government. Through a legal doctrine known as **selective incorporation**, however, the Supreme Court ruled that the due process clause of the Fourteenth Amendment made some provisions of the Bill of Rights applicable to the states as well. Although not all the protections of the Bill of Rights have been incorporated

Exhibit 2.2　**CASES INCORPORATING PROVISIONS OF THE BILL OF RIGHTS INTO THE DUE PROCESS CLAUSE OF THE FOURTEENTH AMENDMENT**

FIRST AMENDMENT

Establishment of religion: *Everson v. Board of Education* (1947)

Free exercise of religion: *Cantwell v. Connecticut* (1940)

Freedom of speech: *Gitlow v. New York* (1925)

Freedom of the press: *Near v. Minnesota* (1931)

Freedom to peaceably assemble: *DeJong v. Oregon* (1937)

Freedom to petition government: *Hague v. CIO* (1939)

SECOND AMENDMENT

Right to bear arms: *McDonald v. City of Chicago* (2010)

FOURTH AMENDMENT

Unreasonable search and seizure: *Wolf v. Colorado* (1949)

Exclusionary rule: *Mapp v. Ohio* (1961)

Warrant requirement: *Ker v. California* (1963)

FIFTH AMENDMENT

Grand jury: Not incorporated

No double jeopardy: *Benton v. Maryland* (1969)

No self-incrimination: *Malloy v. Hogan* (1964)

Compensation for taking private property: *Chicago, Burlington and Quincy Railroad v. Chicago* (1897)

SIXTH AMENDMENT

Speedy trial: *Klopfer v. North Carolina* (1967)

Public trial: *In re Oliver* (1948)

Impartial jury: *Parker v. Gladden* (1966)

Jury trial: *Duncan v. Louisiana* (1968)

Venue: Not incorporated

Notice: *Cole v. Arkansas* (1948)

Confrontation of witnesses: *Pointer v. Texas* (1965)

Compulsory process: *Washington v. Texas* (1967)

Assistance of counsel in capital cases: *Powell v. Alabama* (1932)

Assistance of counsel in noncapital felony cases: *Gideon v. Wainwright* (1963)

Assistance of counsel in most misdemeanor cases: *Argersinger v. Hamlin* (1972)

SEVENTH AMENDMENT

Jury trial in civil cases: Not incorporated

EIGHTH AMENDMENT

No excessive bail: Not incorporated

No excessive fines: *Cooper Industries v. Leatherman Tool Group, Inc.* (2001)

No cruel and unusual punishment: *Robinson v. California* (1962)

NINTH AMENDMENT

Privacy: *Griswold v. Connecticut* (1965). (Note that the word *privacy* does not appear in the Ninth Amendment (nor anywhere else in the Constitution), but in Griswold, several justices viewed the Ninth Amendment as guaranteeing that right.)

SOURCE: Adapted from John Ferdico, Henry F. Fradella, and Christopher Totten, *Criminal Procedure for the Criminal Justice Professional*. 11th ed. Belmont, CA: West/Wadsworth, 2012.

into the Fourteenth Amendment, all of the major protections now apply to the states as well as to the national government (Exhibit 2.2). The major provisions of the Bill of Rights incorporated through the due process clause of the Fourteenth Amendment are protections against unreasonable searches and seizures (Fourth Amendment); protection against self-incrimination (Fifth); the right to counsel and trial by jury (Sixth); and the prohibition against cruel and unusual punishment (Eighth).

CIVIL LAW OVERVIEW

Most disputes that come to court involve private parties. Conflicts over failure to pay money owed or injuries suffered in an automobile accident are settled on the basis of the body of rules collectively known as **civil law**. These suits are brought because the courts possess powers that private parties do not; courts can, for example, order a person to pay money owed under a contract or award monetary damages suffered for an injury received in an automobile accident.

Types of Civil Disputes

A civil suit is brought by a private party. But "private parties" are not limited to individual citizens. They may include groups of citizens (advocacy groups and homeowners' associations, for example) as well as businesses and the government. Given these legal entities, is it best to view civil law as every lawsuit other than a criminal proceeding. Accordingly, civil law is considerably more voluminous than criminal law.

Tort law involves the legal wrong done to another person. Injuries suffered during automobile accidents are a prime example of tort law. When lawyers speak of an injury, however, they do not necessarily mean a physical injury. The term has a broader meaning, including any wrong, hurt, or damage done to a person's rights, body, reputation, or property.

Another type of private law involves **contracts**—agreements between two or more persons involving a promise supported by mutual obligations (termed "consideration"). Money owed on a credit card and bank loans for buying a new car are considered contracts.

Property, which centers on the ownership of things, is another division of private law. Property law regulates three types of property: real property—involving land and real estate; personal property—rights concerning tangible, movable items; and intellectual property—covering original ideas. Intellectual property has grown to be an increasingly important area of the law in the digital age, as it governs the regulation of patents, trademarks, and copyrights.

Domestic relations constitutes a major area of law. These matters of family law mainly involve divorce and related issues such as child custody, child support, and alimony. Some areas of domestic relations overlap with juvenile law (Chapter 17). Domestic disputes are also a common reason that police may be summoned, and at times criminal conduct may be involved (see Chapter 9 for a discussion of domestic violence).

Property received from a person who has died is governed by laws on **inheritance**. The best-known example is a will, a written document telling how a person's property should be distributed after his or her death. But when someone dies without a will, the civil law of *intestacy* determines how possessions should be distributed by a court in *probate proceedings*.

Civil Remedies

Individuals, groups, or governments sue because they want something from another party. What they want is termed a **remedy**. A court's official decision about the rights and claims of each side in a lawsuit is known as a **judgment**. Thus, if the plaintiff wins, the judgment also contains a remedy, which is the relief granted by the court.

Most civil cases involve a request for monetary damages. The **plaintiff** (the person who starts a lawsuit) demands that the **defendant** (the person against whom a lawsuit is brought) pay money to the plaintiff. For example, in a case involving an automobile accident, the injured party may request a sum of money to pay for hospital expenses, doctors' fees, lost wages, and general "pain and suffering." **Monetary damages** are sums of money that a court orders to be paid to a person who has suffered a legal injury. Although there are several types of damages that courts may order, the two pleading types of civil damage awards involve compensatory and punitive damages. *Compensatory damages* are payment for the actual losses suffered by a plaintiff. Punitive damages involve money awarded by a court to a person who has been harmed in a malicious or willful way by another person. The purpose is to warn others.

Another type of remedy occasionally requested is a **declaratory judgment**, which is a judicial determination of the legal rights of the parties. For example, in prisoner litigation, lawyers seek a declaration that prison conditions violate constitutional standards.

A third type of remedy is called an **injunction** (and comes from the type of law found in England termed "equity" or sometimes "chancey" law). An injunction is a court order that requires a

TABLE 2.3 ■ TYPES OF INJUNCTIONS

Temporary restraining order ("TRO")	A temporary injunction lasting only a few days that orders a party to refrain from taking certain action until a hearing can be held, such as not taking a child out of the jurisdiction until a custody hearing can be held.
Preliminary injunction	An injunction issued during the pendency of a civil or criminal case that orders the parties from taking certain actions in order to maintain the *status quo* until there is a final judgment in the case, such as ordering a city not to enforce a local ordinance until its constitutionality can be determined.
Permanent injunction	An injunction entered as part a final judgment ordering a party to refrain from or to perform certain actions, such a ordering a company to permanently stop dumping industrial waste into a river.

© Cengage Learning

person to take an action or to refrain from taking an action. An injunction is a powerful measure that can be enforced by the contempt power of the court (the authority of a court to jail someone for disobeying a court order). Thus, a person who violates an injunction can be fined or sent to jail. Table 2.3 summarizes the three primary types of injunctions.

To qualify for any of these three types of injunctive orders, the plaintiff must demonstrate to the court that irreparable injury will be suffered if the injunction is not issued. In other words, the plaintiff must show that the harm at issue cannot be cured later by monetary compensation and conditions—that once changes are made, things cannot be put back to the way they were before.

Using Civil Remedies to Fight Crime

Civil law is having a growing impact on the criminal justice system. Victims of crime are increasingly resorting to civil litigation, in addition to victim compensation and restitution, as a means of recovering from the ill effects of crime. Moreover, victims' rights advocates are pushing for civil remedies as one way for victims to reassert control (see Chapter 9). In criminal prosecutions, the prosecutor essentially makes all decisions; in civil litigation, though, the plaintiff and plaintiff's lawyer make the decisions.

Although parallel civil and criminal proceedings have been brought for years, they are being used more frequently today than ever before, especially in three areas—civil forfeiture cases related to drug offenses,

lawsuits brought by victims of sexual assault, and civil remedies to compensate victims of white collar crime (Lininger, 2008; McCampbell, 1995).

The overlap between civil and criminal law is highlighted by a number of efforts to fight drug use. Legislators at both the state and national levels are passing laws that allow for the eviction of residents from public housing if they are convicted of drug possession and laws that permit drug testing of employees. Likewise, nuisance-abatement suits have targeted so-called crack houses. These essentially civil laws increase the arsenal of legal weapons that law enforcement officials may use to stop the sale and use of illegal drugs. But some people now wonder whether the use of civil remedies, particularly asset forfeiture, may have gone too far (see "Courts, Controversy, & Reducing Crime: Should Asset Forfeiture Be Limited?").

Rape victims are pursuing justice in the civil courts at a growing rate, seeking damages from almost anyone they can find who may have shared liability for the rape. These lawsuits often proceed on the basis of the legal theory of premises liability, in which the victim alleges that the owner or manager of a property failed to provide adequate security and thereby contributed to the occurrence of the crime. These claims raise issues concerning inadequate security resulting from poorly trained security guards, too few security guards, or environmental design flaws. In short, premises liability lawsuits argue that the crime that occurred was foreseeable and that the defendant had a legal duty to provide adequate security (Gordon & Brill, 1996; Kanter, 2005).

COURTS, CONTROVERSY, & REDUCING CRIME

SHOULD ASSET FORFEITURE BE LIMITED?

Asset forfeiture involves government seizure of the personal assets obtained from, or used in, a crime. Assets refer to property, businesses, cars, cash, and the like. For example, a car used in the distribution of illegal drugs may be forfeited to the government. Asset forfeiture was part of British common law as early as 1660. More recently, it is identified with the Racketeer Influenced and Corrupt Organizations Act (RICO for short), enacted by Congress in 1970. Congress was concerned about the infiltration of organized crime into the regular business marketplace and sought to discourage such activities not only by imposing criminal penalties, but also by making property obtained from the profits of the illegal enterprise subject to forfeiture. Thus, drug dealers who pour their profits into a restaurant can have the restaurant seized by government agents.

But asset forfeiture is not limited to criminal actions. The more potent form of asset forfeiture is civil in nature. The government is proceeding not against a person, but against the property in what is termed an *in rem* procedure (a lawsuit brought against a thing rather than against a person). Through the years, Congress has greatly expanded the scope of asset forfeiture, and nearly all states have enacted asset forfeiture laws. Some cities have even enacted forfeiture laws to confiscate cars used in street racing, operated by drunk drivers, or driven by those with revoked licenses (Worrall, 2008).

The major concern over asset forfeiture laws is that they make it too easy for law enforcement officials to seize the assets of innocent persons, especially since civil forfeiture actions require a low burden of proof. The Supreme Court placed some limits on governmental forfeiture power in *Austin v. United States*, 1993. In that case, a South Dakota man had his mobile home and auto body shop seized after being convicted of selling two grams of cocaine. The Court unanimously ruled that the amount seized—almost $43,000—was disproportionate to the crime. But the Court has nonetheless upheld the seizure of property from innocent owners over due process challenges (*Bennis v. Michigan*, 1996; *United States v. Ursery*, 1996).

After years of debate, Congress passed the Civil Asset Forfeiture Act of 2000. Prior to the Act's passage, property owners had been required to prove that their property was not subject to forfeiture. Today, however, the government must prove—by a preponderance of the evidence—that property is subject to forfeiture. The Act also awards attorneys' fees to those who successfully challenge confiscation of property.

Research concludes that there is no clear answer to whether asset forfeiture encourages policing for profit. However, one study found that local law enforcement agencies circumvent restrictive state laws (those placing limits on the proceeds they can receive) by teaming up with federal officials to receive equitable sharing payments (Worrall & Kovandzic, 2008).

The debate over asset forfeiture crosses traditional ideological lines. Due process advocates want limits on asset forfeiture because they think that innocent people end up being presumed guilty. Similarly, crime control supporters also want strong restrictions on asset forfeiture because they think it improperly gives the government too much authority over important property rights.

What do you think? Should more limits be placed on law enforcement officials' ability to seize assets of suspected wrongdoers? Do large financial incentives like these provide too great a temptation?

Law in Controversy: The Incivility of Civil Justice

In recent years, civil justice has become almost as controversial as criminal justice. Consider, for example, the seemingly endless number of television commercials asking whether viewers took a particular prescription drug and then suffered any of a long list of complications, or asking questions like, "Have you been injured in an accident?" Critics view such product liability and personal injury lawsuits as having corrupted the civil justice system into a type of lottery. In addition, critics point out that tort litigation costs in the United States are two to three times more than they are in many western European countries and that they contribute to the already high cost of health care and automobile insurance. Proponents of the current civil justice system argue against tort reform, however, primarily by pointing out that curtailing civil lawsuits would prevent deserving tort victims from collecting all of the damages to which they are entitled and would interfere with the ability of juries to properly punish wrongdoers (Neubauer & Meinhold, 2013).

Victims who use the civil justice system in an attempt to recover monetary damages from criminal defendants are often motivated to sue seeking vindication of their beliefs with little likelihood of collecting any money. After all, few criminal defendants have the economic resources to make litigation financially worthwhile, as illustrated by the cases of Bernhard Goetz and O.J. Simpson in Table 2.4. On the other hand, as the other cases in Table 2.4 illustrate, most municipalities, governmental agencies, and celebrities have the financial resources to pay large settlements.

Civil Liability of Criminal Justice Officials

In the modern era, not only do criminal defendants find themselves hauled into civil court, but police officers, prosecutors, and prison guards do as well. Criminal justice officials must defend themselves against a variety of civil lawsuits. Perhaps the best known are cases filed by prison inmates under 42 U.S.C. § 1983 (often called "Section 1983 cases") alleging that conditions of confinement constitute cruel and unusual punishment in violation of the Eighth Amendment. These lawsuits have reshaped American prisons in recent years (see Chapter 14).

Other civil lawsuits seek monetary damages for misconduct on the part of law enforcement personnel, such as the Rodney King and Amadou Diallo cases (summarized in Table 2.4). Most commonly, these lawsuits allege that the police used excessive force or were negligent in using deadly force. Conversely, some lawsuits center on the inaction of law enforcement or correctional personnel. For example, local governments have been found liable for

the death of a person in detention when police officers failed to prevent suicide; and prison officials have been held liable for failure to prevent inmate-against-inmate assaults (see Lee, 2011).

Criminal justice officials also find themselves in civil court as defendants in growing numbers of cases filed by their own employees. Some lawsuits allege discrimination in hiring or promotion. Others argue that the plaintiff was sexually harassed. Chapter 3, on federal courts, will explore how a wide range of federal laws shape the internal operations of law enforcement and corrections.

CRIMINAL LAW OVERVIEW

Some disputes are viewed as so disruptive to society that they require special treatment because civil law remedies are not enough. Whereas a breach of the civil law is considered a private matter involving only the individual parties, violations of the criminal law are considered public wrongs. As such, **criminal law** relates to actions that are considered so dangerous, or potentially so, that they threaten the welfare of society as a whole.

A second difference involves prosecution. Unlike civil law, in which private parties file suit in court alleging an infringement of private rights, violations of public wrongs are prosecuted by the state.

The types of penalties imposed on law violators is a third difference. In civil law, the injured party receives compensation. Violators of criminal law, however, are punished. In setting penalties, American law often makes a distinction between a misdemeanor and a felony. In general, a **misdemeanor** is a criminal offense that is less serious than a **felony**. Misdemeanors are generally punishable by a fine or up to a year in jail; felonies usually involve prison sentences of more than a year. The stress on punishment derives from the goal of criminal law to prevent and control crime. It is important to recognize that criminal law is intended to supplement, not supplant, civil law. Thus, as discussed earlier, a person may be prosecuted criminally and the victim may also seek to recover civil damages for the same act. In automobile accidents involving drinking, for example, the drunk driver may be charged criminally with drunk driving and the injured party may also file a civil suit seeking monetary damages.

TABLE 2.4 ▪ PROMINENT EXAMPLES OF CIVIL ACTIONS FOLLOWING CRIMINAL PROSECUTIONS

Person	Criminal Prosecution	Civil Action
Bernhard Goetz	Criminal jury convicted the subway vigilante of illegally having a gun but acquitted him of more serious charges after the 1984 shooting of a youth Goetz claimed was trying to rob him. The shooting had clear racial overtones (Goetz is white; his victim, black).	A 1996 civil jury ordered Goetz to pay $43 million to the man he left paralyzed. It is unlikely that Darrell Cabey, who was paralyzed and suffered brain damage, will be able to collect from the unemployed electrician.
O. J. Simpson	In the televised "trial of the century," the jury acquitted O. J. Simpson of murdering his former wife Nicole Brown Simpson and her friend Ronald Goldman. The verdict divided the nation along racial lines.	A civil jury found Simpson liable for the killings of his ex-wife and her friend. The jury awarded $8.5 million in compensatory damages to Goldman's parents and $25 million in punitive damages. The plaintiff's ability to collect on the judgment is limited because Simpson had placed most of his money in retirement accounts that cannot be seized.
Rodney King	Two Los Angeles police officers were acquitted in state court of beating Rodney King, but they were later convicted in federal court (Chapter 3).	The city of Los Angeles settled the civil lawsuit for $3.8 million.
Randall Weaver	After a months-long standoff, federal agents arrested Randall Weaver at his mountain home in Ruby Ridge, Idaho. During the arrest a firefight broke out, and Weaver's wife and son were killed. A criminal jury acquitted Weaver of a variety of gun charges.	The U.S. Justice Department paid $3.1 million to settle wrongful death claims against federal agents for the 1992 death of Randall Weaver's wife and son.
Amadou Diallo	Four NYPD officers were acquitted of murder. The Justice Department will not file federal charges.	The city of New York settled the case for $3 million.
Kobe Bryant	The prosecutor dropped charges of sexual assault when the victim refused to testify.	Bryant settled out of court for an undisclosed amount of money.
Michael Jackson	The jury acquitted the pop icon of sexually molesting a child at his Neverland ranch.	Media report that Jackson settled out of court at least one earlier case involving improper sexual contact with a minor.

© Cengage Learning

Table 2.5 summarizes several important differences between civil law and criminal law.

Elements of a Crime

In every criminal case, the prosecution must prove what is known as *corpus delicti*, a Latin phrase meaning "body of the crime." *Corpus delicti* refers to the essential elements of a crime that the prosecution must prove beyond a reasonable doubt. In defining the elements of a particular offense, criminal laws are based on five general principles. Most behavior cannot be called criminal unless:

- a guilty act, called an *actus reus* is committed, with

- a particular level of criminal intent, called *mens rea*, and

- the guilty act and the criminal intent are related.

TABLE 2.5 ■ DIFFERENCES BETWEEN CIVIL AND CRIMINAL LAW

	Civil	Criminal
Moving party	Plaintiff	State
Defending party	Defendant	Defendant
Burden of persuasion	Preponderance of the evidence	Beyond a reasonable doubt
Jury verdict rules	Less than unanimous (many states)	Unanimous (most states)
Remedy	Monetary damages	Fine and correctional supervision (in institutions, on probation, or with intermediate sanctions)
Defendant's testimony	May be forced to testify	Constitutional right to silence
Right to counsel	No constitutional right to counsel	Constitutional right to counsel
Prosecution	Must hire own lawyer	The government through the district attorney
Examples	Tort, contract, property, probate	Assault, theft, burglary, murder

© Cengage Learning

- In addition, a number of crimes also require the prosecution to prove additional elements, such as the presence of certain attendant circumstances and/or that the guilty act caused a particular result.

Actus Reus: The Guilty Act

Before there can be a crime, there must be a **guilty act** (*actus reus*). Thus, criminal liability occurs only after a voluntary act that results in criminal harm. The requirement of a guilty act reflects a fundamental principle of American law: No one should be punished solely for bad thoughts. Depending on the crime, there are different types of guilty acts. Most crimes have a voluntary act as the *actus reus*. Thus, a person who strikes another while suffering an epileptic seizure would not be guilty of battery, because the act (hitting) was not voluntary. An omission—a failure to act when there is a legal duty to act—can also qualify as an *actus reus*, such as failing to file income taxes, failing to yield the right of way, and failing to provide adequate care for one's children. The act of possession can also qualify as an *actus reus*, such as the offense of possession of an illegal drug. Differences in the nature of the guilty act account for many gradations of criminal offenses. To choose one obvious example, stealing property is considered separately from damaging property.

An important subdivision of the guilty act is a class of offenses labeled as **attempts** (for example, attempted burglary or attempted murder). The law does not want a person to avoid legal liability merely because someone or something prevented the commission of a crime. Typically, though, the penalties for attempt are less severe than if the act had succeeded. One result is that in some states, defendants often plead guilty in an attempt to reduce the possible severity of the prison sentence.

Mens Rea: Criminal Intent

Most crimes consist of two elements, the guilty act itself and the accompanying mental state. The rationale is that criminal sanctions are not necessary for those who innocently cause harm. As Justice Holmes (1881, p. 3) once pithily put it, "Even a dog distinguishes between being stumbled over and being kicked." The mental state required for a crime to have been committed is referred to as **guilty intent** or *mens rea* ("guilty mind").

Despite its importance in criminal law, guilty intent is difficult to define because it refers to a subjective condition, a state of mind. Some statutes require only general intent (intent to do something that the law prohibits), but others specify the existence of specific intent (intent to do the exact thing charged). Moreover, legislatively defined crimes have added new concepts of mental state to the traditional ones. Thus, crimes differ with respect to the mental state the prosecution must prove existed in order to secure a criminal conviction. Larceny (termed "theft" in some states), for example, typically requires proof of a very great degree of intent; the prosecutor must prove that the defendant intentionally took property to which he knew he was not entitled, intending to deprive the rightful owner of possession permanently. Negligent homicide, on the other hand, is an example of a crime involving a lesser degree of intent; the prosecution need only show that the defendant negligently caused the death of another. Most crimes require that the defendant knew he or she was doing something wrong. Also, the law assumes that people know the consequences of their acts. Thus, a person cannot avoid legal liability by later saying, "I didn't mean to do it."

Union of Act and Intent

Criminal law requires that the guilty act and the guilty intent occur together, a concept often referred to as the *union of actus reus* and *mens rea*. Suppose that you pick up another student's textbook believing it to be your own. Although you take the book—an act that would constitute the *actus reus* for theft—you had no criminal intent; you made an honest and reasonable mistake. Thus, without the union of *actus reus* (the taking of the book) and *mens rea* (the intent to steal), you would not be liable for theft.

Attendant Circumstances

Some crimes require the presence, or absence, of **attendant (accompanying) circumstances**. Driving at a speed of 150 miles per hour would constitute a crime only if it occurred on a public roadway; it would not be a crime to drive at that speed on a racetrack. The location of the speeding is the attendant circumstance for the crime. Attendant circumstances may also be used to define the level or "degree" of crime. For example, most states differentiate between classes of theft on the basis of the amount stolen. The law might provide that a theft of less than $500 be treated as a misdemeanor and a theft of $500 or more be treated as a felony. The amount stolen is the attendant circumstance.

Results

In a limited number of criminal offenses, the **result** of the illegal act plays a critical part in defining the

crime. The difference between homicide and battery, for example, depends on whether the victim died or lived. Similarly, most states distinguish between degrees of battery, depending on how seriously the victim was injured. Note that the concept of results differs from that of intent. In all of the preceding examples, the defendant may have had the same intent. The only difference was how hearty the victim was or perhaps how skillful the defendant was in carrying out his or her intentions.

Defining Crimes

Using the principles of *actus reus, mens rea*, attendant circumstances, and result, legislatures define the elements of crimes in penal codes. The "Law on the Books vs. Law in Action" feature on the next page presents the key characteristics of the most common serious crimes. But because the particular elements combine to provide the technical (that is, legal) definition or *corpus delicti* of a crime, criminal statutes must be read closely; each clause in a penal statute usually constitutes a critical part of the offense.

Criminal Defenses

Individuals may have performed illegal acts, but may nonetheless be not guilty of a crime because of the applicability of legally recognized defenses. **Criminal defenses** derive from the way crime is defined. In most criminal cases, the defense attempts to cast doubt on the defendant's guilt. This is usually accomplished by undercutting the prosecution's case such that the jury has reason to doubt whether the defendant committed all of the elements of the crime(s) charged.

In other cases, however, the defense may assert specific legal doctrines in an attempt to secure an acquittal. An **alibi defense**, for example, permits defendants to argue that they were somewhere else at the time the crime was committed. Witnesses may be called to testify that during the time in question the defendant was drinking beer at a local bar or shopping downtown with some friends. Most states and the federal system require that defendants provide a notice of an alibi defense prior to trial, along with a list of witnesses to be called to support this assertion. A notice of alibi defense gives the prosecution the opportunity to investigate the witnesses' stories before trial. Prosecutors who suspect that

LAW ON THE BOOKS VS. LAW IN ACTION
CHARACTERISTICS OF THE MOST COMMON SERIOUS CRIMES

	LAW ON THE BOOKS	LAW IN ACTION
Murder and nonnegligent homicide	The killing of one human being by another.	Homicide is the least frequent violent crime. Most often murderers are relatives or acquaintances of the victim.
Rape	Sexual intercourse that occurs without the effective consent of the victim.	Contrary to portrayals of sexual assaults by strangers in many movies and television shows, the overwhelming number of such crimes are "acquaintance rapes," in which the victim knows the assailant.
Robbery	The taking or attempting to take anything of value from the care, custody, or control of a person or persons by force or threat of force or violence and/or by putting the victim in fear.	Half of all robberies involve one offender. Half of all robberies involve the use of a weapon.
Assault	*Aggravated assault* is an unlawful attack by one person upon another for the purpose of inflicting severe or aggravated bodily injury. This type of assault is usually accompanied by the use of a weapon or other means likely to produce death or great bodily harm.	Simple assault occurs more frequently than aggravated assault.

Simple assault is the most common type of violent crime. |
	Simple assault is an unlawful attack by one person upon another for the purpose of inflicting less than severe bodily injury. This type of assault does not involve the use of a weapon or other means likely to produce death or great bodily harm.	
Burglary	The unlawful entry into a structure to commit a felony or a theft.	Residential property is targeted in two out of three burglaries.
Larceny (theft)	The unlawful taking, carrying, lending, or riding away of property from possession or constructive possession of another.	Pocket picking and purse snatching occur most frequently inside businesses or on street locations.
Motor vehicle theft	The theft or attempted theft of a motor vehicle. A motor vehicle is self-propelled and runs on the ground or on water, not on rails.	Motor vehicle theft is relatively well reported to the police, but the crime has a low rate of being solved.
Arson	Any willful or malicious burning or attempt to burn, with or without intent to defraud, a dwelling house, public building, motor vehicle, aircraft, or personal property of another.	Single-family residences are the most frequent targets of arson.

SOURCE: Federal Bureau of Investigation. *Uniform Crime Reports.* Washington, DC: Department of Justice, 2011.

witnesses have carefully rehearsed their alibi testimony can use clever cross-examination to ask questions out of sequence, hoping to catch each witness in a series of contradictions. Prosecutors can also call rebuttal witnesses to suggest that the witnesses are longtime friends of the defendant, who may be likely to lie.

Alibi defenses are actually quite rare, since prosecutors generally do not charge suspects who have firm alibis. The sections below present an overview of some of the more common or controversial criminal defenses.

Defenses that Negate Mens Rea

Sometimes people engage in an act that, at first blush might appear to be criminal, but they do so under circumstances demonstrating that they lacked true criminal intent. These defenses are said to negate *mens rea*. The two most common of these defenses include the mistake of fact defense and the defense of necessity.

When a person makes an honest and reasonable mistake regarding a factual matter that, if true, would have justified the act or omission that is the subject of a criminal prosecution, he or she may be able to assert the defense known as mistake of fact if the mistake negates the *mens rea* of the crime with which the defendant is charged. For example, if a student took a book that belonged to a classmate under the mistaken belief that the book was his own, the mistake would negate the crime of theft because there was no intent to steal.

Criminal law recognizes that there are times when someone acts not of his or her own free will, but rather because of the necessary circumstances of the moment or the coercion of another. When such situations exist, the law permits a defendant to argue that his or her conduct should either be excused entirely or mitigated to a less serious charge because *mens rea* was formed under extraordinary circumstances that render it unfair to hold the defendant responsible for the unlawful conduct. Consider the case of *State v. Cole* (1991). The defendant's wife was six months pregnant and had developed pains in her back and stomach. He did not have a telephone to call for help and his only neighbor was not at home. The next closest phone was more than a mile and a half away. So, even though his driver's license had been suspended, he drove to the phone to call for help. The defense of necessity excused his conduct.

Defenses of Justification

Defenses of justification are based on the commission of an act under circumstances the criminal law does not seek to punish, such as using force in self-defense, defense of other persons, or defense of property. Note that it may even be legal to use deadly force to repel an unlawful and potentially deadly attack against oneself or another human being. In contrast, the criminal law never permits deadly force to be used strictly to defend property.

Procedural Defenses

There are a number of procedural defenses that the law recognizes for public policy reasons. These defenses are generally unconcerned with factual guilt. Rather, they focus on compliance with the rules and processes of the criminal justice system, such as the right to a speedy trial and the related defense of the passage of time specified in statutes of limitations (see Chapter 5), the bar against double jeopardy, immunity, and the use of the exclusionary rule to prevent illegally obtained evidence from being used to convict someone (see Chapter 11).

Insanity

Defenses of excuse seek to excuse acts committed by defendants who should not be held criminally responsible for their actions because they were too young (see section on "Delinquency," next) or because their mental state prevented them from understanding the consequences of their actions. The most controversial defense of excuse is insanity.

Contemporary discussions on the insanity defense show marked philosophical divergences within society concerning an individual's responsibility for his or her own acts. The lack of agreement is reflected in major differences among states concerning the extent to which a person's mental faculties must be impaired before he or she is considered legally insane. The standards for insanity vary, but most jurisdictions follow the modern federal formulation of the insanity defense (Fradella, 2007). That version of the insanity defense excuses criminal conduct if, as a result of a severe "mental disease or defect" at the time of the commission of the offense, the defendant was unable to substantially appreciate the wrongfulness of his or her conduct. Although the prosecution must still prove all of the elements of the crime in question, the defense bears the burden of persuasion to prove the defendant's insanity either by a preponderance of the evidence or by clear and convincing evidence, depending on the jurisdiction (see "Case Close-Up" box).

CASE CLOSE-UP

UNITED STATES v. LOUGHNER

On January 8, 2011, Jared Loughner got into a taxicab; went to a local Safeway grocery store in Tucson, Arizona; paid with a $20 bill; and calmly received his change. He then opened fire, killing 6 people, including federal district judge John Roll, and wounding 14 others, including U.S. Congresswoman Gabrielle Giffords (Cloud, 2011). After initial public outrage, some people began to express pity when details of Loughner's mental illness came to light.

Sadly, there were many warning signs that Loughner was seriously mentally ill and dangerous, but nothing was done about it. Loughner displayed several classic symptoms of psychosis, ranging from paranoia and disorganized thoughts and speech to nonsensical outbursts and the inability to function in social situations. In fact, Pima Community College, where Loughner had been a student, dismissed him for behavior that scared his professors and fellow students alike. But he never got any help.

Loughner was indicted on a host of federal charges, including one count of attempted assassination of a member of Congress, two counts of murder of a federal employee (including Judge Roll), two counts of attempting to murder a federal employee, and additional charges of murder and attempted murder, for a total of 49 counts. Because a federal judge was among his victims, all of the members of the federal judiciary in Arizona recused themselves. A federal judge from California was appointed to preside over the case. He ordered that Loughner be transported to a federal psychiatric facility for assessment.

Loughner was diagnosed with schizophrenia, calling into question his **competency** or legal capacity to participate in the court proceedings against him. He was subsequently ruled incompetent to stand trial, meaning that his mental disability impairs Loughner to the extent that he cannot grasp the nature of the charges against him and assist his lawyers in his own defense (see *Dusky v. United States*, 1960). Loughner remained in the psychiatric wing of the U.S. Medical Center for Federal Prisoners in Springfield, Missouri for more than a year. He was forcibly medicated with antipsychotic drugs while there, in an attempt to restore his mental faculties sufficiently such that he was able to be ruled competent to stand trial.

After a court found that Loughner's competence to stand trial had been restored, he pled guilty to avoid facing a possible death sentence. This plea agreement spared Loughner, the families of the victims, and the greater Tucson community going through the trauma of a trial in which the defense is based on insanity. The insanity defense is one of the most hotly debated topics in criminal law. The defense is rooted in a fundamental concept of Anglo-American law: that a person should not be punished for conduct not rooted in criminal intent. But what degree of insanity, mental illness, or mental disease makes a person blameless for otherwise criminal acts? This question has been debated for centuries.

The often heated debate over the insanity defense is largely symbolic. Insanity is pled in less than one-half of 1 percent of all felony cases and, even when it is pled, it is unsuccessful three-quarters of the time (Fradella, 2007). Moreover, several states make incarceration in a mental institution mandatory if the defendant is found not guilty by reason of insanity. Indeed, such defendants are usually held in a mental institution for a longer period of time than they might have been held in prison had they been found guilty of the crime(s) with which they were charged. For these reasons, combined with the great expense of litigating an insanity defense, lawyers consider insanity a defense of last resort.

When the jury found would-be presidential assassin John Hinckley, Jr., "not guilty by reason of insanity," there was a heated outcry against the verdict, even though Hinckley was then confined to a mental institution, where he remains to this day (more than 30 years after he shot Ronald Reagan). Yet, public and professional displeasure produced a rush to reform the insanity defense (Fradella, 2007). For example, some states have greatly altered the traditional insanity defense and made available the verdict "guilty but mentally ill" or "guilty but insane"; other states abolished the defense outright. If Jared Loughner had not pled guilty, but rather had prevailed at trial using the insanity defense, he would not have gone free. Rather, he would have likely spent most of his life in a mental hospital—just as John Hinckley has.

Delinquency

As mentioned previously, the law recognizes youthful age as a criminal defense under certain circumstances. In most states, children under the age of 7 are considered legally incapable of forming criminal intent and therefore cannot be held criminally responsible for their actions, a criminal defense referred to as infancy. After reaching this minimum age, but before becoming an adult, a child's criminal violations are treated as acts of juvenile delinquency. The premise of juvenile delinquency is that people under a certain age have less responsibility for their actions than adults do. The exact age at which a person is no longer considered a juvenile, and can thus be prosecuted as an adult, differs from state to state. As more and more youths are committing violent crimes, states are lowering the age for prosecuting a minor as an adult (see Chapter 17).

EFFECTS OF CRIMINAL LAW ON THE COURTS

Because the criminal code constitutes the basic source of authority for law enforcement agencies, the way crimes are defined has an important bearing on the entire administration of criminal justice. Chapter 5 will consider in greater detail the relationship between law and discretion. For now we will examine the criminal law and inconsistencies, plea bargaining, and sentencing.

Criminal Law and Inconsistencies

Criminal statutes can resemble a crazy quilt of sometimes inconsistent sets of criminal definitions and penalties. Because legislatures change criminal codes piecemeal, the end product is a set of criminal laws with obsolete prohibitions and inconsistent penalties. Typically, such contradictions indicate a lack of agreement in American society about what behavior should be criminalized and what penalties are appropriate.

In practice, judges and prosecutors attempt to rectify these inconsistencies by informally developing a consistent set of penalties. It should be obvious that the courts must apply the law as they find it. The corollary is that the courts often must

rectify inconsistencies in that law. Disparities in possible sentences as provided in state statutes require judges, prosecutors, and defense attorneys to arrive at a workable penalty structure. Society would be outraged if serious crimes elicited the same punishment as minor ones, even if the law technically allowed the two categories of offenses to be treated the same way.

Criminal Law and Plea Bargaining

Variations in the definitions of crimes make the criminal courts fertile ground for plea bargaining. In particular, differences in degrees of seriousness provide the means for charge bargaining (the defendant pleads guilty to a less serious offense than the one charged). For example, in some states, assault and battery involves five degrees (categories). Although the law must attempt to differentiate between, say, a punch thrown in anger and a deliberate gunshot wound that leaves its victim permanently paralyzed, the existence of many different degrees of seriousness facilitates pleas to less serious offenses. Thus, prosecutors may deliberately overcharge in hopes of inducing the defendant to later plead guilty to a lesser charge (see Chapter 12).

Criminal Law and Sentencing

The most obvious way criminal law affects the operations of the criminal courts is in sentencing. As we will discuss in greater detail in Chapter 14, the legislature establishes sentencing options from which judges must choose. Because of the public's concern about crime, pressures are strong to increase penalties. As a result, legislatures increase the harshness of sentencing, and the courts mitigate that harshness. According to Rosett and Cressey (1976, p. 95; see also, Champion, 2007), such legislative action and courthouse reactions follow a predictable pattern:

- Step I. Laws calling for severe punishments are passed by legislatures on the assumption that fear of great pain will terrorize the citizenry into conformity.

- Step II. Criminal justice personnel soften these severe penalties for most offenders: (a) in the interests of justice, (b) in the interests of bureaucracy, and (c) in the interests of gaining acquiescence.

- Step III. The few defendants who then insist on a trial and are found guilty, or who in other ways refuse to cooperate, are punished more severely than those who acquiesce.
- Step IV. Legislatures, noting that most criminals by acquiescing avoid "the punishment prescribed by law": (a) increase the prescribed punishments and (b) try to limit the range of discretionary decision making used to soften the harsh penalties.
- Step V. The more severe punishments introduced in the preceding step are again softened for most offenders, as in Step II, with the result that the defendants who do not acquiesce are punished even more severely than they were at Step III.

This book will return often to the question of whether the legislatures or the courts have adopted the more appropriate stance.

CONCLUSION

What activities should be labeled criminal is a source of constant political discussion. Actions viewed as bad in the past may no longer be considered bad. As society changes, so do public perceptions of public wrongs, and pressures develop to add more activities to the list of officially proscribed ones. Through all of this change, we must not lose sight of the essential fact that law is an integral part of society. Law is not imposed on society; rather, it reflects the sociology, economy, history, and politics of society. Law was created to help society, not the other way around.

Chapter Review

LOI 1. List the four key elements defining law.

Law is defined as: (1) a body of rules, (2) enacted by public officers, (3) in a legitimate manner, and (4) backed by the force of the state.

LO2 2. Identify the three key characteristics of common law.

The three key characteristics of the common law are: (1) judge-made law, (2) precedent, and (3) multiple sources of law.

LO3 3. Explain the importance of the adversary system.

The adversary system seeks to protect individual rights by diffusing governmental power in several actors and insisting that the defendant is presumed innocent until proven guilty.

LO4 4. Name the four amendments of the Bill of Rights that deal specifically with criminal procedure.

Of the first 10 amendments to the U.S. Constitution—collectively known as the Bill of Rights—the Fourth, Fifth, Sixth, and Eighth deal specifically with criminal procedure.

LO5 5. List five major areas of civil law.

The five major areas of civil law are: tort, contract, property, domestic relations, and inheritance/probate.

LO6 6. Identify the major elements of a crime.

Most behavior cannot be criminally unless: (1) an actus reus (a guilty act) is committed, (2) with accompanying mens rea (criminal intent), and (3) the guilty act and the criminal intent are related. In addition, a number of crimes are defined on the basis of: (4) attendant circumstances, and/or (5) specific results.

LO7 7. Identify some of the most important legal defenses in American law.

Some of the most important legal defenses in American law include alibi, necessity, mistake of fact, self-defense, procedural defenses, infancy, and insanity.

LO8 **8.** Discuss the effects of the criminal law on courts.

How the law defines crimes affects the administration of justice in the courts in several important ways, including the need to reconcile inconsistencies in the criminal law, providing the basis for plea bargaining, and the harshness of sentences.

Critical Thinking Questions

1. Constitutional rights of the accused is, of course, a controversial topic. The crime control model, in particular, decries letting the obviously guilty go free on "technicalities," whereas the due process model emphasizes basic rights. What common ground do these two approaches share? Where do they disagree most?

2. Nearly all non–English-speaking industrial democracies use the inquisitorial system rather than the adversary system. In this system, the judge, not the prosecutor and not the defense attorney, calls witnesses and questions them. Would you prefer being tried under the adversary system or the inquisitorial system? Would you have confidence in the willingness of the judge to search out equally evidence for conviction and evidence for acquittal?

3. One of the biggest societal changes in recent years has been the rapid expansion of computer technology. How have legislatures responded to crimes involving the use of computers? How has the Internet changed the debate over pornography?

Key Terms

administrative regulations   32

adversary system   33

affirmative defense   34

alibi defense   46

Anglo-American law   30

attempt   45

attendant (accompanying) circumstances   46

beyond a reasonable doubt   35

Bill of Rights   38

burden of persuasion   34

burden of production   34

civil law   40

clear and convincing evidence   35

common law   30

competency   49

constitution   32

contract   40

corpus delicti   44

criminal defense   46

criminal law   43

declaratory judgment   40

defendant   40

defenses of excuse   48

defenses of justification   48

domestic relations   40

due process of law   38

elements of a crime   44

felony   43

guilty act (*actus reus*)   45

guilty intent (*mens rea*)   45

infancy   50

inference   34

inheritance   40

injunction   40

in rem   42

insanity defense   48

judge-made law   30

judgment   40

juvenile delinquency   50

law   29

misdemeanor   43

mistake of fact   48

monetary damage   40

municipal ordinance   32

necessity   48

plaintiff   40

precedent   30

preponderance of the evidence   35

presumption   34

presumption of innocence   34

presumption of sanity   34

probable cause   34

procedural defenses   48
procedural law   33
property   40
reasonable, articulable
   suspicion   34

remedy   40
result   46
selective incorporation   38
self-defense   48
stare decisis   30

statute   32
substantive law   33
tort   40
union of *actus reus* and
   mens rea   46

Web Resources

Go to the *America's Courts and the Criminal Justice System* companion website at
http://www.cengage.com/criminaljustice/neubauer,
where you will find more resources to help you study.
Resources include web exercises, quizzing, and flash cards.

For Further Reading

Ferdico, John, Henry F. Fradella, and Christopher Totten. *Criminal Procedure for the Criminal Justice Professional.* 11th ed. Belmont, CA: Wadsworth, 2012.

Kappeler, Victor. *Police Civil Liability: Supreme Court Cases and Materials.* Long Grove, IL: Waveland Press, 2006.

Neubauer, David. *Debating Crime: Rhetoric and Reality.* Belmont, CA: Wadsworth, 2001.

Neubauer, David, and Stephen Meinhold. *Judicial Process: Law, Courts, and Politics in the United States.* 6th ed. Belmont, CA: Wadsworth, 2013.

Owen, Stephen S., Henry F. Fradella, Tod W. Burke, & Jerry Joplin, 2012. The *Foundations of Criminal Justice.* New York: Oxford University Press.

Payne, Dennis. *Police Liability: Lawsuits against the Police.* Durham, NC: Carolina Academic Press, 2002.

Pollock, Joycelyn. *Ethical Dilemmas and Decisions in Criminal Justice.* 6th ed. Belmont, CA: Wadsworth, 2010.

Ross, Darrell. *Civil Liability in Criminal Justice.* 5th ed. Cincinnati: Anderson, 2009.

3 Federal Courts

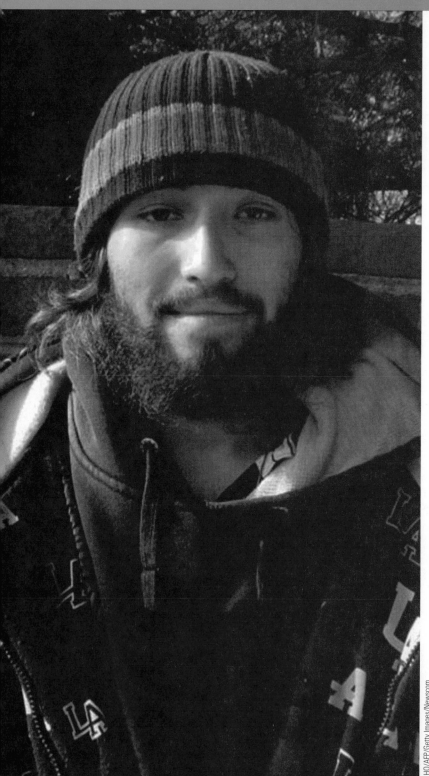

HO/AFP/Getty Images/Newscom

Oscar Ramiro Ortega-Hernandez is alleged to have fired a semi-automatic rifle at the White House in an attempt to assassinate President Barak Obama on November 11, 2011. Ballistic tests confirmed that two bullets and one bullet jacket recovered from White House grounds were fired from a rifle found in Ortega-Hernandez's car. Although President Obama was not in Washington, D.C., at the time of the shooting, Ortega-Hernandez faces life in prison for the attempted assassination of the U.S. president. A federal magistrate judge ordered Ortega-Hernandez held without bond pending indictment because he posed both a potential flight risk and a danger to the community. ■

BASIC PRINCIPLES OF COURT ORGANIZATION
Dual Court System
Jurisdiction
Differentiating Trial and Appellate Courts

Courts, Controversy, & the Administration of Justice
Should the Double Jeopardy Clause Prohibit Parallel State and Federal Prosecutions?

HISTORY OF THE FEDERAL COURTS
The Constitutional Convention
The Judiciary Act of 1789
1789–1891
Court of Appeals Act of 1891
Federal Courts Today

U.S. MAGISTRATE JUDGES
Caseload of U.S. Magistrate Judges

U.S. DISTRICT COURTS
Caseload of U.S. District Courts
Diversity Jurisdiction
Federal Questions

U.S. COURTS OF APPEALS
Caseload of U.S. Courts of Appeals

U.S. SUPREME COURT
Granting Cert: The Rule of Four
Caseload of U.S. Supreme Court
Circuit Justices

SPECIALIZED FEDERAL COURTS
Military Justice
Enemy Combatants

Courts, Law, & Media
The Response (2010)

Foreign Intelligence Surveillance Court

CASE CLOSE-UP: *Was Zacarias Moussaoui The 20th Hijacker?*

FEDERAL JUDICIAL ADMINISTRATION
Chief Justice
Judicial Conference of the United States
Administrative Office of the U.S. Courts
Federal Judicial Center
Judicial Councils
U.S. Sentencing Commission

CASELOADS IN THE FEDERAL COURTS
Increase the Number of Federal Judges?
Reduce Federal Jurisdiction?

CONSEQUENCES OF FEDERAL INVOLVEMENT IN THE CRIMINAL JUSTICE SYSTEM
Forum for Symbolic Politics
Federal Dollars

Federal Courts • Federal Courts • Federal Courts • Federal Courts • Federal Courts • Federal Courts • Federal Courts

Learning Objectives

After reading this chapter, you should be able to:

LO1 Define the four primary types of jurisdiction: geographical, subject matter, personal, and hierarchical.

LO2 Compare and contrast the tasks of trial and appellate courts.

LO3 Explain the historical evolution of the federal courts into their present structure and operations.

LO4 Analyze the different responsibilities and workloads of U.S magistrate judges, district judges, circuit judges, and Supreme Court justices.

LO5 Analyze the impact the federal courts have on the administration of criminal justice at the state and local levels through their federal question jurisdiction.

LO6 Differentiate the jurisdiction and functions of Article III courts from those of Article I courts and other specialized federal courts.

LO7 Distinguish the various agencies and their hierarchical responsibilities for the administration of the federal court system.

LO8 Evaluate the major problems facing the federal courts and the strengths and weaknesses of the major solutions that have been proposed to address these problems.

Alfonso Lopez, Jr., a 12th-grader at Edison High School in San Antonio, Texas, thought he had found an easy way to make a quick buck. "Gilbert" would pay him $40 to take a .38-caliber pistol to school and deliver it to "Jason," who planned to use it in a "gang war." Based on an anonymous tip, school officials confronted Lopez, who admitted carrying the unloaded weapon (but he did have five bullets on his person). Lopez was charged in federal court with violating the Gun-Free School Zones Act of 1990. After a bench trial, Lopez was found guilty and sentenced to 6 months in prison. The Supreme Court reversed the conviction, however, concluding that the U.S. Congress had no authority to outlaw guns in schools.

The Supreme Court's decision in *United States v. Lopez* first attracts our attention because it deals with gun control—one of the truly hot button issues of American politics. But a closer probing raises other, even more important questions. What should be a federal crime? After all, weapons offenses are usually violations of state law, and indeed Mr. Lopez was initially charged in state court; but these charges were dropped after federal officials stepped in. How is it that five conservative judges, appointed by Republican presidents and pledged to getting tough on crime, reversed a conviction that was certainly popular with the American public? After all, Republicans have accused liberal federal judges (seemingly those appointed by Democratic presidents) of being soft on crime.

The issues, both direct and indirect, raised in *United States v. Lopez* trace their origins to the early days of the Republic. The founding fathers were deeply divided over which cases federal courts should hear. Indeed, the drafters of the U.S. Constitution were deeply divided over whether there should be any federal courts besides the U.S. Supreme Court. A principal task of this chapter, therefore, is to discuss how the current federal judicial structure—magistrate, district, and appellate courts and the Supreme Court—is a product of more than 200 years of political controversy and compromise about the proper role of the federal judiciary. The remainder of the chapter focuses on the specialized courts and their administrative structures. Most important, we will discuss the contemporary debate over how many cases are too many for the federal courts to handle, thus illustrating that the controversies continue. But first, to establish some common ground about the often confusing topic of court organization, we begin this chapter by examining some basic principles.

BASIC PRINCIPLES OF COURT ORGANIZATION

Even lawyers who regularly use the courts sometimes find the details of court organization confusing. Court nomenclature includes many shorthand phrases that mean something to those who work in the courts daily but can be quite confusing to the outsider. Learning the language of courts is like learning any foreign language—some of it can come only from experience. Before studying the specifics of federal courts in this chapter and state courts in Chapter 4, it is helpful to understand the basic principles of court organization within the dual court structure that exists in the United States.

Dual Court System

The United States has a **dual court system**: one national court system plus separate court systems in each of the 50 states and the District of Columbia. The result is more than 51 separate court systems. Figure 3.1 illustrates the structure of the dual court system in the United States. The division of responsibilities is not as clear-cut as it looks, however. State and federal courts sometimes have **concurrent** **jurisdiction** (meaning that they share some judicial powers) over certain types of cases. For example, selling drugs or robbing banks are crimes under federal law and under the laws of most states, which means the accused could be tried in either federal court or state court. Moreover, litigants in purely state court proceedings may appeal to the U.S. Supreme Court, a federal court, if a federal question is presented, such as a question of federal constitutional law.

One of the most immediate consequences of the dual court system is the complexity it adds to the criminal justice system. In essence, the framers of the U.S. Constitution created two parallel criminal justice systems consisting of their own law enforcement, court structure, and correctional systems. Of all the levels of complexity created by the dual court system, perhaps the most confusing is the application of the constitutional prohibition against double jeopardy (see "Courts, Controversy, & the Administration of Justice: Should the Double Jeopardy Clause Prohibit Parallel State and Federal Prosecutions?").

Jurisdiction

Court structure is largely determined by limitations on the types of cases a court may hear and decide. **Jurisdiction** is the power of a court to decide on a dispute. A court's jurisdiction can be further classified according to four subcomponents: geographical jurisdiction, subject matter jurisdiction, personal jurisdiction, and hierarchical jurisdiction.

Geographical Jurisdiction and Venue

Courts are authorized to hear and decide disputes arising within a specified **geographical jurisdiction** (sometimes referred to as "territorial jurisdiction"). Geographical jurisdiction in criminal cases is primarily concerned with a sovereign's power to punish conduct that violates its criminal laws. Thus, the courts of California have no jurisdiction to try a person accused of committing a crime in Oregon; Oregon has such power, since the accused is alleged to have violated its criminal law. But which courts within the state of Oregon would hear the case? That is a matter of venue.

Venue is the particular location or area in which a court having geographic jurisdiction may

United States Supreme Court
The High Court of Last Resort in the United States
The most powerful court in the world. It has virtually complete control of the cases it hears by exercising its discretionary appellate jurisdiction over decisions of the U.S. Courts of Appeals and the decisions of the highest courts in the state systems if a question of federal law (including federal constitutional law) is presented. Usually hears fewer than 90 cases each term, less than third of which typically involve criminal cases.

The Federal Courts
Hears cases throughout the United States. Decides roughly 78,000 criminal cases and 13,500 criminal appeals each year.

The State Courts
Important variations from state to state. Decides roughly 6.6 million adult criminal cases each year.

United States Courts of Appeals
Mandatory appellate jurisdiction over the decisions of the U.S. District Courts.
12 Regional Circuits and 1 Federal Circuit that hears appeals from specialized trial courts like the U.S. Court of International Trade, the U.S. Claims Court, and the U.S. Court of Veterans' Appeals.
The last stop for the vast majority of defendants convicted in federal court, very few of which win a significant victory.

State High Courts of Last Resort
Mandatory and discretionary appellate jurisdiction over decisions rendered by lower state courts. Major policy maker for the state. Final decider for questions of state law. Typically decides a handful of criminal appeals each year.

United States District Courts
Trial courts of original jurisdiction over federal cases. 94 federal districts (including territorial ones in the District of Columbia, Puerto Rico, Guam, the U.S. Virgin Islands, and the Northern Mariana Islands). Mandatory appellate jurisdiction over decisions by non-Article III courts.
Adjudicates all federal crimes like drug smuggling, mail fraud, robbery of FDIC-insured banks. Also adjudicates civil lawsuits like civil right cases, claims of federal civil law (e.g., copyright and trademark infringement), and state civil law claims involving diversity of citizenship, such as torts.
U.S. Magistrate Judges are responsible for preliminary stages of all federal felony cases. Magistrates also hear many minor criminal cases and assist with the processing of *habeas corpus* petitions and other civil lawsuits.

State Intermediate Appellate Courts
(40 out of 50 states)
Mandatory appellate jurisdiction over decisions by the state's major trial courts. Few criminal appellants win a significant victory.

State Major Trial Courts
Superior Courts/Courts of Common Pleas/District Courts
Trial courts of general jurisdiction that are usually arranged by county or groups of counties to hear felonies (murder, rape, robbery) and civil cases that do not involve small claims (accident cases, contract disputes). Sometimes they have appellate jurisdiction over state's minor trial courts.

Non-Article III Courts
U.S. Bankruptcy Courts, U.S. Tax Court, decisions of U.S. Magistrate Judges, and Administrative Law Judges (ALJ) in various federal agencies like the FCC, Social Security Administration, EEOC, NLRB, FTC, etc.

State Minor Trial Courts
Municipal Courts/Justice of the Peace Courts/ Magisterial District Courts
Limited original jurisdiction to hear misdemeanor cases (petty theft, public drunkenness, disorderly conduct), civil and criminal traffic violations, local ordinance violations, and small claims of a civil nature.

© Cengage Learning

Figure 3.1 ■ **Overview of the Dual Court Structure of the United States**

hear a case. Proper venue is based on statutorily defined geographic subdivisions. These subdivisions are often determined by city or county boundaries, although other boundaries can be set that are unrelated to city or county lines. Divisions in the federal system are a good example of this. Washington is a large and populous state. Instead of having one federal district coterminous with the boundaries of the state, there are two federal districts in Washington, the eastern district and the western district. Larger states are subdivided even further; California, for example, has a northern, eastern, central, and southern district. A federal case that arises from an act in Sacramento is properly tried in the northern district of California; the other districts in California would lack proper venue.

A defendant can waive venue in the district or county where a crime was committed by consenting to be tried in a venue in another district or county. In state courts, venue can generally be transferred only to another district or county within a particular state, since only the courts of that particular state would have geographic jurisdiction over alleged violations of its own criminal law. In contrast, venue can be changed between districts of the federal system since the offense is against the United States—the same sovereign in federal courts across the country.

Changes of venue in the federal courts are typically granted for one of two reasons. First, venue may be transferred to another location that is much more convenient for the parties and witnesses than the intended place of trial. Second, a change of venue is appropriate when a defendant is unlikely to get a fair and impartial trial in the federal district where the crime is alleged to have taken place. Intense pretrial publicity, for example, may have prejudiced the local jury pool. Since the right to a fair trial is guaranteed by the Sixth Amendment, a federal court should transfer venue to another federal district where the jury pool is less affected by pretrial publicity. For example, Timothy McVeigh, the defendant in the Oklahoma City bombing case, was tried for his crimes outside Oklahoma, even though that is where he committed the offenses. The extensive pretrial publicity and the intense personal connection to the case of the potential jurors in Oklahoma City made it very likely that the defendant could not get a fair and impartial trial in Oklahoma. The case was

therefore transferred to Denver, Colorado, where the jury pool was less personally involved and more likely to meet the constitutional due process guarantees of a fair and impartial jury.

One major complication arising from geographical jurisdiction occurs when a person is arrested in one state for committing a crime in another state.

Extradition involves the surrender by one state of an individual accused of a crime outside its own territory and within the territorial jurisdiction of the other state. If an American fugitive has fled to a foreign nation, the U.S. Secretary of State will request the return of the accused under the terms of the extradition treaty the United States has with that country (a few nations of the world do not have such treaties).

Subject Matter Jurisdiction

Court structure is also determined by **subject matter jurisdiction**. Trial courts of *limited or special jurisdiction* are restricted to hearing a limited category of cases, typically misdemeanors and civil suits involving small sums of money. State courts typically have traffic courts or juvenile courts, both of which are examples of subject matter jurisdiction. The federal courts are all courts of limited jurisdiction, since they are limited to adjudicating certain types of cases (to be discussed later in this chapter). In contrast to trial courts of limited/special jurisdiction, trial courts of *general jurisdiction* are empowered to hear all other types of cases within the geographical jurisdiction of the court. In the state court systems (to be discussed in the next chapter), the county trial court fits here.

Personal Jurisdiction

Personal jurisdiction (sometimes called "*in personum* jurisdiction") refers to a court's power over an individual person or corporation. A court gains power over a particular defendant by virtue of the defendant's having done some act within the place where the court is located or having had some contact with the place in which the court is located. In criminal cases, personal jurisdiction refers to a court's authority to try a defendant for violating the state's criminal law. While a bit of an oversimplification, courts obtain personal jurisdiction over a

COURTS, CONTROVERSY, & THE ADMINISTRATION of JUSTICE

SHOULD THE DOUBLE JEOPARDY CLAUSE PROHIBIT PARALLEL STATE AND FEDERAL PROSECUTIONS?

On May 7, 1985, 27-year-old Army Sergeant Timothy Hennis responded to a classified ad placed by a North Carolina woman who was trying to sell a dog. A few days later, authorities found the bodies of the woman and two of her three children in their home. The woman had been raped and stabbed fifteen times.

A community member told police that a few days earlier, he had seen a seen a man (whom he later identified as Hennis) wearing a black "Members Only" jacket leaving the family's driveway with a garbage bag slung over his shoulder. The Friday after the murders, Hennis had taken a black "Members Only" jacket to a local dry cleaner's. The following day, Hennis's neighbors saw him burning a bonfire in a 55-gallon drum for at least 5 hours. Fingerprints and pubic hair were found at the crime scene; none of them belonged to the family members. And none of evidence or the semen found in the victim were a match with Hennis.

Hennis was charged with three counts of murder and one count of rape. He was convicted and sentenced to death. His conviction was set aside on appeal because of evidentiary rulings that may have inflamed and biased the jury at Hennis's trial. Hennis was acquitted on all counts at this second trial, due, in large part, to two factors. First, the unduly prejudicial evidence erroneously used in the first trial was excluded from the second trial. Second, defense attorneys were able to discredit the testimony of the community member who had previously identified Hennis. This

witness first described the man he had seen as one shorter and slighter than himself, but then revised his description to match Hennis' build—one considerably taller and heavier than the witness's own. After his acquittal, Hennis reenlisted in the Army, apparently serving exemplarily until he retired in July 2005.

In the mid-1980s, forensic science was much less precise than it is today and DNA technology had not yet been used for law enforcement purposes. In the spring of 2005, however, 20 years after the murders, a homicide detective sent the semen sample recovered from the crime scene for DNA testing. It was a match for Tim Hennis. The Double Jeopardy Clause of the Fifth Amendment to the U.S. Constitution prevents the same sovereign from trying a criminal defendant on the same charges after acquittal. Thus, North Carolina could not try Hennis again for either the rape or the murders. But the federal government is a different sovereign and, therefore, is not technically bound by double jeopardy in the Hennis case. With that in mind, the Army recalled Hennis to active service in September 2006. His court martial trial in a federal, military court began in March 2010. The following month, and after only 3 hours of deliberation, a jury convicted Hennis. He was sentenced to death and currently has appeals pending. According to the Death Penalty Information Center, Hennis is the only person in U.S. history to have been exonerated after a capital conviction and then returned to death row for the same crime.

Some scholars have argued that that the Army violated the spirit—if not the precise letter—of the Constitution's prohibition on double jeopardy. What do you think? Are federal prosecutions after failed state prosecutions a good way to remedy miscarriages of justice, or are the rights of defendants unnecessarily placed in jeopardy?

defendant by the defendant having violated the law of the particular sovereign while within the forum state. This is relatively straightforward for traditional crimes against a person such as assault, rape, or murder. In contrast, establishing personal jurisdiction over a criminal defendant accused of fraud or cybercrimes who was not physically present

in the forum state at the time the alleged crime occurred can be quite complicated (see Kerr, 2008).

Hierarchical Jurisdiction

The third subcomponent of jurisdiction is hierarchical jurisdiction, which refers to differences in the courts' functions and responsibilities. **Original jurisdiction** means that a court has the authority to try a case and decide it. **Appellate jurisdiction** means that a court has the power to review cases that have already been decided by another court. Trial courts are primarily courts of original jurisdiction, but they occasionally have limited appellate jurisdiction—for example, when a trial court hears appeals from lower trial courts such as a municipal court or a justice of the peace court (Chapter 4). Appellate courts often have very limited original jurisdiction. The U.S. Supreme Court has original jurisdiction involving disputes between states, and state supreme courts have original jurisdiction in matters involving disbarment of lawyers.

Differentiating Trial and Appellate Courts

Virtually all cases begin in a **trial court** that has original jurisdiction. In a criminal case, the trial court arraigns the defendant, conducts a trial (or takes a guilty plea) and, if the defendant is found guilty, imposes sentence. In a civil case, the trial court operates in much the same way, ensuring that each party is properly informed of the complaint and conducting a trial or accepting an out-of-court settlement. Because only trial courts hear disputes over facts, witnesses appear only in trial courts. Trial courts are considered finders of fact, and the decision of a judge (or jury) about a factual dispute is very difficult to challenge on appeal (Chapter 16).

The losing party in the trial court generally has the right to request an appellate court to review the case. The primary function of the **appellate court** is to ensure that the trial court correctly interpreted the law. But appellate courts may also make new law.

Appellate and trial courts operate very differently because their roles are not the same. Appellate courts exercising appellate jurisdiction do not hear testimony from witnesses, conduct trials, or use juries. Those actions occur in a trial court exercising original jurisdiction. Moreover, instead of a single judge deciding, as in trial courts, a group of judges makes appellate court decisions; there may be as few as 3 or as many as 28 judges. (For more details on appellate courts and the appeals process, see Chapter 16.)

HISTORY OF THE FEDERAL COURTS

At first glance, the history of the federal courts appears to be a debate over details of procedure. But a closer look reveals that the political controversies that have shaped the federal judiciary go to the heart of the federal system of government, often involving the allocation of power between the national and state governments. Thus, any discussion of the federal courts in the early 21st century must begin with two 18th-century landmarks—Article III of the U.S. Constitution and the Judiciary Act of 1789. Although there have been important changes since, the decisions made at the beginning of the Republic about the nature of the federal judiciary have had a marked impact on contemporary court structure.

The Constitutional Convention

One major weakness of the Articles of Confederation was the absence of a national supreme court to enforce federal law and resolve conflicts and disputes between courts of the different states. Thus, when the delegates gathered at the Constitutional Convention in Philadelphia in 1787, a resolution was unanimously adopted that "a national judiciary be established." There was considerable disagreement, however, on the specific form that the national judiciary should take. Article III was one of the most hotly debated sections of the Constitution.

The dominant question of whether there should be a federal court system separate from the state systems produced two schools of thought. Advocates of states' rights (later called "Anti-Federalists") feared that a strong national government would weaken individual liberties. More specifically, they saw the creation of separate federal courts as a threat to the power of state courts. As a result, the Anti-Federalists believed that federal law should be adjudicated first by the state courts; the U.S. Supreme Court should be limited to hearing appeals only from state courts. On the other hand, the Nationalists (who later called themselves "Federalists" because they favored ratification of the Constitution) distrusted the provincial prejudices of the states and favored a strong national government that could provide economic and political unity for the struggling new nation. As part of this approach, the Nationalists viewed state courts as incapable of developing a uniform body of federal law that would allow businesses to flourish. For these reasons, they backed the creation of lower federal courts.

The conflict between Federalists and Anti-Federalists was resolved by one of the many compromises that characterized the Constitutional Convention. Article III is brief, providing only an outline of a federal judiciary: "The judicial Power of the United States, shall be vested in one Supreme Court, and in such inferior Courts as the Congress may from time to time ordain and establish." The brevity of this provision left Congress with the task of filling in much of the substance of the new judicial system.

The Judiciary Act of 1789

Once the Constitution was ratified, action on the federal judiciary came quickly. Indeed, the first bill introduced in the Senate dealt with the unresolved issue of inferior federal courts. The congressional debate included many of the same participants, who repeated all the arguments involved in the judiciary debates at the Constitutional Convention. After extensive debate, Congress passed the Judiciary Act of 1789, which laid the foundation for our current national judicial system. The Judiciary Act of 1789 represented a major victory for the Federalists; they were successful in creating separate federal district courts. At the same time, the act was a compromise that allayed some of the Anti-Federalists' fears. The organization of the federal judiciary supported state interests in three ways (LaCroix, 2007; Richardson & Vines, 1970).

First, the boundaries of the district courts were drawn along state lines; no district encompassed more than one state. Thus, from the outset, the federal judiciary was "state-contained." Even though district courts enforced national law, they were organized along local lines, with each district court responsible for its own work under minimal supervision.

Second, by custom the selection process ensured that federal district judges would be residents of their districts. Although nominated by the president, district judges were to be (and are today) local residents, presiding in their home area, and therefore

subject to the continuing influence of the local social and political environment (see Chapter 8).

Third, the act gave the lower federal courts only limited jurisdiction. The Federalists wanted the full range of federal jurisdiction granted by the Constitution to be given to district and circuit courts. However, to achieve a lower federal court system, they were forced to reduce this demand greatly. But this issue would reappear repeatedly over the next 100 years.

1789–1891

The Judiciary Act of 1789 provided only a temporary compromise on the underlying disagreements between Federalists and Anti-Federalists. The Federalists immediately pushed for expanded powers for the federal judiciary. These efforts culminated in the passage of the Judiciary Act of 1801, which created many new judgeships and greatly extended the jurisdiction of the lower courts. The Federalist victory was short-lived, however. With the election of Thomas Jefferson as president, the Anti-Federalists in Congress quickly repealed the act and returned the federal judiciary to the basic outlines of the previous court system. The 1801 law is best remembered for the resulting lawsuit of *Marbury v. Madison* (1803), in which Chief Justice John Marshall declared that the U.S. Constitution granted courts the power of judicial review—the authority to invalidate acts of Congress as unconstitutional (for more on judicial review, see Appendix D).

Between 1789 and 1891 there was general agreement on the inadequacy of the federal judicial system, but the underlying dispute persisted. Congress passed numerous minor bills modifying the system in a piecemeal fashion. Dissatisfaction centered on two principal areas: circuit riding and the appellate court workload.

One of the most pronounced weaknesses of the 1789 judicial structure was circuit riding. The Supreme Court justices, many of them old and ill, faced days of difficult and often impossible travel. In 1838, for example, the nine justices traveled an average of 2,975 miles. There were numerous complaints from the justices about the intolerable conditions that circuit-riding duties imposed on them.

Beyond the personal discomforts some justices encountered, the federal judiciary confronted a more systemic problem—mounting caseloads.

Initially, the federal judges of the newly created trial courts had relatively little to do because their jurisdictions were very limited. The Supreme Court likewise had few cases to decide. But the initially sparse workload began to expand as the growth of federal activity, the increase in corporate business, and the expansion of federal jurisdiction by court interpretation created litigation for a court system that was ill equipped to handle it. From the end of the Civil War until 1891, it was not uncommon for an appeal to wait 2 or 3 years before it was argued before the Supreme Court. This was because the high court had to decide every case appealed to it.

Court of Appeals Act of 1891

At first glance, the creation of the court of appeals in 1891 appears to have been an automatic response to increased federal litigation resulting from a rapidly expanding population and the growth of business following the Civil War. A closer look indicates that it was the culmination of "one of the most enduring struggles in American political history" (Richardson & Vines 1970, p. 26). There was no debate over the difficulties facing the federal court system. All parties to the controversy agreed that the federal judiciary needed relief; what was in dispute was the nature of the relief.

To solve the burden of mounting litigation in the federal courts, the supporters of states' rights wanted to return cases to the state level by reducing the jurisdiction of federal courts. The supporters of national power, on the other hand, argued for expanding the jurisdiction of federal courts by creating a system of federal appellate courts that would take a great deal of the burden off the high court and also allow the trial courts to function as true trial courts.

The landmark Court of Appeals Act of 1891 represented the climactic victory of the Nationalists' interests. The law created new courts known as circuit courts of appeals. Under this new arrangement, most appeals of trial decisions went to a circuit court of appeals. In short, the creation of the circuit courts of appeals released the high court from hearing many types of petty cases. The high court now had much greater control over its workload and could concentrate on deciding major cases and controversies.

Federal Courts Today

In 1925, Congress passed the Judges Bill, which among other things gave the Supreme Court much greater control over its docket. In 1988, Congress eliminated even more mandatory appeals to the high court. Other important changes that have shaped the development of the federal courts are presented in box titled, "Key Developments in the Federal Judiciary."

The current structure of federal courts is best understood in terms of four layers of courts: magistrate, district, appellate, and Supreme Court. In addition, the federal judiciary includes specialized courts and administrative structures.

KEY DEVELOPMENTS IN THE FEDERAL JUDICIARY

U.S. Constitution	1787	Article III creates U.S. Supreme Court and authorizes lower federal courts.
Judiciary Act of 1789	1789	Congress establishes lower federal courts.
Marbury v. Madison	1803	The Court has the authority to declare an act of Congress unconstitutional.
Courts of Appeals Act	1891	Modern appellate structure is created.
Judges Bill	1925	Supreme Court is given control over its docket.
Court Packing Plan	1937	FDR's attempt to pack the Court is defeated.

© Cengage Learning

Continued on next page

Continued from previous page

Administrative Office Act	1939	Current administrative structure is created, including judicial conference and judicial councils.
Federal Judicial Center	1967	Research and training unit is created.
Federal Magistrate Act	1968	Commissioners are replaced by U.S. magistrates (later, the name is changed to "magistrate judges").
Multidistrict Litigation Act	1968	Created the Judicial Panel on Multidistrict Litigation and gave it the power to transfer to a single district court the pretrial proceedings for civil cases involving common questions of fact, such as litigation regarding airplane crashes, product liability, patent infringements, and securities fraud.
Bankruptcy Reform Act	1978	Conferred original bankruptcy jurisdiction on the U.S. district courts and established a bankruptcy court in each judicial district to exercise bankruptcy jurisdiction.
Foreign Intelligence Surveillance Act	1978	Authorized the chief justice of the United States to designate seven federal district court judges to review applications for warrants related to national security investigations on a special court named the "Foreign Intelligence Surveillance Court." The Act also created the U.S. Foreign Intelligence Surveillance Court of Review, a special appellate court whose only function is to review denials by the Foreign Intelligence Surveillance Court of applications for electronic surveillance warrants.
Federal Courts Improvement Act	1982	Congress combined the jurisdictions of the U.S. Court of Customs and Patent Appeals and the U.S. Court of Claims into one court, the U.S. Court of Appeals for the Federal Circuit.
Sentencing Commission	1984	Commission is charged with developing sentencing guidelines.
Congressional Act of 1988	1988	Some mandatory appeals to the Supreme Court are eliminated.
Antiterrorism and Effective Death Penalty Act (AEDPA)	1996	Right of state prisoners to file *habeas corpus petitions* in federal court is severely limited.
USA PATRIOT Act	2001	The government's ability to gather domestic antiterrorism intelligence is expanded, allowing for less court scrutiny and closing some court proceedings to the public.
Military Trials for Enemy Combatants Act	2006	The president was empowered to identify enemy combatants and detain them indefinitely without their being able to obtain federal court review of their detentions through *habeas corpus* proceedings, a right traditionally afforded to prisoners.
House v. Bell	2006	Created a narrow exception to the AEDPA by allowing prisoners with evidence of actual innocence to obtain *habeas corpus* review if a "miscarriage of justice" would occur with the court's review.
Boumediene v. Bush and Al Odah v. United States	2008	The Supreme Court invalidated the provision of the Military Trials for Enemy Combatants Act that deprived the detainees of their constitutional right to *habeas corpus* review in the federal courts.

U.S. MAGISTRATE JUDGES

Congress created **U.S. magistrate judges** in 1968 to replace the former position of U.S. commissioners. The purpose was to provide a new type of judicial officer in the federal judicial system to alleviate the increased workload of the U.S. district courts (Anderson, 2007). Technically, magistrate judges and their courts are a subcomponent of federal district courts; their duties and workload, however, merit separate discussion.

Magistrate judges perform quasi-judicial tasks and work within the judicial branch of government. They are not, however, Article III judges. Magistrate judges are selected by district court judges. Full-time magistrate judges are appointed for 8-year terms, and part-time magistrate judges for 4 years. They may, however, be removed for "good cause." Except in special circumstances, all must be lawyers. According to the Administrative Office of the U.S. Courts, there are currently 571 full-time magistrate judges and 44 part-time magistrate judges.

Magistrate judges are authorized to perform a wide variety of duties. In felony cases, they are responsible for preliminary proceedings, including holding initial appearances, conducting preliminary hearings, appointing counsel for indigents, setting bail, and issuing search warrants. In misdemeanor and petty offense cases, the jurisdiction of magistrate judges is more extensive; they may preside over trials, accept pleas of guilty, and also impose sentences. On the civil side, they supervise discovery, review Social Security disability benefit appeals, and even conduct full civil trials with the consent of the litigants. In short, under specified conditions and controls, magistrate judges may perform virtually all tasks carried out by district court judges, except trying and sentencing felony defendants (*Gonzales v. United States*, 2008).

Caseload of U.S. Magistrate Judges

Magistrate judges play an increasingly important role in helping district court judges dispose of their growing caseloads. In a typical year, for example, magistrate judges handle approximately 1.03 million matters for the federal courts, including being involved in some way in roughly 560,000 felony matters. In addition, they dispose of approximately 117,000 misdemeanor and petty offenses and 21,900 prisoner litigation cases. Magistrate judges are also involved in assisting with nearly 261,000 civil matters, although they preside over only about 5 percent of all civil trials in federal courts.

U.S. DISTRICT COURTS

Congress has created 94 **U.S. district courts**, of which 89 are located within the 50 states. There is also a district court in the District of Columbia and four territorial district courts located in Guam, Puerto Rico, the Virgin Islands, and the Northern Mariana Islands.

There is at least one district court in each state; moreover, based on the compromise that produced the Judiciary Act of 1789, no district court crosses state lines. Some states have more than one district court: California, New York, and Texas, for instance, each have four. Because district courts often encompass large geographical areas, some hold court in various locations, or divisions. Some districts have only one division, while others have several.

Congress has created 678 district court judgeships for the 94 districts. The president nominates district judges, who must then be confirmed by the Senate (see Chapter 8). Once they take the oath of office, they serve during "good behavior," which for practical purposes means for life. The number of judgeships in each district depends on the amount of judicial work as well as the political clout of the state's congressional delegation; the number ranges from 3 active district judges in sparsely populated Wyoming to 28 in densely inhabited Manhattan (officially called the U.S. District Court for the Southern District of New York).

Judges are assisted by an elaborate supporting cast of clerks, secretaries, law clerks, court reporters, probation officers, pretrial services officers, and U.S. marshals. The larger districts also have a federal public defender. Another important actor at the district-court level is the U.S. attorney. There is one U.S. attorney (see Chapter 6) in each district, nominated by the president and confirmed by the Senate, but unlike the judges, he or she serves at the pleasure of the president.

The work of the district judges is significantly assisted by 352 **bankruptcy judges**. Although bankruptcy judges are adjuncts of the district courts, they are appointed for 14-year terms by the court of appeals in which the district is located. In 2005, bankruptcy filings reached an astonishing level, with more than 1.78 million petitions filed. The vast majority of these bankruptcy filings were non–business-related, typically involving consumers who cannot pay their bills; the others were filed by businesses big and small. That same year, however, Congress passed the Bankruptcy Abuse Prevention and Consumer Protection Act of 2005. The law made it more difficult for consumers to discharge debts that they were having trouble paying. As a result, the number of bankruptcy petitions filed dropped to around 800,000 per year by 2007. In the wake of the economic downturn since then, however, bankruptcy filings have risen again, to nearly 1.6 million petitions.

Caseload of U.S. District Courts

In the federal system, the U.S. district courts are the federal trial courts of original jurisdiction. Table 3.1 provides an overview of case volume in the federal courts. The volume of cases is large and growing in complexity.

The district courts are the trial courts for all major violations of federal criminal law. Each year, U.S. attorneys file approximately 78,000 criminal cases, primarily for drug violations, embezzlement, and fraud. For many years, federal prosecutions remained fairly constant (roughly 30,000 per year), only to shoot up beginning in 1980. A major part of this upsurge has been the dramatic increase in drug prosecutions, which, as Figure 3.2 illustrates, account for more than 20 percent of all federal criminal cases. Moreover, trials of criminal cases are now more frequent (and also longer) than in years past. Thus, although civil, not criminal, cases

account for most of the work of the district courts, in some districts criminal filings are limiting the ability of these courts to decide civil cases.

Civil lawsuits consume considerably more of the federal courts' time than criminal cases do. Although only a small number of all civil cases are filed in federal courts as compared with state courts, federal civil cases typically involve considerably larger sums of money than the cases filed in state court. This is due, in part, to the types of cases over which the federal courts have jurisdiction. Federal courts are permitted to hear only civil cases involving diversity of citizenship and several types of cases that involve questions of federal law, including prisoner petitions.

Diversity Jurisdiction

Diversity of citizenship cases involve suits between citizens of different states or between a U.S. citizen and a foreign country or citizen. For example, a citizen from California claims to be injured in an automobile accident in Chicago with an Illinois driver and sues in federal court in Illinois because the parties to the suit are of "diverse citizenship." Pursuant to the Supreme Court's decision in *Erie Railroad Co. v. Tompkins* (1938), federal courts apply state—not federal—law when adjudicating state claims in federal court under their diversity of citizenship jurisdiction.

From the 1980s through the mid-1990s, diversity cases constituted approximately 25 percent of the civil docket of the district courts, thus making a significant contribution to the workload of the district courts. In an effort to restrict the types of minor disputes that may be filed in federal court, Congress in 1996 raised the amount-in-controversy to $75,000 under 28 U.S.C. § 1332(a). At first, this

TABLE 3.1 ▪ CASE FILINGS IN THE U.S. COURTS

	2002	2007	2010
U.S. Supreme Court	8,255	8,241	7,857
U.S. Circuit Courts of Appeals	57,555	58,410	55,992
U.S. District Courts	341,841	325,920	361,323
U.S. Bankruptcy Courts	1,547,669	801,269	1,596,355

© Cengage Learning

Traffic offenses on federal land
4,432 (6%)

Regulatory offenses
1,743 (2%)

Violent felonies
2,252 (3%)

Other, nonviolent crimes
1,739 (2%)

Property crimes
13,340 (17%)

Immigration offenses
28,435 (36%)

Drug offenses
16,109 (20%)

Firearms & explosives
7,183 (9%)

Justice system offenses
823 (1%)

Sex offenses
3,041 (4%)

Figure 3.2 ■ Federal Criminal Prosecutions

SOURCE: Federal Judicial Center. *Caseload Statistics* 2011, Table D-2. Washington, DC: Administrative Office of the U.S. Courts.

change in jurisdictional amount decreased the number of diversity cases filed in federal courts each year such that diversity cases were reduced to 18.7 percent of the federal civil caseload in 2000. However, the effects of the change in the amount-in-controversy were short-lived. Since 2005, diversity filings have constituted between 25 and 36 percent of the federal civil case load. Given the burdensome workload that diversity jurisdiction brings to the federal courts, combined with the fact that the exercise of diversity jurisdiction requires the federal courts to apply state law—a task that is arguably better performed in state courts—both judges and legal scholars have called for the abolition of diversity of citizenship jurisdiction in the federal courts. If that were to occur, the federal courts would be able to focus on federal questions. However, Congress has not heeded such calls. Rather, Congress may have decided to maintain the status quo because it agreed with the overwhelming sentiment of lawyers in private practice that state courts are

biased against out-of-state defendants (Underwood, 2006). Alternatively, Congress may simply have opted to continue using the federal courts to resolve interstate disputes.

Federal Questions

Article III provides that federal courts may be given jurisdiction over "Cases, in Law and Equity, arising under this Constitution, the Laws of the United States, and Treaties made, or which shall be made under their authority." Cases that fall under this type of jurisdiction are generally referred to as involving a **federal question**. Although some federal question cases present issues concerning the interpretation or application of the U.S. Constitution, most federal question cases concern the application or interpretation of a statute enacted by Congress as illustrated in Exhibit 3.1. Some of these laws—and the decisions of the federal courts interpreting them—significantly affect the operation of the criminal justice system.

Exhibit 3.1   FEDERAL QUESTION JURISDICTION CASES

- Suits between states—Cases in which two or more states are parties.

- Cases involving ambassadors and other high-ranking public figures—Cases arising between foreign ambassadors and other high-ranking public officials.

- Federal crimes—Crimes defined by or mentioned in the U.S. Constitution or those defined and/or punished by federal statute. Such crimes include treason against the United States, piracy, counterfeiting, crimes against the law of nations, and crimes relating to the federal government's authority to regulate interstate commerce. However, most crimes are state matters.

- Bankruptcy—The statutory procedure, usually triggered by insolvency, by which a person is relieved of most debts and undergoes a judicially supervised reorganization or liquidation for the benefit of the person's creditors.

- Patent, copyright, and trademark cases:

  (1) Patent—The exclusive right to make, use, or sell an invention for a specified period (usually 17 years), granted by the federal government to the inventor if the device or process is novel, useful, and non-obvious.

  (2) Copyright—The body of law relating to a property right in an original work of authorship (such as a literary, musical, artistic, photographic, or film work) fixed in any tangible medium of expression, giving the holder the exclusive right to reproduce, adapt, distribute, perform, and display the work.

  (3) Trademark—A word, phrase, logo, or other graphic symbol used by a manufacturer or seller to distinguish its product or products from those of others.

- Admiralty—The system of jurisprudence that has grown out of the practice of admiralty courts: courts that exercise jurisdiction over all maritime contracts, torts, injuries, and offenses.

- Antitrust—The body of law designed to protect trade and commerce from restraining monopolies, price fixing, and price discrimination.

- Securities and banking regulation—The body of law protecting the public by regulating the registration, offering, and trading of securities and the regulation of banking practices.

- Other cases specified by federal statute—Any other cases specified by an applicable federal statute, such as of civil rights, labor relations, environmental cases, and cases arising under the Americans with Disabilities Act.

SOURCE: "Understanding Federal and State Courts." Available online at http://www.uscourts.gov/EducationalResources/FederalCourtBasics/CourtStructure/UnderstandingFederalAndStateCourts.aspx

The Constitutionalization of Criminal Procedure

Under Chief Justice Earl Warren, the U.S. Supreme Court sparked a due process revolution, giving defendants the right to counsel (Chapter 7), broadening notions of a fair trial (Chapter 13), and expanding the right to appeal (Chapter 16). The federal courts have also set standards regulating how local and state law enforcement officers gather evidence and interrogate suspects (Chapter 11). And the federal courts continue to impact greatly the sentencing and punishment of criminal offenders (Chapter 14). Violations of these constitutional rights as interpreted in relevant federal court precedent can lead to a conviction being overturned either on direct appeal or collaterally in *habeas corpus* proceedings (Chapter 16).

Discrimination Laws and Civil Rights Cases

Federal laws prohibit discrimination on the basis of race, religion, sex, age, or national origin in domains such as employment, welfare, housing, and voting. For example, except in rare instances, employers are required to ignore gender when hiring or promoting, provide equal pay to all employees, and treat pregnancy like any other temporary disability (Kruger, 2007). Bona fide occupational qualifications, however, are exempt. Thus, valid job-related requirements necessary to normal business operations are allowed. Criminal justice agencies, though, should avoid height and weight requirements that are not legitimately related to job performance.

Similarly, the roughly 43 million people with disabilities in the United States are protected against discrimination in employment and in their use of public facilities and services under the Americans with Disabilities Act. These protections affect the design and functionality of police departments, courthouses, and correctional facilities to accommodate the special needs of the disabled. In *Yeskey v. Pennsylvania Department of Corrections* (1998), the U.S. Supreme Court held that the Americans with Disabilities Act applies to the ways in which police officers and correctional officials interact with people with disabilities. As a result, police may be civilly liable for arresting someone because they confuse the effects of a disability with criminally aggressive behavior or because they fail to accommodate a person's disability during investigation, interrogation, or arrest (Osborn, 2008). Similarly, the Court held in *United States v. Georgia* (2006) that states and municipalities can be held civilly liable for failing to maintain correctional facilities that accommodate the special needs of disabled prisoners.

Prisoner Petitions

In spite of a criminal conviction, inmates in local, state, and federal custody all retain certain constitutional rights. The Supreme Court emphasized this point in *Wolff v. McDonnell* (1974), when it said, "There is no iron curtain drawn between the Constitution and the prisons of this country" (pp. 555–556). To enforce their rights, prisoners are permitted to file several types of civil lawsuits, which are collectively referred to as **prisoner petitions**. The four primary types of prisoner petitions that the federal courts adjudicate are summarized in Table 3.2.

Prisoner petitions have grown steadily and now account for a considerable portion of the workload of the federal courts. Collectively, civil rights cases from state and federal inmates have increased significantly, from about 3,500 filings in 1960 to a record high of more than 68,235 cases in 1996. These numbers were driven, in large part, by the sharp increase in the prison population over the corresponding period. The following year, prisoner petitions began to decrease as a result of Congress enacting the Prison Litigation Reform Act (PLRA) of 1996. The PLRA made it more difficult for prisoners to file Section 1983 cases by requiring them to exhaust administrative remedies before filing a federal case, by making them pay certain fees from which they had previously been exempt, and by barring them from filing subsequent cases if they had prior Section 1983 cases dismissed for being frivolous or malicious.

U.S. magistrate judges greatly assist federal district judges with *habeas* petitions and prisoner civil rights. But, because they are not Article III judges, magistrates generally write a report to the U.S. district judge to whom the case is formally assigned. The report concludes with a recommendation for how to rule in the case. The report and recommendation is usually adopted by the district judge who ultimately orders the final judgment in the case.

Discrimination and Civil Rights Caseload in the Federal Courts

Nonprisoner civil rights filings doubled in U.S. district courts from 1990 (18,922 filings) to 1997 (43,278 filings). This increase in the civil rights caseload of the federal courts was due, in large part, to the major expansion of federal civil rights by various acts of Congress, most especially the passage of the Americans for Disabilities Act of 1990 and the Civil Rights Act of 1991, which amended several older employment discrimination laws, including, among others, Title VII of the Civil Rights Act of 1964 and the Age Discrimination in Employment Act of 1973. In the early 2000s, civil rights filings stabilized at around 40,500 cases per year. Since then, however, they have declined to around 36,500 filings, thereby accounting for approximately 12.5 percent of all civil cases filed in the federal courts.

TABLE 3.2 ▪ PRISONER PETITIONS IN U.S. DISTRICT COURTS IN 2011

Prisoner Petition		Number Filed	Percent of Prisoner Petitions	Percent of Total Civil Docket
Type	Description			
Habeas Corpus	Typically filed under 28 U.S.C. § 2254, habeas corpus cases are those in which inmates may collaterally challenge their convictions (after exhausting all available state remedies to do so) by arguing that their trial was constitutionally defective.	20,880	39.16%	7.09%
Motions to Vacate Sentence	Allow a federal prisoner to try to get a sentence set aside or corrected because the sentence was imposed contrary to law. Such motions might allege that the court lacked jurisdiction to impose a criminal sentence or that the sentence was in excess of that allowed under the law.	6,178	11.59%	2.10%
Mandamus Petitions	Seeks a court order to compel a public entity or official to do something that is owed to the plaintiff as a matter of constitutional or statutory right.	989	1.85%	0.34%
Section 1983 and Bivens Civil Rights actions	Against state actors: 42 U.S.C. § 1983 allows individual persons to sue those who act under color of state law to redress alleged deprivations of constitutional rights. Typical claims are use of excessive force, illegal searches and seizures, interference with Fifth and/or Sixth Amendment rights to counsel during interrogations (Chapter 11), denials of First Amendment rights, interference with the Sixth Amendment right to access the courts, and violations of the Eighth Amendment's guarantee against cruel and unusual punishment based on claims of excessive force, lack of medical care, or inhumane conditions of confinement. Against federal actors: Bivens v. Six Unknown Agents of the Federal Bureau of Narcotics (1971), permits private persons to sue those who act under color of federal authority (e.g., federal law enforcement or correctional officers) for alleged deprivations of constitutional rights.	25,276	47.40%	8.59%

SOURCE: Federal Judicial Center. Caseload Statistics 2011, Table C-2. Washington, DC: Administrative Office of the U.S. Courts.

U.S. COURTS OF APPEALS

As mentioned previously, Congress created the U.S. courts of appeals in 1891 to relieve the Supreme Court from hearing the growing number of appeals. The courts of appeals are the intermediate appellate courts of the federal system. Originally called "circuit courts of appeal,"

they were renamed and are each now officially known as the U.S. Court of Appeals for the _____ Circuit. Each circuit hears appeals from specific district courts. At present, there are 14 circuits: 11 numbered circuits (each containing at least three states); a Circuit Court of Appeals for the District of Columbia; the Court of Appeals for the Federal Circuit; and the Court of Appeals for the Armed Forces.

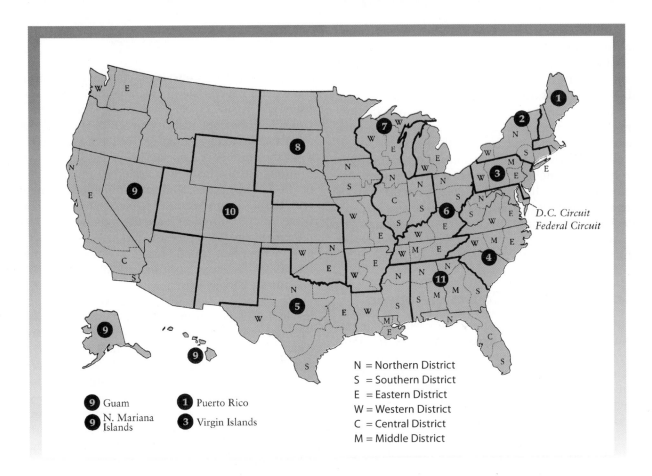

N = Northern District
S = Southern District
E = Eastern District
W = Western District
C = Central District
M = Middle District

9 Guam
9 N. Mariana Islands
1 Puerto Rico
3 Virgin Islands

Figure 3.3 ■ Geographic Boundaries of the Federal Courts

SOURCE: Russell Wheeler and Cynthia Harrison. *Creating the Federal Judicial System.* 2nd ed. Washington, DC: Federal Judicial Center, 1994, p. 26.

As illustrated in Figure 3.3, the numbered circuits and the Circuit Court of Appeals for the District of Columbia are geographically arranged. All 12 of these circuit courts are empowered to review all final decisions of U.S. district courts, as well as certain interlocutory decisions of district courts (see Chapter 16). They also have the power to review and enforce orders of many federal administrative bodies. In contrast, the Federal Circuit is the only civilian judicial circuit whose jurisdiction is based on subject matter rather than geographical boundaries. It was created by an act of Congress in 1982 and granted nationwide jurisdiction to hear specialized appeals concerning certain types of government contracts, patents, trademarks, certain nontort money claims against the U.S. government, federal personnel, and veterans' benefits. Finally, the Court of Appeals for the Armed Forces hears appeals only from cases decided in military courts and tribunals concerning members of the U.S. armed forces on active duty and other persons subject to the Uniform Code of Military Justice.

The courts of appeals are staffed by 179 judges nominated by the president and confirmed by the Senate. As with the district courts, the number of judges in each circuit varies, from 6 (the First Circuit) to 29 (the Ninth Circuit), depending on the volume and complexity of the caseload. Each circuit has a chief judge who performs administrative duties in addition to hearing cases. As a rule, the judge who has served on the court the longest and who is under 65 years of age is designated as the chief judge. Several staff positions aid the judges in conducting the work of the courts of appeals. A circuit executive assists the chief judge in administering the circuit. The clerk's office maintains the records. Each judge is also allowed to hire three law clerks. In addition, each circuit has a central legal staff that screens appeals and drafts memorandum opinions.

In deciding cases, the courts of appeals normally use rotating three-judge panels. Along with active judges in the circuit, these panels often include visiting judges (primarily district judges from the same circuit) and senior judges. By majority vote, all the judges in the circuit may sit together to decide a case or rehear a case already decided by a panel. Such *en banc* hearings are relatively rare, however; in a typical year fewer than 100 are held throughout the entire nation.

Caseload of U.S. Courts of Appeals

Over the past five decades, the caseload of the courts of appeals has skyrocketed. This dramatic increase in caseload has not been matched by an equivalent increase in judgeships, however. In 1960, there were 68 judgeships whose workload involved hearing 172 cases per three-judge panel. Today, there are 179 circuit court judges who hear more than 1,000 cases per three-judge panel.

The number of appeals filed annually in the federal courts has varied between 54,679 in 2000 to a high of 68,473 in 2005. That number has fallen, as 55,753 appeals were filed in 2011, the most recent year for which statistics are available. Appeals from criminal convictions in the U.S. district courts constitute about 29 percent of the workload of the courts of appeals. Appeals from decisions in prisoner petition cases comprise 25.4 percent of the federal appellate caseload. Thus, criminal and prisoner petitions account for nearly 55 percent of the appeals filed each year, while civil appeals, including bankruptcy appeals and appeals from administrative agencies, account for the remainder.

A decision by the court of appeals exhausts the litigant's right to one appeal. The losing party may request that the Supreme Court hear the case, but such petitions are rarely granted. As a result, the courts of appeals are the "courts of last resort" for virtually all federal litigation. Their decisions end the case; only a tiny percentage will be heard by the nation's highest court.

U.S. SUPREME COURT

The **U.S. Supreme Court** is the court of last resort in the federal court system, meaning that it is a court from which no appeal is possible. The Supreme Court has one chief justice and a number of associate justices fixed by Congress. By act of Congress in 1948, the number of associate justices is eight. Power to nominate the justices is vested in the president of the United States, and appointments are made with the advice and consent of the Senate. Once confirmed to the Supreme Court, there is no mandatory retirement age for Supreme Court justices; so as long as they maintain "good behavior," the justices may remain on the court until their death or until they voluntarily choose to retire.

The Constitution grants the Supreme Court original jurisdiction in a limited number of cases. In other words, the Supreme Court acts as a trial court in certain types of cases, such as controversies between the United States and a state, between two states, or between foreign ministers or ambassadors. Such cases are quite rare; so in the overwhelming majority of cases, the Supreme Court exercises its appellate jurisdiction, reviewing the decisions of the lower federal courts and the highest state courts.

With a few limited exceptions, the appellate jurisdiction of the Supreme Court is discretionary rather than mandatory. In other words, the Court has great discretion with regard to the appeals it elects to hear and decide. The Supreme Court exercises this discretion through the granting of a **writ of** *certiorari*, which means that the Court, upon petition by a party, agrees to review a case decided by one of the circuit courts of appeals or the highest court of a state. The writ of certiorari is an order issued by the Supreme Court to a lower court to send the case records so that the Supreme Court can determine whether the law has been correctly applied.

Granting Cert: The Rule of Four

A vote of four Supreme Court justices is required to grant *certiorari* to review a case. This is often referred to as the **rule of four**. The rule of four is not contained in any law or formal rule of the Court;

rather, it is a custom that has been observed since the Supreme Court gained the ability to control its own docket with the creation of the circuit courts of appeal in 1891 (Fang, Johnson, & Roberts, 2007). The rule of four is remarkable in that it is a device through which "a minority of the Court can impose on the majority a question that the majority does not think it appropriate to address" (Kurland & Hutchinson, 1983, p. 645). This power of a minority of justices appears to make a difference in about 25 percent of the Court's cases; for the other three-quarters of their caseload, a majority of justices agree that a case presents an issue that the Court should address through plenary review (Fang et al., 2007).

Whether *certiorari* is granted by four justices or more, the Court's discretion is always guided by whether a case presents questions that have some general "importance beyond the facts and parties involved" (*Boag v. MacDougall* 1982, p. 368) (Rehnquist, J., dissenting). For example, the Court may grant *certiorari* in cases involving important and unsettled questions of federal law or in situations involving a conflict among state high courts or the federal circuits concerning the interpretation of federal law, most especially one ruling on a question of interpretation of the U.S. Constitution. Note that failure to grant *certiorari* is not an affirmation in disguise of the lower court's decision. It simply means that the petitioner failed to persuade four of the nine justices to hear the appeal.

Caseload of U.S. Supreme Court

Only a small percentage of the requests for a *writ of certiorari* (or *cert*, as it is often called) is granted. In particular, the legal issue must involve a "substantial federal question." This means state court interpretations of state law can be appealed to the Supreme Court only if there is an alleged violation of either federal law or the U.S. Constitution. For example, a suit contending that a state supreme court has misinterpreted the state's divorce law would not be heard because it involves an interpretation of state law and does not raise a federal question. The same is true for decisions of state high courts recognizing controversial rights, such as the right for same-sex couples to marry, when the decisions are based entirely on their state constitutions. As a result of this limitation that cases

must raise a substantial federal question, the vast majority of state cases are never reviewed by the Supreme Court.

By statute, the Supreme Court begins its annual term on the first Monday in October and it continues until late June or early July of the following year. Each term is comprised of rotating intervals of sittings and recesses, each of which lasts approximately 2 weeks. During *sittings*, the justices hear cases and deliver opinions. During *recesses*, they study the cases on their docket and work on researching and writing their opinions. In addition, each week, the justices evaluate roughly 130 petitions for writs of certiorari.

Through its discretionary powers to hear appeals, the Supreme Court limits itself to deciding about 80 cases a year. With the exception of capital cases, the Court does not really act as an error-correction court. Rather, the Court marshals its time and energy to decide the most important policy questions of the day (see Chapter 16).

Circuit Justices

Each justice on the Supreme Court is assigned to serve as a **circuit justice**. While the function of circuit justices has varied over time, their role today is concerned primarily with addressing certain requests for extension of time and ruling on requests for stays in cases coming from the circuit (or circuits) to which the justice is assigned. A **stay** is a court order that temporarily suspends activity in a case. If the circuit justice thinks that there is merit in a case such that the full Supreme Court should have an opportunity to decide whether to hear the case, the circuit justice may grant the stay. This is particularly important in capital cases, in which a stay of execution can keep a death-row prisoner alive until the full Court can review the case.

SPECIALIZED FEDERAL COURTS

The magistrate, district, appeals courts, and Supreme Court handle the bulk of federal litigation and therefore are a principal focus of this book. To round out our discussion of the federal judicial system, however, we also need to discuss briefly several additional courts that Congress has periodically created. These courts are called "specialized federal courts" because they are authorized to hear only a limited range of cases—taxes or patents, for example. They are created for the express purpose of helping administer a specific congressional statute.

Table 3.3 gives an overview of the specialized federal courts and highlights two important distinctions. First, most specialized courts have permanent, full-time judges appointed specifically to that court. A few specialized courts, however, temporarily borrow judges from federal district courts or courts of appeals as specific cases arise (Baum, 2011).

The second distinction relates to the specialized courts' constitutional status. Judicial bodies established by Congress under Article III are known as **constitutional courts**. The Supreme Court, courts of appeals, and district courts are, of course, constitutional courts. Judicial bodies established by Congress under **Article I** are known as **legislative courts**. Courts presided

over by bankruptcy judges and U.S. magistrate judges are examples of legislative courts. The constitutional status of federal courts has important implications for judicial independence. Article III (constitutional court) judges serve for a period that amounts to a lifetime appointment, but Article I (legislative court) judges are appointed for a specific term of office. Moreover, Article III judges are protected against salary reductions while in office. Article I judges enjoy no such constitutional protection. In short, constitutional courts have a greater degree of independence from the other two branches of government than do the legislative courts. The specialized federal courts are overwhelmingly civil in their orientation, handling such matters as patents and tariffs on imported goods. But two specialized courts bear directly on criminal matters, the military courts and the Foreign Intelligence Surveillance Act Court. In addition, a murky legal area has arisen because of the capture of those who are called "military noncombatants"; it is not clear in which courts they will be tried.

TABLE 3.3 ■ SPECIALIZED FEDERAL COURTS

COURT	AUTHORITY	LEVEL	JURISDICTION
Courts with Permanent Judges			
Tax Court	Article I	Trial	Tax disputes
Court of Federal Claims	Article I	Trial	Monetary claims against the federal government
Court of Veterans Appeal	Article I	Trial	Federal veterans' benefits
U.S. Court of International Trade	Article III	Trial	Imports of foreign goods
U.S. Court of Appeals of the Armed Forces	Article III	Appellate	Uniform Code of Military Justice
Court of Appeals for the Federal Circuit	Article III	Appellate	Trademarks, patents, foreign trade, claims against the federal government
Courts with Judges Borrowed from Other Federal Courts			
Alien Terrorist Removal Court	Article I	Trial	Decides whether an alien should be removed from the United States on the grounds of being an alien terrorist
Foreign Intelligence Surveillance Court	Article III	Trial	Electronic surveillance of foreign intelligence agents
Foreign Intelligence Surveillance Court of Review	Article III	Appellate	Electronic surveillance of foreign intelligence agents

SOURCE: Adapted from Lawrence Baum, *Specializing the Courts*. Chicago: University of Chicago Press, 2011. For further details on these courts visit the Federal Judicial Center at http://www.fjc.gov/history/home.nsf/page/courts.html.

Military Justice

Congress adopted the Uniform Code of Military Justice in 1950, extending significant new due process rights in courts-martial. Congress also created the U.S. Court of Appeals for the Armed Forces, composed of five civilian judges appointed by the president for 15-year terms. The intent was clearly to extend civilian influence to military law. The Military Justice Act of 1968 contributed to the further civilianization of courts-martial. The code covers criminal acts, but can also punish acts that are not criminal for civilians (for example, disrespect of an officer). Moreover, on a military base, military justice applies not only to members of the armed services but also to civilian employees, and it covers acts committed by military personnel on and off a military base (Fidell, Hillman, & Sullivan, 2012).

As with other systems of criminal law, the objective of military justice is to provide a forum for determining guilt or innocence. In addition, however, courts-martial serve the purpose of enforcing order and discipline in the military. In the words of the U.S. Military (U.S. Joint Service Committee on Military Service 2008, p. I–1): "The purpose of military law is to promote efficiency and effectiveness in the military establishment, and thereby to strengthen the national security of the United States." Thus, although military justice is not exempt from the Constitution, it is certainly distinctive. Military justice differs from state and federal justice in the following ways:

- Proceedings are open to military society.
- The burden of proof is less demanding.
- Three- and five-person juries are used.
- The jurors are military personnel.
- A two-thirds majority is sufficient to convict.
- Convictions are automatically appealed to a higher military court.

The principal concern with military courts is that jurors may be unduly influenced by military commanders.

In recent years, a few high-profile cases have thrust military justice into the news. Some of the more prominent cases include these:

- Seven Marines and a Navy corpsman were charged with premeditated murder of an innocent civilian in the Iraqi town of Haditha.

Charges against several of these military personnel were ultimately dropped, but at least one has been convicted so far.

- Several Army personnel were found guilty of abusing inmates in Iraq's notorious Abu Ghraib prison.
- Seven U.S. soldiers from an elite Airborne division were charged with knowingly engaging in sex for money on a public website.
- At the age of 39, psychiatrist and Army Major Nidal Malik Hasan went on a shooting rampage at Fort Hood, killing 13 people and wounding 29 others. His trial is scheduled to take place in 2012.
- Charges are currently pending against Pfc. Bradley Manning, who has been accused of leaking classified government documents, including a classified military video of an attack in Iraq that was posted online by WikiLeaks. His actions allegedly formed the largest ever intelligence leak in American history.

Enemy Combatants

In response to the attacks of September 11, 2001, the United States invaded Afghanistan, capturing hundreds of persons suspected of being members of the al-Qaeda terrorist organization. The military decided that those captured did not qualify as prisoners of war (and therefore subject to the Geneva Conventions) but instead would be considered **enemy combatants**. Since the War on Terrorism began, nearly 800 people from 48 countries have been imprisoned as enemy combatants at the Navy base in Guantanamo Bay, Cuba; thousands more have been held in military installations in Afghanistan, Iraq, and elsewhere.

The George W. Bush administration asserted that international law did not require any legal process for enemy combatants. Rather, the president, as commander-in-chief, could detain enemy combatants until the War on Terrorism was over. The U.S. Supreme Court rejected this view in *Rasul v. Bush* (2004), ruling that federal courts have jurisdiction to hear the detainees' *habeas corpus* petitions challenging their indefinite detentions.

Less than 2 weeks after the *Rasul* decision, the Department of Defense established Combatant Status Review Tribunals (CSRTs) to review evidence in secret proceedings to determine whether a detainee had been properly classified as an enemy combatant. Within 6 months, over 550 CSRTs were held. (See "Courts, Law, & Media" box below). Ultimately, the U.S. Supreme Court rejected the legality of these military commissions, ruling in *Hamdan v. Rumsfeld* (2006) that they had not been authorized by an act of Congress and that they violated both the Uniform Code of Military Justice and the Geneva Conventions.

Congress responded to the *Hamdan* decision by enacting the Military Commissions Act of 2006 (MCA), which authorized the president to identify enemies, imprison them indefinitely, try them in military commissions, and deprive the federal courts of jurisdiction to hear any *habeas corpus* cases filed by detainees. In doing so, Congress sanctioned past and future decisions of CSRTs and attempted to place enemy combatants beyond the reach of federal courts, processes afforded to

COURTS, LAW, & MEDIA

THE RESPONSE (2010)

The Response is a 30-minute movie depicting a hearing held at the U.S. military's detention camp in Guantanamo Bay, Cuba. Although the film's characters—the detainee and the three members of the military tribunal—are composite characters, the depiction of the legal processes is accurate. In fact, the dialogue in the first 20 minutes of the movie is an amalgamation of actual transcripts from several detainee tribunals. And although the final 10 minutes of the film contain a fictionalized depiction of the private deliberations among the three military tribunal members, the content comes from numerous interviews with officers in the military's Judge Advocate General (JAG) corps.

The suspected enemy combatant is played by Aasif Mandvi, a comic actor known largely for work on *The Daily Show*. His character has been held for 4 years on suspicion of having ties to al-Qaeda.

Tight camera shots of Mandvi's face add to the drama of a tense courtroom scene as he pleads his innocence before three military officials who repeatedly question him about evidence he is forbidden to see. The officials deliberate Mandvi's fate in the following scene. A heated exchange between two of the three military officers, a Colonel Simms, played by Kate Mulgrew, and a Colonel Jefferson, played by Peter Riegert, highlights the film's underlying dilemma.

"Are you willing to keep him locked up based on suspect evidence he can't even hear? If we are fighting

an ideological war, shouldn't we be holding on to an idea worth fighting for, say, like the Constitution on the rule of law?" Jefferson asks. Wary of letting a potential terrorist walk away, Simms responds, "We are compelled to make the best decision we can under the laws we were given. Obviously it's not a perfect solution." (Walsh, 2010, ¶¶ 3–6).

The audience is left to determine what decision the third officer makes, thereby placing the viewer in the position of casting the tie-breaking vote.

The Response ponders:

profound questions about the U.S. justice system in the aftermath of the 9/11 attacks ... [asking] its audience to consider what course of action is fair and just during a war on terror; what kinds of restrictions to civil liberties and human rights are acceptable when it comes to national security; and if information gained during interrogations involving torture can be considered reliable. (Walsh, 2010, ¶ 11).

After viewing the movie, answer the following questions:

- What are the strongest arguments for classifying the detainee as an enemy combatant? What are the strongest arguments against doing so?

- Take a position on whether Congress should close the Guantanamo Bay detention facility, transfer the detainees to a U.S. prison, and then try them in federal courts.

- Considering the role that federal *habeas corpus* proceedings play in the U.S. scheme of justice, what do you think is the proper balance between national security and due process rights of those suspected of being terrorists?

criminal defendants and ordinary prisoners. The Supreme Court declared the MCA unconstitutional in *Boumediene v. Bush* (2008). As a result, a number of enemy combatants have been released by order of the courts reviewing their detention in Guantanamo Bay. In fact, nearly three-quarters of the cases reviewed by federal judges concluded that there was insufficient evidence to hold the petitioners as enemy combatants and, therefore, ordered their release (Cole, 2010, as quoted in Walsh, 2010). As of this writing, however, 171 detainees remain in U.S. custody in Guantanamo Bay.

Foreign Intelligence Surveillance Court

The Foreign Intelligence Surveillance Court has authority over electronic surveillance of foreign intelligence agents. Because it was created by the Foreign Intelligence Surveillance Act (FISA), it is popularly referred to as the FISA Court. This court has no permanent judges; rather, the chief justice appoints 11 justices who hear requests for warrants as needed. The courtroom is inside the U.S. Department of Justice, and only the judge is allowed to review the requests submitted by the Justice Department. By statute, the judge is authorized to sign a search warrant for electronic eavesdropping based on "clear and convincing evidence," a legal standard that is less stringent than that required for a normal search warrant.

For years, the FISA Court labored in obscurity. Indeed, the only visible public role came in year-end reports, which invariably indicated that the court had approved all warrant requests. This lack of public attention changed greatly with the revelation in late 2005 that the National Security Agency was conducting warrantless surveillance of domestic phone conversations of suspected foreign terrorist groups like al-Qaeda. The Bush administration contended that the president had inherent war powers under the Constitution to order eavesdropping without warrants even though some in Congress disputed this interpretation. In the wake of controversy, a republican-controlled Congress enacted the Protect America Act of 2007. The law mandated that telecommunications providers assist the government in intercepting international phone calls and e-mails for national security purposes. The law was upheld in 2008 over a Fourth Amendment challenge (see Chapter 11) by a decision of the Foreign Intelligence Surveillance Court of Review (which has appellate review over decisions of the Foreign Intelligence Surveillance Court), although the decision was not made public until early 2009. The court reasoned that requiring the government to obtain a warrant would impair its ability to gather time-sensitive information, thereby potentially putting national security interests at risk. The opinion concluded by saying that as long as the executive branch has "several layers of serviceable safeguards to protect individuals against unwarranted harms and to minimize incidental intrusions, its efforts to protect national security should not be frustrated by the courts" (*In re Directives Pursuant to Section 105B of the Foreign Intelligence Surveillance Act* 2008, p. 29).

CASE CLOSE-UP

WAS ZACARIAS MOUSSAOUI THE 20TH HIJACKER?

Three weeks before September 11, 2001, Zacarias Moussaoui, a French national of Moroccan descent, was taking flying lessons when he was arrested on immigration charges. After September 11, the government's theory was that Moussaoui was to be the 20th hijacker on that fateful day. The prosecution also argued that Moussaoui should be put to death because he lied to the FBI, thus withholding evidence that would have prevented the terrorist attack.

Throughout the proceedings, Moussaoui seemed more intent on clashing with Judge Leonie Brinkema and his own defense attorneys than seeking to save himself. Some of his statements were so outlandish that he gave

Continued on next page

Continued from previous page

every appearance that he wanted to be a martyr. He often ranted against the judge and refused to cooperate with his court-appointed lawyers. Initially, Judge Brinkema reluctantly let Moussaoui act as his own lawyer, but she ended his self-representation because of inflammatory and unprofessional briefs.

The proceedings were also marked by accusations of governmental misconduct. At one point Judge Brinkema ruled that the federal prosecutors could not seek the death penalty because they refused to grant Moussaoui's lawyers access to certain government evidence (but the Fourth Circuit Court of Appeals sided with the prosecutors and the Bush administration). During the sentencing phase, she showed anger over allegations of witness tampering by government officials.

Moussaoui tried to plead guilty on several occasions, but Judge Brinkema ruled that he did not appear to understand what he was doing. On April 20, 2005, Moussaoui sent the judge a letter saying he wanted to plead guilty and over the objections of his lawyer, he did so. It was then up to a jury to determine his punishment.

The penalty phase was split into two parts. First, the jury had to determine whether this was a death-penalty-eligible case. Testifying against his lawyers' advice, Moussaoui stated he was supposed to hijack a fifth jetliner on September 11 and crash it into the White House. The jury found that Moussaoui's crime was death-penalty-eligible, but then needed to decide if he should actually be sentenced to death.

In addition to victim-impact statements from the surviving family members of those killed on September 11, the jury heard the cockpit voice recording of one of the doomed airliners. Moussaoui again testified against his lawyers' advice, stating that he had "no regret, no remorse" about the attacks. Trying to undermine their own client, the defense called a psychologist to the stand who testified that the defendant was a paranoid schizophrenic with delusions. Several survivors also testified that he should not die (Lewis, 2006). In what many considered a surprising move, the federal jury rejected the death penalty for

Moussaoui, concluding that he played only a minor role in terrorist attacks.

Defiant to the end, Moussaoui boasted "America, you lost . . . I won." But when Moussaoui was formally sentenced, the judge had the last word. "You came here to be a martyr and to die in a great bang of glory. But . . . instead you will die with a whimper. The rest of your life you will spend in prison" (Serrano, 2006). A few days later, before dawn, U.S. marshals flew Moussaoui, now prisoner 51427-054, to the Supermax federal prison in Colorado. He will spend 23 hours a day in his cell with little or no contact with the other notorious criminals imprisoned there.

In many ways, the trial of Zacarias Moussaoui lacked a compelling sense of public drama partly because it dragged on for almost 4 years and partly because there was no live television coverage since federal courts do not allow cameras in the courtroom. But ultimately the trial lacked real drama because the outcome (as to guilt) was never really in doubt. After all, the defendant repeatedly made clear that he wanted to be found guilty and wanted to be executed, thus ensuring that (in his mind at least) he was a martyr to an important cause. Thus, the only real tension in the case came to center on the question of whether or not he should die, and as the trial progressed, that question increasingly became linked to who was Zacarias Moussaoui the person, not what was the role he would have played in the tragic events of September 11. Indeed, in the end, the trial failed to provide closure to the important question of whether Zacarias Moussaoui was indeed the 20th hijacker. Some of his statements were so outlandish and so contradictory, that some close observers of the case came to believe that his claims were simply not believable. Overall, the trial seems to represent only a macabre footnote to a national tragedy. The federal courts have been hearing cases debating the permissible scope of the government's War on Terrorism, but the Moussaoui trial was devoid of any major legal issues. Thus, the trial will be remembered only for the bizarre behavior of the defendant, not for any enduring addition to our nation's legal history.

FEDERAL JUDICIAL ADMINISTRATION

The Administrative Office Act of 1939, which largely created the current administrative structure of the federal judiciary, illustrates the interplay between judicial administration and politics. During the mid-1930s, the conservative majority on the Supreme Court declared many pieces of New Deal legislation unconstitutional. After his reelection in 1936, President Franklin Delano Roosevelt put forth his Court-packing plan: The Court would be expanded from 9 to 15 justices, thus allowing FDR to pack the Court with justices more sympathetic to his policies. There was no legal barrier to such an action because the Constitution fails to specify how many justices shall serve on the Court. But the political obstacles proved insurmountable; many of Roosevelt's backers felt that tampering with the Court was a bad idea. The Court-packing plan never passed, but it did call attention to the president's complaints that the administration of federal courts was inefficient. At the same time, some judges were dissatisfied with the old system of court management because it was located in the Department of Justice, an executive agency. Thus, a movement arose among federal judges and national court reformers to clean their own house. The result was a compromise plan—the Administrative Office Act of 1939. The act expanded the responsibilities of the Judicial Conference, created the Administrative Office of the U.S. Courts, and established the judicial councils. These agencies, along with the office of the chief justice, the Federal Judicial Center, and the more recently created U.S. Sentencing Commission, are the main units involved in administering the federal courts. A summary of their functions, composition, and hierarchical structure is presented in Figure 3.4.

Chief Justice

The chief justice is the presiding officer of the Supreme Court and has supervisory authority over the entire federal judicial system. To fulfill these duties, the chief justice hires a fifth law clerk (one more than the four law clerks allotted to each associate justice) and an administrative assistant to help with the administrative tasks for the Court and for the judicial system as a whole.

At the Supreme Court itself, the chief justice presides over all courtroom proceedings as well as the private conferences in which the justices discuss and vote on cases. As a matter of tradition, the chief justice normally speaks either first or last in these conferences, thereby having significant influence on the discussion. The chief justice assigns associate justices (and himself) to serve as the circuit justice for the various federal circuits. While the chief justice's vote in a case carries no more or less weight than the vote of any of the associate justices, the most senior justice always decides who will write the opinion of the Court in a given case. Since the chief justice is the most senior position on the court (regardless of the number of years the chief justice has actually served on the Court), that means that the when the chief justice votes with the majority of justices in a given case, he possesses the important power to assign the authorship of the majority opinion. This includes the ability to keep important constitutional cases for himself.

Other administrative tasks at the Supreme Court for the chief justice include regulating attorney admissions to the Supreme Court bar; formally opening and closing each court term; supervising and working with the Court's clerk, librarians, and reporter of decisions; budgeting; advocating for the courts before Congress; and serving as a spokesperson not only for the Supreme Court, but also for all of the federal courts. For example, former Chief Justice William Rehnquist often spoke about the need for Congress to increase the number of federal judges, increase the salaries of judges to be competitive with the private practice of law, reduce the workload of the courts, and protect judicial independence. Chief Justice John Roberts has continued to echo all of these sentiments. For example, in an *Annual Report*, Chief Justice Roberts pointed out that the entire judicial system of the United States received only two-tenths of 1 percent of the total federal budget, a figure that causes the courts to "continuously look . . . for ways to do more with less" (2008, p. 4). This chronic underfunding of the courts has led to federal judges' pay being steadily eroded, since they have not been provided with cost-of-living increases for several years, even though Congress has given such increases to all other federal employees (including all members of Congress).

Executive Branch
Participates in legislative process. Transmits appropriations requests. Provides buildings and security. Is represented on rules committees.

Congress
Appropriates funds. Enacts legislation on court organization and jurisdiction. Reviews procedural rule amendments.

Supreme Court
Approves rule amendments.

Chief Justice of the United States

Administrative Office of the U.S. Courts
The chief justice appoints the director and deputy director after consultation with Judicial Conference.
Functions: Provides, under Conference supervision, administrative support to courts (including budget, personnel, space and facilities), staff to Judicial Conference and its committees, legislative coordination, other functions.

Judicial Conference of the United States
Members: Chief justice (chair); chief judge and district judge from the twelve regional circuits; chief judge, Court of Appeals for the Federal Circuit; chief judge, Court of International Trade.
Functions: Sets national administrative policy for the federal judiciary; approves appropriations requests for submission to Congress; recommends changes in rules of procedure to the Supreme Court for submission to Congress; other statutory functions.

Committees of the Judicial Conference
Members: Judges, practicing lawyers, and legal scholars appointed by the chief justice, and ex officio government officials.
Functions: Make recommendations to the Conference and, in a few cases, exercise statutory responsibilities.

Federal Judicial Center
Board: Chief justice (chair); seven judges elected by the Judicial Conference; Administrative Office director. Board appoints Center director and deputy director.
Functions: Provides orientation and continuing education to judges and personnel of courts, research support to courts and Judicial Conference committees.

Chief Judges of the Circuits

U.S. Sentencing Commission
Members: Seven voting members appointed by the president (no more than three of whom may be federal judges) and two nonvoting ex officio members.
Functions: Promulgates sentencing guidelines and otherwise establishes federal sentencing policies as directed by the 1984 Sentencing Reform Act.

Judicial Conferences of the Circuits
Optional circuit-wide meetings, called no more than once a year by the chief circuit judge, about various topics related to the administration of justice. All federal judges may attend, and each court of appeals must adopt rules to provide for participation by members of the bar.

Judicial Councils of the Circuits
Members: Chief judge (chair); circuit and district judges in equal numbers; council size determined by majority vote of all active circuit and district judges.
Functions: (1) Make necessary orders for administration of justice within the circuit (all judges and employees of the circuit are statutorily directed to give effect to council orders); (2) consider complaints of judicial misconduct or disability under if referred by the chief circuit judge; (3) review district court plans in various administrative areas, as required by statute or Judicial Conference.

Courts of Appeals, District Courts, and Bankruptcy Courts
Courts, each with a chief judge and clerk of court, also develop and implement administrative policy in numerous areas within the framework depicted above.

Figure 3.4 ■ Organization of Federal Judicial Administration

SOURCE: Russell Wheeler. *A New Judge's Introduction to Federal Judicial Administration.* Washington, DC: Federal Judicial Center, 2003.

Outside the walls of the Supreme Court, the chief justice has many other ceremonial and administrative responsibilities. By mandate of Article I, Section 3 of the U.S. Constitution, the chief justice presides over impeachment trials of the president of the United States in the U.S. Senate. The chief justice normally administers the oath of office to the president and vice president at inaugurations. He supervises the acquisitions of the law department at the Library of Congress. The chief justice also possesses the significant authority to appoint judges to special tribunals and courts, such the U.S. Foreign Intelligence Surveillance Court and the Judicial Panel on Multidistrict Litigation (a group of seven federal judges who select the venue for the district that coordinates all pretrial proceedings for multiple cases across the country concerning the same basic cause of action with common questions of face, such as mass tort actions resulting from a plane crash or a product-liability case). And the chief justice serves on the boards of three cultural institutions: The Smithsonian (often serving as its Chancellor), the Hirshhorn Museum, and the National Gallery of Art.

In the role of leader of the federal courts system, the chief justice serves as the chair of the Judicial Conference of the United States, supervises the Administrative Office of the U.S. Courts, and serves as the chair of the Federal Judicial Center. All three of these organizations are discussed in greater detail in the following sections.

Judicial Conference of the United States

The Judicial Conference of the United States is the administrative policymaking organization of the federal judicial system. It is comprised of 26 members, including the chief justice, the chief judges of each of the courts of appeals, one district judge from each circuit, and the chief judge of the Court of International Trade. The conference meets semiannually for a 2-day session. Because these short meetings are not sufficient to accomplish a great deal, most of the work is done by about 25 committees. The chief justice of the United States has the power to appointment members to the committees, all of which contain not only members of the Judicial Conference itself, but also other judges, law professors, and practicing attorneys selected by the chief justice.

One of the most important responsibilities of the Judicial Conference is drafting proposed amendments to the rules that govern proceedings in the federal courts. These include the Federal Rules of Civil Procedure, Federal Rules of Criminal Procedure, Federal Rules of Bankruptcy Procedure, Federal Rules of Appellate Procedure, and the Federal Rules of Evidence. Other committees of the Judicial Conference oversee judicial codes of conduct, information technology in the federal courts, and court administration and case management.

The Judicial Conference directs the Administrative Office of the U.S. Courts in administering the judiciary budget and makes recommendations to Congress concerning the creation of new judgeships, increases in judicial salaries, and budgets for court operations. The Judicial Conference also plays a major role in discipline (including impeachment) of federal judges (a topic discussed in greater depth in Chapter 8). In short, the Judicial Conference is a vehicle through which federal judges play a major role in developing policy for the federal judiciary.

Administrative Office of the U.S. Courts

Since its establishment in 1939, the Administrative Office (AO) of the U.S. Courts has been responsible for implementing the policies established by the Judicial Conference by handling the day-to-day administrative tasks of the federal courts. The director of the AO is appointed by the chief justice and reports to the Judicial Conference. Acting as the Judicial Conference's official representative in Congress, the AO's lobbying and liaison responsibilities include presenting the annual budget requests for the federal judiciary, arguing for the need for additional judgeships, and transmitting proposed changes in court rules. The AO also serves as the housekeeping agency of the judiciary, responsible for allotting authorized funds and supervising expenditures. Throughout the year, local federal court staff send the AO a vast array of statistical data on the operations of the federal courts, ranging from the number of filings to the speed of the disposition of cases. The data are published in three separate volumes. The heftiest is the *Annual Report*, which runs to hundreds of pages and is now available on the Internet.

Federal Judicial Center

The Federal Judicial Center is the research and training arm of the federal judiciary. Its activities are managed by a director appointed by a board that consists of the chief justice, the director of the Administrative Office, and judges from the U.S. district court, courts of appeals, and bankruptcy court. One of the principal activities of the Federal Judicial Center is education and training of federal judicial personnel, including judges, probation officers, clerks of court, and pretrial service officers. The center also conducts research on a wide range of topics, including the work of the magistrate judges, ways of measuring the workload of the courts, and causes of delay.

Judicial Councils

The judicial council (sometimes referred to as the "circuit council") is the basic administrative unit of a circuit. The membership consists of both district and appellate judges of the circuit. A judicial council is given sweeping authority to "make all necessary and appropriate orders for the effective and expeditious administration of justice within its circuit." Working within this broad mandate, the councils monitor district court caseloads and judicial assignments. Although the law specifies that "all judicial officers and employees of the circuit shall promptly carry into effect all orders of the judicial council," the councils' actual enforcement powers are limited. The major weapons at their disposal are persuasion, peer group pressure, and publicity directed at the judge or judges who are reluctant to comply with circuit policy. At times, for example, circuit councils have ordered that a district judge receive no new cases until his or her docket has been brought up to date. Judicial councils are also authorized to investigate complaints of judicial disability or misconduct (a topic probed in greater detail in Chapter 8).

U.S. Sentencing Commission

The U.S. Sentencing Commission is an independent agency in the judicial branch of government. It consists of seven members—a chairperson, three vice chairs, and three commissioners appointed by the president of the United States. The Sentencing Commission was created by the Sentencing Reform Act of 1984. Its original purpose was to develop federal sentencing guidelines. Today, the Commission is also charged with evaluating the effects of the sentencing guidelines on the criminal justice system, recommending to Congress appropriate modifications of substantive criminal law and sentencing procedures, establishing a research and development program on sentencing issues, and monitoring the performance of federal probation officers with respect to their roles in recommending sentences to federal judges (see Chapter 14).

CASELOADS IN THE FEDERAL COURTS

The onset of the Industrial Revolution increased the caseload of the federal courts, a trend that was later accelerated by Prohibition, then the New Deal, and even further by federal lawmaking often associated with President Lyndon Johnson's "Great Society" programs. Growing caseloads, in turn, prompted changes and additions to the federal judiciary; appellate courts have been added and specialized courts created.

What is new is the pace of that expansion. For most of our nation's history, the growth in federal cases was gradual. No longer. Over the past 50 years, district court filings have increased more than 6-fold, and court of appeals cases have increased more than 10-fold. According to the Administrative Office of the U.S. Courts, federal judges today are faced with unprecedented levels of work. By and large, federal judges across the country face a greater number of cases each year and, in some instances, are encountering record levels of work.

The caseload problem is particularly acute in some metropolitan jurisdictions, where federal judges must postpone civil trials for months and even years to accommodate criminal trial schedules (particularly of major drug dealers) in accordance with the Speedy Trial Act (see Chapter 5). The solutions most often suggested for the problem of rising federal court caseloads are increasing the number of federal judges and reducing federal jurisdiction.

Increase the Number of Federal Judges?

Through the years, increases in the number of cases filed in federal court have been followed by an increase in the number of federal judgeships.

More recently, however, the dramatic increases in federal court cases have not been accompanied by a corresponding increase in the number of federal judgeships. Particularly at the appellate level, the creation of new judgeships has lagged far behind the increase in filings.

It is unlikely that in the short term the number of federal judgeships will be increased. Only Congress can authorize additional judgeships, and Congress has been locked in a decades-long partisan battle over the federal judiciary. Chapter 8 will explore ongoing political battles between Republicans and Democrats over who should fill existing vacancies on the federal bench. Given this partisan divide, it is unlikely that additional judgeships will be created until one party controls a filibuster-proof majority of the United States (and the president is a member of that party) because new judgeships would become political spoils for the party in control at that time.

Reduce Federal Jurisdiction?

To cope with rising caseloads, federal judges have proposed not only creating more judgeships, but also reducing the types of cases that can be filed in federal court. According to the *Report of the Federal Courts Study Committee* (1990), Congress created most of these problems by unwisely expanding federal court jurisdiction, and therefore Congress should enact remedial legislation. Specifically, the report advocated several jurisdictional reforms. Some of the proposals to limit the ability of prisoners to file civil rights lawsuits under 42 U.S.C. § 1983 until after having exhausted certain state administrative remedies were adopted by Congress as part of the Prisoner Litigation Reform Act of 1996. But no action has been taken with respect to some of the more dramatic recommendations in the 1990 report:

1. Federal diversity jurisdiction should be abolished except in cases by or against citizens of foreign countries, and in complex, multi-state cases arising primarily from large disasters.

2. The crime of illicit drug trafficking is punishable under both state law and federal law. This concurrent jurisdiction should be abolished such that offenses arising out of trafficking on a local basis should be the exclusive province of state criminal law (tried in state courts), leaving the federal courts to handle only large multi-state or even multi-national drug trafficking cases.

3. Congress should create several new Article I legislative courts, such as a Court of Disability Claims, which would hear appeals from decisions by administrative law judges denying claims for disability benefits under the Social Security Act and possibly under other disability statutes as well. The Committee even proposed an Article I court to adjudicate small claims under the Federal Tort Claims Act in which the amount sought in good faith by the plaintiff is $10,000 or less.

Perhaps because Congress was labeled the primary culprit, it is hardly surprising that Congress gave the report a chilly reception (Biskupic, 1993; Underwood, 2006). In short, the nation's top elected lawmakers have been at odds with the nation's top appointed law interpreters for most of the past century, and this disagreement is not likely to be resolved.

Arguments based on numbers of cases stress issues of efficiency, but typically need to be understood within a broader framework of political winners and losers. Thus, some disagreements reflect divisions along the lines of the due process versus crime control models of justice. But other disagreements reflect institutional differences: The views of federal judges (whether appointed by Republican or Democratic presidents) contrast with the views of federal lawmakers. Concurrent federal and state jurisdiction over certain drug-related offenses, to name just one example, illustrates the political nature of the debate over the appropriate scope of federal criminal law.

CONSEQUENCES OF FEDERAL INVOLVEMENT IN THE CRIMINAL JUSTICE SYSTEM

Crime has been a pressing national concern for decades. As a result, national elected officials, whether members of Congress or the president, have often made crime a key campaign issue. In turn, the crime policies of nonelected officials, whether bureaucrats or judges, have been closely scrutinized.

Despite all this clamor at the national level, the role of the federal government in the criminal justice system is limited. Crime remains primarily the responsibility of state and local governments. This imbalance between federal officials' need to be seen as doing something about the crime problem and their limited jurisdiction to do anything explains a good deal of the political dynamics surrounding the role of the federal government (and the federal judiciary) in the criminal justice system.

Forum for Symbolic Politics

In spite of the limited scope of its involvement in crime, the federal government remains the focal point of the national debate. Crime is a powerful issue and, therefore, has attracted a variety of interest groups. Some focus on crime issues directly—for example, the American Correctional Association (ACA), the Police Executive Research Forum (PERF), and Mothers Against Drunk Driving (MADD). Other interest groups, such as the American Civil Liberties Union (ACLU), Lambda Legal, and the National Organization for Women (NOW)—and find that crime and crime issues are related to other concerns.

Interest groups have a major impact on public policy. Most directly, they lobby on behalf of their members for favorable government policies. They can also mount campaigns encouraging their members to write federal officials in favor of (or in opposition to) specific proposals. Some organizations likewise make campaign contributions to selected officials. The National Rifle Association (NRA), for instance, contributes to officials who are dubious about gun control, whereas the Brady Campaign to Prevent Gun Violence supports candidates who favor gun control.

Federal Dollars

A basic rule of American politics is that citizens' demands for services exceed the willingness of voters to raise taxes to pay for those services. Those who one day vocally demand a tax reduction are quick to demand expanded government services the next day. Funding the criminal justice system illustrates this rule. Citizens demand that courts "get tough with criminals" but are unwilling to raise taxes to build new prison cells. Likewise, pleas for more

cops on the beat are seldom followed by requests for increased taxes to pay for such increased personpower. Faced with these limitations, local and state officials often turn to Washington as a source of "free" money (with *free* defined as "no local taxes"). In turn, federal officials find that appropriating federal money is one way of assuring voters that they take the crime problem seriously.

Congress has authorized spending for a variety of anticrime programs. Some are general in nature—for example, block grants for local projects that reduce crime and improve public safety. Similarly, 60 percent of the research budget of the National Institute of Justice—the principal federal agency involved in the war on crime—is spent on developing new technology for law enforcement and the criminal justice system. Other spending programs are targeted toward specific concerns—for example, domestic violence and victim assistance programs (see Chapter 9).

Overall, though, the amount of federal dollars is small compared to what local and state governments spend. Moreover, federal money is often limited to a short period of time (typically 3 years). After federal funding ends, state or local units of government are expected to take over funding, but often these agencies are strapped for cash, leading to the cancellation of successful programs.

CONCLUSION

Offenders like Alfonso Lopez were no doubt on Justice Scalia's mind when he condemned what he called the deterioration of the federal courts. In the 1960s, the federal courts had few judges and small caseloads, but the cases they did hear were "by and large … cases of major importance." In contrast, Justice Scalia argued that while the federal courts now have more judges and larger caseloads, many of these cases are "minor" and "routine," concerning "mundane" matters of less import or even "overwhelming triviality" (quoted in Galanter, 1988). Thus, according to one of the Court's leading conservatives, the federal courts should be returned to their rightful role of deciding major controversies; lesser ones would be banished to state courts.

In the more than two decades since Justice Scalia made those comments, other judges, scholars, and commentators with diverse political viewpoints have echoed his sentiments that the federal courts handle too many routine cases that ought to be handled in state courts so that the federal courts could focus on more important federal questions (*Report of the Federal Courts Study Committee,* 1990). Such concerns are most evident with regard to the seemingly ever-expanding federalization of crimes—most especially drug cases (Husak, 2008; Luna, 2005). But in an era when crime remains a major political issue, rolling back federal jurisdiction to the "good old days" (whenever that might have been) is unlikely to happen. What we learn ultimately is that the jurisdiction of federal courts is determined in no small measure by decisions of elected officials in Congress. In an earlier era, federal officials decided that federal law should cover matters such as prostitution, consumption of alcoholic beverages, gambling, and organized crime. Today they focus more on drug dealers, crooks who use guns, and intimate-partner-violence offenders.

Federal prosecutions often grab the headlines because the crimes are large or audacious or because the accused are people of prominence. In turn, the public by and large identifies the judiciary with federal courts. But we should not be misled. The federal courts are a relatively small part of the nation's judicial system. A major city such as Chicago or Los Angeles prosecutes more felons in a year than the entire federal judiciary. The nature of the crimes brought to federal court differs strikingly from those appearing in state judiciaries, though. State courts handle primarily street crimes that require immediate action—burglary, armed robbery, and murder, for example. By contrast, with the exception of drug-related offenses, federal crimes largely concern immigration offenses, fraud cases, firearms violations, and money laundering. It is to the more common state courts that we turn our attention in the next chapter.

Chapter Review

LO1 **1.** Define the four primary types of jurisdiction: geographical, subject matter, personal, and hierarchical.

Geographical jurisdiction limits the power of courts to adjudicate disputes arising within certain geographic boundaries. Subject matter jurisdiction concerns the types of cases a court may hear and decide. Personal jurisdiction refers to a court's power over a specific person or legal entity (such as a partnership or corporation). Hierarchical jurisdiction concerns whether the court has the power to originally decide a case or to review it on appeal.

LO2 **2.** Compare and contrast the tasks of trial and appellate courts.

Trial courts are primarily concerned with considering evidence to resolve factual decisions within the bounds of the law. Appellate courts primarily review the legal decisions made by trial courts. In doing so, they serve dual purposes: error correction and policy formation (see Chapter 16).

LO3 **3.** Explain the historical evolution of the federal courts into their present structure and operations.

Article III of the U.S. Constitution established the U.S. Supreme Court and gave Congress the power to create lower courts. Congress has exercised its authority under Article III to create inferior courts at different times in U.S. history. Today, the trial courts that primarily exercise original jurisdiction in the federal system are the U.S. District Courts, whereas most appeals are resolved by the U.S. Courts of Appeals.

LO4 **4.** Analyze the different responsibilities and workloads of U.S magistrate judges, district judges, circuit judges, and Supreme Court justices.

U.S. magistrate judges assist U.S. district judges by conducting pretrial criminal matters, supervising discovery in civil cases, and making reports and recommendations concerning the disposition of motions and prisoner petitions. District court judges

preside over trials and write opinions adjudicating many types of civil disputes. Typically sitting in panels of three, circuit judges review the records in cases appealed from district courts and write opinions ruling on the merits of legal arguments raised in those appeals.

LO5 5. Analyze the impact the federal courts have on the administration of criminal justice at the state and local levels through their federal question jurisdiction.

By interpreting the requirements of federal law—especially the U.S. Constitution—the federal courts set the parameters for the operation of the criminal justice system so that police, prosecutors, defense attorneys, and judges honor the individual rights and liberties guaranteed in Constitution.

LO6 6. Differentiate the jurisdiction and functions of Article III courts from those of Article I courts and other specialized federal courts.

Article III courts are empowered to adjudicate "cases and controversies" arising under the U.S. Constitution, federal law, and certain cases between citizens of different states or different counties. Article I courts are tribunals created by Congress to handle specialized types of cases, especially those that arise under the regulatory law of federal agencies. The decisions of Article I courts are generally reviewable in Article III courts. Article III judges are nominated by the president and confirmed to office by the U.S. Senate. Article I judges are not; they are appointed for fixed terms. Article I judges enjoy two protections to foster their independence: life-tenure (unless impeached) and a guarantee that their salaries can never

be decreased. Article I judges do not have these protections.

LO7 7. Distinguish the various agencies and their hierarchical responsibilities for the administration of the federal court system.

The Judicial Conference of the United States sets national administrative policy for the federal judiciary. Under the supervision of the Judicial Conference, the Administrative Office of the U.S. Courts provides administrative support to courts (including budget, personnel, space, and facilities). The Federal Judicial Center provides orientation and continuing education to judges and personnel of courts, as well as research support for courts and Judicial Conference committees. The U.S. Sentencing Commission promulgates sentencing guidelines and otherwise establishes federal sentencing policies as directed by the 1984 Sentencing Reform Act.

LO8 8. Evaluate the major problems facing the federal courts and the strengths and weaknesses of the major solutions that have been proposed to address these problems.

Heavy caseloads are the major problem facing the federal courts. Not only does the heavy workload burden those who work in the courts, but it also affects litigants whose cases may be delayed because of a backlog. Adding more staff, especially more federal judges, could help, but is cost-prohibitive. Reducing the jurisdiction of the federal courts, especially by eliminating diversity of citizenship jurisdiction, could also help, but this has not gained sufficient political support for Congress to have acted on the proposal.

Critical Thinking Questions

1. To what extent are contemporary debates over the role of the federal government similar to, but also different from, the debates in the late 18th century?

2. How would the criminal justice system be different today if the founding fathers had decided not to create a separate system of federal courts and instead allowed federal laws to be enforced in state courts?

3. How would you reduce the federal court caseload? In considering where you would reduce federal court jurisdiction, also consider where you might increase it. What do your choices reflect about your political values?

4. To what extent does the debate over federalization of state crimes cut across traditional ideological values as represented in the due process model and the crime control model?

5. Federal law enforcement is limited in scope but subject to considerable public attention. Why?

Key Terms

appellate court 61

appellate jurisdiction 61

Article I 74

Article III 62

bankruptcy judge 65

Bivens actions 70

concurrent jurisdiction 57

constitutional courts 74

circuit justice 73

diversity of citizenship 66

dual court system 57

en banc 72

enemy combatants 75

extradition 59

federal question 67

geographical jurisdiction 57

Habeas Corpus 70

habeas corpus petitions 70

hierarchical jurisdiction 60

jurisdiction 57

legislative courts 74

mandamus petitions 70

motions to vacate sentences 70

original jurisdiction 61

personal jurisdiction 59

prisoner petitions 69

rule of four 72

Section 1983 70

subject matter jurisdiction 59

stay 73

trial court 61

U.S. courts of appeals 70

U.S. district courts 65

U.S. magistrate judges 65

U.S. Supreme Court 72

venue 57

writ of certiorari 721

Web Resources

Go to the *America's Courts and the Criminal Justice System* companion website at
http://www.cengage.com/criminaljustice/neubauer,
where you will find more resources to help you study.
Resources include web exercises, quizzing, and flash cards.

For Further Reading

Ball, Howard. *Bush, the Detainees and the Constitution: The Battle over Presidential Power in the War on Terror.* Lawrence: University of Kansas Press, 2007.

Brody, David. "The Misuse of Magistrate Judges in Federal Criminal Proceedings: A Look at the Non-Ministerial Nature of Sentencings." *Justice System Journal* 23: 259–262, 2002.

Carp, Robert, Ronald Stidham, and Kenneth Manning. *The Federal Courts.* 5th ed. Washington, DC: CQ Press, 2011.

Chutkow, Dawn. "Jurisdiction Stripping: Litigation, Ideology, and Congressional Control of the Courts." *Journal of Politics* 70: 1053–1064, 2008.

Collins, Paul, Daniel Norton, Kenneth Manning, and Robert Carp. "International Conflicts and Decision Making on the Federal District Courts." *Justice System Journal* 29: 121–144, 2008.

Cross, Frank. *Decision Making in the U. S. Courts of Appeals.* Palo Alto, CA: Stanford University Press, 2007.

Luna, Erik. 2005. "The Overcriminalization Phenomenon." *American University Law Review* 54: 703–746.

Lurie, Jonathan. *Military Justice in America: The U.S. Courts of Appeals for the Armed Forces, 1775–1980.* Lawrence: University of Kansas Press, 2001.

Yackle, Larry. *Federal Courts.* 3rd ed. Durham, NC: Carolina Academic Press, 2009.

4 State Courts

© Oswaldo Paez/AP Photo

Suspected drug traffickers, arrested and handcuffed by the police, walk past packages containing cocaine in Cali, 185 miles southwest of Bogota, Colombia. The cocaine, destined for the United States, was found in brick form, wrapped in brown paper, and hidden in a Cali apartment. While this arrest occurred in Colombia, the world's leading cocaine exporter, similar "drug busts" occur in the United States, especially in cities and towns along the United States–Mexican border. ■

Chapter Outline

HISTORY OF STATE COURTS
Colonial Courts
Early American Courts
Courts in a Modernizing Society

TRIAL COURTS OF LIMITED JURISDICTION: LOWER COURTS
Cases in the Lower Courts

Courts, Controversy, & Reducing Crime
Should DUI and Distracted Driving Prosecutions Be Increased?

Justice of the Peace Courts
Municipal Courts
Sentencing in the Lower Courts
Problems of the Lower Courts
Community Justice

TRIAL COURTS OF GENERAL JURISDICTION: MAJOR TRIAL COURTS

Courts, Law, & Media
American Gangster (2007)

INTERMEDIATE COURTS OF APPEALS

STATE HIGH COURTS OF LAST RESORT

COURT UNIFICATION
Key Components
Analysis

CASE CLOSE-UP: *Ewing v. California* and Three Strikes Laws

PROBLEM-SOLVING COURTS
Drug Courts
Domestic Violence Courts
Mental Health Courts

TECHNOLOGY SHAPES THE COURTROOMS OF THE FUTURE

CONSEQUENCES OF COURT ORGANIZATION
Decentralization and Choice of Courts
Local Control and Local Corruption
Uneven Court Financing

Learning Objectives

After reading this chapter, you should be able to:

LO1 Outline the four layers of a typical state court system.

LO2 Describe the types of cases handled by the trial courts of limited jurisdiction.

LO3 Discuss the similarities and differences between justice of the peace courts and municipal courts.

LO4 List the four primary problems confronting the lower courts in the United States.

LO5 Identify the types of civil and criminal cases filed in trial courts of general jurisdiction.

LO6 Explain briefly the differences between a state high court of last resort in states with and without intermediate courts of appeals.

LO7 List the key components of court unification.

LO8 Identify how problem-solving courts using therapeutic jurisprudence handle cases.

LO9 Discuss the consequences of court organization.

After attending several judicial conferences around the nation, two judges had little trouble identifying the major problem facing the Los Angeles County municipal courts: Soaring drug prosecutions were further crowding jails that were already full. Implementing a solution, however, proved a more troublesome and time-consuming process. To establish a drug court, the judges needed the active cooperation of other judges, the district attorney, the public defender, treatment providers, and the sheriff. To ensure that these agencies had a voice in the process, a coordinating council was formally established. Finally, after months of meeting and planning, two drug courts were created (Torres & Deschenes, 1997).

State Courts • State Courts • State Courts • State Courts • State Courts • State Courts • State Courts • State Courts • State Courts • State Courts • State

Discussions of state courts usually contain references to major cases, such as armed robberies and automobile accidents. But this is only part of their workload. State judges must also adjudicate cases involving wives who want divorces from unfaithful husbands and husbands who physically abuse their wives; juveniles who rob liquor stores and juveniles who simply drink liquor. The contemporary realities reflect an increase in the number of cases placed on the dockets of state courts and rising societal expectations about the administration of justice—while staffing levels remain constant. Thus, although an earlier generation viewed court reform in terms of a neater organizational chart, contemporary discussions are more likely to focus on topics such as finding a better way to handle drug cases.

This chapter examines the structure and functions of state courts. We begin with a discussion of the development of American courts and then divide the somewhat confusing array of state courts into four levels: trial courts of limited jurisdiction, trial courts of general jurisdiction, intermediate courts of appeals, and courts of last resort. (Chapter 16 examines the lower courts in depth, and we will discuss juvenile courts in Chapter 17.) We will examine the efforts of court reformers to reorganize state court structure as well as the consequences of court organization for the administration of justice.

HISTORY OF STATE COURTS

Just as American law borrowed heavily from English common law, the organization of American courts reflects their English heritage. But the colonists and later the citizens of the fledgling new nation that called itself the United States of America adapted this English heritage to the realities of the emerging nation. Issues such as the clash of opposing economic interests, the debate over state versus national power, and outright partisanship have shaped America's 50 diverse state court systems.

Colonial Courts

Early colonial courts were rather simple institutions whose structure replicated English courts in form but not in substance. The numerous, complex,

and highly specialized English courts were ill suited to the needs of a small group of colonists trying to survive on the edge of the wilderness, so the colonists greatly simplified the English procedures. As towns and villages became larger, however, new courts were created so that people would not have to travel long distances to have their cases heard. Moreover, a notion of separation of governmental powers began to emerge. In the early days, the same governmental body often held executive, legislative, and judicial powers. The county courts, for example, stood at the heart of American colonial government. In addition to adjudicating cases, they performed important administrative functions. Gradually, different institutions began to perform these tasks.

Diversity was the hallmark of the colonies, with each colony modifying its court system according to variations in local customs, different religious practices, and patterns of commercial trade. Some of these early variations in legal rulings and court structures have persisted and contribute to the great variety of U.S. court systems today (Friedman 2005; Glick & Vines 1973).

In the northern colonies, biblical codes were often adopted. In the South, laws governing slavery were enacted. Overall, public punishments like the pillory and the stocks were commonly used, but the death penalty was used less often than in England.

Early American Courts

After the American Revolution, the functions of state courts changed markedly. Their governing powers were drastically reduced and taken over by the legislative bodies. The former colonists distrusted lawyers and harbored misgivings about English common law. They were not anxious to see the development of a large, independent judiciary. Thus, state legislatures often responded to unpopular court decisions by removing some judges or abolishing specific courts all together.

A major source of political conflict between legislatures and courts centered on the issue of monetary debtors. Legislators were more responsive to policies that favored debtors, usually small farmers. Courts, on the other hand, reflected the views of creditors, often merchants. Out of this conflict over legislative and judicial power, the courts gradually emerged as an independent political institution.

TABLE 4.1 ▪ CASE FILINGS IN STATE TRIAL COURTS IN 2009

	Traffic	Criminal	Civil	Domestic	Juvenile	Total
Unified trial courts	11,412,497	2,437,408	2,620,043	742,197	241,007	17,453,152
Major trial courts of general jurisdiction	3,442,263	3,802,927	6,591,754	3,406,641	1,011,431	18,255,016
Minor trial courts of limited jurisdiction	43,184,929	14,465,449	10,313,815	1,612,290	724,335	70,300,818
Total	58,039,689	20,705,784	19,525,612	5,761,128	1,976,773	106,008,986

SOURCE: Robert C. Lafountain, Richard Y. Schauffler, Shauna M. Strickland, Sarah A. Gibson, and Ashley N. Mason. *Examining the Work of State Courts: An Analysis of 2009 State Court Caseloads.* Williamsburg, Va: National Center For State Courts, 2011.

In the northern states, European immigration generated cultural and religious tensions between new arrivals and current residents. In the South, the justice system focused on tracking down escaped slaves. Meanwhile, the nation was steadily moving west, and a unique form of frontier justice emerged.

Courts in a Modernizing Society

Rapid industrialization following the Civil War produced fundamental changes in the structure of the American judiciary. Increases in population led to a higher volume of litigation. Just as important, the growing concentration of people in the cities (many of whom were immigrants) meant the courts were faced with a new set of problems. Thus, by the end of the 19th century, the nation had to respond to a new type of social problem—crimes committed by juveniles (see Chapter 17).

The American courts, still reflecting the rural agrarian society of the early 19th century, were inadequate in the face of rising demands for services (Colburn, 2006; Jacob, 1984). States and localities responded to societal changes in a number of ways. City courts were created to deal with new types of cases in the urban areas, including public drunkenness, gambling, and prostitution. Specialized courts were formed to handle specific classes of cases (for example, small claims courts and family relations courts). Additional courts were created, often by specifying the court's jurisdiction in terms of a geographic boundary within the city.

The development of courts in Chicago illustrates the confusion, complexity, and administrative problems that resulted from this sporadic and unplanned growth. In 1931, Chicago had 556 independent courts; the majority were justice of the peace courts, which handled only minor offenses (Glick and Vines, 1973). The jurisdiction of these courts was not exclusive; that is, a case could be brought before a variety of courts, depending on the legal and political advantages that each offered. Moreover, each court was a separate entity; each had a judge and a staff. Such an organizational structure meant that cases could not be shifted from an overloaded court to one with little to do. Each court also produced patronage jobs for the city's political machines.

The sporadic and unplanned expansion of the American court system has resulted in an often confusing structure. Each state system is different. Although some states have adopted a unified court structure, others still have numerous local courts with overlapping jurisdictions. To reduce confusion, we will examine state courts at four levels: trial courts of limited jurisdiction, trial courts of general jurisdiction, intermediate appellate courts, and courts of last resort. Table 4.1 summarizes the tremendous volume of cases decided each year by state courts.

TRIAL COURTS OF LIMITED JURISDICTION: LOWER COURTS

At the first level of state courts are **trial courts of limited jurisdiction**, sometimes referred to as **inferior courts**, or more simply, **lower courts**. The United States has more than 13,500 trial courts of limited jurisdiction, staffed by about 18,500 judicial officers (LaFountain et al., 2008). The lower courts constitute 85 percent of all judicial bodies in the United States. Six U.S. jurisdictions— California, Iowa, Illinois, Minnesota, the District of Columbia, and Puerto Rico—have unified court systems that do not use trial courts of limited jurisdiction. On the other hand, New York has more than 2,900 and Texas has over 2,230 courts of limited jurisdiction.

Variously called district, justice, justice of the peace, city, magistrate's, or municipal courts, the lower courts decide a restricted range of cases. Most of these courts are created by city or county governments and therefore are not part of the state judiciary. Thus, lower courts are typically controlled only by the local governmental bodies that create them and fund them.

Cases in the Lower Courts

The caseload of the lower courts is staggering—more than 70 million cases a year, the overwhelming number of which are traffic cases (more than 43 million in any given year—see Table 4.1). Thus, these are the courts with which the average citizen is most likely to come into contact.

Lower-court judges typically authorize search warrants. In addition, the lower courts are primarily responsible for handling the early stages of felony criminal cases. Thus, after an arrest, a judge in a trial court of limited jurisdiction will hold the initial appearance, appoint counsel for indigent defendants, and conduct the preliminary hearing, if applicable. Later, the case is transferred to a trial court of general jurisdiction for trial (or plea) and sentencing. But the bulk of the work in the lower courts involves several types of nonfelony criminal cases and small claims of a civil nature.

Lower courts typically adjudicate two types of nonfelony criminal cases: misdemeanors and ordinance violations. Lower courts also adjudicate all of the traffic offenses in a jurisdiction.

Nonfelony Criminal Cases

A **misdemeanor** is a crime punishable by a fine, imprisonment (usually in a local jail, for a period of less than 1 year), or both. Misdemeanors are enacted by state legislative bodies and cover the entire state.

Ordinances, on the other hand, are laws passed by a local governing body such as a city council. They are similar in effect to a legislative statute, but they apply only to the locality, and any fine that is assessed for violations goes to the local government, not to the state. It is typical for ordinances to prohibit the same types of conduct (for example, disorderly conduct, public drunkenness) as state misdemeanors. Ordinance violations are technically noncriminal, which means that they are easier to prosecute. At times, police prefer to arrest a suspect for an ordinance violation because it presents fewer legal obstacles to gaining a conviction.

Traffic Offenses

Traffic offenses refer to a group of offenses involving self-propelled motor vehicles. These violations range from parking violations to improper equipment. Speeding is the most common traffic offense, followed by driving without a license, and driving while a license is suspended or revoked.

For a time the number of traffic cases heard in the lower courts was declining, but no longer. During 9 of the last 10 years the volume of traffic cases has increased (LaFountain et al., 2011). New Jersey leads the nation, with more than 5.6 million traffic cases each year, which translates into 64,824 traffic cases per 100,000 people. Overall, as Table 4.1 illustrates, traffic cases constitute nearly 55 percent of lower-court caseloads.

Traffic offenses are typically punishable by fines. But because the volume of these cases is quite large, traffic tickets can be big moneymakers for local governments. Indeed, traffic fines and fees are a multi-billion-dollar business in the United States. The money a driver pays for a typical traffic ticket includes both fines and fees. Revenue generated from fines usually goes to the government that has created the court, either the city, the county, or the state. Typically, this revenue stream is then used to pay the expenses of the court itself (judges, clerks, and the like) as well as the prosecutor's office and the public defender, but not necessarily. Revenue generated from court-imposed fees, on the other hand, goes to the court itself. In some jurisdictions, these fees are used to support important court matters, such as expenses of the public defender's office and reimbursing jurors. These revenues may also be dedicated to programs we have discussed throughout this book, including specialized courts, alternative dispute resolution (ADR) programs, driver education programs, victim-compensation funds, and domestic-violence facilities.

In some jurisdictions, the government makes a considerable profit from court-imposed fines. Over the years, some localities have become known as speed traps. Although this appears to be less true today, there are still some small towns that finance a considerable part of their expenses, including the police department, from tickets issued to out-of-town motorists. In Oklahoma, for example, 15 small towns with populations of fewer than 2,000 people reported more revenue from traffic fines and fees than from sales taxes (Killman, 2006).

When governments, whether state or local, are faced with a budget crisis, one place they often look for additional revenue without having to take the unpopular step of raising taxes is to increase fines and fees on traffic offenses. Florida, for example, facing a major budget shortfall, increased traffic fines by a projected $63 million a year, sparing further budget cuts for courts, prosecutors, and public defenders (Dunkelberger, 2009). At the local level, in 2009 El Paso County, Colorado, reaped 147 percent more from moving violations than the year before thanks to an increase in traffic fines voted by the state legislature (Zubeck, 2009). Legislatures in over 40 states are likewise looking to solve some of their fiscal crisis in a similar manner (Schwartz, 2009b).

Modern technology is making it even easier for local governments to generate more revenue through traffic enforcement. Across the nation, cities are installing cameras at traffic lights that take pictures of cars that run red lights. The result is often a significant increase in the citations generated by the computer and fines billed. In suburban New Orleans, for example, traffic cameras generated over 140,000 tickets and $11 million in fines. If supporters say traffic cameras increase safety, critics say the red-light system is all about seeing green (Waller, 2008). The use of traffic cameras to collect fines has been being challenged in court (Roesler, 2009). One such lawsuit alleged that using photographic evidence to nab speeders and red-light runners violates basic constitutional rights to due process, including the rights to be presumed innocent, to have a hearing before an impartial judicial official, and to have the opportunity to challenge the evidence. But the Ohio Supreme Court unanimously ruled that there were no constitutional violations because these infractions are civil and not criminal (*Mendenhall v. Akron*, 2008).

On the other hand, some driving-related offenses, like driving under the influence (DUI), are serious enough that they are prosecuted as misdemeanors. Repeat or extreme cases of DUI are routinely classified as felonies today (see "Courts, Controversy, & Reducing Crime" on page 95).

Small Claims Civil Cases

On the civil side, the lower courts decide disputes under a set dollar amount; these cases are often referred to as "small claims." **Small claims courts** handle cases involving maximum amounts that range from a low of $2,500 in Arizona, Kentucky, and Rhode Island, to a high of $25,000 in Tennessee (NOLO, 2012). The trend is clearly in an upward direction. The largest number of cases falling under these dollar amounts is debt collection, primarily involving nonpayment for goods purchased or services rendered. Another major category includes landlord–tenant disputes—mostly claims by landlords against tenants concerning past-due rent, evictions, and property damage. A smaller number of small claims cases involve alleged property damage, largely stemming from automobile accidents.

In most states, streamlined procedures have been adopted to provide quick, inexpensive processing by dispensing with strict rules of evidence and the right to trial by jury. Accordingly, small claims cases are less formal and less protracted than other civil cases. Yet, as Table 4.1 illustrates, they comprise roughly 53 percent of the civil cases filed each year in the nation's state courts.

Justice of the Peace Courts

The legal system in the United States is largely county-based, and approximately 80 percent of U.S. counties are rural. In most rural areas, the lower courts are collectively called **justice of the peace courts**. The officeholder is usually referred to simply as a **JP**. This system of local justice traces its origins to 14th-century England, when towns were small and isolated. The JP system developed as a way to dispense simple and speedy justice for minor civil and criminal cases. The emphasis was decidedly on the ability of local landowners, who

COURTS, CONTROVERSY, & REDUCING CRIME

SHOULD DUI AND DISTRACTED DRIVING PROSECUTIONS BE INCREASED?

Drinking and driving has been a problem since the invention of the automobile, but it did not gain recognition as a prominent social concern until the 1980s (Applegate, Cullen, Link, Richards, & Lanza-Kaduce, 1996). The group most responsible for focusing public attention on drinking and driving is Mothers Against Drunk Driving (MADD). Depending on the state, offenses related to driving while under the influence of alcohol or drugs is termed "driving under the influence" (DUI) or "driving while intoxicated" (DWI).

MADD is victim-oriented, with many leaders having themselves experienced a family death due to DUI violations. They are closely related to the victims' rights movement (see Chapter 9). Publicly they are recognized as the leading proponents of increasing the criminal penalties for DUI. The almost sole emphasis on enforcement and punishment differs from other approaches, which stress prevention of early alcohol use and treatment of alcohol dependence as better approaches to prevent drug- and alcohol-related crashes (Hingson, Heeren, & Edwards 2008).

For almost three decades, legislatures—under considerable pressure from MADD and other groups like it—have passed a variety of "get tough with drunk drivers" laws, including:

- Increasing the drinking age to 21
- Lowering from .15 to .08 the blood alcohol content (BAC) level at which a person is presumed legally intoxicated
- Increasing jail penalties for DWI, particularly for repeat offenders
- Mandating that drivers who refuse to take a breathalyzer test will automatically lose their driver's license

But somehow the get-tough laws recently passed never seem to be harsh enough, so in subsequent years legislatures are called upon to crack down even harder on DUI offenders. And when the threats of even more arrests

and harsher punishments do not seem to be working, the agenda is shifted to technology—mandating that even first offenders be required to install a device that tests drivers and shuts down the car if it detects alcohol (MADD, 2009; Wald, 2006). Evolving legislative agendas are crucial for organizations like MADD because they need to constantly motivate their constituents lest the organization lose momentum and also lose members.

To sociologist Joseph Gusfield, groups like MADD engage in symbolic politics, portraying DUI offenders as villains. The difficulty with this approach is that DUI arrestees reflect a range of social backgrounds, including ordinary citizens and at times even prominent members of the community. Moreover, the range of behavior varies greatly from a person barely at .08 and having caused no accident to those measuring near .30 (comatose for most people) who have killed several people. This analysis of MADD is reinforced by the organization's refusal to even discuss lowering the legal drinking age. MADD has long cast underage drinking in black-and-white terms, whereas many college officials see it as impossible gray. Raising the legal drinking age has not stopped student drinking, only displaced it, driving such activity off campus and behind doors, making it even more difficult to deal with (Hoover, 2008).

The absence of criminal stereotypes is compounded by the pervasive role of alcoholic beverages in American social and economic life. As a result, there is considerable societal ambivalence toward drinking and driving. Society is quick to condemn impaired drivers involved in serious accidents, but those who drive after a few drinks often evoke the attitude of "There but for the grace of God go I" (Gusfield, 1981).

The contradictions in societal attitudes toward drinking and driving explain why the enforcement of DUI laws is riddled with loopholes. These contradictions help us understand why actual enforcement of DUI laws blunts the cutting edge of the harsh penalties. Law on the books treats drinking and driving as a serious problem, but law in action sees DUI not as a criminal offense, but as a traffic violation. The end product is not a series of absolutes

Continued on next page

Continued from previous page

propounded by MADD but rather a negotiated reality (Homel, 1988). With the imposition of tougher laws:

- Police do not necessarily make more arrests. Faced with serious crime problems, big-city police forces assign higher priority to violent offenders than to DUI offenders (Mastrofski & Ritti, 1996).

- Prosecutors are pressured to plea-bargain. Given that local jails are already overcrowded and most defendants are not as villainous as public images suggest, pleas to lesser charges such as reckless driving are often arranged.

- Juries are reluctant to convict. As discussed in Chapter 13, if jurors think the penalty is too harsh for the crime, they are less likely to convict.

- As more people go to jail for longer times following DUI convictions, the prisons become overcrowded, which necessitates shortening actual sentences (Vermont Center for Justice Research, 1995).

- Those who lose their licenses may continue to drive, and those previously convicted may continue to drive while impaired. Indeed, one survey found that more than half the persons in local jails charged with DUI had prior sentences for DUI offenses (Cohen, 1992).

Overall, studies of DUI laws tend to be skeptical of a deterrent effect of get-tough legislation (Fradella, 2000). Typically, new, tougher laws are ushered in with announcements of a major crackdown followed by increased arrests for DWI. But over time, levels of drinking and driving return to previous levels as the perceived certainty of punishment declines with experience (Homel, 1988; Ross, 1992). For example, one study found "no evidence that lowering the BAC to .08 reduced fatality rates but other approaches like seat belt laws have been effective" (Freeman, 2007).

What works and what does not in reducing DUI fatalities is now being applied to a major new highway safety threat—texting while driving (Lowy, 2009). The National Transportation Safety Board has declared that texting, e-mailing, or talking on a cell phone while driving is simply too dangerous to be allowed. Indeed, in recent years a number of major accidents have been blamed on such practices (Lowy, 2011). Yet efforts to curb such dangerous practices quickly run into a basic problem—people engage in such behavior because they like to and because they do not think it is dangerous. Thus, these so-called driver distraction laws are often unpopular. And in a democracy, governmental efforts to enforce unpopular laws (which requires expenditures of tax dollars) often proves difficult.

What do you think? Should there be tougher punishments for DUI or are current punishment levels about right? Should more efforts be made to arrest and prosecute impaired drivers or is the current level of effort about right? And what should be done about drivers who operate vehicles while distracted by their cell phones? Overall, how do punishment and enforcement levels of DUI and distracted-driver laws compare with other social problems, such as domestic violence and drug abuse?

---

served as part-time JPs, to decide disputes on the basis of their knowledge of the local community.

The small-town flavor of the JP system persists today (even in large urban places such as Harris County, Texas, which includes Houston, and Maricopa County, Arizona, which includes Phoenix). In the past, the vast majority of JPs were part-time non-lawyers who conducted court at their regular place of business—the back of the undertaker's parlor, the front counter of the general store, or next to the grease rack in the garage. Today, however, JPs tend to be more professional and hold court in a courthouse or another government building. Yet, many JPs are not trained lawyers and, as a result, they often fail to abide by the rules that are supposed to bind them (Mansfield, 1999).

Many JPs are locally elected officials or mayors of small towns who serve *ex officio*. The Office of Justice of the Peace in Texas (2009) lists the following qualifications:

- U.S. citizenship

- At least 18 years of age on the first day of the term or date of appointment

- Not mentally incompetent by a final judgment of a court
- Not finally convicted of a felony
- Continual Texas resident for 12 months; precinct resident for 6 months
- Have no conviction for giving or offering a bribe to procure election or appointment

Critics argue that the JP system has outlived its purpose. It may have met the needs of the small, isolated towns of a century ago, but it is out of step with the modern era. The ultimate goal of judicial reformers is to abolish the JP system altogether. A major defect is that JP courts are not part of the state judiciary; they are controlled only by the local government bodies that create and fund them. Only recently have judicial conduct commissions (see Chapter 8) been granted the authority to discipline or remove local judges who abuse their offices.

Nor are the activities of the lower courts subject to appellate scrutiny. Rarely are trial courts of limited jurisdiction courts of record; no stenographic record is kept of the witnesses' testimony or the judges' rulings. When a defendant appeals, the appeal is heard by a trial court of general jurisdiction. This court must conduct an entirely new trial, taking the testimony of the same witnesses and hearing the same attorneys' arguments as the lower court did. This is called a **trial** *de novo.*

Today, many JPs have been replaced with magistrates, who assume the same kinds of responsibilities as traditional JPs but do not use that title. Magistrates are more likely to be appointed than elected and tend to have better training than JPs. For example, North Carolina has phased out its JPs and replaced them with magistrates who are required to have more education and are appointed by the district court (Neubauer & Meinhold, 2013).

Overall, the issues facing rural courts are qualitatively different from those faced by urban courts (Baehler & Mahoney, 2005). Compared to their big-city counterparts, rural courts exhibit three special features: lower caseloads, lack of resources, and greater familiarity (Bartol, 1996; see also, McKeon & Rice, 2009).

Lower Caseloads

Caseloads in rural courts are lighter than those in suburban or urban courts, largely because of higher crime rates in urban areas as compared with rural ones. This is particularly true of violent offenses, which are more than four times more likely to occurs in urban as opposed to rural areas (Lee, 2008; Thompson, 1996; Weisheit, Falcone, & Wells, 2006). But this does not mean that rural citizens do not experience crime. Over the past decades, rural crimes have increased at the same rate as big-city crimes. And some types of crime—DUI and fraud, for example—are more prevalent in rural areas. Moreover, illegal drug use is increasingly common in rural areas, so much so that that the "scourge of social and criminal problems associated with the methamphetamine epidemic" is putting a stress on rural courts (White, 2008). Treating drug addiction is more difficult in rural areas because of the lack of public transportation, the shortage of treatment facilities, and the additional resources necessary to treat the medical conditions of addicts (Cooper, 2003).

Rural settings present unique problems for domestic violence cases (Pruitt, 2008). And rural areas also tend to harbor hate groups, militia, and others who bill themselves as antigovernment.

Lack of Resources

Although rural courts have lower caseloads, this does not mean that they do not face problems processing their workloads. Rural courts receive less federal money and have a lower local tax base than larger counties (McDonald, Wood, & Pflug 1996; McKeon & Rice, 2009). As a consequence, court facilities are often outmoded and salaries are low.

Lack of resources is a particular problem in criminal cases in which defendants are indigent (Chapter 7). Because few attorneys practice law in rural areas, the defense pool is limited. These built-in limitations have been compounded in recent years by cutbacks in federal funding. Rural areas have been hardest hit by drastic reductions in publicly funded legal services for the poor, resulting in ever dwindling access to justice for nonurban residents (Kerrigan, 2008).

Familiarity

Whereas big-city courts are characterized by the interface of numerous bureaucracies, in rural areas contacts are invariably one-on-one (Weisheit et al.,

2006). The active bar consists of a dozen or fewer members, including the prosecutor, the judge, and the lawyer who represents the local government. Often, there are five or fewer sheriff's deputies and a single probation officer, each of whom is known to the judge. The clerk's office typically consists of two or three long-term employees.

Not only is the number of actors in rural courts small, but their interactions are frequent and long term. By and large, justice is administered by those who grew up in the community, and they are bound together by long-standing social and family networks. As a result, rural courts place greater emphasis on informal mechanisms of social control, whereas urban courts are more legalistic and formal (Weisheit et al., 2006).

Although such comity generally creates a friendly social atmosphere, it also can mean "You scratch my back, and I'll scratch yours." It's not always a conscious thing. The members of the courtroom work group are friends; some may even be related. Thus, some point to a lack of an independent judiciary and a weak adversarial process in many parts of rural America. The danger is that community knowledge is substituted for the Constitution. Some specific types of injustices include capricious arrests, unduly high bonds, rubber-stamping prosecutorial decisions, and pressuring defendants into pleading guilty (Glaberson, 2006; Sitomer, 1985; Waldron, 2008). Defendants who are not part of the community (either socially or geographically) may be at a disadvantage. These courts want to preserve the peace and their community's traditional values; however, doing so sometimes comes at the expense of minorities, the poor, and those considered "outsiders" (Sitomer, 1985; see also, Pruitt, 2006).

Reforming JP Courts

Some reformers would unify state courts into a three-tier system, consisting of a single trial court that handles both major and minor cases, an intermediate appellate court, and a state high court of last resort. This reform would abolish the office of justice of the peace, require all judges to be lawyers, and eliminate the trial *de novo* system. The biggest change occurred in California, which began phasing out its JPs after a landmark 1974 decision in which the Supreme Court of California unanimously

held that it was a violation of federal due process to allow a nonlawyer to preside over a criminal trial that could result in incarceration of the defendant (*Gordon v. Justice Court*, 1974). The remaining justice courts (as well as municipal courts) were eliminated by the passage of Proposition 220 in June 1998, which merged all lower courts within the state judicial branch into the superior courts (the courts of general jurisdiction). Under current California law, all California judges must be licensed attorneys. Notably, the U.S. Supreme Court disagreed with California's analysis of the Fourteenth Amendment in the landmark case of *North v. Russell* (1976), which is why JPs still exist in numerous states.

One major obstacle to abolition is the powerful influence of nonlawyer judges, who do not want their jobs abolished. Another is some people's belief that JPs are easily accessible, whereas more formal courts are miles away. For example, JPs are readily available to sign arrest warrants for the police or to try a motorist accused of driving too fast. JP courts are often viewed as people's courts, forums where people without much money can go to resolve their problems without the necessity of having a lawyer.

Historically, the low pay and equally low status of the JP did not attract highly qualified personnel. One survey showed that between a third and a half of California's lower-court judges were not even high-school graduates (Ashman & Chapin, 1976). Perhaps most shocking of all, the assistant attorney general of Mississippi estimated that "33 percent of the justices of the peace are limited in educational background to the extent that they are not capable of learning the necessary elements of law" (*North v. Russell*, 1976). Although some states have moved to upgrade the quality of the personnel, others have not. In the state of New York, 75 percent of the JPs are not lawyers, and over the past three decades over 1,100 have been reprimanded by the Commission on Judicial Conduct. Some are not even high-school graduates. The problems that arise are perhaps best summed up in a quote from a JP who, after threatening to jail a woman because her dog was running loose, said: "I just follow my own common sense. And the hell with the law" (Glaberson, 2006). And the problems persist. A rural judge has been cited for levying over $11,000 in illegal fines and at least created the appearance he was doing so to provide additional revenue for the city (Gorman, 2009).

High on the judicial reformers' list of priorities has been upgrading the quality of lower-court judges, and they have made major strides. Many states have instituted training programs for lay judges. For example, Texas requires all newly selected JPs to attend a training seminar and provides ample opportunities for continuing judicial education. Indeed, most states now require judges of limited jurisdiction courts to have graduated from law school and passed the state bar. In 1987, only 44 percent of these courts required judges to be licensed attorneys, but today that number is 52 percent (Langton, 2007). But to many reformers, the ultimate goal remains the elimination of nonlawyer judges.

Municipal Courts

The urban counterparts of the justice of the peace courts are **municipal courts**. The overriding reality of municipal courts in the nation's big cities is the press of cases. Accordingly, "obstacles" to speedy disposition—constitutional rights, lawyers, trials— are neutralized. In a process some have labeled an assembly line, shortcuts are routinely taken to keep the docket moving. Thus, the municipal courts more closely resemble a bureaucracy geared to mass processing of cases than an adjudicative body providing consideration for each case.

The emphasis on moving cases begins when the defendant is arraigned. Instead of addressing defendants individually—a time-consuming process—municipal court judges often open court by advising defendants of their constitutional rights as a group. Notification of rights is treated by the court as a clerical detail to be dispensed with before the taking of guilty pleas can begin.

Defense attorneys constitute another potential obstacle to the speedy disposition of cases. Although defendants have a theoretical right to be represented by an attorney, in practice the presence of an attorney in the lower courts is rare except for DUI prosecutions, for which defendants face potentially severe penalties. The general absence of defense attorneys reinforces the informality of the lower courts and the lack of attention to legal rules and procedures.

What of those too poor to hire a lawyer? In *Argersinger v. Hamlin* (1972), the Supreme Court ruled that "absent a knowing and intelligent waiver, no person may be imprisoned for any offense, whether classified as petty, misdemeanor, or felony unless he was represented by counsel." Thus, an indigent defendant may be fined without having a lawyer, but a judge considering imposing a jail term must give the impoverished defendant the opportunity to have a court-appointed counsel at state expense. Compliance, however, has generally been token in nature, meaning that the legal right to counsel in lower courts remains an empty right for many defendants.

In municipal courts, the defendant's initial appearance is usually the final one. Most people charged with a traffic violation or minor misdemeanor plead guilty immediately. The quick plea represents the fatalistic view of most defendants: "I did it—let's get it over with." Realistically, a defendant charged with crimes such as public drunkenness and disorderly conduct probably cannot raise a valid legal defense. What has struck all observers of the lower courts is the speed with which the pleas are processed.

Few trials are held in the lower courts. A defendant has a right to a jury trial only if the offense can be punished by imprisonment for more than 6 months (*Baldwin v. New York*, 1970). The absence of attorneys and the minor nature of the offenses combine to make requests for jury trials rare. If there is a trial, it is a bench trial often conducted in an informal manner.

Assembly-Line Justice and the Courtroom Work Group

The courtroom work group often toils together to keep cases moving quickly. Some courts manipulate bail to pressure defendants into an immediate disposition. During arraignment, each defendant is informed of the right to a full hearing with a court-appointed attorney. But, if the hearing cannot be held for 2 or 3 weeks, during which time the defendant will have to be in jail, it is not surprising that the majority of defendants choose to waive their right to counsel in favor of a speedy disposition.

The routines of the lower courts are threatened, however, by uncooperative defendants. Judges and prosecutors dislike defendants who "talk too much." The accused who unreasonably take up too much of the court's time can expect sanctions. Consider the case of a young, middle-class, white man who made a detailed inquiry into his rights and then gave a relatively lengthy account (roughly 2 minutes) of his alleged offense of vagrancy. Although the defendant was polite, the judge interrupted him with "That will be all, Mr. Jones" and ordered him to jail. Other defendants who "talked too much" received sentences that were longer than normal (Mileski, 1971; see also, Mack & Anleu, 2007).

Sentencing in the Lower Courts

Because few defendants contest their guilt, the lower courts are more sentencing institutions than true trial courts. The courtroom encounter is geared to making rapid decisions about which sentence to impose. The punishments imposed by lower-court judges include many of those found in the major trial courts—fines, probation, and jail. In the misdemeanor courts, however, judges can choose alternative sanctions, including community service, victim restitution, placement in substance-abuse treatment programs, mandatory counseling, and required attendance in education programs such as driver clinics (Meyer & Jesilow, 1997). Despite the diversity of potential sanctions, fines play a predominant role. Few misdemeanor defendants are sentenced to jail.

The sentencing process in the lower courts involves elements of both routinization and individualization. Lower-court judges define their role as "doing justice"; rather than merely being bound by rules of law, judges use their discretion to achieve what they believe to be a fair and just result (Meyer & Jesilow, 1997). In attempting to achieve justice, lower-court judges use readily identifiable characteristics to sort defendants into categories. In the lower courts, sentencing involves a process of quickly determining group averages. The result is a high degree of uniformity; by and large, a defendant gets the same sentence as all others in the same category. To the casual observer, the process appears to be an assembly line, but sentences can also be fitted to the specific defendant. During plea negotiations, there is some individual attention to cases. Despite sentencing consistencies, exceptions are made (Ragona & Ryan, 1983). The most important factors in both the routinization and the individualization of sentencing in the lower courts are

the nature of the event and the defendant's criminal record.

The defendant's prior criminal record is also a key factor in sentencing. First offenders rarely receive a jail term. Indeed, for petty offenses, first offenders may be released without any penalty whatsoever. Repeaters are given more severe sanctions (Mileski, 1971). For example, a study of DUI dispositions in Sacramento, California, highlights the importance of a prior record and the nature of the event (Kingsnorth, Barnes, & Coonley, 1990). For defendants with no prior convictions, the likelihood of a reduction to a charge of reckless driving increased three to four times. Similarly, the probability of receiving a jail sentence increased dramatically for those with a prior record. The nature of the event (measured by the level of blood alcohol) also played a role. A low level of blood alcohol was of primary importance in the decision to reduce charges from DUI to reckless driving. Similarly, for defendants with a high level of alcohol in their systems, not only was a jail sentence much more likely, but also that jail term was probably lengthy. These two factors, of course, operate together. Defendants with no priors and low levels of blood alcohol fared much better than those with prior convictions and high levels of alcohol in their system. Studies like this one, however, rarely enter the public discourse.

Problems of the Lower Courts

For decades, reformers have criticized the lower courts, highlighting a variety of problems. Only a shadow of the adversary model of criminal justice can be found in these courts. Few defendants are represented by an attorney. Trials are rare. Rather than the rules of courtroom procedure, informality predominates. And some defendants have been denied fundamental legal rights, including the right to a trial, an impartial judge, and the presumption of innocence (Glaberson, 2006). Jail sentences are imposed, sometimes with lightning speed and not always in accordance with law (Ashman, 1975; Glaberson, 2006). In short, practices that would be condemned if they occurred in higher courts are commonplace in the lower courts. Is this justice?

Research over the years has focused on four problem areas: inadequate financing, inadequate facilities, lax procedures, and unbalanced caseloads.

Inadequate Financing

In general, lower courts are funded locally. Sparsely populated counties and small municipalities often lack funds to staff and equip their courts adequately. Even when funds are available, there is no guarantee that local governments will spend money on the lower courts. In many cities, these courts are expected to produce revenue for local governments. Indeed, some lower courts generate revenues much greater than their operating expenses, yet they still lack adequate courtrooms and other facilities. Rather, the funds go to pay for city services.

Inadequate Facilities

Lower-court courtrooms are often crowded and noisy, with 100 or more people forced to spend hours waiting for their minute before the judge. Some are makeshift, hastily created in the side of a store or the back of a garage. In the state of New York, "Some of the courtrooms are not even courtrooms: tiny offices or basement rooms without a judge's bench or jury box" (Glaberson, 2006). Such courtroom conditions lack dignity and leave a bad impression, suggesting that the judiciary is more interested in collecting the fine for speeding than bothering to do justice. Such inadequate facilities are detrimental to the attitudes of the defendant, prosecutor, judge, and all others involved in the justice process.

Lax Court Procedures

Besides singling out inadequate facilities, critics of lower courts often cite lax procedures in the day-to-day administration of these courts. Many trial courts of limited jurisdiction do not have written rules for the conduct of cases. Conventional bookkeeping methods are often ignored. How much fine money was collected and how it was spent is often impossible to determine. You can find some information in the city budget but not in the court records; this frustrates any attempts to assess the effectiveness of these courts.

Unbalanced Caseloads

Many lower courts are characterized by moderate to heavy caseloads, but others appear to have little to do. Because of unbalanced caseloads, some courts have huge backlogs that they are ill equipped to handle. But because these courts are locally controlled, there is no way to equalize the workload.

Unbalanced caseloads are the clearest indication that any generalizations about the problems of the lower courts must be coupled with the observation that the nation's lowest tribunals are tremendously varied. From state to state, between one county and its neighboring county, and even within a city, wide discrepancies exist in the quality of justice rendered. There is no easy way to determine what is wrong (or even what is right) about these courts. Because of the wide disparity, it is best to examine rural justice of the peace courts separately from urban municipal courts. Although they share many problems, they are also sufficiently different to warrant separate treatment.

Community Justice

As court activities have been consolidated and streamlined, some of the qualities of locally dispensed justice have been lost. As a result, some court reformers continuously seek ways to reestablish court–community cooperation.

The central target of these community justice efforts is minor disputes between parties in ongoing relationships (domestic partners, neighbors, consumers–merchants, landlords–tenants, employees–employers). Examples include unruly children who annoy neighbors, dogs who defecate on the wrong lawns, owners who neglect their property, and acquaintances who dispute small debts. It is not clear what role the criminal justice system can play in resolving such private disputes. Yet private disagreements between friends, neighbors, and significant others are the steady diet of the police and the lower courts. A trial would only obscure the underlying issues because the problem is either irrelevant or immaterial to the legal action. In such interpersonal disputes, the person who files a complaint may be as "guilty" as the defendant. Many of these private disputes are essentially civil matters, yet criminal justice agencies must deal with them to head off the commission of a more serious crime. In addressing problems such as these, mediation programs seek solutions not in terms of a formal finding by a judge, but rather through compromise and bargaining. The goal is to seek long-term solutions in the hope the disputants will not return. The two most commonly mentioned types of programs are alternative dispute resolution and community courts.

Alternative Dispute Resolution

Efforts at court–community collaboration are but one example of a broader movement termed **alternative dispute resolution (ADR)**, which seeks to settle disputes by less adversarial means than the traditional legal processes (Coltri, 2009; Goldberg, Sander, Rogers, & Cole, 2007; Nolan-Haley, 2008). Many ADR programs function as alternatives to going to court. Others involve efforts to settle court cases after they have been filed but before they are tried by a judge. ADR efforts, such as **arbitration** and **mediation**, most often focus on civil matters, but nonserious criminal matters may also be included.

The rapid growth of ADR programs has produced a second-generation wave of reforms aimed at improving the qualifications of those who serve in these programs, often through the use of specialized community courts (Brown, 2005; Pou, 2005).

Community Courts

Courts across the nation are searching for ways to reach out in order to be more responsive to the needs of specific communities within their geographical jurisdictions. The phrase "justice community" refers to the range of organizations and people within any specific locale who have a stake in the justice system. It includes judges, court personnel, district attorneys, public defenders, private attorneys, probation departments, law enforcement personnel, community organizers, business groups, and others (Borys, Banks, & Parker, 1999; Williams, 2007).

Often these outreach efforts lead to an emphasis on mediation of minor disputes. There are important organizational differences, though, between court-based mediation and community courts.

Community courts, or community mediation programs, as they have sometimes been called, are government-sponsored (by either court or prosecutor) and as a result, these programs receive the bulk of their cases as referrals from criminal justice agencies. The dominant goal is to improve the justice system by removing minor cases from the court. In their view, cases such as simple assault, petty theft, and criminal trespass are prime candidates for mediation and not formal processing in the lower courts.

The "community courts" of today were initially termed "criminal justice–based mediation programs," also known as "multidoor courthouses" or "neighborhood justice centers." Many of these dispute-resolution programs began with a primary emphasis on misdemeanor criminal cases and later added civil matters from the local small claims court and other sources. In a sense, they convert criminal matters to civil ones by treating the cases as matters for discussion between the individual disputants and not for processing between the state and the defendant. The Center for Court Innovation (2012a) stresses that community courts are neighborhood-focused courts that attempt to harness the power of the justice system to address local problems.

The best-known community court in the nation is the Midtown Community Court in New York City. The Midtown experience was born of a profound frustration with quality-of-life crime in the neighborhood, particularly prostitution, graffiti, illegal vending, vandalism, and low-level drug offenses (Center for Court Innovation, 2009). Offenders are sentenced to make restitution to the community through work projects in the neighborhood: removing graffiti, cleaning subway stations, and sorting cans and bottles for recycling. But at the same time, the court attempts to link offenders with drug treatment, health care, education, and other social services. Perhaps one of the most distinctive features is that the courthouse includes an entire floor of office space for social workers to assist offenders referred by the judge in the courtroom a few floors below. Thus, instead of sending an offender to a distant bureaucracy, the courthouse now incorporates helping institutions within its midst. The Midtown Community Court is serving as a prototype for other jurisdictions as well (Clear & Cadora, 2003).

TRIAL COURTS OF GENERAL JURISDICTION: MAJOR TRIAL COURTS

At the second level of state courts are the **trial courts of general jurisdiction**, usually referred to as *major trial courts*. An estimated 2,000 major trial courts in the 50 states and the District of Columbia are staffed by more than 11,000 judges (LaFountain et al., 2008). The term *general jurisdiction* means that these courts have the legal authority to decide all matters not specifically delegated to lower courts. The specific division of jurisdiction between the lower courts and the major trial courts is specified by law—statutory, constitutional, or both. The most common names for these courts are district, circuit, and superior. The specific names used in all states are listed in Table 4.2.

TABLE 4.2 ▪ MAJOR TRIAL COURTS IN DIFFERENT STATES

Circuit Court

Alabama, Arkansas,[a] Florida, Hawaii, Illinois, Indiana,[b] Kentucky, Maryland, Michigan, Mississippi,[a] Missouri, Oregon, South Carolina, South Dakota, Tennessee,[a] Virginia, West Virginia, Wisconsin

Court of Common Pleas

Ohio, Pennsylvania

District Court

Colorado, Idaho, Iowa, Kansas, Louisiana, Minnesota, Montana, Nebraska, Nevada, New Mexico, North Dakota, Oklahoma, Texas, Utah, Wyoming

Superior Court

Alaska, Arizona, California, Connecticut, Delaware,[a] District of Columbia, Georgia, Maine, Massachusetts, New Hampshire, New Jersey, North Carolina, Rhode Island, Vermont,[c] Washington

Supreme Court

New York[d]

[a] Arkansas, Delaware, Mississippi, and Tennessee have separate chancery courts with equity jurisdiction.
[b] Indiana uses superior and circuit courts.
[c] Vermont also uses district courts.
[d] New York also uses county courts.
SOURCE: Based on Data from Court Statistics Project. (2012). State Court Structure Charts. Williamsburg, VA: National Center for State Courts. Available online at http://www.courtstatistics.org/Other-Pages/State_Court_Structure_Charts.aspx.

The geographical jurisdictions of the major trial courts are defined along existing political boundaries, primarily counties. Each court has its own support staff consisting of a clerk of court, a sheriff, and others. In most states, the trial courts of general jurisdiction are also grouped into judicial districts or circuits. In rural areas these districts or circuits encompass several adjoining counties. Here, the trial court judges are true generalists who hear a wide variety of cases as they literally ride circuit, holding court in different counties on a fixed schedule. More populated counties have only one circuit or district for the area. Here, judges are often specialists assigned to hear only certain types of cases, such as criminal, family, juvenile, or civil. Refer to Table 4.1 for some basic workload data on the major trial courts.

As discussed in Chapter 3, the lion's share of the nation's judicial business takes place at the state, not the federal, level. About 35 million cases are filed each year in the major trial courts of the states, more than 95 times the number of similar filings in the federal district courts. Moreover, the types of cases filed in the state courts differ greatly from those filed in the federal courts. Litigants in federal courts are most often big businesses and governmental bodies. In sharp contrast, litigants in state courts are typically individuals and small businesses.

Whereas federal courts hear a high percentage of cases dealing with white-collar crimes and major drug distribution, state courts decide primarily street crimes. The more serious criminal violations are heard in the trial courts of general jurisdiction. The public associates felonies with crimes of violence, such as murder, robbery, and rape, but as Chapter 10 will show, 90 percent of criminal violations involve nonviolent crimes, such as burglary and theft. State courts must also process a rising number of drug-related offenses, ranging from simple possession of small amounts of illicit drugs to the sale of large quantities of cocaine and heroin. Over the past decade and a half, criminal cases filed in general jurisdiction courts (primarily felonies) increased 25 percent. Most criminal cases do not go to trial. Thus, the dominant issue in the trial courts of general jurisdiction is not guilt or innocence, but what penalty to apply to the guilty.

AMERICAN GANGSTER (2007)

COURTS, LAW, & MEDIA

American Gangster contrasts the wealthy Frank Lucas (Denzel Washington) with the looming poverty of Richie Roberts (Russell Crowe), a Newark Police Department Detective. Lucas has made a fortune as Harlem's top heroin dealer largely because he delivers a quality product and has cut out the middleman—he imports his drugs directly from Thailand on U.S. Air Force planes. Roberts, meanwhile, is on the economic brink because of a pending divorce. Financial salvation seems at hand when the detective and his partner discover nearly $1 million in unmarked bills in a car. But he resists temptation and turns in the money, which results in his being ostracized from his precinct. His honesty catches him a break, however, and he is assigned to a newly created drug task force that concentrates on going after high-level drug suppliers, rather than lower-level dealers.

Lucas usually avoids any flashy behavior that might attract unwanted police attention, but to impress a beauty queen (who will soon become his wife) he attends the Muhammad Ali and Joe Frazier fight in a gaudy chinchilla fur coat. Detective Roberts is at the event and spots this unknown person of great wealth who has easy access to the top crime figures of the area. Richie eventually discovers how the drugs are being smuggled into the country and meets with Frank and offers him a deal—go to prison for the rest of your life or get a shorter prison term by cooperating. He chooses cooperation, and his testimony leads to more than 100 drug convictions, the arrest of numerous narcotics cops who have been taking bribes, and the destruction of one of New York City's mafia families. Lucas has his sentence reduced to 4 years and is placed in the witness protection program (but he cannot stay out of trouble).

American Gangster captures the reality of drug dealing, including racial tensions in Harlem, the wars between rival drug dealers, and the waning influence of Italian-based mafias in drug dealing. Indeed the movie trailer proclaims that it is based on a true story. But how true is the portrayal? Federal Judge Sterling Johnson, Jr., who served as a special narcotics prosecutor, describes the film as "one percent reality and ninety-nine percent Hollywood." The real Frank Lucas was "illiterate, vicious, violent, and everything Denzel Washington was not" (CNN, 2008). And in terms of legal ethics, the movie sets an all-time low. Detective Richie graduates from law school and later prosecutes Lucas and still later serves as his defense attorney. This creates a conflict of interest that would not be allowed in any real court.

The deal Lucas strikes with the prosecution raises some troubling policy questions. At one point he is described as the "most dangerous man walking the streets of our city." Yet he is allowed back on the streets for turning in lower-level criminals. Drug dealers are depicted very differently in the 1971 movie *The French Connection,* which stars Gene Hackman as a New York detective trying to break up an organized crime gang smuggling heroin from Turkey through the French port of Marseilles. *The French Connection* presents no moral or policy ambiguities; it is an action movie about a good cop arresting bad guys. Thus, simply busting big-time drug dealers is the end in and of itself. The movie *Traffic* (2000), however, highlights the moral ambiguities of American drug policy. It sparked a national debate on drug policy by offering three separate narratives: the morally hazy world of drug cops in Tijuana, Mexico; the political ambiguity of drug policy makers in Washington, D.C.; and the real source of wealth in a socially snobby country club of La Jolla, California.

American Gangster shows how difficult it is to put a face on the complex issues involved in the War on Drugs. Publicly elected officials treat the War on Drugs like a third rail—touch it and you die. Privately, however, many government officials (some even in law enforcement) have serious doubts that this war is winnable. Amidst these conflicting assessments, America's courts must process approximately 1.7 million drug arrests each year.

INTERMEDIATE COURTS OF APPEALS

A century ago, state court systems included only a single appellate body—the state court of last resort. Like their federal counterparts, however, state courts have experienced a significant growth in appellate cases that threatens to overwhelm the state high court of last resort. State officials in 39 states have responded by creating **intermediate courts of appeals (ICAs)** (Exhibit 4.1). The only states that have not followed suit are sparsely populated ones with a low volume of appeals. The ICAs must hear all properly filed appeals. Subsequent appeals are at the discretion of the higher court. Thus, a decision by the state's intermediate appellate court is the final one for most cases.

The structure of the ICAs varies in several ways. Twenty-four states organize their ICAs on a statewide basis and the rest on a regional basis. In most states, these bodies hear both civil and criminal appeals. Alabama and Tennessee, however, have separate courts of appeals for civil and criminal cases. Like their federal counterparts, these courts typically use rotating three-judge panels for deciding cases.

Exhibit 4.1 | **INTERMEDIATE COURTS OF APPEALS (NUMBER OF JUDGES IN DIFFERENT STATES)**

Appeals Court
Massachusetts (25)

Appellate Court
Connecticut (9), Illinois (52)

Appellate Division of Superior Court
New Jersey (34)

Appellate Divisions of Supreme Court
New York (55)

Appellate Terms of Supreme Court
New York (15)

Commonwealth Court
Pennsylvania (9)

Court of Appeals
Alaska (3), Arizona (22), Arkansas (12), Colorado (16), Georgia (12), Idaho (3), Indiana[a] (15), Iowa (9), Kansas (14), Kentucky (14), Michigan (28), Minnesota (16), Mississippi (10), Missouri (32), Nebraska (6), New Mexico (10), North Carolina (15), Oregon (10), South Carolina (9), Tennessee[b] (12), Utah (7), Virginia (11), Washington (22), Wisconsin (16)

Courts of Appeal
California (105), Louisiana (53), Ohio (68)

Courts of Appeals
Texas (80)

Court of Civil Appeals
Alabama (5), Oklahoma (12)

Court of Criminal Appeals
Alabama (5), Tennessee (12)

Court of Special Appeals
Maryland (13)

District Court of Appeals
Florida (62)

Intermediate Court of Appeals
Hawaii (4)

Superior Court
Pennsylvania (15)

None
Delaware, District of Columbia, Maine, Montana, Nevada, New Hampshire, North Dakota, Rhode Island, South Dakota, Vermont, West Virginia, Wyoming

---

[a] Temporary
[b] Civil only
Source: Bureau of Justice Statistics. 2007. *State Court Organization, 1987–2004*. Washington, DC: U.S. Department of Justice.

The ICAs handle the bulk of the caseload in the appellate system, and their workload has increased dramatically in the past decade. States have created these courts and given them additional judgeships in hopes of relieving the state high courts of last resort of crushing caseloads, only to find that the ICAs experience the same problems.

ICAs will be covered in more detail in Chapter 16, but in general, intermediate courts of appeals engage primarily in error correction; they review trials to make sure that the law was followed. The overall standard is one of fairness—the defendant is entitled to a fair trial but not a perfect one. As a result, defendants find that appellate courts are markedly unsympathetic to their legal arguments; only a small percentage of such appeals results in a victory. Moreover, those victories are often temporary ones, since the handful of defendants who win the right to a new trial are often reconvicted during their second trial. Thus, although the public perceives that appellate courts are prone to release defendants on technicalities, the opposite is true.

As we will shortly see, the intermediate courts of appeals represent the final stage of the process for most litigants. Very few cases make it to the appellate court in the first place, and of those cases, only a handful will be heard by the state's highest appellate court.

STATE HIGH COURTS OF LAST RESORT

The court of last resort is generally referred to as the **state high court of last resort**. The specific names vary from state to state, and to further complicate the picture, Texas and Oklahoma have two courts of last resort—one for civil appeals and another for criminal appeals. The number of state high court judges varies from a low of five to as many as nine (see Exhibit 4.2). Unlike the intermediate appellate courts, these courts do not use panels in making decisions; rather, the entire court participates in deciding each case. All state high courts of last resort have a limited amount of original jurisdiction in dealing with matters such as disciplining lawyers and judges.

In states without an intermediate court of appeals, however, the supreme court has no power to choose which cases will be placed on its docket; in most other states, the high court has a purely discretionary docket. As with the U.S. Supreme Court, the state high courts of last resort select only

---

Exhibit 4.2 **COURTS OF LAST RESORT IN DIFFERENT STATES (NUMBER OF JUDGES)**

Supreme Court

Alabama (9), Alaska (5), Arizona (5), Arkansas (7), California (7), Colorado (7), Connecticut (7), Delaware (5), Florida (7), Georgia (7), Hawaii (5), Idaho (5), Illinois (7), Indiana (5), Iowa (8), Kansas (7), Kentucky (7), Louisiana (7), Michigan (7), Minnesota (7), Mississippi (9), Missouri (7), Montana (7), Nebraska (7), Nevada (7), New Hampshire (5), New Jersey (7), New Mexico (5), North Carolina (7), North Dakota (5), Ohio (7), Oklahoma[a] (9), Oregon (7), Pennsylvania (7), Rhode Island (5), South Carolina (5), South Dakota (5), Tennessee (5), Texas[a] (9), Utah (5), Vermont (5), Virginia (7), Washington (9), Wisconsin (7), Wyoming (5)

Court of Appeals

District of Columbia (9), Maryland (7), New York (7)

Supreme Judicial Court

Maine (7), Massachusetts (7)

Court of Criminal Appeals

Oklahoma[a] (5), Texas[a] (9)

Supreme Court Of Appeals

West Virginia (5)

---

[a] Two courts of last resort in these states.

SOURCE: Bureau of Justice Statistics. 2007. *State Court Organization, 1987–2004*. Washington, DC: U.S. Department of Justice.

a few cases to hear, but these cases tend to have broad legal and political significance. The ability of most state high courts of last resort to choose which cases to hear and which cases not to hear makes them important policy-making bodies. Whereas intermediate appellate courts review thousands of cases each year looking for errors, state high courts of last resort handle a hundred or so cases that present the most challenging legal issues arising in that state.

Nowhere is the policy-making role of state high courts of last resort more apparent than in deciding death penalty cases. In most states with death penalty laws, if the judge imposes the death penalty, then the case is automatically appealed to the state's highest court, thus bypassing the intermediate courts of appeals. Because of the high stakes, state high courts of last resort expend considerable time and energy in reviewing these cases. The outcomes of these reviews, though, vary greatly from state to state; some state high courts of last resort rarely overturn a death penalty decision, but others are very prone to reverse it.

The state high courts of last resort are the ultimate review board for matters involving interpretation of state law. The only other avenue of appeal for a disgruntled litigant is the U.S. Supreme Court, but successful applications are few and must involve important questions of federal law. Chapter 16 will probe why many state high courts of last resort have in recent years emerged as significant governmental bodies. In state after state, the supreme courts are deciding issues that have a major impact on the law and government of their jurisdiction.

COURT UNIFICATION

Historically, court reform focused on organizational structure. To court reformers, the multiplicity of courts is inefficient (because judges cannot be shifted to meet the caseload needs of other courts) and also inequitable (because the administration of justice is not uniform). Thus, traditional court reform has most often identified with implementing a unified court system. Figure 4.1 provides a diagram of a state (Florida) with a unified court system; Figure 4.2 offers a contrasting diagram of a state (Texas) with limited unification.

Key Components

The principal objective of a **unified court system** is to shift judicial administration from local control to centralized management. The loose network of independent judges and courts is replaced by a coherent hierarchy with authority concentrated in the state capital. Although court reformers differ about the exact details of a unified court system, their efforts reflect five general principles: a simplified court structure; centralized administration, rule making, and judicial budgeting; and statewide financing (Berkson & Carbon, 1978).

Simplified Court Structure

Court reformers stress the need for a **simplified court structure** with a simple, uniform court structure for the entire state. In particular, the multiplicity of minor and specialized courts, which often have overlapping jurisdiction, would be consolidated in one county-level court. This would mean that variations between counties would be eliminated and replaced by a similar court structure throughout the state. Overall, the court reformers envision a three-tier system: a state court of last resort at the top, intermediate courts of appeal where the volume of cases makes it necessary, and a single trial court.

Centralized Administration

Reformers envision **centralized administration**, with the state high court of last resort, working through court administrators, providing leadership for the state court system. The state court system would embody a genuine hierarchy of authority, in which local court administrators would be required to follow the policy directives of the central office and would in turn be held accountable by the state high court of last resort. Thus, a centralized state office would supervise the work of judicial and nonjudicial personnel.

Centralized Rule Making

Reformers argue that the state high courts of last resort should have the power to adopt uniform rules to be followed by all courts in the state. Examples of **centralized rule making** include procedures

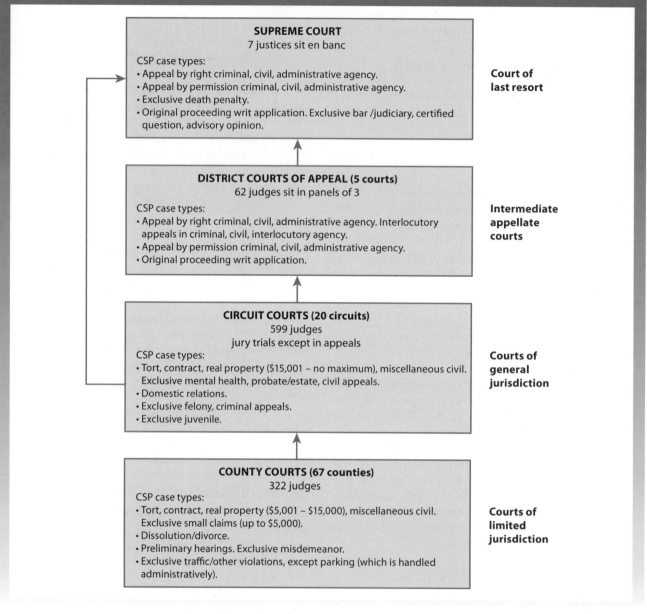

SUPREME COURT
7 justices sit en banc

CSP case types:
• Appeal by right criminal, civil, administrative agency.
• Appeal by permission criminal, civil, administrative agency.
• Exclusive death penalty.
• Original proceeding writ application. Exclusive bar /judiciary, certified question, advisory opinion.

Court of last resort

DISTRICT COURTS OF APPEAL (5 courts)
62 judges sit in panels of 3

CSP case types:
• Appeal by right criminal, civil, administrative agency. Interlocutory appeals in criminal, civil, interlocutory agency.
• Appeal by permission criminal, civil, administrative agency.
• Original proceeding writ application.

Intermediate appellate courts

CIRCUIT COURTS (20 circuits)
599 judges
jury trials except in appeals

CSP case types:
• Tort, contract, real property ($15,001 – no maximum), miscellaneous civil. Exclusive mental health, probate/estate, civil appeals.
• Domestic relations.
• Exclusive felony, criminal appeals.
• Exclusive juvenile.

Courts of general jurisdiction

COUNTY COURTS (67 counties)
322 judges

CSP case types:
• Tort, contract, real property ($5,001 – $15,000), miscellaneous civil. Exclusive small claims (up to $5,000).
• Dissolution/divorce.
• Preliminary hearings. Exclusive misdemeanor.
• Exclusive traffic/other violations, except parking (which is handled administratively).

Courts of limited jurisdiction

© Cengage Learning

Figure 4.1 ■ Example of a State with a Unified Court Structure: Florida Court Structure

for disciplining errant attorneys and time standards for disposing of cases. In addition, judges could be temporarily assigned to other courts to alleviate backlogs and reduce delay. Centralized rule making would shift control from the legislature to judges and lawyers.

Centralized Judicial Budgeting

Centralized judicial budgeting would give the state judicial administrator (who reports to the state high court of last resort) the authority to prepare a single budget for the entire state judiciary and send it directly to the legislature. The

SUPREME COURT
9 justices sit en banc
CSP case types:
• Exclusive appeal by permission civil administrative agency.
• Original proceeding application for writ, certified question. Exclusive bar/judiciary.

COURT OF CRIMINAL APPEALS
9 judges sit en banc
CSP case types:
• Exclusive appeal by permission criminal.
• Exclusive death penalty.
• Original proceeding application for writ, certified question.

Courts of last resort

COURTS OF APPEALS (14 courts)
80 justices sit in panels
CSP case types:
• Appeal by right criminal, administrative agency. Interlocutory appeals in criminal, civil, administrative agency.
• Original proceeding application for writ.

Intermediate appellate courts

DISTRICT COURTS* (499 courts, 499 judges)

DISTRICT COURTS (436 courts, 436 judges) Jury trials	**DISTRICT COURTS** (10 courts, 10 judges) Jury trials
CSP case types: • Tort, contract, real property ($201 – no maximum), probate/estate. • Miscellaneous civil. Exclusive administrative agency appeal. • Juvenile.	CSP case types: • Felony, misdemeanor.

Courts of general jurisdiction

COUNTY-LEVEL COURTS (499 courts, 499 judges)

Constitutional County Courts (254 courts, 254 judges) Jury trials	**Probate Court** (18 courts, 18 judges) Jury trials	**County Court at Law** (227 judges) Jury trials
CSP case types: • Tort, contract, real property ($200–$10,000), probate/estate, mental health, civil trial court appeals, miscellaneous civil. • Misdemeanor, criminal appeals. • Juvenile. • Traffic infractions.	CSP case types: • Probate/estate. • Mental health.	CSP case types: • Tort, contract, real property ($200 – $100,000), probate/estate, mental health, civil trial court appeals, miscellaneous civil. • Misdemeanor, DWI/DUI, criminal appeals. • Juvenile. • Traffic infractions.

Municipal Court** (916 courts, 1,414 judges) Jury trials	**Justice Court**** (821 courts, 821 judges) Jury trials
CSP case types: • Misdemeanor. • Traffic infractions, Exclusive ordinance violation.	CSP case types: • Tort, contract, real property ($0–$10,000), small claims (up to $10,000). • Misdemeanor. • Traffic infractions, parking.

Courts of limited jurisdiction

** Some municipal and justice of the peace courts may appeal to the district court.

© Cengage Learning

Figure 4.2 ■ Example of a State with Limited Court Unification: Texas Court Structure

governor's power to recommend a judicial budget would be eliminated. Likewise, lower courts would be dependent on the state high court of last resort for their monetary needs and unable to lobby local representatives directly. Thus, decisions about allocating funds would be made at the state and not the local level.

Statewide Financing

Along with centralized judicial budgeting, reformers argue for the adoption of **statewide financing** of the judiciary. Although courts are mandated by state law, they are often financed in whole or in part by local governments. Given that courts are often not a high priority for local government, they end up with less-than-adequate local financing. State government, in contrast, has more money and could better support necessary court services.

With the recent economic downturn across the nation, the issue of how to fund the courts has taken on new significance. Faced with mounting deficits, many states are cutting funding for the courts, with potentially serious consequences. In the words of the American Bar Association (2009), judicial independence is "a value that is indispensable to our democratic republic. A large part of that independence lies in courts having consistent, adequate funding to deliver justice." Yet at the same time, public demands for court services are increasing. Faced with these realities, court leaders are being encouraged to examine zero-cost or very-low-cost innovations (Broccolina & Zorza, 2008).

Analysis

The assumptions and philosophy of traditional notions of court reform have been called into serious question. Some scholars believe that the old principles of court reorganization hamper creative thinking about the direction court reform should take (Flango, 1994; Lamber & Luskin, 1992). One concern is that the concept of a unified court system does not allow for a desirable diversity. The standard blueprint of court organization fails to consider, for example, important differences in the working environment of courts in densely populated cities as opposed to those in sparsely inhabited rural areas.

Critics have also charged that traditional concepts of court reform stress abstract ideals of court organization (law on the books) to the neglect of the realities of the courthouse (law in action) (Baar, 1980). As a result, court reformers suffer from elite bias. Their perceptions of the problems of the courthouse extend only to cases with policy significance involving major community actors and rarely extend to ordinary cases affecting average citizens. In the biting words of Laura Nader (1992), court reformers talk about ridding the courts of "garbage cases," which include domestic violence, substance abuse, and neglected children. The solutions proposed by lawyer elites seem unresponsive to the realities of ordinary cases heard in the nation's trial courts. A judiciary with a clearly delineated organizational structure staffed by judges selected on the basis of merit (see Chapter 8) will face the same problems of large caseloads and types of cases— juvenile delinquency, for example—that are difficult to decide. Moreover, courts, no matter how well organized, must cope with public sentiments demanding getting tough with crime (see "Case Close-Up: *Ewing v. California* and Three Strikes Laws").

PROBLEM-SOLVING COURTS

Contemporary court reform concentrates more on improving the quality of justice meted out by American courts and less on providing a neat organizational chart. The modern agenda of court reform includes topics such as reducing trial court delay (Chapter 5), improving the efficiency of the appellate courts (Chapter 16), creating alternative dispute resolution, and establishing community courts.

Contemporary court reform is often identified with problem-solving courts (Wolf, 2007). Although problem-solving courts vary considerably from place to place, they all emphasize addressing the underlying issue of the individual appearing in court. Moreover, these judicial bodies actively collaborate with service providers (Casey & Rottman, 2004).

Contemporary court reform involves the creation of specialized courts to deal with specific types of cases. Initially, these were called "designer courts" or "boutique courts," indicating their specialized nature. Common examples include drug court, domestic violence court, juvenile drug court, gun court, DUI court, elder court, mental health court, and reentry court (which deals with prisoners reentering the community). More recently, these

CASE CLOSE-UP

EWING v. CALIFORNIA AND THREE STRIKES LAWS

Forty-year-old Gary Ewing was caught moments after he attempted to steal three golf clubs, which he had hidden in his pants leg. Under normal circumstances Ewing would have been prosecuted for a misdemeanor violation. But his background of several previous convictions marked the case as unusual. Thus, the Los Angeles District Attorney decided to prosecute Ewing under California's "three strikes and you're out" law; as a result, he was sentenced to 25 years in prison without parole.

Three strikes laws have become an increasingly popular reaction to citizen frustrations over crime. As discussed further in Chapter 14, these laws systematically increase potential prison sentences for defendants who have been convicted of violent offenses. In California, however, only one of the convictions must be for a violent crime, thus adding to the controversy in the nation's most populous state. Critics argue that such laws are fundamentally unfair because the sentence is disproportionate to the actual crime committed. However, in *Ewing v. California* a majority of the U.S. Supreme Court rejected this argument, holding that the sentence was not disproportionate and hence not a violation of the Eighth Amendment prohibition against cruel and unusual punishment.

Justice O'Connor's opinion for the majority stressed that in enacting three strikes laws, the California legislature had made a deliberate policy choice that individuals who repeatedly engage in serious or violent criminal behavior have not been deterred by conventional punishments, and therefore society can protect itself by isolating the defendant. Justice Stevens and three other justices dissented, arguing that a 25-year sentence for such a petty offense was "grossly disproportionate" and therefore constituted cruel and unusual punishment.

These laws increase the volume of criminal prosecutions. Note that Gary Ewing would normally have been tried in a misdemeanor court, where costs are low and trials are few. Instead, he was prosecuted in a more

costly felony court, where trials are more likely and also more time consuming. In California, for example, felony jury trials increased by nearly 10 percent after the state enacted its Three Strikes law (Brown & Jolivette, 2005). The felony trial rate more than quintupled in Los Angeles (Schultz, 2000).

Ample evidence shows that such get-tough policies have resulted in uneven application of the laws. "In some counties, for example, prosecutors seek Three Strikes enhancements only in certain cases, such as for certain types of crimes that are particular problems in their county or when the current offense is serious or violent. In other counties, prosecutors seek Three Strikes enhancements in most eligible cases" (Brown & Jolivette, 2005). Three Strikes laws also give prosecutors enormous leverage in forcing a defendant to accept a plea bargain (Ryan, 2002). The risk of conviction at trial may even lead an innocent person facing a third strike to plead guilty.

In addition, Three Strikes laws contribute to great variations in sentencing. For example, California's Kern County is 13 times more likely to send someone to state prison with a strike enhancement than San Francisco County is (Brown & Jolivette, 2005). Finally, these laws have had a tremendous impact on corrections. Not only have Three Strikes laws increased the number of pretrial inmates being detained in local jails, but also they have resulted in a growing and aging prison population (Brown & Jolivette, 2005; see also Chapter 14).

Supporters of Three Strikes laws point to falling crime rates as evidence of the law's effectiveness. But there is little agreement among researchers about the these laws' impact on crime and public safety. Consider that the "violent crime rate in those counties least likely to send strikers to prison declined by an average of 45 percent, while the violent crime rate in the counties most likely to send strikers to prison declined by an average of 44 percent" (Brown & Jolivette, 2005).

specialized courts have been said to rely on therapeutic jurisprudence (Amendola, 2010; Rosenthal, 2002; Wexler & Winick, 1996). Such courts have five essential elements:

1. Immediate intervention
2. Nonadversarial adjudication
3. Hands-on judicial involvement
4. Treatment programs with clear rules and structured goals
5. A team approach that brings together the judge, prosecutors, defense counsel, treatment provider, and correctional staff (Rottman & Casey, 1999)

Drug courts, domestic violence courts, and mental health courts are prime examples of courts based on the concept of therapeutic jurisprudence.

Drug Courts

The emergence of drug courts illustrates how the judiciary is responding both to increases in caseload and changes in the types of cases being brought to court. In the mid-1980s, drug caseloads increased dramatically in courts throughout the country. As a centerpiece of the so-called war on drugs, elected officials across the nation backed efforts to arrest, prosecute, and imprison persons possessing or selling illegal drugs. As a result, arrests for drug-related violations represent the largest single category of police activity, particularly in the nation's major urban areas.

Faced with a rapidly increasing caseload of types of cases that did not seem to fit the traditional criminal court model, courts began to experiment with new ways of processing cases by creating drug courts. Rather than viewing these defendants as criminals, they saw them as persons with an addiction problem. Drug courts emphasize treatment. The assumption was that treatment would reduce the likelihood that convicted drug offenders would be rearrested.

The first drug court was created in 1989 in Dade County, Florida Circuit Court (in which the city of Miami is located). To be eligible, defendants must have had no prior felony convictions, must have been charged with possession only (not sale), and must have admitted their drug problem and requested treatment. Such offenders were diverted into treatment. A judge, in addition to probation

officers, monitored offenders' progress by requiring participants to report periodically to the court. The judge assessed offenders' progress and moved them through the phases of the program.

Since the advent of the first drug court, these specialized courts have grown to become an important part of the criminal justice system (Belenko, 2001). There are more than 2,600 drug courts operating in the 50 states today (National Drug Court Resource Center, 2011). Early drug courts had the simple goal of reducing drug use and recidivism by monitoring offenders through weekly court visits, drug testing, and supervision by probation officers and judges alike. It soon became clear that offenders needed more in-depth treatment in order to change behavior patterns so that long-term goals of reduced criminal activities and drug use could be maintained after the offender was out of the program (Belenko, 2001).

The Effectiveness of Drug Courts

Initial evaluations of early drug courts found favorable rates of success. For example, as compared with defendants not in the program, offenders in the Dade County drug court treatment program had lower incarceration rates, less frequent rearrests, and longer times to rearrest (Goldkamp & Weiland, 1993). More sophisticated evaluations, however, have highlighted the complex impact of drug courts. In Washington, D.C., participation in a drug court treatment program has been relatively poor—only 41 percent of those eligible chose to participate. Moreover, completion of the program took much longer than anticipated; cases were open an average of 11 months as opposed to the 6 months estimated (Harrell, Cavanagh, & Roman, 2000).

More recent studies support the earlier conclusions that drug courts have a positive impact (Downey & Roman, 2010; Huddleston & Marlowe, 2011). Most drug court studies have found:

- that overall treatment retention is substantially better than in other community- based treatment programs for offenders (Belenko, 2001; Springer & Roberts, 2007; Goldkamp, White, & Robinson, 2001; U.S. Government Accountability Office, 2005);

- lower recidivism rates from drug-court participants than for comparison groups (Banks &

Gottfredson 2004; Belenko, 2001; Gottfredson, Najaka, & Kearley, 2003; Springer & Roberts, 2007); and

- a net cost savings to the criminal justice system by providing offenders with treatment that is much less expensive than incarcerating them (Aos, Miller, & Drake 2006; Belenko, 2001; Carey, Finigan, & Pukstas, 2008; Logan, Hoyt, McCollister, French, Leukefeld, & Minton 2004; Springer & Roberts 2007).

But the impact of drug courts varies by time, manner, and place (Goldkamp, 2002). Moreover, the drug-court model appears to be relatively ineffective when applied to drunk drivers (Bouffard & Richardson 2007). Completion of drug court reduced recidivism among non-DUI offenders but there was no significant reduction in recidivism among chronic DUI offenders (Bouffard, Richardson, and Franklin, 2010).

Juvenile Drug Courts

Some jurisdictions have extended the therapeutic jurisprudence model of drug courts to youthful offenders (Belenko, 2001). Although dramatically fewer in number than adult drug courts, juvenile drug courts "are quickly emerging as one of the most popular means of diversionary treatment within the juvenile justice system" (Miller, Ventura-Miller, and Barnes 2007, pp. 246–247).

Juvenile drug courts use judicial and multiagency teams (e.g., prosecutors, defense attorneys, treatment providers, school officials, etc.) to provide intensive and continuous supervision of participants to ensure "compliance with the court-imposed conditions of participation," such as "treatment program participation, school attendance, drug testing, community service, court appearances" (Cooper, 2001, p. 6). Frequent court appearances for active judicial involvement in case management, juvenile accountability, and a behaviorally based system of rewards and sanctions (especially using community service and curfews) are all key differences from regular juvenile courts. In addition, juvenile drug courts offer earlier and "far more comprehensive assessments of offenders based on an integration of cumulative information, a heavy concentration on family functioning, and highly coordinated services for offenders and their families" (Gilmore, Rodriguez, & Webb, 2005, p. 289; see also, Chassin, 2008).

Most studies have reported that juvenile drug-court participation reduced recidivism (Applegate & Santana, 2000; Shaffer, 2006; Shaw & Robinson, 1998). However, the positive effects of participation in juvenile drug courts appear to "decline when court supervision ends" (Chassin, 2008, p. 170; see also, Belenko & Dembo 2003; Flanzer, 2005). And, the efficacy of drug-court interventions for juveniles is significantly affected by the length of drug use, whether the juvenile is involved in other types of criminal offenses, and the presence of co-occurring psychiatric disorders (Fradella, Fischer, Kleinpeter, & Koob, 2009).

Domestic Violence Courts

Domestic violence courts comprise another type of problem-solving court being created in a growing number of communities across the nation. Domestic violence was once considered a private family matter but is now viewed as a significant social problem (Chapter 9). Changes in how police and prosecutors respond to domestic violence cases have produced changes in how courts respond as well.

In domestic violence courts, the emphasis is on integration. These courts respond to a historical problem in the court system, which required domestic violence victims and their families to appear in different courts before multiple judges, often located in different courthouses in different parts of the county. As a result, a single family could be involved in several courts before several different judges and face the possibility of conflicting court orders (Casey & Rottman, 2004).

Today, practices of domestic violence courts typically include the following:

- A dedicated judge presides over all phases of domestic violence cases, and related cases are consolidated.
- Ongoing monitoring by judge and staff enables the court to hold offenders accountable.
- A resource coordinator prepares information for the judge and is the court's primary liaison with the community.
- On-site victim advocates serve as the primary linkage to social service agencies.
- The emphasis is on a coordinated community response that includes information sharing,

education, and coordination across the criminal justice system (Center for Court Innovation, 2012c).

Operating within this general framework, more than 200 specialized domestic violence courts have been created across the nation and a similar number internationally (Labriola, Bradley, O'Sullivan, Rempel, & Moore, 2009). One example is Manhattan's Specialized Domestic Violence Court (Center for Court Innovation, 2009). By removing domestic violence cases from mixed-docket courts, this specialized court seeks to increase defendant accountability, promote victim safety, and better coordinate the activities of governmental agencies that respond to domestic violence. Also called "integrated domestic violence courts," they are dedicated to the one-family–one-judge concept. Thus, a single judge handles multiple criminal, family court, and divorce cases involving the same defendant (Peterson, 2004).

Most evaluations of domestic violence courts suggest that they are successful in reducing reoffenses of domestic violence. For example, an evaluation of a California domestic violence court found a 62 percent completion rate for a yearlong program and lower recidivism rates among program completers versus noncompleters—specifically 15 percent vs. 25 percent for domestic violence arrests (Petrucci, 2010). Other evaluations of domestic violence court programs in Albuquerque, New Mexico (Pitts, Givens, & McNeeley, 2009) and Lexington County, South Carolina (Gover, McDonald, & Alpert, 2003) similarly found that program completers were significantly less likely to receive subsequent charges for domestic violence, other violent offenses, or any other criminal offense. In contrast, an evaluation of Manhattan's Specialized Domestic Violence Court showed mixed results: Conviction rates did not increase, cases were disposed of more quickly, defendants were more likely to be placed in a batterer-intervention program, and rearrests increased (Peterson, 2004). The mixed results from evaluations of different domestic violence courts may be because completion rates vary dramatically, often as a function of the length of the program (Petrucci, 2002). Still, the evidence indicates that these courts enhance victims' and defendants' satisfaction with the court process and deliver more services to victims and their families (Casey & Rottman, 2004).

Mental Health Courts

Mental health courts (MHCs) are a third type of problem-solving court using the concept of therapeutic jurisprudence. Over the past several years there has been a growing awareness that the mentally ill are overrepresented in the criminal justice system. It is estimated that anywhere from 14.5 percent to 31 percent of those in jail suffer from serious mental illness, a rate that is many times that of the general adult population (Steadman, Osher, Robbins, Case, & Samuels, 2009). Indeed, Los Angeles County Jail and New York's Rikers Island held more people with mental illness than the largest psychiatric hospital inpatient facilities in the United States (Council of State Governments Justice Center, 2008). Not only do mentally ill defendants present special security risks in courts and jails, but they are also more likely to repeatedly recycle through the criminal justice system (Mental Health America, 2012).

The first MHC was established in 1997; since then, a growing number of courts across the nation are establishing MHCs that are remarkably diverse. For example, Mann (2011) found that 85 percent of MHCs accept misdemeanor cases; 75 percent of MHCs handled felony cases (although only 20 percent accepted violent felony cases and only 1 percent handled seriously violent felony cases); and the eligible clinical diagnoses for participation varied significantly across MHCs. Nonetheless, these courts exhibit several key features:

- A specialized court docket is created.
- Mental health screening is available for acceptable candidates.
- Mentally ill defendants voluntarily enroll in the specialize court which, in turn, processes their cases on the basis of therapeutic jurisprudence rather than the adversary style of justice.
- Judges supervise a community-based treatment plan for each defendant, involving a team of court staff and mental health professionals.
- The judge and probation officials periodically review the progress of each defendant and use a system of incentives for compliance and sanctions for noncompliance with the conditions imposed by the court.
- Criteria define a participant's completion (sometimes called "graduation form") of the

program (Council of State Governments Justice Center, 2012; Mann, 2011).

Judge Matthew D'Emic (2009) of the Brooklyn Mental Health Court writes that in the 7 years of that court's operation, over 275 persons have successfully graduated. But he is quick to point out that public policy should not be driven by anecdotes of individual successes, but rather by research that systematically evaluates the effectiveness of the growing number of MHCs. Such evaluations must take into account the difficult population that these courts work with as well as the difficulty of coordinating efforts not just within the criminal justice system but also in the mental health community.

The few empirical evaluations of MHCs to date generally found that these specialized courts are effective (Herinckx, Swart, Ama, Dolezal, & King, 2005; McNiel & Binder, 2007; Moore & Hiday, 2006; Trupin & Richards, 2003). For example, Dirks-Linhorst and Linhorst (2012) found that the rearrest rate of 351 defendants who successfully completed an MHC program was 14.5 percent, as compared with 38 percent among defendants negatively terminated from the program and 25.8 percent among defendants who chose not to participate. But at least two studies have concluded that there is little difference in reoffending levels between MHC graduates and those who do not complete such a program (Christy, Poythress, Boothroyd, Petrila, & Mehra, 2005; Cosden, Ellens, Schnell, & Yamini-Diouf, 2005). The intense variations in the MHC programs may be responsible for these divergent findings.

TECHNOLOGY SHAPES THE COURTROOMS OF THE FUTURE

From the outside looking in, Courtroom 23 in Orange County, Florida, looks like your typical courtroom— a jury box, tables for the lawyers, the judge's bench and the like. But from the inside looking out, Courtroom 23 hardly resembles a traditional courtroom— computer monitors are everywhere, microphones are located around the courtroom, and video monitors are in plain view. Welcome to the modern courtroom, where technology is an integral part of the design, not a retrofitted feature.

Courtroom 23 is billed as the courtroom of the future and is the outgrowth of an earlier effort known as Courtroom 21. Launched in 1993 as a joint effort of the National Center for State Courts and the William and Mary School of Law, Courtroom 21 was the most technologically advanced courtroom in the world (National Center for State Courts, 2012). As technology has evolved, so has the notion of a high-technology courtroom. In the words of DC Superior Court Judge Herbert Dixon (2011), these changes have not always been easy. "Traditional litigators and judges whose skills were honed without the newfangled gadgets were not the fastest to embrace new technologies." As time passed, however, the number of old-time litigators diminished and interest in using new technologies increased.

Based on conducting several complex criminal trials, Judge Dixon highlights several important features of the courtrooms of the future. Evidence cameras, which project images of paper documents and the like, he labels as essential. Witnesses can readily mark vital aspects of the evidence and jurors can easily see it as well. Laptop connections are likewise of key importance. Lawyers can present digital images and sounds without carrying the evidence physically to the courtroom. Overall, jurors rated the use of courtroom technology very positively (Dixon, 2011).

Beyond trials, technology is shaping the future of courts in another important way, through electronic communications. Termed cyber-courts or virtual courts, judges can resolve disputes through electronic communications without the lawyers and parties being physically present. And at the discretion of the judge, proceedings of the cyber-court may be open to the public on the Internet (Global Courts, 2012). In the not-too-distant future, bail hearings and routine arraignments may be routinely conducted in a virtual court.

CONSEQUENCES OF COURT ORGANIZATION

What activities legislatures define as illegal has a major impact on the courts. In turn, how the courts are organized and administered has a profound effect on the way cases are processed and on the type of justice that results.

Decentralization and Choice of Courts

Although people often talk about the American legal system, no such entity exists. Instead, America has 51 legal systems—the federal courts and separate courts in each of the 50 states. Chapter 2 stressed the significant differences in the law among these separate systems. As a result, lawyers sometimes try to maneuver cases so that they are heard in courts that are perceived to be favorable to their clients. For example, some criminal offenses violate both state and federal laws. As a general rule, federal officials prosecute major violations, leaving more minor prosecutions to state officials.

The prosecution of the DC-area snipers illustrates the importance of the choice of courts. During a 3-week shooting spree, John Muhammad and Lee Malvo engaged in 13 shootings, killing 10 people and wounding 3. The U.S. attorney general decided to transfer the defendants to Virginia because that state's law makes the death penalty more likely than in the other jurisdictions where murders occurred— Maryland and the District of Columbia. After both were convicted, Muhammad was sentenced to death, but Malvo (because he was young) was sentenced to life imprisonment.

Local Control and Local Corruption

The 50 state court systems are in actuality often structured on a local basis. The officials who staff these courts—judges and lawyers, prosecutors and defense attorneys—are recruited from the local community they serve and thus reflect the sentiments of that community. As a result, the U.S. system of justice has close ties to local communities and the application of "state" law often has a local flavor. Jurors in rural areas, for example, often have markedly different attitudes toward guns than jurors in suburban areas.

Local control of justice has the obvious advantage of closely linking courts to the people they serve. But local control has also been an incubator of corruption and injustice. Every state invariably has a town or two where gambling and prostitution flourish because the city fathers agree to look the other way. Not surprisingly, they often receive monetary benefits for being so nearsighted. Increasingly, though, such activities attract the attention of state police, state attorneys general, and federal prosecutors.

The locally administered criminal justice system has also been marked by pockets of injustice. At times, the police and the courts have been the handmaidens of the local economic elite. In the South, historically, the police and the courts hindered efforts to exercise civil rights by arresting or harassing those who sought to register to vote, eat at whites-only lunch counters, or simply speak up to protest segregation. The dual court system has provided a safety valve for checking the most flagrant abuses of local justice. Often, it is federal—not state or local—officials who prosecute corrupt local officials.

Uneven Court Financing

The combination of court decentralization and local control of the judiciary results in uneven court financing. As discussed earlier, only a few states have adopted statewide financing of courts. Thus, in most states, courts are financed by a sometimes bewildering array of state taxes, local taxes, court fees, and fines. During normal times, this patchwork system of financing courts provides limited funding for the judiciary. In the words of David Boies, cochair of a commission formed by the American Bar Association to study court budget issues, "The justice system's funding has been decreasing in constant dollars for at least two decades" (Schwartz 2011, p. A18).

During a nationwide financial crisis, like the one that began in 2008, cutbacks in funding the courts have resulted in major reductions in services. A 30-percent reduction in state general funds over a 3-year period in California means that citizens of the nation's largest state will face delays in finalizing divorces, prolonged custody battles, and extended waits for lawsuits to go to trial (Dolan & Kim, 2011). Steep reductions in overtime pay for court employees in the state of New York means that a 3-day trial will now take 4 days, thus backing up the justice system even further (Caher & Keshner, 2011). Across the nation, getting cases, civil or criminal, to trial will prove to be a struggle.

Economic downturns not only reduce court funding but also increase demands for court services. Financial crises, for example, typically result in increased filings of bankruptcy petitions in federal courts (Chapter 3) and mortgage foreclosure cases in state courts (Sommer & Li, 2011).

Beyond the immediate problems of trying to provide the same services with less funding, courts also face long-term limitations in designing new programs to respond to changing social problems. Citizen demands to create or expand problem-solving courts—like drug courts, domestic violence courts, and mental health courts—are stymied because of a lack of funding. Other sectors of the criminal justice system face similar frustrations. Budget cuts, for example, often force prosecutors to provide fewer services for crime victims (Chapter 9) and public defenders to reduce services (Chapter 7).

CONCLUSION

The implementation of drug courts across the nation illustrates a major shift in thinking about court reform in the United States. Whereas traditional court reform emphasized consolidating various judicial bodies, the emerging agenda encourages the creation of specialized courts. Modern court reform also actively encourages working with members of the community, whereas the older tradition stressed notions of professionalism that disdained popular input. Likewise, court reform in the contemporary context stresses the importance of working with other agencies rather than viewing the judge as a lone authority figure. The next chapter focuses on these other agencies, elaborating on the concept of the courtroom work group.

What is perhaps most striking is that the ideas that have dominated discussion of court reform for most of this century are now being quietly buried. Instead of stressing organizational charts and other abstract notions, most efforts to reform the judiciary now focus on more specific matters—reducing court delay and targeting drug cases for special treatment, for example. Thus, today's court reform is marked by tremendous experimentation at the local level. Judges and other court actors identify a problem and seek solutions, adapting local resources and local understandings in the process. This adaptation to change has always been the hallmark of the American judiciary. Perhaps the only differences today are the rapid pace of change and the public attention paid to these ongoing efforts at judicial reform.

Chapter Review

LO1 **1.** Outline the four layers of a typical state court system.

A typical state court system includes lower courts (trial courts of limited jurisdiction), major trial courts (trial courts of general jurisdiction), intermediate appellate courts, and the state high court of last resort.

LO2 **2.** Describe the types of cases handled by the trial courts of limited jurisdiction.

The lower courts handle the preliminary stages of felony cases and also decide a large number of misdemeanor, traffic, and small claims cases.

LO3 **3.** Discuss the similarities and differences between justice of the peace courts and municipal courts.

Both justice of the peace (JP) courts and municipal courts are considered lower courts.

They differ primarily in terms of caseloads. The rurally based JP courts have relatively low caseloads, whereas the urban-based municipal courts have very large caseloads. Different urban and rural tax bases also affect their funding levels.

LO4 **4.** List the four primary problems confronting the lower courts in the United States.

The four major problems confronting the lower courts are inadequate financing, inadequate facilities, lax court procedures, and unbalanced caseloads.

LO5 **5.** Identify the types of civil and criminal cases filed in trial courts of general jurisdiction.

The major trial courts decide felony cases and civil cases including domestic relations, estate, personal injury, and contract cases.

LO6 **6.** Explain briefly the differences between a state high court of last resort in states with and without intermediate courts of appeals.

In states without intermediate appellate courts, state courts of last resort must hear all criminal appeals. In states without intermediate courts of appeals, state courts of last resort have discretion to hear only the cases they decide are the most important.

LO7 **7.** List the key components of court unification.

The key components of court unification include simplified court structure, centralized administration, centralized rule making, centralized judicial budgeting, and statewide financing.

LO8 **8.** Identify how problem-solving courts using therapeutic jurisprudence handle cases.

Courts using therapeutic jurisprudence have five essential elements: (1) immediate intervention, (2) nonadversarial adjudication, (3) hands-on judicial involvement, (4) treatment programs with clear rules, and (5) a team approach to treatment.

LO9 **9.** Discuss the consequences of court organization.

The organization of courts in the United States impacts the processing of cases in several ways, including the decentralization of justice, which at times can mean that there is a choice of courts and that local control has at times resulted in local corruption.

Critical Thinking Questions

1. Although we typically talk of state courts (as opposed to federal courts), would it be better to talk about local courts? To what extent are there major variations within your state?

2. Compare your state's court structure to those in Figures 4.1 and 4.2. How unified is your state court structure?

3. Have there been discussions in your state of court reorganization? What major interest groups are urging court reform, and what advantages do they suggest? What interest groups are opposing court reform, and what disadvantages do they cite?

4. Why do crime control advocates often oppose drug courts, and why do due process proponents support drug courts?

5. Make a list of state and local politicians who have been tried in federal court. Were there parallel state investigations or prosecutions? To what extent would corrupt local officials be better off if federal court jurisdiction were limited?

Key Terms

alternative dispute resolution (ADR) 102

arbitration 102

centralized administration 107

centralized judicial budgeting 108

centralized rule making 107

community courts 102

drug courts 112

inferior court (lower court) 92

intermediate courts of appeals (ICAs) 105

JP 94

justice of the peace courts 94

mediation 102

misdemeanor 93

municipal court 99

ordinance 93

simplified court structure 107

small claims court 94

state high court of last resort 106

statewide financing 110

therapeutic jurisprudence 112

traffic offenses 93

trial court of general jurisdiction 102

trial court of limited jurisdiction (lower court/inferior court) 92

trial de novo 97

unified court system 107

Web Resources

Go to the *America's Courts and the Criminal Justice System* companion website at
http://www.cengage.com/criminaljustice/neubauer,
where you will find more resources to help you study.
Resources include web exercises, quizzing, and flash cards.

For Further Reading

Abadinsky, Howard. *Drug Use and Abuse: A Comprehensive Introduction*. 7th ed. Belmont, CA: Wadsworth, 2011.

Adler, Parericia, Peter Adler, and Patrick O'Brien. *Drugs and the American Dream: An Anthology*. Hoboken, NJ: Wiley-Blackwell, 2012.

Almquist, Lauren, and Elizabeth Dodd. *Mental Health Courts: A Guide to Research Informed Policy and Practice*. Council of State Governments Justice Center, 2009.

American Judicature Society. "The Cost of Justice: Funding State Courts." *Judicature* 88: 158–169, 2005.

Beckett, Katherine, Kris Nyrop, and Lori Pfinst. "Race, Drugs, and Policing: Understanding Disparities in Drug Delivery Arrests." *Criminology* 44: 105, 2006.

Champagne, Anthony. "Judicial Reform in Texas: A Look Back after Two Decades," *Court Review* 43 (2): 68, 2006.

Council of State Governments. 2008 Mental Health Courts: A Primer for Policymakers and Practitioners. Austin: Council of State Governments Justice Center, 2008.

Council of State Governments 2012. "Mental Health Consensus Project." Available online at http://consensusproject.org

Crow, Matthew, Richard Hough, Jason Mosley, John Smykla, and Kimberly Tatum. "Drunk and Alone in a K-Mart Parking Lot: The Pedagogy of Simulations and Contemporary Attitudes toward Drinking and Driving." *Journal of Criminal Justice Education* 19: 417–431, 2008.

Erickson, Patricia, and Steven Erickson. *Crime, Punishment, and Mental Illness*. Piscataway, NJ: Rutgers University Press, 2008.

Federal Judicial Center. "Resources on Courtroom Technology," Available online at http:/www.fjc .gov/public/ home.nsf/autoframe?openform& url_l=/public/home. nsf/inavgeneral? openpage&url_r=/public/home.nsf/ pages/1100

Fell, James, Deborah Fisher, Robert Voas, Kenneth Blackman, and Scott Tippetts. "The Impact of Underage Drinking Laws on Alcohol-Related Fatal Crashes of Young Drivers." *Alcoholism, Clinical, and Experimental Research* 33: 1208–1219, 2009.

Gerber, Rudolph. *Legalizing Marijuana: Drug Policy Reform and Prohibition Politics*. Westport, CT: Praeger, 2004.

Hartley, Roger, and James Douglas. "Budgeting for State Courts." *Justice System Journal* 24: 251–264, 2003.

Lederer, Fredic. 2010. "Wired: What We've Learned about Courtroom Technology." *Criminal Justice* 24: 18–25.

Lightcap, Tracy. "Issue Environments and Institutionalization: Structural Changes in U.S. State Judicial Institutions, 1975–1995." *Justice System Journal* 24: 183–204, 2003.

Nafisi, Terry. "One Hundred Years since Pound: Has Court Reform Mattered?" *Justice System Journal* 27: 223–236, 2006.

Slate, Risdon, and W. Wesley Johnson. *The Criminalization of Mental Illness: Crisis and Opportunity for the Justice System*. Durham, NC: Carolina Academic Press, 2008.

Solomon, Freda. "New York City's Gun Court Initiative: A Pilot Program Study." CJA Research Brief No. 11. New York: New York City Criminal Justice Agency, 2006.

Willrich, Michael. *City of Courts: Socializing Justice in Progressive Era Chicago*. New York: Cambridge University Press, 2003.

Winick, Bruce, and David Wexler, eds. *Judging in a Therapeutic Key: Therapeutic Jurisprudence and the Courts*. Durham, NC: Carolina Academic Press, 2003.

Winkle, John III, and Robert Oswald. "The Role of Trial Judges in State Court Reform: The Case of Mississippi." *Judicature* 91: 288–297, 2008.

5 The Dynamics of Courthouse Justice

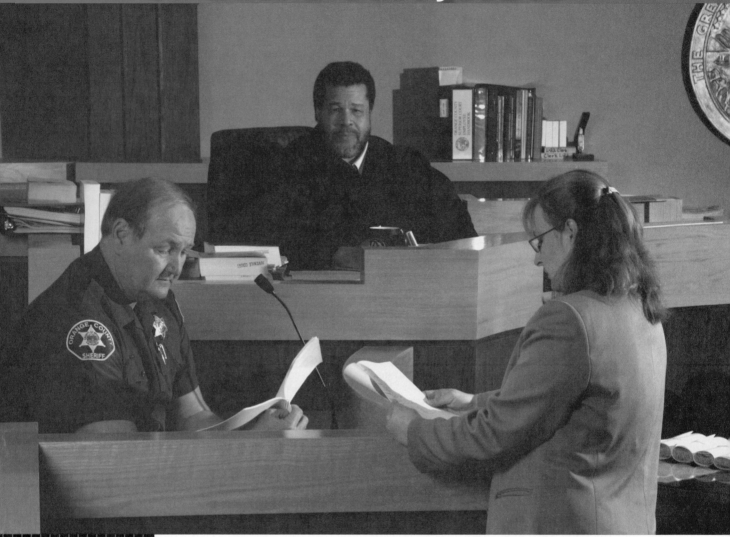

© Spencer Grant/PhotoEdit

A judge watches as a sheriff's deputy checks his notes before answering a question posed to him by a lawyer. While such a scene is typical, the courtroom work group is composed of many people who rarely are depicted in news photos or on television. Rather, the courtroom work group works together "behind-the-scenes" out of shared norms and their mutual interdependence on each other. ∎

THE COURTHOUSE AND THE PEOPLE WHO WORK THERE

The Courthouse
The Courtroom
Behind the Scenes

COURTHOUSE SECURITY AND CHANGING TECHNOLOGIES

Courts, Law, & Media
Law & Order

DYNAMICS OF COURTHOUSE JUSTICE

ASSEMBLY-LINE JUSTICE

Strengths of the Explanation
Weaknesses of the Explanation

DISCRETION

THE COURTROOM WORK GROUP

Mutual Interdependence
Shared Decision Making
Socialization
Normal Crimes

Courts, Controversy, & Gender Equity
Is Gender Bias a Significant Problem in the Courts?

Rewards and Sanctions
Variability in Courtroom Work Groups

THE PROBLEM OF DELAY

Consequences of Delay
Assessing the Costs of Delay

LAW ON THE BOOKS APPROACH TO COURT DELAY

Speedy-Trial Laws
Limits of Speedy-Trial Laws

LAW IN ACTION APPROACH TO COURT DELAY

CASE CLOSE-UP: *Barker v. Wingo* and the Right to a Speedy Trial

Case Scheduling
Efforts at Coordination
Variability in Courtroom Work Groups Revisited

LEGAL ETHICS

The Dynamics of Courthouse Justice • The Dynamics of
use Justice • The Dynamics of Courthouse Justice • The

Learning Objectives

After reading this chapter, you should be able to:

LO1 Have a general sense of who works where in the courthouse.

LO2 Analyze the importance of assembly-line justice.

LO3 Describe why discretion is found in the criminal courts.

LO4 Identify the principal actors in the courtroom work group.

LO5 Indicate why ethics is important to the American legal system.

LO6 Contrast differing understandings of why delay is a problem in the courts.

LO7 Discuss the strengths and weaknesses of speedy-trial laws.

LO8 Explain why law in action approaches to court delay are more effective than law on the books approaches..

Sixteen times, Willie Barker's murder case was set for trial, and sixteen times it was continued. At first the defense readily agreed, gambling that Barker's codefendant would be found not guilty. Thus, some of the continuances were caused by the six separate trials before the codefendant was finally convicted. Other continuances were granted because of the illness of the police investigator. It was not until 5 years after arrest that Barker was convicted of murder. To Barker's lawyer, this lengthy delay clearly violated the Sixth Amendment's right to a speedy trial. The Kentucky prosecutor replied that the delay did not jeopardize Barker's right to a fair trial.

Barker v. Wingo (1972) underscores three key points about criminal-case processing in contemporary courts. First, courts deal with lots of cases. From the perspective of victims and defendants, criminal cases are discrete life events, but from the vantage point of judges, prosecutors, and defense attorneys, the docket consists of numerous cases, each demanding the court's time. The pressure to move cases, often referred to as assembly-line justice, is the first concept discussed in this chapter.

of Courthouse Justice • The Dynamics of Courthouse Justice • Th

s of Courthouse Justice • The Dynamics of Courthouse Justice •

Second, the problems in prosecuting and convicting Barker indicate that discretion is often needed in interpreting the law. After all, the meaning of "speedy trial" is not self-evident. As we shall see, the concept of discretion begins to grapple with the day-to-day realities of courthouse dynamics.

Third, the *Barker* case shows that case dispositions involve far more than the isolated actions of individual judges. From arrest through trial and sentencing, case dispositions require mutual activity on the part of prosecutors and defense attorneys, to say nothing of police officers and probation officers, bail agents, and bailiffs. This chapter uses the concept of the courtroom work group to analyze the complexities of interaction among courthouse regulars.

This chapter examines the dynamics of courthouse justice by analyzing three major explanations for the great difference between textbook images of criminal procedure and the realities of the courtroom. We will then apply these concepts to one of the most often mentioned problems of American justice—delay. As in the *Barker* case, though, we will see that deciding how long is too long is a knotty question. But first let us begin with a tour of a typical U.S. courthouse.

THE COURTHOUSE AND THE PEOPLE WHO WORK THERE

Court jurisdiction and court structure are admittedly intangible concepts. Courthouses, on the other hand, are concrete. From the outside, courthouses appear to be imposing government buildings, but on the inside they are beehives of activity. Most immediately, courthouses are places where you find lawyers arguing before juries, talking to their clients, and conversing with one another. But courthouses also employ numerous nonlawyers who perform vital roles; without clerks and probation officers, bail agents and bailiffs, courthouses could not function. Not to be overlooked, ordinary citizens (whether victims or defendants, witnesses or jurors) also perform important roles in the courthouse.

In trying to understand how lawyers and nonlawyers, regular participants and occasional ones, dispense courthouse justice on a daily basis, it is helpful to start with a walking tour of a courthouse. What goes on inside different courthouses, of course, varies in important ways. In the courthouses of small towns, for example, one finds only a few courthouse regulars who handle many different types of matters. By contrast, in the courthouses of major cities you will find numerous courthouse regulars who specialize in specific duties. Moreover, in some courthouses, civil and criminal cases are heard in the same courtroom at the same time; in other jurisdictions, civil and criminal cases are separated by time and place. These variations aside, the following provides an overview of a typical day in a medium-sized courthouse in the United States.

The Courthouse

Early American courthouses were simple structures with "plain furnishings and finishes" (Sahoo, 2006, p. 9). But by the mid-1800s, major courthouses were designed to be "imposing, grandiose" structures that incorporated "formal architectural elements such as columns, domes, clock towers, and grand entrances" (Sahoo, 2006, p. 9). Today, courthouses in the United States "come in a myriad of designs, from centuries-old stone fortresses to modern-day, multifloor monolithic towers, from the one-room council chambers to the abstract designs of the creative architect" (Zaruba, 2007, p. 46).

The locations of courthouses vary dramatically as well. In some cities, courthouses are landmarks in the center of downtown areas. Such courthouses have served as anchors "for many commercial and community activities" (Sahoo, 2006, p. 9). In sharp contrast, for security reasons, criminal courts of other cities were purposefully constructed near pretrial detention facilities in isolated and inconvenient locations. Clustered nearby are older buildings, occupied by bail agents and defense attorneys. Garish neon signs proclaiming "Bail Bonds, 24-Hour Service" compete with unpainted wooden structures to provide a general sense of urban decay. The courthouse building likewise often has a haggard and unkempt look about it. Beneath the veneer of decades of grime, though, one sees a once grand building built during an era when citizens took great pride in their public buildings. Although criminal court buildings are constructed in a variety of architectural styles, they nevertheless all seem to present an image of solidity and unyielding strength.

In the modern era, court security concerns drive courthouse design, renovation, and function. Entrance is usually gained by climbing an excessive number of steps that lead to a single set of doors through which all people must enter.

> Visitors or employees entering the courthouse are met by CSOs [Court Security Officers] and screened as they pass through a metal detector. Persons setting off a metal detector are scanned by a CSO using a handheld detector. Briefcases, packages, and other items in which dangerous or prohibited items might be stored are X-rayed. The CSOs also hand-check any item deemed suspicious or problematic. Policies regarding the use, or even the presence, of cellular and digital phones, personal digital assistants, or other electronic devices are set by each individual courthouse. (Novak, 2003, p. 24)

In older courthouses, prisoners used the same entrances and circulation paths as judges, jurors, and members of the public. Modern courthouses, however, are designed to transfer prisoners securely from holding facilities into courthouses using different entrances and restricted internal routes so that they are kept separated from the public and courthouse personnel (Novak, 2003; Zaruba, 2007).

Once inside a courthouse, visitors may find themselves in an austere, small area or in a massive lobby with an impressive, high-arched ceiling. Either way, the lobby and hallways typically resound with animated conversations among lawyers, bail agents, bailiffs, defendants, family members, witnesses, and a variety of other interested parties. Indeed, for many bail agents and private criminal lawyers, these hallways are their daytime offices.

The Courtroom

After some difficulty, most first-time visitors manage to locate their courtroom of interest, entering through heavy double doors, which suggests that this is not an ordinary public building. This initial impression of orderliness under law quickly gives way to a sense of social anarchy. One is immediately confronted with a visual and audio reality far different from that portrayed on television or in the movies (Figure 5.1). What is happening inside the courtroom is best viewed in terms of the actors who congregate in different locations.

In the front is an imposing bench that dominates the courtroom, literally elevating the black-robed judge on a pedestal. Court begins by the customary call of the crier: "All rise, the court for ___ County is now in session, the Honorable ___ presiding." On cue, the judge strides mindfully from behind a hidden door, law book or case folder tucked under one arm. Just below the bench sits the clerk of court (sometimes called the "calendar clerk"), who controls the scheduling of cases and keeps the judge apprised of the relevant details of the case. To one side of the bench sits the court stenographer, whose machine mysteriously makes a shorthand record of the proceedings. Also in attendance is a bailiff, who tries to maintain order in the courtroom. The judge's staff also may include a law clerk and a secretary (who guards access to the judge when he or she is not presiding in the courtroom).

About 10 to 20 feet from the front of the bench are two tables reserved for the defense and prosecution, respectively. The district attorney's (DA) table is piled high with case folders needed for the day's activities. Somehow, no matter how high the pile of case folders, a file or part of a file is invariably missing, resulting in last-minute scurrying by frantic assistant DAs trying to rectify the periodic lapses of the prosecutorial bureaucracy. The mountain of files on the public defender's (PD) table nearly matches that of the prosecutor's. The public defender likewise finds that files are missing or incomplete, resulting in scurrying around looking for missing pieces of paper. When a case involving a private criminal lawyer is called, the PD temporarily gives up the seat at the defense table, but the files remain, an indication that it is really the PD who dominates. Between the bench and the lawyers' tables stands a battered wooden podium, which is typically used only for ceremonial occasions—most notably, when the defendant

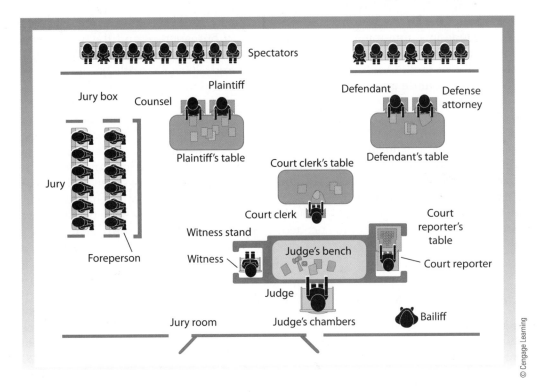

© Cengage Learning

Figure 5.1 ▪ Courtroom

enters a plea of guilty, or the lawyers argue before a jury. Otherwise, lawyers typically argue while sitting behind the table.

To the side of the bench is the jury box. On trial day, jurors occupy these seats; when no jury trial is being conducted, a variety of folks can be found in and around the jury box, waiting, socializing, and occasionally conducting business. Often the easiest to identify are police officers who are in court to provide testimony. Also in attendance are probation officers, substance-abuse counselors, and pretrial services representatives. Bail agents also often drop in to make sure that the persons for whom they have posted bail have indeed arrived as scheduled.

Often sitting in the jury box, too, are defendants who have been detained before trial. Defendants out on bail sit in the public sector, but those in jail sit in brightly colored uniforms with the name of the county jail readily displayed. Often they are manacled together and are temporarily unchained when their cases are called. Surrounding the defendants, hovering like brooding hens, are the sheriff's deputies. The number of deputies

in court provides a pretty good indication of the perceived threat of the defendants; the higher the ratio of guards to prisoners, the more serious the crime and the criminal.

A railing separates the courthouse regulars from the occasional participants. The first row or two are reserved for lawyers waiting for their cases to be called. Sitting in the remaining rows are the defendants (those who have been freed on bond or released on their own recognizance), family members, and perhaps a variety of other observers—for example, senior citizens, who enjoy rooting for the prosecutor. Increasingly in contemporary courthouses, one will also find victim advocates affiliated with organizations such as victim/witness-assistance programs, Mothers Against Drunk Driving, child advocates, and rape crisis centers. Like senior citizens, these people make known their desire for harsh punishments. Table 5.1 summarizes the courthouse actors and their main activities.

What is disconcerting to the newcomer to the courtroom is that these actors seem in constant motion. Small groups form and re-form as cases are called and defendants summoned before the bench. In one corner, an assistant DA can be seen conversing with an assistant PD, while in the back of the room a private defense attorney is engaged in whispered conversations with a defendant and his mother. Moreover, the cast of characters is ever changing. Many actors are in court for a specific case, and when that case has finished, they leave, often walking to another courtroom where they have other cases to attend. Most exasperating of all, the courtroom alternates between bursts of energy and periods of lethargy. Cases are called, only to be put on hold because one of the needed participants is temporarily busy elsewhere in the courthouse.

Behind the Scenes

Outside the great hall of the courthouse and behind the individual courtrooms are areas where visitors seldom venture. What is immediately obvious is that the steady march of people and the accompanying din are absent. Behind the scenes work the actors who provide essential support for courtroom activities.

Courts are paperwork bureaucracies. Even the simplest case requires sheets and sheets of paper: the initial charge, and later, the indictment, bail release forms, pretrial motions, notice of appearance of counsel, and so on. Most of the behind-the-scenes people process this paperwork. Their actions are almost never visible, but their inaction can make headlines.

Other behind-the-scenes actors are managers. A constant complaint is that the courts are mismanaged. Alas, the definition of management in a court setting is elusive. Part of the difficulty is that in many jurisdictions, three distinct sets of court managers—clerks of court, chief judges, and court administrators—are often in competition. Just as important, it is difficult to define what the managers should be doing. A fundamental conflict exists between management (standardized work processes and standard outputs) and the profession of law (individual attention to cases that are fundamentally different). Thus, at the heart of the problem of managing the

courthouse is the tension between the rationality of bureaucracy and the antibureaucratic philosophies of judges (DuPont-Morales, Hooper, & Schmidt 2000; Saari 1982).

The **clerk of court**, variously referred to as *prothonotary, register of probate*, and *clerk,* is pivotal in the administration of local judiciaries. They are responsible for docketing cases, collecting fees, overseeing jury selection, and maintaining court records. These local officials have enormous power. Since they are elected officials in all but six states, they can operate semi-autonomously from the judge. Thus, they have traditionally competed with judges for control over judicial administration (Aikman, 2006; Mays & Taggart, 1986).

Judges are responsible for court administration, but they have most often been ineffective managers. This is primarily due to the unique environment in which the courts operate. Judges may be held responsible, but they seldom have the necessary authority to implement systemic change in a courthouse (Aikman, 2006; Jacob, 1997). Moreover, they are not trained in management. The end result is that the lawyers who become judges are not accustomed to analyzing patterns of case dispositions or managing large dockets—the essential skills a manager needs. These problems are reflected in the position of chief judge. Although the chief judge has general administrative responsibilities, the position is really one of "first among equals." Particularly when the chief judge assumes the position by seniority, as many do, there is no guarantee that the person will be interested in management or will be effective at it.

One of the most innovative approaches to court problems has been the creation of a professional group of trained administrators to assist judges in their administrative duties. In short, management—like law—is a profession; therefore, well-trained managers can give the courts what they have often lacked—managerial skill and bureaucratic knowledge. The development of the professional position of court administrator has been sporadic (Flanders, 1991; Lawson & Howard, 1991). However, by the 1980s, every state had established a statewide court administrator. In the years since then, court administration has become

TABLE 5.1 ■ COURTHOUSE ACTORS

	Actors	Main Activities
Law enforcement	Court security staff	Provide security throughout the courthouse
	Sheriff's deputy	Transports prisoners to and from jail
	Bailiff	Maintains order in the courtrooms; handles evidence
Lawyers	Prosecutor	Government official who prosecutes criminal cases
	Public defender	Government attorney who represents indigent defendants
	Private defense attorney	Lawyer paid by a defendant for representation
Court personnel	Judge	Officer who presides in a court of law
	Law clerk	Performs legal research for the judge
	Clerk of court	Record keeper, often responsible for summoning potential jurors to participate in the jury-selection process
	Court reporter	Makes verbatim transcript of proceedings
	Secretary	Handles routine work of judge's office, including keeping the judge's calendar
	Translator	Renders another language into English and vice versa
	Court administrator	Supervises and performs administrative tasks for the court
	Docket clerk	Prepares and assembles case files; distributes legal documents to attorneys and judges; maintains files and records, including entry of data into computer records
Corrections	Probation officer	Recommends defendants for probation and monitors their activities while on probation
	Pretrial services representative	Handles release of qualified pretrial detainees
	Diversion program representative	Recommends defendants for diversion programs such as drug rehabilitation and anger management programs and monitors progress in them
Public	Bail agent	Secures pretrial release of defendants for a fee
	Reporter	Provides media coverage of key events
	Defendant	Person accused of violating the law
	Victim	Person who has suffered a loss due to crime
	Witness	Anyone who will testify in court
	Jurors	Citizens who will decide whether the defendant is guilty or not guilty
	Rape crisis center representative	Provides counseling and support services for sexual assault victims; provides counseling to rape victims
	Child advocate	Person who speaks up for a child's best interest
	Court watchers	Reporters, researchers, students, retirees, and others who go to court to observe proceedings
	Victim/witness assistance	Public or private agency seeking to improve treatment program of victims and witnesses

increasingly professionalized (Aikman, 2006). Moreover, the profession has expanded significantly; today, most courts (even at the trial court level) routinely employ professional court administrators (Aikman, 2006). The primary duties of these officials are preparing annual reports, summarizing caseload data, preparing budgets, and troubleshooting. Usually, they report to the state supreme court or the chief justice of the state supreme court.

Tension between judges and the court administrator may arise. Some judges are reluctant to delegate responsibility for important aspects of the court's work, such as case scheduling (Aikman, 2006; Mays & Taggart, 1986). In practice, the distinction between administration and adjudication is not clear-cut. A court administrator's proposal to streamline court procedures may be viewed by the judges as an intrusion on his or her role in deciding cases. For example, it is not easy to determine whether transferring a judge from one assignment to another is a judicial or nonjudicial responsibility (Aikman, 2006; Hoffman, 1991; Stott, 1982).

COURTHOUSE SECURITY AND CHANGING TECHNOLOGIES

Upset with the way his divorce and child custody case had been handled, James Ray Palmer, 48, headed back to the Crawford County Courthouse in Van Buren, Arkansas. When the secretary politely informed Palmer that the judge was not available he pulled out a semi-automatic weapon and began firing. The secretary was wounded in the leg but escaped life-threatening injuries. Before he was shot by a sheriff's deputy, Palmer managed to fire 70 rounds from some of the four weapons in his possession (CNN, 2011, September 14).

The shooting in rural Arkansas is but the latest incident of violence in courthouses, and such attacks have greatly changed courthouse security. On a typical morning, you will find long lines of jurors, witnesses, defendants, and litigants waiting to enter the courthouse. Not too long ago, entering a courthouse often meant little more than walking through the door past a bored security officer. No longer. Now metal detectors guarding courthouse doors are an ever-present reminder of how threats of violence have altered American society, courthouses included. Metal detectors and surveillance cameras hardly qualify as modern technologies, because they have been in use for a long time. But what has changed dramatically is how widespread they have become in courthouses in recent years. And changes in airport security are certain to affect courthouse security as well.

Operating a court building today is, by its very nature, a risky business. Governmental buildings, courthouses included, represent important symbolic targets for terrorist groups, whether of domestic or international origin. The bombing of the federal courthouse in downtown Oklahoma City in 1995 exposed external threats to buildings like these. Protecting older courthouses is difficult because they were built for ready access, not protection. But newer courthouses are constructed with safety as a primary focus.

But most attention is focused on internal security threats. Every day, court buildings are visited by a large volume of disgruntled and even lawbreaking citizens (National Center for State Courts, 2010). Gang members trying to intimidate witnesses, defendants charged with domestic violence, and disgruntled spouses litigating a divorce are but three examples of types of people who might explode into violence in the courtroom. No wonder there is often extra security in a courtroom when the judge or jury reaches a verdict.

In some ways security at courthouses is more restrictive than its better-known counterpart at airports. Weapons of course are strictly off limits in both places. But depending on the courthouse, one may not be able to carry in cameras, cell phones, laptop computers, or knitting needles. Moreover, courthouse security is also very concerned about persons smuggling contraband to prisoners.

Beyond the changing technology of courthouse security is a changing mind-set of what *courthouse security* means. Security is no longer merely protecting the people who work in the courthouse,

COURTS, LAW, & MEDIA

LAW & ORDER

Law & Order is the longest-running drama series on network television. First aired in 1990, the show has proven so popular that the producers have spun off shows such as *Law & Order: Special Victims Unit* and *Law & Order: Criminal Intent*. The shows are also aired regularly on cable television. Indeed, it has been estimated that a viewer can watch a full 20 hours of these shows each week.

Part of the popularity of *Law & Order* stems from its "ripped-from-the-headlines" style. Each episode is self-contained. The stripped-down quality means that plot is everything. And the stories often have a twist—the most obvious suspect is not necessarily the one who committed the murder. Although there are continuing characters, there is little effort at character development (Dempsey, 2003). The entrapping sense of reality is reinforced by the video—outdoor scenes are shot on the streets of New York City, and indoor scenes are shot on a soundstage on the Hudson River.

At its best, *Law & Order* (and its numerous spinoffs) is willing to confront social issues, such as sexually transmitted diseases and promiscuous sex, that typically go unmentioned on prime-time television. Unlike stereotypical crime stories in which most characters live stereotypical lives, the episode characters on *Law & Order* are more likely to experience issues associated with interracial dating and illegal immigration. Overall, the series seems best when its plots highlight the complexities of emotionally charged issues such as child molestation and child custody battles.

But how real is *Law & Order*? To scholars, the sense of realism projects a number of dubious images about policing and prosecution. *Law & Order* often distorts policing and prosecution beyond recognition. Investigation

techniques are often bad, as, for example, in the episode in which the police searched the car of the murder victim on the street instead of impounding the vehicle inside a weather-free building. Interrogation techniques are equally faulty. Suspects are interrupted as they make statements instead of being allowed to tell their version before facing more probing questions. Plea-bargaining sessions also represent major distortions of reality. Typically on *Law & Order*, the defendant is in the same room as the prosecutor and the defense attorney. Overall, the program gives the impression that the law (particularly the part related to the constitutional rights of all citizens) is a nuisance. Indeed, disrespect for the law extends to police actions—some episodes show police brutality (minor but often unnecessary force in arresting a suspect).

Television shows such as *Law & Order* have had a major impact on the American legal system. Professors teaching courses like violent crime scene analysis find that they must first help students unlearn what they had learned incorrectly from watching television (Lacks, 2007). Similarly, juries now demand forensic evidence. Moreover, jurors have to be instructed that *Law & Order* is fiction, not fact. Chapter 13 focuses on a closely related show, *CSI: Crime Scene Investigation*. Defense lawyers love the "*CSI* shows because they have caused juries to demand DNA analysis in nearly every two-bit 7-Eleven holdup. Prosecutors, meanwhile, feel hampered by the fact that 10 eyewitnesses are not enough to satisfy *CSI*-watching jurors who crave the supposedly conclusive proof of hair follicles on a knife" (Goehner, Lofaro, & Novack, 2004).

Concerns that fiction might dictate fact are not hypothetical. The Texas Appellate Court reversed the conviction of Andrea Yates (the Houston woman who drowned her children in a bathtub) because the prosecution psychiatrist falsely testified that he had consulted on a *Law & Order* episode with a similar theme (Liptak, 2005). Frequent viewing of television crime dramas significantly increase concerns about crime (Holbrook & Hill, 2005).

judges and lawyers primarily. Notions of courthouse security have expanded to protecting the citizens in the courthouse as well. According to the National Sheriff's Association (2011), courthouses and their immediate areas now need a security component that can only best be described as a police district in and of itself. Thus, courthouse security needs to be concerned about the possibility of physical disagreements between litigants, civil or criminal, in the courthouse and outside as well. And it needs to take into account that courthouse disagreements may lead to retaliation in other places.

Consistent with the theme of this chapter, courthouse actors like the sheriff, court administrator, chief judge, and county boards at times disagree about the adequacy of security. Increasing security sounds good in the abstract but takes on a different tone when the issue turns to who will pay. Sheriffs have been known to plead poverty when it comes to requests for even more deputies assigned to courtroom duty rather than patrol, investigation, or jail duties. There are also important policy disagreements among courthouse actors. Some judges express concerns that too much security lessens public access to the courthouse and often causes major inconvenience to jurors.

Courthouse security varies from place to place, with rural areas like Van Buren, Arkansas, less restrictive than big cities. The courthouse in Van Buren had no metal detector, and an armed deputy was on duty only when the court was in session. But the trend for even more costly and expansive security is sure to continue. On occasion, the news media carry stories about violence in the courthouse, which inevitably leads to even tighter security.

DYNAMICS OF COURTHOUSE JUSTICE

A brief tour of a courthouse indicates that justice is very unlike the dramatizations one sees on TV or in the movies. First-time observers find scant relationship between the dynamics of courthouse justice (law in action) and widely held cultural images (law on the books).

- Expecting to see individual trials, they instead witness a parade of defendants and their cases. In particular, newcomers to the courthouse are often struck by the sheer volume of cases.

- Expecting the law to provide guidance, they instead find that decisions are not necessarily clear-cut and that some leeway is available. How else can one explain disagreements over lengths of prison sentences and terms of probation?

- Expecting to observe the conflict (and perhaps even hostility) projected by the adversarial model, courthouse watchers discover cooperation among judges, prosecutors, and defense attorneys. At times, conversations become animated, but by and large, the verbal exchanges reflect a good amount of badinage.

In exploring these differences, practitioners and scholars have used three concepts—assembly-line justice, discretion, and the courtroom work group (see Table 5.2).

- Assembly-line justice explains why few cases receive individual treatment.

- Discretion emphasizes that decisions, although guided by law, are not totally determined by rules found in statutes or court decisions.

- The courtroom work group concept stresses the importance of the patterned interactions of judges, prosecutors, and defense attorneys.

As we shall see, each of these explanations is useful in understanding the dynamics of courthouse justice.

ASSEMBLY-LINE JUSTICE

The most commonly advanced reason that criminal courts do not administer justice according to the textbook image is assembly-line justice. This explanation was put forth by the President's Commission on Law Enforcement and Administration of Justice (1967, p. 31): "The crux of the problem is that there is a great disparity between the number of cases and the number of judges." Not only judges but also prosecutors, defense attorneys, and probation officers are in short supply. The deluge of cases is reflected in every aspect of the courts' work, from

TABLE 5.2 ▪ THREE CONCEPTS EXPLAINING THE DYNAMICS OF COURTHOUSE JUSTICE

Concept	Definition	Examples
Assembly-line justice	The operation of any segment of the criminal justice system with such speed and impersonality that defendants are treated as objects to be processed rather than as individuals.	The war on drugs has greatly increased case volume. Judges feel pressure to move cases.
Discretion	The authority to make decisions without reference to specific rules or facts.	Prosecutors decide whether to file criminal charges. Judges choose between prison or probation.
Courtroom work group	The regular participants in the day-to-day activities of a particular courtroom; judge, prosecutor, and defense attorney interacting on the basis of shared norms.	Cooperation more than conflict governs the working relationships of courtroom actors. Case disposition requires joint actions of judge, prosecutor, and defense attorney. Rules of thumb guide bail release and sentencing.

© Cengage Learning

overcrowded corridors and courtrooms to the long calendars that judges, prosecutors, and defense attorneys face each day. Although this report was written nearly 50 years ago, sadly, these facts have not changed, as the court system remains grossly underfunded and understaffed today (Broccolina & Zorza, 2008).

Strengths of the Explanation

The assembly-line justice explanation highlights some important features of the contemporary courthouse. No one disputes that the volume of cases is large. Every year, approximately 14 million persons are arrested—3 million for felonies and the rest for misdemeanors. Because of the large volume, overworked officials are often more interested in moving the steady stream of cases along than in individually weighing each case on the scales of justice. Particularly in large cities, tremendous pressures exist to move cases and keep the docket current lest the backlog becomes worse and delays increase. In short, law on the books suggests a justice process with unlimited resources, whereas law in action stresses an administrative process geared toward disposing of a large volume of cases.

To cope with large caseloads, prosecutors, defense attorneys, and judges often apply several mass-production techniques. Thus, actors often specialize in specific tasks. In big-city public defender's offices, for example, one assistant will conduct the initial interview with the defendant, another will represent him or her at the initial appearance, and still another will negotiate the plea. Another mass-production technique is group processing. During the initial appearance, felony defendants are often advised of their rights in one large group rather than individually. Moreover, in the lower courts, sentences are often fixed on the basis of the defendant's membership in a given class rather than on detailed consideration of the individual case.

Weaknesses of the Explanation

Although the assembly-line justice explanation draws our attention to some important aspects of the criminal courts, it also obscures many important considerations. First of all, this orthodox explanation stresses that excessive caseloads are a modern problem. Repeated references are made to the "rise" of plea bargaining and the "decline" of the trial. However, these vivid metaphors distort history. American courts have been faced with caseload pressures for more than a century. Even more important, plea bargaining predates any of the "modern" problems of the courthouse. Indeed, plea bargaining "began to appear during the early or mid-nineteenth century and became institutionalized as a standard feature of American urban criminal courts in the last of the nineteenth century" (Haller, 1979, p. 273; see also, Fisher, 2003). In short, those who try to explain how justice is administered in the courthouse simply in terms of too many cases resulting from the growth of big cities are ignoring the historical evidence.

Emphasizing excessive caseloads also fails to consider the types of cases trial courts must decide. Most trial court cases, criminal or civil, present no disputed questions of law or fact. Rather, most case dispositions reflect **routine administration**: "A matter is routine when a court has no disputed question of law or fact to decide. Routine administration means the processing or approving of undisputed matters" (Friedman & Percival, 1976, p. 267). Most cases, therefore, end with a plea of guilty (rather than a trial), not because the courthouse has too many cases, but because the courts are confronted with a steady stream of routine cases in which the only major question is the sentence to be imposed. This has led some commentators to conclude that the emphasis on due process procedures that "dominated the era between the 1930s and the 1970s, [has been] supplanted by a model . . . in which the focus (both in criminal and civil cases) is on how to achieve resolution without or with little adjudication" (Resnik, 2006, p. 1140).

Although heavy caseloads are part of the conventional wisdom surrounding the operations of criminal courts, several studies cast serious doubt on this proposition. A 1979 study in Connecticut compared two courts—one with a heavy caseload, another with a light one. It would be logical to expect major differences in how cases were processed and in the substance of justice handed out, but the results indicated that the courts were remarkably similar. Neither court had many trials. In neither did the defense attorneys engage in a pitched battle with the prosecution. Both courts set bail in approximately the same amounts and

imposed roughly similar sentences. Each court spent the same amount of time per case, moving through its business "rapidly and mechanically." The only difference was that the busier court was in session longer than the court that had fewer cases (Feeley, 1979). This and other studies clearly suggest that the criminal court process cannot be understood solely on the basis of excessive caseloads, because such an explanation omits too many important considerations—most especially organizational relationships and local legal culture (Heumann, 1975; Lynch, 1994; Nardulli, 1979; Roach-Anleu, 2000).

DISCRETION

Law on the books projects an image of a legal system that seemingly runs by itself—a mechanical process of merely applying rules of law to given cases. Law in action, however, emphasizes a legal system in which the legal actors exercise discretion because choices must be made.

Discretion lies at the heart of the criminal justice process. From the time a crime is committed until after a sentence is imposed, discretion is exercised every time key decisions are made. After arrest, the prosecutor may decide not to prosecute. Once charges have been filed, a lower-court judge must set the amount of bail and decide whether sufficient probable cause exists to hold the defendant for the grand jury. In turn, grand juries have discretion over indictments; trial juries over conviction; and the judge over sentencing.

Discretion is best defined as the lawful ability of an agent of government to exercise choice in making a decision. Viewed from this perspective, discretion has three major subcomponents: legal judgments, policy priorities, and personal philosophies (Cole, 1970; Stith, 2008).

Many discretionary decisions in the criminal court process are made on the basis of legal judgments. An example would be a prosecutor who refuses to file a criminal charge because in her legal judgment, the evidence is insufficient to prove all the elements of the offense. Some legal judgments stem from a prediction about the likely outcome of a case at a later stage in the proceedings. The prosecutor, for example, may believe that the defendant did violate the law but that no jury would convict.

Other discretionary decisions reflect policy priorities. Because criminal laws are so broad and general, they must be selectively enforced. The number of crimes that could be charged is virtually unlimited, but the resources devoted to detecting wrongdoers and processing them through the courts (and later incarcerating them) are limited. Thus, discretionary decisions are often made on the basis of policy priorities. Through policy priorities, court officials try to devote more resources to prosecuting serious crimes, such as murder, rape, and armed robbery, rather than minor offenses.

Other discretionary decisions reflect the decision makers' personal values and attitudes—their personal philosophies. Judges and prosecutors have varying views of what offenses are serious and deserving of a high priority. Differences among judges in the same courthouse are readily apparent. Some differences center on the purpose of the criminal law. Those who believe that the courts can deter crime (through heavy sentences, for example) behave differently from those who discount the role the courts can play in deterrence. Stated another way, the same differences of opinion about crime that characterize society as a whole likewise divide courthouse actors.

THE COURTROOM WORK GROUP

Every day, the same group of courthouse regulars assembles in the same courtroom, sits or stands in the same places, and performs the same tasks as the day before. The types of defendants and the nature of the crimes they are accused of also remain constant. Only the names of the victims and defendants are different. Whereas defendants come and go, the judges, prosecutors, defense attorneys, clerks, and probation officers remain the same. To even the most casual observer, the courthouse regulars occupy a special status. They freely issue instructions to the temporary visitors to the courthouse (don't smoke, don't talk, don't read the newspaper), although they smoke, talk, and read

the newspaper themselves. The ordinary citizens sit on hard benches in the rear of the courtroom and may approach the bench only when specifically requested to. The courthouse regulars, on the other hand, enjoy easy access to the front part of the courtroom.

The activities of the courthouse regulars represent a complex network of ongoing social relationships (Blumberg, 1970; Flemming, Nardulli, & Eisenstein, 1992; Guzik, 2007; Neubauer, 1974b; Sarat & Felstiner, 1995). These relationships are as important as they are complex. James Eisenstein and Herbert Jacob (1977) have proposed that the best way to analyze the network of ongoing relationships among the courthouse actors is through the concept of the **courtroom work group**.

Judges, prosecutors, and defense attorneys are representatives from separate, independent sponsoring institutions. They are drawn together by a common task: Each must do something about a given case. As a result, courthouse regulars work together cooperatively on a daily basis in ways not envisioned by the formal adversary model (Jacob, 1991; Lichtenstein, 1984; Lynch & Evans, 2002). Indeed, in problem-solving courts (especially those subscribing to a therapeutic jurisprudence model) such cooperation forms the philosophical backbone for the courts' existence (Worrall & Nugent-Borakove, 2008). To understand the extent as well as the limits of this cooperation, we need to examine why courtroom work groups form in the first place and their impact on the administration of justice.

Mutual Interdependence

The criminal courthouse is not a single organization but rather a collection of separate institutions that gather in a common workplace. Whereas most large organizations consist of distinct divisions operating under a central leadership, the criminal courthouse consists of separate institutions without a hierarchical system of control. For instance, a judge cannot reward a prosecutor or a public defender who performs well. Rather, each of the courthouse regulars is a representative of a sponsoring institution, which hires and fires them, monitors their activities, and rewards their performance.

None of these actors can perform his or her tasks independently; they must work together. These interactions are critical because none of the courthouse regulars can make decisions independently; each must consider the reactions of others. This is most readily seen in the work of the defense attorney. In representing his or her client, the defense attorney must consider the type of plea agreement the prosecutor may offer, the sentencing tendencies of the judge, and the likelihood of a jury verdict of guilty. Prosecutors and judges are interdependent in similar ways.

Each member of the work group can achieve individual goals and accomplish separate tasks only through work-group participation. The actors come to share common interests in disposing of cases. Hence, cooperation—mutual interdependence—within the work group is viewed to lead to mutual benefits. Assistant prosecutors, for example, are judged by their superiors not so much on how many cases they win but on how few they lose. Thus, to secure their primary goal of gaining convictions, they must depend on defense attorneys to sell their clients on the advantages of the bargain offered and also on judges to impose the agreed-upon settlement.

Shared Decision Making

Courtroom work groups reflect shared decision making. Judges retain the legal authority to make the major decisions, such as setting bail and imposing sentences, but they often rely on others. They routinely follow the bail recommendations of the prosecutor and accept guilty-plea agreements reached by the defense and prosecution. This does not mean that the judge is without power; the other actors must be sensitive to what the judge might do. Prosecutors (and defense attorneys) know the amount of bail a particular judge has set in past situations, so that is what they recommend in the current case.

This shared decision making is highly functional because it diffuses responsibility. Judges, prosecutors, defense attorneys, and others are aware that the decisions they make could turn out to be wrong. Since such dire results cannot be predicted, the members of the courtroom work group share a sense that when one of their members looks bad, they all look bad. Decisions, therefore,

are made jointly. If something later goes wrong, work-group members have protected themselves because everyone thought it was a good idea at the time (Clynch & Neubauer, 1981).

The hallmark of work groups is regularity of behavior. This regularity is the product of shared norms about how each member should behave and what decisions are desirable. Courthouse workers can make their common worksite a fractious and unpredictable place for carrying out assigned tasks or, through cooperation, a predictable place to work. The greater the certainty, the less time and resources they need to spend on each case. Newcomers learn these important informal norms of cooperation through a process referred to as "socialization."

Socialization

A problem common to all organizations, courts included, is the need to break in new members, a process known as **socialization**. Through socialization, newcomers are taught not only the formal requirements of the job (how motions are filed and so on), but also informal rules of behavior. In other words, veteran members of the courtroom work group have to "break in" new members so that they understand the ways things are done (Haynes, Ruback, & Cusick, 2010; Wiseman, 1970).

Thus, newcomers learn not only from their peers but also from other members of the social network. One of the most important things they learn is the importance of shared norms. It is the shared norms that provide structure to what otherwise would appear to be an unstructured, almost chaotic, process. These shared norms allow the members of the courtroom work group to routinely process what are known as "normal crimes."

Normal Crimes

As discussed earlier, most of the matters before the courts are routine. Although each case is unique, most fall into a limited number of categories. Based on similarities among cases, members of the work group develop certain ideas about types of crimes and criminals. A landmark study in 1965 by Sudnow aptly labeled this phenomenon the **normal**

COURTS, CONTROVERSY, & GENDER EQUITY

IS GENDER BIAS A SIGNIFICANT PROBLEM IN THE COURTS?

The past several decades have witnessed a monumental change in the gender composition of the American workforce. Not only are a higher percentage of women working outside the home, but women are also increasingly working in what were once considered male professions. Law most certainly is a case in point. Today, women constitute between 40 and 55 percent of all law students and make up nearly 30 percent of the nation's judges (National Association of Women Judges, 2012).

One of the areas of most concern to the women's rights movement is gender bias. Thirty-six states have created task forces to investigate gender bias in the legal system. Some state task forces define gender bias as making decisions based on stereotypes about men and women; others stress insensitivity toward certain aspects of men's and women's lives; still others emphasize intentional bias and ill will. Regardless of the precise definition, a team of researchers found these reports to be remarkably consistent. The state task forces consistently found gender bias in four areas of the legal system: domestic violence, sexual assault, divorce, and behavior toward female workers and domestic violence (Belknap, Hartman, & Lippen 2010; Hemmens, Strom, & Schlegel, 1997).

Sexual assault is one area in which women experience gender bias. Sexual assaults are underreported for a number of reasons, ranging from the stigma and internalized sense of shame that sexual assault victims often experience (Koss, 2000) to concerns about whether victims will be believed and whether they will be blamed (see Russell, Oswald, & Kraus, 2011). Moreover, many victims fear that reporting their sexual assault will result in revictimization by the justice system when its actors make judgments about the case based on their own attitudes (including sexism and belief in rape myths) and their perceptions of victim credibility, attractiveness, sexual history, attire, and level of intoxication (for a review, see Grubb & Harrower, 2009).

Divorce cases are another area in which the possibility of gender bias looms. State task force reports unanimously found that women suffer from gender bias in terms of awarding alimony, division of property, and child support. The courts, on the other hand, appear to be biased against fathers in child custody awards.

Finally, all the state task force reports found gender bias against female lawyers and court employees. Of principal concern were offensive and intolerable actions toward female participants in the legal system. The most common form of gender bias mentioned was the practice of judges' and attorneys' addressing female lawyers in a demeaning manner. Female lawyers, more so than their male counterparts, were addressed by their first names. Moreover, terms like "sweetie," "little lady lawyer," "pretty eyes," and "dear" were used. Another common form of gender bias suffered by female attorneys (and judges) is sexist remarks or jokes. Gender bias also affects hiring and promotion. Female lawyers perceive that it is harder to get hired, and once hired they are paid less and have fewer opportunities for promotion.

It is important to underscore that these findings are based on reports of specific events ("Have you ever had remarks made about your looks?") as well as perceptions of gender bias or problems. Women consistently reported problem areas at higher levels than men. Answers to questions like those asked in surveys, of course, can be understood in different ways. Perhaps women are oversensitive to these issues (or alternatively, males are oblivious). Another stumbling block is the difficulty in estimating the true extent of the gender-bias problem. Perceptions of bias could be the product of an isolated few who have contact with many female lawyers and judges or they could be the result of persistent practices by numerous male lawyers and judges.

Perceptions of gender bias are a serious matter because they affect litigants' perceptions of the fairness of justice. If litigants and/or their lawyers perceive that they are treated differently, they have less confidence in the process of justice, irrespective of the outcome of the case. It is also important to underscore that the gender-bias issues investigated must be taken seriously because they directly affect the lives of many women and their children as well. Moreover, the issues are some of the most explosive facing the justice system and have become, in a relatively few years, important public issues.

Continued on next page

Continued from previous page

Gender bias is not a problem created by the court system; rather, it is a reflection of prevailing attitudes in society. Although "current laws and affirmative action plans have furthered women's equality, they cannot by themselves change the attitudes of individuals. It is the individual attitudes that require change if gender bias is to be eradicated" (Hemmens et al., 1997, p. 31).

What do you think? Is gender bias a serious problem in the nation's courthouses? Have you seen or experienced biased behavior by lawyers, judges, or other court personnel? If you are troubled by using individual reports to make the case for gender bias, what alternative methods would you use to study the problem?

crime, a term still used today. The legal actors categorize crimes on the basis of the typical manner in which they are committed, the typical social characteristics of the defendants, and the types of victims. Once a case has been placed into one of these categories, it is usually disposed of on the basis of a set pattern. In essence, normal crimes represent a group sense of justice.

Rewards and Sanctions

Actors who violate these rules of personal and professional conduct can expect sanctions from the other members of the work group. A variety of rewards (carrots) are available as benefits to those who follow the rules. For example, defense attorneys who do not unnecessarily disrupt routines are able to negotiate a sentence that is slightly less severe than normal. In turn, some sanctions (sticks) may be applied to those who do not cooperate. Judges can sanction uncooperative private defense attorneys, for instance, by making them wait for their case to be called. By far the more effective approach is the carrot, because it operates indirectly and is less disruptive. The imposition of sanctions can lead to countersanctions, with the result that the network is disrupted even further.

Variability in Courtroom Work Groups

Virtually all criminal courts studied to date exemplify the patterns that were just discussed of how courtroom work groups operate that were just discussed, but some important variations need to be considered. For example, the

stability of the work groups varies—low turnover in some courts promotes stability in the work group, while high turnover in others produces ongoing disruptions of the relationships in the courthouse.

Mavericks can be found in most courthouses. Some defense attorneys engage in hostile relations with prosecutors and exhibit many attributes of adversarial behavior. They do so at a price, however: They are seldom able to negotiate effectively for good deals during plea bargaining (Covey, 2007).

The policy norms vary from community to community. Property crimes are viewed as more threatening in rural areas than in urban ones, so the appropriate penalty for a defendant convicted of burglary in a rural area is more severe than that for a defendant convicted in a big city. In recent years, one set of major concerns about the policy norms relates to gender equity (see "Courts, Controversy, and Gender Equity: Is Gender Bias a Significant Problem in the Courts?").

To the general public, perhaps the most visible variation between work groups concerns delay. Each courthouse has, over time, evolved a set of expectations about the proper pacing of case dispositions. Some courthouses process cases in a timely fashion, others do not.

THE PROBLEM OF DELAY

A commonly mentioned problem affecting many of the nation's courts is that too many cases take too long to reach disposition. The magnitude of the backlog and the length of the delay vary greatly, however, depending on the court involved.

COSCA Case Processing Standards

Civil
- Non-jury trial – 100% within 12 months
- Jury trial – 100% within 18 months

Criminal
- Felony – 100% within 180 days
- Misdemeanor – 100% within 90 days

Juvenile
- Detention and shelter hearings – 100% 24 hours
- Adjudicatory or transfer hearings
- Concerning a juvenile in a detention or shelter facility – 100% within 15 days
- Concerning a juvenile not in a detention or shelter facility – 100% within 30 days

Domestic
- Uncontested – 100% within 3 months
- Contested – 100% within 6 months

ABA Case Processing Standards

Civil
- 90% within 12 months
- 98% within 18 months
- 100% within 24 months

Criminal
- Felony
  - 90% within 120 days
  - 98% within 180 days
  - 100% within 1 year
- Misdemeanor
  - 90% within 30 days
  - 100% within 90 days

Juvenile
- Detention and shelter hearings – 100% 24 hours
- Adjudicatory or transfer hearings
- Concerning a juvenile in a detention or shelter facility – 100% within 15 days
- Concerning a juvenile not in a detention or shelter facility – 100% within 30 days

Domestic
- 90% within 3 months
- 98% within 6 months
- 100% within 1 year

Figure 5.2 ■ Case-Processing Standards

SOURCE: Model Time Standards for State Trial Courts: Williamsburg VA: National Center for State Courts, 2011. Available online at http://www.ncsconline.org. Reprinted by permission.

In a general sense, the term **delay** suggests abnormal or unacceptable time lapses in the processing of cases (Neubauer, Lipetz, Luskin, & Ryan, 1981). The inherent subjectivity of the term becomes apparent when we try to define *unnecessary delay* (Neubauer, 1983; Steelman, 1997). Although the question "How long is too long" varies by both jurisdiction and the complexity of cases, the American Bar Association (ABA) and the Conference of State Court Administrators (COSCA) have both established standards that establish nonbinding expectations for the reasonable processing of cases (Figure 5.2).

Over three-fourths of the states have adopted their own case-disposition targets, some of which aspire to meet the ABA or COSCA standards (Van Duizend, Steelman, & Suskin, 2011). And, many courts are, in fact, meeting these model time standards, as 88 percent of felony defendants in large urban counties have their cases disposed within 1 year (Cohen & Kyckelhahn, 2010). But, as Figure 5.3 illustrates, there is great variability.

From one perspective, the data presented in Figure 5.3 suggest that some courts are not currently meeting the recommended standards. But from a different perspective, perhaps they are, because the data measures time from arrest to disposition, thus including the time that passes in the prosecutor's office as well as in the courts.

Consequences of Delay

Concern that "justice delayed is justice denied" is as old as the common law itself. In the 13th century,

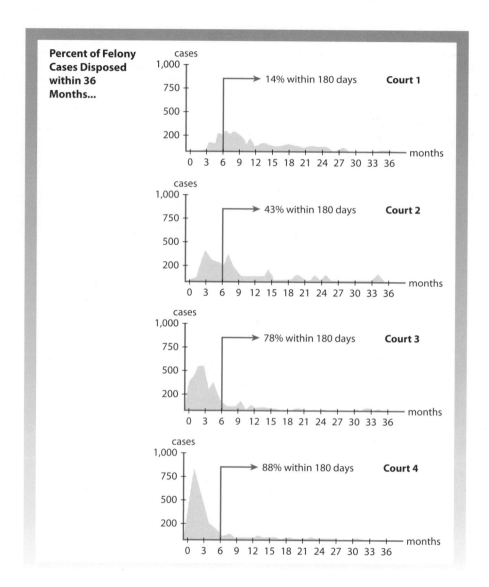

Figure 5.3 ■ A Comparison of Felony Disposition Times in Four Courts

SOURCE: *CourTools: Trial Court Performance Measures.* Williamsburg VA: National Center for State Courts, 2005. Available online at http://www.ncsconline.org/D_Research/CourTools/Images/courtools_measure3.pdf.

the nobles forced King John to sign the Magna Carta and promise not to "deny or delay right or justice." In the 19th century, the novelist Charles Dickens condemned the tortuous process of litigation in the English courts. Today, judicial reformers and critics argue that case delay undermines the values and guarantees associated with the legal system. The three most often cited negative consequences of delays in the courthouse center on defendant, society, and citizen.

Historically, court delay was considered a problem because it jeopardized the defendant's right to a speedy trial. The Sixth Amendment provides that "in all criminal prosecutions, the accused shall enjoy the right to a speedy and public trial. . . ." Defendants may languish in jail for a number of months before guilt or innocence is determined. A number of states have enacted speedy-trial laws premised on the need to protect the defendant's rights.

More recently, delay has been viewed as hampering society's need for a speedy conviction. This view stresses harm done to the prosecution's case. As the case becomes older and witnesses' memories diminish, the defendant's chances of acquittal increase. In short, the state is also viewed as possessing the right to a speedy trial. Thus, in recent years some jurisdictions have enacted speedy-trial laws to try to increase conviction rates.

Regardless of the costs or benefits to either the defense or the prosecution, a third perspective emphasizes that delay erodes public confidence in the judicial process. Citizens lose confidence in the swiftness or certainty of punishment for those who are found guilty. In addition, victims and witnesses may be forced to make repeated, needless trips to the courthouse. Such appearances can cost citizens time and money and ultimately discourage them from prosecuting. Overall, delay in disposing of cases wastes the resources of the criminal justice system.

Assessing the Costs of Delay

Assertions about the costs of delay require careful scrutiny. A general consensus has emerged that delay is a problem facing the courts, with no agreement about the particulars. The three perspectives just described stress different reasons that delay is a problem. Some perceive that lengthy pretrial incarceration forces defendants to enter into detrimental plea bargains. Others, however, portray caseload pressures as forcing prosecutors into offering unduly lenient negotiated agreements.

In 1978, The National Center for State Courts sponsored a landmark study on the problem of delay in criminal cases (Church & McConnell, 1978). The report noted that few of the assertions about the social costs of delay have been subjected to empirical examination. While there was some evidence to indicate that jail overcrowding

and defendants' skipping court appearances (Chapter 10) were related to case delay, the report did not find support for the assertions that case delay causes deterioration of cases or pressures prosecutors to offer lenient plea bargains. Over the decades since then, we have learned more about the problems of court delays. While improved case-flow management implemented in the 1980s and 1990s shortened the median time from arrest to disposition, it is clear that such techniques "can probably never be viewed as a full and final solution to court delay" (Steelman, 1997, p. 158).

LAW ON THE BOOKS APPROACH TO COURT DELAY

The law on the books approach to court delay focuses on resources and procedures. It is an article of faith among many commentators that the problem of delay results from an imbalance between available resources and mounting caseloads (Church & McConnell, 1978). A common response is to supplement resources—add judges, prosecutors, clerks, and so on—although the realities of today's austere budgets often prevent doing so. Beyond adding more resources when financially feasible, traditional court reformers emphasize streamlining procedures. They view procedural stages such as preliminary hearing, grand jury indictment, and pretrial motions as sources of delay. But this conventional wisdom about court delay has been called into serious question (Church, 1982; Gallas, 1976).

In *Justice Delayed* (Church, Carlson, Lee, & Tan, 1978), the National Center for State Courts studied 21 courts across the nation and found that the level of court resources was not associated with court delay. The relative size of court caseloads, for example, bore little relationship to case-processing time. Similarly, court procedures were poor predictors of delay. Courts that emphasized plea bargaining (as opposed to trying cases) were as fast (or as slow) as their opposite numbers (see also, Steelman, 1997).

These findings explain why the law on the books approach—issuing more and more rules and regulations—is often ineffective in speeding up case dispositions and reducing excessive caseloads. Speedy-trial laws are a case in point.

Speedy-Trial Laws

Speedy-trial laws are federal or state statutes that specify time limits for bringing a case to trial after arrest. Some speedy-trial laws specify precise time standards for periods from arrest to arraignment, trial, and or sentencing. These laws supplement the provisions of the U.S. Constitution and 35 state constitutions that have speedy-trial guarantees. These provisions, however, apply only when the delay has been "extensive." What constitutes unnecessary delay, however, is difficult to pinpoint (see "Case Close-Up: *Barker v. Wingo* and the Right to a Speedy Trial"). Given the vagueness of these constitutional standards, legislatures have shown considerable interest in putting some teeth into the guarantee of a speedy trial. The best-known such effort is the Speedy Trial Act of 1974 (amended in 1979), which specifies time standards for the two primary stages in the federal court process. A span of 30 days is allowed from arrest to indictment, and 70 days from indictment to trial. Certain time periods, such as those associated with hearings on pretrial motions and the mental competency of the defendant, are considered excludable time.

Speedy-trial statutes exist in all 50 states (Herman & Chemerinsky, 2006), but they have a different orientation from their federal counterpart. Most state laws are defendant-centered; that is, they are designed to protect defendants from suffering extensive delay, particularly if they are incarcerated prior to trial. By contrast, the federal law is designed to protect the interests of society; that is, a speedy trial is viewed as an important objective irrespective of whether the defendant's interests are in jeopardy.

Limits of Speedy-Trial Laws

Efforts to mandate speedy trials are striking in their lack of specifics. These laws are not based on an analysis of why delay occurs. Moreover, they do not provide for any additional resources (more judges or prosecutors) to aid the courts in complying. This can produce unforeseen consequences. In a number of federal courts, compliance has come at the price of

delaying civil cases. Potential difficulties also arise because not all cases fit easily into the mandated time frames. A major murder case or a large drug-smuggling case takes longer to prepare than an ordinary burglary prosecution.

Researchers approach speedy-trial laws with considerable skepticism. Various studies find that such laws have had limited impact in speeding up the flow of cases through the state criminal court process (Church et al., 1978; Mahoney, Aikman, Casey, Flango, Gallas, Henderson, Ito, Steelman, & Weller, 1988; Nimmer, 1978). The primary reason is that most state laws fail to provide the court with adequate and effective enforcement mechanisms. As a result, the time limits specified by speedy-trial laws are seldom a guide to actual practice. One study found that North Carolina's speedy-trial law did indeed speed up the criminal docket, but Connecticut's law did not (Marvell & Luskin, 1991). The federal speedy-trial law has proven effective. The average criminal case filed in the federal courts in the early 1970s took 7 months to reach a disposition. By the early 1980s, the average case was disposed of in less than 3 months. Thus, the federal approach of court planning followed by fixed standards works to reduce delay (Garner, 1987).

Without adequate resources, however, speedy trials are doomed to failure. Recent budget cuts have increased court delays in California. Officials predict extended waits for lawsuits to reach court, longer custody fights, and even lengthy battles to challenge traffic citations (Dolan & Kim, 2011)

Overall, researchers stress that law in action approaches to reducing court delay are ultimately more effective.

LAW IN ACTION APPROACH TO COURT DELAY

Law on the books approaches to reducing court delay are ineffective because they ignore the dynamics of courthouse justice. All too often, the impression conveyed is that case-flow management is somehow removed from other issues in the criminal court process. Delay is related not to how many cases a court must process but to the choices that the actors make in how they process these

CASE CLOSE-UP

BARKER v. WINGO AND THE RIGHT TO A SPEEDY TRIAL

The police arrested two suspects—Willie Barker and Silas Manning—for beating an elderly couple to death with a tire iron in Christian County, Kentucky. The district attorney had a stronger case against Manning and believed that Barker could not be convicted unless Manning testified against him. Thus, the district attorney first sought a conviction against Manning. The court-appointed lawyer initially had no objection to continuing the trial; after all, an acquittal could only help Barker.

The Commonwealth of Kentucky, however, encountered more than a few difficulties in its prosecution of Manning. Altogether, six trials were conducted. Two ended in hung juries and two others in convictions that were reversed on appeal. Finally, Manning was convicted of murdering one victim, and a sixth trial resulted in a conviction for the other murder.

During these legal maneuverings, Barker was in jail for 10 months, which largely explains why at the time the 12th continuance was requested, the defense filed a motion to dismiss the charges. By the time the Commonwealth was ready to try Barker (after two more continuances), another problem arose: The chief investigator on the case was ill, resulting in two additional continuances. Eventually, the judge announced that the

case would be dismissed if it were not tried at the next scheduled date. The trial finally commenced, with Manning as the chief prosecution witness; Barker was convicted and given a life sentence.

In assessing these lengthy delays, the opinion of the Court notes that "the right to speedy trial is a more vague concept than other procedure rights. It is, for example, impossible to determine with precision when the right has been denied. We cannot definitely say how long is too long in a system where justice is supposed to be swift but deliberate" (*Barker v. Wingo*, 1972, p. 522). In essence, the right to a speedy trial is relative, not absolute. The test would be a balancing test, in which the conduct of both the prosecution and the defendant are weighted. Calling the delay "extraordinary," the Court nonetheless ruled that Barker's case was not seriously prejudiced by the more than 5-year delay.

Only in extraordinary circumstances has the Court ordered criminal charges dismissed for lack of a timely trial. One such situation involved an 8-year gap between indictment and arrest. The government was negligent in making any effort to track down the defendant, and the defendant was entitled to go free without a trial (*Doggett v. United States*, 1992).

cases. Defense attorneys, for example, may seek continuances to avoid harsh judges, to obtain more time to prepare a defense, or even to pressure the client to pay the agreed-upon fee. Prosecutors may use delay to increase the stakes of plea bargaining or to postpone weak cases they are likely to lose. Judges acquiesce to requests for continuances so as not to disrupt the dispositional process (Flemming et al. 1987).

For these reasons, lawyers and judges are generally content with the existing pace of litigation in their courts. Practitioners were asked to provide appropriate case-processing times

for typical cases. Within the four courts studied—the Bronx, Detroit, Miami, and Pittsburgh—there was little systematic disagreement among judges, defense counsel, and prosecutors on the appropriate pace of case dispositions (Church et al., 1978). More recent studies have similarly concluded that "pervasive local legal culture that transcends court jurisdiction, court size, judicial resources, court rules, or calendaring systems as the explanation of differences in the pace of litigation in fast and slow courts" (Gallas, 2005, p. 23). Findings like these show why law in action approaches to court delay seek to alter practitioners' attitudes regarding proper case-disposition times. Improving case scheduling and trying to achieve better coordination among courtroom work-group members are two such approaches.

Case Scheduling

Waiting is one activity in which people at the courthouse inevitably become engaged. A busy courtroom can grind to a halt because an important witness fails to show up or a lawyer is detained in another courtroom. From an administrative perspective, the courts are extremely complex institutions. The disposition of a case often requires the presence of the following individuals: judge, clerk, court reporter, bailiff, defendant, prosecutor, defense attorney, police officer, victim, and witness. Depending on the procedural stage, jurors, a probation officer, a pretrial services representative, and an interpreter may also need to appear.

Many of these people have several different courts to appear in during a single day. For example, defense attorneys, prosecutors, and probation officers may have several cases set for the same time. There can be administrative problems, too. Because of an illegible address, the defendant never receives a notice. Or the jailer may forget to include the needed defendant on the day's list. If just one person is late, the others must wait, and if one person never shows up at all, the hearing must be rescheduled.

Efforts at Coordination

As we have noted previously, the court is actually a collection of agents from separate and independent organizations: judge, police officer, prosecutor, sheriff, clerk, and probation officer. Most of these organizations are headed by elected officials or, like the police, report to elected officials. They have their own bases of power, their own separate legal mandates, and their own scheduling problems. Judges and court administrators, therefore, have only limited control over coordinating interagency schedules and cooperative efforts (although they are often held responsible when something goes wrong).

Variability in Courtroom Work Groups Revisited

The variability in courtroom work groups (discussed earlier in this chapter) has major consequences for how long it takes courts to dispose of cases. A team of researchers associated with the National Center for State Courts studied a blend of urban and rural courts (Ostrom, Ostrom, Hanson, & Kleiman, 2007). In each courthouse, they interviewed the wide range of officials discussed in this chapter. They focused on how cases were managed and how court actors interacted and found four distinctive ways of doing things.

Some courts were characterized as hierarchical because there was a clear chain of command among judges, administrative staff, and courtroom staff. Courts with a hierarchical culture processed felony cases significantly faster than other courts. Other courts were characterized as communal because they valued communication, cooperation, and compromise. Courts with a communal culture processed felony cases more slowly than other courts. The authors caution that no cultural type is necessarily good or bad. Rather, variations in courtroom work groups reflect responses to multiple goals as well as differing ways of managing relations between a diverse set of courthouse actors (Ostrom et al., 2007).

LEGAL ETHICS

Lawyers often suffer from a negative public image, which is one reason the legal profession places considerable emphasis on **legal ethics**. *Ethics* refers to the study and analysis of what constitutes good or bad conduct (Pollock, 2012). Legal ethics represents a specific type of ethics. First, it is an example of applied ethics, in which ethical principles are applied to specific issues. Legal ethics is also an example of professional ethics, because it involves the behavior of a profession, in this case the legal profession. All ethical systems, legal ethics included, have a moral component. But morality and ethics are different. Whereas morality emphasizes a set of moral absolutes, legal ethics involves the difficult task of helping lawyers sort out the best option when perhaps no good options exist.

Legal ethics is of critical importance because the American legal system is based on the adversarial system, which stresses verbal combat. At its basis, this system represents a fight between opposing viewpoints, and the use of legal ethics is one way to regulate this verbal combat to ensure, in essence, a fair fight. At heart, legal ethics emphasizes protecting clients by ensuring that they have competent attorneys to forcefully present their cases. Legal ethics also seeks to promote public respect for the legal system. Thus, lawyers are not allowed to mislead the court, nor can they knowingly allow witnesses for their side to perjure themselves.

Regulation of the legal profession begins with codes of legal ethics and professional responsibilities. The American Bar Association (ABA) adopted the *Model Rules of Professional Conduct* in 1983, which it updates periodically. These rules serve as models for the ethics rules of most states. But, consistent with federalism (see Chapter 3), each state has adopted its own code. Thus, state bar associations, not the national association of lawyers, enforce these codes. Law students are required to take a course in legal ethics, and before they can be admitted to the bar, they must pass a separate test on legal ethics.

The codes of legal ethics promulgated by the legal profession are increasingly supplemented by statutes and court decisions. Most important, the Supreme Court has made significant rulings on when prosecutors must disclose exculpatory information to the defense (Chapter 12) and when prosecutors may not use race as a factor in jury selection (Chapter 13).

The primary responsibility for establishing and enforcing professional standards of conduct for the legal profession rests with the highest court of each state. In turn, state courts of last resort have delegated enforcement to the state bar association, which establishes a specific committee to enforce the provisions. Disciplinary proceedings typically begin with the filing of a complaint by a disgruntled client, although judges, other lawyers, or the committee itself can initiate action. Complaints about attorney misconduct are typically investigated in secret, although a few states mandate a more public process. Most complaints are dismissed because of insufficient evidence. But when evidence of an ethical violation exists, the committee files charges and conducts a private hearing. If the charges are proved, the committee recommends disciplinary actions, which can range from a reprimand (either private or public) to a suspension of the license to practice law for a given period of time to restitution to the client. The most severe sanction is

disbarment, which permanently revokes a lawyer's right to practice law. These recommendations may be appealed to the state supreme court, which, after a public hearing, may accept, modify, or reject them. Bar association sanctions against lawyers are relatively rare, however.

The typical remedy for legal mistakes made during the trial is an appellate court reversal (Chapter 16). Legal ethics is enforced in other ways, as well, including sanctions meted out by judges (Chapter 8) and civil lawsuits for legal malpractice (Chapter 7). Typically though, lawyers working in the criminal justice system enjoy legal immunity, which is to say you cannot sue a prosecutor, defense attorney, or a judge just because you lost your case.

The ethical issues surrounding the three types of lawyers who appear in court vary greatly depending on the role they play. In the next chapters, we will examine some of the legal issues facing prosecutors, defense attorneys, and judges.

CONCLUSION

Discussions of court delay and its consequences all too often are conducted in abstract terms. *Barker v. Wingo,* however, forces one to deal with some of the realities. The Court's opinion is clearly mindful of the fact that to interpret the right to a speedy trial in a manner understood by the drafters of the Constitution would, in all likelihood, result in brutal murderers being set free.

Barker v. Wingo and our discussion of the problem of delay show that the actual operations of the criminal courts differ greatly from official expectations. Three concepts—excessive caseloads, discretion, and the courtroom work group—have been used to explain this gap between the law in action and the law on the books. Although courts are burdened with too many cases, an excess of cases is at best only a partial explanation for the behavior of the criminal courts. More important is the role discretion plays in the court system, shaping the dictates of formal law to the actual cases and defendants that come to the criminal courts. The courtroom–work-group concept emphasizes the interactions among the key actors in court. The next three chapters will examine in greater depth how prosecutors, defense attorneys, and judges work within the courtroom work group, and why.

Chapter Review

LO1 **1.** Have a general sense of who works where in the courthouse.

Bail bondsmen have their offices outside courthouses. Judges, lawyers, clerks, court stenographers, law clerks, and bailiffs work inside the courtroom. Clerks of court and court administrators work behind the scenes.

LO2 **2.** Analyze the importance of assembly-line justice.

The concept of assembly-line justice stresses the high volume of cases in courthouses and the emphasis on moving the docket.

LO3 **3.** Describe why discretion is found in the criminal courts.

At every key stage of the criminal court process, humans must apply the law. Choices are made on the basis of legal judgments, policy priorities, and values and attitudes of the actors.

LO4 **4.** Identify the principal actors in the courtroom work group.

The courtroom work group refers to the regular participants, such as judges, prosecutors, and defense attorneys, who interact on a daily basis.

LO5 **5.** Indicate why ethics is important to the American legal system.

Legal ethics are important because they provide necessary boundaries on conflict represented by the adversary system and also seek to ensure clients that their lawyers are working in their best interests.

LO6 **6.** Contrast differing understandings of why delay is a problem in the courts.

Some see delay as a problem because it works to the disadvantage of the prosecutor, others see delay as a problem because it jeopardizes the rights of defendants, and still others see delay as a problem because it reflects a waste of resources.

LO7 **7.** Discuss the strengths and weaknesses of speedy-trial laws.

Speedy-trial laws reflect a law on the books approach to problem solving. Although these laws have the advantage of calling attention to delay as a problem, they are limited because they provide no mechanisms to deal with discretion.

LO8 **8.** Explain why law in action approaches to court delay are more effective than law on the books approaches.

Law in action approaches to solving the problem of delay can prove effective because they focus on coordinating the activities of the key actors in the courthouse. Without such coordination, the local legal culture is unlikely to be changed.

Critical Thinking Questions

1. Take a tour of your local courthouse. How does your perception of it match the description at the beginning of this chapter? Compare notes with other classmates; perhaps they focused on features that you did not.

2. Place yourself in the position of a felony court prosecutor. In what ways does the cooperation of other members of the courtroom work group work to your benefit? How would your answer be different if you approached the question from the vantage point of the judge or the defense attorney?

3. Of the several consequences of delay, which one do you think is the most important? Which one is the least important?

4. In *Barker v. Wingo*, the U.S. Supreme Court stressed the legitimate reasons for the 16 trial continuances. But is there a danger that prosecutors might illegitimately seek continuances?

Key Terms

assembly-line justice　130

clerk of court　126

courtroom work group　133

delay　137

discretion　132

legal ethics　142

normal crime　134

routine administration　132

socialization　134

speedy-trial laws　140

Web Resources

Go to the *America's Courts and the Criminal Justice System* companion website at

http://www.cengage.com/criminaljustice/neubauer,

where you will find more resources to help you study.

Resources include web exercises, quizzing, and flash cards.

For Further Reading

Aikman, Alexander. *The Art and Practice of Court Administration.* Boca Raton, FL: CRC Press, 2006.

Bach, Amy. *Ordinary Injustice: How America Holds Court.* New York: Holt Paperbacks, 2009.

Barrett, Jimmie. *Protecting Court: A Practitioner's Guide to Court Security.* Minneapolis, MN: Mill City Press, 2009.

Braswell, Michael, Belinda McCarthy, and Bernard McCarthy. *Justice, Crime and Ethics.* 5th ed. Cincinnati: Anderson, 2005.

Burke, Kevin, and Frank Broccolina. 2005. "Another View of Local Legal Culture: More Than Court Culture." *Court Manager* 20: 29.

Castellano, Ursula. 2009. "Beyond the Courtroom Workgroup: Caseworkers as the New Satellite of Social Control." *Law and Policy* 31: 429–462.

Gould, Jon, Roger Hartley, William Raftery, Linda Merola, and James Oleson. "The Challenges and Opportunities of Evidence-Based Management in the Courts." *Judicature* 95: 61–67, 2011.

Haynes, Stacy, Barry Ruback, and Gretchen Cusick. "Courtroom Workgroups and Sentencing: The Effects of Similarity, Proximity, and Stability." *Crime & Delinquency* 56: 126–161, 2008.

Lipetz, Marcia. "Routines and Deviations: The Strength of the Courtroom Workgroup in a Misdemeanor Court."

International Journal of the Sociology of Law 8: 47–60, 1980.

Merritt, Nancy. 2006. *Sentencing Reform and the Influence of Courtroom Communities: Oregon's Measure 11.* Newark: Rutgers, The State University of New Jersey–Newark.

National Association for Court Management. 2011. "Visioning and Strategic Planning." Available online at http://www.nacmnet.org/CCCG/strategic-planning.html

Olin, Dirk, and Rebecca Kourlis. *Rebuilding Justice: Civil Courts in Jeopardy and Why You Should Care.* Golden, CO: Institute for the Advancement of the American Legal System, 2011.

Orlik, Deborah. *Ethics for the Legal Professional.* 7th ed. Upper Saddle River, NJ: Pearson, 2010.

Peak, Kenneth. *Justice Administration: Police, Courts and Corrections Management.* 7th ed. Upper Saddle River, NJ: Pearson, 2012.

Souryal, Sam. *Ethics in Criminal Justice: In Search of the Truth.* 5th ed. Burlington, MA: Anderson, 2011.

Stojkovic, Stan, John Klofas, and David Kalinich. *The Administration and Management of Criminal Justice Organizations.* Long Grove, IL: Waveland Press, 2010.

Wendel, Bradley. 2007. *Professional Responsibility and Explanations.* New York: Aspen.

6 Prosecutors

© HARRY LYNCH/MCT/Landov

Former District Attorney **Mike Nifong,** left, speaks while Duke lacrosse player Reade Seligmann, right, listens in the courtroom at a Durham County, NC, court building in 2006. Instead of trying to find the truth about what happened on March 13, 2006, Nifong set out to prove that three Duke University lacrosse players had raped an exotic dancer. Nifong's conduct led to his being disbarred from the practice of law by the State Bar of North Carolina. But the result of the disciplinary action against Nifong may never be able to erase the stain left by a case that went wrong from the start for Duke lacrosse players Dave Evans, Collin Finnerty, and Reade Seligmann. ■

Chapter Outline

ROLE OF THE PROSECUTOR
Broad Discretion
Charging Decisions

CASE CLOSE-UP: *Connick v. Thompson* and **Prosecutorial Misconduct**

Decentralization

PROSECUTION IN FEDERAL COURTS
Solicitor General
Criminal Division of the Justice Department
U.S. Attorneys

PROSECUTION IN STATE COURTS
State Attorneys General
Chief Prosecutor
Local Prosecutor

THE PROSECUTOR'S OFFICE AT WORK
Assistant District Attorneys
Learning the Job
Promotions and Office Structure

Supervision
Attempts at Greater Supervision

PROSECUTORIAL ETHICS
Prosecutorial Immunity

Ethical Duties of Prosecutors

Courts, Law, & Media
Nancy Grace

PROSECUTORS AND COURTROOM WORK GROUPS
Conflicting Goals and Contrasting Work Groups
Political Styles and Contrasting Work Groups

THE EXPANDING DOMAIN OF THE PROSECUTOR
Improving Police–Prosecutor Relationships
Community Prosecution

Courts, Controversy, & Gender Equity
Are Sexual Assaults against Women Underprosecuted?

Learning Objectives

After reading this chapter, you should be able to:

LO1 Discuss the two major characteristics of prosecutors in the United States.

LO2 Describe the three most important entities in federal prosecution.

LO3 Identify the three somewhat overlapping agencies involved in prosecution in state courts.

LO4 Explain the major factors affecting the work life of assistant district attorneys.

LO5 Analyze the principal factors affecting prosecutorial ethics.

LO6 Outline two major examples of the expanding domain of the prosecutor.

"I wouldn't allow Durham to become known for 'a bunch of lacrosse players from Duke raping a black girl,'" proclaimed Mike Nifong, candidate for district attorney. After a 30-year career as an assistant prosecutor in Durham County, North Carolina, Nifong was running for election as district attorney. His comments fanned the fires of what quickly became a sensational national case.

Following a party thrown by the Duke lacrosse team, three team members were accused of sexually assaulting a woman who had been hired as a stripper. While the case was being investigated and while charges were pending, Nifong made nearly 50 pretrial statements to the press.

> Among the statements, ten were alleged to be improper commentary on the team members' failure or refusal to give information to law enforcement authorities and their invocation of their constitutional rights. Another ten were alleged to be "improper commentary on [his] opinion about the guilt of the accused and/or about his opinion that a crime had occurred." Finally, the bar listed statements that particularly heightened public condemnation of the accused, many of which asserted a racial motivation for the attack. (Mosteller, 2007, p. 1349)

Nifong was apparently motivated to appear in the media as a crusader for racial justice while he was locked in a tight reelection battle. He represented himself as someone fighting to vindicate a young, African-American woman's sexual victimization by White student-athletes of socioeconomic privilege. And his plan worked; Nifong was reelected with strong support from the Black community in the Durham area even though one of his opponents, a Black man, had won some major community endorsements that would typically sway the larger community (Mosteller, 2007). Nifong would win the election, but the rape charges would eventually be dismissed for lack of evidence.

Prosecutors • Prosecutors • Prosecutors • Prosecutors • Prosecutors • Pro
Prosecutors • Prosecutors • Prosecutors • Prosecutors • Prosecutors •

In addition to filing politically motivated charges that were allowed to continue for months even though it had become clear that the defendants were innocent, Nifong concealed exculpatory DNA evidence and made deceptive and misleading statements to the press, the trial court, fellow attorneys, and the state bar. This unethical conduct ultimately resulted in Nifong being hauled before the State Bar of North Carolina for disciplinary proceedings. The State Bar concluded that Nifong violated several provisions of the North Carolina Revised Rules of Professional Conduct, including two parts of Rule 3, which concern pretrial publicity. (These rules are based on the Model Rules of the American Bar Association which have been adopted in more than 40 states.)

- Rule 3.6(a) prohibits a lawyer from making an "extrajudicial statement that the lawyer knows, or reasonably should know, will be disseminated by means of public communication and will have a substantial likelihood of materially prejudicing an adjudicative proceeding in the matter."

- Rule 3.8(f) prohibits prosecutors from making out-of-court statements that have a substantial likelihood of heightening public condemnation of the accused.

Nifong's violation of these rules, among others, ultimately caused him to lose his license to practice law, because the rules are designed to protect criminal defendants' Sixth Amendment right to a fair trial from being eroded by unfair media coverage from a seemingly reliable source (see Chapter 13). But Nifong made some outrageous statements in spite of these ethics rules when he said things like, "The guilty will stand trial" and "I am convinced there was a rape."

Nifong also improperly commented on the lacrosse players' invocation of the right to remain silent and the right to counsel as evidence of their guilt when he said to the media, "If it's not the way it's been reported, then why are they so unwilling to tell us what, in their words, did take place that night?" Nifong also said, "And one would wonder why one needs an attorney if one was not charged and had not done anything wrong."

Although the Duke lacrosse sexual assault case was highly unusual, it illustrates the influential role prosecutors play in the criminal justice system. More so than judges and defense attorneys, the prosecutor is the most powerful official in the criminal courts. From initial arrest to final disposition, how the prosecutor chooses to exercise discretion determines to a large extent which defendants are prosecuted, the type of bargains that are struck, and the severity of the sentence imposed.

This chapter discusses several factors involved in the work of the prosecutor. We begin by examining the prosecutor's role in the criminal justice system and then consider separately the structure of federal and state prosecutors' offices. Our focus then shifts to actual courtroom behavior, looking at prosecutors at work. But prosecutors do not work in isolation. Thus, the later parts of this chapter look at prosecutors within the context of the courtroom work group and their expanding domain in the criminal justice system.

ROLE OF THE PROSECUTOR

The prosecutor is of critical importance because of the office's central position in the criminal justice system. Whereas police, defense attorneys, judges, and probation officers specialize in specific phases of the criminal justice process, the duties of the prosecutor bridge all of these areas. This means that on a daily basis, the prosecutor is the only official who works with all actors of the criminal justice system. As Justice Robert Jackson (1940, p. 18) once remarked, "The prosecutor has more control over life, liberty, and reputation than any other person in America."

Prosecutors stand squarely in the middle of the fragmented nonsystem of criminal justice discussed in Chapter 1. Naturally, the various actors have conflicting views about how prosecutorial discretion should be used—the police push for harsher penalties; defense attorneys, for giving their clients a break; and judges, to clear the docket. Thus, prosecutors occupy a uniquely powerful and highly visible position in a complex and conflict-filled environment. Amid the diffusion of responsibility that characterizes the criminal justice system, power has increasingly been concentrated in the hands of the prosecutor (Misner, 1996; Worrall & Borakove, 2008).

Broad Discretion

A key characteristic of the American **prosecutor** is broad discretion. Although the prosecutor works in the courthouse, the office of prosecutor is part of the executive branch of government. This independence from the judiciary is vital for the proper functioning of the adversary system, since prosecutors at times challenge judicial decisions. The breadth of prosecutorial power stems from numerous court cases since 1833. Typical is *People v. Wabash, St. Louis, and Pacific Railway*, an 1882 decision in which the Illinois Court of Appeals stated that the district attorney (DA) "is charged by law with large discretion in prosecuting offenders against the law. He may commence public prosecutions...and may discontinue them when, in his judgment the ends of justice are satisfied." In decisions like this one, appellate courts have allowed the modern prosecuting attorney to exercise virtually unfettered discretion relating to initiating, conducting, and

terminating prosecutions (Albonetti, 1987; Jacoby, 1980; Sarat & Clarke, 2008). The "Law on the Books vs. Law in Action" feature provides an overview of the role of the prosecutor throughout the criminal justice process.

It is only during the trial itself that appellate courts have placed restrictions on the exercise of prosecutorial power. In the context of the adversary system, the prosecutor is expected to advocate the guilt of the defendant vigorously. But the prosecutor is also a lawyer and is therefore an **officer of the court**; that is, he or she has a duty to see that justice is done. Violations of the law must be prosecuted, but in a way that guarantees that the defendant's rights are respected and protected. In 1935, the Supreme Court spelled out the limitations imposed on prosecutors by their obligation as officers of the court: "He may prosecute with earnestness and vigor—indeed, he should do so. But while he may strike hard blows, he is not at liberty to strike foul ones. It is as much his duty to refrain from improper methods calculated to produce a wrongful conviction as it is to use every legitimate means to bring about a just one" (*Berger v. United States 1935, p. 88*).

In recent years, the Supreme Court has expressed repeated concern about prosecutorial misconduct. Convictions have been reversed because prosecutors were too zealous in their advocacy. But at the same time, the nation's highest tribunal has also decided that prosecutors enjoy absolute immunity from civil lawsuits when acting as courtroom advocates. However, under other conditions, prosecutors may be sued civilly (see "Case Close-Up: *Connick v. Thompson* and Prosecutorial Misconduct").

Charging Decisions

Of all the discretionary decisions prosecutors routinely make, perhaps none is more important than the decision whether to file charges, thereby transforming a suspect into a criminal defendant. There are few, if any, legislative or judicial guidelines to guide prosecutors in the exercise of their discretion in this domain. Indeed, the Supreme Court has made it clear that, "So long as the prosecutor has probable cause to believe that the accused committed an offense defined by statute, the decision whether or not to prosecute, and what charge to file or bring before a grand jury generally rests entirely in his discretion"

LAW ON THE BOOKS VS. LAW IN ACTION
ROLE OF THE PROSECUTOR IN STEPS OF CRIMINAL PROCEDURE

	LAW ON THE BOOKS	LAW IN ACTION
Crime	Must enforce all laws to the fullest.	The impossible legal mandate means that priorities must be established.
Arrest	Little involvement.	In major crimes, may advise the police whether sufficient evidence of probable cause exists to arrest.
Initial appearance	Represents the government.	Manages the chaos in the lower court, where there are many cases and little is known about the crime or the defendant.
Bail	Can make a bail recommendation to the judge.	Typically recommends a high bail amount to the judge.
Charging	Exclusive domain of the prosecutor.	Often decides which defendants will be charged with what crime.
Preliminary hearing	Dominates this step because of the authority to call witnesses.	Highly successful in having defendants bound over for further proceedings.
Grand jury	Acts as legal adviser to the grand jury.	The prosecutor largely decides which cases will be heard; the grand jury tends to "rubber stamp" prosecutorial requests for indictments.
Arraignment	Formally presents the charges against the defendant in open court.	By taking the case this far, the prosecutor has indicated his or her willingness to move forward on a case.
Discovery	Important variations in state law regarding how much information must be disclosed prior to trial.	Informally provides trusted defense attorneys with information to induce a plea of guilty.
Suppression motions	Argues that police acted legally in searching and/or interrogating the suspect.	Argues that police acted legally in searching for evidence to be admitted.
Plea bargaining	District attorneys have considerable discretion in plea bargaining.	Based on normal penalties, dictates the terms under which defendant pleads guilty.
Trial	Presents witnesses proving defendant guilty and urges jury to return a verdict of guilty.	Very successful in gaining convictions.
Sentencing	In many jurisdictions, the district attorneys can make a sentencing recommendation to the judge.	Judge is more likely to follow the district attorney's sentencing recommendation than the defense attorney's.
Appeal	Argues before the appellate court why the lower court conviction should stand, and often wins.	Wins a significant victory in most appeals.

CASE CLOSE-UP

CONNICK v. THOMPSON AND PROSECUTORIAL MISCONDUCT

John Thompson spent 14 years on death row because a prosecutor deliberately withheld evidence that might have led to his acquittal. Should the district attorney's office have to pay for such egregious prosecutorial misconduct? A six-person federal jury decided that the district attorney's office was liable and calculated damages at $1 million per year. Five justices of the Supreme Court reached a very different decision.

John Thompson was charged with the murder of a New Orleans hotel executive, and the extensive publicity surrounding that case resulted in Thompson being charged with an unrelated armed robbery that occurred after the murder. To enhance their chances of getting a guilty verdict in the murder case, the Orleans Parish District Attorney's Office tried Thompson first on the armed robbery charge and secured a conviction. During the subsequent murder trial, the defendant declined to testify because he didn't want the jury to know of his prior felony conviction. Thompson was convicted and sentenced to death.

A month before the scheduled execution, a private investigator found a lab report that clearly showed that Thompson could not have committed the armed robbery—the robber had type B blood; Thompson's blood was type O. Assistant District Attorney Gerry Deegan had checked out the lab report from the police evidence locker but never placed it in the courthouse property room. On his death bed, Deegan confessed to a friend and former prosecutor that he had deliberately withheld the evidence. Under *Brady v. Maryland* (1963), prosecutors must disclose evidence favorable to the defense (see Chapter 11).

Thompson's attempted armed robbery conviction was dismissed and he was retried on the murder charge. This time he took the stand in his own defense and after only 30 minutes of deliberation, the jury acquitted. Thompson filed a Section 1983 civil rights suit (discussed in Chapter 2) in the U.S. District Court for the Eastern District of Louisiana. The $14 million verdict was upheld by the U.S. Fifth Circuit before the Supreme Court decided to hear the appeal from the District Attorney's office.

Writing for the five-judge conservative majority, Justice Thomas overturned the jury verdict arguing that one cannot sue for civil rights violations under Section 1983 for failure to train prosecutors based on a single *Brady* violation. Assistant District Attorney Deegan was viewed as a rogue prosecutor and not typical of prosecutors in the office. Justice Ginsburg's dissent scoffed at such notions of an isolated act, writing that under *Connick* "long-concealed prosecutorial transgressions were neither isolated nor atypical."

The current Orleans Parish district attorney reacted positively to the decision, noting that the $14 million verdict would have crippled his office (Maggi, 2011). Others, however, feared the decision would lead to prosecutorial impunity (Appleton, 2011). An influential article in the online edition of *The Yale Law Journal* argues that this decision means that prosecutors cannot be held accountable. The Court based its decision in part of the availability of other measures to check prosecutorial misconduct but these are ineffective (Keenan, Cooper, Lebowitz, & Lerer, 2011).

Connick v. Thompson is but the latest in a some what tortured line of prosecutorial misconduct decisions. Prosecutors are immune from civil lawsuits when they are performing their prosecutorial role, but they enjoy only qualified immunity outside the judicial arena, in particular when they provide faulty legal advice to the police (*Burns v. Reed,* 1991). The Court revisited the issue 2 years later and laid down a slightly more discernible line of permissible and impermissible conduct. The Court restated that prosecutors have absolute immunity from civil damage suits for actions in connection with the traditional role of courtroom advocacy. But DAs enjoy only "qualified immunity" for other actions. The Court unanimously held that statements made in a news conference were not protected by absolute immunity. But the justices split 5 to 4 on whether investigative actions by the DA were subject to suit (*Buckley v. Fitzsimmons* 1993).

Continued on next page

Continued from previous page

How these cases apply to Mike Nifong in the Duke lacrosse case is unclear. The players sued the former North Carolina prosecutor, but the federal judge ruled that they would have to prove that Nifong "willfully and maliciously prosecuted the players," a high legal hurdle (McDonough, 2008).

After the *Connick* decision, part of the lawsuit was allowed to proceed. But the issue may be moot. Nifong has filed for bankruptcy and even if he were to be found liable in a civil judgment, it is unlikely the plaintiffs would ever recover any monetary damages (Chapter 2).

(*Bordenkircher v. Hayes*, 1975, p. 364). Scholars posit that prosecutorial discretion in charging decisions is guided by a set of *focal concerns* on the practical constraints and consequences regarding both organizational efficiency and the certainty of conviction (Beichner & Spohn, 2005; Ulmer, Kurlychek, & Kramer, 2007).

Focal concerns about organizational efficiency require prosecutors to evaluate the consequences of their charging decisions with the contexts of media scrutiny, their relationships with other members of the courtroom work group, and the limitations of budgets, personnel, and time (Gershman, 2011). In contrast, the focal concern about obtaining a conviction involves a complex interplay of both legal and extralegal factors (factors that are not supposed to be legally relevant).

The *legal factors* prosecutors routinely consider in charging decisions include:

- the seriousness of the offense (Albonetti, 1987; Jacoby, Mellon, Ratledge, & Turner, 1982; Neubauer, 1974a; Spears & Spohn, 1997);

- the strength of the evidence, such as valid eyewitness identifications, victims who are cooperative and willing to testify, and the corroborating physical or forensic evidence (Albonetti, 1987; Jacoby et al., 1982; Spohn & Holleran, 2001);

- the culpability of the defendant, including the number of charges, the accused person's prior criminal history, and the accused person's motives for the offense (Albonetti. 1987; Gershman. 2011; Neubauer, 1974a; Spohn & Holleran 2001);

- the degree of harm caused by the offense and the corresponding proportionality of the potential punishment (Gershman, 2011);

- the degree to which the accused cooperates in prosecuting others (Gershman, 2011); and

- the availability and likelihood of prosecution by another jurisdiction (Gershman, 2011).

The *extralegal factors* are not quite as clear-cut. Most concern either victim or offender characteristics, such as race, sex, age, educational level, employment status, and so on.

- Some studies conclude that race does not influence the decision to prosecute or dismiss a case (e.g., Albonetti, 1986, 1987; Baumer, Mesner, & Felson, 2000; Spears & Spohn, 1997). Other studies disagree, finding that the race of the suspect or the racial differences in the victim–offender dyads (especially if the defendant is Black or Hispanic and the victim is White) significantly affect the charging and dismissal decisions (Baumer, Messner, and Felson 2000; Spohn, Gruhl, and Welch, 1987; Spears and Spohn 1997). And still others report findings that advantage racial and ethnic minorities over Whites, especially in misdemeanor shoplifting (Myers, 1982) and felony drug cases (Barnes & Kingsnorth, 1996; Franklin, 2010; Wooldredge & Thistlethwaite, 2004).

- Researchers have demonstrated that prosecutors are more likely to charge defendants who are male (Nagel & Hagan, 1983; Spohn, Gruhl, & Welch, 1987; Spohn & Spears, 1997) or unemployed (Schmidt & Steury, 1989).

But few people assume that racism, sexism, and other forms of intentional bias are, in and of themselves, responsible for invidious discrimination in charging decisions. Rather, most researchers believe these factors influence prosecutors' predictions of how judges and jurors might assess the background, behavior, and motivations of both suspects and victims (Frohmann, 1997). Indeed, there is ample evidence that prosecutors are more likely to file charges when there is a "stand-up" victim—someone whose personal characteristics align with societal stereotypes concerning who is credible and undeserving of victimization (see Stanko, 1988). These factors are particularly salient in sexual assault cases (see "Courts, Controversy, and Gender Equity: Are Sexual Assaults against Women Underprosecuted?").

Decentralization

Another characteristic of the office of prosecutor is decentralized organization. Although the American prosecutor represents the state in the prosecution of criminal cases, the office is not centralized, as it is in England and most of Europe (Flemming, 1990; Jehle & Wade, 2006). Instead, prosecution is highly decentralized, with more than 8,000 federal, state, county, municipal, and township prosecution agencies.

Commensurate with the nation's often confusing dual court system, separate prosecutors are found in federal and state courts. The structure, however, is not parallel with court structure; that is, each court does not have attached to it a specific prosecutor. DAs, for example, often conduct the trial in the trial court of general jurisdiction and then appeal through both layers of state courts and, on rare occasions, even to the U.S. Supreme Court (a federal judicial body). Moreover, different prosecutors' offices may handle the same case; sometimes, the city attorney conducts the preliminary stages of a felony case in the lower courts, and the district attorney prosecutes in the trial court of general jurisdiction.

Table 6.1 provides a rough overview of typical state and federal prosecutorial structure. Be aware, however, that the apparent hierarchy of prosecutorial structure is an illusion. In the federal courts, the U.S. attorneys enjoy considerable autonomy from the U.S. Justice Department, and in the states, local district attorneys are totally separate from state attorneys general. We will begin with prosecution in federal courts and then turn to the more complex realities of state prosecutions.

TABLE 6.1 ▪ OVERVIEW OF PROSECUTORS IN THE DUAL COURT SYSTEM

Federal	State
Solicitor General	**Attorney General**
• Represents the U.S. government before the U.S. Supreme Court in all appeals of federal criminal cases.	• Chief legal officer of the state.
	• Civil duties more extensive than criminal duties.
• Often appears as amicus in appeals involving state criminal convictions.	• Has limited authority in criminal prosecutions.
Criminal Division	**Chief Prosecutors and Their Assistants**
• Prosecutes a few nationally significant criminal cases.	(see Table 6.2 for varying names)
• Exercises nominal supervision over U.S. attorneys.	• Have great autonomy in prosecuting felony cases.
	• Typically argue cases on appeal.
U.S. Attorneys and Their Assistants	**Local Prosecutors**
• Prosecute the vast majority of criminal cases in federal courts.	• Often handle preliminary stages of felony cases.
• Enjoy great autonomy in actions.	• Prosecute the large volume of cases in the lower courts

NOTE: To learn more about the vast bureaucracies included in the U.S. Department of Justice, go to http://www.usdoj.gov.

© Cengage Learning

PROSECUTION IN FEDERAL COURTS

Prosecutions in federal courts are conducted by the U.S. Department of Justice. Billed as the world's largest law firm, the Department of Justice represents the U.S. government in all legal matters not specifically delegated to other agencies. The department is headed by the **U.S. Attorney General**, who is a member of the president's cabinet. Top-level officials are presidential appointees who reflect the views of the administration on important policy issues. Day-to-day activities are carried out by a large cadre of career lawyers, who enjoy civil service protection and have, over the years, developed invaluable expertise in particular areas of law (Landsberg, 1993; Sisk, Noone, Steadman, & Lester, 2006).

The Department of Justice has grown tremendously in recent years. It is a sprawling series of bureaucracies including investigatory and law enforcement offices such as the Federal Bureau of Investigation, the Drug Enforcement Administration, the U.S. Marshals Service, and the Federal Bureau of Prisons. Also in the Department of Justice is the Office of Justice Programs, which oversees the Bureau of Justice Assistance and other entities.

In terms of prosecution, three entities—solicitor general, criminal division, and U.S. attorneys—are particularly important. We will examine them from the top down, although, as we shall see, the hierarchy does not prevent the exercise of considerable autonomy.

Solicitor General

The **U.S. Solicitor General** is the third highest-ranking official in the Justice Department. The solicitor general's principal task is to represent the executive branch before the Supreme Court. But at the same time, the justices depend on the solicitor general to look beyond the government's narrow interests. Because of the solicitor general's dual responsibility to the judicial and executive branches, the officeholder is sometimes called the Tenth Justice, an informal title that underlines the special relationship with the Supreme Court (Aberbach & Peterson, 2006; Caplan, 1988; Meinhold & Shull, 1993).

The office of the solicitor general is in essence a small, elite, very influential law firm whose client is the U.S. government. The staff consists of 23 of the most able attorneys found anywhere. As the representative of the United States in litigation before the Supreme Court, the solicitor general's office argues all government cases before the Court. For example, the assistant solicitor general argued the major issues in *Burns v. Reed*. But the influence of the office extends further.

Roughly half the work of the solicitor general's office involves coordinating appeals by the federal government. With few exceptions, all government agencies must first receive authorization from the solicitor general to appeal an adverse lower court ruling to the Supreme Court. The office requests Supreme Court review only in cases with a high degree of policy significance and in which the government has a reasonable legal argument. In turn, the solicitor general has a high rate of success in petitioning the Supreme Court and in winning cases argued on their merits.

Criminal Division of the Justice Department

The criminal division formulates criminal law enforcement policies over all federal criminal cases, except those specifically assigned to other divisions. The criminal division, with the U.S. attorneys, has the responsibility for overseeing criminal matters under more than 900 statutes, as well as certain civil litigation. The criminal division is organized into a number of units that handle matters such as fraud, organized crime, and public integrity. Several of the units deal with international matters and have become more visible with the U.S. efforts to fight terrorism.

Criminal division attorneys prosecute many nationally significant cases—for example, the Unabomber and the Oklahoma City bombing cases. In the wake of 9/11, the criminal division has directed prosecutions of several alleged terrorists and overseen the detainment of enemy noncombatants on federal military bases. Through the years, the criminal division has also received extensive press coverage for cases involving corrupt government officials, alleged members of organized crime, and major drug-dealing enterprises.

U.S. Attorneys

The U.S. attorneys serve as the nation's principal litigators under the direction of the Attorney General. 94 U.S. attorneys are stationed throughout the United States, Puerto Rico, the Virgin Islands, Guam, and the Northern Mariana Islands.

U.S. attorneys are appointed by, and serve at the discretion of, the President of the United States, with the advice and consent of the Senate. One U.S. attorney is assigned to each of the judicial districts, with the exception of Guam and the Northern Mariana Islands, where one serves both districts. Each U.S. attorney is the chief federal law enforcement officer of the United States within his or her particular jurisdiction. The 93 U.S. attorneys are assisted by over 6,000 assistant U.S. attorneys, who increasingly have become career employees.

U.S. attorneys represent the federal government in court in many matters. They have three statutory responsibilities:

- Prosecution of criminal cases brought by the federal government
- Initiation and defense of civil cases in which the United States is a party
- Collection of certain debts owed the federal government

The volume of litigation varies considerably among the districts. U.S. attorneys along the Mexican border, for example, initiate a large number of drug prosecutions. Nonetheless, each district handles a mixture of simple and complex litigation.

U.S. attorneys enjoy full authority and control in the areas of personnel management, financial management, and procurement. They exercise wide discretion in the use of their resources to further the priorities of local jurisdictions and the needs of their communities.

Although the criminal division of the U.S. Department of Justice supervises all federal prosecutions, in practice U.S. attorneys enjoy considerable autonomy. This is partly because of their remoteness from Washington, D.C.—the 93 U.S. attorneys are widely dispersed geographically. The selection process also plays a role. Many U.S. attorneys owe their appointments primarily to persons other than the U.S. attorney general or, in some cases, even the U.S. president (Bell, 1993).

Thus, in the vast majority of cases, the decisions are made by U.S. attorneys scattered across the nation rather than by the central office based in Washington, D.C.

PROSECUTION IN STATE COURTS

Decentralization and local autonomy characterize prosecution in state courts. The result is divided responsibility, with state prosecution authority typically found in three separate offices: state, county (or district), and local. At times, the relationship among these separate agencies is marked by competition; various prosecutors jockey to be the first to prosecute a notorious defendant. We will examine the three major state prosecutors from the top down, but bear in mind that each office is separate and not necessarily subject to the dictates of the office above it.

State Attorneys General

The position of Attorney General, the state's chief legal officer, is typically spelled out in the state's constitution. Among the most important duties are providing legal advice to other state agencies and representing the state in court when state actions are challenged. In recent years, attorneys general have focused on their civil responsibilities by emphasizing their role in protecting consumers from various forms of fraud. Thus, the typical home page of the Attorney General of a state proclaims how many individual consumer complaints (many of which involve motor vehicle and home repair fraud) are handled annually. Many state attorneys general have also been visible in filing consumer lawsuits against major U.S. businesses. The biggest of all involves the suits by more than 30 states against the tobacco industry.

State attorneys general have chosen to emphasize their civil responsibilities because they typically have limited authority over criminal matters. Local autonomy is a key characteristic of the office of prosecutor. In general, state officials do not monitor the activities of local prosecutors. Although the state Attorney General is the state's chief law enforcement official, his or her authority, over local criminal procedures is quite limited. Indeed, in a handful of states, the Attorney General has no legal authority to initiate or intervene in local prosecutions. In other states, this authority is limited to extreme situations.

Thus, the state Attorney General exercises virtually no control or supervision over chief prosecutors at the county level. This lack of supervisory power, coupled with the decentralization of the office, means that local prosecutors enjoy almost total autonomy. Only the local voters have the power to evaluate the prosecutor's performance, by means of their votes.

Chief Prosecutor

The American prosecutor has few direct parallels elsewhere in the world (Flemming, 1990; Jehle & Wade, 2006). Compared to their counterparts in England and Europe, American prosecutors enjoy unmatched independence and discretionary powers (Albonetti, 1987).

Variously called the "district attorney," "county attorney," or "prosecuting attorney" (Table 6.2),

the prosecutor is the chief law enforcement official of the community. Altogether, 2,344 chief prosecutors are employed across the nation, with a staff of almost 80,000. Structure and workload differ according to the size of the population. The typical office serves a population of 36,000 people, with 250 adult felony cases in the district, a staff of 9, and a budget of $355,000. But deviations are readily apparent (Perry, 2006). The great majority of the nation's prosecutors' offices are small ones (Table 6.3). Frequently, rural prosecutors are part-time officials who also engage in private law practices.

Elections are a key characteristic of the office of prosecutor, as 95 percent of chief prosecutors are locally elected officials who typically serve 4-year terms. The exceptions are Alaska, Connecticut, Delaware, the District of Columbia, New Jersey, and Rhode Island, where chief prosecutors are either appointed or are members of the state Attorney General's office.

Because of elections, the work of the American prosecutor is deeply set within the larger political process. For a lawyer interested in a political career, the prosecutor's office offers a launching

TABLE 6.2 ■ CHIEF PROSECUTORS WHO HANDLE FELONY CASES IN STATE COURTS

Title	States
District attorney	Alabama, California, Colorado, Georgia, Kansas,^{a} Louisiana, Maine, Massachusetts, Mississippi, Nevada, New Mexico, New York, North Carolina, Oklahoma, Oregon, Pennsylvania, Texas,^{a} Wisconsin, Wyoming^a
County attorney	Arizona, Iowa, Kansas,^{a} Minnesota, Montana, Nebraska, New Hampshire, Texas,^{a} Utah
State's attorney	Connecticut, Florida, Illinois, Maryland, North Dakota, South Dakota, Vermont
Prosecuting attorney	Arkansas, Hawaii, Idaho, Indiana, Michigan, Missouri,^{a} Ohio, Washington, West Virginia
Commonwealth attorney	Kentucky, Virginia
County prosecutor	New Jersey
District Attorney General	Tennessee
County and prosecuting attorney	Wyoming^a
Solicitor	South Carolina
Circuit Attorney	Missouri^a (City of St. Louis)
No local prosecutor	Alaska, Delaware, Rhode Island

^{a}Kansas, Missouri, Texas, and Wyoming use varying names depending on the jurisdiction.
SOURCE: Steven Perry, Prosecutors in State Courts, 2005. Washington, DC: Bureau of Justice Statistics, National Institute of Justice.

TABLE 6.3 ■ STATE COURT PROSECUTORS' OFFICES

	All Offices	Full-Time Offices (By Population Served)				Part-Time Offices
		1 Million or More People	250,000 to 999,999 People	100,000 to 249,999 People	Under 99,999 People	
Number of offices	2,330	43	211	341	1389	346
Mean population served	299,567,000	2,025,000	496,000	158,000	36,000	13,000
Full-time equivalent employees	34,288 attorneys 43,640 staff 77,928 total	244 attorneys 291 staff 535 total	57 attorneys 74 staff 131 total	17 attorneys 22 staff 39 total	4 attorneys 6 staff 10 total	2 attorneys 1 staff 3 total
Felony cases closed	2,906,795 3% by jury verdict	759,057 2% by jury verdict	934,884 3% by jury verdict	622,073 3% by jury verdict	555,050 3% by jury verdict	35,731 3% by jury verdict
Mean budget	$5.8 billion	$49.2 million	$9.9 million	$2.3 million	$562,000	$157,000
Mean salary of chief prosecutor	$98,024	$165,732	$138,017	$121,777	$96,956	$44,981
Entry-level assistant prosecutor salary	$46,330 (full-time) to $55,885 (full-time)	$51,354 to $64,517	$47,580 to $57,759	$44,007 to $55,263	$42,380 to $46,000	$33,460 to $36,712

SOURCE: Steven W. Perry and Duren Banks, *Prosecutors in State Courts, 2007 - Statistical Tables*. Washington, DC: Bureau of Justice Statistics. 2011. Available online at http://bjs.ojp.usdoj.gov/content/pub/pdf/psc07st.pdf.

pad. Indeed, prosecutors "virtually own the politically potent symbols of 'law and order' politics" (Flemming, Nardulli, & Eisenstein, 1992, p. 23).

Numerous government officials—governors, judges, and legislators—have begun their careers as crusading prosecutors. Many prosecutors, however, do not plan to enter politics. Studies in Wisconsin and Kentucky, for example, indicated that more than half of the prosecutors had no further political ambitions. They viewed the office as useful for gaining visibility before establishing a private law practice (Engstrom, 1971; Jacob, 1966). Thus, after serving one or two terms in office, former DAs typically practice private law or assume other positions in the public sector—primarily judge (Jones, 1994).

The tremendous power of the prosecutor means that political parties are very interested in controlling the office. The chief prosecutor has numerous opportunities for patronage. In some communities, partisan considerations play a large role in the hiring of assistant district attorneys (Eisenstein, Flemming, & Nardulli, 1988). Political parties may also want one of their own serving as district attorney to guarantee that their affairs will not be closely scrutinized and to act as a vehicle for harassing the opposition.

Local Prosecutor

Little is known about the activities of local prosecutors—variously called "city attorneys," "solicitors," or the like. In some jurisdictions, local prosecutors are responsible for the preliminary stages of felony cases as they are processed in the lower courts. In these jurisdictions, it is the local prosecutor (not the chief prosecutor) who represents the government at the initial appearance, argues bond amounts, and conducts the preliminary hearing. These decisions may have important consequences for later stages of the felony prosecution, but the chief prosecutor's office has no direct control over these matters.

Local prosecutors, however, are primarily responsible for processing the large volume of minor criminal offenses disposed of in the lower courts. As explained in Chapter 4, public drunkenness, petty theft, disorderly conduct, and minor assaults are the staple of these judicial bodies.

THE PROSECUTOR'S OFFICE AT WORK

In the courtroom, one's attention normally gravitates toward the individual lawyers as they call witnesses, ask questions, and cross-examine the opponent's witnesses. These individual activities, however, must be understood within the larger context in which they occur. As Table 6.3 illustrates, the day-to-day work of the prosecutor's office is executed by nearly 78,000 people—approximately 34,288 attorneys and 43,640 investigators, legal services personnel, victim advocates, and support staff. How these persons are hired, trained, and supervised has a major bearing on the exercise of prosecutorial discretion.

Assistant District Attorneys

Most assistant district attorneys (sometimes called "deputy district attorneys") are hired immediately after graduation from law school or after a short time in private practice. Traditionally, these young attorneys attend local or regional law schools, rather than the nation's most prestigious law schools (whose graduates are usually able to obtain higher-paying jobs in private practice with prestigious law firms). This has changed somewhat in the past decade or two, as competition for positions in major prosecutor's offices has increased significantly, especially since new prosecutors gain valuable trial experience that new lawyers in law firms typically cannot.

In the past, many prosecutors hired assistants on the basis of party affiliation and the recommendations of elected officials. Increasingly, however, greater stress is being placed on merit selection, a trend exemplified by the Los Angeles prosecutor's office—the nation's largest, with more than 1,000 lawyers—where hiring is done on a civil service basis.

The turnover rate among assistant DAs is high. Most serve an average of 3 to 6 years before leaving prosecution to enter private practice, politics, business, or another field. Thirty-five percent of all prosecutors' offices nationwide report significant problems retaining assistant DAs, with low salaries cited as the leading reason for the high turnover (Perry, 2006). Indeed, low salaries were "the primary obstacle cited by prosecutors' offices with recruitment problems (83%) and offices with retention problems (71%)," especially when compared to the higher salaries lawyers earn in private law practice—a disparity that seems to grow over time (Perry, 2006, p. 3).

Turnover is also a product of assistants' growing tired of the job. With its never-ending stream of society's losers, the criminal courthouse can become a depressing place to work. Moreover, regular trial work creates numerous physical and psychological pressures. In the words of a former New Orleans prosecutor, "The average trial assistant leaves work every day with a huge stack of papers under his arm. The grind can really wear you down. There's just too much work" (Perlstein, 1990). In *Bronx D.A.*, Sarena Straus (2006) discussed the day she reached her breaking point. She was a felony prosecutor in the Domestic Violence and Sex Crimes Unit. She had just interviewed a 6-year-old autistic boy who watched his sister get stabbed to death that morning. "When I finished the interview, I went back to my office. It was 7 pm. Everyone else had gone home for the evening. I sat in my office and cried." Realizing she could no longer separate herself from her work, she left the job.

Although many assistants view their job as a brief way station toward a more lucrative and varied private practice, some see it as a permanent career position. In Wisconsin, the average tenure is about 6 years, and perhaps just as important, some assistants advance to become the elected DA in their county, run for the position in a neighboring county, or make other lateral moves (Jones, 1994). Across the nation, a marked trend toward a prosecutorial "civil service" has become obvious, with assistants moving from office to office (Jones, 2001).

Learning the Job

Law schools provide an overview of law on the books—criminal law, criminal procedure, evidence, and constitutional law, to name just a few. But most law schools give their students very little exposure to law in action. Thus, the typical assistant DA comes to the job having little familiarity with the day-to-day realities of the profession. Here is how one lawyer described his first days on the job:

> For the first week or two, I went to court with guys who had been here. Just sat there and watched. What struck me was the amount of things he [the prosecutor] has to do in the courtroom. The prosecutor runs the courtroom. Although the judge is theoretically in charge, we're standing there plea-bargaining and calling the cases at the same time and chewing gum and telling the people to quiet down and setting bonds, and that's what amazed me. I never thought I would learn all the terms. What bothered me also was the paperwork.

> Not the Supreme Court decisions, not the *mens rea* or any of this other stuff, but the amount of junk that's in those files that you have to know. We never heard about this crap in law school. (Heumann, 1978, p. 94)

For decades, training in prosecutors' offices was almost exclusively on the job; it was not unusual for recent law school graduates with no experience to be sent into court on their first day on the job. One assistant summed up the office tradition as follows: "They have a very unique way of breaking people in. They say, 'Here's a file. There's the jury. Go try it'" (Flemming, Nardulli, & Eisenstein, 1992). More recently, large prosecutors' offices have begun to train new employees more systematically. After a week of general orientation to the different divisions of the office, new assistants are allowed to watch various proceedings and observe veteran trial attorneys at work.

Law schools have been under increasing pressure to teach their students more about the actual practice of law. Many have responded by adding more skills-oriented classes to their curricula, problem-based learning within classes, and a host of community-engaged learning activities (such as legal practice clinics and internship placement programs) that are aimed at helping students become more prepared to enter the legal workforce (Bard, 2011). Still, even if one graduates from law school with a more applied than theoretical legal education, there is still much to learn upon entering prosecutorial practice. For example, an important part

of learning law in action involves working with the office clientele. Here is how journalist Gary Delsohn (2003b, p. 13) described the reality of the prosecutor's office in Sacramento, California:

> In an urban prosecutor's office, witnesses you build a case around are often just a shade less unsavory than the defendants you're trying to put away. It's blue-collar law. To succeed, a prosecutor has to be willing and able to deal with all kinds of people.

New assistants quickly learn to ask questions of more experienced prosecutors, court clerks, and veteran police officers. Through this socialization process, assistants learn important unwritten rules about legal practice relating to what types of violations should be punished and the appropriate penalties to be applied to such violations. Assistants also learn that their performance and chances for promotion are measured by how promptly and efficiently they dispose of cases. They become sensitive to hints—for example, if a judge complains that a backlog is developing because prosecutors are bringing too many minor cases, the new assistant usually gets the message that his or her plea-bargaining demands are too high.

Promotions are also related to the candidate's reputation as a trial attorney. Assistants are invariably judged by the number of convictions they obtain. In the courthouse environment, however, not losing a case has a higher value than winning. Thus, assistants learn that if the guilt of the defendant is doubtful or the offender is not dangerous, it is better to negotiate a plea than to disrupt the courtroom routine by attempting to gain a jury conviction.

Promotions and Office Structure

As assistants gain experience and settle into the courthouse routine, they are promoted to more demanding and also more interesting tasks. Promotions are related to office structure (Flemming, Nardulli, & Eisenstein, 1992). Small prosecutors' offices usually use vertical prosecution, in which one prosecutor is assigned responsibility for a case from intake to appeal (Nugent & McEwen, 1988). In these offices, assistants are promoted by being assigned more serious cases. However, such an assignment system is administratively burdensome in large courthouses; assistants would spend much of their time moving from one courtroom to another and waiting for their one or two cases to be called. Therefore, most big-city prosecutors' offices use horizontal prosecution, in which prosecutors are assigned to specific functions, such as initial appearance, charging, preliminary hearing, grand jury, trial, or appeal. On a regular basis, one or two attorneys are systematically assigned to one courtroom with a given judge. Over time, prosecutors come to know the judge's views on sentencing and the like. Under horizontal prosecution, assistants spend a year or more handling misdemeanor offenses before they are promoted by being assigned to courtrooms with felonies.

Over the past decades, specialization has become increasingly common in chief prosecutors' offices, particularly in densely populated jurisdictions. Often it is the most experienced trial attorneys who staff these positions. Specialized units dealing with murder, sexual assault, armed robbery, and major drug crimes are the most prestigious, mainly because trial work is both plentiful and challenging.

Supervision

Assistant district attorneys are supervised by a section head, who is supposed to ensure that they follow office policies. However, for several reasons, assistant DAs enjoy fairly broad freedom.

Office policies are often general and somewhat vague. In small offices, they are seldom even put in writing. Official and unofficial policies are simply part of what the assistant learns informally; for this reason, it is hard for the bureau chief to enforce them. In large offices, decentralized work assignments mean that supervisors can exert only limited control over specific cases or individual assistants. Assistant DAs spend most of their time not in the central office but in the courtroom. Indeed, in crowded courthouses, trial assistants often have offices adjoining the judge's chambers and only rarely appear in the prosecutor's office at all. It is therefore difficult for supervisors to observe and monitor the assistant district attorney's activities. Each assistant has dozens of cases that require individual decisions on the basis of specific facts,

unique witness problems, and so on. A supervisor has no way to monitor such situations except on the basis of what the assistant reports orally or writes in the file. Here, as elsewhere, information is power. Assistants can control their supervisors by selectively telling them what they think they should know (Neubauer, 1974b).

Attempts at Greater Supervision

The traditional form of prosecutorial management is centered on autonomy; each individual assistant DA is granted a great deal of freedom to make his or her own decisions. The Erie, Pennsylvania, DA's office is typical; it "promulgated few formal written policies, gave most of its assistants fairly wide latitude to dispose of cases in ways consistent with the general aim of the office, and relied on informal supervision" (Eisenstein, Flemming, & Nardulli, 1988, p. 215).

Concerned that autonomy allows too much unchecked discretion, some prosecutors have attempted to exert greater supervision by adopting a rigid system of office policies. Some forbid any charge reductions whatsoever for some types of defendants (habitual offenders) and for serious charges such as violent offenses and major drug dealing (Eisenstein, Flemming, & Nardulli 1988). To ensure compliance with these detailed office policies, formal, detailed, bureaucratic enforcement mechanisms are imposed. Typical is DuPage County, Illinois, where the DA's office "was highly centralized, rigidly enforcing the 'bottom-line' pleas established by the indictment committee. The DA's office relied on a formally structured hierarchy to administer its policies" (Eisenstein, Flemming, & Nardulli, 1988, p. 215). Chief prosecutors believe that these management systems monitor prosecutorial discretion, minimize differences among individual assistants, and concentrate scarce crime-fighting resources (Jacoby, 1980).

Attempts by supervisors to control the work of the assistants tend to erode the morale of the office, as the following account from the Sacramento, California, DA's office illustrates. According to one of the top supervisors in the office, second-guessing is rarely worth the trouble, because the deputies tend to "stay pissed" forever. Indeed, one assistant is still furious 7 years after his boss refused to allow him to participate in a meeting involving his case (Delsohn,

2003a,b). Overall, office review of all case files (to ensure that policies have been followed) makes some assistants uncomfortable because they think this means that they are not completely trusted. Reductions in individual discretion increase the general level of tension in the office. One trial assistant related how a colleague was summarily fired on the same day he violated office policy on plea bargaining. All the assistants resented and feared the administrator who fired him (Eisenstein, Flemming, & Nardulli, 1988, p. 215).

PROSECUTORIAL ETHICS

The Duke lacrosse team rape case has become the contemporary poster child for prosecutorial misconduct. But this was a truly exceptional case and needs to be analyzed within an array of legal issues that limit prosecutorial power.

Ethical issues facing prosecutors are very different from those confronting defense attorneys because prosecutors do not represent individual clients. Prosecutors often define their jobs as representing victims of crime (Chapter 9), but these are not typically considered to fit under the attorney–client relationship. Rather, the client of the prosecutor is the government, and for this reason, prosecutors are given special responsibilities. In the

words of the Criminal Justice Standards: "The duty of the prosecutor is to seek justice, not merely to convict" (Standard 3-1.2c, American Bar Association 2012). And, because prosecutors represent the government, they enjoy a great deal of protection from civil lawsuits.

Prosecutorial Immunity

Prosecutors enjoy **absolute immunity**—complete freedom from civil liability—for everything they do with regard to the core prosecutorial functions of initiating criminal charges and pursuing criminal convictions as the government's advocate (*Imbler v. Pachtman*, 1976). Such absolute immunity extends to all actions, even those motivated by ill will or bad faith, concerning filing or declining to file criminal charges, plea bargaining, and presenting arguments or evidence in court (whether before a grand jury, at bail hearings, at preliminary hearings, at trials, or on appeal). Thus, for example, a defendant whose conviction is overturned on appeal (and is later found not guilty) cannot sue the prosecutor for malpractice. The appellate court reversal is viewed as a sufficient remedy.

In contrast, when prosecutors are not acting as the government's advocate in some judicial phase of the criminal justice process, they enjoy

KEY DEVELOPMENTS CONCERNING THE PROSECUTOR

Berger v. United States (1935)	The prosecutor's primary interest is in doing justice, not simply winning cases.
Imbler v. Pachtman (1976)	Prosecutors enjoy absolute immunity from civil liability when initiating and pursuing a criminal prosecution.
Morrison v. Olson (1988)	Independent counsel law is constitutional.
Burns v. Reed (1991)	Prosecutors enjoy only qualified immunity from lawsuits concerning advice given to the police.
Buckley v. Fitzsimmons (1993)	Prosecutors enjoy only qualified immunity from civil lawsuits for actions during criminal investigations and statements made during news conferences.
Kalina v. Fletcher (1997)	A prosecutor may be sued for making false statements of fact in an affidavit in support of an arrest warrant.
Connick v. Thompson (2011)	A district attorney's office may not be held liable under Section 1983 for failure to train prosecutors based on a single *Brady* violation (or perhaps, even a handful of *Brady* violations).

only **qualified immunity** for their actions. Qualified immunity shields prosecutors from civil liability for acts beyond those associated with courtroom advocacy, but still within the scope of their professional duties (such as when advising the police or speaking to the media). However, qualified immunity applies only if prosecutors are acting in good faith that they are not violating any law or ethical rule of which a reasonable person in his or her position would be aware. Examples of situations in which prosecutors enjoy only qualified immunity are presented in the "Key Developments" feature on page 162.

Ethical Duties of Prosecutors

Prosecutors have a number of specific ethical obligations in addition to the overarching prosecutorial duty to seek justice, such as disclosing exculpatory evidence, avoiding conflicts of interest, and refraining from any behavior that would interfere with the fair administration of justice. This section highlights only a few of prosecutors' major ethical responsibilities.

Chapter 11 discusses a series of Supreme Court cases that, like *Brady v. Maryland* (1963), require the prosecutor to hand over to the defense *exculpatory evidence* (evidence that tends to show the innocence of the defendant). But this can be a vague mandate that leads some prosecutors to hand over as little evidence as possible. One result is that appellate courts find that prosecutors sometimes improperly withhold evidence from the defense, and therefore the guilty verdict is reversed and a new trial ordered. Note that this is the typical remedy—appellate reversal—and does not sanction the erring prosecutor. Only on rare occasions do prosecutors face sanctions from the bar association for failure to disclose evidence to the defense.

Conflict of interest is another ethical issue facing prosecutors (and defense attorneys as well). Prosecutors employed part-time, for example, may confront a host of ethical issues. In private practice, a lawyer may represent an individual, but if that person runs afoul of the law, then the prosecutor must recuse himself or herself. Conflicts of interest may also arise when the prosecutor leaves the office for private practice. As a general rule, the now-private lawyer may not represent anyone who was prosecuted while the lawyer was working for the prosecutor's office. Even if he or she had no contact with the case, the lawyer may not represent that individual defendant.

As explained above, prosecutors exercise a tremendous amount of discretion in the charging decision, and several ethical standards relate to how this discretion should be used. Prosecutors are not supposed to institute any criminal charges that are not supported by probable cause, although many prosecutors charge only cases they feel they can win by proving guilt beyond a reasonable doubt. The ambiguous nature of varying legal standards may lead to criticism that prosecutors unfairly failed to prosecute a case. Conversely, prosecutors may be criticized for unfairly prosecuting a defendant based on political motives.

The ethical issues surrounding prosecutors' discretion to seek the death penalty are often debated. Although only a few homicides are eligible for sentence of death (Chapter 14), prosecutors often must make a series of close calls in these cases to decide which defendants should face capital punishment. To ensure that these decisions are made in an evenhanded manner, many big-city prosecutors' offices have a special review process. Moreover, the courts have imposed a proportionality requirement—that is, they seek information that the decision to seek the death penalty in a specific case is proportional to the decision in other cases. Although ethical issues like this one are at the forefront of the debate over capital punishment, appellate courts rarely find that prosecutors abused their discretion.

How much information to release to the public presents another ethical issue for prosecutors (Pollock, 2012). In the modern era, both the prosecution and the defense often try their cases in the press before a jury is picked. For this reason, judges often impose a gag order on high-profile cases (Chapter 13), prohibiting either side from releasing information to the press. In ordinary cases, only on rare occasions have judges found that prosecutors went too far in seeking to convince the public (meaning potential jurors) of the overwhelming guilt of the defendant. But, as the "Courts, Law, & Media" feature on the following page should make clear, even without prosecutorial misconduct, the media can inflame public sentiments through less-than-objective news coverage.

COURTS, LAW, & MEDIA

NANCY GRACE

"I absolutely cannot believe Caylee's death has gone unavenged" opined an obviously upset Nancy Grace. For months, the investigation and trial of Casey Anthony for allegedly killing her daughter and the media coverage of the trial had become so enmeshed it was hard to separate the two (Chapter 1). Indeed Nancy Grace provided the biting description of the defendant as the "tot mom." In announcing the not-guilty verdict, Nancy Grace no doubt expressed the sentiments of many of her viewers. But to her critics, it simply underscored her lack of objectivity—blurring the lines between journalism and advocacy.

According to the official HLN website (2012), *Nancy Grace* is television's only justice themed/interview/debate show, designed for those interested in the "breaking crime news of the day." Before becoming a TV commentator, Grace worked for nearly a decade in the Atlanta-Fulton County, Georgia District Attorney's office as a special prosecutor focusing on felony cases involving serial murder, serial rape, and serial child molestation. Nancy Grace describes the murder of her fiancé in 1979 as the impetus for her career as a prosecutor and victims' right advocate.

Nancy Grace's outspoken style attracts a wide following and good ratings, the key to the survival of any show on TV. But this same aggressive style and an attitude that often comes across as preaching that "the prosecutor is always right" has also drawn condemnation. In the words of a journalist, "the boundaries between illusion and reality, journalism and advocacy, fair trial and free press, all seemed elusive" during Nancy Grace's announcement of the not-guilty verdict in the Casey Anthony trial (Garvin, 2011). One law professor is even harsher accusing her of rushing to prejudice every case, blatantly taking sides, and being intellectually dishonest (Bainbridge, 2011).

Critics also note that Nancy Grace made the wrong calls in other high-profile cases. In the Duke lacrosse case (see chapter opener), she was quick to take the side of the victim. But in the end, the prosecution ended in disaster. Similarly, she rushed to judgment when Dominique Strauss-Kahn—the high ranking French finance minister—was accused of raping a New York hotel employee, only to see that case dropped because of contradictions in the victim's stories (Chapter 9). Moreover, as a prosecutor she was twice cited by the Georgia Supreme Court for prosecutorial misconduct.

Nancy Grace responds to criticism by stating, "If you don't like my coverage then don't watch it" (Alvarez, 2011). And in a strange twist she has defended herself in a book with the improbable title *Objection!: How High-Priced Defense Attorney's Celebrity Defendants, and a 24/7 Media Have Hijacked Our Criminal Justice System* (Grace, 2005). Some wonder if she has confused cause and effect.

Do you think that media distort or sensationalize criminal justice processes? How? In light of the First Amendment protections of free speech and a free press, what might be done to curtail media figures from interfering with the rights of the accused?

PROSECUTORS AND COURTROOM WORK GROUPS

Prosecutors spend most of their time working directly with other members of the courtroom work group. Even when interviewing witnesses or conducting legal research, the prosecutor is anticipating the reactions of judges and defense attorneys. Thus, the activities of prosecutors can be understood only within the setting of the courtroom work group (Worden, 1990).

The prosecutor is the most important member of the work group. Prosecutors set the agenda for judges and defense attorneys by exercising discretion over the types of cases filed, the nature of acceptable plea agreements, and the sentences to be handed out. Prosecutors also control the flow of information about cases by providing access to police arrest reports, laboratory tests, and defendants' criminal histories. By stressing certain information or withholding facts, prosecutors can influence the decisions of judges and defense attorneys.

As the dominant force in the courtroom work group, prosecutors clearly set the tone for plea bargaining. This is how one veteran explained his perspective:

I get so damned pissed off and tired of these guys who come in and cry, "My guy's got a job" or "My guy's about to join the army," when he's got a rap sheet as long as your arm. His guy's a loser, and he's wailing on my desk about what a fine man he is. What really wins me is the guy who comes in and says, "O.K., what are we going to do with my criminal today? I know he has no redeeming social value. He's been a bad son of a bitch all his life, so just let me know your position. But frankly, you know, my feeling is that this is just not the case to nail him on. We all know if he does something serious, he's going." And before long the guy who approaches it this way has you wrapped around his little finger (Carter, 1974, p. 87).

Prosecutors' actions, in turn, are influenced by other members of the courtroom work group.

Through the socialization process, assistant district attorneys internalize the accepted ways of doing things in the courthouse, learning to plead cases out on the basis of normal crimes (discussed in Chapter 5). Prosecutors who stray too far from the shared norms of the courtroom work group can expect sanctions. The judge may informally indicate that the state is pushing too hard for a harsh sentence or may publicly chastise a district attorney in open court, thus threatening the attorney's status among peers. The defense attorney may not agree to a prosecutor's request for a continuance or may use delaying tactics to impair the state's efforts to schedule cases, thus further disrupting the prosecutor's efforts to move cases. (The prosecutor, of course, is not without countersanctions. These will be discussed in the next two chapters.)

Operating within the constraints of the courtroom work group, effective assistant DAs are those who make tactical decisions that maximize their objectives. Experienced prosecutors, for example, know which defense attorneys can be trusted, granting these people greater access to information about the case and listening to them more when the case involves unusual circumstances. Prosecutors also quickly learn the tendencies of the judge. No prosecutor can afford to ignore how the judge wishes the courtroom to be run.

Although the prosecutor is generally the most important member of the courtroom work group, work groups show considerable variability. Differences between one community and the next abound, and in big-city courthouses, these differences often exist from courtroom to courtroom. Conflicting goals and varying political styles are two factors that account for contrasting work groups.

Conflicting Goals and Contrasting Work Groups

On the surface, the goals of prosecutors seem the model of simplicity: Their job is to convict the guilty. But a closer examination shows that the goals are not as clear-cut as they first appear. Prosecutors define their main job in different ways. Some stress working closely with law enforcement agencies. Thus, they serve as police advocates in court and stress punishing the guilty. Others emphasize their role as court-based officials. Thus, they define their job as impartially administering justice and emphasize securing convictions (Delsohn, 2003a,b; Eisenstein, 1978; LaFave, 1965). The uncertainties about which goals should come first have historically produced marked diversity among prosecutors, with some prosecutors' offices focusing on the administration of justice, and others focusing on an adversarial model (McDonald, 1979; Utz, 1979). Such differences in philosophies still exist today (Baker, 1999; Delsohn, 2003a,b), although media attention has often focused on prosecutors whose "win at all costs" mentality has eroded public confidence in those who are supposed to advocate for justice (Roberts & Stratton, 2008).

Political Styles and Contrasting Work Groups

The prosecutor's role within the courtroom work group also needs to be understood within the broader political context in which the office functions. This was the conclusion of Roy Flemming's (1990) study of nine prosecutors' offices in three states. Because they exercise broad discretion (in the context of decentralization and local autonomy), elected prosecutors choose political styles. This choice is both personal and strategic. It depends first on the prosecutor's satisfaction or dissatisfaction with the office's status within the courthouse community. It also depends on the prosecutor's perception of the value of conflict as a means of changing the office's status.

Prosecutors satisfied with the status of the office adopt an "office conservator" style. Office conservators accept the status quo. Continuity is often a key consideration; former assistants are elected with the blessings of the previous officeholder and the support of the local political establishment. Once in office, conservators do not deliberately step on toes; if they push for change, it generally comes as a response to the requests of others. Montgomery County, Pennsylvania, provides an example. The newly elected DA retained the preexisting staff intact. He did fashion some guidelines regarding guilty pleas, but they were flexible, symbolic gestures—signals that a changing of the guard had taken place, not a revolution. Most important, however, the DA tolerated the judges' traditional dominance of the courthouse community.

Prosecutors who are less content with the status of their offices face a more complicated set of choices. They must decide whether conflict is an effective tool for them to use. These "courthouse insurgents" are very dissatisfied with the status quo and are prepared to do battle to change it. They do not shy away from open conflict, nor do they hesitate to challenge the courthouse community in pursuit of their goals. DuPage County, Illinois, is an example. The state's attorney was an outsider to the county who won the office by narrowly defeating the Republican party's favored candidate in a bitterly fought, mudslinging primary. Perceiving that the office failed to stand up to defense attorneys, the new state's attorney turned the office inside out. Immediately after election, he eliminated the part-time staff, hired aggressive assistants, and instituted policies severely restricting plea bargaining. Moreover, the insurgent DA minced no words in publicly criticizing judges and defense attorneys.

"Policy reformers" are also dissatisfied with the status quo, but unlike courthouse insurgents, they are cautious, often conciliatory, in their approach. Upon taking office, they gradually move to tighten their offices' guilty-plea policies, encourage more assertive attitudes among their assistants, and try

to develop innovative approaches to prosecutorial work. They do not shrink from trying to alter their relationships with judges. Erie, Pennsylvania, provides a case in point. Embittered by the decline of the office when he left as an assistant to enter private practice, the new Erie prosecutor bucked the political establishment and decisively trounced the incumbent in the Democratic party primary to win the office. However, his plans to restore the respect of the office clashed with the docket policies of the court. Rather than fighting openly, the Erie DA mounted an indirect campaign to wrest control of the docket from the judges.

Flemming's study highlights two aspects of prosecutorial behavior that are not immediately obvious. First, differences in political styles cross party lines; these are not Republican or Democratic styles. Second, differences in political styles are not necessarily constant through time. In several communities, a district attorney was initially elected as an insurgent or a policy reformer but through the years came to adopt a conservator style.

THE EXPANDING DOMAIN OF THE PROSECUTOR

The domain of the prosecutor has been expanding throughout the past century, and pressures to place greater authority in the hands of the prosecutor are likely to continue (Davis, 2007; Worrall & Borakove, 2008). Within the fragmented, sometimes non-system of criminal justice, the prosecutor is in the best position to provide coordination. Moreover, with crime as a dominant issue in elections, the prosecutor is uniquely able to capitalize on his or her role as the community's chief law enforcement official and to promise the voters to expand crime-fighting efforts.

We will examine two types of programs that exemplify the contemporary expansion of the domain of the prosecutor: improving police–prosecutor relationships and community prosecution.

Improving Police–Prosecutor Relationships

Police and prosecutors are commonly viewed as members of the same crime-fighting team, but a closer look reveals a more complex reality (Harris, 2011). Police and prosecutors have differing perspectives on the law. To the police, the case is closed when the suspect is arrested, but prosecutors stress that they often need additional information to win in court (Stanko, 1981).

Inadequate police reports present a classic illustration of noncoordination within the criminal justice system. The thoroughness of police investigations and the quality of their arrests directly affect the likelihood of the prosecutor's obtaining a conviction. In a survey of 225 (mostly big-city) prosecutors, 66 percent cited inadequate police preparation of crime reports as a major problem in their offices (Nugent & McEwen, 1988). Commonly mentioned problems were that names and addresses of victims and witnesses were lacking, full details of how the crime was committed were missing, and vital laboratory reports were not forwarded on time. Faced with incomplete or inaccurate police reports, the prosecutor may be forced to drop charges (see Chapter 10).

Police and prosecutors in several jurisdictions have adopted strategies to improve coordination and communication between the two groups (Buchanan, 1989). In Indianapolis, for example, the prosecutor has funded a computer messaging system that enables attorneys in the office to transmit notes, case dispositions, and subpoenas directly to police officers at their work locations. In Alameda County, California, and Montgomery County, Maryland, "street jump" narcotics officers and prosecutors consult frequently, both in person and over the telephone, to build cases that meet the requirements of the search-and-seizure law.

A few agencies have gone further, institutionalizing teamwork and making communication between investigators and prosecutors a top priority. In Multnomah County, Oregon, the Organized Crime/Narcotics Task Force has brought together 12 investigators from several area agencies and two prosecutors from the district attorney's office, instituting daily informal contact about the progress of pending cases. Moreover, prosecutors act as consultants to the police during the investigative phase. Thus, investigators can get answers to difficult legal questions in a few minutes, just by walking down the hall.

Programs like these indicate that, despite a long history of difficulties, some agencies apparently are bridging the gap. But a word of caution is in order. No research to date has systematically evaluated these programs to indicate their overall effectiveness. Until such research is conducted, no predictions can be made about which programs are likely to be effective in other communities.

Community Prosecution

The historic image of the district attorney stresses case processing: The DA files charges and doggedly pursues a conviction. But this traditional image is becoming blurred as locally elected prosecutors respond to a wide variety of social problems such as domestic violence (Chapter 9), drug abuse (Chapter 10), disorder on city streets (Chapter 4), and growing numbers of juvenile offenders (Chapter 17). In responding to these types of social problems, which often reflect disintegrating neighborhoods, prosecutors today are more likely to stress problem-oriented approaches (Center for Court Innovation, 2012b). At times, the specifics are hard to pin down because the approaches are truly shaped to local needs rather than to national program guides (Porter, 2011; Coles & Earle, 1996). But these new approaches have three elements in common (Center for Court Innovation 2012b; Jacoby, 1995):

- Prosecutors have the responsibility not only to prosecute cases but also to reduce crime.

- The most effective results are obtained within small, manageable geographic areas, which often means working out of neighborhood offices.

- Change is more likely to occur through cooperative efforts or partnerships rather than through prosecutorial dictates. In many instances, community stakeholders help set the crime-fighting agenda.

The Neighborhood District Attorney approach in Multnomah County (Portland, Oregon) provides a case in point. Business leaders in Lloyd District (an inner-city neighborhood) called for more police protection as well as the assignment of a special prosecutor to the district (for which they provided one year's funding). Citizen demands were invariably expressed in traditional law enforcement terms—more police, more arrests, and more convictions, particularly

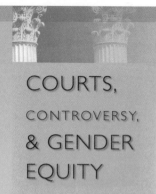

COURTS, CONTROVERSY, & GENDER EQUITY

ARE SEXUAL ASSAULTS AGAINST WOMEN UNDERPROSECUTED?

To many critics, the criminal justice system does not take allegations of rape/sexual assault seriously enough. On the other hand, the Duke lacrosse player sexual assault prosecution serves as a cautionary tale, because in these types of cases, stories of victims can change and the physical evidence does not always corroborate the victim's version of the truth. Similarly, a New York prosecutor was quick to prevent Dominique Strauss-Kahn, the powerful head of the International Monetary Fund, from leaving the country after he was accused of sexual assault by a hotel maid. Three months later, the criminal charges were dropped because the victim told too many inconsistent stories to prosecutors. But Strauss-Kahn's chance to be elected President of France was over (Smith-Spark, 2011).

Sexual assault is one of the most visible gender equity controversies in the criminal justice system. Along with domestic violence (see Chapter 9) and gender bias in the courtroom (Chapter 5), it is the topic that feminists have most identified as involving systematic bias throughout the criminal justice system. A report of the U.S. Senate Judiciary Committee—*The Response to Rape: Detours on the Road to*

Equal Justice (1993)—forcefully concludes that the justice system creates serious barriers to women who are sexually assaulted. Assessing the continuing validity of these arguments approximately 20 years later is difficult because the statistics on the number of sexual assaults each year, the percentage of them reported to the police, the number resulting in criminal charges, and how many cases result in conviction vary widely.

When testifying before a subcommittee of the U.S. Senate's Judiciary Committee, Michelle Dempsey, a professor at Villanova Law School, argued that rape "is one of the most underreported offense in the United States with empirical studies estimating that merely 15-20 percent of cases are reported" (Financial Express, 2010). Professor Dempsey cited the findings of a major study using data collected from the National Violence Against Women Survey (Tjaden & Thoennes, 2006). Official statistics suggest that the reporting rate for the crime of rape has increased by nearly 35 percent in recent years (Truman, 2011). Consider that in 2010, a total of 188,380 rapes were reported in the National Crime Victimization Survey, 84,767 (45 percent) of which were reported to police according to the FBI in its annual publication, *Crime in the United States* (2011). Of course, these statistics are based on official data which, in turn, are affected by police actions.

The reporting rate for rape does not tell the whole story. According to the FBI (2011), only 40 percent of rapes

---

of repeat offenders. The Lloyd District special prosecutor, however, quickly saw that people's concerns were more immediate than he had imagined. "They wanted something done about prostitution, public drinking, drug use, vandalism, [minor] assaults, littering garbage, and 'car prowls' (thefts from cars)" (Boland, 1996, p. 36). Although none of these problems (except thefts from cars) fit traditional notions of serious crime, they nonetheless raise serious concern among citizens. (This approach clearly emphasizes the activities of the local courts, discussed in Chapter 4.)

As the program developed, several distinctive features became apparent. For one, the assistant DA used the laws in new ways, including using civil remedies to fight crime (see Chapter 2).

Perhaps most important, the program was problem-oriented: Rather than focusing on individual arrestees, the Neighborhood District Attorney addressed problems from a larger perspective, with long-term goals in mind. Ultimately, what emerged was an approach, not a program. Rather than being guided by clear-cut procedures, Portland has adopted a highly flexible organization that can meet the different needs of different neighborhoods (Boland, 1996).

Overall, community prosecution stresses a proactive approach: Rather than reacting to crime through prosecution, these programs stress crime prevention (Coles & Kelling, 1999). And often the crimes stressed are minor ones that are nonetheless serious irritants to local residents (Goldkamp, Irons-Guynn, & Weiland, 2002).

reported to police are cleared by arrest. Prosecutors, in turn, file charges in only about half of the cases in which arrests are made (Spohn, Beichner, Frenzel, & Holleran 2002). And, of the cases prosecuted, only half result in a felony conviction (Cohen & Kyckelhahn, 2010). Critics argue that these figures support the conclusion that sexual assaults are underprosecuted. Some research supports this position, while other research does not.

- McCahill, Meyer, and Fischman (1979) and Kerstetter (1990) found that police tend to take reported rapes by strangers more seriously than reports of rapes by people known to the victim. Prosecutors evidence the same bias when deciding whether to prosecute cases (Battelle Memorial Institute Law and Justice Center, 1977; Vera Institute of Justice, 1981). Other researchers, however, have not found support for these propositions (see Spohn & Holleran, 2000).

- Police or prosecutorial discretion in rape cases is often guided by whether the victim is someone whom a judge or jury would find credible. But in assessing credibility, some researchers argue that the character of the victim (and sometimes the accused as well)—are assessed using stereotypes (Stanko, 1988). Similarly, unfair judgments about victims' moral character are often made on the bases of their behavior just prior to the alleged sexual assault, including factors such as how the victim

was dressed or whether the victim consumed alcohol or drugs (McCahill et al., 1979). In contrast, other researchers find little support for victim characteristics influencing prosecutorial charging decisions (Spohn & Holleran, 2000). Rather, legally relevant evidentiary factors, such as the victim's ability to identify the assailant and the presence of physical or medical evidence to corroborate the victim's accusation are the salient factors that explain prosecutorial decisions whether to file or drop charges (Holleran, Beichner, & Spohn, 2010; Horney & Spohn, 1996).

The often ideological debate aside, a new program shows how the legal and medical community can do a better job in sexual assault cases. The SANE (Sexual Assault Nurse Examiners) program began by training hospital nurses in evidence collection, injury-detection methods, and ways of avoiding re-traumatizing a victim during the examination. Researchers found statistically significant increases in guilty pleas or convictions. According to one detective, the program was successful because the quality of the medical forensic exams improved (Bulman, 2009).

What do you think? Are sexual assaults underprosecuted? If so, is the reason because criminal justice officials fail to adequately consider the plight of the victim or because these cases are more likely to have evidence problems?

CONCLUSION

Prosecutors in the United States are powerful, but, as with all other governmental officials, there are limits. In the Duke lacrosse case, the state's Attorney General took over the case and eventually dismissed all charges because of a lack of evidence. Moreover, the North Carolina Bar Association charged Nifong with lying to the judge, withholding key DNA evidence from the defense, and making inflammatory statements to the public. The North Carolina Supreme Court agreed and disbarred him.

The Duke lacrosse case and the Supreme Court decision in *Connick v. Thompson* are examples of prosecutorial misconduct and efforts to control prosecutorial abuse. But these examples must be

assessed within the broader context. For years, courts have granted prosecutors wide-ranging discretionary powers. The exercise of this discretion shapes the dynamics of the courthouse. In effect, all others involved in the criminal courts—judges, defense attorneys, probation officers, juries, witnesses, and so on—must react to the decisions made by the prosecutor. But the law imposes few formal restrictions on the use of these discretionary powers. Prosecutors' offices are decentralized, autonomous, and headed by locally elected officials.

This does not mean that prosecutorial discretion is uncontrolled; rather, it is influenced by other members of the courtroom work group. Through the socialization process and the occasional application of sanctions, new prosecutors are educated in the norms of the courtroom work group.

Chapter Review

LO1 **1.** Discuss the two major characteristics of prosecutors in the United States.

The role of the prosecutor involves broad discretion and decentralization.

LO2 **2.** Describe the three most important entities in federal prosecution.

The three most important entities in federal prosecution are the U.S. Solicitor General, the Criminal Division of the U.S. Department of Justice, and the offices of 94 U.S. Attorneys.

LO3 **3.** Identify the three somewhat overlapping agencies involved in prosecution in state courts.

The three major agencies involved in prosecution in state courts are the state Attorney General, the chief prosecutor and the local prosecutor.

LO4 **4.** Explain the major factors affecting the work life of assistant district attorneys.

Assistant district attorneys are typically young lawyers who must learn how law in action is practiced, seek promotions to prosecuting more serious crimes, and are often loosely supervised.

LO5 **5.** Analyze the principal factors affecting prosecutorial ethics.

As governmental officials, prosecutors are largely immune from civil lawsuits and if an error is made, an appellate court reversal is the typical remedy.

LO6 **6.** Outline two major examples of the expanding domain of the prosecutor.

Programs aimed at improving police–prosecutor relationships and community prosecution are two contemporary examples of the expanding domain of the prosecutor.

Critical Thinking Questions

1. Robert Misner (1996) argued that given the fragmented nature of the criminal justice system (see Chapter 1), over the past 30 years responsibility has increasingly been centralized in the hands of the district attorney. What factors support this assessment?

2. Should state attorneys general be given authority to supervise locally elected district attorneys? How would such increased authority alter the criminal justice system?

3. How much authority should assistant district attorneys be given? As licensed attorneys, should they be given a large amount of discretion to dispose of cases according to

their best judgment, or should they have more limited authority so that the office has a uniform policy?

4. Of the three political styles—office conservator, courthouse insurgent, and policy reformer—which best describes your local prosecutor?

5. Community prosecution stresses the need for the prosecutor to reach out to the community, but what does "community" mean? Is this reform based on a naive assumption that all members of the same geographic entity share similar views? How might different communities within the same city (or perhaps county) stress different law-enforcement priorities?

Key Terms

absolute immunity   162

local prosecutor   158

officer of the court   150

prosecutor   150

qualified immunity   163

state Attorney General   156

U.S. Attorney General   155

U.S. Attorneys   156

U.S. Solicitor General   155

Web Resources

Go to the *America's Courts and the Criminal Justice System* companion website at

http://www.cengage.com/criminaljustice/neubauer,

where you will find more resources to help you study.

Resources include web exercises, quizzing, and flash cards.

For Further Reading

Banks, Cyndi. *Criminal Justice Ethics: Theory and Practice.* Thousand Oaks, CA: Sage, 2008.

Davis, Angela. *Arbitrary Justice: The Power of the American Prosecutor.* New York: Oxford University Press, 2007.

Delsohn, Gary. *The Prosecutors: Kidnap, Rape, Murder, Justice: One Year behind the Scenes in a Big-City DA's Office.* New York: Plume, 2003.

Delsohn, Gary. *The Prosecutors: A Year in the Life of a District Attorney's Office.* New York: Dutton/Penguin, 2003.

Frohman, Lisa. *Prosecutors and Prosecution.* Burlington, VT: Ashgate, 2008.

Heath, Brad, and Kevin McCoy. "Prosecutors' Conduct Can Tip the Scales." *USA Today.* September 23, 2010.

Markovits, Daniel. *A Modern Legal Ethics: Adversary Advocacy in a Democratic Age.* Princeton, NJ: Princeton University Press, 2008.

Mason, Caleb. "The Police-Prosecutor Relationship and the No-Contact Rule: Conflicting Incentives after *Montejo*

v. Louisiana and *Maryland v. Shatzer*. *Cleveland Law Review,* 58: 747–780, 2010.

Sanders, Andrew (Ed.). *Prosecution in Common Law Jurisdictions.* Brookfield, VT: Dartmouth, 1996.

Senjo, Scott. *Sexual Deviancy and the Law: Legal Regulation of Human Sexuality.* Dubuque, IA: Kendall Hunt, 2011.

Straus, Sarena. *Bronx D.A.: True Stories from the Sex Crimes and Domestic Violence Unit.* Fort Lee, NJ: Barricade Books, 2006.

Suthers, John. *No Higher Calling, No Greater Responsibility: A Prosecutor Makes His Case.* Goldon, CO: Fulcrum, 2008.

Train, Arthur. *True Stories of Crime from the District Attorney's Office.* Charleston, SC: BiblioBazar, 2010.

Worrall, John, and M. Elaine Nugent-Borakove (Eds.). *The Changing Role of the American Prosecutor.* Albany, NY: SUNY Press, 2008.

7 Defense Attorneys

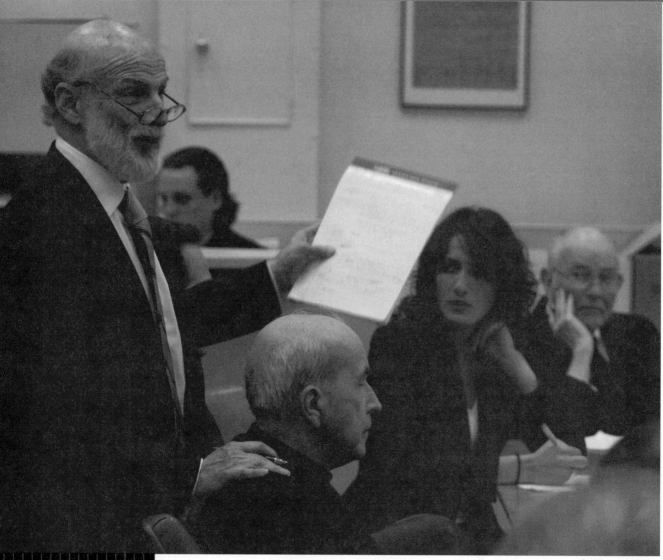

© AP Photo/Andy Morrison

Defense attorney **Alan Konop** addresses the jury with his hand on the shoulder of the Reverend Gerald Robinson, who was accused of killing a nun in a hospital chapel 26 years before his trial date. He was convicted at the age of 68 and sentenced to 15 years to life in prison. His conviction was affirmed by an Ohio appeals court. ■

Chapter Outline

THE RIGHT TO COUNSEL
Nonfelony Criminal Prosecutions
Stages of the Criminal Process

CASE CLOSE-UP: *Gideon v. Wainwright* and the **Right to Counsel**

Ineffective Assistance of Counsel
Self-Representation

DEFENSE ATTORNEYS AND COURTROOM WORK GROUPS
Rewards and Sanctions
Variations in Cooperation
An Assessment

THE CRIMINAL BAR
Diversity and Stratification of the Legal
    Profession
Environment of Practice

PROVIDING INDIGENTS WITH ATTORNEYS
Assigned Counsel
Contract Systems

Courts, Controversy, & Economic Inequality
Are We Spending Too Little or Too Much on Indigent Defense?

Public Defender
Assessing the Merits of Public Defenders

LAWYERS AND CLIENTS
Lawyers' Views on Their Clients
Defendants' Views on Their Lawyers

DEFENSE ATTORNEY ETHICS

Courts, Law, & Media:
Boston Legal (ABC Television, 2004–2008)

Defense Attorneys • Defense Attorneys • Defense Att
Attorneys • Defense Attorneys • Defense Attorneys •

Learning Objectives

After reading this chapter, you should be able to:

LO1 Interpret the four major legal issues surrounding the right to counsel.

LO2 Discuss how the courtroom work group affects how defense attorneys represent their clients.

LO3 Explain why most lawyers do not represent criminal defendants.

LO4 Compare and contrast the three systems of providing indigents with court-appointed attorneys.

LO5 Recognize possible tensions between lawyers and clients.

LO6 Analyze the importance of legal ethics to the defense of criminal defendants.

Clarence Earl Gideon had been in and out of prison since the age of 14. His brushes with the law had been minor—public drunkenness and petty theft primarily—but now he faced a much more serious charge: burglarizing a poolroom in Bay Harbor. As he stood before the judge, he appeared to be a shipwreck of a man; his wrinkled face and trembling hands suggested a person much older than 51. Yet "a flame still burned inside Clarence Earl Gideon ... he had a fierce feeling that the State of Florida had treated him wrongly" (Lewis, 1972, p. 6). He demanded that the court appoint a lawyer to defend him. The trial judge flatly refused; unrepresented by counsel, Gideon was found guilty. But on appeal he was luckier. The Supreme Court plucked this obscure case from the bowels of the criminal justice system to issue a landmark decision: All indigent defendants were entitled to court-appointed counsel in felony trials. *Gideon v. Wainwright* (1963) was not only a victory for Clarence Earl Gideon but, more important, it sent shock waves through the criminal justice system.

The Court's decision in *Gideon* underscores the importance of lawyers in the criminal justice system. But what role do defense attorneys play in representing their clients? Some view defense attorneys as fighting to free falsely accused clients. Others, though, often contrast this favorable image with a less complimentary one of the defense attorney as a conniver who uses legal technicalities to free the guilty.

This chapter assesses these conflicting images in terms of the daily realities of the small proportion of the legal profession who represent defendants accused of violating the criminal law. The picture is a complicated one. Some defense attorneys suffer from the shortcomings mentioned by their critics; others do not. But all face day-to-day problems and challenges not usually encountered by the bulk of American lawyers who represent higher-status clients. The key topics of this chapter are the factors influencing the type of legal assistance available to those who appear in criminal courts: the legal right to counsel, the tasks defense attorneys perform, their relationship with courtroom work groups, the nature of the criminal bar, the relationship between lawyer and client, and finally, the various systems for providing legal assistance to the poor.

THE RIGHT TO COUNSEL

Like many other provisions of the Constitution, the Sixth Amendment has a different meaning today than it did when it was first ratified. In a landmark decision, the U.S. Supreme Court held that, based on the Sixth Amendment's provision of **right to counsel**, indigent defendants charged with a felony are entitled to the services of a lawyer paid for by the government (see "Case Close-Up: *Gideon v. Wainwright* and the Right to Counsel"). Later, the Sixth Amendment right to counsel was extended to juvenile court proceedings as well (*In re Gault*, 1967). But as so often happens, answering one question raised several new ones. In the wake of the *Gideon* decision, the Court wrestled with issues involving the right to counsel with regard to: (1) nonfelony criminal prosecutions, (2) stages of the criminal process, (3) ineffective assistance of counsel, and (4) self-representation. The "Key Development" feature below summarizes key cases affecting the Sixth Amendment right to counsel.

Nonfelony Criminal Prosecutions

The *Gideon* ruling was limited to state felony prosecutions. In *Argersinger v. Hamlin* (1972), the Court refused to extend the newly discovered constitutional right to court-appointed counsel to those accused of minor violations (misdemeanor or ordinance violations), holding that "absent a knowing and intelligent waiver, no person may be imprisoned for any offense, whether classified as petty, misdemeanor, or felony, unless he was represented by counsel." Later, the justices narrowed the *Argersinger* decision, ruling that a defendant is guaranteed the right to legal counsel, paid by the state if necessary, only in cases that actually lead to imprisonment, not in all cases in which imprisonment is a potential penalty (*Scott v. Illinois*, 1979). The net effect of the *Scott* case was to limit the right to counsel in nonfelony prosecutions, particularly if the guilty faced only paying a fine. Nonetheless, indigents are entitled to a court-appointed attorney even if facing only a suspended jail term for a minor charge (*Alabama v. Shelton*, 2002).

We know very little about how local courts actually provide indigents in nonfelony prosecutions with court-appointed counsel, but there is every indication that compliance is less than full. The National Association of Criminal Defense Lawyers (2009) examined seven states and reported that counsel was not being appointed in some cases. Moreover, 30 percent of misdemeanor defendants who were sentenced to incarceration reported that they were not represented by counsel (Hashimoto, 2010).

Stages of the Criminal Process

The *Gideon* ruling spawned another important question: When in the criminal process does the right to counsel begin (and end)? Note that the Sixth Amendment provides for the right to counsel in "all criminal prosecutions," so it is not limited to the trial itself. The Supreme Court adopted a "critical stages" test, under which a defendant is entitled to legal representation at every stage of prosecution "where substantial rights of the accused may be affected," requiring the "guiding hand of counsel" (*Mempa v. Rhay*, 1967). As Table 7.1 summarizes, indigent defendants have a right to court-appointed counsel from the time they first appear before a judge until sentence is pronounced and the first appeal concluded. (The only exception is the grand jury, whose peculiar practices will be examined in Chapter 10.) As a general rule, defendants have a Sixth Amendment

KEY DEVELOPMENTS IN THE RIGHT TO COUNSEL

Sixth Amendment (1791)	"In all criminal prosecutions the accused shall enjoy the right…to have the assistance of counsel for his defence."
Powell v. Alabama (1932)	Indigent defendants in a capital case in state court have a right to court-appointed counsel.
Johnson v. Zerbst (1938)	Indigent felony defendants in federal court are entitled to court-appointed counsel.
Betts v. Brady (1942)	Indigent defendants in a noncapital case in state court have no right to appointed counsel.
Gideon v. Wainwright (1963)	Indigent felony defendants have the right to appointed counsel (*Betts* overruled).
Douglas v. California (1963)	Indigents have a right to court-appointed counsel during the first appeal.
In re Gault (1967)	Juveniles are covered by the Sixth Amendment's right to counsel.
Argersinger v. Hamlin (1972)	Indigent nonfelony defendants have the right to appointed counsel if they are facing jail time.
Faretta v. California (1975)	Defendants have the right to self-representation.
Scott v. Illinois (1979)	Although no indigent criminal defendant may be sentenced to a term of imprisonment unless he or she was afforded the right to assistance of appointed defense counsel, trial courts are not required to appoint counsel for a defendant charged with a statutory offense for which imprisonment upon conviction is authorized, but will not actually be imposed.
Strickland v. Washington (1984)	A defense attorney is ineffective only if proceedings were unfair and the outcome would have been different.
Wiggins v. Smith (2003)	The failure of an inexperienced defense attorney to conduct a reasonable investigation of the defendant's troubled personal background constituted ineffective assistance of counsel.
Halbert v. Michigan (2005)	Indigent defendants who plead guilty are entitled to state-paid legal help on appeal.
Schriro v. Landrigan (2007)	During the penalty phase of a death penalty trial, the defendant refused to allow his attorney to present mitigating evidence about organic brain damage. The defendant was not denied effective assistance of counsel under *Strickland*.
Indiana v. Edwards (2008)	A mentally ill defendant who is nonetheless competent to stand trial is not necessarily competent to dispense with a lawyer and represent himself.
Padilla v. Kentucky (2010)	Failing to inform one's client that a plea carries a risk of deportation constitutes ineffective assistance of counsel under *Strickland*.
Missouri vs. Frye and Lafler vs. Cooper (2012)	Defense counsel has the duty to communicate formal offers from the prosecution to accept a plea on terms and conditions that may be favorable to the accused, and defendants have a right to competent advice from a lawyer on whether to accept or reject such an offer.

CASE CLOSE-UP

GIDEON v. WAINWRIGHT AND THE RIGHT TO COUNSEL

From his prison cell, Clarence Earl Gideon drafted a petition that, despite the garbled prose of a man with no real education, nonetheless raised a major legal principle:

> When at the time of the petitioner's trial he ask the lower court for the aid of counsel, the court refused this aid. Petitioner told the court that this [Supreme] Court made decision to the effect that all citizens tried for a felony crime should have aid of counsel. The lower court ignored this plea. (Lewis, 1972)

Every year thousands of pauper petitions like this are sent to the Supreme Court; few are ever heard. But this petition struck a responsive chord. The Court signaled the importance of the issue when it appointed Abe Fortas, one of the best-known lawyers in Washington, D.C., to represent Gideon. (Fortas would later be appointed to the Court.)

In what became officially known as *Gideon v. Wainwright,* the Court forcefully noted that "in our adversary system of criminal justice, any person, hauled into court, who is too poor to hire a lawyer, cannot be assured a fair trial unless counsel is provided for him. This seems to us to be an obvious truth. . . ."

The Sixth Amendment states that "in all criminal prosecutions, the accused shall enjoy the right . . . to have the assistance of counsel for his defence." As written by the framers more than 200 years ago, this constitutionally protected right to counsel meant only that the judge could not prevent a defendant from bringing a lawyer to court. (In England, defendants had been convicted despite requests to have their lawyers present.) Thus, the Sixth Amendment affected only those who could afford to hire their own lawyers.

Beginning in the 1930s, the Supreme Court took a more expansive view of the right to counsel.

Criminal defendants in federal cases were entitled to a court-appointed lawyer if they were too poor to hire their own. But a different rule prevailed in the state courts. Only defendants accused of a capital offense were entitled to court-appointed counsel; indigent defendants charged with ordinary felonies or misdemeanors were not (*Betts v. Brady*, 1942). Thus, a significant number of defendants in state courts had to face the legal maze of criminal proceedings by themselves.

Gideon v. Wainwright (1963) significantly expanded the legal meaning of the right to counsel. As occasionally happens, the Court reversed its earlier precedent in *Betts*:

> That the government hires lawyers to prosecute and defendants who have the money hire lawyers to defend are the strongest indications of the widespread belief that lawyers in criminal courts are necessities, not luxuries. The right of one charged with crime to counsel may not be deemed fundamental and essential for fair trials in some countries, but it is in ours.

Now, all indigent defendants charged with a felony were entitled to the services of a lawyer paid by the government, irrespective of whether they were on trial in state or federal court.

Gideon proved to be a major transforming event in the American criminal justice system. It was the first major decision of the Warren Court's revolution in criminal justice. But unlike other decisions, it proved not to be controversial. The Court's rationale, focusing on basic fairness and the importance of lawyers, gave it widespread legitimacy. Moreover, *Gideon* focused on the need for a lawyer at the trial itself. Later decisions—*Miranda* in particular—restricted police gathering of evidence and proved to be highly contentious.

TABLE 7.1 ■ RIGHT TO COUNSEL DURING STEPS IN FELONY PROSECUTIONS

	Extent of Right	Supreme Court Case
Arrest	No lawyer required	
Initial appearance	Lawyer required if critical stage	*Rothgery v. Gillespie County* (2008)
Bail	Lawyer required if critical stage	*Coleman v. Alabama* (1970)
Charging	No lawyer required	
Preliminary hearing	Lawyer required	*Coleman v. Alabama* (1970)
Grand jury	No lawyer allowed	
Arraignment	Lawyer required	*Hamilton v. Alabama* (1961)
Interrogation (preindictment)	Lawyer on request	*Miranda v. Arizona* (1966)
Interrogation (postindictment)	Lawyer required	*Massiah v. United States* (1964)
Lineup (preindictment)	No lawyer required	*Kirby v. Illinois* (1972)
Lineup (postindictment)	Lawyer required	*United States. v. Wade* (1967)
Plea bargaining	Lawyer required	*Brady v. United States* (1970); *Tollett v. Henderson* (1973); *Missouri v. Frye* (2012)
Trial	Lawyer required	*Gideon v. Wainwright* (1963)
Sentencing	Lawyer required	*Mempa v. Rhay* (1967)
Probation revocation	Lawyer at court's discretion	*Gagnon v. Scarpelli* (1973)
Parole revocation	Lawyer at board's discretion	*Morrissey v. Brewer* (1972)
First appeal	Lawyer required	*Douglas v. California* (1963)
Discretionary appeal	No lawyer required	*Ross v. Moffitt* (1974)

© Cengage Learning

right to the assistance of counsel once any adversarial proceedings have begun (*Brewer v. Williams,* 1977; *Rothgery v. Gillespie County,* 2008).

The right to counsel in the pretrial stage is much more limited, however. Applying the critical-stages test, subsequent decisions held that defendants have the right to court-appointed counsel during custodial interrogations (*Miranda v. Arizona, 1966)* and police lineups (*Kirby v. Illinois,* 1972; *U.S. v. Wade,* 1967). However, merely being detained by the police is not sufficient grounds to guarantee a right to counsel (*United States v. Gouveia,* 1984). (The controversy surrounding the extension of the right to counsel in the police station will be examined in Chapter 11.)

In the companion cases of *Missouri v. Frye* (2012) and *Lafler v. Cooper* (2012), the Court held that defendants have a right to competent advice from a lawyer on whether to accept an offer to plead guilty in exchange for a lighter sentence. Specifically, defendants must be told of any formal plea offers from prosecutors that would result in a favorable deal and then be given competent advice about the consequences of rejecting a favorable offer.

The right to counsel also extends to certain post-trial proceedings, but as in pretrial proceedings, the right to counsel is more limited. Working on the assumption that a person's right to an appeal can be effective only if counsel is available, the Court held that indigents have the right to court-appointed counsel for the appeal (*Douglas v. California,* 1963), as well as free trial transcripts (*Griffin v. Illinois,* 1956). The Burger Court, however, rejected attempts to extend the *Douglas* ruling beyond the first appeal. Thus, in discretionary appeals and appeals to the Supreme Court, indigent defendants have no right to court-appointed counsel (*Ross v. Moffitt*, 1974).

The *Ross* decision has major consequences in death penalty cases (Chapter 14). The right to court-appointed counsel typically extends only to the first appeal (Chapter 16). But death penalty cases also undergo numerous post-appeal proceedings termed "postconviction remedies." Under *Ross*, defendants sentenced to death often must rely on voluntary counsel in pursuing these postconviction remedies. Some state supreme courts, however, have gone considerably further in mandating counsel for situations in which the Supreme Court has not required counsel under the Sixth Amendment. All states except Alabama provide some level of taxpayer-funded legal assistance (*Maples v. Thomas*, 2012; Mears, 2012).

Ineffective Assistance of Counsel

Is it enough to have a lawyer? Must the lawyer also be competent and effective? The Supreme Court has recognized the effective assistance of counsel as essential to the Sixth Amendment guarantee (*McMann v. Richardson*, 1970). The Court's most significant holding came in 1984 in *Strickland v. Washington*, in which an "objective standard of reasonableness" was set forth as the proper criterion to be applied in making a determination of the ineffectiveness of counsel. Speaking for the Court, former Justice Sandra Day O'Connor emphasized that the "benchmark for judging any claim of ineffectiveness must be whether counsel's conduct so undermined the proper functioning of the adversarial process that the trial cannot be relied on as having produced a just result." It is important to note that an attorney's decisions regarding trial strategy and tactics—such as the order of presentation of evidence; whether to cross-examine an adverse witness; whether to make an objection—all carry a strong presumption of competent performance. Indeed, the Supreme Court has said, "Strategic choices made after thorough investigation of law and facts relevant to plausible options are virtually unchallengeable" (*Knowles v. Mirzayance*, 2009). In short, appellate courts must reverse only if the proceedings were fundamentally

unfair and the outcome would have been different if counsel had not been ineffective.

This standard places a heavy burden on the claimant; few appellate courts reverse decisions on these grounds. Indeed, the Court held that a lawyer's failure to file an appeal did not necessarily constitute ineffective assistance of counsel (*Roe v. Flores-Ortega*, 2000). However, the Court appears to have a higher *Strickland* threshold in death penalty cases. The Court ordered a new sentencing hearing in a death penalty case because the inexperienced defense attorney failed to conduct a reasonable investigation of the defendant's troubled personal background (*Wiggins v. Smith*, 2003). Similarly, the Court overturned a Pennsylvania death sentence because the defense attorney failed to search the record for evidence that could have persuaded the jury to spare the defendant's life (*Rompilla v. Beard*, 2005). But not all appeals on these grounds are successful. During the penalty phase of a death penalty trial, the defendant refused to allow his attorney to present mitigating evidence about organic brain damage. The Court held that the defendant was not denied effective assistance of counsel under *Strickland* (*Schriro v. Landrigan*, 2007).

Self-Representation

Can defendants represent themselves if they wish? An important qualification was added to *Gideon* when the Supreme Court ruled that defendants have a constitutional right to self-representation. This means that criminal defendants have the right to proceed *pro se* (Latin for "on his or her own behalf").

The Court, however, did establish limits. Defendants who wish to represent themselves must show the trial judge that they have the ability to conduct the trial. The defendant need not have the skills and experience of a lawyer, and the judge may not deny self-representation simply because the defendant does not have expert knowledge of criminal law and procedure (*Faretta v. California*, 1975). This decision has been qualified by the Court's recognition that the trial judge may appoint standby counsel when defendants choose to represent themselves (*McKaskle v. Wiggins*, 1984). Standby counsel is available during the trial to consult with the defendant, but it is the defendant, not the standby lawyer, who makes the decisions.

Although self-representation occurs rarely, these cases have the potential to become media spectacles. Perhaps the oddest case of self-representation was that of Colin Ferguson. Ferguson fired into a crowded Long Island Railroad commuter train, killing 6 passengers and wounding 19 others. Ferguson claimed that he acted out of a sense of "black rage;" his lawyer argued he was insane. Ferguson then dismissed his court-appointed lawyer, who objected that the trial would become a complete circus because "a crazy man cannot represent himself." The prediction proved accurate (McQuiston, 1995). Broadcast nationwide, the trial, with its inevitable guilty verdict, was perceived as not a trial but a spectacle and underscored the limits of self-representation. More recently, Dr. Jack Kevorkian represented himself in an assisted suicide case in Michigan, and Zacarias Moussaoui represented himself against charges that he was the 20th participant in the terrorist attack of September 11 (Chapter 3).

A recent case proved that the Court appears ready to limit self-representation in bizarre situations. The Court held that a mentally ill defendant who is nonetheless competent to stand trial is not necessarily competent to dispense with a lawyer and represent himself (*Indiana v. Edwards*, 2008).

An empirical study, however, challenges the conventional wisdom that there is no good reason for a defendant to choose self-representation. *Pro se* defendants fare as well as represented defendants 80 percent of the time, and most do not suffer from mental illness (Hashimoto, 2007).

DEFENSE ATTORNEYS AND COURTROOM WORK GROUPS

Lawyers are expected to be advocates for their clients' cases, arguing for legal innocence. As one defense counsel phrased it, "If the attorney does not appear to be taking the side of the defendant, then no one will" (Neubauer, 1974b, p. 73). But the zealous advocacy of a client's case is not the same thing as winning at all costs. As a member of the

legal profession, a lawyer's advocacy of a client's case is limited by professional obligations. Like prosecutors, defense attorneys are officers of the court, who must fulfill their responsibilities within the framework established by legal ethics. They cannot deliberately mislead the court by providing false information. Nor can they knowingly allow the use of perjurious testimony.

Assessing how well lawyers represent their clients is difficult because of different ways of assessing the work performed. How do we define winning? Our popular culture suggests that winning means an acquittal. But experienced lawyers reject such simplistic notions. A veteran Los Angeles public defender explained:

> What is our job as a criminal lawyer in most instances? Number one is...no kidding, we know the man's done it, or we feel he's done it, he may deny it, but the question is: Can they prove it? The next thing is: Can we mitigate it? Of course you can always find something good to say about the guy—to mitigate it. Those are the two things that are important, and that's what you do. (Mather, 1974b, p. 278)

Thus, many defense attorneys define winning in terms of securing probation, or accepting a plea to a misdemeanor charge. One attorney put it this way: "Given the situation, what is the best that can be done for my client?" (Neubauer, 1974b, p. 74). At virtually all stages of the criminal justice process, defendants may have the guiding hand of counsel (see "Law on the Books vs. Law in Action" feature on the following page).

How defense attorneys seek to reach the best solution possible for their client is directly related to their relationship with other members of the courtroom work group. Usually, assistant public defenders are permanently assigned to a single courtroom and work every day with the same judge, the same prosecutor(s), the same court reporter, and the same clerk of court. Similarly, private defense attorneys—although they practice before several judges—are a permanent fixture in the criminal courts, for a handful of lawyers dominate the representation of fee-paying criminal defendants in any city. This daily interaction of the criminal bar with the court community shapes the type and quality of legal representation received by those accused of violating the law. Whereas the adversary system stresses the combative role of the defense attorney, the day-to-day activities of the courtroom work group stress cooperation.

The legal system, civil and criminal, is based on controversy. Norms of cooperation work to channel such controversy into constructive avenues. All too often, advocacy is falsely equated with antagonism. Although defense attorneys exchange pleasantries with judges and prosecutors, their personal contacts with these officials outside the courtroom are limited.

Another qualification to bear in mind is that cooperative attorneys do not bargain every case;

they also take cases to trial. If the defense attorney thinks the prosecutor is driving too hard a bargain or that the state cannot prove its case to the jury, a trial will be recommended. Furthermore, no evidence exists to show that cooperative attorneys do not argue the case to the best of their abilities during a trial.

Rewards and Sanctions

Defense attorneys who maintain a cooperative stance toward judges, prosecutors, and clerks can expect to reap some rewards. Defense attorneys have limited (in some instances, nonexistent) investigative resources. Prosecutors can provide cooperative defense attorneys with information about the cases by letting them examine the

LAW IN ACTION VS. LAW ON THE BOOKS
THE ROLE OF DEFENSE ATTORNEYS IN A TYPICAL FELONY CASE

	LAW ON THE BOOKS	LAW IN ACTION
Crime		Counsels the client about the crime charged.
Arrest		Rarely present.
Initial appearance	Allowed to be present.	Typically advises client to say nothing during the court proceedings.
Bail	Argues for client's release on bail.	Judge more likely to listen to the district attorney's (DA's) recommended bail.
Charging		May urge the prosecutor to charge the client with a less serious offense.
Preliminary hearing	Allowed to be present but typically cannot call witnesses.	Good opportunity to find out what really happened in the case.
Grand jury	Only in some states may defense attorney be present.	Grand jury transcripts may be useful for discovery.
Arraignment	Allowed to be present.	Chance to talk to the client; may suggest entering a plea of guilty.
Evidence	Requests discovery information from the prosecutor; files motions to suppress confession and/or search and seizure.	Cooperative defense attorneys receive greater discovery information from the DA. Rarely successful in winning suppression motions.
Plea bargaining	Often a direct participant in plea discussions.	Negotiates for most beneficial deal possible.
Trial	Advocate for defendant's rights.	Typically stresses that the prosecutor has not proved the defendant "guilty beyond a reasonable doubt."
Sentencing	Makes a sentencing recommendation to the judge.	Argues for sentence at the low end of the normal penalty scale.
Appeal	Files notice of appeal and writes appellate brief.	Rarely successful on appeal.

© Cengage Learning

police reports, revealing the names of witnesses, and so on.

The court community can also apply sanctions to defense attorneys who violate the norms. Some sanctions work indirectly, by reducing a lawyer's income-generating ability. The clerk may refuse to provide beneficial case scheduling, or the judge may drag out a trial by continuously interrupting it for other business. Other sanctions are more direct. A judge can criticize a lawyer in front of his or her client (thus scaring away potential clients in the courtroom) or refuse to appoint certain attorneys to represent indigents—a significant source of income for some lawyers (Nardulli, 1978). A final category of sanctions involves the prosecutor's adopting a tougher stance during bargaining by not reducing charges or by recommending a prison sentence that is longer than normal.

Sanctions against defense attorneys are seldom invoked, but when they are, they can have far-reaching effects. Every court community can point to an attorney who has suffered sanctions, with the result that the attorney either no longer practices criminal law in the area or has mended his or her ways.

Variations in Cooperation

Defense attorneys are the least powerful members of the courtroom work group. Because of the numerous sanctions that can be applied to defense attorneys, they are forced into a reactive posture.

Prosecutors assess a defense attorney in terms of "reasonableness"—that is, the ability to "discern a generous offer of settlement and to be willing to encourage his client to accept such an offer" (Skolnick, 1967, p. 58). Based on this criterion, Skolnick put attorneys into three categories. One category consisted of defense attorneys who handled few criminal cases. One might suppose that prosecutors would prefer dealing with such inexperienced attorneys, but they did not. Because these attorneys did not know the ropes, they were too unpredictable and often caused administrative problems. In another category were attorneys who had active criminal practices and maintained a hostile relationship with the prosecutor's office. Known as "gamblers," these

attorneys exemplified the aggressive, fighting advocate, but because they either won big or lost big, they also served to show the other attorneys the disadvantage of this posture. The final category of attorneys consisted of public defenders and private attorneys who represented large numbers of defendants. These attorneys worked within the system.

An Assessment

Are criminal defense attorneys, especially public defenders and regular private attorneys, the co-opted agents of a court bureaucracy or simply calculating realists? This question has been a preoccupation of research on defense attorneys for decades (Flemming, 1986b).

Some studies argue that defense attorneys' ties to the court community mean that defendants' best interests are not represented. David Sudnow (1965) argued that public defenders became co-opted when public defenders and prosecutors shared common conceptions of what Sudnow called "normal crimes." Public defenders were more interested that a given case fit into a sociological cubbyhole than in determining whether the event met the proper penal code provisions. As a result, the public defenders seldom geared their work to securing acquittals for their clients. Thus, from the beginning, the presumption of guilt permeated the public defenders' assessment of cases. Similarly, Abraham Blumberg (1967b) concluded that all defense attorney regulars were double agents, working for both their client and the prosecutor. His study of a large New York court likened the practice of law to a confidence game, in which both the defendant and the defense attorney must have larceny at heart; a con game can be successful only if the "mark" is trying to get something for nothing. Judges and prosecutors depended on the defense attorneys to pressure defendants to plead guilty. In short, both Sudnow and Blumberg portray defense attorneys as ideological and as economic captives of the court rather than aggressive advocates.

However, other studies have concluded that defendants' best interests are not eroded when their attorneys adopt a cooperative posture within the courtroom community. Indeed, Jerome

Skolnick (1967) suggested that clients do better as a result of a cooperative posture. Working within the system benefits the client because the prosecutor will be more amenable to disclosing information helpful to the defense, the bargains struck will be more favorable, and the defendant will not be penalized for the hostility of the defense attorney. Furthermore, attorneys identified as agitators may harm their clients' causes because prosecutors and judges will hand out longer sentences. Neubauer's (1974a) study of Prairie City, Illinois, also found that attorneys who remained on good terms with other members of the courtroom work group functioned better as counselors, because they were better able to predict the reactions of the court community to individual cases. In short, the studies by Skolnick (1967), Neubauer (1974a), and Mather (1974b) concluded that attorneys who work within the system are better able to develop a realistic approach to their work, based on experience and knowledge of how their clients will fare.

Little evidence exists, then, that defense lawyers have been co-opted by the criminal justice system. Indeed, a study of what motivates public defenders reaches the opposite conclusion. Based on a study of 48 public defenders in three offices, Weiss (2005) concluded that public defenders are cynical about police, prosecutors, and judges. In the end, a skepticism about justice being done motivates public defenders to vigorously defend their clients.

THE CRIMINAL BAR

Law offices of solo practitioners are a permanent feature of urban architecture. They can be found huddled around the stone edifice of the criminal courts and near the neon lights proclaiming "Harry's 24-Hour Bail Bonds." In Detroit, they are called "the Clinton Street Bar," and in Washington, D.C., "the Fifth Streeters"—titles that are not meant to be complimentary. These lawyers spend little time in their offices; they are most often at the courthouse, socializing with other members of the courtroom work group. Their proximity to the criminal courts and the sparseness of the law books in their offices are good indicators that the law practiced from these offices bears little

resemblance to images of defense attorneys presented on television. A number of factors account for the low economic and professional status of the criminal bar.

Diversity and Stratification of the Legal Profession

Law is a diverse profession based partially on the law school attended and the place of work (Mather & Levin, 2012; Wilkins, 2012). Based on extensive interviews with practicing attorneys, Heinz and Laumann (1982), in *Chicago Lawyers: The Social Structure of the Bar*, reported dramatic differences among several sorts of lawyers, and these differences persist (Heinz, Nelson, Sandefur, & Laumann, 2005).

The most important differentiation within the legal profession involved which clients were served. Some lawyers represent large organizations (corporations, labor unions, or government). Others represent mainly individuals. By and large, lawyers operate in one of these two hemispheres of the profession; seldom, if ever, do they cross the line separating these very different types of legal work. The corporate client sector involves large corporate, regulatory, general corporate, and political lawyers. The personal client sector is divided into personal business and personal plight lawyers (divorce, tort, and so on).

Most of the attorneys who appear in criminal court are drawn from the personal-client sector. They are often referred to as "solo practitioners," because they practice alone or share an office with another attorney. For this group of courtroom regulars, criminal cases constitute a dominant part of their economic livelihood. Thus, studies of private attorneys in different cities report that the bulk of nonindigent defendants are represented by a handful of attorneys (Nardulli, 1986; Neubauer, 1974a).

Environment of Practice

It is no accident that in many large cities, a distinct criminal bar exists. Low status, difficulty in securing clients, and low fees are three factors that affect the availability of lawyers to represent those accused of violating the law.

Most lawyers view criminal cases as unsavory. Representing criminal defendants also produces few chances for victory; most defendants either plead guilty or are found guilty by a judge or jury. Also, despite the legal presumption of innocence, once defendants are arrested, the public assumes they are guilty. As a result, the general public perceives attorneys as freeing known robbers and rapists to return to the streets. "Realistically, a lawyer who defends notoriously unpopular clients becomes identified in the public's mind, and not infrequently in the mind of his own profession, with his client" (Kaplan, 1973).

To earn a living, lawyers first need clients. Attorneys working in the personal-client sector of the legal profession seldom have a regular clientele. Accordingly, a part of their time is spent securing clients. The criminal lawyer's most important commodity in securing clients is his or her reputation, which often develops on the basis of the lawyer's handling of a specific case. A lawyer's reputation is important in several ways. First, defendants want a specific attorney to represent them, not a firm of lawyers. Second, attorneys who do not practice criminal law often refer clients to a specific lawyer who does. Finally, a repeat offender may seek out the previous attorney, if he or she felt the lawyer provided good representation in the past. In securing clients, some defense attorneys rely on police officers, bail agents, and court clerks to give their names to defendants who need counsel (Wice, 1978).

Obtaining clients is only half the problem facing private attorneys who represent criminal clients. The second half is getting paid. "Criminal lawyers are more concerned than other lawyers with collection of the fee—after all, their clients are mostly criminals" (Lushing, 1992, p. 514). The lawyer's fee in a criminal case is generally a flat fee paid in advance. The three most important considerations in setting the fee are the seriousness of the offense, the amount of time it will take the lawyer to deal with the case, and the client's ability to pay. Well-known criminal lawyers, for example, often charge their prosperous clients considerable fees. In the words of a prominent New York City defense attorney, "Reasonable doubt begins with the payment of a reasonable fee" (Gourevitch, 2001, p. 111). The myth that criminal lawyers receive fabulous salaries is mostly untrue; although a few have become

quite wealthy, most earn a modest middle-class living (Wice, 1978). Of course, many defendants are so impoverished that they cannot afford to hire a private attorney at all.

PROVIDING INDIGENTS WITH ATTORNEYS

Indigents are defendants who cannot afford to pay a lawyer and, therefore, are entitled to a lawyer for free. Three quarters of state prison inmates had court-appointed lawyers to represent them for the offense for which they were serving time. In urban courthouses, the indigency rate is a little higher: 82 percent of felony defendants cannot afford to hire their own lawyer (Bureau of Justice Statistics, 2012). Obviously, the Supreme Court's decision in *Gideon*, requiring the state to provide attorneys for indigents, applies to a substantial number of criminal defendants.

Although the Supreme Court has essentially mandated the development of indigent-defense systems, it has left the financing and type of delivery system up to states and counties, which have considerable discretion in adopting programs (Worden & Worden, 1989). As with other aspects of the American dual court system, the characteristics of defense systems for the indigent vary considerably, with some state governments funding virtually all indigent criminal defense services, other state governments sharing the financial costs of providing counsel with counties, and still other jurisdictions in which county funds are used exclusively (Farole & Langton, 2010; Langton & Farole, 2010).

How best to provide legal representation for the poor has been a long-standing issue for the courts and the legal profession. In the United States, the three primary methods are assigned counsel (attorneys appointed by the judge on a case-by-case basis), contract systems (attorneys hired to provide services for a specified dollar amount), and public defender (a salaried public official representing all indigent defendants). The ongoing debate over the advantages and disadvantages of these three systems highlights some important issues about the quality of legal representation provided the poor.

Assigned Counsel

The assigned counsel system reflects the way professions such as law and medicine traditionally respond to charity cases: Individual practitioners provide services on a case-by-case basis. Assigned counsel systems involve the appointment by the court of private attorneys from a list of available attorneys. The list may consist of all practicing attorneys in the jurisdiction or, more commonly, the attorneys who volunteer. The assigned counsel system is used in half of all U.S. counties but serves less than one third of the nation's population. It predominates in small counties, those with fewer than 50,000 residents, where an insufficient volume of cases exists to support the costs of a public defender system.

Critics contend that the assigned counsel system results in the least-qualified lawyers being appointed to defend indigents (Iyengar, 2007). In most counties, the only attorneys who volunteer are either young ones seeking courtroom experience or those who seek numerous appointments to make a living. Even where appointments are rotated among all members of the practicing bar (as in New Jersey and in Houston, Texas), no guarantee exists that the lawyer selected is qualified to handle the increasing complexity of the criminal law; the appointee may be a skilled real estate attorney or a good probate attorney, but these skills are not readily transferable to the dynamics of a criminal trial.

The availability of lawyers willing to serve as assigned counsel is directly related to financial compensation. In the past, a number of jurisdictions expected attorneys to represent indigents as part of their professional responsibility, without being paid (*pro bono*). Today, however, attorneys assigned to represent indigent defendants are paid. Most commonly, lawyers are compensated for such defense work on the basis of separate hourly rates for out-of-court and in-court work. However, hourly fees for in-court felony work usually range far below the fees charged in private practice. Critics contend that inadequate compensation pressures attorneys to dispose of such cases quickly in order to devote time to fee-paying clients.

The widely held assumption that rates of compensation are directly related to the quality of criminal defense representation has been challenged by one study. The extent of effort of lawyers in Michigan who handled appellate representation did not vary significantly in relation to the rate of compensation. Overall, professional role expectations of lawyers may have a greater influence on their work than financial considerations (Priehs, 1999).

Contract Systems

Contract systems involve bidding by private attorneys to represent all criminal defendants found indigent during the term of the contract, in return for a fixed payment (Cohen, 2011; Worden, 1991, 1993). Contract systems are most often found in counties with populations of fewer than 50,000, where the key feature is that they place an absolute budget limit on defense services for the indigent.

The primary advantage of contract systems is that they limit the costs government must pay for indigent defense. Critics counter with two types of concerns. The first is that contract programs will inevitably lead to a lower standard of representation through the bidding system, which emphasizes cost over quality. The second is that the private bar will no longer play an important role in indigent defense (Spangenberg Group, 2000).

The contract system was held unconstitutional in Arizona when the Arizona Supreme Court held that the Mohave County contract system, which assigned defense representation of the indigent to the lowest bidder, violated the Fifth and Sixth Amendments because the system: (1) did not take into account the time the attorney is expected to spend on a case, (2) did not provide for support staff costs, (3) failed to take into account the competence of the attorney, and (4) did not consider the complexity of the case (*Smith v. State*, 1984). Likewise, courts in several other states have found legal defects in contract systems that result in inadequate funding levels (Spangenberg Group, 2000).

Skepticism that contract systems actually save money is growing. Several jurisdictions have been frustrated by contract firms submitting increasingly higher budgets after their initial low bids (Wice, 2005). Moreover, in some markets, contract systems have failed to reduce the costs of indigent defense, and may actually increase such costs,

COURTS,
CONTROVERSY,
& ECONOMIC
INEQUALITY

ARE WE SPENDING TOO LITTLE OR TOO MUCH ON INDIGENT DEFENSE?

Is *Gideon's* promise broken? Fifty years after the Court's landmark right-to-counsel decision, some argue that the promise of equal justice under law has given way to a two-tiered system of criminal representation—one for those with money and another for those without it. Still others contend that the way *Gideon* has been implemented is way too costly.

From the perspective of the due process model, unmanageable caseloads are the single greatest obstacle to effective representation of the indigent (Lefstein, 2011; National Right to Counsel Committee, 2009). In 1973, the National Advisory Commission on Criminal Justice Standards and Goals recommended that a maximum effective felony caseload for a public defender is 150 cases per year. Today, most states have workload standards that recommend a felony caseload of between 50 and 300 cases, with most states continuing to embrace the figure of 150 cases recommended by the National Advisory Commission in 1973 (Spangenberg Group, 2001). Yet, in many jurisdictions, it is typically much higher—sometimes approaching 1,000 clients per year (Cauchon, 1999; Lefstein, 2011). "No more. We can't ethically handle this many cases," argues David Carrol of the National Legal Aid and Defender Association. Typical is Florida's Miami–Dade County, where the public defender's office refused to accept any new lesser-felony cases so they could concentrate on defending current clients (Eckholm, 2008).

The short-term failure to adequately fund indigent defense can prove to be expensive in the long run. The advent of DNA evidence (Chapter 13) has led to the freeing of hundreds of the wrongfully convicted (Chapter 16), but only after major expenditures for lawyers and the like, to say nothing of damage to the reputation of the criminal justice system. Likewise, the lack of attorneys available to defend death row inmates is a major point of contention regarding the death penalty (see Chapter 14).

The problem of out-of-control caseloads is in state courts, not in the federal courts, where funding has long been greater than among the states (Lefstein, 2011). In the wake of the economic downturn of the early 21st century, state after state has often been forced to reduce funding for indigent defense. At issue is who should pay for public defenders. County boards believed that it is the state's responsibility to pay these expenses. But officials of the state countered that its budget was in dire straits, and therefore it was unable to afford such services (Liptak, 2003).

Crime control proponents, on the other hand, have long been concerned that the government is paying too much for indigent defense. As expenditures for defense services for the indigent have risen dramatically (DeFrances, 2001), there has been a noticeable trend toward containing the costs. One technique is the adoption of stringent indigency standards. Traditionally, big-city judges rarely inquired into the financial capabilities of defendants to determine whether they satisfy the court's definition of indigency. However, a report funded by the National Institute of Justice stresses that courts should screen applications "to ensure that only the truly indigent are provided representation at public expense" (Spangenberg, Wilson, Smith, & Lee, 1986, p. 69). However, indigency standards set too high obviously deprive defendants of their constitutional right to court-appointed counsel. This is particularly true in counties that consider making bail in determining indigency—the bail bonds person's fee may exhaust the financial resources to hire a lawyer (Hashimoto, 2010).

Another way of containing government expenses is cost recovery. In screening applications for defense services for the indigent, many courts now distinguish between defendants so poor that they are exempt from paying any costs of their defense and a new category of "partially indigent" defendants who may be able to pay a portion of the costs (Lee, 1992; Spangenberg et al., 1986). Defendants in many jurisdictions may be required to pay application fees for court-appointed counsel (Hashimoto, 2010; Wright & Logan, 2006). It "seems only fair" that defendants be required to pay, argues Jim Rams, president of the National District Attorneys Association. "Since the vast majority of criminal defendants do not get sentenced to jail … their job status and economics can and should change relatively quickly allowing repayment" (quoted in Johnson, 2010). The Brenan Center for Justice counters that in practice these fees often discourage individuals from exercising their constitutional rights, leading to wrongful convictions (Bannon, Nagrecha, & Diller, 2010).

because there are too few attorneys to generate a competitive market (Cohen, 2011; Spangenberg & Beeman, 1995).

Public Defender

The **public defender** is a 20th-century response to the problem of providing legal representation for the indigent. Public defender programs are public or private nonprofit organizations with full- or part-time salaried staff who represent indigents in criminal cases in a jurisdiction.

Started in Los Angeles County in 1914, public defender offices spread slowly. By 1965, the National Legal Aid and Defender Association—the national organization that promotes better legal representation for indigents in civil as well as criminal cases—reported programs in only 117 counties. Since 1965, public defender programs have spread rapidly because of Supreme Court decisions (*Gideon* and later *Argersinger*), as well as increased concern for more-adequate representation of indigents. Today, the public defender system represents approximately 70 percent of all indigents nationwide. It predominates in most big cities and has also been adopted in numerous medium-sized jurisdictions.

The administration and funding of public defender programs occurs at either the state or local level. Twenty-two states have a state public defender program that oversees the policies and practices of the 427 public defender offices located in these states (Langton & Farole, 2010). In another 27 states and the District of Columbia, public defender offices were funded and administered at the local level (Farole & Langton, 2010). Maine is the only state that does not have a public defender office.

Proponents of the public defender system cite several arguments in favor of its adoption. One is that a lawyer paid to represent indigents on a continuous basis will devote more attention to cases than a court-appointed attorney who receives only minimal compensation. Moreover, many members of the practicing bar like the idea that they no longer have to take time away from fee-paying cases to meet their professional obligations.

A second advantage often claimed for the public defender system is that it provides more experienced, competent counsel. Because public defenders concentrate on criminal cases, they can keep abreast of changes in the law, and the day-to-day courtroom work keeps their trial skills sharp. The public defender is also likely to be more knowledgeable about informal norms and is therefore in a better position to counsel defendants and negotiate the best possible deal.

Finally, a public defender system ensures continuity and consistency in the defense of the poor (Silverstein, 1965). Public defenders are usually able to provide early representation, entering the case at the initial appearance. Moreover, issues that transcend individual cases—criteria for pretrial release, police practices, and so forth—are more likely to be considered by a permanent, ongoing organization than under appointment systems.

Assessing the Merits of Public Defenders

Critics contend that public defenders—as paid employees of the state—will not provide a vigorous defense because they are tied too closely to the courtroom work group. Several studies have investigated this concern by comparing the adequacy of representation provided by assigned counsel to that by public defenders' offices. The dominant conclusion is that there is not much difference (Eisenstein, Flemming, & Nardulli, 1988; Flemming, 1989; Hartley, Miller, & Spohn, 2010; Wice, 1985).

Several studies, however, find that defendants represented by assigned counsel attorneys fare less well (Cohen, 2011; Iyengar, 2007; Roach, 2010). Most importantly, though, the research continues to report that clients of private attorneys and public defenders receive similar case outcomes.

The National Center for State Courts drew the following conclusions from the nine jurisdictions it studied:

1. Appointed counsel resolved the cases of their indigent defendants more expeditiously than did privately retained counsel.

2. Appointed criminal defense counsel gained as many favorable outcomes (acquittals, charge reductions, and short prison sentences) for their indigent clients as privately retained attorneys did for their clients.

3. Appointed criminal defense counsel prosecuting attorneys were equally experienced (Hanson, Hewitt, & Ostrom, 1992).

Likewise, the outcomes of criminal appeals do not vary between public defenders and privately retained counsel (Williams, 1995).

The Public Defender: The Practice of Law in the Shadows of Repute offers a radically different view of public defense attorneys. In this book, Lisa McIntyre (1987) demonstrated that public defense lawyers are indeed free to defend their clients zealously. She found that in the courts of Cook County, Illinois, public defenders are adversarial and even combative opponents of the state's prosecutorial apparatus. McIntyre argues, in fact, that the office of the public defender survives because its effective advocacy for its clients bolsters the legitimacy of the court system.

Why, then, does the public defender's image not reflect this? The freedom to defend against the state cannot include the freedom to embarrass it. Hence, the complexity of the public defender's institutional role requires that the office not advertise its successes. McIntyre shows that the public defender's office deliberately retains its image of incompetency in order to guarantee its continued existence. Public defenders may practice good law, but they must do it in the darker shadows of repute.

The long-standing debate over the adequacy of court-appointed counsel is beginning to give way to a new reality—large governmental expenses. Images and myths play a central role in the debate over funding levels for court-appointed lawyers (see "Courts, Controversy, and Economic Inequality: Are We Spending Too Little or Too Much on Indigent Defense?").

The vast majority of public defender agencies attempt to survive from one crisis to the next amid a perpetual flux of inexperienced lawyers. In response to the on going problems of the traditional agencies, some reform defender agencies have emerged. *Public Defenders and the American Justice System* by Paul Wice (2005) focuses on one reform defender system—Essex County (Newark), New Jersey. These reform agencies strive to maintain a group of experienced lawyers by emphasizing their independence from any political or judicial influence. One of their hallmarks is stressing the importance of one-on-one representation for each client.

LAWYERS AND CLIENTS

One of the most important tasks of defense attorneys is counseling. As advocates, defense attorneys are expected to champion their clients' cases. But as counselors, they must advise their clients about the possible legal consequences involved. Lawyers must fully and dispassionately evaluate the strengths and weaknesses of the prosecutor's case, assess the probable success of various legal defenses, and—most important—weigh the likelihood of conviction or acquittal. In appraising risks and outlining options, lawyers interpret the law to their clients, who are often unversed in what the law considers important and what the law demands.

To be an effective advocate and counselor, the lawyer must know all the facts of a case. For this reason, the American legal system surrounds the attorney–client relationship with special protections. Statements made by a client to his or her attorney are considered **privileged communication**, which the law protects from forced disclosure without the client's consent. The attorney–client privilege extends not only to statements made by the client but also to any work product developed in representing the client.

Based on trust and a full exchange of information, the attorney assumes the difficult task of advocating a client's case. In civil litigation, the relationship between lawyer and client is often (but not always) characterized by trust and full disclosure (Cox, 1993). In criminal cases, however, the relationship is more likely to be marked by distrust and hostility. Indeed, more than half of defendants are described by their attorneys as passive participants in the overall defense, and 10 percent are described by their attorneys as recalcitrant—that is, rarely or never accepting the attorney's advice (Bonnie, Poythress, Hoge, Monahan, & Eisenberg, 1996).

In the modern era, high caseloads clearly complicate the ability of lawyers, particularly those appointed by the court to represent indigents, to find time to talk with clients. In the book

Indefensible: One Lawyer's Journey into the Inferno of American Justice, David Feige (2006) reflected on days in court when he was unable to make court appearances because he was busy elsewhere. Given a caseload ranging from 75 to 120 active cases, "the simple matter of where to be when becomes one of the most complicated and taxing puzzles we face. It's not unusual to have six, eight, or even ten different courtrooms to go to in a single day"(p. 87). And on some days, an unexpectedly lengthy appearance in one courtroom means that a lawyer will be unable to meet with a client in another courtroom. In short, becoming a good client manager is something that every public defender has to learn.

Lawyers' Views on Their Clients

Getting along with clients is one of the most difficult tasks of public defenders. One veteran New York City public defender recounts the lecture he received from his boss early on. "If you're working this job looking for appreciation, you're never gonna last," she said. Instead it has to come from inside "even though we lose and lose, and we get creamed every day . . . you have to wake up the next morning and fight your heart out, looking for those few times we can stop it" (Feige, 2006, p. 33). Nonetheless, client disrespect irritates attorneys and sours their associations with clients. As one public defender complained, "It is frustrating to have to constantly sell yourself" to clients. "The standard joke around this county is, 'Do you want a public defender or a real attorney?'" (Flemming, 1986a, pp. 257–258). Many eventually leave the job because of the difficulty of dealing with their clients (Platt & Pollock, 1974).

Refusal to cooperate, deception, and dishonesty are serious problems public attorneys face in dealing with their clients (Flemming, 1986a). At times, defendants tell their attorneys implausible stories, invent alibis, or withhold key information. A veteran public defender observed that in drug cases, the clients all had the same defense—they left home to buy milk or Pampers for the baby. In the end, "when you've heard every defense a thousand times, true or not, they can all start to sound like bullshit" (Feige, 2006, p. 228). The

defendant's lack of candor greatly complicates the job of the attorney in representing him or her. Evasions and deceptions can affect tactical and strategic decisions.

Lynn Mather (1974b) described a case in which a public defender went to trial at the request of a client who claimed she had no prior record. To the attorney's surprise, the defendant's presentence report revealed that she had a 5-year history of similar crimes. She was sentenced to prison. The public defender said that his client "fooled everyone." The lack of trust in the attorney–client relationship may stem from the necessity for the lawyer to prepare the client for less than total victory. The defense attorney may at some point have to inform the defendant that imprisonment is a likely result, given the crime, prior record, facts of the case, and so forth. Since defendants involved in the criminal process often do not look beyond the present, postponing bad news from day to day, such statements are not to their liking. Preparing the client for the possibility of conviction clashes with traditional notions that the attorney should always win.

Ultimately, it is the defendant's choice whether to accept the attorney's advice to plead guilty or to go to trial. Lawyers differ in their ability to influence their clients. Private attorneys find their advice accepted more readily than court-appointed lawyers do. This difference in part reflects the type of commitment the defendant has made. The indigent defendant has no choice in receiving the services of a public defender or assigned counsel, whereas defendants with private attorneys have a choice and have shown their commitment by paying a fee.

Defendants' Views on Their Lawyers

Public clients are skeptical about the skills of their lawyers and are worried about whose side the lawyers are on. Thus, many defendants view their lawyers, whether public or private, with suspicion, if not bitterness. This is particularly the case with court-appointed attorneys, whom many defendants consider the same as any other government-paid attorney. Some defendants think that public defenders will not work hard on their cases because they are paid whether or not they win. To others, the defense attorney has ambitions to become a judge or prosecutor and therefore does not want to antagonize the court system by fighting too hard. Overall, then, many defendants view the public defender as no different from the prosecutor. In prison, PD stands not for "public defender" but for "prison deliverer." In what has become a classic statement, a Connecticut prisoner responded to Jonathan Casper's (1972) question as to whether he had a lawyer when he went to court with the barbed comment, "No, I had a public defender."

A partial explanation for a breakdown of trust between the client and public defender involves the absence of one-to-one contact. Most public defenders' offices are organized on a zone basis. Attorneys are assigned to various courtrooms and/or responsibilities—initial appearance, preliminary hearing, trial sections, and so on. Each defendant sees several public defenders, all of whom are supposed to be working for him or her. This segmented approach to representation for indigents decreases the likelihood that a bond of trust will develop between attorney and client. It also increases the probability that some defendants will be overlooked—that no attorney will work on their cases or talk to them. One can certainly understand the frustration of this 33-year-old accused murderer with no previous record:

> "I figured that with he being my defense attorney, that as soon as that grand jury was over—because he's not allowed in the hearing—that he would call me and then want to find out what went on. After that grand jury I never saw him for two months."
> "You stayed in jail?" "Yeah." (Casper, 1972, p. 8)

Clearly, not all defendants' criticisms of their attorneys are valid. But valid or not, defendants' lack of trust and confidence in their lawyers is a major force in shaping the dynamics of courthouse justice. Defendants try to con their attorneys, and the lawyers respond by exhibiting disbelief when defendants state unrealistic expectations or invent implausible alibis. For an attorney, failure to gain "client control" can lead to a bad reputation in the courthouse and jeopardize his or her own position within the courtroom work group (Eisenstein, Flemming, & Nardulli, 1988).

DEFENSE ATTORNEY ETHICS

Lawyers occupy an ambiguous position in American society. They are admired and respected and at the same time distrusted. These contradictory assessments are reflected in myths about lawyers as either heroes or villains (Wolfram, 1986). Popular culture often portrays lawyers as heroes who valiantly protect clients falsely accused or depicts attorneys as villains for going too far in defending the obviously guilty. Discussions of good lawyers and bad lawyers invariably focus on legal ethics. But this focus often reflects considerable misunderstanding about what lawyers do and what legal ethics is all about.

Years ago, one of the authors was in an Illinois courtroom talking with a top police official. When asked what was wrong with the criminal justice system, he singled out a specific defense attorney. "We arrest the guilty, but he [pointing to a defense attorney] gets them off on a technicality," he opined. Less than a week later, a police officer in his department was accused of manslaughter for shooting an unarmed youth. The police association immediately hired that same lawyer to defend the indicted officer. This saga illustrates the duality of viewpoints about attorneys and perceived ethical problems. More so than the other lawyers in the criminal justice process, defense attorneys are most often identified as having ethical issues.

Defending unpopular clients is the basis for a great deal of criticism of lawyers. People often ask, "How can you defend a person like that?"—a question that implies that lawyers' actions are an offense to morality. But at the core of legal ethics is the notion that every party is entitled to legal representation, even unpopular defendants who have committed heinous crimes or defendants whose guilt is overwhelming.

Each state has adopted its own code of professional responsibility for lawyers licensed within it. All 50 U.S. states, however, have adopted some variation of the American Bar Association's **Model Rules of Professional Conduct**. These rules impose ethical obligations on lawyers to their clients, as well as to the courts, since all attorneys are officers of the court.

The *duty of candor to the tribunal*, as it is known, is the most important responsibility that all lawyers owe to the courts. This ethical rule prohibits lawyers from knowingly making false statements to the court, failing to disclose adverse legal precedents, obstructing access to or tampering with witnesses or evidence, making frivolous discovery requests, and offering any evidence known to be false—including perjurious or misleading testimony. This last restriction can pose a serious ethical issue for defense attorneys, since they are often reluctant to refuse clients' efforts to present their defense. But, as officers of the court, they may not knowingly allow the use of perjured testimony. So, if defense attorneys cannot talk their clients out of taking the stand (particularly if they think that a client is now making the situation worse because the jury will not believe the testimony), the lawyers' duty of candor to the tribunal may require defense attorneys to tell a judge in chambers about such a situation and then let the client testify without the lawyer's help.

Another key responsibility all lawyers owe to the court, including prosecutors and criminal defense attorneys, is refraining from making any out-of-court statements that an attorney knows or reasonably should know will be disseminated to the public and would have a substantial likelihood of prejudicing any judicial proceeding. Recall from Chapter 6 that Mike Nifong, the prosecutor in the Duke lacrosse rape case, was disbarred for violating this duty.

The duties that defense attorneys owe to their clients include:

- zealously representing the client's interests within the bounds of the law;
- abiding by a client's decisions concerning the objectives of representation;
- avoiding providing any counsel that would encourage or assist a client, in conduct that the lawyer knows is criminal or fraudulent (although a lawyer may discuss the legal consequences of any proposed course of conduct with a client and may counsel or assist a client to make a good faith effort to determine the validity, scope, meaning, or application of the law);
- acting with reasonable diligence and promptness in representing a client;
- keeping the client reasonably informed about the status of his or her case;

- maintaining client confidentiality; and
- avoiding conflicts of interest.

The duty of zealous advocacy forms the bedrock of legal ethics. Lawyers are expected to be diligent in asserting valid defenses for their clients. However, this ethical standard does not mean that the lawyers must always do what their clients say. Lawyers are professionals bound by ethical rules of the profession. Within these parameters, people often support the zealous advocacy of their own lawyers, while objecting that the advocacy of opposing counsel goes too far. Conversely, defendants often complain that they lacked competent counsel, which typically translates into a complaint that they were convicted.

Confidentiality is another key component of legal ethics. Based on the attorney–client privilege, the lawyer may not voluntarily disclose what the client confided. Nor may judges, prosecutors, or other officers of the court typically force such disclosure. Holding to this principle may expose the lawyer to charges of obstruction of justice. Consider the case of a client who provided his lawyer a diagram of where he buried the kidnapped baby: The lawyer was severely criticized for failing to show the police where the body was buried. Eventually, a Texas judge ruled that the facts of the case constituted a valid exception to attorney–client privilege (Dzienkowski & Burton, 2006).

Potential conflict of interest is a key ethical issue facing lawyers. Attorneys are prohibited from engaging in representation that would compromise their loyalty to their clients. The most common problem found in the day-to-day practice of law in the criminal courts involves representing two clients who have opposing interests. In a murder case involving more than one defendant, for example, a lawyer may represent only one defendant because the defense might seek to lay the blame solely on another defendant. On the civil side, a lawyer who has represented a couple in various legal matters may be ethically prohibited from representing either party in a divorce proceeding because the lawyer may have learned important details of the couples' finances or other confidential matters.

Lawyers who fail to properly represent their clients may be sued for civil damages (Chapter 2). For

COURTS, LAW, & MEDIA

Boston Legal (ABC Television, 2004–2008)

Welcome to the law firm of Crane, Poole, & Schmidt, the fictional firm at the heart of *Boston Legal*. While the plots of many episodes differ, most of the storylines center around Alan Shore (played by James Spader), an ethically challenged attorney who, with the help of Denny Crane (played by William Shatner), a senior partner in the firm, gains recognition as an attorney of last resort—the guy who can win cases that no other attorney in private practice would ever want to take. Crane, however, possesses an eccentric personality and engages in bizarre conduct as a function of being in the early stages of Alzheimer's. Shirley Schmidt (played by Candice Bergen) is the firm's star litigator and managing partner. In that latter role, she not only has to make major decisions for the firm, but also has to supervise the questionable behaviors of the arrogant and narcissistic team of Shore and Crane.

Crane's own outrageous behavior helps to mentor Shore in his unethical ways. Indeed, it becomes clear that Shore's knack for winning is a function of his highly questionable methods. Shore will not "let trivial things like honesty and integrity get in the way of winning a case" (Smitts, 2004). For example, in one episode, he had an unlicensed physician remove a potentially life-threatening bullet from a client who had refused to seek medical treatment in a hospital for fear that the evidence gathered through traditional medical channels would lead to his being criminally convicted.

Television portrayals of fictional lawyers like Alan Shore and Denny Crane create unreasonable expectations in viewers who may need to hire a lawyer. After all, who would not want to be represented by an attorney-gladiator ready to "fight the battle for them" (Slocum, 2009, p. 516)? But such expectations are not realistic. In real life, attorneys who practiced law the way Alan Shore and Denny Crane did on *Boston Legal* would find themselves in a lot of trouble with judges and their state bar association. Lawyers are bound by codes of professional responsibility and the rules of court to behave in ways that conform to a set of legal ethics.

Despite the media portrayal of lawyers as angry, avenging gladiators, such a role is less common than most clients think. … But in real life, lawyers like the ones we see on TV and in the movies often end up costing their clients money—that kind of "litigation-as-war" mentality usually ratchets up the attacks and counter-attacks, with the clients becoming even angrier and more frustrated as the litigation escalates into all-out war. And the end result is not only that the lawsuit ends up costing both parties a lot of money in legal fees, but also that clients often end up pretty unhappy with the whole legal process, even if they end up getting much of what they wanted in terms of a financial outcome. Far from getting the justice they wanted and believe they deserve, they end up feeling that the legal system let them down (Slocum, 2009, p. 517).

After watching one or more episodes of *Boston Legal*, be prepared to discuss the following questions:

1. Do you think that depictions of the lawyers on *Boston Legal* contribute to the image of unethical criminal defense attorneys? Explain your reasoning.
2. Alan Shore and Denny Crane are just two examples of the media depicting the "win at all costs" defense attorney. Sebastian Stark on *Shark* is another. What other examples of unethical defense attorneys can you find in popular culture?
3. The fictional defense attorneys of yesterday, like Perry Mason, Matlock, or Atticus Finch in *To Kill a Mockingbird*, were consistently depicted as highly ethical attorneys who won cases not by ignoring the rules of professional responsibility, but rather by exercising their superior lawyering skills with uncompromised integrity. Why do you think that media portrayals of fictional defense attorneys have changed so much in a generation or two? What, if anything, does this say about the legal profession?

this reason, lawyers carry legal malpractice insurance. It is important to stress, though, that lawyers are liable only in very limited situations. Just because a lawyer loses a case does not mean that the lawyer is incompetent.

CONCLUSION

From the bleak perspective of his prison cell, Clarence Gideon had no way of knowing that his petition to the Supreme Court would have the impact it did. Overnight, Gideon went from defending himself to having Abe Fortas—one of the nation's most prestigious lawyers—represent him. Following the Supreme Court reversal of his conviction, Clarence Earl Gideon was given a new trial. His court-appointed lawyer discovered evidence suggesting that the man who had accused Gideon of burglarizing the poolroom had himself committed the crime. Moreover, as a result of the *Gideon* decision, thousands of other prison inmates in Florida and elsewhere were freed.

Nor could Gideon have realized that his name would become associated with a landmark Supreme Court decision. He achieved no small degree of legal immortality. His case was chronicled by *New York Times* reporter Anthony Lewis (1964) in the book *Gideon's Trumpet*. *Gideon v. Wainwright* transformed the law, signaling a due process revolution in the rights of criminal defendants. Gideon himself was not transformed, however. He avoided any more major brushes with the law, but he died penniless on January 18, 1972, in Ft. Lauderdale, Florida.

The travails of Clarence Earl Gideon illustrate the importance of legal access to the justice system. Perhaps nowhere else is there a greater contrast between the images and the realities of the criminal court process than in the activities of the defense attorney. Unlike fictional defense attorneys, who always defend innocent clients successfully, most defense attorneys deal with a steady stream of defendants who are in fact guilty, and their representation focuses on plea bargaining.

Chapter Review

LO1 1. Interpret the four major legal issues surrounding the right to counsel.

After *Gideon v. Wainwright* established a right to counsel for indigent felony defendants, courts have wrestled with four areas: (1) right to counsel in nonfelony prosecutions, (2) stages of the criminal process, (3) ineffective assistance of counsel, and (4) self-representation.

LO2 2. Discuss how the courtroom work group affects how defense attorneys represent their clients.

Lawyers who work within the parameters of the courtroom work group receive benefits for their clients, including more case information from prosecutors and perhaps better plea bargains. Lawyers who are less cooperative find that they do not get favorable case-scheduling

considerations and get less favorable plea bargains.

LO3 3. Explain why most lawyers do not represent criminal defendants.

Most lawyers practice civil law because it is more lucrative, they have higher prestige, and they have fewer problems dealing with clients.

LO4 4. Compare and contrast the three systems of providing indigents with court-appointed attorneys.

The three major ways of providing indigents with court appointed attorneys are: (1) assigned counsel, (2) contract systems, and (3) public defender. Studies find no major differences between these three systems in the results achieved.

LO5 **5.** Recognize possible tensions between lawyers and clients.

Lawyers sometimes view their clients as not telling them the whole truth about a case and at times seeking to manipulate their lawyers. Defendants may view their attorneys as not fighting hard enough for them and seeking to accommodate the judge and prosecutor.

LO6 **6.** Analyze the importance of legal ethics to the defense of criminal defendants.

Legal ethics seek to ensure that lawyers will zealously advocate for their clients. Lawyers must assert valid defense and ensure confidentially. But legal ethics places professional limits on how far that advocacy may go, including not using perjured or misleading testimony.

Critical Thinking Questions

1. The public generally views defense attorneys as too zealous in their advocacy of obviously guilty clients, while many scholars portray an image of defense attorneys, particularly public defenders, as too willing to plead their clients guilty. What do you think? What evidence would you cite for either position?

2. In what ways have contemporary decisions by the U.S. Supreme Court modified the original meaning of the Sixth Amendment? Is the original intent of the Sixth Amendment relevant in today's world?

3. What factors hinder a defense attorney in his or her attempt to protect the rights of the defendant? Think of both system factors and individual ones.

4. What are the major contrasts in the workaday world of private defense attorneys and court-appointed lawyers?

5. Should all attorneys be required to provide pro bono defense for indigents? Would such activities improve the image of the bar? Would such activities be in the best interests of the defendants?

6. If you were arrested, which would you rather have: a private lawyer or a public defender?

Key Terms

assigned counsel system 185

contract system 185

indigents 184

Model Rules of Professional Conduct 190

privileged communication 188

pro se 179

public defender 187

right to counsel 175

Web Resources

Go to the *America's Courts and the Criminal Justice System* companion website at http://www.cengage.com/criminaljustice/neubauer, where you will find more resources to help you study. Resources include web exercises, quizzing, and flash cards.

For Further Reading

Davis, Kevin. *Defending the Damned: Inside Chicago's Cook County Public Defender's Office*. New York: Atria, 2007.

Etienne, Margareth. "The Ethics of Cause Lawyering: An Empirical Examination of Criminal Defense Lawyers as Cause Lawyers." *Journal of Criminal Law and Criminology* 95: 1195, 2005.

Gould, Jon. "Indigent Defense—A Poor Measure of Justice." *Judicature* 92: 131, 2008.

Klebanow, Diana, and Franklin Jonas. *People's Lawyers: Crusaders for Justice in American History*. Armonk, NY: Sharpe, 2003.

Mossman, Mary Jane. *The First Women Lawyers: A Comparative Study of Gender, Law, and the Legal Profession*. Oxford, U.K.: Hart, 2006.

The Spangenberg Group. *Keeping Defender Workloads Manageable*. Washington, DC: Bureau of Justice Statistics, 2001.

Williams, Marian. "A Comparison of Sentencing Outcomes for Defendants with Public Defenders versus Retained Counsel in 'Florida Circuit Court.'" *Justice System Journal* 23: 249–258, 2002.

8 Judges

© AP Photo/Brett Coomer.

Texas judge **Belinda Hill** listens to lawyers representing Andrea Yates in her retrial on homicide charges for drowning her five children in a bathtub. Yates was found not guilty by reason of insanity and committed to the maximum-security North Texas State Hospital in Vernon, Texas. Verdicts in high-profile cases like this one often lead to a debate over the role of a judge, including whether judges should be elected or appointed. Although the public often holds judges responsible for all that happens in a courtroom, in reality, judges are often limited by the actions (and inactions) of the other members of the courtroom work group. ■

THE POSITION OF JUDGE
Powers of the Judge
Benefits of the Job
Frustrations of the Job

Courts, Law, & Media
Judge Judy: Justice with an Attitude or Just Plain Nonsense

JUDGES WITHIN THE COURTROOM WORK GROUP

VARYING ROADS TO A JUDGESHIP
Executive Appointments
Election of Judges
Merit Selection

CONSEQUENCES OF JUDICIAL SELECTION
Which System Is Best?
Similarities in Judges' Backgrounds
Diversity and the Judiciary

JUDGING THE JUDGES
Judicial Independence

CASE CLOSE-UP: *Chisom v. Roemer* & Diversity on the Bench

Courts, Controversy, and the Administration of Justice
Is Judicial Independence Being Undermined?

Judicial Misconduct
State Judicial Conduct Commissions
Federal Conduct and Disability Act

JUDICIAL ETHICS

Judges • Judges • Judges • Judges • Judges • Judges • Ju
• Judges • Judges • Judges • Judges • Judges • Judges

After reading this chapter, you should be able to:

LO1 Discuss the role of the judge within the courtroom work group.

LO2 Name the three major ways that judges are selected in the United States.

LO3 Analyze the consequences of different methods of judicial selection.

LO4 Recognize major changes in the composition of the bench over the past several decades.

LO5 Describe the activities of state judicial conduct commissions.

LO6 Explain the difference between the impeachment and the removal of a federal judge.

FACT OR FICTION?

- Facing a $50 million verdict for fraudulent business practices, a coal executive spends $3 million to support a candidate for a seat on the West Virginia Supreme Court; the candidate wins and then casts the deciding vote to overturn the verdict.

- Facing a multi-million-dollar verdict in a toxic waste case, a large chemical company secretly finances a candidate for the Mississippi Supreme Court who is likely to rule in its favor.

One of these cases is based on a recent U.S. Supreme Court decision (*Caperton v. Massey Coal Company*, 2009); the other on the plot of *The Appeal* by popular fiction writer John Grisham (2008), who is also a lawyer. And Grisham admits that his novel is at least partially inspired by the real case. This blending of fact and fiction, life imitating art, offers a very public example of the long-standing debate in the United States over how best to select judges. Should judges be elected directly by the voters, appointed by an elected official (president or governor), or selected by a hybrid system that gives lawyers a direct role in the process?

The debate over how to select judges underscores the important role of the judge in the American legal system. The purpose of this chapter is to untangle the conflicting notions about what judges do and how they do it. The chapter begins by examining the position of judge and how various pressures (the large number of cases, for example) have eroded the ideal image of a judge's power. Next, the judge will be considered as a member of the courtroom community. A judge's actions are shaped and influenced by the actions of prosecutors and defense attorneys, among others. At the same time, the type of justice handed out varies from one judge to another. A persistent concern is whether judges are as qualified as they should be. Therefore, two suggestions for improving the quality of the judiciary will be examined: merit selection and mechanisms for removing unfit judges. The role of judicial ethics will also be examined.

THE POSITION OF JUDGE

For most Americans, the judge is the symbol of justice. Of all the actors in the criminal justice process, the public holds the judge most responsible for ensuring that the system operates fairly and impartially. And most certainly the trappings of office—the flowing black robes, the gavel, and the command "All rise!" when the judge enters the courtroom—reinforce this mystique. As important as these symbols are, they sometimes raise obstacles to understanding what judges actually do and how they influence the criminal justice process.

The vast array of legal powers often causes us to overestimate the actual influence of the judge by ignoring the importance of the other actors in the courtroom work group. At the same time, the mystique of the office often results in an underestimation of the role of the judge. Judges are not merely impartial black-robed umpires who hand down decisions according to clear and unwavering rules. "This view of the judge as an invisible interpreter of the law, as a part of the courtroom with no more individual personality than a witness chair or a jury box, is a fiction that judges themselves have done much to perpetuate" (Jackson, 1974, p. vii).

Powers of the Judge

The formal powers of judges extend throughout the criminal court process. From arrest to final disposition, the accused face judges whenever decisions affecting their futures are made (Table 8.1). Judges set bail and revoke it; they determine whether sufficient probable cause exists to hold defendants; they rule on pretrial motions to exclude evidence; they accept pleas of guilty; if a trial takes place, they preside; and after conviction, they set punishment.

Although we tend to think of judges primarily in terms of presiding at trials, their work is much more varied. In the course of their workday, they conduct hearings, accept guilty pleas, impose sentences, or work in their offices (called **chambers**). In carrying out the responsibilities of the office, judges mainly react to the work of prosecutors and defense attorneys.

Benefits of the Job

In discharging their duties, judges enjoy some distinct benefits of the office. Traditionally, they have been given a high level of prestige and respect. Lawyers address the judge as "your honor," and everyone rises when the judge enters or leaves the courtroom. Judges also enjoy other trappings of the office. Federal judges enjoy life terms, as do judges in a handful of states. More commonly, terms of office for state judges range from 6 to 10 years, considerably longer than those of other public officeholders—a reflection of the independence of the American judiciary.

For many lawyers, a judgeship is the capstone to a successful career. Judicial salaries are not the highest incomes in the legal profession, but they are higher than the average of other criminal justice personnel. Annual salaries of general jurisdiction trial judges range from $104,170 to $180,802 (National Center for State Courts, 2011). The average is about $135,000. For some lawyers, a judicial salary represents an increase over that received in private practice, and it is certainly more secure. For the majority of lawyers, however, a judgeship represents a significant decrease in earning power (Jensen, 2011). For example, it is not at all unusual to find lawyers in federal court who earn much more than the judges before whom they appear in court.

Many judgeships carry with them considerable patronage powers. Court positions—bailiffs, clerks, court reporters, probation officers, and secretaries—must be filled. Because these positions are usually not covered by civil service, judges can award jobs to friends, relatives, campaign workers,

TABLE 8.1 ▪ ROLE OF JUDGES IN THE STEPS OF CRIMINAL PROCEDURE (TYPICAL FELONY CASE)

	Lower Court	Major Trial Court	Appellate Court
Crime			Appellate court opinions are the final word on interpreting criminal laws passed by the legislature.
Arrest	Signs arrest warrants.		Wrestles with legality of police arrest in context of question of illegal search and seizure.
Initial appearance	Informs defendant of pending charges; appoints counsel for indigents.		
Bail	Sets initial bail amount.	May alter bail amount.	Rarely decides that bail is excessive.
Charging	No authority to intervene.	No authority to intervene.	No authority to intervene.
Preliminary hearing	Presides over preliminary hearing.		
Grand jury		Chief judge has nominal supervision over the grand jury.	
Arraignment		Informs defendant of pending charges and enters defendant's plea.	
Evidence	Reviews and authorizes search warrants.	Rules on suppression motions involving illegal search and seizure and custodial interrogation.	Rulings establish boundaries for search and seizure and custodial interrogation.
Plea bargaining	Judges rely on pleas to dispose of items on large dockets.	Some judges actively participate, whereas others are passive.	Rarely rules that plea of guilty was not voluntary.
Trial	Rarely held.	Presides at trial. Rules on admissibility of evidence. Instructs jury as to the law applicable to the case.	Decides whether evidence was properly admitted. Decides whether trial judge properly instructed jury as to the law.
Sentencing	Typically imposes "normal penalties."	Increasingly difficult and controversial task.	In some jurisdictions, must interpret sentencing guidelines.
Appeal	Rare, except in some driving under the influence convictions.	Notice of appeal filed in trial court.	Rarely reverses trial judge.

© Cengage Learning

and party leaders. In some cities, judicial staff positions are significant sources of party patronage.

Frustrations of the Job

Because of the pressures of today's criminal justice system, the ideals surrounding the judge are not always borne out by the reality. One of the most frustrating aspects of being a judge is the heavy caseload and corresponding administrative problems (Rosen, 1987). Thus, instead of having time to reflect on challenging legal questions or to consider the proper sentence for a convicted felon, trial judges must move cases, acting more like administrators in a bureaucracy than as judicial sages. As a New York judge put it:

> It is clear that the "grand tradition" judge, the aloof brooding charismatic figure in the Old Testament tradition, is hardly a real figure. The reality is the working judge who must be politician, administrator, bureaucrat, and lawyer in order to cope with a crushing calendar of cases. A Metropolitan Court Judge might well ask, "Did John Marshall or Oliver Wendell Holmes ever have to clear a calendar like mine?" (Blumberg, 1967a, p. 120)

Although this quote is more than 40 years old, the same judicial frustrations affect judges today (Mayer, 2007).

Moreover, the judge's actions are limited by the system—lawyers are late, court documents get lost, jails are crowded. Added to these general constraints is the overall low prestige of criminal court judges, who occupy the lowest rung within the judicial system. Like the other actors in the criminal justice system, the judge becomes tainted by close association with defendants who are perceived as society's outcasts.

Thus, the frustrations of the criminal trial court judge are many. Some judges prefer the relative peace of civil court, where dockets are less crowded, courtrooms quieter, legal issues more intriguing, and witnesses more honest than in the criminal court atmosphere of too many cases, too much noise, too many routine (and often dull) cases, and too many fabricated stories (Rothwax, 1996). Other judges, however, like the camaraderie of the criminal court.

Despite these frustrations, judges appear to be very satisfied with their jobs. A recent study of trial court judges in New York reports that they were very satisfied with their jobs, enjoyed the activity of judging, and found the work substantively interesting. Their major complaint was the lack of regular pay raises—an overwhelming 94 percent stated they were very dissatisfied with the regularity of pay raises (Jensen, 2011).

COURTS, LAW, & MEDIA

JUDGE JUDY: JUSTICE WITH AN ATTITUDE OR JUST PLAIN NONSENSE?

Straight-talking Judge Judy (Judith Sheindlin) stormed onto the television screen on September 16, 1996, and quickly became the boss of syndicated courtroom television show ratings. Her show is regularly among the top syndicated shows in the country, and you've probably seen it. Before starting her own show, Judge Judy served as a judge in New York, hearing more than 20,000 cases. She is the author of three books for a general audience—*Don't Pee on My Leg and Tell Me It's Raining* (1996); *Beauty Fades, Dumb Is Forever* (1999); *Keep It Simple, Stupid: You're Smarter Than You Look* (2000); and two children's books, *Win or Lose by How You Choose* (2000) and *You Can't Judge a Book by Its Cover: Cool Rules for School* (2001). On the bench, she was known for her outspoken behavior and for being one of New York's toughest judges—attributes she brings to her "syndicourt" (syndicated courtroom) television show with sayings such as "I'm the BOSS, Applesauce."

Some observers see *Judge Judy* and other law-related television shows as beneficial because they reveal to viewers information about how the legal system works. Others disagree and see Judge Judy's behavior and that of her fellow syndicourt show judges as unrepresentative of the real-world job of judging, describing it as "sarcastic, accusatory, and opinionated" (Podlas, 2002, p. 41).

A fair question might be, "What difference does it make who's right? If people enjoy the entertainment, what damage could these shows possibly do?" Kimberlianne Podlas (2002) suggests four troubling implications of these shows: (1) They may reduce respect for the bench; (2) they may lead to general misinterpretation of judicial behavior and temperament; (3) they may alter expectations about the legal system; and (4) they may lead participants in real cases to adopt inappropriate models of behavior.

Continued on next page

Continued from previous page

To test whether any of those negative consequences of watching too much syndicourt TV exist, Podlas conducted a survey of 241 potential jurors in three jurisdictions in the northeastern United States. She asked them about their syndicourt viewing behavior and about their views of judges. Her findings reveal that frequent viewers of syndicourt programs, when compared with nonviewers, are far more likely to believe that "judges should have an opinion regarding the verdict, judges should make their opinion clear, judges should ask questions during trial, judges should be aggressive with litigants or express displeasure with their testimony," and perhaps most shockingly, "a judge's silence indicates belief in a litigant" (Podlas, 2002, p. 41). Moreover, prior court service or experience did nothing to diminish the impact of watching these programs on attitudes about the judiciary.

Judge Judy may have an admirable goal, for she says on her website that for many years, she has "tried to change the way families deal with problems on a very small scale, one case at a time. Now I can use the skills I have developed and take my message to more people every day." But it may also be the case that in taking her message—which is inconsistent with the normal behavior of judges and the actual day-to-day operations of America's courts—that she is doing more harm than good to the credibility and legitimacy of the judiciary. After all, Judge Judy is hardly a model for judicial temperament (Bisceglia, 2007) so in the end, what you get is social condemnation with your justice (Cohn, 2005).

After watching one or more episodes of *Judge Judy*, be prepared to discuss the following:

1. Compare the behavior of Judge Judy with that normally expected of judges as described in this chapter.
2. Write down three things you think you know about the legal system based on your own experience watching law-related shows such as *Judge Judy*, and then discuss whether your observations are indeed true.
3. In what way might the popularity of *Judge Judy* be related to the public desire to be able to see actual courtroom proceedings?

JUDGES WITHIN THE COURTROOM WORK GROUP

The public believes that judges are the principal decision makers in courts. Often they are not. Instead, they are constrained by the actions of other members of the courtroom work group—prosecutors, defense attorneys, and probation officers. Thus, judges often accept bail recommendations offered by prosecutors, plea agreements negotiated by defense attorneys, and sentences recommended by the probation officer. In short, although judges still retain the formal legal powers of their office, they often informally share these powers with other members of the courtroom work group.

Sanctions can be applied against judges who deviate from the consensus of the courtroom work group. Defense attorneys and prosecutors can foul up judges' scheduling of cases by requesting continuances or failing to have witnesses present when required. Particularly in big-city courts, judges who fall too far behind in disposing of the docket feel pressure from other judges, especially the chief judge. Judges who fail to move their docket may be transferred to less desirable duties (for example, traffic court or juvenile court).

By no means are judges totally controlled by the courtroom work group. As the most prestigious members of the group, they can bring numerous pressures to bear on prosecutors, defense attorneys, and others. A verbal rebuke to a defense attorney in open court or an informal comment to the head prosecutor that the assistant is not performing satisfactorily are examples of judicial actions that can go a long way toward shaping how the courtroom work group disposes of cases.

The amount of influence judges actually exert on the other members of the courtroom work group varies. Some judges are active leaders of the courtroom work group; they run "tight ships," pressuring attorneys to be in court on time, for example. These judges participate fully in courthouse dynamics. On the other hand, some judges have a laissez-faire attitude, allowing the attorneys as many continuances as they request.

In large courts, "judge shopping" is a common practice. Through the strategic use of motions for continuances and motions for a change of judge, defense attorneys maneuver to have their clients' cases heard by the judge they perceive as most favorable for their particular cases. Such judge shopping is the most direct evidence of variations among judges. Although organizational pressures work to provide a certain degree of consistency among judges, any examination of a multi-judge court immediately shows that judges differ in terms of the sentences they hand out, the way they run their courtroom, and the number of cases they have pending. Knowledge of these judicial differences is often as necessary for the practicing attorney as mastery of the law and rules of procedure.

VARYING ROADS TO A JUDGESHIP

Which lawyers are selected to be judges is determined by both formal selection methods and informal procedures. Table 8.2 presents the major formal selection methods used in the states, including partisan elections, nonpartisan elections, merit selection (usually referred to as the *Missouri Bar Plan*), and appointment. Note, though, that some states use different selection procedures for different levels of the judiciary.

However, formal selection methods (law on the books) are far less important than informal methods (law in action) in determining which lawyers reach the bench. How selection is conducted establishes the formal routes to who becomes a judge; however, when a judicial vacancy occurs, interim selection methods are needed. And while appointment by governors and merit selection predominate in filling temporary vacancies, who is ultimately selected to serve on an interim basis significantly affects the final outcome for filling a vacancy permanently (Holmes & Emrey, 2006). We will examine the three major methods of judicial selection—executive appointment, popular election, and merit selection—and explore the influence of both formal and informal selection practices.

Executive Appointments

In the early years of the Republic, judges were selected by executive appointment or elected by the legislature. Today, these methods of judicial selection are used in only a handful of jurisdictions.

Three states use election by the legislature, and a few others still use appointment by the governor. All Article III federal judges are selected by executive appointment. A number of studies have examined the political dynamics involved in the selection of federal judges (Goldman, 1997; Holmes & Savchak, 2003).

The U.S. Constitution specifies that the president has the power to nominate judges with the advice and consent of the Senate. Based on this constitutional authorization, both the president and the Senate have a voice in the selection process. When a judgeship becomes vacant, the Office of Legal Policy in the U.S. Department of Justice and the White House Counsel search for qualified lawyers by consulting party leaders of the state in which the vacancy has occurred, campaign supporters, U.S. senators, and prominent members of the bar. This initial private screening has been known to take a year or longer because of conflicts within the president's party regarding who should be selected (Goldman, Slotnick, & Schiovania, 2011).

After the president has submitted a nomination for a vacant judicial post, the process shifts to the Senate. Most nominations are routine. After a hearing by the Senate Judiciary Committee, the full Senate usually confirms, most often without a negative vote being cast. If the nomination is controversial, the committee hearings and Senate vote become the focus of great political activity. Over the past decade, major partisan wrangling has surrounded nominations to the federal bench. Although most of President George W. Bush's nominees to the federal bench were confirmed, Democrats filibustered some nominations to the Courts of Appeals, thus preventing confirmation (Neubauer & Meinhold, 2013). More recently, Republicans in the U.S. Senate have held up a number of President Obama's nominations to the federal bench, resulting in a rising number of vacancies even as caseloads are rising (Wheeler, 2012).

Senators also influence federal judicial selections through the informal power of senatorial courtesy. Senators expect to be consulted before the president nominates a person for a judicial vacancy from their state if the president belongs to the same party. A senator who is not consulted may declare the nominee personally unacceptable, and senators

TABLE 8.2 JUDICIAL SELECTION IN THE STATES

Merit Selection[a]	Gubernatorial (G) or Legislative (L) Appointment	Partisan Election	Nonpartisan Election	Combined Merit Selection and Other Methods
Alaska	California (G)[b]	Alabama	Arkansas	Arizona[c]
Colorado	Maine (G)	Illinois	California[b]	Florida[c]
Connecticut	New Jersey (G)	Louisiana	Georgia	Indiana[d]
Delaware	South Carolina (L)	Michigan	Idaho	Kansas[s]
District of Columbia	Virginia (L)	Ohio	Kentucky	Missouri[e]
Hawaii		Pennsylvania	Minnesota	New York[e]
Iowa		Texas	Mississippi	Oklahoma[c]
Maryland		West Virginia	Montana	South Dakota[e]
Massachusetts			Nevada	Tennessee[e]
Nebraska			North Carolina	
New Hampshire			North Dakota	
New Mexico			Oregon	
Rhode Island			Washington	
Utah			Wisconsin	
Vermont				
Wyoming				

[a] The following eight states use merit plans only to fill midterm vacancies on some or all levels of court: Alabama, Georgia, Idaho, Kentucky, Minnesota, Montana, Nevada, and North Dakota.

[b] California uses gubernatorial appointments for appellate courts, but nonpartisan elections for trial courts.

[c] Merit selection is used for appellate judgeships, while nonpartisan elections are used to fill trial court judgeships.

[d] Merit selection is used for appellate judgeships, while different counties use a variety of approaches to filling trial court judgeship, including merit selection, partisan elections, and nonpartisan elections.

[e] Merit selection is used for appellate judgeships, while either merit selection or partisan elections are used to fill trial court judgeships in different districts.

SOURCE: American Judicature Society. Judicial Selection Methods in the States, 2009. Available online at http://www.ajs.org/selection/sel_state-select-map.asp.

from other states—finding strength in numbers—will follow their colleague's preferences and not approve the presidential nomination. Through this process, senators can recommend persons they think are qualified (former campaign managers come to mind) or exercise a direct veto over persons they find unacceptable (political enemies, for example). But the influence of senators in general over judicial nominations has been declining (Binder & Maltzman, 2004).

Overall the selection process produces federal judges with two defining attributes: They belong to the president's party, and they have often been active in politics.

Although the **American Bar Association (ABA)**, the national lawyers' association, enjoys no formal role in the screening of nominees for the federal bench, it has historically played an influential role through its Standing Committee on the Federal Judiciary. The committee traditionally investigated potential judicial nominees by consulting with members of the legal profession and law professors. It then ranked the candidates as "exceptionally well qualified," "well qualified," "qualified," or "unqualified." Although the president has the sole power to nominate, most presidents did not wish to name someone who would later be declared unqualified. Therefore, the deputy attorney general usually sought the ABA's recommendations prior to nomination, and some potential nominees were eliminated in this way. However, the role of the ABA has diminished over the past decade or so in light of alleged political biases in the ABA's ratings of candidates, as well as criticisms against its "special access" in the nomination process because of the ABA's positions on controversial issues:

> In 1997, Senator Hatch ended the ABA's "quasi-official" role in the Committee process, though ABA representatives continued to testify in confirmation hearings. In 2001, President George W. Bush ended the process of giving the ABA special access to proposed nominees' names in advance of nomination or awaiting its evaluation before making nominations. Although it may be more difficult to elicit candid comments once a nominee is announced, the ABA continues to provide evaluations of whether nominees are professionally qualified, and at least some members of the Senate Judiciary Committee continue to consider the ABA evaluation. (*Georgetown Law Journal*, 2007, pp. 1037–1038)

President Obama restored the traditional role of the ABA and seeks its rankings prior to making a public announcement of a candidate (Neubauer & Meinhold, 2013).

In recent years, the role of the ABA has been eclipsed by that of other interest groups (Scherer, Bartels, & Steigerwalt, 2008). The Federalist Society, Common Cause, NAACP, and the National Women's Political Caucus are examples of interest groups that seek to influence who is selected and confirmed for a federal judgeship. Interest groups from both sides of the ideological spectrum appear to have decided that federal judgeships are critical to their policy agenda and have begun pulling out all the stops to try to influence who is nominated and who is confirmed. (Bell, 2002; Scherer, 2005; Steigerwalt, 2010). Despite the rancorous debate, President Bush

was generally successful, as were his predecessors, in securing the confirmation of his nominees to the federal bench (Dancey, Nelson, & Ringsmuth 2011). Indeed, his two nominations to the U.S. Supreme Court were confirmed after threats of filibusters dissipated. Likewise, President Obama has been successful in securing the confirmation of his nominees to the Supreme Court and most of his other nominations to the federal bench. But after the 2010 election, the pace of confirmation has slowed because 60 votes are required to end a filibuster in the Senate, and Republicans have used this voting rule to delay or defeat some of the president's nominations.

State appointive systems resemble the presidential system for selecting federal judges, except that with **gubernatorial appointments** no equivalent of senatorial courtesy exists at the state level. As with federal appointees, governors tend to nominate those who have been active in their campaigns. At times, governors have been known to make appointments to strengthen their position within a geographical area or with a specific group of voters. In recent years, some governors have allowed bar associations to examine the qualifications of potential nominees. State bar associations are gaining influence, much like the ABA influence on federal judicial appointees. However, governors have greater independence to ignore bar association advice.

Election of Judges

None of the original U.S. states elected its judges (Phillips, 2009). Today, however, approximately 30 states use some sort of election mechanism to select at least some of their judges (see Table 8.2). The concept of an elected judiciary is a uniquely American invention for democratizing the political process, one that arose during Andrew Jackson's presidency. It is based on the notion that an elitist judiciary does not square with the ideology of a government controlled by the people (Dubois, 1980; Streb, 2007). According to this philosophy, there should be no special qualifications for public office; the voters (not the elites) should decide who is most qualified.

In a few states, judges are selected using partisan elections (the nominee's political party is listed on the ballot). Historically, this approach enabled party bosses to use judicial posts as patronage to reward the party faithful. The Supreme Court ruled that party control is constitutional (*New York State Board of Elections v. Lopez Torres,* 2008). But in the majority of states that elect their judges, nonpartisan elections (no party affiliations are listed on the ballot) are used. Nevertheless, even where nonpartisan elections are used, partisan influences are often present (law in action); judicial candidates are endorsed or nominated by parties, receive party support during campaigns, and are readily identified with party labels.

Traditionally, campaigns for American judgeships have been low-key, low-visibility affairs marked by the absence of controversy and low voter turnout (Streb, 2007). Judicial candidates often stressed general themes in their campaigns, such as doing justice and being tough on criminals, thus providing voters few guides to possible differences between the candidates. The general lack of information and the low levels of voter interest give incumbent judges important advantages in running for reelection. The prestigious title "Judge" is often listed on the ballot in front of the judge's name. For this reason, few local lawyers wish to challenge a sitting judge. Once a judge is selected, either through an election or an appointment to fill a midterm vacancy, the chances of being voted out of office are small. Few sitting judges are even opposed for reelection; of those challenged, few are ever voted out of office (Dubois, 1984; Streb, Frederick, & Lafrance, 2007). Indeed one study found that over three-quarters of elections fail to provide voters a choice (Nelson, 2011).

Times are changing, however. In recent years, some judicial elections have become nastier, noisier, and costlier (Barnes, 2007; Bonneau, 2007; Schotland, 1998). Mudslinging and attack advertising have become common in some states (Arbor & McKenzie, 2011). Interest groups backed by business or plaintiff lawyers are spending millions to back their candidates (Goldberg, Holman, & Sanchez 2002). Thus, today's races, particularly at the state high-court level, are hard-fought affairs (Bonneau & Hall 2003; Peters 2008). Moreover, the U.S. Supreme Court ruled that candidates for judicial office are free to announce their views on key issues (*Republican Party v. White,* 2002). One consequence is that incumbent judges are now being defeated for reelection at a higher rate than in the past (although at the trial level, incumbents still often win).

Merit Selection

"Remove the courts from politics" has been the long-standing cry of judicial reformers, who oppose popular election of judges because voters have no way to know which lawyers would make good judges. Moreover, election suggests the appearance of impropriety because it provides an incentive for judges to decide cases in a popular manner. To cure these ills, legal reformers advocate merit selection, also known as the Missouri Bar Plan because that state was the first to adopt it in 1940.

Merit plans are actually hybrid systems incorporating elements from other judicial selection methods: gubernatorial appointment, popular election, citizen involvement, and—most important—a formalized role for the legal profession. Merit selection involves the establishment of a judicial nominating commission composed of lawyers and laypersons, who suggest a list of qualified nominees (usually three) to the governor. The state's chief executive makes the final selection but is limited to choosing from those nominated by the commission.

After a fixed period of service on the bench, the new judge stands uncontested before the voters in a retention election. The length of the initial, probationary appointment varies greatly from state to state, from 1 year in some states to 10 or 12 years in others (American Judicature Society, 2009). The sole question in such a retention election is, "Should Judge X be retained in office?" If the incumbent judge wins a majority of affirmative votes, he or she earns a full term of office (usually 6, 8, or 10 years). Each subsequent term is secured through another uncontested retention ballot. Most judges are returned to the bench by a healthy margin, often receiving 70 percent of the vote. Only a handful of judges have been removed from office (Aspin, 2011). Over a 30-year period, for example, 50 court judges from trial and appellate courts were defeated in 3,912 retention elections in 10 states (meaning that only 1.3% were not retained); 28 of these defeats occurred in Illinois, which requires a judge to receive a minimum of 60 percent of the popular vote to remain on the bench (Aspin, Hall, Bax, & Montoya, 2000; see also, Brody, 2008).

Although backers of the Missouri Bar Plan contend that it will significantly improve the judges selected and remove the courts from politics, studies of the merit selection system in operation have reached different conclusions. The politics of judicial selection have been altered but not removed; in fact, removing politics does not seem possible. What the reformers presumably mean is the removal of "partisan" politics. In operation, the Missouri Bar Plan has reduced the influence of political parties while at the same time greatly increased the power of the legal profession (Taylor, 2009; Watson & Downing, 1969).

Merit selection has won increasing acceptance. A majority of states use the merit system, at least at some level of their state court system (see Table 8.2). In addition, a number of other states have actively considered adopting merit selection. As evidence of the growing importance of merit selection, all states that have altered judicial selection techniques in recent years have adopted some form of the Missouri Bar Plan. Even in states that have not formally adopted merit selection, governors often use "voluntary merit plans" to fill temporary vacancies (Dubois, 1980; Holmes & Emrey, 2006). Typically, though, adoption of merit selection requires a difficult statewide constitutional amendment, which explains why few jurisdictions have adopted merit selection in recent years (Anderson, 2009).

CONSEQUENCES OF JUDICIAL SELECTION

The debate over the best method for selecting state judges has raged for decades. Partisan and nonpartisan elections, used in a majority of states, are supported by those who believe elections are the most appropriate method for guaranteeing the popular accountability of state judicial policymakers. Critics, on the other hand, assert that elections are fundamentally inconsistent with the principle of judicial independence, which is vital for neutral and impartial judicial decision making. Less philosophically, these competing perspectives find expression in tension between the legal profession and political parties over influencing judicial selections. The different methods of judicial selection heighten or diminish the influence of the bar or the influence of political parties. This debate indicates that methods of judicial selection are perceived to have important consequences. Three topics stand out. One centers on which system is "best." The second relates to similarities in judges' backgrounds. The third involves efforts to produce a more diverse judiciary.

Which System Is Best?

In evaluating which selection system is best, a key criterion is whether one system produces better judges than another. Judicial folklore has long held that particular systems may produce superior judges. Several studies have systematically analyzed this folklore. Because it is impossible to evaluate a normative concept such as "best," it is necessary to rephrase the question empirically. That is, do judges selected by one method differ from those selected by others? Researchers use measurable judicial credentials, such as education and prior legal experience, as indicators of judicial quality. These studies point to two different types of conclusions.

From the standpoint of individuals who wish to become judges, methods of judicial selection make a difference, but not much. When legislators appoint judges, it is quite clear that former legislators are more likely to be selected than in other systems. Similarly, when the governor appoints, the system benefits those who have held state office (such as legislators). By contrast, elective systems elevate to the bench a higher proportion of persons who have held local political office—which typically means the district attorney (DA). Under the Missouri Bar Plan and elective systems, former DAs are more often selected as judges. When the executive or legislature makes the selection, fewer DAs become judges. From a broader perspective, methods of judicial selection have only a marginal influence on the types of lawyers who become judges. Whether elected by the voters, appointed by the governor, or selected through merit plans, state judges are more alike than different. In terms of personal background characteristics such as prior political experience, ties to the local community, political party affiliation, and quality of legal education, the systems of judicial selection do not appear to produce very different types of judges (Flango & Ducat, 1979; Goldschmidt, Olson, & Eckman, 2009; Hurwitz & Lanier, 2003).

But what of the quality of judging? Does one method of judicial selection produce higher-quality judges than another? Scholars are divided on this question. Some maintain that no systematic evidence proves that one selection system produces better judges than another (Choi, Gulati, & Posner, 2008; Emmert & Glick, 1987). Others argue that "judicial quality is lower in states that utilize elections to select their judges" (Sobel & Hall, 2007). But putting aside the issue of "quality" in light of its subjective nature, it is important to note the evidence that judges selected in partisan elections react to public opinion with an eye toward their own reelections, whereas those appointed to office are free of this constraint (Brooks & Raphael, 2003; Pinello, 1995). This difference may play a critical role in whether judges are willing to overturn capital convictions (Brace & Boyea, 2007). Evidence also exists that judicial-selection methods may influence case outcomes in particular types of cases. For example, Gryski, Main, and Dixon (1986) reported that decisions upholding sex-discrimination claims occurred far more frequently in states with appointive systems than in those with election systems. Pinello (1995) found that appointed judges reversed criminal convictions for constitutional violations at a significantly higher rate than did elected judges (see also, Epstein, Knight, and Shvetsova, 2002). And Helland and Tabarrok (2002), using a large sample from cases across the country, found that tort awards for in-state plaintiffs against out-of-state defendants were larger in jurisdictions in which judges were elected. Thus, it does appear that the method of judicial selection matters. Which is "best," however, is a matter of interpretation.

Similarities in Judges' Backgrounds

Although the United States uses a variety of methods for selecting judges, it is important to note that judges share some important similarities, which may be of even greater importance than the differences. In general, judges are men from the upper middle class, and their backgrounds reflect the attributes of that class: They are more often White and Protestant, and they are better educated than the average American. Increasingly, though, judges are beginning to more closely resemble the American electorate. Judicial officers on state high courts of last resort, for example, are increasingly women and less likely to be high-status Protestants (Bonneau, 2001).

Another similarity among judges is that most were born in the community in which they serve. Trial court judges are usually appointed from particular districts; the persons appointed were often born in that area and attended local or state colleges before going on to a law school within the state.

Finally, judges are seldom newcomers to political life. Almost three out of four state high court judges have held a nonjudicial political office. Trial court judges also have held prior office—most often district attorney or state legislator. Eighty percent of federal judges had prior government experience. Before becoming judges, they had some familiarity with the range of public issues that government as well as courts must address. Because of these factors, few political mavericks survive the series of screens that precede becoming a judge. The process tends to eliminate those who hold views and exhibit behavior widely different from the mainstream of local community sentiment.

Diversity and the Judiciary

The United States is experiencing a revolutionary change in the composition of the bench. The dominant profile of judges as White males has begun to change. Since the presidency of Jimmy Carter, an increasing number of federal court vacancies have been filled with female judges, a pattern evident during both Republican and Democratic administrations (Goldman & Saronson, 1994; Goldman & Slotnick, 1999; Goldman, Slotnick, Gryski, & Schiavoni, 2007). Eighteen percent of President Clinton's nominations to the federal bench were women (Spill & Bratton, 2001). Republican President George W. Bush was also particularly vocal about his goal of diversity (Solberg, 2005). And Democrat Barack Obama demonstrated his commitment to judicial diversity early in his presidency by nominating the first Latina to the U.S. Supreme Court, Sonia Sotomayor. Later he nominated Elena Kagan, bringing the number of women on the nation's highest court to three. And nearly three-quarters of President Obama's nominees to the federal bench who have been confirmed by the Senate have been women or minorities. As a result, the Federal Judicial Center (2012b) reports that of the 1,208 sitting federal judges (both active and senior judges), 336 (27.8 percent) are women, 177 (14.7 percent) are African-American, 105 (8.7 percent) are Hispanic, and 24 (2 percent) are Asian-American. Only 2 federal judges are of Native-American decent and only 4 are openly gay.

The picture with regard to state judges is significantly more complicated. Until the 20th century, the number of women judges in America was so small that they could be counted on the fingers of one hand. The 20th century began witnessing changes, though not very quickly. By 1950, women had achieved at least token representation on the bench (Carbon, 1984). Today, the National Association of Women Judges (2012) reports that of the roughly 17,500 state court judges in the United States, 4,711 (27 percent) are women. As the number of women serving on the state and federal benches has risen, there has been an understandable interest in probing the "difference" women may bring to the bench (Martin, 1993). Speculation by some has suggested that female judges are likely to be more liberal than male jurists. Some studies reported gender differences in areas like women's rights claims (Palmer, 2001), self-defense by women in homicide cases, and whether to award alimony (Coontz, 2000). But often the differences are at best small.

But other studies find no gender differences among judges (Miller & Maier, 2008). A study of Justice Sandra Day O'Connor, the first woman to serve on the U.S. Supreme Court, concludes, "Overall, the findings presented here do very little to support the assertion that O'Connor's decision making is distinct by virtue of her gender" (Davis, 1993, p. 139). Similarly, an analysis of more than 2,100 written opinions indicated that male and female federal district court judges were not significantly different when it came to their decisions (Stidham & Carp, 1997). These findings have been supported by a study of judicial voting in thousands of cases that show that in most areas of law, the decisions of female and male judges are rarely different. In 12 out of 13 areas of law (sex discrimination is the only exception) male and female judges do not differ in their decisions (Boyd, Epstein, & Martin 2010).

In 1973, slightly more than 1 percent of state judges were African-American; by the mid-1980s, the percentage had increased to 3.8 percent (Graham, 1990). Today, that figure stands at roughly 5.9 percent (American Bar Association, 2009). The underrepresentation of African-Americans on the bench is partially a reflection of the paucity of African-American attorneys. But underrepresentation is also a product of how judges are selected. African-American judges are more likely to be found in states using appointment by either the governor or the legislature; they are less likely to be selected in states using elections (American Judicature Society, 2009; Graham, 1990). In 1991, the Supreme Court held that the Voting Rights Act of 1965, as amended in 1982, applies to judicial elections (*Chisom v. Roemer* and *Houston Lawyers' Association v. Attorney General of Texas*). These rulings pave the way for major changes in the 41 states, particularly in the South, that use elections for at least some of their judges (Smith & Garmel, 1992). On the following page, the "Case Close-Up" explores diversity on the bench.

JUDGING THE JUDGES

Judicial-selection techniques attempt to recruit Solomon-like figures to the bench. Judicial-education programs help beginning judges learn their new roles and keep veteran judges abreast of changes in the law. The troublesome problem remains, however: What should be done about unfit judges? Despite the lack of clarity in what attributes a good judge should possess, one central conclusion stands out: A few judges do not fulfill minimal standards. A few are senile, prejudiced, vindictive, tyrannical, lazy, or sometimes corrupt. Proper judicial conduct is indispensable to people's confidence in their judiciary, confidence that itself is indispensable to the rule of law. In recent years, such confidence has been eroded by questions of judicial misconduct in a variety of states, including California, Illinois, Florida, Louisiana, New York, Oklahoma, Rhode Island, Pennsylvania, and New Hampshire.

Judicial Independence

A critical issue in judging the judges is how to devise a system for removing unfit judges while at the same time guaranteeing **judicial independence**. At times, critics attempt to remove a judge from office not because of his or her misconduct, but solely because of displeasure with the substance of the judge's decisions. Clearly, protections against unpopular court rulings constitute the hallmark of an independent judiciary. Yet judicial independence is not an end in itself. As University of Chicago Law Professor Philip Kurland has put it, "The provisions for securing the independence of the judiciary were not created for the benefit of the judges, but for the benefit of the judged" (quoted in Byrd, 1976, p. 267). The "Courts, Controversy, and the Administration of Justice" feature on page 211 explores the topic of whether judicial independence is being undermined.

CASE CLOSE-UP

CHISOM v. ROEMER AND DIVERSITY ON THE BENCH

Janice Clark had always wanted to be a judge. As a practicing lawyer, she seemed to possess the education and experience necessary to don the black robes, but she still faced an insurmountable barrier. The problem was not gender—after all, women are being elected to the bench on a regular basis all over the United States. Rather, the insurmountable barrier was race. White voters rarely vote for African-American candidates; indeed, as an African-American candidate for a judgeship, Clark received only 3.2 percent of the White vote. So, as lawyers often do, she filed suit in the U.S. District Court for the Middle District of Louisiana. Joined by African-American voters and lawyers throughout Louisiana, her class action lawsuit alleged that electing judges from multimember districts diluted African-American voting strength in violation of the Voting Rights Act.

The lawsuit was joined by local civil rights groups, as well as several national organizations, including the Voter Information Project and the Lawyer's Committee for Civil Rights Under Law. The nominal defendant was the governor of the state and all other government officials connected with judicial elections. Also appearing for the defendants were attorneys representing the Louisiana District Judges Association and the Orleans Trial Judges Association (*Clark v. Edwards*, 1988).

U.S. District Judge John Parker's opinion stressed that of the 156 district court judgeships in Louisiana, only 2 were held by African-Americans. The reason was that judgeships were elected from the entire judicial district, which had the effect of "diluting black voting strength," a violation of the Voting Rights Act.

This case was one of several filed in the federal courts, and the underlying legal issue was eventually settled at the appellate level in *Chisom v. Roemer* (1991) and *Houston Lawyers' Association v. Attorney General of Texas* (1991). The basic legal issue hinged on an interpretation of the Voting Rights Act of 1965 as amended in 1982. The Voting Rights Act covers representatives. Clearly, legislators are considered representatives, but

what of judges? The Fifth Circuit said no, but *Chisom* held otherwise, finding that judges were indeed covered by the Voting Rights Act.

Crossing this important threshold means that, in drawing election districts (either for legislatures or judges), the lines may not dilute minority voting. This conclusion was based on repeated findings of the existence of racially polarized voting, which in an election contest pitting an African-American candidate against a White one, White voters were very unlikely to cast their ballot for the African-American candidate (Engstrom, 1989). But the future of this line of decisions is cloudy. In a 5-to-4 decision, the Supreme Court ruled that race is an impermissible consideration in drawing congressional voting districts (*Miller v. Johnson*, 1995). Nonetheless, challenges to judicial election and selection procedures under the Voting Rights Act have been mounted in 15 states (Scruggs, Mazzola, & Zaug, 1995).

Janice Clark's legal argument eventually became the law of the land. The series of U.S. Supreme Court cases firmly established the principle that judges cannot be elected in ways that place minority candidates at an unfair disadvantage. But the eventual impact is far from certain. Each of the states with a significant minority population differs somewhat in tradition and method of judicial selection, factors that shape the emerging systems of judicial selection. But for Janice Clark, the outcome was both immediate and positive. She ran again for the major trial court bench in Baton Rouge and won, taking the oath of office on January 1, 1993. When a high-ranking state police official publicly complained about one of her decisions, she took to the bench and scolded the official, explaining that the problem was not her interpretation of the law, but how poorly the legislature had written the state's gaming law in the first place. Her unusual candor aside, it will be many years before we know whether minority judges have a long-term impact on the type of justice meted out in courthouses across America.

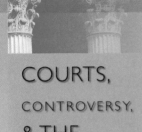

COURTS, CONTROVERSY, & THE ADMINISTRATION of JUSTICE

Is Judicial Independence Being Undermined?

While a candidate for the 2012 Republication nomination for president, former Speaker of the House Newt Gingrich suggested that federal law enforcement agents should arrest federal judges who make controversial decisions in order to compel the judges to justify their decisions before congressional hearings (Gardner & DeLong, 2011). Even though a number of conservatives felt that Gingrich had gone too far, it did symbolize that attacks upon "activist judges" is a recurring theme in the United States.

The most recent Republican attacks came shortly after three justices of the Iowa Supreme Court were voted out of office. A socially conservative group called "Iowa for Freedom" targeted them because they were the only ones facing the electorate during the fall after that court had unanimously voted to legalize same-sex marriages in the state (Aspin, 2011).

In an adversary system, a judge's decision often fails to find favor with the losing party. In the modern era, the losing party is often quick to label the judge an activist. The term activist judges has no legal meaning, but politically it stands for judges who make unpopular decisions. Some worry that in the modern era, attacks on judges seriously undermine judicial independence.

In recent years, both state and federal judges have been the subject of attack (Raftery, 2006).

- Justice Penny White of the Tennessee Supreme Court was voted off the bench in a retention election because she voted in a death penalty case to grant the defendant more leeway to present evidence that might mitigate the sentence imposed in the case (Bright, 1997).

- Jay Bybee, U.S. Court of Appeals for the Ninth Circuit, has been targeted by some for impeachment because of the legal opinions he wrote while head of President Bush's Office of Legal Counsel about harsh treatment of terrorist suspects (Justice at Stake, 2009a).

- The administration of George W. Bush harshly criticized U.S. District Judge Paul Cassell for unduly lenient sentencing even though as a law professor, Cassell was one of the leading academic critics of the Warren Court (Willing, 2003).

Attacks on the federal judiciary are hardly new. President Jefferson tried to remove Justice Samuel Chase as part of a campaign to "reform" the federal judiciary. In the 1960s, a nationwide campaign was launched by the ultraconservative John Birch Society to impeach Chief Justice Earl Warren. Not surprisingly, attacks on federal judges most often occur during election years (Segal, 2000). Thus, during the 1968 presidential election, candidate Richard Nixon attacked the Supreme Court, promising to remake the high court in his own image. But almost invariably, challenges to judicial independence fail (Friedman, 1998). Opposition campaigns are most likely to succeed when there is a clear issue that is important to a large portion of voters (Aspin, 2011).

Attacks on the judiciary, though somewhat predictable, can still exert a chilling effect on judicial independence. Former Chief Justice William Rehnquist voiced concern along these lines: "There is a wrong way and right way to go about putting a popular imprint on the judiciary" (Carelli, 1996). In the same vein, law professor Stephen Burbank (1987) reminded us that judicial independence is a means to an end rather than an end in itself. Criticism is one thing; undermining judicial independence is another. "Courts are not independent when state judges are voted off the bench because of unpopular decisions by their courts, and when federal judges reverse decisions or resign from the bench after a barrage of criticism" (Bright, 1997, p. 167). Judges are concerned that the increasing tendency to verbally attack judges appears to be related to increasing physical threats against judges. According to the U.S. Marshals Service, threats and harassments against federal judges increased 89 percent in just 5 years (Coyle, 2009).

Concerned that recent attacks on judges threaten to alter the delicate balance between judicial independence and judicial accountability, the American Judicature Society has created the Center for Judicial Independence to respond to unwarranted attacks on the judiciary and

Continued on next page

Continued from previous page

to sponsor public education programs on relevant issues ("Issues in Judicial Independence and Accountability," 2004). Similarly, Justice at Stake (http://www.justiceatstake.org) has launched a campaign to protect fair and impartial courts from outside political pressures. Some attacks on judges appear to be ideological in nature. Retired Justice

Sandra Day O'Connor wrote, "What worries me is the manner in which politically motivated interest groups are attempting to interfere with justice" ("After Death Threats," 2009).

What do you think? Where do you draw the line between fair criticism of judges and intimidation?

Judicial Misconduct

Systems for removing or disciplining unfit judges must not only strike a balance between judicial accountability and judicial independence, but they must also grapple with the wide range of misbehavior encompassed by the phrase "judicial misconduct" (Begue & Goldstein, 1987). Most directly, judicial misconduct involves corruption. In recent years, judges in big cities such as Chicago, New York, and Philadelphia have been accused of (and sometimes convicted of) criminal offenses such as taking bribes and fixing traffic tickets. But not all judicial misconduct is so venal; sometimes it involves improper or bizarre behavior on the bench (Goldschmidt, Olson, & Ekman, 2009; Wice, 1991). Exhibit 8.1 summarizes some recent cases that illustrate the range of behavior.

One of the most difficult situations involves judges of advanced years whose mental capacity has become impaired. After years of dedicated service, with exemplary conduct on the bench and no hint of scandal, a judge might become senile. Accordingly, a growing number of states impose mandatory retirement ages for judges. The Supreme Court has ruled that state laws requiring judges to retire at age 70 do not violate the federal Age Discrimination in Employment Act (*Gregory v. Ashcroft*, 1991). In another widely followed case, the nation's highest court upheld the prison sentence of David Lanier, a state judge from Dyersburg, Tennessee. Judge Lanier had been convicted in federal court of sexually attacking five women in his courthouse. He had not been prosecuted in state court, nor had the state's conduct commission taken action—many said because the judge was politically well-connected and his brother was the county prosecutor. The decision in *United States v. Lanier* (1997) strengthened federal civil rights laws (Chapter 3). The "Key Developments" feature on the

following page summarizes some of the leading U.S. Supreme Court cases affecting judges.

Formal methods for removing unfit judges—recall elections and impeachment proceedings—are generally so cumbersome that they have seldom been used. Moreover, these techniques are better directed at corrupt judges than at those whose behavior is improper or whose advanced age has caught up with them. A more workable method for dealing with judicial misconduct is the judicial conduct commission.

State Judicial Conduct Commissions

In 1960, California became the first state to adopt a modern and practical system for disciplining its judges. In response to the mounting public clamor for accountability on the part of government officials, every state has followed California's pioneering lead (Brooks, 1985). Under the California model, a judicial conduct commission is created as an arm of the state's highest court. The commission, made up of judges, lawyers, and prominent laypersons, investigates allegations of judicial misconduct and, when appropriate, hears testimony.

If the commission finds in favor of the judge, the investigation is closed and the matter is permanently concluded (Miller, 1991). Confidentiality is essential, lest a judge's reputation be tarnished by a crank complaint. Many complaints are issued by disgruntled litigants, whose charges amount to simple displeasure that the judge did not rule in their favor (Gray, 2007). If the complaint has merit, the commission may recommend a sanction of private admonishment, public censure, retirement, or removal. The state supreme court retains the final power to discipline errant judges (Gardiner, 1986).

Although commissions are armed with the potent weapon of a public recommendation, they prefer to act more informally. If the information gathered

| Exhibit 8.1 | **EXAMPLES OF ERRANT STATE JUDGES** |

- A veteran town justice in upstate New York was removed from the bench for jailing five defendants without affording them due process (Stashenko, 2012).

- A Luzerne County, Pennsylvania, judge, Mark Ciavarella, Jr., was convicted of 12 criminal counts, including racketeering, receiving bribes, and conspiracy, for his involvement in a scandal that became known as "kids-for-cash." He and a fellow judge, Michael Conahan, accepted nearly $2 million in bribes from developers of juvenile detention centers and, in turn, then sentenced juvenile offenders to those facilities. Shockingly, Ciavarella sentenced thousands of teens to these centers for minor violations that almost never result in sentences of juvenile incarceration, such as a first offense for being in a schoolyard scuffle. He often did so by violating the constitutional rights of the accused teens, ranging from denying them counsel to the right to enter a voluntary, intelligent, and knowing plea. He was sentenced to 28 years in prison in August 2011. Pennsylvania expunged more than 6,000 records of youths Ciavarella sentenced, some for crimes as small as stealing a jar of nutmeg or setting up a MySpace page mocking a school principal (Pitts, 2011).

- Since 2008, at least 16 judges in Georgia have resigned rather than face ethics hearings before the Judicial Qualifications Commission (Torpy & Rankin, 2010).

- David Bradfield of the 36th District announced his retirement, effective immediately, in the face of an indefinite suspension following a spat with a Detroit deputy mayor over a parking place (Schmitt, 2006).

- Rosemarie Williams, the presiding judge of New Jersey's Somerset County's General Equity Part, was reassigned to another county after her conviction for driving under the influence (Toutant, 2006).

- Judge Alan Green of Louisiana's 24th judicial district was sentenced to 51 months in prison after being convicted of taking $10,000 in cash from a local bail bondsman (Krupa, 2006).

- Philadelphia Traffic Court Judge Willie Singletary was charged with misconduct after a YouTube video showed him soliciting campaign funds (Elliott-Engel, 2008).

- Chief Judge Sharon Keller of the Texas Court of Criminal Appeals was charged with incompetence, violating her duties, and casting public discredit on the judiciary for refusing to delay the closing of the clerk's office for an emergency appeal for a man facing the death penalty. The man was executed several hours later (Kovach, 2009).

suggests judicial misconduct, the commission holds a confidential conference and discusses the matter with the judge, who has an opportunity to rebut the charges. The commission may try to correct the matter; a judge with a substance-abuse problem, for example, is encouraged to enroll in a treatment program. If the problems are serious, continuous, or not immediately solvable, the commission usually seeks to force the judge's voluntary retirement. The informal pressures and the threat of bringing public proceedings are often powerful enough to force the judge in question off the bench. The complaints and investigations remain confidential unless the commission finds it necessary to seek a reprimand or removal before the state supreme court.

Federal Conduct and Disability Act

In 1980, Congress passed the Judicial Councils Reform and Judicial Conduct and Disability Act, which lays out a precise mechanism for acting on complaints against federal judges. Complaints are initially heard by the judicial councils (the administrative arm of each U.S. court of appeals). Most result in either a finding of no misconduct or the imposition of nonpublic sanctions. However, if substantial evidence of serious misconduct exists, the judicial council sends a written report to the Judicial Conference, which may recommend that the U.S. House of Representatives begin impeachment procedures.

KEY DEVELOPMENTS CONCERNING JUDGES

Judicial Conduct Commission (1960)	California creates first judicial conduct commission.
Judicial Conduct and Disability Act (1980)	Federal conduct law passed.
Gregory v. Ashcroft (1991)	State laws requiring judges to retire at 70 do not violate the federal Age Discrimination in Employment Act.
Chisom v. Roemer (1991); Houston Lawyers' Association v. Attorney General of Texas (1991)	Judicial elections are covered by the Voting Rights Act.
United States v. Lanier (1997)	State judges are covered by federal civil rights laws.
Republican Party v. White (2002)	In campaigning for a judgeship, a candidate may discuss issues.
Rules for Judicial Conduct and Judicial Disability Proceedings (2008)	Implemented the recommendations of the Breyer Commission to "provide mandatory and nationally uniform provisions" that govern how judicial misconduct proceedings are conducted in the federal circuits.
New York State Board of Elections v. Lopez Torres (2008)	It is not unconstitutional for the state of New York to allow political parties to use a judicial convention system to pick the party's judicial candidates.
Caperton v. Massey Coal (2009)	Judges must recuse themselves from cases when large campaign contributions from interested parties create the appearance of bias.

Article II of the Constitution provides for the removal of the president, vice president, or civil officers of the United States—including federal judges—for crimes of "treason, bribery, or other high crimes and misdemeanors." The House must first vote articles of impeachment specifying the specific charges. Impeachment does not mean conviction, but rather allegations of wrongdoing—roughly equivalent to a grand jury indictment. The trial on the articles of impeachment is conducted before the Senate. Conviction requires a two-thirds vote of the senators present and carries with it removal from office and disqualification from holding any future office. Historically, in functioning as both judge and jury in impeachment trials, all senators observed the testimony and cross-examination of witnesses. But in the modern era, the press of legislative business makes this time-consuming process unworkable. Therefore, in 1986 the Senate made the historic decision to establish a 12-person Impeachment Committee to receive evidence and take testimony prior to the trial on the Senate floor (Heflin, 1987).

An unprecedented series of allegations of misconduct against federal judges since 1981 highlights the interlocking relationships among criminal prosecutions, impeachment, and the new statutory scheme (Exhibit 8.2). The impeachment proceedings against U.S. District Judge Alcee Hastings raised the most difficult questions: Unlike Claiborne and Nixon, he was never convicted of a criminal offense. Hastings, the first African-American federal judge ever appointed in Florida, was indicted for soliciting a $150,000 bribe from two convicted racketeers, but the jury acquitted him. Hastings argued that racial motivations lay behind the impeachment proceedings. In 1989, the Senate removed Hastings from his judicial office, but in a strange twist, Hastings was later elected to the U.S. House of Representatives.

These cases are truly exceptional. Prior to the 1980s, only four federal judges had been removed, the most recent in 1936. But these statistics obscure the fact that many misconduct and disability problems of federal judges are resolved informally by the judiciary itself. Whether the federal courts effectively police themselves, however, is open to debate.

In 2003, an attorney filed an ethical complaint under the Judicial Conduct and Disability Act against U.S. District Judge Manuel Real. The way in which the initial complaint and subsequent complaints against the judge were handled by the Ninth Circuit Court of Appeals caused the case to get the attention of the press, the Judicial Conference, and ultimately, of Congress (Bazelon, 2009). The attention paid to the handling of the allegations against Judge Real, coupled with other instances of ineffective oversight of alleged judicial misconduct, led to the formation of a commission to investigate how the Judicial Conduct and Disability Act of 1980 had been implemented. Because the commission was led by U.S. Supreme Court Justice Stephen Breyer, it came to be known as the Breyer Commission. After 2 years of study, which included details of the botched handling of the complaints against Judge Real, the Breyer Commission issued a 180-page report (2006). While concluding that circuit judges and judicial

councils were "doing a very good overall job in handling complaints" (p. 206), the Breyer Commission found that the federal judiciary mismanaged approximately 35 percent of "high-profile complaints . . . filed by attorneys, court personnel, or public officials," such as the ones against Judge Real (Bazelon, 2009, p. 469). Ultimately, Judge Real was found guilty of misconduct and publicly reprimanded for having made "inaccurate and misleading" comments during the investigation of the complaints filed against him. More significantly, though, most of the recommendations of the Breyer Commission were adopted by the Judicial Conference of the United States in 2008. These changes included 29 new mandatory rules for improving the "consistency and rigor" of disciplinary processes implemented under the Judicial Conduct and Disability Act of 1980 (Bazelon, 2009, p. 474).

Exhibit 8.2 FEDERAL JUDGES WHO HAVE FACED DISCIPLINARY ACTION SINCE 1980

U.S. District Judge Harry Claiborne (District of Nevada) The jury acquitted him on the charge of accepting a bribe in a criminal case over which he was presiding but convicted him of income-tax evasion. While he was serving a 2-year sentence in federal prison, the Senate found Claiborne guilty on three of four impeachment articles by the required two-thirds vote and removed him from the bench (1986).

Chief Judge Walter Nixon (Southern District of Mississippi) The jury convicted him of perjury for falsely denying before a federal grand jury that he had intervened in a state narcotics case involving the son of a friend. While he was serving his sentence at Eglin Air Force Base in Florida, the Senate removed Nixon from the federal bench in 1989.

U.S. District Judge Alcee Hastings (Southern District of Florida) The jury acquitted him of the charge of soliciting a $150,000 bribe from two convicted racketeers. The Eleventh Circuit and the Judicial Conference concluded that Hastings was not guilty but also concluded that he had fabricated his defense. The Senate ousted Hastings from office in 1989, but in a strange twist, Hastings was then elected to Congress.

U.S. District Judge Robert Aguilar (Northern District of California) A jury convicted him of obstruction of justice for telling a friend about a government wiretap in a racketeering investigation. The Ninth Circuit reversed, but the Supreme Court reinstated the wiretap conviction (*United States v. Aguilar*, 1995). After another conviction and yet another appellate reversal, Aguilar resigned from the bench, apparently in exchange for criminal charges being dropped.

U.S. District Judge Robert Collins (Eastern District of Louisiana) A jury convicted him of taking a $100,000 bribe from a drug smuggler. While serving a 7-year prison sentence and facing impeachment proceedings, Collins resigned from the bench before formal Senate action was taken.

U.S. District Judge Brian Duff (Northern District of Illinois) Noted for his temper and for having the highest rate of reversal in the Chicago courthouse, he stepped down amid reports of a Justice Department complaint filed with the Judicial Counsel for the Seventh Circuit. Judge Duff cited medical problems (Robinson, 1996).

Continued on next page

Continued from previous page

U.S. District Judge Edward Nottingham (Colorado) Resigned from the bench amid allegations that he viewed an adult website on his government computer, spent $3,000 in a Denver strip club, and solicited prostitutes using his court-issued cell phone.

U.S. District Judge Samuel Kent (Southern District of Texas) Kent pled guilty to obstruction of justice for lying to judges who investigated sexual misconduct complaints. Sentenced to 33 months in federal prison in May 2009, Kent attempted to retire from the bench, thereby allowing him to draw his salary. The House of Representatives impeached him in June 2009. He resigned from the bench in disgrace, effectively ending his impeachment trial in the Senate.

U.S. District Judge Manuel Real (Central District of California) Amid numerous allegations of bizarre behavior and also taking control of a bankruptcy cases involving a friend, Real faced impeachment hearings in the House of Representatives, but the charges were later dropped. Although publicly censured, the judge who is in his late 80s continues on senior status (a form of semi-retirement in which a judge may opt to hear a reduced caseload).

U.S. Circuit Judge Alex Kozinski (Ninth U.S. Circuit Court of Appeals) Judge Kozinski was formally admonished in June 2009 for having sexually explicit photos and videos on his publicly accessible website. The files were stored on a personal computer at his home that was connected to the Internet using web server software. He claimed that he did not intend for the materials to be publically available. The Judicial Council said that Kozinski had exercised "poor judgment" by failing to take safeguards to prevent the material from becoming publicly accessible, and that his carelessness was "judicially imprudent." Kozinski issued a formal apology for causing "embarrassment to the federal judiciary."

U.S. District Judge Thomas Porteous (Eastern District of Louisiana) Accused of taking cash from lawyers with cases in his court when he was a state judge and repeatedly lying under oath, Porteous was impeached by the House and overwhelmingly convicted by the Senate in 2010.

U.S. District Judge Richard Cebull (District of Montana) At the time this book went to press, Judge Cebull was facing possible disciplinary action by the 9th U.S. Circuit Court of Appeals for a racist and sexist e-mail about President Obama. Cebull admitted forwarding the message to several friends from his judicial e-mail account from the governmental computer in his chambers.

JUDICIAL ETHICS

Because of the special role that judges occupy in the adversary system, they are subject to additional ethical constraints beyond those imposed on lawyers. The American Bar Association developed the Model Canons of Judicial Ethics, similar to the codes of legal ethics, but each state has adopted its own canons of judicial ethics. The purpose of these codes of judicial conduct is to preserve the integrity of the judicial system and to foster public confidence in the system (Gray, 2003).

A study of *A State Judicial Discipline Sanctions* by the Center for Judicial Ethics of the American Judicature Society found that the baseline cases for sanctions involve judges who drive while intoxicated or are unduly slow in issuing decisions (Gray, 2003).

Overall, the study concluded that public assumptions about levels of judicial misconduct are not borne out by the evidence. But state supreme courts can do more to tackle this cynicism by providing thorough, well-reasoned opinions in judicial misconduct cases and making them readily accessible to the public. Interestingly, a failure of the judge to cooperate with the state's judicial conduct commission was a contributing factor to a judge's removal (Gray, 2003).

Accusations of improper conduct by judges often reflect a lack of understanding of the role of judges in the adversary system. Judges face public criticism for reaching decisions that the public finds unpopular. A major obstacle facing judges who are the focus of negative public comments is the judicial conduct standard prohibiting judges from commenting on cases. But some judges find ways to offer appropriate, but nonprejudicial, defenses. A case in point is

Judge Arthur Hunter of New Orleans. The district attorney harshly criticized him for threatening to release defendants because the DA's office could not bring them to trial in a timely manner following Hurricane Katrina. Stressing his credentials as a former police officer, the judge wrote:

> Many people have a gross misconception of the role of judges in the criminal justice system. . . . Judges are like referees in a basketball game. They do not favor either side, but make sure the police, district attorney, and defense attorneys follow all the rules. Judges are not teammates with the district attorney, cheerleaders for the police, or coaches for the defense attorney. (Hunter, 2006)

Prohibition on conduct that brings the judicial office into disrepute is another requirement of canons of judicial ethics. Typically, this applies to situations in which the judge is having an extramarital affair or the like. But occasionally it involves conduct that is not personal but rather judicial. The best-known example is that of Roy Moore, who was elected chief justice of the Alabama Supreme Court. Consistent with his campaign promises, he installed a large granite monument of the Ten Commandments in the courthouse. When a federal court ordered its removal because it violated the First Amendment of the Constitution, the judge refused to comply. His refusal to obey a lawful court order was deemed to bring the judicial office into disrepute, and so he was removed from the bench (Clark, 2005).

The tension between electing judges and appearances of impropriety is emerging as a major issue in judicial ethics. In *Republican Party v. White* (2002), the Supreme Court allowed candidates for judicial office to discuss issues that might come before the court and to criticize past court decisions. The result has been a new dynamic in judicial elections, with some races featuring negative political ads and contentious campaigns (Fortune & White, 2008). Some are concerned that elections erode public perceptions of an impartial judiciary. In the words of Justice at Stake "Can two sides in a lawsuit receive equal justice when one side has spent $3 million to elect the judge deciding the case?" This issue was at the heart of *Caperton v. Massey Coal* (Justice at

Stake, 2009b) in which the Supreme Court held that judges must recuse themselves from cases when large campaign contributions from interested parties create the appearance of bias.

Judges play a key role in enforcing legal ethics. During the course of a lawsuit, a judge may be called on to enforce rules of professional conduct. At times, hearings or trials can become heated. The judge may find that a lawyer went too far in his or her argument or was unduly nasty to opposing counsel. In such cases, the judge may find the lawyer in contempt of court and impose a small fine or a brief jail term. On the civil side, a lawyer may accuse opposing counsel of an ethical violation such as failing to respond in a timely fashion or unnecessarily causing additional work for the lawyer. If the judge agrees, the judge may impose attorney's fees, that is, require the lawyer who caused the misconduct to financially reimburse opposing counsel.

CONCLUSION

In deciding *Caperton v. Massey Coal Company* (2009) the U.S. Supreme Court stressed that the decision addressed an "extraordinary situation": the Court stressed that the owner of Massey Coal spent over $3 million to elect his preferred candidate to the West Virginia Supreme Court, an amount three times more than any of the other candidate's supporters. By emphasizing these facts, the justices of the nation's highest court were apparently trying to separate the case from the fictional basis of the novel *The Appeal*. But where fact ends and fiction begins is always hard to tell. John Grisham is a fiction writer who excels in emphasizing extraordinary situations that, while fictional, are still based on fact. This blending of fact and fiction, life imitating art, provides another chapter in the ongoing national debate over judicial selection. Nor did interest end with the Court decision. A year after *Caperton* a coal mine owned by Massey Energy exploded, leaving 29 dead and reopening the issue of whether the company had systematically cut corners when it came to mine safety (Tavernise, 2012).

In the modern era, displeasure with judges has led to renewed interest in how judges are selected. But no matter how we select our judges and who they are, the workaday world of the trial judge bears little resemblance to the high expectations we have about the role of the judge. The trial judge is expected to dispose of a large caseload but is often frustrated by the attorneys' lack of preparation, missing defendants, misplaced files, little time to reflect, and probably most important, insufficient control over many vital aspects of the case. For these and other reasons, judges depend on other members of the courtroom work group. Some depend heavily on the prosecutors, defense attorneys, and probation officers, feeling content to let them make the difficult decisions. Others are much more active participants and are truly leaders of the courtroom work group.

Chapter Review

LO1 1. Discuss the role of the judge within the courtroom work group.

Judges are the most prestigious members of the courtroom work group, but they are expected to be reasonably responsive to lawyers and are also under pressure to move the docket.

LO2 2. Name the three major ways that judges are selected in the United States.

Judges are appointed by executives (like governors and the president), elected by the voters, or appointed through a merit selection process.

LO3 3. Analyze the consequences of different methods of judicial selection.

The various selection systems produce judges with very similar backgrounds, including local ties and past political involvement. No evidence exists that one selection system consistently produces "better" or "worse" judges than another, although research does reveal some differences in judicial approaches to decision making.

LO4 4. Recognize major changes in the composition of the bench over the past several decades.

Over the past several decades, the composition of the bench has become more diverse, with a significant number of women and some racial and ethnic minorities being elected and appointed to the nation's courts.

LO5 5. Describe the activities of state judicial conduct commissions.

If the state judicial conduct commissions find merit to a complaint about a judge, they often work informally to correct the problem. But if the problem is a serious one, the commission may recommend to the state supreme court that the judge be removed from office.

LO6 6. Explain the difference between the impeachment and the removal of a federal judge.

If the House of Representatives votes articles of impeachment charging a federal judge with serious misconduct, the Senate conducts a trial and may remove the judge from the bench.

Critical Thinking Questions

1. Which method of judicial selection (election, appointment, or merit) do you think is best? What does your choice reveal about your personal attitudes? Stated another way, do you think the legal profession should have more say in judicial selection (merit) or less influence (elections)?

2. For your state, examine judicial selection in terms of both law on the books (formal method of judicial selection) and law in action (actual practices).

3. At what point are efforts to remove "unfit" judges really efforts to remove judges because of decisions they have made?

4. American society has high expectations for judges, yet the actions of judges are constrained by other members of the courtroom work group. To what extent is criticism of judges, whether local or national, really criticism of the actions and inactions of prosecutors and defense attorneys?

5. Does underrepresentation of women on the bench hurt justice? Would citizens' views of the fairness of courts improve if more nontraditional persons became judges?

Key Terms

American Bar Association (ABA) 204
chambers 199
gubernatorial appointment 205

impeachment 214
judicial conduct commission 212
judicial election 206

judicial independence 209
Missouri Bar Plan 206
removal 214

Web Resources

Go to the *America's Courts and the Criminal Justice System* companion website at
http://www.cengage.com/criminaljustice/neubauer,
where you will find more resources to help you study.
Resources include web exercises, quizzing, and flash cards.

For Further Reading

Baum, Lawrence. *Judges and Their Audiences: A Perspective on Judicial Behavior.* Princeton, NJ: Princeton University Press, 2007.

Bonneau, Chris. "Vacancies on the Bench: Open-Seat Elections for State Supreme Courts." *Justice System Journal* 27: 143–160, 2006.

Carns, Teresa. 2009. "The Alaska Merit Selection System at Work, 1984-2007." *Judicature* 93: 102–108.

Epstein, Lee, and Jeffrey Segal. 2005. *Advice and Consent: The Politics of Judicial Appointments.* New York: Oxford University Press.

Geyh, Charles. 2006. *When Courts and Congress Collide: The Struggle for Control of America's Judicial System.* Ann Arbor: University of Michigan Press.

Gray, Cynthia. *Ethical Standards for Judges.* Des Moines, IA: American Judicature Society, 2009.

Hettinger, Virginia, Stefanie A. Lindquist, and Wendy L. Martinek. 2006. *Judging on a Collegial Court:*

Influences on Appellate Decision Making. Charlottesville: University of Virginia Press.

Peabody, Bruce (Ed.). *The Politics of Judicial Independence: Courts, Politics, and the Public.* Baltimore: Johns Hopkins University Press, 2010.

Peters, C. Scott. "Canons, Cost, and Competition in State Supreme Court Elections." *Judicature* 91: 27–35, 2007.

Salokar, Rebecca, D. Jason Berggren, and Kathryn DePalo. "The New Politics of Judicial Selection in Florida: Merit Selection Redefined." *Justice System Journal* 27: 123–142, 2006.

Streb, Matthew (Ed.) *Running for Judge: The Rising Political, Financial, and Legal Stakes of Judicial Elections.* New York: NYU Press, 2007.

Swanson, Rick. "Judicial Roles in State High Courts." *Judicature* 94: 168–177, 2011.

9 Defendants and Victims

AP Photo/Bob Breidenbach, Pool

Sarah Ballard tries to control her emotions as she delivers a victim impact statement in which she described how her life was changed by her mother's death in a nightclub fire in Rhode Island that was caused when indoor fireworks ignited soundproofing foam that had been installed in the club. The owners of the club pled "no contest" to 100 counts of involuntary manslaughter. One was sentenced to 4 years in prison and the other was spared any period of incarceration when he received a suspended sentence and 500 hours of community service. Families of those who died in the fire expressed outrage at the plea-bargained sentence. Stories like this call into question how the criminal justice system treats victims. ■

Chapter Outline

CHARACTERISTICS OF DEFENDANTS
Overwhelmingly Male

Courts, Controversy, & Racial Discrimination
Can Latinos Get Equal Justice under the Law?

Mostly Underclass
Racial Minorities Overrepresented

DEFENDANTS IN COURT
Pro Se Defendants
Social Media Trap

COURTS THROUGH THE EYES OF VICTIMS AND WITNESSES
Frustrations in Coping with the Process
Travails of Testifying
Surprising Support for the System

VICTIMS AND WITNESSES THROUGH THE EYES OF THE COURT
Lack of Cooperation
Witness Intimidation

CHARACTERISTICS OF VICTIMS
Prior Relationships between Defendants and Victims
Domestic Violence

CASE CLOSE-UP: *Thurman v. Torrington* and **Domestic Violence Arrests**

AIDING VICTIMS AND WITNESSES
Victim/Witness Assistance Programs
Victim Compensation Programs
Victims' Bill of Rights
Victim Impact Statements

Courts, Law, & Media
Law and Order: Special Victims Unit (NBC, 1999–present)

AIDING OR MANIPULATING VICTIMS?
The Victims' Rights Movement
Differing Goals
Do Victims Benefit?

*Defendants and Victims • Defendants and Victims • Def
ants and Victims • Defendants and Victims • Defendan*

Learning Objectives

After reading this chapter, you should be able to:

LO1 List the three characteristics of defendants.

LO2 Describe how victims and witnesses view the court process.

LO3 Describe how court actors view victims and witnesses.

LO4 Discuss the prior relationships between defendants and victims and why this is important in domestic violence cases.

LO5 Identify three types of programs that are designed to aid victims and witnesses in coping with the criminal justice process.

LO6 Explain why some view victim programs as aiding victims whereas others view these programs as manipulating victims.

The first officer on the scene described Pervis Tyrone Payne as looking like "he was sweating blood." The officer's partner followed the trail of blood into the kitchen, where he found Charissee Christopher and her two-year-old daughter Lacie butchered to death. After returning a verdict of guilty on two counts of first-degree murder, the trial proceeded to the penalty phase of a capital murder prosecution. The defense called four witnesses, who testified that Payne was a very caring person but had such a low score on an IQ test that he was mentally handicapped. The prosecutor countered by calling the victim's grandmother to the stand, who testified that three-year-old Nicholas (the lone survivor) kept asking why his mother didn't come home, and he cried for his sister. During closing arguments, the prosecutor made maximum use of this emotional testimony, imploring the jury to make sure that Nicholas would know later in life that justice had been done in his mother's brutal slaying. The Memphis, Tennessee, jury imposed the death penalty.

The difficulty with the grandmother's testimony in this case is that, just a couple of years before, the Supreme Court had ruled that such emotional statements are inadmissible because they tend to mislead jurors. But in the interim, the membership of the Court had changed with the addition of two conservatives appointed by Republican presidents. By agreeing to hear the case, the Court was signaling that it might be willing to reverse itself and allow victim impact statements during sentencing.

Payne v. Tennessee directs our attention to both defendants and their victims. All too often, when we think about the criminal courts, our minds immediately focus on the members of the courtroom work group: prosecutors, defense attorneys, and judges. We are less likely to think about the other participants: victims, witnesses, or even defendants. Yet these other actors are also important.

Victims greatly influence workload. Courts are passive institutions. They do not seek out cases to decide; rather, they depend on others to bring matters to their attention. How many cases are filed, as well as what kinds of cases are brought to court, is determined by the decisions of others—police, victims, and those who violate the law in the first place. Thus, the courtroom work group has very little control over its workload. Second, victims, witnesses, and defendants are the consumers of the court process. Democratic governments are expected to be responsive to the wishes and demands of their citizens; victims and witnesses often complain about how the courts handle their cases. Victims and defendants are both subjects and objects of the criminal justice process. Their importance for how the courtroom work group administers justice on a day-to-day basis is the subject of this chapter.

CHARACTERISTICS OF DEFENDANTS

In some ways, those accused of violating the criminal law are a diverse lot. Although many defendants are economically impoverished, their numbers also include high-ranking government officials, businesspeople, and prominent local citizens. An indicator of the diversity of defendants centers on how often they are involved with the criminal justice system. At one end of the spectrum are those who are arrested once and are never involved again. At the other end are a small group of career offenders who are responsible for a disproportionate share of offenses (Tracy, Wolfgang, & Figlio, 1990; Wolfgang, Figlio, & Sellin 1972). In fact, it is estimated that over 70 percent of all serious criminal offenses are committed by roughly 7 percent of offenders, a group commonly referred to as **career criminals,** (DeLisi 2005; Vaughn & DeLisi, 2008). To complicate

TABLE 9.1 ▪ PROFILE OF FELONY DEFENDANTS

Male	82%
Racial or ethnic minorities	71%
At least one prior conviction	61%
Younger than age 35	53%
Under criminal justice supervision at the time of arrest (probation, parole, pretrial release, or in custody)	31%

SOURCE: Thomas H. Cohen and Tracey Kyckelhahn. *Felony Defendants in Large Urban Counties, 2006.* Washington, DC: Bureau of Justice Statistics, 2010. Available online at http://bjs.ojp.usdoj.gov/content/pub/pdf/fdluc06.pdf.

matters further, a generational effect seems to be indicated. Violent offenders are much more likely to have experienced neglect, abuse, or violence in their families (Farrington, 2006; Harlow, 1999). Moreover, conviction of a parent is correlated with the likelihood of a child offending and being convicted (Farrington, 2006; Roettger & Swisher, 2011; Rowe & Farrington 1997). Whether it is possible to predict who will become a career criminal, however, is subject to extensive debate.

Aside from certain aspects of diversity, the majority of violators conform to a definite profile. Compared to the average citizen, felony defendants are significantly younger, overwhelmingly male, disproportionately members of racial minorities, more likely to come from broken homes, less educated, more likely to be unemployed, and less likely to be married (see Table 9.1). Three characteristics of defendants—sex, poverty, and race—figure prominently in discussions of crime and crime policy and therefore deserve expanded treatment.

Overwhelmingly Male

Defendants are overwhelmingly male. In fact, women account for only 25.5 percent of all arrests for all crimes (Federal Bureau of Investigation, 2011). Although these percentages represent a significant increase over the past few decades, it is unclear whether women are actually committing

COURTS, CONTROVERSY, & RACIAL DISCRIMINATION

CAN LATINOS GET EQUAL JUSTICE UNDER THE LAW?

The nomination of Sonia Sotomayor and a recent report of the U.S. Census Bureau (2011) have focused attention on race, ethnicity, and the justice system. More than one-third of our nation's population belongs to a minority group. Sotomayor is the first Hispanic, an ethnic group that constitutes the fastest-growing segment of the U.S. population, to serve on the U.S. Supreme Court. The U.S. Census Bureau reports that Hispanics now constitute nearly one in six residents, or 50.5 million people. Even more telling for the future: 44 percent of children younger than 18 years and 47 percent of children younger than 5 are now from minority families.

Hispanics (the identification adopted by the government) or Latinos (a term some in this group prefer) are diverse in terms of country of origin. Some, like Sonia Sotomayor, are from Puerto Rico, a U.S. territory. Others are Cuban, many of whose parents fled the dictatorship of Fidel Castro. Others are from Mexico, the world's 12th most populous country, with over 114 million people. Others are from other central and South American countries. Although united by the Spanish language, the Latino population is heterogeneous in many ways.

Most importantly for American politics, Hispanics are also diverse in terms of their immigration status. No accurate counts of how many illegal immigrants are in the country exist, but many estimate about 11 million. (Some advocacy groups place the number higher.) The majority of detained immigrants do not have an attorney during their deportation hearings (Hamblett, 2012). Immigration has become a major political issue in the United States, dividing both the American population and the nation's two major political parties. Part of this debate focuses on the role of the criminal justice system.

Hispanics share many of the same social disadvantages as Blacks (Demuth, 2003), including poverty, unemployment, living in neighborhoods with high crime rates and a history of discrimination. But in addition, they face some unique problems surrounding language and cultural heritage. Some Latino victims/defendants speak little if any English, which makes it hard for them to understand what is happening during investigations, arrests, court appearances, and the like. Besides lacking language skills, Latino victims/defendants also often lack a basic understanding of the American justice system. Their heritage is European law, which places less emphasis on the rights of criminal defendants. Moreover, in some of their native countries, the justice system has a history of suppression, which makes them particularly fearful of governmental officials.

The social disadvantages faced by Latinos have several important consequences for the criminal justice system. For one, Latinos express the same levels of lack of confidence in the U.S. criminal justice system as Blacks (Pew Hispanic Center, 2009). Perhaps for this reason, they are less likely to report crimes to the police. In crimes of violence such as

more crimes or whether changes in the criminal justice system itself have occurred. For example, decreases in sexist and paternalistic thought processes might now lead police to arrest and prosecutors to charge female offenders at higher rates than in the past (Pollock & Davis, 2005). According to this view, there has been no major shift in girls' or women's relative violence (Schwartz, Steffensmeier, Zhong, & Ackerman, 2009). On the other hand, there is empirical evidence that the gap between male and female offenders in violent crimes is decreasing (Lauritsen, Heimer, & Lynch, 2009). Whatever the causes, it is clear that rates of female involvement in the justice system have been increasing in recent years, but their absolute numbers still fall well below those of males.

Mostly Underclass

Typical felony defendants possess few of the skills needed to compete successfully in an increasingly technological society. They are drawn from what sociologists call the urban underclass (Jencks & Peterson, 1991). In turn, the more poverty in a community, the higher the amount of crime (Hipp &

assaults, robberies, and rapes, for example, Hispanic women report the crime to authorities just 35 percent of the time, as compared with 51 percent for White women, and 63 percent for Black women (Karmen, 2012). The lack of trust in governmental authorities coupled with a fear of being deported is a major reason Latinos often do not report crimes to the police. In turn, Latinos may be targeted because they are less likely to report the crime.

It is also harder for police and prosecutors to deal with crimes in which Latinos are victims or defendants. Traditionally, the Hispanic population was concentrated in states sharing a border with Mexico and a few big cities. Today, the population has spread across the nation, meaning that many police departments have few if any officers who can take an accurate police report from a Spanish speaker. The same barriers face prosecutors, public defenders, and judges, with justice sometimes lost in the translation. For example, following the slaying of a Hispanic migrant worker, six Spanish-speaking witnesses were held for months in jail as material witnesses, but they had no court-appointed lawyer because no one in the public defender's office could read the letters they wrote (Alexander-Bloch, 2007).

How well or how poorly Latinos fare in the criminal justice system is hard to tell. An extensive body of research has compared White defendants with Black defendants, but relatively little is known about Latino defendants (Martinez, 2007). But we do know that after arrest, Hispanics are more likely to be detained in jail than Blacks or Whites (Demuth, 2003).

The growing Hispanic population and the issues surrounding immigration have strained the U.S. justice system in several important ways (Hsu, 2009). When an immigrant, whether in this country legally or illegally, is arrested, he or she is more likely to be detained in jail because Immigration and Customs Enforcement (ICE) puts a hold on that person for possible deportation. As a result, jail populations increase and local officials demand that the U.S. government pay for the additional costs (Bowes, 2009). Yet ironically, many undocumented immigrants convicted of a minor crime are not deported because the U.S. immigration system is overwhelmed and therefore chooses to deport only those convicted of the most serious offenses (Carroll, 2008). Several states have recently passed major anti-immigration laws that threaten to increase tensions between Latinos the police and the criminal justice system (Martinez, 2010).

The growing number of immigrants has also placed the United States at odds with the international legal community. The Vienna Convention on Consular Relations gives foreign nationals who are accused of a crime the right to talk with the consulate of their home country. The International Court of Justice found that Texas violated the treaty by not informing Jose Medellin, a Texas death row inmate, of these rights. But the Supreme Court refused to follow the decision of the world court, holding that the treaty was not binding on the United States and that rulings of the International Court of Justice are not binding when they contradict states' criminal procedures (*Medellin v. Texas*, 2008). It is also worth noting that the Mexican constitution prohibits that nation from deporting one of its citizens in death penalty cases.

Yates, 2011). The association of crime with poverty helps to explain, in part, why the overwhelming number of crimes—primarily burglary, theft, and drug sale—are committed for economic motives. Although crimes of violence dominate the headlines, most defendants are not dangerous; they are charged with property or drug offenses. As for violent crimes, competing theories offer varying explanations for the fact that the "ghetto poor" are disproportionately involved in violent crime. Anderson (1999, p. 33) argued that the "street code" in such economically depressed areas leads to a subculture with norms that are "conspicuously opposed to those of mainstream society" insofar as they endorse violence as an appropriate response to disrespect (see also, Bourgois, 2003).

Racial Minorities Overrepresented

Race remains a divisive issue in American politics, and nowhere is this more evident than in the area of crime. African-Americans, Hispanics, and Native-Americans are arrested, convicted, and imprisoned at significantly higher rates per capita than Whites. At the same time, it is important to stress that historically Whites constituted the majority of those in prison, a fact conveniently ignored on some radio and TV discussions.

Why minorities are overrepresented in the criminal justice system is a topic of considerable importance (and therefore addressed in several later chapters). To some it is an indication that minorities are more likely to be poor and, therefore, more likely to commit crimes for economic advancement (Haynie, Weiss, & Piquero, 2008). Others counter that discrimination is the reason; minorities are more likely to be targeted by criminal justice officials and also more likely to receive a harsh sentence (Keen & Jacobs, 2009). Whatever the cause, the impact is enormous. An estimated 16.6 percent of African-American males will serve time in state or federal prison in their lifetimes, as compared with 7.7 percent of Latino males and 2.6 percent of White males (Bureau of Justice Statistics, 2007). But no matter the cause, in terms of attitudes about the racial gap in the criminal justice system, Whites and African-Americans are, in Unnever's (2008) words, "two worlds that are far apart" (p. 534).

Altogether, one out of three Americans is a minority, with Hispanics having recently become the largest minority. As explored in the "Courts, Controversy, & Racial Discrimination" feature on page 224, some question whether Latinos can get equal justice under the law.

DEFENDANTS IN COURT

The defendant is supposed to stand at the center of the criminal court drama. Yet typical felony defendants are largely powerless to control their fates; they are more objects to be acted upon than keys to what happens.

Because most defendants are poor and uneducated, they are ill equipped to deal with the technical abstractions of the criminal court process. Many are incapable of understanding even the simplest instructions about the right to bail or the presumption of innocence. Many are too inarticulate to aid their attorneys in preparing a defense. Many hold unfavorable attitudes toward the law and the criminal justice system and thus regard the judge and all other court personnel, including their defense attorneys, with hostility and distrust.

The mental competence of criminal defendants is another significant concern for the courts.

Competency to stand trial concerns itself with a criminal defendant's mental state at the time of trial. If a bona fide issue regarding the defendant's competency to stand trial has been raised, the defendant must be clinically assessed. In *Ake v. Oklahoma* (1985), the Supreme Court held that an indigent criminal defendant had the right to have the state provide a psychiatric evaluation that can be used not only to determine competency to stand trial, but also may be used to help prepare and present an insanity defense, if warranted (see Chapter 14).

Even when the mental competency of a criminal defendant is not in question, the nature of the clientele can make criminal courts a depressing place to work. Judges, prosecutors, and defense attorneys seldom come away from their day's activities with a sense of accomplishment, for many of the criminal cases involve social problems—drug addiction, marital problems, lack of education, and mental illness—over which court personnel have no control. Many cases stem from disputes between people who know one another.

Court personnel have little empathy with or understanding of the types of defendants whose fates they must decide. Members of the courtroom work group are essentially middle class. Little in their backgrounds or training has equipped them to deal with violations of the law committed by the poor.

Pro Se Defendants

In spite of the legal maxim that only a fool has himself as a client, more and more court litigants elect to act *pro se*, meaning they speak on their own behalf by serving as their own attorneys. *Pro se* litigants are far more numerous in civil cases, especially in family law cases, largely because of the high costs of legal assistance and the general unavailability of appointed counsel in most civil cases. And although legal representation is provided free of charge to indigent criminal defendants facing incarceration (see Chapter 7), not all defendants avail themselves of this right.

Although a "right" to self-representation is not explicitly mentioned in the Sixth Amendment, in *Faretta v. California* (1975), the U.S. Supreme Court determined that the right to make one's own defense is necessarily implied by the plain language of the Amendment. To do so, however, one must be mentally competent to waive counsel and serve as one's own attorney. In *Indiana v. Edwards* (2008), the Court held that "the Constitution permits States to insist upon representation by counsel for those competent enough to stand trial . . . but who still suffer from severe mental illness to the point where they are not competent to conduct trial proceedings by themselves" (p. 178).

When a criminal defendant acts *pro se*, courts have the discretion to appoint **standby/shadow counsel** to assistant the defendant as needed. Having a lawyer able to take over the case is desirable if the court revokes the defendant's right to self-representation either because of emerging questions of mental incompetence or if the defendant is abusive, threatening, obstructionist, or the cause of repeated, unnecessary delays.

Pro se litigants can be expensive and time consuming for the courts.

> *Pro se* cases increase the complexity of the duties assigned to judges, magistrates, and other court administrators and personnel and can challenge the impartiality of both judges and clerks. Pro se litigants, meanwhile, increase administrative costs, skip court proceedings or attend proceedings unprepared, and upset court routines. This development has proven to be a "fundamental challenge to many basic assumptions of our adversary system"; a system that built the roles of judges and clerks on the premise that each party is represented. (Thompson, 2010-2011, p. 610)

For example, *pro se* defendants plead "not guilty" and go to trial at significantly higher rates than do felony defendants represented by counsel (Hashimoto, 2007). And because *pro se* litigants are usually unfamiliar with the law, the rules of evidence, and the rule of criminal procedure, they can pose significant challenges for court personnel.

Yet, *pro se* criminal defendants appear to fare reasonably well in state courts. Those who do plead guilty often do so to significantly higher percentages of misdemeanors and lower numbers of felonies (47 percent and 53 percent, respectively) as compared with represented defendants, nearly 84 percent of whom plead guilty to felonies and only 16 percent to misdemeanors (Hashimoto, 2007). Of those who go to trial, acquittal rates for *pro se* defendants are generally the same as those for defendants represented by counsel. In federal courts, however, *pro se* defendants tend to garner less favorable pleas and enjoy only one-third the acquittal rate of represented defendants (Hashimoto, 2007).

Social Media Trap Defendants

"I could win most of my cases if it weren't for the clients. ... They will waltz into the witness-box and blurt out things which are far better left unblurted" complained Horace Rumpole, a fictitious British defense attorney (Mortimer, 1984). Modern American defense attorneys no doubt complain that they could win a few more of their cases if their clients did not text, e-mail, tweet, or otherwise post online what was best untexted, un–e-mailed, untweeted, or unposted.

To be sure defendants enjoy the privilege against self-incrimination, which means they cannot be forced to testify at trial. And this privilege has been extended to include police interrogation, because the police must provide suspects with *Miranda* warnings. But the privilege against self-incrimination does not apply to voluntary statements made by defendants. In the era of social media, what people tweet on Twitter, send by e-mail, or post to Facebook can have major legal repercussions. The conviction of Dharun Ravi for hate crimes is a case in point.

Dharun Ravi, a freshman at Rutgers University, used a web cam to spy on his gay roommate's dorm-room sexual encounters and streamed the video on the Internet (Shallwani, 2012). A few days later, his roommate Tyler Clementi, a talented young musician, committed suicide. These events quickly became the subject of intense national interest and Ravi was charged under New Jersey law with a hate crime, invasion of privacy, witness intimidation, and bias intimidation (but not murder). The government case was based on a pixelated paper trail of twitter feeds, Facebook posts, text messages e-mails, and other chatter. Ravi, for example, widely publicized his actions using social media and deleted texts sent to the prosecution. In the end, the jurors decided that this overwhelming amount of social media data elevated the case from one of a teenager behaving cruelly to a person committing an insensitive crime (Halbringer & Kormanik, 2012).

Social media can also pose a problem for convicted defendants at sentencing, as the case of *People v. Binkerd* (2007) illustrates. The defendant was driving home from a party when she collided into oncoming traffic, killing the friend and coworker who had been her passenger. Her blood alcohol concentration was more than twice the legal limit. At her sentencing for vehicular homicide, the probation officer had recommended a jail sentence of less than 1 year, a sentence the deceased victim's family supported. Yet, the judge sentenced the defendant to 64 months in state prison after seeing pictures of the defendant posted on her MySpace page wearing a t-shirt reading "I ♥Patron" while drinking with friends after the fatal accident. The judge thought that the photos indicated the defendant lacked remorse and therefore deserved a tough sentence (see Chapter 15).

COURTS THROUGH THE EYES OF VICTIMS AND WITNESSES

Traditionally, victims and witnesses have been the forgotten participants in the criminal justice system. Fictional and nonfictional treatments of the court process direct attention to the criminal as victim rather than to the victim as victim (Elias, 1986). More recently, however, a growing number of studies have focused on the victim (Karmen, 2012). These studies have identified ways in which the courts, along with the rest of the criminal justice community, have ignored the interests of victims and witnesses.

Frustrations in Coping with the Process

Crime victims once played a prominent role in the criminal process. Before the American Revolution, victims were the central figures in the criminal justice drama. Criminals' fates were closely tied to their victims' wishes. When crime became viewed as an offense against the state, the victim was assigned a subordinate role. As prosecutorial dominance increased, the power of the victim declined (see Chapter 6). Victims lost control over their cases, and their role was reduced to initiating investigations by complaining to the police and testifying for the prosecution as just another piece of evidence in the state's presentation of damning facts against the accused (Karmen, 2012).

Several studies have documented the hardships victims and witnesses face while participating in the criminal court process (Cannavale & Falcon, 1976; Connick & Davis, 1983; McDonald, 1976).

Although some are minor inconveniences, such as getting to the courthouse and finding a parking place, other hardships are more significant:

- Trial delays, which result in frequent travel and wasted time
- Long waits in uncomfortable surroundings
- Wages lost for time spent going to court
- Fear of the defendant or retaliation from the defendant's associates
- A sense that criminal justice personnel are indifferent to their plight

Travails of Testifying

Victims and witnesses also face major problems while testifying in court. Because few people are accustomed to testifying, lawyers must coach their witnesses ahead of time to answer only the question asked, to speak forcefully (but not belligerently), and not to become rattled by cross-examination. Even after such preparation, many witnesses are uncomfortable during cross-examination, as the defense attorney tests their memory, challenges their veracity, or even suggests that they were somehow responsible for their own victimization. After enduring cross-examination, some victims report feeling as though they, and not the offender, have been portrayed as the criminal.

Most of what we know about the ordeal of testifying in court comes from studies of rape victims (Resick, 1984). The dominant conclusion is that the victim, rather than the defendant, is put on trial. Testifying in court provokes anxiety for several months, exacerbating psychological distress (Steketee & Austin, 1989). Holmstrom and Burgess (1983), both of whom counsel rape victims at Boston City Hospital, followed the cases of 14 women who testified in court during a rape trial. They concluded that the trauma is often significant, because the victim must publicly repeat in detail how the rape occurred. The type of defense used by the defense attorney also has an impact on the victim's adjustment to the crime. A defense claim that the woman consented to sex is injurious, because it puts the victim on trial and calls into question her discouragement of the perpetrator (Steketee & Austin, 1989). Moreover, the defense often seeks to blame the victim by suggesting that she consented, did not resist, was provocatively dressed, and so on. It can take little to discredit the victim. Following the Holmstrom and Burgess study, most states have passed legislation limiting inquiry into a rape victim's past sexual conduct (Caringella, 2008).

Surprising Support for the System

Somewhat surprisingly, despite the problems and frustrations experienced, victims and witnesses still express overall support for the court process (Hagan, 1983). A study conducted in Milwaukee found that victims and witnesses were satisfied or very satisfied with the handling of their cases by the police (81 percent), district attorney (75 percent), and judge (66 percent). Less than 15 percent said that they were dissatisfied (Knudten, Meader, Knudten, & Doerner, 1976). Favorable judgments were independent of whether a victim was satisfied with the eventual outcome of the case. Since that time, courts have grown more responsive to the needs of victims and witnesses. Research suggests that increased levels of victim input into the handling of criminal cases moderately increase victims' satisfaction with the judicial system (Erez & Roberts, 2007). Such findings, however, are contingent upon a variety of factors, such as whether victims even know about their rights to participate in various processes, whether the victim was treated with dignity and respect, and whether there was an admission of guilt or an apology from the perpetrator.

VICTIMS AND WITNESSES THROUGH THE EYES OF THE COURT

The criminal courts confront a double bind with regard to victims. On the one hand, victims are valued for the cases they bring to the system; their misfortunes become the raw material of the court process (see the "Law on the Books vs. Law in Action" feature on the following page). On the other hand, individual victims represent a potential source of irrationality in the process. The personal and often emotional involvement of victims in the crime experience can generate particular demands for case outcomes that have little to do with the public interest. Thus, at times members of the courtroom work group perceive that the victim's demands for public justice

actually mask a desire for private vengeance (Hagan, 1983). Members of the courtroom work group also know that, particularly in violent and gang-related crime, the same individual may, at difference times be a victim, a witnesses, and an offender (Dedel, 2006).

Lack of Cooperation

Many victims and witnesses are reluctant to become involved in the criminal justice process. More than half of all major crimes are never reported to the police; even when they are reported, not all victims wish to prosecute (Chapter 10). Particularly in the low-income, high-crime neighborhoods of the nation's largest cities, victims and witnesses may fail to cooperate with the police. In the words of Captain Sheilah Coley of Newark, New Jersey: "I don't know what frustrates me more. Those knuckleheads killing each other, or the residents who won't cooperate with my officers" (quoted in Jacobs, 2007). When her officers respond to reports of gun fire, potential witnesses respond with blank looks.

Scholars refer to this lack of cooperation as legal cynicism. Youths in a high-crime neighborhood are negatively disposed toward police; this is grounded in the lived experience of negative encounters with law enforcement (Carr, Napoliatano, and Keating 2007). Overall, *legal cynicism* refers to a cultural orientation in which law and the courts are viewed as illegitimate, unresponsive, and ill equipped to ensure public safety (Kirk & Matsuda, 2011).

This lack of cooperation is fueled by hip-hop culture's "stop snitching" mantra. Indeed hip-hop superstar B.G., known for his song "I Ain't Tellin," accepted a longer-than-normal prison term on a federal gun charge rather than snitch (McCarthy, 2011).

Some specific witness-related problems include giving the police incorrect addresses, failing to show up in court, and offering testimony that is confused, garbled, or contradicted by other facts. Witness-related problems result in a significant number of cases in which the prosecutor refuses to file charges or the case is later dismissed (Boland, Brady, Tyson, & Bassler, 1982). But when victims cooperate with the prosecution, the odds that a case will be prosecuted increase dramatically (Dawson & Dinovitzer, 2001).

Not all uncooperative behavior can be blamed on victims and witnesses, however; the court process can be equally at fault. In Washington, D.C., a study focusing on what it called "noncooperative" witnesses reported that 41 percent were never told that they should contact the prosecutor; 62 percent were never notified of court appearances; and 43 percent stated that the police, prosecutor, and judge all failed to explain the witnesses' rights and duties. Other reports have found that the longer the case is delayed, the more likely it is that witnesses will not appear when summoned (Cannavale & Falcon, 1976).

LAW ON THE BOOKS VS. LAW IN ACTION
MAJOR ACTIVITIES OF VICTIMS IN THE STEPS OF THE COURT PROCESS

	LAW ON THE BOOKS	LAW IN ACTION
Crime	No general requirement to report crimes to the police.	Thirty-eight percent of personal and household crimes are reported to the police.
Arrest	A citizen's arrest is the taking of a person into physical custody by a person other than a law enforcement officer for the purpose of delivering the person to the custody of a law enforcement officer.	The vast majority of arrests are made by law enforcement officers. Citizen's arrests may result in injury to the victim and may also result in civil lawsuits.
Initial appearance	Open to the public.	Very unlikely for victim to be present because unlikely to know timing of the event.
Bail	VRA[a] provides that victims have a right to be heard if present and to submit a statement "to determine a release from custody."	Victims are very rarely present.
Charging	Victim has no role, and the VRA states that "nothing in this article shall provide grounds for the victim to challenge the charging decision."	Reluctance or refusal of victims to cooperate is a key reason for case dismissal.
Preliminary hearing	Besides the right to notice and to be present, the VRA is silent on the role of victims during this stage.	Victims rarely testify because hearsay evidence is admissible.
Grand jury	Grand jury can subpoena victim to testify.	In grand jury states, victim is likely to be subpoenaed to testify.
Arraignment	VRA provides that victims of crimes have the right to notice of proceedings like this.	Victims are rarely present.
Evidence	In some jurisdictions, the defense is entitled to see a copy of the victim's statement to the police.	Even if not required, some district attorneys disclose the victim's statement in hopes of inducing a guilty plea.
Plea bargaining	VRA provides that victims may be heard and may submit a statement during an acceptance of a negotiated plea.	Some jurisdictions allow victims to be heard with regard to the plea bargain, but few actually appear.
Trial	If they are to testify, victims generally cannot view the trial (wording in the VRA concerning public proceedings might change this law).	Victim's testimony is a key part of the trial.
Sentencing	VRA provides that victims may be heard and may submit a statement during sentencing.	Victims are unlikely to appear.
Appeal	Like other court proceedings, appellate argument is open to the public.	Victims are very unlikely to be present.

[a]VRA = Proposed Victims' Rights Amendment to the U.S. Constitution.

Witness Intimidation

One form of noncooperation involves witness intimidation. Persons who have been victims of crime, or witnessed a crime, may be pressured not to testify. Witness intimidation may take the form of threats of violence or actual violence against the person in question or his or her friends and family members. Property damage may also be involved. Such pressures may be made by the defendant, members of the defendant's family, other associates, or even gang members (Dedel, 2006). Witness intimidation is often a specific focus of victim/witness assistance programs, discussed later in this chapter.

CHARACTERISTICS OF VICTIMS

In some ways, victims of crimes are a diverse lot, including the rich and the poor, the young and the old, and men as well as women. This diversity aside, however, crime victims are more likely to be young, nonwhite, male, divorced or never married, low-income, and unemployed (Elias, 1986; Truman, 2011). Thus, in many ways, the profile of victims matches that of defendants. Indeed several decades of research have established that offenders and victims often possess the same characteristics and engage in many of the same behaviors (Schreck, Stewart, & Osgood, 2008). The major deviation is that rates of female victimization approaches that of males.

The overlaps of offenders and their victims possess numerous problems for members of the courtroom. Indeed, it is not uncommon to find that a person who appears in court as the defendant was in the past in court in the role of victim. How a case is handled is determined by the identity of the victim as well as that of the offender. Prosecutors allocate their limited resources to the cases they believe constitute the most "trouble" (Hagan, 1983). Not surprisingly, such judgments correlate with the desire for high conviction rates. Prosecutors assume that judges and juries will find the claims of certain kinds of victims credible and acceptable, but not the claims of others (Stanko, 1981–1982). The troubles of older, white, male, employed victims are considered more worthy of public processing (Myers & Hagan, 1979), For example, legal outcomes in murder cases were related to the race, gender, and conduct of victims at the time of the incident (Baumer, Messner, & Felson, 2000).

Prior Relationships between Defendants and Victims

Perhaps the most important victim characteristic that influences case processing is the prior relationship between defendants and victims. The following case is illustrative.

An auxiliary police officer watched a woman approach a man as he emerged from a liquor store. It was dark. The officer thought he saw a knife flash in her hand, and the man seemed to hand her some money. She fled, and the officer went to the aid of the victim, taking him to the hospital for treatment.

The officer saw the woman on the street a few days later and arrested her for first-degree robbery on the victim's sworn complaint. It was presumably a "high-quality" arrest—identification of the perpetrator by an eyewitness, not from mugshots or a lineup, but in a crowd. Yet, shortly thereafter, this apparently airtight case was dismissed on the prosecutor's motion.

What the victim had not explained to the police was that the defendant, an alcoholic, had been his girlfriend for the past five years; that they had been drinking together the night of the incident; that she had taken some money from him and got angry when he took it back; that she had flown into a fury when he then gave her only a dollar outside the liquor store; and that she had slashed at him with a pen knife in anger and run off. He had been sufficiently annoyed to have her charged with robbery, but, as the judge who dismissed the case said, "He wasn't really injured. Before it got into court they had kissed and made up." In fact, the victim actually approached the defense attorney before the hearing and asked him to prevail upon the judge and the assistant district attorney (ADA) to dismiss the charges against his girlfriend. (Vera Institute of Justice, 1981, p. xxii)

This case is one of many cited by the Vera Institute that show the importance of the prior relationship between defendants and victims.

Prior relationships between defendants and victims are more common than generally assumed. In half of all felony arrests in New York, the victim had a prior relationship with the defendant. Prior relationships were frequent in cases of homicide and assault, in which they were expected, but they were also frequent in cases of robbery, in which they were not. Other studies reach a similar conclusion. Nationwide, roughly half of all violent crimes (rape, assault, and robbery) are committed by relatives, friends, or acquaintances of the victim (Truman, 2011). Homicides, in particular, are usually committed not by strangers but by someone the victim knows by sight; in fact, the victim and the perpetrator are strangers in only 14 percent of all murders (Fox & Zawitz, 2007). Criminal court officials often regard crimes involving people who know one another as not very serious, viewing them as private disputes rather than offenses against the entire community.

Domestic Violence

The prior relationship between victims and defendants is most apparent in crimes against women. Women are much more likely than men to experience violence committed by an intimate partner, such as a current or former spouse, lover, or boyfriend or girlfriend, including same-sex relationships. Measuring violence between intimate partners is difficult because it often occurs in private, and victims are often reluctant to report incidents to anyone because of shame or fear of reprisal. Rates of intimate violence have been declining over the past several decades but still remain a significant issue in American society (Catalano, Smith, Snyder, & Rand, 2009).

Domestic Violence and the Police

Historically, police officers made an arrest only as a last resort—if taking the suspect into custody seemed the only way to ensure no more violence that night. Justice-system actors—including police officers, prosecutors, and judges—seemingly believed "that the importance of protecting families from interference outweighed the importance of protecting women from abuse" (Goldfarb, 2008, p. 1495-1496; see also, "Case Close-Up" on *Thurman v. Torrington*). In the

late 1970s through the 1980s, however, this attitude began to change as domestic violence came to be understood as a serious social problem.

Advocacy groups for battered women and victims have worked vigorously for policy changes designed to make the criminal justice system treat domestic violence as a serious offense. Jeffrey Fagan (1996) gave this movement a name in his aptly titled book, *The Criminalization of Domestic Violence*. As a result, there have been significant changes in how the criminal justice system responds to domestic violence. The question of what constitutes the most effective criminal justice response, however, has stirred considerable controversy (Maxwell, Garner, & Fagan, 2002). The prior relationship between victim and offender causes particular problems for law enforcement officials in the area of domestic violence (Buzawa & Buzawa, 1996).

The police have been urged to make more arrests, and prosecutors to file charges, no matter what the wishes of the victim. Mandatory-arrest policies clearly produce higher arrest rates (Hirschel, Buzawa, Pattavina, & Faggiani, 2007). Whether these mandatory-arrest policies are effective in reducing intimate-partner violence has been questioned, however (Hirschel, Hutchison, Dean, & Mills, 1992). Researchers report that arrest reduces domestic violence in some cities but increases it in others (Schmidt & Sherman, 1993). Although some exceptions exist, most studies to date indicate that criminal justice interventions deter intimate-partner violence or improve victim safety (Cosimo, 2011; Spohn, 2008).

Domestic Violence in the Courts

Arrests do not always lead to prosecutions. Many women call the police to stop the violence but later have a change of heart and refuse to sign a complaint. In *Bronx D.A.*, Sarena Straus (2006, p. 31) expressed her frustration as a prosecutor in the sex crimes and domestic violence unit:

> I found that a large percentage of the abused women who came into the Complaint Room refused to press charges, and most of them would return time and time again. Many of these women were known to their local precincts as they were constantly calling 911 for help. . . . The story was often the same. They loved the guy. They knew he wouldn't do it again.

CASE CLOSE-UP

THURMAN v. TORRINGTON AND DOMESTIC VIOLENCE ARRESTS

Between October 1982 and June 1983, Tracey Thurman repeatedly notified the police of threats made on her life and the life of her child by her estranged husband, Charles Thurman. On one of those occasions, Charles screamed threats at Tracey while she was sitting in her car. A police officer watched and did nothing until Charles broke the windshield on the car while Tracey was still inside of it. The officer then arrested Charles. He was convicted of breaching the peace and received a suspended sentence of 6 months. The police continued to ignore Tracey's requests each time she called. Indeed, both she and a neighbor attempted to file criminal complaints against Charles when he violated orders of protection, but police repeatedly ignored her.

On June 10, 1983, Charles appeared at the home of one of Tracey's friends, demanding to speak with Tracey, who remained indoors. The police were called with a request that Charles be picked up for violation of his probation. After about 15 minutes, Tracey went outside to speak to her husband in an effort to persuade him not to take or hurt their son. Soon thereafter, Charles stabbed Tracey 13 times in the chest, neck, and throat.

Approximately 25 minutes after Tracey's call to the Torrington Police Department, and after her stabbing, a single police officer arrived on the scene. He saw Charles holding a bloody knife. Charles dropped the knife and, in the presence of the officer, kicked Tracey in the head and ran into the house. Charles returned from within the residence holding their son. He dropped the child on his wounded mother and then kicked Tracey in the head a second time. Soon thereafter, three more police officers arrived on the scene, but all of them permitted Charles to wander about the crowd and to continue to threaten Tracey. Finally, upon approaching Tracey once again—this time while she was lying on a stretcher—Charles Thurman was arrested and taken into custody.

Miraculously, Tracey survived the attack, although she suffered significant injuries that left her with impaired motor function. She and her son sued the City of Torrington, Connecticut, and 24 of its police officers for their failure to arrest her violent, estranged husband. Tracey alleged that by following a policy of not arresting abusive husbands or boyfriends, Torrington police failed to provide the same protection for abused wives and children as they provided for victims of similar assaults outside a domestic relationship. The court agreed with her.

> City officials and police officers are under an affirmative duty to preserve law and order, and to protect the personal safety of persons in the community. This duty applies equally to women whose personal safety is threatened by individuals with whom they have or have had a domestic relationship as well as to all other persons whose personal safety is threatened, including women not involved in domestic relationships. If officials have notice of the possibility of attacks on women in domestic relationships or other persons, they are under an affirmative duty to take reasonable measures to protect the personal safety of such persons in the community.

$$* * *$$

> [A] police officer may not knowingly refrain from interference in such violence, and may not automatically decline to make an arrest simply because the assailant and his victim are married to each other. Such inaction on the part of the officer is a denial of the equal protection of the laws. (pp. 1527–1528)

Ultimately, Tracey Thurman was awarded $2.3 million in compensatory damages. But perhaps the true legacy of her story is that it prompted Connecticut to revise its domestic violence laws to include mandatory arrest provisions.

He said he was sorry. He bought them flowers. It was their fault because they provoked him.

At times, the district attorneys would pressure the woman to file charges, but often they simply accepted defeat.

The criminalization of domestic violence has also greatly increased the workload of the courts. Between 1989 and 1998, for example, the number of domestic relations cases in state courts across the nation grew by 178 percent (Ostrom & Kauder, 1999) with about a 10 percent increase in the following decade (LaFountain et al., 2008). In response to the growing awareness of domestic violence as a serious social problem, many courts in the United States have created domestic violence courts that emphasize a problem-solving approach (see Chapter 4). An evaluation of one such court found significantly lower rates of re-arrests among defendants processed through the domestic violence court (Gover, MacDonald, & Alpert, 2003).

A growing number of courts rely on batterer programs as the mandate of choice. Some researchers report that batterer programs do not appear to reduce recidivism (Labriola, Rempel, & Davis, 2008), but others argue that these programs are appropriate in most cases (Gondolf, 2012). However, programs involving a coordinated response that involve courts and justice agencies appear to be more effective (Visher, Harrell, Newmark, & Yahner, 2008).

Legal sanctions against domestic violence are not limited to criminal law. Victims of domestic violence may request a **civil protection order**. Recent legislative changes in most jurisdictions now make these court orders easier to obtain. They are no longer limited to women who have filed for divorce, and they may be issued on an emergency basis without the other party present. Half of the women in five Kentucky counties who received a civil protection order experienced no violations; among the half who did experience a violation, the levels of violence and abuse declined significantly (Hawkins, 2010). However, civil protection orders are not self-enforcing; there is even a danger that a civil protection order may induce a false sense of security among some women who are at risk of continued battery from a former intimate. Conversely, some are concerned that protection orders can be abused. In the words of public defender David Feige (2006, p. 182), "Though a fine idea in principle, orders of protection are constantly abused. It is not at all uncommon for vindictive, angry partners to use orders of protection to wreak havoc on each other—using them as substitutes for eviction orders or citing them to justify ignoring child custody agreements."

AIDING VICTIMS AND WITNESSES

For decades, reformers have urged that victims and witnesses be accorded better treatment.

- In 1931, the National Commission on Law Observance and Enforcement concluded that effective administration of public justice required willing witnesses, but testifying in court imposed unreasonable burdens on citizens.

- A 1938 American Bar Association report found that witness fees were deplorably low, courthouse accommodations were uncomfortable, and witnesses were frequently summoned to court numerous times only to have the case continued.

But it was not until the 1960s that attention was seriously devoted to the problems faced by victims and witnesses in court and to ways of improving the situation (Karmen, 2012).

- In 1967, the President's Commission on Law Enforcement and Administration of Justice highlighted a "growing concern that the average citizen identifies himself less and less with the criminal process and its officials."

A few years later, concern for victims and witnesses of crime rose to a crescendo. Crime victims received special attention from the White House.

- In 1982, the President's Task Force on Victims of Crime stressed the need for achieving a balance between the needs and rights of the victim and those of the defendant.

Public and governmental concern over the plight of victims has prompted numerous pieces of legislation (see the "Key Developments" feature on the next page). The Victim and Witness Protection Act, a federal law passed in 1982, required greater protection of victims and witnesses and also mandated guidelines for the fair treatment of victims and witnesses in federal criminal cases. The Victims of Crime Act of 1984 authorized federal funds for state victim programs. Spurred by these concerns, every state has passed comprehensive legislation protecting the interests of victims. In short, a wide variety of programs have been adopted in recent years to improve the treatment crime victims receive from the criminal justice system. The four most common types of initiatives are: (1) victim/witness assistance programs, (2) victim compensation programs, and (3) a victims' bill of rights, and (4) victim impact statements.

Victim/Witness Assistance Programs

Victim/witness assistance programs encourage cooperation in the conviction of criminals by reducing

the inconvenience citizens face when appearing in court (Finn & Lee, 1988). Typical activities include providing comfortable and secure waiting areas, assisting with the prompt return of stolen property that has been recovered, and providing crisis intervention. These programs also provide victims and witnesses with a clearer understanding of the court process by distributing brochures, explaining court procedures, and notifying witnesses of upcoming court dates (Webster, 1988). Of particular concern is victim and witness intimidation. Intimidation can be

KEY DEVELOPMENTS IN LAW RELATING TO VICTIMS

National Crime Victims' Week (1980)	Annual event focusing on the plight of crime victims.
Victim and Witness Protection Act (1982)	Enhance and protect the necessary role of crime victims and witnesses in the criminal justice process.
Victims' Bill of Rights (1982)	California was first state to adopt.
Victim of Crimes Act (1984)	Established Crime Victim Fund from fines, penalties, and bond forfeitures of convicted federal criminals.
***Booth v. Maryland* (1987)**	In capital cases, victim impact statements are unconstitutional because they introduce the risk of imposing the death penalty in an arbitrary and capricious manner.
***South Carolina v. Gathers* (1989)**	Characteristics of the victim are irrelevant during death penalty deliberations.
***Payne v. Tennessee* (1991)**	The Eighth Amendment creates no bar to the introduction of victim impact statements during sentencing.
***Simon & Schuster v. New York State Crime Victims Board* (1991)**	Declared unconstitutional New York's "Son of Sam" law, which sought to prevent criminals from profiting from their crimes.
Violence Against Women Act (1994)	Comprehensive law creating a variety of programs to strengthen law enforcement, prosecution, and victim services in cases involving crimes against women.
The Antiterrorism and Effective Death Penalty Act (1996)	A federal court must impose mandatory restitution, without consideration of the defendant's ability to pay.
Victims' Rights Amendment (VRA 1996)	VRA proposed in the U.S. Congress.
VRA (2000)	VRA withdrawn in face of virtually certain defeat.
Crime Victims' Rights Act (2004)	Federal legislation protecting victims in federal court that parallels the former Victims' Rights Amendment.
***Town of Castle Rock, Colorado v. Gonzales* (2005)**	A victim of domestic violence does not have the right to sue the local police department for failing to enforce a restraining order against her husband, who subsequently murdered her three children.
***Carey v. Musladin* (2009)**	A federal appeals court overstepped its authority when it granted a new trial to a murder defendant whose victim's relatives sat at the trial, in the view of the jury, wearing buttons with the victim's picture on them.

either case-specific—threats or violence intended to dissuade a witness from testifying in a specific case—or communitywide—acts of gangs or drug-selling groups intended to foster a general atmosphere of fear and noncooperation within a neighborhood or community (Healey, 1995).

Today, virtually all jurisdictions of any size have established programs aimed at helping crime victims cope with the hardships of victimization and deal with the often-troublesome demands of the criminal justice system. Most are based in criminal justice agencies (prosecutors', police, and sheriffs' offices). Often the program title is Victim Services. Overall, few victims use these programs, and older victims of violent crimes are more likely to use victim services than are younger victims of nonviolent crimes (Sims, Yost, & Abbott, 2005).

Evaluations of victim/witness assistance programs have yielded mixed results. In some communities, a victim's willingness to cooperate in the future was positively associated with considerate treatment by criminal justice personnel (National Institute of Justice, 1982; Norton, 1983). Thus, victims and witnesses receiving help were more likely to appear when summoned than those who had not been aided. But no such impact was found in other communities (Davis, 1983; Skogan & Wycoff, 1987). Those helped by the program appeared at the same rate as those who were not aided, and there was no change in the rate of case dismissals.

Andrew Karmen (2012) suggests that one explanation for these research findings is that expectations of significant improvements in case outcomes were based on faulty assumptions. The presumption is that the adjudication process is characterized by an adversarial model. The reality is that the courtroom work group has a mutual interest in processing large numbers of cases expeditiously. Thus, whereas victims see their situations as unique events that deserve careful and individual consideration, judges, prosecutors, and defense attorneys see them as routine occurrences, to be disposed of based on "going rates."

Victim Compensation Programs

The criminal justice system in the United States is offender-oriented, focusing on the apprehension, prosecution, and punishment of wrongdoers. While emphasizing the rehabilitation of offenders,

the system has done little to help victims recover from the financial and emotional problems that they suffer.

Civil lawsuits are of little relevance, because most criminal defendants have no money to pay monetary damages for personal injuries or damage to property. An increasingly common technique is restitution, in which the court orders the defendant to pay the victim for the losses suffered (see Chapter 15). But a major shortcoming of restitution is that in many crimes, no offender is convicted. Even if convicted, many defendants have little or no ability to provide adequate compensation to a victim. And once restitution is ordered, the victim's likelihood of collecting is not good (Davis, Smith, & Hillenbrand, 1992).

When restitution by the offender is inadequate or impractical, compensation by a third party (an insurance company, for example) is the only alternative. But many victims, because they are poor, do not have insurance covering medical expenses or property losses. The government is another sort of third party. Victim compensation programs rest on the premise that the government should counterbalance losses suffered by victims of criminal acts. The first compensation program in the United States began in California in 1965. Similar programs quickly emerged in a few other states.

In 1984, Congress passed the Victims of Crime Act, which established a Crime Victims Fund administered by the Office for Victims of Crimes within the U.S. Department of Justice. The fund is financed primarily from fines paid by defendants in federal court (Parent, Auerbach, & Carlson, 1992).

The federal backing has now spurred all states to enact legislation providing compensation for at least certain classes of crime victims. The staffs are small, however, and relatively few claims are filed—fewer than 100,000 during a typical year. Most programs provide for recovery of medical expenses and some lost earnings; none reimburses the victim for lost or damaged property. The maximum amount that can be paid in damages ranges from $1,000 to $50,000.

Victim compensation programs appear to provide clear benefits to victims of crime, but the actual results of such programs require careful scrutiny. Preliminary evaluations of compensation programs have yielded findings that are disappointing for administrators (Karmen, 2012). Cumbersome administrative procedures lead to added frustrations and increased alienation. Moreover, few victims of violent crimes apply for benefits, and even fewer claimants receive any money (Elias, 1986). Eligibility requirements are strict. Most states require that the victim assist in the prosecution of the offender, effectively excluding many domestic violence, child abuse, and sexual assault victims (McCormack, 1991). Similarly, most states also have a "family exclusion" clause, which makes victims living in the same household as the offender ineligible. Crime victims must also be "innocent" victims (those to whom no contributory fault can be ascribed). Indeed, in eight states, all persons with a felony conviction are ineligible for aid, even if their current problem has nothing to do with their past illegal activity (Mitchell, 2008). Overall, these programs are designed to spread the limited funds around, rather than to concentrate on a few badly injured victims.

Victims' Bill of Rights

Nowhere is the awakened concern about victims of crime more readily apparent than in proposals for a victims' bill of rights. Apart from sharing the title, however, these proposals vary markedly, reflecting different philosophies. In 1982, the President's Task Force on Victims of Crime submitted 68 separate recommendations aimed at achieving a balance between the needs and rights of the victim and those of the defendant. Also in 1982, California voters approved Proposition 8 by a 2-to-1 margin. Known as the Victims' Bill of Rights, it added 12 controversial provisions to the state constitution and the criminal code. In 2008, California voters approved Proposition 9, which granted additional rights to the victim at the expense of the defendant (Karmen, 2012). These versions of the victims' bill of rights reflect the rallying cry of the law-and-order movement, which accuses the courts of protecting the rights of defendants rather than those of victims. Premised on the notion that defendants escape too easily from the court process, these proposals stress substantive changes in the law, such as abolishing the exclusionary rule, limiting bail, restricting plea bargaining, and imposing stiffer sentences.

Other proposed victims' bills of rights are less ideological, emphasizing improvements in court procedures to better the lot of victims and witnesses. For example, the National Conference of the Judiciary on the Rights of Victims of Crime adopted a Statement of Recommended Judicial Practices, suggesting: (1) fair treatment of victims and witnesses through better information about court procedures; (2) victim participation and input through all stages of judicial proceedings; and (3) better protection of victims and witnesses from harassment, threats, intimidation, and harm.

Efforts to protect the rights of victims began with the passage in most jurisdictions of victims' rights legislation. These activities soon expanded to include a demand that these protections be given even greater force of law by placing them in state constitutions, and the public has responded with overwhelming support. Nearly two-thirds of the states have passed victims' rights amendments to their state constitutions (National Center for Victims of Crime, 2012a). Having achieved considerable success at the state level, victims' rights groups began pressing for an amendment to the U.S. Constitution. Senator Dianne Feinstein (D-California) was a cosponsor of the proposed amendment, arguing that the Constitution protects the rights of criminal defendants but "crime victims, families, survivors have no rights at all, according to the Constitution of the United States" (Cannon, 1996).

The most fundamental concern expressed about the proposed victims' rights amendment is that its guiding assumption—that victims are being excluded from the judicial process—is patently false. Unlike many nations of the world, in the United States all steps of the criminal process (except grand jury proceedings) are mandated to be open to the public. Victims are excluded from trial only when they will be witnesses, and this is happening more often because of another facet of the victims' rights movement—victim impact statements.

Proposals to amend the U.S. Constitution are frequently offered but rarely adopted. This appears to be the fate of the proposed Victim's Rights Amendment.

Victim Impact Statements

Victim impact statements consist of written or oral information about how the crime impacted the victim and the victim's family. These emotion-filled statements are usually offered in an attempt to sway the sentencing court to impose a severe sentence on the convicted offender, although pleas for leniency do occur from time to time. Today, every state permits victim impact statements as part of the sentencing process (see Chapter 15).

Almost invariably, neither the defendant nor the defense counsel interrupt or make any after-the-fact attempt to rebut the statement. Such silence, however, should not be interpreted as acquiescence. Rather, the rules of procedure in some states prohibit the defense from challenging victim impact statements on cross-examination or otherwise. But even in the handful of states that statutorily grant an opportunity to cross-examine victim impact testimony, the defense runs the risk of alienating those in court since any "attempt by defense counsel to obstruct [a victim impact statement] will surely be met with disapproval, if not disgust, and possibly retaliation by the sentencing authority, particularly where a jury determines the sentence" (Stevens, 2000, p. 17).

Constitutionality of Victim Impact Evidence

In the late 1980s, the U.S. Supreme Court decided two cases, *Booth v. Maryland* (1987) and *South Carolina v. Gathers* (1989), in which the Court held that victim impact statements were unconstitutional in capital cases because they can create an unacceptable risk that a jury may impose the death penalty in an arbitrary and capricious manner. But this approach was short-lived. In *Payne v. Tennessee* (1991), the Court decided that the Eighth Amendment was not a per se bar to victim impact evidence during sentencing, even in death penalty cases.

Still, under some circumstances, *Payne* can serve as the basis for disallowing, on due process grounds, inflammatory and highly prejudicial victim impact evidence. For example, in *Salazar v. State* (2002), the Texas Court of Criminal Appeals invalidated the use of a 17-minute video that displayed 140 photos of the deceased victim, arranged chronologically from infancy through adulthood. The court concluded that the montage, set to the music of Enya and Celine Dion's "My Heart Will Go On," was unfairly prejudicial.

Victim Impact Evidence and Restorative Justice

The National Victim Center and other victims' groups support giving victims a voice in the process, rather than reducing them to a mere statistic. Proponents contend that, consistent with restorative justice principles (see Chapter 14), by allowing victims to vent their feelings, they are better able to get on with their lives. But critics fear that the venting of frustrations can demean the judicial process. Consider, for example, that as a certain death sentence was about to be pronounced against Richard Allen Davis for sexually molesting and then killing Polly Klaas (discussed in Chapter 15), Davis told the court that Polly's father had sexually molested her, a charge that crime-victim advocates labeled outrageous and sickening.

Incidents like this one lead critics to wonder whether victim impact statements help victims; perhaps the possibility of speaking in court at a much later date unnecessarily prolongs their grieving process. Victims are not encouraged to reach a sense of closure until they testify (or in some cases, until the defendant is actually executed). In spite of these concerns, research supports the conclusion that victim impact statements produce a beneficial effect for those making them and increase their satisfaction with both the outcomes of the case and with the criminal justice system as a whole (Alexander & Lord, 1994; Hoyle, 2011).

Effects of Victim Impact Statements on Sentences

In the states that allow for the death penalty, victim impact statements are typically allowed with few procedural restrictions. During the penalty phase of a capital trial, victim impact statements can have a very emotional impact on jurors typically eliciting punitive impulses (Mille et al. 2008).

In non–capital cases, research suggests that victim impact evidence has not dramatically increased defendants' sentences (Davis & Smith, 1994; Erez & Roger, 1999). In fact, victim impact evidence appears to have little effect on overall sentence severity (Villmoare & Neto, 1987), although it can affect judicial imposition of special conductions of probation, "causing the judge to order anger-management treatment, drug and alcohol supervision, domestic violence counseling, or such" (Propen & Schuster, 2008, p. 315). Victim impact statements also appear to have a significant impact on parole hearing outcomes (Morgan & Smith, 2005).

COURTS, LAW, & MEDIA

LAW AND ORDER: SPECIAL VICTIMS UNIT (NBC, 1999–PRESENT)

This long-running television show tells the stories of an elite squad of police detectives who are assigned to a Special Victims Unit ("SVU") in New York City, which investigates sexually related offenses like rape and child molestation. The show, while fictional, often bases its storylines on real cases. Sometimes, the show gets it right; most of the time, however, its depictions of defendants and victims are inaccurate. Britto, Hughes, Saltzman, and Stroh (2007) conducted a content analysis of the fifth season of SVU. Here are the highlights of their findings.

What they get right:

- As in reality, SVU depicts police officers and prosecutors struggling with the difficult subject matter of sexual victimization.
- As in real life, the majority of SVU cases do not involve strangers, but rather involve individuals who know each other.
- "The majority of the victims portrayed on SVU were shown as innocent or blameless and it appeared that the show actively tried to counter the common myth that victims cause sexual assault" (p. 51).

What they get wrong:

- Clearance rates—Sex crimes pose significant problems for the criminal justice system. In Manhattan, "just less than one half of all murder and rape reports are cleared by arrest, and of those cleared by arrest only 51% result in a conviction" (p. 49). In contrast, 100% of suspects on SVU were caught and 92% of them were convicted in court.
- Types of rape—Most of the rapes that occur on SVU are not spousal or date-rapes; in reality, these two types of rape account for the overwhelming majority of rapes.
- Nature of harm—While sexual assaults are clearly violent crimes that inflict a tremendous amount of psychological harm, "victims generally survive and in the majority of cases do not require hospitalization for their physical

injuries" (p. 45). On SVU, however, the crimes are usually extremely violent, resulting in the physical brutalization of victims. Indeed, nearly 60 percent of the victims on the show are dead by the end of an episode.

- Victim age—Nearly half of all SVU victims are under the age of 18. According to the National Crime Victimization Survey (NCVS), "the actual figure is closer to one-quarter of all victims" (p. 46).
- Victim gender—Roughly 40 percent of the victims on SVU are male whereas "only 12 percent of all victims of sexual assault and murder are male" according to the NCVS victimization rates adjusted for the population of Manhattan (p. 46).
- Victim race—Almost two-thirds of the victims on SVU are white, while the majority of sex crime victims in Manhattan are members of racial and ethnic minority groups.
- Offender and gender issues—Females commit approximately 5 percent of the sexual assaults and murders in Manhattan. On SVU, however, females commit more than one-third of these offenses. In contrast, males commit 95 percent of the rapes, murders, and manslaughters in Manhattan, but only 63 percent of the crimes on SVU. Moreover, female offenders on the show are often portrayed "as being particularly manipulative and cruel in their planning and execution of violent crimes" (p. 48). This is especially true for female juvenile offenders who are depicted as "brutal, vindictive," and "petty"; in contrast, "juvenile male offenders were shown as victims of their circumstances" (p. 48). Finally, male offenders were significantly more likely to plea bargain a reduced sentence, whereas female offenders were more likely to go to trial, be convicted, and receive a harsh suggested sentence.

After watching one or more episodes of Law and Order: SVU, be prepared to discuss the following questions:

1. Britto et al. found that although most victims on SVU were portrayed sympathetically, female victims were more likely than men to appear to contribute to their victimization by associating with the wrong crowd,

Continued on next page

Continued from previous page

talking to strangers, or using drugs and alcohol" (p. 45). What are the societal implications of this?

2. Do you think that the overrepresentation of female offenders and male victims on SVU tends to de-gender sex crimes? Why or why not? Because the storylines often illicit sympathy for victims, do you think that these overrepresentations mask issues of gender inequality, patriarchy, and male socialization? Explain your position.

3. Britto et al. argued that because SVU consistently depicts extremely violent rapes that cause severe injuries or death, the show perpetuates the "myth of the sadistic, psychologically disturbed rapist who preys on innocent victims for 'sick' enjoyment" (p. 51). What effect do you think this has on jurors who sit in judgment of real sexual assault cases that lack the extreme brutality that is often portrayed on the show? Why?

AIDING OR MANIPULATING VICTIMS?

After a long period of neglect, aiding victims has become good politics. These efforts are backed by a national movement for the rights of crime victims.

The Victims' Rights Movement

Organizing crime victims is a difficult task. Aside from having been harmed by criminals, victims as a group have very little in common (Karmen, 2012). Despite these obstacles, victim advocacy groups have become a powerful political voice.

The emergence of the victims' rights movement reflects several parallel trends. One is the law-and-order rhetoric of the 1960s, which emphasized the harm criminals do to victims. Another is the women's rights movement, which came to take a special interest in crimes involving women. A key feature of the feminist movement is its emphasis on grassroots activism. Thus, a logical extension of the women's movement was to form local programs to aid women who had been victims of rape or spousal abuse (Weed, 1995).

The victims' rights movement involves people striking back to turn tragedy into action and rage into reform (Office for Victims of Crime, 1998). The best known of these organizations is Mothers Against Drunk Driving (MADD). Founded by Candy Lightner, whose daughter was killed by a drunk driver, MADD has become the nation's largest victim advocacy group (see Chapter 4). A search of the Internet reveals numerous other groups. Many of these groups are local, emphasizing various types of victims ranging from those harmed by drunk drivers to battered women. These grassroots operations function loosely under the national umbrella organization, the National Organization of Victim Assistance, which provides a larger focus for their specialized concerns.

Today, the victims' rights movement involves a loose coalition of local, state, and national organizations with wide-ranging interests. Their activities constitute a full-blown social movement that seeks to place the interests of crime victims into the mainstream of American political discourse. Although diverse in origins, the victims' rights movement shares a common ideology, seeking to demonstrate the triumph of good over evil. Thus, the movement resonates with a moral view of crime held by many average citizens (Weed, 1995).

Differing Goals

The victims' rights movement reflects the mutual interests of a strange set of political bedfellows, which explains why, beneath the rhetoric about aiding victims of crimes, important disagreements over goals and priorities exist (Viano, 1987). A study of a victims' rights organization in Alabama found that the membership was disproportionately white and female, with African-Americans excluded from potential membership. These results suggest that the victims' rights movement is becoming polarized, with some quite concerned about secondary victimization and others more focused on punishment of defendants (Smith & Huff, 1992). Similarly, a study in the state of Washington found that groups supporting the Community Protection Act reflected a punitive orientation toward defendants more than an effort to aid victims of sexual assault (Scheingold, Olson, & Pershing, 1994). These differing goals explain why victims' rights laws and constitutional amendments are so contradictory.

Do Victims Benefit?

Everyone agrees that victims and witnesses should be treated better during the court process. But political rhetoric should not be allowed to obscure some important issues. Although enthusiasm for helping victims is clearly growing, the willingness to pay for the necessary services is not always present. Overall, legislators and other government officials find voting for victim-oriented legislation politically advantageous, but when it comes to voting money for another "welfare program," they are much more hesitant.

Moreover, it is unclear how much aid victims and witnesses receive from these programs. Once enacted, programs do not always work as intended. Elias (1993) concluded that victim compensation laws were exercises in symbolic politics. Few claimants ever received compensation; the laws provided "political placebos," with few tangible benefits for victims (see also, Erez & Roberts, 2007).

Victim/witness assistance programs appear to be important first steps in providing better services to citizens who find themselves thrust into the criminal court process, but not all agree that these programs actually benefit the victim. Sociologist William McDonald (1976, p. 35) charged that "some projects that are billed as 'assisting victims' are more accurately described as assisting the criminal justice system and extending government control over victims. Whether the victims so controlled would regard the project as 'assisting' them is problematic." Some victims do not wish to become involved.

An important question is, at whose expense should victims be compensated? Some versions emphasize protecting the rights of victims by denying privileges and benefits to suspects, defendants, and prisoners. This type of victim's bill of rights is the most recent example of the conflict between the due process model and the crime control model (highlighted in Chapter 1). Other versions emphasize improving the welfare of victims at the expense of the privileges and options

enjoyed by members of the courtroom work group (Karmen, 2012).

CONCLUSION

The future of both Pervis Tyrone Payne and his victim are difficult to predict. Payne is on Tennessee's death row. Having lost on appeal to the Supreme Court, his lawyers hope to set aside the death penalty during further rounds of *habeas corpus* review. Meanwhile, he sits in his cell, wondering whether he will die. Predicting Nicholas's future is even more difficult. At his young age, his mind might be able to block out the memories of seeing his mother and younger sister murdered in his presence. But the chance of flashbacks and antisocial behavior—which psychologists label posttraumatic stress disorder—is good. It is possible that as he grows up, Nicholas will himself shift from victim to defendant. As we learned in this chapter, many defendants arrested for violent crimes were themselves the victims of violent acts as children.

The perhaps troubling future of Nicholas highlights some of the contradictions still apparent in how society reacts to victims. Today, blaming victims (particularly rape victims) for causing their own misfortune is more unusual than in the past. Instead, numerous groups are ready to step forward and call for helping victims. Yet some of these same voices who are quick to champion the cause of victims are just as quick to denounce what has become popularly called the "abuse excuse."

Victims and witnesses provide the raw material for the court process. The complaints they bring, the credibility of their stories, and their willingness to participate directly affect the courtroom work group's activities. But members of the courtroom work group do not respond uncritically to the demands for their services. They find some stories more believable than others and some claims more worthy than others.

The clientele shapes the criminal court process in a less obvious way. Most defendants are young, male, illiterate, impoverished members of minority groups. Many victims share similar traits. They are also poor, unversed in the ways of the courts, and disproportionately members of minority groups. As a result, in the criminal courts, victims and witnesses often exert little influence over the disposition of the cases in which they are involved.

Chapter Review

LO1 **1.** List the three characteristics of defendants.

Defendants are overwhelmingly male and mostly economically underclass, and racial minorities are overrepresented.

LO2 **2.** Describe how victims and witnesses view the court process.

Victims and witnesses face frustrations in coping with the process (long waits and uncomfortable surroundings), experience travails in testifying, but overall exhibit surprising support for the system.

LO3 **3.** Describe how court actors view victims and witnesses.

Members of the courtroom work group become frustrated when victims and witnesses do not cooperate and are intimidated by the defendant or the defendant's friends and family.

LO4 **4.** Discuss the prior relationships between defendants and victims and why this is important in domestic violence cases.

In roughly half of the crimes of violence, the defendant and the victim had a prior relationship. Prior relationships are most notable in domestic violence cases, in which the battered women is not always interested in criminal prosecution.

LO5 **5.** Identify three types of programs that are designed to aid victims and witnesses in coping with the criminal justice process.

Victim/witness assistance programs are designed to help better navigate the court process. Victim compensation seeks to provide economic assistance for victims of crime. And the Victims' Bill of Rights seeks to provide rights for victims because defendants already have rights.

LO6 **6.** Explain why some view victim programs as aiding victims whereas others view these programs as manipulating victims.

Some see the victims' movement as providing much needed support for victims of crime. Others view the victims' movement as manipulating victims by providing symbols but no substance.

Critical Thinking Questions

1. In what ways are victims and defendants similar? In what ways are they different? Is there any difference in the characteristics of victims and defendants when the victim is male as opposed to when the victim is female?

2. Many discussions of crime suggest that smart defendants are able to beat the rap by pleading insanity (see Chapter 14), slanting their testimony at the urging of the defense counsel (see Chapter 7), and exploiting legal loopholes such as the exclusionary rule (see Chapter 12). Given the profile of the typical criminal defendant, how realistic are these assumptions of a smart crook?

3. To some, the victims' rights movement is more an exercise in symbolic politics than a substantive program. Thus, some critics argue that many of these programs are really more interested in severe punishment of the defendant than in helping victims adjust socially, economically, or psychologically to their new role as victim. Which dimensions of helping victims reflect the crime control model? Which dimensions reflect the due process model?

4. Would your views on victim impact statements be different if the U.S. Supreme Court had chosen a less emotional case to consider in deciding their constitutionality? Overall, do you think victim impact statements correctly allow victims a voice in the process or just add unnecessary emotionalism?

Key Terms

career criminals 223

civil protection order 234

defendant 226

pro se 226

standby/shadow counsel 227

victim impact statements 237

Web Resources

Go to the *America's Courts and the Criminal Justice System* companion website at

http://www.cengage.com/criminaljustice/neubauer,

where you will find more resources to help you study.

Resources include web exercises, quizzing, and flash cards.

For Further Reading

Belknap, Joanne. *The Invisible Woman: Gender, Crime and Justice.* 3rd ed. Belmont, CA: Wadsworth, 2007.

Bergelson, Vera. 2009. *Victim's Rights and Victims' Wrongs: Comparative Liability in Criminal Law.* Stanford, CA: Stanford University Press.

Davis, Robert, Arthur Lurgio, and Susan Harmon (Eds.). *Victims of Crime.* 4th ed. Thousand Oaks, CA: Sage, 2012.

Dragiewicz, Molly. *Equality with a Vengeance: Men's Rights Groups, Battered Women, and Antifeminist Backlash.* Boston: Northeastern University Press, 2011.

Hickey, Eric. *Serial Murderers and Their Victims.* 5th ed. Belmont, CA: Wadsworth, 2010.

Humphries, Drew (Ed.). *Women, Violence and the Media: Readings in Feminist Criminology.* Boston: Northeastern University Press, 2009.

Johnson, Michael. *A Typology of Domestic Violence: Intimate Terrorism, Violent Resistance and Situational Couple Violence.* Boston: Northeastern University Press, 2008.

Karmen, Andrew. *Crime Victims: An Introduction to Victimology.* 8th ed. Belmont, CA: Wadsworth, 2012.

Kochel, Tammy Rinehart, David Wilson, and Stephen Mastrofski. "Effect of Suspect Race on Officers' Arrest Decisions." *Criminology*, 49(2), 473–512, 2011.

Mann, Coramae, Marjorie Zatz, and Nancy Rodriguez. *Images of Color, Images of Crime.* 3rd ed. Los Angeles: Roxbury, 2006.

Morin, Jose Luis. *Latino/A Rights and Justice in the United States: Perspectives and Approaches.* 2nd ed. Durham, NC: Carolina Academic Press, 2008.

Ridgway, Delissa (Ed.). "The Unique Challenges of Cross-Cultural Justice. *Judicature* 92: 190–242, 2009.

Schuster, Mary, and Amy Propen. *Victim Advocacy in the Courtroom: Persuasive Practices in Domestic Violence and Child Protection Cases.* Boston: Northeastern University Press, 2011.

Slate, Risdon, and W. Wesley Johnson. *The Criminalization of Mental Illness: Crisis and Opportunity for the Justice System.* Durham, NC: Carolina Academic Press, 2009.

Smith, Erica, and Donald Farole. *Profile of Intimate Partner Violence Cases in Large Urban Counties.* Washington, DC: Department of Justice, Bureau of Justice Statistics, 2009.

Vazquez, Yolanda. "Perpetuating the Marginalization of Latinos: A Collateral Consequences of the Incorporation of Immigration Law into the Criminal Justice System. *Howard Law Journal*, 54(3), 639–674, 2011.

Vogel, Mary (Ed.). *Crime, Inequality and the State.* New York: Routledge, 2007.

Walker, Samuel, Cassia Spohn, and Miriam DeLone. *The Color of Justice.* 5th ed. Belmont, CA: Wadsworth, 2012.

10 From Arrest and Bail through Arraignment

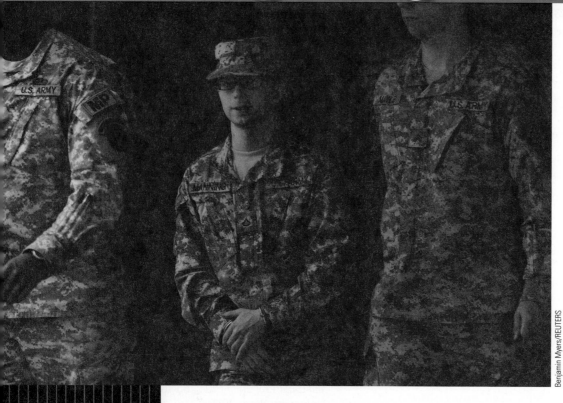

Benjamin Myers/REUTERS

Pfc. Bradley Manning was arrested in Iraq in May 2010 after allegedly having downloaded nearly 700,000 documents, the majority of which were classified, and transferred most of them to WikiLeaks. Manning spent 10 months in solitary confinement until public outcry from legal scholars, Amnesty International, and the public at large led to his being transferred to a military prison in Kansas. From the perspective of the criminal justice wedding cake model, this is a celebrated case for several reasons: the nature of the crime, since Manning is accused of creating the largest breach of classified information in U.S. history; the breakdown in security that enabled a low-ranking, enlisted Army intelligence analyst to obtain a vast quantity of classified documents; the fact that series of violent outbursts and other behaviors caused members in his unit to suspect that Manning was in serious mental distress, but nothing was done about it; and the fact that he was held in pretrial solitary confinement for almost a year even though there is no allegation that any of the material Manning is alleged to have revealed caused any harm other than embarrassment to the United States. ■

Chapter Outline

CRIME
Measuring Crime

ARREST
Quality of Arrests

INITIAL APPEARANCE
CASE CLOSE-UP: *County of Riverside v. McLaughlin* and a Prompt Hearing before a Magistrate

CHARGING
Law on the Books: Prosecutorial Control
Law in Action: Police Influence
Courts and Controversy: Charging Decisions

Courts, Controversy, & Economic Inequality
Are White-Collar Criminals Underprosecuted?

BAIL
Law on the Books: The Monetary Bail System
Law in Action: The Context of Bail Setting
Bail Agents and Bounty Hunters
Effects of the Bail System

PRELIMINARY HEARING
Law on the Books: Weighing Probable Cause
Law in Action: Variations in Using the Preliminary Hearing

GRAND JURY
Law on the Books: Shield and Sword
Law in Action: Prosecutorial Domination
Courts and Controversy: Reform the Grand Jury?

ARRAIGNMENT

LAW IN ACTION PERSPECTIVE: CASE ATTRITION

WHY ATTRITION OCCURS
Legal Judgments
Policy Priorities
Personal Standards of Justice

THE CRIMINAL JUSTICE WEDDING CAKE
Celebrated Cases
Serious Felonies
Lesser Felonies
The Lower Depths

Courts, Law, & Media
Crime on The Nightly News

From Arrest and Bail through Arraignment • From Arrest
From Arrest and Bail through Arraignment • From Arrest

Learning Objectives

After reading this chapter, you should be able to:

LO1 Define the two methods of estimating the amount of crime in the United States.

LO2 Discuss how arrests made by the police impact the criminal court process.

LO3 List the four ways that criminals are formally charged in court and the major actors in each of these important documents.

LO4 List the four most common ways that defendants secure pretrial release.

LO5 Compare and contrast "law on the books" and "law in action" approaches to bail setting, including the overall effects of the bail system on criminal defendants and their cases.

LO6 Explain the role bail agents play in the criminal justice system.

LO7 Contrast how the law on the books approach to criminal justice and the law in action perspective offer contrasting views of the preliminary hearing.

LO8 Explain why some jurisdictions use grand juries extensively and others do not.

LO9 Delineate the three major reasons for case attrition.

LO10 Describe the four layers of the criminal justice wedding cake.

After a warrantless arrest, all people have a right to have a "prompt hearing" at which a neutral judicial officer reviews the arrest to determine whether it was supported by probable cause. In Riverside County, California, arrestees were routinely taken before a judge within 2 days, exclusive of Saturdays, Sundays, or holidays. Thus, many of those arrested on a Friday, like Donald Lee McLaughlin, had to wait in jail at least 3 days before a judge was available to conduct a probable cause hearing. On holiday weekends, the wait could be even longer—4, 5, or even 6 days. The public defender for the County argued that the U.S. Constitution requires a more prompt hearing. Not practical, countered the district attorney, stressing the realities of the contemporary criminal justice system in large urban areas—thousands of arrests, overcrowded jails, and lack of availability of judges, to say nothing of defense attorneys and prosecutors. It is in this context that the U.S. Supreme Court had to decide how prompt a "prompt hearing" needs to be. It settled on 48 hours, including weekends.

County of Riverside v. McLaughlin (1991) highlights the importance of the early stages of a felony prosecution. At first glance, the numerous preliminary stages of a prosecution seem to be of only procedural interest, with cases moving automatically from arrest to charging through preliminary hearing and grand jury before arriving at the major trial court. But a closer look indicates that at numerous stages during these early proceedings, prosecutors, judges, police officers, and victims have the option of advancing a case to the next step, seeking an alternative disposition, or dropping the case altogether. These screening decisions result in significant case attrition, with half of all felony arrests being dropped at some point after arrest and before arraignment.

This chapter examines the early stages of a criminal case, focusing on when and why case attrition occurs. The discussion begins with crimes and the arrests that sometimes follow. Our attention then shifts to events in the courthouse, including initial appearance, charging, bail, preliminary hearing, grand jury, and (for some cases) arraignment in the trial court of general jurisdiction.

CRIME

Beginning in the early 1960s, the United States experienced a dramatic increase in crime. For almost two decades, the number of crimes known to the police increased much faster than the growth in population. In the early 1980s, the crime rate reached a plateau, and since the early 1990s, it has decreased considerably. The peaks and valleys of the official crime figures, however, are largely irrelevant to the general public. Rather, the public continues to perceive (no matter what the official figures say) that crime is on the increase. These fears are reinforced by extensive media coverage, particularly of violent crime.

Measuring Crime

There are two official measures of crime in the United States. The most publicized and widely used measure of crime comes from the Federal Bureau of Investigation's (FBI) **Uniform Crime Reporting (UCR)** Program. Each year, policing agencies voluntarily report summary-based measures of crime within their jurisdictions to the FBI, such as the number of murders in a year. The FBI, in turn, compiles those data and disseminates statistics in a number of publications, the most comprehensive of which is their annual publication *Crime in the United States*. Nearly 18,000 campus, local, tribal, county, and state law enforcement agencies—representing roughly 96 percent of the U.S. population—are active in the UCR program today.

The UCR divides criminal offenses into two categories: Type I and Type II Offenses. As summarized in Table 10.1, there are eight serious **Type I offenses** that are referred to as **index crimes**; Type II offenses are less serious, but more numerous. Still, Type I offenses are the crimes that produce headlines about rising crime rates. Contrary to public perceptions, most felony crimes are for nonviolent offenses involving burglary and larceny. In fact, property crimes outnumber violent offenses by a ratio of 8 to 1. The UCR program also gathers statistics on index offenses that are cleared by the police via arrest, providing a rough measure of police performance in solving crimes.

By the late 1970s, law enforcement recognized that more detailed crime data would be beneficial to crime prevention and analysis. After a pilot study in South Carolina, the FBI began to gather more detailed information for crimes reported to the police in 1988 called the **National Incident Based Reporting System (NIBRS)**. NIBRS is incident-based, rather than summary-based. It tracks all of the same offenses covered in the traditional UCR Type I and Type II categories, plus a few others, such as criminal trespass and passing bad checks. A wealth of data is gathered about each incident, including

- the location of the crime
- whether the crime was completed or attempted (the traditional UCR did not differentiate between attempts and completed crimes)
- the type of weapon used (if any)
- the type and value of properly damaged or stolen
- the personal characteristics of both the offender and the victim (e.g., age, sex, race/ethnicity, marital status, and socioeconomic status)

Another significant difference concerns the so-called **hierarchy rule**. If two or more crimes were committed, the traditional UCR reported the most serious of the crimes. For example, if during the commission of an armed bank robbery, the offender shoots a security guard in the foot then steals a car to escape from the bank, the UCR would count this as a robbery only since robbery is a more serious crime than aggravated assault and motor vehicle theft. NIBRS, on the other hand, would count all three crimes and gather data concerning each of the three distinct offenses.

A major weakness of both the UCR and NIBRS is that they are based only on crimes known to the police. But only a fraction of the number of crimes committed are actually reported to the police. Of the personal and household offenses measured in the National Crime Victimization Survey's yearly sample of households, only half of the violent crimes and almost two thirds of the property crimes were not reported to the police (Rand, 2008). What this means

TABLE 10.1 ▪ A COMPARISON OF TYPE I AND TYPE II UCR OFFENSES

	Part I: Index Crimes	Part II: Other Crimes
Violent crimes	• Murder and nonnegligent manslaughter • Forcible rape • Robbery • Aggravated assault	• Simple assault
Property crimes	• Burglary • Larceny/theft • Motor vehicle theft • Arson	• Embezzlement • Forgery and counterfeiting • Fraud • Stolen property offenses • Vandalism
Other crimes	None	• Disorderly conduct • Driving under the influence • Drug offenses • Drunkenness • Gambling • Liquor law offenses • Loitering • Prostitution • Offenses against the family (e.g., child neglect) • Sex offenses (other than forcible rape) • Vagrancy • Weapons offenses
Status offenses by juveniles	None	• Curfew and loitering offenses • Runaways

© Cengage Learning

is that the official FBI crime statistics underestimate the total amount of crime in the United States.

ARREST

The term *arrest* is difficult to define because it is used in different ways. In its narrow sense (sometimes called a "formal or technical arrest"), **arrest** is defined as the taking of a person into custody for the commission of an offense as the prelude to prosecuting him or her for that offense. In its broader sense, *arrest* means any seizure of a person significant enough that it becomes the functional equivalent of a formal arrest in that the person seized would reasonably not feel free to terminate the encounter (*United States v. Drayton*, 2002).

TABLE 10.2 ■ CLEARANCE RATES FOR UCR TYPE I OFFENSES

Violent Crime Clearance Rates		Property Crime Clearance Rates	
Murder and nonnegligent manslaughter	64.8%	Burglary	12.4%
Forcible rape	40.3%	Larceny/theft	21.1%
Robbery	28.2%	Motor vehicle theft	11.8%
Aggravated assault	56.4%	Arson	19.0%
Overall Clearance Rate for Type I violent crimes	47.2%	Overall Clearance Rate for Type I property crimes	18.3%

© Cengage Learning 2014

Of the crimes known to police, the percentage that is cleared by an arrest varies greatly by the type of offense, as illustrated in Table 10.2.

Collectively, all of the crimes cleared by police each year result in approximately 13.1 million arrests for nontraffic offenses, about 2.2 million of which are for UCR index crimes (see Figure 10.1). Other than a handful of criminal prosecutions that are instituted as a result of a grand jury investigation that results in an indictment, these arrests are the overwhelming

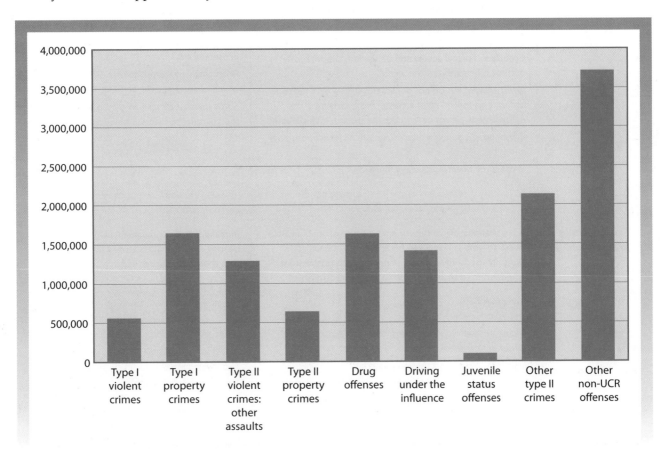

Figure 10.1 ■ Criminal Arrests

SOURCE: Federal Bureau of Investigation, *Crime in The United States—2010.* Washington, DC: Government Printing Office, 2011.

LAW IN ACTION VS. LAW ON THE BOOKS
STEPS IN PRETRIAL CRIMINAL PROCEDURES

	LAW ON THE BOOKS	LAW IN ACTION
Crime	Any violation of the criminal law.	Property crimes outnumber violent crimes by an 8-to-1 ratio.
Arrest	The physical taking into custody of a suspected offender.	Each year, police make more than 13 million arrests for nontraffic offenses, about 2.2 million of which are for UCR index crimes.
Initial appearance	The accused is told of the charges and advised of his or her rights. A neutral judicial officer reviews the arrest to make sure it was supported by probable cause. Preliminary bail may be set. Date for the preliminary hearing is set, if applicable.	Occurs in lower courts. Many misdemeanor defendants plead guilty. May be combined with other judicial proceedings, such as a preliminary hearing, formal bail hearing, or an arraignment, depending on the jurisdiction.
Charging	Formal criminal charges are brought against the defendant, stating which criminal law was violated. *Information*: Formal accusation of a crime made by the prosecutor. *Complaint*: Formal accusation of a crime supported by oath or affirmation of the victim. *Arrest warrant*: An official document, signed by a judge, accusing an individual of a crime and authorizing law enforcement personnel to take the person into custody. Prosecutor is supposed to prosecute all known criminal conduct. Prosecutor controls charging decision.	From arrest to arraignment, half of felony arrests are terminated, downgraded, or diverted in some manner. Complaints very rarely used in felony prosecutions. Prosecutor exercises discretion in deciding which charges should be filed. Some prosecutors allow police input into the charging decision.
Bail	No general right to bail under the Eighth Amendment, but commonly guaranteed as a statutory right.	The average daily jail population is approximately 750,000.
Preliminary hearing	A pretrial hearing to determine whether probable cause exists to hold the accused for further proceedings. Typically used only in jurisdictions that do not require grand juries to make a probable cause determination.	In many jurisdictions, the preliminary hearing is brief, with a strong probability that the case will proceed.
Grand jury	Required for felony prosecutions in 19 states and the federal courts. Grand juries have extensive powers, not possessed by law enforcement, to investigate crimes. *Indictment*: Formal accusation of a crime, made against a person by a grand jury, upon the request of the prosecutor. *Subpoena*: Court order requiring a person to appear before the grand jury and/or produce documents.	Typically not a major decision maker. Prosecutor dominates grand jury proceedings, deciding which cases will be presented and which charges filed. The investigatory powers of the grand jury are most likely to be used in cases involving major drug rings, governmental corruption, and significant white-collar crime.
Arraignment	Stage of the criminal process in which a defendant is formally informed of the charges pending and must enter a plea.	A significant milestone because it indicates that the evidence against the defendant is sufficient to warrant impaneling a jury for trial.

source of work for the criminal courts, since an arrest triggers the first of the steps summarized in the Law in Action vs. Law on the Books box on page 250.

Quality of Arrests

The police have a lot to do with what happens in court after arrest. The strength of the evidence police provide to prosecutors is one of the most important factors influencing whether prosecutors file criminal charges (Holleran, Beichner, & Spohn, 2009). Thus, when police are able to secure tangible evidence and cooperative witnesses for the prosecution (while honoring suspects' constitutional rights), the prosecutor is not only more likely to file charges, but is also more likely to win a conviction (Albonetti, 1987; Forst, Lucianovic, & Cox 1977; Worrall, Ross, & McCord 2006). Conversely, when police conduct incomplete investigations (missing important evidence or witnesses), or improperly seize, mark, or store the items they do gather, prosecutors find themselves without sufficient evidence to prosecute a case successfully, a situation that often puts stress on the relationship between police and prosecutors (Dantzker, 2005). Of course, the quality of law enforcement investigations varies greatly. Not only do individual police officers differ in particular investigatory skills, but also, some police departments, as units, function better than others when conducting investigations because of differences in management, training, resources, procedures, and analytical processes (Keel, Jarvis, & Muirhead, 2009).

INITIAL APPEARANCE

In *Gerstein v. Pugh* (1975, pp. 113–114), the U.S. Supreme Court held that although a police officer's "on-the-scene assessment of probable cause provides legal justification for arresting a person suspected of crime, and for a brief period of detention to take the administrative steps incident to arrest[,] ... the Fourth Amendment requires a judicial determination of probable cause as a prerequisite to extended restraint of liberty following arrest." Thus, after a person has been arrested, a law enforcement officer must take the arrested person before a magistrate for an **initial appearance** (sometimes called a *Gerstein* hearing after the case). Statutes in different jurisdictions require that this

be done promptly, using terms such as "immediately," "without unnecessary delay," "forthwith," or other similar statutory language. These statutes confer a substantial right on the arrestee and create a corresponding duty on law enforcement officers.

The reasons for requiring an initial appearance without unnecessary delay are:

- To verify that the person arrested is the person named in the complaint.

- To advise arrested persons of the charges, so that they may begin to prepare a defense.

- To advise arrested persons of their rights, such as the right to counsel, the right to remain silent, and the right to either a preliminary hearing or a grand jury indictment.

- To protect arrested persons from being abandoned in jail and forgotten by, or otherwise cut off from contact with, people who can help them.

- To prevent secret and extended interrogation of arrested persons by law enforcement officers.

- To give arrested persons an early opportunity to secure release on bail while awaiting the final outcome of the proceedings. If the person has been bailed earlier, the magistrate simply reviews that bail. Release on personal recognizance may also be granted at the initial appearance.

- To give arrested persons an opportunity to speedily conclude proceedings on charges of minor offenses by pleading guilty to the charges, paying fines, and carrying on with their lives.

- To obtain a prompt, neutral "judicial determination of probable cause as a prerequisite to extended restraint of liberty following arrest." (Ferdico, Fradella, & Totten, 2013, p. 54, quoting *Gerstein v. Pugh*, 1975, p. 114)

As a general rule, the Supreme Court expects an initial appearance to occur within 48 hours of a warrantless arrest, inclusive of weekends (*County of Riverside v. McLaughlin*, 1991). Note that in indictment jurisdictions, if a grand jury has already returned an indictment, an initial appearance is not mandated under *Gerstein v. Pugh (1975)*, although some states require an initial appearance for all arrests. Not all states, however, provide for a judicial determination of probable cause at the initial appearance before a magistrate. Some states make a probable cause determination at bail hearings

CASE CLOSE-UP

COUNTY OF RIVERSIDE v. MCLAUGHLIN AND A PROMPT HEARING BEFORE A MAGISTRATE

Beyond the bare fact that he was arrested in Riverside County, California, little is known about Donald Lee McLaughlin. Who he was, why he was arrested, and whatever happened to his case quickly became irrelevant. For whatever reason, the public defender's office decided that the facts of his case made him an ideal candidate to be used as a plaintiff in a suit filed in federal court. The office was prepared to challenge countywide practices; a plaintiff was needed and, at the last minute, McLaughlin's name was inserted. Thus, McLaughlin's name went first in a class action lawsuit filed on behalf of McLaughlin and all other individuals in the same situation.

McLaughlin v. County of Riverside raised the difficult question of how prompt is prompt. California law mandated a probable cause hearing for all those arrested without a warrant within 48 hours of arrest, weekends and holidays excluded. Thus, an individual arrested late in the week might in some cases be held for as long as 5 days before appearing before a neutral judicial official; over the Thanksgiving holiday, a 7-day delay was possible. The U.S. district court agreed with part of McLaughlin's plight and ordered a probable cause hearing within 36 hours of arrest. Having lost in the trial court, the county appealed (hence the names changed place, with the county now listed as the moving party). The Ninth Circuit affirmed the district court's decision, and the county appealed to the U.S. Supreme Court, which granted certiorari.

Although *County of Riverside v. McLaughlin* appears to be a minor quibble over a few hours, the underlying issues are much more fundamental, centering on where to strike the balance between an individual's right to liberty and society's need for effective law enforcement. The Supreme Court has allowed police officers to make arrests, based on their own assessment of probable cause, without first

obtaining a warrant. To counterbalance this privilege, the Court established that an individual arrested without a warrant is entitled to a prompt judicial determination of probable cause afterward. In *Gerstein v. Pugh*, they wrestled with this issue and held that the defendant was entitled to a timely determination. The Court ruled that the 30-day wait in Florida was too long, but failed to be much more specific. As a result, *Gerstein* "created a nationwide divergence in postarrest and pretrial procedures and subjected some individuals to what numerous courts and commentators believed to be unjustifiably prolonged restraints of liberty following their arrests" (Perkins & Jamieson 1995, p. 535).

Justice Sandra Day O'Connor wrote the opinion of the Court, evidencing her ability to strike a compromise. The earlier decision in *Gerstein*, she wrote, provided flexibility to law enforcement, but not a blank check. She recognized that the standard of "prompt" has proved to be vague and therefore has not provided sufficient guidance. In the future, *prompt* shall be defined in most circumstances as 48 hours—a time period she labeled as a "practical compromise between the rights of individuals and the realities of law enforcement." A 24-hour rule would compel local governments across the nation to speed up their criminal justice mechanisms substantially, presumably by allotting local tax dollars to hire additional police officers and magistrates. What is perhaps most striking is how forthright the opinion is in recognizing that law on the books must take into account law in action.

What is most interesting about the four dissenters is their ideological mix. The three moderates agreed with the lower courts that the 36-hour standard was best. But Justice Antonin Scalia, one of the Court's most conservative members, would have fixed the time at 24 hours, a standard he says existed in the common law from the early 1800s.

while other states use preliminary hearings for this purpose. But even in jurisdictions that combine an initial appearance with other pretrial proceedings, judicial probable cause determinations must generally occur within 48 hours of a warrantless arrest (see "Case Close-Up").

Most misdemeanor defendants enter a plea of guilty at their initial appearance and are sentenced immediately (see Chapter 14). For those arrested on a felony, however, a plea is not possible because the initial appearance occurs in a trial court of limited jurisdiction, which has no authority to accept a plea. Thus, the initial appearance is typically a brief affair, as little is known about the crime or the alleged criminal. At times suspects insist on telling their side of the story, but the judge typically cautions that anything said can be used against the defendant. Lawyers provide the same advice.

CHARGING

The criminal court process begins with the filing of a formal written accusation alleging that a specified person or persons committed a specific offense or offenses. The **charging document** includes a brief description of the date and location of the offense. All the essential elements (*corpus delicti*) of the crime must be specified. These accusations satisfy the Sixth Amendment provision that a defendant be given information with which to prepare a defense. Applicable state and federal laws govern technical wording, procedures for making minor amendments, and similar matters.

The four types of charging documents are: complaint, information, arrest warrant, and indictment (which will be discussed later). Which one is used depends on the severity of the offense, applicable state law, and local customs.

A **complaint** must be supported by oath or affirmation of either the victim or the arresting officer. It is most commonly used in prosecuting misdemeanor offenses or city ordinance violations. An **information** is virtually identical in form to the complaint, except that it is signed by the prosecutor. It is required in felony prosecutions in most states that do not use the grand jury. In grand jury states, an information is used for initiating felony charges pending grand jury action. An **arrest warrant** is issued by a judicial officer—usually a lower-court judge. On rare occasions, the warrant is issued prior to arrest, but for most street crimes, the police arrest the suspect and then apply for an arrest warrant. Some states require that the prosecutor approve the request in writing before an arrest warrant can be issued.

Law on the Books: Prosecutorial Control

Through the charging decision, the prosecutor controls the doors to the courthouse. He or she can decide whether charges should be filed and what the proper charge should be. Although the law demands prosecution for "all known criminal conduct," the courts have traditionally granted prosecutors wide discretion in deciding whether to file charges. For example, no legislative or judicial standards govern which cases merit prosecution and which should be declined. Moreover, if a prosecutor refuses to file charges, no review of this decision is possible; courts have consistently refused to order a prosecutor to proceed with a case.

Law in Action: Police Influence

Although the prosecutor has the legal authority to dominate the charging process, the police often influence the prosecutor's decision. Police and prosecutors regularly discuss cases before charges are filed. Sometimes, the police exercise considerable influence by pressuring prosecutors to overcharge defendants or to file charges even though the evidence is weak (Cole, 1970; Skolnick, 1993). Prosecutors, however, rarely need external pressure to overcharge defendants; they do so because it gives them leverage in the plea-bargaining process (see Chapter 12). But in a large number of cases, prosecutors decline to file charges against those arrested by police. In most jurisdictions, the number of police arrests that result in no criminal charges being filed varies between 20 and 50 percent (Boland, Mahanna, & Sones, 1992; Collins, 2007; Neubauer, 1974a; O'Neill 2003).

Courts and Controversy: Charging Decisions

Police departments sometimes object when prosecutors set high standards for charging because they see case rejections as an implicit criticism of the arresting officer for making a "wrong" arrest. Prosecutorial screening can have consequences at the polls. In one jurisdiction where a district attorney refused to file charges in a significant number of arrests, the Fraternal Order of the Police forced the incumbent not to seek reelection (Flemming, Nardulli, & Eisenstein, 1992). But police and prosecutors alike can be subject to public scrutiny for how they use their resources. For example, there is much controversy surrounding whether police and prosecutors devote sufficient attention to white-collar crimes.

COURTS, CONTROVERSY, & ECONOMIC INEQUALITY

ARE WHITE-COLLAR CRIMINALS UNDERPROSECUTED?

Normally, Martha Stewart was at ease before television cameras as she demonstrated the latest in decorating and entertainment ideas, but she was noticeably harried as cameras caught her quick entry into the New York federal courthouse. Martha Stewart became the most recognizable person to be caught up in recent high-profile white-collar crime prosecutions. But the scope of her crime (relatively small) was soon eclipsed by Bernard Madoff, who defrauded investors (some of whom were personal friends) of $50 billion, in the largest Ponzi scheme in American history. Ponzi schemes are named after Charles Ponzi, who in 1919 and 1920 cheated investors out of $10 million. A Ponzi scheme, or pyramid scheme, is a scam in which people are persuaded to invest in a fraudulent operation that promises unusually high returns. The early investors are paid their returns out of money put in by later investors (Lavoie, 2008).

Madoff was ultimately sentenced to 150 years in prison for his crimes. Other prominent persons who have been prosecuted for white-collar crimes are:

- John Rigas and his son Timothy were convicted of fraud and sentenced to 10 years in prison for hiding $2.3 billion in liabilities, reporting inflated earnings, and using millions of corporate dollars for personal use while running Adelphia Communications. Notably, Rigas's other son, Michael, pled guilty to the charges and received a much lighter sentence: 10 months of home arrest and 2 years of probation.

- Sam Waksal, founder of ImClone, was sentenced to 7 years in prison for selling stock in his company the day before a negative ruling from the Food and Drug Administration.

- Ken Lay and Jeffrey Skilling, top executives of Enron, were found guilty of numerous charges of cooking the books, leading to the nation's biggest corporate collapse. (Lay died shortly thereafter, thereby making it more difficult for former employees to pursue restitution in civil court.) Skilling was sentenced to a $45 million fine and 24 years in prison. He appealed his conviction to the U.S. Supreme Court, arguing that he did not receive a fair trial in Enron's home base of Houston, Texas—an argument the high Court rejected.

- Bernie Ebbers, the former top executive at Worldcom, was found guilty of criminal activity after that company was forced into bankruptcy because of approximately $11 billion in fraudulent accounting practices. Ebbers was sentenced to 25 years in prison for his crimes.

- L. Dennis Kozlowski and Mark Swartz, the former heads of Tyco International, were found guilty of stealing hundreds of millions of dollars from the company. Both were sentenced to between 8 and 25 years in prison and ordered to pay $134 million in restitution to Tyco and additional fines of $105 million.

BAIL

Bail is a guarantee. In return for being released from jail, the accused promises to return to court as needed. This promise is guaranteed by posting money or property with the court. If the defendant appears in court when requested, the security is returned. If he or she fails to appear, the security can be forfeited. The practice of allowing defendants to be released from jail pending trial originated centuries ago in England, largely as a convenience to local sheriffs. The colonists brought the concept of bail with them across the Atlantic. It eventually became embedded in the Eighth Amendment, which provides that "excessive bail shall not be required."

Law on the Books: The Monetary Bail System

A careful reading of the Eighth Amendment reveals that the Constitution does not specifically provide that all citizens have a right to bail. Rather, if bail is granted, it must not be "excessive," defined by the Supreme Court in *Stack v. Boyle* (1951), as an amount higher than reasonably calculated to ensure the defendant's presence at trial.

The term *white-collar* is used because it suggests crimes committed by persons of higher economic status, as opposed to the typical street crimes most often associated with the social underclass. As such, the term encompasses a broad range of matters, ranging from crimes against consumers and the environment to securities fraud and governmental corruption (Rosoff, Pontell, & Tillman, 2007). The public, though, remains relatively indifferent to white-collar crimes. One reason is that white-collar crimes lack the drama associated with murders and bank robberies. Another is that the defendants are respectable—they don't look like criminals (whatever that might mean). In the words of David Friedrichs (2009), they are "trusted criminals." Society's contradictory assessments of white-collar criminals are most noticeable when it comes to sentencing: although the crime has negatively affected some individuals, the offenders do not present a physical threat to society. To some, draconian sentences (often amounting to effective life imprisonment) are excessive (Podgor, 2007).

Allegations that white-collar crimes are underprosecuted, however, require close scrutiny. After all, a number of major prosecutions and convictions have occurred over the years. In addition, since the Enron scandal, public attention to white-collar crimes has clearly increased, and Congress passed the Sarbanes–Oxley Act, which, among other things, sharply increased penalties for various forms of fraud ("Go Directly to Jail," 2009). At the federal level, the Justice Department and other federal regulatory agencies such as the Securities and Exchange Commission have large staffs devoted to these matters. At the local

level, though, district attorneys' offices have only small staff devoted to fraud and similar crimes because the office is overwhelmed by the sheer volume of day-to-day street crimes like murder, robbery, and drug offenses. Moreover, convincing a jury to return a guilty verdict in a white-collar crime presents a difficult task to prosecutors. For one, jurors often find it difficult to follow the detailed testimony from accountants. For another, a "smoking gun" seldom points convincingly to guilty intent (Glater & Belson, 2005). But juries are increasingly returning guilty verdicts, particularly in cases like Tyco, where jurors said they did not find the defendants' stories on the witness stand to be credible (Maremont & Bray, 2005). Nor are juries any longer impressed with the "dummy defense," whereby chief executives testify that they were paid millions every year, but knew nothing about the details of their company (Norris, 2005).

On the other hand, the Transactional Records Access Clearinghouse (TRAC) at Syracuse University found that in 2011, the annual total of financial fraud prosecutions was down nearly 29 percent in 5 years and nearly 58 percent from a decade earlier even though financial institution fraud played a major role in the 2008 economic meltdown that paralyzed the U.S. economy. Yet, few corporate or banking executives have faced any criminal charges for their roles in creating deceptive derivative contracts that inflated the real-estate bubble.

What do you think? Are white-collar crimes underprosecuted? Would white-collar crimes be better deterred by more prosecutions or more government regulations?

A right to bail, however, was recognized in common law and in statutes as early as 1789 for all those accused of committing noncapital crimes. In 1966, Congress enacted the Bail Reform Act, thereby creating a statutory presumption favoring pretrial release of federal arrestees.

Bail Procedures

Bail procedures vary by jurisdiction and according to the seriousness of the crime. In the majority of states, those arrested for minor misdemeanors can be released fairly quickly by posting bail at the police station. In most communities, lower-court judges

have adopted a fixed bail schedule (also known as an "emergency bail schedule"), which specifies an exact amount for each offense. In contrast, bail procedures for felony or serious misdemeanor cases are considerably more complex. Depending on the jurisdiction, bail may be set during an initial appearance, a preliminary hearing, or a separate bail hearing. Either way, the arrestee appears before a lower-court judge who must determine whether the arrestee qualifies for release on bail and, if so, what those conditions will be. Accordingly, those accused of serious crimes remain in police custody for a number of hours before they have the opportunity to make bail.

TABLE 10.3 ▪ FORMS OF BAIL

Release on recognizance (ROR)	Judges release a defendant from jail without monetary bail if they believe the person is not likely to flee. Such personal bonds are used most often for defendants accused of minor crimes and for those with substantial ties to the community.
Cash bond	The accused must post either the full amount of cash bail with the court or a percentage of it in the form of a cash bond. All of this money will be returned when all court appearances are satisfied. Because it requires a large amount of cash, this form of bail is seldom used. If, for example, bail is set in the amount of $10,000, most persons cannot raise that much money easily and quickly.
Property bond	Most states allow a defendant (or friends or relatives) to use a piece of property as collateral. If the defendant fails to appear in court, the property is forfeited. Property bonds are also rare, because courts generally require that the equity in the property must be double the amount of the bond. Thus, a $10,000 bond requires equity of at least $20,000.
Bail bond	The arrestee hires a bail agent (often called a bail bondsman), who posts the amount required and charges a fee for services rendered, usually 10 percent of the amount of the bond. Thus, a bail agent would normally collect $1,000 for writing a $10,000 bond; none of that money is refundable.

© Cengage Learning

Forms of Bail

Once bail has been set, a defendant can gain pretrial release in four basic ways, outlined in Table 10.3. Because many of those arrested lack ready cash, do not own property, or lack the needed social clout, the first three options for making bail listed in Table 10.3 are only abstractions, requiring most to post a bail bond.

Preventive Detention

In the American system of monetary bail, those who are rich enough can often buy their freedom while awaiting trial. But the poor await trial in jail. On any given day, there are nearly 750,000 persons in jail (not prison), nearly 63 percent of whom have not been convicted of any crime (Minton & Sabol, 2009). Five out of six of these pretrial detainees "had bail set with financial conditions required for release that were not met" (Cohen & Reaves, 2007, p. 1).

Congress amended the Bail Reform Act in 1984 to make clear that when setting bail, a judge may remand arrestees to preventive detention, effectively holding suspects without bail if they are accused of committing a dangerous or violent crime and locking them up is deemed necessary for community safety. Specifically, the Bail Reform Act of 1984 allows a suspect to be held in jail without bail for up to 90 days pending trial if the judge finds clear and convincing evidence that:

1. there is a serious risk that the person will flee;
2. the person may obstruct justice or threaten, injure, or intimidate a prospective witness or juror; or
3. the offense is one of violence or one punishable by life imprisonment or death.

The law also creates a presumption against pretrial release for major drug dealers (Berg, 1985). The Supreme Court upheld the Bail Reform Act in *United States v. Salerno* (1987), ruling that Congress enacted preventive detention not as a punishment for dangerous individuals, but as a potential solution to the pressing social problem of crimes committed by persons on bail. Approximately 6 percent of all felony defendants are denied bail and held in pretrial detention, a figure that has remained remarkably consistent since the Bail Reform Act of 1984 and its state law counterparts went into effect (Cohen & Reaves, 2007).

Law in Action: The Context of Bail Setting

Deciding whom to release and whom to detain pending trial poses critical problems for American courts. The realities of the bail system in the United States reflect an attempt to strike a balance between the legally recognized purpose of setting bail to ensure reappearance for trial and the working perception that some defendants should not be allowed out of jail until their trial.

Trial court judges have a great deal of discretion in fixing bail. Statutory law provides few specifics about how much money should be required, and appellate courts have likewise spent little time deciding what criteria should be used. Although the Eighth Amendment prohibits excessive bail, appellate courts will reduce a trial judge's bail amount only in the rare event that flagrant abuse can be proved. In practice, then, trial court judges have virtually unlimited legal discretion in determining the amount of bail. The discretion is often guided by the following factors:

- *Risk of flight and other nonappearance:* Considers the suspect's "ties to the community" in terms of stable employment, property ownership, marital status, number of close, stable relationships, length of presence in the community, and such.

- *Risk to self and others:* Considers the suspect's mental condition, the seriousness of the crime(s) for which the suspect was arrested, and the arrestee's prior criminal history.

- *Situational justice:* Considers factors such as how the defendant appears, acts, responds to questions, and the like. Note that the use of situational justice might lead judges to make certain judgments about defendants based on demographic characteristics, resulting in racial, ethnic, gender, and sexual orientation disparities to manifest themselves in bail decisions (Demuth, 2003; Katz & Spohn, 1995; Schlesinger, 2005; Spohn, 2008).

At first blush, these factors might seem straightforward. But uncertainty abounds because typically few details of the alleged crime are available shortly after a warrantless arrest. Similarly, the information about the defendant's mental status, ties to the community, and even criminal history are often in short supply. In many courts, for example, police "rap sheets" (lists of prior arrests) are available, but typically do not contain information about how prior cases were eventually disposed of—dismissal, plea, or imprisonment.

Moreover, each bail decision is risky. In the face of uncertainly (often caused by a lack of complete information), judges must weigh risks such as whether a defendant released on bail will commit another crime and whether police groups, district attorneys, and the local newspapers may criticize a judge severely for granting pretrial release to defendants.

In addition, judges have to worry about jail overcrowding. If a particular arrestee is placed in pretrial detention, might that result in someone else—perhaps someone more dangerous—being released from a jail crowded beyond its capacity?

Bail Agents and Bounty Hunters

If a judge grants bail, many defendants who lack the financial resources to post cash or property as bail turn to the services of commercial **bail agents**—people who, for a nonrefundable fee, post a bond with the court. If the defendant does not appear for subsequent court proceedings, the bail agent is responsible for the full amount of the bond. For assuming this risk, he or she is permitted to charge a fee, usually 10 percent of the face amount of the bond. Rarely, however, do bail agents post cash directly with the court. Instead, they purchase a surety bond from a major insurance company, which charges 30 percent of the bail agent's fee. Thus, if the total amount of the bail is $10,000, the bondsman receives $1,000 from the client and keeps $700 of it.

As a condition of posting bail, bail agents require their clients to sign a contract waiving any protections against extradition and allowing the bail agent or a bounty hunter acting on behalf of the bail agent to retrieve the defendant from wherever he or she may have fled. These powers exceed any possessed by law enforcement officials since bail agents and bounty hunters are private actors; they are not, therefore, bound by the same constitutional constraints placed on law enforcement officers, who act under governmental authority when they seek, apprehend, detain, and transport bail jumpers. The exercise of such broad power has often led to corruption, "excessive use of force, false imprisonment, destruction of property, and arrest of innocent citizens" (Baker, Vaughn, & Topalli, 2008, p. 125). As a result, organizations like the American Bar Association and the National

District Attorneys Association have recommended the abolition of commercial bail, but they have succeeded in only four states (Kentucky, Oregon, Wisconsin, and Illinois). Also, the District of Columbia, Maine, and Nebraska have little commercial bail activity (Cohen & Reaves, 2007). Yet, an estimated 14,000 commercial bail agencies nationwide secure the release of more than 2 million defendants annually (Cohen & Reaves, 2007). But things are slowly changing. Today, largely as a result of state statutory and case law changes,

> Bail bond agents and bounty hunters have jurisdictional constraints placed on their actions, and they must follow the law or be subject to criminal prosecution. . . . For the most part, arbitrary, capricious, and discriminatory actions committed by bail bond agents and bounty hunters are subject to criminal prosecution, although some continue to use their extra-legal authority to flaunt the rule of law. . . . Partly as a result of the threat of criminal prosecution, many states have bail bond societies and associations that are working to professionalize the industry. More jails, and the Sheriff's Offices that run them, require bail bond agents and bounty hunters to be licensed, are using technology to establish early warning systems to monitor potential misbehavior, and require criminal background checks to detect potential wrong-doing within the industry before it spirals out of control into a major scandal. (Baker, Vaughn & Topalli, 2008, p. 129)

Effects of the Bail System

The process of setting bail is not neutral. Defendants who have some access to money are much more likely than poor defendants to be bailed out of jail. The fact that some defendants remain in jail awaiting trial (or plea) has direct and perhaps indirect effects.

Most directly, defendants who cannot make bail face a variety of hardships. Even though defendants detained before trial are presumed innocent until proven guilty, they suffer many of the same disadvantages as those incarcerated after conviction. Economically, they often lose their jobs.

Psychologically, they are subjected to stress, anxiety, and isolation. Physically, they are held in a violence-prone atmosphere. Indeed, some defendants spend time in jail during pretrial detention and are later not convicted.

More indirectly, defendants who cannot make bail may be at a disadvantage during the criminal justice process. Conversely, those who have been released may not appear in court as required. The effects of bail have been an active area of concern for the public, policymakers, and researchers alike. The topics that have received the greatest attention are jail conditions, race and ethnicity, failure to appear, and case disposition.

Jail Conditions

In an influential 1965 book *Ransom: A Critique of the American Bail System*, Ronald Goldfarb described the conditions of jails in the United States as "the ultimate ghetto." Over the past decades, jail conditions have improved greatly; Section 1983 conditions of confinement lawsuits filed in federal courts have played a role in these improvements. Nonetheless, many jails are still substandard, since efforts to improve jail conditions are typically low on the priority list of local officials, who are reluctant to spend taxpayers' dollars and do not want to appear to be coddling criminals.

Race and Ethnicity

Some studies have found clear differences between the defendants who await trial in jail and those who are released. Hispanics are the group most likely to be detained in jail, whites are the least likely to be detained, and African-Americans are in the middle. These differences are partially the product of variation in economic status and the corresponding (in)ability to pay bail. Hispanics face a "triple disadvantage" during the bail-setting process—as a group they are least likely to qualify for ROR, have the highest bail amounts set, and are the least able to pay bail (Demuth, 2003; Schlesinger, 2005). Higher pretrial detention rates for Hispanics may be the product of immigration holds filed by the U.S. Immigration and Customs Enforcement to detain those illegally in the country (Cohen & Reaves, 2007).

Failure to Appear

Defendants who have gained pretrial release do not always appear in court when required. Skipping bail has several consequences. First, bail is forfeited. Second, a warrant is issued for the suspect's arrest. This warrant, termed a **bench warrant** or a *capias*, authorizes the police to take the person into custody. The person must be delivered to the judge issuing the warrant and cannot be released on bail. Finally, failure to appear often subjects the defendant to a separate criminal charge of bond jumping.

How often bailed defendants fail to appear in court is subject to considerable debate. A study of felony defendants in large urban counties reports that 22 percent of the released defendants missed one or more court dates (Cohen & Reaves, 2007). This estimate defined nonappearance as missing a single court date, but the problem of people absconding from bail to become fugitives from the law is real. Some studies estimate that 6 percent of released defendants were still fugitives at the end of a year, whereas other studies have reported that up to 30 percent of felony absconders will remain fugitives for a least a full year (Helland & Tabarok, 2004).

Defendants who fail to appear do not always intend to miss their court dates. Failure-to-appear rates are closely related to practices within the court. A number of defendants do not show up because they were not given clear notice of the next appearance date. Another way in which courts themselves contribute to nonappearances is by lengthy delays in disposing of cases. As the time from arrest to trial increases, the rate of nonappearances rises even faster.

Case Disposition

Pretrial detention has a great impact on the legal processing of defendants:

> Viewed from the perspective of maintaining the plea-bargaining system, pretrial detention and demoralizing conditions in jails are highly functional. They discourage the defendant from bargaining too hard; they place a high price upon filing motions or demanding a trial. … This is not to argue that those in authority consciously plan rotten jails; clearly most are concerned about jail conditions. But it is to

suggest that such conditions are functional, do serve the needs of the production ethic that dominates our criminal justice system. (Casper, 1972, p. 67)

The discriminatory impact of bail has been the subject of considerable research. There is widespread agreement in the literature that jailed defendants are more likely to be convicted and (once convicted) more likely to be sentenced to prison than those who have obtained pretrial release (Ares, Rankin, & Sturz, 1963; Cohen & Reaves, 2007; Phillips, 2007, 2008; Reaves, 2001). What is in dispute is the interpretation of these findings. Do these disparities result because the lack of pretrial release imposes additional burdens on the defendants? Or are these disparities a statistical artifact of a preselection process? Given that bail increases with the severity of the crime and the length of the prior record, one might reasonably expect that these defendants would end up disadvantaged, but for good reason.

John Goldkamp (1980) attempted to answer these difficult questions through a sophisticated analysis of more than 8,000 criminal cases in Philadelphia. Goldkamp found that jailed defendants did not differ from their bailed counterparts in terms of findings of guilt. At all the significant stages—dismissal, diversion, and trial—jailed defendants were as likely as bailed ones to receive a favorable disposition of their cases. When it came to sentencing, however, jailed defendants were more likely to be sentenced to prison, although the length of the sentence was not related to bail status. Another study (Eisenstein & Jacob, 1977) found no uniform impact of bail status on findings of guilt or on sentencing. Does bail status negatively affect the defendant's case? Perhaps the best response is provided by Goldkamp: "It depends." More recently, research in New York City found that in felony (Phillips, 2008) and nonfelony cases (Phillips, 2007) pretrial detention had a small, but statistically significant effect on the likelihood of conviction and also slightly longer sentences.

PRELIMINARY HEARING

In most states, any person who has been arrested for a felony and has not been indicted by a grand jury (and, therefore, has been charged via an information or complaint or similar document filed by a prosecutor), has the right to a preliminary hearing. At the **preliminary hearing** (also called the "preliminary examination"), the magistrate must determine whether **probable cause** exists to believe that a felony was committed and that the defendant committed it. In this context, *probable cause* means a fair probability, under the totality of the facts and circumstances known, that the person arrested committed the crime(s) charged. Usually held before a lower-court judge, the preliminary hearing is designed:

> to prevent hasty, malicious, improvident, and oppressive prosecutions, to protect the person charged from open and public accusations of crime, to avoid both for the defendant and the public the expense of a public trial, to save the defendant from the humiliation and anxiety involved in public prosecution, and to discover whether or not there are substantial grounds upon which a prosecution may be based. (*Thies v. State*, 1922, p. 541)

As stated above, the initial appearance before a magistrate may or may not include a probable cause hearing. If it does not, then a separate preliminary hearing is required unless: (1) the defendant is charged with a petty offense or misdemeanor; (2) the defendant waives the hearing; or (3) a grand jury has already determined that probable cause exists for the defendant to stand felony trial. Rule 5 of the Federal Rules of Criminal Procedure provides that, when the preliminary hearing is required, "[t]he magistrate judge must hold the preliminary hearing within a reasonable time, but no later than 10 days after the initial appearance if the defendant is in custody and no later than 20 days if not in custody."

Law on the Books: Weighing Probable Cause

The preliminary hearing is a formal adversarial proceeding conducted in open court; normally, a transcript of the proceedings is recorded. During a preliminary hearing, the state does not have to prove the defendant guilty beyond a reasonable doubt, as would be required during a trial. Rather,

the prosecutor needs only to establish probable cause that a crime has been committed and that the defendant committed it. If the magistrate finds probable cause to believe that the defendant committed the offense, the magistrate **binds over** the defendant to the trial court for adjudication of the felony charges. The magistrate may admit the defendant to bail at the preliminary hearing or may continue, increase, or decrease the original bail. If the magistrate does not find probable cause, the magistrate dismisses the complaint and releases the defendant. A dismissal at this stage does not invoke the constitutional safeguard against double jeopardy. This means that the prosecution may recharge the defendant and submit new evidence at a later preliminary hearing. Nor does a dismissal prevent the prosecution from going to the grand jury and obtaining an indictment in states that have both grand jury and preliminary hearing procedures. Table 10.4 compares the preliminary hearing with grand jury proceedings.

Law in Action: Variations in Using the Preliminary Hearing

Defense attorneys weigh several factors in deciding whether to demand a preliminary hearing or waive it (Flemming, 1986b; Prosser, 2006). Practices of the local prosecutor are one important consideration. If the district attorney's files are open and plea-bargaining policies are well known, it is viewed as time consuming and redundant to hold a preliminary hearing. Second, strategic and tactical considerations are involved. Waiving the preliminary hearing may reflect an assessment that the information to be gained from holding a preliminary hearing does not outweigh the potential damage to the defendant's case (for example, the publicity that may surround a rape case). A third factor is client control. Defense attorneys sometimes insist on a preliminary hearing to impress on their client the gravity of the situation. Finally, the preliminary hearing gives the defense attorney an overview of the evidence against the client and provides the opportunity for discovery (see Chapter 11).

The tactical decision of holding or waiving the preliminary hearing highlights the complexity of the preliminary hearing from the law in action perspective. Although the legal purpose of the

TABLE 10.4 ■ DIFFERENCES IN PRETRIAL PROCEDURES TO DETERMINE WHETHER PROBABLE CAUSE EXISTS TO MAKE A DEFENDANT STAND TRIAL IN FELONY CASES

Grand Jury Proceedings	Preliminary Hearing
Primary function is to determine whether probable cause exists to believe that the defendant committed the crime or crimes charged.	Primary function is to determine whether probable cause exists to believe that the defendant committed the crime or crimes charged.
If probable cause is found, the grand jury returns an indictment/"true bill" against the defendant that is signed both by the prosecutor and by the foreperson of the grand jury.	If probable cause is found, the judge binds over the defendant for the trial court for adjudication by signing an information.
Held in the grand jury room in a closed session (i.e., secret proceedings not open to the public).	Held in open court (i.e., open to the public).
Informal proceeding in which no judicial officer presides.	Formal judicial proceeding presided over by a judge or magistrate.
Nonadversarial proceeding in which the grand jury hears only evidence presented by the prosecution.	Adversarial proceeding in which both the prosecution and the defense may present evidence to the presiding judicial officer.
Defendant has no right to be present or to offer evidence.	Defendant has the right to be present, to offer evidence, and to cross-examine adverse witnesses.
Defendant has no Sixth Amendment right to counsel.	Defendant has a right to the effective assistance of counsel under the Sixth Amendment.
Grand jury has the power to investigate crimes on its own initiative.	No power to investigate crime.
Grand jury has the power to subpoena witnesses and evidence.	No subpoena power.
Grand jury has the power to grant immunity.	No power to grant immunity.

SOURCE: John Ferdico, Henry F. Fradella, and Christopher Totten. *Criminal Procedure for the Criminal Justice Professional.* 11th ed. Belmont, CA: Wadsworth, 2012.

preliminary hearing is simple, the actual conduct of these hearings is quite complex. In some courts, they may last an hour or more; in others, they consume only a few minutes. In some jurisdictions, preliminary hearings are an important stage in the proceedings; in others, they are a perfunctory step, in which probable cause is found to exist in virtually every case.

This variability makes it difficult to generalize about the importance of the preliminary hearing, but studies do reveal four major patterns. In some jurisdictions, preliminary hearings are almost never held. In many, they are short and routine, lasting but a few minutes with the defendant almost always bound over to the grand jury (Neubauer, 1974b). In most jurisdictions, the preliminary hearing is largely ceremonial, resulting in few cases being

screened out of the criminal process; but in a few courts, it is quite significant (McIntyre & Lippman, 1970; Washburn, 2008).

GRAND JURY

Grand juries make accusations; trial juries decide guilt or innocence. The grand jury emerged in English law in 1176, during a political struggle among King Henry II, the church, and noblemen. At first, criminal accusations originated with members of the grand jury themselves, but gradually this body came to consider accusations from outsiders as well.

After the American Revolution, the grand jury was included in the Fifth Amendment to the Constitution, which provides that "no person shall be held

TABLE 10.5 ▪ VARIABILITY IN STATE USE OF GRAND JURIES

Grand Jury Indictments Required for Most or All Felonies (N = 24)	Grand Jury Indictments Optional for Most Felonies (N = 25)	Grand Jury Indictments Abolished (N = 2)
Alabama, Alaska, Delaware, District of Columbia, Florida, Kentucky, Louisiana, Maine, Massachusetts, Minnesota, Mississippi, Missouri, New Hampshire, New Jersey, New York, North Carolina, North Dakota, Ohio, Rhode Island, South Carolina, Tennessee, Texas, Virginia, and West Virginia	Arizona, Arkansas, California, Colorado, Georgia, Hawaii, Idaho, Illinois, Indiana, Iowa, Kansas, Maryland, Michigan, Montana, Nebraska, Nevada, New Mexico, Oklahoma, Oregon, South Dakota, Utah, Vermont, Washington, Wisconsin, and Wyoming	Connecticut, Pennsylvania

© Cengage Learning 2014

to answer for a capital, or otherwise infamous crime, unless on a presentment or indictment of a grand jury." The archaic phrase "otherwise infamous crime" has been interpreted to mean felonies. This provision, however, applies only to federal prosecutions. In *Hurtado v. California* (1884), the Supreme Court held that states have the option of using either an indictment or an information. Today, grand juries in every U.S. state and the District of Columbia can investigate criminal activity; in contrast, U.S. jurisdictions differ with regard to how grand jury indictments operate as explained in Table 10.5.

Grand juries are impaneled (formally created) for a set period of time—typically varying between 10 days and 24 months. During that time, the jurors periodically consider the cases brought to them by the prosecutor and conduct other investigations. If a grand jury is conducting a major and complex investigation, its time may be extended by the court. The size of grand juries varies greatly, from as few as 5 jurors to as many as 23, with an average size of 17. Grand jurors are normally selected randomly, in a manner similar to the selection of trial jurors. In a handful of states, however, judges, county boards, jury commissioners, or sheriffs are allowed to exercise discretion in choosing who will serve on the grand jury.

Law on the Books: Shield and Sword

The two primary functions of grand juries have been aptly summarized in the phrase "shield and sword" (Zalman & Siegel, 1997). *Shield* refers to the protections the grand jury offers, serving as a buffer between the state and its citizens and preventing the government from using the criminal process against its enemies. *Sword* refers to the investigatory powers of this body (Alpert & Petersen, 1985). If the grand jury believes grounds for holding the suspect for trial are present, they return an **indictment**, also termed a **true bill**, meaning that they find the charges to be true. Conversely, if they find the charges insufficient to justify trial, they return a no bill, or **no true bill**.

Many legal protections found elsewhere in the criminal court process are not applicable at the grand jury stage. One unique aspect of the grand jury is secrecy. Because the grand jury may find insufficient evidence to indict, it works in secret to shield those merely under investigation from adverse publicity. By contrast, the rest of the criminal court process is required to be public. Another unique aspect is that indictments are returned by a plurality vote; in most states, half to two-thirds of the votes are sufficient to hand up an indictment. Trial juries can convict only if the jurors are unanimous (or, in four states, nearly unanimous). Finally, witnesses before the grand jury have no right to representation by an attorney, whereas defendants are entitled to have a lawyer present at all vital stages of a criminal prosecution. Nor do suspects have the right to go before the grand jury to protest their innocence or even to present their version of the facts.

In furtherance of their investigative powers, grand juries have the authority to grant **immunity** from prosecution. The Fifth Amendment protects a person against self-incrimination. In 1893 Congress passed a statute that permitted the granting of **transactional immunity**. In exchange for a witness's testimony, the prosecutor agrees not to prosecute the witness for any crimes admitted—a practice often referred to as "turning state's evidence." The Organized Crime Control Act of 1970 added a new and more limited form of immunity. Under use immunity, the government may not use a witness's grand jury testimony to prosecute that person. However, if the state acquires evidence of a crime independently of that testimony, the witness may be prosecuted. The Supreme Court has held that use immunity does not violate the Fifth Amendment's prohibition against self-incrimination (*Kastigar v. United States*, 1972). Use immunity gives witnesses less protection than does transactional immunity. A witness may not refuse the government's offer of immunity, and failure to testify may result in a jail term for contempt of court.

The investigative powers of the grand jury to gather evidence are also seen in its subpoena power. Under the court's authority, the grand jury may issue a subpoena requiring an individual to appear before the grand jury to testify and/or bring papers and other evidence for its consideration. Failure to comply with a subpoena (or offer of immunity) is punishable as contempt. A person found in contempt of the grand jury faces a fine or being jailed until he or she complies with the grand jury request. Thus, contempt of the grand jury is potentially open ended—as long as the grand jury is in existence and as long as the person refuses to comply, the person can sit in jail. Critics contend that some prosecutors call political dissidents to testify to find out information unrelated to criminal activity.

The contempt power can also be used for punishment. A prosecutor may call a witness, knowing that he or she will refuse to testify, and then have the witness jailed. In this way, a person can be imprisoned without a trial. This has happened mainly to newspaper reporters. In *Branzburg v. Hayes* (1972), the Supreme Court ruled that journalists must testify before a grand jury. Some journalists have gone to jail rather than reveal their confidential sources, because they believe that to do so would erode the freedom of the press protected by the First Amendment.

Law in Action: Prosecutorial Domination

The work of the grand jury is shaped by its unique relationship with the prosecutor. In theory at least, the prosecutor functions only as a legal adviser to the grand jury, but in practice, the prosecutor dominates. Grand jurors hear only the witnesses summoned by the prosecutor, and, as laypeople, they are heavily influenced by the legal advice of the prosecutor. Indeed, the high court has ruled that the government is under no obligation to disclose to the grand jury evidence that would tend to clear the defendant (*United States v. Williams*, 1992). This is one of a number of significant developments in the way criminal procedure has been shaped by the courts, as explained below in the "Key Developments" feature.

The net result is that grand juries often function as a rubber stamp for the prosecutor. One study found that the average time spent per case was only 5 minutes; in 80 percent of the cases, there was no discussion by members of the grand jury; rarely did members voice a dissent; and finally, the grand jury approved virtually all of the prosecutor's recommendations (Carp, 1975). Similarly, federal grand juries rarely return no true bills. In short, grand juries generally indict whomever the prosecutor wants indicted (Gilboy, 1984; Neubauer, 1974b; Washburn, 2008).

Courts and Controversy: Reform the Grand Jury?

The grand jury system has been the object of various criticisms. In theory, the grand jury serves as a watchdog on the prosecutor, but some portray the grand jury as "the prosecutor's darling," a "puppet," or a "rubber stamp." To William Campbell (1973), U.S. District Court judge for the Northern District of Illinois, "The grand jury is the total captive of the prosecutor who, if he is candid, will concede that he can indict anybody at any time, for almost anything, before any grand jury" (p. 174). These concerns have prompted a call for abolition of the grand jury. Early in the 20th century, judicial reformers succeeded in abolishing grand juries in some states. More recently, such abolition efforts have not been successful, however, because they require a constitutional amendment.

Today, critics call for reforming the grand jury (Brenner, 1998; Washburn, 2008). Often these calls are based on concerns that grand jury proceedings have been misused to serve partisan political ends, harassing and punishing those who criticize the government. The leading advocate for federal grand jury reform is the National Association of Criminal Defense Lawyers (2000). This organization advocates a Citizens' Grand Jury Bill of Rights, which among other things would grant witnesses the right to counsel during testimony, require prosecutors to disclose evidence that might exonerate the target, and allow targets of investigations to testify (Lefcourt, 1998).

KEY DEVELOPMENTS CONCERNING CRIMINAL PROCEDURE

Crime *Lanzetta v. New Jersey* (1939)	A law is unconstitutional if it forbids an act in terms so vague that "men of common intelligence must necessarily guess at its meaning."
Arrest *Chimel v. California* (1969)	During a search incident to arrest, the police may search only the person and the area within the immediate vicinity.
Payton v. New York (1980)	Unless the suspect gives consent or an emergency exists, an arrest warrant is necessary if an arrest requires entry into a suspect's private residence.
Arizona v. Gant (2009)	Police may search a vehicle incident to the arrest of its recent occupant after the arrest only if it is reasonable to believe that the arrestee might access the vehicle at the time of the search or that the vehicle contains evidence of the offense of the arrest.
Initial appearance Sixth Amendment (1791)	"In all criminal prosecutions, the accused shall enjoy the right ...to be informed of the nature and cause of the accusation."
Rothgery v. Gillespie County, Texas (2008)	Defendant's initial appearance in which he learns of the charge(s) against him and his liberty is subject to restriction, marks initiation of adversary proceedings that trigger attachment of Sixth Amendment right to counsel.
Charging Sixth Amendment (1791)	"In all criminal prosecutions, the accused shall enjoy the right ...to be informed of the nature and cause of the accusation."
People v. Wabash, St. Louis and Pacific Railway (1882)	Prosecutor has discretion in beginning prosecutions and may terminate them when, in his (or her) judgment, the ends of justice are satisfied.
Burns v. Reed (1991)	Prosecutor enjoys absolute immunity to civil lawsuit for all actions involving the adversarial process.
Bail Eighth Amendment (1791)	Excessive bail shall not be required.
Bail Reform Act of 1984	Upheld in *United States v. Salerno* (1987), this law created a statutory presumption in favor of pretrial release.
Grand jury Fifth Amendment (1791)	"No person shall be held to answer for a capital, or otherwise infamous crime, unless on a presentment or indictment of a grand jury."
Hurtado v. California (1884)	States are not required to use a grand jury in charging felonies.
U.S. Congress (1893)	Prosecutors may grant transactional immunity for testimony a witness is compelled to give before a grand jury.
Organized Crime Control Act (1970)	Prosecutors may grant a witness use immunity for testimony before the grand jury.

© Cengage Learning

Continued on next page

Continued from previous page

Kastigar v. United States (1972)	Use immunity does not violate the Fifth Amendment protection against self-incrimination.
Branzburg v. Hayes (1972)	Journalists have no constitutional right to maintain the confidentiality of their news sources when subpoenaed before grand juries, and are compelled to give testimony.
United States v. Williams (1992)	Prosecutors are under no obligation to present exculpatory evidence to the grand jury.
Campbell v. Louisiana (1998)	A White criminal defendant may challenge his conviction on grounds that African-Americans were discriminated against in the selection of grand jurors.
Arraignment Sixth Amendment (1791)	"In all criminal prosecutions, the accused shall enjoy the right ... to be informed of the nature and cause of the accusation."

ARRAIGNMENT

Arraignment occurs in the trial court of general jurisdiction. During the arraignment, the defendant is formally accused of a crime (either by an information or indictment) and is called upon to enter a plea. Thus, initial appearance and arraignment are similar in that the defendant must be informed with some specificity about the alleged criminal actions. The major difference is that felony defendants are not allowed to enter a plea (either innocent or guilty) in a lower court because that court lacks jurisdiction to take a plea and to sentence.

Procedurally, the arraignment provides the court the opportunity to ensure that the case is on track for disposition. The judge summons the defendant, verifying his or her name and address, and the lawyer provides formal notification to the court that he or she represents the defendant in this matter. Most important, the arraignment means that the defendant must enter a plea. Typically, defendants plead not guilty and a trial date is established. In some jurisdictions, however, a significant proportion of defendants enter a plea of guilty (Neubauer, 1996).

The arraignment is rarely a major decision-making stage in the process. Rather, its real importance is measured more indirectly. The arraignment is important because it signifies to all members of the courtroom work group that the defendant is in all probability guilty and that the likelihood of being found not guilty is now slim. Thus, from the perspective of law in action, the arraignment says something very important about case attrition.

LAW IN ACTION PERSPECTIVE: CASE ATTRITION

The law on the books perspective suggests a mechanical process—cases move almost automatically from one pretrial stage to the next. In sharp contrast, the law in action perspective emphasizes a dynamic process—cases are likely to be eliminated during these early stages.

A detailed picture of case attrition emerges in the research summarized in Figure 10.2. For every 100 arrests, 8 are diverted and 23 are dismissed by the prosecutor through a *nolle prosequi* (no prosecution). When this happens, the case is said to be "nolled," "nollied," or "nol. prossed." Overall, only 69 of the 100 arrests are carried forward to the trial stage, at which 65 are resolved by guilty pleas; only 4 go to trial. These statistics underscore the fact that decisions made during early steps of felony prosecutions are much more important in terminating cases than the later activities of judges and juries. However, important variations arise among courts in the stage at which case attrition occurs. These variations reflect differences in state law, the structure of courts, and local traditions. Thus, a critical stage for case screening and case attrition in one court may be of little importance in another jurisdiction.

Figure 10.2 ■ Case Attrition of Felony Arrests in 75 of the Largest Counties in the United States

SOURCE: Bureau of Justice Statistics. 2010. *Felony Defendants in Large Urban Counties, 2006.* Washington, DC: Department of Justice.

WHY ATTRITION OCCURS

Case attrition is the product of a complex set of factors, including the relationships among the major actors in the criminal justice system, the patterns of informal authority within the courtroom work group, the backlog of cases on the court's docket, and community standards defining serious criminal activity. We can best examine why attrition occurs by using three facets of discretion: legal judgments, policy priorities, and personal standards of justice. As with other attempts to understand discretion, these categories are not mutually exclusive—some screening decisions are based on more than one criterion.

Legal Judgments

Legal judgments are the most important reason that cases drop by the wayside after arrest and before arraignment. Prosecutors, judges, and grand jurors begin with a basic question: Is there sufficient evidence to prove the elements of the offense? (Cole, 1970; Feeney, Dill, & Weir, 1983). One assistant district attorney phrased it this way: "When I examine the police report, I have to feel that I could go to trial with the case tomorrow. All the elements of prosecution must be present before I file charges" (Neubauer, 1974b, p. 118).

The legal-evidentiary strength of the case is the reason cited most often for prosecutors declining to prosecute cases (Albonetti, 1987; Holleran et al., 2009; Jacoby, Mellon, Ratledge, & Turner, 1982; Miller & Wright, 2008). Such problems include noncooperation by victims and witnesses; insufficient evidence to prove the elements of charged crimes; problems with the strength or credibility of witnesses' testimony; and, on rare occasion, problems with the ways in which law enforcement obtained evidence. Lack of cooperation from victims and witnesses poses a particular problem in some urban areas (DeFrances, Smith, & van der Does, 1996; Miller & Wright, 2008).

Focusing on the strength of the state's case introduces an important change in evaluative standards. From an initial concern with *probable cause*, the emphasis shifts to whether it is a *prosecutable case*. At the preliminary hearing, the judge determines whether probable cause exists—that a crime has been committed and that grounds to believe that the suspect committed it are present. From the prosecutor's perspective, however, probable cause is too gross a yardstick; even though probable cause exists, a case may still be legally weak. Thus, a prosecutable case is not one that merely satisfies the probable-cause standard required of police in making an arrest and used by the judge at the preliminary hearing. Rather, it is a case that meets the standards of proof necessary to convict.

Policy Priorities

Case attrition also results from general prosecutorial policies about the priority of cases. Prosecutors devote greater resources to more serious offenses (Gilboy, 1984; Jacoby et al., 1982). At times, these case priorities are reflected in office structure; district attorneys around the nation have established priority prosecution programs that focus on major narcotics dealers, organized crime, sex offenders, and the like. Just as important, prosecutors use informal criteria that govern allocation of scarce resources. For example, some U.S. attorneys will not prosecute bank tellers who embezzle small amounts of money, get caught, and lose their jobs. The stigma of being caught and losing the job is viewed as punishment enough. Similarly, numerous local and state prosecutors have virtually decriminalized possession of small amounts of marijuana by refusing to file charges. Based on informal office policies, district attorneys are reluctant to prosecute neighborhood squabbles and noncommercial gambling. And, of course, politics also plays a role, as district attorneys are much more likely to prosecute property and drug crimes in election years than at other times (Dyke, 2007).

Personal Standards of Justice

Personal standards of justice—attitudes of members of the courtroom work group about what actions should not be punished—constitute the third category of criteria that explain case attrition. Thus,

some cases are dropped or reduced for reasons other than failure to establish guilt (McIntyre, 1968; Miller & Wright, 2008). Even if the evidence is strong, defendants might not be prosecuted if their conduct and background indicate that they are not a genuine threat to society. Across the nation, these reasons for rejection are referred to as "Prosecution would serve no useful purpose" or "interests of justice" (Boland, Mahanna, & Sones, 1992). Often, personal standards of justice are based on a subjective assessment on the part of the prosecutor that the case is not as serious as the legal charge suggests. In most courthouses, officials refer to some cases as "cheap" or "garbage" cases (Rosett & Cressey, 1976). Decisions not to file charges in cheap cases reflect the effort of court officials to produce substantive justice.

THE CRIMINAL JUSTICE WEDDING CAKE

The tyranny of criminal justice statistics is that they treat all cases in the same way in calculating the crime rate. Merely counting the number of criminal events gets in the way of understanding how and why court officials treat cases of murder differently from those of involuntary manslaughter, even though both are homicides. To understand case attrition, Samuel Walker (2011) suggested that it is useful to view criminal justice as a wedding cake (see Figure 10.3).

The wedding cake model is based on the observation that criminal justice officials handle different kinds of cases very differently. The cases in each layer have a high degree of consistency; the greatest disparities are found between cases in different layers. An examination of these layers illuminates the paradox of American criminal justice: "The problem is not that our system is too lenient, or too severe; sadly, it is both" (Zimring, O'Malley, & Eigen, 1976).

Celebrated Cases

The top layer of the criminal justice wedding cake consists of a few celebrated cases. Every year, a few cases dominate media attention because of the number of persons killed, the bizarre nature of the crime, or the prominence of the defendant. Likewise, local communities may have a few celebrated cases, either

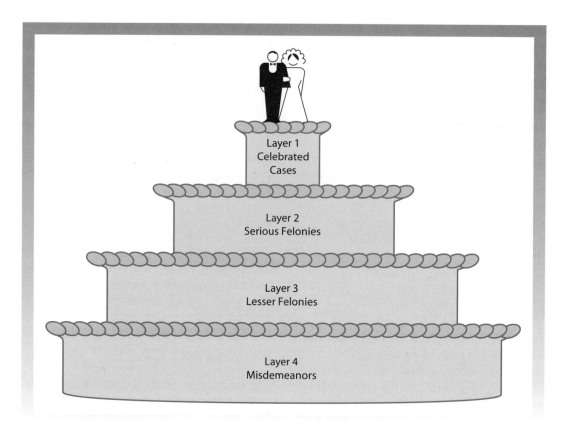

Layer 1
Celebrated
Cases

Layer 2
Serious Felonies

Layer 3
Lesser Felonies

Layer 4
Misdemeanors

Figure 10.3 ■ The Criminal Justice Wedding Cake

SOURCE: Samuel Walker. *Sense and Nonsense about Crime and Drugs: A Policy Guide.* 7th ed. Belmont, CA: Wadsworth, 2011.

because a local notable has been charged with a serious crime or because the crime itself was particularly heinous.

From the moment these cases begin, criminal justice officials treat them as exceptional, making sure that every last detail of the judicial process is followed. The cases are also extraordinary because they frequently involve the rarest of criminal court events—the full jury trial. To the fascination of the viewing and reading public, controversial matters are aired in public. As in morality plays of old and soap operas of today, public attention is focused on the battle between good and evil, although who is playing which role is not always obvious.

These celebrated cases are most likely to be broadcast on television, with some cable stations offering instant analysis and critique. Because of the publicity surrounding them, celebrated cases have a tremendous impact on public perceptions of criminal justice. On one level, these cases reinforce the textbook notion that defendants will receive

their day in court, complete with first-rate defense counsel and an attentive jury. But on another level, celebrated cases highlight the public's worst fears—the rich often get off scot-free because they can afford an expensive attorney. All too many seem to beat the rap. People assume that the court process ordinarily functions this way, but in fact it does not. Celebrated cases are atypical; they do not reflect how the courts operate on a day-to-day basis.

Serious Felonies

The second layer of the wedding cake consists of serious felonies. The courtroom work group distinguishes between this level and the next on the basis of three main criteria: the seriousness of the crime, the criminal record of the suspect, and the relationship between the victim and the offender. The guiding question is, "How much is the case worth?" Serious cases end up in the second layer; the "not-so-serious" ones in the third. Murders, armed robberies, and most rapes are treated by all members of the courtroom work group as serious felonies, resulting in less likelihood that the suspect will be released on bail. In addition, at this level, more pretrial maneuvering (Chapters 10 and 11) means less chance that the sides can reach a plea agreement (Chapter 12), a strong likelihood of trial (Chapter 13), and eventually, an appeal (Chapter 16).

Lesser Felonies

Of course, no automatic formula dictates sorting cases into serious and not-so-serious felonies; the key is a commonsense judgment about the facts of the case. What first appears to be a serious offense might be downgraded because the victim and the offender knew one another. For example, what starts out as an armed robbery might later be viewed as essentially a private disagreement over money owed, with the criminal act a means of seeking redress outside accepted channels. On the other hand, a suspect's long criminal record might transform an otherwise ordinary felony into a serious one, at least in the eyes of the prosecuting attorney.

Analysis of the true seriousness of a case is part of the everyday language of the courthouse actors. Serious cases are routinely referred to as "heavy" cases or "real" crimes, and the less serious ones as "garbage," "bullshit," or simply not real crimes. The practical consequences are that second-layer felonies are given considerable attention, whereas third-layer crimes receive less attention and are treated in a routine and lenient manner.

The Lower Depths

The bottom layer of the criminal justice wedding cake is a world unto itself, consisting of a staggering volume of misdemeanor cases, far exceeding the number of felony cases. As discussed in Chapter 4, about half are "public order" offenses—disorderly conduct, public drunkenness, disturbing the peace, and the like. Only about a third involve crimes against property or persons, many of which are petty thefts or physical disagreements between "friends" or acquaintances. Rarely do these defendants have any social standing. In the eyes of the courtroom work group, few of these cases are worth much, and relatively little time is devoted to their processing. They are usually handled by a different court from the one that handles felony cases and are processed in a strikingly different way. Dispositions are arrived at in a routine manner. Defendants are arraigned en masse. Guilt is rarely contested. Even more rarely are the punishments harsh.

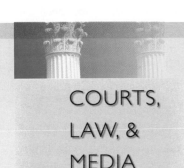

COURTS, LAW, & MEDIA

CRIME ON THE NIGHTLY NEWS

"Violent Weekend in the City"

"Pair Arrested in Deadly Home invasion"

"Guilty on All Counts"

The local nightly news often leads with headlines like these because they attract viewers. In case fictional shows have not provided viewers with their daily fill of cops, crimes, criminals, and courts, the local nightly news provides even more coverage. Indeed, at times it is hard to distinguish the entertainment value of fictional crime shows from the media attention to real crimes. We need to think critically about these matters because how the local nightly news covers crime stories has a major impact on how ordinary citizens view the criminal justice system (Surette, 2010).

The nightly news provides a lot of crime-related stories because they attract viewers. Local television stations generate considerable revenue from locally produced news shows and the higher the ratings, the higher the advertising revenues. The central goal of generating high ratings leads to the mantra of news directions: "If it doesn't bleed, it doesn't lead." As a result, crime coverage features as much blood and violence as possible. Footage of crimes scenes and police investigations are supplemented by interviews with victims, family members, and neighbors, with an emphasis on emotion and cries for vengeance. Conversely, nonviolent crimes merit attention only if the dollar amount is large or a newsworthy person is implicated.

Continued on next page

Continued from previous page

Local TV news devotes a fair amount of time to crimes, but offers less coverage of arrests because arrests by real law enforcement officers are often less dramatic than arrests by fictional cops. Viewers are accustomed to watching TV shows that feature chase scenes and daring arrests. But news cameras are seldom able to capture such action, so TV news often settles for the next best thing—the "perp walk" (perp being short for perpetrator). Police accommodate the media by walking the suspect to jail in front of waiting cameras. TV reporters are quick to ask suspects why they committed such a dastardly crime and suspects are just as quick to respond with a scowl or a profanity-laced diatribe. No matter, the drama has been enhanced. For the police, the perp walk is highly functional because it offers compelling visual evidence that they have done their job—an arrest has been made. For prosecutors, the perp walk is highly valued because the circus-like atmosphere undermines the presumption of innocence—the suspect clearly looks guilty. And, for the media, the perp walk provides dramatic footage.

TV coverage of the arrest often reinforces the image from TV cop shows that the case is now closed, the suspect has been arrested and is in jail awaiting trial. These notions are reinforced because there is considerably less coverage of later court proceedings in the case. Unless the crime was very dramatic, or the case has achieved celebrity status, TV is interested in little more than a brief report on the outcome of the trial. The lack of attention to trials is partly a function of the lack of expertise of reporters, who are seldom trained in the intricacies of legal proceedings, but also a reflection of what viewers want to see. Television viewers who are accustomed to seeing dramatic moments in fictional trials have less patience for watching actual

trials that often proceed at a ponderous pace. If it takes *Law and Order* only an hour to solve the crime, arrest the suspect, and convict him, why does a local municipality or city take days, weeks, months, or even years to accomplish the same thing?

How the local nightly news covers crime, cops, criminals, and courts has several positive features. For one, television provides coverage of one of our nation's most pressing social problems. And in doing so, they put faces on the stories, capturing the emotions of victims, defendants, and their family members. Following a jury verdict, the cameras sometimes capture the joy of victory (a conviction or an acquittal depending on who won) or the agony of defeat (a conviction or an acquittal depending on who lost).

How the local nightly news covers crimes, cops, criminals, and courts also distorts the process in fundamental ways, however. All this news coverage of course reinforces public concern that crime is a serious social problem and out of control. And by concentrating on crimes of violence, the false impression conveyed is that most criminals commit violent offenses. And in the end, all the time local television stations devote to these matters seems to suggest that after the crime footage has been run and the suspect arrested, the case is over. By the time the defendant pleads guilty or goes to trial, there is a sense that the outcome was foreordained. Trials, rather than being forums for assessing innocence or guilt within the framework of law, are reduced to rubber stamps. Not-guilty verdicts in turn are often portrayed as a defect in the system caused by shifty defense attorneys, soft-hearted judges, or dishonorable witnesses. The end result can be a citizenry even more cynical than before the trial.

CONCLUSION

The debate among the nine justices in *Country of Riverside v. McLaughlin* over what constitutes a prompt hearing may seem arcane, but it illustrates the overriding reality of the modern age: At times, the rights of individuals must be considered not just on their own merits but also in the context in which they are raised. Individually providing each defendant a probable cause hearing within 24 hours would cause no disruption to the system. But providing potentially hundreds of suspects a day such a right runs smack into logistical problems—transporting

prisoners from distant jails, hiring more magistrates, making sure that police reports are available quickly, and many other issues. What is ultimately important about *County of Riverside v. McLaughlin* is that it focuses attention on what is otherwise an invisible time period in the history of a felony prosecution.

Bail is another often invisible step in the prosecution of a felony. Bail serves several purposes in the American court system, some legally sanctioned, others definitely extralegal. Bail is used to guarantee a defendant's appearance at trial, to protect society by holding those perceived to be dangerous, to punish those accused (but not yet convicted) of violating the law, and to lubricate the system by softening defendants up to enter a plea of guilty. These varying purposes are partially the result of the tension among conflicting principles. Although the law recognizes that the only legal purpose of bail is to guarantee a suspect's future appearance at trial, court officials perceive a need to protect society. Out of these conflicting principles arise compromises.

The specific steps of criminal procedure are important because they help to ensure fairness in the process. But equally important is the substance of the decisions made. In statistical profile, the process resembles a funnel—wide at the top, narrow at the end. Fewer than half of all crimes are ever reported to the police. Only one in five of the crimes known to the police results in an arrest. Thus, most crimes never reach the courts. Of the small subset of criminal events referred to court officials, half are dropped after prosecutorial screening, preliminary hearings, or grand jury deliberations. Prosecutors and judges decline to prosecute or later dismiss charges that have been filed because the case lacks sufficient evidence, falls too low on the priority list, or is viewed as a "cheap"

case. The wedding cake model highlights this sorting process. Considerable resources are devoted to serious felonies. Lesser felonies receive less attention; they are more likely to be filtered out of the system.

The decisions made at these early points set the tone of cases moving through the criminal court process. Quantitatively, the volume of cases is directly related to screening decisions. In many areas, it is common for roughly half the defendants to have their charges dismissed during these early stages. Qualitatively, screening decisions greatly influence later stages in the proceedings. Most directly, plea bargaining reflects how cases were initially screened. For instance, it is a long-standing practice in many courts for prosecutors to overcharge a defendant by filing accusations more serious than the evidence indicates, in order to give themselves leverage for later offering the defendant the opportunity to plead to a less serious charge. Thus, the important decisions about innocence or guilt are made early in the process by judges and prosecutors—not, as the adversary system projects, late in the process by lay jurors.

Chapter Review

LO1 1. Define the two methods of estimating the amount of crime in the United States.

In the United States the two methods of estimating the amount of crime are the Uniform Crime Reports, based on crimes reported to the police, and the National Crime Victimization Survey, based on self-reports from households.

LO2 2. Discuss how arrests made by the police impact the criminal court process.

Arrests made by the police impact the criminal court process in two ways: (1) if the police fail to gather enough evidence, it will be difficult for the police to gain a conviction, and (2) the increase in the number of arrests has swollen the dockets of the courts.

LO3 3. List the four ways that criminals are formally charged in court and the major actors in each of these important documents.

Defendants are formally charged in court with a violation of the criminal law by: (1) a

complaint signed by the victim, (2) a bill of information filed by the prosecutor, (3) an arrest warrant prepared by the police, or (4) a true bill issued by a grand jury.

LO4 4. List the four most common ways that defendants secure pretrial release.

The four most common ways defendants secure pretrial release are: (1) release on recognizance (ROR), (2) cash bond, (3) property bond, and (4) bail bond through the services of a commercial bail agent.

LO5 5. Compare and contrast "law on the books" and "law in action" approaches to bail setting, including the overall effects of the bail system on criminal defendants and their cases.

Law on the books expresses a strong preference for bail unless clear and convicting evidence establishes that: (1) there is a serious risk that the person will flee; (2) the person may obstruct

justice or threaten, injure, or intimidate a prospective witness or juror; or (3) the offense is one of violence or one punishable by life imprisonment or death. In contrast, law in action affects bail setting in terms of uncertainly, risk, jail overcrowding, and situational justice. How these factors coalesce in a bail decision affects the processing of criminal defendants in terms of jail conditions, disparate impact on racial and ethnic minorities, the failure of some defendants to appear in court as promised, and case disposition.

LO6 6. Explain the role bail agents play in the criminal justice system.

The bail agent provides a specialized form of insurance and makes a profit by focusing on low-risk offenders accused of less serious crimes.

LO7 7. Contrast how the law on the books approach to criminal justice and the law in action perspective offer contrasting views of the preliminary hearing.

The law on the books approach to criminal justice emphasizes that during the preliminary hearing the judge decides whether there is probable cause to hold the defendant, while the law in action perspective emphasizes that in most jurisdictions there is a strong probability that the case will proceed.

LO8 8. Explain why some jurisdictions use grand juries extensively and others do not.

Grand juries are used extensively in jurisdictions where the constitution requires a grand jury indictment in all felonies. In jurisdictions that do not have this constitutional requirement, grand jury indictments are required in only select offenses.

LO9 9. Delineate the three major reasons for case attrition.

The three major reasons for case attrition are: (1) legal judgments (lack of evidence), (2) policy priorities (some cases are considered too minor to be prosecuted), and (3) personal standards of justice (attitudes of the courtroom work group about what actions should or should not be punished).

LO10 10. Describe the four layers of the criminal justice wedding cake.

From the top to the bottom, the four layers of the criminal justice cake are: (1) celebrated cases (which are very atypical), (2) serious felonies (which are treated as meriting major attention), (3) lesser felonies (which are treated as of less importance), and (4) the lower depths (which comprise the large volume of misdemeanor arrests).

Critical Thinking Questions

1. How long can an arrested person be held before being brought before a neutral judicial official? Do you think it was proper for the Court to take into account law in action factors such as case volume in deciding *County of Riverside*?

2. In your community, at what stage does case attrition occur? Do you detect any public displeasure with how the process currently operates?

3. If you were the prosecutor, what arguments would you make to the police chief(s) regarding a policy of careful screening of cases soon after arrest? Conversely, what arguments do you think law enforcement officials would make?

4. In what ways do crime control model advocates approach bail differently than do backers of due process model values?

5. Examine the local papers. Have there been reports of defendants' committing crimes while out on bail? Have there been reports of poor conditions in the local jail? How might these reports affect bail setting?

6. To what extent do the issues of weeding out weak cases cut across ideological dimensions?

7. Do you know of any local crimes that fit the celebrated cases category of the criminal justice wedding cake? Why did these cases receive such attention? Are they similar to or different from cases that receive extensive coverage in the media?

Key Terms

arraignment 265

arrest 248

arrest warrant 253

bail 254

bail agent 257

bail bond 256

bench warrant (*capias*) 259

bind over 260

cash bond 256

charging document 253

complaint 253

contempt (of court) 263

grand jury 261

hierarchy rule 247

immunity 262

index crimes 247

indictment 262

information 253

initial appearance 251

National Incident-Based Reporting System (NIBRS) 247

nolle prosequi 265

no true bill 262

preliminary hearing 260

preventive detention 256

probable cause 260

property bond 256

release on recognizance (ROR) 256

subpoena power 263

transactional immunity 262

true bill 262

Type I offenses 247

Uniform Crime Reports (UCR) 247

use immunity 263

Web Resources

Go to the *America's Courts and the Criminal Justice System* companion website at

http://www.cengage.com/criminaljustice/neubauer,

where you will find more resources to help you study.

Resources include web exercises, quizzing, and flash cards.

For Further Reading

Friedrichs, David. *Trusted Criminals: White Collar Crime in Contemporary Society*. Belmont, CA: Wadsworth, 2009.

Goldkamp, John, and Michael White. "Restoring Accountability in Pretrial Release: The Philadelphia Pretrial Release Supervision Experiments." *Journal of Experimental Criminology* 2: 143–181, 2006.

Holleran, David, and Cassia Spohn. "On the Use of the Total Incarceration Variable in Sentencing Research." *Criminology* 42: 211–240, 2004.

Kingsnorth, Rodney, Randall MacIntosh, and Sandra Sutherland. "Criminal Charge or Probation Violation? Prosecutorial Discretion and Implications for Research in Criminal Court Processing." *Criminology* 40: 554–578, 2002.

Messner, Steven, and Richard Rosenfeld. *Crime and the American Dream*. 4th ed. Belmont, CA: Wadsworth, 2007.

O'Neill, Michael. "Understanding Federal Prosecutorial Declinations: An Empirical Analysis of Predictive Factors." *American Criminal Law Review* 41: 1439, 2004.

Pontell, Henry, and William Black. "White-Collar Criminology and the Occupy Wall Street Movement." *The Criminologist* 37: 1–6.

Rose, Kenneth. "Pretrial Justice: Principles and Practice (NIC Update). *Corrections Today* 69: 72, 2007.

Taylor, Terrance, David Holleran, and Volkan Topalli. "Racial Bias in Case Processing: Does Victim Race Affect Police Clearance of Violent Crime Incidents?" *Justice Quarterly* 26: 562–591, 2009.

Terry, Karen. *Sexual Offenses and Offenders: Theory, Practice, and Policy*. Belmont, CA: Wadsworth, 2006.

11 Disclosing and Suppressing Evidence

Michael Newman/Photo Edit

A police officer reads a suspect his **Miranda rights** after arrest. *Miranda* is the best-known example of the U.S. Supreme Court's "due process revolution" that greatly changed how crimes are prosecuted. To liberals, due process limits on police power are necessary to protect the rights of all citizens, especially those who are wrongfully accused. Conservatives, however, often argue that the myriad rights enjoyed by the criminally accused often allow the guilty to go free. This philosophical debate aside, in reality, judges rarely suppress evidence in criminal cases. ■

Chapter Outline

DISCOVERY
Law on the Books: Rules Requiring Disclosure
Law in Action: Informal Prosecutorial Disclosure
Law and Controversy: Requiring Reciprocal
Disclosure

SUPPRESSING EVIDENCE
The Exclusionary Rule
Fruit of the Poisonous Tree

INTERROGATIONS AND CONFESSIONS
The Voluntariness Standard
The Birth of *Miranda* Warnings
Interrogations and the Sixth Amendment

CASE CLOSE-UP: *Miranda v. Arizona* and Police
Interrogations

Interrogations and the Fourteenth Amendment
Applying the Law of Interrogation

SEARCH AND SEIZURE
Search Warrants
Warrant Exceptions

Electronic Surveillance
Intelligence Surveillance
Applying the Fourth Amendment

THE EXCLUSIONARY RULE AND THE COURTROOM WORK GROUP
Pretrial Motions
Defense Attorney as Prime Mover

Courts, Law, & Media
Minority Report (2002)

The Defensive Posture of the Prosecutor
Trial Judges as Decision Makers
Police Testimony

LAW AND CONTROVERSY: COSTS OF THE EXCLUSIONARY RULE

Courts, Controversy, & Reducing Crime
Should the Exclusionary Rule Be Abolished?

Learning Objectives

After reading this chapter, you should be able to:

LO1 Explain the reasons why the process of discovery exists in both civil and criminal cases, but is significantly curtailed in the latter.

LO2 Differentiate formal and informal discovery and the reasons why both are used in criminal cases.

LO3 Identify the types of evidence subject to mandatory criminal discovery.

LO4 Compare and contrast the exclusionary rule and the fruit of the poisonous tree doctrine.

LO5 Summarize how the decision in *Miranda v. Arizona* regulates the process of police interrogations of suspects.

LO6 Explain the requirements governing the application for search warrants, the issuance of search warrants, and the execution of search warrants.

LO7 Identify the major exceptions to the Fourth Amendment's warrant requirement.

LO8 Analyze the effect of the exclusionary rule on the operations of the courtroom work group.

LO9 Evaluate whether the exclusionary rule should be abolished.

Just before midnight, 18-year-old Lois Ann Jameson (not her real name) left the downtown theater where she worked and walked the two blocks to her normal bus stop. A half-hour later, she arrived in her neighborhood for her usual short walk home. The only unusual event was a strange car, which suddenly veered in front of her. A young Hispanic man got out, grabbed her with one hand, and placed the other over her mouth while dragging her into the parked car. He drove 20 minutes into the desert, where he tore off her clothes and raped her. In a strange twist of circumstances, the assailant drove Lois Ann Jameson back to her neighborhood.

Once she was home, she immediately called the police. To Detective Carroll Cooley, Jameson's story was not only somewhat contradictory but also offered few leads. Jameson couldn't provide a very good description of her attacker. The only lead was her detailed description of the car—an old model, light green, clean on the outside, and dirty brown upholstery on the inside. Moreover, in the backseat of the car was a loop of rope designed to help rear-seat passengers in pulling themselves up. This description eventually led Detective Cooley to a house on the west side of town, where he found a car exactly as described. The subsequent interrogation and conviction of Ernesto Miranda was to change the landscape of American criminal justice.

Suppressing Evidence • Disclosing and Suppressing Evidence • Discl nd Suppressing Evidence • Disclosing and Suppressing Evidence • Di

The *Miranda* warnings are the most controversial part of the Supreme Court's revolution in criminal justice. Responding to criticisms that police procedures were unfair and that the police were not adhering to the procedural requirements of the law, the Supreme Court imposed additional restrictions on police investigative techniques, such as searches, interrogations, and lineups. The Court's decisions resulted in extensive national controversy. Subsequent Courts, dominated by appointees of Republican presidents, have significantly curtailed (but not eliminated) these earlier decisions.

This chapter examines some of the diverse activities that may occur between arraignment and final disposition (either a guilty plea or a trial). The first topic will be the gathering of evidence, which is termed "discovery." Next will be a discussion of how and why some evidence is excluded from trial.

DISCOVERY

The informal and formal exchange of information between prosecution and defense is referred to as **discovery**. Laboratory reports, statements of witnesses, defendants' confessions, and police reports are examples of information that prosecutors often gather and defense attorneys want to know about before trial.

Discovery seeks to ensure that the adversary system does not give one side an unfair advantage over the other. The guiding assumption of the adversary system is that truth will emerge after a struggle at trial. But as Justice William Brennan (1963) asked, should this struggle at trial be a sporting event or a quest for the truth? Historically, civil trials were largely sporting events, in which the outcome depended heavily on the technical skills of the lawyers. In an effort to eliminate the worst aspects of such contests, the Federal Rules of Civil Procedure were adopted in 1938, and most states have since followed the federal example. By these rules, prior to trial, every party in a civil action is entitled to the disclosure of all relevant information in the possession of any person, unless that information is privileged (Friedenthal, Kane, & Miller, 2005). These discovery rules are intended to make a trial "less a game of blind man's bluff and more a fair contest with the basic issues and facts disclosed to the fullest practicable extent" (*United States v. Procter & Gamble Co.*, 1958, p. 682). A long-standing debate, however, has been fought over the extent of pretrial discovery in criminal cases.

Law on the Books: Rules Requiring Disclosure

In contrast to the very broad power of discovery in civil proceedings, "there is no general constitutional right to discovery in a criminal case" (*Weatherford v. Bursey*, 1977, p. 559). However, a series of court decisions, statutes, and court rules provide the framework for the criminal discovery process. Courts have expressed concern that requiring too much prosecutorial disclosure might result in the defendant's taking undue advantage (*State v. Tune*, 1953). For example, the defendant, knowing of the state's case, might procure perjured testimony or might intimidate witnesses who are likely to testify (Mosteller, 2002).

Discovery in federal cases is governed primarily by sections of Rules 12, 16, and 26 of the Federal Rules of Criminal Procedure. Collectively, these rules provide a defendant, upon motion, rights to discovery concerning tangible objects; tape recordings; books, papers, and documents (including written or recorded statements made by the defendants or witnesses) that are relevant to the case; the defendant's prior criminal record, if any; the results or reports of physical examinations, scientific tests, experiments, and forensic comparisons; and summaries of any expert testimony that the government intends to offer in its case-in-chief. These materials may total only a few items and pages, or they may fill many boxes. The rules often afford the government similar reciprocal discovery upon its compliance with the request of the defendant.

In state courts, the type of information that is discoverable varies considerably from state to state. Some jurisdictions allow only limited discovery: The trial court has the discretion to order the prosecutor to disclose the defendant's confession and other physical documents, but that is all. Other jurisdictions take a middle ground: Discovery of confessions and physical evidence is a matter of right, but discovery of other items (witnesses' statements, for example) is more difficult. Finally, a few states have adopted liberal discovery rules: A presumption strongly in favor of prosecutorial disclosure exists, with only certain narrow exceptions.

Because of growing discontent with the discovery system, American courts have cautiously expanded mandatory disclosure by the prosecutor, especially with respect to disclosures of exculpatory evidence and impeachment material. **Exculpatory evidence** is any evidence that may be favorable to the defendant at trial either by tending to cast doubt on the defendant's guilt or by tending to mitigate the defendant's culpability, thereby potentially reducing the defendant's sentence.

Impeachment evidence is any evidence that would cast doubt on the credibility of a witness. The "Key Developments in Criminal Discovery Law" feature summarizes the major case and statutory law governing criminal discovery.

Discovery of Exculpatory Evidence

In *Brady v. Maryland* (1963, p. 87), the U.S. Supreme Court held that "the suppression by the prosecution of evidence favorable to an accused upon request violates due process where the evidence is material either to guilt or punishment, *irrespective of the good faith or bad faith of the prosecution*" (italics added). This is commonly referred to as the *Brady* rule.

The *Brady* rule is limited to admissible evidence. Thus, the prosecution has no obligation to provide the defense potentially exculpatory information that would not be admissible in court. For example, in *Wood v. Bartholomew* (1995), the U.S. Supreme Court held that there is no requirement to turn over the results of a polygraph examination of a witness because polygraph results are inadmissible.

The *Brady* rule applies only to exculpatory evidence that is *material*. Exculpatory evidence is material "only if there is a 'reasonable probability' that, had the evidence been disclosed to the defense, the result of the proceeding would have been different. A 'reasonable probability' is a probability sufficient to undermine confidence in the outcome" (*United States v. Bagley*, 1985, p. 682). Needless to say, this standard requires a judgment call on the part of prosecutors, and in recent years the Court has ruled that prosecutors have been too narrow in their interpretation.

In *Kyles v. Whitley* (1995), the prosecutor failed to disclose the statements of two of four witnesses and other evidence relating to Kyles's car. In a 5-to-4 decision, Justice David Souter wrote that the test was a cumulative one, looking at all the evidence that was not disclosed, not just isolated pieces. Moreover, to gain a new trial, the defense need only show a reasonable probability of a different result (not a preponderance of the evidence). "The question is not whether

the defendant would more likely than not have received a different verdict with the evidence, but whether in its absence he received a fair trial, understood as a trial resulting in a verdict worthy of confidence" (p. 434). Applying this test, the Court ruled that the *Brady* rule had been violated in the case. What made the case particularly challenging, though, was that the prosecution did not know about the exculpatory evidence in the case because the police had not revealed the two witness statements to the prosecutor. According to the Court, though, prosecutors are responsible for ensuring that police communicate relevant evidence to the prosecutor's office. It is worthy to note that on retrial, three juries declined to convict Kyles, and charges were eventually dropped.

Brady does not require the prosecution to make its files available to the defendant for an open-ended "fishing expedition." Nor does *Brady* require the disclosure of inculpatory, neutral, or speculative evidence. However, prosecutors' obligations under *Brady* are not limited to situations in which the defendant specifically requests the evidence. As the "attorney for the sovereign," the prosecutor "must always be faithful to his client's overriding interest that 'justice shall be done'" (*United States v. Agurs*, 1976, pp. 110–111).

Discovery of Impeachment Evidence

In *Jencks v. United States* (1957), the Supreme Court ruled that the government must disclose any prior inconsistent statements of prosecutorial witnesses so that the defense can conduct a meaningful cross-examination of such witnesses. Congress both expanded and limited the holding in *Jencks* when it enacted the Jencks Act. That law requires the prosecutor to disclose, after direct examination of a government witness and on the defendant's motion, any statement of a witness in the government's possession that relates to the subject matter of the witness's testimony. Thus, the Jencks Act requires disclosure of all prior statements of witnesses, even if the prior statements are not inconsistent with any subsequent statement by the witnesses, expanding the holding of *Jencks*. Yet, Congress placed the burden on the defense counsel to ask for the information (unlike *Brady* material, which the prosecutor has an ethical obligation to disclose even if not asked). Congress also limited the time frame for such disclosures such that it need not take place until after the direct examination of a government witness by the prosecution.

In *Giglio v. United States* (1972), the Supreme Court clarified that all impeachment evidence, even if not a prior statement by a witness, must be disclosed to the defense. Thus, *Giglio* mandated that the prosecution disclose any and all information that may be used to impeach the credibility of prosecution witnesses, including law enforcement officers. Impeachment information under *Giglio* includes information such as the prior criminal records or other acts of misconduct of prosecution witnesses, or such information as promises of leniency or immunity offered to prosecution witnesses. As with *Brady* material, the mandates of *Jencks* and *Giglio* do not require the prosecution to make its files available to the defendant for an open-ended fishing expedition.

Law in Action: Informal Prosecutorial Disclosure

Discovery rules are vitally important to defense attorneys. In states that grant defense considerable discovery rights, the lawyer can go straight to the prosecutor's files and obtain the essentials of the state's case against the defendant. By learning

KEY DEVELOPMENTS IN CRIMINAL DISCOVERY LAW

Jencks v. United States (1957)	Prior inconsistent statements of a witness must be made available to defense counsel so that the defense can conduct a meaningful cross-examination of such witnesses.
Jencks Act (1957)	Congress both expanded and limited the holding in *Jencks* by requiring the prosecutor to disclose, after direct examination of a government witness and on the defendant's motion, any statement of a witness in the government's possession that relates to the subject matter of the witness' testimony. Thus, the Jencks Act requires disclosure of all prior statements of witnesses, even if the prior statements are not inconsistent with any subsequent statement by the witnesses, expanding the holding of *Jencks*. Yet, Congress placed the burden on the defense counsel to ask for the information (unlike *Brady* material, which the prosecutor has an ethical obligation to disclose even if not asked). Congress also limited the time frame for such disclosure such that it need not take place until after the direct examination of a governmental witness by the prosecution.
Brady v. Maryland (1963)	Due process of law is violated when prosecutors either willfully or inadvertently conceal evidence that might be favorable to the defense because it is exculpatory.
Williams v. Florida (1970)	Requiring defense to disclose an alibi defense prior to trial does not violate the defendant's privilege against self-incrimination.
Giglio v. United States (1972)	All evidence that would impeach the credibility of any witnesses for the prosecution (including law enforcement officers)—even if not prior statements—must be disclosed, such as a witness's prior criminal acts or promises of leniency or immunity offered to prosecution witnesses.
United States v. Agurs (1976)	*Brady* does not require the prosecution to make its files available to the defendant for an open-ended "fishing expedition." Nor does *Brady* require the disclosure of inculpatory, neutral, or speculative evidence. However, prosecutors' obligations under *Brady* are not limited to situations in which the defendant specifically requests the evidence. As the "attorney for the sovereign," the prosecutor "must always be faithful to his client's overriding interest that 'justice shall be done'" by disclosing evidence that would have been persuasive and produced reasonable doubt about guilt (pp. 110–111).
Weatherford v. Bursey (1977)	There is no general constitutional right to discovery in criminal cases.
United States v. Bagley (1985)	The *Brady* duty to disclose evidence that might be favorable to the defense extends to impeachment evidence (as well as exculpatory evidence).

Continued on next page

Continued from previous page

Kyles v. Whitley (1995)	A *Brady* violation occurs when the government fails to turn over evidence that is known only to police investigators—and not to the prosecutor—because prosecutors have a duty to learn of any favorable evidence known to the others acting on the government's behalf in the case, including the police. However, the test for reversing a conviction for a *Brady* violation is a cumulative one that looks at all the evidence that was not disclosed, not just isolated pieces. To gain a new trial, the defense need only show a reasonable probability of a different result (not a preponderance of the evidence). "The question is not whether the defendant would more likely than not have received a different verdict with the evidence, but whether in its absence he received a fair trial, understood as a trial resulting in a verdict worthy of confidence" (p. 434).
Wood v. Bartholomew (1995)	*Brady* is limited to admissible evidence. Thus, failure of the prosecutor to turn over inadmissible polygraph evidence was not a *Brady* violation.
Strickler v. Greene (1999)	To prevail on a *Brady* violation claim, a defendant must demonstrate prejudice to his or her case. Thus, even when exculpatory evidence is not disclosed in accordance with *Brady's* mandate, there must be a reasonable probability that the conviction or sentence would have been different had the evidence been disclosed to the defense—even when there has not been a request for the information by the defense.
United States v. Ruiz (2002)	A plea agreement requiring a defendant to waive the right to receive any impeachment information is valid since the Constitution does not require the prosecution to disclose impeachment material prior to entering a plea agreement with a criminal defendant.
Youngblood v. West Virginia (2006)	A *Brady* violation occurs when the government fails to disclose evidence materially favorable to the accused, regardless of whether the evidence is better classified as exculpatory evidence or impeachment evidence.

the facts of the prosecutor's case, the defense attorney need not face the difficult task of trying to force his client to voluntarily disclose this information. Across the nation, "nearly all lawyers interviewed felt that clients' veracity is questionable and in need of thorough verification. This forces the attorney to devote extra hours, frequently wasted, verifying a client's version of the facts, which also puts a strain on their relationship—especially when the attorney is forced to confront the defendant with his prevarications" (Wice, 1978, p. 45; see also Sternlight & Robbennolt, 2008).

In jurisdictions that grant limited discovery rights to the defense, defense attorneys must be more resourceful in determining what actually happened. To that end, a variety of proceedings not directly designed for discovery purposes can be used. At the preliminary hearing, intended to test the sufficiency of the evidence for holding the defendant, the defense hears at least part of the story of some critical witnesses. Similarly, during a

hearing on a pretrial motion to suppress evidence, the testimony of key government witnesses may yield important new facts relevant to a trial defense. But eventually, defense attorneys may be forced to confront their clients about inconsistencies (or worse) in their statements, a confrontation that can strain lawyer–client relationships (see Chapter 7).

Some prosecutors have an office policy prohibiting assistant prosecutors from disclosing any information not required by law. But it is more usual that assistant DAs voluntarily disclose certain aspects of the state's case to defense attorneys. Such informal discovery operates within the norms of cooperation of courtroom work groups. Defense attorneys who maintain good relationships with prosecutors and are viewed as trustworthy receive selected information about the case. Conversely, defense attorneys who maintain hostile relationships with the prosecutor, who represent clients who are viewed as troublemakers, or both (the two frequently go together) find the prosecutors holding the cards as tightly to the vest as the law allows.

Informal prosecutorial disclosure does not stem from sympathy for the defendant, but rather from a long-held courthouse theory that an advance glimpse at the prosecutor's case encourages a plea of guilty. From the perspective of the prosecutor, defendants often tell their lawyers only part of what happened. Therefore, the defense attorney who learns what evidence the prosecutor possesses can use it to show the defendant that contesting the matter may be hopeless. At times, though, defense attorneys are often frustrated by the prosecution's control over the discovery process, especially when the prosecution fails to disclose important information until the last possible minute—by which point it has minimal value (Wice, 2005).

Informal prosecutorial discovery greatly encourages pleas of guilty, at least when the prosecution has a strong case. In their classic studies, Milton Heumann (1978) and Paul Wice (1978) reported that in courthouses where prosecutors emphasize closed discovery, there is often a failure to plea-bargain, and a large number of cases go to trial, frequently without a jury. In contrast, they found that in courthouses where prosecutors have adopted open discovery policies, pleas of guilty are entered sooner, resulting in a significantly smaller backlog than is found in most cities with closed discovery. More than three decades later, their findings remain the conventional wisdom, subject to the limitation that the prosecution has a strong case. If, on the other hand, the prosecution's case is weak, then open discovery may serve to embolden a defendant to take his or her chances at trial (Covey, 2007).

Law and Controversy: Requiring Reciprocal Disclosure

Ordinarily, to obtain discoverable information, a party must make a timely motion before the court; must show that the specific items sought are material to the preparation of its case; and that its request is reasonable. Some jurisdictions, however, provide for **reciprocal disclosure**—automatic discovery for certain types of evidence, without the necessity for motions and court orders. Who must disclose what to whom, however, varies significantly, causing controversy in the criminal justice system.

Defense attorneys understandably press for broader discovery laws. But to what extent should the defense be required to disclose relevant materials in its possession to the prosecution? After all, the Constitution limits reciprocal discovery in criminal cases, unlike in civil proceedings, because criminal defendants enjoy the privilege against self-incrimination. Thus, requirements that the defense turn over to the prosecutor statements from expert witnesses that it does not intend to call at trial would probably be unconstitutional. If, however, the defendant intends to call an expert witness at trial, rules such as Federal Rule of Criminal Procedure 16(b) typically require the defense to disclose the expert's identity, qualifications, conclusions, and the bases for having reached those conclusions.

A few states allow the defendant access to discoverable information in the prosecution's possession without the defense having a duty to disclose any information to the prosecution. Even in such jurisdictions, however, the defense would have an obligation to disclose certain evidence in support of select affirmative defenses. For example, an **alibi defense** means that the defendant claims the crime was committed while the defendant was somewhere else, and thus could not have been the perpetrator. The defense would have to disclose a list of witnesses to be called to support the alibi (Federal Rule of Criminal Procedure 12.1(a)(2); *Williams v. Florida*, 1970). Such pretrial notice enables the prosecutor to investigate the backgrounds of these witnesses and thus be prepared to undermine the defendant's contention that he or she was somewhere else when the crime was committed. Similarly, Federal Rule of Criminal Procedure 12.2 and the rules in most states mandate that the defense must disclose to the prosecution prior to trial that an insanity plea will be entered or that expert witnesses will be called.

In contrast to jurisdictions with only limited disclosure requirements for the defense, in some states "a defendant who issues a discovery request to the prosecutor thereby automatically incurs the duty to disclose information to the prosecutor. In still others, a defense discovery request gives the prosecutor the right—presumably almost certain to be exercised—to demand discovery from the defendant" (Easton & Bridges, 2008, p. 6). The state of the law governing discovery is constantly changing, but the trend appears to be in favor of broadening the right of discovery for both the defense and the prosecution. The guiding light, as articulated by prosecutors and law-and-order advocates, is that the trial should be a level playing field for all parties; both sides should be prevented from attempting to conduct a trial by ambush.

SUPPRESSING EVIDENCE

The most controversial of the Supreme Court's criminal justice decisions have concerned how the police gather evidence. For example, the rape conviction of Ernesto Miranda in 1966 was overturned because the police had not advised him of his constitutional right to remain silent before he confessed. In 1961, Dollree Mapp's pornography conviction was reversed because the police had illegally searched her house. In both cases, otherwise valid and trustworthy evidence was excluded from trial. These cases are applications of the exclusionary rule.

The Exclusionary Rule

The **exclusionary rule** prohibits the prosecutor from using illegally obtained evidence during a trial. Under the common law, the seizure of evidence by illegal means did not affect its admissibility in court. Any evidence, however obtained, was admitted as long as it satisfied other evidentiary criteria for admissibility, such as relevance and trustworthiness. That changed when the exclusionary rule was first developed in *Weeks v. United States* (1914). *Weeks*, however, was limited to a prohibition on the use of evidence illegally obtained by federal law enforcement officers. Not until *Wolf v. Colorado* (1949), did the U.S. Supreme Court take the first step toward applying the exclusionary rule to the states by ruling that the Fourth Amendment was applicable to the states through the Due Process Clause of the Fourteenth Amendment. *Wolf v. Colorado*, however, left enforcement of Fourth Amendment rights to the discretion of the individual states; it did not specifically require application of the exclusionary rule. That mandate did not come until the landmark decision of *Mapp v. Ohio* (1961). With *Mapp*, the exclusionary rule became the principle method to deter Fourth Amendment violations by law enforcement officials. The rule was also supported by a normative argument: A court of law should not participate in or condone illegal conduct.

The exclusionary rule is commonly associated with the search and seizure of physical evidence under the Fourth Amendment. But the exclusionary rule is also applicable to interrogations and confessions that violate either the Fifth Amendment privilege against self-incrimination or the Sixth Amendment right to counsel. However, the rule applies differently depending on the type and severity of the underlying constitutional violation. As the U.S. Supreme Court stated in *Dickerson v. United States* (2000), "unreasonable searches under the Fourth Amendment are different from unwarned interrogation under the Fifth Amendment." Thus, for example, a failure to give *Miranda* warnings before a suspect's confession may not trigger the exclusionary rule to other, future incriminating statements by that same suspect.

Finally, it should be noted that the exclusionary rule also applies to the pretrial **confrontations** between witnesses and suspects (show-ups, photo arrays, and lineups) that were either unreliable (therefore violating due process) or that occurred in violation of the accused's Sixth Amendment right to counsel. Thus, for example, if a police lineup is improperly conducted, the identification of the suspect may be excluded from evidence during trial pursuant to the exclusionary rule.

Fruit of the Poisonous Tree

The exclusionary rule is not limited to evidence that is the direct product of illegal police behavior, such as coerced confessions, unnecessarily suggestive lineups, or seizure of items during unconstitutional searches. The rule also requires exclusion of evidence indirectly obtained as a result of a constitutional violation (this type of evidence is sometimes called **derivative evidence**). The exclusionary rule operates to exclude derivative evidence because it is considered to be **fruit of the poisonous tree**. Under this doctrine's metaphors, the poisonous tree is evidence directly obtained as a result of a constitutional violation; the fruit is the derivative evidence obtained because of knowledge gained from the first illegal search, arrest, confrontation, or interrogation. For example, assume that police illegally arrest someone without probable cause and then interrogate the suspect without first administering *Miranda* warnings. During the interrogation, the suspect confesses to a murder and tells the police the location of the body. The exclusionary rule would prevent the confession from being admitted into evidence at trial since it was obtained as a result of two constitutional violations: an illegal arrest and a Fifth Amendment self-incrimination violation. If the police then discovered the body where the suspect told them to look, the body and any evidence on it would also be inadmissible at trial since the police found the body as a result of their illegal interrogation of the suspect. The body itself would be considered fruit of the poisonous tree.

As you might imagine, judges loathe excluding derivative evidence under the exclusionary rule or the fruit of the poisonous tree doctrine. Accordingly, the courts have developed four doctrines, summarized in Table 11.1, that mitigate the harsh effects of preventing the use of both illegally obtained evidence and the fruits derived from the illegality.

INTERROGATIONS AND CONFESSIONS

Since the 1930s, the Supreme Court has struggled to place limits on how police interrogate suspects.

The Voluntariness Standard

Traditionally, English common law routinely admitted all confessions, even those produced by torture. That began to change in the mid-1700s when English courts started to examine the circumstances

TABLE 11.1 ▪ EXCEPTIONS TO THE EXCLUSIONARY RULE

Exception	Key Case(s)	Effect	Example
Independent source	*Nix v. Williams* (1984) *Segura v. United States* (1984)	Evidence that is tainted by a Fourth Amendment violation is admissible if it is also obtained from an independent source—a source that had nothing to do with the underlying constitutional violation.	In *Segura*, police illegally entered an apartment and remained inside for nearly 19 hours until a search warrant arrived. Even though the entry was illegal, the evidence collected during the search was admissible since the warrant was supported by probable cause established by information independent from the illegal entry.
Attenuation	*Nardone v. United States* (1939) *Won Sun v. United States* (1963) *United States v. Ceccolini* (1978)	If evidence is obtained in a manner that is so far removed from a constitutional violation such that the initial illegality is sufficiently attenuated (meaning weakened), then the evidence is admissible.	In *Ceccolini*, police conducted an illegal search that led them to discover a key witness. That witness was allowed to testify at trial in spite of the illegal entry because the witness's voluntary cooperation with the police sufficiently attenuated the original violation from the testimonial evidence.
Inevitable discovery	*Murray v. United States* (1988) *State v. Miller* (Or. 1984).	Allows illegally obtained evidence to be admitted if it would have inevitably been discovered by lawful means.	In *Miller*, police violated a defendant's *Miranda* rights and got him to confess that he had "hurt someone" in his hotel room. During a warrantless search of the room, a dead body was found. The court ruled that the body would have inevitably been discovered by a hotel maid, so evidence from the room (including the body) was admissible in spite of the *Miranda* violation and the warrantless search of the room.
Good faith	*United States v. Leon* (1984) *Arizona v. Evans* (1995)	If a police officer acts in good faith reliance on a warrant that he or she reasonably believes to be valid, but later is determined to be invalid, the officer's good faith should allow the evidence to be admissible. There is no police misconduct to be deterred when an officer does not know that he or she is doing anything wrong.	In *Evans*, police lawfully stopped a motor vehicle and found that there was an outstanding arrest warrant for the driver. The officer therefore arrested the driver and searched the vehicle, finding marijuana. The warrant, however, had been dismissed. Thus, the arrest was invalid. However, because the officer acted in good faith reliance on a warrant believed to be valid, the search of the vehicle was upheld.

SOURCE: Stephen S. Owen, Henry F. Fradella, Tod W. Burke, & Jerry W. Joplin. *Foundations of Criminal Justice*. New York: Oxford University Press, 2012. Used with permission from Oxford University Press.

under which a confession was made. The rule that eventually emerged was that only confessions that were "free and voluntary" would be admitted at trial. Confessions obtained by physical coercion, such as beatings or torture, were no longer allowed into evidence because they were not trustworthy; someone in fear of a beating is likely to say what his or her antagonists want to hear. Relying on the Fourteenth Amendment's Due Process Clause, the U.S. Supreme Court adopted this approach in *Brown v. Mississippi* (1936). Since then, confessions based on physical coercion have been inadmissible in U.S. courts on due process grounds. As a result, such harsh means of interrogation by police in the United States have largely ceased. (As explained in Chapter 3, however, interrogations of "enemy combatants" under the administration of George W. Bush were a notable departure from the trend away from physically coercive techniques.)

The Court was then confronted with the slightly different issue of confessions obtained as a result of lengthy interrogations, psychological ploys, and the like. For example, in *Ashcraft v. Tennessee* (1944), the suspect was interrogated for 36 hours with virtually no break, thereby depriving him of any rest. The Court invalidated the confession as involuntary, reasoning that confessions based on psychological coercion should be rejected just as if they were based on physical coercion, because such statements were not likely to be free and voluntary. But it is not easy to define what constitutes psychological coercion. In numerous cases, the Court sought to spell out what factors the trial court should use in deciding what constitutes psychological coercion, but the standards announced were far from precise.

The Birth of *Miranda* Warnings

In an attempt at greater precision, the Supreme Court under the leadership of Chief Justice Earl Warren adopted specific procedures for custodial police interrogations. In the path-breaking decision *Miranda v. Arizona* (1966), the Court imposed what are widely known as *Miranda* warnings. Before a suspect in custody may be lawfully interrogated, the police are required to tell the suspect:

- You have the right to remain silent.
- Anything you say can and will be used against you in a court of law.

- You have the right to talk to a lawyer and have him or her present with you while you are being questioned.
- If you cannot afford to hire a lawyer, one will be appointed to represent you before any questioning, if you wish.

In addition, the Court shifted the burden of proof from the defense, which previously had to prove that a confession was not "free and voluntary," to the police and prosecutor, who now must prove that they advised the defendant of his or her constitutional rights and that he or she knowingly and voluntarily waived those rights (see "Case Close-Up: *Miranda v. Arizona* and Limiting Police Interrogations").

Miranda is based on the Fifth Amendment's command that "No person . . . shall be compelled in any criminal case to be a witness against himself. . . ." Given the language of the Fifth Amendment's Self-Incrimination Clause, it should come as no surprise that even before *Miranda* was decided, the Supreme Court held that if a defendant exercises his or her right to silence, the prosecutor may not ask the jury to draw an inference of guilt from the defendant's refusal to testify in his or her own defense (*Griffin v. California*, 1965). That rule still applies today.

Even in the liberal Warren Court era, *Miranda* applied only to custodial interrogations. If someone was not "in custody" (they were talking to the police voluntarily and were free to terminate the discussion at any time), *Miranda* warnings were not necessary. Similarly, even if a suspect were in custody, if the police were not engaged in conduct designed to illicit an incriminating response, then *Miranda* was similarly inapplicable. This remains the law to this day.

Another limitation of the *Miranda* rule is that it applies only to "evidence of a testimonial or communicative nature" (*Schmerber v. California*, 1966, p. 761). Thus, *Miranda* warnings do not need to be given before law enforcement officers obtain nontestimonial evidence, such as breath or blood samples, handwriting exemplars, lineup participation, or fingerprints.

Interrogations and the Sixth Amendment

The Sixth Amendment provides that "[i]n all criminal prosecutions, the accused shall enjoy the right . . . to have the Assistance of Counsel for his defense."

CASE CLOSE-UP

MIRANDA v. ARIZONA AND POLICE INTERROGATIONS

By the age of 23, Ernesto Miranda had compiled a long police record. He dropped out of Queen of Peace Grammar School in Mesa, Arizona, after the eighth grade, and shortly thereafter was arrested for car theft. By age 18, his police blotter showed six arrests and four prison sentences. A stint in the military to turn his life around quickly degenerated to mirror his civilian life; after going AWOL, he was given an undesirable discharge. But at 23, he appeared to have turned the corner. His boss at the produce company described him as "one of the best workers I ever had." Indeed, on Wednesday he worked from 8:00 p.m. to 8:00 a.m. and had barely slept an hour when the police knocked on the front door.

Stating that they didn't want to talk in front of his common law wife, the police took him to a Phoenix, Arizona, police station. A lineup of three other Hispanics from the city jail was quickly assembled. Lois Ann Jameson viewed the four men but could state only that Miranda's build and features were similar to those of her assailant. In the interrogation room, Miranda asked how he did, and Detective Cooley replied, "You flunked." After 2 hours of questioning, he signed a written confession admitting guilt. His subsequent trial was short and perfunctory. The only prosecution exhibit was the signed confession. Needless to say, the jury quickly returned guilty verdicts for kidnapping and rape.

The interrogation of Ernesto Miranda was in most ways unremarkable. It most certainly lacked the blatant duress at the center of earlier Supreme Court decisions on the limits of police interrogation. What was missing, however, was any advice to Ernesto about his rights under the Constitution. Indeed, the police testified that they never told Miranda that he didn't have to talk to the police, nor did they advise him of his right to consult with an

attorney. These facts highlighted the giant chasm between the principles of the Constitution and the realities of police stations in America.

By 1966, the Supreme Court had been grappling with the issue of confessions for three decades. Despite numerous cases, the standards for interrogating suspects were still far from clear. Chief Justice Earl Warren's opinion in *Miranda* expressed concern over the "police-dominated" atmosphere of interrogation rooms and held that warnings were required to counteract the inherently coercive nature of station-house questioning. But in reality, *Miranda* created no new rights. Under American law, suspects have never been required to talk to the police, and the right to counsel extends to the police station as well as the courthouse. In essence, the Court held that the Fifth Amendment privilege against self-incrimination was as applicable to interrogation by the police before trial as it was to questioning by the prosecutor during trial.

Miranda v. Arizona is the Warren Court's best known and, arguably, most controversial decision extending constitutional rights to those accused of violating the criminal law. The four dissenting justices criticized the ruling on both constitutional and practical grounds. To Justice Byron White, the *Miranda* rule was "a deliberate calculus to prevent interrogation, to reduce the incidence of confessions, and to increase the number of trials." Police, prosecutors, and public officials likewise criticized the ruling, and it became a key plank in Richard Nixon's law-and-order campaign in 1968. With four Nixon-appointed justices, the Burger Court began narrowing *Miranda*, but the holding itself has not been overturned. Indeed, *Miranda* has now become settled law, deeply imbedded in the constitutional fabric of our nation.

The right to counsel under the Sixth Amendment differs from the right to counsel under *Miranda* that flows from the Fifth Amendment. The sole purpose of the right under *Miranda* is to insure that a suspect's will is not overborne by coercive police interrogation tactics while the suspect is in custody. Thus, it exists to prevent compulsory self-incrimination only when a suspect is subject to custodial interrogation. In contrast, the Sixth Amendment is not concerned with compulsion in the self-incrimination context; rather, it protects those facing criminal adversarial proceedings in court. Thus, the Sixth Amendment right to counsel is triggered ("attaches") when formal criminal proceedings "have been initiated against him whether by way of formal charge, preliminary hearing, indictment, information, or arraignment." (Ferdico, Fradella, & Totten, 2013, p. 522, quoting *Fellers v. United States*, 2004, p. 523)

Once the Sixth Amendment right to counsel attaches and is invoked or asserted, authorities may not engage in any conduct that is designed to elicit an incriminating response from the defendant without the presence or waiver of counsel (*Brewer v. Williams*, 1977). This means that a defendant (whether in custody or not) may not be questioned without the defendant's lawyer being present unless a valid waiver of the Sixth Amendment right to counsel is first obtained. Thus, the Sixth Amendment bars the use of any secret investigatory techniques (such as placing an informant in a jail cell with a suspect), while the Fifth Amendment does not (*United States v. Henry*, 1980).

As with the Fifth Amendment right to counsel under *Miranda*, a defendant may waive his or her right to counsel under the Sixth Amendment. A valid waiver of *Miranda* rights for Fifth Amendment purposes also satisfies the requirements of the Sixth Amendment. Thus, *Miranda* warnings are sufficient to inform a defendant of the right to have counsel present during questioning once the Sixth Amendment right to counsel has attached, as well as the consequences of a decision to waive the

Sixth Amendment right during such questioning (*Patterson v. Illinois*, 1988).

Interrogations and the Fourteenth Amendment

Neither *Miranda* nor any Sixth Amendment right to counsel cases replaced the voluntariness test; rather, the Fifth and Sixth Amendments work in conjunction with that due process requirement. "[T]he failure to provide *Miranda* warnings in and of itself does not render a confession involuntary" (*New York v. Quarles*, 1984, p. 655). However, while satisfaction of *Miranda*'s requirements is a relevant consideration in determining the voluntariness of a confession, it is not conclusive. Statements given after *Miranda* warnings may nonetheless be inadmissible if they were not given voluntarily, but rather were coerced (*Berkemer v. McCarty*, 1984). In *Mincey v. Arizona* (1978), for example, the continued interrogation of an injured, depressed, and medicated suspect who was in extreme pain while being treated in a hospital intensive care unit was held to render his statements involuntary even though he had been Mirandized.

Applying the Law of Interrogation

The feature entitled "Key Developments in Interrogation Law since *Miranda*" summarizes some of the major cases decided after the *Miranda* decision in 1966. With a handful of exceptions, such as *Minnick v. Mississippi* (1990) and *Dickerson v. United States* (2000),

KEY DEVELOPMENTS IN INTERROGATION LAW

Fifth Amendment (1791)	1791 "No person …shall be compelled in any criminal case to be a witness against himself…."
English Common Law (19th century)	Involuntary confessions are not admissible in court.
***Brown v. Mississippi* (1936)**	Use of physical coercion to obtain confessions violates the Due Process Clause of the Fourteenth Amendment.
***Ashcraft v. Tennessee* (1944)**	Psychologically coerced confessions are not voluntary and therefore not admissible in court.
***Griffin v. California* (1965)**	If a defendant exercises his or her right to silence, the prosecutor may not ask the jury to draw an inference of guilt from the defendant's refusal to testify in his own defense.
***Miranda v. Arizona* (1966)**	Suspect's Fifth and Fourteenth Amendment rights were violated because he had not first been advised of his right to remain silent and to have an attorney present during a custodial interrogation.

© Cengage Learning

Continued on next page

Continued from previous page

Harris v. New York (1971)	Voluntary statements taken in violation of *Miranda* are inadmissible only as substantive evidence in the prosecution's case-in-chief to prove the defendant's guilt. However, voluntary statements made by defendants who had not been properly warned of their *Miranda* rights may be used during trial to impeach their credibility if they take the witness stand in their own defense and contradict the earlier statements.
Michigan v. Mosley (1975)	Even though *Miranda* states that the interrogation must cease when the person in custody indicates a desire to remain silent, *Miranda* did not create "a per se proscription of indefinite duration upon any further questioning by any police officer on any subject, once the person in custody has indicated a desire to remain silent" (p. 103). Thus, so long as a suspect's right to cut off questioning is "scrupulously honored" by police, a second attempt at custodial interrogation is permissible so long as a significant amount of time has passed between the first and second interrogation attempts and fresh *Miranda* warnings are administered again.
North Carolina v. Butler (1979)	*Miranda* warnings must be given in language that the person can comprehend and on which the person can act intelligently. The relevant inquiry is whether the words used by the officer, in view of the language skills, age, intelligence, and demeanor of the person being interrogated, convey a clear understanding of all *Miranda* rights. If so, suspects may waive *Miranda* rights, even if they do so impliedly, rather than explicitly.
Rhode Island v. Innis (1980)	A "spontaneous" statement made by a suspect in custody before being Mirandized is admissible so long as the statements were not given in response to police questioning or other conduct by the police likely to illicit an incriminating response.
New York v. Quarles (1984)	Overriding considerations of public safety justified a police officer's failure to provide *Miranda* warnings before asking questions about the location of a weapon apparently abandoned just before arrest.
Oregon v. Elstad (1985)	Absent deliberately coercive or improper tactics in obtaining the initial statement, when a suspect subject to custodial interrogation makes incriminating statements without having been Mirandized, but subsequently repeats those incriminating statements after having been read *Miranda* rights, defendants cannot argue that the fruit of the poisonous tree doctrine bars the admissibility of their second admission or confession as being tainted by the first if the initial statements were knowingly and voluntarily given.
Colorado v. Connelly (1986)	A suspect's personal characteristics (e.g., age; mental capacity; education level; physical or mental impairment from illness, injury, or intoxication; and experience in dealing with the police) are all relevant considerations when determining the voluntariness of an admission or confession. However, "mere examination of the confessant's state of mind can never conclude the due process inquiry. . . . [C]oercive police activity is a necessary predicate to the finding that a confession is not 'voluntary' within the meaning of the Due Process Clause of the Fourteenth Amendment" (p.167).
Kuhlmann v. Wilson (1986)	Neither a defendant's Fifth nor Sixth Amendment rights are violated when someone overhears a defendant make incriminating statements and reports them to the police either voluntarily or through prior arrangement. Rather, a defendant must demonstrate that the police and their informant took some action, beyond merely listening, that was designed deliberately to elicit incriminating remarks.
Illinois v. Perkins (1990)	For Fifth Amendment purposes, a law enforcement officer can pose as a prison inmate and elicit a confession from an actual inmate, even though the officer gives no *Miranda* warnings about the inmate's constitutional rights. Note that such a practice would violate the Sixth Amendment right to counsel if formal criminal proceedings had been initiated.

Continued on next page

Continued from previous page

Minnick v. Mississippi (1990)	Unlike an invocation of the right to remain silent, once a suspect has invoked his or her right to counsel, interrogation must cease and police may not reinitiate interrogation without counsel present—regardless of whether the accused has consulted with an attorney.
Pennsylvania v. Muniz (1990)	Routine questions asked of a suspect to determine whether he or she understands instructions on how to perform physical sobriety tests or breathalyzer tests, as well as routine booking questions regarding the suspect's name, address, eye color, weight, date of birth, and age are not interrogation, and therefore fall outside *Miranda*.
Arizona v. Fulminate (1991)	A coerced confession does not automatically overturn a conviction. Rather, *Miranda* violations must be reviewed for a determination of harmless or harmful error (see Chapter 16).
Davis v. United States (1994)	A suspect's assertion of *Miranda* rights must be clear and unambiguous. Thus, police do not need to stop questioning a suspect who makes an ambiguous statement about wanting to remain silent or wanting an attorney.
Dickerson v. United States (2000)	*Miranda* embodies a constitutional rule that has become embedded in police practices; the Court will not overrule it.
Texas v. Cobb (2001)	The right to counsel under the Sixth Amendment is offense specific it does not necessarily extend to offenses that are "factually related" to those that have actually been charged. Thus, police were able to question a defendant about a murder even though his lawyer in a pending burglary case was not present during the interrogation.
Chavez v. Martinez (2003)	Suspects who are interrogated in violation of the requirements of *Miranda* may not sue police for damages under 42 U.S.C. § 1983 (see Chapter 3) for violations of their Fifth Amendment rights.
United States v. Patane (2004)	The fruit of the poisonous tree doctrine does not apply to physical evidence derived from statements made in violation of *Miranda*, so long as the suspect's unwarned statements were voluntary.
Missouri v. Seibert (2004)	Deliberately questioning a suspect twice, the first time without reading the *Miranda* warnings, is usually improper.
Florida v. Powell (2010)	The warnings need not be given in the exact form used in the *Miranda* decision. All that is necessary is that the words used reasonably convey to a suspect his or her *Miranda* rights.
Maryland v. Shatzer (2010)	When a suspect is released from custody and returned to his normal life for at least 14 days, there is a sufficient break in custody such that the logic of *Minnick* is inapplicable. Thus, if police reapproach a suspect after this waiting period and the suspect waives his or her *Miranda* rights to counsel, the statements will be admissible.
Berghuis v. Thompkins (2010)	Silence in the face of an accusation does not constitute an invocation of *Miranda* rights; a break in silence, however, may constitute a valid implied waiver of them. Thus, even though a suspect was silent during a 3-hour interrogation, when he answered "yes" near the end of the interrogation when asked if he prayed to God to forgive him for the shooting, his statement was admissible.
J.D.B. v. North Carolina (2011)	A suspect's age is a relevant factor in the "totality of the circumstances" when analyzing whether a minor is in custody for *Miranda* purposes (thereby triggering *Miranda* rights) or whether a "reasonable juvenile" would have felt free to terminate the interview and, therefore, was not in custody for *Miranda* purposes.

the Supreme Court has generally limited *Miranda*'s application under the leadership of Chief Justices Warren Burger, William Rehnquist, and John Roberts.

SEARCH AND SEIZURE

The Fourth Amendment provides:

> The right of the people to be secure in their persons, houses, papers, and effects, against unreasonable searches and seizures, shall not be violated, and no Warrants shall issue, but upon probable cause, supported by Oath or affirmation and particularly describing the place to be searched, and the persons or things to be seized.

The first part of the Fourth Amendment is referred to as the *reasonableness clause*. "A search occurs when an expectation of privacy that society is prepared to consider 'reasonable' is infringed. A seizure of property occurs when there is some meaningful interference with an individual's possessory interest in that property." (*United States v. Jacobsen*, 1984, p. 113). Thus, for the protections of the Fourth Amendment to apply, there must be some governmental invasion of a person's actual, subjective expectation of privacy and that expectation of privacy must be objectively reasonable by societal standards (*Katz v. Unites States,* 1967).

An **unreasonable search and seizure** occurs when law enforcement infringes upon a reasonable expectation of privacy by conducting a search or seizure without complying with the second clause of the Fourth Amendment, called the *warrants clause*. Under it, searches and seizures unsupported by probable cause are illegal. Moreover, even if there is probable cause, a warrant is required to conduct a search and seizure unless a recognized warrant exception applies.

Although probable cause is usually necessary to conduct a search, seize evidence, or make an arrest, the Supreme Court has created several notable exceptions to this rule. The first important exception is commonly referred to as a "stop and frisk." Police are permitted to stop suspects based on reasonable suspicion of criminal activity—a lower standard of proof than probable cause. Moreover, if they have reasonable suspicion that the suspect may be armed, they may frisk the suspect for weapons (*Terry v. Ohio*, 1968).

Cursory, *Terry*-like protective sweeps of the passenger compartment of a car may be made if an officer has reasonable suspicion "that the suspect is dangerous and . . . may gain immediate control of weapons" (*Michigan v. Long,* 1983). The same is true for a brief protective sweep of premises (*Maryland v. Buie*, 1990).

One overarching exception to the Fourth Amendment that should be noted concerns exigent circumstances. Exigent circumstances are those "that would cause a reasonable person to believe that entry (or other relevant prompt action) was necessary to prevent physical harm to the officers or other persons, the destruction of relevant evidence, the escape of a suspect, or some other consequence improperly frustrating legitimate law enforcement efforts" (*United States v. McConney,* 1984, p. 1199). This is because the touchstone of the Fourth Amendment is reasonableness, and compliance with the usual requirements of probable cause and a warrant would be unreasonable in such emergency situations.

Search Warrants

A **search warrant** is a written document, signed by a judge or magistrate, authorizing a law enforcement officer to conduct a search. The Fourth Amendment specifies that "no Warrants shall issue, but upon probable cause, supported by Oath or affirmation, and particularly describing the place to be searched and the Persons or things to be seized." In light of the plain language of the Fourth Amendment, search warrants issued by a neutral judicial officer (usually a magistrate or judge) are the preferred mechanism for authorizing and conducting searches and seizures in the United States.

Applying for Search Warrants

Once a police officer decides that a search warrant is necessary, the officer usually goes back to the station house to prepare the application, affidavit, and warrant. Three alternative procedures are used. In a few jurisdictions, search-warrant applications are prepared by a deputy prosecutor on the basis of information provided by the officer. In other localities and in the federal system, the law enforcement officer prepares all the documentation and then submits them to a prosecutor, who systematically reviews them before they are presented to the magistrate. Regardless of who actually prepares the documentation, the application must provide sufficient information to a neutral judicial officer to determine that there is "a fair probability that contraband or evidence of a crime will be found in a particular place" (*Illinois v. Gates,* 1983, p. 238). This information is usually provided in an **affidavit**, a written statement of facts sworn to before the magistrate. Several jurisdictions permit issuance of search warrants over the telephone or by e-mail or facsimile (fax), but still require that the information provided by the police to the magistrate be given under oath and recorded. Law enforcement officers must be careful to include all the relevant information on which probable cause may be based in their written affidavits so that a complete record exists for courts to evaluate the magistrate's decision if the warrant is challenged.

Issuing Search Warrants

Only judicial officers who have been specifically authorized to do so may issue search warrants. Most jurisdictions give this authority to judicial officers, such as, magistrates, complaint justices, justices of the peace, and judges. The vesting of warrant-issuing power in a neutral and detached judicial officer stems from the Supreme Court's mandate that warrants can be issued only by people who are not involved in the "activities of law enforcement" (*Shadwick v. City of Tampa,* 1972, p. 350).

Next, the applicant must contact a neutral judicial officer to approve the warrant based on the application and the affidavit detailing the facts that establish probable cause. This is traditionally done in person at a courthouse. However, if court is not in session, it may occur at the home of a judge or even by telephone. The review seldom takes long. In fact, all of the few empirical studies of the search-warrant process found that the process typically takes only a few minutes (Benner & Samarkos, 2000; Slobogin, 1998). Moreover, outright rejection is rare. A study by the National Center for State Courts reported that most police officers interviewed by the researchers could not remember having a search-warrant application denied (Van Duizend, Sutton, & Carter, 1984). The authors concluded that the warrant-review process

did not operate as it was intended. Research has suggested two reasons for this. Van Duizend and colleagues concluded that the review process was largely perfunctory, as some judicial officers regarded themselves more as allies of law enforcement than as independent reviewers of evidence. And Benner and Samarkos (2000, p. 266) reported that computers have also contributed to the rubber-stamping of search-warrant applications by allowing police to prepare applications by cutting-and-pasting "pre-packaged, boiler-plated affidavits [that] are produced by merely filling in a few blanks."

The Requirement of Particularity

As the text of the Fourth Amendment makes clear, warrants must describe with particularity "the place to be searched and the persons or things to be seized." This requirement means that warrants should be as detailed as possible. Thus, warrants to search premises should use specific addresses when addresses are known. Warrants to search motor vehicles should include information such as the make, body style, color, year, location, license plate number, and owner or operator of the vehicle (to the extent such information is known). Warrants to search particular people should include the person's name or, alternatively, a detailed description of a person whose name is unknown that includes the person's weight, height, age, race, clothing, address, aliases, and so forth. Finally, items to be seized must be described with sufficient particularity so that the officers executing the warrant: (1) can identify the items with reasonable certainty, and (2) are left with no discretion as to which property is to be taken.

Executing Search Warrants

The final step is the execution of the warrant. The officer serves the warrant, conducts the search, and seizes evidence. Officers mainly search private residences and impound vehicles for drugs or stolen goods. Regardless of the area or persons to be searched, a few general rules must be followed during the execution of a search warrant.

1. Search warrants must be executed in a timely manner to prevent the information that established probable cause from going stale.

2. The scope of law enforcement activities during the execution of the warrant must be strictly

limited to achieving the objectives that are set forth with particularity in the warrant. If officers exceed the scope of the authorized invasion under the terms of the warrant, the evidence seized will usually be deemed inadmissible.

3. Search warrants must be executed at a reasonable time of day. This normally means that warrants must be executed during the daytime; however, courts may authorize a nighttime search if the affidavit in support of the warrant sets forth specific facts showing some need to execute the warrant at night.

4. Law enforcement officers are generally required to *knock-and-announce* their presence, authority, and purpose before entering the premises. to execute a search warrant (*Wilson v. Arkansas*, 1995). Courts usually require police officers to wait at least 10 to 20 seconds after announcing their presence before entering the premises. However, police do not need to knock-and-announce their presence "if circumstances present a threat of physical violence, or if there is reason to believe that evidence would likely be destroyed if advance notice were given, or if knocking and announcing would be futile" (*Hudson v. Michigan*, 2006, pp. 589–590). In fact, if such circumstances are known in advance, many states allow for courts to issue "no knock warrants." While violations of the knock-and-announce rule may subject offending officers to civil damages in a lawsuit brought under 42 U.S.C. § 1983 (Chapter 3), *Hudson* held that knock-and-announce violations will not result in application of the exclusionary rule to the evidence seized.

5. In light of the Fourth Amendment's command of reasonableness, courts are also concerned with the amount of time it takes law enforcement personnel to perform a search once it is initiated pursuant to a valid warrant. The police may remain on the premises only for as long as it is reasonably necessary to conduct the search. After all the objects described in a warrant have been found and seized, the authority of the warrant expires and police must leave the premises.

6. Also because of the Fourth Amendment's reasonableness requirement, officers executing a search warrant must be careful to use only a reasonable amount of force when conducting a search, such a breaking down a door. An

otherwise reasonable search may be invalidated if excessive force is used.

7. After a search is completed, statutory law generally requires that the officer file a "return" in court, indicating what items were seized, if any. Courts generally hold that these post-search duties are ministerial acts. Thus, a failure to perform them will usually not result in suppression of any evidence.

Warrant Exceptions

Pursuant to the mandates of the plain text of the Constitution, the Supreme Court held in *Katz v. United States* (1967, p. 357), that **warrantless searches** "are per se unreasonable under the Fourth Amendment subject only to a few specifically established and well-delineated exceptions." Accordingly, warrants play a very important role in criminal procedure. It might therefore come as a surprise to many people that the majority of searches are conducted without a warrant under one of the recognized exceptions to the warrant requirement listed in Table 11.2.

Electronic Surveillance

Searches conducted using wiretaps, bugs, or other devices to overhear conversations or obtain other kinds of information pose unique challenges for balancing privacy interests against the need for effective law enforcement in the area of electronic surveillance. On the one hand, electronic listening, tracking, and recording devices provide a very powerful tool for law enforcement officials in investigating and prosecuting crime. On the other hand, the potential for the abuse of individual rights can be far greater with electronic surveillance than with any ordinary search or seizure. The task of resolving these competing interests has fallen on state legislatures, the U.S. Congress, and ultimately, the courts.

The law governing electronic surveillance is complex. Law enforcement personnel must comply with the requirements of many pieces of legislation, the most important of which is Title III of **Omnibus Crime Control and Safe Streets Act of 1968**. That statute provides greater privacy protections than the Fourth Amendment by:

1. limiting who may apply for wiretaps;

2. requiring multiple levels of administrative and judicial review of wiretap applications;

TABLE 11.2 ▪ EXCEPTIONS TO THE WARRANT REQUIREMENT

Doctrine and Leading Case(s)	Fourth Amendment Holding
Searches incident to lawful arrest *Chimel v. California* (1969) *Arizona v. Gant* (2009)	Police may search someone who is lawfully arrested "to remove any weapons that the latter might seek to use in order to resist arrest or effect his escape." Police may also search for and seize any evidence on the arrestee's person, or in the area within his/her immediate control, "in order to prevent its concealment or destruction." However, law enforcement officers must demonstrate an actual and continuing threat to their safety posed by an arrestee, or a need to preserve evidence related to the crime of arrest from tampering by the arrestee, in order to justify a warrantless vehicular search incident to arrest conducted after the vehicle's recent occupants have been arrested and secured.
Motor vehicle searches *Carroll v. United States* (1925) *California v. Acevedo* (1991) *Florida v. Jimeno* (1991)	The mobility of motor vehicles justifies warrantless searches of them if there is probable cause to believe that the vehicle contains contraband. This includes any location in which the particular contraband might be found, such as the truck, the glove compartment, luggage, and other containers in the vehicle that could hold the contraband.
Consent searches *Schneckloth v. Bustamonte* (1973) *Illinois v. Rodriguez* (1990)	Fourth Amendment rights may be voluntarily waived. Thus, if police ask for permission to search without probable cause and/or a warrant, and permission is granted, any evidence found may be used in a criminal prosecution. The person granting consent need not actually know that s/he may refuse consent; accordingly, unlike in the *Miranda* setting, police do not have to inform people that a request to conduct a consensual search may be denied (i.e., people can refuse to give consent). Moreover, the actual owner need not be the person granting consent; warrantless searches are permitted when police have a reasonable belief that voluntary consent was obtained from a party who possesses common authority over premises.
Border searches *United States v. Ramsey* (1977) *Illinois v. Andreas* (1983) *United States v. Flores-Montano* (2004)	Searches conducted at any international border do not require a warrant, probable cause, or even reasonable suspicion that is required for *Terry* stops. This is based on the "longstanding right of the sovereign to protect itself by stopping and examining persons and property crossing into this country." (*United States v. Ramsey*, p. 616).
Searches of open fields *Cady v. Dombrowski* (1973) *Oliver v. United States* (1984) *United States v. Dunn* (1987)	Because one cannot have a reasonable expectation of privacy in open areas, like fields, forests, open water, vacant lots, and the like, police do not have to comply with the Fourth Amendment's mandates of warrants and probable cause to search open areas, even if "no trespassing" signs are posted. Only those areas within the "curtilage" of one's home (i.e., the areas immediately adjacent to a home that the owner has taken steps to keep private, like a detached garage, a locked shed or barn, etc.) receive Fourth Amendment protection.
Plain view *Harris v. United States* (1968) *Washington v. Chrisman* (1982)	When a law enforcement officer is legally in a place in which s/he sees contraband or other evidence that provides probable cause to believe criminal activity is afoot, the evidence may be seized without a warrant. The plain view doctrine has been expanded to cover other senses, such as "plain smell."
Special needs searches in public schools *New Jersey v. T.L.O.* (1985) *Board of Ed. of Ind. School Dist. 92, Pottawatomie County v. Earls* (2002) *Safford Unified School District v. Redding* (2009)	Although the Fourth Amendment applies to searches and seizures conducted by schoolteachers and administrators, neither probable cause nor a warrant is required. There need be only reasonable "grounds for suspecting that the search will turn up evidence that the student has violated or is violating either the law or the rules of the school." (T.L.O., 1985, p. 342). Moreover, to curb alcohol and drug abuse in schools, random drug testing of students who participate in extracurricular or athletic activities may be conducted without any individualized suspicion or a warrant. Strip searches of students, however, have been held to go too far.

Continued on next page

Continued from previous page

Searches of public employers and/or their work spaces *O'Connor v. Ortega* (1987) *National Treasury Employees Union v. Von Raab* (1989) *Skinner v. Railway Labor Executives' Assoc.* (1989)	Neither probable cause nor a warrant is necessary for public employers to conduct searches either for work-related purposes or for investigations of work-related misconduct. This includes noninvasive seizures of bodily fluids to conduct random drug tests on public employees whose job functions make it particularly important for them to be drug-free, such as federal law enforcement agents and railroad conductors.
Administrative searches *Donovan v. Dewey* (1981) *New York v. Burger* (1981)	Neither probable cause nor a warrant is required to conduct administrative inspections for compliance with regulatory schemes such as fire, health, and safety codes (e.g., inspections of jetliners, mining operations, junk yards, pharmacies, gun stores, etc.).
Abandoned property *California v. Greenwood* (1988)	The Fourth Amendment does not prohibit the warrantless search and seizure of abandoned property, such as garbage left for collection outside a home.
Aerial searches *California v. Ciraolo* (1986) *Florida v. Riley* (1989)	Police do not need a warrant to conduct aerial surveillance of a suspect's property from an aircraft in public airspace, so long as they do so from a reasonable altitude.
Searches of people under correctional supervision *Hudson v. Palmer* (1984) *Sampson v. California* (2006)	Warrantless and suspicionless searches may be conducted of jail or prison cells, as well as of the person or inmates in custody, on probation, or on parole.
Third-party disclosure *United States v. Miller* (1976) *Smith v. Maryland* (1979)	Disclosure of confidential information to third parties destroys any reasonable expectation of privacy for that information. Thus, for example, there is no reasonable expectation of privacy in bank records since they are not a person's private papers, but rather are business records of banks to which bank employees have access. Similarly, there is no reasonable expectation of privacy in the numbers dialed from a telephone since phone company employees have access to such information.

SOURCE: Adapted From Stephen S. Owen, Henry F. Fradella, Tod W. Burke, & Jerry W. Joplin. *The Foundations Of Criminal Justice.* New York: Oxford University Press, 2012.

3. mandating that the wiretap procedures minimize the interception of communications not subject to the wiretap order;

4. requiring law enforcement officers who learn information by listening to intercepted communications to keep the content of what they hear confidential; and

5. requiring that, immediately upon the expiration of a wiretap order, both the interception order and all recordings made pursuant to it be delivered to the judge who issued the order to be sealed. (Putting material *under seal* means it is not accessible to anyone without a special court order.)

Title III applies to private searches and seizures of wire, oral, or electronic communications, not just those involving governmental actors. When its mandates are violated, Title III provides its own statutory remedies, including both criminal and civil penalties for violations of its commands. Title III also provides a statutory exclusionary rule for intercepts that were illegally obtained by either government actors or private persons to which the good-faith exception to the exclusionary rule does not apply.

Eavesdropping and Consent Surveillance

If a conversation takes place in public where other parties can overhear the conversation, there is no reasonable expectation of privacy, because the participants exposed their conversation to the ears of others. Thus, any recording of such a conversation would not violate either the Fourth Amendment or Title III. Moreover, what an employer overhears while monitoring phone conversations over extensions for legitimate business reasons and what family members overhear while eavesdropping on the conversations of other family members using an extension telephone does not implicate Title III.

Title III excludes **consent surveillance** from its regulatory scheme. Therefore, when one party to a communication consents to the interception of the communication, neither Title III nor the Fourth Amendment prevents the use of the communication in court against another party to the communication. Thus, a law enforcement officer or a private citizen who is a party to a communication may intercept the communication or permit a law enforcement official to intercept the communication without violating Title III or the Fourth Amendment (*United States v. Caceres*, 1979). This exception allows a law enforcement officer or agent, an informant, an accomplice or co-conspirator, or a victim to wear a body microphone; act as an undercover agent without being wired; or eavesdrop and/or record a telephone conversation with the permission of the person receiving the call even though the person making the call has no knowledge of this activity. A private citizen, however, may not intercept a communication "for the purpose of committing any criminal or tortious act in violation of the Constitution or laws of the United States or of any State" (18 U.S.C. § 2511(2)(d)).

Electronically Stored Information

Like traditional searches for physical evidence, searches of electronically stored information (ESI) are also governed by the Fourth Amendment. Thus, ESI searches normally require a duly authorized warrant supported by probable cause. Statutory provisions in the **Stored Communications Act**, however, allow law enforcement to access stored communications older than 180 days, such as e-mail and voice mail, using either a search warrant, or, after giving notice to the subscriber, a subpoena (18 U.S.C. § 2703(a)).

Computer files and programs are the most obvious sources of ESI, but ESI can also be found on servers, tablets, thumb/jump drives, CDs and DVDs, floppy disks, memory cards and sticks, tape media, external hard drives, cell phones, PDAs, and other electronic devices with data-storage capacity, such as digital cameras, iPods, voice mail systems, fax machines, and copy machines.

The U.S. Department of Justice has recommended a set of practices to ensure compliance with the particularity requirement of the Fourth Amendment when police conduct searches of ESI. The federal government recommends that an affidavit should not only list "the specific hardware to be seized and searched" but also explain "the techniques that will be used to search only for the specific files related to the investigation, and not every file on the computer" (Jekot, 2007: ¶ 2, citing U.S. Department of Justice, 2002, Part II.C.3).

There are additional requirements law enforcement personnel often need to use technology to monitor telephone conversations on both landlines and cell phones, e-mail communications, pager and text messages, and Internet-based communications that are beyond the scope of this book (see Ferdico, Fradella, & Totten, 2012).

Video Surveillance

Title III does not cover **video surveillance**—the use of video cameras that record only images, not sound. Thus, surreptitious video surveillance without any audio component is analyzed under state invasion of privacy laws and under the Fourth Amendment. Legal analysis under the latter, of course, depends on whether the video surveillance violated an aggrieved person's reasonable expectation of privacy. In contrast, if surveillance contains both audio and video components, then the video sections are controlled by the Fourth Amendment (and state privacy laws) and audio portions are reviewed under Title III and the Fourth Amendment.

Intelligence Surveillance

In 1978, Congress passed the **Foreign Intelligence Surveillance Act (FISA)**. FISA regulates the electronic surveillance of foreign powers and their agents within the United States where a "significant purpose" of the surveillance is to gather foreign intelligence information that cannot reasonably be obtained through normal investigative techniques. FISA also permits surveillance of "lone wolves"— any individual or group that is not linked to a foreign government but who is suspected of terrorism or sabotage.

Any federal agent may apply for a FISA warrant. However, an application must first be approved by the U.S. attorney general and either the assistant to the president for National Security Affairs or the deputy director of the Federal Bureau of Investigation. After these two layers of executive approval, judicial review of an application for a FISA warrant occurs at the Foreign Intelligence Surveillance Court (see Chapter 3). FISA permits the U.S. attorney general to authorize domestic surveillance in an emergency situation in which seeking approval of a warrant application before the Foreign Intelligence Surveillance Court would unnecessarily delay the gathering of necessary evidence.

Applying the Fourth Amendment

Historically, the gathering of physical evidence was governed by the common law rule that "if the constable blunders, the crook should not go free." This meant that if the police conducted an **illegal search and seizure** (such as a search not supported by probable cause), the evidence obtained could still be used if it was reliable, trustworthy, and relevant. How the police obtained the evidence was considered a separate issue. Thus, there were no effective controls on search and seizure; law enforcement officials who searched illegally faced no sanctions. But, as discussed earlier, the Supreme Court modified the common law tradition when it adopted the exclusionary rule for the Fourth Amendment violations in *Weeks v. United States* (1914) and subsequently extended its application to the states in *Mapp v. Ohio* (1961).

Critics and supporters of the exclusionary rule agree on one central point: The grounds for a lawful search are complex and highly technical. Consider, for example, the cases on the next page in the "Key Developments in Search-and-Seizure Law" feature.

THE EXCLUSIONARY RULE AND THE COURTROOM WORK GROUP

The police must often make immediate decisions about searching or interrogating a suspect. In street arrests, officers do not have time to consult an attorney about the complex and constantly evolving law governing these areas. These on-the-spot decisions may later be challenged in court as violations of suspects' constitutional rights. Even though the exclusionary rule is directed at the police, its actual enforcement occurs in the courts, particularly the trial courts.

Pretrial Motions

A defense attorney who believes that his or her client was identified in a defective police lineup, gave a confession because of improper police activity, or was subjected to an illegal search can file a motion to suppress the evidence. Most states require that **suppression motions** be made prior to trial.

During the hearing on these pretrial motions, the defense attorney usually bears the burden of proving that the search was illegal or that the confession was coerced. The only exception involves an allegation that the *Miranda* warnings were not given, in which case the state has the burden of proof. The judge's ruling in the pretrial hearing is binding on the later trial.

Pretrial hearings on a motion to suppress evidence are best characterized as "swearing matches." As one defense attorney phrased it, "The real question in Supreme Court cases is what's going on at the police station" (Neubauer, 1974b, p. 167). Seldom is there unbiased, independent evidence of what happened. The only witnesses are the participants—police and defendant—and, not surprisingly, they give different versions. This dispute over the facts structures and apportions the roles that the police, defense attorneys, judges, and prosecutors play. Because they must search out the issues, defense attorneys are forced into a catalytic role. By virtue of their power as fact finders at hearings, judges become the supreme umpires that legal theory indicates they should be. Prosecutors, in contrast, play a relatively passive role. Although pretrial motions place prosecutors in a defensive posture, they are not at a major disadvantage, because the police are usually able to provide information indicating compliance.

Defense Attorney as Prime Mover

Because defense attorneys have the responsibility of protecting the constitutional rights of their clients,

KEY DEVELOPMENTS IN SEARCH-AND-SEIZURE LAW

Fourth Amendment (1791)	"The right of the people to be secure in their persons, houses, paper, and effects against unreasonable searches and seizures, shall not be violated, and no Warrants shall issue, but upon probable cause, supported by Oath or affirmation, and particularly describing the place to be searched, and the persons or things to be seized."
***Weeks v. United States* (1914)**	The exclusionary rule was established in federal prosecutions.
***Wolf v. Colorado* (1949)**	The exclusionary rule applies to the states as well as to the federal government, but states are not required to adopt the exclusionary rule to sanction noncompliance.
***Mapp v. Ohio* (1961)**	Both states and the federal government are required to use the exclusionary rule to sanction noncompliance with the mandates of the Fourth Amendment (overturning *Weeks* and *Wolf*).
***Katz v. United States* (1967)**	The Fourth Amendment protects people's subjective expectations of privacy only when those expectations are objectively reasonable by societal standards.
***Berger v. New York* (1967)**	The use of electronic devices to capture conversations is a seizure within the meaning of the Fourth Amendment.
***United States v. Calandra* (1974)**	The exclusionary rule does not apply in grand jury proceedings.
***Rakas v. Illinois* (1978)**	A defendant has standing to object to the admission of unconstitutionally seized evidence only if such seizure violated his own Fourth Amendment rights; a defendant may not assert another person's rights.
***Dalia v. United States* (1979)**	Neither Title III nor the Fourth Amendment requires law enforcement officers to obtain judicial authorization to covertly enter premises to install a listening device after an inception order has been issued.
***Smith v. Maryland* (1979)**	The installation and use of a pen register (a device that records all numbers called from a telephone line) is not a search for Fourth Amendment purposes because there is no reasonable expectation of privacy in the destination of outgoing phone calls since the telephone company routinely monitors calls to check billing, detect fraud, and prevent other violations of law.
***Payton v. New York* (1980)**	Absent some exigent circumstances (an emergency), police may not make a warrantless entry into a suspect's home to make an arrest.
***United States v. Mendenhall* (1980)**	A person is "seized" within the meaning of the Fourth Amendment when his or her freedom of movement is restrained by means of physical force or show of authority, and under the circumstances, a reasonable person would believe that he was not free to leave or otherwise terminate the encounter.
***Illinois v. Gates* (1983)**	Whether probable cause exists must be examined under the "totality of the circumstances." Moreover, a trial court's ruling that probable cause exists is to be given substantial deference on appeal.
***Unites States v. Knotts* (1983)**	The warrantless monitoring of a tracking beeper placed inside a container of chemicals did not violate the Fourth Amendment when it revealed no information that could not have been obtained through visual surveillance.

Continued on next page

Continued from previous page

***Tennessee v. Garner* (1985)**	The Fourth Amendment prohibits the use of deadly force to apprehend a fleeing suspect unless the pursuing officer has probable cause to believe that the suspect poses a significant threat of death or serious physical injury to the officer or others.
***Winston v. Lee* (1985)**	A compelled surgical intrusion into an individual's body for evidence of a crime implicates expectations of privacy and security of such magnitude that it cannot be sanctioned as reasonable under the Fourth Amendment.
***Illinois v. Krull* (1987)**	The good-faith exception applies to warrantless searches, even when the state statute authorizing a warrantless search was later found to violate the Fourth Amendment.
***United States v. Sokolow* (1989)**	A suspect fitting a "drug courier profile" (such as using an alias; purchasing airline tickets with cash; not checking any luggage; traveling for only a short period of time to and from a city with a known, large drug distribution network; and appearing nervous) provides reasonable suspicion to stop and question the suspect.
***Michigan Department of State Police v. Sitz* (1990)**	Sobriety roadblocks do not violate the Fourth Amendment. They are a reasonable tool for combating the problem of driving under the influence and they pose only a minimal intrusion on motorists stopped briefly at checkpoints.
***United States v. Ojeda Rios* (1990)**	A failure to comply with Title III's sealing requirement renders intercepted communications inadmissible.
***Florida v. Jimino* (1991)**	A suspect's consent to a search of his or her vehicle extends to closed containers found inside that can hold the object for which police are searching.
***Minnesota v. Dickerson* (1993)**	When a police officer conducting a lawful pat-down for weapons feels something that's contour or mass makes its identity as contraband immediately apparent, the object may be seized even though it is not a weapon. However, if the nature of the object is not immediately recognizable as contraband, the officer may not manipulate the object to determine what it might be since doing so would go beyond a pat-down and into the realm of a full search.
***Arizona v. Evans* (1995)**	The exclusionary rule does not require the suppression of evidence seized during a search incident to the arrest of a driver pursuant to a warrant that was later determined to be invalid since the officer relied in good faith on the warrant that had not been entered properly into the system by a clerk of the court.
***Whren v. United States* (1996)**	Police officers may stop a vehicle for any violation of traffic law even if the underlying traffic offense is only a pretext to investigate other criminal activity.
***Knowles v. Iowa* (1998)**	Issuing a speeding ticket does not give police authority to search the car.
***Illinois v. Wardlow* (2000)**	Fleeing from the sight of police (running away) is a pertinent factor in determining whether reasonable suspicion justifies the police stopping the runner to investigate whether criminal activity is afoot.
***Bond v. United States* (2000)**	Bus and train passengers have a reasonable expectation of privacy in the carry-on luggage they place into overhead racks.
***Florida v. J. L.* (2000)**	Police cannot stop and search someone solely because they have received an anonymous tip. Anonymous tips must possess a moderate level of reliability, including "predictive information" that offers police a means to test the informant's knowledge or credibility.

Continued on next page

Continued from previous page

Kyllo v. United States (2001)	The warrantless use of thermal imaging devices to scan a building to detect the presence of high-intensity lamps used to grow marijuana violates the Fourth Amendment.
Hiibel v. Sixth Judicial District Court of Nevada (2004)	States may enact laws requiring suspects to identify themselves during police investigations without violating either the Fourth or Fifth Amendments.
Illinois v. Caballes (2005)	The Fourth Amendment permits police making a routine traffic stop to use a trained dog to sniff the car for drugs.
Georgia v. Randolph (2006)	The police must have a warrant to look for evidence in a couple's home unless both partners present agree to let them in.
Hudson v. Michigan (2006)	Although police armed with a search warrant are supposed to knock and announce their presence before they can lawfully enter homes to search for and seize evidence, a violation of the knock-and-announce rule will not give rise to the application of the exclusionary rule.
Brendlin v. California (2007)	When a police officer makes a traffic stop, both the driver of the car and his or her passengers are all "seized" within the meaning of the Fourth Amendment. Thus, a passenger may challenge the constitutionality of the stop.
Scott v. Harris (2007)	A police officer who terminated a high-speed chase of a suspect by applying his push bumper to the rear of the suspect's vehicle, causing it to leave the road and crash and rendering the suspect a quadriplegic, did not act unreasonably in using such force and, therefore did not violate the motorist's Fourth Amendment right against unreasonable seizure.
Virginia v. Moore (2008)	A police officer does not violate the Fourth Amendment by making an arrest supported by probable cause for a traffic violation even though arrest is not authorized under state law for such an offense; therefore, evidence seized incident to the arrest is admissible.
United States v. Herring (2009)	The Fourth Amendment does not require the suppression of evidence seized following a search that occurred incident to an illegal arrest when the arrest was based on erroneous information negligently provided by another law enforcement agency, as long as the arresting police officer relied on the erroneous information in good faith.
United States v. Jones (2012)	Police must first obtain a warrant before attaching a GPS device to a vehicle and then monitoring the vehicle's movements.

they are the prime movers in suppression matters. Unless the defense objects, it is assumed that law enforcement officials have behaved properly. Filing a pretrial motion to suppress evidence may produce benefits for the defense. If the motion is granted, the defense wins, because the prosecutor will usually dismiss the case for lack of evidence. Even if the motion is denied, the defense may be able to discover information that may later prove valuable at trial. Moreover, filing a pretrial motion keeps options open; plea bargaining remains a possible course of action.

Despite these apparent advantages, defense attorneys face major barriers in raising objections. Possible violations of *Miranda* or the Fourth Amendment do not come into the lawyer's office prepackaged, just

awaiting a court hearing. Defense attorneys must frame the issue and determine whether enough facts exist to support the contention. According to many defense attorneys, the police follow proper procedures most of the time. Thus, the task of the lawyer is to separate the out-of-the-ordinary situation from the more numerous ones in which the police have not violated Supreme Court rulings.

In deciding whether to make a motion to suppress evidence, defense attorneys are influenced by the informal norms of the courtroom work group. Pretrial motions require extra work, not only for the defense attorney but also for the judge and prosecutor. Defense attorneys who file too many frivolous motions or use them to harass the judge, the

COURTS, LAW, & MEDIA

MINORITY REPORT (2002)

When this 2002 Stephen Spielberg film was released, its tagline read: "What would you do if you were accused of a murder you had not committed … yet?" The film takes place in Washington, D.C., in the year 2054. Crime in the city is practically nonexistent because the "Pre-Crime Unit" of the police force apprehends criminals *before* they actually commit any crimes. John Anderton (played by Tom Cruise) and his fellow pre-crime police officers are able to do so thanks to the information provided to them from three "precogs"—genetically mutated humans who have the ability to see the future. Their visions occur in dreamlike states, complete with the "disjunctions and distortions of regular dreams" (Capers, 2009, p. 798). The precogs project their visions onto a screen so that police can try to make sense of how the crime will unfold, thereby allowing them to make a preemptive arrest. Anderton believes the system to be flawless until the precogs predict that he will commit murder. Thus, the chief of the Pre-Crime Unit becomes a fugitive for a crime he has yet to commit. At the end of the movie, Anderton arrests the person whom the precogs predicted he would kill. Notably, he reads the suspect *Miranda* warnings when making the arrest.

While this fast-paced action film raises a number of philosophical points, it clearly implicates some Fourth Amendment concerns. For one thing, the Washington D.C., of the future has become a surveillance state.

Individuals are tracked via eye scans as they move about the city. Public spaces are surveillance spaces. But then again the same could be said of many cities today. We currently permit such surveillance on the theory that individuals do not have a reasonable expectation of privacy in information that they knowingly expose to the public and also on the theory of consent. Thus, the expectation of privacy we theoretically enjoy behind closed doors, we lose in public spaces, at least in terms of items exposed to public view. In this respect, the surveillance state that exists in *Minority Report* is the surveillance state that current Fourth Amendment law already sanctions. But *Minority Report*, in a scene in which the police use thermal imaging to ascertain the number of individuals in a building and then release mechanical spiders to conduct retinal scans of those individuals in a search for John Anderton, does serve as a cautionary tale of sorts, exposing the steep declivity of a slippery slope. The scene recalls *Kyllo v. United States* (2001), in which the Supreme Court held that thermal imaging directed at a private residence amounted to a search and thus required a warrant supported by probable cause. Except here, the technology seems to have been refined to survive constitutional scrutiny.

In *United States v. Jacobsen* (1984), the Court read the Fourth Amendment as protecting only legitimate activity and thus excluding from its ambit government conduct that could reveal only illegitimate activity. In *United States v. Place* (1983), the Court assumed canine sniffs disclose "only the presence or absence of narcotics, a contraband item" and thus fell within this category. Followed to the extreme, these cases would permit the very mechanical spiders that are used to such effect in *Minority Report*, assuming such spiders are only capable of "seeing" the eyes of, say, a fugitive (Capers, 2009, pp. 800–801).

1. Recall from this chapter that a lawful arrest must be supported by probable cause. What do you think of the idea of preemptive arrests? Do you think that "visions" of the future from a consistently reliable source, such as the fictional precogs, should be sufficient to establish probable cause for an arrest? Does the fact that the precogs were wrong in Anderton's case affect your view?

2. What do you make of Professor Capers's argument that the surveillance depicted in the movie *Minority Report* is of the same qualitative type that is permitted today? Do you think we should reasonably expect any privacy when we are out in public?

3. Professor Capers points out that the thermal imaging scan in *Minority Report* would not be permissible today under the Supreme Court's ruling in *Kyllo v. United States*. However, he cites two additional pieces of precedent that could be interpreted as allowing mechanical spiders to conduct retinal scans. Do you think that type of technology would be an invasion of privacy if used out in public? What about if such devices were used to perform retinal scans of people inside private residences?

4. As stated above, *Miranda* warnings are alive and well in 2054. Why do you think that television shows and movies have embraced *Miranda*? Do you think it is good or bad that these warnings are so engrained in our national psyche that they work their way into science-fiction scripts that depict the future? Why?

prosecutor, or both can be given a variety of sanctions. The prosecutor may refuse to plea-bargain in a given case or may insist on a harsher-than-normal sentence.

The Defensive Posture of the Prosecutor

Suppression motions represent only liabilities for prosecutors. At a minimum, they must do extra work. At worst, they may lose the case entirely. Even if they win the suppression motion, they may have to expend extra effort defending that decision on appeal, at which time they may lose.

Despite these drawbacks, prosecutors maintain the upper hand. For once, they need only defend, because the defense attorney bears the burden of proof. Because the police control the information involved, prosecutors are generally in a favorable position to argue against excluding evidence. For example, the police are usually able to obtain the defendant's signature on the *Miranda* warning form, which indicates compliance with Supreme Court requirements. Similarly, in a search-and-seizure case, the officers are familiar enough with the law to know how to testify in order to avoid suppression of evidence. Of course, the district attorney can dismiss a case that presents potential problems, thus avoiding a public hearing on the matter.

Trial Judges as Decision Makers

The decision to suppress evidence rests with the trial judge. After hearing the witnesses and viewing the physical evidence (if any), the judge makes a ruling based on appellate court decisions. Thus, trial court judges are key policymakers in applying and implementing Supreme Court decisions concerning confessions and search and seizure.

As noted earlier, a pretrial motion is essentially a clash over the facts. The trial court judge possesses virtually unfettered discretion in making findings of fact. Judges' backgrounds predispose them to be skeptical of defense motions to suppress. As noted in Chapter 8, many judges were once prosecutors, whose courtroom arguments supported the police. These inclinations are reinforced by the selection process. Judges are, by and large, either appointed by governors or presidents—who are often critical of appellate court restrictions on the gathering of

evidence by the police—or elected by the public in campaigns that stress crime reduction. For these reasons, trial judges do not regularly grant defense motions to suppress evidence.

On appeal, higher courts examine whether the law was correctly applied by the trial judge, but they rarely scrutinize the facts to which the law was applied. Such deference is based on the trial judge's proximity to the event. Only trial judges have the opportunity to observe directly how witnesses testify—their responsiveness to questions or their attempts at concealment. Such nuances are not reflected in the trial court transcript.

Police Testimony

At the center of court hearings on police practices and defendants' rights are events that happened out in the field or in the police station. Although some jurisdictions now require police to tape interrogations, many do not (Leo, 1996b; Rosen, 2006). What is known in court, therefore, is largely the product of police testimony.

Richard Leo (1996a) observed 122 interrogations in a major urban police department and reported the following. Detectives begin by cultivating the suspect, getting him or her to make eye contact and engage in conversation. The *Miranda* warnings are useful for this purpose because they induce suspects to respond to questions. Thus, three out of four suspects waive their *Miranda* rights. Next, the detective states that his or her job is to discover the truth and typically shares with the suspect some of the evidence in the case. A two-pronged approach is being used. One is the use of negative incentives, tactics that suggest the suspect should confess because no other plausible course of action exists. The other is the use of positive incentives, tactics that suggest the suspect will in some way feel better or benefit if he or she confesses. The results were as follows:

- No incriminating statement (36 percent)
- Incriminating statement (23 percent)
- Partial admission (18 percent)
- Full confession (24 percent)

A suspect's decision to provide detectives with incriminating information was fateful. Those who incriminated themselves were more likely to be charged with a crime, more likely to enter a plea of guilty, more likely to be convicted, and likely to receive more punishment than their counterparts who did not provide incriminating statements.

Police, prosecutors, and defense attorneys often become embroiled in disputes about what occurred during interrogation. These disputes can be ended by using audio and/or video equipment to record everything that occurs during custodial interviews. Although many law enforcement agencies continue to resist such practices, a growing number of jurisdictions are now making these practices a requirement (Rosen, 2006; Sullivan, 2004).

LAW AND CONTROVERSY: COSTS OF THE EXCLUSIONARY RULE

A key issue in the ongoing debate over the exclusionary rule centers on its costs. In a widely cited statement, Chief Justice Burger summed up the critics' position as follows: "Some clear demonstration of the benefits and effectiveness of the exclusionary rule is required to justify it in view of the high price it exacts from society—the release of countless guilty criminals" (*Bivens v. Six Unknown Federal Narcotics Agents*, 1971, p. 416).

One study of police searches in a major American city concluded that 30 percent of the searches failed to pass constitutional muster. Even though the patrol officers knew they were being observed, they still conducted illegal searches. But only a handful of these events were documented in official records because so few resulted in arrest or citation (Gould & Mastrofski, 2004). The lack of official action, therefore, makes it difficult to truly calculate the cost of the exclusionary rule at subsequent stages of the process.

Assessing the number of convictions lost because of the exclusionary rule is difficult, for reasons discussed in Chapter 10. Case attrition occurs at numerous stages of the proceedings and for various reasons. Several studies shed considerable light on the topic.

Exclusionary rules can lead to the freeing of apparently guilty defendants during prosecutorial screening. Prosecutors may refuse to file charges because of a search-and-seizure problem, a tainted confession, or a defective police lineup. However, this occurs very infrequently. The Comptroller General of

the United States (1979) examined case rejections by U.S. attorneys and found that search and seizure was cited as the primary reason for rejection 0.4 percent of the time. Similarly, a study of seven communities reported that an average of 2 percent of the rejections were for *Mapp* or *Miranda* reasons (Boland, Brady, Tyson, & Bassler, 1982). A more controversial study analyzed 86,033 felony cases rejected for prosecution in California. The National Institute of Justice (NIJ) report found that 4.8 percent were rejected for search-and-seizure reasons. The NIJ conclusion that these figures indicated a "major impact of the exclusionary rule" has been challenged as misleading and exaggerated (Davies, 1983). Indeed, compared to lack of evidence and witness problems, *Mapp* and *Miranda* are minor sources of case attrition.

After charges are filed, case attrition can also occur when judges grant pretrial motions to suppress. But in actuality, few pretrial motions to suppress evidence are actually filed. Nardulli (1983) reported that motions to suppress evidence were filed in fewer than 8 percent of the cases. Once filed, pretrial motions are rarely successful, although the success rate has varied significantly in the research from a low of 0.3 percent (Davies, 1983) to a high of 1.5 percent (Uchida & Bynum, 1991).

Piecing together the various stages of the criminal court process leads to the conclusion that the exclusionary rule has a marginal effect on the criminal court system (Nardulli, 1983). Examining case-attrition data from California, Davies (1983) calculated that 0.8 percent of arrests (8 of 1,000) were rejected because of *Mapp* and *Miranda*. As for cases filed, Nardulli calculated that 0.57 percent of convictions (fewer than 6 of 1,000) were lost because of exclusionary rules. Moreover, of the lost convictions, only 20 percent were for serious crimes. Weapons cases and drug cases are those most likely to involve questions about police conduct.

A special panel of the American Bar Association (1988) likewise concluded that constitutional protections of the rights of criminal defendants do not significantly handicap police and prosecutors in their efforts to arrest, prosecute, and obtain convictions for the most serious crimes. Although many people blame the failures of the criminal justice system on judges' concern for defendants' rights, the blame is misplaced. The main problem is that the criminal justice system is stretched too thin, the Association concluded.

COURTS, CONTROVERSY, & REDUCING CRIME

SHOULD THE EXCLUSIONARY RULE BE ABOLISHED?

The exclusionary rule was controversial when it was adopted in 1961 and remains so today. In a 1981 speech, President Reagan's strong words expressed the views of the crime control model in opposition to the exclusionary rule:

The exclusionary rule rests on the absurd proposition that a law enforcement error, no matter how technical, can be used to justify throwing an entire case out of court, no matter how guilty the defendant or how heinous the crime. The plain consequence of treating the wrongs equally is a grievous miscarriage of justice: The criminal goes free; the officer receives no effective reprimand; and the only ones who really suffer are the people of the community.

But to law professor Yale Kamisar (1978), illegal conduct by the police cannot be so easily ignored. Here is how he states the due process model case for the exclusionary rule: "A court which admits [illegally seized evidence] . . . manifests a willingness to tolerate the unconstitutional conduct which produced it."

How can the police and the citizenry be expected to "believe that the government truly meant to forbid the conduct in the first place"? A court that admits the evidence in a case involving a "run of the mill" Fourth Amendment violation demonstrates an insufficient commitment to the guarantee against unreasonable search and seizure.

While the *Mapp* decision remains controversial, the nature of the debate has changed. Initially, critics called for abolition of the exclusionary rule (Oaks, 1970; Wilkey, 1978); now, they just suggest modifications. This shift in thinking is reflected in the Reagan administration's Attorney General's Task Force on Violent Crime (1981). Although composed largely of long-standing critics of the exclusionary rule, the final report called only for its modification, not its abolition.

Among the alternatives proposed, former Chief Justice Warren Burger urged an "egregious violation standard" (*Brewer v. Williams*, 1977). Others have proposed an exception for reasonable mistakes by the police (Fyfe, 1982). To critics, modifications along these lines would reduce the number of arrests lost because of illegal searches, and the sanction would be more proportional to the seriousness of the Fourth Amendment violation. The Supreme Court, however, has recognized an "honest mistake" or a "good-faith" exception to the exclusionary rule only in extremely narrow and limited circumstances (*United States v. Leon*, 1984; *Illinois v. Krull*, 1987).

What do you think? Should the exclusionary rule be abolished outright, given "good-faith" exceptions, or kept in its present form? If one admits that there are problems in its current application, what realistic alternatives might restrain law enforcement from potentially conducting blatant and flagrant searches in violation of the Fourth Amendment?

CONCLUSION

In many ways, Ernesto Miranda fit the pattern of those arrested by the police—a young minority male with little education and few job prospects. But the eventual outcome of his case was hardly typical. His case was heard by the nation's highest court, and he not only won the right to a new trial but also established a new law in the process. Unlike most defendants, whose cases are quickly forgotten, his name became a code word for the rights of criminal defendants.

Although *Miranda* the legal principle endured, Miranda the man was less fortunate. Initially, his chances of gaining an acquittal during retrial looked promising indeed. After all, the state's only evidence—the signed confession—had been ruled to be inadmissible. It turned out, however, that while in jail Ernesto Miranda had admitted details of the crime to his common law wife, who by now had grown afraid of him. She testified for the state, and after an hour and a half of deliberations, the jury found Miranda guilty of rape and kidnapping a second time. After serving his prison term, Ernesto Miranda was living in Phoenix when he became involved in a barroom quarrel over small change in a poker game. A large knife ended his life. It is no small irony that the Phoenix police read Miranda's killer his *Miranda* rights when they arrested him.

This chapter has examined several important aspects of what occurs while cases are being prepared for trial. One is discovery, the formal or informal exchange of information between prosecution and defense. What information is subject to discovery varies greatly. As a rule, defense attorneys who are cooperative members of the courtroom work group receive more information than those who are not cooperative members.

Another important aspect of preparing for trial centers on suppression of evidence. Confessions and physical evidence that have been illegally obtained cannot be used at trial. If the defense believes that there have been illegal actions by the police, it files a pretrial motion to suppress the evidence. Prosecutors are usually in a favorable position to show that the evidence was obtained legally.

Chapter Review

LO1 **1.** Explain the reasons why the process of discovery exists in both civil and criminal cases, but is significantly curtailed in the latter.

Discovery is designed to give both parties to a legal dispute a good idea about the evidence that will be presented at trial. Not only does this exchange of information prevent surprises, but also, it facilitates resolutions without trial, such as the settlement of a civil case or a plea bargain in a criminal case. Discovery, however, is limited in criminal cases, since the prosecution bears the burden of persuasion to prove a defendant guilty beyond a reasonable doubt, and the defendant is protected against being forced to incriminate himself/herself. If the defense had to disclose evidence to the prosecution, the privilege against self-incrimination would be rendered meaningless.

LO2 **2.** Differentiate formal and informal discovery and the reasons why both are used in criminal cases.

Formal discovery in criminal cases concerns the exchange of information mandated either by the rules of procedure or applicable law. The crux of mandatory discovery in criminal cases concerns prosecutorial disclosure of exculpatory evidence to the defense. Informal discovery concerns the disclosure of information not mandated by law. It occurs frequently because it often facilitates a prompt resolution of a dispute without

the need for trial (i.e., either the prosecutor drops the charges in light of exculpatory evidence disclosed to it by the defense, or the defendant pleads guilty once the strength of the prosecution's case becomes evident).

LO3 **3.** Identify the types of evidence subject to mandatory criminal discovery.

All potentially exculpatory evidence must be disclosed to the defense. This includes any prior inconsistent statements of prosecutorial witnesses, as well as all impeachment evidence that might cast doubt on a witness's credibility.

LO4 **4.** Compare and contrast the exclusionary rule and the fruit of the poisonous tree doctrine.

The exclusionary rule bars evidence from being used in the prosecution's case-in-chief if it was obtained in violation of a defendant's constitutional rights. The fruit of the poisonous tree doctrine bars derivative evidence found as a result the violation of a defendant's constitutional right from being used in the prosecution's case-in-chief unless the evidence is so far attenuated from the constitutional violation that its use would not offend due process.

LO5 **5.** Summarize how the decision in *Miranda v. Arizona* regulates the process of police interrogations of suspects.

Before a suspect in police custody is interrogated, the suspect must be informed of his or her rights under the Fifth Amendment's

Self-Incrimination Clause, namely that the suspect has the right to remain silent and the right to have counsel present during an interrogation. Moreover, the suspect must be told that the consequence of voluntarily waving these rights will result in the prosecution being able to use anything the suspect says at trial. If the suspect invokes his or her *Miranda* rights, questioning must stop.

LO6 6. Explain the requirements governing the application for search warrants, the issuance of search warrants, and the execution of search warrants.

When law enforcement officers want to conduct a search for evidence, the Fourth Amendment generally requires them to seek a warrant. They apply for a warrant by swearing to the facts they know, usually in an affidavit. A magistrate then considers those facts to determine whether there is probable cause to authorize the search of a particular place or person for particular evidence connected to a specific crime. If such a warrant is issued, the police must execute the warrant quickly and in a reasonable manner.

LO7 7. Identify the major exceptions to the Fourth Amendment's warrant requirement.

Police may conduct warrantless searches when granted consent to search by someone with actual or apparent authority to grant such consent; when incident to a lawful arrest; when items are in plain view or in open fields; when probable cause exists to search a motor vehicle; or when emergency situations make it impracticable for police to seek and obtain a warrant first.

LO8 8. Analyze the effect of the exclusionary rule on the operations of the courtroom work group.

Because pretrial motions to suppress evidence are relatively rare, the exclusionary rule does not generally impact the operations of the courtroom work group in most cases. However, when questions about the constitutionality of a search or seizure arise, the defense attorney takes charge of the situation by filing a motion to suppress. In somewhat of a role reversal, these motions have the effect of putting the prosecution on the defensive. Moreover, they ultimately cause a judge to have to rule on the credibility of testimony offered by law enforcement officers. Depending on whom the judge believes, the relationships within the courtroom work group can be significantly strained.

LO9 9. Evaluate whether the exclusionary rule should be abolished.

Supporters of the exclusionary rule argue that the rule is the only effective deterrent against police misconduct. Thus, they assert that the rule must be preserved in order to guarantee that our constitutional rights are honored. In contrast, those who want to see the exclusionary rule abolished argue that the threat of civil lawsuits should be enough to deter police misconduct. Moreover, they assert that the rule "costs" too much, in that it operates to prevent juries from considering highly relevant evidence, which, in turn, sometimes operates to allow the guilty to go free.

Critical Thinking Questions

1. In civil cases, each party is entitled to all the information in the possession of the other side (unless that information is privileged). Why are discovery rules in criminal cases different?

2. To what extent do prosecutorial policies that restrict the sharing of information with defense attorneys other than what is legally required represent a contradiction in the crime control model?

3. When the Court announced its decision in *Miranda v. Arizona* in 1966, the decision sparked massive controversy and was a major issue in the 1968 presidential campaign. Yet, over time it has become much more accepted than the Court's decision in *Mapp v. Ohio* regarding search and seizure. What factors might explain this apparent shift in assessments?

4. A number of conservatives call for eliminating or restricting the exclusionary rule in street crimes. Yet some conservatives also call for a stricter rule in white-collar crimes, suggesting that the financial records of a person or a business should be given special protections under the Fourth Amendment. Are these arguments consistent or simply a case of whose ox is being gored? How would these arguments play out if a substantial citizen in the community (whose financial records are being requested) were under investigation for major drug dealings?

5. To what extent is the continuing controversy over search-and-seizure law really a debate over the war on drugs? Recall the controversy in Chapter 8 centering on judicial independence, in which a federal judge in New York suppressed a substantial amount of illegal drugs.

Key Terms

aerial search 293

affidavit 290

alibi defense 281

consent search 292

consent surveillance 294

confrontation 282

custodial interrogation 284

derivative evidence 282

discovery 277

exclusionary rule 282

exculpatory evidence 278

Foreign Intelligence Surveillance Act (FISA) 294

fruit of the poisonous tree 282

illegal search and seizure 295

impeachment evidence 278

motor vehicle searches 292

Omnibus Crime Control and Safe Streets Act of 1968 291

open fields 292

plain view 292

reciprocal disclosure 281

search incident to lawful arrest 292

search warrant 289

Stored Communications Act 294

suppression motions 295

unreasonable search and seizure 289

video surveillance 294

warrantless search 291

Web Resources

Go to the *America's Courts and the Criminal Justice System* companion website at

http://www.cengage.com/criminaljustice/neubauer,

where you will find more resources to help you study.

Resources include web exercises, quizzing, and flash cards.

For Further Reading

Brooks, Peter. *Troubling Confessions: Speaking Guilt in Law and Literature*. Chicago: University of Chicago Press, 2000.

Del Carmen, Rolando, and Craig Hemmens. *Criminal Procedure and the Supreme Court: A Guide to the Major Decisions on Search and Seizure, Privacy, and Individual Rights*. Lanham, MD: Rowman & Littlefield 2010.

Ferdico, John, Henry F. Fradella, and Chris Totten. *Criminal Procedure for the Criminal Justice Professional*, 11th ed. Belmont, CA: Wadsworth, 2012.

Fradella, Henry F., Weston W. Morrow, Ryan G. Fischer, and Connie E. Ireland. 2011. "Quantifying *Katz*: Empirically Measuring 'Reasonable Expectations of Privacy' in the Fourth Amendment Context." *American Journal of Criminal Law*, 38(3): 289–373.

Hilton, Alicia M. "Alternatives to the Exclusionary *Rule after Hudson v. Michigan*: Preventing and Remedying Police Misconduct." *Villanova Law Review* 53: 47–82, 2008.

Horne, Jed. *Desire Street: A True Story of Death and Deliverance in New Orleans*. New York: Farrar, Straus, and Giroux, 2005.

Leo, Richard, and George Thomas. *The Miranda Debate: Law, Justice, and Policing*. Boston: Northeastern University Press, 2000.

Mialon, Hugo M., and Sue H. Mialon. "The Effects of the Fourth Amendment: An Economic Analysis." *Journal of Law, Economics, and Organization* 24: 22–44, 2008.

Sklansky, David Alan. "Is the Exclusionary Rule Obsolete?" *Ohio State Journal of Criminal Law* 5: 567–584, 2008.

12 Negotiated Justice and the Plea of Guilty

Pool/Elaine Thompson/Reuters/Corbis Wire/Corbis

With his lawyers at his side, **Gary Leon Ridgway** looks over papers he is signing in which he pleads guilty to 48 counts of aggravated first-degree murder in the Green River killing cases. Ridgway pleaded guilty as part of a plea bargain with prosecutors in which his life would be spared. To the public, such a plea bargain may appear to be unduly lenient. In reality, though, such agreements are a part of the normal processing of crimes. Without such pleas, prosecutors risk the possibility of offenders like Ridgway being acquitted at trial. Moreover, if trials were the norm, rather than plea bargains, the system would collapse since it lacks both the time and resources to conduct trials in most criminal cases. ■

Chapter Outline

LAW ON THE BOOKS: TYPES OF PLEA AGREEMENTS
Charge Bargaining
Count Bargaining
Sentence Bargaining

LAW IN ACTION: BARGAINING AND CASELOADS

LAW IN ACTION: BARGAINING AND DISCRETION
Presumption of Factual Guilt
Costs and Risks of Trial
What to Do with the Guilty

BARGAINING AND THE COURTROOM WORK GROUP
Prosecutors
Defendants
Defense Attorneys
Judges

DYNAMICS OF BARGAINING
Decision-Making Norms
Why Cases Go to Trial
Jury Trial Penalty

Courts, Law, & Media
American Violet (2008)

COPPING A PLEA
Questioning the Defendant
No Contest and *Alford* Pleas
Acceptance and Withdrawal of Pleas

CASE CLOSE-UP: *Santobello v. New York* and Honoring a Plea Agreement

Effective Assistance of Counsel during Plea Bargaining

LAW IN CONTROVERSY: ABOLISHING PLEA BARGAINING

Courts, Controversy, & the Administration of Justice
Who Benefits from Plea Bargaining?

Are the Changes Implemented?
Is Discretion Eliminated or Just Moved Elsewhere?
Do Offsetting Changes Occur?

Learning Objectives

After reading this chapter, you should be able to:

LO1 Distinguish between the three most common types of plea agreements.

LO2 Discuss the three major factors influencing bargaining and discretion.

LO3 Recognize the importance of *Boykin v. Alabama*.

LO4 List the major reason each of the members of the courtroom work group engages in plea bargaining.

LO5 Indicate why a few cases go to trial but most defendants plead guilty.

LO6 Explain why adherents of the crime control model of criminal justice oppose plea bargaining for different reasons from those of adherents of the due process model of criminal justice.

Charged with two counts of felony gambling, Rudolph Santobello pled guilty to one count of a misdemeanor charge of possessing gambling records. Just as important, the prosecutor agreed to make no recommendation as to the sentence. But Santobello's sentencing hearing was delayed for several months, and in the interim the initial judge retired, and another prosecutor replaced the one who had negotiated the plea of guilty. Apparently ignorant of his colleague's commitment, the new district attorney demanded the maximum sentence, and the new judge agreed, imposing a 1-year jail term. The justices of the U.S. Supreme Court were concerned about the failure of the prosecutor's office to honor the commitment it had made in inducing the guilty plea. Others were no doubt concerned about whether Santobello, who had a long and serious criminal record, should have been allowed to plead guilty with such a light sentence in the first place.

Santobello v. New York highlights the importance of guilty pleas. Although the average American equates criminal justice with trials, only a handful of defendants are ever tried. Instead, most convictions result not from a guilty verdict following a contested trial but rather from a voluntary plea by the accused. Indeed Justice Kennedy recently wrote that our criminal justice system is, "for the most part, a system of pleas, not a system of trials" (*Lafler v. Cooper*, 2012, p. 1388). The simple reality is that "ninety-seven percent of federal convictions and ninety-four percent of state convictions are the result of guilty pleas" (*Missouri v. Frye*, 2012, p. 1407). Views about this common practice differ. To some, it erodes the cornerstones of the adversary system: the presumption of innocence and the right to trial. To others, it enables the guilty to escape with a light penalty. To still others, it is a modern-day necessity if the courts are to dispose of their large caseloads. All agree, however, that it is the most important stage of the criminal court process.

LAW ON THE BOOKS: TYPES OF PLEA AGREEMENTS

Guilty pleas are the bread and butter of the American criminal courts. Between 85 and 95 percent of all state and federal felony convictions are obtained by a defendant entering a negotiated plea of guilt (Covey, 2008; Hashimoto, 2008). The data in Figure 12.1 demonstrate the pervasiveness of guilty pleas for specific types of offenses. **Plea bargaining** can best be defined as the process through which a defendant pleads guilty to a criminal charge with the expectation of receiving some consideration from the state.

Plea bargaining is hardly new. Considerable evidence shows that it became a common practice in state courts sometime after the Civil War (Alschuler, 1979; Friedman, 1979; Sanborn, 1986). In Middlesex County, Massachusetts, for example, plea bargaining had become firmly "normalized" by the 20th century (Fisher, 2003). In federal courts, the massive number of liquor cases stemming from Prohibition led to the institutionalization of plea bargaining in the first third of the 20th century (Padgett, 1990). What is new is the amount of attention plea negotiations now receive. In an earlier era, the issue was discussed only sporadically. The crime surveys of the 1920s reported the dominance of plea bargaining (Moley, 1928), but most courts persistently denied its existence. It was not until the 1960s that plea bargaining emerged as a controversial national issue. Today, however, although specific aspects of plea bargaining may give rise to periodic controversy, the process itself is so widely accepted that it "dominates the modern American criminal process" (Covey, 2008, p. 1238; see also *Lafler v. Cooper* 2012).

Plea bargaining is a general term that encompasses a wide range of practices. Indeed, court officials disagree about what is meant by plea bargaining. Some prosecutors refuse to admit that they engage in bargaining; they simply call it something else (Miller, McDonald, & Cramer 1978). Thus, any discussion of negotiated justice must start with the recognition that important variations exist both in the types of plea agreements negotiated and the process by which such agreements are reached. Typically, plea agreements take one or more of the following three forms: charge bargaining, count bargaining, and sentence bargaining. The "Law on the Books vs. Law in Action" feature on the next page summarizes the different types of plea bargaining.

Charge Bargaining

One type of plea agreement is termed charge bargaining. In return for the defendant's plea of guilty,

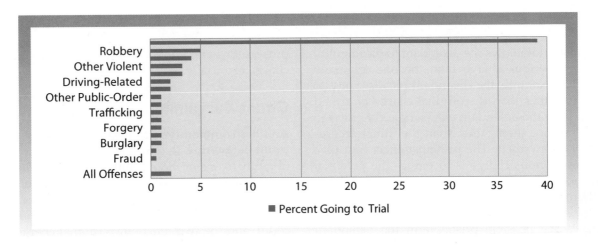

Figure 12.1 ■ Trial Rates for Typical Felonies by Most Serious Arrest Charge

Source: Thomas H. Cohen and Tracey Kyckelhahn. *Felony Defendants in Large Urban Counties, 2006.* Washington, DC: Bureau of Justice Statistics, 2010.

LAW ON THE BOOKS VS. LAW IN ACTION
FORMS OF PLEA BARGAINING

	LAW ON THE BOOKS	LAW IN ACTION
Plea bargaining	The process by which a defendant pleads guilty to a criminal charge with the expectation of receiving some benefit from the state.	The majority of findings of guilt occur because of plea bargaining. The proportion of pleas (as opposed to trials) varies among jurisdictions.
Charge bargaining	The defendant pleads guilty to a less serious charge than the one originally filed. Pleading to a less serious charge reduces the potential sentence the defendant faces.	Courthouse norms control allowable reductions. Some prosecutors deliberately overcharge so it appears that the defendant is getting a break.
Count bargaining	The defendant pleads guilty to some, but not all, of the counts contained in the charging document. Pleading guilty to fewer counts reduces the potential sentence the defendant faces.	Some prosecutors deliberately file additional charges so they can dismiss some later on, making it appear that the defendant got a good deal.
		In multiple-count charges, sentences are typically served concurrently (not consecutively), so the "sentence reduction" the defendant receives is largely illusionary.
Sentence bargaining	The defendant pleads guilty, knowing the sentence that will be imposed. The sentence in the sentence bargain is less than the maximum.	Sentences are based on normal penalties. Because the normal penalty for an offense is less than the maximum, defendants appear to get off lightly.

© Cengage Learning

the prosecutor allows the defendant to plead guilty to a less serious charge than the one originally filed. For example, the defendant pleads guilty to robbery rather than the original charge of armed robbery. Or the defendant enters a plea of guilty to misdemeanor theft rather than the initial accusation of felony theft. The principal effect of a plea to a less serious charge is to reduce the potential sentence.

Some offenses carry a stiff maximum sentence. A plea to a lesser charge therefore greatly reduces the possible prison term the defendant will have to serve. Bargains for reduced charges are most commonly found in jurisdictions where the state's criminal code is rigid or where prosecutors routinely overcharge to begin with. Thus, some charge reductions reflect the probability that the prosecutor would not be able to prove the original charge in a trial.

Count Bargaining

Another common type of plea agreement is called count bargaining. In return for the defendant's plea of guilty to one or more counts in the indictment or information, the prosecutor dismisses the remaining charges. For instance, a defendant accused of three separate burglaries pleads guilty to one burglary count, and the two remaining criminal charges are dismissed.

Like a charge-reduction agreement, a count bargain reduces the defendant's potential sentence, but in a very different way. A person charged with multiple counts theoretically can receive a maximum sentence of something like 135 years, a figure arrived at by multiplying the number of charges by the maximum jail term for each charge and assuming that the judge will sentence the defendant to serve the sentences consecutively (one after another). Such figures are often unrealistic, because sentences are typically imposed concurrently (to run at the same time). In practice, the defendant will often receive the same penalty no matter how few (or how many) charges are involved.

Sentence Bargaining

The third common form of plea agreement is called sentence bargaining. A plea of guilty is entered in exchange for a promise of leniency in sentencing. There may be a promise that the defendant will be placed on probation or that the prison term will be no more than a given figure—say, 5 years. In a sentence bargain, the defendant typically pleads to the original charge (often termed a plea on the nose). In some jurisdictions, however, sentence bargaining operates in conjunction with count bargaining and charge-reduction bargaining.

In sentence bargaining, the defendant invariably receives less than the maximum penalty. To some, this is an indication that defendants get off too easily, but in fact, only defendants with long criminal records who have committed particularly heinous crimes would receive the maximum sentence anyway. In practice, courts impose sentences on the basis of normal penalties for specific crimes involving common types of defendants. In sentence bargaining, the sentence agreed to is the one typically imposed in similar cases.

LAW IN ACTION: BARGAINING AND CASELOADS

The common explanation for plea bargaining is that the courts have too many cases. Plea bargaining is usually portrayed as a regrettable but necessary expedient for disposing of cases. In Chapter 5, it was argued that although this explanation contains some truth, it obscures too many important facets of what the courts do and why they do it. Certainly, the press of cases and lack of

adequate resources shape the criminal court process, plea bargaining included (Worden, 1990). And because prosecutors need to move cases, they agree to more lenient pleas than they might prefer.

But the caseload hypothesis cannot explain why plea bargaining is as prevalent in courts with relatively few cases as it is in courts with heavy caseloads (Eisenstein & Jacob, 1977; Covey, 2009). A comparison of plea rates in a number of courthouses across the nation found high plea rates in suburban counties with low crime rates and below-average caseloads. The vast differences among jurisdictions in the ratio of pleas to trials primarily reflect differences in the prosecution and the police or differences in courtroom workgroup culture, not in disparities concerning crime rates or court resources (Boland & Forst, 1985; Emmelman, 2002).

A similar conclusion emerges from a study that presented the members of the courtroom work group with several hypothetical cases and asked, "Assuming that prosecution, defense, and the court have adequate resources to deal with their caseloads in a fair and expeditious manner, how do you believe this case should be resolved?" (Church. 1985, p. 474). The responses indicated that relatively few of the cases would be disposed of by a trial. Furthermore, there was little support for the notion that practitioners considered negotiated guilty pleas a necessary but illegitimate response to inadequate court system resources (see also, Worden, 2008).

LAW IN ACTION: BARGAINING AND DISCRETION

The principal weakness of the excessive caseload hypothesis is that it assumes a purely mechanical process, ignoring the underlying dynamics. It seems to suggest that if only there were more judges, more prosecutors, more defense attorneys, and more courtrooms, there would be many more trials, and the penalties imposed on the guilty would also increase. Such a view ignores the discretion inherent in the criminal justice process. Plea bargaining is a response to some fundamental issues, the first of which centers on the question of guilt.

Presumption of Factual Guilt

The process of negotiated justice does not operate in isolation from the other stages of the criminal court process. What has gone before—for example, the setting of bail, the return of a grand jury indictment, and the prosecutor's evaluation of the strengths of a case—significantly affects how courts dispose of cases on a plea. The opposite is equally true. Throughout the history of a case, decisions on bail, indictment, and screening have been premised on the knowledge that the majority of defendants end up pleading guilty (Wright & Miller, 2002).

Recall from Chapter 10 that the bulk of legally innocent defendants are removed from the criminal court process during the screening process through the preliminary hearing, the grand jury, or the prosecutor's charging decision. By the time a case reaches the trial stage, the courtroom work group presumes that the defendant is probably guilty. Survival through the prior processing means that prosecutors, defense attorneys, and judges alike perceive that trial defendants are in serious trouble.

One study estimated that about 50 percent of the cases in the major trial court were "hopeless" or devoid of triable issues of law (Schulhofer, 1984). These cases are what some court officials term a "dead bang" or a "slam dunk" case, with very strong evidence against the defendant, who has no credible explanation indicating innocence (Mather, 1974a). More recently, some courts have come to refer to these types of cases as "no-brainers" (Bowen, 2009). One district attorney summarized the strong evidence of guilt in such cases: "The pervasiveness of the facts should indicate to any competent attorney that the element of prosecution is present and a successful prosecution is forthcoming" (Neubauer, 1974b, p. 200).

No two cases are ever the same, of course. Many discussions of plea bargains leave the false impression that the attorneys haggle only over the sentence. In fact, courtroom work groups spend a lot of time discussing and analyzing how the crime was committed, the nature of the victim, the types of witnesses, and the character of the defendant (Emmelman, 2002; Maynard, 1988). In many cases, the likelihood that the defendant will be acquitted outright is small; however, the possibility exists that he or she might be convicted of a less serious offense. The question of what charge the facts will support is an important part of plea bargaining.

Costs and Risks of Trial

The possibility of trial greatly influences negotiations. Trials are a costly and time-consuming means of establishing guilt. For example, to try a simple burglary case typically would take from 1 to 4 days (depending on the jurisdiction) and require the presence of the judge, bailiff, clerk, defense attorney, prosecutor, and court reporter. During this period, none of them could devote much time to the numerous other cases requiring disposition. Also, each would be forced to spend time preparing for this trial. A trial would also require the presence of numerous noncourt personnel: police officers, witnesses, victims, and jurors. For each of these people, a trial represents an unwanted intrusion into their daily lives.

Based on these considerations, all members of the courtroom work group have a common interest in disposing of cases and avoiding unnecessary trials. Their reasons may differ. Judges and prosecutors want high disposition rates in order to prevent case backlogs and to present a public impression that the process is running smoothly. Public defenders prefer quick dispositions because they lack the personnel to handle the caseload. Private defense attorneys depend on a high case turnover to earn a living, because most of their clients can afford only a modest fee. In short, all members of the courtroom work group have more cases to try than the time or resources to try them.

To a large extent, then, a trial is a mutual penalty that all parties seek to avoid through plea bargaining. To be sure, not all trials are avoided. But through plea bargaining, scarce trial resources can be applied to the cases that need to be tried.

What to Do with the Guilty

The adversary proceedings of trial are designed to resolve conflict over guilt or innocence. In practice, however, it is not the issue of legal guilt that is most often in dispute, but rather what sentence to impose on the guilty. Sentencing decisions involve more than the verdict of guilt or innocence presented at trial; they incorporate difficult issues of judgment about the type of crime and the nature of the defendant. Moreover, because of the standards of evidence, information relevant to sentencing is not easily introduced at trial. Unlike a trial, plea bargaining does focus on what to do with an offender—particularly, how much leniency is appropriate.

Criminal statutes are broad; the courtroom work group is called upon to apply these broad prohibitions to specific and variable cases. The participants are concerned with adjusting the penalties to the specifics of the crime and the defendant. In the interest of fairness, they seek to individualize justice.

Consider a case with two co-defendants of unequal culpability: an armed robbery involving an experienced robber who employed a youthful accomplice as a driver. Technically, both are equally guilty, but in the interest of fairness and substantive justice, the prosecutor may legitimately decide to make a concession to the young accomplice but none to the prime mover. In short, members of the courtroom work group seek to individualize justice.

BARGAINING AND THE COURTROOM WORK GROUP

Plea bargaining is a contest involving the prosecutor, defendant, defense counsel, and at times, the judge. Each party has its own objectives. Each attempts to structure the situation to its own advantage by using tactics to improve its bargaining position. Each defines success in terms of its own objectives. Among the conflicting objectives, accommodations are possible, because each side can achieve its objectives only by making concessions on other matters. Plea bargaining is typical of "most bargaining situations which ultimately involve some range of possible outcomes within which each party would rather make a concession than fail to reach agreement at all" (Schelling, 1960, p. 70; see also, Emmelman, 2002).

Plea bargaining typically begins informally, according to two veteran federal prosecutors. When discussing the matter with opposing counsel, prosecutors want to be reassured that the defendant is genuinely interested in pleading guilty and that a reasonable chance exists of reaching an agreement before they invest time and effort in preparing a formal plea agreement. Consistent with our earlier discussion of the courtroom work group (Chapter 5), trust is a critical component of these discussions.

"If the prosecutor and the defense counsel have negotiated plea agreements with each other in the past, expect to do so in the future, and from their past dealings, respect and trust each other, these preliminary, informal discussions are likely to be candid and efficient and may quickly lead to an informal proposed agreement" (Brown & Bunnell, 2006, pp. 1065–1066).

Bargaining is possible because each of the legal actors understands the realities of law in action: the presumption of guilt, the costs and uncertainties of trial, and the concern with arriving at an appropriate sentence. All these factors influence bargaining positions.

Prosecutors

To the prosecutor, a plea bargain represents the certainty of conviction without the risks of trial. Recall that prosecutors emphasize convictions. Because they value the deterrent objectives of law enforcement, they prefer that a guilty person be convicted of some charge rather than to escape with no conviction at all.

The certainty and finality of a defendant's pleading guilty contrast sharply with the potential risks involved in a trial (Covey, 2008; Worden, 1990). During trial, a number of unexpected events can occur, most of which work to the detriment of the prosecutor. The victim may refuse to cooperate. Witnesses' testimony may differ significantly from earlier statements made in investigative reports. A mistrial—the judge ending the trial without a verdict because of a major defect in the proceedings—could be declared. Even after a jury verdict of guilty, the appellate courts may reverse, meaning that the whole process must be repeated.

In seeking a conviction through a guilty plea, the prosecutor is in a unique position to control the negotiating process (Hashimoto, 2008; Holmes, Daudistel, & Taggart, 1992). To begin with, the prosecutor proceeds from a position of strength: In most cases, the state has sufficient evidence for conviction. If, however, the case is weak, the prosecutor can avoid the embarrassment of losing a case at trial by either dismissing it altogether or offering such a good deal that the defendant cannot refuse.

To improve their bargaining position, some prosecutors deliberately overcharge. "Sure, it's a lever," said one San Francisco prosecutor, referring to his office's practice of charging every nonautomobile homicide as murder. With unusual candor, he added, "And we charge theft, burglary, and the possession of burglar's tools, because we know that if we charged only burglary there would be a trial" (Alschuler, 1968, p. 90; see also Davis, 2007).

Prosecutors, of course, control several of the forms of plea bargaining. They are in a position to offer a charge reduction or a count bargain. They can threaten to throw the book at a defendant who does not plead, or they may refuse to bargain at all. If the crime is a serious one and the defendant is viewed as very dangerous, the prosecutor may force the defendant either to plead on the nose, with no sentencing concessions, or to run the risk of trial and a harsher sentence for not having cooperated.

Defendants

If pleas give prosecutors what they want (convictions), why do defendants plead guilty? To understand plea bargaining, it is important to recognize that it is often in the defendant's best interest to give up the right to be presumed innocent at a trial. The primary benefit of a plea is the possibility of a lenient sentence.

Around the courthouse, it is a common perception that defendants who refuse to plead guilty receive harsher sentences. For example, a judge may impose a stiffer sentence because the defendant compounded the crime by lying on the witness stand or getting some friends to perjure themselves. Or a prosecutor may agree not to invoke state "career criminal" provisions, which impose higher penalties for those with a prior felony conviction. Moreover, for defendants who are unable to post bail, a guilty plea can mean an immediate release (either on probation or for time served).

Ultimately, defendants must decide whether to go along with the plea bargain or to take their chances at trial. Few defendants are in a position to make a reasoned choice between the advantages of a plea and those of a trial; most are poor, inarticulate, and have little formal education. For these defendants, the experience in the courts is like their life on the streets: They learn to go along. Often softened up by the experience in jail awaiting trial, many defendants find that entering a plea is the best way to go along and avoid the possibility of even harsher penalties.

Defense Attorneys

If the prosecutor enters negotiations from a position of strength, the opposite is true of defense attorneys, who have few bargaining chips. Over the years prosecutorial power has increased (Bowen, 2009; Chapter 6), which in turns limits the power of defense attorneys. If the chances of winning at trial are not high—and they rarely are—defense attorneys must consider the strong possibility that after a trial conviction the defendant may be penalized with a higher prison sentence.

The decision-making process for defense attorneys involves three phases. First, the defense attorney must assess the offer for a guilty plea, weighing the potential costs of delay against the likely outcome of a trial. Second, the defense attorney negotiates the terms of a plea bargain; if the initial offer is better than average, negotiations are less intense than if it is below average. Third, the defense attorney counsels the defendant, who may or may not accept the offer (Emmelman, 1996, 2002).

The lawyer's main resource in negotiating a plea agreement is his or her knowledge of the courtroom work group—the types of pleas the prosecutor usually enters, the length of sentence the judge normally imposes in similar cases, and so on. Defense attorneys act as classic negotiators, trying to get the best deal possible for their clients while explaining to the clients the realistic alternatives. As noted in Chapter 7, these two roles can conflict. A defense attorney may negotiate what he or she considers the best deal under the circumstances, only to have the client refuse to go along.

Convincing clients to accept a plea is not always easy. Veteran public defender David Feige (2006, p. 119) recalls a lawyer and his client screaming at each other in the jail holding cell. Although other lawyers and clients were present, "No one interferes, no one tried to calm them down, and lawyer and client go on yelling at each for another four or five minutes." Such interactions are constant. "Overworked, underappreciated lawyers and desperate clients are a potent mix. Many lawyers see intimate client relationships as superfluous." As stressed in Chapter 7, some lawyers try to protect their clients from making bad decisions, but lawyers also have to deal with pressures from judges to move the docket.

Judges

Several factors limit a judge's ability to control or supervise plea bargaining. Given the division of powers in the adversary system, judges are reluctant to intrude on prosecutorial discretion. Many of the key bargaining mechanisms—specifically, the charges filed and the charges the defendant is allowed to plead to—are controlled by the prosecutor. Thus, when a prosecutor, defense attorney, and defendant have agreed either to a count bargain or a charge-reduction bargain, the judge has no legal authority to refuse to accept the plea.

Even more fundamentally, the judge knows relatively little about each case. Only the prosecutor, defendant, and defense attorney know the evidence for and against the defendant. Without knowledge of why the parties agreed to plea bargain, it is obviously difficult for a judge to reject a plea agreement. In short, the judge is dependent on the prosecutor and, to a lesser extent, the defense attorney.

Within these constraints, judges have some ability to shape the plea-bargaining process. Judicial involvement in the plea-bargaining process can have important consequences. In Essex, New Jersey, for example, trials are rare, and judges spend a great amount of time dealing with the plea-bargaining process. Indeed, "every defender interviewed recalled being coerced into returning to his client and convincing him or her of the judge's strong desire to resolve the case quickly with a plea" (Wice, 2005, p. 125).

In the federal court system, judges are prohibited from being involved in plea negotiations (Borenstein & Anderson, 2009). The extent to which judges are involved in the process in state courts varies greatly. A survey of state trial court judges (Ryan & Alfini, 1979) revealed four basic patterns.

- A few judges are actively involved in plea negotiations, offering recommendations about case disposition.
- Some judges are indirectly involved, reviewing the recommendations made by defense and prosecutor.
- A small percentage of judges attend plea discussions but do not participate.
- The majority of judges do not attend plea-negotiating sessions. Thus, their role is limited to ratifying agreements reached by others.

A review of the rules of criminal procedure across the United States reveals that these four approaches continue, although a clear preference exists for judges not to participate in the plea-bargaining process other than to ratify or reject plea agreements reached independently by the prosecution and the defense (Borenstein & Anderson, 2009). But even when judicial participation is limited to ratifying plea negotiations, judges can have an important impact on the process. Regular members of the courtroom work group know the sentence the judge is likely to impose. Therefore, they negotiate case dispositions that incorporate these sentencing expectations. On rare occasions, judges may reject a plea agreement. Such rejections serve to set a baseline for future negotiations.

DYNAMICS OF BARGAINING

Negotiating is a group activity, typically conducted in busy, noisy, public courtrooms. In such a courtroom, the initial impression is of constant talking and endless movement. While the judge is hearing a pretrial motion in one case, a prosecutor and defense attorney are engaged in an animated conversation about a charge reduction in another. Meanwhile, in more hushed tones, a public defender is briefing his client about why a continuance will be requested, and nearby a mother is talking to her son who is being held in jail. These numerous conversations occur while other participants continually move in and out. Police officers leave after testifying in a motion to suppress, bail agents arrive to check on their clients, clerks bring in new files, and defense lawyers search for the prosecutor assigned to their case. Occasionally, the noise becomes so loud that the judge or bailiff demands silence—a request that usually produces only a temporary reduction in the decibel level.

On the surface, courtrooms appear disorganized. In fact, there is an underlying order to the diverse activities. For example, when the judge calls a case, the other participants involved in that matter are immediately expected to drop all other business and proceed to the front of the court. Decision-making norms govern the substance of the negotiations. In particular, patterns exist as to why some cases go to trial and about understandings regarding penalties for those who do go to trial.

Decision-Making Norms

Through working together on a daily basis, the members of the courtroom work group come to understand the problems and demands of the others. They develop shared conceptions of how certain types of cases and defendants should be treated. Everyone except the outsider or the novice knows these customs of the courthouse.

As we have seen, plea bargaining is a complex process, but studies in different courts reveal important similarities in shared norms. The most important consideration is the seriousness of the offense. The more serious the crime charged, the harder the prosecutor bargains (Mather, 1979; Nardulli, Flemming, & Eisenstein, 1984; Piehl & Bushway, 2007). The next most important factor is the defendant's criminal record. Those with prior convictions receive fewer concessions during bargaining (Alschuler, 1979; Nardulli, 1978; Piehl & Bushway, 2007; Smith, 1986; Springer, 1983). Another key consideration is the strength of the prosecutor's case. The stronger the evidence against the defendant, the fewer concessions are offered (Adams, 1983; Smith, 1986).

These shared norms structure plea negotiations. In each courtroom work group, the set of allowable reductions is well understood. Based on the way the crime was committed and the background of the defendant, nighttime burglary will be reduced to daytime burglary, drunkenness to disturbing the peace, and so on. Thus, contrary to many popular fears, defendants are not allowed to plead to just any charge (Emmelman, 2002; Feeley, 1979). If a defendant has been charged with armed robbery, the defense attorney knows that the credibility of her bargaining position will be destroyed if she suggests a plea to disturbing the peace. Such a plea would be out of line with how things are normally done.

Courtroom work groups have similar shared norms about sentencing. On the basis of these shared norms, all parties know what is open for bargaining and what is not. The shared norms provide a baseline for disposing of specific cases. Upward or downward adjustments are made, depending on the circumstances of the individual case.

Why Cases Go to Trial

Although most cases are disposed of by a guilty plea, an important 2 to 10 percent of defendants are tried. Cases go to trial when the parties cannot settle a case through negotiation. In large measure, the factors that shape plea bargaining—the strength of the prosecutor's case and the severity of the penalty—are the same ones that enter into the decision to go to trial. Defense attorneys recommend a trial when the risks of trial are low and the possible gains are high.

This broad calculation leads to two very different types of trial cases. In one, the possible gains for the defendant are high because of the chance of an acquittal. There may be reasonable doubt that the defendant committed any crime, or two sets of witnesses may tell conflicting versions of what happened (Neubauer, 1974b). A second category of cases going to trial involves situations in which the prison sentence will be high. Even though a judge or jury is not likely to return a verdict of not guilty, the defendant may still decide that the slim possibility of an acquittal is worth the risk of the trial penalty.

However, not all trial cases are the result of such rational calculations. Some defendants insist on a trial, no matter what. Judges, prosecutors, and defense attorneys label as irrational defendants who refuse to recognize the realities of the criminal justice system and insist on a trial even when the state has a strong case (Bibas, 2004; Neubauer, 1974b). The net effect of these considerations is that some types of cases are more likely to go to trial than others. Property offenses (burglary and larceny) are much less likely to go to trial than homicide, sexual assault, or robbery. Mather (1974a) suggests that property crimes are least likely to go to trial because the state is apt to have a strong case (usually buttressed by the presence of indisputable physical evidence) and the prison sentence will not be long (see also, Bibas, 2004). Serious crimes such as murder, rape, and robbery are much more likely to be tried. In some crimes of violence, reasonable doubt may exist because the victim may have provoked the attack. Moreover, a convicted defendant is likely to serve a long prison term and is therefore more disposed to take a chance on an outright acquittal.

Jury Trial Penalty

Although most defendants plead guilty, a significant minority of cases do go to trial. As previously indicated, it is a common assumption in courthouses around the nation that defendants who do not enter a plea of guilty can expect to receive harsher sentences. Typically called the "jury trial penalty," the notion reflects the philosophy, "He takes some of my time, I take some of his." Here, *time* refers to the hours spent hearing evidence presented to a jury (Bowen, 2009; Heumann, 1978; King, Soulé, Steen, & Weidner, 2005; Uhlman & Walker, 1980).

Several studies provide empirical documentation for these courthouse perceptions (Brereton & Casper, 1981–1982). In a major eastern city, "the cost of a jury trial for convicted defendants in Metro City is high: sentences are substantially more severe than for other defendants" (Uhlman & Walker 1980, p. 337). Similarly in U.S. district courts across the nation, meaningful trial penalties exist after accounting for legal factors like sentencing guidelines and whether the defendant provided substantial assistance to law enforcement (Ulmer, Eisenstein, & Johnson, 2010).

Although a couple of studies have challenged these conclusions (Eisenstein & Jacob, 1977; Rhodes, 1978), more recent research finds that the magnitude of the jury trial penalty is stunningly high. In serious cases, the sentence imposed on a defendant who is found guilty after trial will often be over five times more severe than the expected sentence for the same offense for a guilty plea (King et al., 2005; McCoy, 2003; Ulmer & Bradley, 2006).

AMERICAN VIOLET (2008)

COURTS, LAW, & MEDIA

Dee Roberts (played by Nicole Beharie), is a 24-year-old African-American woman who lives in the housing projects of a small Texas town with her mother, Alma (played by Alfre Woodard), and her four children. At the start of the movie, police conduct one of many military-style, racially motivated drug raids of their housing complex that have been occurring for many years.

Shortly thereafter, Dee is arrested and roughly dragged by the police from the diner where she works as a waitress. She thought she was being taken into custody for not having paid hundreds of dollars in parking tickets. Much to her surprise, however, she is charged with distributing cocaine in a school zone, a serious felony. But Dee has no drug record. She was not carrying any drugs on her at the time of her arrest, nor were any drugs found in her home during the police raid. Yet, she is arrested and prosecuted as a drug dealer on the basis of false information provided by a confidential informant. The local and seemingly racist district attorney, Calvin Beckett (played by Michael O'Keefe), pushes ahead with the prosecution against Dee as part of his self-driven mission of rounding up "black druggies and hauling them off to jail—by any means necessary" (Ragland, 2009, para. 8).

Dee is faced with a difficult choice. If she agrees to plead guilty, she will not have to go to prison. Rather, in exchange for her plea, she would receive a 10-year suspended sentence with a small fine, allowing her to stay at home and raise her children. If, however, Dee rejects the plea offer, she risks a 16- to 25-year prison term and losing custody of her four kids.

Dee's court-appointed lawyer and her mother urge her to take the plea bargain. But Dee refuses to plead guilty to a crime she did not commit. Unlike most people in her situation, Dee eventually receives help from an American Civil Liberties Union lawyer, who ultimately is able to get the cocaine distribution charges dropped.

This movie is based on actual events that occurred in Hearne, Texas, to Ms. Regina Kelly (the person on whom the character of Dee Roberts is based) in 2000. Ms. Kelly's

Continued on next page

Continued from previous page

high-profile case eventually resulted in Texas changing its criminal law so that "cases can no longer be prosecuted based solely on the claims of a single confidential informant" (Barnes, 2009, para. 3).

After you watch this movie, be prepared to answer the following questions:

1. In *American Violet*, the district attorney tells Dee, "If you don't take the plea, we will prosecute you to the fullest extent of the law." Should prosecutors be able to use their power in this way? Is threatening a defendant with the most severe punishment possible if the defendant does not accept a plea a type of extortion? Explain your answer.

2. Dee is pressured by her lawyer and her family to enter a plea bargain even though she is not guilty. Although she fears the "jury trial penalty" that could land her in prison for up to 25 years, she refuses to cave in to the pressure to plead. How often do you think wrongfully accused defendants who lack the resources to mount a solid legal defense accept a plea, even though they are not guilty, in order to avoid incarceration? Why do you think people would do this? Would you?

3. The drug raids in Hearne, Texas had been going on for years. Regina Kelly's case brought them to national attention. Using what you learned in Chapter 11 about constitutional criminal procedure, critique the use of military-style drug sweeps of housing projects inhabited by the poor. Why do you think such raids occur? What are the effects on the justice system as a whole when local law enforcement officials conduct such raids?

4. In the real raids in Hearne, Texas, seven other defendants accepted the plea bargains that were offered to them. While the charges were dropped against Regina Kelly, the charges were never dismissed against those who pled guilty to avoid the risk of spending many years in prison (Watkins, 2009). What do you think about this? Why?

The U.S. Supreme Court has clearly sanctioned the jury trial penalty. A Kentucky defendant accused of forging an $88 check was offered a 5-year prison sentence if he entered a plea of guilty. But the prosecutor indicated that if the defendant rejected the offer, the state would seek to impose life imprisonment because of the defendant's previous two felony convictions. Such stepped-up sentences for habitual criminals were allowed at that time by Kentucky law. The defendant rejected the plea, went to trial, was convicted, and was eventually sentenced to life imprisonment.

In *Bordenkircher v. Hayes* (1978), the high court held, "The course of conduct engaged in by the prosecutor in this case, which no more than openly presented the defendant with the unpleasant alternative of forgoing trial or facing charges on which he was plainly subject to prosecution" did not violate constitutional protections. In dissent, however, Justice Powell noted that the offer of 5 years in prison "hardly could be characterized as a generous offer." He was clearly troubled that "persons convicted of rape and murder often are not punished so severely" as this check forger. See the "Key Developments" feature below for major legal developments involving plea bargaining.

COPPING A PLEA

"Your honor, my client wishes at this time to withdraw his previous plea of not guilty and wishes at this time to enter a plea of guilty." In phrases similar to this one, defense attorneys indicate that the case is about to end; the defendant is ready to plead. A plea of guilty is more than an admission of conduct; it is a conviction that also involves a defendant's waiver of the most vital rights of the court process: presumption of innocence, jury trial, and confrontation of witnesses (*Boykin v. Alabama* 1969).

In an earlier era, the process of entering a plea of guilty was usually brief and informal. Because the courts and the legal process as a whole were reluctant to recognize the existence of plea bargaining, little law guided the process. Under the leadership of Chief Justice Warren Burger, however, the

KEY DEVELOPMENTS INVOLVING PLEA BARGAINING

Boykin v. Alabama (1969)	When a defendant enters a plea of guilty, the judge must determine whether the plea is knowingly entered and completely voluntary.
Brady v. United States (1970)	Even though the defendant pled guilty to avoid the possibility of a death penalty, the plea was voluntary and intelligently made and therefore not coerced.
Alford v. North Carolina (1970)	Given the defendant's desire to avoid the death penalty and the existence of substantial evidence of guilt, the plea of guilty was valid even though the defendant denied guilt.
Santobello v. New York (1971)	When a plea rests in any significant degree on a promise or agreement of the prosecutor, so that it can be said to be a part of the inducement or consideration, such promise must be fulfilled.
Bordenkircher v. Hayes (1978)	It is not a violation of due process for a prosecutor to threaten defendants with other criminal prosecutions so long as the prosecutor has probable cause to believe that the accused has committed the offense.
Ricketts v. Adamson (1987)	The prosecutor allowed the defendant to plead guilty to second-degree murder, contingent upon his testimony against the codefendant. When the defendant refused to so testify, the DA prosecuted him for first-degree murder. The defendant was not protected by double jeopardy because he breached the plea agreement.
Alabama v. Smith (1989)	The defendant was successful in having his original guilty plea vacated. After conviction at trial, though, the judge imposed a substantially more severe sentence than had originally been negotiated in the plea agreement. The Court held that the enhanced sentence was not vindictiveness because the trial judge had more information available as a result of the trial.
United States v. Mezzanatto (1995)	Federal prosecutors may use statements made by a defendant during plea bargaining to cross-examine the defendant at trial.
United States v. Ruiz (2002)	Prior to a plea of guilty, the prosecutor does not have to disclose to the defense as much evidence as before a trial.
Iowa v. Tovar (2004)	When a defendant is *pro se* and, therefore, is acting as his or her own attorney, the court need not inform the defendant that waiving counsel's assistance in deciding whether to plead guilty risks overlooking a viable defense and forgoes the opportunity to obtain an independent opinion on the wisdom of pleading guilty.
Lafler v. Cooper (2012) and *Missouri v. Frye* (2012)	The right to effective assistance of counsel extends to plea bargaining. Thus, when an attorney provides ineffective advice that leads to the rejection of a plea agreement, the defendant is entitled to a hearing to show a reasonable possibility that the outcome of the plea process would have been different with competent advice.

U.S. Supreme Court sought to set standards for the plea-bargaining process (see "Case Close-Up: *Santobello v. New York* and Honoring a Plea Agreement" on page 323).

Following *Santobello,* the plea process has become more formalized. For example, in the U.S. Attorney's Office in the District of Columbia, an initial plea agreement between opposing counsel must first be approved by a senior supervisor. Next, a plea agreement is drafted. "Over the years, written plea agreements have grown longer and more complex as successive generations of prosecutors, defense counsel and judges ... have noticed or exploited ambiguities of the parties' rights and obligations. As a result, federal plea agreements in D.C. now often run ten single-spaced pages or more" (Brown & Bunnell, 2006, p. 1066). Once a plea agreement has been struck, the next step is the courtroom. A pair of recent Supreme Court opinions will likely force state courts to formalize their plea practices along federal lines (see *Lafler v. Cooper* 2012; *Missouri v. Frye* 2012).

Questioning the Defendant

For years, plea negotiations were officially considered taboo. As a result, the taking of a plea was often a sham. The defendant was expected to lie and deny that a deal had been made (Casper, 1972). Today, however, to prevent the possibility of covering up plea bargaining, many courts now require that a plea agreement be placed on the record.

Most defendants plead guilty to one or more charges listed in the charging document. Before a defendant's plea of guilty can be accepted, the judge must question the defendant. This was not always the case; judges once merely accepted the attorney's statement that the defendant wanted to plead guilty. But in *Boykin v. Alabama*, the Supreme Court ruled: "It was error, for the trial judge to accept petitioner's guilty plea without an affirmative showing that it was intelligent and voluntary" (1969, p. 241).

In light of *Boykin*, Rule 11 of the Federal Rules of Criminal Procedure and similar state provisions bars courts from accepting a plea of guilty in felony proceedings unless the court is satisfied, after inquiry, that:

1. the plea is made knowingly, intelligently, and voluntarily;

2. the defendant committed the crime charged; and

3. the defendant is mentally competent to enter the plea and thereby waive important constitutional rights.

Waiver of Rights

Accordingly, Rule 11 requires a judge to "address the defendant personally in open court and determine

that the plea is voluntary and did not result from force, threats, or promises (other than promises [contained] in the plea agreement)." Thus, a judge must ensure that a defendant pleading guilty has not been improperly influenced by the prosecution, law enforcement officials, or the defendant's own attorney.

At a Rule 11 hearing, the judge inquires whether the defendant understands the nature of the charge(s) and the possible penalty upon conviction; whether the defendant is satisfied with the services of defense counsel; and whether the defendant realizes that a plea waives a series of constitutional rights, including:

- the right to a trial by jury;
- the right to confront and cross-examine adverse witnesses;
- the right to compel the attendance and testimony of witnesses;
- the right to testify on one's own behalf;
- the right to be free from being forced to incriminate oneself;
- the right to be presumed innocent until proven guilty beyond a reasonable doubt; and
- the right to appeal one's conviction.

Courts often use a *Boykin* **form** to ensure that defendants have been informed of all the rights they are waiving. *Boykin* forms, a sample of which appears in Figure 12.2, also provide the added benefits of ensuring that a guilty plea reflects the defendant's own choice and that it is made with a general understanding of the charges and consequences of conviction. Finally, the questioning during a Rule 11 hearing and the completion of a *Boykin* form provide an official court record, which prevents defendants from later contending that they were forced to plead guilty or that they did not knowingly and intelligently waive their rights.

Allocution

To satisfy Rule 11's requirement that the court be satisfied that the defendant actually committed the crime charged in order for the court to accept a plea, either a law enforcement officer or the prosecutor states that if a trial were held, the evidence would show the defendant to be guilty

STATE OF WISCONSIN, CIRCUIT COURT, _____ COUNTY | *For Official Use*

State of Wisconsin, Plaintiff
-vs-

**Plea Questionnaire/
Waiver of Rights**

_____ Case No. _____
Name

I am the defendant and intend to plea as follows:

Charge/Statute	Plea	Charge/Statute	Plea
	☐ Guilty ☐ No Contest		☐ Guilty ☐ No Contest
	☐ Guilty ☐ No Contest		☐ Guilty ☐ No Contest

☐ See attached sheet for additional charges.

I am _____ years old. I have completed _____ years of schooling.
I ☐ do ☐ do not have a high school diploma, GED, of HSED.
I ☐ do ☐ do not understand the English language.
I ☐ do ☐ do not understand the charge(s) to which I am pleading.
I ☐ am not ☐ am currently receiving treatment for a mental illness or disorder.
I ☐ have not ☐ have had any alcohol, medications, or drugs within the last 24 hours.

Constitutional Rights
I understand that by entering this plea. I give up the following constitutional rights:

☐ I give up my right to a trial.
☐ I give up my right to remain silent and I understand that my silence could not be used against me at trial.
☐ I give up my right to testify and present evidence at trial.
☐ I give up my right to use subpoenas to require witnesses to come to court and testify for me at trial.
☐ I give up my right to a jury trial, where all 12 jurors would have to agree that I am either guilty or not guilty.
☐ I give up my right to confront in court the people who testify against me and cross-examine them.
☐ I give up my right to make the State prove me guilty beyond a reasonable doubt.
I understand the rights that have been checked and give them up of my own free will.

Understandings
- I understand that the crime(s) to which I am pleading has/have elements that the State would have to prove beyond a reasonable doubt if I had a trial. These elements have been explained to me by my attorney or are as follows: ☐ See Attached sheet.
_____
_____

- I understand that the judge is not bound by any plea agreement or recommendations and may impose the maximum penalty. The maximum penalty I face upon conviction is: _____

- I understand that the judge must impose the mandatory minimum penalty. If any. The mandatory minimum penalty I face upon conviction is: _____

- I understand that the presumptive minimum penalty, if any. I face upon conviction is: _____
_____
The judge can impose a lesser sentence if the judge states appropriate reasons.

CR-277, 11/99 Plea Questionnaire/Waiver of Rights §971.08, Wisconsin Statutes.
This form shall not be modified. It may be supplemented with additional material.
Page 1 of 2

Figure 12.2 ■ A Typical Boykin Form

and then proceeds to summarize the evidence sufficient to prove each of the elements of the offense. The defendant then has the opportunity to offer any corrections or additions, but must allocute—provide a factual basis for the plea—to each charge; in other words, the defendant, in open court, must admit to the conduct central to the criminality of crimes charged unless permission has been granted for the defendant to enter an *Alford* plea (see below). In some jurisdictions, this Rule 11 hearing is therefore called an allocution hearing. This public disclosure allows defendants and attorneys to correct any misunderstandings.

Competency

Rule 11 does not specifically state that a court must ensure that a criminal defendant is competent to waive any constitutional rights. But the Supreme Court has held that because pleading guilty involves waiving the numerous rights discussed earlier, a court may not accept a guilty plea from a defendant who is not mentally competent (*Godinez v. Moran*, 1993).

When a defendant has competently waived the right to counsel and, therefore, is acting as his or her own attorney, the court need not inform the defendant that waiving counsel's assistance in deciding whether to plead guilty risks overlooking a viable defense and forgoes the opportunity to obtain an independent opinion on the wisdom of pleading guilty (*Iowa v. Tovar*, 2004). In other words, the defendant who acts as his own counsel proceeds at his own peril during plea bargaining and is stuck with the consequences of that decision.

No Contest and *Alford* Pleas

There are two types of pleas that do not require a defendant to allocute by giving a factual basis for the crimes to which they are pleading because these two pleas do not involve express admissions of guilt. Rather, they amount to consent to be convicted and punished.

The first such plea is a **no contest** plea, sometimes referred to as a plea of *nolo contendere*— Latin for "I will not contest it." A *nolo contendere* plea is not an express admission of guilt by a defendant. Rather, it serves "as a consent by the defendant that he may be punished as if he were guilty and a prayer for leniency" (*North Carolina v. Alford* 1970, p. 35 n.8). Although a plea of *nolo contendere* has the same results in criminal proceedings as a plea of guilty, it cannot be used in a subsequent civil proceeding as a defendant's admission of guilt. Thus, this plea is usually entered when civil proceedings and liabilities may result.

The second type of plea that does not technically require allocution is an *Alford* **plea**. This plea allows a defendant to plead guilty while claiming innocence. The name of this plea stems from the case of *North Carolina v. Alford* (1970), a capital murder case. The defendant protested

his innocence, but entered a plea of guilty anyway, saying, "I pleaded guilty on second-degree murder because they said there is too much evidence, but I ain't shot no man.... I just pleaded guilty because they said if I didn't they would gas me for it.... I'm not guilty but I pleaded guilty" (p. 29 n.2). The Supreme Court held that given the defendant's desire to avoid the death penalty and the existence of substantial evidence of guilt, the plea of guilty was valid.

The only difference between a *nolo* plea and an *Alford* plea is that the defendant does not maintain he or she is innocent in a *nolo* plea, whereas innocence is asserted in *Alford* pleas. Both, however, have the same effect. They speed up the clogged judicial process by allowing the defendant to "save face," at least superficially. But for all practical purposes, both *nolo* and *Alford* plea have the same effect as a conventional guilty plea and results in roughly the same punishment.

Judges have discretion in deciding whether to accept the defendant's plea of guilty, *nolo contendere,* or *Alford* plea. Some judges refuse to accept *nolo* or *Alford* pleas since they do not require the defendant to fully admit guilt. According to Superior Court Judge Martin McKeever of Connecticut, such pleas fly "in the face of what crime and punishment should be all about." Thus, he does not accept pleas "in cases where culpability is so obvious that the public has a right to know about it" (quoted in Steinberger, 1985). Moreover, such pleas rob "the victim of the opportunity to hear the defendant acknowledge and accept responsibility" for his or her crimes, a deprivation that can impair the psychological recovery of victims (Molesworth, 2008, p. 914).

Acceptance and Withdrawal of Pleas

Even in cases in which a defendant enters a traditional plea of guilt, judges still have the discretion to reject a plea agreement if they find it does not serve the interests of justice. But, as described earlier, most judges do not reject the plea agreements negotiated between prosecutors, defense attorneys, and defendants.

To ensure fairness in negotiations between defense and prosecution, the law now gives defendants a limited right to withdraw a guilty plea. In *Santobello v. New York* (1971), Chief Justice Warren

CASE CLOSE-UP

SANTOBELLO v. NEW YORK AND HONORING A PLEA AGREEMENT

Rudolph Santobello was indicted on two counts: promoting gambling in the first degree and possession of gambling records in the first degree, both felonies under New York law. After negotiations with the prosecutor's office in the Bronx, Santobello entered a plea to the lesser included offense of possession of gambling records in the second degree, and the prosecutor also agreed to make no recommendation as to the sentence. Santobello represented to the judge that the plea was voluntary and that the facts of the case, as described by the Assistant District Attorney, were true. The court accepted the plea and set a date for sentencing.

Months elapsed, though, before sentencing. A new defense attorney was hired, and he moved to suppress the evidence on grounds of an illegal search and seizure. The trial judge retired. Another assistant DA assumed control over the case (it is unclear whether his predecessor was promoted or resigned to take a job in private practice). Months later, when Santobello appeared for sentencing, the new prosecutor recommended the maximum 1-year sentence, thereby breaching the terms of the plea agreement. The new judge, unaware of the terms of plea agreement, quickly imposed this sentence, leaving no doubt of his thoughts about the defendant. Reading the probation report, he said: "I have here a history of a long, long serious criminal record. . . . He is unamenable to supervision in the community. He is a professional criminal." The judge concluded by regretting that a 1-year sentence was all he was allowed to impose.

Chief Justice Warren Burger was beginning his second term on the court. Despite being a product of the law-and-order movement, his decision begins by noting the sloppiness apparent in the DA's office. "This record represents another example of an unfortunate lapse in orderly prosecutorial procedures, in part, no doubt, because of the enormous increase

in the workload of the often understaffed prosecutor's office." But, most notably, he continues the theme of workload by coming out strongly in favor of guilty pleas:

> The disposition of criminal charges by agreement between the prosecutor and the accused, sometimes loosely called "plea bargaining," is an essential component of the administration of justice. Disposition of charges after plea discussions is not only an essential part of the process but a highly desirable part.

The Court therefore vacated Santobello's sentence and remanded the case for resentencing before a different judge.

The Burger Court decision in *Santobello* in essence brought plea bargaining out of the closet. This was the Court's first look at a state non–capital punishment plea. As for the specific issue, "When a plea rests in any significant degree on a promise or agreement of the prosecutor, so that it can be said to be part of the inducement or consideration, such promise must be fulfilled." The net effect was to suggest that state pleas proceed under Rule 11 of the Federal Rules of Criminal Procedure, which requires the parties to disclose in open court the nature of the plea agreement.

In hindsight, what is perhaps most notable is that a justice appointed by President Nixon as representative of his law-and-order philosophy readily embraced plea bargaining. Within just 2 years, Nixon's crime commission denounced the practice and called for the abolition of plea bargaining within 5 years—a call that was doomed to failure from the beginning. Indeed, in 2012, the Supreme Court formally recognized that since the overwhelming majority of criminal cases in the United States are disposed of by plea bargaining, the Sixth Amendment right to effective assistance of counsel applies during plea bargaining (*Lafler v. Cooper*, 2012; *Missouri v. Frye*, 2012).

Burger wrote, "When a plea rests in any significant degree on a promise or agreement of the prosecutor, so that it can be said to be a part of the inducement or consideration, such promise must be fulfilled" (p. 262; see the "Case Close-Up" feature on the next page). Subsequent decisions likewise held that defendants must live up to their end of the plea agreement (*Ricketts v. Adamson*, 1987).

Effective Assistance of Counsel during Plea Bargaining

Decades of seeming Supreme Court indifference to plea-bargaining practices ended with two significant 2012 decisions.

Galin Edward Frye's attorney never told him of plea-bargain offers from prosecutors on charges that he was driving with a revoked license. Frye later pleaded guilty and was sentenced to 3 years in prison. But prosecutors had offered Frye two options for plea bargains. Under the first option, Frye would plead guilty to a felony version of the driving on a revoked license charge (since he already had three misdemeanor convictions for doing so), but he would serve only 10 days of a 3-year jail sentence as so-called shock time (see Chapter 14), with the balance of the 3-year sentence suspended. The second offer was to reduce the charge to a misdemeanor and, if Frye pleaded guilty to it, to recommend a 90-day sentence. Frye's defense attorney, however, never communicated these offers to him. The Court reversed Frye's conviction, ruling that his lawyer failed to provide effective assistance of counsel as guaranteed by the Sixth Amendment (Chapter 7).

Writing for a 5-to-4 majority in *Missouri v. Frye* (2012, p. 1407), Justice Kennedy stressed "In today's criminal justice system . . . , the negotiation of a plea bargain, rather than the unfolding of a trial, is almost always the critical point for a defendant." Quoting from law reviews, he emphasized that "plea bargaining is not some adjunct to the criminal justice system; it *is* the criminal justice system" (p. 1407). The Court held that defense attorneys have a legal duty to communicate formal offers from the prosecution to accept a plea on terms and conditions that may be favorable to the accused.

In *Lafler v. Cooper* (2012), the Court held that the defendant had received ineffective assistance of counsel (Chapter 7) when his attorney recommended against accepting a plea agreement because the jury would not convict Lafler of murder (but it did). Lafler was therefore entitled to a hearing to determine whether there was a reasonable probability that "the outcome of the plea process would have been different with competent advice" (p. 1384).

In a sharply worded dissent, Justice Scalia wrote "the Court today opens a whole new field of constitutionalized criminal procedure: plea-bargaining law. The ordinary criminal process has become too long, too expensive, and unpredictable, in no small part as a consequence of an intricate federal Code of Criminal Procedure imposed on the States by this Court in pursuit of perfect justice" (*Lafler v. Cooper* 2012, p. 1392). The majority of the Court acknowledged that future litigation would examine some details of the process. Whether future litigation results in major changes in plea bargaining practices or some minor adjustments remains to be seen.

LAW IN CONTROVERSY: ABOLISHING PLEA BARGAINING

Chief Justice Burger's opinion in *Santobello* supports plea bargaining because it contributes to the efficiency of the criminal justice processes. But some people find justifying plea bargaining merely on the basis of expediency to be unconvincing. What of justice? some legitimately ask. (See "Courts, Controversy, & the Administration of Justice: Who Benefits from Plea Bargaining?")

Doubts about plea bargaining have resulted in attempts in some jurisdictions to abolish or reform the practice. Such efforts conform to one of the most controversial recommendations of the National Advisory Commission on Criminal Justice Standards and Goals (1973)—abolishing plea bargaining altogether. This recommendation was prompted by the commission's view that plea bargaining produces undue leniency. The main

COURTS, CONTROVERSY, & THE ADMINISTRATION of JUSTICE

WHO BENEFITS FROM PLEA BARGAINING?

Some people within the court system are concerned that plea bargaining reduces the courthouse to a place where guilt or innocence is negotiated in the same way as one might haggle over the price of copper jugs at a Turkish bazaar (Rubin, 1976). Primarily, though, opposition to plea bargaining reflects different ideological preferences. What is particularly interesting is that civil libertarians as well as spokespersons for law and order see plea bargaining as a danger, but often for different reasons.

Supporters of the values of the due process model are concerned that plea bargaining undercuts the protections afforded individuals, may lead to the conviction of innocent defendants, and produces few tangible benefits for defendants. This view is aptly expressed by the leading academic critic of plea bargaining, law professor Albert Alschuler: "Today's guilty plea system leads even able, conscientious, and highly motivated attorneys to make decisions that are not really in their clients' interests" (1975, p. 1180).

A prime concern of due process adherents is that a criminal court process geared to produce guilty pleas negates the fundamental protection of the adversary system—a public trial in which the defendant is presumed innocent—because plea bargaining discourages trials by imposing a penalty on those who may lose at trial. They therefore advocate abolishing bargaining and increasing the number of trials. However, such a position ignores the reality of criminal courts: In most cases, the participants do not substantially disagree over the facts. Moreover, civil libertarian critics look to the jury as the proper forum for separating guilt from innocence. Yet, experienced trial attorneys often

have grave doubts about such an approach. In the words of a Los Angeles public defender: "If you've got an exceptional case—one which is weak and there's a good chance that the defendant may be innocent—then you don't want to take it before a jury because you never know what they'll do" (Mather, 1974a, p. 202).

If advocates of due process are worried that plea bargaining jeopardizes the rights of the individual, the backers of the crime control model express the opposite concern. They believe that plea bargaining allows defendants to avoid conviction for crimes they actually committed, results in lenient sentences, and in general gives criminal wrongdoers the impression that the courts and the law are easily manipulated. In the words of the Pima County, Arizona, prosecutor, "Plea bargains send the wrong message. When criminal offenders are permitted to plead guilty to lesser charges with lesser penalties, the credibility of the entire system is corrupted" (LaWall, 2001).

It is not a difficult task to single out individual cases in which these law enforcement criticisms of plea bargaining have merit. But the argument obscures too much. In particular, it confuses cause with effect. A bargained agreement on reduced charges, for example, may be the product of initial overcharging, of evidence problems that surface later, or both. Moreover, such criticisms suggest that in plea bargaining, anything goes—the prosecutor and judge will make any deal to dispose of a case. In reality, each court uses a more or less consistent approach to what charge or count reductions are customary, plus a set of sentencing rules of thumb.

Many of the law enforcement criticisms of plea bargaining may be reduced to an overall displeasure with the leniency of the courts. Whether sentences are too harsh or too lenient should be a separate issue from the vehicle for reaching these sentencing dispositions.

What do you think? Does plea bargaining sacrifice the rights of the defendant, or do the guilty benefit?

---

weakness of the commission's recommendation to abolish plea bargaining is that it failed to recognize the importance of law in action. The commission seemed preoccupied with an idealized criminal

law that is clear and precise and that does not have to accommodate messy disagreements.

Faced with mounting public criticism and professional concern, prosecutors and judges in a number of American communities have altered traditional plea-bargaining practices. Claims that plea bargaining has been abolished or that major reforms have been instituted require critical analysis. As a result of a growing number of studies of such efforts, some important areas of interest can be highlighted.

Are the Changes Implemented?

In analyzing the impact of changes in plea-bargaining practices, a basic question is whether the changes were indeed implemented. Written policy changes do not always alter the behavior of court actors. For example, some efforts to reform plea bargaining met with resistance from defense attorneys and others. As a result, the programs did not have their intended impact and were later dropped (Covey, 2008; Nimmer & Krauthaus 1977). A similar pattern was observed in a northern California county. After the grand jury publicly criticized plea bargaining for undue leniency, the prosecutor responded by trying to eliminate plea bargaining. The defense attorneys then began to take more cases to trial. After the state lost 12 out of 16 jury verdicts, the prosecutor quietly returned to the old policies (Carter, 1974). Of course, not all efforts at reform are short-lived. In some jurisdictions, efforts at reforming plea bargaining have been successfully implemented (Covey, 2008; Heumann & Loftin, 1979; Nimmer & Krauthaus, 1977).

Is Discretion Eliminated or Just Moved Elsewhere?

Even when programs are successfully implemented, they may not have the impact intended. Discretion in the criminal justice system (see Chapter 5) has been likened to a hydraulic process. Efforts to control discretion at one stage typically result in its displacement to another part of the process. Thus, the result of "abolishing" or "reforming" plea bargaining is often that the activity simply moves elsewhere. Such a hydraulic process occurred in California after the voters approved Proposition 8 in 1982. One of the key provisions of this victim's bill of rights (see Chapter 9) prohibits plea bargaining for 25 of the most serious crimes. The ban applied only to

the major trial court, however. Proposition 8 did not abolish plea bargaining, but rather relocated it to the lower court, where the proportion of bargained cases increased (McCoy, 1984). Indeed, the overall level of plea bargaining increased. Far from helping the victims of crime, the acceleration of plea bargaining prevented both victims and defendants from understanding the reasons for convictions and sentences (McCoy, 1993).

Alaska provides another clear example. In that state, the attorney general forbade assistant prosecutors from engaging in plea bargaining or from making sentencing recommendations to the judge. Judges complained that their responsibilities increased dramatically, meaning they had very little opportunity to give sentencing thorough consideration (Rubenstein & White, 1979, p. 277). The hydraulic process seems to explain why a later reevaluation of Alaska's plea-bargaining ban found clear evidence of both evolution and decay in the policy. For example, charge bargaining had reemerged in most of the state (Carns & Kruse, 1992).

Do Offsetting Changes Occur?

Efforts to abolish or change plea-bargaining practices may produce offsetting changes. This was the conclusion of an excellent in-depth study of a Michigan county (Church, 1976). After a law-and-order antidrug campaign, the newly elected prosecuting attorney instituted a strict policy forbidding charge-reduction plea bargaining in drug-selling cases. One result was an increased demand for trials, although it was not as great as some judges feared. But at the same time, outright dismissals because of insufficient evidence increased. Moreover, a much greater percentage of defendants were sentenced as juveniles rather than adults so that they would not have a felony record. Most important, plea bargaining involving defense attorneys and judges continued in drug cases, and the assistant prosecutor's ability to control the disposition of the cases weakened.

Efforts to increase sentence severity by abolishing or constraining plea bargaining are not always successful. When the Coast Guard effectively eliminated plea bargains in special courts-martial, there was no increase in sentence severity (Call, England, & Talarico, 1983). In short, attempts to abolish plea bargaining often produce a number of offsetting changes because overall policies fail to consider the reasons for negotiations.

CONCLUSION

Most of the Supreme Court decisions highlighted in this book deal with serious crimes and punishments—quite often murder and the death penalty. Perhaps the Court decided to rule on *Santobello* because the underlying charge was a minor one. After all, establishing new rules for plea bargaining would prove less controversial if the crime was not a violent one. Nonetheless, it is still curious that Burger's opinion states so many negatives about *Santobello*, leaving little doubt that this small-time alleged member of one of New York's crime families was hardly a model citizen. As for Santobello the man, little else is known. In covering the case, the *New York Times*

discussed only the legal issues, not the local man whose name is now enshrined in a major Supreme Court pronouncement.

Plea bargaining vividly illustrates the difference between law on the books and law in action. The rules of criminal procedure, decisions of appellate courts, and theories of the adversary system suggest that the trial is the principal activity of the criminal courts. Instead, plea bargaining is the predominant activity. Bargaining is best understood not as a response to the press of cases but as an adaptation to the realities of the types of cases requiring court disposition. In most cases, little question about the defendant's legal guilt exists. A trial is a costly and sometimes risky method of establishing that guilt, and it cannot wrestle with the most pressing issue: what sentence to impose on the guilty. Finally, through plea bargaining, courthouse officials are able to individualize justice. In short, it is neither necessary nor desirable that every defendant have a trial.

Chapter Review

LO1 **1.** Distinguish between the three most common types of plea agreements.

The three most common types of plea agreements are charge bargaining, count bargaining, and sentence bargaining. In a charge bargain, the defendant pleads guilty to a less serious charge than the one originally specified. In a count bargain, the defendant pleads guilty to a few of the charges in the indictment or bill or information. In a sentence bargain, the defendant pleads guilty in anticipation of leniency in sentencing.

LO2 **2.** Discuss the three major factors influencing bargaining and discretion.

The three major factors influencing bargaining and discretion are the presumption of factual guilt, the costs and

risks of trial to all parties, and the question of what sentence to impose upon the guilty.

LO3 **3.** Recognize the importance of *Boykin v. Alabama*.

In *Boykin*, the Court held that a plea of guilty was more than an admission of guilt and also involved the waiver of important constitutional rights. As a result, a defendant must knowingly waive his or her constitutional rights before a plea of guilty is accepted.

LO4 **4.** List the major reason each of the members of the courtroom work group engages in plea bargaining.

Prosecutors engage in plea bargaining because they want to gain convictions, defense attorneys seek leniency for their

clients, and judges feel pressures to move cases.

LO5 **5.** Indicate why a few cases go to trial but most defendants plead guilty.

Defendants and their lawyers will opt for a trial if they think the case factually presents a reasonable doubt or if the prison sentence will be high.

LO6 **6.** Explain why adherents of the crime control model of criminal justice oppose plea

bargaining for different reasons from those of adherents of the due process model of criminal justice.

Adherents of the crime control model of criminal justice oppose plea bargaining because they believe defendants get off too lightly. On the other hand, adherents of the due process model of criminal justice oppose plea bargaining because they believe that innocent defendants might be forced to plead guilty to a crime they did not commit.

Critical Thinking Questions

1. Should a defendant be allowed to plead guilty without fully admitting guilt? Would you limit *Alford* pleas to situations in which the defendant wishes to avoid the death penalty? Would you allow white-collar defendants to enter *Alford* pleas? Some federal judges will not, because they perceive that high-ranking corporate officials want to end the criminal cases without accepting full responsibility for their actions.

2. What types of plea agreements were involved in *Santobello*—charge, count, or sentence? Was the nature of the agreement implicit or explicit? How would you characterize the working relationship between the defense and the prosecution in *Santobello*?

3. Do defendants benefit from plea bargaining in terms of lower sentences, or is plea bargaining largely a shell game in which defendants are manipulated to think they are getting a good deal?

Key Terms

Alford plea   322

allocute/allocution hearing   321

Boykin form   320

charge bargaining   309

count bargaining   310

nolo contendere/no contest   322

plea bargaining   309

plea on the nose   311

sentence bargaining   311

Web Resources

Go to the *America's Courts and the Criminal Justice System* companion website at

http://www.cengage.com/criminaljustice/neubauer,

where you will find more resources to help you study.

Resources include web exercises, quizzing, and flash cards.

For Further Reading

Brown, Mary, and Stevan E. Bunnell. "Negotiating Justice: Prosecutorial Perspectives on Federal Plea Bargaining in the District of Columbia." *American Criminal Law Review* 43: 1063–1094, 2006.

Fisher, George. *Plea Bargaining's Triumph: A History of Plea Bargaining in America.* Stanford, CA: Stanford University Press, 2003.

McCoy, Candace. *Politics and Plea Bargaining: Victim's Rights in California.* Philadelphia: University of Pennsylvania Press, 1993.

Nardulli, Peter, James Eisenstein, and Roy Flemming. *The Tenor of Justice: Criminal Courts and the Guilty Plea Process.* Champaign: University of Illinois Press, 1988.

Nasheri, Hedieh. *Betrayal of Due Process: A Comparative Assessment of Plea Bargaining in the United States and Canada.* Lanham, MD: University Press of America, 1998.

Rauxloh, Regina. "Plea Bargaining—A Necessary Tool for the International Criminal Court Prosecutor." *Judicature* 94: 178–185. 2011.

Vogel, Mary. *Coercion to Compromise: Plea Bargaining, the Courts, and the Making of Political Authority.* New York: Oxford University Press, 2006.

Wright, Ronald, and Marc Miller. "The Screening/Bargaining Tradeoff." *Stanford Law Review* 55: 29–118, 2002.

13 Trials and Juries

Frank Polich/Getty Images

Former Illinois Governor **Rod Blagojevich** was accused of numerous corruption charges, including trying to auction the U.S. Senate seat that opened when Barak Obama became president. After a summer-long trial, the jury deadlocked on all but one count, causing the case to end in a mistrial. Jurors later complained that the wide-ranging charges of racketeering had been too complicated. On retrial, federal prosecutors significantly revamped the way in which they presented their case. Jurors deliberated for 10 days before convicting Blagojevich on 17 of 20 criminal counts, including fraud, extortion, and bribery. The different result in the second trial illustrates the importance of trial strategy. ■

HISTORY OF TRIAL BY JURY
English Roots
Colonial Developments

LAW ON THE BOOKS: THE CONSTITUTION AND TRIAL BY JURY
Jury Size
Unanimity

LAW ON THE BOOKS: SELECTING A FAIR AND UNBIASED JURY
Master Jury List
Summoning the Venire
Venire Eligibility
Voir Dire
Serving on a Jury

CASE CLOSE-UP: *People v. Garcia* Should *Batson* Extend to Sexual Orientation?

LAW IN ACTION: CHOOSING A JURY BIASED IN YOUR FAVOR
Educating Jurors
Jury Consultants

PRESUMPTIONS AND THE BURDEN OF PROOF
Starting Presumptions
Burdens of Proof

OVERVIEW OF BASIC EVIDENCE
Differentiating Direct and Circumstantial Evidence
Types of Evidence
Basic Rules of Evidence

SPECIAL RULES OF EVIDENCE GOVERNING EXPERT WITNESSES
Determining Reliability

FORENSIC SCIENTIFIC EVIDENCE IN THE AGE OF *DAUBERT*
The CSI Effect

OBJECTIONS TO THE ADMISSION OF EVIDENCE

Courts, Law, & Media
CSI: Crime Scene Investigation

Challenging Forensic Evidence

Courts, Controversy, & the Administration of Justice
Should Fingerprint Evidence Be Admissible?

STEPS IN THE TRIAL PROCESS
Opening Statements
Prosecution's Case-in-Chief
Defense's Case-in-Chief
Rebuttal
Closing Arguments
Jury Instructions
Jury Deliberations
The Verdict
Postverdict Motions

LAW IN ACTION: TRIALS AS BALANCING WHEELS
Popular Standards of Justice
Uncertainty

PREJUDICIAL PRETRIAL PUBLICITY
Limited Gag Orders
Change of Venue
Sequestering the Jury

MEDIA IN THE COURTROOM
Changing Views on Cameras in the Courtroom
Current Broadcasting Rules
Technology beyond "Cameras"

Trials and Juries • Trials and Juries • Trials and Juries •
Juries • Trials and Juries • Trials and Juries • Trials and

Learning Objectives

After reading this chapter, you should be able to:

LO1 Trace the history of trials by jury.

LO2 Analyze the scope of the right to a trial by jury in a criminal case.

LO3 Evaluate the impact of differences in jury size and unanimity requirements.

LO4 Explain how a jury is summoned and selected, including the constitutional limitations on these processes.

LO5 Discuss the function of jury consultants in the process of scientific jury selection.

LO6 Distinguish between the presumptions that apply at the start of trials and the burdens of proof applicable to overcoming them.

LO7 Summarize the basic rules of evidence concerning trustworthiness and relevance of evidence.

LO8 Analyze how special limitations on expert witnesses affect the litigation of criminal cases, especially with regard to leading types of forensic evidence.

LO9 Identify the steps in a criminal trial.

LO10 Describe the effects and implications of pretrial publicity and the solutions that courts use to prevent those effects from influencing a criminal trial.

Michael Jackson died in June 2009 of a lethal combination of various sedatives and the clinical anesthetic propofol. Dr. Conrad Murray, Jackson's personal physician, was convicted of involuntary manslaughter for Jackson's death in November 2011. According to testimony at the trial, Murray had been providing the drug to Jackson to help him sleep nearly every night for the past 2 months of his life, even though it is normally used in hospitals to provide anesthesia to patients during surgery.

Trials attract more attention than any other step of the judicial process. The national media provide detailed accounts of the trials of Conrad Murray, Rod Blagojevich, and Casey Anthony (Chapter 1). Local media typically offer extensive coverage of the trials of local notables, brazen murderers, and the like. The media use courtroom encounters to entertain. The importance of trials, however, extends far beyond the considerable public attention lavished on them. They are central to the entire scheme of Anglo-American law. Trials provide the ultimate forum for vindicating the innocence of the accused or the liability of the defendant. For this reason, the right to be tried by a jury of one's peers is guaranteed in several places in the Constitution.

es • Trial and Juries • Trial and Juries • Trial and Juries • Trial and Juries • Trial and Ju
and Juries • Trial and Juries • Trial and Juries • Trial and Juries • Tri

Given the marked public interest in trials, as well as their centrality to American law, we would expect trials to be the prime ingredient in the criminal court process. They are not. Trials are relatively rare events. As Chapter 12 established, upwards of 95 percent of all felony convictions result from guilty pleas. In a fundamental sense, then, a trial represents a deviant case. But at the same time, the few cases that are tried have a major impact on the operations of the entire criminal justice system. Trials are the balance wheel of the process, determining how members of the courtroom work group bargain cases.

HISTORY OF TRIAL BY JURY

The primary purpose of the jury is to prevent oppression by the government and provide the accused a "safeguard against the corrupt or over-zealous prosecutor and against the compliant, biased, or eccentric judge" (*Williams v. Florida*, 1970). Ideally, juries are made up of fair-minded citizens who represent a cross section of the local community. Once selected, their role is to judge the facts of the case. During trial, the judge rules on questions of law, but the jury decides the weight of the evidence and the credibility to give to the testimony of witnesses.

Trial juries are also called **petit juries**, to differentiate them from grand juries. The jury system represents a commitment to the role of laypeople in the administration of justice. The views and actions of judges and lawyers are constrained by a group of average citizens who are amateurs in the ways of the law (Jonakait, 2006; Kalven & Zeisel, 1966).

English Roots

The trial by jury has roots deep in Western history. Used in Athens five or six centuries B.C.E., juries were later used by the Romans. They reappeared in France during the 9th century and were transferred to England from there. The concept of the jury functioning as an impartial fact-finding body was first formalized in the Magna Carta of 1215, when English noblemen forced the king to recognize limits on the power of the Crown:

No Freeman shall be taken or imprisoned, or be disseized of his Freehold, or Liberties, or free Customs, or be outlawed, or exiled or otherwise destroyed, nor will we pass upon him nor condemn him but by lawful judgment of his peers or by Law of the Land.

This protection applied only to nobility ("Freeman"). Its extension to the average citizen occurred several centuries later. Thus, in the centuries after the Magna Carta, the legal status of the jury continued to evolve. Early English juries often functioned more like modern-day grand juries. Only later did they become impartial bodies, selected from citizens who knew nothing of the alleged event.

Colonial Developments

By the time the U.S. Constitution was written, jury trials in criminal cases had been in existence in England for several centuries. This legal principle was transferred to the American colonies and later written into the Constitution. The pivotal role that the right to trial by jury plays in American law is underscored by the number of times it is mentioned in the Constitution.

Article III, Section 2, provides that "the trial of all crimes, except cases of impeachment shall be by jury and such trial shall be held in the state where the said crimes shall have been committed." This section not only guarantees the right to a trial by jury to persons accused by the national government of a crime but also specifies that such trials shall be held near the place of the offense. This prevents the government from harassing defendants by trying them far from home.

The Sixth Amendment guarantees that "in all criminal prosecutions, the accused shall enjoy the right to a speedy and public trial, by an impartial jury." The requirement of a public trial prohibits secret trials, a device commonly used by dictators to silence their opponents.

The Seventh Amendment provides: "In suits at common law . . . the right to trial by jury shall be preserved." This provision is a historical testament to the fact that the framers of the Constitution greatly distrusted the judges of the day.

LAW ON THE BOOKS: THE CONSTITUTION AND TRIAL BY JURY

Throughout most of our nation's history, the three broad constitutional provisions dealing with trial by jury had little applicability in state courts. The U.S. Constitution applied only to trials in federal courts. These practices changed dramatically, however, when the Supreme Court decided *Duncan v.* *Louisiana* (1968), ruling that the jury provisions of the Sixth Amendment were incorporated by the Due Process Clause of the Fourteenth Amendment to apply to state courts, as well. Subsequent decisions grappled with the problem of defining the precise meaning of the right to trial by jury. The most important issues concerned the scope of the right to a jury trial, the size of the jury, and unanimous versus nonunanimous verdicts. The important case law defining the scope of the right to a trial by jury is presented in the "Key Developments" feature below.

KEY DEVELOPMENTS CONCERNING THE RIGHT TO TRIAL BY JURY AFTER THE ADOPTION OF THE BILL OF RIGHTS

Griffin v. California (1965)	The privilege against self-incrimination prohibits the prosecutor from commenting on the defendant's failure to testify during trial.
Sheppard v. Maxwell (1966)	A criminal defendant's Sixth Amendment right to a fair trial is violated when prejudicial pretrial publicity unfairly taints the trial process.
Duncan v. Louisiana (1968)	The due process clause of the Fourteenth Amendment incorporates the Sixth Amendment's right to a jury trial.
Baldwin v. New York (1970)	Defendants accused of petty offenses do not have the right to a trial by jury. In this context, "no offense can be deemed 'petty' for the purposes of the right to trial by jury where imprisonment for more than six months is authorized" (*Baldwin v. New York*, 1970, p. 69). Some state constitutions, however, guarantee a jury trial to anyone facing any criminal charge whatsoever, including traffic offenses.
Williams v. Florida (1970)	State juries are not required by the U.S. Constitution to consist of 12 members.
McKeiver v. Pennsylvania (1971)	Youths prosecuted as juvenile offenders have no right to have their cases heard by a jury.
Johnson v. Louisiana (1972)	Federal criminal juries must be unanimous.
Apodaca v. Oregon (1972)	The U.S. Constitution does not require state juries to reach unanimous verdicts.
Taylor v. Louisiana (1975)	Women cannot be excluded from juries.
Ballew v. Georgia (1978)	Six is the minimum number for a jury.
Burch v. Louisiana (1979)	Six-member criminal juries must be unanimous.
Duren v. Missouri (1979)	Although neither the venire nor the actual petit jury must be "a perfect mirror of the community or accurately reflected the proportionate strength of every identifiable group," the master jury lists from which a venire is summoned must reflect a representative and impartial cross section of the community.
Chandler v. Florida (1981)	The right to a fair trial is not violated by electronic media and still photographic coverage of public judicial proceedings.

© Cengage Learning

Continued on next page

Continued from previous page

Batson v. Kentucky (1986)	The Equal Protection Clause of the Fourteenth Amendment prohibits prosecutors from exercising peremptory challenges in a racially discriminatory manner.
Powers v. Ohio (1991)	A criminal defendant may object to race-based exclusions of jurors through peremptory challenges whether or not the defendant and the excluded jurors share the same race.
Georgia v. McCollum (1992)	As with prosecutors in *Batson,* the Equal Protection Clause of the Fourteenth Amendment also prohibits the defense from exercising peremptory challenges in a racially discriminatory manner.
Daubert v. Merrell Dow Pharmaceuticals (1993)	The trial judge must ensure that any and all scientific evidence is not only relevant, but also reliable.
J.E.B. Petitioner v. Alabama (1994)	Lawyers may not exclude potential jurors from a trial because of their sex.
Victor v. Nebraska (1994)	"A reasonable doubt is an actual and substantial doubt arising from the evidence, from the facts or circumstances shown by the evidence, or from the lack of evidence on the part of the state, as distinguished from a doubt arising from mere possibility, from bare imagination, or from fanciful conjecture."
Kumho Tire v. Carmichael (1999)	*Daubert* standards for scientific testimony apply to nonscientific expert testimony as well.
Portuondo v. Agard (2000)	Prosecutors can tell jurors that the defendant's presence during trial helps them tailor their testimony to fit the evidence.
Snyder v. Louisiana (2008)	Murder conviction in a death penalty case was overturned because the judge sat idly by as prosecutors dismissed all the Blacks in the jury pool.

When there is no right to a jury trial (for example, in most traffic and petty offense cases), a **bench trial** takes place in which a judge serves as both the trier-of-law (as always) and trier-of-fact determining guilt. But bench trials are not limited to cases in which no right to a trial by jury exists. Sometimes, the parties waive the right to a trial by jury and opt for a bench trial instead. For example, a judge might appreciate subtle legal distinctions in a complicated case that a jury may neglect. Other times, either pretrial publicity or the facts of a case might motivate the parties to seek a bench trial. This is especially true in criminal cases in which the defendant has a long criminal history or is accused of a particularly heinous crime since "it may be difficult to empanel a fair and impartial jury" (Peterson, 2011, p. 458). State laws vary considerably on when the prosecution and/or defense may waive a trial by jury in criminal cases.

Jury Size

During the 14th century, the size of English juries became fixed at 12. Although some colonies experimented with smaller juries in less-important trials, the number 12 was universally accepted by the time of the American Revolution. However, in *Williams v. Florida* (1970, p. 102), the Supreme Court declared that the number 12 was a "historical accident, unnecessary to effect the purposes of the jury system and wholly without significance except to mystics," and therefore not required by the U.S. Constitution. The Court concluded that the six-person jury used in Florida in noncapital cases was large enough to promote group deliberations and to provide a fair possibility of obtaining a representative cross section of the community. Attempts to use juries with fewer than six members were struck down by *Ballew v. Georgia* (1978). The defendant's misdemeanor conviction by a five-member jury was reversed because

LAW ON THE BOOKS VS. LAW IN ACTION
GOING TO TRIAL

	LAW ON THE BOOKS	LAW IN ACTION
Trial	The adversarial process of deciding a case through the presentation of evidence and arguments about the evidence.	Only a handful of felonies and even fewer misdemeanors are decided by trial.
Bench trial	Trial before a judge without a jury.	Defense prefers when the issues are either highly technical or very emotional.
Jury trial	A group of average citizens selected by law and sworn in to look at certain facts and determine the truth.	Introduces public standards of justice into the decision-making process.

© Cengage Learning

"the purpose and functioning of the jury in a criminal trial is seriously impaired, and to a constitutional degree, by a reduction in size to below six members."

As Table 13.1 illustrates, many states have specifically authorized juries of fewer than 12 jurors, but most allow these smaller juries only in misdemeanor cases. In federal courts, defendants are entitled to a 12-person jury unless the parties agree in writing to a smaller jury, but 6-member juries in federal civil cases are quite common.

TABLE 13.1 ▪ STATE PROVISIONS ON THE SIZE OF CRIMINAL JURIES

12-member juries required in felony cases	Alabama, Arkansas,^{a} California, Colorado, Delaware, District of Columbia, Georgia, Hawaii, Idaho, Illinois, Iowa, Kansas, Kentucky, Maine, Michigan, Minnesota, Mississippi, Missouri, Montana, Nebraska, Nevada, New Hampshire, New Jersey,^{a} New Mexico, New York, North Carolina, North Dakota, Ohio, Oklahoma, Oregon, Puerto Rico, Rhode Island, South Carolina, South Dakota, Tennessee, Texas, Vermont, Virginia, West Virginia, Wisconsin, Wyoming
12-member juries required in misdemeanor cases	Alabama, Arkansas,^{a} California,^{a} Delaware, District of Columbia, Hawaii,^{a} Illinois, Maine, New Jersey,^{a} Pennsylvania, Puerto Rico, Rhode Island, South Dakota, Tennessee, Vermont
Juries of fewer than 12 authorized for felony cases	Arizona, Connecticut,^{b} Florida,^{c} Indiana, Louisiana,^{c} Massachusetts, Missouri, North Carolina, Pennsylvania,^{a} Utah,^{c} Washington^a
Juries fewer than 12 authorized for misdemeanor cases	Alaska, Arizona, Colorado, Florida, Georgia, Idaho, Indiana, Iowa, Kansas, Kentucky, Louisiana, Massachusetts, Michigan, Minnesota, Mississippi, Montana, Nebraska, Nevada, New Hampshire, New Mexico, New York, North Dakota, Ohio, Oklahoma, Utah, Oregon, Pennsylvania,^{a} South Carolina, Texas, Virginia, Washington, West Virginia, Wisconsin, Wyoming

^{a}The parties may stipulate to a jury that consists of fewer than 12 jurors.

^{b}12-person juries are used in death penalty cases unless the defendant elects to use a smaller jury.

^{c}12-person juries must be used in death-penalty cases.

SOURCE: Adapted from David B. Rottman and Shauna M. Strickland. 2006. *State Court Organization, 2004* (Table 42). Washington, DC: Bureau of Justice Statistics. Available online at http://bjs.ojp.usdoj.gov/content/pub/pdf/sco04.pdf

There has been a good deal of debate over whether small juries provide the defendant with a fair trial (Landsman, 2005; McCord, 2005; Saks, 1996). The debate stems from the fact that social science has produced inconsistent findings on the differences in the conduct of deliberations between 6- and 12-person juries. Some studies have found very few differences (Pabst, 1973; Roper, 1979), while others have reported significant differences (Hastie, Penrod, & Pennington, 1983; Saks & Marti, 1997). In a review of the empirical literature on juries, Smith and Saks (2008) reported that:

- racial, ethnic, religious, and sexual minorities are represented in a smaller percentage of 6-person as compared to 12-person juries

- larger juries deliberate longer than smaller juries

- talking time is more evenly divided among members of smaller juries, allowing for less domination by a strong voice or two as compared with larger juries

- members of larger juries more accurately recall evidence both during deliberation and in individual recall afterward

- 12-person juries recall more probative information and rely on evaluative statements and nonprobative evidence less than 6-person juries

- in the civil context, 6-person juries show more variability in their awards and, on average, give larger awards than 12-person juries

- jurors report more satisfaction in the deliberation process with 12-person juries than with smaller ones

In light of these findings, it is not surprising to learn that hung juries—juries unable to reach a unanimous verdict—occur more frequently with 12-person juries than with 6-person juries (Hannaford-Agor, Hans, Mott, & Munsterman, 2002; Kalven & Zeisel, 1966). However, many other factors affect whether a jury hangs: "weak evidence; police credibility problems … ; juror concerns about fairness; case complexity; and a dysfunctional deliberation process—a catchall phrase indicating poor interpersonal interactions among the jurors" (Hannaford-Agor et al., 2002, p. 85). Yet, the quest to reduce hung juries has resulted in some jurisdictions authorizing a controversial change in the way

juries have historically functioned: nonunanimous verdicts.

Unanimity

The requirement that a jury reach a unanimous decision became a firm rule in England during the 14th century. An agreement by all of the jurors seemed to legitimize the verdict, giving the community a sense that the conclusion must be correct. However, the Supreme Court altered this assumption in a pair of 1972 decisions. It held that verdicts in federal criminal trials must be unanimous, but it affirmed state courts' findings of guilty by votes of 9 to 3 and 10 to 2 (*Johnson v. Louisiana*, 1972; *Apodaca v. Oregon*, 1972). Most state constitutions specifically require unanimous verdicts in criminal trials; only five states (Louisiana, Montana, Oregon, Oklahoma, and Texas) permit nonunanimous criminal verdicts. Of these, only Louisiana and Oregon permit nonunanimous verdicts in serious felony cases. In any case, six-member juries must be unanimous (*Burch v. Louisiana*, 1979).

Opponents of nonunanimous verdicts argue that the Supreme Court misread the history of the jury, with the result that a basic constitutional right is being sacrificed. They point out that proof beyond a reasonable doubt has not been shown if only some of the jurors vote to convict. These concerns receive some empirical support (Zeisel, 1982). A carefully controlled experiment compared unanimous with nonunanimous juries and found that nonunanimous juries tend to be hung less often, deliberate less thoroughly, and result in less-satisfied jurors (Hastie, Penrod, & Pennington, 1984; see also, Smith & Saks, 2008). These findings may be explained by the fact that the deliberation process appears to differ significantly depending on whether a unanimous or majority verdict is permitted.

When juries were not required to be unanimous, they tended to be more verdict driven. That is, they were more likely to take the first formal ballot during the first 10 minutes of deliberation and to vote often until they produced a verdict. In contrast, juries that heard the same case but were required to reach a unanimous verdict tended to delay their first vote and discuss the evidence more thoroughly. These evidence-driven juries rated their deliberations as more serious and thorough. (Diamond, Rose, & Murphy 2006).

LAW ON THE BOOKS: SELECTING A FAIR AND UNBIASED JURY

Before the first word of testimony, trials pass through the critical stage of jury selection. Many lawyers believe that trials are won or lost on the basis of which jurors are selected. Juries are chosen in a process that combines random selection with deliberate choice.

Jury selection occurs in three stages: compiling a master list, summoning the *venire*, and conducting *voir dire.* The "Law on the Books vs. Law in Action" feature below compares perspectives on these jury selection steps. Whether these processes actually produce fair and impartial juries has been the subject of much concern.

Master Jury List

Juries are supposed to be made up of fair-minded laypeople, representatives of the community in which the defendant allegedly committed the crime. Therefore, the first step in jury selection is the development of procedures that will produce a representative cross section of the community. These sentiments are reflected in the Federal Jury Selection and Service Act of 1968, which was designed to ensure that "no citizen shall be excluded from service as a grand or petit juror in the district courts of the United States on account of race, color, religion, sex, national origin, or economic status." This act was prompted by evidence that selection of federal juries was systematically biased. Similar concerns have been expressed about jury selection at the state level (Fukurai, Butler, & Krooth, 1991; Re, 2007).

The first step in jury selection is the compilation of a **master jury list**. Voter registration lists are the most frequently used source for assembling this list (sometimes called a *"jury wheel"* or *"master wheel"*). Voter lists have major advantages: They are readily available, frequently updated, and collected in districts within judicial boundaries. However, basing the master jury list on voter registration tends to exclude the poor, the young, racial minorities, and the less educated (Kairys,

LAW ON THE BOOKS VS. LAW IN ACTION
JURY SELECTION

	LAW ON THE BOOKS	LAW IN ACTION
Jury selection	Process of selecting a fair and impartial jury.	Each side seeks to select jurors who are biased in its favor.
Master jury list	Potential jurors are selected by chance from a list of potential jurors. The list should reflect a representative cross section of the community.	Selecting only from registered voters means that the poor, the young, and minorities are less likely to be called.
Venire	A group of citizens from which jury members are chosen (jury pool).	Judges vary in their willingness to excuse potential jurors because of hardship.
Voir dire	The process by which prospective jurors are questioned to determine whether there is cause to excuse them from the jury.	Lawyers use questioning to predispose jurors in their favor.
Peremptory challenge	Each side may exclude a set number of jurors without stating a reason.	Both sides use peremptory challenges to select a jury favorable to their side.
Challenge for cause	A judge may dismiss a potential juror if the person cannot be fair and objective.	Rarely granted.

Kadane, & Lehorsky, 1977; Re, 2007). Because of these limitations, many jurisdictions use other sources—telephone directories, utility customer lists, or driver's license lists—in drawing up the master list. The use of multiple sources achieves a better cross section of the community on jury panels, although it sometimes creates problems for jury administrators, who have to deal with a high number of duplicates when multiple sources are merged (Randall & Woods, 2008).

Jury panels can be challenged if master jury lists from which the venire was called fail to include racial or other minorities. The Supreme Court has ruled that master jury lists must reflect a representative and impartial cross section of the community (*Duren v. Missouri*, 1979). This does not mean, however, that either the venire or the actual petit jury must be "a perfect mirror of the community or accurately [reflect] the proportionate strength of every identifiable group" (*Swain v. Alabama* 1965, p. 208). Rather, the requirement of a representative cross section of the community applies only to jury pools (*Holland v. Illinois*, 1990).

Summoning the Venire

The second step in jury selection is the drawing of the **venire** (or jury pool). Periodically, the clerk of court or jury commissioner determines how many jurors are needed for a given time. A sufficient number of names is then randomly selected from the master jury list and a **summons** is issued—a court order commanding these citizens to appear at the courthouse for jury duty. Even though people who fail to obey a jury summons can be fined or imprisoned, estimates place the nonresponse rate to jury summonses between 9 percent in some jurisdictions to as high as 66 percent in others (Randall & Woods, 2008; Schwartz, Behrens, & Silverman, 2003). Failing to respond to a jury summons, however, is most unwise, since it can result in a warrant being issued for the scofflaw's arrest; punishments range from fines to jail sentences for contempt of court.

Venire Eligibility

Not all those summoned will actually serve on the venire. Virtually all states have laws that require jurors to be citizens of the United States, residents of the locality, of a certain minimum age, and able to understand English. Most states also disqualify people who, as a result of mental illness, are not competent to adjudicate a case. Thirty-one states also disqualify convicted felons, although that practice has been increasingly criticized as a type of disenfranchisement that disproportionately affects racial and ethnic minorities (Binnall, 2008; Kalt, 2003; Wheelock, 2005). Persons who fail to meet these requirements are eliminated from the venire.

Others will be excused because of **statutory exemptions**. The identities of those exempted from jury duty by statute vary greatly. Historically, those statutorily excluded included government officials (especially police, firefighters, and political officeholders); medical personnel (including paramedics, physicians, nurses, and others); ministers/clergy; educators; lawyers; and full-time students. Today, however, jurisdictions have increasingly been eliminating statutory exemptions.

As Table 13.2 illustrates, all but three states statutorily exempt citizens with previous jury service within a prescribed period of time—usually within the past 12 to 24 months—of being summoned again. And more than half the states allow senior citizens over the age of 65, 70, or 75 to exempt themselves from jury service. Most other statutory exemptions, however, have been eliminated in more than two-thirds of the states.

The people who show up when summoned to court and are eligible to serve on a jury usually check in with a jury administrator (or other clerk of the court staff person) who then directs them to a specific courtroom. The petit jury for a particular trial will be selected from this pool of people. The people in this jury pool, however, may be excused from serving on a jury if they convince the judge that jury duty would entail an undue hardship. People try to get excused quite frequently. As van Dyke observed in 1977, although serving on a jury is "a right and privilege of citizenship, most people consider it a nuisance" and request to be excused (p. 111). The sentiment persists today (Losh & Boatright 2002; Sinclair, Behrens, & Silverman, 2003).

Voir Dire

The final step in jury selection is the **voir dire** (French legal term for "to speak the truth"), which involves the preliminary examination of a prospective juror

TABLE 13.2 ■ CATEGORIES AND FREQUENCY OF STATUTORY EXEMPTIONS FROM JURY SERVICE

Exemption	Number of States
Previous jury service	47
Age (ranging from minimum of 65 to 75)	27
Political officeholder	16
Law enforcement and emergency services personnel	12
Other (most frequently clergy and teachers)	12
Judicial officers	9
Health care professionals	7
Sole caregivers of young children or incompetent adults	7
Licensed attorneys	6
Active military	5

"The median number of statutory exemption categories was three per state. Louisiana is the only state that has no exemptions whatsoever. Twelve states and the District of Columbia provide exemptions only for previous jury service. Florida provides exemptions in nine of the ten categories, the most of any state." (p. 15)

SOURCE: Gregory E. Mize, Paula Hannaford-Agor, & Nicole L. Waters. *The State-of-the-States Survey of Jury Improvement Efforts: A Compendium Report* (Table 10). Williamsburg, VA: National Center for State Courts, 2007. Reprinted by permission.

in order to determine his or her qualifications to serve as a juror. In addition to prospective jurors' names (88.3%) and addresses (sometimes only ZIP codes), most courts "obtain preliminary voir dire information from prospective jurors, such as marital status (64%), occupation (72%), [and the] number and ages of minor children (52%). . . (Mize et al., 2007, p. 26).

The prospective jurors are questioned by the attorneys, the judge, or both about their backgrounds, familiarity with persons involved in the case (defendant, witness, or lawyer), attitudes about certain facts that may arise during trial, and any other matters that may reflect on their willingness and ability to judge the case fairly and impartially. In most cases, questions are posed to the venire as a group, usually with instructions to answer by raising their hands. There are then follow-up questions to individual members of the venire. Prospective jurors are often permitted to respond to sensitive voir dire questions either by written questionnaire or "in the relative privacy of a sidebar conference or in the judge's chambers" (Mize et al., 2007, p. 29).

In high-profile cases, extensive jury questionnaires may be used in an effort to screen out potential biases held by the venire—especially if jury consultants are used (see below). For example, in the trial of Dr. Conrad Murray for the involuntary manslaughter of Michael Jackson, 145 venirepersons completed a 32-page questionnaire about their backgrounds, job history, and, perhaps most critically, their views of Jackson and their exposure to the media coverage of his 2009 overdose.

The Accuracy of Voir Dire

For hundreds of years, the law has considered voir dire to be an inexpensive and efficient way to select a fair and impartial jury. The process, however, may not be a particularly accurate way to detect bias. Although the venire is sworn under oath to answer truthfully, they do not always do so. Sometimes potential jurors refuse to admit to facts or thoughts they find embarrassing to share, such as prior criminal victimization (Hannaford, 2001).

Other reasons may be less personal, but still not be something that potential jurors want to admit in court under oath, such as a predisposition to believe the accused is guilty. Even when venirepersons are not deliberately concealing information, they may unconsciously conceal personal biases or prejudices during voir dire in an attempt to please the court and the attorneys by being "good" jurors (Borgida & Fiske, 2008).

Excusing Jurors through Voir Dire

If a potential juror's responses during questioning (whether honest or not) suggest that the person cannot fairly judge the case, the juror may be challenged for cause by either the defense or the prosecution. Both sides have an unlimited number of **challenges for cause.** The presiding judge rules on the challenge and, if it is sustained, the juror is excused. Strikes for cause generally fall into one of two categories: principal challenges and fact-partial challenges. *Principal challenges* involve strikes of potential jurors because they have some relationship to one of the "principals" or participants in the case. They are presumed to be partial on account of this relationship. *Fact-partial challenges* involve strikes of potential jurors because the subject matter of the dispute presents issues on which the potential juror is biased, prejudiced, or predisposed to a particular outcome because of their belief system or experiences.

Peremptory challenges are the second method used by the prosecution and the defense in influencing who will sit on the jury. Each side has a limited number of peremptory challenges that can be used to exclude a juror. Originally, these challenges were designed and used for a curative purpose—to correct the mistake of a judge for failing to strike a juror for cause. While they are still used in that manner today, they are primarily used to exclude people that the lawyers believe will be hostile to their side of the case. In other words, based on hunches, prejudice, knowledge of psychology, or pseudoscience, attorneys use peremptory strikes—without having to give a reason—to eliminate the jurors they feel might not vote for their side.

Attorneys traditionally enjoyed unrestricted freedom to exercise peremptory challenges. But in *Batson v. Kentucky* (1986), the Supreme Court restricted the ability of prosecutors who used peremptory challenges to keep African-Americans off the jury in any case involving an African-American defendant. If a prosecutor uses peremptory challenges to exclude potential jurors solely on account of their race, the prosecutor must explain his or her actions and may be ordered to change tactics. And in a move backed by prosecutors, the Court held that the defense is also prohibited from excluding jurors based on race (*Georgia v. McCollum*, 1992). Most recently, the Supreme Court has ordered new trials for several death row inmates because of racial bias during jury selection (*Miller-El v. Dretke*, 2005; *Johnson v. California*, 2005; *Snyder v. Louisiana*, 2008).

The Court extended *Batson* to cover gender jury bias, holding that lawyers may not exclude potential jurors from a trial because of their sex (*J.E.B. Petitioner v. Alabama*, 1994). The principle of nondiscrimination at the core of *Batson* and *J.E.B.* has not yet been extended by the Supreme Court to other categories, such as ethnicity, religion, or sexual orientation. But some lower federal courts have done so on their own (see "Case Close-Up" below). For example, the U.S. Court of Appeals of the Second Circuit upheld the application of *Batson* to strikes against Italian-Americans (*United States v. Biaggi*, 1988). Similarly, as the "Case Close-Up" on *People v. Garcia* (2000) illustrates, peremptory challenges on the basis of sexual orientation have been limited in California.

Serving on a Jury

Every year, thousands of Americans are called to serve as jurors. In addition to impaneling the requisite number of jurors (e.g., 6, 9, or 12), it is a common practice in many courts to select several **alternate jurors,** who will serve if one of the regular jurors must withdraw during the trial. Unfortunately, though, many jurors experience great frustration in the process. They are made to wait hours in barren courthouse rooms; the compensation is minimal, and not all employers pay for the time lost from work; and some potential jurors are apprehensive about criminals and courthouses.

In spite of these hardships, most citizens who actually serve on a jury express overall satisfaction with their jury service, viewing their experience

CASE CLOSE-UP

PEOPLE v. GARCIA (CAL. APP. 2000): SHOULD BATSON EXTEND TO SEXUAL ORIENTATION?

Cano Garcia was charged with burglary. During his trial, it somehow became known that two members of the jury venire were lesbians. In fact, they both worked for the same gay and lesbian foundation. After the prosecution excused both women, defense counsel objected, making a Batson-type argument. The trial judge denied the motion, explaining, "Well, I am going to rule that sexual preference is not a cognizable group. ... I don't think that your sexual preference specifically relates to them sharing a common perspective or common social or psychological outlook on human events. Lesbians or gay men vary in their social and psychological outlook on human events and I don't think they fit into this protection. So I'm going to deny your motion."

The appeals court began its analysis by stating the rule of law in California established in the wake of *Batson*: "The right under the California Constitution to a jury drawn from a 'representative cross-section of the community' is violated whenever a 'cognizable group' within that community is systematically excluded from the jury venire" (p. 1275). In concluding that lesbians and gays were such a "cognizable group," the court reasoned:

> It cannot seriously be argued ... that homosexuals do not have a common perspective—"a common social or psychological outlook on human events"— based upon their membership in that community. They share a history of persecution comparable to that of blacks and women. While there is room to argue about degree, based upon their number and the relative indiscernibility of their membership in the group, it is just that: an argument about degree. It is a matter of quantity, not quality.
>
> This is not to say that all homosexuals see the world alike. The Attorney General here derides the cognizability of this class with the rhetorical question, "[W]hat 'common perspective' is, or was, shared by Rep. Jim Kolbe (R–Ariz.), RuPaul, poet William Alexander Percy, Truman Capote, and Ellen DeGeneres?" He confuses "common

perspective" with "common personality." Granted, the five persons he mentions are people of diverse backgrounds and life experiences. But they certainly share the common perspective of having spent their lives in a sexual minority, either exposed to or fearful of persecution and discrimination. That perspective deserves representation in the jury venire, and people who share that perspective deserve to bear their share of the burdens and benefits of citizenship, including jury service.

> The Attorney General also insists "there is no evidence that gays or lesbians have a common social or psychological outlook on human events." But this misperceives the nature of the term "common perspective." Commonality of perspective does not result in identity of opinion. That is the whole reason exclusion based upon group bias is anathema. It stereotypes. It assumes all people with the same life experience will, given a set of facts, reach the same result. Common perspective does no such thing. It affects how life experiences are seen, not how they are evaluated. And inclusion of a cognizable group in the jury venire does not assure any particular position; it assures only that the facts will be viewed from a variety of angles. It assures that as many different life views as possible will be represented in the important decisions of the judicial process. Put more elegantly, the goal of the cross-section rule is to enhance the likelihood that the jury will be representative of significant community attitudes, not of groups per se.

> But we cannot think of anyone who shares the perspective of the homosexual community. Outside of racial and religious minorities, we can think of no group which has suffered such "pernicious and sustained hostility and such immediate and severe opprobrium as homosexuals.

Critique the court's reasoning in *Garcia*. Do you think the same logic should be extended to support a ban on religious discrimination during voir dire? Why, or why not? What about the use of peremptory challenges to systematically excuse people on the basis of age (too young or to old) or weight (too thin or too obese)? Explain your reasoning.

as a precious opportunity of citizenship that generally bolstered their confidence in fellow citizens and public institutions (Gastil, Black, Deess, & Leighter, 2008; Pabst, 1973). Just as important, there is every indication that jurors take their job seriously.

Considerable attention is being devoted to reducing the inconvenience of jury duty. Courts in most states use a juror call-in system. In these jurisdictions, jurors can dial a number to learn whether their attendance is needed on a particular day during their term of service. In addition, an increasing number of courts are reducing the number of days a person remains in the jury pool. Traditionally, jurors were asked to serve for a full 30 days. Although only a few jurors were needed for a particular day, the entire pool had to be present in the courthouse each and every working day. Increasingly, however, jurors are asked to serve for only a few days. An approach known as the one-day/one-trial jury system requires each juror to serve either for one day or for the duration of one trial. The person is then exempt from jury duty for a year or two. The one-day/one-trial jury system is much more efficient than older practices not only because it spares many citizens the inconvenience of waiting in courthouses with no trials to hear, but also because it reduces constraints on judicial resources (Litras & Golmant, 2006; Sinclair, Behrens, & Silverman, 2003).

As a result of some of these reforms, "more than one-third of all Americans (37.6%) are now likely to be impaneled as trial jurors sometime during their lifetime. . . . [Thus], American citizens have first-hand experience with jury service, due to more inclusive master jury lists, shorter terms of service, and other policies designed to make jury service more convenient and accessible for all citizens." (Mize et al., 2007, p. 8).

LAW IN ACTION: CHOOSING A JURY BIASED IN YOUR FAVOR

The National Advisory Commission (1973) has succinctly summarized the official—that is to say, the law on the books—purpose of jury selection as follows: "A defendant is entitled to an unbiased jury; he is not entitled to a jury biased in his favor" (p. 99). Members of the courtroom work group are reluctant to formally question this pious wisdom, but informally their actions are strikingly different. Particularly through selective use of peremptory challenges, lawyers for both prosecution and defense seek jurors predisposed to their side. This is the major reason why in some areas the voir dire has become a time-consuming process. Through educating jurors, trial lawyers seek decision makers who are comfortable with their approach. Through hiring jury consultants, trial lawyers aggressively seek to identify jurors who will be biased in their favor.

Educating Jurors

Attorneys use voir dire for purposes other than eliminating bias. They use the questioning of jurors to establish credibility and rapport with the panel, to educate and sell prospective jurors on their respective theories of the case, and to either highlight or neutralize potential problem areas in the case (Voss, 2005). This, in turn, gives lawyers the opportunity to influence jurors' attitudes and perhaps later their vote.

Jury Consultants

In recent years, jury selection has taken a scientific turn. Rather than relying on personal hunch, attorneys in a few highly publicized cases have employed social scientists to aid them in a more intelligent, systematic use of the voir dire that has come to be called "scientific jury selection."

As described in great detail by Lieberman and Sales (2006), **scientific jury selection** typically involves a small group of experts from a variety of disciplinary backgrounds, including marketing, communications, sociology, and, most especially, psychology. Teams of such **jury consultants** conduct public opinion polls and employ laypeople to participate in focus groups or mock trials. With polls and focus groups, they test which pieces of evidence, witnesses, and arguments might be most effective in convincing people to vote a particular way. With mock trials, they test their whole case and then debrief the mock jurors on why they voted as they did. These processes allow jury consultants to identify the issues in a case that are most relevant to the case outcome, as well as to formulate profiles of the juror characteristics that are likely to affect the trial outcome. Using the information they gather, the jury consultants then design questionnaires to be administered to the potential jurors in an actual case. Once these questionnaires are compiled, the jury consultants are able to advise the lawyers in a case about which potential jurors they should want on the jury, and those whom they should seek to avoid.

Trial consultants are hired most often by defense attorneys, as opposed to the prosecutors. In reality, the consultants try to deselect jurors who are likely to be adverse to their client. Whether this process actually functions any better than attorneys doing traditional jury selection using "pop psychology" and their gut instincts is still being debated both in the empirical literature and by practitioners. Two things, however, seem clear. First, jury consultants can help attorneys develop trial presentations that are clear and convincing. Second, jury consultants appear to be here to stay.

PRESUMPTIONS AND THE BURDEN OF PROOF

Once the jury has been selected and sworn, most courts provide the jurors with some basic instructions concerning juror conduct, such as not to discuss the case until after the trial is concluded and not to form an opinion until all the evidence has been heard. Judges also typically provide an overview of both the relevant presumptions and governing burden of proof.

Starting Presumptions

The trier-of-fact must have an evidentiary starting place at the outset of a trial. In a criminal trial, that starting place usually involves two presumptions. A *presumption* is a conclusion or deduction that the law requires the trier-of-fact to make in the absence of evidence to the contrary. Criminal trials start with two presumptions: the presumption of sanity and the presumption of innocence.

The **presumption of sanity** requires that all defendants be presumed sane unless sufficient

evidence of their insanity is proven. Insanity defense trials, however, are quite rare; in fact, they occur in less than one-half of 1 percent of all felony cases. But, when defendants challenge the presumption of sanity in insanity cases, considerable controversy usually follows.

The **presumption of innocence** requires the trier-of-fact to accept that the defendant is innocent unless the prosecution meets its burden to prove that the defendant is guilty beyond a reasonable doubt. This means that the state must prove all elements of the alleged crime(s); the defendant is not required to prove himself or herself innocent. This difference is a fundamental one. A moment's reflection will give an idea of how hard it would be to prove that something did not happen or that a person did not commit an alleged criminal act, for it is very difficult to rule out all possibilities. Therefore, a defendant is cloaked with the legal shield of innocence throughout all pretrial and trial processes.

Burdens of Proof

The concept of **burden of proof** actually encompasses two separate burdens, the burden of production and the burden of persuasion. If a party has the **burden of production** (often referred to as the "burden of going forward"), they must produce some evidence to put facts in issue. The **burden of persuasion** is the obligation of a party to prove a fact (or facts) to a certain level, either beyond a reasonable doubt, by clear and convincing evidence, or by a preponderance of the evidence.

In meeting its burden of persuasion in a criminal case, the prosecution is required to prove the defendant guilty beyond a reasonable doubt. **Reasonable doubt** is a legal yardstick measuring the sufficiency of the evidence. This burden of proof does not require that the state establish absolute certainty by eliminating all doubt—just reasonable doubt. *Reasonable doubt* is an amorphous term that judges have difficulty fully defining. In her concurring opinion in *Victor v. Nebraska* (1994, p. 24), Justice Ginsburg endorsed the following definition of reasonable doubt as being "clear, straightforward, and accurate":

[T]he government has the burden of proving the defendant guilty beyond a reasonable doubt. Some of you may have served as jurors in civil cases, where you were told that it is only necessary to prove that a fact is more likely true than not true. In criminal cases, the government's proof must be more powerful than that. It must be beyond a reasonable doubt.

Proof beyond a reasonable doubt is proof that leaves you firmly convinced of the defendant's guilt. There are very few things in this world that we know with absolute certainty, and in criminal cases the law does not require proof that overcomes every possible doubt. If, based on your consideration of the evidence, you are firmly convinced that the defendant is guilty of the crime charged, you must find him guilty. If on the other hand, you think there is a real possibility that he is not guilty, you must give him the benefit of the doubt and find him not guilty.

To meet its burden of persuasion, the prosecutor introduces evidence tending to show, either directly or indirectly, the defendant's guilt. The defense may—but is not required to—introduce evidence tending to cast doubt on the defendant's guilt. When doing so, both parties must abide by the rules of evidence.

OVERVIEW OF BASIC EVIDENCE

Evidence consists of physical objects, testimony, or other things offered to prove or disprove the existence of a fact. There are several types of evidence that may be direct or circumstantial evidence depending on how the evidence is used at trial.

Differentiating Direct and Circumstantial Evidence

Direct evidence is first-hand evidence that does not require any inferences to be drawn in order to establish a proposition of fact. The best example of direct evidence is eyewitness testimony. One need not draw any inference from a witness's testimony that she saw something. Note, however, that direct evidence does not necessarily establish truth. Witnesses can be mistaken or misleading Chapter 16.

Circumstantial evidence is indirect evidence. To reach a conclusion, the trier-of-fact would have to reason through the circumstantial evidence and infer the existence of some fact in dispute, such as inferring that the defendant killed the victim because the defendant's fingerprints were found on the murder weapon.

Types of Evidence

Evidence can be classified as testimonial evidence, real or physical evidence, scientific evidence, or demonstrative evidence. **Testimonial evidence** is oral testimony given under oath. **Real evidence** (also referred to as "physical evidence") consists of tangible objects such as documents, drug paraphernalia, clothing, and weapons. The scientific examination of real evidence, in a laboratory, for example, yields **scientific evidence**—the formal results of forensic investigatory and scientific techniques. **Demonstrative evidence** has no evidential value by itself. Rather, it serves as a visual or auditory aid to assist the fact-finder in understanding the evidence. Charts, maps, videos, and courtroom demonstrations are forms of demonstrative evidence.

Basic Rules of Evidence

The presentation of evidence during trial is governed by principles called **rules of evidence**. A trial is an adversarial proceeding in which the rules of evidence resemble the rules of a game, with the judge acting as an impartial umpire. Although they may seem to be a fixed set of legal rules, they are not. Like all other legal principles, they are general propositions that courts must apply to specific instances to advance the trustworthiness and reliability of the evidence used at trial. During such applications, judges use a balancing test, carefully weighing whether the trial would be fairer with or without the piece of evidence in question. Some basics of the rules of evidence are summarized in Table 13.3.

TABLE 13.3 ▪ SUMMARY OF SELECT RULES OF EVIDENCE

Best-evidence rule	The best-evidence rule means that to prove the content of a writing, recording, or photograph, the original is generally required, since a copy is too easily altered.
Chain of custody	The chronological documentation of the seizure, control, transfer, analysis, and disposition of evidence before it can be admitted into evidence at trial.
Competency to testify	A witness must have personal knowledge of the matter about which he or she is testifying; must be capable of understanding the duty to tell the truth—something he or she is required to do by an oath or affirmation; must be capable of expressing himself or herself so as to be understood by the jury either directly or through an interpreter. People who cannot differentiate between truth and nontruth, such as young children and those who are affected by certain types of serious mental illnesses, generally are not competent to be witnesses in court.
Hearsay	Hearsay is secondhand evidence. It is testimony that is not based on personal knowledge, but rather is a repetition of what another person has said: "My brother Bob told me he saw Jones enter the store that evening." The general rule is that hearsay evidence is not admissible because it is impossible to test its truthfulness; there is no way to cross-examine with regard to the truth of the matter. There are numerous exceptions to this rule, however, ranging from dying declarations and ancient writings to statements showing the speaker's state of mind.
Relevancy	Evidence is relevant if it shows the existence of any fact that is of consequence to the determination of the action by making that fact more probable or less probable than it would be without the evidence. Evidence that does not tend to prove or disprove any material fact in dispute is irrelevant and inadmissible. Evidence regarding the accused's motive, intent, ability, and opportunity to commit a crime would all be relevant. In contrast, information about the defendant's character, prior convictions, or a reputation would not normally be relevant and is, therefore, inadmissible.
Cumulative or unduly prejudicial evidence	Even relevant evidence may be inadmissible if its use would be a waste of time because it is cumulative (duplicative of other evidence) or if it could unfairly prejudice, confuse, or mislead the jury.
Privilege	Privileged communications protect confidential discussions in certain relationships in which we want to foster open, honest communications. The law usually recognizes privileges that include communications between attorney and client; clergy-member and penitent; physician and patient; psychotherapist and patient; and husband and wife.
Lay opinions	Since opinions are subjective beliefs, most witnesses are not permitted to give their opinions other than general opinions that are rationally based on their own common perceptions, such as whether someone acted drunk, smelled like alcohol, appeared upset, or looked tired.

©Cengage Learning

SPECIAL RULES OF EVIDENCE GOVERNING EXPERT WITNESSES

In contrast to lay witnesses, expert witnesses are permitted to give opinions on matters about which they have no personal knowledge. Before someone is permitted to give opinions in court, the person must be qualified as an expert witness based on their knowledge, skill, experience, training, or education. But even the opinions of properly qualified experts are not admissible unless they meet other standards for admissibility, such as those specified in Federal Rule of Evidence 702:

1. The expert's scientific, technical, or other specialized knowledge must help the trier-of-fact to understand the evidence or to determine a fact in issue;

2. The expert's testimony must be based on sufficient facts or data that they have either personally observed or been made aware of through reliable second-hand information;

3. The expert's testimony must be the product of reliable principles and methods; and

4. The expert must have reliably applied the principles and methods to the facts of the case.

Determining Reliability

For much of the 20th century, the *Frye* test governed the admissibility of scientific testimony. In *Frye v. United States* (1923), a federal appeals court refused to allow an expert to testify about the results of a lie-detector test because the instrument had not gained general acceptance in the scientific community. The purpose behind the *Frye* test was to prevent unfounded scientific principles or conclusions based on such principles from being used at trial. Shortcomings of the *Frye* test, however, caused the drafters of the federal rules of evidence to replace *Frye* with rules that the U.S. Supreme Court fleshed out in *Daubert v. Merrill-Dow Pharmaceuticals, Inc.* (1993).

Daubert established that trial court judges are supposed to act as gatekeepers who have a special obligation to ensure the reliability of scientific evidence. *Daubert* suggested several factors (that are neither exhaustive nor applicable to every case) that might be used in evaluating whether a particular scientific theory, study, or test is both valid and reliable, including whether it:

- is empirically testable and capable of replication

- has been published and/or subjected to peer review

- has a known or potential rate of error that is acceptably low

- is logical, avoids bias, and has construct validity (how well data fits into preexisting theory)

- adheres to recognized research methods and, if applicable, to proper sampling and statistical procedures for data analysis

- is generally accepted in the relevant scientific community (making *Frye* a part of *Daubert's* test, but not the dispositive factor)

Initially, *Daubert* applied only to scientific evidence. But in *Kumho Tire Co. v. Carmichael* (1999), the Supreme Court held that all expert testimony that involves scientific, technical, or other specialized knowledge must meet the *Daubert* test for admissibility.

FORENSIC SCIENTIFIC EVIDENCE IN THE AGE OF *DAUBERT*

Scientific evidence analyzing materials such as blood, firearms, and fingerprints has been routinely admitted into evidence for years if it met the traditional yardsticks of the rules of evidence—trustworthiness and relevance. But when the technologies for gathering and measuring these forms of evidence first emerged, their use as evidence was far from routine. Moreover, as the *Frye* case illustrated by disallowing polygraph results, not all evidence based on "science" was necessarily admissible. Results from hypnosis have similarly been excluded from evidence. But separating science from pseudoscience has never been an easy task.

Even under *Daubert*, just when a scientific principle or discovery crosses the line between the experimental and reliably demonstrable stages is difficult to define. *Daubert* has been reasonably effective at keeping "junk science" (unreliable findings, often by persons with questionable credentials) out of evidence, especially in civil cases seeking monetary compensation based on scientifically questionable claims (Buchman, 2004). *Daubert's* impact on forensic science in criminal cases, however, has been surprisingly less dramatic (Fisher, 2008; Neufeld, 2005). Indeed, forensic scientific evidence either caused or contributed to wrongful convictions in 116 of the first 225 (52 percent) DNA exoneration cases by the Innocence Project (2011). Troublingly, in more than a quarter of such exonerations, false or misleading testimony by forensic experts contributed to the wrongful convictions (Giannelli, 2007).

Many forensic techniques, such as hair and fiber analysis, toolmark comparisons, and fingerprint analysis, rely upon a simple "match game," whereby a forensic analyst compares a known sample to a questioned sample and makes the highly subjective determination that the two samples originated from the same source. Although lacking a true scientific foundation, this "Sesame Street Science" plays a prominent role in many cases because of the availability of trace evidence, which is easy to leave and easy to find at a crime scene. Other forensic fields, including comparative bullet lead analysis and arson investigation, rely on assumptions that are "under-researched and oversold." (Gabel & Wilkinson, 2008, p. 1002). Table 13.4 summarizes some of the problems with forensic scientific evidence that has been routinely used in criminal trials in the United States.

Due in large part to many of the shortcomings listed in Table 13.4, the National Academies of Sciences (NAS) issued a scathing report on forensic science in the United States in 2009. The report concluded that, among all existing forensic methods, "only nuclear DNA analysis has been rigorously shown to have the capacity to consistently, and with a high degree of certainty, demonstrate a connection between an evidentiary sample and a specific individual or source" (p. 100). In contrast, most other types of forensic analyses lack sufficient systematic research to even "validate the discipline's basic premises and techniques" (p. 22). Accordingly, the NAS called for the creation of an independent federal agency to oversee forensic science in the United States. As of this writing, no such action has been taken.

As the NAS report makes clear, DNA (deoxyribonucleic acid) is the gold standard of forensic science. As a result, prisoners and their representatives are demanding that old cases be reopened so that DNA tests (not available at the time of the original trial) be performed. These requests are most often identified with the issue of innocents on death row Chapter 14. However, in *District Attorney's Office v. Osborne* (2009), the Supreme Court ruled that prisoners have no constitutional right to postconviction DNA testing that might prove their innocence.

There are two limitations to DNA evidence that should be highlighted. First, biological evidence that can be subjected to DNA testing is available in only about 10 percent of criminal cases (Garrett, 2008). Second, even when evidence is available, that evidence may have been contaminated or

otherwise rendered unreliable because of mistakes by police or crime lab personnel, including mix-up of samples, deficiencies in lab-proficiency testing, and problems with or miscalculations of matching criteria—something that jurors often do not understand (Lieberman, Miethe, Carrell, & Krauss, 2008).

The CSI Effect

For many years, most of the techniques outlined in Table 13.4 were known only to scientists and criminal lawyers. But Hollywood changed that in the 1990s when dramas about crime and forensics became a staple of prime-time television. At the height of their popularity, the three different versions of *CSI: Crime Scene Investigation* (Las Vegas, Miami, and New York) each drew between 10 and 30 million viewers per week (Kelley, 2011; Shelton, 2008), with millions more watching other shows such as *NCIS, Dexter, Bones, Forensic Files, The New Detectives, Secrets of Forensic Science, Medical Detectives, Cold Case*, and *Without a Trace*, to name just a few. In these popular, although often inaccurate, shows,

> lab technicians identify a suspect through analysis that isn't—or shouldn't be—possible in the real world. They match bullets to guns to gun owners, they track footprints and fingerprints in unlikely places, they match fibers from the crime scene to a car or piece of clothing. These unreliable methods usually aren't available, and when they are, they've led to wrongful convictions. Prosecutors are right to tell a jury that there's no forensic evidence rather than stretching to make a connection that isn't there (as the scientists in *CSI* might). But then they say juries are skeptical of a case without fancy forensics. (Innocence Project, 2008, ¶ 2)

Prosecutors insist that these television shows created the so-called **CSI effect**, in which jurors wrongfully acquit guilty defendants when no scientific evidence is presented. But research has not empirically validated their anecdotal concerns.

Jurors have come to expect sophisticated forensic evidence in even the most mundane cases (see Figure 13.1).

TABLE 13.4 ■ PROBLEMS WITH FORENSIC SCIENTIFIC EVIDENCE UNDER *DAUBERT*

Hair microscopy	Used since the 19th century, this technique uses a microscope to compare hair samples using characteristics like color, pigment distributions, and texture. The technique has rarely been subjected to rigorous peer review or proficiency testing. Moreover, the few tests that have been performed revealed that error rates are quite high. In an FBI scientific paper entitled "Correlation of Microscopic and - DNA Hair Comparisons," the authors found that even the most competent hair examiners make significant errors. In 11 percent of the cases in which the hair examiners declared two hairs to be "similar," DNA testing revealed that the hairs did not match. In some jurisdictions, hair microscopy is being phased out and replaced by the more sensitive and discriminating mitochondrial DNA typing test. Yet, many local prosecutors continue to rely on the microscope because mitochondrial DNA typing remains relatively expensive and is offered in only a few laboratories. A study of Innocence Project prisoners found nearly 22 percent of prisoners exonerated by DNA evidence had been wrongly convicted based, in large part, on hair comparisons. Yet, results of this technique are routinely used in court.
Serology	Serology is a branch of biochemistry that tests serums found in the human body (in blood, semen, and other bodily fluids). It can be reliable, yet in 40 percent of the DNA-exoneration cases, conventional serology had been used by the prosecutor to secure a conviction. The case transcripts reveal that in the vast majority of these cases, the crime lab serologist misrepresented the data to the advantage of the prosecution.
Fingerprinting	This process compares the impressions of prints from fingers or palms left at a crime scene to known impressions. Empirical studies are just starting to reveal that thousands of misidentification errors are made each year, especially because "non-mate prints can sometimes appear more similar than mate print pairs" to the FBI's automated fingerprint identification system (Cole, Welling, Dioso-Villa, & Carpenter, 2008). Wrongful convictions have also resulted from the misapplication of fingerprint identification. For example, Stephen Cowans was convicted and served 6 years in prison for shooting a Boston police officer. Two fingerprint experts told a jury during the trial that a thumbprint left by the perpetrator was "unique and identical" to Cowans's print because it matched at 16 points. Post-conviction DNA testing excluded Cowans as the perpetrator.
Compositional analysis of bullet lead	This technique compares the quantity of various elements that comprise a lead slug recovered from a crime scene with the composition of the lead found in unused bullets seized from a suspect. In criminal cases, to say that two samples are similar can be very misleading. In fact, the National Research Council of the National Academies of Sciences (2004) concluded that variations in the manufacturing process rendered this technique "unreliable and potentially misleading." The FBI has discontinued the use of this technique accordingly, but hundreds, if not thousands, of criminal defendants may have been convicted based, in part, on this faulty pseudo-science.
Firearm, toolmark, bitemark, and forensic document comparisons	Like examinations of hair samples, these types of forensic analyses rely on an examiner to make comparisons between a crime scene sample and a known exemplar. Thus, they are subject to the same human errors based on subjective judgments as these other techniques. The reliability of these techniques is questionable in light of either unestablished or unacceptably high error rates. For example, a classic study (Risinger, Denbeaux, & Saks, 1989) reported that forensic-document examiners were correct between 36 and 45 percent of the time, that they erred partially or completely 36 to 42 percent of the time, and were unable to draw a conclusion in 19 to 22 percent of cases. Experts have recently noted that there is little empirical evidence to support the uniqueness of teeth marks, shoeprints, or weapon markings (Moriarty, 2007). Saks and Koehler (2005) reported error rates as high as 64 percent for bite-mark comparison, a 40-percent error rate for handwriting comparison, and a 12-percent error rate for microscopic hair comparison.

SOURCES: Jessica D. Gabel and Margaret D. Wilkinson. 2008. "'Good' Science Gone Bad: How the Criminal Justice System Can Redress the Impact of Flawed Forensics." *Hastings Law Journal* 59: 1001–1030; Peter J. Neufeld, 2005. "The (Near) Irrelevance of *Daubert* to Criminal Justice and Some Suggestions for Reform." *American Journal of Public Health* 95: S107–S113.

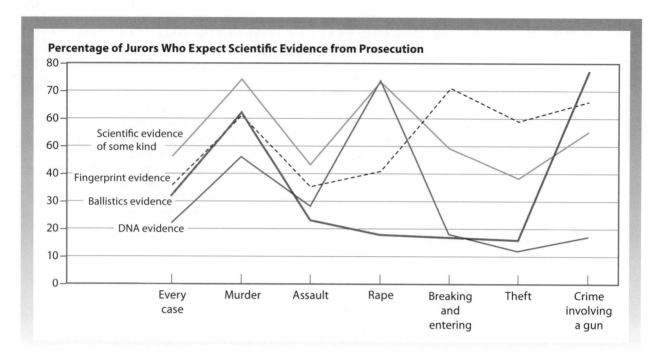

Percentage of Jurors Who Expect Scientific Evidence from Prosecution

Scientific evidence of some kind

Fingerprint evidence

Ballistics evidence

DNA evidence

Every case · Murder · Assault · Rape · Breaking and entering · Theft · Crime involving a gun

Figure 13.1 ■ Juror Expectations for Forensic Evidence

SOURCE: Donald Shelton, 2008. "The 'CSI Effect': Does It Really Exist?" *National Institute of Justice Journal* 259. Available online at http://www.nij.gov/nij/journals/259/csi-effect.htm

However, these higher expectations for forensic evidence did not significantly affect conviction or acquittal voting patterns (Shelton, Kim, & Barak, 2009). In fact, Schweitzer and Saks (2007) found that *CSI* viewers were actually more critical of the forensic evidence presented in a simulated trial, finding it less believable, than people who did not watch *CSI*. Yet, the verdicts of *CSI* viewers and nonviewers did not differ significantly.

It may be fair to blame *CSI*-type shows for misleading people into believing many misconceptions about forensic science (see "Courts, Law, & Media" on the next page). But blaming forensics on television for the CSI effect may be too simplistic. Television notwithstanding, the advancement of science and technology has "heightened juror expectations and demands for scientific evidence in almost every respect" (Shelton, Kim & Barak, 2009, p. 2). Forensic science on television appears to be only one factor in increasing juror expectations for scientific evidence in a wide range of criminal cases.

OBJECTIONS TO THE ADMISSION OF EVIDENCE

During trial, attorneys must always be alert, ready to make timely **objections** to the admission of evidence. After a question is asked but before the witness answers, the attorney may object if the evidence is irrelevant or hearsay. The court then rules on the objection, admitting or barring the evidence. The judge may rule immediately or may request the lawyers to argue the legal point out of the hearing of the jury (this is termed a "*sidebar conference*").

Occasionally, inadmissible evidence will inadvertently be heard by the jury. For example, in answering a valid question, a witness may overelaborate. When this occurs and the attorney objects, the judge will instruct the jury to disregard the evidence. If the erroneous evidence is deemed so prejudicial that a warning to disregard is not sufficient, the judge may declare a **mistrial**.

COURTS, LAW, & MEDIA

CSI: Crime Scene Investigation (CBS, 2000–present)

This fictional crime drama chronicles a team of forensic scientists who work for the Las Vegas Police Department. Although the television show has been wildly popular, it is widely criticized because it lacks any basis in reality. Consider these discrepancies between forensic fact and fiction.

- In reality, crime scene investigators certainly process crime scenes as the team on *CSI* does, but forensic experts do not engage in police activities like pursuing suspects, conducting interrogations, staging sting operations, conducting raids, and so on. "The actors playing forensic personnel portrayed on television, for instance, are an amalgam of police officer/detective/forensic scientist—this job description does not exist in the real world. Law enforcement, investigations and forensic science are each sufficiently complex that they demand their own education, training and methods" (Houck, 2006, ¶ 11).

- The crime laboratories on television have a dazzling array of forensic equipment and technology at their disposal. But some of the technologies that are depicted on *CSI*—upwards of 40 percent according to some experts—do not really exist (Houck, 2006). Real crime labs, on the other hand, are often understaffed, lack all of the scientific equipment they need, and cannot perform all types of forensic analyses, "whether because of cost, insufficient resources, or rare demand" (Houck, 2006, ¶ 12).

- On *CSI*, a handful of forensic personnel possess an incredible range of scientific expertise. In real crime labs, however, different types of forensic examinations are performed by specialists in the given forensic subfield.

- The *CSI* investigators are seemingly able to lift fingerprints off of almost anything. In reality, prints can be lifted off of only certain surfaces under certain conditions. Moreover, on *CSI*, the prints are uploaded into a computer database and a screen nearly instantly appears with a photo of the person to whom the fingerprint belongs. In reality, many latent fingerprints lifted from crime scenes are not good enough to use for identification purposes. But even when

a set of prints can be run through the FBI's Integrated Automatic Fingerprint Identification System (IAFIS), the computerized database provides a list of potential matches. This process is not instantaneous; it typically takes up to 2 hours (Federal Bureau of Investigation, 2008). And while the IAFIS has the capacity to store and distribute photos, it does not provide pop-up photographic identifications when a set of fingerprints is potentially matched. A human trained in fingerprint comparison must then compare the latent prints with a set of known exemplars.

- On *CSI*, crime-scene evidence is tested immediately, resulting in cases being solved quickly and efficiently. Real crime labs across the United States are seriously backlogged.

- DNA solves many cases on *CSI*. But evidence on which DNA tests can be run is recovered in only about 10 percent of criminal cases (Garrett, 2008). And even when there is evidence to test, the results take several days at best (often several weeks), not the mere minutes in which genetic tests are run on *CSI*. Most importantly, DNA is not infallible, even though *CSI* presents DNA results as 100 percent foolproof.

- *CSI* routinely overstates the probative value of forensic evidence. "In one episode, for example, investigators perform a remarkable 'reverse algorithm and enhancement' of an audiotaped ransom demand. Using a spectrograph to match the sound waves from the ransom recording to those from a different voice recording, they are able to conclusively identify the kidnapper" (Tyler, 2006, p. 1070). While this makes for great fiction, the shortcomings of voice identification are legion, as current technology simply cannot "conclusively identify" a voice to the exclusion of others.

1. Recall from the text of this chapter that several common forensic techniques may be unreliable or prone to either high or unknown error rates. Why do you think that *CSI* presents its storylines in terms of scientific fact rather than exploring the indeterminate nature of several forensic techniques?

2. Were you aware of all of the above differences between forensic fact and forensic science fiction? If so, how did you learn of the reality? If not, what is your opinion of the show now that you know more about the truth?

3. What effect do you think forensically based shows like *CSI* have on criminals? Do you think these shows have influenced how they commit some crimes? Why, or why not?

COURTS, CONTROVERSY, & THE ADMINISTRATION of JUSTICE

SHOULD FINGERPRINT EVIDENCE BE ADMISSIBLE?

Since *Daubert* was decided in 1993, nearly every court that has reviewed fingerprinting evidence has concluded that expert testimony using fingerprint identification is admissible. But is this the correct result? Many of the courts reviewing the "science" of fingerprinting merely cite other courts for the proposition that fingerprint identification is reliable, making it more of a judicially certified practice than one validated by science (Cole, 2010).

The NAS report on forensic science (2009) called into question the premises upon which fingerprint identifications are based. First, although there is some scientific evidence supporting the presumption that each fingerprint is unique, this assumption has not been sufficiently empirically validated. Second, there are generally no objective standards for declaring a fingerprint to be a "match" that have been scientifically validated, especially because examiners of latent prints often receive only partial fingerprints of variable quality. The standards for fingerprint comparison under such circumstances are subjective, as are the declarations of a match. Thus, in contrast to DNA evidence, there are no generally accepted statistical models "that would permit the likelihood that two prints came from the same person to be expressed in probabilistic terms" (Mnookin, 2008, p. 129; see also, NAS, 2009, p. 139). And third, not only have the claims that fingerprint analyses have error rates near zero unsubstantiated, but also, they are "not scientifically plausible" (p. 142).

Critics of fingerprint identification also point out that unlike the extensive education, training, and certification undergone by DNA analysts, most fingerprint examiners "receive the majority of their training on the job, without either a formal structure of topics covered or formal assessment of success in meeting training goals. Variation in training means that variation in the use of a method must also occur" (Haber & Haber, 2008, p. 94). Similarly, neither the reliability nor the validity of the proficiency tests used to certify analysts has ever been established. Indeed, one leading analyst referred to the prints used in the FBI proficiency test as being "so easy" that "they are a joke" (Haber & Haber, 2008, p. 95, quoting Bayle, 2002).

Collectively, these shortcomings have led leading scholars of the forensic sciences to conclude that the leading current method of fingerprint analysis (the ACE-V [accuracy, comparison, evaluation, and verification] method) is "both untested and untestable" (Haber & Haber, 2008, p. 87).

In a highly controversial ruling in 2002, a federal district judge ruled that fingerprint identification evidence did not meet the *Daubert* test and, therefore, experts could not express an opinion as to whether a particular latent fingerprint found at a crime scene could be attributed to the defendant in the case (*United States v. Llera Plaza*). The ruling caused such an outcry that the judge reversed his own decision (see Moenssens, 2002).

Latent fingerprints continue to be collected from crime scenes, and the results of their analysis play a large part in the investigation of crimes. But given the current state of scientific knowledge about fingerprint analysis, should fingerprinting analysts be permitted to testify as experts in criminal trials that the defendant's prints "match" those found at a crime scene? Most police and prosecutors answer this question with a resounding "yes" and have been quite successful in convincing courts to agree with them. But the National Academies of Science and numerous scholars with expertise in the intersection of law and forensic science cast doubt on the courts' routine acceptance of fingerprint evidence for the purposes of individualizing identifications. Where do you stand on the matter? Explain your reasoning.

Challenging Forensic Evidence

During the 8-month murder trial of O. J. Simpson in 1995, the defense team stressed the mishandling of evidence, suggesting that any subsequent analysis, no matter how precise, was not believable. This case thrust crime labs under the microscope, and the results were not always flattering.

Significant errors in laboratory testing have been documented not only at the FBI crime lab, but also in numerous state and local crime labs, especially in Texas, Virginia, and West Virginia

(Giannelli, 2007, 2011; Moriarty, 2007). Part of the problem lies with workload, as crime labs have become victims of their own success with requests for scientific tests growing faster than their budgets. But negligence or outright misconduct in crime labs is clearly also to blame (Giannelli, 2011; Thompson, 2006). As a result, some cases have been dismissed, and some convictions reversed, because testimony concerning scientific evidence proved unreliable. The Supreme Court has made challenging scientific evidence easier, holding that crime laboratory reports may not be introduced as evidence unless the person responsible for creating them gives testimony and is subject to cross-examination (*Melendez-Diaz v. Massachusetts*, 2009). But, as explored in the "Courts, Controversy, & the Administration of Justice" feature on the previous page, applying the rigors of *Daubert* to techniques long used for crime solving can cause quite an uproar.

STEPS IN THE TRIAL PROCESS

The order in which different components of a trial unfold differs from jurisdiction to jurisdiction (and even sometimes from courtroom to courtroom within the same courthouse). For example, some courts provide jurors with legal instructions at the start of a case; others do so at the end of the presentation of evidence but before closing arguments; and still other courts provide jury instructions after closing arguments. Such minor differences aside, most criminal trials follow the sequence outlined in the "Law on the Books vs. Law in Action" feature on the next page. Each of the steps in the trial process is explored in detail in the following sections.

Opening Statements

Once the jury has been selected and sworn, the trial begins with **opening statements** by both sides, outlining what they believe the evidence in the case will prove. The purpose of an opening statement is to advise the jury of what the attorney intends to prove. Opening statements are not evidence; the attorneys offer the jurors "road maps" to guide them through the case. It is important to note that these road maps must be limited to statements of what the attorneys

actually believe will be presented as the trial progresses (*United States v. Dinitz*, 1976); an opening statement, therefore, must be rooted in some degree of fact. A detailed and well-organized opening statement presents the jury with a *schema*—a thematic framework through which to view the trial. If done well, opening statements may be case-determinative. Research has repeatedly demonstrated that even though jurors are admonished not to make up their minds until the conclusion of trial after having given fair and impartial consideration to all the evidence, many jurors make a preliminary decision with regard to the outcome of the case after hearing opening statements (Kalven & Zeisel, 1966; Spiecker & Worthington 2003).

Prosecution's Case-in-Chief

After opening statements, the prosecutor presents the state's *case-in-chief*, calling witnesses and introducing other forms of evidence to bolster the prosecution's allegation that the defendant is guilty. The prosecutor conducts a **direct examination** by asking open-ended, nonleading questions to prosecutorial witnesses, focusing on questions that get at who, what, when, where, how, and why. A fundamental tenet of the adversary system is the need to test evidence for truthfulness, and the primary means of testing the truthfulness of witnesses is **cross-examination**. Thus, the defense has the right to cross-examine any witnesses for the prosecution. Because such witnesses are presumed to be hostile to the defense, closed-ended or leading questions are permissible on cross-examination (such as, "Isn't it true that. . . .").

Motion for Judgment of Acquittal

At the conclusion of the prosecution's case-in-chief, the defense may make a **motion for judgment of acquittal**. The court must enter such a judgment whenever the prosecution fails to introduce sufficient evidence to sustain a conviction as a matter of law. These motions are very rarely granted, since it is unusual for prosecutors to present a case that is so weak that no reasonable jury could determine that the defendant committed the crime(s) charged.

LAW ON THE BOOKS VS. LAW IN ACTION
STEPS OF THE PROCESS: TRIALS

	LAW ON THE BOOKS	LAW IN ACTION
Opening statements	Lawyers discuss what the evidence will show.	Lawyers use to lead the jury to a favorable verdict.
Prosecution's case-in-chief	The main evidence offered to prove the defendant guilty beyond a reasonable doubt.	Defense suggests that the prosecution has not met its burden of proof.
Witness	A person who makes a statement under oath about the events in question.	Through cross-examination, the defense undermines the credibility of the witness.
Expert witness	A person who possesses special knowledge or experience who is allowed to testify not only about facts but also about the opinions he or she has drawn from a review of the facts.	Some expert witnesses testify only for one side or the other. Some types of forensic evidence in criminal cases may not be reliable enough to pass the *Daubert* test.
Motion for judgment of acquittal	Defense argues that no reasonable jury could convict the defendant based on the evidence presented by the prosecution.	Judges almost never grant this motion, largely because prosecutors rarely fail to present insufficient evidence to sustain a conviction.
Defense's case-in-chief	Evidence that defense may present. Because the defendant is innocent until proven guilty, the defense is not required to present evidence.	The defense may rest without calling witnesses, but jurors expect to hear reasons why they should not convict.
Defendant as witness	The defendant may waive his or her privilege against self-incrimination and testify.	Defense attorneys are reluctant to call the defendant to the stand, particularly if there is a prior conviction.
Rebuttal	Evidence that refutes or contradicts evidence given by the opposing party.	The prosecutor will call witnesses to undermine a defendant's alibi.
Renewed motion for judgment of acquittal	Defense argues that in light of the evidence presented by both sides, no jury could reasonably convict the defendant.	Trial judges almost never grant this motion.
Closing arguments	After all the evidence has been presented, each side sums up the evidence and attempts to convince the jury why their side should win.	Many trial attorneys believe that a good closing argument will win the case.
Jury instructions	Explanations by the judge informing the jury of the law applicable to the case.	Legal language difficult for average citizens to follow.
Jury deliberations	Jurors deliberate in private. Jurors select a foreperson and discuss the case. Jurors take an oath to follow the law as instructed by the judge.	Some juries introduce popular law into the decision-making process. On rare occasions, a juror might refuse to follow the law in a particular case.

Continued on next page

Continued from previous page

Verdict	Decision that the defendant is either guilty or not guilty (acquittal).	Juries convict three out of four times. Jury verdicts often reflect a compromise.
Hung jury	Jury is unable to reach a verdict.	Defense attorneys consider a hung jury an important victory.
Postverdict motions	Motions filed by the defense after conviction and before sentencing.	Judge must accept a verdict of not guilty.
Renewed motion for judgment of acquittal	Defense argues that the jury could not have reasonably convicted the defendant based on the evidence presented.	Trial judges are very reluctant to second-guess jury verdicts and almost never grant this motion.
Motion for a new trial	Defense argues that the trial judge made mistakes and therefore a new trial should be held.	On very rare occasions, trial judges admit that an error occurred and set aside a jury verdict of guilty.

Defense's Case-in-Chief

Once the prosecutor rests, the defense must choose whether to put on its case-in-chief or to rest. Because the defendant is presumed innocent, the defense does not have to call any witnesses or introduce any evidence. But, if the defense chooses to present its side of the case to the jury, it does so following the same procedure the prosecution used: conducting direct examination of defense witnesses and introducing other forms of evidence. The prosecutor has the right to cross-examine any defense witnesses.

At times, defense attorneys present a classic defense—self-defense, intoxication, entrapment, insanity, alibi, frame-up, mistake, and so on. But more often than not, the defense instead seeks to undermine whether the prosecutor did indeed prove the defendant guilty *beyond a reasonable doubt*. But many experienced defense attorneys consider this to be the weakest kind of defense. They believe that to gain an acquittal, the defense must give the jury something to "hang their hat on." Thus, they must consider whether to let the defendant testify.

The Defendant as Witness

The Fifth Amendment protection against **self-incrimination** means that the defendant cannot be compelled to be a witness against himself or herself. If the defendant chooses not to testify, no comment or inference may be drawn from this fact. The prosecutor cannot argue before the jury, "If he is innocent, why doesn't he take the stand and say so?" (*Griffin v. California*, 1965). Nonetheless, jurors are curious about the defendant's version of what happened. They expect the defendant to profess innocence; in the secrecy of the jury room, they may ponder why the defendant refused to testify.

Defendants may, of course, waive the privilege against self-incrimination and take the stand in their own defense. In deciding whether the defendant should testify, the defense attorney must consider whether the story is believable. If it is not, the jury will probably dismiss it, thus doing more harm to the defendant's case than if he or she had not testified at all.

Like any other witness, a defendant who takes the stand is subject to cross-examination. Cross-examination usually ensures that the defendant cannot tell only a part of the story and conceal the rest. Once the defendant chooses to testify, the state can bring out all the facts surrounding the events to which the defendant testifies. Just as important, once the defendant has taken the stand, the state can **impeach** the defendant's credibility by introducing into evidence any prior felony convictions and, in some circumstances, other prior misconduct. The defense attorney must make the difficult decision about whether to arouse the jury's suspicion by not letting the accused testify or letting the defendant testify and be subjected to possibly damaging cross-examination.

"Damned if they do, damned if they don't" is the conclusion of a research project that interviewed jurors in capital murder trials. In general, jurors wanted the defendants to testify during trial and were confused when they did not. But when defendants chose to testify, jurors concluded that they were lying and showed no remorse (Antonio & Arone, 2005).

Renewed Motion for Judgment of Acquittal

At the conclusion of the defense's case-in-chief, the defense may make another motion for a judgment of acquittal, arguing that no reasonable jury could convict based upon the totality of the evidence presented. Given this high standard, these motions are very rarely granted. Moreover, most judges do not want to impinge upon the province of the jury to make a factual determination concerning the defendant's guilt.

Rebuttal

After the defense rests its case, the prosecution may call rebuttal witnesses, whose purpose is either to discredit the testimony of a previous witness or to discredit the witness. The prosecutor may call a **rebuttal** witness to show that the previous witness could not have observed what she said she did because she was somewhere else at the time. Or the prosecutor may call witnesses or otherwise present evidence to show that the previous witnesses have dishonorable reputations. The rules of evidence regarding rebuttal witnesses are complex. In general, evidence may be presented in rebuttal that could not have been used during the prosecution's main case. For example, the prosecution may legitimately inform the jury of the previous convictions of defendants who take the stand, in an attempt to impeach their credibility.

Closing Arguments

After the prosecution and defense have rested (that is, completed the introduction of evidence), each side has the opportunity to make a closing argument to the jury. **Closing arguments** allow each side to sum up the facts in its favor and indicate why it believes a verdict of guilty or not guilty is in order.

In most jurisdictions, the prosecutor goes first, carefully summing up the facts of the case and tying together into a coherent pattern what appeared during the trial to be isolated or unimportant matters. The prosecutor calls upon the jurors to do their duty and punish the defendant, who has committed the crime. The defense attorney goes next, highlighting the evidence favorable to the defendant, criticizing the witnesses for the state, and showing why they should not be believed. The defense also calls upon the jurors to do their sworn duty and return a not-guilty verdict. Because the prosecutor bears the burden of proof, he or she has the opportunity to make one last statement to the jury, refuting the defense arguments.

Closing arguments are often the most dramatic parts of the trial. However, there is a fine line between persuasiveness and unnecessary emotionalism. Jury verdicts have been reversed on appeal because the prosecutor interjected prejudicial statements into the closing argument.

Jury Instructions

Although in jury trials the jury is the sole judge of the facts of the case, the judge alone determines the law. Therefore, the court instructs the jury as to the meaning of the law applicable to the facts of the case. These **jury instructions** begin with discussions of general legal principles (innocent until proven guilty, guilty beyond a reasonable doubt, and so forth). They follow with specific instructions on the elements of the crime in the case and what specific actions the government must prove before there can be a conviction. If the defendant has raised a defense such as insanity or duress, the judge instructs the jury as to the meaning of the defense according to the law in that jurisdiction. Finally, the judge instructs the jury on possible verdicts in the case and provides a written form for each verdict of guilty and not guilty. Often juries have the option of choosing alternative forms of guilty verdicts, called *"lesser included offenses."* In a murder case, for example, the jury may find the defendant guilty of murder in the first degree, murder in the second degree, or manslaughter—or they may acquit on all charges.

The judge and the trial attorneys prepare the jury instructions during a special **charging conference** that precedes jury deliberations. Each side drafts suggested instructions, and the judge chooses the most appropriate ones. If the judge rejects a given instruction, the lawyer enters an objection on the record, thus preserving the issue for later appeal. The instructions are written out, signed by the judge, and then read to the jury. Some judges allow the jurors to take a copy of the instructions into the jury room as a guide.

Jury instructions represent a formal, detailed lecture on the law. Because faulty jury instructions are a principal basis for appellate court reversal, judges are careful in their wording. However, given the complexity of the law, juror comprehension of jury instructions is pitifully low (Ogloff & Rose, 2007). For example, given jury instructions stressing that a defendant is presumed innocent until proven guilty by the evidence beyond any reasonable doubt, only 50 percent of the jurors understood that the defendant did not have to present any evidence of innocence and 10 percent were still uncertain what the presumption of innocence was (Strawn & Buchanan, 1976; see also, Frank & Broschard, 2006). The major difficulty in improving jury comprehension is the complexity of the law itself; it is difficult to translate into plain English the subtleties of meaning of certain legal terms and the intentional vagueness of the law ("reasonable person" and "preponderance of the evidence" come quickly to mind) (Ogloff & Rose, 2007; Steele & Thornburg, 1991).

Jury Deliberations

How juries decide has long fascinated lawyers and laypeople alike. There is a great deal of curiosity about what goes on behind the locked jury room door. During the trial, jurors are passive observers who are not allowed to ask questions and are usually prohibited from taking notes. But after the judge reads the jury instructions, the lawyers, judges, and defendants must wait passively, often in tense anticipation, for the jury to reach a verdict. The only hints of what is happening during **jury deliberations** occur on the rare occasions when the jurors request further instructions from the judge about the applicable law or ask to have portions of the testimony read in open court.

Sometimes, juries deliberate for a significant period of time but are unable to reach a verdict. In such circumstances, a judge might opt to call the jury into the courtroom and read them an *Allen* **charge** (sometimes referred to as a "dynamite charge"). This strongly worded jury instruction encourages jurors to continue deliberations until a verdict is reached. If, however, the jury is unable to reach a verdict, the jury is declared *deadlocked* and the trial ends with a **hung jury**. The prosecutor then has the option of trying the defendant again. Despite recent concerns, the rate of hung juries is low and has been stable for years (Hannaford, Hans, & Munsterman, 1999). Nationwide, juries are unable to reach a decision only 6 percent of the time (National Center for State Courts, 2003).

Are Juries Biased?

Juries are supposed to decided cases based on two factors: the evidence presented during a trial and the legal instructions they receive from a judge. More than a century ago, the U.S. Supreme Court stated:

> The entire effort of our trial procedure is to secure . . . jurors who do not know . . . anything of either the character [of the parties] or events [on trial]. . . . The zeal displayed in this effort to empty the minds of the jurors . . . [is a sign] that the jury . . . is an impartial organ of justice. (*Patterson v, Colorado*, 1907, p. 462)

The sentiment expressed in the preceding quote is known as the *tabula rasa* theory—Latin for "clean slate." Jurors are not supposed to consider any **extralegal factors**—information not admitted into evidence during a trial. But jurors do not actually come to court with an "empty mind." And if they did, would we really want them on a jury? Mark Twain commented on this paradox after he observed jury selection in a murder case. Twain noted that several intelligent potential jurors were dismissed since they had read newspaper accounts of the case even though each of them said they would be able to put aside the information they had read and decide the case fairly and impartially on the evidence. Twain concluded "ignoramuses alone could mete out unsullied justice" (1913, pp. 56–57).

Media attention is not the only factor that interferes with the *tabula rasa* theory. Even in run-of-the-mill cases that have received no media attention, jurors will inevitably still bring their own knowledge and experiences to the deliberation process. "All adults have beliefs, values, and prejudices which make impartiality in the *tabula rasa* sense impossible" (Gobert, 1988, p. 271). For example, in spite of the voir dire process,

- Jurors are less likely to convict a defendant on a charge involving conduct in which the jurors had personally engaged in the past, such as gambling or reckless driving (Kalven & Zeisel, 1966).

- Emotional arousal often based on images or descriptions of particularly gruesome bodily harm affects juror biases toward guilt (Bright & Goodman-Delahunty, 2006).

- Jurors intuitively value some types of evidence more than others. Specifically, they routinely undervalue circumstantial evidence and "overvalue direct evidence (eyewitness identifications and confessions) when making verdict choices, even though false-conviction statistics indicate that the former is normally more probative and more reliable than the latter" (Heller, 2006, p. 241). However, in cases in which DNA evidence is presented as circumstantial evidence, jurors tend to give it much greater weight than other types of evidence (Lieberman et al., 2008).

- Some jurors are inclined to credit or disregard testimony by police (Dorfman, 1999).

- The victim's or defendant's attractiveness (especially in sex-crime cases) or how sympathetic the defendant appears to the jury have both been found to be a significant factor in jurors' determinations of guilt (Kalven & Zeisel, 1966; Patry, 2008; Sigall & Ostrove, 1975).

- And demographic characteristics of the victim and defendant, including their race, gender, socioeconomic class, and sexual orientation, all affect juror decision making as well (see Devine, Clayton, Dunford, Seying, & Pryce, 2001; Levett et al., 2005; Sommers, 2007). Biases on account of race and ethnicity, whether purposeful or unconscious, have especially pronounced effects in death penalty cases (Chapter 14).

The answer to the question of whether juries are biased depends on what is meant by "biased." Most research suggests that modern juries in the United States appear to perform remarkably well on the whole, deciding cases primarily on the basis of legal factors rather than extralegal ones (Ford, 1986; Garvey et al., 2004; Mills & Bohannon, 1980). Even in trials involving emotional issues such as sexual assault, evidence is the primary factor in decision making. Jurors were influenced by extralegal factors, but these effects were largely limited to weak cases in which the state presented little hard evidence (Reskin & Visher, 1986). This is not to say that racism, sexism (including gender stereotypes), homophobia, and the like do not enter into juror decision making; they do. However, the effects of these biases appear to be minimal because they are significantly moderated by legal factors—especially the strength of the evidence (Diamond, 2006; Garvey et al., 2004; Mitchell, Haw, Pfeifer, & Meissner, 2005).

The Verdict

Once the jury informs the judge that a decision has been reached, the lawyers and the defendant gather in the courtroom. Typically, the foreperson announces the **verdict**. How often do juries convict? Given that the vast majority of cases have already been dismissed or disposed of by a plea of guilty, one might expect that the defendant's chances of winning at trial are roughly 50–50, but the real odds against acquittal are significantly higher. In federal courts, juries convict 82 percent of the time in nondrug cases. Data from the National Center for State Courts (Ostrom, Kauder, & LaFountain, 2001) point in the same direction; juries convict about three-quarters of the time in state criminal cases.

Do juries view cases differently from judges? Harry Kalven and Hans Zeisel (1966) found that judges and juries agree more than three out of four times. When judge and jury disagree, the judge is more likely to convict and the jury to acquit. Subsequent studies have replicated these findings (Eisenberg et al., 2004). But this pattern is tied to several factors, including the severity of the charge, whether the defendant takes the stand to testify in his or her own defense and a jury learns that the defendant has no prior convictions, and whether the defense merely challenges the sufficiency of the state's case or presents its own witnesses to disprove the prosecution's version of the case (Eisenberg et al., 2004; Givelber & Farrell, 2008; Levine, 1983).

Postverdict Motions

A trial verdict of **acquittal** (not guilty) ends the case; the defendant can leave the courthouse a free person. A verdict of guilty, however, means that further proceedings will occur; the defendant must be sentenced (Chapter 14) and in all likelihood will appeal (Chapter 16).

If the jury returns a verdict of guilty, the defendant still has certain legal options remaining. A guilty defendant may file **postverdict motions**, which are heard prior to sentencing. These motions give the defense attorney the opportunity to reargue alleged mistakes made at trial. The trial judge may have a change of mind and become convinced that some ruling made against the defendant was erroneous. For example, the defense might try making another motion for a judgment of acquittal. Another common postverdict motion is the *motion for a new trial*. It asserts that serious errors were made at trial (either by the trial judge or by the prosecutor), so the guilty verdict should be set aside and a new trial granted. Postverdict motions are largely a formality; few are ever granted.

LAW IN ACTION: TRIALS AS BALANCING WHEELS

Trials exert a major influence on the operation of the entire criminal court process. This process resembles a balance. A balance wheel regulates or stabilizes the motion of a mechanism. Although only a handful of cases go to trial, the possibility of trial operates as a balancing wheel on all other cases. Most important, the likelihood of conviction determines the negotiating position of lawyers during plea bargaining. Thus, jury trials must be measured not only in terms of their impact on specific cases but also on how the decisions reached affect similar cases in the future.

Popular Standards of Justice

Juries introduce the community's commonsense judgments into judicial decisions. The University of Chicago jury project (Broeder, 1959) found that popular standards of justice are by far the major reason for disagreement between judge and jury.

The result is jury legislation—a jury's deliberate modification of the law to make it conform to community views of what the law ought to be (Kalven & Zeisel, 1966).

One example of how juries introduce popular standards into the criminal court process involves prosecutions for hunting violations. Rural juries are dubious about laws that restrict hunting privileges. Thus, federal defendants accused of shooting too many birds (and the like) have a good chance of finding friendly juries ready to come to their rescue (Levine, 1983).

In recent years, the importance of juries' introducing popular standards into the justice system has been associated with the concept of **jury nullification**—the right of juries to nullify or refuse to apply law in criminal cases despite facts that leave no reasonable doubt that the law was violated. Some advocates of jury nullification base their ideas on a perceived need to reduce government intrusion into citizens' lives; others are motivated by concern over racial injustice (Brooks, 2004; Brown, 1997; Butler, 1995). Judges are quick to denounce jury nullification because they feel that the rule of law is undermined. But others counter that juries have been refusing to follow the law for centuries, and they have every right to send a message by not following a law they find, for whatever reason, to be flawed. Contemporary discussions focus on whether juries should be told they have the right to disregard the judge's jury instructions and substitute their own views and, if so, what the effects of doing so may be (Diamond, 2007; Dunn, 2007; Galiber et al., 1993; Horowitz, Kerr, Park, & Gockel, 2006).

Uncertainty

Jury trials also affect the criminal court system by introducing uncertainty into the process. Stories about irrational juries form part of the folklore of any courthouse. Here are two examples. During jury deliberations in a drug case, two jurors announced that "only God can judge" and hung the jury by refusing to vote. After an acquittal in a burglary case, a juror put her arm around the defendant and said, "Bob, we were sure happy to find you not guilty, but don't do it again" (Neubauer, 1974b, p. 228). Legal professionals resent such intrusions into their otherwise ordered world; they seek to reduce such uncertainties by developing the norms of cooperation discussed throughout this book. Viewed in this light, plea bargaining serves to shield the system from a great deal of the uncertainty that results when lay citizens are involved in deciding important legal matters.

PREJUDICIAL PRETRIAL PUBLICITY

Two provisions of the U.S. Constitution often come into conflict in high-profile criminal cases. On one hand, the Sixth Amendment guarantees the accused a fair trial. On the other, the First Amendment guarantees the press the ability to cover criminal trials (*Richmond Newspapers v. Virginia*, 1980). But extensive media coverage can cause **prejudicial pretrial publicity**. This term refers to the media's ability to taint the venire so that potential jurors are incapable of rendering a fair and impartial verdict based on the evidence presented in court because pretrial publicity has already shaped their opinions of the case.

Two cases in the 1960s caused the U.S. Supreme Court to overturn convictions based on prejudicial pretrial publicity having interfered with the defendants' right to a fair trial (*Irvin v. Dowd*, 1961; *Sheppard v. Maxwell, 1966). The Sheppard* case, in particular, received national attention. Dr. Sam Sheppard stood accused of bludgeoning his wife to death in her bedroom. Intensive media coverage both before and during the trial contributed to the jurors' verdict of conviction. Sheppard spent 10 years in prison before the Supreme Court ruled that the media publicity had denied Sheppard a fair trial. Prosecutors retried him and, the second time around, he was acquitted. His story was later chronicled both on television and in the movie, *The Fugitive*.

In the wake of the *Sheppard* case, trial judges attempted to preserve defendants' Sixth Amendment rights to a fair trial by imposing **gag orders** on the press. Because violations of gag orders are punishable as **contempt of court** (disobeying a judge's order), they prevented the press from reporting on pretrial criminal proceedings—or subjected them to jail time for doing so. But in *Nebraska Press Association v. Stuart* (1976), the Supreme Court ruled that such gag orders were unconstitutional violations of the First Amendment rights of the press.

Research supports the Supreme Court's reasoning that publicity does, in fact, affect jurors. In a classic study, a team of researchers provided one set of "jurors" with prejudicial news coverage of a case and a control group with "nonprejudicial" information. After listening to an identical trial involving a case in which the guilt of the defendant was greatly in doubt, the study found that the "prejudiced jurors" were more likely to convict than the "nonprejudiced jurors" (Padawer-Singer & Barton, 1975). These results have been replicated many times such that it is now widely accepted that even modest pretrial publicity can prejudice potential jurors against a defendant (Moran & Cutler, 1991; Studebaker & Penrod, 2007).

Historically, very few criminal trials involved prejudicial pretrial publicity. But with the advent of 24-hour cable news channels and the ease of information access through the Internet, pretrial publicity affects more cases today than ever before. When there is extensive pretrial publicity, the jury-selection process is greatly strained. Voir dire is geared to ferreting out ordinary instances of unfairness or prejudice, not to correcting the possibility of a systematic pattern of bias. For example, if an attorney excuses all jurors who have heard something about the case at hand, he or she runs the risk of selecting a jury solely from the least attentive, least literate members of the general public. On the other hand, if an attorney accepts jurors who assert that they will judge the case solely on the basis of testimony in open court, he or she is still not certain that the juror—no matter how well-intentioned—can hear the case with a truly open mind.

In trying to reconcile conflicting principles of a fair trial and freedom of the press, trial courts use (singly or in combination) three techniques: limited gag orders, change of venue, and sequestering of the jury. Each of these methods suffers from admitted drawbacks.

Limited Gag Orders

The First Amendment forbids the court from censoring what the press writes about a criminal case, but it says nothing about restricting the flow of information to the media. Thus, in cases in which it seems likely that selecting a jury may be difficult, judges now routinely issue *limited gag orders* forbidding those involved in the case—police, prosecutor, defense attorney, and defendant—from talking to the press. Since these people know the most about the case (and often have the most to gain from pretrial publicity), the net effect is to dry up news leaks. However, consistent with the First Amendment, the press is free to publish any information it discovers. The greatest difficulty is that one of the people involved in the case may secretly provide information, in violation of the judge's order. The judge can then subpoena the reporter and order disclosure of the source. Reporters believe that identifying their sources will dry up the flow of information, so they refuse to testify. They are cited for contempt and go to jail. Thus, the court may infringe on freedom of the press when its intent is simply to guarantee another Bill of Rights protection—the right to a fair trial.

Change of Venue

Recall from Chapter 2 that **venue** refers to the place where a case is tried. If the court is convinced that a case has received such extensive publicity that picking an impartial jury is impossible, the trial may be shifted to another part of the state. If a case has received statewide coverage, however, such a change is of limited use. Defense attorneys face a difficult tactical decision in deciding whether to request a **change of venue**. They must weigh the effects of prejudicial publicity against the disadvantages of having a trial in a more rural and conservative area, where citizens are hostile to big-city defendants (particularly if they are African-American). Prosecutors generally oppose such moves because they believe that the chances of conviction are greater in the local community. To justify this position, prosecutors cite the expense of moving witnesses, documents, and staff to a distant city for a long trial.

Sequestering the Jury

A prime defect in the trial of Dr. Sheppard was the failure to shield the jury from press coverage of the ongoing trial. Indeed, jurors read newspaper stories of the trial, which included inadmissible evidence. One remedy that is common in trials involving extensive media coverage is to **sequester** the jury. The jurors live in a hotel, take their meals together, and participate in weekend recreation together. Sheriff's deputies censor newspapers and shut off television news. The possibility of being in virtual quarantine for a number of weeks makes many citizens reluctant to serve. When sequestering is probable, the jury selected runs the risk of including only citizens who are willing to be separated for long periods of time from friends and family, who can afford to be off work, or who look forward to a Spartan existence. At a minimum, sequestration is a trying experience for the jurors.

MEDIA IN THE COURTROOM

The rise of electronic media has added a new dimension to the defendant's right to a fair trial. Trials, of course, are open to the public, and journalists are free to observe and report on courtroom proceedings. But what tools the public, journalists, and even jurors can use in the courtroom has been the subject of controversy for nearly a century. The debate is frequently framed around "cameras in the courtroom." But in this sense, the term "cameras" is used more broadly than still photography equipment; it also includes recording and broadcasting devices.

Changing Views on Cameras in the Courtroom

Since the sensational Lindbergh trial of the 1930s, radio and television coverage of the judicial process has been limited. In that case, German immigrant Bruno Hauptman was accused of kidnapping and murdering the son of the famous aviator Charles Lindbergh. Because it was perceived that the daily press coverage of the trial was excessive, rules of court came to forbid cameras or recording devices in the courthouse. Indeed, in *Estes v. Texas* (1965), the Supreme Court overturned a conviction on due process grounds when a criminal case was televised in spite of the defendant's objections. In his concurring opinion, Justice Harlan stressed the Court's reasoning: televised trials "possess such capabilities for interfering with the even course of the judicial process that they are constitutionally banned" (p. 595).

In 1978, the American Bar Association proposed allowing television coverage of courtroom proceedings when it would not be obtrusive. As a result, some states began to change their rules. Three years later, the Supreme Court changed its view when it unanimously held that electronic media and still photographic coverage of public judicial proceedings do not violate a defendant's right to a fair trial (*Chandler v. Florida*, 1981). Since then, the barriers against cameras in the courtroom have fallen in state after state.

A 2009 C-SPAN Supreme Court Survey found that 61 percent of Americans would like to see cameras in the courtroom (Penn, Schoen, & Berland Associates, 2009). But some people complain that televising trials distorts the process by encouraging the participants to play to the camera (Thaler, 1994). They also argue that by covering only sensational trials and presenting only the most dramatic moments of hours of testimony, television stations fail to portray the trial process accurately. And as recently as 2010, the Supreme Court expressed concern about the "the intimidating effect of cameras on some witnesses and jurors" (*Hollingsworth v. Perry*, 2010, p. 712).

Others argue that cameras in the courtroom have a valuable educational role, providing the public with a firsthand view of how court proceedings operate (Alexander, 1991; Raymond, 1992). As to the possibility of the camera's disrupting judicial proceedings, a detailed study in Florida concluded: "Broadcast journalists who follow state guidelines present coverage which, upon close examination by presiding judges, participating attorneys and jurors, is perceived as undistorted" (Alexander, 1991).

Current Broadcasting Rules

In 1996, the U.S. Judicial Conference adopted a resolution prohibiting electronic media coverage in federal district courts, but allowing each court of appeals to decide whether cameras should be allowed. As of this writing, only the Second and Ninth Circuit allow their proceedings to be broadcast. And cameras are not permitted in the U.S. Supreme Court. Indeed, during the highly unusual 3 days of hearings that the U.S. Supreme Court devoted to reviewing President Obama's health

care law, not only were television cameras banned as per the Court's usual rules, but all electronic devices were also banned, effectively preventing anyone in the courtroom from texting, e-mailing, or using social media such as Twitter or Facebook to send real-time updates about the arguments (see Ingram, 2012).

Congress has proposed a series of bills that would allow electronic media coverage in federal judicial proceedings, but to date, none of these proposed pieces of legislation has been passed. Things are quite different, however, in state courts.

> State restrictions on broadcasting and cameras in the court generally fall into three groups. The first group includes nineteen states that allow the broadest coverage, giving broad discretion to the presiding judge. The second group includes sixteen states that prohibit coverage of important types of cases, or when witnesses object to broadcasting their testimony. The third group includes fifteen states that allow appellate coverage only, or that have such restricting trial coverage rules which essentially prohibit coverage. Most of these states only allow appellate court coverage or coverage at the consent of all parties. (Cervantes, 2010, p. 143).

In most of the states that allow broadcast media coverage in courtrooms, there are specific restrictions designed to prevent disruptions of the proceedings. For example, the number of cameras in the courtroom is usually limited, and camera operators are prohibited from moving around the courtroom while the court is in session.

Technology beyond "Cameras"

In May 2008, the California Supreme Court invalided state laws that limited marriage to opposite-sex couples (*In re Marriage Cases*, 2008). As a result, same-sex couples were able to be legally married in California. But in November 2008, by a 52-to-48-percent margin, voters passed Proposition 8, amending the California state constitution to prohibit the legal recognition of same-sex marriages in the state. In 2009, the constitutionality of Prop 8 was then challenged on federal constructional law grounds. When the case came to a bench trial in January 2010, the presiding federal district judge, Vaughn R. Walker, authorized its "broadcast live via streaming audio and video to a number of federal courthouses around the country." By a 5-to-4 vote, the Supreme Court ordered Judge Walker to reverse his decision granting permission for the Proposition 8 trial to be digitally recorded and broadcast (*Hollingsworth v. Perry*, 2010). The Court found that the change in the local court rules that would have allowed for such a broadcast had occurred too quickly and without sufficient time for public comment.

Judge Walker ultimately allowed reporters to broadcast the trial through live "tweets" using Twitter. "Tweeters like '@FedCourt Junkie' were followed by more than a thousand people who wanted to stay instantly updated on the trial proceedings but who would not be able to actually go to the courtroom" (Cervantes, 2010, p. 134). Other courts have also embraced the use of Twitter as a means of increasing the transparency of the judicial process, but other courts disallow the use of all social media in their courtroom.

Technology surely has the potential to assist the public in learning more about America's courts. But technology also poses a threat to the fairness of the trial process. Jurors are using smartphones to obtain information relevant to the case that was not actually presented or was expressly excluded from the jury (Schwartz, 2009a). In one widely reported case, a judge was forced to declare a mistrial after it was revealed that 8 of the 12 jurors used Google—some from home and some from cell phones—to conduct their own research on the defendants and the pharmaceutical medications discussed during trial. But even without any juror misconduct using technology, there is no question that media coverage of certain cases can distort the trial process. Consider what one commentator had to say about cameras in the courtroom after the Casey Anthony trial (see Chapter 1):

> [T]he Casey Anthony case has made me realize the destructive nature of cameras in the courtroom. For months, Americans sat staring at their TV screens catching snippets of the Anthony trial. They saw

only the best highlights from the arguments, the most compelling of the witness testimonies, and a host of evidence (only some of which was ever admitted in court and presented to the jury). Then Americans sat in their living rooms, pieced together everything they saw, and convicted Casey Anthony in the court of public opinion. . . . But twelve people sat in that courtroom for weeks and listened to every argument and heard every bit of testimony and saw only the admissible evidence. They sat and listened. Then they convened and discussed what they saw, and all of them agreed—unanimously—that they could not say beyond a reasonable doubt that Casey Anthony killed her daughter. It's pretty hard to get twelve people to agree on anything, but in this case they were all certain. They did not have enough evidence to convict Casey Anthony, even of manslaughter. (Ferguson, 2011, ¶¶ 2-4).

Cases involving celebrities present even more challenging questions about how much information should be available to the public and what should be withheld. The widely televised trial of O. J. Simpson clearly caused some rethinking about cameras in the courtroom. Perceptions that lawyers were playing to the cameras apparently had an impact in several highly publicized cases that followed. Similarly, journalists complained that in the Michael Jackson child molestation case, the California judge sealed almost all of the records (Deutsch, 2004). In the rape trial of NBA star Kobe Bryant, the Colorado judge restricted inquiries into the alleged victim's prior sex life (Savage & Dolan, 2004). In short, celebrity justice cases force judges and the media to walk a fine line between full reporting and turning the case into a spectacle (Hubler, 2005).

CONCLUSION

After the initial screening of the venire in the case involving Michael Jackson's death, "every potential juror said they had some knowledge of the involuntary manslaughter case against Murray" (Ryan, 2011, ¶ 3). But an extensive questionnaire used to prescreen members of the venire led the judge to limit voir dire questioning to 1 minute per potential juror. In the end, the petit jury impaneled in the case took less than 2 days of deliberations to convict Murray, who was subsequently sentenced to imprisonment for 4 years.

In many ways, highly publicized jury trials for defendants like Conrad Murray, Rod Blagojevich, and Casey Anthony (see Chapter 1) are the high point of the judicial process. Indeed, along with Lady Justice, jury trials stand as the primary symbol of justice. In turn, many Supreme Court decisions emphasize the importance of adversarial procedures at trial. Yet, in examining the realities of trial, we are presented with two contradictory perspectives: Full-fledged trials are relatively rare, yet trials are an important dimension of the court process. Although only a smattering of cases is ever tried, the possibility of trial shapes the entire process. Thus, long after trials have declined to minimal importance in other Western nations, the institution of the jury trial remains a vital part of the American judicial process.

Chapter Review

LO1 1. Trace the history of trials by jury.

The right to a trial by jury can be traced to the Magna Carta in 1215. This right was incorporated into Article III, Section 2, of the U.S. Constitution with respect to the federal government, and in the Sixth Amendment, with respect to the states.

LO2 2. Analyze the scope of the right to a trial by jury in a criminal case.

The right to a trial by jury applies to all nonpetty criminal offenses, usually interpreted as offenses punishable by a term of imprisonment of 6 months or more. The right may be waived by a defendant, who may opt for a bench trial in lieu of a jury trial.

LO3 3. Evaluate the impact of differences in jury size and unanimity requirements.

Common law juries have consisted of 12 people since the 14th century. The Supreme Court, however, authorized smaller juries in noncapital cases, but juries with less than 6 members are not permitted in criminal cases. Since that ruling, many states have specifically authorized juries of fewer than 12 jurors, but most allow these smaller juries only in misdemeanor cases. Some studies have found very few differences between 6- and 12-person juries, while others have reported significant differences.

LO4 4. Explain how a jury is summoned and selected, including the constitutional limitations on these processes.

Potential jurors are summoned to court using master jury lists. The people who are summoned, called the "venire," come to court to participate in voir dire, a process designed to select a fair and impartial petit jury by asking members of the venire about potential biases concerning the case. Those who cannot serve as fair and impartial jurors are excused for cause. A few other members of the venire may be excused by either party using peremptory challenges so long as these challenges are not used in a discriminatory manner that violates the constitutional guarantee of equal protection.

LO5 5. Discuss the function of jury consultants in the process of scientific jury selection.

Jury consultants use social scientific research methods to profile jurors in an attempt to help attorneys select members of the venire for petit jury service who are likely to be predisposed to their side of the case.

LO6 **6.** Distinguish between the presumptions that apply at the start of trials and the burdens of proof applicable to overcoming them.

The two presumptions that apply to every criminal trial are the presumption of innocence and the presumption of sanity. It is the responsibility of the prosecution to introduce sufficient evidence over the course of a trial to overcome or rebut the presumption of innocence by proving a defendant's guilt beyond a reasonable doubt. In insanity defense cases, the defense usually must prove that the defendant was insane at the time of the commission of a crime by clear and convincing evidence.

LO7 **7.** Summarize the basic rules of evidence concerning trustworthiness and relevance of evidence.

Only relevant evidence is admitted at trial— evidence that tends to prove or disprove a fact in dispute. Relevance, however, is not enough. Evidence must also be reliable. Thus, hearsay evidence, lay opinion, speculative testimony, and copies of documents (when originals are available) are generally all inadmissible.

LO8 **8.** Analyze how special limitations on expert witnesses affect the litigation of criminal cases, especially with regard to leading types of forensic evidence.

Historically, and in some jurisdictions even today, expert testimony had to be based on scientific facts that were generally accepted in the relevant scientific community. However, under the *Daubert* standard, reliability is the linchpin to admissibility. Because the reliability of a number of forensic techniques is unknown, the continued use of these techniques has been called into question.

LO9 **9.** Identify the steps in a criminal trial.

After a jury is selected through the voir dire process, the prosecution and then the defense usually deliver their respective opening statements. The prosecution then calls witnesses and conducts direct examination of its witnesses, some of whom will introduce physical or scientific evidence. The defense has the opportunity to cross-examine each of the prosecution's witnesses. When the prosecution rests, the defense may call its witnesses and introduce its evidence. The prosecution then has the opportunity to cross-examine the defense witnesses. At the conclusion of the trial, both parties make closing arguments. The judge instructs the jury with regard to the applicable law and then the jury deliberates until it reaches a verdict.

LO10 **10.** Describe the effects and implications of pretrial publicity and the solutions that courts use to prevent those effects from influencing a criminal trial.

Pretrial publicity can taint the potential jury pool by exposing them to information that is inaccurate or inadmissible as evidence. When that occurs, the defendant may be deprived of his or her Sixth Amendment right to a fair and impartial jury. To reduce the chances of the media tainting potential jurors, judges may issue limited gag orders forbidding those involved in the case—police, prosecutor, defense attorney, and defendant—from talking to the press. But even still, venire members may have heard media reports that could have influenced their views on a case. The voir dire process is supposed to screen out potential jurors who have already been tainted. In high-profile cases, a change of venue might be necessary to find a pool of potential jurors who could render a fair and impartial verdict, free from the taint of pretrial publicity. During a trial, however, courts routinely instruct jurors not to read newspapers, magazines, or watch television news shows that may report on the trial. Sometimes, to shield jurors from such media influence, the jury may be sequestered.

Critical Thinking Questions

1. What impact does the jury system have on the rest of the criminal justice system? How would criminal justice function differently if defendants had no right to a trial by a jury of their peers, which is the situation in virtually all of the non–common-law nations of the world?

2. If you are in a federal courthouse and observe a six-member jury, what type of case is being tried? How do you know this?

3. Compare two recent trials in your community. What were the similarities and differences in terms of jury selection, the prosecutor's case-in-chief, the defense strategy, and the verdict? If possible, compare a murder trial with one involving another major felony. In what ways is a murder trial different from, say, a trial for armed robbery or rape?

4. In the wake of the O. J. Simpson verdict of not guilty, many commentators spoke about the collapse of the jury system. Were these sentiments driven by the one verdict, or were there other reasons?

5. Why are some jury verdicts popular and others not? To what extent do differences of opinion over the fairness of a jury verdict reinforce notions that equate justice with winning?

Key Terms

acquittal 359
Allen charge 357
alternate jurors 341
bench trial 335
best-evidence rule 346
burden of persuasion 344
burden of production 344
burden of proof 344
chain of custody 346
challenge for cause 341
change of venue 361
charging conference 356
circumstantial evidence 345
closing argument 356
contempt of court 360
cross-examination 353
CSI effect 348
demonstrative evidence 345
direct evidence 345
direct examination 353
evidence 345

extralegal factors 357
gag order 360
hearsay 346
hung jury 357
impeach 355
irrelevant 346
jury consultants 343
jury deliberations 357
jury instructions 356
jury nullification 359
master jury list 338
mistrial 350
motion for judgment of acquittal 353
objection 350
opening statement 353
peremptory challenge 341
petit jury 333
petty offense 334
postverdict motions 359

prejudicial pretrial publicity 360
presumption of innocence 344
presumption of sanity 344
real evidence 345
reasonable doubt 344
rebuttal 356
rules of evidence 345
scientific evidence 345
scientific jury selection 343
self-incrimination 355
sequester 361
statutory exemptions 339
summons 339
tabula rasa 357
testimonial evidence 345
venire 339
venue 361
verdict 358
voir dire 339

Web Resources

Go to the *America's Courts and the Criminal Justice System* companion website at
http://www.cengage.com/criminaljustice/neubauer,
where you will find more resources to help you study.
Resources include web exercises, quizzing, and flash cards.

For Further Reading

Borgida, Eugene, and Susan T. Fiske. *Beyond Common Sense: Psychological Science in the Courtroom.* Malden, MA: Blackwell, 2008.

Brewer, Neil, and Kipling D. Williams. *Psychology and Law: An Empirical Perspective.* New York: Guildford Press, 2007.

Burns, Robert. *The Death of the American Trial.* Chicago: University of Chicago Press 2009.

Cherry, Michael, and Edward Imwinkelried. "Questions about the Accuracy of Fingerprint Evidence." *Judicature* 92: 158–159, 2009.

Clarke, George (Woody), and Janet Reno. *Justice and Science: Trials and Triumphs of DNA Evidence.* New Brunswick, NJ: Rutgers University Press, 2008.

Fisher, Jim. *Forensics under Fire: Are Bad Science and Dueling Experts Corrupting Criminal Justice?* New Brunswick, NJ: Rutgers University Press, 2008.

Gardner, Thomas, and Terry Anderson. *Criminal Evidence: Principles and Cases.* 7th ed. Belmont, CA: Wadsworth, 2010.

Jonakait, Randolph N. *The American Jury System.* New Haven: Yale University Press, 2006.

Levine, James, and Steen Zeidman. "The Miracle of Jury Reform in New York." *Judicature* 88: 178–184, 2005.

Moriarty, Jane Campbell. "'Misconvictions,' Science, and the Ministers of Justice." *Nebraska Law Review* 86: 1–42, 2007.

National Academies of Sciences. *Strengthening Forensic Science in the United States: A Path Forward.* Washington, DC: National Research Council, 2009.

Pole, J.R. *Contract and Consent: Representation and the Jury in Anglo-American Legal History.* Charlottesville, VA: University of Virginia Press.

Robinson, Paul. *Would You Convict? Seventeen Cases That Challenged the Law.* New York: New York University Press, 1999.

Smith, Alisa, and Michael J. Saks. "The Case for Overturning *Williams v. Florida* and the Six-Person Jury: History, Law, and Empirical Evidence." *Florida Law Review* 60: 441–470, 2008.

Vidmar, Neil, and Valerie Hans. *American Juries: The Verdict.* New York: Prometheus Books, 2007.

Vidmar, Neil, James Coleman, Jr., and Theresa Newman. "Rethinking Reliance on Eyewitness Confidence." *Judicature* 94: 16–19. 2010.

14 Sentencing Options

© Darrin Klimek/Jupiter Images

A man stands behind the bars of a prison cell. Prison populations are at an all-time high in the United States, with 2.26 million inmates in state and federal custody. Many state prisons are so overcrowded that inmates have won significant victories in federal courts, which have ordered states to improve the conditions of confinement on Eighth Amendment grounds. As a result, many states face major financial challenges in trying to house the growing number of prisoners at a time when the cost of doing so continues to rise. Should this have an effect on sentencing options? ■

Chapter Outline

WHY DO WE SENTENCE?
Retribution
Deterrence
Rehabilitation
Incapacitation
Restoration
Competing Sentencing Philosophies

WHO SHOULD DECIDE THE SENTENCE?
Legislative Sentencing Responsibility
Judicial Sentencing Responsibility
Executive Sentencing Responsibility

WHAT SENTENCE SHOULD BE IMPOSED?
Imprisonment
Probation
Fines
Restitution
Intermediate Sanctions

Courts, Law, & Media
Intermediate Sanctions and Lindsay Lohan

THE DEATH PENALTY
Eighth Amendment Standards
Death-Qualified Juries

Courts, Controversy, & Judicial Administration
Should a Moratorium on the Death Penalty Be Imposed?

Narrowing Death-Eligible Cases
Lengthy Appeals

CASE CLOSE-UP: *Roper v. Simmons:* Should Juveniles Be Sentenced to Death?

Cost Concerns

Learning Objectives

After reading this chapter, you should be able to:

LO1 Distinguish between the five major sentencing philosophies.

LO2 Describe how the three branches of government are involved in sentencing.

LO3 List at least three major issues related to imprisonment as a sentence in the United States.

LO4 Identify the major alternatives to imprisonment.

LO5 Summarize the two U.S. Supreme Court rulings from the 1970s on capital punishment that led to the bifurcated process for death penalty sentencing.

LO6 Indicate how the U.S. Supreme Court has narrowed the list of death-eligible cases and offenders.

LO7 Discuss the major differences between the due process model of criminal justice and the crime control model of justice with regard to the death penalty.

When he was 17 years old, Christopher Simmons and a 15-year-old friend broke into a neighbor's house, hogtied her with duct tape, and then shoved her over a railroad trestle into the Meramec River near St. Louis, Missouri. After the jury convicted Simmons of first-degree murder, they imposed the death penalty. The Supreme Court had earlier ruled that 17-year-olds could be put to death (*Stanford v. Kentucky*, 1989), but the rationale for that decision had more recently been undermined when the Court declared that the mentally retarded could not be executed (*Atkins v. Virginia*, 2002). But the justices waited almost 3 years to address for a second time the issue of the juvenile death penalty.

In 1972, by the slimmest of margins, the Court declared all existing death penalty laws unconstitutional, and in the process irrevocably altered the debate over what punishments are appropriate for those who violate the criminal law. Since then, the nation's highest court, like the rest of the nation, has been wrestling with the moral issue of who deserves to die at the hands of the state, and like the rest of the nation, it is deeply divided over the matter.

tions • Sentencing Options • Sentencing Options • Sentencing Op
ns • Sentencing Options • Sentencing Options Sentencing Opti

The debate over the death penalty is the most obvious example of the unprecedented attention the nation has devoted to crime over the past few decades. In large measure, the public holds judges, from the Supreme Court on down, responsible for high rates of crime. Understanding the dissatisfaction with sentencing and the sentencing reforms that have resulted requires an understanding of the legal basis of sentencing.

WHY DO WE SENTENCE?

No consensus exists on how the courts should punish the guilty, perhaps because five different philosophical principles guide sentencing in the United States: retribution, deterrence, rehabilitation, incapacitation, and restoration. These sentencing philosophies differ in important ways. Some focus on past behavior, whereas others are future oriented. Some stress that the punishment should fit the crime, whereas others emphasize that the punishment should fit the criminal. These issues influence contemporary thinking about sentencing.

Retribution

The idea that offenders deserve punishment lies at the heart of **retribution**. This philosophy toward criminal punishment can be traced back to ancient Babylonia in the Code of Hammurabi, one of the oldest written codifications of laws ever discovered. The code relied heavily on the principle of *lex talionis*—"an eye for an eye, a tooth for a tooth"— a revenge-based conceptualization of retributive punishment.

What is most distinctive about retribution is its focus on past behavior; the severity of the punishment is directly tied to the seriousness of the crime. This concept is based on strongly held moral principles: Individuals are held responsible for their own actions. Because they have disregarded the rights of others, criminals are wicked people and therefore deserve to be punished. Punishing wrongdoers also reflects a basic human emotion, the desire for revenge: Because the victim has suffered, the criminal should suffer as well.

The concept of retribution clearly stands for punitive sentencing, but a closer probing reveals important subtleties involving limits on sentencing.

Because society as a whole is punishing the criminal, individuals are not justified in taking the law into their own hands. Moreover, in applying sanctions, the severity of the punishment is limited to the severity of the injury to the victim.

From biblical times through the 18th century, retribution provided the dominant justification for punishment. Beginning with the Enlightenment, however, revenge lost much of its influence as a justification for criminal punishment. In fact, criminal penalties based on revenge came to be viewed as barbaric. A new, more humane view of retribution evolved that focused on deserved punishment, or **just deserts**. It embodied two distinct but interrelated principles. First, the offender justly deserves to be punished for having wronged another person in violation of the law. Second, society has not only the right, but also the obligation to punish proportionally all transgressions of the criminal law because such acts should be viewed as offenses against society as a whole (e.g., Kant, 1790). The approach to retributive punishment is alive and well in modern times.

The just deserts approach to retributive punishment is predicated on the notion of **proportionality.** While "offenders are punished simply because they deserve to be, . . . the severity of their punishment should be no more and no less than they deserve" (Frase, 2005, p. 73). In short, the severity of the sanction should be proportionate to the gravity of the defendant's criminal conduct (Banks, 2009; Carlsmith, Darley, & Robinson, 2002).

Saint Augustine (c. 426) and, later, Saint Thomas Aquinas (c. 1273) and other theologians posited a third conceptualization of retribution based on **expiation**—atonement for sin through deserved suffering. In their opinion, retributive punishment should cause offenders to suffer, but not to achieve revenge or to balance the scales of justice for wrongs committed against individual victims or even society as a whole. Rather, through such suffering, offenders would come to see the errors of their ways, repent, and, ultimately, be forgiven for their sins.

As a sentencing philosophy, retribution suffers from several limitations. Its focus on crimes of violence offers little apparent guidance for sentencing the far more numerous defendants who have committed property violations. Its moralistic emphasis on individual responsibility does not fit well with modern explanations of human behavior based on social, physical, and psychological factors. Its emphasis on vengeance does not easily square with constitutional limits on governmental power (individual rights) that are fundamental to a representative democracy. Most important, though, it emphasizes the past behavior of the defendant and exhibits no concern for future criminal activity. Indeed, extended periods of custody may actually have unintended criminogenic effects, thereby increasing the likelihood that inmates might commit future criminal acts rather than be deterred by the sentence they received (see Austin & Hardyman, 2004). Thus, sentencing on the basis of retribution may prove to be contrary to the goal of crime reduction.

Deterrence

"Let this sentence be a warning to others." Phrases like this reflect one of the more modern and also most widely held justifications for punishment. According to deterrence theory, the purpose of punishment is the prevention of future crimes. Deterrence is not content to punish the given wrongdoer; rather, it seeks to prevent other potential offenders from committing crimes. Deterrence, however, does not propose to change offenders— just deter them. Much like rehabilitation, deterrence argues that the punishment should fit the criminal. Note that this is a different concern from that of retribution theory, in which the punishment should fit the crime.

Building on the work of 18th-century criminologist Cesare Beccaria (1764), Jeremy Bentham, a 19th-century British lawyer, reformer, and criminologist, articulated a coherent theory of deterrence (1830) that still influences us today. To Bentham, punishment based on retribution was pointless and counterproductive. Instead, he argued that sanctions should be used to further society's goal of preventing crime. Bentham believed that human behavior is governed by individual calculation: People seek to maximize pleasure and minimize pain—a principle he referred to as the hedonistic calculus. Under this utilitarian theory, the basic objective of punishment is to discourage crime by making it painful. Because people seek to minimize pain, they will refrain from activities, such as crimes, that result in painful sanctions.

Deterrence theory suggests that the criminal justice system can effectuate two types of deterrence: general and specific. The general deterrence goal of criminal punishment presumes that the threat of punishment will prevent the general population from engaging in the proscribed conduct. The specific deterrence goal of criminal punishment postulates that those for whom the general deterrent of law was insufficient to prevent them from having engaged in the proscribed conduct should be subjected to punishment so that they will be personally discouraged from engaging in the proscribed conduct again.

Both Beccaria and Bentham in their classical deterrence models argued for the existence of several factors that would influence the effectiveness of punishment as a general deterrent. Much scholarly research has demonstrated that the effectiveness of law as a deterrent is dependent on three primary factors: severity, certainty, and celerity (i.e., swiftness). Severity of punishment is concerned with how severe the punishment is. The theory postulates that the more severe the punishment, the less likely the actor is to engage in the proscribed conduct. The second factor, certainty of punishment, is concerned with how likely the actor is to get away with the crime as opposed to being caught. According to deterrence theory, the more likely it is that the actor is going to be caught, the less likely he or she is to engage in the conduct. Finally, celerity of punishment is the factor that looks at the swiftness of punishment. The theory suggests that the faster the punishment is inflicted after the offense, the less likely the person is to engage in the proscribed conduct. Conversely, the later or further off the punishment, the less likely is the person to be deterred.

Notions of deterrence form the core of contemporary discussions about sentencing. In a general sense, many people refrain from committing illegal acts because they fear the consequences of being convicted. After a party, for example, an intoxicated guest may take a taxi home rather than run the risk of being arrested and disgraced by a drunken driving conviction. In this situation, one can easily argue that the threat of punishment does deter. However, what of the person who drinks and drives? Perhaps such an actor has weighed the costs and benefits and decided that the low likelihood of being caught makes the behavior worth the risk. Alternatively, one could argue that drinking and driving is, in itself, an irrational behavior since it puts the lives of the driver and others on the road in jeopardy. This reveals one of the most significant shortcomings of deterrence theory: the threat of severe, certain, and swift punishment is likely to deter only those who are thinking rationally. Those who are thinking irrationally (whether due to mental illness, disability, the effects of drugs or alcohol, or other reasons) are unlikely to be deterred, because their abilities to engage in the hedonistic calculus is impaired. This is particularly true for many crimes of violence that are committed on the spur of the moment or during the "heat of passion."

An extensive literature examines deterrence but reaches no firm conclusions. Some studies find a deterrent effect, and others do not (Levitt, 2006; Nagin, 1998; Webster, Doob, & Zimring, 2006). Although discussions of deterrence are usually coupled with calls for increasing the severity of sentences, some research suggests that the perceived certainty of punishment is more of a deterrent than the perceived severity of punishment (Cullen, Wright, & Blevins, 2006; Wilson, 1983). Moreover, because deterrence rests on the assumption of rational, calculating behavior, and this precondition is absent in many crimes (as described above), many observers question whether court sentences—particularly severe ones—do indeed deter.

Rehabilitation

Another modern justification for imposing punishment concerns helping offenders assume a constructive place in society through vocational, educational, or therapeutic treatment. The idea of rehabilitation assumes that criminal behavior is the result of social or psychological disorders, and that the treatment of such disorders should be the primary goal of corrections. Success means assessing the needs of the individual and providing a program to meet those needs. Ultimately, then, offenders are not being punished but treated, not only for their own good but also for the benefit of society. Under rehabilitation, sentences should fit the offender rather than the offense.

The concept of rehabilitation dominated thinking about sentencing throughout much of the 20th century, providing the intellectual linchpin for important developments such as probation and

parole, as well as the concept of pretrial diversion—an alternative to prosecution that seeks to divert certain offenders from traditional criminal justice processing into programs of supervision and rehabilitative services. Most court personnel and correctional officials have strongly favored rehabilitation. It has also enjoyed widespread public support; almost three out of four persons favor the idea that the main emphasis in prisons should be to help the offender become a productive citizen.

The rehabilitative ideal has been challenged on both normative and empirical grounds. Some commentators have voiced concern that the rehabilitative ideal grants too much discretion to judges and corrections personnel. As a result of this discretion, the humanitarian goal of rehabilitation can serve to mask punishment. But such normative concerns appear to be taking a back seat to the empirical data concerning rehabilitation.

Starting in the mid-1970s, evidence revealed that rehabilitative programs did not substantially reduce the later criminality of their clients (Blumstein, Cohen, Martin, & Tonry, 1983; Martinson, 1974). California, for example, where the rehabilitative model had been most completely incorporated, was also marked by high rates of *recidivism* (repeat criminal behavior). To some, the key weakness of rehabilitation is that people cannot be coerced to change. Some prisoners participate in prison rehabilitation programs, such as counseling, job training, and religious services, in order to gain an early release—not because they wish to change their behavior.

More recently, though, empirical studies have found that rehabilitation can indeed be effective (see Cullen, 2005). Much of the research supporting the rehabilitative model comes from studies that have evaluated the effectiveness of different correctional interventions. An ever-growing number of modern correctional policies are being crafted in light of the empirical evidence produced by these evaluation studies, a movement called evidence-based corrections (MacKenzie, 2006; Robinson, 2008). As a result, resources are being put into interventions that research has demonstrated to be effective, such as "using behavioral and cognitive approaches, occurring in the offenders' natural environment, being multi-modal and intensive enough to be effective, encompassing rewards for pro-social behavior, targeting high-risk and high-criminogenic need individuals, and matching the learning styles and abilities of the offender" (Listwan, Cullen, & Latessa, 2006, p. 20). In contrast, rehabilitative strategies that have proven to be largely ineffective, such as psychodynamic therapies and "scared straight" programs, are slowly being abandoned (Cullen, Blevins, & Trager, 2005; MacKenzie, 2006).

The reemergence of rehabilitation as a viable basis for criminal punishment has also been fueled, in part, by the severe economic downturn in the later part of the first decade of the 21st century. The extremely high costs of incarcerating so many people—especially nonviolent drug offenders—caused many commentators to question the sustainability of the punitive, "get tough" policies of the 1980s and 1990s (Steen & Bandy, 2007). In other words, from a cost–benefit standpoint, the harsh economic reality of the prison-industrial complex has led to a renewed focus on rehabilitative strategies (Robinson, 2008). California, for example, is undergoing **prison realignment**—transferring the state's responsibility for lower-level drug offenders, thieves, and other nonviolent convicts to the county level. Counties, in turn, would house these offenders in jails and in-home detention and work crew assignments. State officials hope that county-level services can provide better rehabilitation and job-training services that might improve on the state's dismal 70 percent recidivism record. But critics fear that the lack of financial resources at the county level (including insufficient bed space in jails) will lead to more criminals being out on the street rather than incarcerated. Time will tell whether this experiment proves to be a success or failure (see Krisberg & Taylor-Nicholson, 2011).

Incapacitation

"Lock them up and throw away the key." Average citizens, outraged by a recent, shocking crime, often express sentiments like this. The assumption of **incapacitation** is that crime can be prevented if criminals are physically restrained. The theory of isolating current or potential criminals differs from the theory of retribution in two important ways. First, it is future oriented; the goal is to prevent future crimes, not punish past ones. Second, it focuses on the personal characteristics of the offender; the type of person committing the

crime is more important than the crime committed. Unlike rehabilitation, however, incapacitation has no intention of reforming the offender.

Since ancient times, societies have banished persons who have disobeyed the rules. England transported criminals to penal colonies, such as Georgia and Australia. Russia exiled dissidents to cold, distant Siberia, where they could not threaten the government. More commonly, nations have used prisons to isolate guilty offenders, preventing them from committing additional crimes in the community. Some people likewise justify the death penalty on the basis that it prevents future crimes.

Incapacitation is probably the most straightforward justification offered for punishing wrongdoers. As a sentencing philosophy, however, it suffers from important limitations. It cannot provide any standards about how long a sentence should be. Indeed, the goal of crime prevention may be used to justify severe sanctions for both trivial and serious offenses. Moreover, isolation without efforts directed toward rehabilitation may produce more severe criminal behavior once the offender is released. Prisons protect the community, but that protection is only temporary. Applying the incapacitation theory to the fullest would require the building of many more prisons, at great expense.

The incapacitation theory of sentencing has never been well articulated. Its assumptions about crime and criminals are simplistic. But in recent years a more focused variant, **selective incapacitation,** has received considerable attention (Goodman-Delahunty, ForsterLee, & ForsterLee, 2007). Research has shown that a relatively small number of criminals are responsible for a large number of crimes (DeLisi, 2005; Haapanen, 1989). These findings have led to an interest in targeting dangerous offenders (Chaiken & Chaiken, 1990). Some studies estimate that sending serious offenders to prison for longer periods of time will result in a significant reduction in crime (Shinnar & Shinnar, 1975; Spelman, 2000). Not all researchers agree, however, that selective incapacitation will greatly reduce crime because predictions of who will commit crimes in the future are very unreliable (Auerhahn, 2006; Cunningham, Reidy, & Sorensen, 2008). "Offenders commit crimes at different rates and individuals' offending rates evolve over their life course. Therefore, estimating how many crimes are averted . . . must depend crucially on when in individuals' lives and at what point in their criminal careers the incarceration occurs" (Bhati, 2007, p. 357). Moreover, critics argue that even though some offenders may be incapacitated through imprisonment, other people on the verge of criminality are ready to take their places (Auerhahn, 1999; Visher, 1987). And still other critics argue that the costs of imprisonment typically exceed the benefits gained from preventing certain criminals from recidivating by keeping them incapacitated (Blokland & Nieuwbeerta, 2007).

Restoration

After imposing a prison sentence on a rapist, an Australian judge observed a victim who remained as upset as she had been throughout all of the judicial proceedings. So, he asked her to approach the bench. Speaking quietly, he said, "You understand that what I have done here demonstrates conclusively that *what happened was not your fault*." Hearing these words, she burst into tears and ran from the courtroom. Several days later, he called the family and learned that his words provided a sense of "vindication for the woman; they marked the beginning of her psychological recovery. Her tears had been tears of healing" (Van Ness & Strong, 2006, p. 3).

The restorative justice movement seeks to replace retribution with **restoration**. Restorative justice is based on three distinct elements (Galaway & Hudson, 1996):

1. Crime is primarily a conflict between individuals, which results in injuries (physical and/or psychological) to victims, the community, and the offender as well. Therefore, crime is only secondarily a violation of governmental laws.

2. The principal aim of the criminal justice system should be to repair these injuries. Therefore, promoting peace and reconciling parties is much more important than punishing the guilty.

3. The criminal justice system should facilitate involvement of victims, offenders, and the community. Therefore, lay citizens should play a central role in the criminal justice system, and

professionals (police, prosecutors, and probation officers, for example) should play less of a role.

Proponents of restorative justice reject retributive punishment because they view vengeance as counterproductive. Similarly, they see the rehabilitative model as being too narrow—targeting offenders but providing no healing for victims.

Skeptics voice concern that restorative justice means considerably different things to different people. Indeed, by stressing abstract concepts rather than pointing to specific programs, proponents make it somewhat difficult to discuss restorative justice because many of the examples singled out as demonstrating successful implementation are drawn from other countries.

If skeptics seem somewhat receptive to this new idea, critics express open hostility about subjecting a victim to another, possibly equally damaging, encounter with the defendant. Typical was the person on an Internet discussion list who wanted to know why victims should be forced to bargain with a person who has caused them harm. Perhaps victims do not want to go through the process because of legitimate concerns (unnecessarily revisiting the original trauma) or out of shortsightedness (holding on to the role of victim is comfortable). Overall, it is clear that the restorative justice understanding of victims is far different from those views that stress punishment.

Restorative justice programs have become increasingly common in the justice system, but relatively little is known about their effectiveness. Some of the early studies have been characterized as using weak research designs. A rigorous study of the Indianapolis Restorative Justice Experiment is important, therefore, because the results were largely positive. Youths who were assigned to family group conferences (as opposed to a control group) were less likely to be rearrested (McGarrell & Hipple, 2008).

Competing Sentencing Philosophies

Of the five major philosophies outlined above—retribution, incapacitation, deterrence, rehabilitation, and restoration—none alone is adequate; the various goals must be balanced. Therefore, elements of each of these philosophies have been incorporated into society's efforts to control crime.

As a result, sentencing decisions reflect ambivalent expectations about the causes of crime, the nature of criminals, and the role of the courts in reducing crime. Moreover, debates about the morality and effectiveness of each philosophical perspective resulted in widespread sentencing reforms, many of which focus on who should have the authority to impose a sentence and what limits should be placed on that authority.

WHO SHOULD DECIDE THE SENTENCE?

From the inside looking out, sentencing is a judicial function. With a few exceptions, only the judge has the legal authority to send the guilty to prison or to grant probation. From the outside looking in, however, sentencing responsibility involves all three branches of government—legislative, executive, and judicial.

Throughout most of the 20th century, sentencing was exercised within broad limits set by the legislature, which prescribed maximum sentences. The judicial branch of government had primary authority over who went to prison, and an executive agency—**parole boards**—controlled the length of the prison term. Since the mid-1970s, dramatic changes have been made in the laws under which offenders are sent to prison and in the mechanisms that control how long they stay there. Legislatures have increased their control over the sentencing process, and the judiciary and the parole boards have taken steps to formalize and regularize their exercise of discretion in applying sanctions. The result has been a significant narrowing of sentencing discretion in most states.

Legislative Sentencing Responsibility

Legislatures are initially responsible for creating sentencing options in the criminal codes they enact. Legislatures specify terms of imprisonment in two different ways. Consistent with the goal of rehabilitation, which dominated correctional thinking through most of the 20th century, state legislatures adopted **indeterminate sentences** (often called *"indefinite sentences"*), based on the idea that correctional personnel must have discretion to release an offender when treatment has been successful. States

with indeterminate sentences stipulate a minimum and maximum amount of time to be served in prison—1 to 5 years, 3 to 10 years, 20 years to life, and so on. At the time of sentencing, the offender knows the range of the sentence and knows that parole is a possibility after the minimum sentence, minus good time (discussed below), has been served. How long the person actually remains in prison is determined by the parole authority, based on its assessment of the offender's progress toward rehabilitation.

Because of the growing disillusionment with the rehabilitative model in the 1970s, along with evidence that indeterminate sentences often produced disparate sentencing outcomes for similar crimes, determinate sentences grew in popularity. **Determinate sentences** (sometimes called *"fixed sentences"*) consist of a specified number of years rather than a range of years. For example, the judge must sentence the defendant to imprisonment for 5 years, 10 years, or whatever the legislature specifies for a particular offense.

Judicial Sentencing Responsibility

Although other members of the courtroom work group may recommend a criminal sentence (especially probation officers), with limited exceptions only a judge has the authority to choose among the sentencing options provided by the legislature. Wide judicial discretion in sentencing reflects the rehabilitative model, which stresses that the punishment should fit the criminal. No two crimes or criminals are exactly alike; sentences should therefore be individualized, with judges taking these differences into account. But no agreement has been reached on what factors should increase or reduce the penalty.

By the mid-1970s, wide judicial discretion had come under attack from both ends of the political spectrum. Advocates of the due process model of criminal justice expressed concern that judicial sentencing discretion was too broad, resulting in inequities such as racial discrimination. Conversely, proponents of the crime control model expressed concern that too much judicial discretion led to unduly lenient sentences. These two political movements, although contradictory, led legislatures to greatly reduce judicial sentencing discretion. Thus, an increasing number of jurisdictions are narrowing judicial discretion over sentencing in some manner.

Executive Sentencing Responsibility

Sentences imposed by judges are typically carried out by officials of the executive branch. Of particular importance is the impact of executive officials on prison populations. How long an offender will be imprisoned depends not only on the length of the sentence imposed by the judge, but also on the decisions made by governors, parole boards, and departments of corrections. Only about a quarter of prisoners serve their full sentences and are then released unconditionally. The remainder are conditionally released from prison to serve the balance of their sentences in the community as a function of one of three early release programs: parole, good time, and (to a much lesser extent) executive clemency.

Parole is the conditional release of an inmate from incarceration, under supervision, after a portion of the prison sentence has been served. A parole officer supervises the conditions of release, and any rule violations or new crimes can result in a return to prison for the balance of the unexpired term. Parole boards, which are usually appointed by the governor, vary greatly in their discretionary authority. Approximately 840,000 persons are currently on parole in the United States (Bureau of Justice Statistics, 2011).

Another way in which decisions made by the executive branch affect how long an inmate must stay in prison is **good time**; in many states, prisoners are awarded days off their minimum or maximum terms as a reward for good behavior or for participation in various vocational, educational, and treatment programs. The amount of good time that can be earned varies from 5 days a month to 45 days a month in some states. Correctional officials find these sentence-reduction provisions necessary for the maintenance of institutional order and as a mechanism to reduce overcrowding. They usually have discretion in awarding good time.

State governors, as well as the president of the United States, have the power to pardon any prisoner in their respective jurisdictions, reduce sentences, or make prisoners eligible for parole (Moore, 1989; Ruckman, 1997). **Pardons** are not a common method of prisoner release, however; only a small group of inmates receive executive clemency each year.

The early release of prisoners through the use of parole and good time has come under heavy political attack in recent years. The result has been significant changes in some jurisdictions. The federal government and one-third of the states have abolished parole board authority to release offenders, and another four have abolished parole board authority for releasing violent offenders. Similarly, legislatures in many states have reduced or eliminated good time for certain types of prisoners. Despite efforts to reduce the use of parole and curb the awarding of good time, burgeoning prison populations increasingly force correctional officials to use parole as a backdoor solution to prison overcrowding.

The failure rate for ex-prisoners, whether released on parole or after the expiration of their sentence, is dishearteningly high (Wallman, 2005). Each year more than two-thirds of the inmates who return to their communities are likely to be re-arrested within 3 years (Mears, Wang, Hay, & Bales, 2008). Considerable attention is now being paid to prisoner reentry (MacKenzie, 2006; National Governors Association, 2009; Travis, 2005). Whether high failure rates are the result of bad behavior on the part of the ex-prisoners or bad public policy is an open question (Wilson, 2005).

WHAT SENTENCE SHOULD BE IMPOSED?

What types of sentences should be imposed upon the guilty? Today, answers center on prison and probation, with a hot debate over the death penalty. But throughout history, sentences were very different. Flogging, the stocks, exile, chopping off a hand, and branding are just a few examples of punishments historically inflicted on the guilty. Today, such sanctions are viewed as violating the Constitution's prohibition against **cruel and unusual punishment**. In their place, we use imprisonment, probation, intermediate sanctions, fines, and restitution. Many states also make formal provisions for capital punishment, but the death penalty is rarely used. In essence, these forms of punishment are tools created under the sentencing structure to advance society's theories of punishment. They are the options from which the sentencing judge must choose.

LAW ON THE BOOKS VS. LAW IN ACTION
SENTENCING OPTIONS

	LAW ON THE BOOKS	LAW IN ACTION
Prison	A correctional facility for housing adults convicted of felony offenses, usually under the control of state government.	Approximately 1.5 million U.S. adults are in prison. About 7 percent of inmates are female. Of male prisoners, 39 percent are African-American, 31 percent are White, and 23 percent are Hispanic.
Parole	Adults conditionally released to community supervision after serving part of a prison term. The parolee is subject to being returned to prison for rule violations or other offenses.	More than 840,600 are on parole from state or federal prison. Twelve percent of parolees are women. Of male parolees, 42 percent are White, 39 percent are African-American, and 18 percent are Latino.
Probation	Punishment for a crime that allows the offender to remain in the community without incarceration but subject to certain conditions.	More than 4.1 million adults are under federal, state, or local jurisdiction on probation. Half of those offenders are on probation for felonies.
Intermediate sanctions	A variety of punishments that are more restrictive than traditional probation but less stringent than incarceration.	Much less costly than imprisonment. Community service requires the offender to perform a public service such as street cleaning or hospital volunteer work.
Fines	A sum of money to be paid to the government by a convicted person as punishment for an offense.	Often used in misdemeanors. Recent research shows that it can be effectively used in select felonies.
Restitution	Requirement that the offender pay to the victim a sum of money to make good the loss.	Most defendants are so poor that they cannot reasonably be expected to make restitution.
Capital punishment	The use of the death penalty (execution) as the punishment for the commission of a particular crime.	More than 3,150 prisoners are on death row. In 2010, 46 executions were carried out. Of death row inmates, 55 percent are White and 42 percent are African-American.

One can approach the question of which penalty should be imposed upon the guilty from either a micro or a macro perspective. The micro perspective focuses on a specific defendant convicted of a crime. It is from this perspective that victims often view sentencing, and from this vantage point they are often critical of the judge's (or sometimes the legislature's) choice, arguing that the sentence is too lenient. It is vitally important, however, to assess such criticisms from a macro perspective. From this vantage point, prisons are already overcrowded and

the caseloads of probation officers overwhelming. It is for this reason that judges occasionally address crime victims and explain the painfully obvious—to send this defendant to prison will require correctional officials to release someone who is possibly an even greater threat to the community.

Imprisonment

Although it has been used from time to time throughout history, **imprisonment** (incarceration) has become the dominant form of punishment only during the past two centuries. The United States imprisons a larger share of its population than any other nation. More than 2.26 million inmates are currently housed in prisons and jails (Bureau of Justice Statistics, 2011).

The high rate of imprisonment is not without its critics (Listwan, Johnson, Cullen, & Latessa, 2008). In *Big Prisons, Big Dreams*, Michael Lynch (2007) argues that the dramatic growth in our prison population has not reduced crime because we are not targeting the worst offenders. Prison populations are comprised of the poor, and many are incarcerated for nonviolent drug offenses or for relatively minor offenses. In *Imprisoning Communities: How Mass Incarceration Makes Disadvantaged Neighborhoods Worse*, Todd Clear (2007) adds that high rates of incarceration contribute to the very social problems it is intended to solve: It breaks up families and erodes economic and social networks in economically disadvantaged communities.

One reason for this high rate of imprisonment is the length of sentences. Prison sentences in the United States are quite long as compared with those imposed in Europe, where it is rare for a defendant to be sentenced to more than 5 years.

Overcrowding

Jail and prison overcrowding has become the dominant reality of criminal justice policy. The numbers of people on probation and parole have also risen sharply. Figure 14.1 shows how the size of the correctional population has skyrocketed in recent years, but the trend is starting to change. Record high numbers of prisoners were reported every year for nearly four decades. In 2010, though, the number of people incarcerated in U.S. prisons and jails dropped for the first time since 1972.

Conditions of Confinement Lawsuits

The numbers of prisoners provide only part of the picture. Rapid increases in the size of the correctional population occurred during the same time that federal courts began to demand improvements in jail and prison conditions, which have often been described as substandard.

Traditionally, courts followed a hands-off policy regarding correctional institutions, choosing not to interfere in their internal administration. But this policy began to change in 1964 (*Cooper v. Pate*). By the 1970s, the federal courts began to scrutinize the operations of correctional institutions to ensure

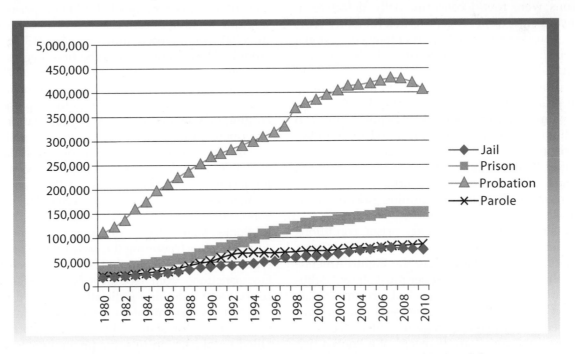

Figure 14.1 ■ Adults under Correctional Supervision in the United States

SOURCE: Persons under Correctional Supervision: National Estimates (Table 6.1). *Sourcebook of Criminal Justice Statistics*, 2010.

compliance with the Eighth Amendment's protection against cruel and unusual punishment (DiIulio, 1990). Prisoners have sued under 42 U.S.C. § 1983 (see Chapter 2), in what are often termed **conditions of confinement lawsuits**. The lawsuits contend that local, county, or state officials have deprived them of their constitutional rights, such as adequate medical treatment and protection against excessive force by correctional officers and violence by other inmates (Hanson & Daley, 1995). Unfortunately, though, inmates have also abused their rights to access the courts to redress legitimate grievances by suing over frivolous matters as a means of harassing correctional staff, taking revenge on the courts, or passing the time while incarcerated (Fradella, 1999). The volume of meritless suits led Congress to restrict inmates' ability to sue in 1996, when it enacted the Prison Litigation Reform Act. The law was effective in significantly reducing the number of civil rights cases filed by prisoners. Critics, however, point out that in limiting the number of frivolous lawsuits that can clog the courts, Congress may have also made it more difficult for prisoners to file and win meritorious suits (Schlanger, 2003).

The entire prison systems of at least nine states were declared unconstitutional, and individual prisons were found constitutionally defective in many others. The net effect was that for many years most states operated all or part of their correctional systems under a federal court order. Federal judges in virtually all states ordered state governments to alter dramatically the way in which they operated their prisons and jails. These court orders specified a maximum prison population, required physical conditions to be upgraded, increased the number of prison guards, and mandated minimal medical facilities (Chilton, 1991; Crouch & Marquart, 1990; Taggart, 1989). These federal court orders have had a significant effect in transforming prison conditions (Feeley & Rubin, 1998).

It is now harder to challenge prison conditions in federal court, however. The Rehnquist Court created a new standard under the Eighth Amendment, holding that the prisoner must show "deliberate indifference" on the part of prison officials (*Wilson v. Seiter*, 1991). The Court later clarified that "deliberate indifference" requires subjective recklessness—the conscious disregard of a known risk (*Farmer v. Brennan*, 1994).

Overall, the nation's highest court has limited the conditions under which federal courts will recognize violations of a prisoner's rights (Mushlin & Galtz, 2009). And the Prison Litigation Reform Act of 1996 significantly limited the federal courts' supervisory powers over state prisons. Nonetheless, state correctional officials are aware that slipping back to old practices will result in future litigation.

High Costs

Getting tough on criminals is popular, yet public opinion polls show that spending money for more prisons is not a high priority for the general public. Prisons are costly to build and even more costly to maintain (Spelman, 2009). Estimates of the costs of constructing a single cell exceeds $100,000 (Clear, Cole & Reisig, 2009). The costs of incarcerating a prisoner (clothes, food, and guards, primarily) depend on the level of confinement and also vary from state to state, ranging from $20,000 to $30,000 per prisoner per year.

Faced with swelling prison populations and federal court orders over conditions of confinement, state legislatures have been faced with spending enormous sums of money to build new prisons and upgrade existing ones. Prison construction during the 1990s was a growth industry, with 213 state and federal prisons built during the first 5 years, at an estimated cost of $30 billion ("In '90s, Prison," 1997). Despite large expenditures, few states have been able to build prisons fast enough to keep ahead of surging prison admissions. Across the nation, prisons operated at averages between 99% and 115% of capacity during the last year for which data are available, with Alabama and Illinois reporting the highest levels of overcrowding at 196% and 144% of their respective capacities (Guerino, Harrison, & Sabol, 2011).

Some states have declared an emergency situation, thus triggering the early release of certain types of prisoners. States that fail to take such action face sanctions from federal judges. Contempt of court, hefty fines, and judicially mandated release of prisoners are some of the remedies federal judges have imposed on state and local officials who have failed to take action to solve prison overcrowding (Clear, Cole, & Reisig, 2009).

KEY DEVELOPMENTS CONCERNING IMPRISONMENT

Eighth Amendment (1791)	Excessive bail shall not be required, nor excessive fines imposed, nor cruel and unusual punishments inflicted.
***Ex Parte Hull* (1941)**	A state prison rule abridging or impairing a prisoner's right to apply to the federal courts for a writ of *habeas corpus* is invalid.
***Robinson v. United States* (1962)**	The Eighth Amendment's prohibition against cruel and unusual punishment applies to the states as well as the federal government.
***Cooper v. Pate* (1964)**	Prisoners can sue correctional officials in federal court under 42 U.S.C. § 1983.
***Procunier v. Martinez* (1974)**	Prisoners retain First Amendment free speech rights while incarcerated. Restrictions on their speech must be narrowly tailored to achieve a compelling penological interest, such as maintaining security.
***Wolf v. McDonnell* (1974)**	When facing administrative segregation or a sanction that would extend their incarcerating length, inmates have due process rights in disciplinary proceedings that include the rights to be notified of charges, to call witnesses, and to an impartial decision maker.
***Estelle v. Gamble* (1976)**	Deliberate indifference to serious medical needs of prisoners constitutes the unnecessary and wanton infliction of pain, and thus violates the Eighth Amendment.
***Bounds v. Smith* (1977)**	Because inmates retain a Sixth Amendment right to access the courts, correctional authorities must provide inmates access to trained legal professionals or to a law library.
***Bell v. Wolfish* (1979)**	Correctional practices implemented in the genuine interest of institutional security, such as restrictions on reading materials and required body-cavity searches, are constitutionally permissible, even when applied to pretrial detainees.
***Ruiz v. Estelle* (1980)**	A U.S. District Court declared a wide range of conditions of confinement in the Texas prison system unconstitutional, such as overcrowding, lack of access to health care, and abusive security practices. The court orders entered in the case led the court to oversee the Texas system for more than 25 years.
***Rhodes v. Chapman* (1981)**	Double-celling and crowding do not necessarily constitute cruel and unusual punishment.
***Smith v. Wade* (1983)**	Inmates are entitled to punitive damages in § 1983 cases in which the defendant's conduct involves reckless or callous indifference to the plaintiff's federally protected rights, or when it is motivated by evil motive or intent.
***Hudson v. Palmer* (1984)**	Prisoners have no reasonable expectation of privacy in their prison cells entitling them to Fourth Amendment protection.
***Whitley v. Albers* (1986)**	A prisoner shot in the leg during a riot does not suffer cruel and unusual punishment if the action was taken in good faith to maintain discipline rather than for the mere purpose of causing harm.
***Turner v. Safely* (1987)**	Prisoners maintain the right to marry while incarcerated.

Continued on next page

Continued from previous page

Wilson v. Seiter (1991)	Prisoners contesting conditions of confinement in federal court must show that prison officials acted with "deliberate indifference" to prisoner needs and living conditions.
Prison Litigation Reform Act (1996)	Congress limits the authority of federal courts to supervise the operations of correctional institutions and limits the ability of inmates to file civil rights actions.
Pennsylvania Department of Corrections v. Yeskey (1997)	Correctional institutions must abide by the mandates of the Americans with Disabilities Act by making reasonable accommodations for disabled inmates.
Miller v. French (2000)	Upheld the Prison Litigation Reform Act, saying Congress could lawfully impose a 90-day time limit to rule on prison-condition lawsuits.
Correctional Services Corp. v. Malesko (2001)	Inmates may not file Bivens actions for damages against private entities acting under color of federal law.
Hope v. Pelzer (2001)	Tying a prisoner to a hitching post for punitive purposes violates the Eighth Amendment.
Brown v. Plata (2011)	Federal courts may place limits on prisoner populations to remedy Eighth Amendment violations that occur due to excessive overcrowding (such as the California prison system holding nearly twice as many inmates as it was designed to accommodate).

The long-standing political debate over sentencing has now given way to the overriding reality of a severe shortage of prison cells. State after state is discovering that the political rhetoric of the late 20th century to get tough on criminals by sending more people to prison for longer periods must give way to the fiscal realities of the 21st century—adjusting sentencing policies to fit prison capacity. The economic recession that began in December 2007 has greatly reduced state tax revenues, forcing states to reexamine how much they can spend on prisons when other important governmental services, such as education, face major budget reductions. Almost out of desperation, states are now turning to alternative penalty programs that resemble ideas that were tried and largely discarded a decade ago.

Probation

Unlike incarceration, probation is designed as a means of maintaining control over offenders while permitting them to live in the community (under supervision). The major justification for probation is that prisons are inappropriate places for some defendants and that limited supervision is a better way to rehabilitate criminals. Youthful or first-time offenders may only become embittered if mixed in prison with hardened criminals; they may end up learning more sophisticated criminal techniques. But most important, probation is significantly less expensive than imprisonment.

Probation is the principal alternative to imprisonment. It is also the most commonly used sanction in the United States; indeed, more than two times as many adults are on probation as are housed in state and federal prisons (Glaze, 2011). Altogether, about 4 million adults are on probation, a number that represents a doubling in about two decades. The increasing use of probation is a direct reflection of the serious problem of prison overcrowding. Ironically, it has resulted in a significant amount of "probation crowding"—the overload of the probation system equivalent to prison overcrowding (Byrne, Lurigio, & Baird 1989). Recall from Figure 14.1 that the number of people on probation rose almost as dramatically as the number in prison. As a result, probation officers often must handle excessive caseloads.

State and federal laws grant judges wide discretion in deciding whether to place a defendant on probation. In general, statutes allow probation when it appears that:

1. The defendant is not likely to commit another offense.

2. The public interest does not require that the defendant receive the penalty provided for the offense.

3. The rehabilitation of the defendant does not require that he or she receive the penalty provided for the offense.

Legislative provisions regarding who may be placed on probation vary considerably from state to state. Some states have statutes prohibiting certain types of offenders—typically violent offenders—from receiving probation.

Offenders placed on probation must agree to abide by certain rules and regulations prescribed by the sentencing judge. Termed "conditions of probation," these rules typically include keeping a job, supporting the family, avoiding places where alcoholic beverages are sold, reporting periodically to the probation officer, and not violating any law. Because probation is a judicial act, the judge can revoke probation and send the defendant to prison if the conditions of probation are violated. Chapter 15 will discuss in greater detail the key role probation officers play in managing the probation population (Lurigio, Olson, & Snowden, 2009).

Fines

The imposition of a fine is one of the oldest and also one of the most widely used forms of punishment. Fines are used extensively for traffic offenses and minor ordinance violations, generating well over $1 billion annually for local governments (Clear, Cole, & Reisig, 2009). Judges in the lower courts impose a fine alone or in combination with other sanctions in about 86 percent of their cases. But the imposition of fines is not confined to the lower courts. In the major trial courts, a fine, either alone or together with other sanctions, is imposed in almost 45 percent of the cases. First offenders with a known ability to pay are most likely to be sentenced in this way (Cole, Mahoney, Thornton, & Hanson, 1988).

The limited use of fines as punishment in felony cases contrasts sharply with practices in some Western European countries (Shoham, Beck, & Kett 2007). Some countries have adopted sentencing policies that explicitly make fines the sentence of choice for many offenses, including some crimes of violence that would result in jail sentences in many American courts. In Germany, for example, a major legislative goal is to minimize the imposition of jail terms of less than 6 months. Instead, German courts make extensive use of day fines, which enable judges to set fines at amounts reflecting the gravity of the offense but also taking into account the financial means of the offender (Hillsman & Mahoney, 1988). In the United States, the day fine concept has been relabeled "structured fines" and is being recommended as a less-costly sentencing option than imprisonment (Bureau of Justice Statistics, 1996). In some respects structured fines reflect a "Robin Hood" approach to criminal justice—the rich pay more (DeLisi & Conis, 2010).

American judges frequently cite the poverty of offenders as an obstacle to the broader use of fines as sanctions (Gillespie, 1988–1989). Nonetheless, some courts regularly impose fines on persons whose financial resources are extremely limited and are successful in collecting those fines. Some research suggests that fines can be collected. Performance can be improved substantially if administrators systematically apply collection and enforcement techniques that already exist and have been proven effective (Cole, 1992; Klaversma, 2008; Turner & Greene, 1999).

Restitution

Restitution is the requirement that the offender provide reparation to the victim for the harm caused by the criminal offense. Requiring defendants to compensate victims (giving something back) for their losses was customary in ancient civilizations. But as the government replaced the victim as the principal party in criminal prosecution, restitution fell into decline; offenders paid fines to the government rather than restitution to the victim (Tobolowsky, 1993). Beginning in the mid-1960s, the idea of restitution became the focus of renewed interest and became touted as one of the criminal justice system's more creative responses to crime. Nearly all states have enacted laws providing for the collection and distribution of restitution funds.

Restitution efforts generally take one of two forms—direct or symbolic (Galaway, 1988). In **direct restitution**, the offender is required, as a condition of probation, to make monetary payments to the victim. As a criminal sanction, it is largely restricted to property crimes, since it has little relevance if violence figured in the commission of the offense. Since 1996, Congress has required the federal court to impose mandatory restitution, without consideration of the defendant's ability to pay. But that approach may only increase victim dissatisfaction if the offender fails to pay (Davis & Bannister, 1995). A study of the Government Accountability Office of five major white-collar cases in federal court found that only 7 percent of court-ordered payments were ever collected (Schwartz, 2007).

In symbolic restitution, the offender makes reparation for the harm done in the form of good works benefiting the entire community rather than the particular individual harmed. Such work is often called *"community service."* This sanction is most often used when there is no direct victim of the offense—for example, in convictions for drunk driving. Community service will be discussed more fully in the next section.

Intermediate Sanctions

Concern is growing that the United States relies much too heavily on imprisonment and probation. Prison is viewed as too harsh (as well as unavailable) for many defendants, whereas high caseloads often leave too many probationers without adequate supervision. Alternative sentences that lie somewhere between prison and probation are often referred to as **intermediate sanctions**. In their influential book, *Between Prison and Probation: Intermediate Punishments in a Rational Sentencing System*, Norval Morris and Michael Tonry (1990) put it this way: "Prison is used excessively; probation is used even more excessively; between the two is a near vacuum of purpose and enforced punishments" (p. 3). This is particularly true of nonviolent offenders who commit one or more minor crimes—the expensive option of prison seems best reserved for more serious offenders, but minor penalties like probation have not worked well in the past.

Intermediate sanctions are based on the concept of continuum of sanctions—the range of punishments vary from low control to high control (see

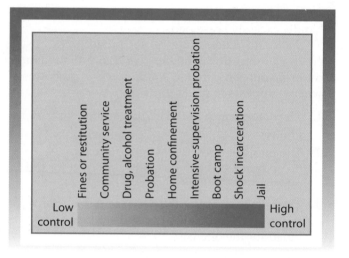

Figure 14.2 ■ Continuum of Sanctions

SOURCE: Adapted from Todd Clear, George Cole, and Michael Reisig, *American Corrections*. 7th ed. Belmont, CA: Wadsworth, 2006.

Figure 14.2). At one end of the continuum are fines and community service, which reflect low control over the activities of the guilty person; at the other end are punishments like home confinement, intensive-supervision probation, and boot camps, which reflect high control just short of the maximum level of control—jail or prison. The importance of drug and alcohol treatment has already been stressed in Chapter 4 in the discussion of drug courts. In the following sections, we explore some of these other intermediate sanctions.

Community Service

Community service is based on the theory of **symbolic restitution**—the offender has injured the community and therefore should compensate the community for that injury. Thus, a person sentenced to **community service** is required to provide a specified number of hours of free labor in some public service, such as street cleaning, repairing substandard housing, or volunteering in a hospital. In the eyes of the general public, community service is most visible when it is imposed on celebrities like actors and athletes (see "Courts, Law, & Media" on page 386).

The effectiveness of community service is mixed. It does not appear to reach its major goal of reducing prison populations because virtually all of those sentenced to community service would have received probation (not a prison sentence). Nor does community service appear to be particularly effective in reducing criminal behavior—those who participate have higher failure rates than those who receive regular supervision (Allen & Treger, 1994). Nonetheless, one study suggests that overall offenders given community service have lower re-arrest rates than would be expected if they had been sentenced differently (Caputo, 1999).

Intensive-Supervision Probation

Given the high number of persons on probation, the amount of an offender's contact with a probation officer is typically very limited—perhaps a brief meeting once a month. **Intensive-supervision probation** (ISP) involves strict reporting, with the offender required to meet with a probation officer briefly every day. ISP targets offenders who are most likely to be facing imprisonment for their next violation.

Early evaluation of ISP programs found that intensive supervision did reduce re-arrest rates. But at the same time, these offenders were more likely to be found in violation of their conditions of probation largely because they were being more closely supervised. As a result, even minor violations like arrests for disorderly conduct could result in the offender being in violation of his or her probation and sent to prison. In short, ISP might not be achieving its goal of sending fewer people to prison but instead might actually lead to a larger prison population. Despite questions about its effectiveness, the ISP approach remains popular with judges, prosecutors, corrections officials, and the public (Clear, Cole, & Reisig 2009).

Home Detention with Electronic Monitoring

Another alternative to incarceration that helps to reduce jail and prison overcrowding, as well as the costs of punishment, is **home detention** (sometimes referred to as "house arrest"). This punishment confines offenders to their homes under specific terms and conditions. Typically, offenders are permitted to leave their home for only explicit, preauthorized reasons, such as to obtain health care (including court-mandated treatment), to shop for groceries and other necessities, to attend religious services, and to go to work and/or school—but only if such activities have been authorized. Home arrest is enforced by unannounced field visits (usually by probation or parole officers) at all times of the day and night. And, starting in the 1980s and growing in use to the present, enforcement has been aided by **electronic monitoring (EM).**

Today, nearly all states use a variety of EM technologies to surveil and control offenders including "home monitoring devices, wrist bracelets, ankle bracelets, field monitoring devices, alcohol testing devices, and voice verification systems" (National Law Enforcement and Corrections Technology Center, 1999). Most offenders under EM wear a device that transmits a unique code that, once relayed, allows both computer and monitoring specialists to track compliance with house arrest and highly regimented, limited scheduled departures from the home that may be allowed in a particular case (DeMichele & Payne, 2009). Some EM devices can even detect alcohol consumption through skin pores (see "Courts, Law, & Media" on the next page).

Not surprisingly, most offenders prefer to serve their time at home rather than in jail or prison, even though they still experience incarceration in the home as punitive (Gainey& Payne, 2000; Martin, Hanrahan, & Bowers, 2009). This allows them to sleep in their own beds, wear their own clothes, watch television, and spend time with friends and family. Still, most offenders under house arrest report that the combination of technological and human supervision transforms their homes into prison-like environments—places of confinement into which corrections official intrude with intense invasions of privacy that burden not only the offender, but also the others living with the offender. Indeed, they report that house arrest with electronic monitoring is quite punitive because surveillance is near total. This "creates and sustains 'a particular kind of tension between the home world and the institutional world' and uses this persistent tension 'as strategic leverage in the management of' offenders" (Staples & Decker, 2010, p. 17, quoting Goffman, 1961, p. 13).

House arrest with EM offers the benefit of access to more rehabilitative opportunities (Gainey & Payne, 2000) while avoiding the criminogenic and often dangerous environment found in many jails

COURTS, LAW, & MEDIA

INTERMEDIATE SANCTIONS AND LINDSAY LOHAN

After a series of accidents and a brief stint in a rehab program, actress, singer, and model Lindsay Lohan was arrested in 2007 for driving under the influence (DUI). She returned to rehab and less than 2 weeks after she left the program, she was arrested again for driving under the influence of alcohol, driving on a suspended license, and possession of narcotics. After she was formally charged with seven counts stemming from her two DUI arrests, she reached a plea agreement that allowed her to serve 1 day in jail, do 10 days of community service, complete an 18-month drug and alcohol education program while on 3 years of probation, and complete a 3-day program at the county coroner's office that required her to visit a morgue to talk with the families of victims of drunk-driving accidents.

Lohan struggled on probation. Not only did she relapse into substance abuse, but also she failed to complete her drug and alcohol education program as required, causing the judge supervising her case to extend Lohan's probation for a year. She then violated the terms of her probation by consuming alcohol, leading the judge to require Lohan to wear an alcohol-monitoring bracelet. But after the judge determined Lohan was missing required counseling sessions, Lohan was sentenced to 90 days in jail and 90 days in rehab. But jail overcrowding led to her release after just 23 days. She subsequently failed a random drug test and returned to rehab, spending 3 months in the Betty Ford Clinic. Within weeks of her release from rehab, though, Lohan allegedly stole a necklace valued at $2,500 from a jewelry store, leading to her being charged with felony grand theft (a charge subsequently reduced to misdemeanor theft).

Lohan was sentenced to 120 days in jail for violating the terms of her DUI probation by being charged with theft. She was also ordered to perform 480 hours of community service at a women's center in downtown Los Angeles and at the county morgue. But, again because of overcrowding, Lohan was released from jail after less than a week and allowed to serve the remainder of her term under house arrest with electronic monitoring. While under house arrest, she again failed a random drug test. Even though that failure did not result in additional sanctions, Lohan subsequently failed to complete her community service at the woman's shelter. A judge imposed a 300-day jail sentence, but required Lohan to complete only 30 days of that sentence, during which time she was not eligible for house arrest, electronic monitoring, or any other early release program "other than that required by law" (Oldenburg, 2011, ¶ 3). Upon her release, Lohan was to resume her community service.

Lohan's repeated violations of the terms of her probation, even when other intermediate sanctions were added to her criminal sanctions, seemingly failed to control her behavior. Moreover, her case raises two important questions about intermediate sanctions. First, through many stages of her continued struggles with the criminal law, Lohan has had to post hundreds of thousands of dollars as bail. Average people would not likely be able to buy their freedom after so many repeated violations of the terms and condition of probation in the same way that a celebrity like Lohan could afford to do. Do you think that Lohan's case serves as evidence that "celebrity justice" is qualitatively different from "criminal justice"? Explain your reasoning. Second, do you think that Lohan's repeated failures call into question the legitimacy and usefulness of intermediate sanctions? Why or why not?

and prisons (Payne & Gainey, 2004). This in turn can lead EM participants to have lower recidivism rates than those on traditional probation with community service (Killias, Gilliéron, Kissling & Villettaz, 2010) and those imprisoned (Bonta, Wallace-Capretta & Rooney, 2000). That finding, however, is likely due, in part, to EM programs having lower-risk offenders. When risk is controlled for, there are no significant recidivism differences between parolees and EM offenders (see also, MacKenzie, 2006; Renzema & Mayo-Wilson, 2005). But since EM generally costs a fraction of what it would cost to incarcerate offenders in institutions (Crowe, Sydney, Bancroft, & Lawrence, 2002), its primary benefit as an alternative to incarceration may be cost savings.

GPS Monitoring

EM programs have traditionally been used with relatively low-risk offenders, such as those convicted of drug possession, driving under the influence, driving on a suspended license, petty theft, and certain white-collar crimes (Gable & Gable, 2005). But today's most sophisticated EM devices can monitor an offender's location every second of the day using global positioning satellites (GPS). The second-generation of GPS-EM technology allows for greater control of higher-risk offenders, such as some sex offenders and intimate-partner violence offenders. GPS-EM can be used to monitor offenders on house arrest as an alternative to incarceration or as part of an intensive-supervision program after they are paroled (Erez & Ibarra, 2007; Payne & DeMichele, 2011).

GPS-EM offers much higher levels of control over offenders than traditional EM alone. This appears to have real benefits in monitoring higher-risk offenders (Padgett, Bales, & Blomberg, 2006), although limited research exists regarding the effectiveness of GPS-EM as compared to other forms of intermediate sanctions, especially for higher-risk offenders. But there are some serious drawbacks to the technology. In addition to being very expensive to operate and monitor, the technology relies on wireless data service coverage. These concerns detract from the cost-savings benefit associated with more traditional EM programs.

Boot Camps and Shock Incarceration

To some, the deterrent effect of incarceration loses its impact after a short time, which leads some to advocate shock incarceration—the offender is sentenced to a brief jail or prison sentence (typically 30 to 90 days) and then released on probation, which may be combined with other intermediate sanctions, such as home detention or electronic monitoring. The assumption is that the offender will find the experience so unpleasant that he or she will be motivated to "stay clean."

The best-known example of shock incarceration is the boot camp, in which offenders serve a short sentence that includes a rigorous, paramilitary regimen designed to develop discipline and respect for authority. Proponents of boot camps argue that many young offenders are involved in crime because they have little discipline in their disordered lives. Thus, a relatively brief, quasi-military experience is designed to send the offender off in more productive directions. Critics, however, argue that the military-style physical training and the harshness of the program do little to overcome the problems facing inner-city youths who are in trouble with the law. Evaluations of boot camp graduates show that they do no better than other offenders after release (Cullen, Blevins, & Trager, 2005; Parent, 2003). To be effective, boot camp programs must be carefully designed, target the right types of offenders, and provide rehabilitative services (Kurlychek & Kempinen, 2006). Findings like these, coupled with the high costs, have led some state and local officials to close their boot camps.

THE DEATH PENALTY

Of all the forms of punishment, the death penalty is by far the most controversial, but it is also the least used; only a handful of offenders potentially face the ultimate sanction society can impose on the guilty. Since the Supreme Court ushered in the modern era of the death penalty in 1976, approximately 1,280 executions have been carried out in the United States.

Capital punishment was once almost the only penalty applied to convicted felons. By the time of the American Revolution, the English courts had defined more than 200 felonies, all of which were capital offenses. However, many death penalties were not carried out; instead, offenders were pardoned or banished to penal colonies. Over time, courts and legislatures began to recognize other forms of punishment, such as imprisonment and probation.

As Figure 14.3 illustrates, the number of executions in the United States fell steadily from the 1930s to the 1970s. From 1967 to 1972, an unofficial moratorium on executions existed. In 1976, the numbers increased once again, reaching a peak of 98 in 1998. Since then, however, the number of executions has been falling.

As of this writing, 17 U.S. states, the District of Columbia, and the Commonwealth of Puerto Rico, do not have a death penalty. Of the 35 U.S. jurisdictions (including the federal government and the U.S. military) with capital punishment, there are currently just over 3,150 prisoners under

Figure 14.3 ■ Persons Executed in the United States, 1930–2011

SOURCE: Bureau of Justice Statistics. 2011. Number of Persons Executed in the United States: Capital Punishment Statistical Tables, 1930-2011. Washington, DC: Author.

sentences of death. Southern states account for both the most capital sentences and the most executions (Figure 14.4).

Abolition of the death penalty has been a hot political issue. Opponents contend that it is morally wrong for the state to take a life; it has no deterrent value and is inherently discriminatory. These arguments have led all Western democracies except the United States to abolish the death penalty. Supporters counter that retribution justifies the taking of a life and that the death penalty does deter; they are generally unconcerned or unconvinced about allegations of discriminatory impact. In the United States, a series of Supreme Court opinions interpreting the Eight Amendment ushered in the modern era of death penalty jurisprudence.

Eighth Amendment Standards

In *Trop v. Dulles* (1958), the Supreme Court explained that the scope of the Cruel and Unusual Punishments Clause of the Eighth Amendment to the U.S. Constitution is not static, but rather should be interpreted on the basis of "evolving standards of decency in a maturing society" (p. 101). Since that time, the

Court has been repeatedly called upon to determine whether particular capital punishment laws or their application in particular cases are consistent with the Eighth Amendment as viewed from the perspective of "evolving standards of decency in a maturing society." Applying this standard in its 1972 landmark decision in *Furman v. Georgia*, the Court invalidated all 37 then-existing state death penalty statutes. The Court was deeply divided, however, with every justice writing a separate opinion.

Method of Decision Making

Furman v. Georgia raised more questions than it answered, and state legislatures attempted to write new capital punishment laws consistent with the Eighth Amendment. By 1976, a total of 37 states had enacted new legislation designed to avoid the arbitrary application of capital punishment. These laws took two forms. Some states passed mandatory death penalty laws, which removed all discretion from the process by requiring that anyone convicted of a capital offense be sentenced to death. Other states enacted guided discretion statutes, which required judges and juries to weigh various

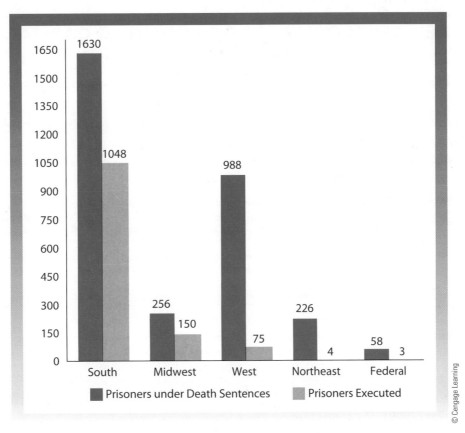

© Cengage Learning

Figure 14.4 ■ Death Sentences by U.S. Region

aggravating and mitigating circumstances in deciding whether or not a particular defendant should receive the death penalty (Blankenship, Luginbuhl, Cullen, & Redick, 1997).

These new laws were tested in five companion cases, collectively known as the death penalty cases (*Gregg v. Georgia*, 1976). Again, the Court was badly divided, but a seven-justice majority agreed that the death penalty did not constitute cruel and unusual punishment under all circumstances. Next, the Court considered under what circumstances the death penalty was unconstitutional. Mandatory death penalty laws in 21 states were struck down because they failed to focus on the circumstances of the case. Guided-discretion death penalty laws, on the other hand, were upheld: "The concerns expressed in *Furman* that the penalty of death not be imposed in an arbitrary or capricious manner can be met by a carefully drafted statute that ensures that the

sentencing authority is given adequate information and guidance" (p. 195).

For a death penalty law to be constitutional, the high court ruled, it must provide for a **bifurcated trial** process. During the first, or guilt, phase of the trial, the jury considers only the issue of guilt or innocence. If the jury unanimously convicts for a crime carrying the death penalty, then the jury reconvenes. During the second, or penalty, phase of the trial, the jury considers aggravating and mitigating circumstances and then decides whether to impose the death penalty. If the death penalty is not imposed, the defendant is usually sentenced to life imprisonment.

Method of Execution

A variety of forms of execution have been used in the United States. Since *Gregg*, most states have used electrocution, gas poisoning, hanging, firing

KEY DEVELOPMENTS CONCERNING CAPITAL PUNISHMENT AFTER *GREGG*

Coker v. Georgia (1977)	The imposition of the death penalty for rape is a disproportionate punishment that violates the Eight Amendment.
Pulley v. Harris (1984)	The Eighth Amendment does not require states to compare with other cases to assess whether a sentence of death is proportional.
Lockhart v. McCree (1986)	Potential jurors may be excluded if they oppose the death penalty. Thus, a death-qualified jury was upheld.
McClesky v. Kemp (1987)	Statistical studies about racial disparities in capital sentences do not sufficiently establish an Equal Protection Clause violation. Rather, to prevail on such claims, capital defendants must show that purposeful discrimination had a discriminatory effect in their particular trials.
Stanford v. Kentucky (1989)	It is not unconstitutional to apply the death penalty to persons who were convicted of murder when they were 17.
Simmons v. South Carolina (1994)	Defense may tell jurors that the only alternative to a death sentence is life imprisonment without parole.
Harris v. Alabama (1995)	States may give judges the power to sentence a capital defendant to death even if the jury votes not to impose the death penalty.
Ramdass v. Angelone (2000)	Even if jurors are not told that defendant is not be eligible for parole if sentenced to life in prison, that does not render a death sentence unconstitutional.
Williams v. Taylor (2000)	Upheld a section of the Antiterrorism and Effective Death Penalty Act intended to shorten the time between sentencing and execution.
Ring v. Arizona (2002)	The Sixth Amendment entitles defendants in capital cases to a jury determination of any aggravating factors that increase their maximum punishment from life imprisonment to death.
Atkins v. Virginia (2002)	The Eighth Amendment bars the execution of mentally retarded criminal defendants with IQs of 70 or less.
Roper v. Simmons (2005)	The Eighth Amendment forbids the imposition of the death penalty on offenders who were under age 18 when their crimes were committed, overruling *Stanford v. Kentucky*.
Hill v. McDonough (2006)	Challenges to the method of execution are properly filed in federal court under 42 U.S.C. § 1983, not in *habeas corpus* proceedings.
Kansas v. Marsh (2006)	Upheld Kansas law requiring that when juries find that the arguments for and against capital punishment carry equal weight, the automatic sentence must be death.
Uttecht v. Brown (2007)	A juror in the capital murder trial was properly excused for cause because a reading of the transcript of the voir dire indicates he expressed reservations about the death penalty.
Baze v. Rees (2008)	Because the lethal injection process is not intended to cause unnecessary pain and suffering, it does not create an "objectively intolerable risk of harm" that qualifies as cruel and unusual punishment under the Eighth Amendment.
Kennedy v. Louisiana (2008)	The death penalty is unconstitutional punishment for the rape of a child.

squad, and lethal injection. When people challenge the proposed method of their execution as cruel and unusual, the courts apply *Trop's* perspective of "evolving standards of decency in a maturing society."

In *Hill v. McDonough* (2006), the Court opened the door to whether the chemicals used in lethal injections are too painful and therefore constitute an Eighth Amendment violation. In the aftermath of *Hill*, many states halted executions and sought to change their practices. In Missouri, for example, a federal judge barred executions in that state amid resistance from the medical profession over whether doctors should be involved at all in meting out lethal injections (Davey, 2006). Two years, later, however, the Court squarely addressed the issue in *Baze v. Rees* (2008). The Court upheld lethal injection, reasoning that, "Simply because an execution method may result in pain, either by accident or as an inescapable consequence of death, does not establish the sort of 'objectively intolerable risk of harm' that qualifies as cruel and unusual" (p. 50). But few think that the issue of method of execution has been settled because many questions of state law remain (Fulkerson & Suttmoeller, 2008).

Death-Qualified Juries

One long-standing issue has been the exclusion of persons opposed to the death penalty from juries in capital cases. The Warren Court rejected the classic "hanging jury," holding in *Witherspoon v. Illinois* (1968) that states cannot exclude from juries in capital cases any persons who voice general objections to the death penalty or express religious scruples against its imposition. However, the more conservative Rehnquist Court limited *Witherspoon* in *Wainwright v. Witt* (1985), ruling that the Constitution does not prohibit the removal for cause of prospective jurors whose opposition to the death penalty is so strong that it would prevent or substantially impair the performance of their duties as jurors at the sentencing phase of the trial (*Lockhart v. McCree*, 1986). More recently, the Roberts Court held that a juror in a capital murder trial was properly excused for cause because a reading of the transcript of the voir dire indicated that he expressed reservations

about the death penalty (*Uttecht v. Brown*, 2007). Decisions like this make it easier for prosecutors to weed out jurors who have concerns about the death penalty, meaning that juries will be more prone to convict (Butler & Moran, 2007a,b; Haney, 1984, 2005; Moran & Comfort, 2006). In fact, a wealth of social scientific data support the notion that so-called **death-qualified juries** differ from regular juries in several important ways:

First, death-qualified jurors are demographically unique. When compared with excludables, they are more likely to be male, Caucasian, moderately well educated, politically conservative, Catholic or Protestant, and middle-class. Second, death-qualified jurors are dispositionally unique. When compared with excludables, they are more likely to have a high belief in a just world (i.e., feel the world is a fair and just place), espouse legal authoritarian beliefs (i.e., believe the rights of the government should supersede the rights of the individual), exhibit an internal locus of control (i.e., feel that internal factors control the events in their lives), and have a low need for cognition (i.e., lack the tendency to engage in and enjoy effortful cognitive activity). Third, death-qualified jurors are attitudinally unique. When compared with excludables, they are more likely to weigh aggravating circumstances (i.e., arguments for death) more heavily than mitigating circumstances (i.e., arguments for life), evaluate ambiguous expert scientific testimony more favorably, be skeptical of defenses involving mental illness (including the insanity defense), and are more susceptible to the pretrial publicity that inevitably surrounds capital cases. [And], death-qualified jurors are more likely to believe in the infallibility of the criminal justice process and less likely to agree that even the worst criminals should be considered for mercy. Fourth, death-qualified jurors are behaviorally unique with respect to their decision-making processes. When compared with excludables, they are more likely to find capital defendants guilty as well as sentence them to death.

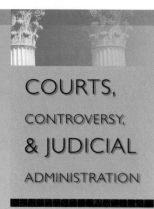

COURTS, CONTROVERSY, & JUDICIAL ADMINISTRATION

SHOULD A MORATORIUM ON THE DEATH PENALTY BE IMPOSED?

Anthony Porter was 2 days away from dying by lethal injection when the Illinois Supreme Court intervened, holding that his IQ of 51 dictated that his mental competency be examined. Northwestern University professor David Protess and his journalism students delved into Porter's case and found that he had not committed the pair of 1982 murders he was convicted for (McCormick, 1999). Another suspect later confessed.

In the wake of the Porter case, Illinois governor George Ryan, a Republican, declared a temporary halt to executions in his state, saying "I now favor a moratorium, because I have grave concerns about our state's shameful record of convicting innocent people and putting them on death row." The thorough review of the death penalty in Illinois would result in some death row prisoners' being freed altogether because DNA evidence, witnesses who recanted, or independent investigations showed their innocence. Moreover, according to the *Chicago Tribune*, 33 death row inmates were defended by attorneys who were later disbarred or suspended, and 46 convictions were obtained through the questionable testimony of jailhouse informants (Stern, 2000). Just days before stepping down as governor, Ryan commuted the sentences of the remaining 167 inmates on death row to life imprisonment.

Over the years, different groups—most notably, the American Bar Association—have called for moratoriums on the death penalty. Illinois and Maryland, however, have been the only states to actually implement a moratorium. Indeed, governors in other states have shown little inclination to follow the lead of the Land of Lincoln. In 2007, however, New Jersey became the first state since 1965 to vote for abolition. Some scholars continue to call for a moratorium (Acker, 2007) as do groups like the Death Penalty Information Center. Occasionally, these efforts attract new supporters, such as long-time conservative Richard Viguerie (Death Penalty Information Center, 2009).

The focus on innocents on death row represents the latest round in a long-running debate over the death penalty. Not surprisingly, profound ideological differences exist on the three central issues in the death penalty debate: morality, deterrence, and fairness. To advocates of the due process model of criminal justice, the death penalty is immoral because the state should not take a life. To proponents of the crime control model, the death penalty is moral because the defendant has already taken a life.

To advocates of the due process model, the death penalty is not a deterrent, because many of those who commit murder are incapable of rational calculation. To proponents of the crime control model, the death penalty is a deterrent, because some who might murder refrain from doing so because they know they might themselves die.

To advocates of the due process model, the death penalty is unfairly administered. They stress that members of racial minorities are more likely than Whites to be executed. They also believe that in too many cases, people on death row are innocent or their trials involved procedural irregularities. To this, the proponents of the crime control model respond that the fairness of the death penalty is unimportant or unproven. They believe that African-Americans are no more likely to be executed than Whites. They also argue that the review process works because appeals have freed the few innocents who were wrongfully convicted.

These issues form the background for the debate by the justices of the Supreme Court over how death penalty cases should be decided (*Kansas v. Marsh*, 2006). At the end of its 2005–2006 term, the four liberal justices stopped short of calling for an end to capital punishment, but they pointed to studies finding that dozens of people condemned to death were later exonerated (see Chapter 16). Justice David Souter stressed that we are in a period of new empirical argument about how capital punishment is different. Justice Antonin Scalia responded that these studies were not proven. "Those ideologically driven to ferret out and proclaim a mistaken modern execution have not a single verifiable case to point to, whereas it is easy as pie to identify plainly guilty murderers who have been set free."

What do you think? Of the three main issues in the death penalty debate—morality, deterrence, and fairness—which provides the best argument for abolishing the death penalty? Which one offers the best grounds for keeping the death penalty? Do you think that the issue of innocents on death row justifies a moratorium on the death penalty?

[And fifth], death-qualified venirepersons exhibited . . . higher levels of homophobia, modern racism, and modern sexism. (Butler, 2007, pp. 857, 858–859)

Yet, in spite of these many differences, constitutional challenges to the composition of death-qualified juries have been rejected by the federal courts for more than 40 years.

Narrowing Death-Eligible Cases

Part of the national debate over capital punishment has focused on what crimes deserve the ultimate punishment. The term **death-eligible** refers to crimes that are punishable by death. Today, very few crimes are considered death-eligible, but this was not always the case. Over the years, persons were executed for committing a wide variety of crimes besides murder, including rape, robbery, and stealing horses. Legislators have played a major role in narrowing the scope of death-eligible offenses. Today, the focus is on the U.S. Supreme Court. In the wake of *Gregg v. Georgia*, the Supreme Court has placed important limits on what types of crimes and offenders are death-eligible.

Crime Limitations

State efforts to make nonhomicide cases death-eligible have been rejected. According to the Supreme Court, rape is not a grave enough offense to justify the imposition of the death penalty (*Coker v. Georgia*, 1977). More recently, the Court ruled that the death penalty is unconstitutional as the punishment for the rape of a child (*Kennedy v. Louisiana*, 2008). Whether the Court would uphold the death penalty for treason is unclear. Under federal law, treason is also a death-eligible offense, but since no one has been sentenced to death for espionage since the 1950s, the status of this penalty has not been determined.

Developmental Limitations

The Supreme Court has also placed important developmental limitations on when the death penalty may be imposed both in terms of chronological age and mental functioning.

For many years, the minimum age varied from 12 to 18, with a few states not specifying a minimum age. In fact, George Junius Stinney, Jr., a 14-year-old African-American boy, was executed in South Carolina in 1944 after having been dubiously convicted of killing two White girls, ages 8 and 11. Jury selection to verdict took less than 8 hours; the trial itself took only 3 hours and jury deliberations lasted only 10 minutes.

In 1988, the Supreme Court applied its first age-related limitation to the death penalty when it ruled that defendants who were 15 or younger at the time they committed murder could not be executed (*Thompson v. Oklahoma*, 1988). Later, the Court refused to set aside the death penalty for defendants who were 17 at the time of the crime (*Stanford v. Kentucky*, 1989). But in *Roper v. Simmons*, the Supreme Court ruled that evolving standards of decency required that the Eighth Amendment be interpreted as barring the execution of all juvenile offenders who were younger than age 18 at the time of their offense.

Lengthy Appeals

"Death is different" wrote Justice Thurgood Marshall about death penalty cases in general and death penalty appeals in particular (*Ford v. Wainwright*. 1986, p. 411). One way to assess how death penalty cases are different is to examine case-processing time.

Like all defendants found guilty, those sentenced to death are entitled to appellate court review. In death penalty cases, however, special provisions govern appeal. In all except two states, convictions for capital cases are automatically reviewed by the state's highest appellate court (Hurwitz, 2008). In the other two, the intermediate appellate courts first hear the appeals. If the conviction is upheld, the next step is filing a writ of *certiorari* with the U.S. Supreme Court. Even though the chances of four justices voting to hear the case are not high, they are much higher than for ordinary criminal appeals. Having exhausted these appellate remedies, defendants sentenced to death often file numerous writs of *habeas corpus* in state and federal courts, although this practice changed greatly in 1996 (see Chapter 16).

CASE CLOSE-UP

ROPER v. SIMMONS: SHOULD JUVENILES BE SENTENCED TO DEATH?

The jurors in *Roper v. Simmons* (2005) wrestled with a truly difficult question: Did Christopher Simmons deserve to live or die? No doubt, his crime was heinous—he and his friend deliberately drowned a neighbor girl who had befriended them. But at 17, was he too young to truly understand the dreadful crime that he had committed?

In *Roper v. Simmons,* the Court held that the Eighth Amendment forbids the imposition of the death penalty on offenders who were under the age of 18 when their crimes were committed. The Court's decision affected 72 inmates on death row in 20 states. It also impacted untold numerous current and future murder prosecutions.

Writing for the five-judge majority, Justice Kennedy argued that capital punishment must be limited to those offenders who commit "a narrow category of the most serious crimes" and whose extreme culpability makes them "the most deserving of execution." Those under 18 cannot with reliability be classified among the worst offenders. Citing factors like juveniles' susceptibility to immature and irresponsible behavior, the Court concluded: "The differences between juvenile and adult offenders are too marked and well understood to risk allowing a youthful person to receive the death penalty." In finding a national consensus opposing the execution of juveniles, the Court set the age of 18 on the basis of state legislative determinations of the age one is old enough to vote, marry, and serve on a jury (Bradley, 2006).

The decision in *Roper v. Simmons* highlights major differences of opinion over how the Constitution should be interpreted. Six of the justices expressed support for continuing to interpret the Eighth Amendment on the basis of "evolving standards of decency in a maturing society" (*Trop v. Dulles,* 1958). In short, the meaning of the Bill of Rights was not frozen when it was originally drafted but should be interpreted in a common law manner. To Scalia, Rehnquist, and Thomas, the interpretation of the Bill of Rights and other provisions of the Constitution should be based on their original meaning. Doctrines like evolving standards make interpretation too subjective, they argue.

In a fiery dissent, Justice Scalia (joined by Rehnquist and Thomas) blasted the majority opinion, arguing that it made a mockery of the vision of the federal judiciary set forth by the Founding Fathers and also that it ignored state legislatures. In short, the majority was off base by proclaiming itself the sole arbiter of our nation's moral standards. The finding of a national consensus was based on the flimsiest of grounds, the dissent argued.

The decision in *Roper v. Simmons* also highlights major differences of opinion over the role of international law in interpreting the Constitution. The court's opinion observed that only seven other countries—Iran, Pakistan, China, Saudi Arabia, Yemen, Nigeria, and Congo—allow the execution of juveniles. They concluded that "the overwhelming weight of international opinion against the juvenile death penalty is not controlling here, but provided respected and significant confirmation of the Court's determination that the penalty is disproportionate punishment for offenders under 18." This position provoked strong condemnation from the Court's three most conservative members, who thought that the basic premise of the Court's argument—that American law should conform to the laws of the rest of the world—ought to be rejected out of hand.

Some people's mental functioning, especially those with serious developmental problems, is far less than their chronological age. In *Penry v. Lynaugh* (1989), the Supreme Court ruled that in spite of cognitive impairments, the Eight Amendment did not bar the execution of mentally retarded people convicted of capital murder. In *Atkins v. Virginia* (2002), however, the Court reversed *Penry,* holding that the Eighth Amendment bars persons with an IQ of 70 or lower from being executed. State and federal courts, though, continue to struggle to apply this principle in practice, mainly because the decision in *Atkins* did not provide a functional definition of mental retardation. Rather, *Atkins*

left each state on its own to solve the problems presented by the holding—from formulating a definition

Continued on next page

Continued from previous page

of mental retardation to determining the applicable burden of proof and upon whom that burden falls. As a result, amongst the states there is neither a uniform definition of mental retardation nor a uniform procedure for determining whether a defendant is mentally retarded, and some state legislatures have declined to act on this issue at all. (Hagstrom, 2009, p. 242)

Relying on the definition of mental retardation provided by the American Psychiatric Association and the American Association on Intellectual and Developmental Disabilities, some states automatically prohibit the execution of someone with an IQ of less than 70 (Covarrubias, 2009). Other states set the bar lower; for example, Arizona bars execution of those with IQs of 65 or lower (Gottsfield & Alcorn, 2009). And other jurisdictions consider factors in addition to IQ to determine whether a nexus exists between a capital defendant's IQ and the causation of his or her crime (*Tennard v. Dretke*, 2004). Although mental retardation should not be diagnosed solely on the basis of IQ in light of variations in test results across time, the examination of a person's adaptive functioning leaves much subjectivity in diagnosing mental retardation—especially for people with borderline IQ scores (Fabian, 2006; Hagstrom, 2009).

The review process in death penalty cases is quite lengthy, mainly because of the numerous issues that federal and state courts have dealt with since *Gregg*. Among prisoners executed in the 20-year period between 1990 and 2010, the average time from imposition of sentence to execution was more than 11.2 years (Bureau of Justice Statistics, 2011). This time is nearly double what it had been in the two decades before that.

At the state level, the initial appeal in capital cases averages 2½ years, but with significant geographical differences. In Virginia, for example, the median time for a capital appeal was 295 days, as compared with 1,331 days in Ohio. How long cases took for the initial appeal also varied in terms of the types of cases. More complex cases, a reversal of the trial court verdict, and the presence of dissenting opinions all increased case-processing time (Cauthen & Latzer, 2008). After appellants have exhausted this initial appeal, they can turn to federal court. Federal court capital *habeas* petitions now take twice as long to complete as they did a decade ago. However, the time these cases take shows important geographical differences. The U.S. district courts in Texas, for example are speedier in their reviews than their counterpart in California (Gould, 2008). Conservatives have objected to allowing condemned prisoners repeated opportunities to file challenges in appellate courts. Congress has responded by limiting federal appellate review (Chapter 16).

Cost Concerns

After decades of debate over the morality, fairness, and effectiveness of the death penalty, a major new concern has been voiced—cost. In the words of retired California Judge Donald McCartin, who was known as "The Hanging Judge of Orange County" because he sentenced nine men to death row, "It's 10 times more expensive to kill them than to keep them alive" (quoted in Hastings, 2009). While some might disagree with McCartin's precise cost estimates, few doubt that death penalty prosecutions and appeals are more expensive than noncapital felony prosecutions because they often require extra lawyers, and the appellate process takes years to complete. The high cost of defending capital cases has strained public defender budgets and the courts as well.

To assess how cost concerns might affect the death penalty, researchers interviewed prosecutors in South Carolina, where economic issues are particularly important because local governments, not the state, pay for prosecutions. While local prosecutors recognized that cost might be a concern, they claimed that money issues do not influence their decisions regarding whether to file capital charges. An analysis of statistical data, however, showed a different pattern—the wealthier the county, the greater the death penalty caseloads (Douglas & Stockstill, 2008).

CONCLUSION

In *Furman v. Georgia,* the Supreme Court set in motion a national debate over the death penalty when it struck down all existing state death penalty laws because they violated the Eighth Amendment prohibition against "cruel and unusual punishment." Forty years later, the debate continues. Most recently, the Court has held that those under 18 cannot be put to death and that the method of execution can also be challenged in federal courts. No one doubts that in the coming years, the Supreme Court will write new chapters to this debate.

Although public support for the death penalty has increased, we as a nation execute very few people. Often unrecognized is the fact that murder (the only crime for which the death penalty is allowed) constitutes only a tiny percentage of crime. The public's demands that something be done about "rising" crime rates has directly and indirectly affected the why, who, and what of sentencing.

During the past three decades, there has been an unprecedented public debate over *why* we sentence. The previously dominant goal of rehabilitation has come under sharp attack, and many voices urge that punishment should instead be based on the principle of just deserts. After 40 years of stability, the indeterminate sentencing system has been rejected in state after state.

Intense interest in crime has also produced major alterations in *who* has the authority to sentence. The mix of sentencing responsibilities has changed in major ways. Legislators have inserted themselves more directly in the sentencing process, reducing the sentencing discretion of judges in many jurisdictions. Legislatures have also restricted parole board authority over early release in some jurisdictions and abolished parole altogether in a few areas.

The *what* of punishment has likewise come under intense scrutiny. Prison overcrowding has become the dominant issue. Probation overcrowding is an equally pressing, if less visible, problem. Perhaps more pressing than the debate over capital punishment is the lack of a national debate over prison overcrowding. Our nation's emphasis on getting tough on criminals is apparently a policy without costs, until we total the bill for building and maintaining prisons. Although citizens and public officials want to send even more offenders to prison, they are unwilling to expend large sums of tax dollars to build the needed facilities. Thus, sentencing is likely to remain an important public policy issue for the foreseeable future.

Chapter Review

LOI **1.** Distinguish between the five major sentencing philosophies.

The five major sentencing philosophies are retribution, which seeks to punish wrongdoers; incapacitation, which is aimed at removing offenders from the community; deterrence, whose goal is to prevent the commission of future crimes; rehabilitation, which emphasizes restoring the offender to a constructive place in society; and restoration, which attempts to promote the victim's healing.

L02 **2.** Describe how the three branches of government are involved in sentencing.

The legislative branch of government defines the range of possible punishment for a given crime. The judicial branch of government has discretion in choosing the specific sentence for the individual criminal. The executive branch of government is responsible for carrying out the actual sentence, including running prisons, pardons, and parole.

L03 **3.** List at least three major issues related to imprisonment as a sentence in the United States.

The three issues most directly related to the use of imprisonment as a sentence in the United

States are prison overcrowding, which limits how many guilty defendants may be sentenced to prison; conditions of confinement lawsuits, which impact living conditions in prison; and the high costs of incarcerating prisoners.

L04 **4.** Identify the major alternatives to institutional incarceration.

The major alternatives to imprisonment include probation, which is often used in felonies; fines, which are rarely used in felonies; restitution, which is increasingly imposed after a misdemeanor and or felony conviction; and intermediate sanctions, such as community service, house arrest, intensive-supervision probation, boot camp, and electronic monitoring.

L05 **5.** Summarize the two U.S. Supreme Court rulings from the 1970s on capital punishment that led to the bifurcated process for death penalty sentencing.

In *Furman v. Georgia* (1972), the Court declared that most U.S. death penalty laws were unconstitutional because of their arbitrary nature. In *Gregg v. Georgia* (1976), the Court upheld death penalty laws that specified aggravating and mitigating circumstances for when the death penalty may be applied and also provided for separate phases of the trial, one to determine guilt and the other to decide on the penalty.

L06 **6.** Indicate how the U.S. Supreme Court has narrowed the list of death-eligible cases and offenders.

The Court has narrowed the list of death-eligible cases by striking down death penalty provisions for most crimes, such as rape—even of a child—and upholding capital punishment only in homicide cases thus far; treason remains an open question. The Court has also narrowed the list of death-eligible offenders by declaring that developmental issues, such as age less than 18 years at the time of the crime or mental retardation, preclude execution.

L07 **7.** Discuss the major differences between the due process model of criminal justice and the crime control model of justice with regard to the death penalty.

The due process model of criminal justice believes the death penalty should be abolished because it is morally wrong for the state to take a life, the death penalty is not a deterrent to crime, and the death penalty is unfairly administered. The crime control model of criminal justice believes that the death penalty should be retained because it is morally acceptable to take the life of a person who has already taken another person's life, the death penalty is a deterrent, and issues of fairness are either unimportant or unproven.

Critical Thinking Questions

1. In what ways is restorative justice similar to the four dominant sentencing philosophies of retribution, incapacitation, deterrence, and rehabilitation? In what ways is restorative justice different from these four sentencing philosophies?

2. Should the punishment fit the crime, or should the punishment fit the criminal? In what ways do the four sentencing philosophies provide different answers to this question?

3. What is the mix of legislative, judicial, and executive sentencing responsibilities in your state?

What changes, if any, have occurred over the past decade in the balance of sentencing responsibilities?

4. Public criticism of lenient sentencing tends to occur in a select number of violent crimes or highly unusual circumstances. In what ways do such discussions deflect attention from the question of what the appropriate sentence should be for the bulk of defendants convicted of nonviolent crimes (burglary and theft, for example) and drug-related crimes?

Key Terms

bifurcated trial 389

boot camp 387

capital offense 387

capital punishment 387

celerity of punishment 372

certainty of punishment 372

community service 384

conditions of confinement
lawsuit 380

cruel and unusual
punishment 377

day fine 383

death-eligible 393

death penalty 387

death-qualified juries 391

determinate sentence 376

deterrence theory 372

direct restitution 384

electronic monitoring (EM) 385

evidence-based corrections 373

expiation 371

fine 383

Furman v. Georgia 388

general deterrence 372

good time 377

Gregg v. Georgia 398

hedonistic calculus 372

home detention 385

imprisonment 378

incapacitation 374

indeterminate sentence 376

intensive-supervision
probation 385

intermediate sanctions 384

just deserts 371

lex talionis 371

pardon 377

parole 377

parole board 376

pretrial diversion 373

prison realignment 374

probation 382

proportionality 371

rehabilitation 373

restitution 383

restoration 375

retribution 371

selective incapacitation 374

severity of punishment 372

shock incarceration 387

specific deterrence 372

symbolic restitution 384

Web Resources

Go to the *America's Courts and the Criminal Justice System* companion website at
http://www.cengage.com/criminaljustice/neubauer,
where you will find more resources to help you study.
Resources include web exercises, quizzing, and flash cards.

For Further Reading

Abbott, Geoffrey. *Lords of the Scaffold: A History of the Executioner*. New York: St. Martin's Press, 1991.

Bazemore, Gordon. "Whom and How Do We Reintegrate? Finding Community in Restorative Justice." *Criminology and Public Policy* 4: 131–148, 2005.

Bedau, Hugo Adam, and Paul Cassell. *Debating the Death Penalty: Should America Have Capital Punishment? The Experts on Both Sides Make Their Case*. New York: Oxford University Press, 2005.

Bureau of Justice Assistance. "Building an Offender Reentry Program: A Guide for Law Enforcement." Washington, DC, U.S. Department of Justice. 2006.

Clear, Todd. *Imprisoning Communities: How Mass Incarceration Makes Disadvantaged Neighborhoods Worse*. New York: Oxford University Press, 2007.

Clear, Todd, George Cole, and Michael Reisig. *American Corrections*. 8th ed. Belmont, CA: Wadsworth 2009.

Ewald, Alec, and Marnie Smith. "Collateral Consequences of Criminal Convictions in American Courts: The View from the State Bench." *Justice System Journal* 29: 145–164, 2008.

Gainey, Randy, Sara Steen, and Rodney Engen. "Exercising Options: An Assessment of the Use of Alternative Sanctions for Drug Offenders." *Justice Quarterly* 22: 488–520, 2005.

Gottschalk, Marie. *The Prison and the Gallows: The Politics of Mass Incarceration in America*. New York: Cambridge University Press, 2006.

Haney, Craig. *Capital Punishment as a Social Psychological System*. New York Oxford University Press, 2005.

Huebner, Beth, and Timothy Bynum. "An Analysis of Parole Decision Making Using a Sample of Sex Offenders: A Focal Concerns Perspective." *Criminology* 44: 961–991, 2006.

Johnstone, Gerry, and Daniel Van Ness (eds.). *Handbook of Restorative Justice*. Devon, United Kingdom: Willan, 2006.

Lanier, Charles, William Bowers, and James Acker (eds.). *The Future of America's Death Penalty: An Agenda for the Next Generation of Capital Punishment Research*. Durham, NC: Carolina Academic Press, 2009.

Latzer, Barry. *Death Penalty Cases*. 2nd ed. Boston: Butterworth-Heineman, 2002.

Lin, Ann Chih. *Reform in the Making: The Implementation of Social Policy in Prison*. Princeton, NJ: Princeton University Press, 2000.

Lynch, Michael. *Big Prisons, Big Dreams: Crime and the Failure of America's Penal System*. Piscataway, NJ: Rutgers University Press, 2007.

Mays, G. Larry, and L. Thomas Winfree. *Essentials of Corrections*. 4th ed. Belmont, CA: Wadsworth. 2009.

McCord, David (symposium editor). "The Effects of Capital Punishment on the Administration of Justice." *Judicature* 8: 248–305, 2006.

Paternoster, Raymond, Robert Brame, and Sarah Bacon. *The Death Penalty: America's Experience with Capital Punishment*. New York: Oxford University Press, 2007.

Petersilla, Joan. *When Prisoners Come Home: Parole and Prisoner Reentry*. New York: Oxford University Press, 2003.

Rice, Stephen, Danielle Dirks, and Julie Exline. "Of Guilt, and Repentance: Evidence from the Texas Death Chamber." *Justice Quarterly* 26: 295–326, 2009.

Santos, Michael. *Inside: Life Behind Bars in America*. New York: St. Martin's Press, 2006.

Shepherd, Joanna. "The Imprisonment Puzzle: Understanding How Prison Growth Affects Crime." *Criminology and Public Policy* 5: 285–298, 2006.

Simon, Jonathan. *Poor Discipline: Parole and the Social Control of the Underclass, 1890–1990*. Chicago: University of Chicago Press, 1994.

Travis, Jeremy, and Christy Visher (eds.). *Prisoner Reentry and Crime in America*. New York: Cambridge University Press, 2005.

Unnever, James, Francis Cullen, and John Bartkowski. "Image of God and Public Support for Capital Punishment: Does a Close Relationship with a Loving God Matter?" *Criminology* 44: 835–866, 2006.

Wasby, Stephen, and Robert Howard (eds.). "Special Issue: Court-Related Aspects of Capital Punishment. *Justice System Journal* 29: 243–440, 2008.

White, Welsh. *Litigating in the Shadow of Death: Defense Attorneys in Capital Cases*. Ann Arbor: University of Michigan Press, 2006.

Winfree, L. Thomas, and Howard Abadinsky. *Understanding Crime: Essentials of Criminological Theory*. 3rd ed. Belmont, CA: Wadsworth, 2010.

15 Sentencing Decisions

© AP Photo/Casper Star-Tribune/Dan Cepeda

Amid growing concern that the nation relies too heavily on imprisonment, intermediate sanctions are growing in popularity. One example is intensive-supervised probation. In this photo, probation officer Bridget Wiggins fills out her report as her probationer looks on. He had been in the Intensive-Supervision Probation program in Casper, Wyoming, for six months at the time. ■

THE COURTROOM WORK GROUP AND SENTENCING DECISIONS
Probation Officers
Prosecutors
Defense Attorneys
Judges

Courts, Law, & Media
Using Mitigation Videos at Sentencing

NORMAL PENALTIES AND SENTENCING DECISIONS
Seriousness of the Offense
Prior Record
Aggravating or Mitigating Circumstances
Law in Controversy: Uncertainty and Public Opinion

DIFFERENCES IN SENTENCING OUTCOMES
Imbalance versus Discrimination
Sentencing Disparities
Discrimination in Noncapital Sentencing
Discrimination and Capital Punishment

CHANGING SENTENCING STRUCTURES
Law in Controversy: Reducing Judicial Discretion
Law on the Books: Variations of Determinate Sentencing Return

STRUCTURED SENTENCING SCHEMES
Presumptive Sentencing in the States
State Sentencing Guidelines
Federal Sentencing Guidelines
Law in Action: Diverse Impacts

CASE CLOSE-UP: *Kimbrough v. United States* **and Federal Sentencing Guidelines in Crack Cocaine Cases**

INCREASING THE SEVERITY OF THE PENALTY
Law on the Books: Mandatory Minimum Sentences

Courts, Controversy, & Reducing Crime
Are "Three Strikes and You're Out" Laws Fair?

Law in Action: Nullification by Discretion
Law in Controversy: Negative Side Effects

Learning Objectives

After reading this chapter, you should be able to:

LO1 Define the concept of normal crimes, and indicate the two most important factors in determining normal penalties.

LO2 Distinguish between the concepts of sentencing disparities and discrimination.

LO3 Explain how scholars approach the issue of racial discrimination differently than the general public and the implications these differing approaches have for the conclusions reached.

LO4 Indicate why the offender–victim dyad is important in studies of racial discrimination in capital punishment.

LO5 List the two major factors related to disparities and sentencing.

LO6 Recognize the main objective of changes in sentencing structure beginning in the late 1960s and the major consequences of these changes.

LO7 Outline how the U.S. Supreme Court has limited state sentencing guidelines.

LO8 Identify the most recent changes in how the U.S. Supreme Court has responded to federal sentencing guidelines

LO9 Explain the law in action perspective on researching the impact of mandatory minimum sentences.

Twelve-year-old Polly Klaas was kidnapped from a slumber party in her home while her mother and little sister slept in the next room. Her two friends were found a short time later, bound and gagged, and were able to provide a general description of the bearded intruder. For 9 weeks, hundreds of law enforcement officers and thousands of volunteers attempted to find the girl, but to no avail. Just before Christmas, the bad news came: Polly had been killed shortly after her abduction.

The police arrest of parolee Richard Allen Davis did little to calm an angry public. The kidnapping and murder of Polly Klaas was blamed on a badly flawed criminal justice system that failed to keep a dangerous person like Davis behind bars. The murder of Polly Klaas, and the extensive national media coverage that surrounded it, sparked another round of get-tough-with-crooks legislation. Whereas earlier laws resulted in mandatory minimums, abolition of parole, and sentencing guidelines, the focus now shifted to "three strikes and you're out" laws.

Decisions • Sentencing Decisions • Sentencing Decisions • Senten
Decisions • Sentencing Decisions • Sentencing Decisions • Sent

While public attention focuses on the sentences handed out in the handful of sensational cases such as the Polly Klaas murder (refer to the wedding cake analogy used in Chapter 10), judges must wrestle with the sentence to impose on the more than 1 million felons convicted each year. The problems members of the courtroom work group face in reaching these sentencing decisions are captured by the powerful symbol of Lady Justice. Held high in her right hand are the scales of justice, symbolizing fairness in the administration of justice. Draped across her eyes is a blindfold, suggesting that all who come before her will receive impartial justice. Grasped low in her left hand is a sword, standing for the power and might of law. Replicas of Lady Justice adorn the exteriors of many American courthouses, but whether the sentencing process inside the courtrooms lives up to those high ideals is open to question.

The scales of justice are the starting point in examining sentencing. This chapter begins by focusing on who is and who is not sentenced to prison, granted probation, or executed. First, we need to know what factors judges and other members of the courtroom work group weigh in deciding between prison and probation. Normal penalties are the most important consideration in sentencing. Based on the seriousness of the offense and the defendant's prior record, courthouses have developed going rates, which are used as parameters in fine-tuning a sentence for a given offender.

The blindfold is the next major topic. Sentences imposed on the guilty are expected to be fair and just. Many observers argue that they are not; disparities and discrimination in sentencing are major topics of concern. Numerous studies probe the extent to which economic status, age, gender, and race improperly pierce the judicial blindfold when sentences are imposed.

The sword of justice will also be discussed. Whereas some worry that the scales of justice are tipped, others are concerned that the sword of justice is sheathed. Frustration over rising crime rates has given rise to charges that judges are too lenient. Demands that sentences be more certain as well as more severe have become a staple of American politics. Legislators have responded by increasing the severity of some punishments and altering sentencing structures in hopes of producing greater predictability in sentencing. Sentencing guidelines are now the centerpiece in discussions of increasing the predictability of sentencing as well as increasing the severity of penalties.

THE COURTROOM WORK GROUP AND SENTENCING DECISIONS

Sentencing is a joint decision-making process. Although only judges possess the legal authority to impose a sentence, other members of the courtroom work group are also influential, as the "Law on the Books vs. Law in Action" feature on the following page makes clear.

The extent of this influence varies from jurisdiction to jurisdiction and from judge to judge. Where sentence bargaining predominates, for example, the judge almost invariably imposes the sentence that the prosecutor and defense attorney have already agreed upon. Where count and charge bargaining are used, the actors reach agreements based on past sentencing patterns of the judge. The most significant actors in sentencing are probation officers, prosecutors, defense attorneys, and (of course) judges.

Probation Officers

Probation officers perform two major functions in the sentencing process. One is the supervision of offenders after a sentence of probation has been imposed. The other is investigation prior to sentencing.

The primary purpose of a **presentence investigation (PSI)** is to help the judge select an appropriate sentence by providing information about the crime and the criminal. Most often, the PSI is ordered by the court following the defendant's conviction. A date is set for sentencing the offender, and meanwhile the probation officer conducts the investigation. The presentence report is designed to give the judge, who must select the proper sentence, an appropriate database. This is particularly important when the defendant has entered a plea of guilty, because in these cases the judge knows little about the particulars of the crime or the background of the offender.

Historically, the presentence report has been based on police reports, prosecutor's records, an

LAW ON THE BOOKS VS. LAW IN ACTION
THE COURTROOM WORK GROUP AND SENTENCING

	LAW ON THE BOOKS	LAW IN ACTION
Probation officer	Conducts presentence investigation (PSI).	Judges most often follow the recommendation in PSI. Studies disagree about whether the sentencing decision is guided by PSI or provides a paper rationale for an already agreed-upon sentence.
Prosecutor	In most jurisdictions, the district attorney (DA) makes a sentencing recommendation to the judge.	Judges are more likely to impose the sentence recommended by the DA than that recommended by the defense attorney.
Defense attorney	During the sentencing hearing, the defense attorney argues for the court to show leniency to the defendant.	Pleas for leniency are viewed as efforts to impress the client and the client's family and therefore are often ignored. Defense attorneys with good working relationships with the other members of the courtroom work group are influential in achieving lenient sentences in selected instances.
Judge	By law, the judge is the only person who can impose a sentence. Mandatory sentences and sentencing guidelines restrict judges' discretion in a growing number of jurisdictions.	Judges most often sentence within the normal penalty structure. Judges often criticize legislatures for restricting judicial sentencing discretion.

interview with the offender, and perhaps a talk with the defendant's family as well. Using the information gathered from these sources, probation officers typically prepare a presentence report containing a description of the offense, the defendant's version of the crime, the person's prior criminal record and social history, and a psychological evaluation (if needed). But as sentencing systems have become more determinate, these reports

> have become more succinct, including less offender information. Now, in many jurisdictions, the primary role of the PSI is merely to determine the applicable mitigating and aggravating circumstances. In some states PSIs are no longer required at all, having been replaced by worksheets that calculate prescribed sentences under statutory or administrative guidelines. (Warren, 2009, p. 608)

Beyond providing background information, many presentence reports also include a recommendation for an appropriate sentence. However, some judges will not allow a recommendation, claiming that this is the prerogative solely of the court. Even without an explicit recommendation, most PSIs leave little room for doubt about what the probation officer thinks the sentence should be. If probation is recommended, the report usually includes a suggested level of supervision (ranging from intensive through regular to minimal), a listing of special conditions of probation, a plan for treatment, and an assessment of community resources available to facilitate rehabilitation.

Probation officers clearly play a significant role in the sentencing process. Judges are very likely to impose the sentence recommended in the PSI. Indeed, one study found a 95-percent rate of agreement between the judge and the probation report when probation was recommended and an 88-percent rate of agreement when the report opposed probation (Carter & Wilkins, 1967). Studies have replicated these results with respect to first-time offenders, but found that probation officers recommended incarceration for recidivists almost twice as often as judges imposed it (Campbell, McCoy, & Osigweh, 1990; Hagan, 1977). Thus, although sentencing judges are not required to follow such recommendations, they usually do.

However, considerable disagreement exists over the actual influence of probation officers in the sentencing process. Some studies suggest that judges seriously consider the recommendations and use them to guide their decisions—that judges lean heavily on the professional advice of probation officers (David, 1980; Walsh, 1985). Others report that judges skim these reports and read only the sections they deem most important (Leiber, Reitzel, & Mack, 2011; Norman & Wadman, 2000; Rush & Robertson, 1987). And still other researchers argue that probation officers have little real influence on the sentencing process—that probation recommendations have been supplanted by plea bargaining (Clear, Harris & Baird, 1992). Prosecutors and defense attorneys usually talk to the probation officer before the PSI is submitted to the court. The conversation indicates what information should be stressed to justify the sentence already agreed upon (Kingsnorth & Rizzo, 1979). By and large, recommendations by probation officers "do not influence judicial sentencing significantly but serve to maintain the myth that criminal courts dispense individual justice" (Rosencrance, 2004). This, however, may be changing because of the evidence-based corrections movement.

Recall that the criminal justice system has slowly been examining "what works" through a scientific lens. Evidence-based corrections refers to the correctional practices and interventions "that are supported by the best research evidence . . . derived from clinically relevant research . . . based on systematic reviews, reasonable effect sizes, statistical and clinical significance, and a body of supporting evidence" (Warren, 2009, p. 597). Evidence-based sentencing makes use of such data by using risk assessment instruments that have been validated by empirical research to help determine whether a particular defendant would be a suitable candidate for a particular correctional rehabilitation or treatment program. A few states,

notably Virginia and Arizona, pioneered incorporating such risk assessment into their presentence investigation processes (Warren, 2009). A few other states have followed their lead, successfully reducing incarceration rates, recidivism, and correctional expenditures through sentencing offenders to interventions tailored to meet their rehabilitative needs (Aos, Miller & Drake, 2006; Kimora, 2008; Warren, 2009).

Prosecutors

Prosecutors influence the sentencing decision in several important ways. By agreeing to a count or charge bargain, prosecutors limit the maximum penalty the judge may impose. During the sentencing hearing, prosecutors can bring to the court's attention factors that are likely to increase the penalty—for example, that the victim was particularly vulnerable or that the defendant inflicted great harm on the victim. Alternatively, prosecutors can bring out factors that would lessen the penalty—for example, the defendant's cooperation with the police.

Finally, prosecutors may make a specific sentencing recommendation. If, for example, there has been a sentence bargain, the prosecutor will indicate the penalty agreed on, and the judge will usually adopt that recommendation as the sentence. When such prosecutorial recommendations are based on office policy, they can have the positive effect of muting sentencing disparities among the different judges. In some courts, however, prosecutors are not allowed to make sentencing recommendations, because sentencing is viewed solely as a judicial responsibility.

Defense Attorneys

The defense attorney's role in sentencing begins early in the history of a case. The decision whether to go to trial or to enter a guilty plea is partially based on the attorney's assessment of the sentence likely to be imposed. Based on the knowledge of what sentences have been handed out to past defendants accused of similar crimes and with similar backgrounds, the attorney must advise the client as to the probable sentence.

At the same time, the defense attorney seeks to obtain the lightest sentence possible. One way to

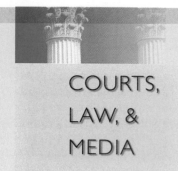

COURTS, LAW, & MEDIA

USING MITIGATION VIDEOS AT SENTENCING

In the wake of decisions that dramatically increased judicial discretion in sentencing defendants convicted in federal cases, U.S. district court judge John Kane stated that a criminal defense attorney's primary responsibility and greatest challenge was to "[m]ake the judge suffer" (as cited in Passon, 2010, p. 981). The logic underlying this bold assertion stemmed from the fact that sentencing had largely been a dispassionate exercise since the Federal Sentencing Guidelines had reduced the practice to a cookie-cutter process. But with the Guidelines now being advisory, Judge Kane argued that defense lawyers need to make judges understand the plight of their clients and impose sentences from a perspective of empathy.

In response to Judge Kane's position, federal public defender Doug Passon argued that defense attorneys should turn to the power of media to inform and persuade judges. Specifically, he asserted that defense attorneys should create emotionally charged sentencing documentaries that "tell a unique story using compelling characters and powerful visuals" (p. 1002).

> Just as every good writer knows that story is the primary vehicle for conveying fundamental truths about life, every good lawyer knows that story is the most effective tool of courtroom persuasion. The best lawyers consistently use story as a means to bring to life the truth of film. Movies connect us to, and reshape our views about, people, places, and issues. So, if great movies have the power to, literally, change the world—it follows that great sentencing movies have the power to change your client's world. With the increasing prevalence of technology in the courtroom, and the accessibility of inexpensive and user-friendly equipment, the widespread use of film in courtroom persuasion is inevitable. (p. 983).

At first blush, one might think that the rules of procedure or rules of evidence might bar the use of such media. But that is not the case. The rules of evidence do not apply at sentencing hearings, and Federal Rule of Criminal Procedure 32(i)(4) requires that before imposing a sentence, the judge *must* allow a defendant to "speak or present *any information* to mitigate the sentence" (emphasis added). The federal sentencing statute (18 U.S.C. § 3661) goes even further: "*No limitation* shall be placed on the information concerning the background, character, and conduct of a person convicted of an offense which a court of the United States may receive and consider for the purpose of imposing an appropriate sentence" (emphasis added).

Passon also asserts that the use of movies at sentencing offers additional benefits to defense lawyers. For one thing, the video-editing process allows for much greater control over

---

accomplish this goal is to maneuver the case before a judge with a lenient sentencing record. Another way is to discuss the case with the prosecutor in hopes that he or she will agree to (or at least not oppose) a recommendation of probation in the presentence investigation. Defense attorneys also try to emphasize certain circumstances that make the defendant look better in the eyes of the judge, prosecutor, and probation officer. They may try to downplay the severity of the offense by stressing the defendant's minor role in the crime or the fact that the victim was not without blame; or they may have friends or employers testify about the defendant's general good character and regular employment.

Overall, though, defense attorneys are less influential than prosecutors. Judges and prosecutors typically view defense attorneys' arguments for leniency as efforts to impress their clients with the fact that they tried as hard as they could.

Judges

Courtroom work groups impose informal limits on how judges exercise their formal legal authority to impose sentences. Judges are well aware that the

the content, pace, and emotional tone of a sentencing hearing, especially since it greatly reduces, if not eliminates, surprises that might occur when a witness testifies on the stand.

Passon admits that crafting the type of documentary that is likely to truly make a sentencing judge feel empathy for a criminal defendant is tricky, since judges will not tolerate being manipulated through the use of "dramatic voice-over narrations, flashy editing tricks, overbearing or melodramatic music, gratuitous scenes of crying loved ones, pointless inclusion of children, cheesy re-enactments, and so forth" (pp. 987–988). Instead, Passon asserts that the key to creating effective sentencing videos is giving the judge reasons to relate to the defendant in spite of his or her criminal acts by emphasizing character traits with which the judge will personally connect. Passon uses the character of Dr. Hannibal Lecter in *The Silence of the Lambs* as an example of such empathy at work.

> Lecter is a serial killer who eats his victims. It is hard to imagine a more disturbing, unlikable character. Yet, the audience is drawn to him. In fact, many who see this movie are actually quite satisfied at the end when (spoiler alert) Lecter escapes and announces his intention to devour Dr. Chilton, the sadistic psychiatrist who tortured him for years at the prison insane asylum. Why is it that audiences rally behind this crazed killer? The writer, Ted Tally, masterfully infused this complicated character with traits most people respect or admire. Lecter was brilliant. He was persecuted. He cooperated with law enforcement to help catch another serial killer. He demonstrated the capacity to care for other human beings, as demonstrated

by his relationship with the protagonist, Clarice Starling (played by Jodie Foster). He was fearless and in control. These are the kinds of qualities people see in themselves, either in truth or in desire. (p. 990).

Passon points to Melvin Udall (Jack Nicholson) in *As Good As It Gets*, Tony Soprano (James Gandolfini) in *The Sopranos*, and Ratso Rizzo (Dustin Hoffman) in *Midnight Cowboy*, as additional examples of troubled characters that nonetheless evoke empathy from the audience. Similarly, the documentary *March of the Penguins* is another example of how viewers can be made to connect with even nonhuman characters, since "at its core, [it] was about family and the struggles parents endure in order to provide for and protect their children" (p. 991).

Of course, defense attorneys are not filmmakers and, therefore, probably lack the skill set necessary to craft effective documentaries. Even if they developed such skills, in light of the heavy caseloads and insufficient funding issues facing most appointed counsel (Chapter 7), there are serious questions as to whether lawyers would have the time either to produce such videos themselves or to hire a private video production firm to create such movies—especially since they routinely cost tens of thousands of dollars.

What do you think? If you were a criminal defendant, would you want your defense lawyer to use this approach? Why or why not? As a student of the criminal judicial process, what do you see as the benefits and drawbacks of using customized media as part of sentencing? Can you think of any unintended consequences of criminal defense attorneys taking this approach? Explain your reasoning.

disposition of cases is related to plea bargaining, which in turn depends on being able to anticipate the sentencing tendencies of judges. Judges share in a framework of understandings, expectations, and agreements that are relied on to dispose of most criminal cases. If a judge strays too far from expectations by imposing a sentence substantially more lenient or more severe than the one agreed on by the defendant, defense lawyer, and prosecutor, it becomes more difficult for the prosecutor and defense counsel to negotiate future agreements.

In working within the limits established by the consensus of the courtroom work group, judges

are also constrained because the other members of the work group have more thorough knowledge about the details of the defendant and the nature of the crime. In particular, a judge's sentencing decision is restricted by the bargains struck between prosecution and defense. Indeed, judges who enjoy stable relationships with the prosecutors who practice before them are more likely to defer to those prosecutors' sentencing recommendations.

Judges, though, are not without influence. They are the most experienced members of the courtroom team, so their views carry more weight than those of relatively inexperienced prosecutors or defense attorneys. The particular judge's attitudes about sentencing are reflected in the courtroom work group's common understanding of what sentences are appropriate.

NORMAL PENALTIES AND SENTENCING DECISIONS

Sentencing involves a two-stage, decision-making process. After conviction, the first decision is whether to grant probation or to incarcerate the defendant. If incarceration is chosen, the second decision is determining how long the sentence should be. Making these sentencing decisions is

not an easy task; many judges say that sentencing is the most difficult part of their job. The frustrations of sentencing stem in part from the need to weigh the possibility of rehabilitation, the need to protect the public, popular demands for retribution, any potential deterrent value in the sentence, and restoration of the victim to the extent possible (see Chapter 13). Of course, courtroom work groups do not consider these competing perspectives in the abstract. They must sentence real defendants found guilty of actual crimes. Each defendant and crime is somewhat different. Sentences are expected to be individualized—to fit the penalty to the crime and the defendant.

In seeking individualized sentences, courtroom work groups use normal penalties (Spohn, 2008;

TABLE 15.1 ▪ TYPES OF SENTENCED IMPOSED BY CONVICTION OFFENSE

Conviction Type	Percent Sentenced to:			
	Prison	Jail	Probation	Other
All Offenses	41	28	27	4
Violent Offenses	54	23	20	3
Murder & Nonnegligent Manslaughter	93	2	3	2
Sexual Assault	64	18	16	3
Robbery	71	14	13	2
Aggravated Assault	43	30	25	3
Property Offenses	38	29	29	4
Burglary	49	24	24	3
Larceny	34	34	28	3
Motor Vehicle Theft	42	41	15	2
Fraud, Forgery, & Embezzlement	32	27	35	6
Drug Offenses	38	28	30	4
Possession	33	31	33	4
Trafficking	41	26	29	4
Weapons Offenses	45	28	25	2

Source: Sean Rosenmerkel, Matthew Durose, & Donald Farole. *Felony Sentences in State Courts*, 2006. Washington, DC: Department of Justice, Bureau of Justice Statistics, 2010. Available online at http://bjs.ojp.usdoj.gov/content/pub/pdf/fssc06st.pdf

Sudnow, 1965). Based on the usual manner in which crimes are committed and the typical backgrounds of the defendants who commit them, courtroom work groups develop norms of what penalties are appropriate for given categories (see Table 15.1). The normal sentences are not used mechanically; rather, they guide sentencing. It is within the context of these normal penalties that individualization occurs. Upward and downward adjustments are made. Normal penalties governing appropriate sentences for defendants take into account the seriousness of the crime, the prior criminal record, and any aggravating or mitigating circumstances.

Seriousness of the Offense

The most important factor in setting normal penalties is the seriousness of the offense (Spohn, 2009; Spohn & DeLone, 2000; Steffensmeier, Ulmer, & Kramer, 1998). The more serious the offense, the less likely the defendant will be granted probation. Also, the more serious the offense, the longer the prison sentence. These conclusions are hardly surprising. Society expects that convicted murderers will be punished more severely than defendants found guilty of theft. What is important is how courtroom work groups go about the task of deciding what offenses are serious.

When weighing the seriousness of the offense, courtroom work groups examine the harm or loss suffered by the crime victim in what they perceive to be the "real offense" (what really happened, not the official charge). For example, by examining the prior relationship between the defendant and the victim, the courtroom work group may perceive that the underlying crime is a squabble among friends and therefore less serious than the official charge indicates (Vera Institute of Justice 1977; Wilmot & Spohn, 2004).

Sentencing on the basis of seriousness is one of the principal ways courts attempt to arrive at consistent sentences. Most courts use a rank ordering that incorporates the full range of offenses—from the most serious crimes of armed robbery and rape, through middle-level crimes of domestic violence, to the lowest level of forgery, theft, and burglary. One reason that sentences appear to critics to be lenient is that most cases are ranked at the lowest of these levels.

Prior Record

After the seriousness of the offense, the next most important factor in sentencing is the defendant's prior record (Albonetti, 1997; Spohn, 2009; Ulmer, 1997). As the prior record increases, so does the sentence. In choosing between probation and imprisonment, the courtroom work group carefully considers the defendant's previous criminal involvement. If the decision has been made to sentence the offender to prison, the prior record also plays a role in setting the length of incarceration. In general, a previous incarceration increases the length of the sentence (Crow, 2008; DeLisi, 2001; Welch & Spohn, 1986).

How courts assess prior records varies. Some consider only previous convictions, whereas others look at arrests as well. In addition, courtroom work groups often consider the length of time between the current offense and the previous one. If there has been a significant gap, the defendant will often receive a sentence more lenient than normal. On the other hand, if the previous conviction is a recent one, this is often taken as an indication that the defendant is a "bad actor," and the severity of the punishment will increase. Finally, the prior record is assessed within the context of the severity of the crime itself. When the crime is perceived as being less serious, individual factors such as prior record seem to be given relatively more weight than when the crime is more serious.

Aggravating or Mitigating Circumstances

In passing sentence, judges and other members of the courtroom work group consider not only the formal charge but also the way the crime was committed. Prosecutors and defense counsel engage in a careful calculation of moral turpitude, examining the nature of the crime and the role of the victim. Some of the aggravating circumstances that lead to a higher penalty are the use of a weapon and personal injury to the victim.

Mitigating factors include lack of mental capacity and role (principal or secondary actor) in the crime. One of the most important mitigating factors is the perceived social stability of the defendant. Marital status, relationship with the family, length of employment, and prior alcohol or drug abuse are considered to be indicators of social stability or instability. Social stability is a particularly important predictor of judges' sentencing, especially when probation is being considered.

The youth of the defendant is often considered a mitigating factor. In *Graham v. Florida* (2009), the U.S. Supreme Court ruled that the Cruel and Unusual Punishment Clause of the Eighth Amendment to the U.S. Constitution does not permit a juvenile offender to be sentenced to life in prison without parole for a nonhomicide crime.

Law in Controversy: Uncertainty and Public Opinion

Sentencing is more art than science. Judges, prosecutors, probation officers, and defense attorneys are well aware that they will make mistakes in considering the seriousness of the offense, the prior record of the defendant, aggravating or mitigating circumstances, and the stability of the defendant. Uncertainty is ingrained in the process. They may send someone to prison who should not be there or impose a prison sentence that is longer than necessary. Or they may err in the opposite direction: A defendant recently granted probation may commit a serious and well-publicized crime. Note that only the second type of error will reach public attention; mistakes of the first kind may appear, but only well after the fact.

The uncertainties inherent in sentencing are particularly important at a time when public opinion is critical of the courts and sentencing. For a long time, the majority of Americans felt that sentences were too lenient. In response, legislatures increased the severity of sentences and courts sentenced a higher proportion of defendants to prison. This caused the average sentence length in the United States to nearly double between the 1970s and the mid-2000s. In fact, by 2004, 1 out of 11 prison sentences being served in the United States was a life sentence without the possibility of parole (Mauer, King & Young, 2004). This, in turn, led prisons to become overcrowded, adding further complexity to the difficult task of arriving at a fair and appropriate sentence.

In 2010, though, the incarceration rate in the United States fell for the first time in 40 years (see Figure 14.1). This change appears to be a function of a slow shifting in sentencing policy in response

to a number of factors, including lower crime rates, the implementation of evidence-based policies, a renewed focus on rehabilitation for prisoner reentry into society, and a series of sentencing reforms that have begun to scale back some of the harsh "get tough" policies enacted in the past few decades—such as mandatory minimum sentences, as discussed below (Mauer, 2011). And there can be no doubt that this shift has also been driven by the high costs of mass incarceration during a period of economic strain. But some changes have also been prompted by recognition of racial, ethnic, and socioeconomic differences in sentencing outcomes (Cole, 2011; Mauer, 2011).

DIFFERENCES IN SENTENCING OUTCOMES

The ideal of equal justice under the law means that all persons convicted of the same offense should receive identical sentences. But not all deviations from equality are unwarranted. The law also strives for individualized dispositions, sometimes reflecting varying degrees of seriousness of the offense, sometimes reflecting varying characteristics of the offender. What one person may perceive as unfairness, another may see as justifiable variation.

Discussions about unwarranted variation in sentencing involve two widely used terms: *disparity* and *discrimination*. Although widely used, these terms are rarely defined consistently. Moreover, the concepts overlap somewhat. Nonetheless, for our purposes they should be treated as involving distinct phenomena.

Disparity refers to inconsistencies in sentencing; the decision-making process is the principal topic of interest. **Discrimination**, on the other hand, refers to illegitimate influences on the sentencing process; defendants' attributes are the primary focus. Legal factors such as the seriousness of the offense and the prior criminal record of the defendant are considered legitimate factors that contribute to disparities. But sentencing discrimination exists when some illegitimate attribute is associated with sentencing outcomes after all other relevant variables are adequately controlled. These objectionable influences are referred to as "extralegal variables" (Walker, Spohn, & DeLone, 2007).

Imbalance versus Discrimination

No one doubts that the criminal justice system reflects an imbalance in terms of the types of people caught in its web. Whether we examine arrests, prosecutions, convictions, or sentences, the statistical profile highlights the same imbalance—poor, young minority males are disproportionately represented.

Evidence of imbalance in outcomes, however, is not proof of discrimination. Imbalance could be the result of the legally relevant factors discussed earlier in this chapter (such as seriousness of the offense and prior record). In making claims about discrimination, researchers want to make sure they are comparing cases that are truly similar. By way of illustration, consider two defendants of different races who have received different sentences. One of the defendants is a first offender who pled guilty to burglary and received 1 year of probation. The other has two prior felony convictions and was convicted by a jury of simple robbery and sentenced to 3 years in prison. Irrespective of which offender was white or African-American, we would not conclude solely on this evidence that the sentences were discriminatory. Rather, we would want to compare a number of cases involving similar crimes and defendants with similar backgrounds.

In trying to ensure that like cases are being compared, researchers use statistical controls. A variety of statistical procedures allows researchers to compare first offenders to other first offenders, and burglars to other burglars. Only after legally relevant variables have been held constant can claims about the existence (or absence) of discrimination be made. Earlier studies often failed to incorporate appropriate statistical controls. They considered only the single variables of race and sentencing, for example, and found racial discrimination in the sentencing. When these studies were reanalyzed, Hagan (1974) found that claims of racial discrimination were not supported by the data.

Sentencing Disparities

The most commonly cited types of sentencing disparity involve geography (variations across jurisdictions) and judicial backgrounds and attitudes (variations among judges within the same jurisdiction).

The Geography of Justice

What counts against defendants is not only what they do but also where they do it. Significant variations in the sentencing patterns of judges in different judicial districts within the same political jurisdiction is referred to as the "geography of justice" or "community effects" (Fearn, 2005). The frequency of fines, probation, or imprisonment varies from county to county. Urban courts, for example, make greater use of probation and shorter prison terms than their rural counterparts (Austin, 1981). Capital sentences provide another example, as executions are concentrated in certain regions (primarily the South). Figure 15.1 illustrates the differences among the states in convicts imprisoned per 100,000 people.

Geographic sentencing patterns demonstrate that court officials, drawn as they are from the local communities, vary in their views of what offenses are the most serious as well as what penalty is appropriate (Myers & Reid, 1995; Myers & Talarico, 1986b). These geographic differences also extend to the federal courts, where the applications of the federal sentencing guidelines vary (Johnson, Ulmer & Kramer, 2008; Tiede, 2009). "In sum, substantial evidence exists that what kind of sentence one gets, and the factors that predict why one gets it, in significant part depends on where one is sentenced" (Ulmer, 2012, p. 14).

Judges' Backgrounds and Attitudes

What counts against defendants is not only what they do and where they do it, but also which judge imposes the sentence. Sentencing disparities among judges have fascinated social scientists for decades. A classic study of female shoplifting defendants placed on probation ranged from a low of 10 percent for one judge to a high of 62 percent for another in the same Chicago courthouse (Cameron, 1964). Similarly, downward departures in federal sentencing for certain types of offenders are routine in some districts and rare in others (Johnson, Ulmer & Kramer, 2008). Although such sentencing disparities are due, in part, to variations in the seriousness of the cases heard, differences in judges' backgrounds and attitudes are major contributing factors.

Judges come to the bench from a variety of backgrounds. We might reasonably expect these differences to be reflected in varying patterns of judicial behavior, and studies of judicial decision making support this proposition.

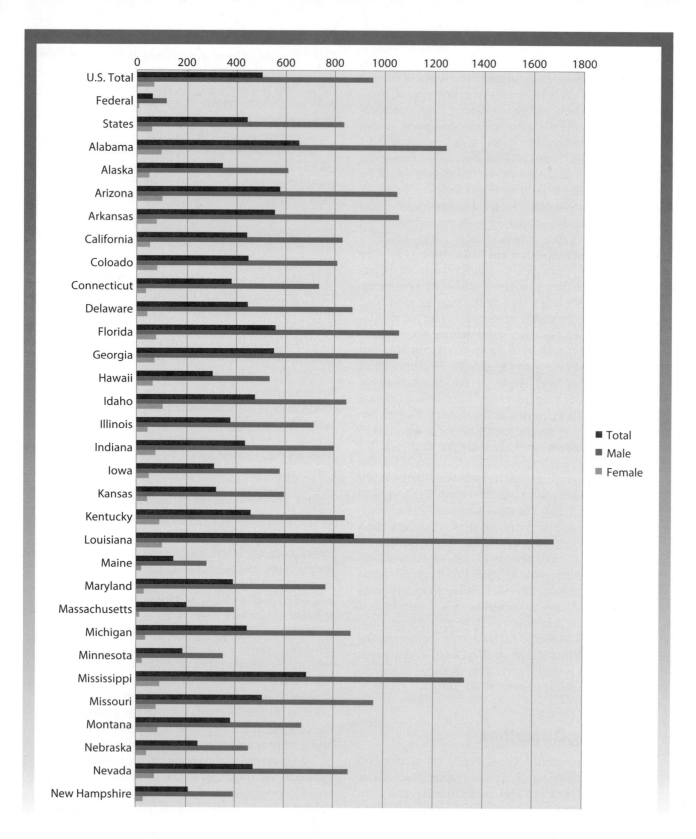

Continued on next page

Continued from previous page

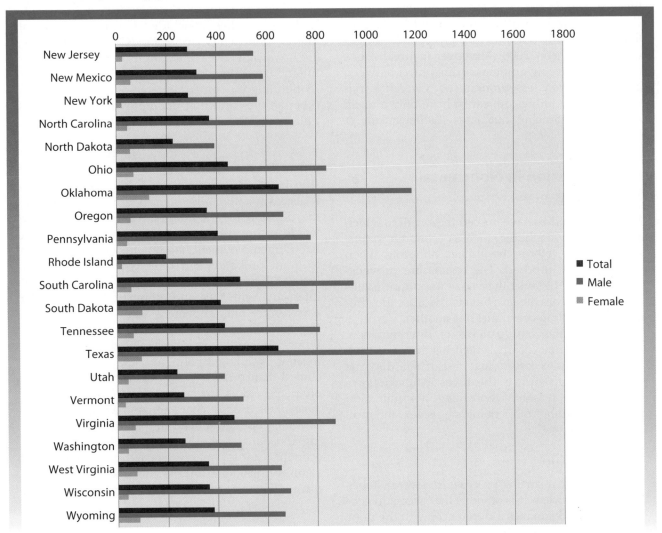

Figure 15.1 ■ Prisoners in Custody per 100,000 Civilian Population

SOURCE: Paul Guerino, Paige M. Harrison, and William J. Sabol. *Prisoners in 2010.* Washington, DC: Department of Justice, Bureau of Justice Statistics 2011.

Variations in judges' backgrounds are associated with different perceptions of what crimes are serious as well as the relative weights to be assigned to conflicting sentencing goals. For example, judges who stress deterrence are more likely to favor prison sentences, while judges who are more treatment oriented are more likely to impose suspended sentences or relatively short jail sentences (Hogarth, 1971).

Although the public views judges as either harsh or lenient sentencers, detailed studies indicate that the pattern is far more complex (Myers & Talarico, 1987). It is an accepted fact that judges

have different sentencing tendencies. Some have reputations for handing out stiff sentences. "Maximum Max" or "Mean Geraldine" are examples of the colorful labels used by members of the courtroom work group to characterize such judges. Others are known for lenient sentences. "Cut 'em Loose Bruce" is one name given such a judge by courthouse regulars. The sentences of most judges fall somewhere in between these extremes (Partridge & Eldridge, 1974). Because they are less distinctive, these courtroom actors seldom get colorful nicknames. One study of judges in Pennsylvania underscores this point. After statistically controlling for a wide range of factors, minority judges were found to be a little more lenient in the sentences imposed, but interestingly, female judges were not (Johnson, 2006). Moreover, in jurisdictions that use sentencing guidelines, differences between judges are even less pronounced. Overall variations between judges appear to have only a weak effect on sentencing outcomes (Steffensmeier & Hebert, 1999).

Discrimination in Noncapital Sentencing

Numerous studies have probed the extent to which a defendant's attributes, such as economic status, sex, and race, pierce the judicial blindfold when sentences are imposed. The results are provocative, not only because they raise important issues of equality before the law, but also because they frequently appear to contradict one another.

Some studies find patterns of discrimination, and others do not. Clearly, sentencing discrimination involves complex issues, and researchers disagree over how best to study it. The discussion that follows examines the research concerning discrimination under the headings of economic status, sex, and race.

Economic Status

The courts are a sorting process. At several stages during the process, it is obvious that access to economic resources makes a difference, with the poor receiving less-preferential treatment. For example, the poor are less likely to be released on bail prior to trial and also are less likely to be able to hire a private attorney. These differences during processing carry over to sentencing: Defendants who are not released on bail or are represented by a court-appointed attorney are granted probation less often and are given longer prison sentences.

Outcome differences based on economic status are, therefore, readily apparent in sentencing. The provocative title of a book by Jeffrey Reiman (2007), *The Rich Get Richer and the Poor Get Prison*, reflects this fact. Prisons are arguably the modern equivalent of the poorhouse. Do these patterns indicate that courts discriminate against the poor in sentencing, or are they the product of other, legally

permissible, factors? A number of studies yield conflicting and complex answers.

Some studies conclude that unemployment affects sentencing decisions (Chiricos & Bales, 1991; Walsh, 1987). For example, judges may assess unemployed persons as being at higher risk for reoffending (Spohn & Holleran, 2000). In contrast, other studies find that unemployment has no significant influence on sentencing (Clarke & Koch, 1976; Myers & Talarico, 1986a).

A comprehensive study comparing two cities highlights the complexity of the relationship between economic status and sentencing. In Kansas City, unemployment had a direct effect on the decision to grant probation but none on the length of imprisonment. In Chicago, on the other hand, unemployment had no effect on the decision to grant probation but directly affected sentence length. Perhaps most important, unemployment interacted with race and ethnicity. If the offender was white, unemployment status had no effect. For African-American or Hispanic young males, though, unemployment was related to harsher sentencing. Nobiling, Spohn, and DeLone (1998) concluded that certain types of unemployed offenders are perceived as "social dynamite." The term *social dynamite* is used to characterize the segment of the deviant population seen as particularly threatening and dangerous. Viewed from this perspective, economic status appears to be a dimension of social stability considered by the courtroom work group during sentencing (see also, LaFrenz & Spohn 2006).

Sex

Crime, as Chapter 9 emphasized, is predominantly (but not exclusively) a male enterprise. Of all adults convicted each year, 82 percent are male, meaning only 18 percent are women (Cohen & Kyckelhahn, 2010). The marked imbalance between male and female defendants complicates efforts to examine gender-based differences in sentencing outcomes.

Some empirical research suggests that women are less likely to be incarcerated in jail or prison than men, and when they are incarcerated, women receive shorter sentences than men even when sentencing guidelines are in effect that should reduce such gender disparities (Blackwell, Holleran, & Finn, 2008). Other studies found that when the sexes are in similar circumstances and are charged with similar offenses, no significant gender-based differences are found (Crew, 1991; Spohn & Spears, 1996; Steffensmeier, Kramer, & Streifel, 1993).

In *The Invisible Woman*, Joanne Belknap (2007) aptly summarized the three competing hypotheses concerning the treatment of women by the criminal justice system: (1) chivalry or paternalistic treatment, (2) the evil woman, and (3) equal treatment.

The chivalry/paternalism hypothesis stresses that "women are awarded leniency in sentencing as a result of their inherent biological weaknesses and consequently, their need to be protected and coddled both as offenders and as victims" (Franklin & Fearn, 2008, p. 279). Paternalism emphasizes the notion that women are childlike, and therefore "women are incapable of achieving, nor are they in fact held to, the same standards of personal responsibility as are men" (Rapaport, 1991, p. 368). In essence, gender stereotypes lead predominantly male criminal justice officials to treat women in a protective manner.

The evil woman hypothesis focuses on traditional sex-role expectations. This hypothesis emphasizes that women lose the advantages normally provided by chivalry and paternalism when they are convicted of "manly" crimes such as robbery or assault. This evil woman view argues that women might actually be treated more harshly than men when they deviate from stereotypical sex-role expectations (Griffin & Wooldredge, 2006; Weisheit & Mahan, 1988).

The third hypothesis is that men and women are actually treated equally during sentencing. Pennsylvania sentencing data indicate that "when men and women appear in (contemporary) criminal court in similar circumstances and are charged with similar offenses, they receive similar treatment" (Steffensmeier, Kramer, & Streifel, 1993). Studies in other jurisdictions likewise report no significant gender-based differences (Crew, 1991; Spohn & Spears, 1996), although an Ohio study found that after sentencing guidelines were implemented in that state, women were sentenced more leniently than males, even though the sexes were convicted at the same rates (Griffin & Wooldredge, 2006). Boritch (1992, p. 293) wrote that "some of the less severe treatment of women is attributable to the fact that women usually are less serious offenders than men," and therefore studies using appropriate statistical controls for legally relevant variables find less evidence of differential leniency in the severity of sanctions.

In *Gender, Crime, and Punishment*, Kathleen Daly (1994) fleshed out this argument. She selected 40 male–female pairs of apparently similar crimes and then analyzed transcripts of the court proceedings. She concluded that women were involved in less serious crimes, and this factor (not gender) explained "lenient" treatment.

Most contemporary researchers now explicitly reject the evil woman explanation. The continued viability of the chivalry/paternalism hypothesis, however, is still being debated. The hypothesis continues to find empirical support insofar as male offenders who target female victims continue to receive the most severe sanctions as compared with any of the other offender–victim gender dyads (Franklin & Fearn, 2008). Regardless of the theoretical explanations, concern remains that different criteria influence the legal processing of male and female offenders. Some studies report that gender-role expectations and stereotypes guide parole decision making (Erez, 1992), and that a form of gender bias exists in capital punishment laws (Rapaport, 1991).

Race

Critics of the criminal justice system view the high rates of arrest and imprisonment for African-Americans and other minorities as evidence of racial discrimination. Although the law contains no racial bias, these critics claim that, because criminal justice officials exercise discretion, discrimination can and often does occur.

More studies have been done of racial discrimination at the sentencing stage than at any other decision point in the criminal justice system. Studies conducted from the 1930s through the 1960s often reported that extralegal factors such as race were responsible for differences in sanctions. These original findings, however, have not stood up to further analysis, because they failed to use appropriate statistical techniques. When Hagan (1974) reexamined the data from early studies, he found that the relationship between the race of the offender and the sentence handed out was not statistically significant. Contemporary research using appropriate statistical techniques has produced conflicting findings.

Some researchers conclude that African-Americans are sentenced more harshly than Whites (Spohn & Holleran, 2000; Steffensmeier, Ulmer, & Kramer, 1998; Zatz, 1984). A prominent example of this type of conclusion was based on a study of six American cities. In three southern cities, African-Americans were sentenced to prison more often than Whites. No such differences were found in northern jurisdictions (Welch, Spohn, & Gruhl, 1985). A meta-analysis of 71 studies that examined the effects of race on criminal sentencing concluded that even when legal factors (such as criminal history and severity of the offense), were statistically controlled, "on average African-Americans were sentenced more harshly than Whites," although racial differences were generally small (Mitchell, 2005, p. 462; see also, Crow & Johnson, 2008; Spohn & Cederblom, 1991). More recent studies have also found racial disparities in sentencing outcomes for Hispanic offenders, especially in drug-related cases (Brennan & Spohn, 2008).

In contrast, another group of studies failed to find a link between race and sentencing (D'Alessio & Stolzenberg, 2009; Klein, Petersilia, & Turner, 1990; Kramer & Steffensmeier, 1993; McDonald & Carlson 1993; Myers & Talarico, 1986a; Wooldredge, 2012). Research in diverse geographical locations reported the absence of consistent evidence of systematic racial discrimination in sentencing. Perhaps typical is a study of sentencing in federal courts (McDonald & Carlson 1993), which found that from 1986 to 1988 "White, Black, and Hispanic offenders received similar sentences, on average, in Federal District Courts." After sentencing guidelines were imposed in 1989, Hispanic and African-American offenders were slightly more likely than White offenders to be sentenced to prison, but these apparent racial differences were directly attributable to characteristics of offenses and offenders.

Finally, a few studies concluded that African-Americans are sentenced more leniently than Whites (Bernstein, Kelly, & Doyle, 1977; Walker, Spohn, & DeLone, 2007).

At first blush, the findings on the studies of racial and ethnic effects on sentencing outcomes may appear to be inconsistent, making it difficult to draw firm conclusions. But the results of the most recent and methodologically sophisticated studies evidence that the contemporary sentencing process, while not characterized by "a widespread systematic pattern of discrimination" (Blumstein, Cohen, Martin, & Tonry, 1983, p. 93), is nonetheless not racially neutral.

Some research has noted that the impact of race on sentencing disparities can be mediated by the racial composition of the courtroom work group. Specifically, more racially diverse courtroom work groups—especially within prosecutors' offices—appear to reduce sentencing disparities (Ward, Farrell, & Rousseau, 2009; King, Johnson & McGeever, 2010).

Interaction Effects

Although research continues to examine the effects of specific legal and extralegal factors on sentencing decisions, most contemporary research has demonstrated that the interaction between these variables produces the most significant differences. Thus, as discussed above, research has demonstrated racial and ethnic differences in sentencing outcomes; however, these disparities are magnified when other extralegal variables, such as age, gender, educational level, employment, and socioeconomic status are taken into account (Franklin & Fearn, 2008; LaFrenz & Spohn, 2006; Spohn & Holleran, 2000; Ulmer & Johnson, 2004; Wooldredge, 2012). Collectively, the research supports the proposition that young, poor, African-American males and Hispanic males are sentenced more harshly than any other group (Curry & Corral-Camacho, 2008; Spohn & DeLone, 2000; Steffensmeier et al., 1998).

Discrimination and Capital Punishment

Capital punishment has figured prominently in studies of racial discrimination in sentencing. Marked racial differences in the application of the death penalty in the South provide the most obvious historical evidence of racial discrimination in sentencing. From 1930 to 1966, 72 percent of the prisoners executed in the South were African-American. This proportion is dramatically higher than the ratio of African-Americans in the overall population or the ratio of African-Americans convicted of capital offenses. The racial gap was even more pronounced in rape cases. Only the South executed rapists, and 90 percent of those executed for rape were African-American. Those most likely to be executed were African-Americans who had raped white women (Wolfgang & Riedel, 1973). Recall from Chapter 14 that in the modern era, rape is no longer a death-eligible offense. But the evolution of capital punishment law has not eliminated racial disparities in death penalty cases.

Offender–Victim Dyad

The executions in the South clearly show major racial differences. As indicated earlier, however, racial imbalances in outcomes do not necessarily prove discrimination. Interestingly, many studies found that the most obvious factor—race of the defendant—was not as important as the race of the offender in combination with the race of the victim. The offender–victim dyad, ordered according to the perceived seriousness of the offense, is:

1. Black offender, White victim
2. White offender, White victim
3. Black offender, Black victim
4. White offender, Black victim

Research on the offender–victim dyad established that Blacks killing or raping Whites were the most likely to be executed; conversely, Whites killing or raping Blacks were the least likely to receive the death penalty. These findings have been interpreted as indicating that severe punishments were motivated by a desire to protect the White social order. Some also argue that Black lives were not valued as much as White lives. A variety of studies indicated that the use of the death penalty in the South was racially discriminatory (Baldus, Pulaski, & Woodworth, 1983; Hindelang, 1972; Ralph, Sorensen, & Marquart, 1992). A different conclusion emerged for the North. Studies of the death penalty in northern states found no evidence of racial discrimination (Kleck, 1981).

Evidence of Discrimination since Gregg

Major racial differences in execution rates, together with studies finding racial discrimination in the application of the death penalty, figured prominently in the opinions of several justices when the Supreme Court struck down state death penalty laws in 1972 (*Furman v. Georgia*). The Court later upheld guided discretion statutes designed to reduce or eliminate the arbitrariness with which the death penalty is imposed. Since *Gregg v. Georgia* in 1976, several studies have reported evidence of racial discrimination in the application of post-*Gregg* death penalty laws.

Research on the use of the death penalty post-*Gregg* continue to find that the race of the defendant is rarely associated with the imposition of a death sentence (Williams, Demuth, & Holcomb, 2007). Rather, studies that find evidence of discrimination in the modern era report that Black defendants who kill White victims are more likely to receive adverse treatment than those with similarly situated cases with non-Black defendant–White victim cases (Paternoster & Brame, 2008). Conclusions like this have emerged in states as diverse as Maryland, Florida, South Carolina, Georgia, and Colorado (Spohn, 2009).

One stage in the process at which discrimination occurs, according to these studies, is the decision of the prosecutor to charge the defendant with a capital homicide, rather than a homicide that typically carries a life sentence (Radelet & Pierce, 1985; Sorensen & Wallace, 1999; Weiss, Berk, & Lee, 1996). In South Carolina, for example, the race of the victim was found to be a significant factor structuring the district attorney's decision to request capital punishment. For African-American offenders who killed White victims, the prosecutor was 40 times more likely to request the death penalty than in the case of African-American defendants accused of killing other African-Americans (Paternoster, 1984). Similarly, in Colorado prosecutors were more likely to seek the death penalty for homicides with White female victims (regardless of the race of the defendant) and that the probability of death being sought was 4.2 times higher for those who killed Whites than for those who killed Blacks (Hindson, Potter, & Radelet, 2006).

These studies also found that jurors are more likely to choose a sentence of death rather than life imprisonment during the penalty phase of the trial. Indeed, when the U.S. General Accounting Office (1990, p. 6) reviewed the body of literature on racial discrimination in capital litigation in the post-*Gregg* era, it reported that in "82 percent of the studies, race of the victim was found to influence the likelihood of being charged with capital murder or receiving the death penalty, i.e., those who murdered whites were found to be more likely to be sentenced to death than those who murdered blacks." More recent studies have confirmed that this pattern has continued (Baldus & Woodworth, 2003; Baldus, Woodworth, Grosso, & Christ, 2002; Jacobs & Kent, 2007; Jacobs, Qian, Carmichael, & Kent, 2007; Paternoster & Brame, 2008).

Evidence of No Discrimination since Gregg

Findings that the application of the death penalty remain racially biased despite the apparent protections required by *Gregg* were challenged by a study of all death-eligible cases appealed to the Louisiana Supreme Court (Klemm, 1986). The initial analysis revealed the impact of extralegal variables. The chance of receiving a death sentence steadily decreased as one moved down the scale of offender–victim dyads. These findings clearly paralleled earlier ones in other states. More sophisticated analysis, however, highlighted the importance of legal variables.

Unlike previous researchers, Klemm also examined how the crime was committed. The prior relationship of the offender to the victim emerged as an important factor. *Primary homicides* are crimes of passion involving persons who knew each other. *Nonprimary homicides* occur during the commission of another felony (most typically, armed robbery), and the victim is a total stranger. Those convicted of nonprimary homicides were more likely to receive a sentence of death, regardless of the race of the offender or the race of the victim. Thus, the chances of receiving a death sentence were greater if the victim was a stranger.

Overall, the race of the victim had only an indirect effect in Louisiana. Likewise, a study of the use of the death penalty in Texas prior to *Furman* found some remarkable parallels to the findings from Louisiana. In particular, nonprimary homicides were more likely to result in the imposition of the death penalty (Ralph, Sorensen & Marquart, 1992).

The importance of examining not just the victim but the nature of the homicide as well emerges in recent research on victim gender. In murder cases, defendants who victimize women are punished more harshly. The three victimization factors were rape, forcing the victim to disrobe, and killing an unclothed victim (Williams et al., 2007).

McCleskey v. Kemp Rejects Social Science Evidence

The Supreme Court squarely addressed the issue of racial discrimination in capital punishment in a controversial 1987 decision, *McCleskey v. Kemp*. At issue was a study in Georgia that the application of capital punishment was related to the offender–victim dyad. Defendants convicted of killing a White victim were four times more likely to receive a sentence of death than those found guilty of slaying an African-American victim. These racial differences remained even after controls for relevant factors such as prior record and type of homicide were introduced. The authors concluded that Georgia had a dual system of capital punishment, based on the race of the victim (Baldus et al., 1983).

By a 5-to-4 vote, the majority rejected claims that statistical studies indicated that the state's death penalty law was "wanton and freakish" in application. To Justice Lewis Powell, "Disparities are an inevitable part of our criminal justice system." The opinion argued that the statistics do not prove that race enters into any capital sentencing decisions or that race was a factor in McCleskey's case. To be clear, though, the Supreme Court emphasized that racial discrimination in the imposition of the death penalty violates the Fourteenth Amendment's guarantees of due process and equal protection. However, proof of such discrimination cannot rest on statistical evidence of racially disparate sentencing outcomes. Rather, a defendant must prove that a specific state actor (or group of actors) intentionally discriminated against him or her in the specific case—a task that is often virtually impossible (Paternoster & Brame, 2008).

Overall, as the Court has become more supportive of the death penalty, it has become less inclined to consider social science evidence that might show patterns of racial discrimination (Acker, 1993; Fradella, 2004). Nonetheless, critics continue to point to patterns of discrimination in the application of the death penalty.

CHANGING SENTENCING STRUCTURES

During the late 1960s and early 1970s, an unusual (and temporary) political coalition developed between liberals and conservatives. Both sides found considerable fault in existing sentencing practices. Although their reasons reflected fundamentally different concerns, liberals and conservatives defined the problem in similar terms: The criminal laws permitted too much latitude in sentencing, providing judges with little or no guidance on how to determine the proper sentence for each individual case. This coalition therefore sought greater predictability in sentencing. The result was a fundamental change in how defendants are sentenced (see Chapter 14).

Law in Controversy: Reducing Judicial Discretion

Adherents of the due process model were concerned that excessive discretion resulted in a lack of fairness in sentencing. They perceived that criminal justice officials, ranging from police officers to parole boards, were making decisions in a discriminatory manner, especially on the basis of race. They were also concerned that judges' sentencing discretion resulted in sentencing disparities. Thus, the political left saw determinate sentences as a means of reducing individual discretion and thereby (presumably) reducing disparity and discrimination (e.g., Frankel, 1972; von Hirsch, 1976).

Adherents of the crime control model were far more concerned that excessive discretion resulted in a lack of effective crime control. They perceived that criminal justice officials were making decisions that produced undue leniency. Concern about disparity or discrimination was not part of the agenda. In particular, they viewed trial judges as all too ready to impose sentences well below the statutory maximum. They perceived that parole boards were too willing to release prisoners early; they were shocked that prisoners were back on the streets on parole well before the maximum sentence had expired. To conservatives, the essential problem was that sentencing was not reducing crime (e.g., Wilson, 1975). In an effort to make sentencing more effective, a "justice" model of sentencing came into increasing prominence. Wrongdoers should be punished on the principle of just deserts, which implies a certainty and uniformity of punishment (see Chapter 14).

Law on the Books: Variations of Determinate Sentencing Return

In response to criticisms of the rehabilitation model, with its emphasis on indeterminate sentences and discretionary parole release, a number of states returned to sentencing schemes intended to provide more legislative control over imprisonment decisions. The systems put in place are based on the assumption that judges should give offenders a specific amount of time to serve rather than an indeterminate period of incarceration between some minimum and maximum sentence. But the varying approaches to doing so use different means to accomplish the desired ends. **Structured sentencing** schemes target sentencing decisions by judges. In contrast, true **determinate sentencing** schemes control release decisions, usually by abolishing boards and requiring offenders be released after serving the term imposed (or a high percentage of the term imposed, such as 85 percent), less any reductions through "good time" credits and similar programs (Stemen & Rengifo, 2011).

Table 15.2 summarizes the major approaches to controlling discretion with regard to whether a particular offender should be incarcerated and, if so, how long that offender will actually serve. It should be noted, though, that the states differ substantially in their statutory systems for structured and determinate sentencing schemes. We will then explore each of these variations in detail.

STRUCTURED SENTENCING SCHEMES

Early efforts to impose structured sentencing suffered from a serious weakness: Legislative bodies had neither the time nor the skills to enact detailed sentencing rules. Therefore, since the 1980s, efforts to provide certainty and consistency in sentencing have taken a different form. Legislatures have created commissions to devise detailed sentencing rules, and the legislatures have then enacted these guidelines into law (Griset, 1995).

Presumptive Sentencing in the States

Under unstructured sentencing law, states typically provided a wide sentencing range for felony offenses. For example, a judge might be authorized to impose a sentence of 2 to 10 years. To reduce judicial discretion and sentencing disparities, some states opted to put in place a series of **presumptive sentences**. Under this approach, legislatures specified a presumptive term of imprisonment for

TABLE 15.2 ■ KEY CHARACTERISTICS OF DIFFERENT STRUCTURED SENTENCING SCHEMES

Sentencing Scheme	Description	Departures and Appellate Enforcement
Presumptive sentences	A *required* structured sentencing system that provides a single recommended prison term within a wider statutory sentence range for each felony offense, with the recommended term based solely on the offense committed.	Judges may legally impose a term different from the recommended term only by finding aggravating or mitigating circumstances. Departures are reviewable on appeal to ensure that presumptive sentences are followed.
Presumptive sentencing guidelines	A *required* structured sentencing system of multiple recommended sentences and dispositions for each offense class determined by both the severity of the offense and the prior criminal history of the offender.	Judges may legally impose a term different from the recommended term only by finding aggravating or mitigating circumstances. Departures are reviewable on appeal to ensure that presumptive sentences are followed.
Voluntary sentencing guidelines	A *recommended* structured sentencing system of multiple recommended sentences and dispositions for each offense class determined by both the severity of the offense and the prior criminal history of the offender.	Judges may legally impose a term different from the recommended. Departures are not reviewable on appeal.
Determinate sentencing	A *required* sentencing system of multiple recommended sentences and dispositions for each offense class determined by both the severity of the offense and the prior criminal history of the offender. Parole is abolished and release occurs only at the expiration of serving a fixed percentage of the sentence imposed.	Judges may legally impose a term different from the recommended term only by finding aggravating or mitigating circumstances. Departures are reviewable on appeal to ensure that presumptive sentences are followed.
Mandatory minimum sentencing	A *required* sentencing system of determinate sentencing that mandates judges impose a fixed, minimum prison sentence and prohibits release until after the statutory minimum period of incarceration has been served.	Judges have no discretion to impose a term different from the required minimum mandatory sentence. Because departures are illegal, they are reviewable on appeal to ensure that mandatory minimum sentences are followed.

SOURCE: Don Stemen and Andres F. Rengifo, "Policies and Imprisonment: The Impact of Structured Sentencing and Determinate Sentencing on State Incarceration Rates, 1978–2004." *Justice Quarterly*, 28(1): 174–201, 2011. Reprinted by permission of Taylor & Francis Ltd., http://www.tandf.co.uk/journals.

a particular criminal offense. Thus, instead of an indeterminate term of 2 to 10 years, a presumptive sentence of 4 years' imprisonment would be specified for a particular felony. Judges may legally impose a term different from the recommended term only by finding aggravating or mitigating circumstances. Departures are reviewable on appeal to ensure that presumptive sentences are followed.

This approach to sentencing is based solely on the offense committed. Presumptive sentences do not take into account variations in offenders' backgrounds. This led only seven states to adopt presumptive sentencing schemes between 1975 and 2004 (Stemen & Rengifo, 2011). Many more states opted for a different approach to sentencing reform: sentencing guidelines.

Severity Level of Conviction Offense (Common offenses listed in italics)		Criminal History Score						
		0	1	2	3	4	5	6 or more
Murder, 2nd Degree (intentional murder; drive-by-shootings)	XI	306 261-367	326 278-391	346 295-415	366 312-439	386 329-463	406 346-480[2]	426 363-480[2]
Murder, 3rd Degree Murder, 2nd Degree (unintentional murder)	X	150 128-180	165 141-198	180 153-216	195 166-234	210 179-252	225 192-270	240 204-288
Assault, 1st Degree Controlled Substance Crime, 1st Degree	IX	86 74-103	98 84-117	110 94-132	122 104-146	134 114-160	146 125-175	158 135-189
Aggravated Robbery, 1st Degree Controlled Substance Crime, 2nd Degree	VIII	48 41-57	58 50-69	68 58-81	78 67-93	88 75-105	98 84-117	108 92-129
Felony DWI	VII	36	42	48	54 46-64	60 51-72	66 57-79	72 62-84[2]
Controlled Substance Crime, 3rd Degree	VI	21	27	33	39 34-46	45 39-54	51 44-61	57 49-68
Residential Burglary Simple Robbery	V	18	23	28	33 29-39	38 33-45	43 37-51	48 41-57
Nonresidential Burglary	IV	12[1]	15	18	21	24 21-28	27 23-32	30 26-36
Theft Crimes (Over $5,000)	III	12[1]	13	15	17	19 17-22	21 18-25	23 20-27
Theft Crimes ($5,000 or less) Check Forgery ($251-$2,500)	II	12[1]	12[1]	13	15	17	19	21 18-25
Sale of Simulated Controlled Substance	I	12[1]	12[1]	12[1]	13	15	17	19 17-22

☐ Presumptive commitment to state imprisonment. First-degree murder has a mandatory life sentence and is excluded from the guidelines by law. See Guidelines Section II.E., Mandatory Sentences, for policy regarding those sentences controlled by law.

■ Presumptive stayed sentence; at the discretion of the judge, up to a year in jail and/or other non-jail sanctions can be imposed as conditions of probation. However, certain offenses in this section of the grid always carry a presumptive commitment to state prison. See, Guidelines Sections II.C. Presumptive Sentence and II.E. Mandatory Sentences.

Figure 15.2 ■ Minnesota Sentencing Guidelines

SOURCE: Minnesota Sentencing Guidelines Commission, 2008, p. 57

State Sentencing Guidelines

Statewide sentencing guidelines are mentioned most frequently as the procedures for ensuring fairness and appropriate severity in sentencing. Twenty-one states adopted sentencing guidelines between 1975 and 2004 (Kauder & Ostrom, 2008) and other states seriously considered this approach (Reitz, 2001).

Sentencing guidelines direct the judge to specific actions that should be taken. The sample sentencing grid in Figure 15.2 illustrates how they operate. The far left column ranks the seriousness of the offense according to 10 categories. The top row provides a seven-category criminal history score for the defendant based on number of previous convictions, employment status, educational achievement, drug or alcohol abuse, and so on. Having determined the offense severity ranking and the criminal history score, the judge finds the recommended sentence in the cell where the applicable row and column meet. The cells below the bold black line call for sentences other than state imprisonment; these numbers specify months of supervision (that is, probation). The cells above the bold line contain the guideline sentence expressed in months of imprisonment. The single number is the recommended sentence. The range (shown below the single number) varies by plus or minus 5 to 8 percent from the guideline sentences and can be used for upward or downward adjustments.

The Continuum of Voluntary to Required Use

Of the 21 states that adopted sentencing guidelines, 11 required judges to sentence within the presumptive sentencing guidelines while 10 states made judicial compliance with sentencing guidelines voluntary (Stemen & Rengifo, 2011). But this dichotomy is a bit misleading. State sentencing guidelines are best viewed as ranging along a continuum of more voluntary on one side and more mandatory on the other (Kauder & Ostrom, 2008).

Under *voluntary sentencing guidelines,* recommended sentencing ranges were derived by empirically analyzing the sanctions judges in the jurisdiction have usually imposed in various types of cases in the past. Thus, descriptive guidelines codify past sentencing practices as standards for future cases. Once adopted, these guidelines may voluntarily be used by judges, but they are advisory only. Thus, voluntary sentencing guidelines do not have the force of law. Noncompliance by a judge creates no right to appeal a sentence. As one would expect, not all judges actually use the guidelines when imposing sentences (Miethe & Moore, 1989). Over the years some voluntary sentencing guidelines have fallen into such disuse that it is not always clear whether a particular state's guideline system is still operational (Kauder & Ostrom, 2008).

In contrast to a voluntary compliance approach with sentencing guidelines, other states adopted *presumptive sentencing guidelines* that require judges

to impose sentences in accordance with the directives in the guidelines. In most states using this approach, the legislature delegates the authority for developing detailed sentencing criteria to a sentencing commission (Kramer, Lubitz & Kempinen, 1989). The resulting guidelines are prescriptive—that is, they express what sentence *should* be imposed, irrespective of existing practices. Once adopted, these guidelines have the force of law; they must be followed by sentencing judges. If a sentence is imposed outside the guidelines, the judge must provide reasons for the deviation. Both defendants and prosecutors have the right to have the judge's explanation reviewed by an appellate court.

The Constitutionality of State Sentencing Guidelines

Since 2000, the U.S. Supreme Court has raised serious doubts about the constitutionality of many state sentencing guidelines, holding that other than a prior conviction, any fact that increases the penalty for a crime beyond the statutory maximum must be tried before a jury (*Apprendi v. New Jersey,* 2000). Based on this reasoning, in 2004 the Court struck down sentencing guidelines in the State of Washington, holding that the Sixth Amendment gives juries (and not judges) the power to make a finding of fact beyond a reasonable doubt (*Blakely v. Washington,* 2004). The dissenters argued that the decision will serve only to increase judicial discretion and lead to less uniformity in sentencing, perhaps leading to increasing racial discrimination.

Some state high courts of last resort held that *Blakely* did not apply to their state sentencing schemes (Lankford, 2006), only to be firmly rebuffed when the Supreme Court struck down the California sentencing laws, holding that the statute gave judges authority that the U.S. Constitution places with juries (*Cunningham v. California,* 2007). Since *Cunningham,* it is clear that *Blakely* applies to state sentencing laws. But a failure to submit a sentencing factor to a jury is not "structural" error, which always invalidates a conviction. Rather, *Blakely* violations are subject to harmless error review (see Chapter 16).

Blakely limited judicial discretion in sentencing even more than mandatory sentencing guidelines did. It does not appear that the shift from judicial to jury decision making when imposing sentences more severe than those set forth in sentencing guidelines has increased sentencing disparities (Iannacchione & Ball, 2008). But it also does not appear to have reduced sentencing disparities either. Rather, extralegal factors that impact the imposition of a sentence above the maximum range of sentencing guidelines appear to affect both jury and judicial decision making, especially age and sex (Iannacchione & Ball, 2008).

Federal Sentencing Guidelines

The legal and political factors leading to the creation of state sentencing guidelines likewise led to the creation of federal sentencing guidelines, which have become more visible and also more controversial than their state counterparts. In 1984, Congress created the U.S. Sentencing Commission (Chapter 3) and charged it with developing guidelines for sentencing federal offenders. These standards became law in 1987. The Supreme Court upheld their legality in 1989 (*Mistretta v. United States*), only to rule them unconstitutional in 2005 (*United States v. Booker*).

The federal sentencing guidelines proved to be highly controversial (Stith & Cabranes, 1998). Indeed, many federal judges, probation officers, defense attorneys, and even some prosecutors resent and resist the guidelines (Tiede, 2009). According to Michael Tonry (1993), the federal sentencing guidelines "are a failure and should be radically revised or repealed." In support of this conclusion, he offers the following arguments: First, the guidelines are unduly harsh and as a result have produced a dramatic increase in the federal prison population. Second, the guidelines have failed to achieve their primary goal of reducing unwarranted disparities in federal sentencing. Indeed, the guidelines contribute to unfairness in sentencing because they are rigid and complex.

In *United States v. Booker* (2005), the Supreme Court greatly altered how federal guidelines are used. The first part of the complex opinion struck down federal sentencing guidelines as unconstitutional for the same reasons used to declare state sentencing guidelines unconstitutional—Congress improperly allowed judges and not juries to make key factual decisions in sentencing. But the second part of the opinion allows federal judges to continue to use the guidelines as advisory, and appellate courts can review for reasonableness.

The impact of *Booker* on federal sentencing practices was not as dramatic as some hoped and others feared. At the district court level, the rate of within-range sentences remained the same and average sentence lengths remained constant. There were more downward departures, but these were largely due to actions of U.S. attorneys and not the judges (Hofer, 2007). The U.S. courts of appeals varied in their approaches: Some adopted a wait-and-see attitude; others held that *Blakely* did not apply to the federal sentencing guidelines, and still others held that the guidelines were unconstitutional (Hurwitz, 2006). The Court revisited the issues, holding that sentences within the guidelines may be presumed "reasonable" but did not require appellate courts to do so (*Rita v. United States*, 2007). Amid confusion about the impact of *Rita*, the Court again considered the issues, this time making it more difficult for appeals courts to reverse a trial judge who imposes a sentence more lenient than the guideline recommendations (*Gall v. United States*, 2007). At the same time, the high court, by a vote of 7 to 2, held that trial judges may narrow the sentencing gap between crack cocaine and powder cocaine (*Kimbrough v. United States*, 2007; see the "Case Close-Up" on *Kimbrough*). Although these decisions clearly restored some of the sentencing discretion taken away by the sentencing guidelines, they will likely result in only limited sentencing leniency. In all likelihood, specialists in sentencing law predict, federal judges will continue to use their sentencing power relatively sparingly (Liptak, 2007). Moreover, in upcoming sessions, Congress might attempt to enact a new statutory sentencing scheme. Consider, for example, that several of these U.S. Supreme Court decisions prompted Congress to revise the drug laws in 2010 to reduce the disparities in sentencing that some thought was racially discriminatory. And the U.S. Sentencing Commission voted to apply these changes retroactively, meaning that over 12,000 persons in federal prison may have their crack-related sentences reduced (Gresko, 2011).

The short-term impact of *Booker* is unclear because the Court failed to state whether the decision was retroactive (potentially meaning that appellate courts must review past sentences). Likewise, the long-term impact of *Booker* is unclear because Congress might attempt to enact a new statutory sentencing scheme. Meanwhile, the

CASE CLOSE-UP

KIMBROUGH v. UNITED STATES AND FEDERAL SENTENCING GUIDELINES IN CRACK COCAINE CASES

According to his former lawyer, Derrick Kimbrough was leading a "pretty unremarkable" life until he fell into a drug habit. In his early 20s, Kimbrough enlisted in the Marines, fought in Operation Desert Storm, and received an honorable discharge. He then moved to Norfolk, Virginia, where he worked construction. Kimbrough's life took a decided turn for the worse when the Norfolk police spotted Kimbrough and another man sitting in a car in a drug-plagued neighborhood. The police questioned the two and then searched the car, with Kimbrough's consent. They found 56 grams, or about 2 ounces, of crack cocaine and 92 grams of powder cocaine, plus an illegal handgun (McGlone, 2007a). Although the state charges were dropped, Kimbrough was indicted in U.S. District Court for the Eastern District of Virginia, where he pled guilty to the four counts in the indictment.

Based on the federal sentencing guidelines, the U.S. attorney sought a prison term between 19 and 22 years, but U.S. District Judge Raymond Jackson balked. If Kimbrough had been in possession of only powder cocaine, he would have faced no more than a total of 8 years in prison, the judge noted. Jackson, a federal judge for nearly 14 years, and—according to the local paper—not noted for a history of being lenient, decided to take a stand. "The Justice Department has yet to recognize the disproportionate and unjust effect that crack cocaine guidelines have in sentencing." He added "I find it absolutely ridiculous that the Department of Justice demands the heart and lungs, feet and everything else in a case on these facts" (quoted in McGlone, 2007b). Jackson concluded that the statutory minimum of 15 years was "clearly long enough."

The government appealed the downward departure as unreasonable and appealed to the Fourth Circuit of Appeals based in nearby Richmond, Virginia—a circuit that has the reputation of being one of the nation's most conservative judicial bodies when it comes to defendant's rights. In an unpublished opinion, the court vacated the sentence, writing that a sentence "outside the guideline's range is per se unreasonable when it is based on a

disagreement with the sentencing disparity for crack and powder cocaine offenses."

Justice Ruth Bader Ginsburg authored the Supreme Court's majority opinion. She focused heavily on the contradictions in American drug policy. Working on the assumption that crack cocaine was more harmful than its powder form, the Anti-Drug Abuse Act of 1986 adopted a "100-to-1 ratio" that treated every gram of crack cocaine as the equivalent of 100 grams of powder cocaine. Although the intent of the law was to punish drug dealers more severely than drug users, the anomalous result of the 100-to-1 ratio was that retail crack dealers received longer sentences than the wholesale drug distributors who supplied the powder cocaine from which the crack is produced.

Extending its previous decision in *Booker* (2005), which held that federal sentencing guidelines were unconstitutional if mandatory, but judges could still refer to them as advisory, the Court held that the Fourth Circuit erred in vacating Kimbrough's sentence because district judges are not bound by the sentencing guidelines in crack cocaine cases.

The public debate over crack cocaine versus powder cocaine has focused heavily on the issue of racial disparities. And, to be sure, concerns about race clearly underpin the *Kimbrough* case. Although Kimbrough is never identified as being African-American, a picture in the *Norfolk-Pilot* clearly leads to that conclusion. Moreover, an *amicus* brief filed by the NAACP Legal Defense Fund focuses on racial disparities in cocaine cases ("LDF Applauds Supreme Court," 2007). The Court's opinion, however, mentions race only in passing. Without expressing a position, the Court's opinion cites a report of the U.S. Sentencing Commission that the crack/powder sentencing differential "fosters disrespect for and lack of confidence in the criminal justice system" because of a widely held perception that it promotes unwarranted disparity based on race.

After *Kimbrough* was decided, Congress changed the sentencing laws with regard to different forms of cocaine. The new law, the Fair Sentencing Act of 2010,

Continued on next page

Continued from previous page

reduced the sentencing disparity between crack and power contain from a 100:1 ratio to an 18:1 ratio. This change in sentencing law created a new problem for the courts. By its terms, the new law was effective only against those who committed their drug offenses after the law became effective on August 3, 2010. Those who committed their offenses before that date, but had not yet been sentenced, could have benefited from the reduced sentencing disparity. As of this writing, the Supreme Court has granted *certiorari* in two cases testing the applicability of the 2010 law. Whatever the outcome of those cases, though, the disparate statutory treatment of offenses involving crack versus powder cocaine still remains. The Obama administration believes that the disparity in sentencing between crack and powder cocaine is unwarranted and must be eliminated (Cose, 2009). Thus, as with many other topics, politics, and not the law, may finally bring about a resolution of this divisive issue.

courts of appeals are applying *Booker* in fundamentally different ways. Some have indicated that the guidelines are not enforceable, but others are enforcing them. However, the limited empirical research on the impact of federal judges being freed from the requirement of following the federal sentencing guidelines suggests that sentencing disparities based on extralegal factors have not increased (Ulmer, Light & Kramer, 2011).

Law in Action: Diverse Impacts

The application of sentencing guidelines is complex (Kramer & Ulmer, 2009). One major question asked by researchers and policy makers is whether structured or determinate sentencing schemes do indeed result in fairer sentences. Not surprisingly, the answer to that question might depend on one's interpretation of the data. Some adherents hoped that these laws would increase the certainty of punishment; others feared that prison populations would swell. Several studies investigated the impact of these sentencing schemes and found that the impacts were diverse. In one state, an offender's chance of receiving probation declined, but there was no change in another (Covey & Mande, 1985; McCoy, 1984). Likewise, in some states there was a projected 50 percent increase in the actual length of sentence for first offenders, yet in another jurisdiction only a modest increase was foreseen (Clarke, 1984; Clear, Hewitt & Regoli, 1979).

Certain structured and determinate sentencing approaches help to reduce disparities, at least for a while. A three-state study concluded that in states that use sentencing guidelines, offenders are sentenced with more predictability, in a less discriminatory manner, and with increased transparency (Ostrom, Ostrom, Hanson, & Kleinman, 2008). Earlier studies reached similar conclusions. Racial, ethnic, and gender differences in sentencing generally decline (Kramer & Ulmer, 1996; Parent, Dunworth, McDonald, & Rhodes, 1996). Disparity reductions, though, tend to erode somewhat over time. Studies in Minnesota (Koons-Witt, 2002) and Ohio (Griffin & Wooldredge, 2006) found only short-term reductions in gender-based dispositions in felony cases. Not surprisingly, presumptive sentencing guidelines are more likely to reduce sentencing disparities than voluntary sentencing guidelines.

Although the specific impacts of these laws varied from state to state, the general pattern became quite clear—the overall prison populations increased. An early study in California (Casper, Brereton & Neal, 1982) reported a significant increase in the number of prisoners incarcerated there, a finding replicated in other states as well (Carroll & Cornell, 1985; Kramer, Lubitz & Kempinen, 1989; Tonry, 1987). By the mid-1990s, the inescapable conclusion was that changes in sentencing structure begun in the late 1960s and early 1970s resulted in major increases in the prison population across the nation (Marvell & Moody, 1996). As discussed in Chapter 14, the increase in prison populations did not begin to level off until about 2005.

By themselves, structured sentencing schemes appear to have little impact on overall incarceration rates (Stemen & Rengifo, 2011). In contrast,

COURTS, CONTROVERSY, & REDUCING CRIME

Are "Three Strikes and You're Out" Laws Fair?

The kidnapping and murder of 12-year-old Polly Klaas focused the nation's attention on violent, predatory criminals. The man convicted of the crime, Richard Allen Davis, was an ex-con who had recently been released from prison on parole. The news coverage of the kidnapping and eventually the arrest fed the nation's fears that no one was safe, not even those who lived in a tranquil small town like Petaluma, California. But not just criminals like Davis were at fault; the system that paroled him was too (Surette, 1996). Faced with an unsettled public, elected officials sought to reassure them by taking dramatic action. Thus, the murder of Polly Klaas became the reference event for passing "three strikes and you're out" legislation. These laws imprison someone for life, without the possibility of parole, upon conviction of a third qualifying felony.

The basic arguments advanced by proponents of the three strikes concept parallel the crime control model. Incapacitating chronic offenders who have demonstrated by their acts that they are both dangerous and unwilling to reform will protect the public. Moreover, repeat offenders will be deterred because they will be off the streets.

Critics counter that substantial increases in the use of imprisonment over the past decades have had little if any effect on violent-crime rates. Life terms for three-time felons will require the allotment of expensive prison cells to offenders who are well past the peak age of criminal conduct. These adherents of the due process model argue that spending the same amount of money in other areas would produce a much greater reduction in crime than three strikes laws (Greenwood et al., 1996).

Court arguments aside, public support for three strikes laws was overwhelming, and in quick order elected officials in 24 states and the federal government enacted new laws using the "three strikes" moniker. What was left largely unspoken during the debate was that for many years most states have had provisions in their laws for enhanced sentencing of repeat offenders (Clark, Austin & Henry, 1998). Thus, outside of California, three strikes provisions rarely applied. These laws have had minimal impact because they were drafted to apply to only the most violent repeat offenders, the very defendants already covered by habitual offender laws and also the very offenders who fare the worst under existing normal penalties (Clark, Austin & Henry, 1997).

"determinate sentencing laws alone, through the abolition of discretionary parole release, can lead to lower incarceration rates," since they limit the ability of correctional officials to deny parole (Stemen & Rengifo, 2011, p. 194). In other words, although structured sentencing schemes limit judicial discretion, the discretion parole boards exercise can undo the intended standardization of incarceration periods by controlling release (see also, Bushway & Piehl, 2007). The combination of both presumptive sentencing guidelines and determinate sentencing schemes offers the most control over incarceration rates by impacting both sentencing and release decisions (Stemen & Rengifo, 2011). But there is another factor that significantly affects incarceration rates: the increasing severity of criminal penalties.

INCREASING THE SEVERITY OF THE PENALTY

For many years, the majority of Americans have believed that prison sentences are too lenient (Cullen, Fisher & Applegate, 2000; Krisberg, 1988; Rossi & Berk, 1997), and elected officials often express these views (Thomson & Ragona, 1987). Thus, when confronted with a crime problem, legislators responded by sounding a clarion call to get tough with criminals. Accordingly, criminal punishments grew harsher throughout the 1980s and 1990s. But the economic crisis in the late 2000s may have caused the American public to rethink its ever-more-punitive stance. Opinion research finds that the public "overwhelmingly favors spending more

California's law potentially has greater impact because it was more loosely drafted. Because any felony can be a third strike, life sentences can be imposed for relatively nonviolent crimes. Thus, the California law applies to criminals with a record of one or more violent or serious felonies. After one such crime ("strike"), the sentence for any new felony is doubled. After two strikes, a new felony requires a term of 25 years to life (Criminal Justice Consortium, 1997).

Three strikes laws are the most recent example of spasmodic attempts by the public, and the politicians they elect, to respond in an extreme manner to what is perceived as skyrocketing crime rates and an unduly lenient criminal justice system. These outbursts are followed by adaptation by members of the courtroom work group (Feeley & Kamin, 1996; Harris & Jesilow, 2000). Adaptive behavior is readily apparent in the California Supreme Court's decision holding that judges do not have to impose life sentences on repeat criminals if they think the punishment is too harsh (*San Diego County v. Romero*, 1996). Later, the court held that juvenile convictions likewise need not be counted (*San Diego County v. Garcia*, 1999). In essence, the California high court held that the law went too far and that judges should use discretion. Judges, however, clearly differ in their approach to exercising discretion when deciding whether

a conviction "counts" as a strike, as illustrated by *Ewing v. California* (2002).

Gary Ewing was convicted of stealing three golf clubs, valued at $399 each. At the time of the theft, Ewing was on parole for convictions in three burglaries and one robbery. Under California's three strikes law, another felony conviction would require a sentence of 25 years to life. In sentencing Ewing under the three strikes law, the trial court refused to exercise its discretion to reduce the conviction to a misdemeanor under a state law that permits certain offenses, known as "wobblers," to be classified as either misdemeanors or felonies. The court also refused to exercise its discretion to not count his nonviolent burglary as a relevant conviction. On appeal, Ewing argued that the sentence of 25 years to life was grossly disproportionate to the crime and therefore violated the Eighth Amendment's Cruel and Unusual Punishment Clause. The U.S. Supreme Court rejected this argument and affirmed Ewing's conviction, reasoning that the three strikes law served the state's legitimate crime control interests.

What do you think? Are three strikes laws an appropriate and effective response to violent crimes by predators? Or do you think that these laws are overreactions? Given that adaptation by the courtroom work group seems inevitable, why do legislatures periodically pass such laws?

---

on policing, crime prevention programs for young people, and drug treatment for nonviolent offenders," while they oppose additional funding for prisons (Gottschalk, 2009, p. 456; see also, Cohen, Rust & Steen, 2006). States have been experimenting with different sentencing formulas aimed at rehabilitation, especially for nonviolent offenders (Gottschalk, 2009; King, 2008). But there can be no doubt that the increased severity of criminal penalties over the past 30 years or so still causes the United States to incarcerate more people per capita than any other country in the world.

Increasing the severity of penalties is premised on the notion that these harsher penalties will deter criminals and reduce crime. These ideas are more often justified by philosophical claims than by valid scientific evidence. Indeed, researchers

are skeptical that this type of deterrent effect actually exists.

Law on the Books: Mandatory Minimum Sentences

Mandatory minimum sentencing laws are one method legislatures use to increase the severity of sentencing. These types of laws are typically enacted in response to allegations that lenient judges are allowing many serious offenders—particularly violent ones—to go free. The "proof" of this proposition is often limited to one or two highly publicized cases. Although fewer than half the states have adopted determinate sentencing laws, virtually all states and the federal government have enacted a particular type of determinate sentencing law mandating minimum sentences for certain offenses.

Typically, **mandatory minimum sentencing** laws require that offenders convicted of certain offenses must be sentenced to a prison term of not less than a specified period of years, and nonprison sentences (such as probation) are expressly precluded. In short, a term of imprisonment is mandated regardless of the circumstances of the offense or the background of the individual.

In recent years, the most popular mandatory minimum laws are so-called **three strikes laws**, which supposedly target violent offenders with previous felony convictions (see "Courts, Controversy & Reducing Crime: Are 'Three Strikes and You're Out' Laws Fair?"). Through the years, legislative bodies have also enacted mandatory minimums for crimes that are particularly unpopular at the moment, including convicted felons in possession of a firearm, repeat drunk drivers, and those in possession of certain drugs (such as cocaine) with intent to sell.

In addition, some states enacted so-called **truth in sentencing laws**, which require offenders to serve a substantial portion of their prison term (often 85 percent) before release (Ditton & Wilson, 1999). Truth in sentencing laws were prompted by the 1994 Crime Act, a law that provided federal funds to help states expand their prisons to house violent offenders on their having such a law. But few states actually enacted such laws, and funding was discontinued in 2002 (Turner, Greenwood, Fain, & Chiesa, 2006). As a result of skyrocketing prison costs, some states, most notably Iowa, have decreased the time inmates are required to serve to facilitate earlier release through parole (Public Safety Performance Project, 2007). And other states, like California, are attempting to reduce the number of inmates in state prisons by shifting responsibility to counties for the custody, treatment, and supervision of individuals convicted of specified nonviolent, nonserious, nonsex crimes.

Law in Action: Nullification by Discretion

Mandatory minimum sentencing laws have proved popular because they promise certainty of punishment. "If Every Criminal Knew He Would Be Punished If Caught" is the title of an article by neoconservative James Q. Wilson (1973). But researchers caution that administering the law is seldom that automatic.

Sharp increases in formal penalties tend to be sidestepped by those who apply the law. At a variety of points in the application of legal sanctions—police arrest, prosecutorial discretion, jury conviction, and judicial sentencing—discretion may be exercised to offset the severity of the penalty (McCoy, 1984; Stith, 2008).

A reduction in the number of arrests is one type of discretionary reaction that may occur when the severity of the penalty is increased. This clearly occurred when Connecticut's governor tried to crack down on speeders by imposing a mandatory loss of the driver's license; arrests for speeding decreased after the severe penalties were announced, because the police and other legal officials perceived that the penalty was too severe for the offense (Campbell & Ross, 1968).

An increase in prosecutorial discretion may also compensate for an increase in the harshness of sentencing. Prosecutors often respond to new legislative actions by reducing the number of charges for that category. In 1994, Oregon voters approved Measure 11, which imposed long mandatory prison terms for 16 designated violent and sex-related offenses. This measure had fewer negative system impacts than had been anticipated by many criminal justice administrators, largely because prosecutors exercised the discretion provided to them by the law. As a result, fewer mandatory-eligible cases were prosecuted. At the same time, more nonmandatory-sentence offenses were brought to court (Merritt, Fain & Turner, 2006). Thus, prosecutors may choose to file charges for an offense that does not carry the most severe penalties when they anticipate that judges and juries will be reluctant to convict.

A decrease in the number of convictions may also occur when legislators increase the severity of punishment. The most commonly cited example is capital punishment in late 18th- and early 19th-century England, when most felonies were punishable by death. Judges often strained to avoid convicting defendants by inventing legal technicalities (Hall, 1952). Similarly, in New York State, after a tough drug law was passed, the number of convictions dropped.

KEY DEVELOPMENTS IN NONCAPITAL SENTENCING SINCE THE SENTENCING REFORM ACT OF 1984

***Mistretta v. United States* (1989)**	Federal sentencing guidelines and Sentencing Commission do not violate constitutional separation of powers.
***Mitchell v. United States* (1999)**	A defendant may plead guilty, assert the privilege against self-incrimination at the sentencing hearing, and not have a judge draw an adverse inference from the defendant's sentence.
***Apprendi v. New Jersey* (2000)**	Other than the fact of a prior conviction, any fact that increases the penalty for a crime beyond the prescribed statutory maximum must be submitted to a jury and proved beyond a reasonable doubt.
***United States v. Johnson* (2000)**	A term of supervised release does not begin until an individual is actually released from imprisonment. Therefore, the length of supervised release is not reduced by excess time served in prison.
***Ewing v. California* (2002)**	Three strikes laws do not violate the Eighth Amendment prohibition against cruel and unusual punishment.
***Connecticut v. Doe* (2002)**	Affirmed Connecticut's "Megan's Law" requiring convicted sex offenders to register and have their names published in a registry.
***Blakely v. Washington* (2004)**	Under the Sixth Amendment, juries, not judges, have the power to make a finding of guilty beyond a reasonable doubt for facts used in state sentencing guidelines.
***United States v. Booker* (2005)**	The first part of the opinion struck down federal sentencing guidelines as unconstitutional for the reasons expressed in *Blakely*. The second part of the opinion allows federal judges to continue to use federal sentencing guidelines as advisory.
***Washington v. Recuenco* (2006)**	Failure to submit a sentencing factor to a jury is not "structural" error, which always invalidates a conviction. Rather, *Blakely* violations may be subject to harmless error review.
***Rita v. United States* (2007)**	Sentences that fall within the range established by the Federal Sentencing Guidelines may be presumed to be "reasonable," but appellate courts are not required to consider such sentences reasonable under the facts and circumstances of any particular case.
***Gall v. United States* (2007)**	In reviewing a sentence imposed by a U.S. district judge that is more lenient than the guideline recommendations, the courts of appeal should be deferential and reverse only if the trial judge abused his or her discretion.
***Kimbrough v. United States* (2007)**	U.S. district court judges are not bound by federal sentencing guidelines that require offenses involving crack cocaine to be punished more harshly than offenses involving powder cocaine.
***Greenlaw v. United States* (2008)**	An appeals court is not permitted to order an increase in a defendant's sentence when the government did not appeal the sentence.
***Graham v. Florida* (2009)**	The Cruel and Unusual Punishment Clause of the Eighth Amendment to the U.S. Constitution does not permit a juvenile offender to be sentenced to life in prison without parole for a nonhomicide crime.
***Pepper v. United States* (2011)**	When a defendant's sentence has been set aside on appeal, a district court at resentencing may consider evidence of the defendant's postsentencing rehabilitation and such evidence may, in appropriate cases, support a downward variance from the now-advisory Federal Sentencing Guidelines.
***Tapia v. United States* (2011)**	The Sentencing Reform Act precludes a sentencing court from imposing or lengthening a prison term in order to promote a criminal defendant's rehabilitation.

After conviction, judges are reluctant to apply a severe penalty (Ross & Foley, 1987). When Chicago traffic court judges sought to crack down on drunk drivers by voluntarily agreeing to impose a 7-day jail term, the penalty was rarely applied (Robertson, Rich & Ross, 1973).

Clearly, a relationship exists between punishment policy and the system that administers it. The more severe the penalty, the less likely it will be imposed when its severity exceeds what is viewed as appropriate. In other words, increasing the severity of the punishment does not increase the certainty of punishment; in fact, the threat of punishment may even be reduced by increasingly severe punishments. At this point, however, it should be clear that judicial discretion in sentencing is limited by a number of factors (Chapter 14 summarized key cases affecting capital sentencing. The "Key Developments" feature on page 429 summarizes important cases affecting noncapital sentencing since Congress enacted the Sentencing Reform Act of 1994.) Thus, the discretionary actions of police, prosecutors, and juries may be nullifying harsh penalties as much as, if not more than, discretionary decision making by judges.

Law in Controversy: Negative Side Effects

One reason legislators find raising penalties so attractive is that they appear to be fighting crime without having to increase appropriations. It is a policy apparently without costs; the public will be appeased without the painful necessity of voting for higher taxes. But a number of studies suggest that increasing the severity of the punishment produces negative side effects (referred to by economists as "hidden costs" and by others as "unanticipated consequences")—that is, harsher laws have impacts, but often not the ones intended.

One negative side effect of increasing the severity of punishments centers on the greater time, effort, and money courts must expend. Faced with severe sanctions, defendants demand more trials, which consume more court time. A backlog of cases results, delays increase, and the certainty and speed of conviction decline.

Critics are also concerned that mandatory minimum sentencing legislation results in a rigid and inflexible overreaction to problems of judicial discretion. Requiring every single defendant convicted under the same statute to serve the identical sentence threatens to create a system so automatic that it may operate in practice like a poorly programmed robot. In the words of U.S. District Court Judge Vincent Broderick, "The most frustrating aspect of mandatory minimum prison sentences is that they require routinely imposing long prison terms based on a single circumstance, when other circumstances in the case cry out for a significantly different result. The same sentence is mandated for offenders with very different criminal backgrounds and whose roles differ widely one from another" (Vincent & Hofer, 1994).

CONCLUSION

Whether the "three strikes and you're out" laws passed in the aftermath of the Polly Klaas kidnapping and murder will have a lasting impact is open to question. The essential difficulty is that the criminals who figure prominently in the media bear little resemblance to the ones who appear before U.S. judges every day. Although the replica of Lady Justice outside the courthouse contemplates justice in the abstract, judges inside the courthouse must pass judgment on real-life defendants, not the stereotypical villains who dominate the rhetoric of elected officials. In deciding whether to send an offender to prison or grant him or her probation, the scales of justice require the judge (and other members of the courtroom work group) to weigh the normal penalty for the offense, the seriousness of the crime, and the defendant's prior record and social stability. The resulting decisions have become the focus of heated public debate.

To some, American courthouses do not mete out fair and impartial justice. These critics find that the blindfold is improperly pierced by sentences that are discriminatory, disparate, or both. To others, American courthouses hand out sentences that are too lenient. These critics argue that wielding the sword of justice will protect the public from crime.

These dual concerns have prompted numerous changes since the mid-1970s. Determinate sentencing laws, mandatory minimum sentencing provisions, and sentencing guidelines are the most prominent changes undertaken. Sentencing is likely to remain on the nation's political agenda.

All too often, members of the public, as well as elected officials, have ignored an important reality: Prison populations are swelling. The United States sends more people to prison than any other Western nation, and the rate of incarceration is growing steadily. The result is severe prison overcrowding, compounded by federal court orders requiring major improvements in prison conditions. Limitations on the capacity and quality of prisons create a political dilemma. Although citizens and public officials want to send even more offenders to prison for longer periods of time, they are unwilling to spend large sums of tax dollars to build the needed facilities. Sentencing is thus likely to remain an important public policy issue for the foreseeable future. Alas, in the end, Lady Justice appears to cost more than the public is able or willing to spend.

Chapter Review

LO1 **1.** Define the concept of normal crimes and indicate the two most important factors in determining normal penalties.

The concept of normal crimes refers to the group norms about the typical manner in which crimes are committed and the typical characteristics of defendants who commit those crimes. The seriousness of the offense and the prior record of the defendant are the most important factors in determining normal penalties.

LO2 **2.** Distinguish between the concepts of sentencing disparities and discrimination.

The concepts of disparity and discrimination highlight unwarranted variations in sentencing but point to different types of factors. *Disparities* refer to inconsistencies resulting from the decision-making process. By contrast, *discrimination* refers to illegitimate influences on the sentencing process related to the characteristics of the defendant being sentenced.

LO3 **3.** Explain how scholars approach the issue of racial discrimination differently than the general public and the implications these differing approaches have for the conclusions reached.

Evidence of racial imbalance in prison populations is not evidence of racial discrimination in the sentencing process. When studies analyze sentences in terms of the severity of the crime and the defendant's prior record, they generally conclude that sentencing is not characterized by a widespread pattern of discrimination.

LO4 **4.** Indicate why the offender–victim dyad is important in studies of racial discrimination in capital punishment.

The offender–victim dyad refers to the race of the defendant and the race of the victim. Studies have consistently found that the race of the defendant alone plays little, if any, role in the decision to apply the death penalty; however, members of racial and ethnic minorities who are convicted of murdering Whites are most likely to receive a sentence of death.

LO5 **5.** List the two major factors related to disparities and sentencing.

The two major factors involved in sentencing disparities are the geography of justice and judges' backgrounds and attitudes.

LO6 **6.** Recognize the main objective of changes in sentencing structure beginning in the late 1960s and the major consequences of these changes.

The main objective of changes in sentencing structure beginning in the late 1960s was a reduction in judicial discretion in sentencing. The major consequence of these changes has been a major increase in the number of persons in prison in the United States.

LO7 **7.** Outline how the U.S. Supreme Court has limited state sentencing guidelines.

Beginning in 2000, the U.S. Supreme Court has raised serious constitutional doubts about the constitutionality of state sentencing guidelines. In particular the Court has held that juries and not judges have the authority to decide on important facts (other than prior record) that determine sentencing.

LO8 **8.** Identify the most recent changes in how the U.S. Supreme Court has responded to federal sentencing guidelines.

In *United States v. Booker* (2005), the Supreme Court held that the federal sentencing guidelines are unconstitutional but judges may use them as advisory information. In later cases, the Court held that judges may indeed sentence defendants more leniently than the guidelines prescribe, particularly in crack-cocaine cases.

LO9 **9.** Explain the law in action perspective on researching the impact of mandatory minimum sentences.

A law on the books approach to mandatory minimum sentences stresses certainty of punishment, whereas a law in action approach stresses nullification by discretion. Researchers find that at a number of stages in the process, including police arrest, prosecutorial charging, trial convictions, and judicial sentencing, discretionary changes occur in the process that nullify the impact of these laws.

Critical Thinking Questions

1. Within the courtroom work group, which actor is the most influential in sentencing decisions? Why? How might influence vary from one courtroom to the next?

2. In what ways do the crime control model and the due process model differ over the issues of disparity and discrimination in sentencing?

3. In what ways do sentencing guidelines reflect normal penalties? In what ways do they differ?

4. To what extent can slight variations in the defendant's background produce markedly different sentences? In Figure 15.2, calculate the recommended sentence for a defendant convicted of second-degree assault. How much does the sentence change if the criminal history score is a 2 or a 3? Do you think this is too much variation to be determined by a mathematical calculation?

5. How have public demands to "get tough with crooks" changed the sentencing process in the past two decades? Why do courtroom work groups resist such efforts and often subvert them?

Key Terms

aggravating circumstances   409

mitigating factors   409

determinate sentencing   419

discrimination   410

disparity   410

mandatory minimum sentencing   428

normal penalties   408

presentence investigation (PSI)   403

presumptive sentences   419

sentencing guidelines   421

structured sentencing   419

three strikes laws   428

truth in sentencing laws   428

Web Resources

Go to the *America's Courts and the Criminal Justice System* companion website at
http://www.cengage.com/criminaljustice/neubauer,
where you will find more resources to help you study.
Resources include web exercises, quizzing, and flash cards.

For Further Reading

Alozie, Nicholas, and C. Wayne Johnson."Probing the Limits of the Female Advantage in Criminal Processing: Pretrial Diversion of Drug Offenders in an Urban County."*Justice System Journal* 21: 239–259, 2000.

Austin, James, and John Irwin. *It's about Time: America's Imprisonment Binge*. 3rd ed. Belmont, CA: Wadsworth, 2001.

Bosworth, Mary, and Jeanne Flavin (Eds.). *Race, Gender, and Punishment: From Colonialism to the War on Terror*. Piscataway, NJ: Rutgers University Press, 2007.

Cole, David."Turning the Corner on Mass Incarceration?" *Ohio State Journal of Criminal Law*, 9(1), 27–51, 2011.

Cole, David. *No Equal Justice*. New York: New Press, 1999.

Engen, Rodney, Randy Gainey, R. Crutchfield, and J. Weiss. "Discretion and Disparity under Guidelines: The Role of Departures and Structured Sentencing Alternatives." *Criminology* 41: 99–130, 2003.

Ewald, Alec, and Marnie Smith."Collateral Consequences of Criminal Convictions in American Courts: The View from the State Bench."*Justice System Journal* 29: 145–164, 2008.

Finn, Peter, and Sarah Kuck. *Stress among Probation and Parole Officers and What Can Be Done about It*. Washington, DC: National Institute of Justice, 2005.

Foglia, Wanda."They Know Not What They Do: Unguided and Misguided Discretion in Pennsylvania Capital Cases."*Justice Quarterly* 20: 103–107, 2003.

Gabbidon, Shaun, and Helen Green. *Race and Crime*. Thousand Oaks, CA: Sage, 2009.

Grana, Sheryl. *Women and (In)Justice*. Boston: Allyn and Bacon, 2002.

Hartley, Richard, Sean Maddan, and Cassia Spohn. "Prosecutorial Discretion: An Examination of Substantial Assistance Departure in Federal Crack-Cocaine and Powder-Cocaine Cases."*Justice Quarterly* 24: 381–406, 2007.

Johnson, Robert. *Hard Time: Understanding and Reforming Prison*. 3rd ed. Belmont, CA: Wadsworth, 2002.

Keen, Bradley, and David Jacobs."Racial Threat, Partisan Politics, and Racial Disparities in Prison Admissions Panel Analysis."*Criminology* 47: 209–238, 2009.

Kramer, John, and Jeffrey Ulmer. *Sentencing Guidelines: Lessons from Pennsylvania*. Boulder, CO: Lynne Rienner, 2009.

Lynch, Michael, E. Brit Patterson, and Kristina Childs (Eds.). *Racial Divide: Racial and Ethnic Bias in the Criminal Justice System*. Monsey, NY: Criminal Justice Press, 2008.

Mann, Coramae Richey, and Marjorie Zatz. *Images of Color, Images of Crime*. Los Angeles: Roxbury, 1998.

Marquart, James, Sheldon Edland-Olson, and Jonathan Sorensen. *The Rope, the Chair, and the Needle: Capital Punishment in Texas*, 1923–1990. Austin: University of Texas Press, 1994.

Mauer, Marc."Sentencing Reform Amid Mass Incarcerations—Guarded Optimism."*Criminal Justice*, 26(1), 27–36, 2011.

Myers, Martha. Race, *Labor and Punishment in the New South*. Columbus: Ohio State University Press, 1998.

Pager, Devah. *Marked: Race, Crime, and Finding Work in an Era of Mass Incarceration*. Chicago: University of Chicago Press, 2007.

Pollock, Jocelyn. *Women, Prison, and Crime*. 2nd ed. Belmont, CA: Wadsworth, 2002.

Sharp, Susan, Meghan McGhee, Trina Hope and Randall Coyne."Predictors of Support of Legislation Banning Juvenile Executions in Oklahoma: An Examination by Race and Sex."*Justice Quarterly* 24: 133–155, 2007.

Tarver, Marsha, Steve Walker, and Harvey Wallace. *Multicultural Issues in the Criminal Justice System*. Boston: Allyn and Bacon, 2002.

Tonry, Michael."Crime and Human Rights—How Political Paranoia, Protestant Fundamentalism, and Constitutional Obsolescence Combined to Devastate Black America."*Criminology* 46: 1–34, 2008.

Vandiver, Margaret. *Lethal Punishment: Lynchings and Legal Executions in the South*. New Brunswick, NJ: Rutgers University Press, 2006.

16 Appellate and *Habeas Corpus* Review

© Handout/MCT/Newscom.

The U.S. Supreme Court at the start of its 2011–2012 session. Front row (from left to right): Clarence Thomas, Antonin Scalia, John Roberts, Anthony Kennedy, and Ruth Bader Ginsburg. Back row: Sonia Sotomayor, Stephen Breyer, Samuel Alito, Jr., and Elena Kagan. ■

Chapter Outline

NATURE OF THE APPELLATE PROCESS
The Purposes of Appeal
Limitations on the Right to Appellate Review
Appellate Standards of Review

APPELLATE COURT PROCEDURES
Notice of Appeal
Appellate Court Record
Appellate Briefs
Oral Argument
Written Opinion
Disposition
Reversible vs. Harmless Error
Rising Caseloads and Expedited Appeals

CRIMINAL APPEALS
Law on the Books: Expanded Opportunity to Appeal Criminal Convictions
Law in Action: Defendants Rarely Win on Appeal

Courts, Law, & Media
The Amanda Knox Case

POSTCONVICTION REVIEW

CASE CLOSE-UP: *House v. Bell* and Federal Court Scrutiny of State Death Row Inmates

How Postconviction Remedies Differ from Appeals

Courts, Controversy, & the Administration of Justice
Should Federal Courthouse Doors Be Closed to State Prisoners?

Judicial Expansion and Contraction of *Habeas* Access for State Prisoners
Congress Greatly Restricts *Habeas* Access
Habeas Corpus Relief for Federal Prisoners

WRONGFUL CONVICTIONS
How Many Wrongful Convictions Are There?
Why Do Wrongful Convictions Occur?
Reducing Wrongful Convictions

STATE COURTS OF LAST RESORT
Law on the Books: State High Courts and Discretionary Dockets
Law in Action: State High Courts as Policy Makers
Law in Controversy: State High Courts and Death Penalty Cases

THE U.S. SUPREME COURT AND CRIMINAL JUSTICE POLICY
The Warren Court (1953–1969)
The Burger Court (1969–1986)
The Rehnquist Court (1986–2005)
The Roberts Court (2005–)

THE SUPREME COURT IN BROAD PERSPECTIVE

Appellate and Habeas Corpus Review • Appellate and Ha
view • Appellate and Habeas Corpus Review • Appell

Learning Objectives

After reading this chapter, you should be able to:

LO1 Explain how appeals and appellate processes differ from trials and trial processes.

LO2 Describe the two primary functions of appeals.

LO3 Explain how Double Jeopardy limits appeals by the prosecution in criminal cases.

LO4 Define the contemporaneous objection rule and explain its impact on appeals.

LO5 Differentiate between mandatory and discretionary appellate jurisdiction.

LO6 Identify the different appellate standards of review and evaluate their impact on the criminal appeals.

LO7 Describe the six customary phases in the appeals process.

LO8 Compare and contrast plain error, reversible error, and harmless error.

LO9 Analyze the reasons why most criminal appeals result in convictions being affirmed.

LO10 Compare and contrast appeals and postconviction review processes.

LO11 Identify the leading causes of wrongful convictions.

LO12 Analyze how state courts of last resort and the U.S. Supreme Court exercise their discretion to set justice policy.

For 20 years, Paul House sat on death row proclaiming his innocence. A Tennessee jury had found him guilty for murder and sentenced him to death on the basis of forensic evidence—primarily bloodstains and semen. His case had already been reviewed by numerous courts, but along the way, he and his lawyers had failed to raise key points in their earlier court papers. But then new evidence, some of it based on DNA testing, cast doubt on the jury's verdict.

Should House be entitled to yet another hearing in federal court? Proponents of the crime control model argue that *House* is a textbook example of endless appeals, and therefore he should not be allowed yet one more review. Supporters of the due process model, on the other hand, counter that basic fairness is far more important than failure to comply with a narrow technical requirement.

House v. Bell (2006) highlights the importance of appellate court decisions. To be sure, appellate courts decide far fewer cases than the trial courts. Nonetheless, the relatively small numbers of cases decided by the appellate courts are critically important for the entire judicial process. Appellate courts subject the trial court's action to a second look, examining not a raw dispute in the course of being presented, but rather a controversy already decided. This second look provides a degree of detachment, by a group of judges who can examine the process to see whether mistakes were made. Appellate courts are important for a second reason: Through written opinions, appellate judges engage in significant policy making.

Ultimately, the decisions of a group of judges not only determine the results of specific cases (the fate of individual defendants like Paul House) but also, and more important, they shape the law by providing the reasons for the decisions reached. *House v. Bell* also symbolizes how a relative handful of death penalty decisions receives a disproportionate share of appellate court time and attention.

NATURE OF THE APPELLATE PROCESS

One of the few aspects of the American judicial process about which consensus exists is that every loser in a trial court should have the right to appeal to a higher court. Yet, the appeals process is widely misunderstood. In the United States, an appeal is not a retrial of the case, nor is it ordinarily a reexamination of factual issues decided by a trial court. U.S. appellate courts hear no new testimony and consider no new evidence. Rather, they focus on how decisions were made in the trial court, basing their review on the appellate court record. Thus, an appellate court's function is primarily to review the questions of law presented in a case.

Appellate courts were created in part because of the belief that several heads are better than one when examining such legal questions. In essence, the decisions of a single judge on matters of the law are subjected to review by a panel of judges who are removed from the heat engendered by the trial and are consequently in a position to take a more objective view of the legal questions raised. They operate as multimember or collegial bodies, with decisions made by a group of judges. In the courts

of last resort, all judges typically participate in all cases. On intermediate appellate courts, decisions are typically made using rotating three-judge panels, but in important cases, all judges may participate (this is termed an *en banc* hearing).

In unraveling the complexities of the review process, it is helpful to begin by asking why appellate courts exist and why dissatisfied litigants are permitted to appeal.

The Purposes of Appeal

The most obvious function of appellate courts is **error correction**. During trial, a significant portion of the decision making is "spur of the moment." As one trial judge phrased it, "We're where the action is. We often have to 'shoot from the hip' and hope you're doing the right thing. You can't ruminate forever every time you have to make a ruling. We'd be spending months on each case if we ever did that" (quoted in Carp & Stidham, 1990, p. 256). Fortunately, judges' quickly made decisions are often surprisingly accurate, although sometimes, mistakes do occur (Guthrie, Rachlinski, & Wistrich, 2007). As reviewing bodies, appellate courts oversee the work of the lower courts, ensuring that the law was correctly interpreted. Thus, the error-correction function of appellate review protects against arbitrary, capricious, or mistaken legal decisions by a trial court judge.

The other primary function of appellate courts is **policy formulation**. The lawmaking function focuses on situations in which appellate courts fill in the gaps in existing law, clarify old doctrines, extend existing precedent to new situations, and on occasion even overrule previous decisions. Thus, through policy formulation, appellate courts shape the law in response to changing conditions in society. Stated another way, error correction is concerned primarily with the effect of the judicial process on individual litigants, whereas policy formulation involves the impact of the appellate court decision on other cases (see Cooper & Berman, 2000).

Limitations on the Right to Appellate Review

A basic principle of U.S. law is that the losing party has the **right to one appeal**. So long as the person seeking to appeal the decision of a lower court follows the rules for perfecting an appeal (such as filing a timely notice of appeal and meeting all appellate court deadlines), that initial appeal is guaranteed as a right. However, once a criminal defendant has been convicted at trial, the legal shield of innocence is gone. The individual is no longer considered innocent until proven guilty but rather now stands guilty in the eyes of the law. This has important implications for bail. Guilty defendants no longer have a right to bail; courts may set a bail amount (typically in higher amounts than prior to trial), but many defendants wait out their appeal in prison.

Although U.S. law recognizes the right to one appeal, the right to appellate review is subject to several important limits and exceptions. Appeals, for example, may be filed only by parties who have lost in the lower court. In *Kepner v. United States* (1904), the U.S. Supreme Court held that the prosecution is not permitted to appeal an acquittal. This is because the Fifth Amendment guarantees, "Nor shall any person be subject for the same offense to be twice put in jeopardy of life or limb." This provision protects citizens from **double jeopardy** (a second prosecution of the same person for the same crime by the same sovereign after the first trial). Thus, once a not-guilty verdict is returned, a prosecutor cannot appeal the acquittal, even if the original trial was littered with serious mistakes (*Sanabria v. United States*, 1978). Prosecutors may, however, appeal questions of law that would not result in a defendant being put in jeopardy again. For example, if a judge made a serious error in an evidentiary ruling, the prosecution could appeal so that there would be appellate precedent on the books; therefore, trial court judges would know not to make a similar mistake again in the future. Alternatively, if a defendant was never really in jeopardy because a trial was conducted fraudulently (for example, if the defendant bribed the judge or a juror), then double jeopardy will not prohibit a prosecutor from appeals for a new trial (*Aleman v. Judges of the Criminal Division, Circuit Court of Cook County, IL*, 1998).

Appeals are also discretionary; that is, the losing party is not required to seek appellate court review. The lone exception involves capital punishment cases; when a jury imposes a sentence of death, the case must be appealed regardless of the defendant's wishes. Typically, this automatic review is heard directly by a state court of last resort, thereby bypassing any intermediate courts of appeals a state may have. The mandatory appeal requirements in capital

punishment cases aside, in all other cases, civil and criminal, appeals are discretionary.

When cases may be appealed is limited. As a general rule, the losing party may appeal only from a final judgment of the lower court. In this context, a judgment is considered final when a final decision has been reached in the lower court. In very limited situations, however, litigants may appeal certain types of **interlocutory** (nonfinal) orders. Prosecutors may file an interlocutory appeal on certain pretrial rulings that substantially hinder the state's ability to proceed to trial. For example, if the trial court suppresses a defendant's confession or excludes physical evidence because of an illegal search and seizure, the prosecution may file an interlocutory appeal arguing that the judge's ruling was in error.

Appeals are also confined to issues properly raised in the trial court. Recall from Chapter 13 that during trial, attorneys must make timely objections to the judge's rulings on points of law, or the objection will be deemed waived. This is called the **contemporaneous objection rule**. Thus, an attorney making an objection and the trial judge overruling it constitutes a disagreement over a point of law, properly preserving the issue for appeal.

Appeals in criminal cases have also historically been limited in the United States to legal rulings that led to a conviction. That is, a defendant was not able to appeal the sentence imposed as being too harsh, nor could the prosecutor appeal a sentence as being too lenient. This restriction, however, has changed slowly over time. Several states now allow defendants to appeal the sentence imposed by the trial judge. Defendants are also permitted to appeal illegally imposed sentences, such as sentences that fall outside a statutorily authorized sentencing range. And, under a string of U.S. Supreme Court rulings discussed in Chapter 15 (e.g., *Apprendi v. New Jersey*, 2000; *Blakely v. Washington*, 2004; *Cunningham v. California*, 2007), defendants may appeal sentences if penalty enhancements (other than those based on prior convictions) were applied by a judge without the facts underlying such aggravating factors having been proved to a jury beyond a reasonable doubt.

Finally, the right to appeal is limited to a single appeal, within which all appealable issues have to be raised. Appeals from U.S. district courts and most appeals from state courts of general jurisdiction are heard by intermediate courts of appeals. In the less-populous states, which do not have intermediate appellate bodies, the initial appeal is filed with the court of last resort (see Chapter 4). These courts have **mandatory appellate jurisdiction,** which means they must hear all properly filed appeals. But after the first reviewing body has reached a decision, the right to one appeal has been exhausted. The party that loses the appeal may request that a higher court review the case again, but such appeals are discretionary; the higher court does not have to hear the appeal. The U.S. Supreme Court and most state high courts of last resort have largely **discretionary appellate jurisdiction,**

which means that they can pick and choose which cases they will hear. The overwhelming number of appeals is decided by intermediate courts of appeals; only a small fraction of appeals is heard by state courts of last resort and even fewer will be decided by the U.S. Supreme Court. Table 16.1 shows the appellate court structure of the states.

Appellate Standards of Review

Appeals courts approach appellate decision making in different ways, depending on the types of

TABLE 16.1 ▪ STATE APPELLATE COURT STRUCTURE

Court of Last Resort Only	Court of Last Resort and One Intermediate Appellate Court		One Court of Last Resort and Two Intermediate Appellate Courts	Two Courts of Last Resort and One Intermediate Appellate Court
Delaware	Alaska	Michigan	Alabama (one civil and one criminal)	Oklahoma^a (one civil and one criminal)
District of Columbia	Arizona	Minnesota	Indiana (one for tax cases and one for all other appeals)	Texas (one civil and one criminal)
Maine	Arkansas	Mississippi	New York^b	
Montana	California	Missouri	Pennsylvania	
Nevada	Colorado	Nebraska	Tennessee (one civil and one criminal)	
New Hampshire	Connecticut	New Jersey		
North Dakota	Florida	New Mexico		
Rhode Island	Georgia	North Carolina		
South Dakota	Hawaii^a	North Dakota^a		
Vermont	Idaho^a	Ohio		
West Virginia	Illinois	Oregon		
Wyoming	Iowa^a	Puerto Rico		
	Kansas	South Carolina^a		
	Kentucky	Utah		
	Louisiana	Virginia		
	Maryland	Washington		
	Massachusetts	Wisconsin		

^{a}Court of last resort assigns cases to intermediate appellate court.

^{b}New York has established two intermediate appellate courts only in certain parts of the state.

SOURCE: David Rottman and Shauna M. Strickland. *State Court Organization 2004.* Williamsburg, VA: National Center for State Courts, 2006.

questions presented for review on appeal. Sometimes appellate courts are very deferential to what happened in lower courts, while other times they give no deference at all. How much deference (or conversely, scrutiny) an appellate court will afford to the decisions of a judge, jury, or administrative agency in an appeal is referred to as the **standard of review**. The most frequently used standards of review in criminal cases are presented in Table 16.2.

Given these standards of review, criminal appeals rarely involve questions of fact decided by a judge or jury. Because they have not been directly exposed to the evidence, appellate courts are reluctant to second-guess findings of fact made in lower courts.

Factual findings, whether by the trial court judge or the jury, are rarely a basis for reversal. . . . Absent certain types of error, it is improper for the reviewing court to substitute its judgment for that of the jury; having guilt or innocence decided by the community is a central tenet of the American legal system. The rationale for the principle that it is the exclusive province of the fact-finder to determine credibility is that the fact-finder had the opportunity to see the witness(es) testify at trial, and is therefore in a much better position to determine credibility issues. Equally cogent is the idea of judicial economy—that the already overburdened judicial system simply cannot afford to retry every case on appeal. (TerBeek, 2007, p. 36)

TABLE 16.2 ■ STANDARD OF APPELLATE REVIEW IN CRIMINAL CASES (FROM LEAST DEFERENTIAL TO MOST DEFERENTIAL)

Type of Question Presented	Standard of Review	Level of Deference	Test	Example
Questions of law	*De novo* (anew)	None	Plenary review of a legal issue for a second time with no deference to prior decision	Whether a judge erred in interpreting a statute Whether hearsay evidence was properly admitted or excluded
Mixed questions of law and fact	Mixture of *de novo* and clear error	Moderate	Underlying factual findings are given substantial deference (reviewed for clear error), but the legal consequences of those facts are reviewed *de novo*.	Whether a suspect was subjected to "custodial interrogation" Whether a defendant knowingly, intelligently, and voluntarily waived a constitutional right
Questions of fact decided by a judge	Clear error	High	Trial court's factual findings are to be upheld unless they are so clearly erroneous that they have no support in the record.	Whether a criminal defendant is competent to stand trial Whether a criminal defendant is guilty beyond a reasonable doubt (in a bench trial)
Questions of fact decided by a jury	Reasonableness/ substantial evidence	High	Jury's decision is upheld if it is reasonable in light of the evidence in the record; support for the jury's conclusion is adequate.	Whether a criminal defendant is guilty beyond a reasonable doubt Whether a defendant has proven his/her insanity by clear and convincing evidence
Discretionary decisions by a judge	Abuse of discretion	Very high	Trial court's decision will be upheld unless arbitrary, capricious, or manifestly unfair in light of any reasonable justification under the circumstances.	Whether a judge abused his/her discretion when denying a continuance, limiting the scope of cross-examination, or refusing to dismiss a juror for cause

In contrast to the highly deferential appellate review of factual issues, questions of law are reviewed without deference on appeal. Questions of law (or mixed questions of fact and law) that are commonly raised on appeal include defects in jury selection, improper admission of evidence during the trial, and mistaken interpretations of the law. The appellant may also claim constitutional violations, including illegal search and seizure or improper questioning of the defendant by the police (see Chapter 11). Finally, some defendants who have pled guilty may seek to set aside the guilty plea because of ineffective assistance of counsel or because the plea was not voluntary.

APPELLATE COURT PROCEDURES

Appellate court procedures reflect numerous variations among the nation's 51 legal systems. Nonetheless, each judicial system uses essentially the same six steps to start an appeal from a trial court judgment. The "Law on the Books vs. Law in Action" feature summarizes the appeals process.

Notice of Appeal

An appeal does not follow automatically from an adverse trial court judgment. Rather, the **appellant** (the losing party in the lower court) must take

LAW IN ACTION VS. LAW ON THE BOOKS
STEPS IN THE APPELLATE PROCESS

	LAW ON THE BOOKS	LAW IN ACTION
Appeal	Legal challenge to a decision by a lower court.	Virtually certain if the defendant is convicted at trial.
Mandatory	Appellate court must hear the case.	Many appeals are "routine," which means they have little likelihood of succeeding.
Discretionary	Appellate court may accept or reject.	Appellate courts hear a very small percentage of discretionary appeal cases.
Notice of appeal	Written statement notifying the court that the defendant plans to appeal.	Standards for indigent defenders mandate that an appeal must be filed.
Appellate court record	The transcript of the trial along with relevant court documents.	Some appellate courts prefer a focused record of contested matters, whereas others want the entire record.
Appellate brief	Written statement submitted by the attorney arguing a case in court.	Defense lawyers make numerous arguments in hopes that one will be successful.
Oral argument	Lawyers for both sides argue their cases before appellate court justices, who have the opportunity to question lawyers.	Judges often complain that they learn little during oral argument. To expedite decision making, some courts limit oral argument to select cases.
Written opinion	Reasons given by appellate courts for the results they have reached.	Only appellate court opinions are considered precedent.
Disposition		
Affirmed	Appellate court decision that agrees with the lower court decision.	Seven out of eight criminal appeals are affirmed.
Remanded	Case is sent back to the lower court for a hearing on a specific issue.	Often an indication that the appellate court is troubled by the judge's action but does not wish to reverse.
Reversed	The lower court decision is set aside, and further proceedings may be held.	Defendants are very often remanded and reconvicted following retrial.

© Cengage Learning

Notice of Appeal to a Court of Appeals from a Judgment or Order of a District Court

File Number _____

United States of America, Plaintiff |
   v. | Notice of Appeal
[Name], Defendant |
_____ |

Notice is hereby given that [insert name], the Defendant in the above named case, hereby appeals to the United States Court of Appeals for the Second Circuit from the final judgment entered in this action on the _____ day of _____, 20__.

_____
Attorney for Defendant
Address:_____

Figure 16.1 ■ Sample Notice of Appeal

affirmative action to set an appeal in motion. The first step consists of filing a **notice of appeal** with the trial court. As illustrated by Figure 16.1, a notice of appeal is short and simple. However, to trigger one's right to an appeal, the appellant must file a notice of appeal in a timely manner. The rules of appellate procedure in a particular jurisdiction fix the precise period—usually 10, 30, or 60 days.

Keep in mind that the filing of a notice of appeal initiates the appellate process for the first appeal—the appeal that is guaranteed as a right. In contrast, the party that loses a first appeal generally does not have a right to any subsequent appeals. Rather, the loser of a first appeal must usually seek permission to initiate any subsequent discretionary appeals. To do so, they do not file another notice of appeal. Rather, as described in Chapter 3, they file a petition for a **writ of** *certiorari*. From that point forward, the party seeking another appeal is usually known as the **petitioner,** since they are filing a petition seeking another round of appellate review.

Appellate Court Record

After the notice of appeal has been filed, the next step is preparing and transmitting the record. The **appellate court record** consists of the materials that advance to the appellate court. Many of

these items—papers and exhibits—are already in the case file. A major item not in the clerk's office is the transcript of the testimony given at the trial. To include this in the record, the court reporter prepares a typewritten copy and files it with the court.

Appellate Briefs

The third step in the appeal process consists of writing briefs. An **appellate brief** is a written argument that sets forth the party's view of the facts of the case, the issues raised on appeal, and the precedents supporting their position. Many commentators have noted that the term *brief* is an oxymoron in this context because appellate briefs are usually not "brief" at all; they are usually quite long.

The length of an appellate brief notwithstanding, first, the appellant files an *opening brief*, which lists alleged errors on questions of law that were made at trial. Next, the winning party in the lower court (termed the **appellee** during the initial appeal and the **respondent** in any subsequent, discretionary appeals, since they are responding to a petition for discretionary review) files a *response brief* setting forth arguments as to why the original decision of the lower court was legally correct and should stand. The appellant then has the option of filing a *reply brief*. Briefs are arguably the most important part of the appellate process because roughly three-quarters of all appeals are decided by appeals courts based on the briefs without the benefit of oral argument.

In some cases, various nonparties may seek to influence an appellate court's decision making by seeking leave to file a brief as a "friend of the court," typically referred to in Latin as *amicus curiae*. Such *amicus* briefs are commonly filed by the American Bar Association, the American Medical Association, the American Psychological Association, and similar organizations with specialized knowledge that they feel might help an appellate court make a decision in a case.

Oral Argument

Oral argument provides an opportunity for face-to-face contact between the appellate judges and lawyers. The lawyers for both parties are allotted a limited time to argue their side of the case before the appellate court panel. The appellant's oral argument, for example, briefly discusses the facts on which the cause of action is based, traces the history of the case through the lower courts, and presents legal arguments as to why the decision of the trial court was erroneous. In this phase, judges typically ask lawyers questions about particular issues in the case.

Many judges view oral arguments as not particularly helpful in deciding routine cases (Hellman, 2006; Wasby, 1982). Thus, some courts have eliminated oral arguments altogether in straightforward cases. By ruling solely on the basis of the appellate court record and the briefs, judges can decide cases more quickly. In some states, however, the litigants are entitled to oral arguments before an appeals court either if requested in a timely manner by one of the parties or by rule in certain types of cases (Binford et al., 2007).

Written Opinion

After the case has been argued, the court recesses to engage in group deliberations. Decisions are made in private conference, with one judge in the majority assigned the task of writing the opinion, which summarizes the facts of the case and discusses the legal issues raised on appeal. If the case is an easy one, the **opinion** of the court may be short, perhaps no more than a page or two. But if the legal issues are important or complex, the court's opinion may run dozens of pages. The decisions of appellate courts are compiled and published in books of reported court decisions, which can be found in law libraries.

Attorneys and judges use these reported decisions as authorities for arguing and deciding future cases that raise issues similar to those already decided.

Some decisions are *per curium* **opinions**, those written "by the court" without attribution to a specific judicial author. But most of the time, judges sign their opinions. Judges who disagree with the majority often write **dissenting opinions**, explaining why they believe their fellow judges reached the wrong conclusions. In some cases, judges who agree with the case outcome on appeal might elect to write a **concurring opinion**. Judges who write concurring opinions may do so to emphasize particular points, or they may express disagreement with a portion of the rationale expressed in the majority decision. In courts of last resort, where multiple appellate judges review a case, sometimes so many judges write concurring opinions that a true majority cannot be reached. For example, assume that six justices on the U.S. Supreme Court believe that a defendant petitioning to have his conviction reversed should win. Of those six votes, three justices sign a concurring opinion expressing their reasoning, and three others sign a separate concurring opinion expressing different reasons why they think the conviction should be overturned (leaving three justices in the dissent). In such cases with no majority decision, the decision is called a **plurality opinion**. Although a plurality decision may resolve a particular case, it generally has limited or no precedential value. In other words, the rationale expressed in a plurality decision has no *stare decisis* effect.

Opinion preparation consumes more of appellate judges' time than any other activity, and for this reason the opinion-writing process is a prime candidate for increasing the efficiency of appellate courts. Some appellate courts are therefore deciding some cases by summary affirmation, in which the court affirms the decision of the lower court without providing a written opinion and often without granting oral argument (Binford et al., 2007; Neubauer, 1985).

Many courts are reluctant to take the drastic step of not writing opinions, even in selected cases. Therefore, a more common practice is curtailing opinion publication; the litigants are given written reasons for the decision reached, but the opinion is not published. Unpublished opinions are used in error-correction cases when the court is applying existing law (Songer, 1990). They save considerable judicial time because unpublished opinions need not be as polished as published opinions. Because unpublished opinions have limited precedential authority since they merely apply existing law, a number of courts prohibited citation to unpublished cases as precedent for many years. But the Judicial Conference of the United States banned this practice in the federal courts effective January 1, 2007, when it enacted Federal Rule of Appellate Procedure 32.1(a), prohibiting courts from restricting the citation of persuasive precedential authority. While roughly half of the states do not allow citation to unpublished cases, the modern trend is clearly away from such bans and toward the new federal rule that allows citation to all available precedents regardless of whether or not the opinion was formally published (Payne, 2008).

Disposition

The court's opinion ends with a disposition of the case. The appellate court may **affirm** (uphold) the judgment of the lower court. Or the court may *modify* the lower court ruling by changing it in part but not totally reversing it. Alternatively, the previous decision may be **reversed** (set aside) with no further court action required. A disposition of **reversed and remanded** means that the decision of the lower court is overturned and the case is sent back to the lower court for further proceedings, which may include holding a hearing or conducting a new trial. Often the defendant is tried a second time, but not always. Finally, the case may be **remanded** to the lower court with instructions for further proceedings. What the ultimate disposition of a case will be on appeal will turn on whether a majority (or plurality) of the appellate judges hearing the case find a reversible error under the applicable standard of review.

Reversible vs. Harmless Error

Appellate courts modify, reverse, remand, or reverse and remand only if they find **error**—that is, a mistake made during the trial. If the error is substantial, it is called **reversible error** by the higher court. If the error is minor, it is called **harmless error**. This distinction means that an appellate court may find error, but may nonetheless affirm the lower court decision anyway if the mistake was not significant enough to have had a prejudicial effect on the ultimate outcome of the case.

Recall that the contemporaneous objection rule bars an appellate court from considering any claim on appeal to which a timely objection was not made. However, one exception to this rule is for mistakes that constitute **plain error**. Plain errors are defects that seriously affect substantial rights that are so prejudicial to a jury's deliberations "as to undermine the fundamental fairness of the trial and bring about a miscarriage of justice" (*United States v. Polowichak*, 1986, p. 416).

On the other hand, even when an appellant preserves a claim by timely objection and the appellate court finds that the trial court erred, the appellate court may still affirm the conviction if it finds that the error was harmless. This harmless error rule avoids the "setting aside of convictions for small errors or defects that have little, if any, likelihood of having changed the result of the trial" (*Chapman v. California*, 1967). If the error was of constitutional dimensions, the appellate court must determine "beyond a reasonable doubt that the error complained of did not contribute to the verdict obtained" (p. 23). If the error was not of constitutional dimensions, the appellate court must determine with "fair assurance after pondering all that happened without stripping the erroneous action from the whole that the judgment was not substantially swayed by the error" (*Kotteakos v. United States,* 1946, p. 765).

Most types of error are subject to harmless error analysis, including classic trial errors involving the erroneous admission of evidence (*Arizona v. Fulminante*, 1991). Some types of error, however, involve rights so basic to a fair trial that they can never be considered harmless, such as conflicts of interest in representation (*Holloway v. Arkansas*, 1978); denial of the right to an impartial judge (*Chapman v. California*, 1967); racial, ethnic, or sex discrimination in grand jury or petit jury selection (*Vasquez v. Hillery*, 1986; *Batson v. Kentucky*, 1986; *J.E.B. v. Alabama ex rel. T.B.*, 1994); and a failure to inquire whether a defendant's guilty plea is voluntary (*United States v. Gonzalez*, 1987).

Rising Caseloads and Expedited Appeals

In recent years, traditional appellate court procedures have been modified because of exponential increases in appellate court filings. Appellate court caseloads have been increasing more rapidly than those of the trial courts. By way of illustration, appeals filed in the U.S. courts of appeals increased by a whopping 705 percent from 1961 through 1983, and then increased another 131 percent from 1983 through 2005, a year in which a record high of more than 68,400 cases were filed in federal appellate courts. That caseload began to drop slightly in 2006 and 2007; by 2011, nearly 56,000 appeals were filed in federal appellate courts (Administrative Office of the U.S. Courts, 2012).

Appeals in state courts have likewise grown rapidly. Today, the National Center for State Courts (2012) reports that roughly 230,000 appeals are filed in state appellate courts every year. To accommodate this volume of appeals, reviewing bodies now often use expedited processing for some cases, such as shortening the period for submitting briefs, waiving the submission of formal briefs, denying extensions of time, and eliminating oral argument (Binford et al., 2007).

CRIMINAL APPEALS

The bulk of trial court filings are never appealed because the case is settled without a trial—civil cases are negotiated and criminal cases are plea-bargained. As a result, only a small percentage of state trial court cases are reviewed by higher courts. The majority of appeals involve civil cases, but the number of criminal appeals has increased dramatically since the 1960s.

Law on the Books: Expanded Opportunity to Appeal Criminal Convictions

For decades, most defendants found guilty by judge or jury did not appeal because they could not afford the expense. This pattern changed significantly in the early 1960s. A series of important Warren Court decisions held that economically impoverished defendants cannot be barred from effective appellate review. Indigent defendants, therefore, are entitled to a free trial court transcript (*Griffin v. Illinois*, 1956) and a court-appointed lawyer (*Douglas v. California*, 1963). Indigents, however, are not normally provided free legal service to pursue discretionary appeals (*Ross v. Moffitt*, 1974).

As a result of these rulings, it is now rare for a convicted defendant not to appeal a trial verdict of guilty. Indeed, indigent defendants have everything to gain and nothing to lose by filing an appeal. For example, if the appeal is successful but the defendant is reconvicted following a new trial, the sentencing judge cannot increase the sentence out of vindictiveness (*North Carolina v. Pearce*, 1969; *Texas v. McCullough*, 1986). However, if a convicted defendant's lawyer fails to file a timely appeal, that does not necessarily violate the Sixth Amendment right to effective assistance of counsel (*Roe v. Flores-Ortega*, 2000).

The decisions expanding the opportunity for indigent defendants to appeal produced an exponential increase in the number of criminal appeals filed. Whereas criminal appeals composed only 10 to 15 percent of total appeals before 1963, they now constitute approximately 35 percent of appeals adjudicated in state high courts of last resort and 50 percent of the appellate volume in state intermediate appellate courts (National Center for State Courts, 2012).

Law in Action: Defendants Rarely Win on Appeal

For many years, criminal appeals were drawn from a fairly narrow stratum of the most serious criminal convictions in the trial courts (Davies, 1982). For example, more than half the criminal appeals contested convictions for crimes of violence (primarily homicides and armed robberies). Moreover, these appeals cases often involved substantial sentences (Chapper & Hanson, 1990). In short, criminal appeals were fairly atypical of crimes prosecuted in the trial courts. However, over the past 30 years or so, penalties for all sorts of crimes have increased, especially for drug offenses, as penal social control has been increasingly used to incapacitate criminal offenders (Tonry, 2004). This has led to a broader range of criminal cases being appealed, as illustrated by Figure 16.2, which shows a recent distribution of the types of criminal cases appealed in the federal system.

Criminal appeals are generally routine because they seldom raise meritorious issues (Primus, 2007; Wold & Caldeira, 1980). Current standards of effective assistance of counsel often force lawyers to appeal, no matter how slight the odds of appellate court reversal. As a result, a significant number of

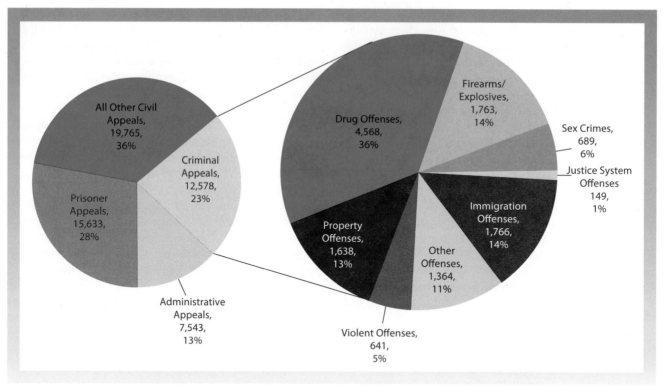

Figure 16.2 ■ Distribution of Types of Criminal Appeals in the Federal Appellate Courts, 2011

SOURCE: Administrative Office of the U.S. Courts. 2012. *Federal Judicial Statistics*, 2011. Washington, DC: Author. Available online at http://www.uscourts.gov/Statistics/FederalJudicialCaseloadStatistics/FederalJudicialCaseloadStatistics2011.aspx

criminal appeals lack substantial merit. According to one intermediate appellate court judge, "If 90 percent of this stuff were in the United States Post Office, it would be classified as junk mail" (Wold, 1978). Although this quote is more than 30 years old, the sentiment expressed appears to be valid today (see Miner, 1999; Stogel, 2002). Consider, for example, that of the roughly 5,125 written dispositions in criminal appeals filed by defendants in the California Court of Appeals in 2010, the court reversed only 226 (4%) convictions (Judicial Council of California, 2011).

Why do criminal appeals rarely succeed? The answer is twofold. First, as illustrated in Table 16.2, the appellate standards of review applicable to most decision making during criminal trials are highly deferential to trial court outcomes (Primus, 2007). Thus, the rules of appeals are designed not to disturb the results of a criminal trial unless a serious, reversible error has occurred. Second, appellate courts often find that no reversible error was committed during

the trial court proceedings. That is due, in large part, to the harmless error doctrine. Accordingly, the vast majority of criminal appeals affirm the conviction.

Roughly speaking, defendants win cases on appeal less than 10 percent of the time. A closer look, though, indicates that an appellate court reversal often produces only minor victories for many criminal defendants. For example, some "reversals" produce a modification but do not otherwise disturb the conviction or even order a new trial (Burke-Robertson, 2008; Neubauer, 1992). Moreover, if the appellate court reverses and remands the case to the lower court for a new trial, many defendants will be convicted a second time. In fact, the few studies that have examined retrials following successful appeals found that roughly half resulted in reconviction (Neubauer, 1991, 1992; Roper & Melone, 1981).

The types of cases in which reversals occur are also interesting. Neubauer (1991) found that defendants convicted of nonviolent offenses and who

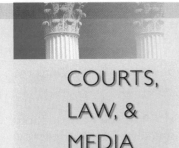

THE AMANDA KNOX CASE

COURTS, LAW, & MEDIA

Amanda Knox, a Seattle native, was a junior at the University of Washington when she decided to study Italian, German, and creative writing at the University for Foreigners in Perugia, Italy, for a year. While there, Amanda lived in a house with two Italian women and Meredith Kercher, a British citizen who was also studying abroad. On November 1, 2007, Kercher was murdered in the house she shared with Amanda and the other two women. Amanda and her Italian boyfriend at the time, Rafaelle Sollecito, were subsequently charged with her murder, and their cases received extensive press coverage here and in Italy.

At trial, Italian prosecutors presented evidence that they argued proved Sollecito's and Knox's guilt. According to CNN (2010), this evidence included:

- a knife found in Sollecito's house that allegedly had the DNA of both Amanda Knox and Meredith Kercher on the blade
- a bra clasp from Kercher's bra that allegedly had Sollecito's DNA on it
- two incriminating statements Knox made during her interrogation
- a bloody footprint in the bathroom prosecutors said was made by Sollecito
- a broken window staged as fake evidence of a break-in as a cover for the murder

Sollecito and Knox asked for an independent examination of the forensic evidence. Their requests were denied and they were convicted. They appealed, arguing that shoddy police work led to contamination of key evidence. In the United States, judges sit on appellate courts and decide appeals based on the trial court record; there is no jury in an appeal and the appellate judges generally do not review new evidence. In Italy, however, the first appeal serves as a second trial in which jurors decide a case.

During the appeal/second trial, Sollecito and Knox were granted the independent examination of the forensic evidence that they had been denied during their initial trial. The defense introduced crime scene video showing "investigators sometimes not wearing gloves or hair coverings, prodding their fingers in Kercher's wounds, leaving key pieces of evidence at the scene for weeks and moving them around, and at one point breaking a window for no reason." Defense forensic experts also demonstrated how the bloody footprint was not likely to have been made by Sollecito since he had a hammer toe which would have left a different type of imprint. And Knox's incriminating statements were also thrown out because she was confused and pressured while being interrogated without a lawyer present.

These arguments proved persuasive to the jury, leading it to reverse the initial convictions of both Sollecito and Knox, but only after both had served more than 4 years in jail between their pretrial detention before their initial trial and the reversal of their conviction.

The Amanda Knox case became the focus of worldwide media coverage. Supporters of Knox criticized Italian newspapers' coverage of the case as constituting character assassination while some in Italy argue that a rich girl got away with murder.

1. Do you think that Amanda Knox was innocent or guilty? Explain your answer.
2. Compare and contrast the Italian system's method of handling criminal appeals with a second trial before a jury with the U.S. system of judges reviewing a trial court record. Which system do you think is better? Why?

received a relatively lenient sentence were the most likely to win on appeal; conversely, defendants convicted of violent offenses and sentenced to lengthy prison terms were the least likely to win on appeal. He concluded that this pattern of winners and losers is far from random. Rather, the appellate court justices strained to find ways to affirm convictions for crimes such as murder and armed robbery when the defendant had a long criminal record. For an interesting exception to these usual patterns that garnered international attention, read the "Courts, Law, & Media" box on the Amanda Knox case.

POSTCONVICTION REVIEW

After the appellate process has been exhausted, state as well as federal prisoners may challenge their convictions in federal courts on certain limited grounds. These postconviction remedies are termed **collateral attacks**, because they are attempts to avoid the effects of a prior court decision by bringing a different (collateral) action in new court proceedings. Although they are filed by prisoners who have been convicted of a criminal offense, they are technically civil matters. Thus, they are usually filed against a prison

warden or the chief administrator of a state's department of corrections. The "Case Close-Up: *House v. Bell* and Federal Court Scrutiny of State Death Row Inmates" illustrates this point. When Paul House appealed, the case title was *House v. State of Tennessee*. But after the right to appeal had been exhausted, he later filed a *habeas* petition in federal court, and the case was captioned *House v. Bell*. The warden, Ricky Bell, is considered a nominal respondent because no actions on his part are at issue. Bell is merely a stand-in; the defendant contends he is being illegally detained because of the actions of the trial judge.

CASE CLOSE-UP

HOUSE v. BELL AND FEDERAL COURT SCRUTINY OF STATE DEATH ROW INMATES

Carolyn Muncey disappeared from her rural Tennessee home on Saturday night, July 13, 1984. The next day, two local residents found her body concealed amid brush and tree branches roughly 100 yards from her house. The police later arrested Paul House, a convicted sex offender who lived in the area. During House's 1985 capital murder trial, several witnesses testified about Mrs. Muncey's disappearance and discovery, but no one could directly link House to the murder. Central to the state's case was what FBI testing showed (or seemed to show). Lab experts testified that the semen found on her nightgown and panties was consistent with House's blood type, and that small bloodstains on House's blue jeans were consistent with Carolyn Muncey's blood type. The jury convicted House and sentenced him to death.

On appeal, the Tennessee Supreme Court concluded the evidence was circumstantial but "quite strong." The U.S. Supreme Court refused to grant *certiorari*, thus ending House's appeals. His lawyers then filed successive writs of *habeas corpus* in both state and federal courts. At a key point in these protracted legal proceedings, House procedurally defaulted, that is, he failed to properly preserve issues for *habeas corpus* review. He now faced a very high legal hurdle—to proceed further, he had to prove actual innocence before a federal court would grant his *habeas corpus* petition seeking a new trial (*Schlup v. Delo*, 1995).

Since House's 1985 conviction, DNA evidence has increasingly been introduced during trial (Chapter 13) and also used to overturn convictions on appeal and/or during postconviction relief (see the discussion in this chapter). No such testing had been done for the original trial because DNA testing did not exist then. But was it relevant in House's case? A majority of the Supreme Court said yes.

Justice Kennedy, the swing vote on the Roberts Court, wrote the opinion of the court stressing that DNA testing showed that the semen found on Mrs. Muncey did not come from the defendant. Similarly, the testimony based on bloodstains was suspect because of poor evidence control by the state crime lab—the samples were not properly preserved and were possibly contaminated during testing. The court's opinion also emphasized that not only did the new evidence tend to undermine the state's claim of guilt, but it also seemed to point to a different suspect—Carolyn Muncey's husband. The court concluded that "this is the rare case where—had the jury heard all the conflicting testimony—it is more likely than not that no reasonable jury viewing the record as a whole would lack reasonable doubt."

Chief Justice Roberts concurred in the judgment in part and dissented in part. He was joined by the other two conservatives, but Justice Alito did not participate because the case was argued before he was confirmed. The dissenters were unconvinced that the newly discovered

Continued on next page

Continued from previous page

DNA evidence was as important as the majority concluded, arguing "the case against House remains substantially unaltered from the case presented to the jury." As a result, Roberts wrote, "I do not find it probable that no reasonable juror would vote to convict him." In short, the threshold for federal review of state court convictions in matters like this should remain high.

In the end, the Court sided with House, but the holding is a narrow one. Future appellants will continue to face a high hurdle in convincing a reviewing court that they are actually innocent and therefore are entitled to federal court relief when they procedurally default in state court. Perhaps what is most important about this case is that for the first time the Supreme Court dealt with postconviction appeals based on DNA testing. For this reason, death penalty opponents view the case as a major victory. Peter Neufeld, co-director of the Innocence Project, concluded that *House* "recognizes that scientific advances have transformed our criminal justice system and must be weighed heavily in determining whether innocent people have been wrongly convicted" (quoted in Mauro, 2006).

How Postconviction Remedies Differ from Appeals

Postconviction remedies differ from appeals in several ways that have important implications for the criminal justice system. First, they may be filed only by those actually in custody. Second, they may raise only constitutional defects, not technical ones. Third, they may be somewhat broader than appeals, which are usually limited to objections made by the defense during the trial absent plain error. Postconviction petitions can bring up issues not raised during trial, as well as assert constitutional protections that have developed since the original trial under certain circumstances. Finally, many state court systems allow unlimited postconviction remedies; thus, a prisoner could file numerous petitions in state court as well as seek postconviction relief in the various levels of the federal court system.

House v. Bell illustrates these factors. House was eligible to file because he was in prison. Second, his postconviction relief petitions raised issues that had not been properly preserved at trial or on direct appeal. Finally, the petition had been filed in two state courts and the U.S. District Court for the Eastern District of Tennessee, had been reviewed by the Sixth Circuit Court of Appeals, and was now being considered by yet another federal court—the U.S. Supreme Court.

The most common type of postconviction relief is *habeas corpus* (Latin for "you have the body"). Protected by the U.S. Constitution, it is a judicial order to someone holding a person to bring that person immediately before the court. Article I provides that "the Privilege of the Writ of Habeas Corpus shall not be suspended unless when in Cases of Rebellion or Invasion the public Safety may require it." This provision traces its roots to 17th-century England, when the king's officers often detained citizens without ever filing charges. The writ of *habeas corpus* has been described as the "great writ," because it prevents the government from jailing citizens without ever filing charges. Many totalitarian regimes have no such protections; even some Western democracies allow the police or prosecutors to detain a person suspected of a crime for up to a year without formally accusing the person of any wrongdoing. Note that a state prisoner who challenges the conditions of confinement or attempts to obtain damages for violations of constitutional rights should seek relief by means of a civil action under 42 U.S.C. § 1983, not by filing a petition for a writ of *habeas corpus*.

Originally, *habeas corpus* was regarded as an extraordinary means to determine the legality of detention prior to trial. But the great writ of liberty has undergone considerable transformation in recent decades. See "Courts, Controversy, & the Administration of Justice: Should Federal Courthouse Doors Be Closed to State Prisoners?"

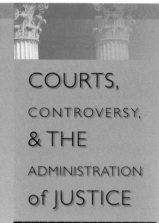

COURTS, CONTROVERSY, & THE ADMINISTRATION of JUSTICE

SHOULD FEDERAL COURTHOUSE DOORS BE CLOSED TO STATE PRISONERS?

The right of convicted offenders to seek review through *habeas corpus* proceedings has sparked a heated debate. Some people would keep the doors of the federal courts wide open to state prisoners; others would slam the doors firmly shut in most cases.

Some proposals to restrict *habeas corpus* relief are based on problems of judicial administration. Postconviction petitions contribute to the heavy caseload of the federal courts, are sometimes frivolous, and undermine the value of a final determination of guilt.

But most restrictive efforts are anticrime proposals. Typical is the letter President Reagan wrote to Congress urging passage of remedial legislation: "As a result of judicial expansion of the habeas corpus remedy, state prisoners are now free to relitigate their convictions and sentences endlessly in the lower federal courts" (quoted in Remington, 1988). Conservatives stress that a criminal trial is a procedure that determines the defendant's guilt or innocence, not a game in which the accused may elude justice for any imperfection (Fein, 1994).

Writs of *habeas corpus* play a particularly important role in capital punishment cases. After exhausting appellate remedies, defendants engage in lengthy challenges to the sentence of death by filing multiple writs of *habeas corpus* in various state and federal courts. Chief Justice William Rehnquist criticized his colleagues for providing capital offenders with "numerous procedural protections unheard of for other crimes" and "for allowing endlessly drawn out legal proceedings" (*Coleman v. Balkcom*, 1981, pp. 958, 960, Rehnquist, J., dissenting).

Others counter that the death penalty is qualitatively different from other types of sanctions, so multiple scrutiny of such cases is more than justified. The argument for keeping the federal courthouse doors open was forcefully stated by Justice John Paul Stevens, who noted that federal *habeas* proceedings reveal deficiencies in 60 to 70 percent of the capital cases (*Murray v. Giarratano*, 1989). Advocates of this policy also argue that not only should there be no rush to judgment, but also that death row inmates should have access to legal assistance, yet often do not. The majority of postconviction cases are *pro se*—the prisoner is appearing on his or her own behalf. Recall from Chapter 7 that the Court has held that defendants have no right to counsel after the first appeal has been exhausted. Many death row defendants must rely on overworked volunteer attorneys (Applebome, 1992).

The Antiterrorism and Effective Death Penalty Act of 1996 restricted both the time periods during which prisoners' must file *habeas corpus* petitions and the number of petitions they may file. As Table 3.2 illustrates, 20,000 such petitions were filed in 2011, comprising approximately 7 percent of the federal courts' civil docket. This marks a dramatic decrease in *habeas* access at roughly the same time as national attention began to focus on innocents on death row. Thus, some now question whether the law went too far in denying federal court access to inmates—particularly death row inmates—who may be innocent.

Justices of the U.S. Supreme Court have expressed increasing concern that the lower federal courts have become too cursory in reviewing death penalty appeals (Greenhouse, 2004). Writing for the majority, Justice Kennedy said that while Congress has instructed the federal courts to accord greater deference to state-court decisions, "deference does not imply abandonment or abdication of judicial review" (*Miller-El v. Cockrell*, 2003, p. 340). In particular, the Court has often been critical of the Fifth Circuit Court of Appeals for being too willing to uphold death penalty cases. Overall, the court has shown a willingness in recent years to reverse death penalty cases on the basis of ineffective assistance of counsel (Chapter 7), failure of prosecutors to disclose exculpatory evidence to the defense Chapter 11), bias in jury selection (Chapter 13), and DNA evidence (this chapter).

What do you think? Should the federal courthouse doors be reopened to state prisoners, particularly those on death row, to ensure that justice is not short-circuited? Or should the federal courthouse doors remain as they are now, with only one federal review (unless the case presents an extraordinary issue)? Asked another way, where should the line be drawn between the interests of justice (ensuring that only the truly guilty are executed) and the need for finality (many of the *habeas* petitions raise issues that are very unlikely to succeed)?

Judicial Expansion and Contraction of *Habeas* Access for State Prisoners

In the 1950s and 1960s, the U.S. Supreme Court greatly expanded the application of *habeas corpus*, making it much easier for state prisoners to seek judicial relief in the federal courts (see "Key Developments in Federal *Habeas Corpus* Law, 1953–1996"). These decisions opened the floodgate for federal review, dramatically increasing the number of *habeas corpus* petitions filed in federal courts. But the more conservative Burger, Rehnquist, and Roberts Supreme Courts have narrowed the scope of federal *habeas* relief.

Congress Greatly Restricts *Habeas* Access

For more than two decades Congress considered proposed changes in *habeas corpus* proceedings (Smith, 1995). This inconclusive debate was shattered by the Oklahoma City bombing in 1995. Victims were anxious to channel their grief into tangible reform, and one avenue was *habeas corpus* reform (Gest, 1996). Thus, as the 1996 elections loomed, Congress passed the Antiterrorism and Effective Death Penalty Act. In terms of *habeas corpus* actions filed in federal courts, the act:

- Created 1-year deadlines for filing *habeas* petitions
- Limited successive petitions
- Restricted the review of petitions by state prisoners if the claim was adjudicated on the merits in state courts
- Required a "certificate of appealability" before a *habeas* petition could be appealed to a federal court of appeals
- Provided that decisions of a federal appellate panel are not appealable by writ of *certiorari* to the Supreme Court

Moving with unusual speed, the U.S. Supreme Court agreed to hear a challenge to the new law within 2 months of its passage. A unanimous Court held that the law was constitutional in *Felker v. Turpin* (1996).

Violations of state law are not valid grounds for a *habeas* action unless such violations are of constitutional magnitude. For example, *Brown v. Sanders* (2006) held that *habeas* relief was unavailable when a jury had considered a state sentencing guideline that was later invalidated by a state high court of last resort because the claim did not present any violation of a constitutional right.

As the "Key Developments" feature on the next page indicates, prisoners must exhaust available state remedies before a federal court will consider their constitutional claim on *habeas corpus*. This rule means that, if an appeal or other procedure to hear a claim is still available by right in the state court system, the prisoner must pursue that procedure before a federal *habeas corpus* application will be considered. Federal *habeas corpus* review may likewise be barred if a defendant is unable to show cause for noncompliance with a state procedural rule and to show some actual prejudice resulting from the alleged constitutional violation (*McCleskey v. Zant*, 1991; *Dretke v. Haley*, 2004).

Habeas Corpus Relief for Federal Prisoners

In 1948, Congress enacted a statute that was designed to serve as a substitute for *habeas corpus* for federal prisoners. The primary purpose of the statute was to shift the jurisdictions of the courts hearing *habeas corpus* applications. The statute did not change the basic scope of the remedy that had been available to federal prisoners by *habeas corpus*. That statute, 28 U.S.C. § 2255, provides, in relevant part:

> Federal custody; remedies on motion attacking sentence. A prisoner in custody under sentence of a court established by Act of Congress claiming the right to be released upon the ground that the sentence was imposed in violation of the Constitution or laws of the United States, or that the court was without jurisdiction to impose such sentence, or that the sentence was in excess of the maximum authorized by law, or is otherwise subject to collateral attack, may move the court which imposed the sentence to vacate, set aside, or correct the sentence.

> * * *

An application for a writ of habeas corpus in behalf of a prisoner who is authorized to apply

KEY DEVELOPMENTS IN FEDERAL *HABEAS CORPUS* LAW, 1953–1996

Brown v. Allen (1953)	Established *de novo* standard of review for federal courts conducting *habeas* review of state court convictions.
Fay v. Noia (1963)	Although the doctrine of *procedural default* requires petitioners to have presented *habeas* claims to state courts on direct appellate review first before having those claims reviewed in federal *habeas* proceedings, the federal courts may waive the doctrine of procedural default to grant *habeas* relief if the facts of a case establish that a conviction was obtained unconstitutionally.
Townsend v. Sain (1963)	*Habeas* courts may "receive evidence and try the facts anew."
Sanders v. United States (1963)	*Habeas* courts may consider previously rejected claims if doing so serves "the ends of justice."
Stone v. Powell (1976)	Removed all claims of Fourth Amendment search and seizure violations from the scope of federal *habeas* review.
Wainwright v. Sykes (1977)	Overruled *Fay v. Noia* by holding that petitioners must show good cause and actual prejudice to his or her case for not complying with state procedural rules.
Patton v. Yount (1984)	Overruled *Brown v. Allen* by requiring federal courts to afford deference to state court findings of fact.
Kimmelman v. Morrison (1986)	*Stone v. Powell* does not bar a Sixth Amendment ineffective assistance of counsel *habeas* claim based on mishandling or failing to raise a valid Fourth Amendment issue.
Teague v. Lane (1989)	An individual may not seek to enforce a new rule of law in federal *habeas corpus* proceedings if the new rule was announced after the petitioner's conviction became final or if the petitioner is seeking to establish a wholly new rule or to apply a settled precedent in a novel way that would result in the creation of a new rule.
Coleman v. Thompson (1991)	Elaborating on *Wainwright v. Sykes*, federal *habeas* courts generally may not review a state court's denial of a state prisoner's federal constitutional claim if the state court's decision rests on a state procedural default that is independent of the federal question and adequate to support the prisoner's continued custody.
McCleskey v. Zant (1991)	A *habeas* court must honor state procedural default rules unless the petitioner can show cause and prejudice for his or her procedural default.
Keeney v. Tamayo-Reyes (1992)	Overruled *Townsend v. Sain* by holding that *habeas* courts may not try facts anew, but rather may consider facts not presented in state court proceedings only if the petition can establish good cause and prejudice for not having fully developed the facts in state court.
Herrera v. Collins (1993)	Claims of actual innocence are not valid *habeas* actions unless there is an independent constitutional violation in the underlying criminal proceedings that led to the state prisoner's wrongful conviction. However, a "truly persuasive demonstration of 'actual innocence' made after trial" can render the execution of an innocent defendant unconstitutional.
Schlup v. Delo (1995)	A petitioner establishes actual innocence by making a showing that, in light of all the evidence, "it is more likely than not that no reasonable juror would have convicted."
Murray v. Carrier (1996)	An innocent petitioner's failure to show cause and prejudice for procedural default should not prevent a court from granting a writ.

for relief by motion pursuant to this section, shall not be entertained if it appears that the applicant has failed to apply for relief, by motion, to the court which sentenced him, or that such court has denied him relief, unless it also appears that the remedy by motion is inadequate or ineffective to test the legality of his detention.

A Section 2255 motion is, therefore, the correct mechanism for a federal prisoner to challenge the validity of a federal criminal conviction. The statute recognizes four grounds upon which an inmate in federal custody may seek relief:

1. that the sentence was imposed in violation of the Constitution or laws of the United States
2. that the court was without jurisdiction to impose such sentence
3. that the sentence was in excess of the maximum authorized by law
4. that the sentence is "otherwise subject to collateral attack."

Although the final criterion may appear broad, Section 2255 relief may be granted under it only if a violation of federal law caused a "fundamental defect which inherently results in a complete miscarriage of justice [or] an omission inconsistent with the rudimentary demands of fair procedure" (*Davis v. United States*, 1974, p. 346).

Section 2255 is similar in many respects to the *habeas* remedy for state prisoners, including in terms of time limitations. Section 2255 motions, for example, must usually be filed within 1 year of the date on which a judgment of conviction becomes final, such as the day after the deadline for filing a petition for *certiorari* or when such a petition is denied. There are, however, some significant distinctions between state and federal *habeas*-type relief that that are beyond the scope of this text.

WRONGFUL CONVICTIONS

In spite of the many procedural protections afforded to the criminally accused prior to and during trial, it is clear that some defendants are wrongfully convicted of crimes they did not actually commit. Paul House's case is just one example.

How Many Wrongful Convictions Are There?

One might think that the appeals and postconviction review processes would routinely correct situations in which a defendant was wrongfully convicted, but that is clearly not the case. Up until the mid-1990s, public perception was that criminal defendants had gained too many rights during the Warren era, and, as a result, far too many criminal defendants escaped criminal punishment on technicalities (Uphoff, 2006). Such perceptions led many—including judges and several Supreme Court justices—to deny that wrongful convictions were a major problem (see *Herrera v. Collins*, 1993). Moreover, such sentiments caused legislators to sharply curtail "the avenues available to convicted defendants to challenge their convictions, including appellate review after a certain period (Rosen, 2006, pp. 238–239). And the Antiterrorism and Effective Death Penalty Act's curtailment of *habeas corpus* review further complicated defendants' pursuit of judicial remedies for alleged wrongful convictions.

Since 1989, though, over 280 inmates have been exonerated by DNA evidence, largely due to the efforts of the Innocence Project, the Death Penalty Information Center, and similar organizations (Zalman, Smith & Kiger, 2008). As a result of these exonerations—and media portrayals of them—nearly 40 states have changed their laws to allow for appellate or postconviction review on the grounds of actual innocence, especially when supported by new DNA evidence (Zalman, 2006). The federal government similarly enacted the Innocence Protection Act of 2004, which expands judicial review of convictions on the basis of evidence that tends to exonerate.

It is impossible to get an accurate count of the number of innocent people who are wrongfully convicted each year. Using different methods (each with their own flaws), estimates of the rate of wrongful convictions range between a low of 0.5 percent and a high of 15 percent, with between 1 percent and 3 percent being the estimate with the most empirical support (Zalman, Smith, & Kiger, 2008). But it should be noted that most of what we know about wrongful convictions comes from exoneration cases, 95 percent of which occur in murder and rape cases (Gross & O'Brien, 2008).

Since murder and rape cases account for only 2 percent of all felony convictions, exoneration cases are treated "as an imperfect proxy for a subset of likely wrongful convictions" (Gould & Leo, 2010, p. 826).

Why Do Wrongful Convictions Occur?

One of our leading sources of knowledge about wrongful convictions comes from the work of the Innocence Project. Since it first started operations in 1989, the Innocence Project has exonerated more than 280 wrongfully convicted defendants using DNA, including 17 who had erroneously been sentenced to death (Innocence Project, 2012). An examination of these cases and of the results of several leading empirical studies of wrongful convictions reveals much about how and why they occur.

Mistaken Eyewitness Identifications

According to the Innocence Project (2012), eyewitness misidentification is *the* leading cause of wrongful convictions, playing a role in 75 percent of the DNA exonerations to date. However, as Wells and Quinlivan (2009, p. 2) explain,

> There are several reasons why the true numbers would have to be dramatically higher. . . . First, in a large percentage of the old cases (in which convicted persons claim to have been misidentified) the biological evidence for DNA testing has deteriorated, has been lost, or has been destroyed. Moreover, virtually all DNA exoneration cases involved sexual assault because those are the cases for which definitive biological evidence (contained in semen) is available to trump the mistaken identification. Such biological evidence is almost never available for murders, robberies, drive-by shootings, and other common crimes that have relied on eyewitness identification evidence. A recent study of lineups in Illinois indicates that only 5% of lineups conducted in Chicago, Evanston, and Joliet were sexual assault cases (Mecklenburg, 2006). Most lineup identifications were for non-sexual

assaults, robberies, and murders for which there is almost no chance that DNA would be available to trump a mistaken identification. In addition, we would normally expect sexual assault victims to be among the most reliable of eyewitnesses because sexual assault victims usually have a longer and closer look at the culprit than other crime witnesses (compared to robberies, for instance). For these reasons, the DNA exoneration cases can only represent a fraction, probably a very small fraction, of the people who have been convicted based on mistaken eyewitness identification.

(See also, Gross et al., 2005.)

Flowe, Mehta, and Ebbesen (2011) empirically confirmed Wells and Quinlivan's intuitive logic. They examined a random sample of 725 felony cases from the archives of a district attorney's office in a large, southwestern U.S. city. They found that one out of every three suspects had positive ID evidence in their case. Moreover, eyewitness identifications by both strangers and acquaintances was associated with increased odds of prosecution.

Misidentifications can be caused by a number of natural psychological errors in human judgment that involve the complex interplay of perception and memory (see Fradella, 2007). Social scientists generally classify the primary contributors to such psychological errors into two main categories: estimator variables and system variables.

Estimator variables are those that cannot be controlled by the criminal justice system. They include simple factors like the lighting when the crime took place or the distance from which the witness saw the perpetrator. Estimator variables also include more complex factors, including race (identifications have proven to be less accurate when witnesses are identifying perpetrators of a different race), the presence of a weapon during a crime, and the degree of stress or trauma a witness experienced while seeing the perpetrator.

System variables are those that the criminal justice system can and should control. They include all of the ways that law enforcement agencies retrieve and record witness memory, such as lineups, photo arrays, and other identification procedures. System variables that substantially impact the accuracy of identifications include the type of lineup used, the selection of "fillers" (or members of a lineup or photo array who are not the actual suspect), blind administration, instructions to witnesses before identification procedures, administration of lineups or photo arrays, and communication with witnesses after they make an identification. (The Innocence Project, 2012, ¶¶ 9–10)

"[D]espite its inherent unreliability, much eyewitness identification evidence has a powerful impact on juries. . . . All evidence points rather strikingly to the conclusion that there is almost nothing more convincing than a live human being who takes the stand, points a finger at the defendant, and says, 'That's the one!'" (*Watkins v. Sowders*, 1981, p. 352). Yet, mistaken identifications are the leading cause of wrongful convictions (Huff, Rattner, & Sagarin, 2003). Moreover, in 38 percent of the eyewitness misidentifications identified by the Innocence Project, multiple eyewitnesses misidentified the same innocent person. Of these cases, two eyewitnesses misidentified an innocent person 25 percent of the time and three eyewitnesses misidentified an innocent person in 13 percent of the exoneration cases.

Improper Forensic Evidence

Recall from Chapter 13 that DNA testing is the "gold standard" of forensic science because it was developed by leading scientists and subjected to rigorous, peer-reviewed empirical validation. In contrast, many other forensic techniques, such as hair and fiber analysis, toolmark comparisons, and fingerprint analysis, rely on subjective determinations that the two samples are consistent with having originated from the same source, while comparative bullet lead analysis and many arson investigation techniques have been disproven (see Table 13.4). And even forensic analyses that have been scientifically validated can be improperly conducted, due to shoddy laboratory

practices, or conducted on contaminated samples, due to shoddy police work (see Garret & Neufeld, 2009). Collectively, invalidated and improper forensic evidence contribute to roughly 50 percent of wrongful convictions (Innocence Project, 2012).

False Confessions

False confessions occur when people confess to crimes they did not commit. At first blush, it may seem unfathomable that someone would incriminate themselves in this manner, but both empirical research and police practice demonstrate that the phenomenon is actually fairly common. In fact, false confessions contributed to approximately 25 percent of the wrongful convictions identified through the Innocence Project's DNA exonerations. Many false confessions occur as a result of psychologically coercive police interrogation tactics (Ofshe & Leo, 1997; Leo, 2008).

In a candid 2008 op-ed piece for the *Los Angeles Times*, D.C. Police Detective Jim Trainum detailed how he unwittingly coaxed a false confession out of a 34-year-old woman he suspected of murder. She even revealed details about the crime that could only have been known to police investigators and the killer. But Trainum later discovered that the woman couldn't possibly have committed the crime. When he reviewed video of his interrogation, he realized that he had inadvertently provided the woman with those very specific details, which she then repeated back to him when she was ready to confess. (Balko, 2011, ¶ 44).

The Innocence Project (2012, ¶ 4) summarized the leading factors that contribute to false confessions as follows:

- duress
- coercion
- intoxication
- diminished capacity
- mental impairment
- ignorance of the law
- fear of violence
- the actual infliction of harm

- the threat of a harsh sentence
- misunderstanding the situation

Unreliable Informants

People who are not in law enforcement but provide information to law enforcement are called **informants**. One particularly unreliable type of informant is commonly known as the *jailhouse snitch*. These jailhouse informants are criminals who, while in custody, claim to overhear incriminating information from a fellow inmate and then pass that information along to police and prosecutors, often in the hopes that it will help their own situations. But these informants are notoriously unreliable. "With little or nothing to lose, and everything to gain, cunning and unscrupulous jailhouse snitches invent narratives and crime details that mislead law enforcement officers and contribute to appalling miscarriages of justice" (The Justice Project, 2007, p. 1). As a result, jailhouse informants are one of the leading contributors to wrongful convictions.

Fabricated testimony by unreliable informants accounted for 33.4 percent of wrongful convictions in a classic study (Bedau & Radelet, 1987), 21 percent in another study (Dwyer, Neufeld, & Scheck, 2000), and 45.9 percent in another (Warden, 2004). In a particularly comprehensive study of 340 exonerations in the United States from 1989 through 2003, Gross and his colleagues (2005, pp. 543–544) reported that "the real criminal lied under oath to get the defendant convicted" in 5.6 percent of cases and in 28.5 percent of exonerations, "a civilian witness who did not claim to be directly involved in the crime committed perjury—usually a jailhouse snitch or another witness who stood to gain from the false testimony."

Tunnel Vision and Misconduct by Justice Professionals

The more police, prosecutors, and forensic analysts become convinced of a conclusion, such as the guilt of a particular suspect, the more likely they are to focus only on factors that support that conclusion while conversely, the less likely they are to consider alternative explanations. This process is commonly referred to as **tunnel vision**. It occurs at both conscious and unconscious levels

when justice professionals "select and filter the evidence that will 'build a case' for conviction, while ignoring or suppressing evidence that points away from guilt" (Findley & Scott, 2006, p. 292).

Tunnel vision is exacerbated by the emphasis the criminal justice system places on obtaining convictions, especially for police who are evaluated by their clearance rates through arrests and prosecutors whose performance is evaluated by their conviction rates (see Chapter 6).

> [P]rosecutors may engage in overly suggestive witness coaching, offer inappropriate and incendiary closing arguments, or fail to disclose critical evidence to the defense, all of which may raise the prospect of a wrongful conviction. In research on wrongful convictions, the most commonly established transgression is the prosecution's failure to turn over exculpatory evidence. Sometimes police officers do not provide prosecutors with this evidence in order to make it available to the defense, or prosecutors may not be aware that they have such information in their files. In other cases, though, the misdeeds are intentional. (Gould & Leo, 2010, pp. 854–855)

Recall from Chapter 6 that prosecutors are absolutely immune from civil liability for their misconduct when prosecuting a case. Of course, they may be subject to criminal liability and professional sanctions for misconduct, but either type of sanction is quite rare. Consider that Ridolfi and Possley identified 782 acts of prosecutorial misconduct in 707 California criminal cases between 1997 and 2009—"on average, about one case a week" (2010, p. 2). Only six of these cases resulted in the state bar taking any disciplinary action against the at-fault prosecutors. Figure 16.3 illustrates the types of misconduct Ridolfi and Possley found.

One might assume that appellate courts would take steps to fix the problems caused by any type of governmental misconduct that may have tainted a verdict. But two factors already discussed in this chapter limit the effectiveness of appeals in doing so. First, the clearly erroneous standard of review governs appellate evaluations of factual determinations at trial. Thus, appeals courts rarely second-guess a jury's determination based on the

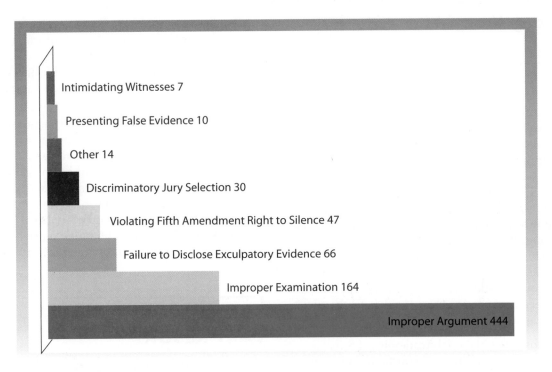

Intimidating Witnesses 7

Presenting False Evidence 10

Other 14

Discriminatory Jury Selection 30

Violating Fifth Amendment Right to Silence 47

Failure to Disclose Exculpatory Evidence 66

Improper Examination 164

Improper Argument 444

Figure 16.3 ■ Types and Frequency of Prosecutorial Misconduct

*Improper argument "includes vouching for a witness's truthfulness, testifying for an absent witness, misstating the law, arguing facts not in evidence, mischaracterizing evidence, impugning the defense, arguing inconsistent theories of prosecution, appealing to religious authority, offering personal opinion and shifting the burden of proof" (Ridolfi & Possley, 2010, p. 25).

SOURCE: Kathleen Ridolfi and Maurice Possley. *Preventable Error: A Report on Prosecutorial Misconduct in California, 1997–2009*. Santa Clara, CA: Santa Clara University School of Law's Northern California Innocence Project.

evidence in a criminal case. Second, governmental misconduct is often dismissed as harmless error on appeal, especially when other factors implicating the defendant's guilt are present, even though those factors may be highly suspect themselves (such as invalid forensic evidence or unreliable eyewitness identifications). Consider, for example, that convictions were upheld on appeal under the harmless error rule in 548 (77.5%) of the 707 misconduct cases Ridolfi and Possley identified. Garrett (2008) found that of the first 200 DNA exoneration cases, only 18 convictions had been reversed by appellate courts.

As explained in Chapter 13, misconduct by forensic scientific personnel has been well documented. Sometimes this misconduct takes the form of sloppy, improperly conducted forensic analyses (Giannelli, 2007). Other times, it takes the form of inaccurate or misleading trial testimony (Garrett

& Neufeld, 2009). And, in rare but egregious cases, forensic analysts have outright fabricated results (Garrett & Neufeld, 2009). All of these types of forensic misconduct contribute to wrongful convictions.

Inadequate Defense Representation

As detailed in Chapter 7, upwards of 80 percent of all criminal defendants are represented by court-appointed defense attorneys. Many of these lawyers are chronically overworked and do not have the resources to perform their duties effectively. Bad lawyering clearly contributes to wrongful convictions. In fact, a leading study of capital appeals found that "ineffective defense lawyering was the biggest contributing factor to the wrongful conviction or death sentence of criminal defendants in capital cases over a 23-year period" (Gould & Leo, 2010, p. 855, citing Liebman, Fagan, & West, 2000).

Reducing Wrongful Convictions

Traditional wisdom held that the courts can do only so much to combat wrongful convictions. After all, courts make decisions based on the evidence presented. Neither participants in a trial nor judges in an appellate court may be aware of problems with faulty evidence. Thus, the most significant ways to combat wrongful convictions lie with reforms in other areas of the criminal justice system. These include changing the ways in which pretrial identifications are conducted to minimize the risk of misidentification; videotaping interrogations of criminal suspects to help reduce the incidence of false confessions; and improving the collection, handling, preservation, and analysis of forensic evidence (National Academies of Science, 2009; Rosen, 2006; Uphoff, 2006). But conventional wisdom is slowly giving way to select policy recommendation that could help the courts reduce the number of wrongful convictions.

1. In light of the National Academies of Science (2009) report on forensics, courts should rigorously apply *Daubert* to exclude or limit the use of unreliable forensic techniques (see Chapter 13; see also Giannelli, 2011).

2. As Fradella (2007) argued, rather than just relying on cross-examination and jury instructions, judges should admit expert testimony from witnesses who specialize in the ways in which memory, perception, and even a variety of crime-scene variables can affect the reliability of eyewitness identifications (see *State v. Clopten*, 2009).

3. Attorney discipline is the province of the courts. State high courts of last resort should be more active in disciplining attorneys who engage in misconduct in the course of criminal prosecutions in both state and federal courts.

4. The courts have recognized the inherent unreliability of snitches who testify in exchange for reduced sentences or other such consideration. Even the U.S. Supreme Court has stated, "[t]he use of informers, accessories, accomplices, false friends, or any of the other betrayals which are 'dirty business' may raise serious questions of credibility" (*On Lee v. United States*, 1952 p. 757). At least 18 states now require that "snitch" testimony from an alleged accomplice be corroborated by other evidence (American Bar Association, 2005). But no such corroboration is required for jailhouse informants. Without such corroboration, courts should exclude such testimony as unreliable and unduly prejudicial under Rule 403 of the Federal Rules of Evidence and its state-law counterparts.

5. Finally, appellate courts need to be more aware of the ways in which the leading causes of wrongful conviction interact with each other—especially when applying the harmless error rule. Specifically, when examining whether any particular type of mistake in a criminal case constitutes harmless or prejudicial error, appeals courts should be hesitant to rely on any other factor that contributes to wrongful convictions.

STATE COURTS OF LAST RESORT

No typical state court of last resort exists. While some are referred to as state supreme courts, some go by other names, such as the *state court of appeals, supreme judicial court, court of criminal appeals,* or *supreme court of appeals.* More important, the role that state high courts play is affected by the control these judicial bodies exercise over their dockets. Perhaps just as important is the exact wording of the state constitution. But these legal factors only partially explain the policy-making role of state supreme courts. Perhaps nowhere is this more obvious than in death penalty appeals.

Law on the Books: State High Courts and Discretionary Dockets

In states that have not created intermediate courts of appeals, the responsibility for appellate review falls directly on the state court of last resort. In such circumstances, the state's highest court finds itself relegated to dealing with a succession of relatively minor disputes, devoting its energies to error correction rather than to more time-consuming efforts to shape the law of the state.

By contrast, in the District of Columbia and in the 40 or so states that have created intermediate courts of appeals, it is the intermediate appellate courts that are primarily concerned with error correction.

This leaves the state's highest court free to devote more attention to cases that raise important policy questions (Scott, 2006; Tarr & Porter, 1988). This high level of discretion not only yields low caseloads, but also transforms the nature of the judicial process. The high court is no longer merely reacting to disputes brought to it by disgruntled litigants; that is the job of the intermediate court of appeals. Rather, the high court exercises its considerable discretion to carefully select disputes in which it chooses to participate, usually for reasons of advancing public policy. In sum, the architecture of the system tells the judges of the top court to be creative (Carrington, Meador, & Rosenberg, 1976; Scott, 2006).

Law in Action: State High Courts as Policy Makers

In recent years, state high courts have become important policy makers in a number of contentious areas, such as tort reform, same-sex marriages, and parental rights in divorce cases. No wonder that elections for state high court judgeships have become nastier, noisier, and costlier (Neubauer & Meinhold, 2013).

Applying U.S. Supreme Court decisions is one way that state high courts participate in policy making. Although in theory federal law is supreme over conflicting state law, in practice state courts of last resort do not invariably follow authoritative pronouncements of the nation's highest court (Bloom, 2008; Tarr, 1982). For example, noncompliance was pronounced in race relations cases, with southern state high courts often aiding and abetting their states' massive resistance to desegregation (Garrow, 2008; Tarr & Porter, 1988). Noncompliance has also occurred in a variety of states in areas such as the constitutionality of executing juveniles (*State ex rel Simmons v. Roper*, 2003); the constitutionality of executing a rapist (*State v. Kennedy*, 2007); the scope of Fourth Amendment search-and-seizure requirements (*State v. Kimbro*, 1985; see also, Comparato & McClurg, 2007); the role the doctrine of proportionality plays in limiting criminal sentencing (*Andrade v. Attorney General of State of California*, 2001); school districts' responses to school prayer decisions (*Murray v. Curlett*, 1962; see also, Abel & Hacker, 2006); and how warning requirements for interrogation announced in *Miranda* would be applied (*Alvord v. State*, 1975; see also, Epstein, Cameron, Segal & Westerland, 2006; Gruhl, 1981).

Interpretation of state constitutional provisions is another way that state supreme high courts act as important government policymakers. The phrase new judicial federalism refers to the movement in the state supreme courts to reinvigorate state constitutions as sources of individual rights over and above the rights granted by the U.S. Constitution. New judicial federalism occurred partially as a response to the Burger Court's unwillingness to continue the Warren Court's understanding of civil liberties (Friedman, 2000; Galie, 1987). Just as important, though, new judicial federalism reflects the growing understanding that the federal Constitution establishes minimum guarantees of individual rights rather than maximum protections (Emmert & Traut, 1992; Friedman, 2000). In some instances, for example, state high courts have interpreted provisions regarding criminal procedures in the state's bill of rights more expansively than the equivalent sections of the U.S. Bill of Rights. Researchers have identified hundreds of state high-court decisions that interpret state charters as more rights-generous than their federal counterpart (Bloom & Massey, 2008; Fino, 1987). For example, reasoning that garbage was abandoned property, the U.S. Supreme Court ruled in *California v. Greenwood* (1988), that the Fourth Amendment to the U.S. Constitution does not require law enforcement to obtain a search warrant before searching someone's garbage. The high courts of New Jersey and Washington state, however, held that search warrants were required for police to search garbage in those states because their state constitutions afforded more privacy rights than the Fourth Amendment (*State v. Hempele, 1990; State v. Boland*, 1990).

Law in Controversy: State High Courts and Death Penalty Cases

State courts of last resort reveal pronounced differences in their handling of death penalty cases. For example, before New Jersey abolished the death penalty in 2007, the state had not executed anyone since 1963, partially because the New Jersey Supreme Court had invalidated 27 of the 28 death sentences it had reviewed (Bienen, 2008). At the other extreme, the high courts of Texas and Virginia routinely uphold the imposition of death sentences (Smith, 2008). Consider, for example, that the Texas Court of Criminal Appeals upheld a death sentence for a criminal defendant whose lawyer slept through major portions of the trial, ruling that such behavior did not rise to the level of ineffective assistance of counsel (*Ex parte McFarland*, 2005). Other states fit somewhere in between. Illinois and the Carolinas, for example, have thrown out roughly half of the sentences of death they reviewed while upholding the other half (Liebman et al., 2000).

Differences in how state courts of last resort respond to death penalty appeals is not random. Justices on high courts in states with competitive judicial elections are more likely to uphold death sentences (Brace & Hall, 1997; Brooks & Raphael, 2003). In particular, liberal justices facing reelection with possibly close margins of victory are more likely to conceal their opposition to the death penalty; they cast votes reflecting their constituents' opinions.

THE U.S. SUPREME COURT AND CRIMINAL JUSTICE POLICY

"I'll appeal all the way to the Supreme Court" is a familiar phrase. Alas, it is not very realistic. The jurisdiction of the U.S. Supreme Court is almost exclusively discretionary; that is, it can pick and choose the cases it wishes to decide. Most of the time it decides not to decide. Of the roughly 92 million lawsuits filed in the United States every year, only about 7,000 will ever be appealed to the nation's highest court; and from this small number, the justices will select a mere handful, between 80 and 90 in recent years. Of these, most are civil cases, as the Supreme Court tends to review only between 20 and 35 criminal cases each year.

Scholars refer to Court eras according to the chief justice. Thus, the Warren Court refers to the period from 1953 to 1969, when Earl Warren (a former Republican governor of California appointed by President Eisenhower) was chief justice. Because the associate justices change, however, these references provide only informal guides to the dominant thinking of the Court. Nonetheless, an examination of the Warren Court, Burger Court, Rehnquist Court, and now the Roberts Court offers a useful summary of major differences in the direction of criminal justice policy.

We begin with the Warren Court because it decided so many cases that shaped contemporary criminal justice policy in the United States, such as the extension of the exclusionary rule to the states in *Mapp v. Ohio* (1961). It should be noted, though,

that earlier Supreme Courts decided many key cases that affected subsequent Courts. For example, *Mapp's* exclusionary rule holding was based largely on *Weeks v. United States* (1914). *Brown v. Mississippi* (1936), *Chambers v. Florida* (1940), and *Ashcraft v. Tennessee* (1944) prohibited the use of confessions obtained through coercion, laying the groundwork for *Miranda. Johnson v. Zerbst* (1938) made clear that the Sixth Amendment entitled a person charged with crime in a federal court to appointed defense counsel, laying the groundwork for *Gideon v. Wainwright*, which in 1963 extended the right to counsel to state felony trials. The scope of First Amendment right to free speech is still greatly affected today by the fighting words doctrine announced in *Chaplinsky v. New Hampshire* (1942). The foundations of the right to privacy were formed in *Meyer v. Nebraska* (1923) and *Pierce v. Society of Sisters* (1925). Even before the historic *Brown v. Board of Education* (1954) case, earlier Courts began to whittle away at legalized racial discrimination on equal protection grounds (e.g., *Shelley v. Kraemer*, 1948). And the power of judicial review—the ability of courts to review the constitutionality of acts by the executive and legislative branches of government—dates back to *Marbury v. Madison* in 1803).

The Warren Court (1953–1969)

The Warren Court (1953–1969) commands attention because in the areas of civil liberties and civil rights, it remains the benchmark against which subsequent periods of the Supreme Court are measured. The Warren Court revolutionized constitutional law and American society as well, giving to minorities victories they had not been able to obtain from reluctant legislatures and recalcitrant executives.

The Warren Court first captured national attention with its highly controversial 1954 decision invalidating racial segregation in the public schools (*Brown v. Board of Education*, 1954). In addition, the Court first confronted the difficult problem of defining obscenity and considerably narrowed the grounds for prosecution of obscene material (*Roth v. United States*, 1957). What produced the greatest controversy, however, was the adoption of a series of broad rules protecting criminal defendants.

During the 1960s, the Supreme Court for the first time attempted to exercise strong policy control over the administration of criminal justice. The nation's highest court began to apply to state courts some of the more specific requirements of the Bill of Rights. Earlier opinions enunciating vague standards of "due process" were replaced by decisions specifying precise rules. The Bill of Rights was seemingly transformed from a collection of general constitutional principles into a code of criminal procedure. These sweeping changes in constitutional interpretation have been called the "due process revolution." Many of the leading cases of the due process revolution have been covered throughout this book.

The Burger Court (1969–1986)

Many of the Warren Court's criminal justice decisions were far from popular. The Supreme Court's attempt to nationalize and constitutionalize the criminal justice system came at a time of increasing crime in the streets, riots in big cities, political violence protesting the Vietnam War, and most tragically of all, assassinations of American leaders. To the public, there appeared to be a connection between the new trends of what was seen as judicial permissiveness and the breakdown of law and order. Supreme Court justices were accused of "coddling criminals" and "handcuffing the police." This controversy became the focus of national debate.

During the 1968 presidential campaign, Republican candidate Richard Nixon made the Warren Court's decisions on criminal procedure a major issue. He promised to appoint "strict constructionists" to the Court, and after his election he made good on this promise. With his four appointments, Nixon achieved remarkable success in remodeling the Court. After Warren Burger, Harry Blackmun, Lewis Powell, and William Rehnquist took the bench, support for civil liberties quickly began to diminish (Segal & Spaeth, 1989).

Although on balance the Burger Court (1969–1986) was more conservative than its predecessor, there was no constitutional counterrevolution, only modest adjustment. The withdrawal from Warren Court decisions was most apparent in criminal justice. *Miranda* was weakened, but not overturned. Similarly, despite clamor by conservatives, *Mapp* was not overruled, although the Court began creating "good faith" exceptions to the exclusionary rule (see Chapter 11). To be sure, the death penalty was reinstated, but overall the Burger Court did not cut back on Warren Court criminal procedure rulings as much as had been expected.

The Rehnquist Court (1986–2005)

Presidents Ronald Reagan and George H. W. Bush continued the Republican policy of appointing conservatives to the court. The Rehnquist Court (1986–2005) officially began when William Rehnquist was elevated from associate justice to chief justice. Unofficially, it can be dated from the 1988 appointment of Anthony Kennedy, who provided a conservative vote far more dependably than did his predecessor Lewis Powell. Thus, it was during the 1988 term that the Rehnquist Court seemed to come of conservative age by cutting back abortion rights, condoning mandatory drug testing, and permitting capital punishment for juveniles and developmentally impaired persons who were convicted of murder. And as emphasized in this chapter, it significantly curtailed *habeas corpus* relief.

But other Rehnquist Court decisions cannot be so easily categorized as conservative. For example, the Court announced a new constitutional right grounded in the Eighth Amendment's prohibitions against excessive fines; these limits place brakes on the government's aggressive use of its authority under the drug forfeiture laws.

The retirement of Byron White gave President Clinton the opportunity to become the first Democratic president in 26 years to make an appointment to the Supreme Court. He chose Ruth Bader Ginsburg. With his second appointment, he elevated Stephen Breyer to the high court. Both have been moderately liberal and have often forged an alliance with the centrist justices.

Decisions reflect shifting alliances of the justices. Firmly on the right were Antonin Scalia, Clarence Thomas, and William Rehnquist, with Anthony Kennedy often joining them. Arrayed more to the left were John Paul Stevens, Ruth Bader Ginsburg, Stephen Breyer, and David Souter. It was Sandra Day O'Connor who often held the balance of power. These shifting alliances were reflected in two controversial 2003 decisions in which the Court declared unconstitutional a state law prohibiting intimate sexual conduct between persons of the same sex (*Lawrence v. Texas*) and upheld some types of race-based diversity programs in university admissions (*Grutter v. Bollinger*).

For 11 years, the same nine justices sat on the Supreme Court, but this changed quickly in the summer of 2005. First, Sandra Day O'Connor announced her retirement, followed 2 months later by the death of the chief justice. Amid considerable public attention, President George W. Bush now had his long-anticipated opportunity to try to move the Court further to the right (Neubauer & Meinhold, 2013).

The Roberts Court (2005–)

The Roberts Court (2005–) began on the first Monday in October 2005, when John Roberts officially assumed his duties as the nation's 17th chief justice. In selecting Roberts, President George W. Bush clearly stated his desire to make the Court more conservative. Although some Democrats viewed Roberts as too conservative, he was confirmed. But all eyes were on the next nominee. Bush eventually nominated Samuel Alito to replace O'Connor. Alito's record as a conservative appellate judge caused some Democrats to consider filibustering his nomination. But Alito was eventually confirmed by the Senate by a relatively narrow margin of 58 to 42.

Democratic President Barack Obama has made two appointments to the U.S. Supreme Court. Sonia Sotomayor, the nation's first Latina justice, replaced Justice David Souter when he retired in 2009. And Elena Kagan, the first female Dean of Harvard Law School and the first female solicitor general, replaced Justice John Paul Stevens when he retired in 2010.

Because both Souter and Stevens were largely considered to be liberal, their replacements by Sotomayor and Kagan did not change the balance of power significantly on the Supreme Court. Table 16.3 presents information about the justices on the Supreme Court as of the publication of this book.

To date, the Roberts Court appears to be slightly more conservative than the Rehnquist Court, but how much more conservative still remains to be seen. "Empirical scrutiny of the Court's voting patterns reveals no significant distinctions between the Rehnquist and Roberts Courts" thus far; rather, the Court appears to be in a state of "relative continuity" rather than dramatic change (Epstein, Martin, Quinn, & Segal, 2008, pp. 651–652). The difference, however, is that Justice Kennedy has replaced Justice Sandra Day O'Connor as the Court's key swing vote. For example, Justice Kennedy was the key fifth vote in *Boumediene v. Bush* (2008). This important case held that the "enemy combatants" being held as prisoners by the U.S. government at the U.S. Naval Station at Guantanamo Bay, Cuba, on suspicion of involvement in terrorist activities had the right to challenge their detention in civilian courts in *habeas corpus* proceedings even though Congress had enacted laws to prevent the prisoners from doing so. The Court ruled that Congress acted unconstitutionally when they enacted the laws that attempted to suspend the writ of *habeas corpus* for enemy combatants. The Court also ruled that the detainees had the right to be informed about the specific grounds

TABLE 16.3 ▪ SUPREME COURT JUSTICES IN ORDER OF SENIORITY

Name	Year of Birth	Home State	Religion	Year of Appointment	Appointed by	Senate Vote
John Roberts	1955	Indiana	Catholic	2005	George W. Bush	78–22
Antonin Scalia	1936	New York	Catholic	1986	Ronald Reagan	98–0
Anthony Kennedy	1936	California	Catholic	1988	Ronald Reagan	97–0
Clarence Thomas	1948	Georgia	Catholic	1991	George H. W. Bush	52–48
Ruth Bader Ginsburg	1933	New York	Jewish	1993	Bill Clinton	96–3
Stephen Breyer	1938	Massachusetts	Jewish	1994	Bill Clinton	87–9
Samuel Alito, Jr.	1950	New Jersey	Catholic	2006	George W. Bush	58–42
Sonia Sotomayor	1954	New York	Catholic	2009	Barack Obama	68–31
Elena Kagan	1960	New York	Jewish	2010	Barack Obama	63–37

for their being kept in custody. Justice Kennedy also sided with the Court's "liberal wing" in holding that defendants have the right to effective assistance of counsel during plea bargaining (*Lafler v. Cooper*, 2012; *Missouri v. Frye*, 2012). Conversely, Justice Kennedy sided with the four conservative justices in *Hudson v. Michigan* (2006) when the Court ruled that the exclusionary rule was not an appropriate remedy for violations of the requirement that police officers knock and announce their presence before executing a search warrant (see Chapter 11).

In some closely watched death penalty cases, Justice Kennedy has sided with both ideological factions of the Court. On the so-called liberal side, Kennedy wrote the majority opinion that allowed a Tennessee death row inmate to use DNA evidence in a federal *habeas corpus* hearing (see "Case Close-Up: *House v. Bell* and Federal Court Scrutiny of State Death Row Inmates" on page 448). He also joined with the "liberal" branch of the Court in invalidating the use of capital punishment against a child rapist (*Kennedy v. Louisiana*, 2008). Yet, he sided with conservatives in several other death penalty cases. With Justice Kennedy writing for the majority in *Ayers v. Belmontes* (2006), the Court ruled that juries need not consider forward-looking mitigating circumstances during death-sentence deliberations. Justice Kennedy also provided the key votes in *Schriro v. Landrigan* (2007), which upheld a death sentence over an ineffective assistance of counsel claim; *Uttecht v. Brown* (2006), which upheld a trial court's dismissal of three venirepersons because they were opposed to the death penalty over an objection that such dismissals violated the right to an impartial jury guaranteed by the Sixth and Fourteenth Amendments; and *James v. United States* (2007), which held that an attempted burglary qualified as a "violent felony" for triggering a 15-year mandatory sentence under the federal Armed Career Criminal Act. The future direction of the Court will depend on the political balance between the president and the U.S. Senate.

THE SUPREME COURT IN BROAD PERSPECTIVE

Newspaper coverage of the Supreme Court tends to resemble the play-by-play commentary for an athletic event, with each decision in the term described as a "victory" or "defeat" for conservatives or liberals. Unfortunately, what gets lost in this commentary is the broader perspective.

Overall, the decisions of the Supreme Court swing back and forth much like a pendulum. Far from being random, however, these swings reflect major political movements in the nation. Most directly, this occurs because of the swing of electoral politics; presidential appointments control the composition of the bench and may temper the speed, if not shift the direction, of the Court. More indirectly, public opinion also affects the justices' lives and may serve to curb them when they threaten to go too far or too fast in their rulings. "But changes in the direction of the Court are ultimately moderated by its functioning as a collegial body, in which all nine justices share power and compete for influence" (O'Brien, 1988, p. 13; see also, Devins, 2008). The Court thus generally shifts direction gradually, incorporating and accommodating the views of new appointees. Ultimately, these long-term trends, more than individual decisions, have the most influence.

CONCLUSION

"This is not a case of conclusive exoneration," wrote Justice Kennedy. Paul House was entitled to another hearing in federal district court, but with no guarantee as to the outcome of that hearing. In the end, the prosecutor chose not to retry the case. As a result, Paul House was released after spending 24 years on death row. Whether this decision will offer much hope to other inmates sitting on death row remains to be seen. But *House v. Bell* only adds a new chapter to the long-running debate over federal review of state court convictions, particularly federal court review of state death penalty cases. To some, allowing multiple reviews only introduces unnecessary complexities into the process, thus eroding the deterrent value of punishment. To others, though, allowing multiple reviews properly introduces multiple perspectives, thus ensuring that justice is done.

The right to one appeal is being increasingly used. Appellate court caseloads have grown dramatically in recent years. The explosive growth in appellate court caseloads not only reflects the greater willingness of litigants to ask reviewing bodies to correct errors but also represents the greater role appellate courts play in policy making. U.S. Supreme Court decisions have important impacts on the criminal justice system. But the nine justices are often as divided over the correct answer to a legal problem as is society. Thus, predicting specific case outcomes is difficult; indeed, the conservative Rehnquist Court did not always rule in a predictably conservative manner, and it remains to be seen whether the Roberts Court will consistently rule as conservatively as predicted.

Chapter Review

LO1 **1.** Explain how appeals and appellate processes differ from trials and trial processes.

Unlike trial courts, appeals courts do not hear evidence at trials. Thus, witnesses do not provide testimony at appeals. Rather, lawyers for both sides appear before a panel of judges to argue about the law applicable to the case.

LO2 **2.** Describe the two primary functions of appeals.

The two primary functions of appeals are error correction and policy formation.

LO3 **3.** Explain how double jeopardy limits appeals by the prosecution in criminal cases.

Although the prosecution can file an appeal over a question of law, the Double Jeopardy Clause of the Fifth Amendment to the U.S. Constitution prevents the prosecution from seeking to have a "not guilty" verdict overturned on appeal.

LO4 **4.** Define the contemporaneous objection rule and explain its impact on appeals.

When lawyers think an error is being made at trial, they must object in order to give the trial court judge the opportunity to correct the error. If the attorneys fail to object, then their objection is deemed waived and, therefore, cannot form the basis of a legal argument on appeal.

LO5 **5.** Differentiate between mandatory and discretionary appellate jurisdiction.

Mandatory appellate jurisdiction concerns the cases that an appeals court must hear. Discretionary appellate jurisdiction concerns the cases that an appeals court may elect to hear, but is not required to adjudicate.

LO6 **6.** Identify the different appellate standards of review and evaluate their impact on the criminal appeals.

Questions of law are reviewed *de novo*, questions of fact are reviewed for clear error, and discretionary rulings by judges are reviewed for an abuse of discretion. The *de novo* standard allows an appellate court to consider any legal question without regard or deference to the decision made by a lower court. The other standards of review require appellate courts to give deference to the decisions of a trial court.

LO7 **7.** Describe the six customary phases in the appeals process.

Appeals are started by the appellant's filing a notice of appeal. The parties then designate the record on appeal and the trial court transmits the designated materials to an appellate court. The parties then brief their cases. The appeals court may then opt to hear oral arguments. The decision of the appellate court is memorialized in a written opinion that concludes with an order disposing of the case.

LO8 **8.** Compare and contrast plain error, reversible error, and harmless error.

Plain errors are severe defects in trial proceedings that require reversal of a conviction and remand for a new trial in order to avoid a miscarriage of justice. All other errors are subject to the harmless error rule. If the mistakes are minor such that they probably did not affect the outcome of the case, they are deemed "harmless" and, therefore, do not provide grounds for the reversal of a conviction on appeal. In contrast, if the errors likely contributed to a defendant being convicted, then they are deemed

prejudicial and, therefore, require that a conviction be reversed.

LO9 **9.** Analyze the reasons why most criminal appeals result in convictions being affirmed.

Most criminal cases are affirmed on appeal because of the harmless error rule and the standards of review applied by appellate courts.

LO10 **10.** Compare and contrast appeals and postconviction review processes.

So long as criminal defendants file a notice of appeal within the specified time limits, they are guaranteed the right to have an appellate court directly examine their convictions for all types of alleged errors. Postconviction reviews, however, collaterally attack convictions in civil court. The grounds for such postconviction reviews are usually much narrower than the grounds that can form the basis of a direct appeal.

LO11 **11.** Identify the leading causes of wrongful convictions.

The leading causes of wrongful convictions include mistaken identifications, improper forensic evidence, false confessions, unreliable informants, tunnel vision and misconduct by justice professionals, and inadequate defense representation.

LO12 **12.** Analyze how state courts of last resort and the U.S. Supreme Court exercise their discretion to set justice policy.

High courts of last resort help to set justice policy through their exercise of their discretionary appellate jurisdiction. They accept only cases that present significant public policy questions while rejecting petitions that merely allege the need for error correction.

Critical Thinking Questions

1. In the public's mind, at least, appeals drag on endlessly and result in a lack of finality in the process. Do you think this is a significant problem, or is it merely one of appearance?

2. How does the appeal-and-review process in a capital murder case differ from the appeal-and-review process in a serious felony?

3. Why are most findings of guilt at the trial level not appealed? In what ways are appellate cases unrepresentative of trial court cases?

4. Based on material in this chapter and earlier ones, what have been the significant differences in decisions among the Warren Court, the Burger Court, the Rehnquist Court, and now the Roberts Court? In particular, consider Court decisions related to right to counsel (Chapter 7), bail (Chapter 10), right to trial (Chapter 13), the death penalty (Chapter 14), and *habeas corpus*.

Key Terms

affirm   444

amicus curiae   443

appellant   441

appellate brief   442

appellate court record   442

appellee   442

Burger Court   461

collateral attack   448

concurring opinion   443

contemporaneous objection
   rule   438

discretionary appellate
   jurisdiction   439

dissenting opinion   443

double jeopardy   438

en banc   437

error   444

error correction   437

estimator variables   454

habeas corpus   449

harmless error   444

informants   456

interlocutory   438

mandatory appellate
    jurisdiction   439

new judicial federalism   459

notice of appeal   442

opinion   443

oral argument   443

per curium opinion   443

petitioner   442

plain error   444

plurality opinion   443

policy formulation   437

Rehnquist Court   461

respondent   442

remand   444

reverse   444

reversed and remanded   444

reversible error   444

right to one appeal   437

Roberts Court   462

standard of review   440

system variables   454

tunnel vision   456

Warren Court   460

writ of *certiorari*, petition for   442

Web Resources

Go to the *America's Courts and the Criminal Justice System* companion website at
http://www.cengage.com/criminaljustice/neubauer,
where you will find more resources to help you study.
Resources include web exercises, quizzing, and flash cards.

For Further Reading

Belbot, Barbara, and Craig Hemmens. *The Legal Rights of the Convicted*. El Paso: LFB Scholarly. 2010.

Bierman, Luke. "Three Views of State Intermediate Appellate Courts: Introduction." *Justice System Journal* 26: 93–97, 2005.

Binford, W. Warren H., Preston C. Greene, Maria C. Schmidlkofer, Robert M. Wilsey, and Hillary A. Taylor. "Seeking Best Practices Among Intermediate Courts of Appeal: A Nascent Journey." *Journal of Appellate Practice and Process* 9: 37–119, 2007.

Bonneau, Chris. "Vacancies on the Bench: Open-Seat Elections for State Supreme Courts." *Justice System Journal* 27: 143–159, 2006.

Diascro, Jennifer Segal. "The Legacy of Chief Justice Rehnquist: A View from the Small Screen." *Judicature* 92: 106–117, 2008.

Eakins, Keith. "Agenda Setting in an Elected Supreme Court: The Case of Ohio." *Justice System Journal* 27: 160–179, 2006.

Eggers, David, and Lola Vollen (Eds.). *Serving Justice: America's Wrongfully Convicted and Exonerated*. San Francisco: McSweeney's, 2006.

Garrett, Brandon. *Convicting the Innocent: Where Criminal Prosecutions Go Wrong*. Cambridge, MA: Harvard University Press. 2011.

King, Nancy, and Joseph Hoffman. *Habeas for the Twenty-first Century: Uses, Abuses, and the Future of the Great Writ*. Chicago: University of Chicago Press. 2011.

Matthew, Jonathan. *Inside Appellate Courts: The Impact of Court Organization on Judicial Decision Making in the United States Courts of Appeals*. Ann Arbor: University of Michigan Press, 2002.

Maveety, Nancy. *Queens' Court: Judicial Power in the Rehnquist Era*. Lawrence: University of Kansas Press, 2009.

Merriner, James. *The Man Who Emptied Death Row: Governor Ryan and the Politics of Crime*. Carbondale: Southern Illinois University Press, 2008.

O'Brien, David. *Storm Center: The Supreme Court in American Politics*. 9th ed. New York: Norton, 2011.

Perry, Barbara. "The 'Bush Twins?' Roberts, Alito, and the Conservative Agenda." *Judicature* 92: 302–311, 2009.

Scott, Kevin M. "Understanding Judicial Hierarchy: Reversals and the Behavior of Intermediate Appellate Judges." *Law and Society Review* 40: 163–191, 2006.

Williams, Jimmy. "Type of Counsel and the Outcome of Criminal Appeals: A Research Note." *American Journal of Criminal Justice* 19: 275–285, 1995.

Zalman, Marvin, Brad Smith, and Angie Kiger. "Officials' Estimates of the Incidence of 'Actual Innocence' Convictions." *Justice Quarterly* 25: 72–100, 2008.

17 Juvenile Courts

© Shelley Gazin/CORBIS

A lawyer meets with her young client in a juvenile detention facility. The bleakness of the wire divider suggests not just a physical separation (perhaps he is a violent offender), but also a societal separation. Juvenile courts were created about 100 years ago to separate youthful from adult offenders, but some argue that the current juvenile justice system does not deal effectively with contemporary problems. ■

Chapter Outline

JUVENILE COURTS 100 YEARS AGO
Industrialization, Cities, and Crime
The Child Savers and the Progressive Movement
Parens Patriae

HOW JUVENILE COURTS DIFFER FROM ADULT COURTS
Emphasis on Helping the Child
Informal Proceedings
Proceedings Based on Civil Law
Secret Proceedings
Absence of Jury Trials

THE ORGANIZATION OF JUVENILE COURTS
Juvenile Court as a Separate Court
Juvenile Court as Part of Family Court
Juvenile Court as a Unit of Trial Court
Law in Action: The Impact of Structure

JUVENILE COURT JURISDICTION: SUBJECT MATTER
Juvenile Delinquency
Status Offenses
Children in Need of Supervision
Law in Action: One-Pot Jurisdiction

JUVENILE COURT JURISDICTION: AGE
Age Limits for Original Jurisdiction over
   Delinquency Matters
Age Limits beyond Original Jurisdiction

TRANSFERS TO ADULT COURT
Types of Transfers
Corrective Mechanisms
Use of Waivers

Courts, Controversy, & Reducing Crime
Should Juveniles Be Tried as Adults?

DUE PROCESS IN JUVENILE COURTS
Key Court Decisions
Important Congressional Acts

CASE CLOSE-UP: *In re Gault* and Due Process in Juvenile Courts

COURTROOM WORK GROUP
Judges
Hearing Officers
Prosecutors
Defense Attorneys
Probation Officers

STEPS OF THE JUVENILE COURT PROCESS
Delinquency (Crime)
Summons (Arrest)
Intake (Initial Hearing)
Detention Hearing
Petition
Conference
Evidence: Gathering and Suppressing
Plea Bargaining
Adjudicatory Hearing
Disposition

Courts, Law, & Media
Dog Pound (2010)

Appeal

THE FUTURE OF JUVENILE COURTS
Crime Control Model: More Adult Penalties
Due Process Model: More Youth Crime
   Prevention

Juvenile Courts • Juvenile Courts • Juvenile Courts •
Courts • Juvenile Courts • Juvenile Courts • Juvenile

Learning Objectives

After reading this chapter, you should be able to:

LO1 Describe the child-saving movement and its relationship to the doctrine of *parens patriae*.

LO2 List the five ways in which juvenile courts differ from adult courts.

LO3 Discuss how states vary in terms of when a juvenile may be transferred to adult court for prosecution.

LO4 Contrast the three major types of cases that are heard in juvenile court.

LO5 Identify and briefly describe the single most important Supreme Court case with respect to juvenile justice.

LO6 Explain the difference between a juvenile case that is petitioned and one that is nonpetitioned.

LO7 Compare and contrast how adherents of the crime control model and proponents of the due process model of criminal justice see the future of juvenile courts.

Gerald Gault was charged with making a lewd phone call. If he had been an adult, the maximum sentence was on the lenient side—a fine of $50 and 2 months in jail. But because he was 15 years old, the sentence was potentially much stiffer—up to 6 years in the state industrial school. These substantive differences mirrored important procedural contrasts as well. If he had been an adult, Gerald Gault would have had the right to confront the witness making the accusation and also the right to have a lawyer present. But because he was a juvenile, none of these basic legal protections applied.

In re Gault (1967) highlights the duality of juvenile court, which is part court of law and part social welfare agency. It sometimes operates formally, but more often its procedures are informal. These contrasts produce a series of contradictions, which are highlighted in the words of a former judge of the Denver Juvenile Court:

> It is law, and it is social work; it is control, and it is help; it is the good parent and, also, the stern parent; it is both formal and informal. It is concerned not only with the delinquent, but also with the battered child, the runaway, and many others.... The juvenile court has been all things to all people. (Rubin, 1989, pp. 79–80)

The historic mandate of juvenile court was to rescue children from a criminal life by providing the care and protection normally afforded by the natural parents. Thus, helping a child was far more important than protecting constitutional rights. But in certain instances, helpful benevolence has been replaced by harsh punishments.

Juvenile Courts • Juvenile Courts • Juvenile Courts • Juvenile
Juvenile Courts • Juvenile Courts • Juvenile Courts • Juvenile

In deciding In re Gault, the Supreme Court confronted the difficult task of determining the relationship between the social welfare functions of juvenile court and basic due process so important to the American court system. The best starting point in unraveling these dualities is an examination of the past 100 years of juvenile court.

JUVENILE COURTS 100 YEARS AGO

Juvenile courts are a distinctly 20th-century development. The major economic and social changes of the late 19th century prompted a rethinking of the role of youth. The result was the creation of specialized courts to deal with what were thought to be distinctly youth-oriented problems. Many of the issues that arose 100 years ago remain with us today, shaping the thinking that will affect juvenile courts for years to come.

Industrialization, Cities, and Crime

By the last third of the 19th century, the United States was well on its way to becoming the world's greatest industrial nation. What had once been a nation of small farmers was rapidly becoming a nation of city dwellers. The factories were located in the cities, and the workers for these factories were partially drawn from those who wished to escape the hard work of farming. But most of the new jobs were filled by immigrants from foreign lands who sought freedom from political oppression or economic want in their home countries. The result was a tremendous growth in cities. Indeed, the population of the nation almost doubled, growing from 40 million in 1870 to 76 million in 1900.

America's emerging big cities were truly diverse. The residents spoke different languages, ate strange foods, dressed differently, and worshiped in a variety of churches. The White Anglo-Saxon Protestants who controlled the institutions of the United States at the time did not extend a cordial welcome to these new immigrants. On the contrary, the immigrant urban masses were associated with the poverty, social disorder, and crime of the emerging big cities. Protecting society from the "dangerous poor"

became a pressing social concern. Then, as now, there was confusion over what was poverty and what was crime.

The Child Savers and the Progressive Movement

Beginning around 1890, members of the Progressive movement advocated a variety of political, economic, and social reforms. They were genuinely concerned about the economic disparities, social disorders, and excesses of industrialization, particularly as they affected children.

Progressives denounced the evils of child labor and pushed for legislation banning the practice. They were likewise appalled by the violent and exploitive conditions of reform schools. The fact that orphans were thrown into reform schools for the uncontrollable circumstance of having no parents shocked the Progressives' moral values. Taking up the plight of the children of the urban immigrant poor, they argued that these children were not bad, but were corrupted by the environment in which they grew up.

The Progressives' concern for the plight of the urban masses was also motivated by self-interest. They were largely middle class, and their position in society was threatened by the growth of a competing urban class composed of the poor and the working poor. These Anglo-Saxon Protestants found the culture of the Southern European Catholics shocking. Anthony Platt's (1969) classic study, *The Child Savers*, notes the types of behavior the Progressives sought to punish—drinking, fighting, begging, frequenting dance halls, staying out late at night, and sexual license. Within a generation, many of the social forces unleashed by the Progressive movement would lead to Prohibition, which was directed squarely at the growing political power of big-city Catholic immigrants, whose power base was the neighborhood tavern.

Thus, from its origins, the juvenile court movement reflected class distinctions: The children of the poor were processed through the system, but those of the more well-to-do were handled informally. These class differences would mark juvenile court activities throughout the century.

Then, as now, there was confusion over what was genuine social concern and what was self-serving class interest.

Parens Patriae

The Progressives' efforts to save the children of the urban masses reflected a major shift in thinking about children. Historically, children had been viewed as miniature adults. Children under the age of 7 were presumed to be incapable of criminal intent and were therefore exempt from prosecution. Those 8 or older were considered adults in the eyes of the law, prosecuted as adults, convicted as adults, and served their sentences in the same prison cells as adults.

By the end of the 19th century, the notion of children as miniature adults was giving way to a very different conceptualization—children as persons with less than fully developed moral and cognitive capacities. This shift in thinking was reflected in the emerging legal doctrine of *parens patriae* (state as parent). No longer were parents considered to have sole and exclusive legal responsibility over their children. If the parents failed in their responsibility to raise a child properly, the state could intervene to protect children's welfare. This doctrine also meant that in extreme circumstances, parents' rights over their children could be terminated altogether.

Then, as now, there was confusion over the right of parents to raise their children in their own image and the need of the state to limit social disorder.

HOW JUVENILE COURTS DIFFER FROM ADULT COURTS

The juvenile court is a continuing legacy of the Progressive movement. Not content to tinker with existing procedures, the Progressives insisted on a radical departure from past practices. Adopting the legal doctrine of *parens patriae* resulted in juvenile judicial proceedings that differed greatly from those used in adult courts.

The unique legal dimensions of **juvenile court** are reflected in the legal terms used. Whereas adults are arrested, tried, and sentenced to prison, juveniles are taken into custody, have an adjudicatory hearing, and are committed to residential placement. For additional coverage of the legal

terms used to distinguish juvenile and adult criminal court processes, see the "Law on the Books vs. Law in Action" feature later in this chapter on page 489.

Juvenile courts differ from adult courts in five important ways: They emphasize helping the child, they are informal, they are based on civil law, they are secret, and they rarely involve a jury.

Emphasis on Helping the Child

Prosecution of adults at the turn of the 20th century sought to achieve punishment. By contrast, the newly created juvenile courts emphasized helping the child. Benevolence and rehabilitation, not punishment, were of paramount importance.

The doctrine of *parens patriae* became the underlying philosophy of juvenile court; the state should deal with a child who broke the law much as a wise parent would deal with a wayward child. The Progressives sought to use the power of the state to save children from a life of crime. Juvenile courts would provide flexible procedures for the treatment of the underlying social problems that were seen as the basis of juvenile crime. Guidance would be the norm.

Informal Proceedings

Criminal prosecutions involving adults are formal and adversarial in nature. By contrast, juvenile court proceedings emphasize informality. Although key elements of due process have been integrated into juvenile court in recent years, juvenile proceedings nonetheless retain their informal nature. As a result, rules of evidence and rules of procedure, so important in adult criminal courts, have little relevance in juvenile proceedings.

Flowing from the premise that juvenile courts are meant to help the child, the creators of juvenile court viewed procedural safeguards not only as unnecessary, but also as harmful. The concern was that a legal technicality might allow a child to avoid getting help (Sanborn, 1993). In essence, the substance of the decision (helping the child) was more important than the procedures used to reach that decision.

Proceedings Based on Civil Law

Prosecutions of adults are based on the criminal law (Chapter 2). In contrast, juvenile court proceedings are based on the civil law (Chapter 2). This is why the legal terminology used in adult and juvenile courts differs so greatly. The terms *summons* and *commitment,* for example, are borrowed directly from civil practice.

Using civil rather than criminal law reinforced the key notion that juvenile courts were intended to rehabilitate, not punish. It is for this reason, for example, that a child's juvenile court record is not admissible in adult court. Regardless of the frequency or severity of the offenses committed by a juvenile, once he or she becomes an adult in the eyes of the criminal law, the person starts over with no prior record.

Over the years, the Supreme Court, state courts, and legislatures have added some procedural due process features of adult courts to juvenile proceedings. And over the years, both punishment and protection of the community have joined rehabilitation as objectives of juvenile delinquency proceedings. Thus, today it is probably best to view juvenile proceedings as quasi-criminal—a blend of civil and criminal law quite different from the original ideals of the early juvenile courts (Morierty, 2008).

Secret Proceedings

Criminal proceedings involving adults are open to the public (except grand jury proceedings, and, on the rarest of rare occasions, part of jury selection in ultrasensitive cases). By contrast, juvenile court proceedings have historically been secret. This means that crime victims who are interested in what happens in their case, or ordinary citizens who are simply curious about what goes on in the courthouse, may freely attend sessions involving adults but not those involving juveniles. In most jurisdictions, it is illegal for law enforcement personnel or juvenile court officials to release the names of juveniles to the media. Moreover, even if the media are able to find out the names, journalistic ethics prohibit that information from being printed or broadcast.

The secrecy of juvenile proceedings is changing in some jurisdictions. Currently, 14 states open delinquency hearings to the general public, and 21 others have passed statutes that open such hearings for certain types of cases. However, judges often retain the authority to close hearings at their discretion (Snyder & Sickmund, 2006).

To its supporters, the secrecy of juvenile court proceedings is essential in meeting the key goal of working with children in trouble to prevent future criminal behavior. To critics, this secrecy merely reinforces the informality of the process and prevents much-needed public scrutiny.

Absence of Jury Trials

Adults accused of violating the criminal law have the right to a trial by a jury of their peers. By contrast, juveniles have no such constitutional right. To be sure, a few states have created, often by statute, an extremely limited right to a trial by jury in some matters concerning juveniles. Nonetheless, the central point is clear: Whereas the possibility of a jury trial structures the disposition of adult offenders, the likelihood of a jury trial almost never enters into the discussion in juvenile court.

The absence of jury trials reinforces the informal nature of the proceedings. It also strengthens the control of juvenile court personnel—both judges and probation officers. In adult courts, the views of ordinary citizens may prove to differ from those of judge or prosecutor, but there is no such possibility in juvenile court.

THE ORGANIZATION OF JUVENILE COURTS

Today, all states have juvenile courts, but their organizational relationship to other judicial bodies varies greatly. In some ways the term *juvenile court* is a misnomer. Only a few states have created juvenile courts that are completely separate from other judicial bodies.

As Chapter 4 emphasized, important variations exist in state court organization. Nowhere is this diversity more apparent than in the organization of juvenile courts. Along a continuum from the most to the least distinctive, juvenile courts are organized in one of three ways: a separate court, part of family court, or a unit of the trial court.

Juvenile Court as a Separate Court

In a few jurisdictions, juvenile court is completely separate from other judicial bodies. This is the case in the states of Connecticut, Rhode Island, and Utah. A juvenile court as a separate statewide entity means that it has its own administration, judges, probation officers, clerks of court, and other employees. Stated another way, matters concerning juveniles are its exclusive jurisdiction. A few large cities, such as Boston and Denver, also separate juvenile courts from other judicial bodies.

Juvenile Court as Part of Family Court

A second organizational arrangement is for juvenile court to be a part of family court, which has broad responsibility over family matters. One major type of case is divorce and related issues, including child custody, child support, alimony, and property settlement. In addition, the jurisdiction of family courts encompasses paternity matters and adoption of children. Most important for our purposes, family-court jurisdiction also typically includes matters concerning juveniles (delinquency, status offenses, and child-victim cases).

Six states and the District of Columbia have authorized family courts on a statewide basis. In Delaware, New York, Rhode Island, and South Carolina, family courts are separately organized. In the District of Columbia, Hawaii, and New Jersey, family courts are a separate division of the trial court of general jurisdiction.

Juvenile Court as a Unit of Trial Court

The third place that juvenile courts are housed organizationally is as part of a trial court. Typically, juvenile court is part of the jurisdiction of the major trial court, but on occasion it is in the minor trial court.

Beyond the legal considerations of jurisdiction, the question of where matters concerning juveniles are heard is largely a function of case volume. In rural areas with few cases, they most often are a type of case on the judge's calendar, much like tort and contract. But most areas have sufficient cases to justify one or more judges who devote themselves full-time to matters concerning juveniles. This specialization is dictated partly by case volume, but also by the requirement that juvenile proceedings be conducted in secret. Administratively, therefore, a separate section of court (sometimes in a different courthouse) makes it easier to keep juvenile proceedings closed to the public.

Law in Action: The Impact of Structure

Since juvenile courts were first established, there has been a debate over the appropriate place in the judicial hierarchy for this new judicial body. Where a state ended up placing its juvenile court was largely determined by broader debates over court organization.

Court reformers recommend that juvenile court be part of family court. But whether this structural arrangement results in "better" justice is, at best, hard to document. There is some evidence, for example, that the more the judge is a juvenile court specialist, the more likely the judge will handle cases informally rather than conduct a full hearing (Sosin, 1978). Similarly, specialists are less likely to find a youth to be a delinquent (Johnson & Secret, 1995). The structural differences, however, appear to be far less important than the social environment in which the juvenile court operates; juvenile courts in big cities march to a different drummer than those in rural or suburban areas (Sanborn, 1994).

JUVENILE COURT JURISDICTION: SUBJECT MATTER

Of the children brought before juvenile court, there is enormous variation in the types of cases. Felons and misdemeanants, petty offenders, and truants are all under the jurisdiction of the juvenile court because of their age. And to complicate matters even further, some juveniles are before the court because of neglect or abuse by their parents.

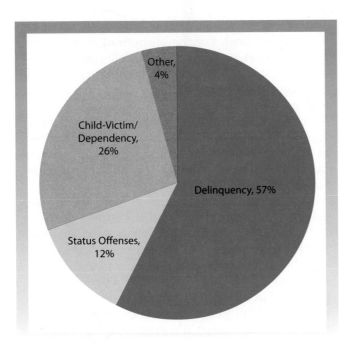

Figure 17.1 ■ Caseload of the Juvenile Courts

Source: Robert C. LaFountain, Richard Y. Schauffler, Shauna M. Strickland, Sarah A. Gibson, and Ashley N. Mason. 2011. *Examining the Work of State Courts: An Analysis of 2009 State Court Caseloads*. Williamsburg, VA: National Center for State Courts.

Juvenile court matters fall into three major categories: delinquency, status offenses, and children in need of supervision (sometimes called "child-victims"). The distribution of cases across these three categories is presented in Figure 17.1.

Juvenile Delinquency

Delinquency is a violation of a criminal law that would be a crime if the act were committed by an adult. Common examples include theft, burglary, sale or possession of drugs, and criminal damage to property. Thus, in a juvenile delinquency matter, there is no age difference in the substance of the criminal law, but the procedures are considerably different.

A juvenile delinquent may be placed on probation or committed to a juvenile institution. The period of confinement may exceed that for an adult charged with the same act.

Status Offenses

Status offenses involve acts that are illegal only for juveniles. Common examples include running away from home, truancy, possession of alcohol, incorrigibility/ungovernability, and curfew violations. Each year, juvenile courts handle approximately 240,000 such cases, or 12 percent of the overall juvenile court docket (LaFountain et al., 2011). Traditionally, juveniles found to be status offenders could be sent to the same juvenile correctional institutions as those found to be delinquent, but this is changing. In recent years, some states have decriminalized some of these behaviors; offenders are now treated as dependent children, and child protective service agencies are given the primary responsibility for addressing the problem.

Children in Need of Supervision

Juvenile courts also deal with children in need of supervision, sometimes referred to as child-victims. Such children are before the court through no fault of their own. These types of cases generally involve issues of child abandonment, child abuse (such as battered children), or child neglect (such as children who are not receiving proper education or medical care).

Clearly, the types of issues in cases concerning children in need of supervision present different issues from those in which juveniles are before the court because of their own actions. For example, children in need of supervision are not placed in juvenile detention facilities. Rather, juvenile courts have a broad mandate to order social services, foster home or group home care, or medical or mental health services for abused or neglected children (DiPietro, 2008). Because of the complexities inherent in the distinctive nature of these cases, further discussion of these cases is beyond the scope of this book.

Law in Action: One-Pot Jurisdiction

The broad subject-matter jurisdiction of juvenile courts complicates the task of addressing the problems facing juvenile justice. At any given time in juvenile court, the judge, prosecutor, probation officer, and police officer are simultaneously dealing with a wide variety of problems. This has been called the "one-pot" jurisdictional approach, in which youths who commit serious crimes, status offenders, and deprived children are put into the same "pot" (Springer, 1986).

Consider the following three hypothetical cases, all of which would meet a given state's age criteria:

- A juvenile who has burglarized a liquor store
- A juvenile who has been stopped by the police for possessing liquor
- A juvenile whose parents drink so heavily that they have given up any efforts to raise their child

The first is a delinquent, the second a status offender, and the third a child-victim. Yet, all three kinds of children were thought to be the products or victims of bad family and social environments; consequently, it was thought that they should be subject, as the wards of the court, to the same kind of solicitous, helpful care (Springer, 1986, pp. 62–63).

It is this broad diversity of juvenile problems that members of the courtroom work group must confront in trying to dispense juvenile court's version of justice.

JUVENILE COURT JURISDICTION: AGE

For adults, court jurisdiction is largely determined by the nature of the criminal offense. For juveniles, on the other hand, jurisdiction is normally determined by their age. But different states provide complex sets of criteria relating to the age at which juvenile courts have jurisdiction over children and young adults.

Age Limits for Original Jurisdiction over Delinquency Matters

In most states, the juvenile court has original jurisdiction over all youth charged with a violation of criminal law who were younger than age 18 at the time of the offense, arrest, or referral to court. Age 18, however, hardly constitutes a consensus among the states for the upper age of jurisdiction (when

a child becomes an adult, at least in the eyes of the criminal law). For the purpose of establishing juvenile court jurisdiction over delinquency matters, two states established the upper age of juvenile court jurisdiction at 15, nine others at age 16, and the remaining states at 17 (see Figure 17.2). Note, however, that many states have higher upper ages of juvenile court jurisdiction for other types of cases, such as in abuse, neglect, or dependency matters—typically through age 20 (Snyder & Sickmund, 2006).

The adjoining states of New York and Pennsylvania illustrate this complex national pattern. In New York, a 16-year-old is considered an adult and is prosecuted in the adult criminal justice system. But move across the border, and Pennsylvania treats that same 16-year-old as a juvenile to be processed in the juvenile court system. This difference in laws of jurisdictions sometimes no more than a few feet apart illustrates the tremendous diversity of American law, which is highlighted in Chapter 4.

There is even more variation at the other end of the spectrum for establishing the lower age of jurisdiction for a juvenile court to exercise delinquency jurisdiction. Most states rely on case law or the common law tradition, which holds that children under a certain age (usually 7 or 8) are incapable of forming criminal intent and, therefore, are exempt from prosecution, even in delinquency proceedings. But, as Table 17.1 illustrates, 16 states have statutorily established a minimum age for juvenile court jurisdiction over delinquency matters.

Age Limits beyond Original Jurisdiction

In most states, once original jurisdiction over delinquency proceedings has been established, juvenile courts may retain jurisdiction over youth who have reached the age at which original juvenile court jurisdiction ends. In fact, as Table 17.2 illustrates, legislation in more than two-thirds of the states permits juvenile courts to continue exercising jurisdiction over young adults "to provide sanctions and services for a duration of time that is in the best interests of the [youth] and the public," at least for certain types of offenses (Snyder & Sickmond, 2006, p. 103).

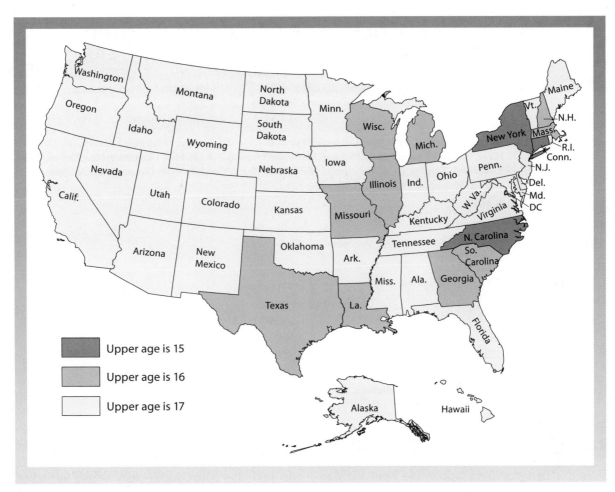

Figure 17.2 ■ Upper Age of Juvenile Court Jurisdiction over Delinquency Matters

SOURCE: Charles Puzzanchera, Benjamin Adams, and Melissa Sickmund. 2011. *Juvenile Court Statistics*, 2008. Pittsburgh: National Center for Juvenile Justice.

TABLE 17.1 ■ LOWEST AGE OF JUVENILE COURT JURISDICTION OVER DELINQUENCY MATTERS

Youngest Age	State
6	North Carolina
7	Maryland, Massachusetts, New York
8	Arizona
10	Arkansas, Colorado, Kansas, Louisiana, Minnesota, Mississippi, Pennsylvania, South Dakota, Texas, Vermont, Wisconsin

SOURCE: Howard N. Snyder and Melissa Sickmond. 2006. *Juvenile Offenders and Victims*: 2006 *National Report.* Washington, DC: Department of Justice, Office of Juvenile Justice and Delinquency Prevention.

TABLE 17.2 ■ OLDEST AGE OF JUVENILE COURT JURISDICTION OVER DELINQUENCY MATTERS

Oldest Age	State
18	Alaska, Iowa, Kentucky, Nebraska, Oklahoma, Tennessee
19	Mississippi, North Dakota
20	Alabama, Arkansas, Connecticut, Delaware, District of Columbia, Georgia, Idaho, Illinois, Indiana, Louisiana, Maine, Maryland, Massachusetts, Michigan, Minnesota, Missouri, Nevada, New Hampshire, New Mexico, New York, North Carolina, Ohio, Pennsylvania, Rhode Island, South Carolina, South Dakota, Texas, Utah, Vermont, Virginia, Washington, West Virginia, Wyoming
21	Florida
22	Kansas
24	California, Montana, Oregon, Wisconsin
Until the full term of the disposition order	Colorado, Hawaii, New Jersey

SOURCE: Howard N. Snyder and Melissa Sickmond. 2006. *Juvenile Offenders and Victims*: 2006 *National Report*. Washington, DC: Department of Justice, Office of Juvenile Justice and Delinquency Prevention.

TRANSFERS TO ADULT COURT

Although a fairly uniform upper age limit for the exercise of original juvenile court jurisdiction in delinquency proceedings has been established in the United States, there is far less uniformity involving lower age limits for juveniles charged with serious offenses, or who have a history of repeated offenses, who may be tried as adults. Transfer to criminal court (alternatively referred to as certification or waiver) refers to the process whereby the jurisdiction over a juvenile delinquent is moved to adult court.

Types of Transfers

There are four primary mechanisms for juvenile transfers to adult criminal courts: judicial waivers, prosecutorial waivers, statutory/legislative waivers, and automatic waivers.

Judicial Waivers

Judicial waiver laws permit—and sometimes even require—juvenile court judges to transfer a juvenile to adult court for criminal prosecution. Cases are filed in juvenile court pursuant to their original jurisdiction. At a special transfer hearing, though, the juvenile court judge can waive jurisdiction based on the facts and circumstances of a particular case, thereby transferring jurisdiction in the case to criminal court.

Judicial waivers are the oldest form of transfers. They are also the most common type of waiver, as 45 states use some form of judicial waiver (Griffin, Addie, Adams, & Firestine, 2011). Only 15 states, however, rely exclusively on judicial waivers; thus, 30 states use more than one mechanism to transfer juveniles to adult courts.

In most states that use judicial waivers, transfers to adult court are discretionary. When judicial waivers are discretionary, the discretion exercised by juvenile court judges is guided by certain standards set forth in statutory law. For example, most states with juvenile waiver laws set a minimum age and a specified type of offense (see Exhibit 17.1). In contrast, a handful of states—Alaska, Kansas, and Washington, for example—allow judicial waiver of juvenile court jurisdiction in nearly all types of delinquency cases.

In 15 states, judicial waivers are presumptive for certain types of offenses. This means that for a class of offenses, the juvenile court judge is expected to transfer cases to adult court barring exceptional circumstances. Often, the burden of proof to show those exceptional circumstances lies with the juvenile, who (usually through counsel) must rebut the presumption that the case should be tried in criminal court (Griffin et al., 2011).

Fifteen states deprive juvenile court judges of discretion over whether to waive certain types of cases because waivers are mandatory for certain offenses. Mandatory judicial waivers function just like statutory waivers (see below), but the juvenile court handles preliminary matters such as appointing counsel and deciding whether the juvenile should be held in detention pending adjudication of the case in criminal court.

Prosecutorial Waivers

For certain offenses in 15 states, prosecutors have the option of filing delinquency petitions in juvenile court or filing criminal charges in adult court. Since either the juvenile courts or the criminal courts may handle such cases depending on the court in which the prosecutor elects to file the case, **prosecutorial waivers** are sometimes called "concurrent jurisdiction waivers."

Because this decision to waive juvenile court jurisdiction is vested within the discretion of the prosecutor, no hearings are held on this determination. And unlike laws that set forth factors to guide the exercise of judicial discretion in judicial waivers, "prosecutorial discretion laws are usually silent regarding standards, protocols, or appropriate considerations for decisionmaking" (Griffin et al., 2011, p. 5). Rather, as with other charging decisions (see Chapter 10), prosecutorial discretion is largely unfettered.

Statutory/Legislative Waivers

Nearly 30 states have enacted laws that grant exclusive jurisdiction over certain crimes to adult court regardless of the age of the offender. These laws effect **statutory/legislative waivers**. As with mandatory judicial waivers, juvenile courts have no power to hear such cases. However, unlike with mandatory judicial waiver cases, even the preliminary aspects of a case are handled in criminal courts. Murder is the most frequent offense subject to statutory waiver, although other violent felonies are included under the laws of some states.

Automatic Waivers

A special form of automatic transfer operates in about 34 states for youth who have already been prosecuted as adults in the past. These so-called **automatic waivers** are built on the premise of "once an adult, always an adult." Automatic waiver laws are generally comprehensive in nature in that they typically require criminal courts to handle all subsequent offenses allegedly committed by a juvenile after an initial transfer to adult court. But some states limit the application of these automatic transfers only to subsequent felonies or to juveniles who have reached the age of 16 (Griffin et al., 2011).

Corrective Mechanisms

At first blush, mandatory judicial waivers, statutory waivers, and automatic waivers may seem particularly harsh insofar as they seemingly prevent any individualized judicial consideration of the transfer decision. About half the states have attempted to compensate for this by enacting some mechanisms that can mitigate the one-size-fits-all approach of such waivers. The most common of these are called **reverse waivers**. This process allows a juvenile to petition the criminal court to transfer jurisdiction to a juvenile court.

Another corrective mechanism some states have enacted is called **blended sentencing**. In the nearly 20 states that have enacted such laws, criminal court judges can impose juvenile dispositions under certainly circumstances, rather than imposing standard criminal sentences.

Use of Waivers

Every year, only a very small proportion of juveniles are transferred to adult court. Indeed, as Figure 17.3 depicts later in this chapter, only about 1 percent of all juvenile delinquency cases are transferred to criminal court. The cases that are

Exhibit 17.1   **MINIMUM AGES AND OFFENSES FOR JUDICIAL TRANSFERS TO ADULT CRIMINAL COURTS**

	Most States Allow Juvenile Court Judges to Waive Juridiction over Certain Cases and Transfer Them to Criminal Court							
State	Any Criminal Offense	Certain Felonies	Capital Crimes	Murder	Certain Person Offenses	Certain Property Offenses	Certain Drug Offenses	Certain Weapon Offenses
Alabama	14							
Alaska	NS							
Arizona		NS						
Arkansas		14	14	14	14			14
California	16							
Colorado		12		12	12			
Delaware	NS							
Dist. of Columbia	16	15						NS
Florida	14							
Georgia	15		13		13			
Hawaii		14		NS				
Idaho	14	NS		NS	NS	NS	NS	
Illinois	13							
Indiana		14		10			16	
Iowa	14							
Kansas	10							
Kentucky		14	14					
Louisiana				14	14			
Maine		NS						
Maryland	15		NS					
Michigan		14						
Minnesota		14						
Mississippi	13							
Missouri		12						
Nevada	14	14						
New Hampshire		15		13	13			
New Jersey	14			14	14	14	14	14
North Carolina		13						

Continued on next page

State	Any Criminal Offense	Certain Felonies	Capital Crimes	Murder	Certain Person Offenses	Certain Property Offenses	Certain Drug Offenses	Certain Weapon Offenses
North Dakota	16				14			
Ohio		14						
Oklahoma		NS						
Oregon		15		NS	NS	15		
Pennsylvania		14						
Rhode Island	NS	16	NS					
South Carolina	16	14		NS	NS		14	14
South Dakota		NS						
Tennessee	16			NS	NS			
Texas		14	14				14	
Utah		14						
Vermont				10	10	10		
Virginia		14						
Washington	NS							
West Virginia		NS		NS	NS	NS	NS	
Wisconsin	15	14		14	14	14	14	
Wyoming	13							

NOTES: Any entry in the column for an offense category means that there is at least one offense in that category for which youth may be transferred from juvenile court to criminal court at the at indicated. The number indicates the youngest possible age at which a juvenile accused of an offense in that category may be waived. "NS" means no age restriction is specified for an offense in that category. Table information is as of the end of the 2009 legislative session.

SOURCE: Patrick Griffin, Sean Addie, Benjamin Adams, and Kathy Firestine. 2011. "Trying Juveniles as Adults: An Analysis of State Transfer Laws and Reporting." Washington, DC: Department of Justice, Office of Juvenile Justice and Delinquency Prevention.

transferred generally involve juveniles accused of murder, armed robbery, or another particularly violent felony.

The number of juveniles transferred to criminal court peaked in 1994 at 13,700 cases but since then has declined by 35 percent to about 8,900 cases a year (Puzzanchera, Adams, & Sickmund, 2011). The decrease in violent crime by juveniles has driven much of this decline (Adams & Addie, 2011). A disproportionate number of juveniles transferred to adult criminal court are male African-Americans (Puzzanchera et al., 2011; Snyder & Sickmund, 2006). Figures like these lead youth advocacy groups like the Center for Children's Law and Policy (2012) to conclude that young people of

color are overrepresented and that states have not done enough to address racial disparities.

How juvenile transfer laws actually operate is complex. For example, transferred juveniles, particularly those convicted of violent offenses, typically receive longer sentences than those sentenced in the juvenile court for similar crimes. However, they may be released on bail for a considerable period of time while they await trial in the criminal court (Meyers, 2005; Redding, 2008; Steiner, 2009).

The Office of Juvenile Justice and Delinquency Prevention evaluated changes in Wisconsin, New Mexico, and Minnesota (Torbet, Griffin, Hurst, & MacKenzie, 2000). The final report highlights the following lessons learned:

COURTS, CONTROVERSY, & REDUCING CRIME

SHOULD JUVENILES BE TRIED AS ADULTS?

Public concerns about juvenile crime, particularly violent crimes committed by juveniles, are often fueled by headlines about juveniles committing brazen or senseless crimes. And at one time the crime statistics seemed to bear out this public concern. Beginning in the mid-1980s the juvenile crime rate increased, with juvenile arrests more than doubling in the span of a decade or so (Cannon, 1997). What attracted the most public attention is the increase in violent juvenile crime, which shot up 93 percent (as compared with a 22 percent increase in property crimes).

To some observers, a juvenile crime wave was on the horizon. Newspaper headlines proclaimed, "Youth Violence Explosion Likely to Worsen" (Bass, 1995) and "Violent Children Straining Limit of Justice System" (Hallinan, 1993). These concerns were bolstered by the realization that the juvenile population would increase from 27 million to 39 million by 2010.

But these dire predictions failed to materialize. Beginning in 1995, arrests for violent juvenile crimes declined significantly (Puzzanchera and Adams, 2011; "Statistical Briefing Book," 2009). Thus, what some had predicted to be a juvenile crime wave now appears to have been only a ripple.

The commonly held belief that juvenile delinquents are becoming younger as a group and committing more serious crimes at earlier ages than in the past does not hold up to scrutiny. The Office of Juvenile Justice and Delinquency Prevention (1996) compared the characteristics of young offenders arrested in the 1990s with those arrested in 1980 and concluded that serious and violent juvenile offenders were not significantly younger than those of 10 or 15 years earlier.

But downward trends in juvenile crime have apparently had little impact on the public dialogue. The U.S. Congress and numerous states have responded to public perceptions that violent juvenile crime is a growing menace. The typical legislative response has been to make it easier to transfer juveniles. Since the 1990s, for example, at least 40 states and the District of Columbia have changed their transfer statutes to make it easier to waive juveniles to adult courts (Griffin et al., 2011; Snyder & Sickmund, 2006). Some of these efforts involve lowering the age of transfer. Others involve increasing the list of crimes for which juveniles may be transferred. Others seek to mandate transfers in certain situations.

But do these laws work? A review of the major studies on this topic concludes that the answer is no. In terms of specific deterrence (stopping a particular person from committing another crime), several major studies find higher recidivism rates among juveniles convicted for violent offenses in criminal court as compared with similar offenders tried in juvenile court. The limited literature on general deterrence (deterring others from committing crime) is somewhat inconsistent but tentatively suggests that transfer laws do not deter crime (Redding, 2008).

Even though the number of juveniles in the United States is increasing, the percentage of cases being transferred to adult court is declining. One reason is cost—faced with a major budget deficit linked to the 2008 recession, many states are saving money by closing older, razor-wire juvenile detention centers (Richmond, 2010). Another is the 2005 Supreme Court decision in *Roper v. Simmons* that highlighted the general difference between young juveniles and older ones (Secret, 2011).

What do you think? Should juveniles be prosecuted as adults? If you answer yes, under what conditions should juveniles be prosecuted as adults, and for what crimes? In what ways are your standards similar to or different from existing practices? If you answer no, what would you suggest to strengthen rehabilitative efforts in juvenile court? In what ways are your recommendations similar to or different from existing practices? In forming your answer, also consider the following question: Do you think that the recent decrease in juvenile crime, particularly violent crime, is temporary or long term?

- A disconnect exists between legislative intent and the actual implementation of new laws.

- The new sentencing laws encourage plea bargaining.

- Judicial and prosecutorial discretion expand.

- Local application of new laws varies widely.

- New sentencing laws have a disproportionate impact on minorities.

Recent research tends to confirm these findings (Griffin et al., 2011). Stated another way, alterations of laws on the books do not necessarily produce the intended changes in law in action.

Public pressure to try juveniles as adults is spawned by concerns over violent juvenile crimes. Reality, though, does not match the expectations of elected officials or the public. (See "Courts, Controversy, & Reducing Crime: Should Juveniles Be Tried as Adults?")

DUE PROCESS IN JUVENILE COURTS

Juvenile court statutes set forth two standards for deciding the appropriate disposition for a child: the best interests of the child and the best interests of the community. Because the concept of the juvenile court was to aid—not punish—children, the due process guarantees of the adult criminal court were absent. Procedures were more administrative than adversarial, stressing the informal, private, and noncombative handling of cases. It is for this reason that juvenile cases are often captioned *In re,* a Latin phrase meaning "in the matter of." But at what point do juveniles obtain benefits from the special procedures applicable to them that offset the disadvantage of denial of due process?

Key Court Decisions

The nature of the juvenile court process remained unchanged until the 1960s. When the Warren Court began to scrutinize procedures in adult criminal courts, its attention turned also to juvenile courts. In a groundbreaking decision, the Supreme Court held in *In re Gault* (1967) that the due process

clause of the Fourteenth Amendment applied to juvenile court proceedings. The court emphasized that "under our Constitution the condition of being a boy does not justify a kangaroo court." The opinion specified that juveniles have: (1) the right to notice, (2) the right to counsel, (3) the right to confront witnesses, and (4) privilege against self-incrimination. (See "Case Close-Up: *In re Gault* and Due Process in Juvenile Courts.") Three years later, the Court ruled that when a juvenile is charged with an act that would be a crime if committed by an adult, then every element of that criminal act must be proved beyond a reasonable doubt (*In re Winship,* 1970).

The *Gault* and *Winship* decisions point to the constant tension within the juvenile court system between those who think that children should be given all the due process guarantees accorded adults and those who reason that children must be handled in a less adversarial, more treatment-oriented manner so that legal procedures will not interfere with efforts to secure the justice that is in the children's best interests.

Gault and *Winship* signaled that the juvenile court must become a real court and its procedures must be regularized in accordance with constitutional requirements. Juvenile courts, however, afford far fewer due process rights than their adult counterparts. Following the two landmark cases, however, the more conservative Burger and Rehnquist Courts were less enthusiastic about extending due process (see the "Key Developments" feature on page 485). Juvenile delinquents, for example, have no constitutional right to a trial by jury (*McKeiver v. Pennsylvania,* 1971), and preventive detention is allowed (*Schall v. Martin,* 1984).

In recent years, the Court has wrestled with the difficult question of the appropriate punishment for juveniles who commit serious crimes. In a path-breaking decision, the Court held that the death penalty may not be imposed on offenders who commit crimes before they are 18 years old (*Roper v. Simmons,* 2005). Applying the same logic, the Court held that sentencing juvenile offenders to life without the possibility of parole violates the Eighth Amendment's ban on cruel and unusual punishment, but only for crimes that did not involve killings (*Graham v. Florida,* 2010).

CASE CLOSE-UP

IN RE GAULT AND DUE PROCESS IN JUVENILE COURTS

The sheriff of Gila County, Arizona, took 15-year-old Gerald Francis Gault into custody for making a lewd phone call to a neighbor. As to what was actually said, the Supreme Court would only say, "It will suffice for purposes of this opinion to say that the remarks or questions put to her were of the irritatingly offensive, adolescent, sex variety."

Gault was transported to the Children's Detention Home, and no effort was made to contact his parents. Over the next couple of weeks, several brief hearings were held, but no record exists of what happened. What is known, though, is that there is some dispute about whether Gerald Gault actually made the phone call. According to one version, he dialed the number, but his friend did the talking. Whatever may have transpired, the hearing would not be able to determine, because the witness was never present.

After another brief hearing, Gerald was found to be a juvenile delinquent and committed to the State Industrial School "for the period of his minority [that is, until 21] unless sooner discharged by due process of law." This harsh sentence was probably influenced by the fact that at the time, he was on 6 months' probation as a result of having been in the company of another boy who had stolen a woman's purse.

It was the lack of procedural regularity in cases like this one that concerned the American Civil Liberties Union (ACLU). Through a series of complex maneuvers, the ACLU was able to get the case before the Arizona Supreme Court and then the U.S. Supreme Court (Manfredi, 1998).

In deciding Gault, the Court was essentially writing on a blank slate concerning juveniles. A year earlier, the Court had ever so tentatively imposed some due process requirements for juveniles accused of serious felonies (Kent v. United States, 1966). But now the Court was ready to confront head-on the basic question about juvenile courts: Does the Bill of Rights apply to juveniles, or are children's best interests protected by informal and paternalistic hearings? Justice Abe Fortas's opinion underscored the lack of procedural regularity, stressing that "Due process of law is the primary and indispensable foundation of individual freedom."

At the same time, the opinion in Gault supports the purposes of the juvenile court: A juvenile court proceeding is one "in which a fatherly judge touched the heart and conscience of the erring youth by talking over his problems, by paternal advice and admonition" to save him from a downward career. The goodwill and compassion of the juvenile court will not, however, be diminished by due process of law. In one bold stroke, In re Gault carved out the following four new constitutional rights in juvenile proceedings:

- Juveniles have the right to timely notice of charges. In the future, parents must be informed that their child has been taken into custody, and written charges must be filed.

- Juveniles have the right to counsel. Following Gideon, the Court held that juveniles, like adults, have the right to have an attorney present during the proceedings, and if they are indigent, to have a lawyer appointed.

- Juveniles have the right against self-incrimination. Miranda, decided by the Court just a year before, greatly extended the right for adults, and many of the same strictures were now extended to juveniles.

- Juveniles have the right to confront and cross-examine complainants and other witnesses.

The Court's opinion in Gault was supported by seven justices and partially by an eighth. Only Justice Potter Stewart dissented outright. He viewed the decision as "a long step backwards into the 19th century." The danger he saw was that abolishing the flexibility and informality of the juvenile courts would cause children to be treated as adults in courts.

The Court continued the trend of holding that delinquent youth cannot be punished in the same manner as adult criminals when it decided the companion cases of Miller v. Alabama and Jackson v. Hobbs in 2012. In those cases, the Court held that automatic sentences of life in prison without parole for juveniles who commit crimes that would be capital offenses if committed by an adult constituted cruel and unusual punishment. Rather, the offender's youthful age must be considered.

Important Congressional Acts

Congress has also imposed key mandates on the juvenile justice process. The Juvenile Justice and Delinquency Prevention Act of 1974 mandated deinstitutionalization of status offenders by stating that juveniles not charged with acts that would

be crimes for adults shall not be jailed. Similarly, the law specifies that juveniles charged with criminal acts shall not be detained in any institution in which they have contact with adult inmates (Snyder & Sickmund, 2006). There is little doubt that this law has fundamentally changed the way our nation deals with troubled youth.

KEY DEVELOPMENTS CONCERNING JUVENILE COURTS

Ex parte Crouse (1839)	Philadelphia Supreme Court uses term *parens patriae*.
Illinois Juvenile Court Act (1899)	First juvenile court created in Cook County, Illinois.
Juvenile Court Act (1938)	Federal government adopts principles of juvenile court movement.
Wyoming (1945)	Last state to create a juvenile court.
Kent v. United States (1966)	Court establishes conditions of waiver to criminal court.
In re Gault (1967)	Juveniles are entitled to due process guarantees.
In re Winship (1970)	Proof must be established "beyond a reasonable doubt" in classifying juveniles as delinquent.
McKeiver v. Pennsylvania (1971)	Juvenile delinquents are not entitled to a jury trial.
Juvenile Justice and Delinquency Prevention Act (1974)	Mandates deinstitutionalization of status offenders.
Schall v. Martin (1984)	Court departs from trend of increasing juvenile rights, upholding the general notion of *parens patriae*.
Thompson v. Oklahoma (1988)	Execution of a person under the age of 16 at the time of his or her crime is unconstitutional.
Stanford v. Kentucky (1989)	It is not unconstitutional to apply the death penalty to persons who were convicted of murder when they were 17.
Roper v. Simmons (2005)	The Eighth Amendment forbids the imposition of the death penalty on offenders who were under the age of 18 when their crimes were committed (reversing *Thompson v. Oklahoma* and *Stanford v. Kentucky*).
Graham v. Florida (2010)	Sentencing juvenile offenders to life without the possibility of parole violates the Eighth Amendment's ban on cruel and unusual punishment, but only for crimes that did not involve killings.
J.D.B. v. North Carolina (2011)	A child's age is part of the custody analysis of *Miranda*.
Miller v. Alabama (2012) and *Jackson v. Hobbs* (2012)	Imposing a mandatory sentence of life without possibility of parole on an offender who was 14 at the time he committed capital murder violates the Eighth Amendment's Cruel and Unusual Punishment Clause.

Congressional mandates, coupled with *Gault* and other Supreme Court rulings, have had a marked effect on juvenile-court procedures. "Today's juvenile court is constantly discarding many of its traditional and fundamental characteristics, and it is adopting many of the features customarily associated with criminal court" (Sanborn, 1993; see also, Moriearty, 2008). Indeed, as juvenile courts have become more formal institutions of law, the benevolent *parens patriae* character that distinguished it from the adult criminal system has eroded. In recognition of this fact, the highest court in the state of Kansas took a radical step in 2008 by declaring that the rationale upon which the U.S. Supreme Court's decision in *McKeiver* was premised (namely benevolence, parental concern, rehabilitation, and sympathy) was no longer valid. Thus, the Kansas Supreme Court ruled that juveniles have a constitutional right to a trial by jury not only under their own state constitution, but also under the Sixth and Fourteenth Amendments to the U.S. Constitution (*In re L.M.*, 2008). It remains to be seen whether other states or the U.S. Supreme Court will follow Kansas's lead or whether the *In re L.M.* decision will be invalidated. Regardless of which path is ultimately taken, it is clear that the juvenile court system in the United States has changed dramatically in philosophy and operation from its original form.

COURTROOM WORK GROUP

At first glance, members of juvenile courtroom work groups are similar to those found in adult courts—prosecutors bring charges, defense attorneys attempt to get the best deal possible for their clients, and judges decide matters that others have not successfully negotiated. These parallels, though, can be deceiving because the tasks of juvenile and adult courts are not the same. More so than courts dealing with adults accused of violating the law, juvenile courts grant judges and other officials unusually wide latitude in making discretionary decisions intended to "individualize justice." Moreover, although the Supreme Court has imposed minimal due process requirements, juvenile courts remain judicial bodies in which informal processing still dominates.

Shared norms are the hallmark of courtroom work groups, as Chapter 5 argued. In assessing the worth of a case, members of the juvenile court work group incorporate many of the same factors as those in adult courts—the severity of the offense and the prior record of the offender. The juvenile-court tradition of individualized treatment, though, encourages the consideration of another important factor—the characteristics of the family. The control the parent or parents have over the youth is a major consideration in deciding the disposition of the case (Fader, Harris, Jones, & Poulin, 2001). Similarly, members of the juvenile-court work group also consider family structure. Youths whose families are perceived to be dysfunctional were much more likely to receive an out-of-home placement than youths whose families were not perceived to be dysfunctional (Rodriguez, Smith, & Zatz, 2009).

The legally trained members of the courtroom work group rely heavily on the professional judgments of nonlawyers in assessing both the background of the youth and the characteristics of the family. This affects the juvenile court work group in a critical way. Whereas in adult court the skills of lawyers are of fundamental importance, in juvenile court they are secondary. Judges, lawyers, and defense attorneys have been trained to interpret and apply the law, but these skills provide little help in making the key decisions in juvenile court cases. Instead, social workers, psychologists, and counselors have been trained to assess the child's problem and devise a treatment plan.

Judges

Judges are the central authority in the juvenile court system. More so than their counterparts in criminal court, they have wide discretion over detention, the adjudicatory hearing, disposition, and other matters. Depending on the size of the court and the rotation system, an individual judge may spend only a little time or a great deal of time in juvenile court.

In many jurisdictions, assignment to the juvenile court is not a highly sought-after appointment. Although some judges like the challenges of juvenile court, to others it is a dead-end assignment. Judges who specialize in juvenile-court matters are often those who enjoy the challenges of working with people rather than those who are intrigued by nuances of legal interpretations. But even judges deeply committed to the juvenile system may seek rotation to other sections to advance their judicial careers (Krisberg & Austin, 1993).

Hearing Officers

In many jurisdictions, judges are assisted by *hearing officers* (sometimes known as *referees, masters*, or *commissioners*). Typically, hearing officers are attorneys appointed by the court to serve on a full- or part-time basis to hear a range of juvenile-court matters. These hearing officers enter findings and recommendations that require confirmation by the judge to become an order.

Prosecutors

Over the past several decades, the power and influence of the prosecutor have grown in U.S. courthouses (Chapter 6). Rising crime rates, coupled with Supreme Court decisions requiring more due process, have contributed to the growing role of the prosecutor in juvenile courts (Kupchik, 2006; Shine & Price, 1992).

Prosecutors now dominate the intake-processing stage in most jurisdictions. At times, intake officers make the initial decision and the prosecutor later reviews that determination. But increasingly, prosecutors are the chief decision makers (with input from others, of course). Similarly, prosecutors, more so than judges, are typically the ones who negotiate the disposition of all but the most serious juvenile delinquency cases.

Although the role of the prosecutor's office has increased in juvenile court, an assignment to a section of juvenile court is not a sought-after promotion. On the contrary, the newly hired assistant DAs fresh out of law school tend to be the ones assigned to juvenile court. Thus, much like judges, assistant DAs typically hope for a promotion to a felony unit, where they can practice "real law," trying and convicting "real criminals" (Kupchik, 2006).

Defense Attorneys

In re Gault (1967) held that juveniles were entitled to representation by defense counsel in delinquency proceedings. Yet, defense attorneys play a secondary role in the juvenile court (Burruss & Kempf-Leonard, 2002). Studies reveal great disparities in the number of juveniles who are actually represented by a lawyer, ranging from a low of 15 percent to a high of 95 percent (Guevara, Herz, & Spohn, 2008). Contrary to what some may intuitively believe, studies reveal that youths represented by counsel actually receive a harsher disposition than those who appear in court without an attorney (Guevara et al., 2008), a fact that might explain why so many juveniles waive their right to counsel, thereby keeping proceedings more informal. Yet, being unrepresented by counsel may compromise the due process rights guaranteed by *Gault* (Puritz, Burrell, Schwartz, Soler, & Warboys, 1995; Young, 2000). The American Bar Association has been working with other advocacy groups to ensure that juvenile offenders are competently represented by attorneys with "particularized training in youth development and juvenile law" and who are assisted by interdisciplinary support services (Shepherd, 2003, p. 27). Minnesota has mandated appointment of counsel in juvenile cases, but law in action lags significantly behind law on the books (Feld & Schaefer, 2010).

Lack of representation by a lawyer partially reflects the nature of the caseload—many of the cases are minor. As we saw with adults in misdemeanor court, few have lawyers because the penalties are so light. The same holds true for juveniles—most cases will receive some form of probation, supervision, and/or restitution irrespective of whether a lawyer is, or is not, present.

The role of the defense attorney is further limited by the informality of juvenile courts. In contrast to adult court, juvenile-court proceedings place little emphasis on the privilege against self-incrimination. From the initial police contact (and often arrest) through the intake proceedings, juveniles are urged to tell the truth. It should be no surprise, therefore, to learn that fewer than 10 percent of juveniles assert their right to remain silent (Grisso, 1981).

Defense attorneys, when they are present at all, become involved after their client has cooperated with police and prosecutor, and perhaps the probation officer and judge as well. For the cases in which there is only weak evidence, the defense strategy is to seek a dismissal. For the vast majority of cases in which there is strong evidence, defense attorneys negotiate, based on the norms of the work group, the best possible deal for their client. Since most of the cases are, by adult standards, relatively minor, the dispositions reached tend to be on the lenient side—primarily probation, restitution, and community service.

Probation Officers

From the beginning, probation officers were a key part of juvenile court. In fact, probation in adult court traces its heritage to these developments. Juvenile probation takes several forms. In some states, probation officers are part of the judicial branch (either locally or statewide); in other jurisdictions, they are part of the executive branch (either locally or statewide).

As in adult court, probation officers in juvenile court conduct background reports and supervise those placed on probation. What is strikingly different, though, is the stage at which they become involved. In adult courts, probation officers are brought into the process after the defendant has entered a plea of guilty or been found guilty. In juvenile courts, they become involved at the early stages of the process. Thus, the probation officer, not a judge or prosecutor, is often the first court official to have contact with the child. Indeed, it is often the probation officer who recommends an informal disposition to the case. Moreover, in more serious cases, the probation officer's recommendation, along with the social worker's, most often becomes the order of the court.

STEPS OF THE JUVENILE COURT PROCESS

From the perspective of law on the books, the steps of the juvenile court process resemble those for adult courts. Although the terminology is slightly different, juveniles accused of violating the law appear to be treated the same as adults in the same situation. From the perspective of law in action, however, the steps of the juvenile court process are strikingly different from their adult counterparts. More than mere differences in terminology, what makes the processing of juveniles so distinctive is

the heavy emphasis on informal decision making. The vast majority of decisions are reached not by lawyers and defendants standing before a judge in open court but rather by a juvenile, a parent, and a probation officer sitting around a desk discussing what will happen next.

Delinquency (Crime)

How many crimes are committed by juveniles (as opposed to adults) is impossible to determine with any great precision. As discussed in Chapter 10, the FBI's Uniform Crime Reports are based on crimes reported to the police, and most crime victims have no way of knowing the age of the person responsible. Juvenile crime increased steadily beginning in 1985, but this increase declined dramatically after 1995. Two important features related to juvenile crime are worth noting:

- Crimes against juveniles are less likely to be reported to the police.
- Juveniles are 2.5 times as likely as adults to be victims of serious violent crime (Snyder & Sickmund, 2006).

Summons (Arrest)

A summons is a legal document requiring an individual (in this case, a juvenile) to appear in court at a certain time and on a certain date. Although the summons is the official term used in juvenile court, it is informally referred to as an arrest. In the latest year for which data are available (Puzzanchera & Adams, 2011), law enforcement agencies in the United States made an estimated 1.9 million arrests of persons under 18, a number that has deceased over the years. Overall, juveniles were involved in 12 percent of all violent-crime index arrests and 17 percent of all property-crime index arrests. Juvenile arrest statistics include two noteworthy features:

- 30 percent of juvenile arrests were of females, and the female proportion of arrests has grown in recent years (Puzzanchera & Adams, 2011; Shaffner, 2006; Zahn, Hawkins, Chiancone, & Whitworth, 2008).
- Juvenile arrests disproportionately involve minorities.

LAW ON THE BOOKS VS. LAW IN ACTION
STEPS OF THE JUVENILE COURT PROCESS

	LAW ON THE BOOKS	LAW IN ACTION
Crime	*Delinquency:* Acts or conduct in violation of criminal laws. *Status offense:* Behavior that is considered an offense only when committed by a juvenile.	Juveniles are more likely than adults to be victims of violent crime. Poor, young, minority males are disproportionately at risk of being victims of violent crime.
Arrest	*Summons:* A legal document ordering an individual to appear in court at a certain time on a certain date.	Some 1.9 million juveniles are arrested yearly. Juveniles are arrested primarily for property offenses.
Initial appearance	*Initial hearing:* An often informal hearing during which an intake decision is made.	There are 2 million juvenile cases a year. Fifty seven percent of juvenile filings involve delinquency.
Bail	*Detention:* Holding a youth in custody before case disposition.	There are 81,000 offenders in public and private juvenile detention facilities.
Charging	*Intake decision:* The decision made by juvenile court that results in the case being handled either informally at the intake level or more formally and scheduled for an adjudicatory hearing. *Nonpetitioned:* Cases handled informally by duly authorized court personnel. *Petition:* A document filed in juvenile court alleging that a juvenile is delinquent or a status offender and asking that the court assume jurisdiction over the juvenile.	Intake decisions are often informal. Courtroom work group norms govern decision making. Forty-five percent of juvenile delinquency cases are handled informally (nonpetitioned). Fifty-five percent of juvenile delinquency court cases are handled formally. Older juveniles with more serious charges are more likely to be handled formally.
Preliminary hearing	*Conference:* Proceeding during which the suspect is informed of rights and a disposition decision may be reached.	In the vast majority of petitioned cases, the juvenile admits guilt during the conference.
Grand jury	Not applicable in juvenile proceedings.	Few juvenile cases are transferred to adult court, where grand jury right may attach.
Arraignment	Occurs during the conference.	Fifty-five percent of juvenile delinquency cases are handled formally (petitioned).
Evidence	Juveniles have the same constitutional protections as adults with regard to interrogation and unreasonable search and seizure.	Police gathering of evidence is very rarely contested.
Plea bargaining	*Plea bargaining:* Formal and informal discussions resulting in juvenile's admitting guilt.	Even more than in adult court, dispositions in juvenile court are the product of negotiations.

© Cengage Learning

Continued on next page

Continued from previous page

Trial	*Adjudicatory hearing:* Hearing to determine whether a youth is guilty or not guilty.	Adjudicatory hearings are more informal than adult trials.
Sentencing	*Disposition:* A court decision on what will happen to a youth who has not been found innocent.	The disposition is often referred to as a treatment plan.
	Placement: Cases in which juveniles are placed in a residential facility or otherwise removed from their homes.	More than 100,000 juveniles are placed in residential facilities each year.
	Probation: Cases in which youths are placed under informal/voluntary or formal/court-ordered supervision.	More than 385,000 youths receive court supervision each year.
	Dismissal: Cases dismissed (including those warned, counseled, and released) with no further disposition anticipated.	Even case dismissals may include a treatment plan or restitution.
	Other: Miscellaneous dispositions including fines, restitution, and community service.	Teen courts are a modern version of other dispositions.
Appeal	*Appeal:* Request that a higher court review the decision of the lower court.	Appeals are very rare in juvenile proceedings.

Intake (Initial Hearing)

Delinquency cases begin with a referral. Arrests by law enforcement personnel are by far the biggest source of these referrals—82 percent in a typical year. Referrals, though, may originate from several other sources; for example, some juvenile court cases stem from petitions filed by teachers, neighbors, merchants, or even parents unable to control their children. But mainly they follow after a juvenile has been arrested by the police.

These arrests and other referrals produce about 2 million juvenile court cases every year. Best estimates indicate that 57 percent of juvenile filings involve delinquency, 26 percent involve dependency cases, and 12 percent status offenses (see Figure 17.1).

Juvenile court cases have decreased significantly in recent years even though the juvenile population is growing. Indeed, the National Center for State Courts estimates that over the past decade juvenile caseloads decreased by 17 percent

in the population adjusted rate (LaFountain et al., 2011).

Soon after referral to juvenile court, an initial hearing (sometimes called a "preliminary inquiry") is held. As with much of the terminology of juvenile court, *hearing* is often a misnomer. A hearing implies a formal setting in front of a judge, but more typically it is an informal exchange involving the police officer, probation officer, child, and parent.

Detention Hearing

Police make the first detention decision shortly after taking the juvenile into custody. Typically, the police release the youth to the custody of his or her parents (or guardians). If the crime is serious, however, the police may detain the youth in a police lockup or local jail. In an earlier era, juveniles were held in the same facilities as adult offenders, but no longer. Federal law mandates that juveniles be held in facilities separated by sight and sound from detention facilities for adults. In many communities, the number of cells is limited, so even serious violators may be returned to the streets.

A second detention decision may occur after the juvenile has been referred to the juvenile court. Intake personnel review the case and determine whether the youth should be released to the parents or detained. Juveniles may be detained if they are thought to be dangerous to themselves or others if released. Statutes in most states now mandate that if the juvenile is to be detained, a detention hearing must be held before a judge or other hearing officer within 24 to 48 hours of arrest.

In a typical year, one out of five juveniles is detained prior to the adjudicatory hearing (Snyder & Sickmund, 2006). On any given day, 81,000 youths are held in public and private juvenile detention facilities (Hockenberry, Sickmund, & Sladky, 2011). Overall non-Whites are more likely to be detained (Armstrong & Rodriguez, 2005).

Petition

During the initial hearing, a decision is made not only about detention but also about whether the case will be handled formally (petition) or informally (nonpetitioned). This decision is most often referred to as the **intake decision** (the juvenile equivalent of the charging decision for adults accused of violating the criminal law).

As Figure 17.3 shows, about 44 percent of delinquency cases are handled informally (termed **nonpetitioned cases**). An informal process is used when the decision makers (police, probation officers, intake workers, and prosecutors) believe that accountability and rehabilitation can be achieved without the use of formal court intervention. Informal sanctions are voluntary. At times, they involve no more than a warning and counseling, but more often they consist of voluntary probation, restitution, and community service.

Juvenile cases that are handled formally are referred to as **petition** cases (or petitioned). Figure 17.3 indicates that approximately 56 percent of delinquency cases and 59 percent of status offense cases receive such treatment. Intake

officers are more likely to petition in delinquency cases if:

- Juveniles are older and have longer court histories.
- The delinquency is serious (involves violence, for example).

Conference

The **conference** is roughly equivalent to a preliminary hearing in an adult proceeding. The more minor the transgression, the more likely the conference will be held at the same time as the initial hearing and the detention hearing. In more serious matters, particularly if the decision has been made to file a petition, the conference is more likely to be held in closed court.

During the conference, the judge informs the respondent of the charges in the petition. The person is also informed of constitutional protections, including the right to counsel, the right to free counsel, the right to subpoena witnesses for the defense, and the opportunity to cross-examine prosecution witnesses.

Vast numbers of juveniles admit to their offense during the conference, waiving the right to counsel and the right to trial. Others request counsel, adjourn to the hallway of the courthouse, and after 5 or 10 minutes with an attorney come back before the judge and admit their offense (Rubin, 1989).

Evidence: Gathering and Suppressing

Challenges to how the police gathered evidence play a very minor role in juvenile cases. The presumption is that the child is in trouble (with the juvenile delinquency charge an indicator of that trouble). This presumption makes it difficult to challenge evidence gathering—the judge might conclude that there is insufficient evidence to find the child a delinquent but still enough to conclude that the child is in need of supervision. Moreover, the informal nature of the entire proceeding discourages legal challenges. The general absence of defense attorneys likewise discourages raising issues associated with *Mapp* and *Miranda*. However, as Chapter 11 should make clear, the protections of the Fourth, Fifth, and Sixth

Amendment certainly apply to juveniles. Moreover, as cases like *J.D.B. v. North Carolina* (2011) illustrate, law enforcement officers must take special care to make sure that they are honoring the constitutional rights of juvenile suspects.

Plea Bargaining

The informality of juvenile court makes it somewhat difficult to focus on plea bargaining as a distinct phase, because often it is not. Rather, the discretion that runs throughout the juvenile court process is really plea bargaining by a different name (Dougherty, 1988; Kupchik, 2006).

Efforts to negotiate the matter typically begin during the intake process. Parent, child, and probation officer discuss the matter and often arrive at a solution satisfactory to all parties. Thus, a significant proportion of the 44 percent of juvenile delinquency cases that are nonpetitioned clearly represent what in adult court would be labeled as plea bargaining.

Efforts to negotiate a settlement continue after a petition is filed. As Figure 17.3 underscores, 38 percent of petitioned delinquency cases are in the "nonadjudicated" category. Yet, approximately 35 percent of juveniles not adjudicated delinquent are nonetheless sanctioned, representing another substantial percentage of cases that are plea bargained. Figure 17.3 demonstrates that similar resolutions by plea bargains (albeit involving lower numbers) occur in status offense cases.

Adjudicatory Hearing

The **adjudicatory hearing** is equivalent to the trial in adult court. The purpose is to determine whether the allegations contained in the petition are supported by a "preponderance of the evidence" (for status offenses) or "beyond a legal doubt" (for juvenile delinquency).

One of the key changes growing out of the due process revolution associated with *In re Gault* is that juveniles have the right to present evidence in favor, which includes cross-examining the government's witnesses and subpoenaing defense witnesses. The juvenile also maintains the privilege against self-incrimination.

Figure 17.3 illustrates that 61 percent of petitioned delinquency cases and 59 percent of status offense cases are **adjudicated**. This seems like a high "trial" rate, but a closer look indicates that this is not the case. Adjudicatory hearings are much less formal than adult trials. This is due in part to the lack of juries (except in a few exceptional cases in a handful of states). The rules of evidence Chapter 13 are designed to keep certain information from lay jurors lest they place undue emphasis on some information. But since there are usually no juries, these rules have considerably less applicability. Of course, if the holding of *In re L.M.* (2008) is adopted beyond the state of Kansas, the formality of juvenile proceedings across the county will grow exponentially.

Disposition

The more serious the crime and/or the longer the juvenile has been in trouble with the law, the more likely it is that a formal probation report will be prepared. Like its adult counterpart, the probation report (sometimes called the "predisposition report") is prepared by the probation officer; it is based on interviews with the juvenile, the parents, school officials, and others. The report chronicles the juvenile's prior history with the court and also may estimate the economic harm suffered by the victim. Finally, the report makes a **disposition** recommendation.

The most common disposition is a **dismissal**. Cases dismissed (including those warned, counseled, and released), with no further disposition anticipated, are most likely to occur among cases that are handled informally.

The second most common disposition is **probation**. Probation allows the juvenile to be released into the custody of a parent or guardian while being placed under the supervision of a juvenile probation officer. The range of probation dispositions is quite broad. Some youths participate in informal/voluntary probation with low levels of monitoring, while others are monitored more closely under terms of formal, court-ordered supervision. Many juveniles on probation are ordered to undergo some form of training, education, or counseling as part of the terms of their probation.

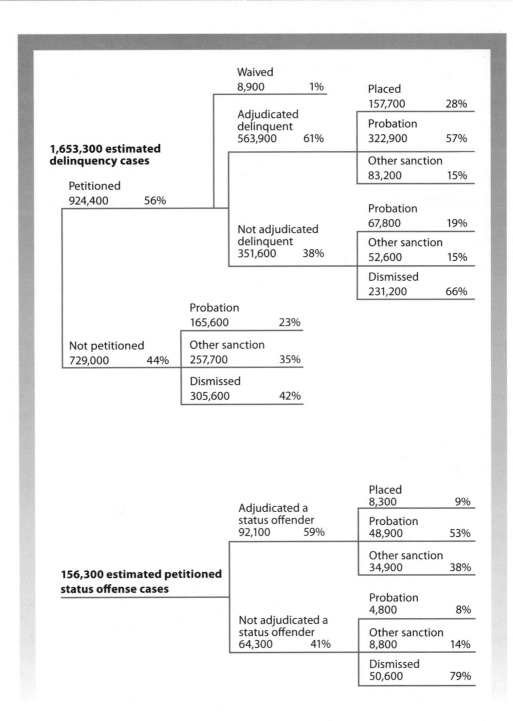

Figure 17.3 ■ **Juvenile Court Processing of Delinquency and Status Offenses Cases**
Cases are categorized by their most severe or restrictive sanction. Numbers may not add
to totals because of rounding.

SOURCE: Charles Puzzanchera, Benjamin Adams, and Melissa Sickmund. 2011. *Juvenile Court Statistics*, 2008. Pittsburgh: National Center for Juvenile Justice.

COURTS, LAW, & MEDIA

DOG POUND (2010)

This hard-hitting drama depicts the experiences of three teenagers sentenced to the Enola Vale Correctional Facility, a juvenile facility in Montana. Davis (Shane Kippel) is an affable and somewhat vulnerable 16-year old convicted of drug possession with intent to sell. Shy and quiet Angel (Mateo Morales) is a 15-year-old sentenced for both assault and car theft. And the dangerous 17-year-old Butch (Adam Butcher) is serving time at Enola Vale after having viciously beaten a correctional officer at another facility.

Officer Goodyear (played by Lawrence Banks), is the stern, but fair prison guard who tries to convince the three boys to abide by the rules while serving their time so that they can earn early release. Although Goodyear is largely well-intentioned, he and his fellow guards are unable to make a real difference for many of the kids under his supervision. In fact, Dog Pound reveals a sense of hopelessness for correctional staff like Goodyear, seemingly fighting a losing battle against the nature of the young men they are trying to reform. Indeed, drug use runs rampant and psychological terror and violence—especially at the hands of inmate bullies—rule the day. One particularly sadistic inmate, Banks (Taylor Poulin) leads a campaign of violence against the new inmates. As the toughest and most criminally experienced of the three, Butch assumes the role of protector over his new friends. But Butch is brutally beaten, just as the other boys were. Davis gets raped and eventually kills himself. This leads Butch to start a riot. The guards use riot gear and tear gas in an attempt to end the violence, but turn violent themselves. In fact, Butch attempts to escape during the pandemonium, but is taken down violently by the guards.

Although a fictional movie based on Alan Clarke's British movie Scum (1979), Dog Pound delivers an authentic look at life inside a juvenile detention facility, doing so, in part, by the director (Kim Chapiron) having cast actual inmates in many of the film's roles. The movie does not really have a plot, per se. Rather, it gives the appearance of being a documentary-style video diary of the dreadful life inside the walls of a particularly tough juvenile detention center. In the end, the movie is less concerned with the oppressive existence of institutional life than it is with the type of predatory characters who find ways to survive within its gloomy, regimented confines. This dark view of teen convicts led a reviewer for Variety magazine to write, "The characters seem to possess little potential for compassion, empathy or insight that the film could be a PSA [Public Service Announcement] promoting life without parole for juvenile offenders" (Anderson, 2010).

Watching Dog Pound is both uncomfortable and disturbing. After viewing the movie, what are your thoughts about confining teenage boys to such detention facilities? Do you think their young age should serve to mitigate the seriousness of their offenses? Might alternatives to incarceration be a more viable sentence for offenders like Davis and Angel?

What do you make of Anderson's comment about the movie serving as a strong argument to lock up youth like Butch and Banks for life? Such a sentence would be unconstitutional under Graham v. Florida (2009), since neither character committed a homicide. But what about a sentence of life in prison for juveniles who kill? In the companion cases of Miller v. Alabama (2012) and Jackson v. Hobbs (2012), the Court ruled that the mandatory imposition of such a punishment was unconstitutional. Both cases involved automatic life sentences on boys who killed when they were 14 years old. But what if the sentences had not been mandatory? Do you think that a court, in exercising its discretion, should be able to impose a sentence of life without parole on a juvenile who commits a homicide at such a young age? Explain your reasoning.

As depicted in Figure 17.3, in approximately 9 percent of status offense cases and 28 percent of cases in which the juvenile is adjudicated a delinquent, the youth is ordered into some formal **placement**. Consistent with the nonpunishment orientation of the juvenile process, juveniles are not sentenced to prison, but rather are placed in a residential facility for delinquents or status offenders, or otherwise removed from their homes and placed in a training school, camp, ranch, or group home. However, as the "Courts, Law, & Media" feature on the next page, regarding the movie *Dog Pound* explores, life in a juvenile correctional facility has come to resemble life in prisons in spite of the supposed different philosophy of the juvenile justice system.

The most recent statistics indicate that 81,015 juvenile offenders are in juvenile residential facility, which represents a 12-percent decline from just a few years before (Hockenberry et al., 2011).

Finally, a significant number of dispositions that do not fall under the previous three categories are referred to simply as other dispositions. These include fines, restitution, community service, and referrals outside the court for services with minimal or no further court involvement anticipated.

In making disposition decisions, juvenile-court judges focus primarily on offense characteristics and are influenced only marginally by the offender's social characteristics. These findings are more consistent with the view that juvenile courts are becoming more like adult criminal courts than with the view that individualized justice is the goal (Applegate, Turner, Sanborn, Latessa, & Moon, 2000).

Juvenile courts in urban areas tend to send proportionally fewer delinquents to state detention facilities than do courts serving less populous areas (Rubin, 1989). Officials in rural areas are sometimes quicker to "pull the string" and send less-serious delinquency cases to state placement—partially because they have fewer institutional resources to deal with these youths, but also because the equivalent event is viewed as more harmful in small towns than in big cities.

Appeal

Juveniles have a right to appeal in nearly all states. The opinion in *Gault* discussed the importance of appeals for due process rights, but declined to make it a constitutional requirement. Prompted, however, by the possibility that the Supreme Court might indeed make it a constitutional right, state legislatures have passed laws granting juveniles the right to appeal. Thus, today the common practice is to give juveniles the same rights to appeal that apply to adults. By statute, juveniles also have the right to a transcript and a right to counsel for the first appeal.

The right to appeal is primarily limited to juveniles (and their parents). The state may appeal only in limited circumstances, and this right is seldom exercised.

THE FUTURE OF JUVENILE COURTS

Juvenile courts, which were once virtually invisible judicial bodies, have in recent years become a major focus in the debate over crime. Amid the constantly evolving war on crime (Chapter 1), there are cross-cutting pressures to change the nature of juvenile court justice. Indeed, some critics argue that this grand experiment has been a failure and should be scrapped.

More than a century after the founding of juvenile courts, it is appropriate to ask, what will juvenile courts be like 50 or 100 years from now? The debate over the future reflects basic disagreements along the lines of the crime control versus due process models.

Crime Control Model: More Adult Penalties

The crime control model begins with the premise that crime is the product of moral breakdown. This is clearly the theme sounded by Darlene Kennedy (1997) of the National Center for Public Policy Research. "Let's hold juveniles responsible for their crimes," she argued, blaming undue leniency of juvenile court for violent juvenile crimes. "The solution is greater deterrence through expected punishments. Children who commit crimes should be punished like adults."

One version of more adult penalties for juvenile offenders involves increasing the number of transfers to adult court. According to the National District Attorneys Association (2007): "Very few juveniles are prosecuted and sentenced as adults in America. . . . In those cases where adult court prosecution does occur, the simple fact of the matter is that adult court prosecution is clearly warranted. . . . "

Some go so far as to argue that it is time to abolish juvenile court altogether. As far back as 1990, Marvin Wolfgang argued that: "The dual system of juvenile and criminal justice that prevents the sharing of information and permits a serious, chronic violent juvenile to become a virgin offender after his 19th birthday is a strange cultural invention" (quoted in Bureau of Justice Statistics, 1990, p. 18). This line of thought led Peter Reinharz, chief of New York City's juvenile prosecution unit, to argue, "It's time to sell everything off and start over" (quoted in Butterfield, 1997). Chronic overcrowding of juvenile justice facilities is one problem often mentioned, but it is unclear how merely shuffling the overcrowding problems of juvenile facilities to already overcrowded adult courts and adult prisons will alleviate the problem. Public opinion, however, supports the continued operation of a separate juvenile justice system in the United States, although there are disagreements about the details of its operation, ranging from the age at which juveniles should be treated as adults to the appropriateness of harsh punishments over more rehabilitative efforts (Mears, Hay, Gertz, & Mancini, 2007).

In short, a sharp increase in the public's fear of juvenile crime, particularly gangs, drugs, and violence, has added impetus to a get-tough attitude toward juvenile criminals.

Due Process Model: More Youth Crime Prevention

The due process model starts with the premise that crime is a reflection of social problems. Punishment alone, therefore, is not necessarily the answer and might even be counterproductive. Placing juveniles in the same prisons as adults, for example, might simply make the youths more-hardened and more-accomplished crooks.

Amid numerous voices arguing that the juvenile court created more than 100 years ago is now outmoded, some respond that the nation should return to those roots. The Progressive movement was concerned about mistreatment of juveniles at the turn of the previous century, and we should have the same concern today, argue groups like the American Civil Liberties Union. The core of the argument is that crime prevention works. Instead of pouring increasing amounts of public dollars into prisons (both adult and juvenile), we need to put more into education and prevention.

In "A Call to Action for Juvenile Justice" the American Civil Liberties Union (2008) outlined

three priorities for the juvenile court system. Priority one is to keep children out of the criminal justice system. In particular, end the disparity in punitive sentences given to youths of color. Priority two is protect the rights of incarcerated children. Ensuring access to counsel and the courts is very important. Priority three is reintegrating children into communities. All too often juvenile adjudications can follow children for decades, hampering their ability to find employment.

CONCLUSION

The charge against Gerald Gault—making a lewd telephone call—seems tame compared with today's concerns about preteens committing violent crimes. Nonetheless, this irritating but hardly life-threatening behavior was to usher in a new era. Whereas the Progressives saw procedural rights as an impediment to helping children in need, a later generation viewed due process as providing an important safety net against high-handed behavior by government officials.

Court decisions like *In re Gault* and changing patterns of youthful behavior—to say nothing of the types of crimes committed by youths today—could not have been foreseen by the Progressive movement. Whether the founders of juvenile court would recognize their innovation more than 100 years later is debatable. Initially, juvenile court was supposed to make decisions based on the "best interests" of the child. Today, a get-tough attitude has come to dominate discussions of juvenile court. Holding the youth accountable to community standards now plays a major role in the dispositions reached.

The future of juvenile courts is rapidly unfolding. To some observers, juvenile courts need to provide more adult-like due process. To others, juvenile courts need to provide more adult-like sentences. Still others would stress the need for new and creative ways of dealing with contemporary problems of American youth. The Progressive movement, after all, responded to changing conditions in society produced by the Industrial Revolution. To many, the current challenge is to respond to the changing conditions of society produced by the information age.

Chapter Review

LO1 1. Describe the child-saving movement and its relationship to the doctrine of *parens patriae*.

Under the legal doctrine of *parens patriae* (state as parent) the government can intervene to protect the child if the parents are failing in their responsibilities. The child-saving movement, which began around 1890, believed that juvenile offenders required treatment, not punishment.

LO2 2. List the five ways in which juvenile courts differ from adult courts.

Juvenile courts emphasize helping the child; the proceedings are informal, the process is based on civil law, the proceedings are secret, and jury trials are not allowed.

LO3 3. Discuss how states vary in terms of when a juvenile may be transferred to adult court for prosecution.

Most states consider children to be juveniles until they reach their 18th birthday but some set this upper age as low as 15. Juveniles accused of serious offenses, or who have a history of repeated offenses, may be tried as adults. Some states set no lower age for transfer while others set the lower limit at 14 or 16.

LO4 4. Contrast the three major types of cases that are heard in juvenile court.

In juvenile delinquency cases, the child is charged with a violation of the criminal law that is not based on age. In status offenses, the child is charged with an activity that is illegal only for juveniles. In child-victim cases, the child has committed no crime but the parents are accused of neglect or the like.

LO5 5. Identify and briefly describe the single most important Supreme Court case with respect to juvenile justice.

The Supreme Court decided *In re Gault* in 1967. Gault was arrested for making an obscene phone call, but his parents were not notified of his arrest or told of the court hearing. The Supreme Court held that juveniles are entitled to many of the same due process rights of adults, including the right to notice, the right to counsel, the right to confront witnesses, and the privilege against self-incrimination.

LO6 6. Explain the difference between a juvenile case that is petitioned and one that is nonpetitioned.

In juvenile court, charging occurs during the intake decision. Less-serious cases are nonpetitioned and handled informally. Petition cases are handled formally and often result in a finding of juvenile delinquency.

LO7 7. Compare and contrast how adherents of the crime control model and proponents of the due process model of criminal justice see the future of juvenile courts.

Adherents of the criminal control model of criminal justice stress that juveniles should face more adult-like penalties and that the juvenile courts should either be abolished or more juveniles transferred to adult court for prosecution. Proponents of the due process model of criminal justice stress that juveniles need more crime prevention programs and that juvenile courts should be less punishment oriented.

Critical Thinking Questions

1. In what ways do juvenile courts differ from courts that process adults accused of violating the criminal law? In what ways are juvenile courts similar?

2. What are the key features of the juvenile courts in your state? How are they organized, what is the upper age limit, and what is the lower age limit?

3. What advantages do you see in adding due process rights to juvenile court? What disadvantages do you see? To what extent are discussions over this matter influenced by atypical cases?

4. Compare the courtroom work groups of adult court and juvenile court. Which actors are the same? Which actors are different? Do the members of the courtroom work group function the same way in juvenile court as in adult court?

5. Compare the steps of the adult court process with the steps of juvenile court. In what ways are they similar? In what ways are they different?

6. What do you think juvenile courts will look like 100 years from now? Will they incorporate more adult due process? Will they stress more adult penalties? Or will they develop more innovative helping programs?

Key Terms

adjudicated   492

adjudicatory hearing   492

automatic waiver   479

blended sentencing   479

child-victims   475

children in need of supervision   475

conference   491

delinquency   475

detention   490

dismissal   492

disposition   492

initial hearing   490

intake decision   491

judicial waiver laws   478

juvenile   476

juvenile court   472

lower age of jurisdiction   476

nonpetitioned case   491

other dispositions   495

parens patriae   472

petition   491

placement   494

probation   492

probation officer   488

prosecutorial waiver   479

referral   490

reverse waivers   479

status offense   475

statutory/legislative waiver   479

summons   488

transfer to criminal court   478

upper age of jurisdiction   476

Web Resources

Go to the *America's Courts and the Criminal Justice System* companion website at

http://www.cengage.com/criminaljustice/neubauer,

where you will find more resources to help you study.

Resources include web exercises, quizzing, and flash cards.

For Further Reading

Feld, Barry. *Bad Kids: Race and the Transformation of the Juvenile Court.* New York: Oxford University Press, 1999.

Flynn, Nicole, Roma Hanks, and Lindsey Gurley. "Stirred, Shaken, or Blended: Gender Differences in Processing and Treatment of Juvenile Offenders." *Women and Criminal Justice* 18 (4): 17–36, 2008.

Gaarder, Emily, and Joanne Belknap. "Tenuous Borders: Girls Transferred to Adult Court." *Criminology* 40: 481–518, 2002.

Gaarder, Emily, Nancy Rodriguez, and Marjorie Zatz. "Criers, Liars, and Manipulators: Probation Officers' Views of Girls." *Justice Quarterly* 21: 548–563, 2004.

Getis, Victoria. *The Juvenile Court and the Progressives.* Champaign: University of Illinois Press, 2000.

Goodkind, Sara Amy. *From Delinquent Daughters to Independent Mothers: Gendered Expectations in Juvenile Justice and Alternative Programs for Girls.* Ann Arbor, MI: Proquest/UMI, 2006.

Greenwood, Peter. *Changing Lives: Delinquency Prevention as Crime-Control Policy*. Chicago: University of Chicago Press, 2006.

Hess, Karen. *Juvenile Justice*. 5th ed. Belmont, CA: Cengage 2010.

Kupchik, Aaron. *Judging Juveniles: Prosecuting Adolescents in Adult and Juvenile Courts*. New York: NYU Press, 2006.

Paik, Leslie. *Discretionary Justice: Looking Inside a Juvenile Drug Court*. New Brunswick, NJ: Rutgers University Press, 2011.

Rubin, H. Ted. *Juvenile Justice: Policies, Practices, and Programs*. Kingston, NJ: Civic Research Institute, 2012.

Shaffner, Laurie. *Girls in Trouble with the Law*. Piscataway, NJ: Rutgers University Press, 2006.

Shelden, Randall, Sharon Tracy and William Brown. *Youth Gangs in American Society*. 4th ed. Belmont, CA: Cengage 2012.

Siegel, Larry, and Brandon Welsh. *Juvenile Delinquency: Theory, Practice, and Law*. 11th ed. Belmont, CA: Wadsworth, 2012.

Tannenhaus, David. *Juvenile Justice in the Making*. New York: Oxford University Press, 2004.

Tapia, Mike. *Juvenile Arrest in America: Race, Social Class, and Gang Membership*. El Paso: LFB Scholarly Press 2012.

Criminal Court Landmarks

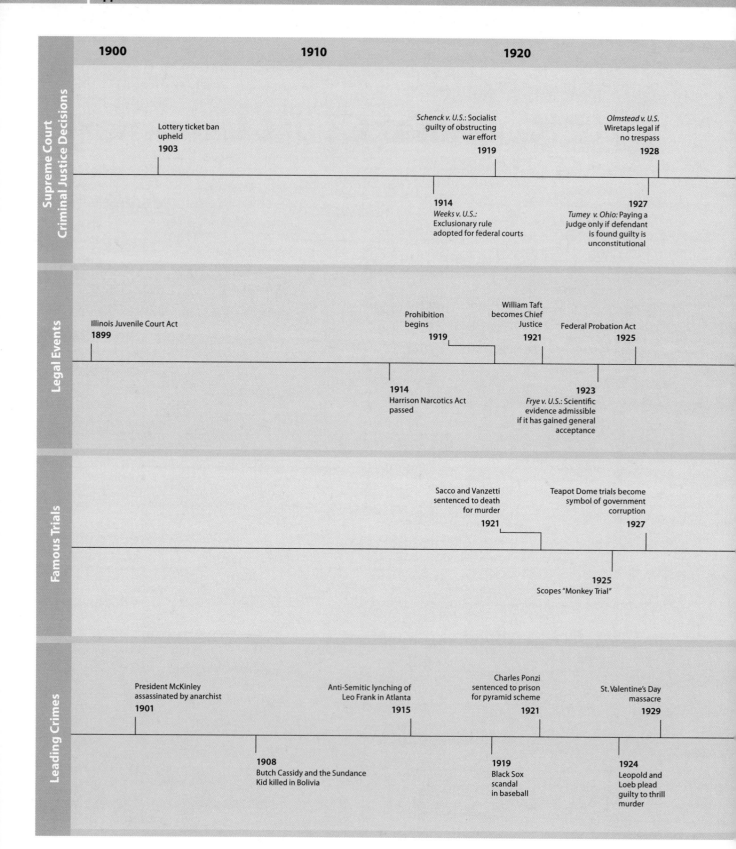

Supreme Court Criminal Justice Decisions

1900 — 1910 — 1920

Lottery ticket ban upheld
1903

Schenck v. U.S.: Socialist guilty of obstructing war effort
1919

Olmstead v. U.S. Wiretaps legal if no trespass
1928

1914
Weeks v. U.S.: Exclusionary rule adopted for federal courts

1927
Tumey v. Ohio: Paying a judge only if defendant is found guilty is unconstitutional

Legal Events

Illinois Juvenile Court Act
1899

Prohibition begins
1919

William Taft becomes Chief Justice
1921

Federal Probation Act
1925

1914
Harrison Narcotics Act passed

1923
Frye v. U.S.: Scientific evidence admissible if it has gained general acceptance

Famous Trials

Sacco and Vanzetti sentenced to death for murder
1921

Teapot Dome trials become symbol of government corruption
1927

1925
Scopes "Monkey Trial"

Leading Crimes

President McKinley assassinated by anarchist
1901

Anti-Semitic lynching of Leo Frank in Atlanta
1915

Charles Ponzi sentenced to prison for pyramid scheme
1921

St. Valentine's Day massacre
1929

1908
Butch Cassidy and the Sundance Kid killed in Bolivia

1919
Black Sox scandal in baseball

1924
Leopold and Loeb plead guilty to thrill murder

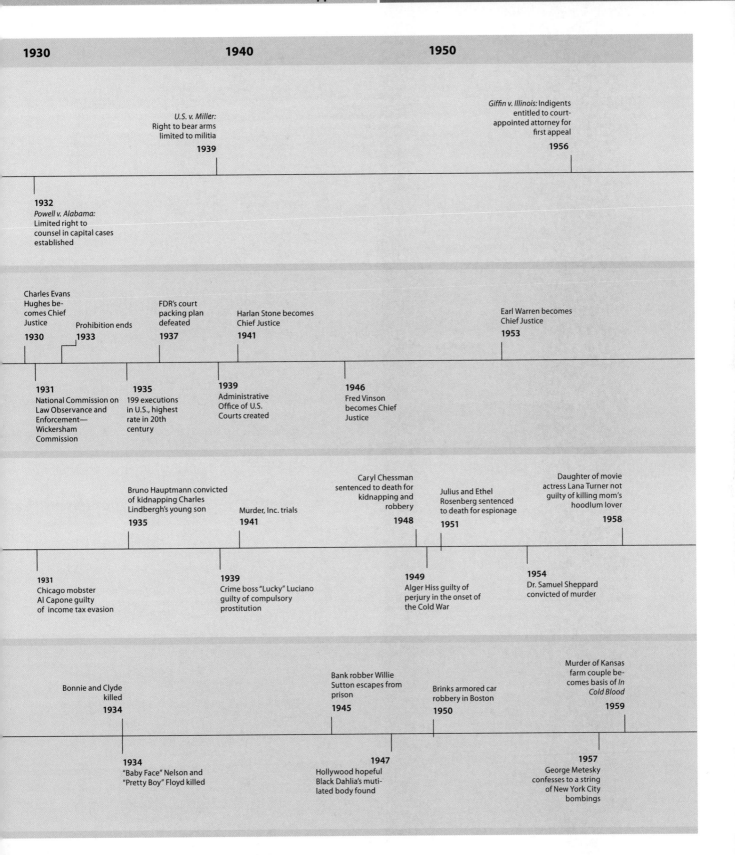

1930 **1940** **1950**

U.S. v. Miller: Right to bear arms limited to militia
1939

Giffin v. Illinois: Indigents entitled to court-appointed attorney for first appeal
1956

1932
Powell v. Alabama: Limited right to counsel in capital cases established

Charles Evans Hughes becomes Chief Justice
1930

Prohibition ends
1933

FDR's court packing plan defeated
1937

Harlan Stone becomes Chief Justice
1941

Earl Warren becomes Chief Justice
1953

1931
National Commission on Law Observance and Enforcement—Wickersham Commission

1935
199 executions in U.S., highest rate in 20th century

1939
Administrative Office of U.S. Courts created

1946
Fred Vinson becomes Chief Justice

Bruno Hauptmann convicted of kidnapping Charles Lindbergh's young son
1935

Murder, Inc. trials
1941

Caryl Chessman sentenced to death for kidnapping and robbery
1948

Julius and Ethel Rosenberg sentenced to death for espionage
1951

Daughter of movie actress Lana Turner not guilty of killing mom's hoodlum lover
1958

1931
Chicago mobster Al Capone guilty of income tax evasion

1939
Crime boss "Lucky" Luciano guilty of compulsory prostitution

1949
Alger Hiss guilty of perjury in the onset of the Cold War

1954
Dr. Samuel Sheppard convicted of murder

Bonnie and Clyde killed
1934

Bank robber Willie Sutton escapes from prison
1945

Brinks armored car robbery in Boston
1950

Murder of Kansas farm couple becomes basis of *In Cold Blood*
1959

1934
"Baby Face" Nelson and "Pretty Boy" Floyd killed

1947
Hollywood hopeful Black Dahlia's mutilated body found

1957
George Metesky confesses to a string of New York City bombings

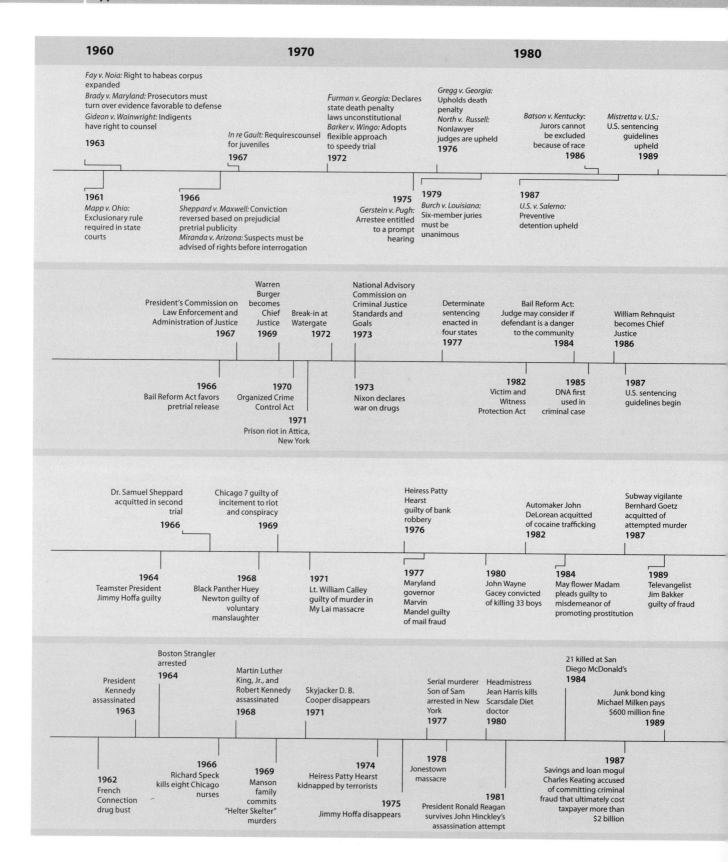

1960 — **1970** — **1980**

Fay v. Noia: Right to habeas corpus expanded
Brady v. Maryland: Prosecutors must turn over evidence favorable to defense
Gideon v. Wainwright: Indigents have right to counsel
1963

In re Gault: Requires counsel for juveniles
1967

Furman v. Georgia: Declares state death penalty laws unconstitutional
Barker v. Wingo: Adopts flexible approach to speedy trial
1972

Gregg v. Georgia: Upholds death penalty
North v. Russell: Nonlawyer judges are upheld
1976

Batson v. Kentucky: Jurors cannot be excluded because of race
1986

Mistretta v. U.S.: U.S. sentencing guidelines upheld
1989

1961 *Mapp v. Ohio:* Exclusionary rule required in state courts

1966 *Sheppard v. Maxwell:* Conviction reversed based on prejudicial pretrial publicity
Miranda v. Arizona: Suspects must be advised of rights before interrogation

1975 *Gerstein v. Pugh:* Arrestee entitled to a prompt hearing

1979 *Burch v. Louisiana:* Six-member juries must be unanimous

1987 *U.S. v. Salerno:* Preventive detention upheld

President's Commission on Law Enforcement and Administration of Justice
1967

Warren Burger becomes Chief Justice
1969

Break-in at Watergate
1972

National Advisory Commission on Criminal Justice Standards and Goals
1973

Determinate sentencing enacted in four states
1977

Bail Reform Act: Judge may consider if defendant is a danger to the community
1984

William Rehnquist becomes Chief Justice
1986

1966 Bail Reform Act favors pretrial release

1970 Organized Crime Control Act

1973 Nixon declares war on drugs

1982 Victim and Witness Protection Act

1985 DNA first used in criminal case

1987 U.S. sentencing guidelines begin

1971 Prison riot in Attica, New York

Dr. Samuel Sheppard acquitted in second trial
1966

Chicago 7 guilty of incitement to riot and conspiracy
1969

Heiress Patty Hearst guilty of bank robbery
1976

Automaker John DeLorean acquitted of cocaine trafficking
1982

Subway vigilante Bernhard Goetz acquitted of attempted murder
1987

1964 Teamster President Jimmy Hoffa guilty

1968 Black Panther Huey Newton guilty of voluntary manslaughter

1971 Lt. William Calley guilty of murder in My Lai massacre

1977 Maryland governor Marvin Mandel guilty of mail fraud

1980 John Wayne Gacey convicted of killing 33 boys

1984 May flower Madam pleads guilty to misdemeanor of promoting prostitution

1989 Televangelist Jim Bakker guilty of fraud

Boston Strangler arrested
1964

President Kennedy assassinated
1963

Martin Luther King, Jr., and Robert Kennedy assassinated
1968

Skyjacker D. B. Cooper disappears
1971

Serial murderer Son of Sam arrested in New York
1977

Headmistress Jean Harris kills Scarsdale Diet doctor
1980

21 killed at San Diego McDonald's
1984

Junk bond king Michael Milken pays $600 million fine
1989

1962 French Connection drug bust

1966 Richard Speck kills eight Chicago nurses

1969 Manson family commits "Helter Skelter" murders

1974 Heiress Patty Hearst kidnapped by terrorists

1975 Jimmy Hoffa disappears

1978 Jonestown massacre

1981 President Ronald Reagan survives John Hinckley's assassination attempt

1987 Savings and loan mogul Charles Keating accused of committing criminal fraud that ultimately cost taxpayer more than $2 billion

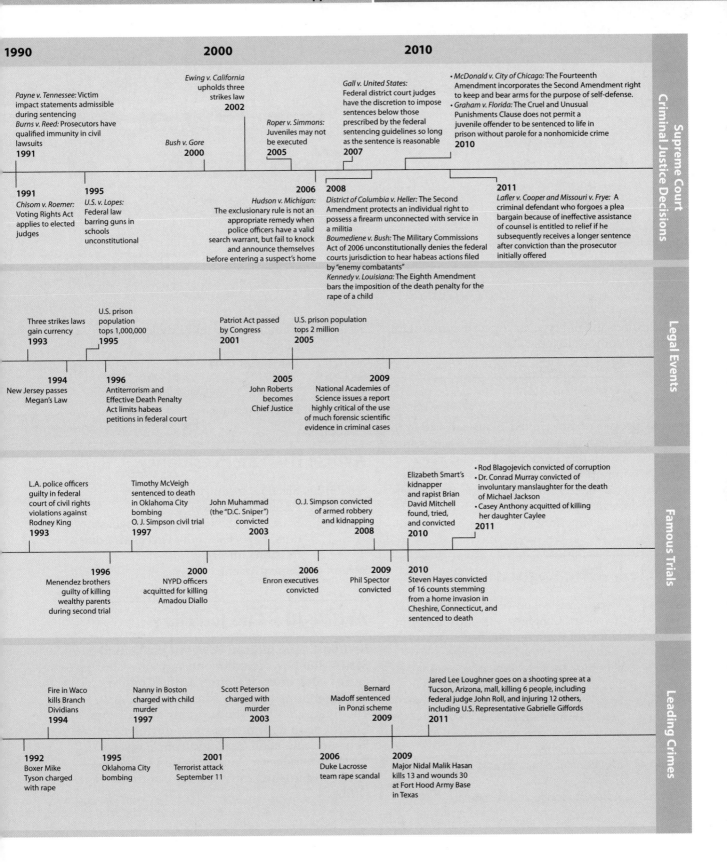

Supreme Court Criminal Justice Decisions

Payne v. Tennessee: Victim impact statements admissible during sentencing
Burns v. Reed: Prosecutors have qualified immunity in civil lawsuits
1991

Ewing v. California upholds three strikes law
2002

Bush v. Gore
2000

Roper v. Simmons: Juveniles may not be executed
2005

Gall v. United States: Federal district court judges have the discretion to impose sentences below those prescribed by the federal sentencing guidelines so long as the sentence is reasonable
2007

• *McDonald v. City of Chicago:* The Fourteenth Amendment incorporates the Second Amendment right to keep and bear arms for the purpose of self-defense.
• *Graham v. Florida:* The Cruel and Unusual Punishments Clause does not permit a juvenile offender to be sentenced to life in prison without parole for a nonhomicide crime
2010

1991
Chisom v. Roemer: Voting Rights Act applies to elected judges

1995
U.S. v. Lopes: Federal law barring guns in schools unconstitutional

2006
Hudson v. Michigan: The exclusionary rule is not an appropriate remedy when police officers have a valid search warrant, but fail to knock and announce themselves before entering a suspect's home

2008
District of Columbia v. Heller: The Second Amendment protects an individual right to possess a firearm unconnected with service in a militia
Boumediene v. Bush: The Military Commissions Act of 2006 unconstitutionally denies the federal courts jurisdiction to hear habeas actions filed by "enemy combatants"
Kennedy v. Louisiana: The Eighth Amendment bars the imposition of the death penalty for the rape of a child

2011
Lafler v. Cooper and Missouri v. Frye: A criminal defendant who forgoes a plea bargain because of ineffective assistance of counsel is entitled to relief if he subsequently receives a longer sentence after conviction than the prosecutor initially offered

Legal Events

Three strikes laws gain currency
1993

U.S. prison population tops 1,000,000
1995

Patriot Act passed by Congress
2001

U.S. prison population tops 2 million
2005

1994
New Jersey passes Megan's Law

1996
Antiterrorism and Effective Death Penalty Act limits habeas petitions in federal court

2005
John Roberts becomes Chief Justice

2009
National Academies of Science issues a report highly critical of the use of much forensic scientific evidence in criminal cases

Famous Trials

L.A. police officers guilty in federal court of civil rights violations against Rodney King
1993

Timothy McVeigh sentenced to death in Oklahoma City bombing
O. J. Simpson civil trial
1997

John Muhammad (the "D.C. Sniper") convicted
2003

O. J. Simpson convicted of armed robbery and kidnapping
2008

Elizabeth Smart's kidnapper and rapist Brian David Mitchell found, tried, and convicted
2010

• Rod Blagojevich convicted of corruption
• Dr. Conrad Murray convicted of involuntary manslaughter for the death of Michael Jackson
• Casey Anthony acquitted of killing her daughter Caylee
2011

1996
Menendez brothers guilty of killing wealthy parents during second trial

2000
NYPD officers acquitted for killing Amadou Diallo

2006
Enron executives convicted

2009
Phil Spector convicted

2010
Steven Hayes convicted of 16 counts stemming from a home invasion in Cheshire, Connecticut, and sentenced to death

Leading Crimes

Fire in Waco kills Branch Dividians
1994

Nanny in Boston charged with child murder
1997

Scott Peterson charged with murder
2003

Bernard Madoff sentenced in Ponzi scheme
2009

Jared Lee Loughner goes on a shooting spree at a Tucson, Arizona, mall, killing 6 people, including federal judge John Roll, and injuring 12 others, including U.S. Representative Gabrielle Giffords
2011

1992
Boxer Mike Tyson charged with rape

1995
Oklahoma City bombing

2001
Terrorist attack September 11

2006
Duke Lacrosse team rape scandal

2009
Major Nidal Malik Hasan kills 13 and wounds 30 at Fort Hood Army Base in Texas

1990   **2000**   **2010**

Overview of the Constitution of the United States of America

Note: Portions in **bold type** are especially important to criminal courts and judicial processes.

Preamble

We the people of the United States, in order to form a more perfect union, establish justice, insure domestic tranquility, provide for the common defense, promote the general welfare, and secure the blessings of liberty to ourselves and our posterity, do ordain and establish this Constitution for the United States of America.

Article I—The Legislative Branch

Section 1 Vests legislative power in a bicameral (two-part) Congress

Section 2 House of Representatives—minimum age 25; 2-year terms; representation by state to be proportional to population; members elect their own Speaker; sole power of impeachment

Section 3 Senate—minimum age 30; 6-year terms; two senators per state; tries all impeachments

Section 4 Elections of Senators and Representatives

Section 5 Rules of House and Senate

Section 6 Compensation and Privileges of Members

Section 7 Passage of Bills

Section 8 Scope of Legislative Power

Section 9 Limits on Legislative Power

Section 10 Limits on States

Article II—The Presidency

Section 1 Election, Installation, Removal

Section 2 Presidential Power

Section 3 State of the Union, Receive Ambassadors, Laws Faithfully Executed, Commission Officers

Section 4 Impeachment

Article III—The Judiciary

Section 1. **The judicial Power of the United States, shall be vested in one supreme Court, and in such inferior Courts as the Congress may from time to time ordain and establish. The Judges, both of the supreme and inferior Courts, shall hold their Offices during good Behavior, and shall, at stated Times, receive for their Services a Compensation which shall not be diminished during their Continuance in Office.**

Section 2. Clause 1: The judicial Power shall extend to all Cases, in Law and Equity, arising under this Constitution, the Laws of the United States, and Treaties made, or which shall be made, under their Authority; to all Cases affecting Ambassadors, other public Ministers and Consuls; to all Cases of admiralty and maritime Jurisdiction; to Controversies to which the United States shall be a Party; to Controversies between two or more States; between a State and Citizens of another State; between Citizens of different States; between Citizens of the same State claiming Lands under Grants of different States, and between a State, or the Citizens thereof, and foreign States, Citizens or Subjects. (This section was modified, in part, by Amendment XI.)

Clause 2: In all Cases affecting Ambassadors, other public Ministers and Consuls, and those in which a State shall be Party, the supreme Court shall have original Jurisdiction. In all the other Cases before mentioned, the supreme Court shall have appellate Jurisdiction, both as to Law and Fact, with such Exceptions, and under such Regulations as the Congress shall make.

Clause 3: The Trial of all Crimes, except in Cases of Impeachment, shall be by Jury; and such Trial shall be held in the State where the said Crimes shall have been committed; but when not committed within any State, the Trial shall be at such Place or Places as the Congress may by Law have directed.

Section 3. Treason against the United States, shall consist only in levying War against them, or in adhering to their Enemies, giving them Aid and Comfort. No Person shall be convicted of Treason unless on the Testimony of two Witnesses to the same overt Act, or on Confession in open Court.

The Congress shall have power to declare the Punishment of Treason, but no Attainder of Treason shall work Corruption of Blood,[1] or Forfeiture except during the Life of the Person attainted.

Article IV—The States

Section 1. Full Faith and Credit
Section 2. Privileges and Immunities, Extradition, Fugitive Slaves
Section 3. Admission of States
Section 4. Guarantees to States

Article V—The Amendment Process

Article VI—Legal Status of the Constitution

Clause 1: All Debts contracted and Engagements entered into, before the Adoption of this Constitution, shall be as valid against the United States under this Constitution, as under the Confederation.

Clause 2: This Constitution, and the Laws of the United States which shall be made in Pursuance thereof; and all Treaties made, or which shall be made, under the Authority of the United States, shall be the supreme Law of the Land; and the Judges in every State shall be bound thereby, any Thing in the Constitution or Laws of any State to the Contrary notwithstanding.

Clause 3: The Senators and Representatives before mentioned, and the Members of the several State Legislatures, and all executive and judicial Officers, both of the United States and of the several States, shall be bound by Oath or Affirmation, to support this Constitution; but no religious Test shall ever be required as a Qualification to any Office or public Trust under the United States.

Article VII—Ratification

Amendment I

"Congress shall make no law respecting an establishment of religion, or prohibiting the free exercise thereof; or abridging the freedom of speech, or of the press; or the right of the people peaceably to assemble, and to petition the Government for a redress of grievances" (1791).

Amendment II

"A well regulated Militia, being necessary to the security of a free State, the right of the people to keep and bear Arms, shall not be infringed" (1791).

Amendment III

"No Soldier shall, in time of peace be quartered in any house, without the consent of the Owner, nor in time of war, but in a manner to be prescribed by law" (1791).

Amendment IV

"The right of the people to be secure in their persons, houses, papers, and effects, against unreasonable searches and seizures, shall not be violated, and no Warrants shall issue, but upon probable cause, supported by Oath or affirmation, and particularly describing the place to be searched, and the persons or things to be seized"(1791).

Amendment V

"No person shall be held to answer for a capital, or otherwise infamous crime, unless on a presentment or indictment of a Grand Jury, except in cases arising in the land or naval forces, or in the Militia, when in actual service in time of War or public danger; nor shall any person be subject for the same offense to be twice put in jeopardy of life or limb; nor shall be compelled in any criminal case to be a witness against himself, nor be deprived of life, liberty, or property, without due process of law; nor shall private property be taken for public use, without just compensation"(1791).

Amendment VI

"In all criminal prosecutions, the accused shall enjoy the right to a speedy and public trial, by an impartial jury of the State and district wherein the crime shall have been committed, which district shall have been previously ascertained by law, and to be informed of the nature and cause of the accusation; to be confronted with the witnesses against him; to have compulsory process for obtaining witnesses in his favor, and to have the Assistance of Counsel for his defence"(1791).

Amendment VII

"In Suits at common law, where the value in controversy shall exceed twenty dollars, the right of trial by jury shall be preserved, and no fact tried by a jury, shall be otherwise re-examined in any Court of the United States, than according to the rules of the common law" (1791).

Amendment VIII

"Excessive bail shall not be required, nor excessive fines imposed, nor cruel and unusual punishments inflicted"(1791).

Amendment IX

"The enumeration in the Constitution, of certain rights, shall not be construed to deny or disparage others retained by the people" (1791).

Amendment X

"The powers not delegated to the United States by the Constitution, nor prohibited by it to the States, are reserved to the States respectively, or to the people" (1791).

Amendment XI

"The Judicial power of the United States shall not be construed to extend to any suit in law or equity, commenced or prosecuted against one of the United States by Citizens of another State, or by Citizens or Subjects of any Foreign State" (1795).

Amendment XII

Election of President and Vice-President (1804).

Amendment XIII

Abolition of Slavery (1865).

Amendment XIV

Section 1. All persons born or naturalized in the United States, and subject to the jurisdiction thereof, are citizens of the United States and of the State wherein they reside. No State shall make or enforce any law which shall abridge the privileges or immunities of citizens of the United States; nor shall any State deprive any person of life, liberty, or property, without due process of law; nor deny to any person within its jurisdiction the equal protection of the laws.

Section 5. The Congress shall have power to enforce, by appropriate legislation, the provisions of this article (1868).

Amendment XV

Rights Not to Be Denied on Account of Race (1870).

Amendment XVI

Income Tax (1913).

Amendment XVII

Election of Senators (1913).

Amendment XVIII

Prohibition (1919).

Amendment XIX

Women's Right to Vote (1920).

Amendment XX

Presidential Term and Succession (1933).

Amendment XXI

Repeal of Prohibition (1933).

Amendment XXII

Two Term Limit on President (1951).

Amendment XXIII

Presidential Vote in D.C. (1961).

Amendment XXIV

Poll Tax (1964).

Amendment XXV

Presidential Succession (1967).

Amendment XXVI

Right to Vote at Age 18 (1971).

Amendment XXVII

Compensation of Members of Congress (1992).

Appendix C
Constitution of the United States

We the People of the United States, in Order to form a more perfect Union, establish Justice, insure domestic Tranquility, provide for the common defence, promote the general Welfare, and secure the Blessings of Liberty to ourselves and our Posterity, do ordain and establish this Constitution for the United States of America.

Article I

Section 1. All legislative Powers herein granted shall be vested in a Congress of the United States, which shall consist of a Senate and House of Representatives.

Section 2. The House of Representatives shall be composed of Members chosen every second Year by the People of the several States, and the Electors in each State shall have the Qualifications requisite for Electors of the most numerous Branch of the State Legislature.

No Person shall be a Representative who shall not have attained to the age of twenty five Years, and been seven Years a Citizen of the United States, and who shall not, when elected, be an Inhabitant of that State in which he shall be chosen.

Representatives and direct Taxes shall be apportioned among the several States which may be included within this Union, according to their respective Numbers, which shall be determined by adding to the whole Number of free Persons, including those bound to Service for a Term of Years, and excluding Indians not taxed, three fifths of all other Persons. The actual Enumeration shall be made within three Years after the first Meeting of the Congress of the United States, and within every subsequent Term of ten Years, in such Manner as they shall by Law direct. The Number of Representatives shall not exceed one for every thirty Thousand, but each State shall have at Least one Representative; and until such enumeration shall be made, the State of New Hampshire shall be entitled to chuse three, Massachusetts eight, Rhode-Island and Providence Plantations one, Connecticut five, New-York six, New Jersey four, Pennsylvania eight, Delaware one, Maryland six, Virginia ten, North Carolina five, South Carolina five, and Georgia three.

When vacancies happen in the Representation from any State, the Executive Authority thereof shall issue Writs of Election to fill such Vacancies.

The House of Representatives shall chuse their Speaker and other Officers; and shall have the sole Power of Impeachment.

Section 3. The Senate of the United States shall be composed of two Senators from each State, chosen by the Legislature thereof, for six Years; and each Senator shall have one Vote.

Immediately after they shall be assembled in Consequence of the first Election, they shall be divided as equally as may be into three Classes.

The Seats of the Senators of the first Class shall be vacated at the Expiration of the second Year, of the second Class at the Expiration of the fourth Year, and the third Class at the Expiration of the sixth Year, so that one third may be chosen every second Year; and if Vacancies happen by Resignation, or otherwise, during the Recess of the Legislature of any State, the Executive thereof may make temporary Appointments until the next Meeting of the Legislature, which shall then fill such Vacancies.

No Person shall be a Senator who shall not have attained to the Age of thirty Years, and been nine Years a Citizen of the United States and who shall not, when elected, be an Inhabitant of that State for which he shall be chosen.

The Vice President of the United States shall be President of the Senate, but shall have no Vote, unless they be equally divided.

The Senate shall chuse their other Officers, and also a President pro tempore, in the Absence of the Vice President, or when he shall exercise the Office of President of the United States.

The Senate shall have the sole Power to try all Impeachments. When sitting for that Purpose, they shall be on Oath or Affirmation. When the President of the United States is tried, the Chief Justice shall preside: And no Person shall be convicted without the Concurrence of two thirds of the Members present.

Judgment in Cases of Impeachment shall not extend further than to removal from Office, and disqualification to hold and enjoy any Office of Honor, Trust or Profit under the United States: but the Party convicted shall nevertheless be liable and subject to Indictment, Trial, Judgment and Punishment, according to Law.

Section 4. The Times, Places and Manner of holding Elections for Senators and Representatives, shall be prescribed in each State by the Legislature thereof; but the Congress may at any time by Law make or alter such Regulations, except as to the Places of chusing Senators.

The Congress shall assemble at least once in every Year, and such Meeting shall be on the first Monday in December, unless they shall by Law appoint a different Day.

Section 5. Each House shall be the Judge of the Elections, Returns and Qualifications of its own Members, and a Majority of each shall constitute a Quorum to do Business; but a smaller Number may adjourn from day to day, and may be authorized to compel the Attendance of absent Members, in such Manner, and under such Penalties as each House may provide.

Each House may determine the Rules of its Proceedings, punish its Members for disorderly Behaviour, and, with the Concurrence of two thirds, expel a Member.

Each House shall keep a Journal of its Proceedings, and from time to time publish the same, excepting such Parts as may in their Judgment require Secrecy; and the Yeas and Nays of the Members of either House on any question shall, at the Desire of one fifth of those Present, be entered on the Journal.

Neither House, during the Session of Congress, shall, without the Consent of the other, adjourn for more than three days, nor to any other Place than that in which the two Houses shall be sitting.

Section 6. The Senators and Representatives shall receive a Compensation for their Services, to be ascertained by Law, and paid out of the Treasury of the United States. They shall in all Cases, except Treason, Felony and Breach of the Peace, be privileged from Arrest during their Attendance at the Session of their respective Houses, and in going to and returning from the same; and for any Speech or Debate in either House, they shall not be questioned in any other Place.

No Senator or Representative shall, during the Time for which he was elected, be appointed to any civil Office under the Authority of the United States, which shall have been created, or the Emoluments whereof shall have been encreased during such time: and no Person holding any Office under the United States, shall be a Member of either House during his Continuance in Office.

Section 7. All Bills for raising Revenue shall originate in the House of Representatives; but the Senate may propose or concur with Amendments as on other Bills.

Every Bill which shall have passed the House of Representatives and the Senate, shall, before it become a Law, be presented to the President of the United States; if he approve he shall sign it, but if not he shall return it, with his Objections to that House in which it shall have originated, who shall enter the Objections at large on their Journal, and proceed to reconsider it. If after such Reconsideration two thirds of that House shall agree to pass the Bill, it shall be sent, together with the Objections, to the other House, by which it shall likewise be reconsidered, and if approved by two thirds of that House, it shall become a Law. But in all such Cases the Votes of both Houses shall be determined by Yeas and Nays, and the Names of the Persons voting for and against the Bill shall be entered on the Journal of each House respectively. If any Bill shall not be returned by the President within ten Days (Sundays excepted) after it shall have been presented to him, the Same shall be a Law, in like Manner as if he had signed it, unless the Congress by their Adjournment prevent its Return, in which Case it shall not be a Law.

Every Order, Resolution, or Vote to which the Concurrence of the Senate and House of Representatives may be necessary (except on a question of Adjournment) shall be presented to the President of the United States; and before the Same shall take Effect, shall be approved by him, or being disapproved by him, shall be repassed by two thirds of the Senate and House of Representatives, according to the Rules and Limitations prescribed in the Case of a Bill.

Section 8. The Congress shall have Power To lay and collect Taxes, Duties, Imposts and Excises, to pay the Debts and provide for the common Defence and general Welfare of the United States; but all Duties, Imposts and Excises shall be uniform throughout the United States;

To borrow Money on the credit of the United States;

To regulate Commerce with foreign Nations, and among the several States, and with the Indian Tribes;

To establish an uniform Rule of Naturalization, and uniform Laws on the subject of Bankruptcies throughout the United States;

To coin Money, regulate the Value thereof, and of foreign Coin, and fix the Standard of Weights and Measures;

To provide for the Punishment of counterfeiting the Securities and current Coin of the United States;

To establish Post Offices and post Roads;

To promote the Progress of Science and useful Arts, by securing for limited Times to Authors and Inventors the exclusive Right to their respective Writings and Discoveries;

To constitute Tribunals inferior to the Supreme Court;

To define and punish Piracies and Felonies committed on the high Seas, and Offences against the Law of Nations;

To declare War, grant Letters of Marque and Reprisal, and make Rules concerning Captures on Land and Water;

To raise and support Armies, but no Appropriation of Money to that Use shall be for a longer Term than two Years;

To provide and maintain a Navy;

To make Rules for the Government and Regulation of the land and naval Forces;

To provide for calling forth the Militia to execute the Laws of the Union, suppress Insurrections and repel Invasions;

To provide for organizing, arming, and disciplining, the Militia, and for governing such Part of them as may be employed in the Service of the United States, reserving to the States respectively, the Appointment of the Officers, and the Authority of training the Militia according to the discipline prescribed by Congress;

To exercise exclusive Legislation in all Cases whatsoever, over such District (not exceeding ten Miles square) as may, by Cession of particular States, and the Acceptance of Congress, become the Seat of the Government of the United States, and to exercise like Authority over all Places purchased by the Consent of the Legislature of the State in which the Same shall be, for the Erection of Forts, Magazines, Arsenals, dock-Yards, and other needful Buildings;—And

To make all Laws which shall be necessary and proper for carrying into Execution the foregoing Powers, and all other Powers vested by this Constitution in the Government of the United States, or in any Department or Officer thereof.

Section 9. The Migration or Importation of such Persons as any of the States now existing shall think proper to admit, shall not be prohibited by the Congress prior to the Year one thousand eight hundred and eight, but a Tax or duty may be imposed on such Importation, not exceeding ten dollars for each Person.

The Privilege of the Writ of Habeas Corpus shall not be suspended, unless when in Cases of Rebellion or Invasion the public Safety may require it.

No Bill of Attainder or ex post facto Law shall be passed.

No Capitation, or other direct, Tax shall be laid, unless in Proportion to the Census or Enumeration herein before directed to be taken.

No Tax or Duty shall be laid on Articles exported from any State.

No Preference shall be given by any Regulation of Commerce or Revenue to the Ports of one State over those of another: nor shall Vessels bound to, or from, one State, be obliged to enter, clear or pay Duties in another.

No Money shall be drawn from the Treasury, but in Consequence of Appropriations made by Law; and a regular Statement and Account of Receipts and Expenditures of all public Money shall be published from time to time.

No Title of Nobility shall be granted by the United States: And no Person holding any Office of Profit or Trust under them, shall, without the Consent of the Congress, accept of any present, Emolument, Office, or Title, of any kind whatever, from any King, Prince, or foreign State.

Section 10. No State shall enter into any Treaty, Alliance, or Confederation; grant Letters of Marque and Reprisal; coin Money; emit Bills of Credit; make any Thing but gold and silver Coin a Tender in Payment of Debts; pass any Bill of Attainder, ex post facto Law, or Law impairing the Obligation of Contracts, or grant any Title of Nobility.

No State shall, without the Consent of the Congress, lay any Imposts or Duties on Imports or Exports, except what may be absolutely necessary for executing it's inspection Laws: and the net Produce of all Duties and Imposts, laid by any State on Imports or Exports, shall be for the Use of the Treasury of the United States; and all such Laws shall be subject to the Revision and Controul of the Congress.

No State shall, without the Consent of Congress, lay any Duty of Tonnage, keep Troops, or Ships of War in time of Peace, enter into any Agreement or Compact with another State, or with a foreign Power, or engage in War, unless actually invaded, or in such imminent Danger as will not admit of delay.

Article II

Section 1. The executive Power shall be vested in a President of the United States of America. He shall hold his Office during the Term of four Years, and, together with the Vice President, chosen for the same Term, be elected, as follows:

Each State shall appoint, in such Manner as the Legislature thereof may direct, a Number of Electors, equal to the whole Number of Senators and Representatives to which the State may be entitled in the Congress: but no Senator or Representative, or Person holding an Office of Trust or Profit under the United States, shall be appointed an Elector.

The Electors shall meet in their respective States, and vote by Ballot for two Persons, of whom one at least shall not be an Inhabitant of the same State with themselves. And they shall make a List of all the Persons voted for, and of the Number of Votes for each; which List they shall sign and certify, and transmit sealed to the Seat of the Government of the United States, directed to the President of the Senate. The President of the Senate shall, in the Presence of the Senate and House of Representatives, open all the Certificates, and the Votes shall then be counted. The Person having the greatest Number of Votes shall be the President, if such Number be a Majority of the whole Number of Electors appointed; and if there be more than one who have such Majority, and have an equal Number of Votes, then the House of Representatives shall immediately chuse by Ballot one of them for President; and if no Person have a Majority, then from the five highest on the List the said House shall in like Manner chuse the President. But in chusing the President, the Votes shall be taken by States, the Representation from each State having one Vote; A quorum for this Purpose shall consist of a Member or Members from two thirds of the States, and a Majority of all the States shall be necessary to a Choice. In every Case, after the Choice of the President, the Person having the greatest Number of Votes of the Electors shall be the Vice President. But if there should remain two or more who have equal Votes, the Senate shall chuse from them by Ballot the Vice President.

The Congress may determine the Time of chusing the Electors, and the Day on which they shall give their Votes; which Day shall be the same throughout the United States.

No Person except a natural born Citizen, or a Citizen of the United States, at the time of the Adoption of this Constitution, shall be eligible to the Office of President; neither shall any Person be eligible to that Office who shall not have attained to the Age of thirty five Years, and been fourteen Years a Resident within the United States.

In Case of the Removal of the President from Office, or of his Death, Resignation, or Inability to discharge the Powers and Duties of the said Office, the Same shall devolve on the Vice President, and the Congress may by Law provide for the Case of Removal, Death, Resignation or Inability, both of the President and Vice President, declaring what Officer shall then act as President, and such Officer shall act accordingly, until the Disability be removed, or a President shall be elected.

The President shall, at stated Times, receive for his Services, a Compensation, which shall neither be encreased nor diminished during the Period for which he shall have been elected, and he shall not receive within that Period any other Emolument from the United States, or any of them.

Before he enter on the Execution of his Office, he shall take the following Oath or Affirmation:—"I do solemnly swear (or affirm) that I will faithfully execute the Office of President of the United States, and will to the best of my Ability, preserve, protect and defend the Constitution of the United States."

Section 2. The President shall be Commander in Chief of the Army and Navy of the United States, and of the Militia of the several States, when called into the actual Service of the United States; he may require the Opinion, in writing, of the principal Officer in each of the executive Departments, upon any Subject relating to the Duties of their respective Offices, and he shall have Power to grant Reprieves and Pardons for Offences against the United States, except in Cases of Impeachment.

He shall have Power, by and with the Advice and Consent of the Senate, to make Treaties, provided two thirds of the Senators present concur; and he shall nominate, and by and with the Advice and Consent of the Senate, shall appoint Ambassadors, other public Ministers and Consuls, Judges of the supreme Court, and all other Officers of the United States, whose Appointments are not herein otherwise provided for, and which shall be established by Law: but the Congress may by Law vest the Appointment of such inferior Officers, as they think proper, in the President alone, in the Courts of Law, or in the Heads of Departments.

The President shall have Power to fill up all Vacancies that may happen during the Recess of the Senate, by granting Commissions which shall expire at the End of their next Session.

Section 3. He shall from time to time give to the Congress Information of the State of the Union, and recommend to their Consideration such Measures as he shall judge necessary and expedient; he may, on extraordinary Occasions, convene both Houses, or either of them, and in Case of Disagreement between them, with Respect to the Time of Adjournment, he may adjourn them to such Time as he shall think proper; he shall receive Ambassadors and other public Ministers; he shall take Care that the Laws be faithfully executed, and shall Commission all the Officers of the United States.

Section 4. The President, Vice President and all civil Officers of the United States, shall be removed from Office on Impeachment for, and Conviction of, Treason, Bribery, or other high Crimes and Misdemeanors.

Article III

Section 1. The judicial Power of the United States, shall be vested in one supreme Court, and in such inferior Courts as the Congress may from time to time ordain and establish. The Judges, both of the supreme and inferior Courts, shall hold their Offices during good Behaviour, and shall, at stated Times, receive for their Services, a Compensation, which shall not be diminished during their Continuance in Office.

Section 2. The judicial Power shall extend to all Cases, in Law and Equity, arising under this Constitution, the Laws of the United States, and Treaties made, or which shall be made, under their Authority;—to all Cases affecting Ambassadors, other public Ministers and Consuls;—to all Cases of admiralty and maritime Jurisdiction;—to Controversies to which the United States shall be a Party;—to Controversies between two or more States;—between a State and Citizens of another State;—between Citizens of different States;— between Citizens of the same State claiming Lands under Grants of different States, and between a State, or the Citizens thereof, and foreign States, Citizens or Subjects.

In all Cases affecting Ambassadors, other public Ministers and Consuls, and those in which a State shall be Party, the supreme Court shall have original Jurisdiction. In all the other Cases before mentioned, the supreme Court shall have appellate Jurisdiction, both as to Law and Fact, with such Exceptions, and under such Regulations as the Congress shall make.

The Trial of all Crimes, except in Cases of Impeachment, shall be by Jury; and such Trial shall be held in the State where the said Crimes shall have been committed; but when not committed within any State, the Trial shall be at such Place or Places as the Congress may by Law have directed.

Section 3. Treason against the United States, shall consist only in levying War against them, or in adhering to their Enemies, giving them Aid and Comfort. No Person shall be convicted of Treason unless on the Testimony of two Witnesses to the same overt Act, or on Confession in open Court.

The Congress shall have Power to declare the Punishment of Treason, but no Attainder of Treason shall work Corruption of Blood, or Forfeiture except during the Life of the Person attainted.

Article IV

Section 1. Full Faith and Credit shall be given in each State to the public Acts, Records, and judicial Proceedings of every other State. And the Congress may by general Laws prescribe the Manner in which such Acts, Records, and Proceedings shall be proved, and the Effect thereof.

Section 2. The Citizens of each State shall be entitled to all Privileges and Immunities of Citizens in the several States.

A Person charged in any State with Treason, Felony, or other Crime, who shall flee from Justice, and be found in another State, shall on Demand of the executive Authority of the State from which he fled, be delivered up, to be removed to the State having Jurisdiction of the Crime.

No Person held to Service or Labour in one State, under the Laws thereof, escaping into another, shall, in Consequence of any Law or Regulation therein, be discharged from such Service or Labour,

but shall be delivered up on Claim of the Party to whom such Service or Labour may be due.

Section 3. New States may be admitted by the Congress into this Union; but no new States shall be formed or erected within the Jurisdiction of any other State; nor any State be formed by the Junction of two or more States, or Parts of States, without the Consent of the Legislatures of the States concerned as well as of the Congress.

The Congress shall have Power to dispose of and make all needful Rules and Regulations respecting the Territory or other Property belonging to the United States; and nothing in this Constitution shall be so construed as to Prejudice any Claims of the United States, or of any particular State.

Section 4. The United States shall guarantee to every State in this Union a Republican Form of Government, and shall protect each of them against Invasion; and on Application of the Legislature, or of the Executive (when the Legislature cannot be convened) against domestic Violence.

Article V

The Congress, whenever two thirds of both Houses shall deem it necessary, shall propose Amendments to this Constitution, or, on the Application of the Legislatures of two thirds of the several States, shall call a Convention for proposing Amendments, which, in either Case, shall be valid to all Intents and Purposes, as Part of this Constitution, when ratified by the Legislatures of three fourths of the several States, or by Conventions in three fourths thereof, as the one or the other Mode of Ratification may be proposed by the Congress; Provided that no Amendment which may be made prior to the Year One thousand eight hundred and eight shall in any Manner affect the first and fourth Clauses in the Ninth Section of the first Article; and that no State, without its Consent, shall be deprived of its equal Suffrage in the Senate.

Article VI

All Debts contracted and Engagements entered into, before the Adoption of this Constitution, shall be as valid against the United States under this Constitution, as under the Confederation.

This Constitution, and the Laws of the United States which shall be made in Pursuance thereof; and all Treaties made, or which shall be made, under the Authority of the United States, shall be the supreme Law of the Land; and the Judges in every State shall be bound thereby, any Thing in the Constitution or Laws of any State to the Contrary notwithstanding.

The Senators and Representatives before mentioned, and the Members of the several State Legislatures, and all executive and judicial Officers, both of the United States and of the several States, shall be bound by Oath or Affirmation, to support this Constitution; but no religious Test shall ever be required as a Qualification to any Office or public Trust under the United States.

Article VII

The Ratification of the Conventions of nine States, shall be sufficient for the Establishment of this Constitution between the States so ratifying the Same.

Done in Convention by the Unanimous Consent of the States present the Seventeenth Day of September in the Year of our Lord one thousand seven hundred and Eighty seven and of the Independence of the United States of America the Twelfth

In witness whereof, We have hereunto subscribed our Names,

George Washington—President and deputy from Virginia
New Hampshire: John Langdon, Nicholas Gilman
Massachusetts: Nathaniel Gorham, Rufus King
Connecticut: William Samuel Johnson, Roger Sherman
New York: Alexander Hamilton
New Jersey: William Livingston, David Brearly, William Paterson, Jonathan Dayton
Pennsylvania: Benjamin Franklin, Thomas Mifflin, Robert Morris, George Clymer, Thomas FitzSimons, Jared Ingersoll, James Wilson, Gouverneur Morris
Delaware: George Read, Gunning Bedford, Jr., John Dickinson, Richard Bassett, Jacob Broom
Maryland: James McHenry, Daniel of Saint Thomas Jenifer, Daniel Carroll
Virginia: John Blair, James Madison, Jr.
North Carolina: William Blount, Richard Dobbs Spaight, Hugh Williamson

South Carolina: John Rutledge, Charles Cotesworth Pinckney, Charles Pinckney, Pierce Butler
Georgia: William Few, Abraham Baldwin

Amendment I

Congress shall make no law respecting an establishment of religion, or prohibiting the free exercise thereof; or abridging the freedom of speech, or of the press; or the right of the people peaceably to assemble, and to petition the Government for a redress of grievances.

Amendment II

A well regulated Militia, being necessary to the security of a free State, the right of the people to keep and bear Arms, shall not be infringed.

Amendment III

No Soldier shall, in time of peace be quartered in any house, without the consent of the Owner, nor in time of war, but in a manner to be prescribed by law.

Amendment IV

The right of the people to be secure in their persons, houses, papers, and effects, against unreasonable searches and seizures, shall not be violated, and no Warrants shall issue, but upon probable cause, supported by Oath or affirmation, and particularly describing the place to be searched, and the persons or things to be seized.

Amendment V

No person shall be held to answer for a capital, or otherwise infamous crime, unless on a presentment or indictment of a Grand Jury, except in cases arising in the land or naval forces, or in the Militia, when in actual service in time of War or public danger; nor shall any person be subject for the same offence to be twice put in jeopardy of life or limb; nor shall be compelled in any criminal case to be a witness against himself, nor be deprived of life, liberty, or property, without due process of law; nor shall private property be taken for public use, without just compensation.

Amendment VI

In all criminal prosecutions, the accused shall enjoy the right to a speedy and public trial, by an impartial jury of the State and district wherein the crime shall have been committed, which district shall have been previously ascertained by law, and to be informed of the nature and cause of the accusation; to be confronted with the witnesses against him; to have compulsory process for obtaining witnesses in his favor, and to have the Assistance of Counsel for his defence.

Amendment VII

In Suits at common law, where the value in controversy shall exceed twenty dollars, the right of trial by jury shall be preserved, and no fact tried by a jury, shall be otherwise re-examined in any Court of the United States, than according to the rules of the common law.

Amendment VIII

Excessive bail shall not be required, nor excessive fines imposed, nor cruel and unusual punishments inflicted.

Amendment IX

The enumeration in the Constitution, of certain rights, shall not be construed to deny or disparage others retained by the people.

Amendment X

The powers not delegated to the United States by the Constitution, nor prohibited by it to the States, are reserved to the States respectively, or to the people.

Amendment XI

The Judicial power of the United States shall not be construed to extend to any suit in law or equity, commenced or prosecuted against one of the United States by Citizens of another State, or by Citizens or Subjects of any Foreign State.

Amendment XII

The Electors shall meet in their respective states, and vote by ballot for President and Vice-President, one of whom, at least, shall not be an inhabitant of the same state with themselves; they shall name in their ballots the person voted for as President, and in distinct ballots the person voted for as Vice-President, and they shall make distinct lists of all persons voted for as President, and of all persons voted for as Vice-President, and of the number of votes for each, which lists they shall sign and certify, and transmit sealed to the seat of the government of the United States, directed to the President of the Senate;—The President of the Senate shall, in the presence of the Senate and House of Representatives, open all the certificates and the votes shall then be counted;—The person having the greatest number of votes for President, shall be the President, if such number be a majority of the whole number of Electors appointed; and if no person have such majority, then from the persons having the highest numbers not exceeding three on the list of those voted for as President, the House of Representatives shall choose immediately, by ballot, the President. But in choosing the President, the votes shall be taken by states, the representation from each state having one vote; a quorum for this purpose shall consist of a member or members from two-thirds of the states, and a majority of all the states shall be necessary to a choice. And if the House of Representatives shall not choose a President whenever the right of choice shall devolve upon them, before the fourth day of March next following, then the Vice-President shall act as President, as in the case of the death or other constitutional disability of the President. The person having the greatest number of votes as Vice-President, shall be the Vice-President, if such number be a majority of the whole number of Electors appointed, and if no person have a majority, then from the two highest numbers on the list, the Senate shall choose the Vice-President; a quorum for the purpose shall consist of two-thirds of the whole number of Senators, and a majority of the whole number shall be necessary to a choice. But no person constitutionally ineligible to the office of President shall be eligible to that of Vice-President of the United States.

Amendment XIII

Neither slavery nor involuntary servitude, except as a punishment for crime whereof the party shall have been duly convicted, shall exist within the United States, or any place subject to their jurisdiction.

Congress shall have power to enforce this article by appropriate legislation.

Amendment XIV

Section 1. All persons born or naturalized in the United States, and subject to the jurisdiction thereof, are citizens of the United States and of the State wherein they reside. No State shall make or enforce any law which shall abridge the privileges or immunities of citizens of the United States; nor shall any State deprive any person of life, liberty, or property, without due process of law; nor deny to any person within its jurisdiction the equal protection of the laws.

Section 2. Representatives shall be apportioned among the several States according to their respective numbers, counting the whole number of persons in each State, excluding Indians not taxed. But when the right to vote at any election for the choice of electors for President and Vice President of the United States, Representatives in Congress, the Executive and Judicial officers of a State, or the members of the Legislature thereof, is denied to any of the male inhabitants of such State, being twenty-one years of age, and citizens of the United States, or in any way abridged, except for participation in rebellion, or other crime, the basis of representation therein shall be reduced in the proportion which the number of such male citizens shall bear to the whole number of male citizens twenty-one years of age in such State.

Section 3. No person shall be a Senator or Representative in Congress, or elector of President and Vice President, or hold any office, civil or military, under the United States, or under any State, who, having previously taken an oath, as a member of Congress, or as an officer of the United States, or as a member of any State legislature, or as an executive or judicial officer of any State, to support the Constitution of the United States, shall have engaged in insurrection or rebellion against the same, or given aid or comfort to the enemies thereof. But Congress may by a vote of two-thirds of each House, remove such disability.

Section 4. The validity of the public debt of the United States, authorized by law, including debts incurred for payment of pensions and bounties for services in suppressing insurrection or rebellion, shall not be questioned. But neither the United States nor any State shall assume or pay any debt or obligation incurred in aid of insurrection or rebellion against the United States, or any claim for the loss or emancipation of any slave; but all such debts, obligations and claims shall be held illegal and void.

Section 5. The Congress shall have power to enforce, by appropriate legislation, the provisions of this article.

Amendment XV

The right of citizens of the United States to vote shall not be denied or abridged by the United States or by any State on account of race, color, or previous condition of servitude.

The Congress shall have power to enforce this article by appropriate legislation.

Amendment XVI

The Congress shall have power to lay and collect taxes on incomes, from whatever source derived, without apportionment among the several States, and without regard to any census or enumeration.

Amendment XVII

The Senate of the United States shall be composed of two Senators from each State, elected by the people thereof, for six years; and each Senator shall have one vote. The electors in each State shall have the qualifications requisite for electors of the most numerous branch of the State legislatures.

When vacancies happen in the representation of any State in the Senate, the executive authority of such State shall issue writs of election to fill such vacancies: Provided, That the legislature of any State may empower the executive thereof to make temporary appointments until the people fill the vacancies by election as the legislature may direct.

This amendment shall not be so construed as to affect the election or term of any Senator chosen before it becomes valid as part of the Constitution.

Amendment XVIII

Section 1. After one year from the ratification of this article the manufacture, sale, or transportation of intoxicating liquors within, the importation thereof into, or the exportation thereof from the United States and all territory subject to the jurisdiction thereof for beverage purposes is hereby prohibited.

Section 2. The Congress and the several States shall have concurrent power to enforce this article by appropriate legislation.

Section 3. This article shall be inoperative unless it shall have been ratified as an amendment to the Constitution by the legislatures of the several States, as provided in the Constitution, within seven years from the date of the submission hereof to the States by the Congress.

Amendment XIX

The right of citizens of the United States to vote shall not be denied or abridged by the United States or by any State on account of sex.

Congress shall have power to enforce this article by appropriate legislation.

Amendment XX

Section 1. The terms of the President and Vice President shall end at noon on the 20th day of January, and the terms of Senators and Representatives at noon on the 3d day of January, of the years in which such terms would have ended if this article had not been ratified; and the terms of their successors shall then begin.

Section 2. The Congress shall assemble at least once in every year, and such meeting shall begin at noon on the 3d day of January, unless they shall by law appoint a different day.

Section 3. If, at the time fixed for the beginning of the term of the President, the President elect shall have died, the Vice President elect shall become President. If a President shall not have been chosen before the time fixed for the beginning of his term, or if the President elect shall have failed to qualify, then the Vice President elect shall act as President until a President shall have qualified; and the Congress may by law provide for the case wherein neither a President elect nor a Vice President elect shall have qualified, declaring who shall then act as President, or the manner in which one who is to act shall be selected, and such person shall act accordingly until a President or Vice President shall have qualified.

Section 4. The Congress may by law provide for the case of the death of any of the persons from whom the House of Representatives may choose a President whenever the right of choice shall have devolved upon them, and for the case of the death of any of the persons from whom the Senate may choose a Vice President whenever the right of choice shall have devolved upon them.

Section 5. Sections 1 and 2 shall take effect on the 15th day of October following the ratification of this article.

Section 6. This article shall be inoperative unless it shall have been ratified as an amendment to the Constitution by the legislatures of three-fourths of the several States within seven years from the date of its submission.

Amendment XXI

Section 1. The eighteenth article of amendment to the Constitution of the United States is hereby repealed.

Section 2. The transportation or importation into any State, Territory, or possession of the United States for delivery or use therein of intoxicating liquors, in violation of the laws thereof, is hereby prohibited.

Section 3. This article shall be inoperative unless it shall have been ratified as an amendment to the Constitution by conventions in the several States, as provided in the Constitution, within seven years from the date of the submission hereof to the States by the Congress.

Amendment XXII

Section 1. No person shall be elected to the office of the President more than twice, and no person who has held the office of President, or acted as President, for more than two years of a term to which some other person was elected President shall be elected to the office of the President more than once. But this article shall not apply to any person holding the office of President when this article was proposed by the Congress, and shall not prevent any person who may be holding the office of President, or acting as President, during the term within which this article becomes operative from holding the office of President or acting as President during the remainder of such term.

Section 2. This article shall be inoperative unless it shall have been ratified as an amendment to the Constitution by the legislatures of three-fourths of the several states within seven years from the date of its submission to the states by the Congress.

Amendment XXIII

Section 1. The District constituting the seat of government of the United States shall appoint in such manner as the Congress may direct: A number of electors of President and Vice President equal to the whole number of Senators and Representatives in Congress to which the District would be entitled if it were a state, but in no event more than the least populous state; they shall be in addition to those appointed by the states, but they shall be considered, for the purposes of the election of President and Vice President, to be electors appointed by a state; and they shall meet in the District and perform such duties as provided by the twelfth article of amendment.

Section 2. The Congress shall have power to enforce this article by appropriate legislation.

Amendment XXIV

Section 1. The right of citizens of the United States to vote in any primary or other election for President or Vice President, for electors for President or Vice President, or for Senator or Representative in Congress, shall not be denied or abridged by the United States or any state by reason of failure to pay any poll tax or other tax.

Section 2. The Congress shall have power to enforce this article by appropriate legislation.

Amendment XXV

Section 1. In case of the removal of the President from office or of his death or resignation, the Vice President shall become President.

Section 2. Whenever there is a vacancy in the office of the Vice President, the President shall nominate a Vice President who shall take office upon confirmation by a majority vote of both Houses of Congress.

Section 3. Whenever the President transmits to the President pro tempore of the Senate and the Speaker of the House of Representatives his written declaration that he is unable to discharge the powers and duties of his office, and until he transmits to them a written declaration to the contrary, such powers and duties shall be discharged by the Vice President as Acting President.

Section 4. Whenever the Vice President and a majority of either the principal officers of the executive departments or of such other body as Congress may by law provide, transmit to the President pro tempore of the Senate and the Speaker of the House of Representatives their written declaration that the President is unable to discharge the powers and duties of his office, the Vice President shall immediately assume the powers and duties of the office as Acting President.

Thereafter, when the President transmits to the President pro tempore of the Senate and the Speaker of the House of Representatives his written declaration that no inability exists, he shall resume the powers and duties of his office unless the Vice President and a majority of either the principal officers of the executive department or of such other body as Congress may by law provide, transmit within four days to the President pro tempore of the Senate and the Speaker of the House of Representatives their written declaration that the President is unable to discharge the powers and duties of his office. Thereupon Congress shall decide the issue, assembling within forty-eight hours for that purpose if not in session. If the Congress, within twenty-one days after receipt of the latter written declaration, or, if Congress is not in session, within twenty-one days after Congress is required to assemble, determines by two-thirds vote of both Houses that the President is unable to discharge the powers and duties of his office, the Vice President shall continue to discharge the same as Acting President; otherwise, the President shall resume the powers and duties of his office.

Amendment XXVI

Section 1. The right of citizens of the United States, who are 18 years of age or older, to vote, shall not be denied or abridged by the United States or any state on account of age.

Section 2: The Congress shall have the power to enforce this article by appropriate legislation.

Amendment XXVII

No law varying the compensation for the services of the Senators and Representatives shall take effect until an election of Representatives shall have intervened.

Legal Reasoning

Adjudication is the formal process by which legal disputes are judicially resolved in courts of law. Adjudication involves numerous processes, some of which are procedural in nature and some of which are mental insofar as they involve decision making. Collectively, the mental components of adjudication are commonly referred to as **legal reasoning**.

Legal reasoning is a complicated process. In its most broad sense, it represents the ways in which judges (and sometimes jurors) make decisions in legal cases. Those decisions tend to involve three distinct types of rational thought processes: analogical, inductive, and deductive reasoning. But, to be sure, legal reasoning is not limited to the use of these logical forms of reasoning. Legal reasoning is more complicated than using logic to resolve factual disputes under the law. It also must take into account other elements of persuasion, such as current events and contemporary morals and values (Carter & Burke, 2007).

Types of Logical Reasoning

Reasoning by Analogy

Reasoning by analogy, or **analogical reasoning**, is a type of inductive reasoning that involves comparing and contrasting things to find key similarities. An analogy is usually expressed in the form of one thing being like another (X is like Y; A is similar to B). You are probably most familiar with analogies

used on standardized exams that test vocabulary. Here is a simple example:

Dolphin is to ocean as . . .
    A. Ant is to jungle   B. Salami is to lunch
    C. Camel is to desert   D. Pencil is to lead

The correct answer would be "C"—camel is to desert. This is because a dolphin lives in the ocean like a camel lives in the desert. Ants may be found in jungles, but also live in many other places. Salami does not "live" anywhere; it may be eaten for lunch, but it may be eaten for other meals as well. And pencils may contain lead, but pencils to do not "live" in lead. In this example, where the dolphin lives is what makes it most similar to the camel living in the desert. Selecting where the animal lives is the logical connection from which we draw the analogy. It is important to note, though, that there are other similarities upon which we could base a logical connection. For example, a dolphin and camel are both animals, while an ant is an insect, salami is a type of food, and a pencil is an inanimate object.

Let's try a slightly more complex analogy. Is an apple more like an orange or a banana? While all three are fruit, there are a number of characteristics upon which these fruits may be compared and contrasted.

Using the information in Table D.1, we find that apples and oranges are alike on only two of our selected dimensions: neither has edible seeds and both are round. Similarly, we find that apples

TABLE D.1
An Example of Reasoning By Analogy

Characteristics for Comparison	Apple		Orange	Banana
Edible seeds	No		No	Yes
Shape	Round		Round	Oblong
Edible skin	Yes		No	No
Peelable without a knife	No		Yes	Yes
Citrus family	No		Yes	No
Color when ripe	Variable (red, orange, yellow, green)		Orange	Yellow

Source: Adapted from Edward C. Martin (n.d.). *Thinking like a lawyer.* http://www.samford.edu/schools/netlaw/dh2/logic

and bananas are alike in only one way under our selected criteria for comparison: neither fruit is a member of the citrus family. Since apples and oranges are alike in two ways while apples and bananas are alike in only one, it would be a valid conclusion to say that apples are more like oranges than bananas. But what is critical to the analogy here is that we have selected six characteristics for comparison, one of which—color when ripe—is of no help whatsoever in comparing apples to the other two fruits. This illustrates one of the major shortcomings of analogical reasoning. It is dependent upon the criteria used for comparison.

Let's now apply this analogy in a legal framework. Supposed that a state prohibited the importation of "oranges and similar fruits," but allowed "bananas and similar fruits" to be imported into the state. Can apples be imported into this state? If you use shape as the basis for comparison, apples may not be imported. But if you use the criterion of whether the fruit belongs to the citrus family, then apples may be imported into the state. Both outcomes would be equally valid from the standpoint of logic. But only one outcome is likely to be correct under the law. Given the ambiguity in the statutory law of this state, it would likely fall on the courts to figure out whether apples could be legally imported into the state. To make that determination, the courts would consider the arguments by analogy offered by the lawyers in the case and try to make as logical a ruling as possible.

In summary, analogical reasoning allows us to make comparisons. The validity of those comparisons depends upon the criteria or characteristics selected as the basis for the comparisons.

In the end, though, analogical reasoning does not allow us to declare any general conclusions that may be used to support other arguments. That is where inductive and deductive reasoning come into play.

Inductive Reasoning

Inductive reasoning is the process of forming a generalization from a list of similar examples. The generalization is called a "conjecture."

The process of inductive reasoning begins by assembling a series of examples from a necessarily limited number of observations (because it is not possible to observe every example on the planet). This process uses analogical reasoning in order to group similar examples together. For example, suppose you observed the following types of fruit: apples, oranges, grapes, plums, tangerines, grapefruits, cranberries, cherries, coconuts, and lemons. From this limited set of examples, what generalization might you make about fruit? If you said, "all fruit are round," that would be an excellent conjecture based on the limited number of examples you had available to you. However, as you know, not all fruits are, in fact, round. Bananas, for example, are oblong. So, your conjecture, although logical in light of your list of examples, would not be valid. This example illustrates the importance of having a sufficient number of examples that are drawn from a representative sample—something that is key to the scientific method. Determining whether the sample is representative is dependent, in part, on there being a sufficient number of examples that are comparable. Whether the examples are sufficiently alike as to warrant a logical comparison is dependent upon the criteria used to compare them. As discussed above, that comparison process involves analogical reasoning.

What color are swans? For thousands of years, all examples of swans in Europe led people to conclude that all swans were white. But they learned that all swans were not white when black swans were discovered in Australia in the late 1600s (Taleb 2007). These Australian counter-examples demonstrated that the conjecture "all swans are white" was not true. But it took going to a distant continent after centuries of first-hand observations to invalidate a conjecture that was assumed to be valid for centuries.

Let's examine an inductive argument as applied to legal reasoning. Suppose that you examined the facts and outcomes of a series of 20 murder cases from a single state in a given year (State A). In each case, the defendant intentionally killed the victim without the victim having done anything to provoke the killing. And, in each case of the 20 cases, the defendant was convicted. From this limited set of 20 examples, a good conjecture would be: "All people who intentionally kill another human being without any provocation will be convicted of murder."

Suppose you then studied 80 more murder cases—20 from each of four other states (States B, C, D, and E) that occurred in the same year from which you drew your sample of 20 cases in State A. In all 80 of these cases, the defendant intentionally killed the victim without the victim having done anything to provoke the killing. Again, in each case of these 80 cases, the defendant was convicted. When added to the 20 murder cases from State A, you would be justified in having more confidence in your conjecture at this point because you not only examined more examples, but you diversified the representativeness of your sample by studying cases from four additional states. At this point, your conjecture could be called a legal precept—a generalized legal conclusion drawn from a reasonably representative list of examples. But your legal precept could not yet be considered a rule of law because it has not yet been established over time in a sufficient number of cases. For that to occur, you would need to examine many more murder cases from more states from a variety of years. See Exhibit D.1 for an illustration of the process of inductive reasoning as it applies within a legal framework.

Suppose, for example, that you studied a random sample of 200 cases drawn from 20 different states over a 50-year period of time. In all 200 cases, the defendant intentionally killed the victim without the victim having done anything to provoke the killing. Again, in each case of these 200 cases, the defendant was convicted (either by a jury or through a guilty plea). At this point, you may feel comfortable saying that your legal precept is a rule of law because the conjecture you made from your study of more than 200 cases was formed from a large number of examples drawn from a cross-section of states over a long period of time. In spite of these facts, though, you would be mistaken if you were to conclude that: "All people who kill another human being without any provocation will be convicted of murder."

Assume that you continued to gather data by looking at more cases in more states from different years. In one of the cases in State J, the defendant intentionally killed the victim without the victim having done anything to provoke the killing. However, the defendant in that case was not convicted because he was determined to be legally insane. Your conjecture/legal precept is now invalidated by this single counter-example. Therefore, the alleged "rule of law" must also be invalid as currently phrased. As you do more research, you find more cases in which mentally ill people were not convicted of murder for the intentional killing of another human being, some of which involved acquittals on the basis of insanity, others of which involved convictions of less serious forms of homicide after a determination of diminished capacity. You would have to refine your legal precept to take into account these examples. You might do so by forming the following inductive conjecture/legal precept: "All people who intentionally kill another human being without any provocation or legally recognized excuse will be convicted of murder."

Deductive Reasoning

In contrast to inductive reasoning, which goes from specific examples to a generalization, deductive reasoning goes from a generalization to a specific conclusion. The most simple and logically sound deductive argument takes the form of a "deductive syllogism." The syllogism allows us to compare

Exhibit D.1 ■ Flowchart of Inductive Reasoning in the Law

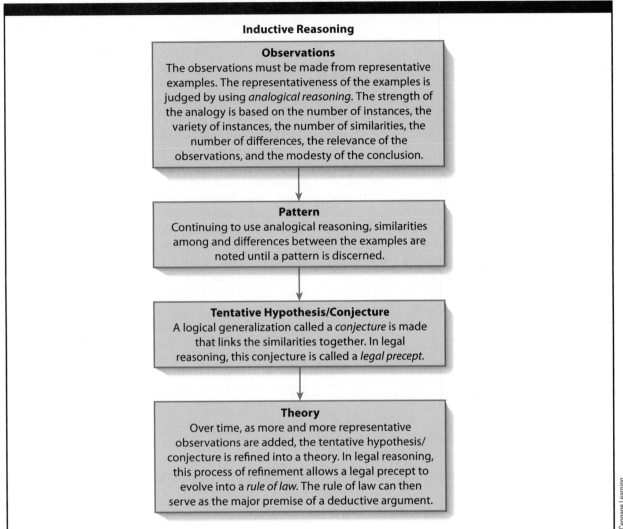

Inductive Reasoning

Observations
The observations must be made from representative examples. The representativeness of the examples is judged by using *analogical reasoning*. The strength of the analogy is based on the number of instances, the variety of instances, the number of similarities, the number of differences, the relevance of the observations, and the modesty of the conclusion.

Pattern
Continuing to use analogical reasoning, similarities among and differences between the examples are noted until a pattern is discerned.

Tentative Hypothesis/Conjecture
A logical generalization called a *conjecture* is made that links the similarities together. In legal reasoning, this conjecture is called a *legal precept*.

Theory
Over time, as more and more representative observations are added, the tentative hypothesis/conjecture is refined into a theory. In legal reasoning, this process of refinement allows a legal precept to evolve into a *rule of law*. The rule of law can then serve as the major premise of a deductive argument.

© Cengage Learning

the logical relationship between two arguments if arranged in a particular form. This form is as follows:

Major Premise	A generalized statement formed through induction.
Minor Premise	A statement capturing the essence of a particular example that relates to the generalization in the major premise.
Conclusion	A statement that is logically consistent with both the major and minor premises.

Here is a classic example of a deductive syllogism:

Major Premise	All men are mortal.
Minor Premise	Socrates is a man.
Conclusion	Socrates is mortal.

The form of the deductive syllogism is key to the validity of its conclusion. There are a number of rules that must be met in order for a deductive syllogism to be validly formed[1] that are beyond the scope of this appendix. For our purposes, it is sufficient to say that a properly formed deductive syllogism guarantees the accuracy of the conclusion, assuming the truth of its premises. Recall, for example, the belief regarding the color of swans.

Major Premise	All swans are white.
Minor Premise	Daphne is a swan.
Conclusion	Daphne is white.

If, however, Daphne was one of the black swans discovered in Australia, then the logical form of the deductive syllogism is useless in providing a valid conclusion because one of the premises is false.

Let's apply the deductive syllogism to a legal example. Recall from the section above on inductive reasoning the generalization that we formed after examining murder cases in many states across a number of years. We eventually refined our inductive conjecture into a rule of law. That rule of law would serve as the major premise in a deductive syllogism.

Major Premise	All people who intentionally kill another human being without any provocation or legally recognized excuse will be convicted of murder.
Minor Premise	John intentionally killed another human being without any provocation or legally recognized excuse.
Conclusion	John will be convicted of murder.

There are two limitations to using deductive reasoning in the law that should be obvious at this point. First, as mentioned above, the conclusion will be invalid if either one of the premises is invalid. Thus, if it is not true that all people who intentionally kill other human beings without any provocation or legally recognized excuse will be convicted of murder, then we cannot know whether or not John will be convicted. Similarly, if John did not kill without provocation or legally recognized excuse, again we cannot form a valid conclusion about the outcome of his trial using the form of the deductive syllogism.

Second, the law rarely presents situations that can be reduced to the form of a pure deductive syllogism. There are clearly rules of law, but most of those rules have exceptions and some of those exceptions have even more specialized exceptions. Thus, it becomes quite difficult to form universal legal statements that can serve as the major premise of a deductive argument. Take, for example, the major premise concerning murder liability that we have been using in this appendix. "A person who intentionally kills another human being without any provocation or legally recognized excuse will be convicted of murder." This statement is fairly close to being an accurate statement of the law. But the problem is that we cannot say that all such people "will be convicted." Some people will be acquitted due to lack of evidence; others may be acquitted due to the sympathies of the jury; others may never even be caught and put on trial. Simply put, legal syllogisms are rarely, if ever, based upon absolute truths. Legal reasoning, therefore, is more complicated than the rules of logic.

Logic as Part of Legal Reasoning

Analogical, inductive, and deductive reasoning all play important roles in the process of legal reasoning. But, as stated above, legal reasoning involves more than these forms of logic. The process of legal reasoning rests upon an important principle in law known as *stare decisis*—Latin for "to stand by decided matters." This principle stands for the proposition that prior cases should serve as precedent for deciding future cases that are factually and legal similar. This is especially important in the hierarchy of court structure. A decision of a higher court serves as binding precedent on a lower court within a particular jurisdiction. Thus, for example, a decision of the Supreme Court of Texas is binding on the lower appellate and trial courts of that state. That decision, however, is not binding on the courts of any other state. In our federal system, the decisions of the U.S.

---

[1]E.g., there must be three and only three terms; at least one of the terms must be distributed using a universal term (like "all" or "none"); the conclusion cannot contain any term that is not distributed by a universal statement in one of the premises; if a negative universal term (like "none") is used to distribute one premise, then the other premise cannot also be phrased using a negative distributor; if either premise is negative, the conclusion must also be negative; and a syllogism with two universal premises cannot have a particular conclusion. For more information, see Martin. (n.d.)

Supreme Court are binding on all lower courts, both state and federal, when it comes to interpretations of federal law (especially constitutional law). But state courts are free to interpret their state laws differently so long as they do not infringe upon the minimal baselines of federal constitutional protections as interpreted by the U.S. Supreme Court.

Given the roles of precedent and the principle of *stare decisis*, legal reasoning in the U.S. common law tradition brings a certain amount of stability to the law. It helps us to organize cases, using analogical reasoning, into legal precepts because we assume that the result in prior similar cases should guide the result in future similar cases. Moreover, the stability of law that *stare decisis* facilitates allows us to refine

legal precepts over time into rules of law. These rules of law may then be deductively applied in new cases to produce reasonably predictable outcomes. The results in these cases then are added to the body of precedent to serve as even more examples to which analogies may be made in subsequent cases. This circular process is graphically represented in Figure D.1.

While stability in law is one of the benefits of reasoning from precedent within the principle of *stare decisis*, that stability can also have a downside. Because lower courts are bound to follow the precedents of higher courts, "bad precedent" must be overruled by the court that established it. It usually takes many years before courts recognize that one of its decisions was poor (or wrong) and, therefore,

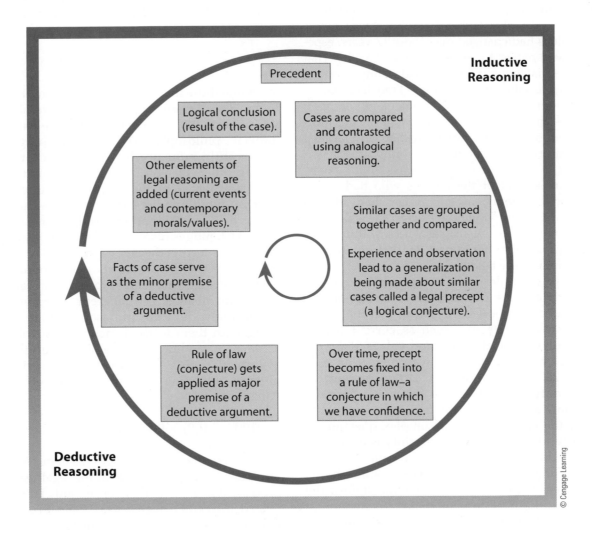

Figure D.1 ■ **The Circular Process of Legal Reasoning**

should not be retained as valid precedent. Part of what transpires over those years may be shifts in social conscience. After all, social norms evolve with time. For example, it took the Supreme Court nearly 60 years to overrule its decision in *Plessy v. Ferguson* (1896), which upheld the racial segregation on the "separate but equal" principle. By the time the Court declared the "separate but equal" unconstitutional in *Brown v. Board of Education of Topeka* (1954), much had changed about the ways race was perceived in the United States.

Similarly, in 2003, the Supreme Court invalidated the nation's sodomy laws (i.e., laws criminalizing consensual oral or anal sex) on due process grounds when it decided *Lawrence v. Texas*. But only 17 years earlier, the Court had upheld the constitutionality of sodomy laws over a due process challenge in *Bowers v. Hardwick* (1986). Certainly, social mores and values had changed over those 17 years, especially with regard to views on homosexuality. That shift in social thought certainly had an impact on the Court's reasoning in *Lawrence* (see Fradella 2003).

Sometimes the passage of time is not enough; perhaps there needs to be a change in the judicial composition of court such that new judicial officials bring a different philosophy of decision making to subsequent cases. Consider, for example, that several of the justices who had voted to uphold sodomy laws in *Bowers* had left the Supreme Court by the time *Lawrence* was decided and were replaced by justices who saw things differently, perhaps due in part, to different judicial philosophies (see below).

These examples illustrate that although the principle of stare decisis brings stability to the law, it does not necessarily mean that the law is stagnant. Other factors such as current events and evolving social norms and values also play an important role in legal reasoning (Carter & Burke 2007). This brings a certain amount of uncertainty to the law. You can never be quite sure how a court will rule in a case—especially when the case involves a complex question of constitutional law. This uncertainty is especially prominent when cases go to high courts, like the U.S. Supreme Court, since it is not bound by its own precedents. In light of such uncertainty, the politics of judicial decision making is frequently an issue when governors and the president select judges or justices.

Jurisprudence and Legal Reasoning

There are many different theories of jurisprudence that collectively form the philosophy of law (see Table D.2).

A judge's belief in one of these schools of jurisprudential thought over another may have a significant effect on the outcome of case. But as Table D.2 should make clear, other factors clearly enter into the decision-making process. Carter and Burke (2007) posit that the decision in a given case is a product of a judge's views on (1) the law governing a particular type of dispute (L); (2) the relevant facts of a case (F); (3) current events (E); and (4) widely shared contemporary morals and values (V).

$$L + F + E + V \mapsto D$$

While these four factors clearly form the basis for most legal reasoning as illustrated in Table D.2, it is important to keep in mind that the particular judicial philosophy (P) of any judge can significantly influence his or her interpretation of any other variable. One judge might find a particular fact to be the legally operative fact in the case, while another judge may view that same fact as being less important. And, as presented in Table D.2, judges also clearly differ with respect to how to interpret the law, especially ambiguities in the law. And, finally, most of us recognize that current events and contemporary morals and values are all subject to different interpretations. Accordingly, judicial philosophy that judges bring with them to the bench clearly will have some effect on how they legally reason through a particular case. Collectively, these principles of legal reasoning may be represented by the equation:

$$f[P(L) + P(F) + P(E) + P(V)] \mapsto D$$

Finally, how the judge perceives his or her own role also plays an important role in the legal reasoning process. While perceptions of the judicial role are related, to a certain degree, to a certain jurisprudential schools of thought, they are distinct, as we shall now explore.

TABLE D.2
Major Schools of Jurisprudential Thought

School	Summary of Major Beliefs	Descriptors	Equation Analogy
Natural Law	Human/Positive law (L) ought to reflect the law of nature or "nature law," which some would consider to be "God's Law." Decisions (D) should be a function (f) of moral principles (M) that are universally applied to promote human life, knowledge, community, friendship, and faith. Ambiguities in law must be resolved to harmonize positive law with natural law.	Static Infallible Humanistic	$f[EP(L + F) \mapsto D$
Legal Formalism	Judges apply the relevant positive law (L) to the pertinent facts of a case (F) and arrive at the correct legal decision (D). Normative or policy considerations are irrelevant. Thus, judges should be guided by the plain meaning of the words in a law, not by their interpretation of what the law should be. Ambiguities in the law should be resolved in accordance with the original meaning of the words and, if known, the intent of those who wrote the words.	Static Fallible Logical	$L + F \mapsto D$
Legal Realism	Law (L) is indeterminate. Law cannot be applied to the facts of a case (F) to reach a result without judges drawing on other extralegal considerations (ELC), especially the judge's personal experiences. ELC may go unstated in a legal opinion, but most often manifest themselves as part of the process of analogical reasoning process when judges decide which cases present the best "fit" to be followed as precedent.	Flexible Fallible Somewhat Idiosyncratic	$L + F + ELC \mapsto D$
Legal Process	Procedural consistency must guide legal reasoning. Decisions are a function (f) of applying positive law (L) to the facts of a case in accordance with certain neutral principles (NP) that restrain the discretion of any individual judge such as deference to legislative and/or executive intent, or widely shared ethical principles of societal goals as expressed in the plain language of positive law. Ambiguities in law should be interpreted in light of which neutral principle (NP) is consistently applied in such cases.	Somewhat Flexible Fallible Consistent	$f[NP(L + F)] \mapsto D$
Law and Economics	Legal decisions (D) should be a function (f) of laissez faire economic principles (EP) being applied to the facts of the case (F) and the governing law. Ambiguities in law should be resolved to promote economic efficiency and maximize wealth.	Somewhat Flexible Fallible Consistent	$f[EP(L + F)] \mapsto D$
Rights-Based Jurisprudence	Legal decisions (D) should be a function (f) of interpreting the facts of a case (F) and the applicable law (L) in ways that produce just outcomes and fair public policies. Ambiguities in law should be resolved to maximize individual rights and liberties (R) while simultaneously promoting social justice (J) and equality (E).	Highly Flexible Fallible Pragmatic and Humanistic	$f[(R + J + E) (L + F)] \mapsto D$
Critical Legal Studies and Postmodern Jurisprudence	Law (L) represents a political and hegemonic device (i.e., it perpetuates the status quo) that is used promote social stratification in a manner that, overall, benefits certain groups of people over others. Indeed, judges interpret both the facts of a case (F) and the law as a function (f) of their indoctrination into ideologies that promotion deeply ingrained structural inequalities (SI) in society on the basis of socio-economic status, race (critical race theory), sex (feminist jurisprudence), and sexual identify (queer legal theory).	Somewhat Static Flawed Hegemonic and Illegitimate	$f[SI(L + F)] \mapsto D$

Judicial Philosophies and Legal Reasoning

One of the most salient philosophical distinctions in legal reasoning stems from how a judge perceives his or her own role. Some judges believe that they should avoid making law through the common law process, and instead restrict themselves to narrow questions of law presented in the cases they adjudicate. This philosophy, most frequently associated with socially conservative judges, is referred to as judicial restraint (Carter & Burke 2007). Those who subscribe to judicial restraint generally believe that judges ought to focus on the original intent of a constitution or a statute. In doing so, they tend to strictly construe a legal provision by focusing on the actual meaning of the words used in a constitution or statute. Judges who subscribe to this point of view tend to be uncomfortable with the courts being used as agents of social change. Instead, they prefer for changes in the law to occur as a result of legislative actions.

In contrast, other judges see their roles as facilitating social change. They feel that they should make new laws in accordance with the changing needs of society. This philosophy, most commonly associated with liberal or moderate judges, is often referred to as judicial activism. Judges who subscribe to this perspective tend to view the language of constitutions and statutes as lenses through which interpretations can be made. To them, the law is as an evolving framework for courts to solve social problems that the other branches of government have neglected or refused to address.

It should be noted that the differences between the philosophies of judicial restraint and judicial activism might produce some false dichotomies, especially with respect to liberals and conservatives. Indeed, in their book *Battle Supreme*, Neubauer and Meinhold (2005) say that perceptions of judicial activism depends on whose ox is being gored.

> Historically, conservatives have tended to interpret legal doctrines quite flexibly, or actively, when it suited their purposes—for example, to extend more power to the executive branch, the police,

and employers. Liberals have tended to read the Constitution quite strictly, or with restraint, when an amendment in is line with their beliefs—for example, the First Amendment stipulation that Congress make no law restricting freedom of speech. (Friedrichs, 2006, p. 58)

Consider, for example the Supreme Court's decision in *District of Columbia v. Heller* (2008). In that case, four conservative justices (Scalia, Roberts, Thomas, and Alito) were joined by one moderate justice (Kennedy) when they ruled that the Second Amendment to the U.S. Constitution grants an individual person the right to possess and use a firearm for lawful purposes, such as self-defense within the home. The Second Amendment provides: "A well regulated Militia, being necessary to the security of a free State, the right of the people to keep and bear Arms, shall not be infringed." They gave the Second Amendment an expansive (liberal?) reading when they decided that the introductory phrase regarding a militia was nothing more than a "prefatory clause" that in no way limited the "operative clause" of the Amendment—the one concerning the right to bear arms. In contrast, four liberal to moderate justices (Stevens, Breyer, Ginsburg, and Souter) dissented in the case by giving the Second Amendment a narrow, strict constructionist (conservative?) reading. They asserted the language used in the text of prefatory clause to the Amendment, as well as the original intent of the Framers, evidenced that the Amendment provided for the right of military and police use of firearms, not any right of private citizens to have and use such weapons. Since the outcome of the case was not in accordance with usual liberal/conservative principles of judicial decision making, that tells us something about the role of judicial philosophy in the constitutional adjudication process. In short, legal reasoning is more complex than a reductionist label. Rather, it is a function of judicial philosophies, jurisprudential theories, current events, morals, and values as they collectively apply to the facts of a particular case and the interpretation of laws which, all too frequently, leave room for disagreement as to their meaning.

Box D.1 ■ An Exercise in Legal Reasoning

Assume that you and your friend Tom are in a bar together. Tom makes eye contact with an attractive young woman who, unbeknownst to him, is Scott's girlfriend. Scott, a very jealous person, sees this and immediately comes over to Tom and hits him over the head with a beer bottle without saying a word. As a result, Tom sustains a concussion and needs ten stitches to repair his injuries. And, for the first time in his life, Tom also starts to suffer severe headaches as a result of the injuries inflicted by Scott. Both you and Tom want Scott brought to justice. In light of your knowledge of criminal justice, Tom asks you what you think will happen to Scott. To answer Tom, you decide to go to a law library in search of some answers.

First, you would need to determine which body of precedent to consult in order to find guiding legal precepts and binding rules of law. In doing so, you would disregard contract disputes, child custody cases, cases involving the probate of wills, and so on. Instead, you would be looking for criminal law cases.

Thus, the type of legal dispute would be the organizing characteristic upon which we separate cases using analogical reasoning.

Once you identified criminal law as the subfield you needed to research, you would then need to engage in more analogical reasoning to find cases most similar to Tom's. Accordingly, you would not likely concern yourself with reading cases concerning homicides, thefts, or sexual assaults. Rather, you would look for cases involving the crime of battery—cases in which the victim sustained physical injuries without being killed.

Once you found a group of cases concerning battery, you would want to locate the ones with facts that are most similar to Tom's case. Again, this process would use analogical reasoning. Ideally, you would hope to find a case in which someone had been hit over the head with a beer bottle while in a bar. If you found such a case, you would be excited because the facts of that case would be nearly identical to yours. Unfortunately, you are unable to find such a case. However, you do find several cases that you think will help you answer Tom's questions.

Case 1: During an argument, the defendant hit the victim over the head with a tire iron, causing the victim to sustain permanent brain damage. The incident took place in an auto repair shop. That defendant was convicted of aggravated battery and sentenced to 8 years in prison.

Case 2: During an argument, the defendant used a chainsaw to sever the arm of the victim. The incident took place in the street in a residential neighborhood. The defendant was convicted of mayhem and sentenced to 12 years in prison.

Case 3: After walking into his own bedroom to find a friend of his in bed with his wife, the defendant shot both his wife and his friend. Both victims lived, but required surgery to save their lives. The defendant was acquitted of attempted voluntary manslaughter, but was convicted of two counts of aggravated battery with a deadly weapon. He was sentenced to 5 years in prison.

Case 4: During an argument that occurred in a bar, the defendant punched the victim in the face, breaking his nose. The defendant was convicted of battery and sentenced to 6 months in jail.

Case 5: The defendant slapped the victim across the face during an argument that occurred in a university dining hall. The defendant was suspended from school and was also criminally convicted of battery for which the defendant was placed on 6 months of probation.

- Which case is most like the one involving Tom and Scott? Why?
- Which case is most unlike the one involving Tom and Scott? Why?
- After reviewing these and other cases, you feel confident that Scott committed either a battery or an aggravated battery.
- Which crime do you think Scott committed? Explain your answer. What types of reasoning did you use to arrive at this answer?

You then look up the statute in your state governing the crimes of battery and aggravated battery. You find that simple battery is punishable by a term of probation to a maximum of 12 months in jail. The crime of aggravated battery, however, is punishable by a term of 5 to 10 years in prison.

- Based upon the case law and statutory research you did as summarized above, what do you think is the most likely outcome of the criminal case against Scott? Will he be convicted of a crime? If so, which one? What do you think the most likely sentence will be?
- As you no doubt surmised, you had to consider other factors in addition to the technical definition of the crimes of battery and aggravated battery in order to make a prediction about the likely outcome of Scott's case and the sentence he is likely to receive. What were those factors?

A

absolute immunity Complete immunity from civil lawsuits. In the case of prosecutors, absolute immunity shields them from all civil liability for actions taken in connection with the traditional role of courtroom advocacy on behalf of the government.

actus reus **(guilty act)** Requirement that, for an act to be considered criminal, the individual must have committed a voluntary act, omission, or state of knowing possession prohibited by the criminal law. See *elements of a crime*.

acquittal The decision of the judge or jury that the defendant is not guilty.

adjudicated Judicial determination (judgment) that a youth is a delinquent or status offender.

adjudicatory hearing Court hearing to determine whether a youth is responsible for an offense and, therefore, should be adjudicated a delinquent.

adjournment When a court ends a session.

administrative regulations Rules and regulations, adopted by administrative agencies, that have the force of law.

adversary system A proceeding in which the opposing sides have the opportunity to present their evidence and arguments.

aerial search A search conducted from an aircraft, usually a helicopter or a small, low-flying plane.

affidavit A written statement of facts, which the signer swears under oath are true.

affirm In an appellate court, to reach a decision that agrees with the result reached in the case by the lower court.

affirmative defense A defense in which the defendant bears the burden of production and/or persuasion to prove that extenuating or mitigating circumstances, such as insanity, self-defense, or entrapment, should result in a not-guilty verdict.

aggravating circumstances Factors that increase the seriousness of a crime and, therefore, tend to increase the severity of the sentence imposed.

Alford **plea** A plea that allows a defendant to plead guilty while nonetheless maintaining his or her innocence.

alibi defense A defense alleging that the defendant was elsewhere at the time that the crime with which he or she is charged was committed.

Allen **charge** A type of jury instruction in which a judge strongly encourages deadlocked jurors to continue deliberations until a verdict is reached.

allocute/allocution hearing (1) The statement made by a defendant at the time he or she admits to the commission of a crime as a condition of the court accepting a guilty plea. (2) The statement made by a defendant at his/her sentencing hearing.

alternate jurors Jurors chosen in excess of the minimum number needed, in case one or more jurors is unable to serve for the entire trial.

alternative dispute resolution (ADR) Less adversarial means of settling disputes that may or may not involve a court.

American Bar Association (ABA) The largest voluntary organization of lawyers in the United States.

amicus curiae Latin for "friend of the court," the term used to refer to an advocacy brief filed in court by a nonparty urging a particular outcome and/or rationale.

Anglo-American law The American legal system. See *common law*.

appellant (petitioner) The party, usually the losing one, that seeks to overturn the decision of a lower court by appealing to a higher court.

appellate brief A formal document submitted to an appellate court setting forth the legal arguments in support of a party's case on appeal. When a brief is filed in support of a motion at the trial court level, it is sometimes referred to as a "memorandum of points and authorities."

appellate court A court that hears appeals from trial courts on points of law.

appellate court record Papers, documents, and exhibits, as well as the transcript of the trial, that are submitted to the appellate court for review.

appellate jurisdiction The authority of a court to hear, determine, and render judgment in an action on appeal from an inferior court.

appellee (respondent) A party, usually the winning party, against whom a case is appealed.

arbitration A form of *alternative dispute resolution (ADR)*, for resolving legal disputes outside the courts in which arbitrators generally act similarly to judges, making decisions that can be binding or nonbinding.

arraignment The stage of the criminal process in which the defendant is formally told the charges and allowed to enter a plea.

arrest The act of depriving a person of his or her liberty, most frequently accomplished by physically taking the arrestee into police custody for a suspected violation of criminal law.

arrest warrant A document issued by a judicial officer authorizing the arrest of a specific person.

Article I Section of the U.S. Constitution concerning the legislative branch of the national government.

Article III Section of the U.S. Constitution concerning the judicial branch of the national government.

assembly-line justice The operation of any segment of the criminal justice system in which excessive workloads result in decisions being made with such speed and impersonality that defendants are treated as objects to be processed rather than as individuals.

assigned counsel system Arrangement that provides attorneys for persons who are accused of crimes and are unable to hire their own lawyers. The judge assigns a member of the bar to provide counsel to a particular defendant.

attempt An act done with the specific intent to commit a crime; an overt act toward the commission of a crime, the failure to complete the crime, and the apparent possibility of committing it.

attendant (accompanying) circumstances Conditions surrounding a criminal act—for example, the amount of money stolen in a theft.

attorney general The chief law enforcement officer of a jurisdiction.

automatic waiver Premised on the notion of "once an adult, always an adult," automatic waiver laws require adult criminal courts to handle all subsequent offenses allegedly committed by a juvenile after an initial transfer to adult court.

B

bail The security (money or bail bond) given as a guarantee that a released prisoner will appear at trial.

bail agent (bail bondsperson) A person whose business it is to effect release on bail for persons held in custody by pledging to pay a sum of money if a defendant fails to appear in court as required.

bail bond A bond for the amount of bail set by a court that is posted by a bail agent to secure the pretrial release of a defendant in exchange for a fee the defendant pays.

bankruptcy judge Judicial officer who presides over the legal procedure under federal law by which a person is relieved of all debts after placing all property under the court's authority. An organization may be reorganized or terminated by the court in order to pay off creditors.

bench trial Trial before a judge without a jury.

bench warrant (*capias*) An order issued by the court itself, or from the bench, for the arrest of a person; it is not based, as is an arrest warrant, on a probable cause showing that a person has committed a crime, but only on the person's failure to appear in court as directed.

best-evidence rule Rule requiring that someone coming into court must bring the best available original evidence to prove the questions involved in the case.

beyond a reasonable doubt Proof that leaves jurors firmly convinced of the defendant's guilt in a criminal case.

Bill of Rights The first ten amendments to the U.S. Constitution, guaranteeing certain rights and liberties to the people.

bind over If at the preliminary hearing the judge believes that sufficient probable cause exists to hold a criminal defendant, the accused is said to be bound over for trial.

***Bivens* actions** The class of civil lawsuits that may be filed against federal officials for an alleged deprivation of one's constitutional rights.

bifurcated trial A trial split into two phases, such as the guilty and penalty phases of a capital prosecution.

blended sentencing A sentencing scheme that allows criminal court judges to impose juvenile dispositions on youthful offenders transferred to criminal court under certain circumstances, rather than imposing standard criminal sentences.

boot camp A physically rigorous, disciplined, and demanding regimen emphasizing conditioning, education, and job training, typically designed for young offenders.

***Boykin* form** Document intended to show that the defendant entered a guilty plea voluntarily and intelligently, understanding the charges and consequences of conviction (*Boykin v. Alabama* 1969).

brief See *appellate brief*.

burden of persuasion The level or quantum of evidence necessary to convince a judge or jury of the existence of some fact in dispute. In a criminal case, the prosecution bears the burden of persuasion to prove each and every element of a crime beyond a reasonable doubt.

burden of production The responsibility of a party in a legal action to introduce sufficient evidence in support of an assertion such that a factual decision needs to be made at a trial or hearing to determine the truth of the assertion, as opposed to having a court summarily reject the assertion on the grounds of insufficient proof.

burden of proof The requirement to introduce evidence to prove an alleged fact or set of facts. See *burden of persuasion and burden of production.*

Burger Court The Supreme Court under the leadership of Chief Justice Warren Burger (1969–1986).

C

capital offense Any crime punishable by death.

capital punishment Use of the death penalty as the punishment for the commission of a particular crime.

career criminals Those people who commit a sequence of delinquent and criminal acts across the lifespan from childhood through adolescence and into adulthood.

cash bond Requirement that money be posted to secure pretrial release.

celerity of punishment The swiftness with which punishment is imposed on a criminal offender. Celerity is a central component of deterrence theory, such that the more swift the punishment, the more the threatened punishment should deter the violation of law.

centralized administration The state supreme court, working through court administrators, provides leadership for the state court system.

centralized judicial budgeting The state judicial administrator (who reports to the state supreme court) has the authority to prepare a single budget for the entire state judiciary and send it directly to the legislature.

centralized rule making The power of the state supreme court to adopt uniform rules to be followed by all courts in the state.

certainty of punishment A core concept of deterrence theory that posits that the more certain it is that an offender will be caught, convicted, and punished, the less likely would-be offenders are to violate the law.

challenge for cause Method for excusing a potential juror because of specific reasons such as bias or prejudgment; can be granted only by the judge.

chambers The private office of a judge.

chain of custody The chronological documentation of the seizure, control, transfer, analysis, and disposition of evidence.

change of venue The removal of a case from one jurisdiction to another. It is usually granted if the court believes that, due to prejudice, a defendant cannot receive a fair trial in the area where the crime occurred.

charge bargaining In return for the defendant's plea of guilty, the prosecutor allows the defendant to plead guilty to a less-serious charge than the one originally filed.

charging conference Meeting attended by judge, prosecutor, and defense attorney during which the judge's instructions to the jury are discussed.

charging document An information, indictment, or complaint that states the formal criminal charge against a named defendant.

child-victims See *children in need of supervision.*

children in need of supervision A type of juvenile court case involving a child who has been abused and/or neglected by parents or legal guardians.

circumstantial evidence An indirect method of proving the material facts of a case; testimony that is not based on the witness's personal observation of the material events.

circuit justice The justice of the U.S. Supreme Court assigned to issue temporary rulings for a judicial circuit until such time as the full court can decide whether to grant a stay or enter another type of judicial order.

civil law Law governing private parties; other than criminal law.

civil protection order Court order requiring a person to stay away from another person.

clear and convincing evidence A more exacting level of proof than preponderance of the evidence, but less demanding than proof beyond a reasonable doubt. This level of proof leaves the trier-of-fact reasonably satisfied as to the existence of a fact, yet there may be some doubts.

clerk of court An elected or appointed court officer responsible for maintaining the written records of the court and for supervising or performing the clerical tasks necessary to conduct judicial business.

closing argument Statement made by an attorney at the end of the presentation of evidence in which the attorney summarizes the case for the jury.

collateral attack An attempt to overturn the outcome of a court case by challenging it in a different proceeding or court.

common law Law developed in England by judges who made legal decisions in the absence of written law. Such decisions served as precedents and became "common" to all of England. Common law is judge-made, it uses precedent, and it is found in multiple sources.

community courts Neighborhood-focused, problem-solving courts that deal with local crime and safety concerns.

community service Compensation for injury to society, by the performance of service in the community.

competency The mental capacity of an individual to participate in legal proceedings.

complaint In civil law, the first paper filed in a lawsuit. In criminal law, a charge signed by the victim that a person named has committed a specified offense.

concurrent jurisdiction When two courts (e.g., both state and federal courts or both state criminal courts and juvenile courts) share some judicial powers to adjudicate certain types of cases.

concurrent sentence In contrast to *consecutive sentence*, a criminal sentence in which a judge allows a convicted defendant to serve the punishments for two or more separate offenses at the same time.

concurring opinion A written opinion in which a judge agrees with the outcome of a case on appeal, but wishes to emphasize different points or rationales than those used by the judges who sign on to the majority decision.

conditions of confinement lawsuit Lawsuit brought by a prisoner contesting prison conditions.

conference Juvenile court proceeding roughly equivalent to a preliminary hearing, in which the suspect is informed of his or her rights and a disposition decision may be reached.

confrontation A process by which a witness "confronts" a suspect in a lineup, a photo array, or even in person (i.e., a show-up) for the purpose of attempting to identify a suspect.

consecutive sentence In contrast to *concurrent sentence*, a criminal sentence in which a judge requires a convicted defendant to serve the punishments for one offense before starting to serve the punishment on another offense.

consent search A person, place, or movables may be lawfully searched by an officer of the law if the owner gives free and voluntary consent.

consent surveillance A situation in which one or more parties to a communication consents to the interception of the communication. Neither Title III nor the Fourth Amendment prevents the use of such communications in court against a nonconsenting party to the communication.

constitution The fundamental rules that determine how those who govern are selected, the procedures by which they operate, and the limits to their powers.

constitutional courts Federal courts created by Congress by virtue of its power under Article III of the Constitution to create courts inferior to the Supreme Court.

contemporaneous objection rule The requirement that an objection be made at a hearing or trial at the time of the alleged error in order for the mistake to qualify as the basis for an appeal.

contempt (of court) The failure or refusal to obey a court order; may be punished by a fine or imprisonment.

contract A legally enforceable agreement between two or more parties.

contract system Method of providing counsel for indigents under which the government contracts with a law firm to represent all indigents for the year in return for a set fee.

corpus delicti The body or substance of a crime, composed of two elements—the act and the criminal agency producing it.

count bargaining The defendant pleads guilty to some, but not all, of the counts contained in the charging document, which reduces the potential sentence.

courtroom work group The regular participants in the day-to-day activities of a particular courtroom; judge, prosecutor, and defense attorney interacting on the basis of shared norms.

court unification The combination of courts of limited and general jurisdiction into a unified entity for administrative purposes such as budgeting, rulemaking, and leadership.

crime control model A perspective on the criminal justice process based on the proposition that the most important function of criminal justice is the repression of crime, focusing on efficiency as a principal measure.

criminal defense Legally recognized justification for illegal actions, or acceptance that individuals were not legally responsible for their actions.

criminal justice system Agencies and institutions directly involved in the implementation of public policy concerning crime, mainly the law enforcement agencies, courts, and corrections.

criminal law Laws passed by government that define and prohibit antisocial behavior.

cross-examination At trial, the questions of one attorney put to a witness called by the opposing attorney.

cruel and unusual punishment Governmental punishment that is prohibited by the Eighth Amendment.

CSI effect The phenomenon in which technology has heightened juror expectations and demands for scientific evidence. Anecdotal evidence suggests that this effect causes jurors to wrongfully acquit guilty defendants when no scientific evidence is presented, a claim not supported by empirical research.

custodial interrogation Any questioning (or its functional equivalent) by law enforcement offers after a suspect has been arrested or otherwise deprived of his or her freedom in any significant way, thereby requiring that the suspect be informed of his or her Fifth Amendment rights as set forth in *Miranda*.

D

day fine A type of graduated fine structure that is based, in part, on the offender's ability to pay as a function of daily personal income.

death-eligible Crimes that are punishable by death.

death-qualified juries Juries that sit in judgment of a defendant in a capital trial and are comprised of members (selected through the *voir dire* process) who are not morally opposed to voting to impose the death penalty.

death penalty Capital punishment, or executions by the state for purposes of social defense.

declaratory judgment Judicial pronouncement declaring the legal rights of parties involved in an actual case or controversy.

defendant The person or party against whom a lawsuit or prosecution is brought.

defenses of excuse Criminal defenses that excuse criminal conduct because of some impairment, such as youthful age or insanity, that significantly mitigates criminal responsibility.

defenses of justification Criminal defenses that justify the use of force under limited circumstances, such as defending oneself or another person.

deferred prosecution An agreement, often reached as part of a plea agreement, in which a prosecutor agrees to grant amnesty in exchange for the defendant agreeing to fulfill certain requirements.

delay Postponement or adjournment of proceedings in a case; lag in case-processing time.

delinquency An act committed by a juvenile that would require an adult to be prosecuted in a criminal court. Because the act is committed by a juvenile, it falls within the jurisdiction of the juvenile court. Delinquent acts include crimes against persons or property, drug offenses, and crimes against public order.

demonstrative evidence Evidence created for demonstration purposes at trial, such as photos, maps, and computer simulations.

deposition A type of discovery in which a witness is questioned under oath and the proceedings are recorded and transcribed.

derivative evidence Secondary evidence derived from primary evidence obtained as a result of an illegal search or seizure.

detention Holding a youth in custody before case disposition.

determinate sentence A term of imprisonment, imposed by a judge, that has a specific number of years.

deterrence theory The view that certain, severe, and swift punishment will discourage others from similar illegal acts.

direct evidence Evidence derived from one or more of the five senses.

direct examination The questioning of witnesses, using primarily open-ended questions, to adduce evidence as part of a party's case-in-chief.

direct restitution The defendant pays money directly to the victim of the crime.

discovery Pretrial procedure in which parties to a lawsuit ask for and receive information such as testimony, records, or other evidence from each other.

discretion The lawful ability of an agent of government to exercise choice in making a decision.

discretionary appellate jurisdiction Jurisdiction that a court may accept or reject particular cases. The Supreme Court has discretionary jurisdiction over most cases that come to it.

discrimination Illegitimate influences in the sentencing process based on the characteristics of the defendants.

dismissal Cases terminated (including those warned, counseled, and released) with no further disposition anticipated.

disparity Unequal sentences resulting from the sentencing process itself.

disposition A court decision about what will happen to a youth who has not been found innocent.

dissenting opinion An opinion written by a judge of an appellate court in which the judge states the reasons for disagreeing with the majority decision.

district attorney The lead prosecutorial officer of a jurisdiction. The prosecutors reporting to the district attorney are often referred to as assistant district attorneys or deputy district attorneys.

diversion See *Pretrial diversion.*

diversity of citizenship When parties on the opposite sides of a federal lawsuit come from different states, the jurisdiction of the U.S. district courts can be invoked if the case involves a controversy concerning $75,000 or more in value.

domestic relations Relating to the home; the law of divorce, custody, support, adoption, and so on.

domestic violence A pattern of abusive behaviors by one partner against another in an intimate relationship such as marriage, dating, family, or cohabitation.

double jeopardy Fifth Amendment prohibition against a second prosecution after a first trial for the same offense.

drug courts Specialty courts with jurisdiction over cases involving illegal substances. Drug courts typically stress treatment rather than punishment.

dual court system A court system consisting of a separate judicial structure for each state in addition to a national structure. Each case is tried in a court of the same jurisdiction as that of the law or laws involved.

due process model A philosophy of criminal justice based on the assumption that an individual is innocent until proven guilty and has a right to protection from arbitrary power of the state.

due process of law A right guaranteed in the Fifth and Fourteenth Amendments of the U.S. Constitution and generally understood to mean the due course of legal proceedings according to the rules and forms established for the protection of private rights.

duress Unlawful pressure on a person to do what he or she would not otherwise have done.

E

electronic monitoring The use of technologies to surveil and control offenders, including wrist and ankle bracelets, field monitoring devices, alcohol testing devices, and voice verification systems.

elements of a crime Five principles of a crime that are critical to the statutory definition of crimes: guilty act, guilty intent, relationship between guilty act and guilty intent, attendant circumstances, and results.

en banc French term referring to the session of an appellate court in which all the judges of the court participate, as opposed to a session presided over by three judges.

enemy combatants People the United States regards as unlawful combatants, a category of persons who do not qualify for prisoner-of-war status under the Geneva Conventions.

entrapment The act of a government official or agent inducing a person to commit a crime that the person would not have committed without the inducement.

error A mistake made by a judge in the procedures used at trial, or in making legal rulings during the trial, that allows one side in a lawsuit to ask a higher court to review the case.

error correction Appellate courts seek to correct legal errors made in lower courts.

estate The interest a person has in property; a person's right or title to property.

estimator variables Variables at the scene of a crime, such as lighting and race, that cannot be controlled by the criminal justice system.

evidence Any kind of proof offered to establish the existence or nonexistence of a fact in dispute—for example, testimony, writings, other material objects, or demonstrations.

evidence-based corrections The use of rehabilitative programs, practices, and techniques in correctional settings that have been empirically evaluated and determined to be effective interventions.

exclusionary rule A rule created by judicial decisions holding that evidence obtained through violations of the constitutional rights of the criminal defendant must be excluded from the trial.

exculpatory evidence Evidence that casts doubt on the guilt of a criminally accused person.

expiation Atoning for sin through deserved suffering.

extradition Legal process whereby officials of one state or country surrender an alleged criminal offender to officials of the state or country in which the crime is alleged to have been committed.

extralegal factors Factors, such as race, ethnicity, sex, and socioeconomic status, that are associated with differential treatment by the criminal justice system even though they are not supposed to affect case processing, outcomes, and sentences.

F

federal question Case that contains a major issue involving the U.S. Constitution or U.S. laws or treaties.

felony The more serious of the two basic types of criminal behavior, usually bearing a possible penalty of 1 year or more in prison.

fine A sum of money to be paid to the state by a convicted person as punishment for an offense. See also *day fine*.

Foreign Intelligence Surveillance Act (FISA) A federal statute that regulates the electronic surveillance of foreign powers and their agents within the United States where a "significant purpose" of the surveillance is to gather foreign intelligence information that cannot reasonably be obtained through normal investigative techniques. FISA also permits surveillance of "lone wolves"—any individual or group that is not linked to a foreign government but who is suspected of terrorism or sabotage.

fruit of the poisonous tree The poisonous tree is evidence directly obtained as a result of a constitutional violation; the fruit is the derivative evidence obtained because of knowledge gained from the first illegal search, arrest, confrontation, or interrogation.

Furman v. Georgia Supreme Court ruling that statutes leaving arbitrary and discriminatory discretion to juries in imposing death sentences are in violation of the Eighth Amendment.

union of *actus reus* and *mens rea* Criminal law generally requires that the guilty intent (*mens rea*) and the guilty act (*actus reus*) occur together. See *elements of a crime*.

G

gag order A judge's order that lawyers, witnesses, or members of law enforcement not discuss the trial with outsiders.

general deterrence The theory that posits that rational, self-interested people will be deterred from committing crimes by the threat of certain, severe, and swift punishment.

geographical jurisdiction Geographical area over which courts can hear and decide disputes.

good faith exception An exception to the exclusionary rule that allows illegally seized evidence to be admitted at trial if law enforcement officers acted in good faith, relying on a defective search warrant or a law subsequently determined to be unconstitutional.

good time A reduction of the time served in prison as a reward for not violating prison rules.

GPS monitoring A particular type of electronic monitoring that uses ground positioning satellites to monitor the location of an offender or to surveil a vehicle, suspect, or item.

grand jury A group of citizens who decide whether persons accused of crimes should be indicted (true bill) or not (no true bill).

Gregg v. Georgia Supreme Court ruling that: (1) the death penalty is not, in itself, cruel and unusual punishment, and (2) a two-part proceeding—one for the determination of innocence or guilt and the other for determination of the sentence—is constitutional and meets the objections noted in *Furman v. Georgia*.

gubernatorial appointment Method of judicial selection in which the governor appoints a person to a judicial vacancy without an election.

guilty act See *actus reus*.

guilty intent See *mens rea*.

H

habeas corpus Latin phrase meaning "you have the body"; a writ inquiring of an official who has custody of a person whether that person is being lawfully imprisoned or detained.

harmless error An error made at trial that is insufficient grounds for reversing a judgment.

hearsay An out-of-court assertion or statement, made by someone other than the testifying witness, which is offered to prove the truth of testimony. Hearsay evidence is excluded from trials unless it falls within one of the recognized exceptions and does not otherwise violate the Sixth Amendment's Confrontation Clause.

hedonistic calculus A principle of utilitarian philosophy that posits that humans seek pleasure and avoid pain. This principle plays an important role in deterrence theory insofar as rational thinkers will seek to avoid the pain that criminal punishment will inflict upon them by avoiding lawbreaking behaviors if and only if the pain of punishment outweighs the pleasure that would be gained through the commission of crime.

hierarchical jurisdiction Refers to differences in the functions of courts and involves original as opposed to appellate jurisdiction.

hierarchy rule A UCR rule that records only the most serious crime to occur during an event in which two or more crimes were committed, rather than recording each crime.

home detention An intermediate sanction that confines offenders to their homes under specific terms and conditions. It may be used independently or in combination with *electronic monitoring.*

hung jury A jury that is unable to reach a verdict.

I

illegal search and seizure See *unreasonable search and seizure.*

immunity A grant of exemption from prosecution in return for evidence or testimony.

impeach To question the truthfulness of a witness's testimony.

impeachment Official accusation against a public official brought by a legislative body seeking his or her removal.

impeachment evidence Any evidence that would cast doubt on the credibility of a witness.

imprisonment Placing a person in a prison, jail, or similar correctional facility as punishment for committing a crime.

incapacitation Sentencing philosophy that stresses crime prevention through isolating wrongdoers from society.

incorporation The theory that the Bill of Rights has been incorporated or absorbed into the due process clause of the Fourteenth Amendment, thereby making it applicable to the states.

indeterminate sentence A sentence that has both a minimum and a maximum term of imprisonment, the actual length to be determined by a parole board.

index crimes The specific crimes used by the FBI when reporting the incidence of crime in the United States in the *Uniform Crime Reports;* also called "Type I offenses."

indictment A formal accusation of a criminal offense made against a person by a grand jury.

indigents Defendants who are too poor to pay a lawyer and therefore are entitled to a lawyer for free.

infancy A criminal defense based on the young age of an offender, preventing the formation of *mens rea.*

inference A logical conclusion that the trier-of-fact may make in light of the evidence.

inferior court (lower court) Term for a trial court of limited jurisdiction; also may refer to any court lower in the judicial hierarchy.

informants People who are not in law enforcement, but provide information to law enforcement personnel.

information A formal accusation charging someone with the commission of a crime, signed by a prosecuting attorney, which has the effect of bringing the person to trial.

inheritance Property received from a dead person, either by effect of intestacy or through a will.

initial appearance Shortly after arrest, the suspect is brought before a judicial official, who informs the person of the reason for the arrest and makes an initial determination about whether there was probable cause for the arrest. In some jurisdictions, a preliminary determination regarding bail may also be made.

initial hearing In juvenile court, an often informal hearing during which an intake decision is made.

injunction A court order directing someone to do something or to refrain from doing something.

in rem Against a thing; a legal proceeding instituted to obtain decrees or judgments against property.

insanity defense A criminal defense that excuses criminal conduct if a severe mental disease or defect substantially impaired the defendant's ability to appreciate the wrongfulness of his or her conduct.

intake decision The decision made by a juvenile court that results in the case being handled either informally at the intake level or more formally by petition and scheduled for an adjudicatory or transfer hearing.

intensive-supervision probation (ISP) Probation granted under conditions of strict reporting to a probation officer with a limited caseload.

interlocutory Provisional; temporary; while a lawsuit is still going on.

intermediate courts of appeals (ICAs) Judicial bodies falling between the highest, or supreme, tribunal and the trial court; created to relieve the jurisdiction's highest court of hearing a large number of cases.

intermediate sanctions Variety of sanctions that lie somewhere between prison and probation.

irrelevant Testimony that has no bearing on the issue of a trial.

J

judge-made law The common law as developed in form and content by judges or judicial decisions.

judgment The official decision of a court concerning a legal matter.

judicial conduct commission An official body whose function is to investigate allegations of misconduct by judges.

judicial election Method of judicial selection in which the voters choose judicial candidates in a partisan or nonpartisan election.

judicial independence Normative value that stresses a judge should be free from outside pressure in making a decision.

judicial waiver Laws that permit—and sometimes even require—juvenile court judges to transfer jurisdiction over a juvenile delinquency case to adult court for criminal prosecution.

jurisdiction The power of a court to hear and adjudicate a case.

jury consultants Professionals who assist lawyers in selecting juries through the use of behavioral scientific principles and techniques.

jury deliberations The action of a jury in determining the guilt or innocence, or the sentence, of a defendant.

jury instructions Directions given by a judge to the members of the jury informing them of the law applicable to the case.

jury nullification The idea that juries have the right to refuse to apply the law in criminal cases despite facts that leave no reasonable doubt that the law was violated.

just deserts Punishment for criminal wrongdoing should be proportionate to the severity of the offense.

justice of the peace (JP) A low-level judge, sometimes without legal training, typically found in rural areas of some states, empowered to try petty civil and criminal cases and to conduct the preliminary stages of felony cases.

juvenile Youth at or below the upper age of juvenile court jurisdiction.

juvenile court Any court that has jurisdiction over matters involving juveniles.

juvenile delinquency An act committed by a juvenile for which an adult could be prosecuted in a criminal court.

L

law Body of rules enacted by public officials in a legitimate manner and backed by the force of the state.

legal ethics Codes of conduct governing how lawyers practice law and how judges administer justice.

legislative courts Judicial bodies created by Congress under Article I (legislative article) and not Article III (judicial article).

legislative waiver See *statutory waiver*.

lex talionis Latin for "the law of retaliation," this is the philosophical principle that punishments should be equal to the harm caused by the commission of a crime as embodied in the phrase, "an eye for an eye; a tooth for a tooth; an arm for an arm; a life for a life."

local prosecutors General term for lawyers who represent local governments (cities and counties, for example) in the lower courts; often called "city attorneys" or "solicitors."

lower age of jurisdiction Minimum age at which a youth may be transferred to adult court.

M

mandamus petitions A type of lawsuit in which a plaintiff seeks a court order commanding someone to perform an act or duty imposed by law as an obligation.

mandatory appellate jurisdiction Jurisdiction that a court must accept. Cases falling under a court's mandatory jurisdiction must be decided officially on their merits, though a court may avoid giving them full consideration.

mandatory minimum sentencing Minimum required penalty specified for a certain crime.

master jury list A list of potential jurors in a court's district, from which a representative cross section of the community in which a crime allegedly was committed can be selected for a trial. It is usually compiled from multiple sources, such as voter registration lists, driver's license lists, utility customer lists, and telephone directories. Also called "jury wheel" or "master wheel."

mediation A form of *alternative dispute resolution (ADR)* in which a mediator acts, not as a judge, but rather as someone who facilitate discussion and resolution of the dispute.

mens rea **(guilty intent)** Latin for "evil mind," it refers to the mental state of intent required for a crime.

misdemeanor Lesser of the two basic types of crime, usually punishable by no more than 1 year in jail.

Missouri Bar Plan The name given to a method of judicial selection combining merit selection and popular control in retention elections.

mistake of fact A criminal defense asserting that the defendant was mistaken about a fact that, if honest and reasonable, negates the *mens rea* for the crime charged.

mistrial Invalid trial.

mitigating circumstances Factors that mitigate the seriousness of a crime and, therefore, tend to reduce the severity of the sentence imposed.

Model Rules of Professional Conduct The American Bar Association's set of model rules that impose ethical obligations on lawyers to their clients and to the courts. Some variation of these rules have been adopted in all 50 states.

monetary damage Compensatory damages—payment for actual losses suffered by a plaintiff. Punitive damages—money awarded by a court to a person who has been harmed in a malicious or willful way.

motion for judgment of acquittal A motion made by a criminal defendant at the close of the government's case (or at the close of all evidence) that asks a judge to enter a verdict of "not guilty" because no legally sufficient evidentiary basis has been established on which a reasonable jury could return a guilty verdict.

motions to vacate sentences Filings by prisoners who seek to have their sentences set aside or changed on the grounds that the sentence was imposed in violation of the Constitution or laws of the United States.

motor vehicle searches The warrantless search of a motor vehicle when there is probable cause to believe that the vehicle contains contraband or evidence of a crime.

municipal court A trial court of limited jurisdiction created by a local unit of government.

municipal ordinance Law passed by a local unit of government.

N

National Incident-Based Reporting System (NIBRS) An incident-based, rather than summary-based, system for tracking criminal offenses with significantly more detail than the UCR.

necessity A criminal defense in which the defendant asserts that in an emergency situation not caused by the defendant, he or she had no choice but to break the law in order to avoid more serious harm than that caused by the commission of the crime.

new judicial federalism Movement in state supreme courts to reinvigorate states' constitutions as sources of individual rights over and above the rights granted by the U.S. Constitution.

no true bill The decision of a grand jury not to indict a person for a crime.

nolle prosequi The ending of a criminal case because the prosecutor decides or agrees to stop prosecuting. When this happens, the case is "nollied," "nolled," or "nol. prossed."

nolo contendere/**no contest** Latin phrase meaning "I will not contest it." A plea of "no contest" in a criminal case means that the defendant does not directly admit guilt but submits to sentencing or other punishment.

nonpetitioned case A case handled informally by duly authorized court personnel.

normal crime Categorization of crime based on the typical manner in which it is committed, the type of defendant who typically commits it, and the typical penalty to be applied.

normal penalties Norms for proper sentencing based on the crime committed and the defendant's prior record.

notice of appeal Written document filed with the clerk of court stating that the defendant in the criminal case plans to appeal.

O

objection The act of taking exception to a statement or procedure during a trial.

officer of the court Lawyers are officers of the court and, as such, must obey court rules, be truthful in court, and generally serve the needs of justice.

open fields The doctrine that allows law enforcement to search open lands without a warrant.

Omnibus Crime Control and Safe Streets Act of 1968 A federal statute, Title III of which provides greater privacy protections than the Fourth Amendment by regulating both law enforcing and private searches and seizures of wire, oral, or electronic communications.

opening statement Address made by attorneys for both parties at the beginning of a trial in which they outline for the jury what they intend to prove in their case.

opinion The reasons given for the decision reached by an appellate court.

oral argument The part of the appellate court decision-making process in which lawyers for both parties plead their case in person before the court.

ordinance A law enacted by a local government body for the regulation of some activity within the community.

original jurisdiction Jurisdiction in the first instance; commonly used to refer to trial jurisdiction as opposed to appellate jurisdiction. Appellate courts, however, have limited original jurisdiction.

other dispositions Miscellaneous dispositions, including fines, restitution, community service, and referrals outside the court for services, with minimal or no further court involvement anticipated.

P

pardon An act of executive clemency that has the effect of releasing an inmate from prison and/or removing certain legal disabilities from persons convicted of crimes.

parens patriae The state as parent; the state as guardian and protector of all citizens (such as juveniles) who are unable to protect themselves.

parole Early release from prison on the condition of good behavior.

parole board An administrative body whose members are chosen by the governor to review the cases of prisoners eligible for release on parole. The board has the authority to release such persons and to return them to prison for violating the conditions of parole.

per curium **opinion** Latin for "by the court," a decision by an appellate court that is not attributed to a specific author.

peremptory challenge Method for excusing a potential juror without cause, so long as the reasons for doing so are not based on racial or gender discrimination.

personal injury Negligence lawsuits, often involving automobile accidents.

personal jurisdiction The power of a court over a particular person or legal entity (such as a partnership or corporation).

petit jury A trial jury, as distinguished from a grand jury.

petition A document filed in juvenile court alleging that a juvenile is a delinquent or a status offender and asking that the court assume jurisdiction over the juvenile or that an alleged delinquent be transferred to criminal court for prosecution as an adult.

petitioner The party filing a petition in a court of law. It is most commonly used to refer to the party seeking discretionary appellate review through filing a petition for a writ of *certiorari*.

petty offense A minor criminal offense that does not entitle the defendant to a trial by jury.

placement Cases in which youths are placed in a residential facility or otherwise removed from their homes and placed elsewhere.

plain error An exception to the contemporary objection rule in which a highly prejudicial error substantially affects the rights of the accused such that a failure to correct the error on appeal, even if an objection was not made at the hearing or trial at the time of the alleged error, would result in a miscarriage of justice.

plain view If police happen to come across something while acting within their lawful duty, that item may be used as evidence in a criminal trial, even if the police did not have a search warrant.

plaintiff The person or party who initiates a lawsuit.

plea bargaining The process by which a defendant pleads guilty to a criminal charge with the expectation of receiving some benefit from the state.

plea on the nose The defendant pleads guilty to the charges contained in the indictment or bill of information.

plurality opinion A decision, usually of an appellate court, in which no single opinion received the support of a majority of the court.

policy formulation Function of appellate courts to make new law and adjust existing law to changing circumstances.

postverdict motions Various motions made by the defense after a jury conviction in hopes of gaining a new trial.

precedent A case previously decided that serves as a legal guide for the resolution of subsequent cases.

prejudicial pretrial publicity Prejudicial information, often inadmissible at trial, that is circulated by the news media before a trial and that reduces the defendant's chances of a trial before an impartial jury.

preliminary hearing A pretrial hearing to determine whether there is probable cause to bind a defendant over for felony trial.

preponderance of the evidence In civil law, the standard of proof required to prevail at trial. To win, the plaintiff must show that the greater weight, or preponderance, of the evidence supports his or her version of the facts.

presentence investigation (PSI) Investigation by a probation department into circumstances surrounding a crime in order to help judges make appropriate sentencing decisions.

presumption A conclusion that the law requires the trier-of-fact to accept as true.

presumption of innocence Presumption that whenever a person is charged with a crime, he or she is innocent until proved guilty. The defendant is presumed to be innocent, and the burden is on the state to prove guilt beyond a reasonable doubt.

presumption of sanity The rebuttable presumption that a criminal defendant was legally sane at the time of the commission of the crime(s) for which he or she is charged. To overcome this presumption, most U.S. jurisdictions require the defense to prove that the defendant was insane by clear and convincing evidence.

presumptive sentencing A required structured sentencing system that provides a single recommended prison term within a wider statutory sentence range for each felony offense, with the recommended term based solely on the offense committed.

presumptive sentencing guidelines A required structured sentencing system of multiple recommended sentences and dispositions for each offense class determined by both the severity of the offense and the prior criminal history of the offender.

pretrial diversion An alternative to prosecution that seeks to divert certain offenders from traditional criminal justice processing into a program of supervision and services, especially ones run by a department of probation.

preventive detention Holding a defendant in custody pending trial in the belief that he or she is likely to commit further criminal acts or flee the jurisdiction.

prison realignment A shift of correctional resources, primarily associated with California, in which the state's responsibility for lower-level drug offenders, thieves, and other nonviolent convicts is transferred to the county level, where services might better provide for rehabilitation and job training services that reduce recidivism.

prisoner petition Civil lawsuit filed by a prisoner alleging violations of his or her rights during trial or while in prison.

privileged communication A recognized right to keep certain communications confidential or private.

pro se Acting as one's own attorney in court; representing oneself.

probable cause Standard used to determine whether a crime has been committed and whether there is sufficient evidence to believe a specific individual committed it.

probation Punishment for a crime that allows the offender to remain in the community without incarceration but subject to certain conditions.

probation officer Employee of probation agency, responsible for supervision of convicted offenders who have been released to the community under certain conditions of good behavior.

procedural defenses Defenses for crimes that are not concerned with factual guilt, but rather are rooted in violations of the rules or processes of the criminal justice system, such as the right to a speedy trial.

procedural law Law that outlines the legal processes to be followed in starting, conducting, and finishing a lawsuit.

property Legal right to use or dispose of particular things or subjects.

property bond Use of property as collateral for pretrial release.

proportionality A philosophical principle positing that criminal punishment should be proportional to the harm caused by the offense committed.

prosecutor A public official who represents the state in a criminal action.

prosecutorial waiver Laws granting prosecutors the discretion to file delinquency petitions in juvenile court or file criminal charges in adult court.

public defender An attorney employed by the government to represent indigent defendants.

Q

qualified immunity A justice actor's partial immunity from civil liability for acts within the scope of their professional duties and sanctioned by law. For prosecutors, such immunity applies only when they are acting in good faith that they are not violating any law or ethical rule of which a reasonable person in the prosecutor's position would be aware.

R

real evidence Objects, such as fingerprints, seen by the jury.

reasonable doubt The state of mind of jurors when they are not firmly convinced of a defendant's guilt because they think there is a real possibility that he or she is not guilty.

reasonable, articulable suspicion The reasons a law enforcement officer is able to articulate for being suspicious of criminal activity. It is the level of proof necessary to conduct a brief, limited investigative detention (also known as a "Terry stop").

rebuttal The introduction of contradictory evidence.

reciprocal disclosure Automatic discovery for certain types of evidence, without the necessity for motions and court orders.

referral A request by a law enforcement agency, governmental agency, parent, or individual that a juvenile court take jurisdiction of a youth. A referral initiates court processing.

rehabilitation The notion that punishment is intended to restore offenders to a constructive role in society; based on the assumption that criminal behavior is a treatable disorder caused by social or psychological ailments.

Rehnquist Court The Supreme Court under the leadership of Chief Justice William Rehnquist (1986–2005).

release on recognizance (ROR) The release of an accused person from jail on his or her own obligation rather than on a monetary bond.

remand In an appellate court, to send a case back to the court from which it came for further action.

remedy Vindication of a claim of right; a legal procedure by which a right is enforced or the violation of a right is prevented or compensated.

removal To dismiss a person from holding office.

respondent The party responding to a petition. It is most commonly used to refer to the party responding to the filing of a petition for a writ of *certiorari*.

restitution To restore or to make good on something—for example, to return or pay for a stolen item.

restoration/restorative justice A philosophy of justice positing that the principal aim of the criminal justice system should be to repair the various physical, psychological, and community harms caused by crime. Promoting peace and reconciling parties is, therefore, considered to be more important than punishing the guilty.

result A consequence; an outcome.

retribution A concept that implies the payment of a debt to society and thus the expiation of one's offense.

reverse In an appellate court, to reach a decision that disagrees with the result reached in the case by the lower court.

reverse waiver A process that allows a juvenile to petition a criminal court to transfer jurisdiction over an offense to a juvenile court.

reversed and remanded Decision of an appellate court that the guilty verdict of the lower court be set aside and the case be retried.

reversible error An error made at trial serious enough to warrant a new trial.

right to counsel Right of the accused to the services of a lawyer paid for by the government, established by the Sixth Amendment and extended by the Warren Court (*Gideon v. Wainwright*) to indigent defendants in felony cases.

right to one appeal U.S. law generally grants the loser in trial court the right to a single appeal, which the upper court must hear.

Roberts Court The Supreme Court under the leadership of Chief Justice John Roberts (2005–).

routine administration A matter that presents the court with no disputes over law or fact.

rule of four The rule that four of the nine justices on the U.S. Supreme Court must vote in favor of granting a petition for a writ of *certiorari* in order for the Court to actually issue the writ, thereby accepting discretionary jurisdiction over an appeal.

rules of evidence Rules that govern whether, when, how, and for what purposes certain forms of proof may be placed before the trier-of-fact for consideration at a hearing or trial.

S

scientific jury selection The use of social scientific techniques and expertise to select venirepersons to serve as petit jurors who are likely to be favorably disposed to one's side of a case.

scientific evidence The formal results of forensic investigatory and scientific techniques.

search incident to arrest The ability of law enforcement to conduct a warrantless search of a person and the area around the arrestee's immediate control when making a lawful arrest.

search warrant A written order, issued by judicial authority, directing a law enforcement officer to search for personal property and, if found, to bring it before the court.

Section 1983 The shorthand way of referring to 42 U.S.C. § 1983, a statute that allows a person to sue someone acting under color of state law for an alleged deprivation of constitutional rights.

selective incorporation An approach to constitutional law that posits that select rights guaranteed by Bill of Rights to the U.S. Constitution are so fundamental to the concept of liberty that they are incorporated into the Fourteenth Amendment's due process clause and, therefore, are applicable to the states.

selective incapacitation Sentencing philosophy that stresses targeting dangerous offenders for lengthy prison sentences.

self-defense The right to use physical force against another person who is committing a felony, threatening the use of physical force, or using physical force.

self-incrimination Forcing a suspect to provide evidence against himself or herself; prohibited by the Fifth Amendment.

sentence bargaining The defendant pleads guilty knowing the sentence that will be imposed; the sentence in the sentence bargain is less than the maximum.

sentencing guidelines Sentences based on the severity of the crime and the defendant's prior record in an attempt to ensure fair and consistent sentencing. The structure of sentencing guidelines varies on a continuum from voluntary (meaning that they merely recommend a sentence) to presumptive to mandatory.

sequester To isolate members of a jury from the community until they have reached a final verdict.

severity of punishment A key component of deterrence theory concerned with how severe a criminal sentence may be. The theory posits that the more severe the punishment, the less likely people are to violate the law.

shock incarceration A short period of incarceration (the "shock"), followed by a sentence reduction.

simplified court structure A simple, uniform court structure for the entire state.

small claims court A lower-level court whose jurisdiction is limited to a specific dollar amount—for example, damages not exceeding $1,500.

socialization As used in the court setting, the process in which new members of the courtroom work group learn the norms, values, behaviors, and skills expected of them in a professional position.

specific deterrence The notion that the experience of criminal punishment should be unpleasant enough to deter an offender from committing future criminal acts.

speedy-trial laws Federal or state statutes that specify time limits for bringing a case to trial after arrest. Some speedy-trial laws specify precise time standards for periods from arrest to arraignment, trial, and or sentencing.

standard of review The amount of deference an appellate court gives to the determinations made by a lower court.

standby/shadow counsel The lawyer appointed by a court to shadow a *pro se* defendant. The defendant may consult with the lawyer while representing himself or herself. The lawyer may also take over the case if the court revokes the defendant's right to self-representation either because of emerging questions of mental incompetence or if the defendant is abusive, threatening, obstructionist, or the cause of repeated, unnecessary delays.

stare decisis Latin phrase meaning "let the decision stand." The doctrine that principles of law established in earlier judicial decisions should be accepted as authoritative in similar subsequent cases.

state attorney general The chief legal officer of a state, representing that state in civil and, under certain circumstances, criminal cases.

state high court of last resort General term for the highest court in a state.

statewide financing Courts financed by the state government as opposed to local government.

status offense Behavior that is considered an offense only when committed by a juvenile—for example, running away from home.

statute A written law enacted by a legislature.

statutory exemptions Rules adopted by legislatures exempting certain types of persons or occupations from jury duty.

statutory/legislative waivers Laws that grant exclusive jurisdiction over certain offenses to adult criminal courts regardless of the age of the offender.

stay The temporary suspension of a case or of specific proceedings within a case.

Stored Communications Act A federal statute that governs law enforcement access to stored communications, such as those in e-mail, voice mail, computer files, and cell phones.

structured sentencing Sentencing schemes that seek to curtail judicial discretion in sentencing by classifying offenders on the basis of the severity of the crime committed and on the extent and gravity of their prior criminal record.

subject matter jurisdiction Types of cases courts have been authorized to hear and decide.

subpoena (power) An order from a court directing a person to appear before the court and to give testimony about a cause of action pending before it.

substantive law Law that deals with the content or substance of the law—for example, the legal grounds for divorce.

summons A legal document ordering an individual to appear in court at a certain time on a certain date.

suppression motion Request that a court of law prohibit specific statements, documents, or objects from being introduced into evidence in a trial.

symbolic restitution The defendant performs community service.

system variables Variables under the control of the criminal justice system that substantially impact the accuracy of identifications, such as the ways in which lineups or photo arrays are conducted.

T

tabula rasa Latin for "blank slate," it is a largely discredited view of jury decision making that posits that jurors come to trials without any preconceived notions that would interfere with their abilities to deliberate to a verdict based solely on the evidence presented in court.

testimonial evidence The giving of evidence by a witness under oath.

therapeutic jurisprudence Judicial bodies such as drug courts that stress helping defendants in trouble through nonadversarial proceedings.

three strikes laws Statutes that mandate increased sentences for repeat offenders, often requiring a mandatory sentence of 20 years or more in prison for those convicted of a third qualifying felony.

tort A private or civil wrong, not arising as the result of a breach of contract, in which the defendant's actions cause injury to the plaintiff or to property.

traffic offenses A group of offenses, including infractions and minor misdemeanors, relating to the operation of self-propelled motor vehicles.

transactional immunity Absolute protection against prosecution for any event or transaction about which a witness is compelled to give testimony or furnish evidence.

transfer to criminal court A case is moved to a criminal court because of a waiver or transfer hearing in the juvenile court.

trial court Judicial body with primarily original jurisdiction in civil or criminal cases. Juries are used, and evidence is presented.

trial court of general jurisdiction A trial court responsible for major criminal and civil cases.

trial court of limited jurisdiction A lower-level state court, such as a justice of the peace court, whose jurisdiction is limited to minor civil disputes or misdemeanors.

trial *de novo* A new trial at a higher level of court.

true bill A bill of indictment by a grand jury.

trustworthiness Basic criterion for the admissibility of evidence, which seeks to ensure that only the most reliable and credible facts, statements, and testimony are presented to the fact-finder.

truth in sentencing laws Laws that require offenders to serve a substantial portion of their prison terms (often 85 percent) before release.

tunnel vision The conscious and unconscious process through which justice professionals select and filter evidence to build a case for conviction against a particular suspect while ignoring or suppressing exculpatory evidence.

Type I offenses Serious crimes of homicide, rape, arson, aggravated assault, robbery, burglary, auto theft, and larceny, according to the FBI's *Uniform Crime Reports*; also called "index crimes."

U

unified court system A simplified state trial court structure with rule making centered in the supreme court, system governance authority vested in the chief justice of the supreme court, and state funding of the judicial system under a statewide judicial budget.

Uniform Crime Reports A program conceived in 1929 by the International Association of Chiefs of Police to meet a need for reliable, uniform crime statistics for the nation. Today, the FBI collects and compiles several annual statistical publications produced from the data collected from law enforcement agencies across the United States..

U.S. attorney general Head of the Department of Justice; nominated by the president and confirmed by the Senate.

U.S. attorneys Officials responsible for the prosecution of crimes that violate the laws of the United States; appointed by the president and assigned to a U.S. district court.

U.S. courts of appeals Intermediate appellate courts in the federal judicial system.

U.S. district courts Trial courts established in the respective judicial districts into which the United States is divided. These courts are established for the purpose of hearing and deciding cases in the limited districts to which their jurisdiction is confined.

U.S. magistrate judges Judicial officers appointed by the U.S. district courts to perform the duties formerly performed by U.S. commissioners and to assist the court by serving as special masters in civil actions, conducting pretrial or discovery proceedings, and conducting preliminary review of applications for post-trial relief made by individuals convicted of criminal offenses.

U.S. solicitor general Third-ranking official in the U.S. Department of Justice; conducts and supervises government litigation before the Supreme Court.

U.S. Supreme Court The nation's highest court, composed of nine justices nominated by the president and confirmed by the Senate.

unreasonable search and seizure The Fourth Amendment provides for protection against unreasonable searches and seizures, or the illegal gathering of evidence, but was not very effective until the adoption of the exclusionary rule, barring the use of evidence so obtained (*Mapp v. Ohio*, 1961).

upper age of jurisdiction The oldest age at which a juvenile court has original jurisdiction over an individual for behavior that violates the law.

use immunity A witness may not be prosecuted based on grand jury testimony he or she provides but may be prosecuted based on evidence acquired independently of that testimony.

V

venire A group of citizens from which members of the jury are chosen.

venue The geographic location of a trial, which is determined by constitutional or statutory provisions.

verdict The decision of a trial court.

victim impact statement Written or oral statements communicating information about how a crime impacted the victim and the victim's family.

video surveillance The use of video cameras that record only images, not sound and, therefore, is beyond the reach of Title III of the Omnibus Crime Control and Safe Streets Act of 1968.

voir dire French legal phrase meaning "to speak the truth." The process by which prospective jurors are questioned to determine whether there is cause to excuse them from the jury.

voluntary sentencing guidelines A recommended structured sentencing system of multiple recommended sentences and dispositions for each offense class determined by both the severity of the offense and the prior criminal history of the offender.

W

warrantless search Search without a search warrant.

Warren Court The Supreme Court under the leadership of Chief Justice Earl Warren (1953–1969).

writ of *certiorari* Order issued by an appellate court for the purpose of obtaining from a lower court the record of its proceedings in a particular case.

writ of *certiorari*, petition for The petition a party files asking an appellate court to exercise its discretionary appellate jurisdiction to review a case.

Abel, C.F., and Hans J. Hacker. 2006. "Local Compliance with Supreme Court Decisions: Making Space for Religious Expression in Public Schools." *Journal of Church and State* 48: 355–378.

Aberbach, Joel D., and Mark A. Peterson. 2006. *The Executive Branch*. New York: Oxford University Press.

Acker, James. 1993. "A Different Agenda: The Supreme Court, Empirical Research Evidence, and Capital Punishment Decisions, 1986–1989." *Law and Society Review* 27: 65–86.

Acker, James R. 2007. "Impose an Immediate Moratorium on Executions." *Criminology & Public Policy* 6: 641–650.

Adams, Benjamin, and Sean Addie. 2011. "Delinquency Cases Waived to Criminal Court, 2008." Washington, DC: Department of Justice, Office of Justice Programs.

Adams, Kenneth. 1983. "The Effect of Evidentiary Factors on Charge Reduction." *Journal of Criminal Justice* 11: 525–538.

Administrative Office of the U.S. Courts. 2012. *Federal Judicial Caseload Statistics: 20112*. Washington, DC: Author. Available online at http://www.uscourts .gov/Statistics/FederalJudicialCaseloadStatistics/ FederalJudicialCaseloadStatistics2011.aspx.

"After Death Threats, O'Connor Responds to GOP Attacks on Judges." 2009. Available online at http://www .perrspectives.com/blog/archives/001415.htm.

Aikman, Alexander B. *The Art and Practice of Court Administration*. Boca Raton, FL: CRC Press.

Albonetti, Celesta A. 1986. "Criminality, Prosecutorial Screening, and Uncertainty: Toward a Theory of Discretionary Decision Making in Felony Case Processings." *Criminology* 24(4): 623–644.

Albonetti, Celesta A. 1987. "Prosecutorial Discretion: The Effects of Uncertainty." *Law & Society Review* 21: 291–313.

Albonetti, Celesta. 1997. "Sentencing under the Federal Sentencing Guideline: Effects of Defendant Characteristics, Guilty Pleas, and Departures on Sentence Outcomes for Drug Offenses, 1991–1992." *Law and Society Review* 31: 789–822.

Alexander, Ellen, and Janice Harris Lord. 1994. *Impact Statements—A Victim's Right to Speak . . . A Nation's Responsibility to Listen*. Arlington, VA: National Center for Victims.

Alexander, S. L. 1991. "Cameras in the Courtroom: A Case Study." *Judicature* 74: 307–313.

Alexander-Bloch, Benjamin. 2007. "Justice Can Be Lost in Translation." *Times-Picayune*, December 2.

Allen, G. Frederick, and Harvey Treger. 1994. "Fines and Restitution Orders: Probationers' Perceptions." *Federal Probation* 58: 34–38.

Alpert, Geoffrey, and Thomas Petersen. 1985. "The Grand Jury Report: A Magic Lantern or an Agent of Social Control?" *Justice Quarterly* 2: 23–50.

Alschuler, Albert. 1968. "The Prosecutor's Role in Plea Bargaining." *University of Chicago Law Review* 36: 50–112.

Alschuler, Albert. 1975. "The Defense Attorney's Role in Plea Bargaining." *Yale Law Journal* 84: 1179–1314.

Alschuler, Albert. 1979. "Plea Bargaining and Its History." *Law and Society Review* 13: 211–246.

Alvarez, Alex. 2011. "Nancy Grace Blasts Her Critics." July 8. Available online at http://www.mediaite.com/online/ nancy-grace-blasts-her-critics-i-suggest-if-they-dont- like-my-coverage-then-dont-watch-it.

Amendola, Andrew. 2010. "New Perspectives in Negotiation: A Therapeutic Jurisprudence Approach." *Harvard Negotiation Law Review* 15. Available online at http://www.hnlr.org/2010/01/new-perspectives-in -negotiation-a-therapeutic-jurisprudence-approach.

American Bar Association. 1988. *Criminal Justice in Crisis*. Chicago: Author.

American Bar Association. 2004. *Gideon's Broken Promise: America's Continuing Quest for Equal Justice*. Chicago: Author.

American Bar Association. 2005. Section of *Criminal Justice, Report to the House of Delegates*. Chicago: Author.

American Bar Association. 2009. National Database on Judicial Diversity in State Courts. Chicago: Author. Available online at http://www.abanet.org/judind/diversity/ national.html.

American Bar Association. 2012. *ABA Criminal Justice Standards*. Chicago: American Bar Association. Available online at://www.americanbar.org/groups/criminal_justice/ policy/standards.html.

American Civil Liberties Union. 1996. *ACLU Fact Sheet on Juvenile Crime*. Available online at http://www .aclu.org/racial-justice/aclu-fact-sheet-juvenile- justice-syst.

American Civil Liberties Union. 2008. "A Call to Action for Juvenile Justice." Available online at http://www.aclu .org/images/asset_upload_file183_37705.pdf.

American Judicature Society. 2009. *Judicial Selection in the States: Appellate and General Jurisdiction Courts: Initial Selection, Retention, and Term Length*. Des Moines, IA: Author. Available online at http://www .judicialselection.us/uploads/documents/Selection_ Retention_Term_1196092850316.pdf.

Anderson, Elijah. 1999. *Code of the Street: Decency, Violence, and the Moral Life of the Inner City*. New York: Norton.

Anderson, John. 2010. "Film Reviews: Dog Pound." *Variety*. April 5.

Anderson, Lawrence O. 2007. "United States Magistrate Judge: The Utility Fielder of the Federal Courts." *Arizona Attorney*, 43, 10–14.

Anderson, Seth (Moderator). 2009. "Anatomy of a Merit Selection Victory." *Judicature* 93: 6–13.

Antonio, Michael, and Nicole Arone. 2005. "Damned If They Do, Damned If They Don't: Jurors' Reaction to

Defendant Testimony or Silence During a Capital Trial." *Judicature* 89: 60–66.

Aos, Steve, Marna Miller, and Elizabeth Drake. 2006. *Evidence-Based Adult Corrections Programs: What Works and What Does Not*. Olympia: Washington State Institute for Public Policy.

Applebome, Peter. 1992. "Indigent Defendants, Overworked Lawyers." *New York Times*, September 18.

Applegate, Brandon, Francis Cullen, Bruce Link, Pamela Richards, and Lonn Lanza-Kaduce. 1996. "Determinants of Public Punitiveness toward Drunk Driving: A Factorial Survey Approach." *Justice Quarterly* 13: 57–79.

Applegate, Brandon K., and Shannon Santana. 2000. "Intervening with Youthful Substance Abusers: A Preliminary Analysis of a Juvenile Drug Court." *The Juvenile Justice System Journal* 21: 281–300.

Applegate, Brandon, Michael Turner, Joseph Sanborn, Edward Latessa, and Melissa Moon. 2000. "Individualization, Criminalization, or Problem Resolution: A Factorial Survey of Juvenile Court Judges' Decisions to Incarcerate Youthful Felony Offenders." *Justice Quarterly* 17: 309–332.

Appleton, Mike. 2011. "*Connick v. Thompson* and Prosecutorial Immunity." Guest blog published on JonathanTurley.org, April 10. Available online at http://jonathanturley.org/2011/04/10/connick-v-thompson-and-prosecutorial-impunity.

Aquinas, Thomas. c. 1273. *Summa Theologica*. Fathers of the English Dominican Province (transl.). Notre Dame, IN: Christian Classics.

Arbor, Brian, and Mark McKenzie. 2011. "Campaign Messages in Lower-Court Elections after Republican Party of Minnesota vs. White." *Justice System Journal* 32: 1–23.

Ares, Charles, Ann Rankin, and Herbert Sturz. 1963. "The Manhattan Bail Project: An Interim Report on the Use of Pretrial Parole." *New York University Law Review* 38: 67–92.

Armstrong, Gaylene, and Nancy Rodriguez. 2005. "Effects of Individual and Contextual Characteristics in Preadjudication Detention of Juvenile Delinquents." *Justice Quarterly* 22: 521–538.

Ashman, Allan. 1975. *Courts of Limited Jurisdiction: A National Survey*. Chicago: American Judicature Society.

Ashman, Allan, and Pat Chapin. 1976. "Is the Bell Tolling for Nonlawyer Judges?" *Judicature* 59: 417–421.

Aspin, Larry. 2011. "The 2010 Judicial Retention Elections in Perspective: Continuity and Change from 1964 to 2010." *Judicature* 94: 218–232.

Aspin, Larry, William Hall, Jean Bax, and Celeste Montoya. 2000. "Thirty Years of Judicial Retention Elections: An Update." *Social Science Journal* 37: 1.

Attorney General's Task Force on Violent Crime. 1981. *Final Report*. Washington, DC: Department of Justice.

Auerhahn, Kathleen. 1999. "Selective Incapacitation and the Problem of Prediction." *Criminology* 37: 703–734.

Auerhahn, Kathleen. 2006. "Selective Incapacitation and the Problem of Prediction." *Criminology* 37: 703–734.

Augustine. c. 1426. *The City of God*. R.W. Dyson (transl.) Cambridge, United Kingdom: Cambridge University Press, 1998.

Austin, James, and Patricia L. Hardyman. 2004. "The Risks and Needs of the Returning Prisoner Population." *Review of Policy Research* 21: 13–29.

Austin, Thomas. 1981. "The Influence of Court Location on Types of Criminal Sentences: The Rural–Urban Factor." *Journal of Criminal Justice* 9: 305–316.

Baar, Carl. 1980. "The Scope and Limits of Court Reform." *Justice System Journal* 5: 274–290.

Baehler, Aimee, and Barry Mahoney. 2005. "Strengthening Rural Courts." Denver, CO, Justice Management Institute. Available online at http://www.jmijustice.org/Data/DocumentLibrary/Documents/1159370501.66/JMI%20SJI%20Strengthening%20Rural%20Courts%20June%202005.pdf.

Bainbridge, Stephen. 2011. "Musing on Nancy Grace." *Stephen Bainbridge's Journal of Law, Politics, and Culture*. July 6. Available online at http://www.professorbainbridge.com/professorbainbridgecom/2011/07/musing-on-nancy-grace.html.

Baker, Mark. 1999. *D.A: Prosecutors in Their Own Words*. New York: Simon & Shuster.

Baker, Shannon M., Michael S. Vaughn, and Volkan Topalli. 2008. "A Review of the Powers of Bail Bond Agents and Bounty Hunters: Exploring Legalities and Illegalities of Quasi-Criminal Justice Officials." *Aggression and Violent Behavior* 13: 124–130.

Baldus, David, Charles Pulaski, and George Woodworth. 1983. "Comparative Review of Death Sentences: An Empirical Study of the Georgia Experience." *Journal of Criminal Law and Criminology* 74: 661–753.

Baldus, David C., and George Woodworth. 2003. "Race Discrimination in the Administration of the Death Penalty: An Overview of the Empirical Evidence with Special Emphasis on the Post-1990 Research." *Criminal Law Bulletin* 39: 194–226.

Baldus, David C., George A. Woodworth, Catherine M. Grosso, and Aaron M. Christ. 2002. "Arbitrariness and Discrimination in the Administration of the Death Penalty: A Legal and Empirical Analysis of the Nebraska Experience (1973–1999)." *Nebraska Law Review* 81: 486–754.

Balko, Radley. 2011. "Wrongful Convictions: How Many Innocent Americans Are Behind Bars?" *Reason*. Available online at. http://reason.com/archives/2011/06/07/wrongful-convictions/singlepage.

Banks, Cyndi. 2009. *Criminal Justice Ethics: Theory and Practice*. Thousand Oaks, CA: Sage.

Banks, Duren, and Denise Gottfredson. 2004. "Participation in Drug Treatment Court and Time to Rearrest." *Justice Quarterly* 21: 637–658.

Bannon, Alicia, Mitali Nagrecha, and Rebekah Diller. 2010. *Criminal Justice Debt: A Barrier to Reentry*. New York: Brenan Center.

Bard, Jennifer S. 2011."Practicing Medicine and Studying Law": How Medical Schools Used to Have the Same Problems We Do and What We Can Learn from Their Efforts to Solve Them." *Seattle Journal for Social Justice* 10: 135–209.

Barnes, Brooks. 2009. "*American Violet* to Premier in Texas Town Where Story Occurred." *The Carpetbagger: The Hollywood Blog of the New York Times* (March 12). Available online at http://carpetbagger.blogs.nytimes.com/2009/03/12/american-violet-to-premier-in-texas-town-where-story-occurred/#more-3725.

Barnes, Carole Wolff, and Rodney Kingsnorth. 1996. "Race, Drug, and Criminal Sentencing: Hidden Effects of the Criminal Law." *Journal of Criminal Justice* 24(1): 39–56.

Barnes, Robert. 2007. "Judicial Races Now Rife with Politics." *Washington Post*, October 28.

Bartol, Anne. 1996. "Structures and Roles of Rural Courts." In: Thomas McDonald, Robert Wood, and Melissa Pflug (Eds.). *Rural Criminal Justice: Conditions, Constraints, and Challenges* (pp. 79–92). Salem, WI: Sheffield.

Bass, Alison. 1995. "Youth Violence Explosion Likely to Worsen." *Times-Picayune*, July 2, p. A14.

Battelle Memorial Institute Law and Justice Center. 1977. *Forcible Rape: A National Survey of the Response by Prosecutors*. National Institute on Law Enforcement and Criminal Justice. Washington, DC: Government Printing Office.

Baum, Lawrence. 2011. *Specializing the Courts*. Chicago: University of Chicago Press.

Baumer, Eric, Steven Messner, and Richard Felson. 2000. "The Role of Victim Characteristics in the Disposition of Murder Cases." *Justice Quarterly* 17: 281–308.

Bayle, Allan. (2002). Testimony in *United States v. Llera Plaza*, 188, R. Suppl. 2d, *Daubert* Hearing.

Bazelon, Lara A. 2009. "Putting the Mice in Charge of the Cheese: Why Federal Judges Cannot Always Be Trusted to Police Themselves and What Congress Can Do About It." *Kentucky Law Journal* 97: 439–503.

Bedau, Hugo Adam, & Michael L. Radelet. 1987. "Miscarriages of Justice in Potentially Capital Cases." *Stanford Law Review* 40: 21–173.

Beccaria, Cesare. 1764. "On Crimes and Punishments." In: Aaron Thomas (Ed. and transl.). *On Crimes and Punishments and Other Writings*. Toronto, ON: University of Toronto Press, 2008.

Begue, Yvette, and Candace Goldstein. 1987. "How Judges Get into Trouble." *Judges Journal* 26: 8.

Beichner, Dawn, & Cassia C. Spohn. 2005. "Prosecutorial Charging Decisions in Sexual Assault Cases: Examining the Impact of a Specialized Prosecution Unit." *Criminal Justice Policy Review* 16: 461–498.

Belenko, Steven. 2001. *Research on Drug Courts: A Critical Review: 2001 Update*. New York: National Center on Addiction and Substance Abuse at Columbia University.

Belenko, Steven, and Richard Dembo. 2003. "Treating Adolescent Substance Abuse Problems in the Juvenile Drug Court." *Journal of Law and Psychiatry* 26: 87–110.

Belknap, Joanne. 2007. *The Invisible Woman: Gender, Crime, and Justice*. 2nd ed. Belmont, CA: Wadsworth.

Belknap, Joanne, Jennifer Hartman, and Victoria L. Lippen. 2010. "Misdemeanor Domestic Violence Cases in the Courts." In: Vanessa Garcia and Janice Clifford (Eds.). *Female Victims of Crime: Reality Reconsidered* (pp. 259–278). Columbus, OH: Prentice Hall.

Bell, Griffin. 1993. "Appointing United States Attorneys." *Journal of Law and Politics* 9: 247–256.

Bell, Laura Cohen. 2002. *Warring Factions: Interest Groups, Money, and the New Politics of Senate Confirmation*. Columbus: Ohio State University Press.

Benner, Laurence A., and Charles T. Samarkos. 2000. "Searching for Narcotics in San Diego: Preliminary Findings from the San Diego Search Warrant Project." *California Western Law Review* 36: 221–266.

Bentham, Jeremy. 1830. "Principles of Penal Law: Rationale of Punishment. In: John Bowring (Ed.). *The Works of Jeremy Bentham*, Vol. 1 (pp. 365–398). Edinburgh, Scotland: W. Tait (published 1843).

Berg, Kenneth. 1985. "The Bail Reform Act of 1984." *Emory Law Journal* 34: 687–740.

Berkson, Larry, and Susan Carbon. 1978. *Court Unification: History, Politics, and Implementation*. Washington, DC: National Institute of Law Enforcement and Criminal Justice.

Bernstein, Ilene Nagel, William R. Kelly, and Patricia A. Doyle. 1977. "Societal Reaction to Deviants: The Case of Criminal Defendants." *American Sociological Review* 42(5): 743–755.

Bertram, Eva, et al. 1996. *Drug War Politics: The Price of Denial*. Berkeley: University of California Press.

Bhati, Avinash Singh. 2007. "Estimating the Number of Crimes Averted by Incapacitation: An Information Theoretic Approach." *Journal of Quantitative Criminology* 23: 355–375.

Bibas, Stephanos. 2004. "Plea Bargaining Outside the Shadow of Trial." *Harvard Law Review*, 117: 2463–2547.

Bienen, L. B. 2008. "Anomalies: Ritual and Language in Lethal Injection Regulations." *Fordham Urban Law Journal* 35: 857–881.

Binder, Sarah, and Forest Maltzman. 2004. "The Limits of Senatorial Courtesy." *Legislative Studies Quarterly* 29: 5–22.

Binford, W. Warren H., Preston C. Greene, Maria C. Schmidlkofer, Robert M. Wilsey, and Hillary A. Taylor. 2007. "Seeking Best Practices among Intermediate Courts of Appeal: A Nascent Journey." *Journal of Appellate Practice and Process*, 9: 37–119.

Binnall, James M. 2008. "EG1900 . . . The Number They Gave Me When They Revoked My Citizenship: Perverse Consequences of Ex-Felon Civic Exile." *Willamette Law Review* 44: 667–697.

Bisceglia, Joseph. 2007. "CSI, Judge Judy and Civic Education." *Illinois Bar Journal* 95: 508.

Biskupic, Joan. 1993. "Congress Cool to Proposals to Ease Load on Courts." *Congressional Quarterly* (April 7): 1073–1075.

Blackwell, Brenda Sims, David Holleran, and Mary A. Finn. 2008. "The Impact of the Pennsylvania Sentencing Guidelines on Sex Differences in Sentencing." *Journal of Contemporary Criminal Justice* 24: 399–418.

Blankenship, Michael, James Luginbuhl, Francis Cullen, and William Redick. 1997. "Juror Comprehension of Sentencing Instructions: A Test of Tennessee's Death Penalty Process." *Justice Quarterly* 14: 325–357.

Blokland, Argan A. J., and Paul Nieuwbeerta. 2007. "Selectively Incapacitating Frequent Offenders: Costs and Benefits of Various Penal Scenarios." *Journal of Quantitative Criminology* 23: 327–353.

Bloom, Frederic M. 2008. "State Courts Unbound." *Cornell Law Review* 93: 501–554.

Bloom, Robert M., and Hillary J. Massey. 2008. "Accounting for Federalism in State Courts: Exclusion of Evidence Obtained Lawfully by Federal Agents." *University of Colorado Law Review* 79: 381–420.

Blumberg, Abraham. 1967a. *Criminal Justice*. Chicago: Quadrangle Books.

Blumberg, Abraham. 1967b. "The Practice of Law as a Confidence Game." *Law and Society Review* 1: 15–39.

Blumberg, Abraham. 1970. *Criminal Justice*. New York: Quadrangle Books.

Blumstein, Alfred, Jacqueline Cohen, Susan Martin, and Michael Tonry (Eds.). 1983. *Research on Sentencing: The Search for Reform*. Washington, DC: National Academies Press.

Boland, Barbara. 1996. "What Is Community Prosecution?" *National Institute of Justice Journal* 231: 35–40.

Boland, Barbara, Elizabeth Brady, Herbert Tyson, and John Bassler. 1982. *The Prosecution of Felony Arrests*. Washington, DC: Institute for Law and Social Research.

Boland, Barbara, and Brian Forst. 1985. "Prosecutors Don't Always Aim to Pleas." *Federal Probation* 49: 10–15.

Boland, Barbara, Paul Mahanna, and Ronald Sones. 1992. *The Prosecution of Felony Arrests, 1988*. Washington, DC: U.S. Department of Justice, Bureau of Justice Statistics.

Bonneau, Chris. 2001. "The Composition of State Supreme Courts." *Judicature* 85: 26–31.

Bonneau, Chris. 2007. "The Effects of Campaign Spending in State Supreme Court Elections." *Political Research Quarterly* 60: 489.

Bonneau, Chris, and Melinda Gann Hall. 2003. "Predicting Challengers in State Supreme Court Elections: Context and Politics of Institutional Design." *Political Research Quarterly* 56: 337–349.

Bonnie, Richard, Norman Poythress, Steven Hoge, John Monahan, and Marlene Eisenberg. 1996. "Decision-Making in Criminal Defense: An Empirical Study of Insanity Pleas and the Impact of Doubted Client Competence." *Journal of Criminal Law and Criminology* 87: 48–77.

Bonta, James, Suzanne Wallace-Capretta, and Jenniffer Rooney. 2000. "Can Electronic Monitoring Make a Difference? an Evaluation of Three Canadian Programs." *Crime and Delinquency* 46(2): 61–75.

Borenstein, Isaac and Erin J. Anderson. 2009. "Judicial Participation in Plea Negotiations: The Elephant in Chambers." *Suffolk Journal of Trial and Appellate Advocacy* 14: 1–34.

Borgida, Eugene, and Susan T. Fiske. 2008. *Beyond Common Sense: Psychological Science in the Courtroom*. Oxford, UK: Wiley-Blackwell.

Boritch, Helen. 1992. "Gender and Criminal Court Outcomes: An Historical Analysis." *Criminology* 30: 293–317.

Borys, Bryan, Cynthia Banks, and Darrel Parker. 1999. "Enlisting the Justice Community in Court Improvement." *Judicature* 82: 176–185.

Bouffard, Jeffrey, and Katie Richardson. 2007. "The Effectiveness of Drug Court Programming for Specific Kinds of Offenders: Methamphetamine- and DWI-Offenders versus Other Drug-Involved Offenders." *Criminal Justice Policy Review* 18: 274–293.

Bouffard, Jeffrey, Katie Richardson, and Travis Franklin. 2010. "Drug Courts for DWI Offenders? The Effectiveness of Two Hybrid Drug Courts on DWI Offenders." *Journal of Criminal Justice* 38: 25-33.

Bourgois, Philippe. 2003. *In Search of Respect: Selling Crack in El Barrio*. 2nd ed. New York: Cambridge University Press.

Boyd, Christina, Lee Epstein and Andrew Martin. 2010. "Untangling the Casual Effects of Sex on Judging." *American Journal of Political Science* 54: 389–411.

Bowden, Deborah. 2011. "Social Media's Effect on the Casey Anthony Trial." *Fox 13 News*, July 19.

Bowen, Deirdre. 2009. "Calling Your Bluff: How Prosecutors and Defense Attorneys Adapt Plea Bargaining Strategies to Increased Formalization." *Justice Quarterly* 26: 1–29.

Bowes, Mark. 2009. "Localities Recoup Incarceration Costs." *Richmond Times-Dispatch*, January 12.

Brace, Paul, and Brent D. Boyea. 2007. "Judicial Selection Methods and Capital Punishment in the American States." In: Matthew Justin Streb (Ed.). *Running for Judge: The Rising Political, Financial, and Legal Stakes of Judicial Elections* (pp. 186–203). New York: New York University Press.

Brace, Paul, and Melinda Gann Hall. 1997. "The Interplay of Preferences, Case Facts, Context, and Rules in the Politics of Judicial Choice." *Journal of Politics* 59: 1206–1241.

Bradley, Craig. 2006. "The Right Decision on the Juvenile Death Penalty." *Judicature* 89: 302–303.

Brennan, Pauline K., and Cassia Spohn. 2008. "Race/Ethnicity and Sentencing Outcomes among Drug Offenders in North Carolina." *Journal of Contemporary Criminal Justice* 24: 371–398.

Brennan, William. 1963. "The Criminal Prosecution: Sporting Event or Quest for Truth?" *Washington University Law Quarterly* 279–294.

Brenner, Susan. 1998. "Is the Grand Jury Worth Keeping?" *Judicature* 81: 190–199.

Brereton, David, and Jonathan Casper. 1981–1982. "Does It Pay to Plead Guilty? Differential Sentencing and the Functioning of Criminal Courts." *Law and Society Review* 16: 45–70.

Breyer, Stephen, et al. 2006. "Implementation of the Judicial Conduct and Disability Act of 1980: A Report to the Chief Justice." Washington, DC: The Judicial Conduct and Disability Act Study Committee. Available online at http://www.supremecourtus.gov/publicinfo/breyercommitteereport.pdf.

Bright, David A., and Jane Goodman-Delahunty. 2006. "Gruesome Evidence and Emotion: Anger, Blame, and Jury Decision-Making." *Law and Human Behavior* 30: 183–202.

Bright, Stephen. 1997. "Political Attacks on the Judiciary." *Judicature* 80: 165–173.

Britto, Sarah, Tycy Hughes, Kurt Saltzman, and Colin Stroh. 2007. "Does 'Special' Mean Young, White and Female? Deconstructing the Meaning of 'Special' in *Law & Order: Special Victims Unit*." *Journal of Criminal Justice and Popular Culture* 14(1): 39–57.

Broccolina, Frank, and Richard Zorza. 2008. "En$uring Access to Ju$tice in Tough Economic Times." *Judicature* 92(3): 124–128.

Brody, David C. 2008. "The Use of Judicial Performance Evaluation to Enhance Judicial Accountability, Judicial Independence, and Public Trust." *Denver University Law Review* 86: 115–156.

Broeder, D. W. 1959. "The University of Chicago Jury Project." *Nebraska Law Review* 38: 744–760.

Brooks, Daniel. 1985. "Penalizing Judges Who Appeal Disciplinary Sanctions: The Unconstitutionality of 'Upping the Ante.'" *Judicature* 69: 95–102.

Brooks, Richard R. W. and Stephen Raphael. 2003. "Life Terms or Death Sentences: The Uneasy Relationship between Judicial Elections and Capital Punishment." *Journal of Criminal Law and Criminology* 92: 609–640.

Brooks, Thom. 2004. "A Defence of Jury Nullification." *Res Publica* 10: 401–423.

Brown, Brian, and Greg Jolivette. 2005. *A Primer: Three Strikes—The Impact after More Than a Decade*. Sacramento: California Legislative Analyst's Office.

Brown, Darryl. 1997. "Jury Nullification within the Rule of Law." *Minnesota Law Review* 81: 1149–1200.

Brown, Gina. 2005. "A Community of Court ADR Programs: How Court-Based ADR Programs Help Each Other Survive and Thrive." *Justice System Journal* 26: 327–341.

Brown, Mary, and Steven Bunnell. 2006. "Negotiated Justice: Prosecutorial Perspectives on Federal Plea Bargaining in the District of Columbia." *American Criminal Law Review* 43: 1063.

Buchanan, John. 1989. "Police–Prosecutor Teams: Innovations in Several Jurisdictions." *NIJ Reports* 214: 2–8.

Buchman, Jeremy. 2004. "The Legal Model and *Daubert's* Effect on Trial Judges' Decisions to Admit Scientific Testimony." Paper presented at the annual meeting of the Midwest Political Science Association, Chicago.

Bulman, Philip. 2009. "Increasing Sexual Assault Prosecution Rates." *NIJ Journal* 264, November.

Burbank, Stephen. 1987. "Politics and Progress in Implementing the Federal Judicial Discipline Act." *Judicature* 71: 13–28.

Bureau of Justice Statistics. 1990. *Juvenile and Adult Records: One System, One Record?* Washington, DC: Department of Justice.

Bureau of Justice Statistics. 1996. *How to Use Structured Fines (Day Fines) as an Intermediate Sanction*. Washington, DC: Government Printing Office.

Bureau of Justice Statistics. 1997. *Correctional Populations in the United States, 1995*. Washington, DC: Department of Justice.

Bureau of Justice Statistics. 2002. "Criminal Victimization 2001: Changes 2000–2001 with Trends." Available online at http://www.prisonpolicy.org/scans/bjs/cv01.pdf.

Bureau of Justice Statistics. 2006. "Criminal Victimization in the United States; Rape/Sexual Assault Tables, 1996–2005." Available online at http://www.bjs.gov/content/pub/html/cvus/rape_sexual_assault.cfm.

Bureau of Justice Statistics. 2007. "Criminal Offender Statistics."

Bureau of Justice Statistics. 2011. "Justice Expenditure and Employment Extracts Series." Available online at http://bjs.ojp.usdoj.gov/index.cfm?ty=dcdetail&iid=286.

Bureau of Justice Statistics. 2011. *Number of Persons Executed in the United States: Capital Punishment Statistical Tables, 1930-2011*. Washington, DC: Author.

Bureau of Justice Statistics. 2012. *Indigent Defense Systems*. Washington, DC: Department of Justice, Bureau of Justice Statistics. Available online at http://bjs.ojp.usdoj.gov/index.cfm?ty=tp&tid=28#indigent.

Burke-Robertson, C. 2008. "Judging Jury Verdicts." *Tulane Law Review* 83: 157–218.

Burruss, George, and Kimberly Kempf-Leonard. 2002. "The Questionable Advantage of Defense Counsel in Juvenile Court." *Justice Quarterly* 19: 37–68.

Bushway, Shawn, and Anne Morrison Piehl. 2007. "Social Science Research and the Legal Threat to Presumptive Sentencing Guidelines." *Criminology and Public Policy* 6: 461–482.

Butler, Brooke. 2007. "Death Qualification and Prejudice: The Effect of Implicit Racism, Sexism, and Homophobia on Capital Defendants' Right to Due Process." *Behavioral Sciences and the Law* 25: 857–867.

Butler, Brooke, and Gary Moran. 2007a. "The Impact of Death Qualification, Belief in a Just World, Legal Authoritarianism, and Locus of Control on Venirepersons' Evaluations of Aggravating and Mitigating Circumstances in Capital Trials." *Behavioral Sciences and the Law* 25: 57–68.

Butler, Brooke, and Gary Moran. 2007b. "The Role of Death Qualification and Need for Cognition in Venirepersons' Evaluations of Expert Scientific Testimony in Capital Trials." *Behavioral Sciences and the Law* 25: 561–571.

Butler, Paul. 1995. "Racially Based Jury Nullification: Black Power in the Criminal Justice System." *Yale Law Journal* 105: 677–725.

Butterfield, Fox. 1997. "Justice Besieged: With Juvenile Courts in Chaos, Critics Propose Their Demise." *New York Times*, July 21.

Buzawa, Eve, and Carl Buzawa. 1996. *Domestic Violence: The Criminal Justice Response*. 2nd ed. Thousand Oaks, CA: Sage.

Byrd, Harry. 1976. "Has Life Tenure Outlived Its Time?" *Judicature* 59: 266–277.

Byrne, James, Arthur Lurigio, and Christopher Baird. 1989. "The Effectiveness of the New Intensive Supervision Programs." *Research in Corrections* 2: 1–15.

Caher, John, and Andrew Keshner. 2011. "Deep Overtime Cuts Bring Delay, Rethinking of Case Presentation." *New York Law Journal*, November 28.

Call, Jack, David England, and Susette Talarico. 1983. "Abolition of Plea Bargaining in the Coast Guard." *Journal of Criminal Justice* 11: 351–358.

Cameron, Mary. 1964. *The Booster and the Snitch*. Glencoe, IL: Free Press.

Campbell, Curtis, Candace McCoy, and Chimezie Osigweh. 1990. "The Influence of Probation Recommendations on Sentencing Decisions and Their Predictive Accuracy." *Federal Probation* 54: 13–21.

Campbell, Donald, and H. Laurence Ross. 1968. "The Connecticut Crackdown on Speeding: Time-Series Data in Quasi-Experimental Analysis." *Law and Society Review* 3: 33–54.

Campbell, William. 1973. "Eliminate the Grand Jury." *Journal of Criminal Law and Criminology* 64: 174–182.

Cannavale, F., and W. Falcon. 1976. *Witness Cooperation*. Lexington, MA: Heath.

Cannon, Angie. 1996. "Bill Spells Out Rights of Victims." *Times-Picayune*, April 23.

Cannon, Angie. 1997. "Violent Teen Crime Rate Drops Two Years in a Row." *Times-Picayune*, October 3.

Capers, I. Bennett. 2009. "Legal Outsiders in American Film: Notes on Minority Report." *Suffolk University Law Review* 42: 795–807.

Caplan, Lincoln. 1988. *The Tenth Justice: The Solicitor General and the Rule of Law*. New York: Vintage.

Caputo, Gail. 1999. *Evaluation of CAES CSP Program*. New York: Vera Institute of Justice.

Carbon, Susan. 1984. "Women in the Judiciary." *Judicature* 65: 285.

Carelli, Richard. 1996. "Independent Judiciary Vital, Rehnquist Says." *Times-Picayune*, April 27.

Carey, Shannon M., Michael W. Finigan, and Kimberly Pukstas. 2008. *Exploring the Key Components of Drug Courts: A Comparative Study of 18 Adult Drug Courts on Practices, Outcomes and Costs*. Portland, OR: NPC Research.

Caringella, Susan. 2008. *Addressing Rape Reform in Law and Practice*. New York: Columbia University Press.

Carlsmith, Kevin, John Darley, and Paul Robinson. 2002. "Why Do We Punish? Deterrence and Just Deserts as Motives for Punishment." *Journal of Personality and Social Psychology* 83: 284–299.

Carns, Teresa White, and John Kruse. 1992. "Alaska's Ban on Plea Bargaining Reevaluated." *Judicature* 75: 310–317.

Carp, Robert. 1975. "The Behavior of Grand Juries: Acquiescence or Justice?" *Social Science Quarterly* 55(4): 855–870.

Carp, Robert, and Ronald Stidham. 1990. *Judicial Process in America*. Washington, DC: Congressional Quarterly Press.

Carr, Patrick, Laura Napolitano, and Jessica Keating. 2007. "We Never Call the Cops and Here Is Why: A Qualitative Examination of Legal Cynicism in Three Philadelphia Neighborhoods." *Criminology* 45: 445.

Carrington, Paul, Daniel Meador, and Maurice Rosenberg. 1976. *Justice on Appeal*. St. Paul, MN: West.

Carroll, Leo, and Claire Cornell. 1985. "Racial Composition, Sentencing Reforms, and Rates of Incarceration, 1970–1980." *Justice Quarterly* 2: 473–490.

Carroll, Susan. 2008. "A System's Fatal Flaws." *Houston Chronicle*, November 16.

Carter, Lief H., and Tom F. Burke. 2007. *Reason in Law* (7th ed.) Upper Saddle River, NJ: Pearson/Longman.

Carter, Lief. 1974. *The Limits of Order*. Lexington, MA: Heath.

Carter, Robert, and Leslie Wilkins. 1967. "Some Factors in Sentencing Policy." *Journal of Criminal Law, Criminology and Police Science* 58: 503–514.

Casey, Pamela, and David Rottman. 2004. *Problem-Solving Courts: Models and Trends*. Williamsburg, VA: National Center for State Courts.

Casper, Jonathan. 1972. *American Criminal Justice: The Defendant's Perspective*. Englewood Cliffs, NJ: Prentice Hall.

Casper, Jonathan, David Brereton, and David Neal. 1982. *The Implementation of the California Determinate Sentencing Law*. Washington, DC: Department of Justice.

Catalano, Shannan, Erica Smith, Howard Snyder, and Michael Rand. 2009. "Female Victims of Violence." Washington, DC: Department of Justice, Bureau of Justice Statistics.

Cauchon, Dennis. 1999. "Indigents' Lawyers: Low Pay Hurts Justice?" *USA Today*, February 3.

Cauthen, James, and Barry Latzer. 2008. "Why So Long? Explaining Processing Time in Capital Appeals." *Justice System Journal* 29: 298–312.

CBS News. 2004. "Scott Practiced Testifying." www.cbsnews.com (October 22.)

Center for Children's Law and Policy. 2012. "Models for Change." Available online at http://www.cclp.org/modelsforchange.php.

Center for Court Innovation. 2009. "Manhattan Community Court." Available online at http://www.courtinnovation.org.

Center for Court Innovation. 2011. "Problem-Solving Justice." Available online at http://www.courtinnovation.org/topic/problem-solving-justice.

Center for Court Innovation. 2012a. "Community Court." Available online at http://www.courtinnovation.org/topic/community-court.

Center for Court Innovation. 2012b. "Community Prosecution." Available online at http://www.courtinnovation.org/topic/community-prosecution.

Center for Court Innovation. 2012c. "Domestic Violence Courts." Available online at http://www.courtinnovation.org/project/domestic-violence-courts.

Cervantes, Adriana C. 2010. "Will Twitter Be Following You in the Courtroom?: Why Reporters Should Be Allowed to Broadcast During Courtroom Proceedings." *Hastings Communications and Entertainment Law Journal* 33: 133–157.

Chaiken, Marcia, and Jan Chaiken. 1990. *Redefining the Career Criminal: Priority Prosecution of High-Rate Dangerous Offenders*. Washington, DC: Department of Justice.

Champion, Dean J. 2007. *Sentencing: A Reference Handbook*. Santa Barbara, CA: ABC-CLIO.

Chapper, Joy, and Roger Hanson. 1990. "Understanding Reversible Error in Criminal Appeals." *State Court Journal* 14: 16–24.

Chassin, Laurie. 2008. "Juvenile Justice and Substance Use." *Juvenile Justice: The Future of Children*, 18(2), 165–183.

Chilton, Bradley. 1991. *Prisons under the Gavel: The Federal Takeover of Georgia Prisons*. Columbus: Ohio State University Press.

Chiricos, Theodore, and William Bales. 1991. "Unemployment and Punishment: An Empirical Assessment." *Criminology* 29: 701–724.

Choi, Stephen J., G. Mitu Gulati, and Eric A. Posner. 2008. "Professionals or politicians: The uncertain empirical case for an elected rather than appointed judiciary." *Journal of Law, Economics, and Organization*.

Christy, Annette, Norman G. Poythress, Roger A. Boothroyd, John Petrila, Shabnam Mehra. 2005. "Evaluating the Efficiency and Community Safety Goals of the Broward County Mental Health Court." *Behavioral Sciences and the Law*, 22: 227–243.

Church, Thomas. 1976. "Plea Bargains, Concessions and the Courts: Analysis of a Quasi-Experiment." *Law and Society Review* 10: 377–389.

Church, Thomas. 1982. "The 'Old' and the 'New' Conventional Wisdom of Court Delay." *Justice System Journal* 7: 395–412.

Church, Thomas. 1985. "Examining Local Legal Culture." *American Bar Foundation Research Journal* 449–518.

Church, Thomas, Alan Carlson, Jo-Lynne Lee, and Teresa Tan. 1978. *Justice Delayed: The Pace of Litigation in Urban Trial Courts*. Williamsburg, VA: National Center for State Courts.

Church, Thomas, and Virginia McConnell. 1978. *Pretrial Delay: A Review and Bibliography*. Williamsburg, VA: National Center for State Courts.

Clark, John, James Austin, and D. Alan Henry. 1997. "*Three Strikes and You're Out*": *A Review of State Legislation*. Washington, DC: National Institute of Justice.

Clark, John, James Austin, and D. Alan Henry. 1998. "'Three Strikes and You're Out': Are Repeat Offender Laws Having Their Anticipated Effects?" *Judicature* 81: 144–154.

Clark, Tom. 2005. "A Note on the Moore Case and Judicial Administration." *The Justice System Journal* 26: 355–361.

Clarke, Stevens. 1984. "North Carolina's Determinate Sentencing Legislation." *Judicature* 68: 140–152.

Clarke, Stevens, and Gary Koch. 1976. "The Influence of Income and Other Factors on Whether Criminal Defendants Go to Prison." *Law and Society Review* 11: 57–92.

Clear, Todd R., and Eric Cadora. 2003. *Community Justice*. Belmont, CA: Wadsworth.

Clear, Todd R., George Cole, and Michael Reisig. 2009. *American Corrections*. 8th ed. Belmont, CA: Wadsworth.

Clear, Todd R., John Hewitt, and Robert Regoli. 1979. "Discretion and the Determinate Sentence: Its Distribution, Control and Effect on Time Served." *Crime and Delinquency* 24: 428–445.

Clear, Todd. R., Patria M. Harris, and S. Christopher Baird. 1992. "Probationer Violations and Officer Response." *Journal of Criminal Justice* 20: 1–12.

Clear, Todd. 2007. *Imprisoning Communities: How Mass Incarceration Makes Disadvantaged Neighborhoods Worse*. New York: Oxford University Press.

Cloud, John. 2011. "The Troubled Life of Jarod Loughner." *Time*, January 24.

Clynch, Edward, and David Neubauer. 1981. "Trial Courts as Organizations: A Critique and Synthesis." *Law and Policy Quarterly* 3: 69–94.

CNN. 2008. "Is 'American Gangster' Really All That 'True'?"

CNN. 2010. The Evidence against Amanda Knox. June 11. Available online at http://www.cnn.com/2010/CRIME/06/11/amanda.knox.evidence/index.html.

CNN. 2011, September 14.. "Police Shoot Arkansas Courthouse Gunman Dead." Available online at http://articles.cnn.com/2011-09-14/justice/arkansas.courthouse.shooting_1_fort-smith-police-metal-detectors-arkansas?_s=PM:CRIME.

Cohen, Mark A., Roland T. Rust, and Sara Steen. 2006. "Prevention, Crime Control or Cash? Public Preferences Towards Criminal Justice Spending Priorities." *Justice Quarterly* 23: 317–335.

Cohen, Robyn. 1992. *Drunk Driving: 1989 Survey of Inmates of Local Jails*. Washington, DC: Bureau of Justice Statistics.

Cohen, Thomas. 2011. "Who's Better at Defending Criminals? Does Type of Defense Attorney Matter in Terms of

Producing Favorable Case Outcomes." Available online at http://ssrn.com/abstract=1876474.

Cohen, Thomas, and Tracey Kyckelhahn. 2010. *Felony Defendants in Large Urban Counties, 2006*. Washington, DC: Bureau of Justice Statistics.

Cohen, Thomas, and Brian Reaves. 2007. *Pretrial Release of Felony Defendants in State Courts*. Washington, DC: Bureau of Justice Statistics.

Cohn, Adam. 2005. "Want Social Condemnation with Your Justice? Tune in Judge Judy." *New York Times*, October 9.

Colburn, Jamison E. 2006. "Localism's Ecology: Protecting and Restoring Habitat in the Suburban Nation." *Ecology Law Quarterly* 33: 945–1014.

Cole, David. 2011. "Turning the Corner on Mass Incarceration." *Ohio State Journal of Criminal Law* 9: 27–51.

Cole, George. 1970. "The Decision to Prosecute." *Law and Society Review* 4: 313–343.

Cole, George. 1992. "Using Civil and Administrative Remedies to Collect Fines and Fees." *State Court Journal* 16: 4–10.

Cole, George, Barry Mahoney, Marlene Thornton, and Roger Hanson. 1988. "The Use of Fines by Trial Court Judges." *Judicature* 71: 325–333.

Cole, Simon A. 2010. "Who Speaks for Science? A Response to the National Academies of Science Report on Forensic Science." *Law, Probability & Risk* 9: 25–46.

Cole, Simon A., Max Welling, Rachel Dioso-Villa, and Robert Carpenter. 2008. "Beyond the Individuality of Fingerprints: A Measure of Simulated Computer Latent Print Source Attribution Accuracy." *Law, Probability, & Risk* 7: 165–189.

Coles, Catherine, and George Kelling. 1999. "Prevention through Community Prosecution." *The Public Interest* 36: 69.

Collins, Reed. 2007. "Strolling While Poor: How Broken-Windows Policing Created a New Crime in Baltimore." *Georgetown Journal on Poverty Law and Policy* 14: 419–439.

Coltri, Laurie. 2009. *Alternative Dispute Resolution: A Conflict Approach*. 2nd ed. Upper Saddle River, NJ: Pearson.

"Community Prosecution." 2008. Cambridge, MA: Program in Criminal Justice Policy and Management, Kennedy School of Government, Harvard University. Available online at http://www.hks.harvard.edu/criminaljustice/research/community_prosecution.htm.

Comparato, Scott A., and Scott D. McClurg. 2007. "A Neo-institutional Explanation of State Supreme Court Responses in Search and Seizure Cases." *American Politics Research* 35(5): 726–754.

Comptroller General of the United States. 1979. *Impact of the Exclusionary Rule on Federal Criminal Prosecutions*. Washington, DC: General Accounting Office.

Congressional Quarterly. 1996. "House Republicans Advance Six Anti-Crime Bills." *1995 Congressional Quarterly Almanac*. Washington, DC: Author.

Connick, Elizabeth, and Robert Davis. 1983. "Examining the Problems of Witness Intimidation." *Judicature* 66: 438–447.

Coontz, Phyllis. 2000. "Gender and Judicial Decisions: Do Female Judges Decide Cases Differently than Male Judges?" *Gender Issues* 18: 59–73.

Cooper, Caroline. 2003. "Rural Drug Courts." Washington, DC: American University, Bureau of Justice Assistance Drug Court Clearinghouse. Available online at http://www1.spa.american.edu/justice/documents/2014.pdf

Cooper, Caroline S. 2001. "Juvenile Drug Court Programs." *Juvenile Accountability Incentive Block Grants Program Bulletin*. Washington, D.C.: Office of Juvenile Justice and Delinquency Prevention.

Cooper, Jeffrey O., and Douglas A. Berman. 2000. "Passive Virtues and Casual Vices on the Federal Courts of Appeals." *Brooklyn Law Review* 66: 712–754.

Corman, Hope, and Naci Mocan. 2005. "Carrots, Sticks, and Broken Windows." *The Journal of Law and Economics*, 48: 235–266.

Cosden, Merith, Jeffrey Ellens, Jeffrey Schnell, and Yasmeen Yamini-Diouf. 2005. "Efficacy of a Mental Health Treatment Court with Assertive Community Treatment." *Behavioral Sciences and the Law* 23: 199–214.

Cose, Ellis. 2009. "Closing the Gap: Obama Could Fix Cocaine Sentencing." *Newsweek*, July 20.

Cosimo, S. Deborah. 2011. *Domestic Violence: Legal Sanctions and Recidivism Rates among Male Perpetrators*. El Paso, TX: LFB Scholarly.

Council of State Governments Justice Center. 2008. *Mental Health Courts: A Primer for Policymakers and Practitioners*. New York: Author. Available online at http://consensusproject.org/mhcp/mhc-primer.pdf.

Council of State Governments Justice Center 2012. *Mental Health Consensus Project*. Available online at http://consensusproject.org.

Court Statistics Project. 2011. "Court Structure Charts." Williamsburg, VA: National Center for State Courts. Available online at http://www.courtstatistics.org/Other-Pages/State_Court_Structure_Charts.aspx.

Covarrubias, Rebecca J. 2009. "Lives in Defense Counsel's Hands: The Problems and Responsibilities of Defense Counsel Representing Mentally Ill or Mentally Retarded Capital Defendants." *Scholar* 11: 413–468.

Covey, Herbert, and Mary Mande. 1985. "Determinate Sentencing in Colorado." *Justice Quarterly* 2: 259–270.

Covey, Russell. 2007. Reconsidering the Relationship between Cognitive Psychology and Plea Bargaining." *Marquette Law Review* 91: 213–247.

Covey, Russell D. 2008. "Fixed Justice: Reforming Plea Bargaining with Plea-Based Ceilings." *Tulane Law Review* 82: 1237–1290.

Covey, Russell D. 2009. "Signaling and Plea Bargaining's Innocence Problem." *Washington and Lee Law Review* 66: 73–130.

Cox, Gail. 1993. "Hellish Clients, Big Trouble." *National Law Journal* 15: 1.

Coyle, Marcia. 2009. "Written, Verbal Threats to Federal Judges Jump." *The National Law Journal*. Available online at http://www.law.com/jsp/nlj/PubArticleNLJ.jsp?id=1202429189887.

Crew, B. Keith. 1991. "Sex Differences in Criminal Sentencing: Chivalry or Patriarchy?" *Justice Quarterly* 8: 59–84.

Criminal Justice Consortium. 1998. "Count of Prisoners Sentenced for Third and Second Strike Cases." Oakland: California Department of Corrections.

Crouch, Ben, and James Marquart. 1990. "Resolving the Paradox of Reform: Litigation, Prisoner Violence, and Perceptions of Risk." *Justice Quarterly* 7: 103–123.

Crow, Matthew S. 2008. "The Complexities of Prior Record, Race, Ethnicity, and Policy Interactive Effects in Sentencing." *Criminal Justice Review* 33: 502–523.

Crow, Matthew S., and Katherine A. Johnson. 2008. "Race, Ethnicity, and Habitual-Offender Sentencing: A Multilevel Analysis of Individual Contextual Threat." *Criminal Justice Policy Review* 19: 63–83.

Crowe, Ann H., Linda Sydney, Pat Bancroft, & Beverly Lawrence. 2002. *Offender Supervision with Electronic Technology: A User's Guide*. Lexington, KY: American Probation and Parole Association. Available online at http://www.ncjrs.gov/pdffiles1/nij/grants/197102.pdf.

Cullen, Francis T. 2005. "The Twelve People Who Saved Rehabilitation: How the Science of Criminology Made a Difference." *Criminology* 43: 1–42.

Cullen, Francis T., Kristie R. Blevins, and Jennifer S. Trager. 2005. "The Rise and Fall of Boot Camp: A Case Study in Common-Sense Corrections." *Journal of Offender Rehabilitation* 40: 53–70.

Cullen, Francis, Bonnie Fisher, and Brandon Applegate. 2000. "Public Opinion about Punishment and Corrections." *Crime and Justice* 27: 1–79.

Cullen, Francis T., John Paul Wright, and Kristie R. Blevins. 2006. *Taking Stock: The Status of Criminological Theory*. Edison, NJ: Transaction.

Cunningham, Mark D., Thomas J. Reidy, and Jon R. Sorensen. 2008. "Assertions of 'Future Dangerousness' at Federal Capital Sentencing: Rates and Correlates of Subsequent Prison Misconduct and Violence." *Law and Human Behavior* 32: 46–63.

Currie, Elliot. 1985. *Confronting Crime: An American Challenge*. New York: Pantheon.

Currie, Elliot. 1989. "Confronting Crime: Looking toward the Twenty-First Century." *Justice Quarterly* 6: 5–15.

Currie, Elliott. 1993. *Reckoning: Drugs, the Cities, and the American Future*. New York: Hill and Wang.

Curry, Theodore R., and Guadalupe Corral-Camacho. 2008. "Sentencing Young Minority Males for Drug Offenses: Testing for Conditional Effects Between Race/Ethnicity, Gender and Age during the U.S. War on Drugs." *Punishment and Society* 10: 253–276.

D'Alessio, Stewart, and Lisa Stolzenberg. 2009. "Racial Animosity and Interracial Crime." *Criminology* 47: 269–296.

Daly, Kathleen. 1994. *Gender, Crime, and Punishment*. New Haven, CT: Yale University Press.

Dancey, Logan, Kjersten Nelson and Eve Ringsmuth. 2011. "'Strict Scrutiny' The Content of Senate Judicial Confirmation Hearings during the George W. Bush Administration." *Judicature* 95: 126–135.

Dantzker, M.L. 2005. *Understanding Today's Police*. Monsey, NY: Criminal Justice Press.

Davey, Monica. 2006. "Missouri Says It Can't Hire Doctor for Executions." *New York Times*, July 15.

David, James R. 1980. *The Sentencing Dispositions of New York City Lower Court Criminal Judges*. Ph.D. dissertation, New York University.

Davies, Thomas. 1982. "Affirmed: A Study of Criminal Appeals and Decision-Making Norms in a California Court of Appeal." *American Bar Foundation Research Journal* 7(3): 543–648.

Davies, Thomas. 1983. "A Hard Look at What We Know (and Still Need to Learn) about the 'Costs' of the Exclusionary Rule: The NIJ Study and Other Studies of 'Lost Arrests.'" *American Bar Foundation Research Journal* 8(3): 611–690.

Davis, Angela. 2007. *Arbitrary Justice: The Power of the American Prosecutor*. New York: Oxford University Press.

Davis, Robert C.. 1983. "Victim/Witness Noncooperation: A Second Look at a Persistent Phenomenon." *Journal of Criminal Justice* 11: 287–299.

Davis, Robert C., and Tanya Bannister. 1995. "Improving Collection of Court-Ordered Restitution." *Judicature* 79: 30–33.

Davis, Robert, C., and Barbara E. Smith, 1994. "The Effects of Victim Impact Statements on Sentencing Decisions: A Test in an Urban Setting." *Justice Quarterly* 11: 453–469.

Davis, Robert C., Barbara Smith, and Susan Hillenbrand. 1992. "Restitution: The Victim's Viewpoint." *Justice System Journal* 15: 746–758.

Davis, Sue. 1993. "The Voice of Sandra Day O'Connor." *Judicature* 77: 134–139.

Dawson, Myrna, and Ronit Dinovitzer. 2001. "Victim Cooperation and the Prosecution of Domestic Violence in a Specialized Court." *Justice Quarterly* 18: 593–649.

Death Penalty Information Center. 2009. "Prominent Conservative Calls for Death Penalty Moratorium." Available online at http://www.deathpenaltyinfo.org/new-voices-prominent-conservative-calls-death-penalty-moratorium.

Dedel, Kelly. 2006. *Witness Intimidation*. Washington, DC: U.S. Department of Justice, Office of Community Oriented Policing Services.

D'Emic, Matthew. 2009. "A Courtroom Miracle: Mental Health Court." MIWatch.org. Available online at http://www.miwatch.org/2009/01/a_courtroom_miracle_mental_health_court.html.

DeFrances, Carol. 2001. "State-Funded Indigent Defense Services, 1999." *Special Report*. Washington, DC: Bureau of Justice Statistics.

DeFrances, Carol, Steven Smith, and Louise van der Does. 1996. "Prosecutors in State Courts, 1994." *Bulletin*. Washington, DC: Bureau of Justice Statistics.

DeLisi, Matt. 2001. "Extreme Career Criminals." *American Journal of Criminal Justice* 25: 239–252.

DeLisi, Matt, and Peter Conis. 2010. *American Corrections*. Sudbury, MA: Jones and Bartlett.

DeLisi, Matt. 2005. *Career Criminals in Society*. Thousand Oaks, CA: Sage.

Delsohn, Gary. 2003a. *The Prosecutors: Kidnap, Rape, Murder, Justice: One Year behind the Scenes in a Big-City DA's Office*. New York: Plume.

Delsohn, Gary. 2003b. The Prosecutors: *A Year in the Life a District Attorney's Office*. New York: Dutton/Penguin.

DeMichele, Matthew, and Brian Payne. 2009. "Using Technology to Monitor Offenders: A Community Corrections Perspective." *Corrections Today*, August.

Dempsey, John. 2003. "Wolf Pack Leads Cable with 'Law and Order.'" *Variety*, October 6, p. 26.

Demuth, Stephen. 2003. "Racial and Ethnic Differences in Pretrial Release Decisions and Outcomes: A Comparison of Hispanic, Black, and White Felony Arrestees." *Criminology* 41: 873–907.

Deutsch, Linda. 2004. "Two-Tiered Justice Favors Famous." Associated Press, July 25.

Devine, Dennis J., Laura D. Clayton, Benjamin B. Dunford, Rasmy Seying, and Jennifer Pryce. 2001. "Jury Decision Making: 45 Years of Empirical Research and Deliberating Groups." *Psychology, Public Policy, and Law* 7: 622-727.

Devins, Neal. 2008. "Ideological Cohesion and Precedent (Or Why the Court Only Cares about Precedent When Most Justices Agree with Each Other)." *North Carolina Law Review* 86: 1399–1442.

Diamond, Shari Seidman. 2006. "Beyond Fantasy and Nightmare: A Portrait of the Jury." *Buffalo Law Review* 54: 717–763.

Diamond, Shari Seidman. 2007. "Dispensing with Deception, Curing with Care." *Judicature* 91: 20–25.

Diamond, Shari Seidman, Mary R. Rose, and Beth Murphy. 2006. "Revisiting the Unanimity Requirement: The Behavior of the Non-Unanimous Civil Jury." *Northwestern University Law Review* 100: 201–230.

DiIulio, John (Ed.). 1990. *Courts, Corrections, and the Constitution: The Impact of Judicial Intervention on Prisons and Jails*. New York: Oxford University Press.

Dill, Forrest. 1975. "Discretion, Exchange and Social Control: Bail Bondsmen in Criminal Courts." *Law and Society Review* 9: 639–674.

DiPietro, Susanne. 2008. "From the Benches and Trenches: Evaluating the Court Process for Alaska's Children in Need of Aid." *Justice System Journal* 29: 187–208.

Dirks-Linhorst, P. Ann, and Donald M. Linhorst. 2012. "Recidivism Outcomes for Suburban Mental Health Court Defendants." *American Journal of Criminal Justice* 37: 76–91.

Ditton, Paula, and Doris Wilson. 1999. *Truth in Sentencing in State Prisons*. Washington, DC: Bureau of Justice Statistics.

Dixon, Herbert. 2011. "The Evolution of a High-Technology Courtroom." Williamsburg, VA: National Center for State Courts. Available online at http://www.ncsc.org/sitecore/content/microsites/future-trends/home/Technology/1-4-Evolution-of-high-tech-courtroom.aspx.

Dolan, Maura, and Victoria Kim. 2011. "Budget Cuts to Worsen California Court Delays, Officials Say." *Los Angeles Times*, July 20.

Dorfman, David N. 1999. "Proving the Lie: Litigating Police Credibility." *American Journal of Criminal Law* 26: 455–503.

Dougherty, Joyce. 1988. "Negotiating Justice in the Juvenile Justice System: A Comparison of Adult Plea Bargaining and Juvenile Intake." *Federal Probation* 52: 72–80.

Douglas, James, and Helen Stockstill. 2008. "Starving the Death Penalty: Do Financial Considerations Limit Its Use?" *Justice System Journal* 29: 326–337.

Downey, P. Mitchell, and John K. Roman. 2010. *A Bayesian Meta-Analysis of Drug Court Cost-Effectiveness*. Washington DC: The Urban Institute. Available online at http://www.dccrimepolicy.org/costbenefitanalysis/images/12-10-Bayesian-Cost-Benefit-Drug-Court_2.pdf.

Dubois, Philip. 1980. *From Ballot to Bench: Judicial Elections and the Quest for Accountability*. Austin: University of Texas Press.

Dubois, Philip. 1984. "Voting Cues in Nonpartisan Trial Court Elections: A Multivariate Assessment." *Law and Society Review* 18: 395–436.

Dunkelberger, Lloyd. 2009. "Fast Lane Offers Financial Fast Fix." *Sarasota Herald Tribune*, January 10.

Dunn, B. Michael. 2007. "'Must Find the Defendant Guilty' Jury Instructions Violate the Sixth Amendment." *Judicature* 91: 12–19.

DuPont-Morales, M.A., Michael Hooper, Judy H. Schmidt. *Handbook of Criminal Justice Administration*. Boca Raton, FL: CRC Press.

Dwyer, Jim, Peter Neufeld, and Barry Scheck. 2000. *Actual Innocence: Five Days to Execution and Other Dispatches from the Wrongly Convicted*. New York: Doubleday.

Dyke, Andrew. 2007. "Electoral Cycles in the Administration of Criminal Justice." *Public Choice* 133: 417–437.

Dzienkowski, John, and Amon Burton. 2006. *Ethical Dilemmas in the Practice of Law*. St. Paul, MN: Thomson/West.

Easton, Stephen D., and Kaitlin A. Bridges. 2008. "Peeking behind the Wizard's Curtain: Expert Discovery and Disclosure in Criminal Cases." *American Journal of Trial Advocacy* 32: 1–56.

Eckholm, Erik. 2008. "Public Defenders' Offices Refuse to Take New Cases." *New York Times*, November 9.

Eisenberg, Theodore, Paula Hannaford-Agor, Valarie Hans, Nicole Mott, G. Thomas Munsterman, Stewart Schwab, and Martin Wells. 2004. "Judge-Jury Agreement in Criminal Cases: A Partial Replication of Kalven and Zeisel's *The American Jury*." *Journal of Empirical Legal Studies* 2: 171–207.

Eisenstein, James. 1978. *Counsel for the United States: U.S. Attorneys in the Political and Legal System*. Baltimore: Johns Hopkins University Press.

Eisenstein, James, and Herbert Jacob. 1977. *Felony Justice: An Organizational Analysis of Criminal Courts*. Boston: Little, Brown.

Eisenstein, James, Roy Flemming, and Peter Nardulli. 1988. *The Contours of Justice: Communities and Their Courts*. Boston: Little, Brown.

Elias, Robert. 1986. *The Politics of Victimization: Victims, Victimology and Human Rights*. New York: Oxford University Press.

Elias, Robert. 1993. *Victims Still: The Political Manipulation of Crime Victims*. Thousand Oaks, CA: Sage.

Elliott-Engel, Amaris. 2008. "Judge Charged with Misconduct after YouTube Video Shows Him Soliciting Campaign Funds." *The Legal Intelligencer*, June 20.

Emmelman, Debra. 1996. "Trial by Plea Bargain: Case Settlement as a Product of Recursive Decision Making." *Law and Society Review* 30: 335–360.

Emmelman, Debra S. 2002. "Trial by Plea Bargain: Case Settlement as a Product of Recursive Decision-Making." In: Mark Pogrebin (Ed.). *Qualitative Approaches to Criminal Justice* (pp. 219–236). Thousand Oaks, CA: Sage.

Emmert, Craig, and Henry Glick. 1987. "Selection Systems and Judicial Characteristics: The Recruitment of State Supreme Court Judges." *Judicature* 70: 228–235.

Emmert, Craig, and Carol Ann Traut. 1992. "State Supreme Courts, State Constitutions, and Judicial Policymaking." *Justice System Journal* 16: 37–48.

Engstrom, Richard. 1971. "Political Ambitions and the Prosecutorial Office." *Journal of Politics* 33: 190.

Engstrom, Richard. 1989. "When Blacks Run for Judge: Racial Divisions in the Candidate Preferences of Louisiana Voters." *Judicature* 73: 87–89.

Epstein, Lee, Andrew D. Martin, Kevin M. Quinn, and Jeffrey A. Segal. 2008. "The Bush Imprint on the Supreme Court: Why Conservatives Should Continue to Yearn and Liberals Should Not Fear." *Tulsa Law Review* 43: 651–671.

Epstein, Lee, Charles M. Cameron, Jeffrey Segal, and Chad Westerland. 2006. "Lower Court Defiance of (Compliance with) the U.S. Supreme Court." Available online at http://ssrn.com/abstract=929018.

Epstein, Lee, Jack Knight, and Olga Shvetsova. 2002. "Selecting Selecting Systems." In: Stephen B. Burbank & Barry Friedman (Eds.). *Judicial Independence at the Crossroads: An Interdisciplinary Approach.* Philadelphia: American Academy of Political and Social Science/Sage.

Erez, Edna. 1992. "Dangerous Men, Evil Women: Gender and Parole Decision-Making." *Justice Quarterly* 9: 105–126.

Erez, Edna, & Peter R. Ibarra. 2007. "Making Your Home a Shelter." *British Journal of Criminology* 47: 100–120.

Erez, Edna, and Julian Roberts. 2007. "Victim Participation in the Criminal Justice Systems." In: Robert Carl Davis, Arthur J. Lurigio, and Susan Herman (Eds.). *Victims of Crime*. Thousand Oaks, CA: Sage.

Erez, Edna, and Linda Rogers. 1999. "Victim Impact Statements and Sentencing Outcomes and Processes. The Perspectives of Legal Professionals." *British Journal of Criminology*, 39(2), 216–239.

Fabian, John M. 2006. "State Supreme Court Responses to *Atkins v. Virginia*: Adaptive Functioning Assessment in Light of Purposeful Planning, Premeditation, and the Behavioral Context of the Homicide." *Journal of Forensic Psychology Practice* 6: 1–25.

Fader, Jamie, Philip Harris, Peter Jones, and Mary Poulin. 2001. "Factors Involved in Decisions on Commitment to Delinquency Programs for First-Time Juvenile Offenders." *Justice Quarterly* 18: 323–341.

Fagan, Jeffrey. 1996. *The Criminalization of Domestic Violence: Promises and Limits*. Washington, DC: National Institute of Justice.

Fang, Songying, Timothy R. Johnson, Jason M. Roberts. 2007. "Will of the Minority: Rule of Four on the United States Supreme Court." (July 5, 2007). Available at SSRN: http://papers.ssrn.com/sol3/papers.cfm?abstract_id=998492.

Farole, Donald and Lynn Langton. 2010. *County-based and Local Public Defender Offices, 2007*. Washington, DC: Department of Justice, Bureau of Justice Statistics.

Farrington, David P. 2006. "Family Background and Psychopathy." In C.J. Patrick (Ed.). *Handbook of Psychopathy* (pp. 229–250). New York: Guilford.

Fearn, Noelle. 2005. "A Multilevel Analysis of Community Effects on Criminal Sentencing." *Justice Quarterly* 22: 452–486.

Federal Bureau of Investigation. 2011. *Crime in the United States: 2010*. Washington, D.C.: Author. Available online at http://www.fbi.gov/about-us/cjis/ucr/crime-in-the-u.s/2010/crime-in-the-u.s.-2010.

Federal Bureau of Investigation. 2008. *Integrated Automated Fingerprint Identification System*. Available online at http://www.fbi.gov/hq/cjisd/iafis.htm.

Federal Judicial Center. 2012a. *Caseload Statistics 2011*. Washington, DC: Administrative Office of the U.S. Courts.

Federal Judicial Center. 2012b. *Judges of the United States*. Available online at http://www.fjc.gov/public/home.nsf/hisj.

Feeley, Malcolm. 1979. *The Process Is the Punishment: Handling Cases in a Lower Criminal Court*. New York: Russell Sage Foundation.

Feeley, Malcolm, and Sam Kamin. 1996. "The Effect of 'Three Strikes and You're Out' on the Courts: Looking Back to See the Future." In: David Shichor and Dale Sechrest (Eds.). *Three Strikes and You're Out: Vengeance as Public Policy*. Thousand Oaks, CA: Sage.

Feeley, Malcolm, and Edward Rubin. 1998. *Judicial Policy Making and the Modern State: How the Courts Reformed America's Prisons*. New York: Cambridge University Press.

Feeney, Floyd, Forrest Dill, and Adrianne Weir. 1983. *Arrests without Conviction: How Often They Occur and Why*. Washington, DC: Department of Justice, National Institute of Justice.

Feige, David. 2006. *Indefensible: One Lawyer's Journey into the Inferno of American Justice*. New York: Little, Brown.

Fein, Bruce. 1994. "Don't Play Criminals' Game." *USA Today*, April 15, p. 11.

Feld, Barry, and Shelly Schaefer. 2010. "The Right to Counsel in Juvenile Court: The Conundrum of Attorneys as an Aggravating Factor at Disposition." *Justice Quarterly* 27: 713–740.

Ferdico, John, Henry F. Fradella, and Christopher Totten. 2013. *Criminal Procedure for the Criminal Justice Professional*. 11th ed. Belmont, CA: Wadsworth.

Ferguson, Russ. 2011. "Cameras in the Courtroom." The American Spectator. July 19. *Available at* http://spectator.org/archives/2011/07/19/cameras-in-the-courtroom.

Fidell, Eugene R., Elizabeth Lutes Hillman, and Dwight Hall Sullivan. 2012. *Military Justice: Cases and Materials* (2d ed.). Cincinnati: Lexis-Nexis.

Financial Express. 2010. "Rape Remains Underprosecuted in U.S. Agencies." September 15.

Findley, Keith & Michael Scott. 2006. "The Multiple Dimensions of Tunnel Vision in Criminal Cases." *Wisconsin Law Review* 2006: 291–397.

Finn, Peter, and Beverley Lee. 1988. *Establishing and Expanding Victim–Witness Assistance Programs*. Washington, DC: National Institute of Justice.

Fino, Susan. 1987. *The Role of State Supreme Courts in the New Judicial Federalism*. Westport, CT: Greenwood.

Fisher, George. 2003. *Plea Bargaining's Triumph: A History of Plea Bargaining in America*. Stanford, CA: Stanford University Press.

Fisher, Jim. 2008. *Forensics under Fire: Are Bad Science and Dueling Experts Corrupting Criminal Justice?* New Brunswick, NJ: Rutgers University Press.

Flanders, Steven. 1991. "Court Administration and Diverse Judiciaries: Complementarities and Conflicts." *Justice System Journal* 15: 640–651.

Flango, Victor. 1994. "Court Unification and Quality of State Courts." *Justice System Journal* 16: 33–56.

Flango, Victor Eugene, and Craig Ducat. 1979. "What Differences Does Method of Judicial Selection Make? Selection Procedures in State Courts of Last Resort." *Justice System Journal* 5: 25–44.

Flanzer, Jerry. 2005. "The Status of Health Services Research on Adjudicated Drug-Abusing Juveniles: Selected Findings and Remaining Questions." *Substance Use and Misuse* 40: 887–911.

Flemming, Roy. 1986a. "Client Games: Defense Attorney Perspectives on Their Relations with Criminal Clients." *American Bar Foundation Research Journal* 253–277.

Flemming, Roy. 1986b. "Elements of the Defense Attorney's Craft: An Adaptive Expectations Model of the Preliminary Hearing Decision." *Law and Policy* 8: 33–57.

Flemming, Roy. 1989. "If You Pay the Piper, Do You Call the Tune? Public Defenders in America's Criminal Courts." *Law and Social Inquiry* 14: 393–405.

Flemming, Roy. 1990. "The Political Styles and Organizational Strategies of American Prosecutors: Examples from Nine Courthouse Communities." *Law and Policy* 12: 25.

Flemming, Roy, Peter Nardulli, and James Eisenstein. 1992. *The Craft of Justice: Politics and Work in Criminal Court Communities*. Philadelphia: University of Pennsylvania Press.

Flowe, Heather D., Amrita Mehta, and Ebbe B. Ebbesen. 2011. "The Role of Eyewitness Identification Evidence in Felony Case Dispositions." *Psychology, Public Policy, and Law* 17: 140–159.

Ford, Marilyn. 1986. "The Role of Extralegal Factors in Jury Verdicts." *Justice System Journal* 11: 16–39.

Forst, Brian, J. Lucianovic, and S. Cox. 1977. *What Happens after Arrest? A Court Perspective of Police Operations in the District of Columbia*. Washington, DC: Law Enforcement Assistance Administration.

Fortune, William, and Penny White. 2008. "Judicial Campaign Oversight Committees' Complaint Handling in the 2006 Elections: Survey and Recommendations." *Judicature* 91: 232–237.

Fox, James Alan, and Marianne W. Zawitz. 2007. *Homicide Trends in the United States*. Washington, DC: Bureau of Justice Statistics.

Fradella, Henry F. 1999. "In Search of Meritorious Claims: A Study of the Processing of Prisoner Civil Rights Cases in a Federal District Court." *Justice Systems Journal* 21: 23–55.

Fradella, Henry F. 2000. "Minimum Mandatory Sentences: Arizona's Ineffective Tool for the Social Control of DUI." *Criminal Justice Policy Review* 11: 113–135.

Fradella, Henry F. 2003. *Lawrence v. Texas*: Genuine or illusory progress for gay rights in America? *Criminal Law Bulletin*, 39: 597–607.

Fradella, Henry F. 2004. "A Content Analysis of Federal Judicial Views of the Social Science 'Researcher's Black Arts.'" *Rutgers Law Journal* 35: 103–170.

Fradella, Henry F. 2007. *Mental Illness and Criminal Defenses of Excuse in Contemporary American Law*. Bethesda, MD: Academica Press.

Fradella, Henry F. 2007. "Why Judges Should Admit Expert Testimony on the Unreliability of Eyewitness Identifications." *Federal Courts Law Review* 2(1), 2–25.

Fradella, Henry F., Ryan G. Fischer, Christine Kleinpeter, and Jeffrey Koob. 2009. "Latino Youth in the Juvenile Drug Court of Orange County, CA." *Journal of Ethnicity in Criminal Justice* 7: 271–292.

Fradella, Henry F., Weston Morrow, Ryan G. Fischer, and Connie Ireland. 2011. "Quantifying *Katz*: Empirically Measuring Reasonable Expectations of Privacy in the Fourth Amendment Context." *American Journal of Criminal Law* 38(3): 289–373.

Frank, Mitchell J., and Dawn Broschard. 2006. "The Silent Criminal Defendant and the Presumption of Innocence: In The Hands of Real Jurors, Is Either of Them Safe?" *Lewis and Clark Law Review* 10: 237–285.

Frankel, Marvin E. 1972. *Criminal Sentences: Law without Order*. New York: Hill and Wang.

Franklin, Cortney A., and Noelle E. Fearn. 2008. "Gender, Race, and Formal Court Decision-Making Outcomes: Chivalry/Paternalism, Conflict Theory or Gender Conflict?" *Journal of Criminal Justice* 36: 279–290.

Franklin, Travis W. 2010. "The Intersection of Defendants' Race, Gender, and Age in Prosecutorial Decision Making." *Journal of Criminal Justice* 38(2): 185–192.

Frase, Richard S. 2005. "Punishment Purposes." *Stanford Law Review* 58: 67–83.

Freeman, Donald. 2007. "Drunk Driving Legislation and Traffic Fatalities: New Evidence on BAC 08 Laws." *Contemporary Economic Policy* 25: 293–310.

Friedenthal, Jack H., Mary Kay Kane, and Arthur R. Miller. 2005. *Civil Procedure, Hornbook Series*. 4th ed. Eagan, MN: West.

Friedman, Barry. 1998. "Attacks on Judges: Why They Fail." *Judicature* 81: 150–156.

Friedman, Lawrence. 1979. "Plea Bargaining in Historical Perspective." *Law and Society Review* 13: 247–259.

Friedman, Lawrence. 1984. *American Law: An Introduction*. New York: Norton.

Friedman, Lawrence. 2000. "The Constitutional Value of Dialogue and the New Judicial Federalism." *Hastings Constitutional Law Quarterly* 28: 93–144.

Friedman, Lawrence, and Robert Percival. 1976. "A Tale of Two Courts: Litigation in Alameda and San Benito Counties." *Law and Society Review* 10: 267–302.

Friedrichs, David. 2006. *Law in our Lives: An Introduction*. 2nd ed. Los Angeles, CA: Roxbury.

Friedrichs, David. 2009. *Trusted Criminals: White Collar Crime in Contemporary Society*. Belmont, CA: Wadsworth.

Frohmann, Lisa. 1997. "Convictability and Discordant Locales: Reproducing Race, Class, and Gender Ideologies in Prosecutorial Decision-Making." *Law and Society Review* 31: 531–556.

Fukurai, Hiroshi, Edgar Butler, and Richard Krooth. 1991. "Cross-Sectional Jury Representation or Systematic Jury Representation? Simple Random and Cluster Sampling Strategies in Jury Selection." *Journal of Criminal Justice* 19: 31–48.

Fulkerson, Andrew, and Michael Suttmoeller. 2008. "Current Issues Involving Lethal Injection." *Criminal Justice Studies* 21: 271–282.

Fyfe, James. 1982. "In Search of the 'Bad Faith' Search." *Criminal Law Bulletin* 18: 260–265.

Gabel, Jessica D., and Margaret D. Wilkinson. 2008. "'Good' Science Gone Bad: How the Criminal Justice System Can Redress the Impact of Flawed Forensics." *Hastings Law Journal* 59: 1001–1030.

Gable, Ralph Kirkland, and Robert S. Gable. 2005. "Electronic Monitoring: Positive Intervention Strategies." *Federal Probation* 69(1): 21–25.

Gainey, Randy R., and Payne, Brian K. 2000. "Understanding the Experience of House Arrest with Electronic Monitoring: An Analysis of Quantitative and Qualitative Data." *International Journal of Offender Therapy and Comparative Criminology* 44(1): 84–96.

Galanter, Marc. 1988. "The Life and Times of the Big Six: or, The Federal Courts since the Good Old Days." Working Paper 9:2. Madison: University of Wisconsin, Institute for Legal Studies.

Galaway, Burt. 1988. "Restitution as Innovation or Unfilled Promise?" *Federal Probation* 52: 3–14.

Galaway, Burt, and Joe Hudson (Eds.). 1996. *Restorative Justice: International Perspectives*. Monsey, NY: Criminal Justice Press.

Galiber, Joseph, Barry Latzer, Mark Dwyer, Jack Litman, H. Richard Uviller, and G. Roger McDonald. 1993. "Law, Justice, and Jury Nullification: A Debate." *Criminal Law Bulletin* 29: 40–69.

Galie, Peter. 1987. "State Supreme Courts, Judicial Federalism and the Other Constitutions." *Judicature* 71: 100–110.

Gallas, Geoff. 1976. "The Conventional Wisdom of State Court Administration: A Critical Assessment and an Alternative Approach." *Justice System Journal* 2: 35.

Gallas, Geoff. 2005. "Local Legal Culture: More than Court Culture." *Court Manager* 20: 23–28.

Gardiner, John. 1986. "Preventing Judicial Misconduct: Defining the Role of Conduct Organizations." *Judicature* 70: 113–121.

Gardner, Amy, and Matt DeLong. 2011. "Newt Gingrich's Assault on 'Activist Judges' Draws Criticism, Even from the Right." *Washington Post*, December 18.

Garner, Joel. 1987. "Delay Reduction in the Federal Courts: Rule 50(b) and the Federal Speedy Trial Act of 1974." *Journal of Quantitative Criminology* 3: 229–250.

Garrett, Brandon L. 2008. "Judging Innocence." *Columbia Law Review* 108: 55–142.

Garrett, Brandon L., and Peter J. Neufeld. 2009. "Invalid Forensic Science Testimony and Wrongful Convictions." *Virginia Law Review* 95: 1–97.

Garrow, David J. 2008. Bad Behavior Makes Big Law: Southern Malfeasance and the Expansion of Federal Judicial Power, 1954-1968. *Saint John's Law Review* 82: 1–38.

Garvey, Stephen P., Paula Hannaford-Agor, Valerie P. Hans, Nicole L. Mott, G. Thomas Munsterman, and Martin T. Wells. 2004. "Juror First Votes in Criminal Trials in Four Major Metropolitan Jurisdictions." *Journal of Empirical Legal Studies* 1: 371–398.

Garvin, Glenn. 2011. "Casey Anthony's Acquittal Prompts Critics to Blame the Media." *Miami Herald*, July 7.

Gastil, John, Laura W. Black, E. Pierre Deess, and Jay Leighter. 2008. "From Group Member to Democratic Citizen: How Deliberating with Fellow Jurors Reshapes Civic Attitudes." *Human Communication Research* 34: 137–169.

Georgetown Law Journal. 2007. "The Judicial Nomination Process Over Time: Some Historic Background." *Georgetown Law Journal* 95: 1028–1039.

Gershman, Bennett L. 2011. "Prosecutorial Decisionmaking and Discretion in the Charging Decision." *Hastings Law Journal* 62: 1259–1283.

Gest, Ted. 1996. "The Law That Grief Built." *U.S. News & World Report*, April 29, p. 58.

Giannelli, Paul C. 2007. "Wrongful Convictions and Forensic Science: The Need to Regulate Crime Labs." *North Carolina Law Review* 86: 163–235.

Giannelli, Paul C. 2011. "Daubert and Forensic Science: The Pitfalls of Law Enforcement Control of Scientific Research." *University of Illinois Law Review* 2011: 53–90.

Gilboy, Janet. 1984. "Prosecutors' Discretionary Use of the Grand Jury to Initiate or to Reinitiate Prosecution." *American Bar Foundation Research Journal* 1–81.

Gillespie, Robert. 1988–1989. "Criminal Fines: Do They Pay?" *Justice System Journal* 13: 365–378.

Gilmore, Amna Saddick, Nancy Rodriguez, and Vincent J. Webb. 2005. "Substance Abuse and Drug Courts: The Role of Social Bonds in Juvenile Drug Courts." *Youth Violence and Juvenile Justice* 3: 287–315.

Givelber, Daniel, and Amy Farrell. 2008. "Judges and Juries: The Defense Case and Differences in Acquittal Rates." *Law and Social Inquiry* 33: 31–52.

Glaberson, William. 2006. "In Tiny Courts of N.Y., Abuses of Law and Power." *New York Times*, September 25.

Glater, Jonathan, and Ken Belson. 2005. "In White-Collar Crimes, Few Smoking Guns." *New York Times*, March 12.

Glaze, Lauren E. 2011. *Correctional Population of the United States, 2010.* Washington, DC: Department of Justice, Bureau of Justice Statistics.

Glick, Henry, and Kenneth Vines. 1973. *State Court Systems.* Englewood Cliffs, NJ: Prentice Hall.

Global Courts. 2012. "Electronic Courtrooms." Available online at http://www.globalcourts.com/text/e_courtrooms.html.

"Go Directly to Jail: White Collar Sentencing after the Sarbanes–Oxley Act. 2009. *Harvard Law Review* 122: 1728.

Gobert, James J. 1988. "In Search of the Impartial Jury." *Journal of Criminal Law and Criminology* 79: 269–327.

Goehner, Amy, Lina Lofaro, and Kate Novack. 2004. "Where *CSI* Meets Real Law and Order." *Time*, November 8, p. 69.

Goffman, Ervin. 1961. *Asylums: Essays on the Social Situation of Mental Patients and Other Inmates.* Garden City, NY: Anchor.

Goldberg, Deborah, Craig Holman, and Samantha Sanchez. 2002. "The New Politics of Judicial Elections." Available online at http://www.justiceatstake.org/files/JASMoneyReport.pdf.

Goldberg, Stephen, Frank Sander, Nancy Rogers, and Sarah Cole. 2007. *Dispute Resolution: Negotiation, Mediation, and other Processes.* 5th ed. New York: Aspen.

Goldfarb, Ronald. 1965. *Ransom: A Critique of the American Bail System.* New York: Harper & Row.

Goldfarb, Sally F. 2008. "Reconceiving Civil Protection Orders for Domestic Violence: Can Law Help End the Abuse Without Ending the Relationship?" *Cardozo Law Review*, 29, 1487–1551.

Goldkamp, John. 1980. "The Effects of Detention on Judicial Decisions: A Closer Look." *Justice System Journal* 5: 234–257.

Goldkamp, John. 2002. "The Importance of Drug Courts: Lessons from Measuring Impact." Paper presented at the American Society of Criminology, Chicago.

Goldkamp, John, Cheryl Irons-Guynn, and Doris Weiland. 2002. *Community Prosecution Strategies: Measuring Impact.* Washington, DC: Bureau of Justice Assistance.

Goldkamp, John, and Doris Weiland. 1993. "Assessing the Impact of Dade County's Felony Drug Court." *National Institute of Justice Research in Brief.* Washington, DC: Department of Justice.

Goldkamp, J.S., M.D. White, & J.B. Robinson, (2001). "Do Drug Courts Work? Getting Inside the Drug Court Black Box." *Journal of Drug Issues, 31(1).*

Goldman, Sheldon. 1997. *Picking Federal Judges: Lower Court Selection from Roosevelt through Reagan.* New Haven, CT: Yale University Press.

Goldman, Sheldon, and Matthew Saronson. 1994. "Clinton's Nontraditional Judges: Creating a More Representative Bench." *Judicature* 78: 68–73.

Goldman, Sheldon, and Elliot Slotnick. 1999. "Clinton's Second Term Judiciary: Picking Judges under Fire." *Judicature* 82: 264–285.

Goldman, Sheldon, Elliot Slotnick, Gerard Gryski, and Sara Schiavoni. 2007. "Picking Judges in a Time of Turmoil: W. Bush's Judiciary during the 109th Congress. *Judicature* 90: 252.

Goldman, Sheldon, Elliot Slotnick, and Sara Schiovania. 2011. "The Confirmation Drama Continues." *Judicature* 94: 262–303.

Goldschmidt, Jona, David Olson, and Margaret Ekman. 2009. "The Relationship between Method of Judicial Selection and Judicial Misconduct." *Widener Law Journal* 18: 455–481.

Gondolf, Edward. 2012. *The Future of Batterer Programs: Reassessing Evidence-Based Practice.* Boston: Northeastern University Press.

Goodman-Delahunty, Jane, Lynee ForsterLee, and Robert ForsterLee. 2007."Dealing with Guilty Offenders."In: Neil Brewer and Kipling Williams (Eds.). *Psychology and the Law: An Empirical Perspective*. New York: Guilford Press.

Gordon, Corey, and William Brill. 1996. *The Expanding Role of Crime Prevention through Environmental Design in Premises Liability*. Washington, DC: National Institute of Justice.

Gorman, Sean. 2009."Bedford Judge Admonished for Doling Out Excessive Traffic Fines."*LoHud.com* (New York's Lower Hudson Valley), July 30.

Gottfredson, Denise, Stacy Najaka, and Brook Kearley. 2003. "Effectiveness of Drug Treatment Courts: Evidence from a Randomized Trial."*Criminology and Public Policy* 2: 171–196.

Gottschalk, Marie. 2009. "The Long Reach of the Carceral State: The Politics of Crime, Mass Imprisonment, and Penal Reform in the United States and Abroad." *Law and Social Inquiry* 34: 439–472.

Gottsfield, Robert L., and Marianne Alcorn. 2009."The Capital Case Crisis in Maricopa County: What (Little) We Can Do About It."*Arizona Attorney* 45: 22–30.

Gould, Jon. 2008. "Justice Delayed or Justice Denied? A Contemporary Review of Capital Habeas Corpus." *Justice System Journal* 29: 273–287.

Gould, Jon, and Stephen Mastrofski. 2004."Suspect Searches: Assessing Police Behavior under the U.S. Constitution."*Criminology and Public Policy* 3: 315–362.

Gould, Jon B., & Richard A. Leo. 2010."One Hundred Years Later: Wrongful Convictions After a Century of Research." *Journal of Criminal Law and Criminology* 100: 825–868.

Gourevitch, Philip. 2001."The Crime Lover."*The New Yorker*, February 19, pp. 160–173.

Gover, Angela, John MacDonald, and Geoffrey Alpert. 2003. "Combating Domestic Violence: Findings from an Evaluation of a Local Domestic Violence Court." *Criminology and Public Policy* 3: 109–132.

Grace, Nancy. 2005. *Objection!: How High-Priced Defense Attorney's Celebrity Defendants, and a 24/7 Media Have Hijacked Our Criminal Justice System*. New York: Hyperion.

Graham, Barbara Luck. 1990. "Do Judicial Selection Systems Matter? A Study of Black Representation on State Courts."*American Politics Quarterly* 18: 316–336.

Gray, Cynthia. 2003."State Supreme Courts Play Key Role in Judicial Discipline."*Judicature* 86: 267–268.

Gray, Cynthia. 2007. "How Judicial Conduct Commissions Work."*The Justice System Journal* 28: 405–418.

Greenhouse, Linda. 2004."Death Sentence Overturned in Texas."*New York Times*, February 25.

Greenwood, Peter, C. Peter Rydell, Allan Abrahamse, Jonathan Caulkins, James Chiesa, Karyn Model, and Stephen Klein. 1996."Estimated Benefits and Costs of California's New Mandatory Sentencing Law."In: David Shichor and Dale Sechrest (Eds.). *Three Strikes and You're Out: Vengeance as Public Policy*. Thousand Oaks, CA: Sage.

Gresko, Jennifer. 2011. "New Crack Cocaine Sentencing Guidelines May Apply to Old Cases." Huffington Post, May 31. Available online at http://www.huffingtonpost.com/2011/05/31/crack-cocaine-sentencing-guidelines_n_869450.html.

Griffin, Patrick, Sean Addie, Benjamin Adams, and Kathy Firestine. 2011."Trying Juveniles as Adults: An Analysis of State Transfer Laws and Reporting."Washington, DC: Department of Justice, Office of Juvenile Justice and Delinquency Prevention.

Griffin, Timothy, and John Wooldredge. 2006. "Sex-Based Disparities in Felony Dispositions before versus after Sentencing Reform in Ohio."*Criminology* 44: 893–923.

Griset, Pamala. 1995."Determinate Sentencing and Agenda Building: A Case Study of the Failure of a Reform."*Journal of Criminal Justice* 23: 349–362.

Grisham, John. 2008. *The Appeal*. New York: Doubleday.

Grisso, Thomas. 1981. *Juveniles' Waiver of Rights*. New York: Plenum.

Gross, Samuel R., Kristen Jacoby, Daniel J. Matheson, Nicholas Montgomery, and Sujata Patil. 2005. Exonerations in the United States 1989 through 2003."*Journal of Criminal Law and Criminology* 95: 523–560.

Gross, Samuel R., and Barbara O'Brien. 2008. "Frequency and Predictors of False Conviction: Why We Know So Little, and New Data on Capital Cases." *Journal of Empirical Legal Studies*, 5(4), 927–962.

Grubb, Amy Rose, and Julie Harrower. 2009."Understanding Attribution of Blame in Cases of Rape: An Analysis of Participant Gender, Type of Rape and Perceived Similarity to the Victim."*Journal of Sexual Aggression* 15(1): 63–81.

Gruhl, John. 1981."State Supreme Courts and the U.S. Supreme Court's Post-*Miranda* Rulings."*Journal of Criminal Law and Criminology* 72: 886–913.

Gryski, Gerard S., Eleanor C. Main, and William J. Dixon. 1986 "Models of State High Court Decision Making in Sex Discrimination Cases."*Journal of Politics* 48: 143–155.

Guerino, Paul, Paife M. Harrison, and William J. Sabol. 2011. *Prisoners in 2010*. Washington, DC: Department of Justice, Bureau of Justice Statistics.

Guevara, Lori, Denis Herz, and Cassia Spohn. 2008. "Race, Gender, and Legal Counsel: Differential Outcomes in Two Juvenile Courts."*Youth Violence and Juvenile Justice* 6: 83–104.

Gupta, Sanjay. 2011."Rx Drug Deaths Triple in Decade."*The Chart*, November 1. Available online at http://thechart.blogs.cnn.com/2011/11/01/40-die-daily-in-rx-drug-epidemic-cdc-says/?iref=allsearch.

Gusfield, Joseph. 1981. *The Culture of Public Problems: Drinking-Driving and the Symbolic Order*. Chicago: University of Chicago Press.

Guthrie, C., J.J. Rachlinski, and A.J. Wistrich. 2007."Blinking on the Bench: How Judges Decide Cases."*Cornell Law Review* 93: 1–43.

Guzik, Keith. 2007. "The Forces of Conviction: The Power and Practice of Mandatory Prosecution upon

Misdemeanor Domestic Battery Suspects." *Law and Social Inquiry* 32: 41–74.

Haapanen, Rudy. 1989. *Selective Incapacitation and the Serious Offender: A Longitudinal Study of Criminal Career Patterns.* New York: Springer.

Haber, Lyn, and Ralph Normal Haber. 2008. "Scientific Validation of Fingerprint Evidence Under *Daubert.*" *Law, Probability & Risk* 7: 87–109.

Hagan, John. 1974. "Extra-Legal Attributes and Criminal Sentencing: An Assessment of a Sociological Viewpoint." *Law and Society Review* 8: 357–381.

Hagan, John. 1977. "Criminal Justice in Rural and Urban Communities: A Study of the Bureaucratization of Justice." *Social Forces* 55: 597–612.

Hagan, John. 1983. *Victims before the Law: The Organizational Domination of Criminal Law.* Toronto: Butterworth's.

Hagan, John, John Hewitt, and Duane Alwin. 1979. "Ceremonial Justice: Crime and Punishment in a Loosely Coupled System." *Social Forces* 58: 506–527.

Hagstrom, Anna M. 2009. "*Atkins v. Virginia*: An Empty Holding Devoid of Justice for the Mentally Retarded." *Law and Inequality: A Journal of Theory and Practice* 27: 241–276.

Hakim, Simon, George Rengert, and Yochanan Shachmurove. 1996. "Estimation of Net Social Benefits of Electronic Security." *Justice Quarterly* 13: 153–170.

Halbringer, David, and Beth Kormanik. 2012. "In Digital Record, Jurors Say, They Found Reasons to Convict." *New York Times*, March 17.

Hall, Jerome. 1952. *Theft, Law and Society.* Indianapolis: Bobbs-Merrill.

Haller, Mark. 1979. "Plea Bargaining: The Nineteenth-Century Context." *Law and Society Review* 13: 273–280.

Hallinan, Joe. 1993. "Violent Children Straining Limit of Justice System." *Times-Picayune*, October 31, p. A24.

Hamblett, Mark. 2012. "Summit Participants Discuss Efforts to Find Competent Lawyers for Poor N.Y. Immigrants." *New York Law Journal*, January 30.

Haney, Craig. 1984. "On the Selection of Capital Juries: The Biasing Effects of the Death-Qualification Process." *Law and Human Behavior* 8: 121–132.

Haney, Craig. 2005. Death by Design: *Capital Punishment as a Social Psychological System.* New York: Oxford University Press.

Hannaford, Paula L. 2001. "Safeguarding Juror Privacy: A New Framework for Court Policies and Procedures." *Judicature* 85: 18–25.

Hannaford, Paula, Valerie Hans, and G. Thomas Munsterman. 1999. "How Much Justice Hangs in the Balance? A New Look at Hung Jury Rates." *Judicature* 83: 59–67.

Hannaford-Agor, Paula L., Valerie P. Hans, Nicole L. Mott, and G. Thomas Munsterman. 2002. *Are Hung Juries a Problem?* Washington, DC: The National Center for State Courts.

Hanson, Roger, and Henry Daley. 1995. *Challenging the Conditions of Prisons and Jails.* Washington, DC: Department of Justice, Bureau of Justice Statistics.

Hanson, Roger, William Hewitt, and Brian Ostrom. 1992. "Are the Critics of Indigent Defense Counsel Correct?" *State Court Journal* (Summer): 20–29.

Harlow, Caroline. 1999. *Prior Abuse Reported by Inmates and Probationers.* NCJ 172879. Washington, DC: Department of Justice, Office of Justice Programs.

Harrell, Adele, Shannon Cavanagh, and John Roman. 2000. "Evaluation of the D.C. Superior Court Drug Intervention Programs." Washington, DC: National Institute of Justice.

Harris, David. 2011. "The Interaction and Relationship between Prosecutors and Police Officers in the U.S., and How this Affects Police Reform Efforts." In: Erik Luna and Marianne Wad (Eds.). *The Prosecutor in Transnational Perspective.* New York: Oxford University Press.

Harris, John, and Paul Jesilow. 2000. "It's Not the Old Ball Game: Three Strikes and the Courtroom Workgroup." *Justice Quarterly* 17: 185–204.

Hashimoto, Erica. 2007. "Defending the Right to Self-Representation: An Empirical Look at the Pro Se Felony Defendant." *North Carolina Law Review* 85: 423–487.

Hashimoto, Erica. 2008. "Toward Ethical Plea Bargaining." *Cardozo Law Review* 30: 949–963.

Hastie, Reid, Steven Penrod, and Nancy Pennington. 1984. *Inside the Jury.* Cambridge, MA: Harvard University Press.

Hastings, Deborah. 2009. "Money May Decide Execution Debate." Associated Press, March 8.

Hartley, Richard, Holly Miller, and Cassia Spohn. 2010. "Do You Get What You Pay for? Type of Counsel and Its Effect on Criminal Court Outcomes." *Journal of Criminal Justice* 38: 1063–1070.

Hashimoto, Erica J. 2010. *Assessing the Indigent Defense System.* Washington, DC: The American Constitution Society for Law and Policy.

Hawkins, Nikki. 2010. "Perspectives on Civil Protective Orders in a Domestic Violence Cases: The Rural and Urban Divide." *NIJ Journal* 266: 4–8.

Haynes, Stacy Hoskins, Barry Ruback, and Gretchen Ruth Cusick. 2010. "Courtroom Workgroups and Sentencing: The Effects of Similarity, Proximity, and Stabilty." *Crime & Delinquency*, 56(1), 126–161.

Haynie, Dana, Harald Weiss, and Alex Piquero. 2008. "Race, the Economic Maturity Gap, and Criminal Offending in Young Childhood." *Justice Quarterly* 25: 595–622.

Healey, Kerry. 1995. *Victim and Witness Intimidation: New Developments and Emerging Responses.* Washington, DC: National Institute of Justice.

Heflin, Howell. 1987. "The Impeachment Process: Modernizing an Archaic System." *Judicature* 71: 123–125.

Heinz, John, and Edward Laumann. 1982. *Chicago Lawyers: The Social Structure of the Bar.* New York: Russell Sage Foundation.

Heinz, John, Robert Nelson, Rebecca Sandefur, and Edward Laumann. 2005. *Urban Lawyers: The New Social Structure of the Bar.* Chicago: University of Chicago Press.

Helland, Eric, and Alexander Tabarrok. 2002. "The Effect of Electoral Institutions on Tort Awards." *American Law and Economics Review* 4: 341–370.

Helland, Eric, and Alexander Tabarrok. 2004. "The Fugitive: Evidence on Public Versus Private Law Enforcement from Bail Jumping." *Journal of Law and Economics* 47: 93–122.

Heller, Kevin Jon. 2006. "The Cognitive Psychology of Circumstantial Evidence." *Michigan Law Review* 105: 241–305.

Hellman, Arthur D. 2006. "The View from the Trenches: A Report on the Breakout Sessions at the 2005 National Conference on Appellate Justice." *Journal of Appellate Practice and Process* 8(1): 141–205.

Hemmens, Craig, Kristin Strom, and Elicia Schlegel. 1997. "Gender Bias in the Courts: A Review of the Literature." Paper presented at the Academy of Criminal Justice Sciences, Louisville, KY.

Herinckx Heidi A., Sandra C. Swart, Shane M. Ama, Cheri D. Dolezal, and Steve King. 2005. "Rearrest and Linkage to Mental Health Services among Defendants of the Clark County Mental Health Court Program." *Psychiatric Services* 56(7): 853–857.

Herman, Susan N., and Erwin Chemerinsky. 2006. The *Right to a Speedy and Public Trial: A Reference Guide to the United States Constitution*. Westport, CT: Greenwood.

Heumann, Milton. 1975. "A Note on Plea Bargaining and Case Pressure." *Law and Society Review* 9: 515–528.

Heumann, Milton. 1978. *Plea Bargaining: The Experience of Prosecutors, Judges, and Defense Attorneys*. Chicago: University of Chicago Press.

Heumann, Milton, and Colin Loftin. 1979. "Mandatory Sentencing and the Abolition of Plea Bargaining: The Michigan Felony Firearm Statute." *Law and Society Review* 13: 393–430.

Hillsman, Sally, and Barry Mahoney. 1988. "Collecting and Enforcing Criminal Fines: A Review of Court Processes, Practices, and Problems." *Justice System Journal* 13: 17–36.

Hindelang, Michael. 1972. "Equality under the Law." In: Charles Reasons and Jack Kuykendall (Eds.). *Race, Crime and Justice* (pp. 312–323). Pacific Palisades, CA: Goodyear.

Hindson, Stephanie, Hillary Potter, and Michael Radelet. 2006. "Race, Gender, Region, and Death Sentencing in Colorado, 1980-1999." *Colorado Law Review* 77: 549–574.

Hingson, Ralph, Timothy Heeren, and Erika Edwards. 2008. "Age at Drinking Onset, Alcohol Dependence, and Their Relation to Drug Use and Dependence, Driving under the Influence of Drugs, and Motor-Vehicle Crash Involvement Because of Drugs." *Journal of Studies on Alcohol and Drugs* 69: 192–201.

Hipp, John, and Daniel K. Yates. 2011. "Ghettos, Thresholds, and Crime: Does Concentrated Poverty Really Have an Accelerating Increase Effect on Crime?" *Criminology* 49: 955–990.

Hirschel, David, Eve Buzawa, April Pattavina, and Don Faggiani. 2007. "Domestic Violence and Mandatory Arrest Laws: To What Extent Do They Influence Police Arrest Decisions?" *Journal of Criminal Law and Criminology* 98: 255.

Hirschel, J. David, Ira Hutchison, Charles Dean, and Anne-Marie Mills. 1992. "Review Essay on the Law Enforcement Response to Spouse Abuse: Past, Present and Future." *Justice Quarterly* 9: 247–284.

HLN. 2012. http://nancygrace.blogs.cnn.com.

Hockenberry, Sarah, Melissa Sickmund, & Anthony Sladky. 2011. "Juvenile Residential Facility Census, 2008: Selected Findings." Washington, DC: Department of Justice, Office of Juvenile Justice and Delinquency Prevention.

Hofer, Paul. 2007. "*United States v. Booker* as a Natural Experiment: Using Empirical Research to Inform the Federal Sentencing Debate." *Criminology and Public Policy* 6: 433–460.

Hoffman, Richard. 1991. "Beyond the Team: Renegotiating the Judge–Administrator Partnership." *Justice System Journal* 15: 652–666.

Hogarth, John. 1971. *Sentencing as a Human Process*. Toronto: University of Toronto Press.

Holbrook, R. Andrew, and Timothy Hill. 2005. "Agenda-Setting and Priming in Prime Time Television: Crime Dramas as Political Cues." *Political Communication* 22: 277–295.

Holleran, David, Dawn Beichner, and Cassia Spohn. 2009. "Examining Charging Agreement between Police and Prosecutors in Rape Cases." *Crime and Delinquency* 56: 385–413.

Holmes, Lisa M., and Jolly A. Emrey. 2006. "Court Diversification: Staffing the State Courts of Last Resort through Interim Appointments." *Justice Systems Journal* 27: 1–12.

Holmes, Lisa, and Elisha Savchak. 2003. "Judicial Appointment Politics in the 107th Congress." *Judicature* 86: 240–250.

Holmes, Malcolm, Howard Daudistel, and William Taggart. 1992. "Plea Bargaining and State District Court Caseloads: An Interrupted Time Series Analysis." *Law and Society Review* 26: 139–160.

Holmes, Oliver Wendell, Jr. 1881. *The Common Law*. Boston: Little, Brown.

Holmes, Oliver Wendell. 1920. *Collected Legal Papers*. Boston: Harcourt.

Holmstrom, Lynda, and Ana Burgess. 1983. *The Victim of Rape: Institutional Reactions*. New Brunswick, NJ: Transaction.

Hoover, Eric. 2008. "For MADD, the Legal Drinking Age Is Not for Debate." *The Chronicle of Higher Education* 55(11).

Horney, Julie, and Cassia Spohn. 1996. "The Influence of Blame and Believability Factors on the Processing of Simple versus Aggravated Rape Cases." *Criminology* 34: 135–162.

Horowitz, Irwin A., Norbert L. Kerr, Ernest S. Park, and Christine Gockel. 2006. "Chaos in the Courtroom

Reconsidered: Emotional Bias and Juror Nullification." *Law and Human Behavior* 30: 163–181.

Houck, Max M. 2006. "CSI: Reality." *Scientific American* 295: 84–89.

Houck, Max M., and Bruce Budowle. 2002. "Correlation of Microscopic and Mitochondrial DNA Hair Comparisons." *Journal of Forensic Science* 47(5): 964–967.

Hoyle, Carolyn. 2011. "Empowerment through Emotion: The Use and Abuse of Victim Impact Evidence." In Edna Erez, Michael Kilching, and Joanne Wemmers (eds.), *Therapeutic Jurisprudence and Victim Participation in Justice: International Perspectives*. Durham, NC: Carolina Academic Press.

Hsu, Spencer. 2009. "U.S. to Expand Immigration Checks to all Local Jails." *Washington Post*, May 19.

Hubler, Shawn. 2005. "Spectacle Supplants Law as Focus of Jackson Trial." *Los Angeles Times*, June 13.

Huddleston, West, and Douglas Marlowe. 2011. *Painting the Current Picture: A National Report on Drug Courts and other Problem-Solving Court Programs in the United States*. New York: National Drug Court Institute. Available online at http://www.ndci.org/sites/default/files/nadcp/PCP%20Report%20FINAL.PDF.

Huff, C. Ronald, Arye Rattner, and Edward Sagarin, 2003. *Convicted but Innocent: Wrongful Conviction and Public Policy*. Thousand Oaks, CA: Sage.

Hunter, Arthur. 2006. "Judges Are Like Referees, Guarding Citizen Rights." *Times-Picayune*, July 20.

Hurwitz, Mark. 2006. "Much Ado About Sentencing: The Influence of *Apprendi*, *Blakely*, and *Booker* in the U.S. Courts of Appeals." *Justice System Journal* 27: 81–94.

Hurwitz, Mark. 2008. "Give Him a Fair Trial, Then Hang Him: The Supreme Court's Modern Death Penalty Jurisprudence." *Justice System Journal* 29: 243–256.

Hurwitz, Mark S. and Dew Noble Lanier. 2003. "Explaining Judicial Diversity: The Differential Ability of Women and Minorities to Attain Seats on State Supreme and Appellate Courts." *State Politics and Policy Quarterly*, 3: 329–352.

Husak, Douglas N. 2008. *Overcriminalization: The Limits of the Criminal Law*. New York: Oxford University Press.

Iannacchione, Brian, and Jeremy D. Ball. 2008. "The Effect of *Blakely v. Washington* on Upward Departures in a Sentencing Guideline State." *Journal of Contemporary Criminal Justice* 24(4): 419–436.

"In '90s, Prison Building by States and U.S. Government Surged." 1997. *New York Times*, July 24, p. A14.

Ingram, David. 2012. "Twitter Coverage of US Court Gets Stuck Down." *Reuters Online: U.S. Edition*. March 27. Available online at: http://www.reuters.com/article/2012/03/27/usa-healthcare-twitter-idUSL2E8ERWED20120327.

Innocence Project. 2008. "Innocence Blog: The 'CSI Effect' on Both Sides of the Courtroom." June 20. Available online at http://www.innocenceproject.org/Content/The_CSI_effect_on_both_sides_of_the_courtroom.php.

Innocence Project, The. 2011. "Know the Cases: Search the Profiles." http://www.innocenceproject.org/know/Search-Profiles.php.

Innocence Project. 2012. Available online at http://www.innocenceproject.org.

"Issues in Judicial Independence and Accountability." 2004. *Judicature* 88: 114–121.

Iyengar, Radha. 2007. *An Analysis of the Performance of Federal Indigent Defense Counsel*. Cambridge, MA: National Bureau of Economic Research, Harvard University.

Jackson, Donald. 1974. *Judges*. New York: Atheneum.

Jackson, Robert H. 1940. "The Federal Prosecutor—His Temptations." *Journal of the American Judicature Society* 24:,18–25.

Jacob, Herbert. 1966. "Judicial Insulation: Elections, Direct Participation, and Public Attention to the Courts in Wisconsin." *Wisconsin Law Review* 812.

Jacob, Herbert. 1984. *Justice in America*. 4th ed. Boston: Little, Brown.

Jacob, Herbert. 1991. "Decision Making in Trial Courts." In: John Gates and Charles Johnson (Eds.). *The American Courts: A Critical Assessment* (pp. 211–233). Washington, DC: CQ Press.

Jacob, Herbert. 1997. "Governance by Trial Court Judges." *Law and Science Review* 31: 3–37.

Jacobs, Andrew. 2007. "Newark Battles Murder and its Accomplice, Silence." *New York Times*, May 29.

Jacobs, David, and Stephanie Kent. 2007. "The Determinants of Execution Since 1951: How Politics, Protests, Public Opinion and Social Divisions Shape Capital Punishment." *Social Problems* 54: 297–318.

Jacobs, David, Zhenchao Qian, Jason Carmichael, and Stephanie Kent. 2007. "Who Survives on Death Row? An Individual and Contextual Analysis." *American Sociological Review* 72: 610–362.

Jacobson, Michael. 2005. *Downsizing Prisons: How to Reduce Crime and End Mass Incarceration*. New York: NYU Press.

Jacoby, Joan. 1980. *The American Prosecutor: A Search for Identity*. Lexington, MA: Heath.

Jacoby, Joan. 1995. "Pushing the Envelope: Leadership in Prosecution." *Justice System Journal* 17: 291–308.

Jacoby, Joan, Leonard Mellon, Edward Ratledge, and Stanley Turner. 1982. *Prosecutorial Decisionmaking: A National Study*. Washington, DC: Department of Justice, National Institute of Justice.

Jefferson, David. 2005. "America's Most Dangerous Drug." *Newsweek*, August 8, pp. 40–48.

Jehle, Jörg-Martin, and Marianne Wade. 2006. *Coping with Overloaded Criminal Justice Systems*. New York: Springer.

Jekot, Wayne. 2007. "Computer Forensics, Search Strategies, and the Particularity Requirement." *University of Pittsburgh Journal of Technology Law and Policy* 12(2): 2–48.

Jencks, Christopher, and Paul Peterson, eds. 1991. *The Urban Underclass*. Washington, DC: Brookings Institution.

Jensen, Jennifer. 2011. "Career Satisfaction and State Trial Court Judges' Plans to Leave the Bench." *Judicature* 95:116–125.

Johnson, Brian D. 2006. "The Multilevel Context of Criminal Sentencing: Integrating Judge- and County-Level Influences." *Criminology* 44: 259–298.

Johnson, Brian, Jeffrey Ulmer, and John Kramer. 2008. "The Social Context of Guidelines Circumvention: The Case of Federal District Courts." *Criminology* 46: 737–783.

Johnson, James, and Philip Secret. 1995. "The Effects of Court Structure on Juvenile Court Decisonmaking." *Journal of Criminal Justice* 23: 63–82.

Johnson, Kevin. 2010. "Imposing Fees." *USA Today*, October 31.

Jonakait, Randolph N. 2006. *The American Jury System*. New Haven: Yale University Press.

Jones, David. 1994. "Prosecutorial Tenure in Wisconsin." Paper presented at the Midwest Criminal Justice Association Meeting, Chicago.

Jones, David. 2001. "Toward a Prosecutorial 'Civil Service': A Wisconsin Case Study." Paper presented at the annual meeting of the American Society of Criminology, Atlanta.

Judicial Council of California. 2011. *2011 Court Statistics Report: Statewide Case Trends through 2010*. San Francisco, CA: California Administrative Office of the Courts.

The Justice Project. 2007. *Jailhouse Snitch Testimony: A Policy Review*. Washington, DC: Author.

Justice at Stake. 2009a. "Bybee Invited to Testify by Leahy." April 30. Available online at http://www.gavelgrab.org/?cat=8.

Justice at Stake. 2009b. "*Caperton v. Massey* Resource Page." Available online at http://www.justiceatstake.org/resources/in_depth_issues_guides/caperton_resource_page.

Kairys, David, Joseph Kadane, and John Lehorsky. 1977. "Jury Representativeness: A Mandate for Multiple Source Lists." *California Law Review* 65: 776–827.

Kalt, Brian C. 2003. "The Exclusion of Felons from Jury Service." *American University Law Review* 53: 65–189.

Kalven, Harry, and Hans Zeisel. 1966. *The American Jury*. Boston: Little, Brown.

Kamisar, Yale. 1978. "Is the Exclusionary Rule an 'Illogical' or 'Unnatural' Interpretation of the Fourth Amendment?" *Judicature* 78: 83–84.

Kant, Immanuel. 1790. *The Science of Right*. (W. Hastie, trans.). Available online at http://philosophy.eserver.org/kant/science-of-right.txt.

Kanter, Lois H. 2005. "Invisible Clients: Exploring Our Failure to Provide Civil Legal Services to Rape Victims." *Suffolk University Law Review* 38: 253–289.

Kaplan, John. 1973. *Criminal Justice: Introductory Cases and Materials*. Mineola, NY: Foundation Press.

Karmen, Andrew. 2012. *Crime Victims: An Introduction to Victimology*. 7th ed. Belmont, CA: Wadsworth.

Katz, Charles M., and Cassia C. Spohn. 1995. "The Effect of Race and Gender on Bail Outcomes: A Test of an Interactive Model." *American Journal of Criminal Justice* 19: 161–184.

Kauder, Neal, and Brian Ostrom. 2008. *State Sentencing Guidelines: Profiles and Continuum*. Williamsburg, VA: National Center for State Courts.

Keel, Timothy G., John P. Jarvis, and Yvonne E. Muirhead. 2009. "An Exploratory Analysis of Factors Affecting Homicide Investigations: Examining the Dynamics of Murder Clearance Rates." *Homicide Studies* 13: 50–68.

Keen, Bradley, and David Jacobs. 2009. "Racial Threat, Partisan Politics, and Racial Disparities in Prison Admissions: A Panel Analysis." *Criminology* 47: 209–238.

Keenan, David, Deborah Jane Cooper, David Lebowitz, and Tamar Lerer. 2011. "The Myth of Prosecutorial Accountability after *Connick v. Thompson*: Why Existing Professional Responsibility Measures Cannot Protect against Prosecutorial Misconduct." *Yale Law Journal Online* 121:

Kegley, Josh. 2011. "Lexington Police Are Writing Fewer Traffic Tickets, Records Show." *Lexington Herald Leader*, December 31.

Kelley, Matt. 2011. "Innocence Blog: Is the 'CSI Effect' Real?" Innocence Project, June 24. Available online at http://www.innocenceproject.org/Content/Is_the_CSI_Effect_Real.php.

Kennedy, Darlene. 1997. "Let's Hold Juveniles Responsible for Their Crimes." National Center for Public Policy Research. Available online at http://www.nationalcenter.org/NPA166.html.

Kerr, Orin S. 2008. "Criminal Law in Virtual Worlds." University of Chicago Legal Forum, 2008: 415-42, GWU Law School Public Law Research Paper No. 391. Available online at http://ssrn.com/abstract=1097392.

Kerr, Orin S. 2008. "Criminal Law in Virtual Worlds." *University of Chicago Legal Forum* 2008: 415-430.

Kerrigan, Tim. 2008. "No Money? No Problem. Legal Aid Lawyers Find Innovative Ways to Serve the Rural Poor." *Public Interest Law Reporter* 13: 133–139.

Kerstetter, Wayne A. 1990. "Gateway to Justice: Police and Prosecutorial Response to Sexual Assaults Against Women." *Journal of Criminal Law and Criminology* 81: 267–313.

Killias, Martin, Gwladys Gilliéron, Izumi Kissling, and Patrice Villettaz. 2010. "Community Service versus Electronic Monitoring—What Works Better?" *British Journal of Criminology* 50: 1155-1170.

Killman, Curtis. 2006. "Pushing the Limits: Towns Cash in on Traffic Fines." *Tulsa World*, August 6.

Kimora. 2008. "The Emerging Paradigm in Probation and Parole in the United States." *Journal of Offender Rehabilitation* 46: 1–11.

King, Nancy J., David A. Soulé, Sara Steen, and Robert R. Weidner. 2005. "When Process Affects Punishment: Differences in Sentences after Guilty Plea, Bench Trial, and Jury Trial in Five Guidelines States." *Columbia Law Review* 105: 959–1009.

King, Ryan D., Kecia R. Johnson, and Kelly McGeever. 2010. "Demography of the Legal Profession and Racial Disparities in Sentencing." *Law & Society Review* 44(1), 1–32.

King, Ryan S. 2008. *The State of Sentencing 2007: Developments in Policy and Practice*. Washington, DC: The Sentencing Project.

Kingsnorth, Rodney, and Louis Rizzo. 1979. "Decision-Making in the Criminal Courts: Continuities and Discontinuities." *Criminology* 17: 3–14.

Kingsnorth, Rodney, Carole Barnes, and Paul Coonley. 1990. "Driving under the Influence: The Role of Legal and Extralegal Factors in Court Processing and Sentencing Practices." Unpublished manuscript, Department of Sociology, California State University, Sacramento.

Kirk, David S., and Mauri Matsuda. 2011. "Legal Cynicism, Collective Efficacy, and the Ecology of Arrest." *Criminology* 49: 443–472.

Klaversma, Laura. 2008. *Courts and Collections*. Williamsburg, VA: National Center for State Courts.

Kleck, Gary. 1981. "Racial Discrimination in Criminal Sentencing: A Critical Evaluation of the Evidence with Additional Data on the Death Penalty." *American Sociological Review* 46: 783–805.

Klein, Stephen, Joan Petersilia, and Susan Turner. 1990. "Race and Imprisonment Decisions in California." *Science* 247: 812–816.

Klemm, Margaret. 1986. "The Determinants of Capital Sentencing in Louisiana, 1979–1984." Unpublished doctoral dissertation, University of New Orleans.

Knudten, Richard, Anthony Meader, Mary Knudten, and William Doerner. 1976. "The Victim in the Administration of Criminal Justice: Problems and Perceptions." In: William McDonald (Ed.). *Criminal Justice and the Victim* (pp. 115–146). Newbury Park, CA: Sage.

Koons-Witt, Barbara. 2002. "The Effect of Gender on the Decision to Incarcerate before and after the Introduction of Sentencing Guidelines." *Criminology* 40: 297–328.

Kovach, Gretel. 2009. "Mixed Opinions of a Judge Accused of Misconduct." *New York Times*, March 8.

Kramer, John, Robin Lubitz, and Cynthia Kempinen. 1989. "Sentencing Guidelines: A Quantitative Comparison of Sentencing Politics in Minnesota, Pennsylvania, and Washington." *Justice Quarterly* 6: 565–587.

Kramer, John, and Darrell Steffensmeier. 1993. "Race and Imprisonment Decisions." *Sociological Quarterly* 34: 357–376.

Kramer, John, and Jeffrey Ulmer. 1996. "Sentencing Disparity and Departures from Guidelines." *Justice Quarterly* 13: 81–106.

Kramer, John, and Jeffrey Ulmer. 2009. *Sentencing Guidelines: Lessons from Pennsylvania*. Boulder, CO: Lynne Rienner.

Krisberg, Barry. 1988. "Public Attitudes about Criminal Sanctions." *Criminologist* 13: 1–21.

Krisberg, Barry, and James Austin. 1993. *Reinventing Juvenile Justice*. Newbury Park, CA: Sage.

Krisberg, Barry, and Eleanor Taylor-Nicholson. 2011. *Research Brief: Criminal Justice Realignment: A Bold New Era in California Corrections*. Berkeley, CA: The Chief Justice Earl Warren Institute on Law and Social Policy.

Kruger, Karen J. 2007. "Pregnancy & Policing: Are They Compatible? Pushing the Legal Limits on Behalf of Equal Employment Opportunities." *Wisconsin Women's Law Journal*, 22, 61–89.

Krupa, Michelle. 2006. "Ex-Judge Is Given Term of 51 Months." *Times-Picayune*, February 9.

Kupchik, Aaron. 2006. *Judging Juveniles: Prosecuting Adolescents in Adult and Juvenile Courts*. New York: New York University Press.

Kurland, Philip B., and Dennis J. Hutchinson. 1983. "The Business of the Supreme Court, O.T. 1982." *University of Chicago Law Review*, 50, 628–651.

Kurlychek, Megan, and Cynthia Kempinen. 2006. "Beyond Boot Camp: The Impact of Aftercare on Offender Reentry." *Criminology and Public Policy* 2: 363–388.

Kyckelhahn, Tracey, and Thomas H. Cohen. 2008. *Felony Defendants in Large Urban Counties, 2004*. Washington, DC: Bureau of Justice Statistics.

Labriola, Melissa, Sarah Bradley, Chris O'Sullivan, Michael Rempel, and Samantha Moore. 2009. *A National Portrait of Domestic Violence Courts*. New York: Center for Court Innovation.

Labriola, Melissa, Michael Rempel, and Robert Davis. 2008. "Do Batterer Programs Reduce Recidivism? Results from a Randomized Trial in the Bronx." *Justice Quarterly* 25: 251–282.

Lacey, Marc. 2011. "Police Officers Find That Dissent on Drug Laws May Come with a Price." *New York Times*, December 2, p. A11.

Lacks, Robyn Diehl. 2007. "The "Real" *CSI*: Designing and Teaching a Violent Crime Scene Class in an Undergraduate Setting." *Journal of Criminal Justice Education* 18: 2.

LaCroix, Alison L. 2007. "The New Wheel in the Federal Machine: From Sovereignty to Jurisdiction in the Early Republic." *Supreme Court Review*, 2007, 345–394.

LaFave, Wayne. 1965. *Arrest: The Decision to Take a Suspect into Custody*. Boston: Little, Brown.

LaFountain, Robert C., Richard Y. Schauffler, Shauna M. Strickland, Sarah A. Gibson, and Ashley N. Mason. 2011. *Examining the Work of State Courts: An Analysis of 2009 State Court Caseloads*. Williamsburg, VA: National Center for State Courts.

LaFountain, Robert, Richard Schauffler, Shauna Strickland, William Raftery, Chantal Bromage, Cynthia Lee, and Sarah Gibson. 2008. *Examining the Work of State Courts, 2007*. Williamsburg, VA: National Center for State Courts.

LaFrenz, C.D., and Cassia Spohn. 2006. "Who Is Punished More Harshly in Federal Court? The Interaction of Race/Ethnicity, Gender, Age, and Employment Status in the Sentencing of Drug Offenders." *Justice Research and Policy* 8: 25–56.

Lamber, Julia, and Mary Luskin. 1992. "Court Reform: A View from the Bottom." *Judicature* 75: 295–299.

Landsberg, Brian. 1993. "The Role of Civil Service Attorneys and Political Appointees in Making Policy in the Civil Rights Division of the U.S. Department of Justice." *Journal of Law and Politics* 9: 275–289.

Landsman, Stephan. 2005. "In Defense of the Jury of 12 and the Unanimous Decision Rule." *Judicature* 88: 301–305.

Langton, Lynn. 2007. *State Court Organization, 1987–2004*. Washington, DC: Department of Justice, Bureau of Justice Statistics.

Langton, Lynn, and Donald Farole. 2010. *State Public Defender Programs, 2007*. Washington, DC: Department of Justice, Bureau of Justice Statistics.

Lankford, Jefferson. 2006. "The Effect of *Blakely* v. *Washington* on State Sentencing." *Justice System Journal* 27: 96–104.

Lauritsen, Janet, Karen Heimer, and James Lynch. 2009. "Trends in the Gender Gap in Violent Offending: New Evidence from the National Crime Victimization Survey." *Criminology* 47: 361–400.

Lavoie, Denise. 2008. "Successful Schemers Know How to Charm Their Victims." *Times-Picayune*, December 20.

LaWall, Barbara. 2001. "Should Plea Bargaining Be Banned in Pima County?" Pima County (Arizona) Attorney's Office.

Law Enforcement Against Prohibition. 2012. "Welcome to Law Enforcement Against Prohibition." Available online at://www.leap.cc.

Lawson, Harry, and Dennis Howard. 1991. "Development of the Profession of Court Management: A History with Commentary." *Justice System Journal* 15: 580–605.

"LDF Applauds Supreme Court Decision in *Kimbrough v. United States*." 2007. *US Newswire*, December 10.

Lee, David W. 2011. *Handbook of Section 1983 Litigation, 2011 Edition*. Frederick, MD: Wolters Kluwer Law & Business.

Lee, Matthew. 2008. "Civic Community in the Hinterland: Toward a Theory of Rural Social Structure and Violence." *Criminology* 46: 447–463.

Lee, Monica. 1992. "Indigent Defense: Determination of Indigency in the Nation's State Courts." *State Court Journal* (Spring): 16–23.

Lefcourt, Gerald. 1998. "Curbing the Abuse of the Grand Jury." *Judicature* 81: 196–197.

Lefstein, Norman. 2011. *Securing Reasonable Caseloads: Ethics and Law in Public Defense*. Chicago: American Bar Association.

Leiber, Michael, John Reitzel & Kristin Mack. 2011. "Probation Officer Recommendations for Sentencing Relative to Judicial Practice: The Implications for African Americans." *Criminal Justice Policy Review* 22: 301–329.

Liebman, James S., Jeffrey Fagan, and Valerie West. 2000. "Capital Attrition: Error Rates in Capital Cases, 1973-1995." *Texas Law Review* 78: 1839–1865.

Leo, Richard. 1996a. "Inside the Interrogation Room." *Journal of Criminal Law and Criminology* 86: 266–303.

Leo, Richard. 1996b. "The Impact of *Miranda* Revisited." *Journal of Criminal Law and Criminology* 86: 621–692.

Leo, Richard A. 2008. *Police Interrogation and American Justice*. Cambridge, MA: Harvard University Press.

Levett, Lora M., et al. 2005. "The Psychology of Jury and Juror Decision Making." In Neil Brewer & Kipling D. Williams eds., *Psychology and Law: An Empirical Perspective* (pp. 365-406). Guilford, NC: The Guilford Press.

Levine, James. 1983. "Using Jury Verdict Forecasts in Criminal Defense Strategy." *Judicature* 66: 448–461.

Levitt, Steven. 2006. "The Case of the Critics Who Missed the Point: A Reply to Webster et al." *Criminology and Public Policy* 5: 449–460.

Lewis, Anthony. 1964. *Gideon's Trumpet*. New York: Vintage Books/Random House.

Lewis, Neil. 2006. "Moussaoui Given Life Term by Jury over Link to 9/11." *New York Times*, May 4.

Lichtenstein, Michael. 1984. "Public Defenders: Dimensions of Cooperation." *Justice System Journal* 9: 102–110.

Lieberman, Joel D., and Bruce Dennis Sales. 2006. *Scientific Jury Selection*. Washington, DC: American Psychological Association.

Lieberman, Joel D., Terance D. Miethe, Courtney A. Carrell, and Daniel A. Krauss. 2008. "Gold versus Platinum: Do Jurors Recognize the Superiority and Limitations of DNA Evidence Compared to Other Types of Forensic Evidence?" *Psychology, Public Policy, and Law* 14: 27–62.

Lininger, Tim. 2008. "Is It Wrong to Sue for Rape?" *Duke Law Journal* 57: 1557–1640.

Liptak, Adam. 2003. "County Says It's Too Poor to Defend the Poor." *New York Times*, April 15.

Liptak, Adam. 2005. "New Trial for a Mother Who Drowned 5 Children." *New York Times*, January 7.

Liptak, Adam. 2007. "Given the Latitude to Show Leniency, Judges May Not." *New York Times*, December 11.

Listwan, Shelley, Francis T. Cullen, and Edward Latessa. 2006. "How to Prevent Prison Re-entry Programs from Failing: Insights from Evidence-Based Corrections." *Federal Probation* 70: 19–25.

Listwan, Shelley, Cheryl Johnson, Francis Cullen, and Edward Latessa. 2008. "Cracks in the Penal Harm Movement: Evidence from the Field." *Criminology and Public Policy* 7: 423–465.

Litras, Marika, and John R. Golmant. 2006. "A Comparative Study of Juror Utilization in U.S. District Courts." *Journal of Empirical Legal Studies* 3: 99–120.

Logan, T.K., William H. Hoyt, Kathryn E. McCollister, Michael T. French, Carl Leukefeld, & Lisa Minton. 2004. "Economic Evaluation of Drug Court: Methodology, Results, and Policy Implications." *Evaluation and Program Planning*, 27(4), 381–396.

Losh, Susan C., and Robert G. Boatright. 2002. "Life-Cycle Factors, Status, and Civil Engagement: Issues of Age and Attitudes toward Jury Service." *Justice System Journal* 23: 221–234.

Lowy, Joan. 2009. "Summit to Focus on Driver Phone Use." *Times-Picayune*, August 5.

Lowy, Joan. 2011. "Feds Propose a Total Cellphone Ban for Drivers." Associated Press, December 14.

Luna, Erik. 2005. "The Overcriminalization Phenomenon." *American University Law Review* 54: 703–746.

Lurigio, Arthur, David Olson, and Jessica Snowden. 2009. "The Effects of Setting, Analyses and Probation Status." *Corrections Compendium* 34: 1–16.

Lushing, Peter. 1992. "The Fall and Rise of the Criminal Contingent Fee." *Journal of Criminal Law and Criminology* 82: 498–568.

Lynch, David. 1994. "The Impropriety of Plea Agreements: A Tale of Two Counties." *Law & Social Inquiry* 19: 115–134.

Lynch, David R., and T. David Evans. 2002. "Attributes of Highly Effective Criminal Defense Negotiators." *Journal of Criminal Justice* 30: 387–396.

Lynch, Michael. 2007. *Big Prisons, Big Dreams: Crime and the Failure of America's Penal System*. Piscataway, NJ: Rutgers University Press.

Mack, Kathy, and Sharyn Roach Anleu. 2007. "'Getting Through the List': Judgecraft and Legitimacy in the Lower Courts." *Social Legal Studies* 16: 341–361.

MacKenzie, Doris L. 2006. *What Works in Corrections: Reducing the Criminal Activities of Offenders and Delinquents*. New York: Cambridge University Press.

MADD. 2009. "Support Ignition Interlocks for all Convicted Drunk Drivers." Available online at https://secure2.convio.net/madd/site/Advocacy?JServSessionIdr004=08v7ubeh61.app7a &pagename=homepage&id=477.

Mahoney, Barry, with Alexander Aikman, Pamela Casey, Victor Flango, Geoff Gallas, Thomas Henderson, Jeanne Ito, David Steelman, and Steven Weller. 1988. *Changing Times in Trial Courts*. Williamsburg, VA: National Center for State Courts.

Manfredi, Christopher. 1998. *The Supreme Court and Juvenile Justice*. Lawrence: University Press of Kansas.

Mann, Jim. 2011. "Delivering Justice to the Mentally Ill: Characteristics of Mental Health Courts." *Southwest Journal of Criminal Justice* 8(1): 44–58.

Mansfield, Cathy Lesser. 1999. "Disorder in the Court: Rethinking the Role of Non-Lawyer Judges in Limited Jurisdiction Court Civil Cases." *New Mexico Law Review* 29: 119–174.

Maremont, Mark, and Chad Bray. 2005. "Tyco Trial Jurors Say Defendants Weren't Credible." *Wall Street Journal*, June 20.

Martin, Edward C. (n.d.), Thinking Like a Lawyer. Available online at http://www.samford.edu/schools/netlaw/dh2/logic.

Martin, Elaine. 1993. "Women on the Bench: A Different Voice?" *Judicature* 77: 126–128.

Martin, Jamie S., Kate Hanrahan, and James H. Bowers, Jr. 2009. "Offenders' Perceptions of House Arrest and Electronic Monitoring." *Journal of Offender Rehabilitation* 48: 547–570.

Martinez, Ramiro. 2007. "Incorporating Latinos and Immigrants into Policing Research." *Criminology and Public Policy* 6: 57–64.

Martinez, Ramiro. 2010. "Economic Conditions and Racial/Ethnic Variations in Violence: Immigration, the Latino Paradox, and Future Research." *Criminology and Public Policy* 9: 707–714.

Martinson, Robert. 1974. "What Works? Questions and Answers about Prison Reform." *Public Interest* 35: 22–54.

Marvell, Thomas, and Mary Luskin. 1991. "The Impact of Speedy Trial Laws in Connecticut and North Carolina." *Justice System Journal* 14: 343–357.

Marvell, Thomas, and Carlisle Moody. 1996. "Determinate Sentencing and Abolishing Parole: The Long-Term Impacts on Prisons and Crime." *Criminology* 34: 107–128.

Mastrofski, Stephen, and R. Richard Ritti. 1996. "Police Training and the Effects of Organization on Drunk Driving Enforcement." *Justice Quarterly* 13: 291–320.

Mather, Lynn. 1974a. "Some Determinants of the Method of Case Disposition: Decision-Making by Public Defenders in Los Angeles." *Law and Society Review* 8: 187–216.

Mather, Lynn. 1974b. "The Outsider in the Courtroom: An Alternative Role for the Defense." In: Herbert Jacob (Ed.). *The Potential for Reform of Criminal Justice*. Newbury Park, CA: Sage.

Mather, Lynn. 1979. *Plea Bargaining or Trial?* Lexington, MA: Heath.

Mather, Lynn, and Leslie Levin. 2012. "Why Context Matters." In: Leslie Levin and Lynn Mather (Eds.). *Lawyers in Practice: Ethical Decision Making in Context*. Chicago: University of Chicago Press.

Mauer, Marc. 2011. "Sentencing Reform Amid Mass Incarceration—Guarded Optimism." *Criminal Justice* 26(1), 27–36.

Mauer, Marc, Ryan S. King & Malcolm C. Young. 2004. *The Meaning of "Life": Long Prison Sentences in Context*. Washington, DC: The Sentencing Project.

Mauro, Tony. 2006. "Court Backs Death Row Inmates." *Legal Times*, June 19.

Maxwell, Christopher, Joel Garner, and Jeffrey Fagan. 2002. "The Preventive Effects of Arrest on Intimate Partner Violence: Research, Policy, and Theory." *Criminology and Public Policy* 2: 51–80.

Mayer, Martin. 2007. *The Judges*. New York: Macmillan.

Maynard, Douglas. 1988. "Narratives and Narrative Structure in Plea Bargaining." *Law and Society Review* 22: 449–481.

Mays, G. Larry, and William Taggart. 1986. "Court Clerks, Court Administrators, and Judges: Conflict in Managing the Courts." *Journal of Criminal Justice* 14: 1–7.

McCahill, Thomas W., Linda C. Meyer, Arthur M. Fischman. 1979. *The Aftermath of Rape*. Lexington, VA; Lexington Books.

McCampbell, Robert. 1995. "Parallel Civil and Criminal Proceedings: Six Legal Pitfalls." *Criminal Law Bulletin* 31: 483–501.

McCarthy, Brendan, 2011. "B.G. Pleads Guilty While Refusing to "Snitch.'" *The Times-Picayune* December 8.

McCord, David. 2005. "Juries Should Not Be Required to Have 12 Members or to Render Unanimous Verdicts." *Judicature* 88: 301–305.

McCormack, Robert. 1991. "Compensating Victims of Violent Crime." *Justice Quarterly* 8: 329–346.

McCormick, John. 1999. "Coming Two Days Shy of Martyrdom." *Newsweek*, February 15.

McCoy, Candace. 1984. "Determinate Sentencing, Plea Bargaining Bans, and Hydraulic Discretion in California." *Justice System Journal* 9: 256–275.

McCoy, Candace. 1993. *Politics and Plea Bargaining: Victim's Rights in California*. Philadelphia: University of Pennsylvania Press.

McCoy, Candace. 2003. "Bargaining under the Hammer: The Trial Penalty in the USA." In: Douglas Koski (Ed.). *The Criminal Jury Trial in America*. Raleigh, NC: Carolina Academic Press.

McDonald, Douglas, and Kenneth Carlson. 1993. *Sentencing in the Federal Courts: Does Race Matter? The Transition to Sentencing Guidelines, 1986–1990*. Washington, DC: Bureau of Justice Statistics.

McDonald, Thomas, Robert Wood, and Melissa Pflug (Eds.) 1996. *Rural Criminal Justice: Conditions, Constraints, and Challenges*. Salem, WI: Sheffield.

McDonald, William (Ed.). 1976. *Criminal Justice and the Victim*. Newbury Park, CA: Sage.

McDonald, William. 1979. "The Prosecutor's Domain." In: William McDonald (Ed.). *The Prosecutor*. Newbury Park, CA: Sage.

McDonough, Molly. 2008. "Judge Dismisses Nifong from Duke Player's Civil Suit, for Now." *ABA Journal*, January 30.

McGarrell, Edmund, and Natalie Kroovand Hipple. 2008. "Family Group Conferencing and Re-Offending among First-Time Juvenile Offenders: The Indianapolis Experiment." *Justice Quarterly* 24: 221–246.

McGlone, Tim. 2007a. "Judge's Stand on Norfolk Man's Sentencing Heads to Supreme Court." *The Virginian-Pilot*, September 29.

McGlone, Tim. 2007b. "Supreme Court Hears Case on Norfolk Drug Sentencing." *The Virginian-Pilot*, October 3.

McIntyre, Donald. 1968. "A Study of Judicial Dominance of the Charging Decision." *Journal of Criminal Law, Criminology and Police Science* 59: 463–490.

McIntyre, Donald, and David Lippman. 1970. "Prosecutors and Disposition of Felony Cases." *American Bar Association Journal* 56: 154–1159.

McIntyre, Lisa. 1987. *The Public Defender: The Practice of Law in the Shadows of Repute*. Chicago: University of Chicago Press.

McKeon, John C., and David G. Rice. 2009. "Administering Justice in Montana's Rural Courts." *Montana Law Review* 70: 201–220.

McNiel Dale E., and Renée L. Binder. 2007. "Effectiveness of a Mental Health Court in Reducing Criminal Recidivism and Violence." *American Journal of Psychiatry* 164(9): 1395–1403.

McQuiston, J. T. 1995. "In the Bizarre L.I.R.R. Trial, Equally Bizarre Confrontations." *New York Times*, February 5.

Mears, Bill. 2012. "Justices Rule for Death Row Inmate after Legal Mistakes." *CNN* January 18. Available online at http://www.cnn.com/2012/01/18/justice/scotus-alabama-inmate/index.html?iref=allsearch.

Mears, Daniel P., Carter Hay, Marc Gertz, and Christina Mancini. 2007. "Public Opinion and the Foundation of the Juvenile Court." *Criminology* 45: 223–257.

Mears, Daniel, Zia Wang, Carter Hay, and William Bales. 2008. "Social Ecology and Recidivism: Implications for Prisoner Reentry." *Criminology* 46: 301–348.

Mecklenburg, Sheri. 2006. "Addendum to the Report to the Legislature of the State of Illinois: The Illinois Pilot Program on Sequential Double-Blind Identification Procedures." Available online at http://www.chicagopolice.org/Addendum%20to%20IP-Report.pdf.

Meinhold, Stephen, and Steven Shull. 1993. "Policy Congruence between the President and the Solicitor General." Paper presented at the annual meeting of the Midwest Political Science Association, Chicago.

Mental Health America. 2012. *Position Statement 53: Mental Health Courts*. Available online at http://www.nmha.org/go/position-statements/53.

Merritt, Nancy, Terry Fain, and Susan Turner. 2006. "Oregon's Get Tough Sentencing Reform: A Lesson in Justice System Adaptation." *Criminology and Public Policy* 5: 5–36.

Meyer, Jon'a, and Paul Jesilow. 1997. *Doing Justice in the People's Court: Sentencing by Municipal Court Judges*. Albany: State University of New York Press.

Meyers, David. 2005. *Boys among Men: Trying and Sentencing Juveniles as Adults*. Westport, CT: Praeger.

Miethe, Terance, and Charles Moore. 1989. "Sentencing Guidelines: Their Effect in Minnesota." Washington, DC: Department of Justice, Bureau of Justice Statistics.

Mileski, Maureen. 1971. "Courtroom Encounters: An Observation Study of a Lower Criminal Court." *Law and Society Review* 5: 473–538.

Miller, Benjamin. 1991. "Assessing the Functions of Judicial Conduct Organizations." *Judicature* 75: 16–19.

Miller, Herbert, William McDonald, and James Cramer. 1978. *Plea Bargaining in the United States*. Washington, DC: National Institute of Law Enforcement and Criminal Justice.

Miller, J. Mitchell, Holly Ventura-Miller, and J.C. Barnes. 2007. "The Effect of Demeanor on Drug Court Admission." *Criminal Justice Policy Review* 18: 246–259.

Miller, Marc L., and Ronald Wright. 2008. "The Black Box." *Iowa Law Review* 94: 125–196.

Miller, Susan L. and Shana L. Maier. 2008. "Moving Beyond Numbers: What Female Judges Say about Different Judicial Voices." *Journal of Women, Politics & Policy* 29: 527–559.

Mills, Carol, and Wayne Bohannon. 1980. "Jury Characteristics: To What Extent Are They Related to Jury Verdicts?" *Judicature* 64: 22–31.

Miner, Roger J. 1999. "Professional Responsibility in Appellate Practice: A View from the Bench." *Pace Law Review* 19: 323–344.

Minton, Todd D., and William J. Sabol. 2009. *Jail Inmates at Midyear 2008*. Washington, DC: Bureau of Justice Statistics.

Misner, Robert. 1996. "Recasting Prosecutorial Discretion." *Journal of Criminal Law and Criminology* 86: 717–758.

Mitchell, Josh. 2008. "Victims Fund Assists Felons." *Baltimore Sun*, March 16.

Mitchell, Ojmarrh. 2005. "A Meta-Analysis of Race and Sentencing Research: Explaining the Inconsistencies." *Journal of Quantitative Criminology* 21: 439–466.

Mitchell, Tara L., Ryann M. Haw, Jeffrey E. Pfeifer, and Christian A. Meissner. 2005. "Racial Bias in Mock Juror Decision-Making: A Meta-Analytic Review of Defendant Treatment." *Law and Human Behavior* 29: 621–637.

Mize, Gregory E., Paula Hannaford-Agor, and Nicole L. Waters. 2007. *The State-of-the-States Survey of Jury Improvement Efforts: A Compendium Report*. Williamsburg, VA: National Center for State Courts. Available online at http://www.ncsconline.org/D_Research/cjs/pdf/SOSCompendiumFinal.pdf.

Mnookin, Jennifer L. 2008. "The Validity of Latent Fingerprint Identification: Confessions of a Fingerprinting Moderate." *Law, Probability & Risk* 7: 127–141.

Moenssens, André. 2002. "The Reliability of Fingerprint Identification: A Case Report." Forensic Evidence.com. Available at http://www.forensic-evidence.com/site/ID/pollak2002.html.

Molesworth, Claire L. 2008. "Knowledge versus Acknowledgment: Rethinking the *Alford* Plea in Sexual Assault Cases." *Seattle Journal for Social Justice* 6: 907–942.

Moley, Raymond. 1928. "The Vanishing Jury." *Southern California Law Review* 2: 97.

Moore, Kathleen Dean. 1989. *Pardons: Justice, Mercy and the Public Interest*. New York: Oxford University Press.

Moore Marlee E., and Virgina Aldigé Hiday. 2006. "Mental Health Court Outcomes: A Comparison of Re-Arrest and Re-Arrest Severity Between Mental Health Court and Treatment Court Participants." *Law and Human Behavior* 30: 659–674.

Moran, Gary, and Brian Cutler. 1991. "The Prejudicial Impact of Pretrial Publicity." *Journal of Applied Social Psychology* 21: 345–367.

Moran, Gary, and John C. Comfort. 1986. "Neither 'Tentative' nor 'Fragmentary': Verdict Preference of Impaneled Felony Jurors as a Function of Attitude toward Capital Punishment." *Journal of Applied Psychology* 71: 146–155.

Morgan, Kathryn, and Brent Smith. 2005. "Victims, Punishment, and Parole: The Effects of Victim Participation on Parole Hearings." *Criminology and Public Policy* 4: 333–360.

Moriarty, Jane Campbell. 2007. "'Misconvictions,' Science, and the Ministers of Justice." *Nebraska Law Review* 86: 1–42.

Moriearty, Perry L. 2008. "Combating the Color-Coded Confinement of Kids: An Equal Protection Remedy." *New York University Review of Law and Social Change* 32: 285–343.

Morris, Norval, and Michael Tonry. 1990. *Between Prison and Probation: Intermediate Punishments in a Rational Sentencing System*. New York: Oxford University Press.

Mortimer, John. 1984. "Rumpole and the Confession of Guilt." *Rumpole for the Defence*. New York: Penguin Books.

Mosteller, Robert P. 2002. "Discovery in Criminal Cases." *Encyclopedia of Crime and Justice*. Farmington Hills, MI: Gale/Cengage.

Mosteller, Robert P. 2007. "The Duke Lacrosee Case, Innocence, and False Identifications: A Fundamental Failure to 'Do Justice.'" *Fordham Law Review* 76: 1337–1412.

Mushlin, Michael. 2007. "Bound and Gagged: The peculiar Predicament of Professional Jurors." *Yale Law and Policy Review* 25: 239–287.

Mushlin, Michael, and Naomi Galtz. 2009. "Getting Real about Race and Prisoner Rights." *Fordham Urban Law Journal* 36: 27–53.

Myers, Laura, and Sue Titus Reid. 1995. "The Importance of County Context in the Measurement of Sentencing Disparity: The Search for Routinization." *Journal of Criminal Justice* 23: 233–241.

Myers, Martha. 1982. "Common Law in Action: The Prosecution of Felonies and Misdemeanors." *Sociological Inquiry* 52: 1–15.

Myers, Martha, and John Hagan. 1979. "Private and Public Trouble: Prosecutors and the Allocation of Court Resources." *Social Problems* 26: 439–451.

Myers, Martha, and Susette Talarico. 1986a. "The Social Contexts of Racial Discrimination in Sentencing." *Social Problems* 33: 237–251.

Myers, Martha, and Susette Talarico. 1986b. "Urban Justice, Rural Injustice? Urbanization and Its Effect on Sentencing." *Criminology* 24: 367–391.

Myers, Martha, and Susette Talarico. 1987. *The Social Contexts of Criminal Sentencing*. New York: Springer.

Nader, Laura. 1992. "Trading Justice for Harmony." *National Institute for Dispute Resolution Forum* (Winter): 12–14.

Nagel, Irene, and John Hagan. 1983. "Gender and Crime: Offense Patterns and Criminal Court Sanctions." In: Michael Tonry and Norval Morris (Eds.). *Crime and Justice: An Annual Review of Research* (vol. 4, pp. 91–144). Chicago: University of Chicago Press.

Nagin, Daniel. 1998. "Criminal Deterrence Research at the Outset of the Twenty-First Century." In: Michael Tonry (Ed.). *Crime and Justice: A Review of Research*. Vol. 23. Chicago: University of Chicago Press.

Nardulli, Peter. 1978. *The Courtroom Elite: An Organizational Perspective on Criminal Justice*. Cambridge, MA: Ballinger.

Nardulli, Peter. 1979. "The Caseload Controversy and the Study of Criminal Courts." *Journal of Criminal Law and Criminology* 70: 89–101.

Nardulli, Peter. 1983. "The Societal Cost of the Exclusionary Rule: An Empirical Assessment." *American Bar Foundation Research Journal* 8(3): 585–609.

Nardulli, Peter. 1986. "'Insider' Justice: Defense Attorneys and the Handling of Felony Cases." *Journal of Criminal Law and Criminology* 77: 379–417.

Nardulli, Peter, Roy Flemming, and James Eisenstein. 1984. "Unraveling the Complexities of Decision Making in Face-to-Face Groups: A Contextual Analysis of Plea-Bargained Sentences." *American Political Science Review* 78: 912–928.

National Academies of Sciences. 2009. *Strengthening Forensic Science in the United States: A Path Forward*. Washington, DC: National Research Council.

National Advisory Commission on Criminal Justice Standards and Goals. 1973. *Report on Courts*. Washington, DC: Government Printing Office.

National Association of Criminal Defense Lawyers. 2000. "Citizens Grand Jury Bill of Rights." Available online at http://www.criminaljustice.org

National Association of Criminal Defense Lawyers. 2009. *Minor Crimes, Massive Waste: The Terrible Toll of America's Broken Misdemeanor Courts*. Washington, DC: Author.

National Association of Women Judges. 2012. "2012 Representation of United States State Court Women Judges." Available online at http://www.nawj.org/us_state_court_statistics_2012.asp.

National Center for State Courts. 2003. "A Profile of Hung Juries." *Caseload Highlights* 9: 1.

National Center for State Courts. 2010. "Guidelines for Implementing Best Practices in Court Building Security Costs, Priorities, Funding Strategies, and Accountability." Available online at http://contentdm.ncsconline.org/cgi-bin/showfile.exe?CISOROOT=/facilities&CISOPTR=153.

National Center for State Courts. 2011. *Survey of Judicial Salaries* (Vol. 36). Williamsburg, VA: Author.

National Center for State Courts. 2012. "High Tech Courtrooms: Resource Guide." Available online at http://www.ncsc.org/Topics/Technology/High-Tech-Courtrooms/Resource-Guide.aspx.

National Center for Victims of Crime. 2012. "Issues: Victims' Bill of Rights." Available online at http://www.ncvc.org

National District Attorneys Association. 2007. "Statement in Response to the Proposed Resolution Concerning Sentence Mitigation for Youthful Offenders." Available online at http://www.ndaa.org.

National Drug Court Resource Center. 2011. "How Many Drug Courts Are There?" Available online at http://www.ndcrc.org/node/348.

National Governors Association. 2010. "Prisoner Reentry Policy." Available online at http://www.nga.org/cms/home/nga-center-for-best-practices/center-issues/page-hsps-issues/col2-content/main-content-list/prisoner-reentry-policy-academy.html.

National Institute of Justice. 1982. *Exemplary Projects: Focus for 1982—Projects to Combat Violent Crime*. Washington, DC: Department of Justice.

National Law Enforcement and Corrections Technology Center. 1999. *Keeping Track of Electronic Monitoring*. Available at http://www.justnet.org/Lists/JUSTNET%20Resources/Attachments/859/Elec-Monit.pdf.

National Research Council, Committee on Scientific Assessment of Bullet Lead Elemental Composition Comparison. 2004. *Forensic Analysis: Weighing Bullet Lead Evidence*. Washington, DC: National Academies Press.

National Right to Counsel Committee. 2009. *Justice Denied: America's Continuing Neglect of Our Constitutional Right to Counsel*. Washington, DC: The Constitution Project.

National Sheriff's Association. 2011. "History of Court Security." Available online at http://www.sheriffs.org/content/court-security.

Nelson, Michael. 2011. "Uncontested and Unaccountable? Rates of Contestations in Trial Court Elections." *Judicature* 94: 208–217.

Neubauer, David. 1974a. "After the Arrest: The Charging Decision in Prairie City." *Law and Society Review* 8: 495–517.

Neubauer, David. 1974b. *Criminal Justice in Middle America*. Morristown, NJ: General Learning Press.

Neubauer, David. 1983. "Improving the Analysis and Presentation of Data on Case Processing Time." *Journal of Criminal Law and Criminology* 74: 1589–1607.

Neubauer, David. 1985. "Published Opinions versus Summary Affirmations: Criminal Appeals in Louisiana." *Justice System Journal* 10: 173–189.

Neubauer, David. 1991. "Winners and Losers before the Louisiana Supreme Court: The Case of Criminal Appeals." *Justice Quarterly* 8: 85–106.

Neubauer, David. 1992. "A Polychotomous Measure of Appellate Court Outcomes: The Case of Criminal Appeals." *Justice System Journal* 16: 75–87.

Neubauer, David. 1996. "A Tale of Two Cities: A Comparison of Orleans and Jefferson Parish, Louisiana." Paper presented at the annual meeting of the Academy of Criminal Justice Sciences, Louisville, KY.

Neubauer, David. 2001. *Debating Crime: Rhetoric and Reality*. Belmont, CA: Wadsworth.

Neubauer, David, Marcia Lipetz, Mary Luskin, and John Paul Ryan. 1981. *Managing the Pace of Justice: An Evaluation of LEAA's Court Delay Reduction Programs*. Washington, DC: Government Printing Office.

Neubauer, David W., and Stephen S. Meinhold. 2013. *Judicial Process: Law, Courts, and Politics in the United States*. 6th ed. Belmont, CA: Wadsworth.

Neubauer, David, and Stephen Meinhold. 2006. *Battle Supreme: The Confirmation of Chief Justice John Roberts and the Future of the Supreme Court*. Belmont, CA: Wadsworth.

Neufeld, Peter J. 2005. "The (Near) Irrelevance of *Daubert* to Criminal Justice and Some Suggestions for Reform." *American Journal of Public Health* 95: S107–S113.

Nimmer, Raymond. 1978. *The Nature of System Change: Reform Impact in the Criminal Courts*. Chicago: American Bar Foundation.

Nimmer, Raymond, and Patricia Krauthaus. 1977."Plea Bargaining Reform in Two Cities." *Justice System Journal* 3: 6–21.

Nobiling, Tracy, Cassia Spohn, and Miriam DeLone. 1998. "A Tale of Two Counties: Unemployment and Sentence Severity." *Justice Quarterly* 15: 459–485.

Nolan-Haley, Jacqueline. 2008. Alternative Dispute Resolution in a *Nutshell. St. Paul,* MN: West.

NOLO. 2012. "How Much Can I Sue for in Small Claims Court?" Available online at http://www.nolo.com.

Norman, Michael D., and Robert C. Wadman. 2000."Utah Presentence Investigation Reports: User Group Perceptions of Quality and Effectiveness." *Federal Probation* 64: 7–12.

Norris, Floyd. 2005."Chief Executive Was Paid Millions, and He Never Noticed the Fraud?" *New York Times*, January 7.

Norton, Lee. 1983. "Witness Involvement in the Criminal Justice System and Intention to Cooperate in Future Prosecutions." *Journal of Criminal Justice* 11: 143–152.

Novak, Lisa. 2003."Federal Courts Adapt for Maximum Security." *The Judges' Journal* 42: 22–24.

Nugent, Hugh, and Thomas McEwen. 1988. *Prosecutor's National Assessment of Needs*. Washington, DC: Department of Justice, National Institute of Justice.

O'Brien, David. 1988."The Supreme Court: From Warren to Burger to Rehnquist." *PS* 20: 13.

O'Neill, Michael Edmund. 2003."When Prosecutors Don't: Trends in Federal Prosecutorial Declinations." *Notre Dame Law Review* 79: 221–290.

Oaks, Dallin. 1970. "Studying the Exclusionary Rule in Search and Seizure." *University of Chicago Law Review* 37: 665–753.

Office for Victims of Crime. 1998. *From Pain to Power: Crime Victims Take Action*. Washington, DC: Department of Justice.

Office of Juvenile Justice and Delinquency Prevention. 1996. *Female Offenders in the Juvenile Justice System*. Washington, DC: Department of Justice.

Office of Justice of the Peace in Texas. 2009. Brazos County, Texas. Available online at http://www.co.brazos.tx.us.

Ofshe, Richard J. & Richard A. Leo. 1997."The Social Psychology of Police Interrogation: The Theory and Classification of True and False Confessions." *Studies in Law, Politics, and Society* 16: 189-254.

Ogloff, James R.P., and V. Gordon Rose. 2007. "The Comprehension of Judicial Instructions." In Neil Brewer and Kipling D. Williams. *Psychology and Law: An Empirical Perspective*. New York: Guildford Press.

Oldenburg, Ann. 2011."Lindsay Lohan Ordered to 30 Days in Jail." *USA Today*, November 2.

Oran, Daniel. 2000. *Law Dictionary for Nonlawyers*. 3rd ed. St. Paul, MN: West.

Osborn, Elizabeth Hervey. 2008. "What Happened to "Paul's Law"?: Insights on Advocating for Better Training and Better Outcomes in Encounters Between Law Enforcement and Persons with Autism Spectrum Disorders." *University of Colorado Law Review* 79: 333–397.

Ostrom, Brian, and Neal Kauder. 1999. *Examining the Work of State Courts*, 1998. Williamsburg, VA: National Center for State Courts.

Ostrom, Brian J., Neal B. Kauder and Robert C. LaFountain. 2001. *Examining the Work of State Courts, 2001: A National Perspective from the Court Statistics Project*. Washington: National Center for State Courts.

Ostrom, Brian, Charles Ostrom, Jr., Roger Hanson, and Matthew Kleiman. 2007. *Trial Courts as Organizations*. Philadelphia: Temple University Press.

Ostrom, Brian, Charles Ostrom, Roger Hanson, and Matthew Kleinman. 2008. *Assessing Consistency and Fairness in Sentencing: A Comparative Study in three States*. Williamsburg, VA: National Center for State Courts.

Owen, Stephen S., Henry F. Fradella, Tod W. Burke, and Jerry Joplin. 2012. *The Foundations of Criminal Justice*. New York: Oxford University Press.

Pabst, William. 1973. "What Do Six-Member Juries Really Save?" *Judicature* 57: 6–11.

Packer, Herbert. 1968. *The Limits of the Criminal Sanction*. Palo Alto, CA: Stanford University Press.

Padawer-Singer, Alice, and Alice Barton. 1975."The Impact of Pretrial Publicity on Jurors' Verdicts." In: Rita James Simon (Ed.). *The Jury System in America: A Critical Overview*. Beverly Hills, CA: Sage.

Padgett, John. 1990."Plea Bargaining and Prohibition in the Federal Courts, 1908–1934." *Law and Society Review* 24: 413–450.

Padgett, Kathy G., William D. Bales, and Thomas G. Blomberg. 2006."Under Surveillance: An Empirical Test of the Effectiveness and Consequences of Electronic Monitoring." *Criminology and Public Policy* 5(1): 61–92.

Palmer, Barbara. 2001. "Women in the American Judiciary: Their Influence and Impact." *Women and Politics* 23: 89.

Parent, Dale. 2003. *Correctional Boot Camps: Lessons from a Decade of Research*. Washington, DC: Department of Justice.

Parent, Dale, Barbara Auerbach, and Kenneth Carlson. 1992. *Compensating Crime Victims: A Summary of Policies and Practices*. Washington, DC: Department of Justice, National Institute of Justice.

Parent, Dale, Terence Dunworth, Douglas McDonald, and William Rhodes. 1996. *The Impact of Sentencing Guidelines*. Washington, DC: National Institute of Justice.

Partridge, Anthony, and William Eldridge. 1974. *The Second Circuit Sentencing Study: A Report to the Judges of the Second Circuit*. Washington, DC: Federal Judicial Center.

Passon, Doug. 2010."Using Mitigation Videos to Bridge the Cultural Gap at Sentencing." Chapter 23 of *Cultural Issues in Criminal Justice*. Huntington, NY: Juris.

Paternoster, Raymond. 1984. "Prosecutorial Discretion in Requesting the Death Penalty: A Case of Victim-Based Racial Discrimination." *Law and Society Review* 18: 437–478.

Paternoster, Raymond, and Robert Brame. 2008. "Reassessing Race Disparities in Maryland Capital Cases." *Criminology* 46: 971–1007.

Patry, Marc W. 2008. "Attractive but Guilty: Deliberation and the Physical Attractiveness Bias." *Psychological Reports* 102: 727–733.

Payne, Brian, and Randy R. Gainey. 2000. "Electronic Monitoring: Philosophical, Systemic, and Political Problems." *Journal of Offender Rehabilitation* 31: 93–112.

Payne, Brian, and Randy R. Gainey. 2004. "The Electronic Monitoring of Offenders Released from Jail or Prison: Safety, Control, and Comparisons to the Incarceration Experience." *The Prison Journal* 84: 413–435.

Payne, Brian K., and Matthew DeMichele. 2011. "Probation Philosophies and Workload Considerations." *American Journal of Criminal Justice* 36: 29–43.

Payne, Shenoa L. 2008. "The Ethical Conundrums of Unpublished Opinions." *Willamette Law Review* 44: 723–760.

Penn, Schoen & Berland Associates. 2012. "C-SPAN Supreme Court Survey." *C-Span*, July 9. Available at http://www.c-span.org/uploadedFiles/Content/Documents/CSPAN-HCR-SCOTUS-Poll.pdf.

Penney, Steven. 1998. "Theories of Confession Admissibility: A Historical Overview." *American Journal of Criminal Law*, 25, 309–383.

Perkins, David, and Jay Jamieson. 1995. "Judicial Probable Cause Determinations after *County of Riverside v. McLaughlin*." *Criminal Law Bulletin* 31: 534–546.

Perlstein, Michael. 1990. "DA's Office Suffers as Prosecutors Flee to Better Pay, Hours." *Times-Picayune*, July 22, p. B1.

Perry, Steven. 2006. *Prosecutors in State Courts*, 2005. Washington, DC: Bureau of Justice Statistics, National Institute of Justice.

Perry, Steven W. and Duren Banks, *Prosecutors in State Courts, 2007—Statistical Tables*. Washington, DC: Bureau of Justice Statistics. 2011. Available online at://bjs.ojp.usdoj.gov/content/pub/pdf/psc07st.pdf.

Peterson, Richard. 2004. "Manhattan's Specialized Domestic Violence Court." Research Brief No. 7. New York: New York City Criminal Justice Agency.

Peterson, Richard L. 2011. "Unintelligent Jury Waivers: A Call to Amend Federal Rule of Criminal Procedure 23A." *George Mason University Civil Rights Law Journal* 21: 441–470.

Petrucci, Carrie. J. 2002. "Respect as a Component in the Judge-Defendant Interaction in a Specialized Domestic Violence Court That Utilizes Therapeutic Jurisprudence." *Criminal Law Bulletin* 38(2), 263–295.

Petrucci, Carrie J. 2010. "A Descriptive Study of a California Domestic Violence Court: Program Completion and Recidivism." *Victims and Offenders* 5: 130–160.

Pew Hispanic Center. 2009. "Hispanics and the Criminal Justice System: Low Confidence, High Exposure." Available at http://pewresearch.org/pubs/1182/hispanic-confidence-in-criminal-justice-system-low.

Phillips, Mary. 2007. "Bail, Detention and Nonfelony Case Outcomes." *Research Brief #14*. New York: New York City Criminal Justice Agency.

Phillips, Mary. 2008. "Bail, Detention and Felony Case Outcomes." *Research Brief #18*. New York: New York City Criminal Justice Agency.

Phillips, Thomas R. 2009. "The Merits of Merit Selection." *Harvard Journal of Law and Public Policy* 32: 67–96.

Piehl, Anne Morrison, and Shawn D. Bushway. 2007. "Measuring and Explaining Charge Bargaining." *Journal of Quantitative Criminology* 23: 105–125.

Pinello, Daniel. 1995. *The Impact of Judicial-Selection Method of State-Supreme-Court Policy: Innovation, Reaction and Atrophy*. Westport, CT: Greenwood Press.

Pitts, Leonard, Jr. 2011. "Justice for an Awful Judge." *The Stump*, February 28. Available online at http://www.oregonlive.com/opinion/index.ssf/2011/02/justice_for_an_awful_judge.html.

Pitts, Wayne, Eugena Givens, and Susan McNeeley. 2009. "The Need for a Holistic Approach to Specialized Domestic Violence Court Programming: Evaluating Offender Rehabilitation Needs and Recidivism." *Juvenile and Family Court Journal* 60(3), 1–21.

Platt, Anthony. 1969. *The Child Savers: The Invention of Delinquency*. Chicago: University of Chicago Press.

Platt, Anthony, and Randi Pollock. 1974. "Channeling Lawyers: The Careers of Public Defenders." In: Herbert Jacob (Ed.). *The Potential for Reform of Criminal Justice*. Newbury Park, CA: Sage.

Podgor, Ellen. 2007. "The Challenge of White Collar Sentencing." *Journal of Criminal Law and Criminology*. 97: 731.

Podlas, Kimberlianne. 2002. "Should We Blame Judge Judy? The Messages TV Courtrooms Send Viewers." *Judicature* 86: 38–43.

Pollock, Joycelyn M. 2012. *Ethical Dilemmas and Decisions in Criminal Justice*, 7th ed. Belmont, CA: Wadsworth.

Pollock Joycelyn M., and Sareta M. Davis. 2005. "The Continuing Myth of the Violent Female Offender." *Criminal Justice Review* 30: 5–29.

Porter, Rachael. 2011. *Choosing Performance Indicators for Your Community Prosecution Initiative*. Washington, DC: Association of Prosecuting Attorneys. Available online at http://www.courtinnovation.org/sites/default/files/documents/Choosing_Performance_Indicators.pdf.

Pou, Charles. 2005. "Scissors Cut Paper: A 'Guildhall' Helps Maryland's Mediators Sharpen Their Skills." *Justice System Journal* 26: 307–325.

President's Commission on Law Enforcement and Administration of Justice. 1967. *Task Force Report: The Courts*. Washington, DC: Government Printing Office.

Priehs, Richard. 1999. "Appointed Counsel for Indigent Criminal Appellants: Does Compensation Influence Effort?" *Justice System Journal* 21: 57–79.

Primus, Eve B. 2007. "Structural Reform in Criminal Defense: Relocating Ineffective Assistance of Counsel Claims." *Cornell Law Review* 92: 679–732.

Propen, Amy and Mary Lay Schuster. 2008. "Making Academic Work Advocacy Work: Technologies of Power in the Public Arena." *Journal of Business and Technical Communications* 22: 299–329.

Prosser, Mary. 2006. "Reforming Criminal Discovery: Why Old Objections Must Yield to New Realities." *Wisconsin Law Review* 2006: 541–614.

Provine, Doris Marie. 2007. *Unequal Under Law: Race and the War on Drugs*. Chicago: University of Chicago Press.

Pruitt, Lisa R. 2006. "Rural Rhetoric." *Connecticut Law Review* 39: 159–240.

Pruitt, Lisa R. 2008. "Gender, Geography, and Rural Justice." *Berkeley Journal of Gender, Law & Justice* 23: 338–391.

Public Safety Performance Project. 2007. *Public Safety, Public Spending: Forecasting America's Prison Population 2007–2011*. Washington, DC: The Pew Charitable Trust.

Puritz, Patricia, S. Burrell, R. Schwartz, M. Soler, and L. Warboys. 1995. *A Call for Justice: An Assessment of Access to Counsel and Quality of Representation in Delinquency Proceedings*. Washington, DC: American Bar Association.

Puzzanchera, Charles, and Benjamin Adams. 2011. *Juvenile Arrests 2009*. Washington, DC: Department of Justice, Office of Justice Programs.

Puzzanchera, Charles, Benjamin Adams, and Melissa Sickmund. 2011. *Juvenile Court Statistics, 2008*. Pittsburgh: National Center for Juvenile Justice.

Radelet, Michael, and Glenn Pierce. 1985. "Race and Prosecutorial Discretion in Homicide Cases." *Law and Society Review* 19: 587–621.

Raftery, William. 2006. "The Legislatures, the Ballot Boxes and the Courts." *Court Review* 4: 102–107.

Ragland, James. 2009. "*American Violet* Tells Story of Ill-Fated Hearne Drug Raids." *Dallas Morning News* (March 13). Available online at http://www.dallasnews.com/sharedcontent/dws/dn/localnews/columnists/jragland/stories/031409dnmetragland.33ada80.html.

Ragona, Anthony, and John Paul Ryan. 1983. "Misdemeanor Courts and the Choice of Sanctions: A Comparative View." *Justice System Journal* 8: 199–221.

Ralph, Paige, Jonathan Sorensen, and James Marquart. 1992. "A Comparison of Death-Sentenced and Incarcerated Murderers in Pre-*Furman* Texas." *Justice Quarterly* 9: 185–209.

Rand, Michael. 2008. *Criminal Victimization*. 2007. Washington, DC: Department of Justice, Bureau of Justice Statistics.

Randall, Ronald, and James A. Woods. 2008. "Racial Representativeness of Juries: An Analysis of Source List and Administrative Effects on the Jury Pool." *Justice System Journal* 29: 71–82.

Rapaport, Elizabeth. 1991. "The Death Penalty and Gender Discrimination." *Law and Society Review* 25: 367–384.

Raymond, Paul. 1992. "The Impact of a Televised Trial on Individuals' Information and Attitudes." *Judicature* 75: 204–209.

Re, Richard M. 2007. "Re-Justifying the Fair Cross-Section Requirement: Equal Representation and Enfranchisement in the American Criminal Jury." *Yale Law Journal* 116: 1568–1614.

Reaves, Brian. 2001. *Felony Defendants in Large Urban Counties, 1998*. Washington, DC: Bureau of Justice Statistics.

Redding, Richard. 2008. "Juvenile Transfer Laws: An Effective Deterrent to Delinquency?" Washington, DC: Department of Justice , Office of Justice Programs.

Reiman, Jeffrey. 2007. *The Rich Get Richer and the Poor Get Prison: Ideology, Class, and Criminal Justice*. 8th ed. Boston: Pearson/Allyn & Bacon.

Reitz, Kevin. 2001. "The Status of Sentencing Guidelines Reforms in the United States." In: Michael Tonry (Ed.). *Penal Reform in Overcrowded Times*. New York: Oxford University Press.

Remington, Frank. 1988. "Post-Conviction Review: What State Trial Courts Can Do to Reduce Problems." *Judicature* 72: 53–57.

Renzema, Marc, and Evan Mayo-Wilson. 2005. "Can Electronic Monitoring Reduce Crime for Moderate to High-Risk Offenders?" *Journal of Experimental Criminology* 1: 215–237.

Resick, Patricia. 1984. "The Trauma of Rape and the Criminal Justice System." *Justice System Journal* 9: 52–61.

Reskin, Barbara, and Christine Visher. 1986. "The Impacts of Evidence and Extralegal Factors in Jurors' Decisions." *Law and Society Review* 20: 423–439.

Resnik, Judith. 2006. "Whither and Whether Adjudication?" *Boston University Law Review* 86: 1101–1154.

Rhodes, William. 1978. *Plea Bargaining: Who Gains? Who Loses?* Washington, DC: Institute for Law and Social Research.

Ribovich, Donald J., and Anthony Martino. 2007. "Technology, Crime Control, and the Private Sector in the 21st Century." *In New Technology of Crime, Law and Social Control*, edited by James Michael Byrne and Donald J. Ribovich, pp. 49–79. Monsey, NY: Criminal Justice Press.

Richardson, Richard, and Kenneth Vines. 1970. *The Politics of Federal Courts*. Boston: Little, Brown.

Richmond, Todd. 2010. "Many States Closing Their Juvenile Jails." Associated Press, June 7.

Ridolfi, Kathleen, and Maurice Possley. 2010. "Preventable Error: A Report on Prosecutorial Misconduct in California, 1997–2009." Santa Clara, CA: Santa Clara University School of Law's Northern California Innocence Project. Available online at http://law.scu.edu/ncip/file/ProsecutorialMisconduct_BookEntire_online%20version.pdf.

Risinger, D. Michael, Mark P. Denbeaux, and Michael J. Saks. 1989. "Exorcism of Ignorance as a Proxy for Rational

Knowledge: The Lessons of Handwriting Identification 'Expertise.'" *University of Pennsylvania Law Review* 137(3): 731–792.

Roach, Michael. 2010. "Explaining the Outcome Gap between Different Types of Indigent Defense Counsel: Adverse Selection and Moral Hazard Effects." Available online at http://ssrn.com/abstract=1839651.

Roach-Anleu, Sharyn L. 2000. *Law and Social Change*. Thousand Oaks, CA: Sage.

Roberts, Paul Craig, and Lawrence M. Stratton. 2008. *The Tyranny of Good Intentions: How Prosecutors and Law Enforcement Are Trampling the Constitution in the Name of Justice*. New York: Three Rivers Press/Random House.

Robertson, Leon, Robert Rich, and H. Laurence Ross. 1973. "Jail Sentences for Driving While Intoxicated in Chicago: A Judicial Action That Failed." *Law and Society Review* 8: 55–68.

Robinson, Gwen. 2008. "Late-Modern Rehabilitation: The Evolution of a Penal Strategy." *Punishment and Society* 10: 429–445.

Robinson, Mike. 1996. "Abrasive, Erratic Judge Sidelined." *Times-Picayune*, October 12.

Roberts, John G., Jr. 2008. *Year-End Report on the Federal Judiciary*. Available online at http://www.supremecourt .gov/publicinfo/year-end/2008year-endreport.pdf.

Rodriguez, Nancy, Hilary Smith, and Marjorie Zatz. 2009. "'Youth Is Enmeshed in a Highly Dysfunctional Family System': Exploring the Relationship among Dysfunctional Families, Parental Incarceration, and Juvenile Court Decision Making." *Criminology* 47: 177–206.

Roesler, Richard. 2009. "Drivers Sue 19 Cities over Traffic Camera Fines." *Spokesman-Review*, June 24.

Roettger, Michael, and Raymond Swisher. 2011. "Association of Father's History of Incarceration with Sons' Delinquency and Arrest among Black, White and Hispanic Males in the United States." *Criminology* 49(4): 1109–1147.

Roper, Robert. 1979. "Jury Size: Impact on Verdict's Correctness." *American Politics Quarterly* 7: 438–452.

Roper, Robert, and Albert Melone. 1981. "Does Procedural Due Process Make a Difference? A Study of Second Trials." *Judicature* 65: 136–141.

Rosen, Ellen. 1987. "The Nation's Judges: No Unanimous Opinion." *Court Review* 24: 5.

Rosen, Richard A. "Reflections on Innocence." *Wisconsin Law Review* 2006: 237–290.

Rosencrance, John. 2004. "Maintaining the Myth of Individualized Justice: Probation Presentence Reports." In: George Cole, Mark Gertz, and Amy Bunger (Eds.). *The Criminal Justice System: Politics and Policies*. 9th ed. Belmont, CA: Wadsworth.

Rosenmerkel, Sean, Matthew Durose, & Donald Farole. *Felony Sentences in State Courts, 2006*. Washington, DC: Department of Justice, Bureau of Justice Statistics, 2010. Available online at http://bjs.ojp.usdoj.gov/content/pub/pdf/fssc06st.pdf.

Rosenthal, John. 2002. "Therapeutic Jurisprudence and Drug Treatment Courts: Integrating Law and Science." In: James Nolan (Ed.). *Drug Courts in Theory and Practice*. Hawthorne, NY: de Gruyter.

Rosett, Arthur, and Donald Cressey. 1976. *Justice by Consent: Plea Bargaining in the American Courthouse*. Philadelphia: Lippincott.

Rosoff, Stephen, Henry Pontell, and Robert Tillman. 2007. *Profit without Honor: White-Collar Crime and the Looting of America*. 4th ed. Upper Saddle River, NJ: Prentice Hall.

Ross, H. Laurence, and James Foley. 1987. "Judicial Disobedience of the Mandate to Imprison Drunk Drivers." *Law and Society Review* 21: 315–323.

Ross, H. Laurence. 1992. "The Law and Drunk Driving." *Law and Society Review* 26: 219–230.

Rossi, Peter, and Richard Berk. 1997. *Public Opinion on Sentencing Federal Crimes*. Washington, DC: United States Sentencing Commission.

Rothwax, Harold J. 1996. Guilty: *The Collapse of Criminal Justice*. New York: Random House.

Rottman, David, and Pamela Casey. 1999. "Therapeutic Jurisprudence and the Emergence of Problem-Solving Courts." *National Institute of Justice Journal* July: 12–19.

Rottman, David B., and Shauna M. Strickland. 2006. *State Court Organization, 2004*. Washington, DC: Bureau of Justice Statistics. Available online at http://bjs.ojp .usdoj.gov/content/pub/pdf/sco04.pdf.

Rowe, David C., and David P. Farrington. 1997. "The Familial Transmission of Criminal Convictions." *Criminology* 35: 177–201.

Rubenstein, Michael, and Teresa White. 1979. "Plea Bargaining: Can Alaska Live without It?" *Judicature* 62: 266–279.

Rubin, Alvin. 1976. "How We Can Improve Judicial Treatment of Individual Cases without Sacrificing Individual Rights: The Problems of the Criminal Law." *Federal Rules of Decisions* 70: 176.

Rubin, H. Ted. 1989. "The Juvenile Court Landscape." In: Albert Roberts (Eds.). *Juvenile Justice: Policies, Programs and Services*. Chicago: Irwin.

Ruckman, P. S. 1997. "Executive Clemency in the United States: Origins, Development, and Analysis (1900–1993)." *Presidential Studies Quarterly* 27: 251–271.

Rush, Christina, and Jeremy Robertson. 1987. "Presentence Reports: The Utility of Information to the Sentencing Decision." *Law and Human Behavior* 11: 147–155.

Russell, Brenda L., Debra L. Oswald, and Shane W. Kraus. 2011. "Evaluations of Sexual Assault: Perceptions of Guilt and Legal Elements for Male and Female Aggressors Using Various Coercive." *Violence & Victims* 26(6): 799–815.

Ryan, Joan. 2002. "Do We Count Strikes or Justice?" *San Francisco Chronicle*, November 5.

Ryan, John Paul, and James Alfini. 1979. "Trial Judges' Participation in Plea Bargaining: An Empirical Perspective." *Law and Society Review* 13: 479–507.

Saari, David. 1982. *American Court Management: Theories and Practice*. Westport, CT: Quorum Books.

Sahoo, Smita . 2006. "Exploring Transient Security: A Case Study of the Alachua County Courthouse Entrance Lobby in Gainesville, Florida." Master's Thesis, University of Florida, Gainesville.

Saks, Michael. 1996. "The Smaller the Jury, the Greater the Unpredictability." *Judicature* 79: 263–265.

Saks, Michael J., and Jonathan J. Koehler. 2005. "The Coming Paradigm Shift in Forensic Identification Science." *Science* 309: 892–895.

Saks, Michael J., and Mollie Weighner Marti. 1997. "A Meta-analysis of the Effects of Jury Size." *Law and Human Behavior* 21: 451–467.

Sanborn, Joseph. 1986. "A Historical Sketch of Plea Bargaining." *Justice Quarterly* 3: 111–138.

Sanborn, Joseph. 1993. "The Right to a Public Jury Trial: A Need for Today's Juvenile Court." *Judicature* 76: 230–238.

Sanborn, Joseph. 1994. "The Juvenile, the Court, or the Community: Whose Best Interests Are Currently Being Promoted in Juvenile Court?" *Justice System Journal* 17: 249–266.

Sarat, Austin, and Conor Clarke. 2008. "Beyond Discretion: Prosecution, the Logic of Sovereignty, and the Limits of Law." *Law and Social Inquiry* 33: 387–416.

Sarat, Austin, and William Felstiner. 1995. *Divorce Lawyers and Their Clients: Power and Meaning in the Legal Process*. New York: Oxford University Press.

Savage, David, and Maura Dolan. 2004. "New Media Struggle to Keep Ground Rules from Changing." *Los Angeles Times*, August 2.

Scheingold, Stuart, Toska Olson, and Jana Pershing. 1994. "Sexual Violence, Victim Advocacy, and Republican Criminology: Washington State's Community Protection Act." *Law and Society Review* 28: 729–763.

Schelling, Thomas. 1960. *The Strategy of Conflict*. Cambridge, MA: Harvard University Press.

Scherer, Nancy. 2005. *Scoring Points: Politicians, Political Activists and the Lower Federal Court Appointment Process*. Stanford, CA: Stanford University Press.

Scherer, Nancy, Brandon Bartels, and Amy Steigerwalt. 2008. "Sounding the Fire Alarm: The Role of Interest Groups in the Lower Federal Court Confirmation Process." *The Journal of Politics* 70: 1026–1039.

Schlanger, Margo. 2003. "Inmate Litigation." *Harvard Law Review* 116: 1555–1706.

Schlesinger, Traci. 2005. "Racial and Ethnic Disparity in Pretrial Criminal Processing." *Justice Quarterly* 22: 170–192.

Schmidt, Janell, and Lawrence Sherman. 1993. "Does Arrest Deter Domestic Violence?" *American Behavioral Scientist* 36: 601–615.

Schmidt, Janell, and Ellen H. Steury. 1989. "Prosecutorial Discretion in Filing Charges in Domestic Violence Cases." *Criminology* 27: 487–510.

Schmitt, Ben. 2006. "Embattled Judge, Facing Suspension, Calls It Quits." *Detroit Free Press*, June 1.

Schotland, Roy. 1998. "Comment." *Law and Contemporary Problems* 61: 149–150.

Schreck, Christopher, Eric Stewart, and D. Wayne Osgood. 2008. "A Reappraisal of the Overlap of Violent Offenders and Victims." *Criminology* 46: 871–906.

Schulhofer, Stephen. 1984. "Is Plea Bargaining Inevitable?" *Harvard Law Review* 97: 1037–1107.

Schultz, David. 2000. "No Joy in Mudville Tonight: The Impact of 'Three Strike' Laws. . . ." *Cornell Journal of Law and Public Policy* 9: 557.

Schwartz, Emma. 2007. "A Debt Hard to Collect: Only 7 Percent of Restitution Orders Get Paid." *U.S. News & World Report*, December 24, 143: 29.

Schwartz, Jennifer, Darrell Steffensmeier, Hua Zhong, and Jeff Ackerman. 2009. "Trends in the Gender Gap in Violence: Reevaluating NCVS and other Evidence." *Criminology* 47: 401–425.

Schwartz, John. 2009a. "As Jurors Turn to Google and Twitter, Mistrials Are Popping Up." *New York Times*, March 18.

Schwartz, John. 2009b. "Pinched Courts Push to Collect Fees and Fines." *New York Times*, April 7.

Schwartz, John. 2011. "Critics Say Budget Cuts for Courts Risk Rights." *New York Times*, November 26, p. A18.

Schwartz, Victor E., Mark A. Behrens, and Cary Silverman. 2003. *The Jury Patriotism Act: Making Jury Service More Appealing and Rewarding to Citizens*. Washington, DC: American Legislative Exchange Council.

Schweitzer, N. J., and Michael J. Saks. 2007. "The 'CSI-effect': Popular Fiction about Forensic Science Affects the Public's Expectations about Real Forensic Science." *Jurimetric*, 47: 357–364.

Scott, Kevin M. 2006. "Understanding Judicial Hierarchy: Reversals and the Behavior of Intermediate Appellate Judges." *Law and Society Review* 40: 163–191.

Scruggs, Anna, Jean-Claude Mazzola, and Mary Zaug. 1995. "Recent Voting Rights Act Challenges to Judicial Elections." *Judicature* 79: 34–41.

Secret, Mos. 2011. "States Prosecute Fewer Teenagers in Adult Courts." *New York Times*, March 5.

Segal, Jeffrey, and Harold Spaeth. 1989. "Decisional Trends on the Warren and Burger Courts: Results from the Supreme Court Data Base Project." *Judicature* 73: 103–107.

Segal, Jennifer. 2000. "Judicial Decision Making and the Impact of Election Year Rhetoric." *Judicature* 84: 26–33.

Serrano, Richard. 2006. "With Case Closed, Moussaoui Silenced." *Times-Picayune*, May 5.

Shaffer, Deborah Koetzle. 2006. *Reconsidering Drug Court Effectiveness: A Meta-Analytic Review*. Doctoral dissertation, University of Cincinnati, Cincinnati.

Shaffner, Laurie. 2006. *Girls in Trouble with the Law*. Piscataway, NJ: Rutgers University Press.

Shallwani, Pervaiz. 2012. "Hate-Crimes Conviction." *Wall Street Journal*, March 17, at A.17 (Greater New York edition).

Shaw, Michelle, and Kenneth Robinson. 1998. "Summary and Analysis of the First Juvenile Drug Court Evaluations:

The Santa Clara County Drug Treatment Court and the Delaware Juvenile Drug Court Diversion Program." *National Drug Court Institute Review* 1(1), 73–85.

Sheindlin, Judy. 1996. *Don't Pee on My Leg and Tell Me It's Raining: America's Toughest Family Court Judge Speaks Out*. New York: HarperCollins.

Sheindlin, Judy. 1999. *Beauty Fades, Dumb Is Forever*. New York: HarperCollins.

Sheindlin, Judy. 2000. *Keep It Simple, Stupid: You're Smarter Than You Look*. New York: Cliff Street Books/HarperCollins.

Sheindlin, Judy. 2000. *Win or Lose by How You Choose*. New York: HarperCollins.

Sheindlin, Judy. 2001. *You Can't Judge a Book by Its Cover: Cool Rules for School*. New York. HarperCollins.

Shelton, Donald E. 2008. "The 'CSI Effect': Does It Really Exist?" *National Institute of Justice Journal* 259. Available online at http://www.nij.gov/nij/journals/259/csi-effect .htm.

Shelton, Donald E., Young S. Kim, and Gregg Barak. 2009. "An Indirect-Effects Model of Mediated Adjudication: The CSI Myth, the Tech Effect, and Metropolitan Jurors' Expectations for Scientific Evidence." *Vanderbilt Journal of Entertainment and Technology Law* 12(1): 1–43. Available online at http://law.vanderbilt.edu/ publications/journal-entertainment-technology-law/ archive/index.aspx.

Shepherd, Robert E., Jr. 2003. "Still Seeking the Promise of Gault: Juveniles and the Right to Counsel." *Criminal Justice* 18: 22–27.

Shine, James, and Dwight Price. 1992. "Prosecutors and Juvenile Justice: New Roles and Perspectives." In: Ira Schwartz (Ed.). *Juvenile Justice and Public Policy: Toward a National Agenda*. New York: Lexington Books.

Shinnar, Shlomo, and Reuel Shinnar. 1975. "The Effects of the Criminal Justice System on the Control of Crime: A Quantitative Approach." *Law and Society Review* 9: 581–611.

Shoham, S. Giora, Ori Beck, and Martin Kett. 2007. *International Handbook of Penology and Criminal Justice*. Boca Raton, FL: CRC Press.

Sigall, Harold, & Nancy Ostrove. 1975. "Beautiful but Dangerous: Effects of Offender Attractiveness and Nature of the Crime on Juridic Judgment." *Journal of Personality and Social Psychology* 31(3): 410-414.

Silverstein, Lee. 1965. *Defense of the Poor*. Chicago: American Bar Foundation.

Sims, Barbara, Berwood Yost, and Christina Abbott. 2005. "Use and Nonuse of Victim Services Programs: Implications from a Statewide Survey of Crime Victims." *Criminology and Public Policy* 4: 361–384.

Sinclair, J. Walter, Mark A. Behrens, and Cary Silverman. 2003. "Making Jury Duty a Little Friendlier." *Advocate* 46: 23–26.

Sisk, Gregory C., Michael F. Noone, John Montague Steadman, and Urban A. Lester. 2006. *Litigation with the Federal Government*. 4th ed. Chicago: ALI-ABA.

Sitomer, Curtis. 1985. "Rural Justice Affects Many, but May Serve Few." *Christian Science Monitor*, May 28, p. 23.

Skogan, Wesley, and Mary Ann Wycoff. 1987. "Some Unexpected Effects of a Police Service for Victims." *Crime and Delinquency* 33: 490–501.

Skolnick, Jerome. 1967. "Social Control in the Adversary System." *Journal of Conflict Resolution* 11: 52–70.

Skolnick, Jerome. 1993. *Justice without Trial*. 3rd ed. New York: Macmillan.

Skolnick, Jerome H., and James J. Fyfe. 1993. *Above the Law: Police and the Excessive Use of Force*. New York: Free Press.

Slobogin, Christopher. 1998. *Criminal Procedure: Regulation of Police Investigation*, Charlottesville, VA: Lexis.

Slocum, R.W. 2009. "The Dilemma of the Vengeful Client: A Prescriptive Framework for Cooling the Flames of Anger." *Marquette Law Review*, 92: 481–549.

Smith, Alisa, and Michael J. Saks. 2008. "The Case for Overturning *Williams v. Florida* and the Six-Person Jury: History, Law, and Empirical Evidence." *Florida Law Review* 60: 441–470.

Smith, Brent, and C. Ronald Huff. 1992. "From Victim to Political Activist: An Empirical Examination of a Statewide Victims' Rights Movement." *Journal of Criminal Justice* 20: 201–215.

Smith, Christopher. 1995. "Federal Habeas Corpus Reform: The State's Perspective." *Justice System Journal* 18: 1–11.

Smith, Douglas. 1986. "The Plea Bargaining Controversy." *Journal of Criminal Law and Criminology* 77: 949–957.

Smith, Nancy, and Julie Garmel. 1992. "Judicial Election and Selection Procedures Challenged under the Voting Rights Act." *Judicature* 76: 154–155.

Smith, S. F. 2008. "The Supreme Court and the Politics of Death." *Virginia Law Review* 94: 283–383.

Smith-Spark, Laura. 2011. "Strauss-Kahn Case: What Next for Accuser and Accused?" *CNN World News*, August 24. Available online at http://articles.cnn.com/2011-08-24/ world/us.france.dsk.case_1_tristane-banon-strauss- kahn-case-martine-aubry?_s=PM:WORLD.

Smitts, Todd. 2004. "Plot Summary for *Boston Legal.*" *Internet Movie Database*. Available online at http://www .imdb.com/title/tt0402711/plotsummary.

Snyder, Howard, and Melissa Sickmund. 2006. *Juvenile Offenders and Victims: 2006 National Report*. Washington, DC: Department of Justice, Office of Juvenile Justice and Delinquency Prevention.

Sobel, Russell S., and Joshua C. Hall. 2007. "The Effect of Judicial Selection Processes on Judicial Quality: The Role of Partisan Politics." *Cato Journal* 27: 69–82.

Solberg, Rorie Spill. 2005. "Diversity and George W. Bush's Judicial Appointments: Serving Two Masters." *Judicature* 88: 276–283.

Sommer, Udi, and Quan Li. 2011. "Judicial Decision Making in Times of Financial Crises." *Judicature* 95: 68–77.

Sommers, Samuel. 2007. "Race and the Decision Making of Juries." *Legal and Criminological Psychology* 12: 171–187.

Songer, Donald. 1990. "Criteria for Publication of Opinions in the U.S. Courts of Appeals: Formal Rules versus Empirical Reality." *Judicature* 73: 307–313.

Sorensen, Jon, and Donald Wallace. 1999. "Prosecutorial Discretion in Seeking Death: An Analysis of Racial Disparity in the Pretrial Stages of Case Processing in a Midwestern County." *Justice Quarterly* 16: 559–578.

Sosin, Michael. "Parens Patriae and Dispositions in Juvenile Courts." Madison, WI: Institute for Research on Poverty.

Spangenberg Group. 2000. *Contracting for Indigent Defense Services: A Special Report*. Washington, DC: Bureau of Justice Statistics.

Spangenberg, Robert, and Marea Beeman 1995. "Indigent Defense Systems in the United States." *Law and Contemporary Problems* 58: 31–50.

Spangenberg, Robert, Richard Wilson, Patricia Smith, and Beverly Lee. 1986. *Containing the Cost of Indigent Defense Programs: Eligibility Screening and Cost Recovery Procedures*. Washington, DC: Department of Justice, National Institute of Justice.

Spears, Jeffrey, and Cassia Spohn. 1997. "The Effect of Evidence Factors and Victim Characteristics on Prosecutors' Charging Decisions in Sexual Assault Cases." *Justice Quarterly* 14: 501–524.

Spelman, William. 2000. "What Recent Studies Do (and Don't) Tell Us about Imprisonment and Crime. *Crime and Justice* 27: 419–494.

Spelman, William. 2009. "Crime, Cash, and Limited Options: Explaining the Prison Boom." *Criminology and Public Policy* 8: 29–77.

Spiecker Shelley C., and Debra L. Worthington. 2003. "The Influence of Opening Statement/Closing Argument Organizational Strategy on Juror Verdict and Damage Awards." *Law and Human Behavior* 27: 437–456.

Spill, Rorie, and Kathleen Bratton. 2001. "Clinton and Diversification of the Federal Judiciary." *Judicature* 84: 256–261.

Spohn, Cassia C. 2009. *How Do Judges Decide?* (2nd ed.). Thousand Oaks, CA: Sage.

Spohn, Cassia, Dawn Beichner, Erika Davis Frenzel, and David Holleran. 2002. *Prosecutors' Charging Decisions in Sexual Assault Cases: A Multi-Site Study, Final Report to the National Institute of Justice*. Available online at https://www.ncjrs.gov/pdffiles1/nij/grants/197048.pdf

Spohn, Cassia, and Jerry Cederblom. 1991. "Race and Disparities in Sentencing: A Test of the Liberation Hypothesis." *Justice Quarterly* 8: 305–328.

Spohn, Cassia, and Miriam DeLone. 2000. "When Does Race Matter? An Analysis of the Conditions under Which Race Affects Sentence Severity." *Sociology of Crime, Law and Deviance* 2: 3–37.

Spohn, Cassia, John Gruhl, and Susan Welch. 1987. "The Impact of the Ethnicity and Gender of Defendants on the Decision to Reject or Dismiss Felony Charges." *Criminology* 25: 175–191.

Spohn, Cassia, and David Holleran. 2000. "The Imprisonment Penalty Paid by Young, Unemployed Black and Hispanic Male Offenders." *Criminology* 38: 281–307.

Spohn, Cassia, and Jeffrey Spears. 1996. "The Effect of Offender and Victim Characteristics on Sexual Assault Case Processing Decisions." *Justice Quarterly* 13: 649–679.

Springer, Charles. 1986. *Justice for Juveniles*. Washington, DC: Office of Juvenile Justice and Delinquency Prevention.

Springer, J. Fred. 1983. "Burglary and Robbery Plea Bargaining in California: An Organizational Perspective." *Justice System Journal* 8: 157–185.

Springer, D. W., & A. R. Roberts (Eds.), *Handbook of Forensic Mental Health With Victims and Offenders: Assessment, Treatment, and Research*. New York: Springer.

Stanko, Elizabeth. 1981. "The Arrest versus the Case." *Urban Life* 9: 295–414.

Stanko, Elizabeth. 1981–1982. "The Impact of Victim Assessment on Prosecutors' Screening Decisions: The Case of the New York County District Attorney's Office." *Law and Society Review* 16: 225–239.

Stanko, Elizabeth. 1988. "The Impact of Victim Assessment on Prosecutor's Screening Decisions: The Case of the New York County District Attorney's Office." In: G. Cole (Ed.), *Criminal Justice: Law and Politics*. Pacific Grove, CA: Brooks-Cole.

Staples, William G., and Stephanie K. Decker. 2010. "Between the 'Home' and 'Institutional' Worlds: Tensions and Contradictions in the Practice of House Arrest." *Critical Criminology* 18: 1–20.

Statistical Briefing Book. 2009. "Juvenile Arrests Rates for All Crimes, 1980-2007." Washington, DC: Office of Juvenile Justice and Delinquency Prevention.

Steadman Henry J, Fred C. Osher, Pamela Clark Robbins, Brian Case, and Steven Samuels. 2009. "Prevalence of Serious Mental Illness among Jail Inmates." *Psychiatric Services* 60(6): 761–765.

Stashenko, Joel. 2012. "Commission Backs Removal of Justice in Last Days of Term." *New York Law Journal*, February 14.

Steele, Walter, and Elizabeth Thornburg. 1991. "Jury Instructions: A Persistent Failure to Communicate." *Judicature* 74: 249–254.

Steelman, David C. 1997. "What Have We Learned About Court Delay, 'Local Legal Culture,' and Caseflow Management Since the Late 1970s?" *Justice Systems Journal* 19: 145–161.

Steen, Sara, and Rachel Bandy. 2007. "When the Policy Becomes the Problem: Criminal Justice in the New Millennium." *Punishment & Society* 9: 5–26.

Steffensmeier, Darrell, and Chris Hebert. 1999. "Women and Men Policymakers: Does the Judge's Gender Affect the Sentencing of Criminal Defendants?" *Social Forces* 77: 1163.

Steffensmeier, Darrell, John Kramer, and Cathy Streifel. 1993. "Gender and Imprisonment Decisions." *Criminology* 31: 411–446.

Steffensmeier, Darrell, Jeffrey Ulmer, and John Kramer. 1998. "The Interaction of Race, Gender, and Age in

Criminal Sentencing: The Punishment Cost of Being Young, Black, and Male." *Criminology* 36: 763–798.

Steigerwalt, Amy. 2010. *Battle over the Bench: Senators, Interest Groups, and Lower Court Confirmations*. Charlottesville: University of Virginia Press.

Steinberger, Barbara. 1985. "*Alford* Doctrine Popular in State's Courts." *New Haven Register*, June 9.

Steiner, Benjamin. 2009. "The Effects of Juvenile Transfer to Criminal Courts on Incarceration Decisions." *Justice Quarterly* 26: 77–106.

Steketee, Gail, and Anne Austin. 1989. "Rape Victims and the Justice System: Utilization and Impact." *Social Service Review* 63: 285–303.

Stemen, Don, & Andres F. Rengifo. 2011. "Policies and Imprisonment: The Impact of Structured Sentencing and Determinate Sentencing on State Incarceration Rates, 1978–2004." *Justice Quarterly*, 28(1): 174–201.

Stern, Andrew. 2000. "Illinois Governor Halts Executions Pending Review." Reuters, January 23.

Sternlight, Jean R., and Jennifer Robbennolt. 2008. "Good Lawyers Should Be Good Psychologists: Insights for Interviewing and Counseling Clients." *Ohio State Journal on Dispute Resolution* 23: 437–548.

Stevens, Mark. 2000. "Victim Impact Statements Considered in Sentencing: Constitutional Concerns." *California Criminal Law Review*, 3. Available online at http://www.boalt.org/CCLR/v2/v2stevensnf.htm.

Stidham, Ronald, and Robert Carp. 1997. "Judges' Gender and Federal District Court Decisions." Paper presented at the Southwestern Political Science Association, New Orleans.

Stith, Kate. 2008. "The Arc of the Pendulum: Judges, Prosecutors, and the Exercise of Discretion." *Yale Law Journal* 117: 1420–1496.

Stith, Kate, and Jose Cabranes. 1998. *Fear of Judging: Sentencing Guidelines in the Federal Courts*. Chicago: University of Chicago Press.

Stogel, Christopher. "Note, *Smith v. Robbins*: Appointed Criminal Appellate Counsel Should Watch for the *Wende* in their Hair." *Southwestern University Law Review* 31: 281–304.

Stott, E. Keith. 1982. "The Judicial Executive: Toward Greater Congruence in an Emerging Profession." *Justice System Journal* 7: 152–179.

Stout, David. 2007. "Crack Sentences Will Get Review." *New York Times*, December 12.

Straus, Sarena. 2006. *Bronx D.A.: True Stories from the Sex Crimes and Domestic Violence Unit*. Fort Lee, NJ: Barricade Books.

Strawn, David, and Raymond Buchanan. 1976. "Jury Confusion: A Threat to Justice." *Judicature* 59: 478–483.

Streb, Matthew J. 2007. *Running for Judge: The Rising Political, Financial, and Legal Stakes of Judicial Elections*. New York: New York University Press.

Streb, Matthew, Brian Frederick, and Casey Lafrance. 2007. "Contestation, Competition, and Potential for Accountability in Intermediate Appellate Court Elections." *Judicature* 91: 71–78.

Studebaker, Christina A., and Steven D. Penrod. 2007. "Pretrial Publicity and Its Influence on Juror Decision Making." In: Neil Brewer and Kipling D. Williams (Ed.). *Psychology and Law: An Empirical Perspective*. New York: Guildford Press.

Sudnow, David. 1965. "Normal Crimes: Sociological Features of the Penal Codes in a Public Defender Office." *Social Problems* 12: 254–264.

Sullivan, Thomas. 2004. "Police Experiences with Recording Custodial Interrogations." *Judicature* 38: 132–136.

Surette, Ray. 1996. "News from Nowhere, Policy to Follow: Media and the Social Construction of 'Three Strikes and You're Out.'" In: David Shichor and Dale Sechrest (Eds.). *Three Strikes and You're Out: Vengeance as Public Policy,*. Thousand Oaks, CA: Sage.

Surette, Ray. 2010. *Media, Crime, and Criminal Justice: Images and Realities* (4th ed.). Belmont, CA: Wadsworth, Cengage.

Taggart, William. 1989. "Redefining the Power of the Federal Judiciary: The Impact of Court-Ordered Prison Reform on State Expenditures for Corrections." *Law and Society Review* 23: 241–272.

Tarr, G. Alan. 1982. "State Supreme Courts and the U.S. Supreme Court: The Problem of Compliance." In: Mary Cornelia Porter and G. Alan Tarr (Eds.). *State Supreme Courts: Policymakers in the Federal System*. Westport, CT: Greenwood.

Tarr, G. Alan, and Mary Cornelia Porter. 1988. *State Supreme Courts in State and Nation*. New Haven, CT: Yale University Press.

Tavernise, Sabrina. 2012. "Mine Superintendent Charged in 2010 Disaster." *New York Times*, February 22.

Taylor, Clifford W. 2009. "Merit Selection: Choosing Judges Based on their Politics under the Veil of a Disarming Name." *Harvard Journal of Law and Public Policy* 32: 97–101.

TerBeek, Calvin. 2007. "A Call for Precedential Heads: Why the Supreme Court's Eyewitness Identification Jurisprudence Is Anachronistic and Out-of-Step with the Empirical Reality." *Law and Psychology Review* 31: 21–51.

Thaler, Paul. 1994. *The Watchful Eye: American Justice in the Age of the Television Trial*. Westport, CT: Praeger.

Thompson, Kevin. 1996. "The Nature and Scope of Rural Crime." In: Thomas McDonald, Robert Wood, and Melissa Pflug (Eds.). *Rural Criminal Justice: Conditions, Constraints, and Challenges* (pp. 3–18). Salem, WI: Sheffield.

Thompson, Timothy D. 2010-2011. "Non-Prisoner Pro Se Litigation in the United States District Court for the Eastern District of Kentucky: Analyzing 2004 and 2007 Cases from Filing to Termination." *Kentucky Law Journal* 99(3): 601–635.

Thompson, William C. 2006. "Tarnish on the 'Gold Standard': Recent Problems in Forensic DNA Testing." *The Champion* 30: 10–16.

Thomson, Douglas, and Anthony Ragona. 1987. "Popular Moderation versus Governmental Authoritarianism: An

Interactionist View of Public Sentiments toward Criminal Sanctions." *Crime and Delinquency* 33: 337–357.

Tiede, Lydia. 2009. "The Impact of the Federal Sentencing Guidelines and Reform: A Comparative Analysis." *Justice System Journal* 30: 34–49.

Tjaden, Patricia, and Nancy Thoennes. 2006. *Extent, Nature, and Consequences of Rape Victimization: Findings from the National Violence Against Women Survey*. Washington, DC: National Institute of Justice.

Tobolowsky, Peggy. 1993. "Restitution in the Federal Criminal Justice System." *Judicature* 77: 90–95.

Tonry, Michael. H. 1987. *Sentencing Reform Impacts*. Washington, DC: Government Printing Office.

Tonry, Michael. H. 1993. "The Failure of the U.S. Sentencing Commission's Guidelines." *Crime and Delinquency* 39: 131–149.

Tonry, Michael. H. 2004. *Thinking about Crime: Sense and Sensibility in American Penal Culture*. New York: Oxford University Press.

Torbet, Patricia, Patrick Griffin, Hunter Hurst, and Lynn MacKenzie. 2000. *Juveniles Facing Criminal Sanctions: Three States That Changed the Rules*. Washington, DC: Department of Justice, Office of Juvenile Justice and Delinquency Prevention.

Torpy, Bill, and Bill Rankin. 2010. "Off the Bench, In Disgrace." *The Atlanta Journal-Constitution*, August 22.

Torres, Sam, and Elizabeth Piper Deschenes. 1997. "Changing the System and Making It Work: The Process of Implementing Drug Courts in Los Angeles County." *Justice System Journal* 19: 267–290.

Toutant, Charles. 2006. "Censure, Transfer in Store for Judge Who Drove Drunk." *New Jersey Law Journal*, July 24.

Tracy, Paul E., Marvin E. Wolfgang, & Robert M. Figlio. 1990. *Delinquency Careers in Two Birth Cohorts*. New York: Plenum.

Travis, Jeremy. 2005. *But They All Come Back: Facing the Challenges of Prisoner Reentry*. Washington, DC: Urban Institute Press.

Truman, Jennifer L. 2011. *Criminal Victimization, 2010*. Washington, DC: Bureau of Justice Statistics.

Trupin Eric, and Henry Richards. 2003. "Seattle's Mental Health Courts: Early Indicators of Effectiveness." *International Journal of Law and Psychiatry* 26(1): 33–53.

Turley, Jonathan. 2012. "Huguely's Failure to Speak." *USA Today*, February 29.

Turner, Susan, and Judith Greene. 1999. "The FARE Probation Experiment: Implementation and Outcomes of Day Fines for Felony Offenders in Maricopa County." *Justice System Journal* 21: 1–21.

Turner, Susan, Peter W. Greenwood, Terry Fain, and James R. Chiesa. 2006. "An Evaluation of the Federal Government's Violent Offender Incarceration and Truth-in-Sentencing Incentive Grants." *Prison Journal* 86: 364–385.

Twain, Mark. 1913. *Roughing It* (Vol. 2). New York: Harper & Brothers.

Tyler, Tom R. 2006. "Viewing CSI and the Threshold of Guilt: Managing Truth and Justice in Reality and Fiction." *Yale Law Journal* 115: 1050–1085.

U.S. Census Bureau. 2011. "The Hispanic Population: 2010." Available online at www.census.gov/prod/cen2010/briefs/c2010br-04.pdf.

U.S. Department of Justice. 2002. Searching and Seizing Computers and Obtaining Electronic Evidence in Criminal Investigations. Washington, DC: Author.

U.S. General Accounting Office. 1990. "Death Penalty Sentencing: Research Indicated a Pattern of Racial Disparities." Gaithersburg, MD: Author. Available online at http://archive.gao.gov/t2pbat11/140845.pdf.

U.S. Government Accountability Office. 2005. *Adult Drug Courts: Evidence Indicates Recidivism Reductions and Mixed Results for Other Outcomes*. Available online at: http://www.gao.gov/new.items/d05219.pdf.

U.S. Joint Service Committee on Military Justice. 2008. *Manual for Courts-Martial-United States*. Available online at http://www.dod.gov/dodgc/images/mcm2008.pdf.

U.S. Senate Judiciary Committee. 1993. *The Response to Rape: Detours on the Road to Equal Justice*. Washington, DC: Author.

U.S. Sentencing Commission. 2003. *Federal Sentencing Statistics by State, District and Circuit*. Available online at http://www.ussc.gov/Data_and_Statistics/Federal_Sentencing_Statistics/State_District_Circuit/index.cfm.

Uchida, Craig, and Timothy Bynum. 1991. "Search Warrants, Motions to Suppress and 'Lost Cases': The Effects of the Exclusionary Rule in Seven Jurisdictions." *Journal of Criminal Law and Criminology* 81: 1034–1066.

Uhlman, Thomas, and Darlene Walker. 1980. "'He Takes Some of My Time: I Take Some of His': An Analysis of Judicial Sentencing Patterns in Jury Cases." *Law and Society Review* 14: 323–342.

Ulmer, Jeffrey. 1997. *Social Worlds of Sentencing: Court Communities under Sentencing Guidelines*. Albany: State University of New York Press.

Ulmer, Jeffery T. 2012. "Recent Developments and New Directions in Sentencing Research." *Justice Quarterly* 29(1): 1-40.

Ulmer, Jeffrey, and Mindy Bradley. 2006. "Variations in Trial Penalties among Serious Violent Offenses." *Criminology* 44: 631–658.

Ulmer, Jeffery, James Eisenstein, and Brian Johnson. 2010. "Trial Penalties in Federal Sentencing: Extra-Guidelines Factors and District Variation." *Justice Quarterly* 27: 560–592.

Ulmer, Jeffery and Brian D. Johnson. 2004. "Sentencing in Context: A Multilevel Analysis." *Criminology* 42: 137–177.

Ulmer, Jeffrey T., Megan C. Kurlychek, and John H. Kramer. 2007. "Prosecutorial Discretion and the Imposition of Mandatory Minimum Sentences." *Journal of Research in Crime and Delinquency* 44: 427–458.

Ulmer, Jeffery T., Michael T. Light & John Kramer. 2011. "The 'Liberation' of Federal Judges' Discretion in the Wake of the Booker/Fanfan Decision: Is There Increased Disparity and Divergence between Courts?" *Justice Quarterly* 28(6): 799–837.

Underwood, James. M. 2006."The Late, Great Diversity Jurisdiction."*Case Western Reserve Law Review*, 57, 179–222.

Unnever, James. 2008."Two Worlds Far Apart: Black-White Differences in Beliefs about Why African-American Men Are Disproportionately Imprisoned." *Criminology* 46: 511–538.

Uphoff, R. 2006."Convicting the Innocent: Aberration or Systemic Problem?"*Wisconsin Law Review* 2006: 739–842.

Utz, Pamela. 1979. "Two Models of Prosecutorial Professionalism."In: William McDonald (Ed.). *The Prosecutor.* CA: Sage.

Van Duizend, Richard, David Steelman and Lee Suskin. 2011. *Model Time Standards for State Trial Courts.* Williamsburg, VA.: National Center for State Courts.

Van Duizend, Richard, L. Paul Sutton, and Charlotte Carter. 1984. *The Search Warrant Process.* Williamsburg, VA: National Center for State Courts.

van Dyke, Jon. 1977. *Jury Selection Procedures: Our Uncertain Commitment to Representative Panels.* Cambridge, MA: Ballinger.

von Hirsch, Andrew. 1976. *Doing Justice: The Choice of Punishment.* New York: Hill and Wang.

Van Ness, Daniel, and Karen Heetderks Strong. 2006. *Restoring Justice.* 3rd ed. Cincinnati: Anderson.

Vaughn, Michael G., and Matt DeLisi. 2008. "Were Wolfgang's Chronic Offenders Psychopaths? On the Convergent Validity between Psychopathy and Career Criminality."*Journal of Criminal Justice* 36: 33–42.

Vera Institute of Justice. 1977. *Felony Arrests: Their Prosecution and Disposition in New York City's Courts.* New York: Author.

Vera Institute of Justice. 1981. *Felony Arrests: Their Prosecution and Disposition in New York City's Courts.* Rev. ed. New York: Longman.

Vermont Center for Justice Research. 1995."DUI Adjudication and BAC Level: An Assessment."*DataLine: The Justice Research Bulletin* 4 (May).

Viano, Emilio. 1987."Victim's Rights and the Constitution: Reflections on a Bicentennial." *Crime and Delinquency* 33: 438–451.

Villmoare, Edwin, and Virginia N. Neto. 1987. "Executive Summary, Victim Appearances at Sentencing Hearings under the California Victims' Bill of Rights."Washington, DC: National Institute of Justice, Department of Justice.

Vincent, Barbara, and Paul Hofer. 1994. *The Consequences of Mandatory Minimum Prison Terms: A Summary of Recent Findings.* Washington, DC: Federal Judicial Center.

Visher, Christy. 1987. "Incapacitation and Crime Control: Does a 'Lock 'Em Up' Strategy Reduce Crime?" *Justice Quarterly* 4: 513–544.

Visher, Christy, Adele Harrell, Lisa Newmark, and Jennifer Yahner. 2008. "Reducing Intimate Partner Violence: An Evaluation of a Comprehensive Justice System-Community Collaboration." *Criminology and Public Policy* 7: 495–524.

Voss, Jansen. 2005."The Science of Persuasion: An Exploration of Advocacy and the Science Behind the Art of Persuasion in the Courtroom."*Law and Psychology Review* 29: 301–327.

Wald, Matthew. 2006."A New Strategy to Discourage Driving Drunk."*New York Times,* November 19.

Waldron, Jeremy. 2008."Lucky in Your Judge."*Theoretical Inquiries in Law* 9: 185–216.

Walker, Samuel. 2011. *Sense and Nonsense about Crime and Drugs: A Policy Guide.* 7th ed. Belmont, CA: Wadsworth.

Walker, Samuel, Cassia Spohn, and Miriam DeLone. 2007. *The Color of Justice: Race, Ethnicity, and Crime in America.* 4th ed. Belmont, CA: Wadsworth.

Waller, Mark. 2008."Officials Say Jefferson's Traffic Cameras Increase Safety, but Critics Say the Red-Light System Is All about Seeing Green."*Times-Picayune,* December 10.

Wallman, Joel. 2005. "Unpacking Recidivism." *Criminology and Public Policy* 4: 479–484.

Walsh, Anthony. 1985."The Role of the Probation Officer in the Sentencing Process." *Criminal Justice and Behavior* 12: 289–303.

Walsh, Anthony. 1987."The Sexual Stratification Hypothesis and Sexual Assault in Light of the Changing Conceptions of Race."*Criminology* 25: 153–173.

Walsh, Colleen. 2010. "Film Explores Military Tribunal." *Harvard Gazette,* May 6. Available online at http://news .harvard.edu/gazette/story/2010/05/film-explores-military-tribunal.

Ward, Geoff, Amy Farrell, and Danielle Rousseau. 2009 "Does Racial Balance in Workforce Representation Yield Equal Justice? Race Relations of Sentencing in Federal Court Organizations."*Law & Society Review* 43(4): 757–806.

Warden, Rob. 2004. *The Snitch System: How Snitch Testimony Sent Randy Steidl and Other Innocent Americans to Death Row.* Chicago: Northwestern University School of Law, Center on Wrongful Convictions.

Warren, Roger K. 2009. "Evidence-Based Sentencing: The Application of Principles of Evidence-Based Practice to State Sentencing Practice and Policy." *University of San Francisco Law Review* 43: 585–634.

Wasby, Stephen. 1982. "The Functions and Importance of Appellate Oral Argument: Some Views of Lawyers and Federal Judges."*Judicature* 65: 340–353.

Washburn, Kevin K. 2008."Restoring the Grand Jury."*Fordham Law Review* 76: 2333–2388.

Watkins, Matthew. 2009. "Screening Stirs Community." (March 17). Available online at http://www.theeagle .com/local/Screening-stirs-community

Watson, Richard, and Ronald Downing. 1969. *The Politics of the Bench and Bar: Judicial Selection under the Missouri Nonpartisan Court Plan.* New York: Wiley.

Webster, Barbara. 1988. *Victim Assistance Programs Report Increased Workloads.* Washington, DC: National Institute of Justice.

Webster, Cheryl, Anthony Doob, and Franklin Zimring. 2006. "Proposition 8 and Crime Rates in California: The Case of the Disappearing Deterrent." *Criminology and Public Policy* 5: 417–448.

Weed, Frank. 1995. *Certainty of Justice: Reform in the Crime Victim Movement*. New York: Aldine de Gruyter.

Weis, Joseph F. et al. *1990. Report of the Federal Courts Study Committee*. Washington, DC: Federal Judicial Center. Available online at http://www.fjc.gov/public/pdf.nsf/lookup/repfcsc.pdf/$file/repfcsc.pdf.

Weisheit, Ralph, David Falcone, and L. Edward Wells. 2006. *Crime and Policing in Rural and Small-Town America*. Long Grove, IL: Waveland Press.

Weisheit, Ralph, and Sue Mahan. 1988. *Women, Crime and Criminal Justice*. Cincinnati: Anderson.

Weiss, Michael. 2005. *Public Defenders: Pragmatic and Political Motivations to Represent the Indigent*. New York: LFB Scholarly.

Weiss, Robert, Richard Berk, and Catherine Lee. 1996. "Assessing the Capriciousness of Death Penalty Charging." *Law and Society Review* 30: 607–638.

Welch, Susan, and Cassia Spohn. 1986. "Evaluating the Impact of Prior Record on Judges' Sentencing Decisions: A Seven-City Comparison." *Justice Quarterly* 3: 389–408.

Welch, Susan, Cassia Spohn, and John Gruhl. 1985. "Convicting and Sentencing Differences among Black, Hispanic and White Males in Six Localities." *Justice Quarterly* 2: 67–80.

Wells, Gary. L., & Deah S. Quinlivan. 2009. "Suggestive Eyewitness Identification Procedures and the Supreme Court's Reliability Test in Light of Eyewitness Science: 30 Years Later." *Law and Human Behavior* 33(1):1–24.

Wexler, David B., and Bruce J. Winick (Eds.). 1996. *Law in a Therapeutic Key: Developments in Therapeutic Jurisprudence*. Durham, NC: Carolina Academic Press.

Wheeler, Russell. 2012. *Judicial Nominations and Confirmations after Three Years—Where Do Things Stand?* Washington, DC: Brookings Institute.

Wheelock, Darren. 2005. "Collateral Consequences and Racial Inequality: Felon Status Restrictions as a System of Disadvantage." *Journal of Contemporary Criminal Justice* 21: 82–90.

White, John Valery. 2008. "A Time for Change." *Nevada Lawyer* 16: 38.

Wice, Paul. 1978. *Criminal Lawyers: An Endangered Species*. Newbury Park, CA: Sage.

Wice, Paul. 1991. *Judges and Lawyers: The Human Side of Justice*. New York: HarperCollins.

Wice, Paul. 2005. *Public Defenders and the American Justice System*. Westport, CT: Praeger.

Wickersham Commission. 1931. National Commission on Law Observance and Enforcement, Publication no. 11, Report on Lawlessness in Law Enforcement.

Wilkey, Malcolm. 1978. "The Exclusionary Rule: Why Suppress Valid Evidence?" *Judicature* 62: 214–232.

Wilkins, David. 2012. "Some Realism about Legal Realism for Lawyers: Assessing the Role of Context In Legal Ethics." In: Leslie Levin and Lynn Mather (Eds.). *Lawyers in Practice: Ethical Decision Making in Context*. Chicago: University of Chicago Press.

Williams, Frank V. 2007. "Reinventing the Courts: The Frontiers of Judicial Activism in the State Courts." *Campbell Law Review* 29: 591–735.

Williams, Jimmy. 1995. "Type of Counsel and the Outcome of Criminal Appeals: A Research Note." *American Journal of Criminal Justice* 19: 275–285.

Williams, Marian, Stephen Demuth, and Jefferson Holcomb. 2007. "Understanding the Influence of Victim Gender in Death Penalty Cases: The Importance of Victim Race, Sex-Related Victimization, and Jury Decision Making." *Criminology* 45: 865–891.

Willing, Richard. 2003. "Judges Go Softer on Sentences More Often." *USA Today*, August 28, p. 1.

Wilmot, Keith Alan, and Cassia Spohn. 2004. "Prosecutorial Discretion and Real-Offense Sentencing: An Analysis of Relevant Conduct under the Federal Sentencing Guidelines." *Criminal Justice Policy Review* 15: 324–343.

Wilson, James. 2005. "Bad Behavior or Bad Policy? An Examination of Tennessee Release Cohorts, 1993–2001." *Criminology and Public Policy* 4: 485–518.

Wilson, James Q. 1973. "If Every Criminal Knew He Would Be Punished if Caught." *New York Times Magazine*, January 28.

Wilson, James Q. 1975. *Thinking about Crime*. New York: Basic.

Wilson, James Q. 1983. *Thinking about Crime: A Policy Guide*. 2nd ed. New York: Basic Books.

Wiseman, Jacqueline. 1970. *Stations of the Lost: The Treatment of Skid Row Alcoholics*. Englewood Cliffs, NJ: Prentice Hall.

Wold, John. 1978. "Going through the Motions: The Monotony of Appellate Court Decisionmaking." *Judicature* 62: 58–65.

Wold, John, and Greg Caldeira. 1980. "Perceptions of 'Routine' Decision-Making in Five California Courts of Appeal." *Polity* 13: 334–347.

Wolf, Robert V. 2007. *Principles of Problem-Solving Justice*. New York: Center for Court Innovation.

Wolfgang, Marvin E., Robert M. Figlio, and Thorsten Sellin. 1972. *Delinquency in a Birth Cohort*. Chicago: University of Chicago Press.

Wolfgang, Marvin, and Marc Riedel. 1973. "Race, Judicial Discretion, and the Death Penalty." *Annals of the American Academy of Political and Social Science* 407: 119–133.

Wolfram, Charles. 1986. *Modern Legal Ethics*. St. Paul, MN: Thomson/West.

Wooldredge, John. 2012. "Distinguishing Race Effects on Pre-Trial Release and Sentencing Decisions." *Justice Quarterly* 29(1): 41–75.

Wooldredge, John, and Amy Thistlethwaite. 2004. "Bilevel Disparities in Court Dispositions for Intimate Assault." *Criminology* 42: 417–456.

Worden, Alissa Pollitz. 1990. "Policymaking by Prosecutors: The Uses of Discretion in Regulating Plea Bargaining." *Judicature* 73: 335–340.

Worden, Alissa Pollitz. 1991. "Privatizing Due Process: Issues in the Comparison of Assigned Counsel, Public Defender, and Contracted Indigent Defense Systems." *Justice System Journal* 14: 390–418.

Worden, Alissa Pollitz. 1993. "Counsel for the Poor: An Evaluation of Contracting for Indigent Criminal Defense." *Justice Quarterly* 10: 613–637.

Worden, Alissa Pollitz. 2008. "Courts and Communities: Toward a Theoretical Synthesis." In: David Duffee and Edward R. Maguire (Eds.). *Criminal Justice Theory* (pp. 181–222). New York: Routledge.

Worden, Alissa Pollitz, and Robert Worden. 1989. "Local Politics and the Provision of Indigent Defense Counsel." *Law and Policy* 11: 401–424.

Worrall, John L. 2008. "Asset Forfeiture." *Problem-Oriented Guides for Policy Response Guides Series No. 7.* Washington, DC: Department of Justice, Office of Community Oriented Policing Services. Available online at http://www.cops.usdoj.gov/files/RIC/Publications/e1108-Asset-Forfeiture.pdf.

Worrall, John, and M. Elaine Nugent-Borakove (Eds.). 2008. *The Changing Role of the American Prosecutor.* Albany, NY: SUNY Press.

Worrall, John, and Tomislav Kovandzic. 2008. "Is Policing for Profit? Answers from Asset Forfeiture." *Criminology and Public Policy* 2: 219–244.

Worrall, John L., Jay W. Ross, and Eric S. McCord. 2006. "Modeling Prosecutors' Charging Decisions in Domestic Violence Cases." *Crime & Delinquency* 52: 472–503.

Wright, Ronald, and Marc Miller. 2002. "The Screening/Bargaining Tradeoff." *Stanford Law Review* 55: 29–118.

Young, Malcolm. 2000. "Providing Effective Representation for Youth Prosecuted as Adults." Washington, DC: Department of Justice, Bureau of Justice Assistance Bulletin.

Zahn, Margaret, Stephanie Hawkins, Janet Chiancone, and Ariel Whitworth. 2008. *The Girls Study Group—Charting the Way to Delinquency Prevention for Girls.* Washington, DC: Department of Justice, Office of Justice Programs.

Zalman, Marvin. 2006. "Criminal Justice System Reform and Wrongful Conviction: A Research Agenda." *Criminal Justice Policy Review* 17(4): 468–492.

Zalman, Marvin, Brad Smith, and Amy Kiger. 2008. "Officials' Estimates of the Incidence of 'Actual Innocence' Convictions." *Justice Quarterly* 25(1): 72–100.

Zalman, Marvin, and Larry Siegel. 1997. *Criminal Procedure: Constitution and Society.* 2nd ed. Belmont, CA: Wadsworth.

Zaruba, John E. 2007. "Courthouse Security: A Direction or a Destination?" *Justice System Journal,* 28(1), 46-49.

Zatz, Marjorie. 1984. "Race, Ethnicity, and Determinate Sentencing: A New Dimension to an Old Controversy." *Criminology* 22: 147–171.

Zeisel, Hans. 1982. "The Verdict of Five Out of Six Civil Jurors: Constitutional Problems." *American Bar Foundation Research Journal* 141–156.

Zimring, Franklin, Sheila O'Malley, and Joel Eigen. 1976. "Punishing Homicide in Philadelphia: Perspectives on the Death Penalty." *University of Chicago Law Review* 43: 227–252.

Zubeck, Pam. 2009. "El Paso County Reaps Bonanza in Traffic Fines." *Gazette,* July 20.

Italic page numbers indicate material in exhibits, figures, or tables.

A

Agurs; United States v., 427 U.S. 97 (1976), 278, *279*
Alabama v. Shelton, 535 U.S. 654 (2002), 175
Alabama v. Smith, 490 U.S. 794 (1989), *319*
Aleman v. Judges of the Criminal Division, Circuit Court of Cook County, IL, 138 F.3d 302 (7th Cir.), *cert. den.* 525 U.S. 868 (1998), 438
Alford v. North Carolina, 400 U.S. 25 (1971), *318*
Al Odah v. United States. See Boumediene v. Bush
Alvord v. State, 322 So.2d 533 (Fla. 1975), 459
Andrade v. Attorney General of State of California, 270 F.3d 743 (9th Cir. 2001), *rev'd sub nom., Lockyer v. Andrade*, 538 U.S. 63 (2003), 459
Apodaca v. Oregon, 406 U.S. 404 (1972), *334*, 337
Apprendi v. New Jersey, 530 U.S. 466 (2000), 422, 429, 438
Argersinger v. Hamlin, 407 U.S. 25 (1972), *39*, 99, 175, *176*
Arizona v. Evans, 514 U.S. 1 (1995), 283, 297
Arizona v. Fulminate, 499 U.S. 279 (1991), *288*, 444
Arizona v. Gant, 556 U.S. 332 (2009), *264*, 292
Ashcraft v. Tennessee, 322 U.S. 143 (1944), 284, *286*
Atkins v. Virginia, 536 U.S. 304 (2002), 370, *390*, *394*
Austin v. United States, 509 U.S. 602 (1993), 42
Ayers v. Belmontes, 549 U.S. 7 (2006), 463

B

Bagley; United States v., 473 U.S. 667 (1985), 278, *279*
Baldwin v. New York, 399 U.S. 66 (1970), 99, *334*
Ballew v. Georgia, 435 U.S. 223 (1978), 334, 335
Barker v. Wingo, 407 U.S. 514 (1972), 122, 123, *141*, 143, *504*
Batson v. Kentucky, 476 U.S. 79 (1986), *335*, 341, *342*, 444, *504*
Baze v. Rees, 553 U.S. (2008), *390*, 391
Bennis v. Michigan, 516 U.S. 442 (1996), 517 U.S. 1163, 42
Benton v. Maryland, 395 U.S. 784 (1969), *39*
Berger v. New York, 388 U.S.41 (1967), 296
Berger v. United States, 295 U.S. 78 (1935), 150, *162*
Berghuis v. Thompkins, 130 S. Ct. 2250 (2010), *288*
Betts v. Brady, 316 U.S. 455 (1942), *176*, 177
Biaggi; United States v., 853 F.2d 89 (2d Cir. 1988), 341
Bivens v. Six Unknown Agents of the Federal Bureau of Narcotics, 403 U.S. 388 (1971), *70*, 301
Blakely v. Washington, 543 U.S. 296 (2004), 422, 429, 438
Board of Ed. of Ind. School Dist. 92, Pottawatomie County v. Earls, 536 U.S. 822 (2002), 292
Bond v. United States, 529 U.S. 334 (2000), *297*
Booker; United States v., 543 U.S. 220 (2005), 423, *429*
Booth v. Maryland, 482 U.S. 496 (1987), *235*, 238
Bordenkircher v. Hayes, 434 U.S. 357 (1978), 153, *319*
Boumediene v. Bush, 553 U.S. 723 (2008), *64*, 77, 462, *505*
Boykin v. Alabama, 395 U.S. 238 (1969), *318*, 320
Brady v. Maryland, 373 U.S. 83 (1963), *152*, 163, 278, *279*

Brady v. United States, 397 U.S. 742 (1970), *178*, *318*
Branzburg v. Hayes, 408 U.S. 665 (1972), 263, *265*
Brendlin v. California, 551 U.S. 249 (2007), *298*
Brewer v. Williams, 430 U.S. 387 (1977), *178*, 286, *302*
Brown v. Board of Education, 349 U.S. 294 (1954), 528
Brown v. Mississippi, 297 U.S. 278 (1936), *16–17*, 284, *286*, 460
Buckley v. Fitzsimmons, 509 U.S. 259 (1993), *162*
Burch v. Louisiana, 441 U.S. 130 (1979), *334*, 337, *504*
Burns v. Reed, 500 U.S. 478 (1991), 155, *162*, 264

C

Cady v. Dombrowski, 413 U.S. 433 (1973), *292*
Calandra; United States v., 414 U.S. 338 (1974), *296*
California v. Acevedo, 500 U.S. 565 (1991), *292*
California v. Ciraolo, 476 U.S. 207 (1986), *293*
California v. Greenwood, 486 U.S. 35 (1988), *293*, 459
Campbell v. Louisiana, 523 U.S. 392 (1998), *265*
Cantwell v. Connecticut, 310 U.S. 296 (1940), *39*
Caperton v. Massey Coal, 556 U.S. 868 (2009), *198*, *214*, 217
Carey v. Musladin, 549 U.S. 70 (2005), *235*
Carroll v. United States, 486 U.S. 35 (1925), *292*
Ceccolini; United States v., 435 U.S. 268 (1978), *283*
Chandler et al. v. Florida, 449 U.S. 560 (1981), *334*, 362
Chapman v. California, 386 U.S. 18 (1967), 444
Chavez v. Martinez, 486 U.S. 35 (2003), *288*
Chicago, Burlington and Quincy Railroad v. Chicago, 166 U.S. 226 (1897), *39*
Chimel v. California, 395 U.S. 752 (1969), *264*, 292
Chisom v. Roemer, 501 U.S. 380 (1991), 210, 214, *505*
Clark v. Edwards, 725 F. Supp. 285 (M.D. La. 1988), 210
Coker v. Georgia, 483 U.S. 584 (1977), *390*, 393
Cole v. Arkansas, 333 U.S. 196 (1948), *39*
Coleman v. Alabama, 399 U.S. 1 (1970), *178*
Coleman v. Balkcom, 451 U.S. 949 (1981), *on denial of cert.*, *450*
Coleman v. Thompson, 501 U.S. 722 (1992), *452*
Colorado v. Connelly, 479 U.S. 157 (1986), *287*
Connick v. Thompson, 131 S. Ct. 1350 (2011), *152–153*, *162*, 169
Cooper Industries v. Leatherman Tool Group, Inc., 532 U.S. 424 (2001), *39*
Cooper v. Pate, 378 U.S. 546 (1967), 379, *381*
County of Riverside v. McLaughlin, 500 U.S. 44 (1991), 246, 251, 252, 270
Crouse, Ex parte, 4 Whart. 9 (Pa. 1838), *485*
Cunningham v. California, 549 U.S. 270 (2007), 422, 438

D

Dalia v. United States, 441 U.S. 238 (1979), *296*
Daubert v. Merrell Dow Pharmaceuticals Co., 509 U.S. 579 (1993), *335*, 347–350, *349*, 458

Davis v. United States, 512 U.S. 452 (1994), *288*, 453
DeJong v. Oregon, 299 U.S. 353 (1937), *39*
Dickerson v. United States, 530 U.S. 428 (2000), 282, 286, *288*
Dinitz; United States v., 424 U.S. 600 (1976), 353
Directives Pursuant to Section 105B of the Foreign Intelligence Surveillance Act of 2008, In re, 551 F.3d 1004 (For. Intel. Surv. Rev. 2008), 77
District Attorney's Office v. Osborne, 557 U.S. 52 (2009), 348
District of Columbia v. Heller, 554 U.S. 570 (2008), *505*, 530
Doggett v. United States, 505 U.S. 647 (1992), *141*
Donovan v. Dewey, 452 U.S. 594 (1981), *293*
Douglas v. California, 372 U.S. 353 (1963), *176*, 178, *178*, 445
Drayton; United States v., 536 U.S. 194 (2002), 248
Duncan v. Louisiana, 391 U.S. 145 (1968), *39*, 334, *334*
Dunn; United States v., 480 U.S. 294 (1987), *292*
Duren v. Missouri, 439 U.S. 357 (1979), *334*, 339

E

Erie Railroad Co. v. Tompkins, 304 U.S. 64 (1938), 68
Estelle v. Gamble, 429 U.S. 97 (1976), *381*
Estes v. Texas, 381 U.S. 532 (1965), 361
Everson v. Board of Education, 330 U.S. 1 (1947), *39*
Ewing v. California, 538 U.S. 11 (2003), *111*, *427*, *429*, *505*
Ex parte. See name of party

F

Faretta v. California, 422 U.S. 806 (1975), *176*, 179, 226
Fay v. Noia, 372 U.S. 391 (1963), *452*, *504*
Felker v. Turpin, 518 U.S. 651 (1996), 451
Flores-Montano; United States v., 541 U.S. 149 (2004), *292*
Florida v. J.L., 529 U.S. 266 (2000), *297*
Florida v. Jimino, 500 U.S. 248 (1991), *292*, *297*
Florida v. Powell, 130 S. Ct. 1195 (2010), *288*
Florida v. Riley, 488 U.S. 445 (1989), *293*
Ford v. Wainwright, 477 U.S. 399 (1986), 393
Frye v. United States, 293 F.2d 1013 (D.C. Cir. 1923), 347
Furman v. Georgia, 408 U.S. 238 (1972), 388, 396, 417, *504*

G

Gagnon v. Scarpelli, 411 U.S. 778 (1973), *178*
Gall v. United States, 552 U.S. 38 (2007), 423, *429*, *505*
Gault, In re, 387 U.S. 1 (1967), 175, *176*, 470, 483, *484*, *485*, 496, *504*
Georgia; United States v., 546 U.S. 151 (2006), 69
Georgia v. McCollum, 505 U.S. 42 (1992), *335*, 341
Georgia v. Randolph, 547 U.S. 103 (2006), *298*
Gerstein v. Pugh, 387 U.S. 1 (1975), 251, 252, *504*
Gideon v. Wainwright, 372 U.S. 335 (1963), *39*, 174, 175, *176*, *177*, *178*, 193, 460
Giglio v. United States, 405 U.S. 150 (1972), *279*, *279*
Gitlow v. New York, 268 U.S. 652 (1925), *39*

Gonzalez; United States v., 820 F.2d 575 (2d Cir. 1987), 444
Gordon v. Justice Court, 12 Cal. 3d 323 (1974), 98
Gouveia; United States v., 467 U.S. 180 (1984), 178
Graham v. Florida, 130 S. Ct. 2011 (2010), 410, *429*, *485*, *505*
Gregg v. Georgia, 428 U.S. 153 (1976), 389, 393, 417, *504*
Gregory v. Ashcroft, 501 U.S. 452 (1991), 212, *214*
Griffin v. California, 380 U.S. 609 (1965), 284, *286*, *334*, 355
Griffin v. Illinois, 351 U.S. 12 (1956), 178, 445, *503*
Griswold v. Connecticut, 381 U.S. 479 (1965), *39*
Grutter v. Bollinger, 539 U.S. 306 (2003), 461

H

Hague v. CIO, 307 U.S. 496 (1939), *39*
Halbert v. Michigan, 545 U.S. 605 (2005), *176*
Hamdan v. Rumsfeld, 548 U.S. 557 (2006), 76
Hamilton v. Alabama, 368 U.S. 52 (1961), *178*
Harris v. Alabama, 513 U.S. 504 (1995), *390*
Harris v. New York, 401 U.S. 222 (1971), *287*
Harris v. United States, 390 U.S. 234 (1968), *292*
Herrera v. Collins, 506 U.S. 390 (1993), *452*
Herring; United States v., 555 U.S. 135 (2009), *298*
Hiibel v. Sixth Judicial District Court of Nevada, 542 U.S. 177 (2004), *298*
Hill v. McDonough, 547 U.S. 573 (2006), *390*, 391
Holland v. Illinois, 493 U.S. 474 (1990), 339
Hollingsworth v. Perry, 130 S. Ct. 705 (2010), 362, 363
Holloway v. Arkansas, 435 U.S. 475 (1978), 444
House v. Bell, 386 F.3d 668 (6th Cir. 2004), *rev'd*, 547 U.S. 518 (2006), *64*, 437, *448–449*, 463
Houston Lawyers' Association v. Attorney General of Texas, 501 U.S. 419 (1991), *214*
Hudson v. Michigan, 547 U.S. 586 (2006), 291, *298*, 463, *505*
Hudson v. Palmer, 468 U.S. 517 (1984), *293*, *381*
Hull, Ex Parte, 312 U.S. 546 (1941), *381*
Hurtado v. California, 110 U.S. 516 (1884), 262, *264*

I

Illinois v. Caballes, 543 U.S. 405 (2005), *298*
Illinois v. Gates, 462 U.S. 213 (1983), 290, *296*
Illinois v. Krull, 480 U.S. 340 (1987), *297*, 302
Illinois v. Perkins, 496 U.S. 292 (1990), *287*
Illinois v. Rodriguez, 497 U.S. 177 (1990), *292*
Imbler v. Pachtam, 424 U.S. 409 (1976), 162, *162*
Indiana v. Edwards, 554 U.S. 164 (2008), *176*, 180, 226–227
In re. See name of party
Iowa v. Tovar, 541 U.S. 77 (2004), *319*, 322
Irvin v. Dowd, 366 U.S. 717 (1961), 360

J

Jackson v. Hobbs, 132 S. Ct. 2455 (2012), 484, *485*
James v. United States, 550 U.S. 192 (2007), 463
J.D.B. v. North Carolina, 131 S. Ct. 2394 (2011), *288*, *485*, 492

J.E.B. Petitioner v. Alabama ex rel. T.B., 511 U.S. 127 (1994), *335, 341, 444*

Jencks v. United States, 353 U.S. 657 (1957), 278, *279*

Johnson v. California, 545 U.S. 162 (2005), 341

Johnson v. Louisiana, 406 U.S. 356 (1972), *334, 337*

Johnson v. Zerbst, 304 U.S. 458 (1938), *176, 460*

Jones; United States v., 132 S. Ct. 945 (2012), *298*

K

Kalina v. Fletcher, 522 U.S. 118 (1997), *162*

Kansas v. Marsh, 548 U.S. 163 (2006), *390*

Kastigar v. United States, 406 U.S. 441 (1972), 263, *265*

Katz v. United States, 389 U.S. 347 (1967), 289, 291, *296*

Keeney v. Tamayo-Reyes, 504 U.S. 1 (1992), *452*

Kennedy v. Louisiana, 554 U.S. 407 (2008), *390, 393, 463, 505*

Kent v. United States, 383 U.S. 541 (1966), *485*

Kepner v. United States, 195 U.S. 100 (1904), 438

Ker v. California, 374 U.S. 23 (1963), *39*

Kimbrough v. United States, 552 U.S. 85 (2007), 423, *429*

Kirby v. Illinois, 406 U.S. 682 (1972), 178, *178*

Klopfer v. North Carolina, 386 U.S. 213 (1967), *39*

Knotts; United States v., 460 U.S. 276 (1983), *296*

Knowles v. Iowa, 525 U.S. 113 (1998), *297*

Knowles v. Mirzayance, 525 U.S. 113 (2009), 179

Kotteakos v. United States, 328 U.S. 750 (1946), 444

Kuhlmann v. Wilson, 477 U.S. 436 (1986), *287*

Kumho Tire v. Carmichael, 526 U.S. 137 (1999), *335, 347*

Kyles v. Whitley, 514 U.S. 419 (1995), 278, *280*

Kyllo v. United States, 533 U.S. 27 (2001), *298*

L

Lafler v. Cooper, 132 S.Ct. 1376 (2012), *176, 178, 319,* 320, 324, 463, *505*

Lanier; United States v., 520 U.S. 259 (1997), 212, *214*

Lanzetta v. New Jersey, 306 U.S. 451 (1939), *264*

Lawrence v. Texas, 539 U.S. 558 (2003), 461, 528

Leon; United States v., 468 U.S. 897 (1984), *283*

L.M., In re, 186 P.3d 164, 165 (Kan. 2008), 486, 492

Lockhart v. McCree, 476 U.S. 162 (1986), *390,* 391

Lopez; United States v., 514 U.S. 549 (1995), 56–57, *505*

Loughner; United States v. (2011), *49* No. 11CR0187 TUC LAB (D. Ariz. 2011).

M

Malloy v. Hogan, 378 U.S. 1 (1964), *39*

Maples v. Thomas, 132 S. Ct. 912 (2012), 179

Mapp v. Ohio, 367 U.S. 643 (1961), 13, *39,* 282, 295, *296, 302,* 460, *504*

Marbury v. Madison, 5 U.S. (1 Cranch) 137 (1803), 62, *63,* 460

Maryland v. Shatzer (2010), *288*

Massiah v. United States, 377 U.S. 201 (1964), *178*

McCleskey v. Kemp, 481 U.S. 279 (1987), *390,* 418

McCleskey v. Zant, 499 U.S. 467 (1991), 451, *452*

McDonald v. City of Chicago, 130 S. Ct. 3020 (2010), *39, 505*

McFarland, Ex parte, 163 S.W.3d 743 (Tex. Crim. App. 2005), 460

McKaskle v. Wiggins, 465 U.S. 168 (1984), 179

McKeiver v. Pennsylvania, 403 U.S. 528 (1971), *334,* 483, *485,* 486

McMann v. Richardson, 397 U.S. 759 (1970), 179

Medellin v. Texas, 554 U.S. 759 (2008), *225*

Melendez-Diaz v. Massachusetts, 557 U.S. 305 (2009), 353

Mempa v. Rhay, 389 U.S. 128 (1976), 175, *178*

Mendenhall v. Akron, 881 N.E.2d 255 (Ohio 2008), 94

Mendenhall; United States v., 446 U.S. 544 (1980), *296*

Mezzanatto; United States v., 513 U.S. 196 (1995), *319*

Michigan v. Mosley, 423 U.S. 96 (1975), *287*

Michigan Department of State Police v. Sitz, 496 U.S. 444 (1990), *297*

Miller-El v. Cockrell, 537 U.S. 322 (2003), *450*

Miller-El v. Dretke, 545 U.S. 231 (2005), 341

Miller v. Alabama, 132 S.Ct. 2455 (2012), 484, *485*

Miller v. French, 530 U.S. 327 (2000), *382*

Miller v. Johnson, 515 U.S. 900 (1995), *210*

Miller; United States v., 425 U.S. 435 (1976), *293*

Minnesota v. Dickerson, 508 U.S. 366 (1993), *297*

Minnick v. Mississippi, 498 U.S. 146 (1990), 286, *288*

Miranda v. Arizona, 384 U.S. 436 (1966), 13, *31,* 178, *178,* 284, *285,* 286, *286, 504*

Missouri v. Frye, 132 S. Ct. 1399 (2010), *176,* 178, *178, 319,* 320, 324, 463

Missouri v. Seibert, 542 U.S. 600 (2004), *288*

Mistretta v. United States, 488 U.S. 361 (1989), 423, *429, 504*

Morrison v. Olson, 487 U.S. 654 (1988), *162*

Morrissey v. Brewer, 408 U.S. 471 (1972), *178*

Murray v. Curlett, 179 A.2d 698 (Md. 1962), *rev'd sub nom., School Dist. of Abington Tp., Pa. v. Schempp*, 374 U.S. 203 (1963), 459

Murray v. Giarratano, 492 U.S. 1 (1989), *450*

Murray v. United States, 487 U.S. 533 (1988), *283*

N

Nardone v. United States, 308 U.S. 338 (1939), *283*

National Treasury Employees Union v. Von Raab, 489 U.S. 656 (1989), *293*

Near v. Minnesota, 283 U.S. 697 (1931), *39*

New Jersey v. T.L.O., 469 U.S. 325 (1985), *292*

New York State Bd. Elections v. López Torres, 552 U.S. 196 (2008), 206, *214*

New York v. Burger, 482 U.S. 691 (1981), *293*

New York v. Quarles, 467 U.S. 649 (1984), 286, *287*

Nix v. Williams, 467 U.S. 431 (1984), *283*

North Carolina v. Butler, 441 U.S. 369 (1979), *287*

North v. Russell, 427 U.S. 328 (1976), 98, *504*

O

O'Connor v. Ortega, 480 U.S. 709 (1987), *293*
Ojeda Rios; United States v., 495 U.S. 257 (1990), *297*
Oliver, In re, 333 U.S. 257 (1948), *39*
Oliver v. United States, 466 U.S. 170 (1984), *292*
Oregon v. Elstad, 470 U.S. 298 (1985), *287*

P

Padilla v. Kentucky, 130 S. Ct. 1473 (2010), *176*
Parker v. Gladden, 385 U.S. 363 (1966), *39*
Patane; United States v., 542 U.S. 630 (2004), *288*
Payne v. Tennessee, 501 U.S. 808 (1991), 222, 235, 238, *505*
Payton v. New York, 445 U.S. 573 (1980), *264, 296*
Pennsylvania Dep't of Corrections v. Yeskey, 524 U.S. 206 (1998), 69, *382*
Pennsylvania v. Muniz, 496 U.S. 582 (1990), *288*
Penry v. Lynaugh, 492 U.S. 302 (1989), *394*
People v. Binkerd, 155 Cal. App. 4th 1143 (2007), 227–228
People v. Garcia (Cal. App. 2000), *342*
People v. Wabash, St. Louis and Pacific Railway, 12 Ill. App. 263 (1882), 150, *264*
Pointer v. Texas, 380 U.S. 400 (1965), *39*
Polowichak; United States v., 783 F.2d 410 (4th Cir. 1986), 444
Portuondo v. Agard, 529 U.S. 61 (2000), *335*
Powell v. Alabama, 287 U.S. 45 (1932), *176, 503*
Powers v. Ohio, 499 U.S. 400 (1991), *335*
Procter and Gamble Co.; United States v., 356 U.S. 677 (1958), 277
Pulley v. Harris, 465 U.S. 37 (1984), *390*

R

Rakas v. Illinois, 439 U.S. 128 (1978), *296*
Ramdass v. Angelone, 530 U.S. 156 (2000), *390*
Republican Party of Minn. v. White, 536 U.S. 765 (2002), 206, *214,* 217
Rhode Island v. Innis, 446 U.S. 291 (1980), *287*
Rhodes v. Chapman, 452 U.S. 337 (1981), *381*
Richmond Newspapers v. Virginia, 448 U.S. 555 (1980), 360
Ricketts v. Adamson, 483 U.S. 1 (1987), *319*
Ring v. Arizona, 536 U.S. 584 (2002), *390*
Rita v. United States, 551 U.S. 338 (2007), 423, *429*
Robinson v. California, 370 U.S. 660 (1962), *381*
Roe v. Flores-Ortega, 528 U.S. 470 (2000), 179, 445
Rompilla v. Beard, 545 U.S. 374 (2005), 179
Roper v. Simmons, 543 U.S. 551 (2005), *390,* 393, *394–395, 482, 485, 505*
Ross v. Moffitt, 417 U.S. 600 (1974), *178,* 179, 445
Roth v. United States, 354 U.S. 476 (1957), 460
Rothgery v. Gillespie County, 554 U.S. 191 (2008), 178, *178*
Ruiz; United States v., 536 U.S. 622 (2002), 280, *319*

S

Safford Unified School District v. Redding, 557 U.S. 364 (2009), *292*
Salazar v. State (2002), 238
Salerno; United States v., 481 U.S. 739 (1987), 256, *504*
Sampson v. California, 547 U.S. 843 (2006), *293*
Sanabria v. United States, 437 U.S. 54 (1978), 438
Sanders v. United States, 373 U.S. 1 (1963), *452*
Santobello v. New York, 404 U.S. 257 (1971), 308, 319, *319,* 322–324, *323,* 327
Schall v. Martin, 467 U.S. 253 (1984), 483, *485*
Schlup v. Delo, 513 U.S. 298 (1995), *452*
Schneckloth v. Bustamonte, 412 U.S. 218 (1973), *292*
Schriro v. Landrigan, 550 U.S. 465 (2007), *176,* 463
Scott v. Harris, 550 U.S. 372 (2007), *298*
Scott v. Illinois, 440 U.S. 367 (1979), 175, *176*
Segura v. United States, 468 U.S. 796 (1984), *283*
Shadwick v. City of Tampa, 407 U.S. 345 (1972), 290
Sheppard v. Maxwell, 384 U.S. 333 (1966), *334,* 360, *504*
Simmons v. South Carolina, 512 U.S. 154 (1994), *390*
Simon & Schuster v. New York State Crime Victims Bd, 502 U.S. 105 (1991), *235*
Skinner v. Railway Labor Executives' Assoc., 489 U.S. 602 (1989), *293*
Smith v. Maryland, 442 U.S. 735 (1979), *293, 296*
Smith v. State, 681 P.2d 1374 (Ariz. 1984), 185
Snyder v. Louisiana, 552 U.S. 472 (2008), *335,* 341
Sokolow; United States v., 490 U.S. 1 (1989), *297*
South Carolina v. Gathers, 490 U.S. 805 (1989), 235, 238
Stack v. Boyle, 342 U.S. 1 (1951), 254
Stanford v. Kentucky, 492 U.S. 361 (1989), 370, *390,* 393, *485*
State v. Boland, 800 P. 2d 1112 (Wash. 1990), 459
State v. Clopten, 223 P.3d 1103 (Utah 2009), 458
State v. Hempele, 576 A.2d 793 (N.J. 1990), 459
State v. Kennedy, 957 So.2d 757 (La. 2007) *rev'd,* 554 U.S. 407 (2008), 459
State v. Kimbro, 496 A.2d. 498 (Conn. 1985), 459
State v. Miller, 680 P.2d 676 (Or. 1984), *283*
State v. Tune, 98 A.2d 881 (N.J. 1953), 277
State ex rel Simmons v. Roper, 112 S.W.3d 397 (Mo. 2003), *aff'd,* 543 U.S. 551 (2005), 459
Stone v. Powell, 428 U.S. 465 (1976), *452*
Strickland v. Washington, 446 U.S. 668 (1984), *176,* 179
Strickler v. Greene, 527 U.S. 263 (1999), *280*
Swain v. Alabama, 380 U.S. 202 (1965), *overruled in part by Batson v. Kentucky,* 476 U.S. 79 (1986), 339

T

Taylor v. Louisiana, 419 U.S. 522 (1975), *334*
Tennessee v. Garner, 471 U.S. 1 (1985), *297*
Terry v. Ohio, 392 U.S. 1 (1968), 34, 289
Texas v. Cobb, 532 U.S. 162 (2001), *288*
Texas v. McCullough, 475 U.S. 134 (1986), 445
Thompson v. Oklahoma, 487 U.S. 815 (1988), 393, *485*

Thurman v. Torrington, 595 F. Supp. 1521 (D. Conn. 1984), *233*
Tollett v. Henderson, 411 U.S. 258 (1973), *178*
Town of Castle Rock, Colo. v. Gonzales, 545 U.S. 748 (2005), *235*
Townsend v. Sain, 372 U.S. 391 (1963), *452*
Trop v. Dulles, 356 U.S. 86 (1958), 388
Turney v. Ohio, 273 U.S. 510 (1927), *502*

U

United States. See name of opposing party
Ursery; United States v., 518 U.S. 267 (1996), *42*
Uttecht v. Brown, 551 U.S. 1 (2007), *390, 391*, 463

V

Vasquez v. Hillery, 474 U.S. 254 (1986), 444
Victor v. Nebraska, 511 U.S. 1 (1994), 35, *335*, 344
Virginia v. Moore, 553 U.S. 164 (2008), *298*

W

Wade; United States v., 388 U.S. 218 (1967), *178*
Washington v. Chrisman, 455 U.S. 1 (1982), 292
Washington v. Texas, 388 U.S. 14 (1967), *39*

Weatherford v. Bursey, 429 U.S. 545 (1977), 277, *279*
Weeks v. United States, 232 U.S. 383 (1914), 282, 295, *296*, 460, *502*
Whitley v. Albers, 475 U.S. 312 (1986), *381*
Whren et al. v. United States, 517 U.S. 806 (1986), *297*
Wiggins v. Smith, 539 U.S. 510 (2003), *176*, 179
Williams v. Florida, 399 U.S. 78 (1970), *279*, 333, *334*, 335
Williams v. Taylor, 529 U.S. 362 (2000), *390*
Williams; United States v., 504 U.S. 36 (1992), 263, *265*
Wilson v. Arkansas, 514 U.S. 927 (1995), 291
Wilson v. Seiter, 501 U.S. 294 (1991), 380, *382*
Winship, In re, 397 U.S. 358 (1970), 483, *485*
Winston v. Lee, 470 U.S. 753 (1985), *297*
Witherspoon v. Illinois, 391 U.S. 510 (1968), 391
Wolf v. Colorado, 338 U.S. 25 (1949), *39*, 282, *296*
Wolff v. McDonnell, 418 U.S. 539 (1974), 69, *381*
Won Sun v. United States, 371 U.S. 471 (1963), *283*
Wood v. Bartholomew, 516 U.S. 1 (1995), 278, *280*

Y

Yeskey v. Pennsylvania Department of Corrections (1998), 69
Youngblood v. West Virginia, 547 U.S. 867 (2006), *280*

Italic page numbers indicate material in exhibits, figures, or tables.

A

Abandoned property, *293*
Absolute immunity, 162
Abuse excuse, 241
Abuse of discretion review, *440*
Accompanying circumstances, 46
Accused, rights of, 36–43
ACLU. *See* American Civil Liberties Union
Acquaintance crimes, 231–232
Acquittal, 359, 438
Acquittal motions, 353, *354*, *355*, 356
Actors in courthouses, 10–11, *10*, 125–126, *127*
   behind-the-scenes, 126–128
   coordination and, 142
   types of, 10–11, *10*, *127*
   See also Courtroom work groups; *specific actors, e.g. judges, prosecutors*
Actus reus, 44, 45
Adjudicated, 492, *493*
Adjudicatory hearings, *490*, 492
Administration
   centralized, 107
   court administrators, 126–128
   federal judicial, 79–82, *80*
Administrative Office Act of 1939, *64*, 79
Administrative Office of the U.S. Courts, 79, *80*, 81
Administrative regulations, 32
Administrative searches, *293*
Admiralty cases, jurisdiction and, *68*
ADR (alternative dispute resolution), 102
Adult courts. *See* Lower courts; Trial courts of general jurisdiction; Trial courts of limited jurisdiction
Adversary system, 33–35, 277
   professional ethics and, 142–143
AEDPA. *See* Antiterrorism and Effective Death Penalty Act
Aerial searches, *293*
Affidavit, 290
Affirmative defenses, 34
Affirmed by appellate court, *441*, 444
African-Americans
   as felony defendants, 11
   as judges, 209, 214

juveniles transferred to adult court, 481
sentencing decisions and, 414, 415–416
See also Discrimination; Racial issues
Age
   juvenile court jurisdiction and, *476*, *477*, *478*
   as mitigating factor, 410
Age Discrimination in Employment Act of 1973, 69, 212
Aggravating circumstances, 409–410
Aguilar, Robert, *215*
Alford plea, 322
Alibi defense, 46–48, 281
Alito, Samuel, Jr., *434*, 462, *462*
Allen charge, 357
Allocute/allocution hearings, 320–321
al-Qaeda , 75
Alschuler, Albert, *325*
Alternate jurors, 341
Alternative dispute resolution (ADR), 102
Amendments to U.S. Constitution. *See specific numbered amendments*
American Bar Association, 204
   case-processing standards, 137, *137*
   on commercial bail, 257–258
   on court funding, 116
   on death penalty moratorium, *392*
   on electronic media in courtrooms, 362
   on exclusionary rule, 301
   judicial selection and, 204–205
   legal ethics and, 190–192
   Model Canons of Judicial Ethics, 216
   Model Rules of Professional Conduct, 190–191
   witnesses, treatment of, 234
American Civil Liberties Union (ACLU), 84, 496
American Gangster (movie), *104*
Americans with Disabilities Act, *68*, 69
American Violet, 317–318
Amicus curiae, 443
Analogical reasoning, 522–523, *523*

Anglo-American law, 30
Annual Report (AO), 81
Anthony, Casey, 2, 4–5, 6, 8, 22, *164*, 363
   charging of, 11
   evidence in the case, 18, *22*, 23
   trial, *22*, 23
   verdict, 10, 18, *505*
Anthony, Caylee, 4, 5, 6, 8, 18, 22, *164*
Anthony, Cindy, 5, 22
Anthony, George, 5
Anti-Federalists, 61–62
Antiterrorism and Effective Death Penalty Act (AEDPA), *64*, *235*, *450*, 451
Antitrust cases, jurisdiction and, *68*
The Appeal (Grisham), 198, 217
Appeals
   overview of, 437–441
   briefs for, *441*, 442–443
   constitutional safeguards and, *38*
   crime, types and, *446*
   criminal, 445–447, *446*
   in death penalty cases, 393–395
   defendants' chance of winning, 445–447
   defense attorneys' role and, *181*
   defined, *441*
   judges' role and, *200*
   juvenile courts and, *490*, 495
   limitations on, 437–439
   procedures/steps in, 441–445, *441*
   prosecutors' role and, *151*
   purposes of, 437
   records for, *441*, 442
   right to counsel and, 178, *178*
   right to one appeal, 437–439, 463
   victims' role and, *230*
   See also Appellate courts
Appeals courts. *See* Appellate courts
Appellants, 441
Appellate briefs, *441*, 442–443
Appellate court records, *441*, 442
Appellate courts, 9, 61, 434–466
   overview of, 437
   caseloads and, 444–445, 463
   as courts of last resort, *9*, *58*, 72, 458–460
   creation of, 437
   criminal appeals in, 445–447, *446*
   discretion and, *441*, 458–459

Appellate courts (*Continued*)
disposition of cases, *441*, 444
error correction by, 437, 444
function of, 61
intermediate courts of appeals
(state), 105–106, *105*, 458–459
judges' role in, *200*
jurisdiction of, 439
limitations on right to review by,
437–439
mandatory vs. discretionary
review, *441*
policy formulation by, 437, 459
postconviction review and,
448–453, *450*
procedures in, 441–445, *441*
process in, 437–441
purposes of, 437
standards of review, 439–441, *440*
state court structure, *439*
success rate in, 445–447
trial courts compared, 61
U.S. Courts of Appeal, *9*, 70–72
written opinions, *441*, 443–444
wrongful convictions and,
453–458
See also Supreme Court, U.S.; U.S.
Circuit Courts of Appeal
Appellate jurisdiction, 61, 439
Appellate process, 437–441
Appellees, 442
Arbitration, 102
Arraignment, 265
overview of, 13, *250*, 265
constitutional safeguards and, *38*
defense attorneys' role and, *181*
defined, 265
judges' role and, *200*
juvenile courts and, *489*
key developments concerning,
265
as procedural step, 265
prosecutors' role and, *151*
right to counsel and, *178*
Sixth Amendment and, *265*
victims' role and, *230*
Arrest, 248–251
overview of, 12, 248–251
constitutional safeguards and, *38*
defense attorneys' role and, *181*
defined, 248, *250*
judges' role and, *200*
of juveniles, 488, *489*
key developments concerning, *264*

number of, 249, *249*
prosecutors' role and, *151*
quality of, 251
right to counsel and, *178*
victims' role and, *230*
Arrest warrants, *250*, 253
Arson, characteristics of, *47*
Article I of the U.S. Constitution, 32,
38, 449, 506, 510–513
Article I courts, 74, *74*, 83
Article I judges, 74
Article II of the U.S. Constitution,
214, 506, 513–514
Article III of the U.S. Constitution,
32, 62, 333, 506–507, 514–515
Article III courts, 74, *74*
as constitutional courts, 74
creation of, *63*
federal question jurisdiction and,
67–69, *68*
Article III judges, 74, 203
Articles of Confederation, 61
Assault, characteristics of, *47*
Assembly-line justice, 130–132, *131*
Asset forfeiture, 41, *42*
Assets, *42*
Assigned counsel system, 184–185
Assistant district attorneys, 159, 161
Attempt, 45
Attendant circumstances, 46
Attorney-client privilege, *346*
Attorney general, *154*, 155
Attorney General's Task Force on
Violent Crime, *302*
Attorneys, *10*, 11, *127*
city attorneys, 158
conflicts of interest and, 163, 191
disciplinary proceedings against,
143
high-profile/celebrity, *36–37*
ineffective assistance by, 179, 457
misconduct by, 143, 456–457, *457*
as officers of the court, 150, 180,
190–191
right to, 175–180, *176*, 193
U.S. Attorneys, 65, *154*, 156
See also Defense attorneys;
Prosecutors
Attrition of cases, 265–267, *266*
Automatic waiver, 479

B

Bail, 254–259
overview of, 12–13, *250*

appeals and, 438
case disposition and, 259
commercial, 257–258
defendant's characteristics and,
254–259
defense attorneys' role and, *181*
defined, 254
discretion and, 257
effects of system for, 258–259
Eighth Amendment and, 254, 257,
264, 508
excessive, protection against, 254,
257
extradition and, 257
factors influencing, 257
failure to appear and, 259
forms of, 256, *256*
functions of, 270–271
judges' role and, *200*, 257
key developments concerning,
264
law in action perspective and,
250, 256–257
law on the books perspective and,
250, 254–256
monetary bail system, 254–256
preventive detention and, 256
procedures for, 255
prosecutors' role and, *151*
Reform Acts, 256, *264*
right to counsel and, *178*
victims' role and, *230*
Bail agents (bondsmen), 257–258
Bail bonds, *256*
Bailiff, 124, *127*
Bail Reform Act of 1984, 256, *264*, *504*
Ballard, Sarah, *220*
Bankruptcy Abuse Prevention and
Consumer Protection Act of 2005,
66
Bankruptcy courts, case filing
in, *66*
Bankruptcy judges, 65–66
Bankruptcy petitions, 116
Bankruptcy Reform Act of 1978, *64*
Barker, Willie, 122–123, *141*, 143
Beccaria, Cesare, 372
Belknap, Joanne, 415
Bench, in courtrooms, 124, *125*
Bench trials, 14, 335, *336*
Bench warrant, 259
Bentham, Jeremy, 372
Bertram, Eva, *21*
Best-evidence rule, *346*

Between Prison and Probation: Intermediate Punishments in a Rational Sentencing System (Morris and Tonry), 384
Beyond a reasonable doubt, 35, *35*, 344–345
Bifurcated trial, 389
Big Prisons, Big Dreams (Lynch), 379
Bill of Rights, 38–39, *39*
   application to states, 38–39
   See also specific numbered amendments; U.S. Constitution
Bind over, 260
Bitemark comparison evidence, *349*
Bivens actions, *70*
Blackmun, Harry, 461
Blagojevich, Rod, *330*, 364, *505*
Blended sentencing, 498
Blindfold of justice, 403, 430
Blumberg, Abraham, 182
Boies, David, 116
Bonds, cash, *256*
Bonds, property, *256*
Boot camps, 387
Border searches, *292*
Boston Legal, 192
Bounty hunters, 257–258
Boykin forms, 320, *321*
Bradfield, David, *213*
Brady rule, *152*, 278, *279–280*
Breyer, Stephen, 215, *434*, 461, *462*
Breyer Commission, *214*, 215
Briefs, appellate, *441*, 442–443
Brinkema, Leoni, *77–78*
Broderick, Vincent, 430
Bronx D.A. (Straus), 159, 232–234
Bryant, Kobe, *44*, 363
Bullet lead, compositional analysis of, 347, *349*
Burden of persuasion, 34, 344–345
   See also Burdens of proof
Burden of production, 344
Burdens of proof, 34–35, *35*, 344–345
   in asset forfeiture cases, *42*
   for grand juries, 13
   levels of, 34–35, *35*
   Miranda warnings and, 384
   suppression of evidence, 295
Burger, Warren, 322–324, 461
Burger Court, 461
   criminal justice policy and, 461
   exclusionary rule and, 301
   Miranda and, *285*, 289

plea bargaining and, 319, 322–324, *323*, 327
   right to counsel and, 178–179
Burglary, characteristics of, *47*
Bush, George H. W., 461
Bush, George W., 21, 75, 203, 205, 208, *211*, 284, 462
Bybee, Jay, *211*

C

California
   judicial conduct commissions, 212, *214*
   Proposition 8, *235*, 237, 326, 362
"A Call to Action for Juvenile Justice," 496
Cameras
   in courtrooms, 361–362
   evidence cameras, in high-technology courtroom, 115
   surveillance, in courthouses, 128
   traffic cameras, 94
Campbell, William, 263
Capias (bench warrant), 259
Capital offenses, 387
   See also Death penalty
Capital punishment. *See* Death penalty
Career criminals, 223, 314
Carter, Jimmy, 208
Case attrition, 265–267, *266*
Case-in-chief, 353–356, *354*
Case law. *See* Common law
Caseloads
   appellate courts and, 444–445, 463
   assembly-line justice and, 131, 132
   civil rights cases, 69
   delay in court system and, 143
   of District Courts, 66
   domestic violence and, 234
   federal courts, 82–83
   felonies, 131
   of judges, 200
   of juvenile courts, 475
   of lower courts, *92*, 93, 97, 101
   of magistrate judges, 65
   plea bargaining and, 311
   probation officers and, 378, 383
   rural courts, 97
   sentencing decisions and, 18
   of Supreme Court, *66*, 73
   of trial courts of general jurisdiction, *92*

of trial courts of limited jurisdiction, *92*, 93
   U.S. Court of Appeals, 72
Case-processing standards, 137, *137*
Case scheduling, 142
Cash bonds, *256*
Cassell, Paul, *211*
Cebull, Richard, *216*
Celebrated cases, 267–268, *268*
Celerity of punishment, 372
Center for Judicial Independence, *211–212*
Centralized administration, 107
Centralized judicial budgeting, 108–110
Centralized rule making, 107–108
Certainty of punishment, 372
Certiori, writs for, 72–73, 393, 442
Challenges for cause, *338*, 341
Chambers, 199
Changes of venue, 59, 361
Charge bargaining, 309–310, *310*
Charging, 253
   defined, *250*
   juvenile courts and, *489*
   key developments concerning, *264*
   overcharging, 313–314
   as procedural step, 253
   See also Charging decisions
Charging conferences, for jury instructions, 356–357
Charging decisions
   overview of, *250*, 253
   defense attorneys' role and, *181*
   judges' role and, *200*
   law in action perspective and, *250*, 253
   law on the books perspective and, *15*, *250*, 253
   prosecutors' role and, 150–154, *151*, 253
   right to counsel and, *178*
   victims' role and, *230*
Charging documents, 253
Chase, Samuel, *211*
Chicago (movie), *36–37*
Chicago Lawyers: The Social Structure of the Bar (Heinz and Laumann), 183
Chief judges, *200*, 202
Chief Justice of U.S. Supreme Court, 72, 79–81
Chief prosecutors, *154*, 157, *157*, 160
   See also District attorneys

Children. *See headings beginning with juvenile*
Children in need of supervision, 475
The Child Savers (Platt), 471
Child savers movement, 471–472
Child-victims, 475
Chivalry/paternalism hypothesis, 415
Christopher, Charissee, 222
Ciavarella, Mark, Jr., *213*
Circuit councils, *80*, 82
Circuit Courts of Appeal, U.S.. *See* U.S. Courts of Appeals
Circuit justice, 73
Circuit riding, 62
Circumstantial evidence, 345
Citizen's Grand Jury Bill of Rights, 264
City attorneys, 158
Civil Asset Forfeiture Act of 2000, *42*
Civil cases and civil law
overview, 39–40, 61
after criminal prosecutions, *44*
asset forfeiture, *42*
burden of proof in, 34–35, *35*
controversies in, 42–43
crime, fighting with, 41
criminal law compared, *45*
defined, 40
judge-made law, 30, 33
remedies in, 40–41
small claims courts, 94
types of, 40
victim compensation and, 236
Civil protection orders, 234
Civil Rights Act of 1964, 69
Civil Rights Act of 1991, 69
Civil rights cases, 68–69, *70*
Claiborne, Harry, *215*
Clark, Janice, *210*
Clear, Todd, 379
Clearance rates, *249*
Clear and convincing evidence, 35, *35*, 77
Clear error, *440*
Clerk of court, 126, *127*
Clinton, William, 208, 461
Closing arguments, *354*, 356
Cocaine, crack vs. powder, *424–425*
Code of legal ethics, 143
Coercion, 282, 284
Coley, Sheilah, 229
Collateral attack, 448
Collins, Robert, *215*
Colonial courts, 91, 333

Combatant Status Review Tribunals (CSRTs), 75–77
Commissioners, for juvenile court, 487
Committees of the Judicial Conference, *80*
Common law, 30–33
confessions and interrogation and, 283, *286*
evidence admissibility and, 282
search and seizure and, 282
Community courts, 102
Community justice, 101–102
Community prosecution, 167–168
Community service, 384–385
Comparison evidence, *349*
Compensatory damages, 40
Competency, 49, 322
Competency to stand trial, 226
Competency to testify, *346*
Complaints, criminal, *250*, 253
Compositional analysis of bullet lead, 347, *349*
Computer files, 294
Conahan, Michael, *213*
Concurrent jurisdiction, 57
Concurring opinions, 443
Conditions of confinement lawsuits, 379–380
Conditions of probation, 383
Conference, for juvenile court, *489*, 491
Confessions, 283–289
exclusionary rule and, 282
false, 455–456
voluntariness standard for, 283–284, *286*
See also Interrogations
Confidentiality, 191
Conflicts of interest, 163, 191
Confrontation
pretrial, 282
right of, 282
Congress, *80*
Congressional Act of 1988, *64*
Consent searches, *292*
Consent surveillance, 293–294
Constitutional Convention, 61–62
Constitutional courts, 74
See also Article III courts
Constitutions as source of law, 32
See also specific numbered amendments; U.S. Constitution
Contemporaneous objection rule, 438
Contempt of court, 263, 360

Contracts, 40
Contract system, for defense attorneys, 185–187
Controversy in courts, 18–22
asset forfeiture, limits on, 42
cameras in courtrooms, 361–362
charging decisions, 253
civil justice and, 42–43
crack cocaine sentencing, *424–425*
death penalty and, *392*, *450*
double jeopardy and, *60*
DUI and distracted driving prosecutions, *95–96*
exclusionary rule, 301, *302*
federal courts, 57
gender bias, *135–136*
grand jury reform, 263–264
habeas corpus review, *450*
indigent defense spending, *186*
judicial discretion, 419
juveniles tried as adults, *482*
Latinos, equal justice and, *224–225*
plea bargaining, 324–327, *325*
reciprocal disclosure, 281–282
Three Strikes and You're Out laws, *426–427*
uncertainties in sentencing, 410
war on drugs, *21*
white-collar crime prosecution rates, *254–255*
Convictions
in federal vs. state court trials, 358
plea bargaining and, 308
severity of punishment and, 428–430
wrongful, 453–458
Cooperation, 101–102, 182
lack of, 229–230
Coordination, 142, 167
Copyright cases, 40, *68*
jurisdiction and, *68*
Corpus delicti, 44, 46, 253
Corrections, 7
See also Jails; Prisons
COSCA. *See* State Court Administrators (COSCA)
Counsel, right to, 175–180, *176*, 284–286
See also Right to counsel
Count bargaining, 310–311, *310*
Court administration, 126–128
Court administrators, 126–128

Court-appointed attorneys, *See also* Defense attorneys

Courthouse justice, dynamics of, 120–145
  See also Courthouses; Delay in court system

Courthouses, 120–145
  overview of, 123–124
  actors in, 125–126, *127*
  courtrooms in, 124–126, *125*
  courtroom work groups and, *131*, 133–136
  dynamics of, 130–136, *131*
  physical characteristics of, 123–124
  security in, 124, 128–130
  See also Courtrooms

Court of appeals. *See* U.S. Courts of Appeals

Court of Appeals Act of 1891, 63, *63*

Court of Appeals for the Armed Forces, 71, *74*

Court Packing Plan, *63, 79, 503*

Courtrooms, 124–126, *125*
  Courtroom 23, Orange County, Florida, 115
  lower courts, 101
  media in, 361–363
  technology and, 115

Courtroom work groups, 133–136, 143
  overview of, *131*, 133–136
  bail agents and, 257–258
  decision-making norms, 316
  defense attorneys as members of, 180–183
  defined, 133
  delay in court system and, 136–139
  exclusionary rule and, 295–301
  informal discovery and, 279–281
  judges as members of, 202–203
  juvenile courts and, 486–488
  lower courts and, 99–100
  mutual interdependence, 133–134
  plea bargaining and, 312, 313–315, 316
  prosecutors as members of, 164–166
  rewards and sanctions, 136, 181–182
  sentencing decisions and, 403–408, *404*
  sentencing norms and, 409

shared decision making, 134
shared norms, 409, 486
socialization and, 134
variability in, 136, 142
See also specific actors in, e.g. judges, prosecutors

Courts
  overview of, 8–10, *9*
  as component of criminal justice system, 6–8, *7*
  crime and, 2–25
  criminal law, effect on, 50–51
  federal vs. state, 8–9, *9*
  fragmentation of, 7–8
  hierarchical vs. communal culture in, 142
  independence of, 5
  specialized courts, 73–77, *74*, 110–115
  staff for, 65, 71–72
  types of, 8–10, *9*
  See also Criminal justice system; Delay in court system; Reform of courts; *specific courts and types of courts*; State courts

Courts-martials, 75

Courts of last resort
  federal, 72
  See also Supreme Court, U.S.
  state, *58*, *106*, 458–460

Court unification, 107–110, *108–109*

Crack cocaine, *424–425*

Crack houses, 41

Crawford County Courthouse, Arkansas, 128, 130

Crime, 2–25, 247–248
  overview of, 12, *248*
  amount of, 12
  categories of, 12
  constitutional safeguards and, *38*
  cost of fighting, 6
  courts and, 5–6
  death-eligible, 393
  defense attorney' role and, *181*
  defined, 46, *250*
  elements of, 44–46, 253
  FBI statistics on, 247–248
  fighting with civil remedies, 41
  index crimes, 247, *248*
  judges' role and, *200*
  key developments concerning, *264*
  landmarks and timeline of cases, *502–505*

measuring, 247–248, *248*
normal crimes, 134–136
as political issue, 83–84
prosecutors' role and, *151*
rhetoric about, 5–6
right to counsel and, *178*
serious, *47*, 409
Type I vs. Type II offenses, 247, *248*
types of, 12, 247, *248*
victims' role and, 228, *230*
See also Defenses to crimes

Crime control model, 19
  overview of, 19, *19*
  asset forfeiture and, *42*
  indigent defense and, *186*
  judicial sentencing discretion, 419
  juvenile courts and, 495–496
  plea bargaining and, *325*

Crime Victims Fund, 236

Crime Victims' Rights Act (2004), *235*

Criminal appeals, 445–447, *446*

Criminal bar, 183–184

Criminal defense, 46–50
  See also Defenses

Criminal division of the justice department, *154*, 155

Criminal intent, 45–46

The Criminalization of Domestic Violence (Fagan), 232

Criminal justice system
  as adversary system, 33–35
  asset forfeiture and, *42*
  burden of proof in, 34–35, *35*, 344–345
  complexity of, 57
  components of, 6–8, *7*
  constitutional safeguards in, *38*
  controversies in, 18–22
  costs of, 6
  defined, 6
  fragmentation of, 7–8, 150
  funding for, 6, 84
  interdependence of, 7, 133–134
  landmarks and timeline of cases, *502–505*
  as a nonsystem, 8
  public perceptions about, 6
  rights of the accused in, 36–43
  shifting balance in, 20
  steps of process, 11–14, *12*, *15*, *250*
  tensions and conflicts, 8
  wedding cake model of, 267–269, *268*

Criminal law, 43–50, *45*
  effects on the courts, 50–51
  inconsistencies in, 50
  plea bargaining and, 50, 309–311
  sentencing and, 50–51
Criminal procedure, 244–273
  case attrition and, 265–267, *266*
  constitutionalization of, 68
  constitutional provisions dealing with, *38*
  discovery and, 277
  judges' role and, *200*
  key developments concerning, *264–265*
  law on the books vs. law in action perspectives on, *250*
  right to counsel and, 175–179, *176, 178*
  steps of, 11–14, *12, 15,* 244–273, *250*
  See also specific steps, e.g. arrest initial appearance
Critical legal studies and postmodern jurisprudence, *529*
Cross-examination, 353, 355
  right of, 33
Cruel and Unusual Clause
  conditions of confinement lawsuits, 380
  death penalty and, 388–391, 396
  Section 1983 cases, *70*
  sentencing options and, 377, 410
  text of, 508
CSI: Crime Scene Investigations, 5, *129,* 348–350, *351*
CSI Effect, 5, 348–350, *351*
Cumulative or unduly prejudicial evidence, *346*
Custodial interrogations, 284
Cyber-courts, 115
Cynicism, legal, 229

D

Dade County, Florida, Circuit Court, 112
Daly, Kathleen, 415
Damages, 40–41
Daubert test, 347–350
Davis, Richard Allen, 238, 402, *426*
Day fines, 383
Deadlocked juries, 357
Deadly force, 48
Death-eligible cases, 393
Death penalty, 14, 387–395

overview of, *378,* 387–388
  abolition of, 388
  Antiterrorism and Effective Death Penalty Act, *64, 235, 450,* 451
  appeals and, 393–395
  bifurcated trials and, 389
  costs of, 395
  defined, 387
  developmental limitations on, 393
  discrimination and, 416–418
  DNA testing and, *448–449*
  double jeopardy and, *60*
  Eighth Amendment standards and, 388–391, 396
  eligibility for, limiting, 393
  habeas corpus petitions and, 393, *450*
  history of, 387–388
  ineffective assistance of counsel and, 179
  juries and, 391–393
  juveniles and, 370, 393
  key developments concerning, *390,* 417
  lethal injection and, 391
  mandatory laws vs. discretion in, 388–389
  mentally retarded people and, *394–395*
  method of execution, 389–391
  minimum age for, 393
  moratorium on, *392*
  number of people executed, 387, *388*
  offender-victim dyads and, 417
  proportionality requirement and, 163
  prosecutorial ethics and, 163
  for rape, 416
  state high courts and, 459–460
  stays and, 73
  time from sentence to execution, 395
  use of, *378,* 389
  victim impact statements and, 238
Death Penalty Information Center, 453
Death-qualified juries, 391–393
Decentralization, 116, 154
Decisions; Sentencing options; U.S. Sentencing Commission
Declaratory judgment, 40
Deductive reasoning, 524–526
Deegan, Gerry, *152*

Defendants, *127,* 220–228, 241
  overview of, 223–226, *223*
  as actors in judicial system, 11
  bail and, 254–259
  binding over, 260
  career criminals and, 223, 314
  characteristics of, 223–226, *223*
  in court, 226–228
  defined, 40, 226
  diversity of, 223
  domestic violence and, 232–234
  gender and, 223–224, *223*
  indigent, 99, 174–179, 184–188, 226
  ineffective assistance of counsel and, 179, 457
  plea bargaining and, 314
  power vs. powerlessness of, 226–228
  prior records and, 409
  prior relationship with victims and, 231–232
  pro se, 226–227
  questioning, in plea agreements, 320–322
  race and, *223,* 225–226, *225*
  rights of, generally, 226–228
  right to counsel and, 175–180, *176*
  self-representation by, 179–180, 226–227
  social media trap and, 227–228
  talking too much by, 99–100
  testimony by, 355–356
  as underclass, 224–225
  views on lawyers, 189–190
  waiver of rights by, 286, 300, 320
  as witness, *354,* 355–356
  See also Indigents; Plea bargaining
Defense attorneys, 172–195
  overview of, 11, 175–180
  adversary system, role in, 34
  assessment of, 182–183
  assigned counsel system for, 184–185
  case-in-chief, *354,* 355–356
  conflicts of interest and, 191
  contract systems for, 185–187
  cooperation and, 182
  counseling role, 188–189
  in courtroom, 124, *125*
  courtroom work groups, as members of, 180–183
  criminal bar and, 183–184
  disclosure of evidence by, 281–282

duties of, 190–193
ethics and, 190–193
"fishing expedition" by, 278, 279
ineffective assistance of counsel
    by, 179, 457
juvenile courts and, 487–488
law in action perspective and, *181*
law on the books perspective and,
    181
liability of, 191–193
obtaining clients and getting paid,
    183–184
as officers of the court, 180,
    190–191
plea bargaining and, 314
preliminary hearings and, *181*,
    260–261
public defenders, 187–188, 189
rewards and sanctions for,
    181–182
right to counsel and, 175–180, *176*
role in stages of judicial process,
    181
self-representation by defendants
    and, 179–180
sentencing decisions and, *181*,
    404, 405–406
solo practitioners, 183
styles of, 182
suppression motions and, 295–300
trial process and, *181*, *354*,
    355–356
views on clients, 189
See also Plea bargaining
Defenses to crimes, 46–50
    affirmative defenses, 34
    alibi defense, 46–48, 281
    defenses of excuse, 48
    delinquency/age as, 50
    insanity defense, 48–50
    justification defenses, 48
    negation of *mens rea*, 48
    procedural defenses, 38
Delay in court system, 136–142, 143
    overview of, 136–139
    case-processing standards and,
        137, *137*
    consequences of, 137–138
    costs of, 139
    defense attorneys and, 141
    defined, 137
    law in action perspective, 140–142
    law on the books perspective,
        139–140

prosecutors and, 141
unnecessary, 137
victims and witnesses and, 228, 230
See also Specialized courts
Delinquency, 475, 489
See also Juvenile delinquency
Delsohn, Gary, 160
D'Emic, Matthew, 115
Democracies, rights in, 36–37
Demonstrative evidence, 345
Dempsey, Michelle, *168*
De novo review, *440*
Department of Justice, U.S., 155
Deportation, *225*
Derivative evidence, 282
Detention, 490
    home detention, 385–386
    of juveniles, 490–491
    pretrial, 12–13, 259
Detention hearings, 490–491
Determinate sentencing, 419, *420*,
    425–426, 430
Deterrence, 372–373
Diallo, Amadou, 44, *505*
Dickens, Charles, 138
Direct evidence, 345
Direct examination, 353
Direct restitution, 384
Disabilities
    Americans with Disabilities Act,
        68, 69
    legal protections and, 69
    mental health courts, 114–115
    mentally retarded people, *394–
        395*
    self-representation and mental
        illness, 180
Disbarment, 143
Disciplinary proceedings, 143
Discovery, 277–282, 303
    overview of, 13, 277
    in civil vs. criminal cases, 277
    defined, 277
    of exculpatory evidence, 278
    formal, 277–279
    of impeachment evidence,
        278–279
    inevitable, *283*
    informal, 279–281
    key developments in, *279–280*
    law in action perspective and,
        279–281
    law on the books perspective and,
        277–279

prosecutors' role and, *151*,
    277–281
reciprocal disclosure, 281–282
witness lists, 281
Discretion, 132–133, 143
    overview of, *131*, 132–133
    abuse of discretion review, *440*
    appeals and, 438–439
    bail and, 257
    case attrition and, 266–267
    defined, 132
    nullification by, 428–430
    plea agreements and, 309–311,
        310, 322
    plea bargaining and, 311–313
    prosecutors and, 149, 150, 169,
        266–267, 271, 428
    in sentencing, 376–377, 419
Discretionary appellate jurisdiction,
    438, 439
Discretionary dockets, 63, 358–359
Discrimination
    bail and, 259
    death penalty and, 416–418
    defined, 410
    economic status and sentencing,
        414
    gender and sentencing, 414–415
    imbalance vs., 411
    laws against, 68–69
    in noncapital sentencing, 414–416
    race and sentencing, 415–416
    sentencing, generally, 410, 411–414
    See also Racial issues
Dismissal, *490*, 492
Disparity in sentencing, 410, 411–414
Disposition of appellate cases, *441*,
    444
Disposition of juvenile cases,
    492–495, *492*
Dissenting opinion, 443
Distracted driving prosecutions,
    95–96
District attorneys, 157, *157*
    assistant, 159, 161
    in courtroom, 124, *125*
    Neighborhood District Attorney
        approach, 167–168
    See also Chief prosecutors;
        Prosecutors
District Courts, U.S., *9*, 65–69
    overview of, *58*, 65–69
    caseload of, *66*, *70*
    magistrate judges and, 65

Diversity jurisdiction, 66–67, 83
Diversity of citizenship, 66–67
Diversity of judges, 208–209, *210*
Divorce cases, gender bias and, *135*
Dixon, Herbert, 115
DNA evidence, *22*, 347, *504*
  as gold standard, 348, 455
  House, Paul and, 436, *448–449*
  limitations of, 348, 455
  wrongful convictions and, 347, *392*, 453–454, 457
Dog Pound (movie), 494
Domestic relations cases, 40, 232–234, *233*
Domestic violence, 232–234, *233*
Domestic violence courts, 113–114, 234
Double jeopardy, 438
  acquittal and, 438
  dual court system and, *60*
  Fifth Amendment, *60*, 438
  preliminary hearings and, 260
Drug courts, 90, 112–113, 117
Drugs
  drug busts, 88
  federal vs. state courts for, 83, 85
  pretrial detention and, 256
  War on Drugs, *21*, *104*
  See also Drunk driving
Drug War Politics: The Price of Denial (Bertram et al.), *21*
Drunk driving
  increasing prosecution of, *95–96*
  Lohan, Lindsay, and intermediate sanctions, *386*
  MADD and, 11, 84, *95*, 240
  sentencing and, 100
  See also Drugs
Dual court system
  overview of, 57, *58*
  defined, 8–9
  double jeopardy and, *60*
  prosecutors and, 154, *154*
Due process, 37–38, 68
  in juvenile courts, 483–486, *484*
  "revolution in," 274
  See also Due Process Clause; Due process model
Due Process Clause, *39*, 282, 334, 508
Due process model, 19–20, *19*
  asset forfeiture and, *42*
  death penalty and, 436
  indigent defense and, *186*
  judicial sentencing discretion, 419

plea bargaining and, *325*
  youth crime prevention, 496
Due process of law, 38
Duff, Brian, *215*
DUI. *See* Drunk driving
Duke lacrosse sexual assault case, 146, *148–149*, *153*, 162, 169
DuPage County, Illinois, DA's office, 161, 166
DWI. *See* Drunk driving

E

Eavesdropping, 293–294
Ebbers, Bernie, *254*
Economics, law and, *529*
Economic status
  defense and indigency, 174–179, 184–188
  sentencing decisions and, 414
  white-collar crimes and, *254–255*
  See also Indigents
Eighth Amendment, *39*, 380, *381*
  bail and, *38*, 254, 257, *264*, 508
  death penalty and, 388–391, *394–395*, 396
  text of, 508
  See also Cruel and Unusual Clause
Elections
  of judges, *204*, 205–206
  of prosecutors, 157
Electronically stored information (ESI), 294
Electronic media, in courtroom, 361–363
Electronic monitoring, 385–386
Electronic surveillance, 77, 291–294
Elements of crimes, 44–46, 253
En banc hearings, 72, 437
Enemy combatants, 75–77, 284, 462–463
Enron, *254*, *505*
Equity, 40
Erie, Pennsylvania, DA's office, 161, 166
Error, 444
  reversible vs. harmless, 444
Error correction, by appellate courts, 437, 444
Estimator variables, 454
Ethics
  defense attorneys and, 190–193
  defined, 143
  judges and, 216–217
  legal, 142–143

professional, 142–143, 190–193
  prosecutors and, 162–163
Evidence, 274–305, 345
  overview of, 345, *346*
  best-evidence rule, *346*
  case attrition and, 266–267
  chain of custody, *346*
  circumstantial, 345
  clear and convincing, 35, *35*
  common law and, 282
  comparison, *349*
  constitutional provisions and, *38*
  cumulative or unduly prejudicial, *346*
  Daubert ruling, 347–350
  defense attorneys' role and, *181*
  defined, 345
  derivative, 282
  direct, 345
  disclosure by prosecutors, 163, 277–281
  discovery and, 277–282
  DNA, *22*, 347
  exculpatory, 163, 278
  expert witnesses, 346–347, 458
  forensic, 347–350, *349*, *350*, 455
  Frye test and, 347
  hearsay, *346*
  illegally obtained, 282–283, 295
  interrogations and confessions, 283–289
  judges' role and, *200*
  juvenile courts and, *489*, 491–492
  motions about, 13
  nontestimonial, 284
  objections to, 350–353
  preponderance of, 35, *35*
  prosecutors' role and, *151*
  reliability of, 347
  rules of, *283*, 345, *346*
  scientific, *22*, 345, 347–350, *349*
  search and seizure and, 289–295
  suppression of, 282–283, *283*, 295–300
  types of, 345
  victim impact, 237–238
  victims' role and, *230*
  See also Confessions; Discovery; DNA evidence; Search warrants; Suppression motions
Evidence-based corrections, 373, 405
Evidence cameras, in high-technology courtroom, 115
Evil woman hypothesis, 415

Ewing, Gary, *111*
Exclusionary rule, 282–283, 295, 460
　overview of, 282
　Burger Court and, 301
　controversy over, 301, *302*
　courtroom work groups and,
　　295–301
　exceptions to, *283*
　good-faith exception to, *283, 302*
Exculpatory evidence, 163, 278
Excuse, defenses of, 48
Executive appointments of judges,
　203–205, *204*
Executive branch, *80*
Executive responsibility, in
　sentencing, 377
Exemptions from jury duty, 339, *340*
Exigent circumstances, 289
Expert witnesses, 281, 346–347, *354*,
　458
Expiation, 371
Extradition, 59, 257
Extralegal factors, 357, 410
Eyewitness identifications, mistaken,
　454–455

F

Facebook, 227
Fact-partial challenges, 341
Fagan, Jeffrey, 232
Failure to appear, 259
Fair Sentencing Act of 2010, *424–425*
Family court, 474
FBI. *See* Federal Bureau of
　Investigation
Federal Bureau of Investigation
　(FBI), 155
　crime statistics, 247–248
Federal Circuit, 70–72
Federal courts, 54–87
　overview of, 57–61, *58*
　administration, 79–82, *80*
　case filings in, *70*
　caseloads, 82–83
　consequences of involvement for,
　　83–84
　criminal prosecutions, types and
　　percentages of, *67*
　discovery in, 277
　diversity jurisdiction, 66–67, 83
　double jeopardy and, *60*
　dual court system, as part of, 57,
　　58
　federal questions and, 67–69, *68*

Foreign Intelligence Surveillance
　Court, *74*, 77
　funding and, 79, 84
　habeas corpus petitions and, *450*
　history of, 61–63, *63–64*
　judges, number of, 82–83
　judicial appointments, 203–204
　Judiciary Act of 1789 and, 62, *63*
　jurisdiction, 57–61
　jurisdiction, reduction of
　　(considered), 83
　key developments in, *63–64*
　layers of, 63
　organization of, 57–61, *58, 80*
　plea bargaining, judges and, 315
　postconviction review and,
　　448–453
　prosecutors in, 155–156
　role of, 84–85
　sentencing and, 68
　specialized, 73–77, *74*
　state courts compared, 8–9, *9*, 103
　unanimity of juries, 337
　U.S. Courts of Appeals, 70–72
　U.S. magistrate judges, 65
　U.S. Supreme Court, 72–73
　See also specific courts
Federal Courts Improvement Act, *64*
Federalists, 61–62
Federal judicial administration,
　79–82, *80*
Federal Judicial Center, *64, 80*, 82
Federal Jury Selection and Service
　Act of 1968, 338
Federal Magistrate Act, *64*
Federal question, 67–69, *68*, 73
Federal Rules of Civil Procedure, 277
Federal Rules of Criminal Procedure,
　281, 320
Fees, collecting, 184
Feige, David, 189, 234, 314
Feinstein, Dianne, 237
Felonies, 12
　caseloads and, 131
　conviction rate for, 11, 309
　initial appearance for, 252–253
　overview of stages in cases of, *12*
　prior relationships and, 232
　profile of defendants, *223*
　race and, 11
　right to counsel and, *178*
　trial rates for, *309*
　wedding cake model and,
　　268–269, *268*

Ferguson, Colin, 180
Fifth Amendment, *38*, 39, *39, 286*,
　508
　double jeopardy clause, 60, 438
　Due Process Clause and, *39*, 508
　exclusionary rule and, 282
　grand juries and, 261–262, *264*
　Miranda warnings and, 284, *285*
　self-incrimination and, 39, *39*, 282,
　　284, 355
　text of, 508
　use immunity and, 263
Fines
　day fines, 383
　defined, *378*
　Eighth Amendment and, 508
　revenue from, 94
　as sentencing option, *378*, 383
　traffic offenses, 93–94
Fingerprinting, *349, 352*
Firearms comparison evidence, *349*
First Amendment, *39*, 360, 508
First appeals, right to counsel for,
　178
FISA, 294–295
FISA Court, *64, 74, 74*, 77
Fixed sentences, 376, *420*
Flemming, Roy, 165–166
Florida
　court system, 6, *108*
　Dade County Circuit Court, 112
　high-technology courtrooms in,
　　115
Foreign Intelligence Surveillance Act
　(FISA), *64*, 294–295
Foreign Intelligence Surveillance
　Court, *64, 74, 74*, 77
Foreign Intelligence Surveillance
　Court of Review, *64, 74*
Forensic document comparison
　evidence, *349*
Forensic scientific evidence, 347–350,
　349, 350
　challenging, 352–353
　improper, 455
Forfeiture of assets, 41, *42*
Formal discovery, 277–279
Fourteenth Amendment, 38–39, *39*
　Due Process Clause of, 282, 334
　exclusionary rule and, 282
　interrogations and, 286
　selective incorporation and,
　　38–39, *39*
　text of, 509

Fourth Amendment, *38*, 39, *39*, 282, 289, *296*, 508
  reasonableness clause, 289, 291
  warrants clause, 289
  See also Search and seizure; Search warrants
Fragmentation of criminal justice system, 7–8, 150
Fraud prosecutions, *254–255*
Freedom of the press, 360
The French Connection (movie), *104*
Friedman, Lawrence, 29
Fruit of the poisonous tree, 282–283
Frye test, 324, 347
The Fugitive, 360
Funding
  federal courts, 79, 84
  state courts, 100, 110, 116–117
Fusion of guilty acts and guilty intent, 44–45

G

Gag orders, 360–361
Garbage, searches of, 459
Gault, Gerald, 470, *484*, 496
Gender, Crime, and Punishment (Daly), 415
Gender and gender bias
  of defendants, 223–224, *223*
  gender equity, law on, 69
  juvenile arrests and, 488
  as problem for courts, *135–136*
  sentencing decisions and, 414–415
  See also Sexual assault
General deterrence goal, 372
General jurisdiction, 103
  See also Trial courts of general jurisdiction
Geneva Conventions, 75, 76
Geographical jurisdiction, 57–59
Geography of justice, 411, *412–413*
Geragos, Mark, *36–37*
Gerstein hearings, 251–253, *252*
  See also Initial appearance
Gideon, Clarence Earl, 174, *177*, 193
Gideon's Trumpet (Lewis), 193
Giffords, Gabrielle, 28, *49*
Gingrich, Newt, *211*
Ginsburg, Ruth Bader, 344–345, *424*, *434*, 461, *462*
Goetz, Bernhard, *44*
Goldkamp, John, 259
Goldman, Ronald, *44*
Good faith, *283*, 302

Good time, to reduce sentence, 377
Google, 363
GPS monitoring, 387
Grace, Nancy, *37*, *164*
Grand juries, 261–264
  overview of, 13, *250*, 261–262, *261*
  burden of proof, 13
  constitutional safeguards and, *38*
  defense attorneys' role and, *181*
  history of, 261
  immunity of, 262–263
  indictments by, 13, *250*, 262
  judges' role and, *200*
  juvenile cases and, *489*
  key developments concerning, *264–265*
  law in action perspective and, *250*, 263
  law on the books perspective and, 262–263
  powers of, *250*, *261*, 263
  probable cause, preliminary hearings compared, *261*
  prosecutors' role and, *151*, 263
  reform of, 263–264
  right to counsel and, *178*
  secrecy and, 262
  size of, 262
  variability in state use of, *262*
  victims' role and, *230*
Great writ, *habeas corpus* as, 449
Green, Alan, *213*
Grisham, John, 198, 217
Guantanamo Bay, 76, 77, 462–463
Gubernatorial appointments of judges, *204*, 205
Guilt, presumption of factual, 312
Guilty act (*actus reus*), 44, 45
Guilty intent (*mens rea*), 44, 45–46
Guilty pleas, 13, 178, 309–311, *310*, 319–324, 358
  informal prosecutorial discovery and, 281
  See also Plea bargaining
Guilty verdicts, *49*, 346
Gusfield, Joseph, *95*

H

Habeas corpus, writ of, 32, 393, 449, *450*, 452
  for enemy combatants, 462–463
  as great writ, 449
Habeas corpus petitions, 68, *70*, 75, 449, *450*

congressional restriction of, 451
  federal prisoners and, 451–453
  judicial expansion and contraction of, 451, 461
  key developments on, *452*
Hair microscopy, *349*
Harmless error, 444
Harrison Narcotics Act of 1914, *21*, 502
Hasan, Nidal Malik, 75
Hastings, Alcee, 214, *215*
Hatch, Orin, 205
Hauptman, Bruno, 361
Hearing officers, 487
Hearsay, *346*
Hedonistic calculus, 372
Hennis, Timothy, *60*
Heumann, Milton, 281
Hierarchical jurisdiction, 60–61
Hierarchy rule, 247
Hill, Belinda, *196*
Hinckley, John, Jr., *49*
Hip-hop culture, 229
Hispanics, *224–225*, 226
  bail and, 258
  as felony defendants, 11, *225*
  pretrial detention and, 258
  sentencing decisions and, 414
  on Supreme Court, *224*
Holmes, Oliver Wendell, 30, 45
Home detention, 385–386
Homicide, 11, *47*, 418
  negligent, 45, 47
  See also Death penalty
House, Paul, 436, *448–449*, 463
Hung juries, 337, *355*, 357
Hunter, Arthur, 217

I

ICAs. *See* Intermediate courts of appeals
ICE (Immigration and Customs Enforcement), *225*
Illegal search and seizure, 295, 301
Illinois, DuPage County DA's office, 161, 166
Illinois Juvenile Court Act, *485*
Immigrants, legal issues and, *224–225*
Immigration and Customs Enforcement (ICE), *225*
Immunity, 162–163, 262–263
  See also Prosecutorial misconduct
Impeachment, 214

evidence, 278–279, 355
of judges, 213–214
of U.S. president, 81, 214
*Imprisoning Communities: How
Mass Incarceration Makes
Disadvantaged Neighborhoods
Worse* (Clear), 379
Imprisonment, 378–380, *378*
costs of, 380–382
key developments concerning,
381–382
numbers of people confined, *379*
See also Jails; Prisons
Incapacitation, 374–375
*Indefensible: One Lawyer's Journey
into the Inferno of American Justice*
(Feige), 189
Indeterminate sentences, 376
Index crimes, 247, *248*
Indictments, 13, *250*, 262
See also Grand juries
Indigents, 99, 174–179, *176, 177*
appeals and, 445
defined, 184
providing with attorneys,
184–188, *186*, 445
rights as defendants, 226
See also Defendants; Economic
status
Individualization of sentences, 100
Inductive reasoning, 523–524, *525*
Ineffective assistance of counsel, 179,
457
Infancy, 50
Inference, 34
Inferior courts, 92
See also Lower courts; Trial courts
of limited jurisdiction
Informal discovery, 279–281
Informants, 456
snitches, 229, 456, 458
Information, *250*, 253
Inheritance, 40
Initial appearance, 251–253
overview of, 12, *250*, 251–253
constitutional safeguards and, *38*
defense attorneys' role and, *181*
defined, *250*
judges' role and, *200*
key developments concerning,
264
prosecutors' role and, *151*
right to counsel and, *178*
timing of, 251, *252*, 270

victims' role and, *230*
See also Preliminary hearing
Initial hearing, *489*, 490
Injunctions, 40–41, *41*
Inmates. *See* Defendants; Jails;
Prisons
Innocence, presumption of, 34, 35,
344, 355
Innocence Project, 347, 453, 455
In personum jurisdiction, 59–60
In rem, 42
Insanity defense, 48–50
for indigent defendants, 226
Intake, *489*, 490
Intake decisions, *489*, 490
Intellectual property, 40, *68*
Intelligence surveillance, 294–295
Intensive supervision probation, 385,
400
Intent, 45–46
Interest groups, 84, 205, *211–212*
Interlocutory orders, 438
Intermediate courts of appeals
(ICAs), 105–106, *105*, 458–459
See also Appellate courts
Intermediate sanctions, *378*, 384–387,
386, 400
International Court of Justice, *225*
Interrogations, 283–289
custodial, 284
of enemy combatants, 284
exclusionary rule and, 282
Fifth Amendment and, 282
Fourteenth Amendment and, 286
key developments in law,
286–289, *286–288*
Miranda warnings and, 284–286,
285, 300
police testimony and, 300–301
right to counsel and, *178*, 284–286
Sixth Amendment and, 284–286
See also Confessions
Intestacy, 40
Intimidation of victims and
witnesses, 231
The Invisible Woman (Belknap), 415
Irrelevant, 346
Irreparable injury, 41
Italy, Amanda Knox case in, *447*

J

Jackson, Michael, *36, 37, 44*, 332, 340,
363–364
Jackson, Robert, 150

Jails
bail and, 258, 259
overcrowding in, 379, 396
See also Prisons
Jefferson, Thomas, 62, *211*
Jencks Act, 278, *279*
John Birch Society, *211*
Johnson, Lyndon, 82
JP (justice of the peace), 94–99
Judge Judy, *201–202*
Judge-made law, 30, 33
Judges, 196–219
overview of, 11, 199–202
activist, *211*, 530
as actors in judicial system, 11
adversary system, role in, 33–34
Article III vs. Article I, 74, 203
assessment of, 209–215
attacks on, *211–212*
backgrounds of, 208, 411–414
benefits of being, 199–200
campaign contributions and, 217
caseloads of, 200
chief judges, *200*, 202
conduct commissions and laws,
212–215, *214*
court administration and, 71–72,
79
courtroom work groups, as
members of, 202–203
for courts of appeals, 437
diversity of, 208–209, *210*
ethics and, 216–217
federal, 82–83
federal, disciplinary actions
against, *215–216*
federal vs. state, 11
frustrations of, 200–201
independence of, 209, *211–212*
judge shopping, 203
jury verdicts, agreement with, 358
for juvenile courts, 486–487
key development concerning, *214*
legal reasoning by, 528, *529*
mandatory retirement ages for, 212
misconduct by, 209, 212, *213*
nonlawyers as, 96, 98–99
plea bargaining and, 315, 322
political opinions, expression of,
211–212
powers of, 199, *200*
role in criminal procedure, *200*
sanctions and, 212
selection methods for, 203–207, *204*

Judges (*Continued*)
  sentencing decisions and, 14, *404*, 406–407, 411–414
  sentencing discretion and, 376–377, 419
  staff for, 65, 126–128
  state conduct commissions and, 212–213, *214*
  suppression motions and, 300
  Supreme Court, current, *434, 462*
  See also Judicial selection; *specific types of judges*
Judges Bill of 1925, *63*
Judge shopping, 203
Judgment, 40
Judgments, declaratory, 40
Judicial activism, 530
Judicial Conduct and Disability Act (1980), 213–215, *214*
Judicial conduct commissions, state, 212–213, *214*
Judicial Conference of the United States, *80*, 81, 444
Judicial Conferences of the Circuits, *80*
Judicial Councils of the Circuits, *80*, 82
Judicial Councils Reform and Judicial Conduct and Disability Act, 213–215
Judicial elections. *See* Judicial selection
Judicial federalism, new, 459
Judicial independence, 209, *211–212*
Judicial misconduct, 212, *213*, 456–457
Judicial restraint, 530
Judicial review
  creation of, 62
  standards of, 439–441, *440*
  See also Appellate courts
Judicial selection, 203–207, *204*
  ABA Standing Committee on, 204–205
  backgrounds of judges and, 208
  consequences of, 207–209
  diversity and, 208–209
  elections for, *204*, 205–206, 217
  evaluation of methods, 207–209
  executive appointments, 203–205, *204*
  federal courts, 62, 65, 203–204
  gubernatorial appointments, *204*, 205

interest groups and, 205
  legislative appointments, *204*
  merit selection, *204*, 206–207
  retention elections, 206
  Senate confirmation of judges, 65, 203–204
  Supreme Court, 72
Judicial waiver laws, 478–479
Judiciary Act of 1789, 62, *63*
Judiciary Act of 1801, 62
Judy, Judge, *201–202*
Juries, 338–344
  alternate jurors, 341
  bias of, 343–344, 357–358
  challenges, in jury selection, *338*, 341
  deadlocked, 357
  death-qualified, 391–393
  deliberations by, *354*, 357–358
  educating jurors, 343
  excusing jurors through voir dire, 341
  exemptions from jury duty, 339, *340*
  expectations about scientific evidence, 348–350, *350*
  federal vs. state courts, 334, 337
  hung juries, 337, *355*, 357
  instructions to, *354*, 356–357
  juror requirements, 339
  jury consultants, 343–344
  master jury list, 338–339, *338*
  media and, 357
  nullification of, 359
  petit juries, 333
  pretrial publicity and, 360–361
  scientific jury selection, 343–344
  selection process for, 338–343, *338*
  sequestering of, 361
  service on, 341–343
  size of, 335–337, *336*
  television shows, effect on, *202*
  unanimity and, 337
  venire, *338*, 339
  voir dire, *338*, 339–341
  See also Trials by jury
Jurisdiction, 57–61
  age and juvenile court, 476, 477, *478*
  appellate, 61, 439, 460
  concurrent, 57
  diversity, 66–67
  extradition and, 59
  federal question, 67–69, *68*

general, 103
  geographical, 57–59
  hierarchical, 60–61
  original, 61
  personal, 59–60
  subject matter, 59, 474–476
  venue and, 57–59
Jurisprudence and legal reasoning, 528, *529*
Jury. *See* Juries
Jury box, 125, *125*
Jury consultants, 343–344
Jury deliberations, *354*, 357–358
Jury instructions, *354*, 356–357
Jury legislation, 359
Jury nullification, 359
Jury trial penalty, 317
Just deserts, 371
Justice, as omitted from definition of law, 29
Justice at Stake, *212*, 217
Justice community, 102
Justice Delayed (Church et al.), 139
Justice of the peace courts, 94–99
  reforming, 98–99
Justices of Supreme Court, *434, 462*
  See also specific justices by name
Justification defenses, 48
Juvenile courts, 468–499
  overview of, 472–473
  adult courts compared, 472–473
  adult court, transfers to, 478–483, *480–481*
  adults, treatment as, *482*, 495–496
  age, jurisdiction based on, 476, *477, 478*
  caseloads, *475*
  civil law and, 473
  congressional acts and, 485–486
  court decisions, key, 483–485, *485*
  court process, steps in, 488–495, *489–490*
  courtroom work groups and, 486–488
  drug courts, 113
  due process and, 483–486, 496
  future of, 495–496
  helping emphasis of, 472
  history of, 471–472
  informal proceedings in, 472
  organization of, 473–474
  parens patriae doctrine and, 472, 486
  processing of cases, *493*

secrecy and, 473
subject matter jurisdiction,
474–476
waivers and, 478–483
See also Juvenile Delinquency;
Juveniles
Juvenile delinquency, 475, 488, 489
as a defense, 50
age limits, jurisdiction and, 476,
477, 478
defined, 475
premise of laws on, 50
rate of, 488, 493
See also Juvenile Courts; Juveniles
Juvenile Justice and Delinquency
Prevention Act of 1974, 485, 485
Juveniles
crime prevention for, 496
death penalty and, 370, 393
status offenses by, 248, 475, 493
transfers to adult court, 478–483
treatment as adults, 482, 495–496
as victims, 475, 488
See also Juvenile courts; Juvenile
Delinquency

K

Kagan, Elena, 208, 434, 462, 462
Kamisar, Yale, 302
Keller, Sharon, 213
Kennedy, Anthony, 324, 434, 448, 461,
462, 463
Kennedy, Darlene, 495
Kent, Samuel, 216
Kevorkian, Jack, 180
"Kids for cash" scandal, 213
Kimbrough, Derrick, 423–425
King, Rodney, 44
Klaas, Polly, 238, 402–403, 426
Knock-and-announce, 291
Knox, Amanda, 447
Konop, Alan, 172
Kozinski, Alex, 216
Kozlowski, L. Dennis, 254
Kurland, Philip, 209

L

Lady Justice, 403, 430
Lanier, David, 212
Larceny (theft), 45, 47
Latinos, 224–225
See also Hispanics
Law, 29–33
basis of, 29

practice of, 183–184
sources of, 32–33
See also Common law; Laws
Law & Order, 129
Law and economics, 529
Law and Order: Criminal Intent, 129
Law and Order: Special Victims Unit,
129, 239–240
Law Dictionary for Nonlawyers (Oran),
29
Law in action perspective
overview of, 15, 17–18, 18
appellate policymaking, 459
appellate process, 441
assembly-line justice and, 131
bail and, 250, 256–257
characteristics of serious crimes,
47
charging decisions and, 253
criminal appeals and, 445–447
criminal procedure and, 250
defense attorneys' role and, 181
delay in court system and,
140–142
discovery, 279–281, 279–280
grand juries and, 263
informal discovery and, 279–281
jury selection and, 338
juvenile courts and, 474, 475–476,
489–490
law on the books compared, 15,
18, 47
nullification by discretion,
428–430
plea bargaining, 310, 311–313
preliminary hearings and,
260–261
pretrial criminal procedure and,
250
probable cause and, 260–261
prosecutors' role and, 151
sentencing, 378, 404
state high courts, 459
trial process and, 336, 354–355
trials as balancing wheels,
359–360
victims' role and, 230
Law on the books perspective
overview of, 14, 15
appellate policy making, 459
appellate process, 441
assembly-line justice and, 131
bail and, 250, 254–256
characteristics of serious crimes, 47

charging decisions and, 253
criminal appeals and, 445
defense attorneys' role and, 181
defined, 14
delay in court system and,
139–140
determinate sentencing, 419, 420
discovery, 277–279
grand juries and, 262–263
jury selection and, 338
juvenile court process, steps in,
489–490
law in action compared, 15,
18, 47
plea agreements, 309–311, 310
preliminary hearings and, 260
pretrial criminal procedure and,
250
probable cause and, 260
prosecutors' role and, 151
sentencing decisions and, 404
sentencing options, 378
state high courts, 458–459
trial by jury and, 334–337
trial process and, 336, 354–355
victims' role and, 230
Laws
Administrative Office Act of 1939,
64, 79
Age Discrimination in
Employment Act of 1973, 69,
212
Americans with Disabilities Act,
68, 69
Antiterrorism and Effective Death
Penalty Act (AEDPA), 64, 235,
450, 451
Bail Reform Act of 1984, 256, 264,
504
Bankruptcy Abuse Prevention
and Consumer Protection Act
of 2005, 66
Bankruptcy Reform Act of 1978,
64
Civil Asset Forfeiture Act of 2000,
42
Civil Rights Acts of 1964 and
1991, 69
Congressional Act of 1988, 64
Court of Appeals Act of 1891, 63
Fair Sentencing Act of 2010,
424–425
Federal Jury Selection and Service
Act of 1968, 338

Laws (*Continued*)
  Harrison Narcotics Act of 1914, *21*, *502*
  Jencks Act, 278, *279*
  Judges Bill of 1925, *63*
  Judicial Conduct and Disability Act, 213, *214*
  Judiciary Act of 1789, 62, *63*
  Judiciary Act of 1801, 62
  Juvenile Court Act of 1938, *485*
  Juvenile Justice and Delinquency Prevention Act of 1974, 485, *485*
  Military Commissions Act (MCA) of 2006, 76–77
  Military Justice Act of 1968, 75
  Military Trials for Enemy Combatants Act, *64*
  Multidistrict Litigation Act, *64*
  Omnibus Crime Control and Safe Streets Act of 1968, 291–293
  Organized Crime Control Act of 1970, 263, *264*, *504*
  Prison Litigation Reform Act (PLRA) of 1996, 69, 380, *382*
  Protect America Act of 2007, 77
  Racketeer Influenced and Corrupt Organizations Act (RICO), *42*
  relating to victims, *235*
  Sentencing Reform Act of 1984, 82, *429*
  for speedy trial, *38*, *39*, 82, 140
  Speedy Trial Act of 1974, 82, 140
  Three Strikes and You're Out, *111*, 402, 426–427, 428, 430
  USA Patriot Act, *64*
  Victims of Crime Act (1984), 234, *235*, 236
  Violence Against Women Act of 1994, *235*
  Voting Rights Act of 1965, 209, *210*
Lawyers. *See* Attorneys
Lay, Ken, *254*
Lay opinions, *346*
Legal citations, *31*
Legal cynicism, 229
Legal defenses, 46–50
Legal ethics, 142–143
Legal events, timeline for landmarks in, *502–505*
Legal formalism, *529*
Legal judgments, case attrition and, 266–267

Legal malpractice, 143, 193
Legal process, *529*
Legal realism, *529*
Legal reasoning, 522–531
  adjudication, as part of, 522
  by analogy, 522–523, *523*
  circular process of, 527–528, *527*
  deductive, 524–526
  inductive, 523–524, *525*
  judicial philosophies and, 530
  jurisprudence and, 528, *529*
  logic as part of, 526–528
Legislative courts (Article I courts), 74, *74*
Legislatures
  judicial appointments and, *204*
  sentencing and, 50–51, 376
Lesser included offenses, 346
Lethal injections, 391
Lewis, Anthony, 193
Lex talionis, 371
Liability of criminal justice officials, 69, 150, *152*
Lie detectors (polygraphs), 347
Lightner, Candy, 240
Limited jurisdiction, trial courts of, *9*, 92–102
Lindbergh trial, 361
Lineups, 178, *178*, 282
Lloyd District, Portland, Oregon, 167–168
Local prosecutors, 158–159
Logic as part of legal reasoning, 526–528
Lohan, Lindsay, *386*
Lopez, Alfonso, Jr., 56–57, 84
Loughner, Jared Lee, *26*, 28–29, *49*, *505*
Lower age of jurisdiction, 476, *477*
Lower courts, 9, 92–102
  caseloads and, *92*, 93, 97, 101
  community cooperation with, 101–102
  courtroom work groups and, 99–100
  judges' role in, *200*
  jurisdiction, 59
  justice of the peace courts, 94–99
  juvenile courts compared, 472–473
  municipal courts, 99–100
  nonfelony criminal cases in, 93
  problems of, 100–101
  sentencing in, 100

small claims, 94
  types of cases in, 93–94
  See also Trial courts of limited jurisdiction
Lucas, Frank, *104*
Lynch, Michael, 379

M

MADD (Mothers Against Drunk Driving), 11, 84, *95*, 240
Madoff, Bernard, *254*
Magistrate courts, *9*
Magistrate judges, U.S., *58*, 65, 69
Magna Carta, 138, 333
Major trial courts, 102–103, *103*
  judges' role in, *200*
Malpractice, 143
Malpractice insurance, 193
Malvo, Lee, 116
Mandamus petitions, *70*
Mandatory appellate jurisdiction, 439
Mandatory minimum sentences, *420*, 427–428
Manhattan's Specialized Domestic Violence Court, 114
Manning, Bradley, 75, *244*
Mapp, Dollree, 282
Marshall, Thurgood, 393
Master jury list, 338–339, *338*
Masters, for juvenile court, 487
McCartin, Donald, 395
McIntyre, Lisa, 188
McKeever, Martin, 322
McLaughlin, Donald Lee, 246, *252*
McVeigh, Timothy, *505*
Medellin, Jose, *225*
Media, 5, 20–23
  in the courtroom, 361–363
  defense attorneys in, *192*
  distortion of reality by, 20–22, 23
  gag orders and, 360–361
  intermediate sanctions and Lindsay Lohan, *386*
  juries, effect on, 357
  Minority Report, 299
  mitigation videos and, *406–407*
  myths perpetuated by, 130
  Nancy Grace, *164*
  nightly news, *269–270*
  sensationalism of, 5, *164*
  trial coverage by, 332
  See also Movies and television
Mediation, 102

Megan's Law, *505*
Mens rea, 44, 45–46
  negation of, 48
Mental competence, 226
Mental health courts, 114–115
Mental illness, self-representation
  and, 180
Mentally retarded people, *394–395*
Mere suspicion (burden of proof),
  34, *35*
Merit selection of judges, *204*,
  206–207
Metal detectors, 128
Midtown Community Court, New
  York City, 102
Military Commissions Act (MCA) of
  2006, 76–77
Military justice, 75–77
  double jeopardy and, *60*
Military Justice Act of 1968, 75
Military noncombatants, 74
Military Trials for Enemy
  Combatants Act, *64*
Minnesota sentencing guidelines,
  421
Minorities. *See* Racial issues; *specific
  minorities*
Minority Report (movie), *299*
Minors. *See headings beginning with
  Juvenile*
Miranda, Ernesto, 276, 282, *285*
  fate of, 302
Miranda warnings
  overview of, 284
  burden of proof, 284
  content of, 284
  for custodial interrogations, 284
  defendant's signature on, 300
  Fifth Amendment and, 284, *285*
  Miranda case specifics, 274, 277,
    285
  sample of, 284
  trend toward limiting, 286–289
  voluntary statements and, 227
  waiver of *Miranda* rights, 286, 300
Misconduct, 456–457
  of attorneys, 143
  of judges, 209, 212, *213*
  prosecutorial, *162*, 169, 456–457,
    457
Misdemeanors, 12, 43, 93
  defined, 93
  wedding cake model and, *268*,
    269

Misidentifications, 454–455
Missouri Bar Plan, 206–207
Mistake of fact, 48
Mistrial, 350
Mitigating factors, 409–410
Mitigation videos, *406–407*
Model Canons of Judicial Ethics, 216
Model Rules of Professional Conduct
  (ABA), 190–191
Monetary damages, 40, 43
Montgomery County, Pennsylvania,
  DA's office, 166, 167
Moore, Roy, 217
Morris, Norval, 384
Mortgage foreclosure cases, 116
Mothers Against Drunk Driving
  (MADD), 11, 84, *95*, 240
Motions
  for judgment of acquittal, 353,
    354, *355*, 356
  for new trial, *355*
  postverdict, *355*, 359
  pretrial, 13, 295–300
  to suppress, 13, 295–300
  to vacate sentences, *70*
Motor vehicle searches, *292*
Motor vehicle theft, characteristics
  of, *47*
Moussaoui, Zacarias, *77–78*, 180
Movies and television
  American Gangster, 104
  American Violet, 317–318
  Boston Legal, 192
  Chicago, 36–37
  CSI: Crime Scene Investigations, 5,
    129, 348–350, *351*
  Dog Pound, 494
  effects on judicial system of, *129*,
    202
  The French Connection, 104
  The Fugitive, 360
  Judge Judy, 201–202
  Law & Order, 129
  Law and Order: Criminal Intent, 129
  *Law and Order: Special Victims
    Unit*, 129, 239–240
  myths perpetuated by, 130
  Nancy Grace, 164
  NCIS, 348
  Nightly news, 269–270
  The Response (2010), 76
  Silence of the Lambs, 407
  Traffic, 104
  See also Media

Muhammad, John, 116, *505*
Multidistrict Litigation Act, *64*
Multnomah County, Oregon,
  167–168
Muncey, Carolyn, *448*
Municipal courts, 99–100
Municipal ordinances, 32
Murder. *See* Homicide
Murray, Dr. Conrad, 332, 340,
  363–364, *505*

N

National Association of Criminal
  Defense Lawyers, 264
National Commission on Law
  Observance and Enforcement,
  234, *503*
National Conference of the Judiciary
  on the Rights of Victims of Crime,
  237
National Crime Victims' Week, *235*
National District Attorney's
  Association, 258
National Incident Based Reporting
  System (NIBRS), 247
National Institute of Justice, 84, 301
Nationalists (Federalists), 61–62, 63
National Organization of Victim
  Assistance, 240
National Rifle Association (NRA), 84
Natural law school of thought, *529*
NCIS, 348
Necessity, 48
Neglect of children, 475
  See also Juvenile courts
Negotiated justice. *See* Plea
  bargaining
Neighborhood District Attorney,
  167–168
Neubauer, David, 183
New judicial federalism, 459
NIBRS. *See* National Incident Based
  Reporting System
Nifong, Mike, *146, 148–149, 153*, 169,
  191
Nightly news, *269–270*
Ninth Amendment, *39*, 508
Nixon, Richard, *285*, *323*, 461
Nixon, Walter, *215*
No bill, 13, 262
No contest plea, 322
Nolle prosequi, 265
Nolo contendere, 322
Non-Article III Courts, *58*

Nonfelony criminal prosecutions, 175
Nonpetitioned cases, *489*, 491
Nonprimary homicides, 418
Normal crimes, 134–136, 182
Normal penalties, 408–410, *408*
Norms
    decision-making, 316
    policy, 136
    shared, 182, 409, 486
Notice of appeal, 441–442, *441*, *442*
No true bill, 13, 262
Nottingham, Edward, *216*
Nullification by discretion, 428–430

O

Obama, Barack, 462
    assassination attempt, 54
    cocaine sentencing distinctions and, *425*
    judicial nominations of, 203, 205, 208
Objection(s), 350–353
Objection! (Grace), *164*
Obscenity, definition of, 460
O'Connor, Sandra Day, *111*, 209, *212*, 461, 462
Offender-victim dyads, 417
"Office conservator" style, 166
Office of Juvenile Justice and Delinquency Prevention, 481
Officers of the court, attorneys as, 150, 180, 190–191
Oklahoma City bombing, 155, 451, *505*
Omission, 45
Omnibus Crime Control and Safe Streets Act of 1968, 291–293
One-day/one-trial jury system, 343
One-pot jurisdictional approach to juvenile courts, 475–476
Open fields, searches of, *292*
Opening statements, 353, *354*
Opinions, written, *441*, 443–444
Oral arguments, *441*, 443
Oran, Daniel, 29
Ordinances, 93
Organized Crime Control Act of 1970, 263, *264*, *504*
Original jurisdiction, 61
Ortega-Hernandes, Oscar Ramiro, *54*
Other dispositions in juvenile court, *490*, 495
Overcharging by prosecutors, 313–314

P

Packer, Herbert, 18
Palmer, James Ray, 128
Pardons, 377
Parens patriae doctrine, 472, 486
Parole, 377, *378*
Parole boards, 376, 377
Parole revocation, *178*
Passon, Doug, *406–407*
Patent cases, 40, *68*
Paternalism in sentencing, 415
Patriot Act, *64*
Payne, Pervis Tyrone, 222–223, 241
Pennsylvania, Erie County DA's office, 161, 166
Pennsylvania, "kids for cash" scandal, *213*
Pennsylvania, Montgomery County DA's office, 166, 167
Per curium opinion, 443
Peremptory challenges, *338*, 341
Permanent injunctions, *41*
Personal jurisdiction, 59–60
Peterson, Scott, *36*, *37*
Petition, in juvenile court cases, *489*, 491
Petition cases, *489*, 491
Petitioners, 442
Petit juries, 333
Petty offenses, 334
Placement of juveniles, *490*, *492*, *493*
Plain error, 444
Plaintiffs, 40
Plain view doctrine, *292*
Plain view searches, *292*
Platt, Anthony, 471
Plea agreements, types of, 309–311, *310*
Plea bargaining, 306–329
    overview of, 13–14, 309–311
    abolishing, controversy over, 324–327, *325*
    acceptance and withdrawal of pleas, 322–324
    caseloads and, 311
    conviction rate and, 308
    courtroom work groups and, 312, 313–315, 316
    courts, effects on, 50
    decision-making norms and, 316
    defendants and, 314
    defense attorneys' role and, *181*, 314
    defined, 309, *310*

    discretion and, 311–313
    dynamics of, 315–317
    factors influencing, 311–313
    formalization of, 319–320
    guilty pleas, 319–324
    history of, 309
    honoring commitment to, 308
    judges' role and, *200*, 315
    juvenile courts and, *489*, 492
    key developments in, *318–319*
    law in action perspective and, *310*, 311–313
    law on the books and, 309–311, *310*
    no contest and *Alford* pleas, 322
    presumption of guilt and, 312
    prosecutors' role and, *151*, 313–314
    questioning of the defendant, 320–322
    right to counsel and, *178*, 323, 324, 463
    types of agreements, 309–311, *310*
    victims' role and, *230*
    See also Overcharging by prosecutors
Plea on the nose, 311
Pleas, 13–14
    See also Guilty pleas
PLRA (Prison Litigation Reform Act) of 1996, 69, 380, *382*
Plurality opinions, 443
Podlas, Kimberlianne, *201*
Police
    charging decisions and, 253
    as component of criminal justice system, 6–7, *7*
    domestic violence cases and, 232, *233*
    evidence and quality of arrests, 251
    good faith actions of, *283*
    liability of, 69
    prosecutors, interaction with, 166–167
    search procedures and, 289–290, 295
    testimony of, 300–301
    See also Interrogations
Police lineups, 178, *178*, 282
Policy formulation, appellate courts and, 437, 459
"Policy reformer" style, 166
Polly's Law, *426–427*

Polygraphs, 347
Ponzi, Charles, *254, 502*
Ponzi scheme, *254*
Poor. *See* Indigents
Popular culture. *See* Media; Movies and television
Popular standards of justice, 359
Porteous, Thomas, *216*
Postconviction review, 448–453
Postmodern jurisprudence, *529*
Postverdict motions, *355*, 359
Powell, Lewis, 418, 461
Precedent, 30–31
Predisposition reports, 492
Prejudicial or cumulative evidence, *346*
Prejudicial pretrial publicity, 360–361
Preliminary hearings, 259–261
    overview of, 13, *250*
    constitutional safeguards and, *38*
    defense attorneys' role and, *181*, 260–261
    defined, *250*, 260
    double jeopardy and, 260
    judges' role and, *200*
    for juvenile courts, *489*, 491
    law in action perspective and, *250*, 260–261
    law on the books perspective and, *250*, 260
    probable cause and, 260, *261*
    probable cause, grand juries compared, *261*
    prosecutors' role and, *151*
    right to counsel and, *178*
    time frame for, 246, 251, 270
    victims' role and, *230*
Preliminary injunction, *41*
Premises liability, rape and, 41
Preponderance of the evidence, 35, *35*
Presentence investigation (PSI), 403–404, *404*
President, power of judicial nomination, 204, 205
President's Commission on Law Enforcement and Administration of Justice, 130, 234
President's Task Force on Victims of Crime, 234, 237
Presumptions
    defined, 34, 344
    of innocence, 34, 35, 344, 355
    of sanity, 34, 344

Presumptive sentencing, 419–420, *420*
Pretrial diversion, 373
Pretrial motions, 13, 295–300
Pretrial publicity, *149*, 360–361
Pretrial right to counsel, 178
Preventive detention, 256
Primary homicides, 418
Principal challenges, 341
Prior record, 409
Prisoner petitions, 69, *70*
Prison Litigation Reform Act of 1996, 69, 380, *382*
Prison realignment, 374
Prisons, 378–380, *378*
    composition of population in, *378*
    conditions of confinement lawsuits, 379–380
    costs of, 380–382
    defined, *378*
    early release from, 380
    key developments concerning, *381–382*
    number of people in, *379*, 380
    overcrowding in, 14, 378, 379, 380, 396, 431
    sentencing options and, 378–380
    women in, 414
    See also Habeas corpus petitions; Jails
Privacy, expectation of, 289
Private parties, 40
Privilege, *346*
Privileged communications, 188
Probable cause, 34–35, *35*, 260
    defined, 260
    grand juries vs. preliminary hearings and, *261*
    initial appearance and, 251–252, *252*, 260
    law in action perspective and, 260–261
    law on the books perspective and, 260
    McLaughlin case and, *252*
    search and seizure and, 289
    search warrants and, 289–291
Probable cause hearing, 260, *261*
Probate cases, 40
Probation, *378*, 382–383
    conditions of, 383
    defined, *378*, 382
    intensive supervision probation, 385, *400*

for juveniles, *490, 492, 493*
    numbers of adults in system, *379*
    revocation of, *178*
Probation crowding, 382
Probation officers, *127*, 403–405, *404*
    juvenile courts and, 488
Problem-solving courts, 110–115
    See also Specialized courts
Pro bono, 185
Procedural defenses, 48
Procedural law, 33
    See also Criminal procedure
Professional ethics, 142–143, 190–193
Progressive movement, 471–472
Property, 40
Property bonds, *256*
Property crimes, 12, *248*, 316
Proportionality, 371
Proposition 8 (California), *235, 237*, 326, 362
Proposition 9, 237
Pro se (self-representation), 179–180, 226–227
Prosecutable cases, 266–267
Prosecutorial misconduct, *162*, 169, 456–457, *457*
Prosecutorial waivers, 479
Prosecutors, 146–171
    overview of, 11, 150–154, *151*
    adversary system, role in, 34
    appeals by, 438
    case-in-chief, 353, *354*
    charging decisions by, 150–154, 163, 313–314
    chief prosecutors, *154, 157, 157*, 160
    community prosecution and, 167–168
    courtroom work groups and, 164–166
    decentralized organization of, 154, *154*
    disclosure of evidence and, *152*, 163, 277–281
    discretion by, 149, 150, 169, 266–267, 271, 428
    dual court system and, 154, *154*
    duties of, 163
    ethics and, 162–163
    expanding domain of, 166–167
    in federal court, 155–156
    functioning at work, *158, 159*–162
    grand juries and, *151*, 263
    immunity and, 162–163
    independence of, 150

Prosecutors (*Continued*)
  informal discovery and, 279–281
  juvenile courts and, 487
  key developments concerning, *162*
  learning on the job, 159–160
  liability of, 150, *152*
  limitations on, 150, 169
  local prosecutors, 158–159
  misconduct of, *162*, 169, 456–457, *457*
  "office conservator" style by, 166
  as officers of the court, 150
  overcharging by, 313–314
  plea bargaining and, 313–314
  police, interaction with, 166–167
  "policy reformer" style by, 166
  power of, 150, 158, 169, 228
  promotions and, 160–161
  role of, 150–154, *151*
  sentencing, discretionary nullification and, 428
  sentencing decisions and, *404*, 405
  sexual assault cases, *168–169*
  specialization of, 160
  in state courts, 156–159, *157*, *158*
  supervision of, 161–162
  suppression motions and, 300
  trial process and, 353, *354*
  types of, *154*
  victims and witnesses and, 228
Protect America Act of 2007, 77
Protection orders, 234
Prothonotary (clerk of court), 126
PSI (pre-sentence investigation), 403–404, *404*
Public defenders, 187–188, 189, 312
  See also Defense attorneys
Public Defenders and the American Justice System (Wice), 188
The Public Defender: The Practice of Law in the Shadows of Repute (McIntyre), 188
Public schools/employers, search and seizure and, *292–293*
Punishment
  celerity of, 372
  certainty of, 372
  severity of, 372, 426–430
  See also Sentencing

Q

Qualified immunity, 163
Questions of fact, 440–441, *440*
Questions of law, *440*, 441

R

Racial issues
  bail and, 258
  defendants, percentage of minorities, 11, *223*, 225–226
  school segregation, 460
  sentencing and, 415–416
  See also Discrimination; *specific minorities*
Racketeer Influenced and Corrupt Organizations Act (RICO), *42*
Rape
  blaming the victim, 228–229, 241
  characteristics of, *47*
  civil remedies and, 41
  death penalty and, 416
  premises liability and, 41
  reporting and prosecution of, *168–169*
  testimony, difficulty of, 228–229
  See also Sexual assault
Rap sheets. *See* Prior record
Ravi, Dharun, 227
Reagan, Ronald, *49*, *302*, *450*, 461
Real evidence, 345
Real, Manuel, 215, *216*
Reasonable, articulable suspicion, 34, *35*
Reasonable doubt, 35, *35*, 44, 344–345
Reasonableness clause (Fourth Amendment), 289, 291
Reasonable probability, in evidence disclosure, 278
Reasoning. *See* Legal reasoning
Rebuttal, *354*, 356
Rebuttal witnesses, 47
Recidivism, 377, 386
Reciprocal disclosure, 281–282
Records
  appellate court, *441*, 442
  prior record, 409
Referees, for juvenile court, 487
Referrals to juvenile court, 490
Reform of courts
  problem-solving courts and, 110–115
  specialized courts and, 110–115
  state courts, 107–110, 117
  unified court system and, 107–110, *108–109*
Register of probate (clerk of court), 126
Rehabilitation, 373–374
Rehnquist, William, 79, *211*, 461
Rehnquist Court, 461–462

conditions of confinement lawsuits, 380
criminal justice policy and, 461–462
death penalty juries and, 391
habeas corpus petitions, 461
Miranda warnings and, 289
Reiman, Jeffrey, 414
Reinharz, Peter, 495
Release on recognizance (ROR), *256*
Relevancy, of evidence, *346*
Remanded by appellate court, *441*, 444
Remedies, 40–41
Removal, 214
Repeat offenders, 100
Report of the Federal Courts Study Committee, 83
Respondents, 442
The Response (2010), 76
Restitution, 236, *378*, 383–384
Restoration, 375
Restorative justice, 238, 375
Results (of illegal acts), 46
Retention elections, 206
Retribution, 371–372
Reversed and remanded by appellate court, *441*, 444
Reversed by appellate court, *441*, 444
Reverse waivers, 479
Reversible error, 444
Rewards in courtroom work groups, 181–182
Rhode Island nightclub fire, 220
The Rich Get Richer and the Poor Get Prison (Reiman), 414
RICO (Racketeer Influenced and Corrupt Organizations Act), *42*
Ridgeway, Gary Leon, *306*
Rigas, John, *254*
Rights-based jurisprudence, *529*
Rights of the accused, generally, 36–43
Rights, waiver of, 286, 300, 320
Right to counsel, 39, 175–180, *176*
  overview of, 11, 175–180
  during plea bargaining, *178*, *323*, 324, 463
  exclusionary rule and, 282
  felony prosecutions, *178*
  ineffective counsel, 179
  key developments in, *176*
  Miranda warnings and, 284
  nonfelony criminal prosecutions, 175

self-representation and, 179–180
Sixth Amendment and, 175, *176*, 284–286, *323*
in stages of criminal process, 175–179, *178*
Right to one appeal, 437–439, 463
Right to remain silent, 36, 284
Right to trial by jury, 36
Robbery, characteristics of, *47*
Roberts, John, 79, *434*, *448–449*, 462, *462*
Roberts Court, 462–463
criminal justice policy and, 462–463
death penalty juries and, 391, 463
Miranda warnings and, 289
Robinson, Gerald, 172
Roll, John, *49*
Roosevelt, Franklin Delano, 79, *503*
ROR (release on recognizance), *256*
Routine administration, 132
Routinization of sentencing, 100
Rule 11 hearings, 320–322
Rule of four to grant certiori, 72–73
Rules of evidence, *283*, 345, *346*, *406*
Rural justice, 94–99
Ryan, George, *392*

S

Sacramento, California, DA's office, 161
Safeguards, of adversary system, 33–34
Same-sex marriage, 362–363
Sanctions
attorney, 143
continuum of, *384*
in courtroom work groups, 181–182
defense attorneys and, 181–182
intermediate sanctions, *378*, 384–387, *386*
judges and, 212
SANE (Sexual Assault Nurse Examination) program, *169*
Sanity, presumption of, 34, 344
Santobello, Rudolph, 308, *323*
Sarbanes-Oxley Act, *255*
Scales of justice, 403
Scalia, Antonin, 84, *252*, 324, *392*, *434*, 461, *462*
Scheduling of cases, 142
Schema, 353
Schools, search and seizure and, *292*

Scientific evidence, *22*, 345, 347–350, *349*
challenging, 352–353
Daubert ruling, 347–350
Frye test and, 347
jurors' expectations about, 348–350, *350*
Scientific jury selection, 343–344
Search and seizure, 289–295
common law and, 282
electronic surveillance, 291–294
Fourth Amendment and, *38*, 39, 289, 295, *296*
illegal, 295, 301
incident to arrest, 292
intelligence surveillance, 294–295
key developments in law on, *296–298*
knock-and-announce, 291
probable cause and, 289
types of searches, *292–293*
unreasonable, 289
warrantless searches, 291, *292–293*
See also Search warrants
Search incident to arrest, 292
Search warrants, 289–291
affidavit for, 290
application for, 289–290
defined, 289
exceptions to, 289, 291, *292–293*
execution of, 290–291
Fourth Amendment and, 291
for garbage, 459
issuance of, 290
knock-and-announce, 291
particularity requirement, 290
Second Amendment, *39*, 508, 530
Section 1983 cases, *70*
conditions of confinement lawsuits, 379–380
Section 2255 motions, 451–453
Securities cases, *254–255*
jurisdiction and, *68*
Security in courthouses, 124, 128–130
Selective incapacitation, 374
Selective incorporation, 38–39, *39*
Self-defense, 48
Self-incrimination, 355
Fifth Amendment and, 39, *39*, 227, 282, 284, *286*, 355
social media use and, 227
Self-representation, 179–180, 226–227
Senate confirmation of judges, 65, 203–204

Senate Judiciary Committee, 203
Sentencing, 368–399
overview of, 14, *378*
constitutional safeguards and, *38*
courts, effects on, 50–51
defense attorneys' role and, *181*
determinate sentences, 419, *420*, 425–426
deterrence and, 372–373
evidence-based, 373, 405
Fair Sentencing Act (2010), *424–425*
incapacitation theory of, 374–375
indeterminate sentences, 376
as individualized, 100
judges' role and, 14, *200*, 376–377
jury trial penalty and, 317
in juvenile cases, 492–495, *492*
key developments in, *429*
mitigation videos and, *406–407*
overcrowding in prisons and, 14, 378, 396, 431
philosophies of, 371–376
plea bargaining and, 314
proportionality in, 371
prosecutors' role and, *151*
reasons for, 371–376, 396
restoration and, 375
retribution and, 371–372
right to counsel and, *178*
sentence bargaining, *310*, 311
Sentencing Reform Act (1984), 82, *429*
social media and, 227–228
truth in sentencing laws, 428
uncertainty and, 410
vacating, motions for, *70*
victim impact statements and, 222, 238
victims' role and, *230*
See also Death penalty; Sentencing decisions; Sentencing options; U.S. Sentencing Commission
Sentencing Commission. *See* U.S. Sentencing Commission
Sentencing decisions, 400–433
aggravating or mitigating circumstances and, 409–410
caseloads and, 18
changing structures for, 418–419
competing philosophies and, 375–376
courtroom work group and, 403–408, *404*

Sentencing decisions (*Continued*)
  death penalty, *378*, 387–395
  defense attorney and, *404*,
    405–406
  determinate sentences, 419, *420*,
    425–426
  differences in outcomes, 410–418
  discrimination and, generally,
    410, 411–414
  discrimination in capital cases,
    416–418
  discrimination in noncapital
    cases, 414–416
  disparity in, 410, 411–414
  drunk driving and, 100
  executive responsibility and, 377
  factors in, 312–313
  gender and, 414–415
  geographic disparity in, 411,
    412–413
  impact of, 425–426
  judges and, 14, *404*, 406–407,
    411–414
  judicial responsibility and
    discretion, 376–377
  legislatures and, 50–51, 376
  length of sentences, 379, 408, *408*
  lower courts and, 100
  mandatory minimum sentences,
    420, 427–428
  mitigation videos and, *406–407*
  normal penalties, 408–410, *408*
  nullification by discretion,
    428–430
  presentence investigation and,
    403–404, *404*
  presumptive sentencing, 419–420,
    420
  prior record and, 409
  probation officer and, 403–405,
    404
  prosecutors and, *404*, 405
  public opinion about, 410,
    426–427
  recidivism and, 377
  severity of penalty, increasing of,
    426–430
  side effects of, 430
  structured sentencing, 419–426,
    420
  Three Strikes and You're Out
    laws, *111*, *426–427*, 428
  See also Sentencing; Sentencing
    guidelines; Sentencing options

Sentencing guidelines, 419–426, *420*,
    504
  crack cocaine and, *424–425*
  federal guidelines, 82, 423–425
  mandatory minimum, *420*,
    427–428
  Minnesota, *421*
  presumptive guidelines, *420*, 422
  state guidelines, 421–423, *421*
  voluntary, *420*, 422
Sentencing hearings, rules of
  evidence and, *406*
Sentencing options, 377–387
  overview of, *378*
  cruel and unusual punishment
    and, 377, 396
  executive responsibility for, 377
  fines, *378*, 383
  imprisonment, 378–380, *378*,
    381–382
  incapacitation, 374–375
  intermediate sanctions, *378*,
    384–387, *386*
  judicial responsibility for, 376–377
  law on the books vs. law in
    action, *378*
  legislative responsibility and,
    50–51, 376
  macro perspective on, 378
  micro perspective on, 378
  parole, 377, *378*
  prison overcrowding and, 14, 378,
    380, 396
  probation, *378*, 382–383
  rehabilitation, 373–374
  restitution, *378*, 383–384
  restorative justice, 375
  retribution, 371–372
  See also Death penalty;
    Sentencing; Sentencing
    decisions
Sentencing Reform Act of 1984, 82,
    429
Sentencing rehabilitation and,
    373–374
September 11, 2001, 5, 155
Sequestering the jury, 361
Serology, *349*
Seventh Amendment, *38*, *39*, 333, 508
Severity of punishment, 372, 426–430
Sexual assault
  civil remedies for, 41
  Duke lacrosse case, 146, *148–149*,
    153, 162, 169

gender bias and, *135*
  prosecution of, 5, *168–169*
  SANE (Sexual Assault Nurse
    Examination) program, *169*
  See also Rape
Sexual orientation, *342*
Shared norms (normal crimes), 182,
    409, 486
Sheindlin, Judy, *201–202*
Sheppard, Samuel, 360, *503*
Shield and sword, grand juries as,
    262–263
Shock incarceration, 387
Sidebar conference, 350
Silence, right to, 36, 284
Silence of the Lambs, 407
Simmons, Christopher, 370
Simplified court structure, 107
Simpson, Nicole Brown, 44
Simpson, O.J., *37*, 44, 352, 363, *505*
Singletary, Willie, *213*
Sixth Amendment, *39*, 508
  arraignment and, *265*
  charging and, *38*
  cross-examination, right of, 33
  exclusionary rule and, 282
  interrogations and, 284–286
  jury trial, right to, 334, 360
  procedural developments and,
    264
  right to counsel and, 39, 175, *176*,
    177, 284–286, *323*
  speedy trial and, 122, 138–139,
    333
  text of, 508
Skilling, Jeffrey, *254*
Skolnick, Jerome, 182–183
Small claims courts, 94
Snitching, 229, 456, 458
Social dynamite, 414
Socialization, 134
Social media, 227–228
Society as a whole, protection of, 6,
    19
Sodomy laws, 528
Solicitor general, *154*, 155
Solicitors, 158
Solo practitioners, 183
Sotomayor, Sonia, 208, *224*, *434*, 462,
    462
Souter, David, 278, *392*, 461, 462
Specialized courts, 73–77, *74*, 110–115
Special or limited jurisdiction, *9*,
    92–102

specific deterrence, 372
Speedy conviction, 139
Speedy trial
    Barker v. Wingo and, 122, 123, *141*, 143
    Sixth Amendment right to, 82, 140
Speedy Trial Act of 1974, 82, 140
Speedy trial laws, *38, 39*, 82, 140
    limits of, 140
Standards of justice
    personal, 267
    popular, 359
Standards of review, appellate, 439–441, *440*
Standby/shadow counsel, 179–180, 227
Standing Committee on Federal Judiciary, ABA, 204
Stare decisis, 30, 443, 527
State attorneys general, 156–157
State Court Administrators (COSCA), case-processing standards, 137, *137*
State courts, 88–119
    overview of, *58*
    case filings in, *92*, 93–94
    caseloads, *92, 93*, 445
    courts of last resort, *58, 106*, 458–460
    decentralization, choice of courts and, 116
    delay in, 139
    discovery in, 277
    double jeopardy and, *60*
    dual court system, as part of, 57, *58*
    federal courts compared, 8–9, *9*, 103
    funding/financing for, 100, 110, 116–117
    history of, 91–92
    intermediate courts of appeal, 105–106, *105*, 458–459
    jury size and, *336*
    local control and corruption and, 116
    lower courts, 92–102
    major trial courts, 102–103, *103*
    organization, consequences of, 115–117
    problem-solving courts, 110–115
    prosecutors in, 156–159, *157, 158*
    reform of, 107–110, 117
    subject matter jurisdiction, 59

technology in, 115
    unified court system and, 107–110, *108–109*
    See also Lower courts; Trial courts of general jurisdiction; Trial courts of limited jurisdiction
State sentencing guidelines, 421–423, *421*
State sentencing patterns, 411, *412–413*
Statewide financing for state courts, 110
Status offenses, *248*, 475, *493*
Statutes, 32
    See also Laws
Statutory exemptions, 339, *340*
Statutory/legislative waivers, 479
Stays, 73
Steps of criminal process, 11–14, *12, 15, 250*
    right to counsel during, 175–179, *176, 178*
    See also Criminal procedure
Stevens, John Paul, *450*, 461, 462
Stewart, Martha, *254*
Stop and frisk, 34, 289
Stored Communications Act, 294
Straus, Sarena, 159, 232–234
Strauss-Kahn, Dominique, *168*
Structured sentencing, 419–426, *420*
Subject matter jurisdiction, 59, 474–476
Subpoena, *250*
Subpoena power, 263
Substantial federal question, 73
Substantive law, 33
Sudnow, David, 182
Summary affirmations, 443
Summons for jury duty, 339
Summons for juvenile court, 488, *489*
Suppression motions, 13, 295–300
    burden of proof, 295
    case attrition and, 301
    defense attorney and, 295–300
    judges and, 300
    prosecutors' role and, *151*, 300
Suppression of evidence, 282–283, 295–300, 303
    exclusionary rule, 282–283, *283*
    fruit of the poisonous tree, 292–293
Supreme Court, U.S., 9, *58*, 72–73, 460–463
    overview of, 72–73, 460–463

annual term of, 73
appellate jurisdiction of, 72
caseload of, *66*, 73
chief justice of, 72, 79–81
constitutional interpretation by, 33
control over docket, 72–73
Court Packing Plan and, *63*, 79, *503*
creation of, 62
criminal justice policy and, 277
current justices on, *434, 462*
granting *certiorari*; rule of four, 72–73
as high court of last resort, *58*
importance of, 9–10, 14
jurisdiction, discretionary, 460
Latina on, *224*
no appeal possible from, 72
original jurisdiction of, 61
photo of, *434*
shifting alliances in, 461, 463, 530
state noncompliance with, 459
timeline for landmarks in, *502–505*
women on, 208, *224*
    See also Burger Court; Rehnquist Court; Roberts Court; Warren Court; *and specific justices by name*
Supreme Court Reporter, 31
Supreme Court Reports, 31
Surveillance
    electronic, 291–294
    intelligence, 294–295
Susteren, Greta Van, *37*
Swartz, Mark, *254*
Sword and shield, grand juries as, 262–263
Sword of justice, 403
Symbolic politics, 84, *95*, 241
Symbolic restitution, 384
System variables, 454–455

T

Tabula rasa, 357
Technology
    courthouse security, 128–130
    in the courtroom, 115, 361–363
Television shows. *See* Movies and television
Temporary restraining order (TRO), *41*
Ten Commandments, courthouse monument and, 217

Terry stops, 34, 289
Testimonial evidence, 345
Testimony, 228–229
    competency to testify, *346*
    hearsay, *346*
    of police, 300–301
    snitching and, 229, 456, 458
Texas court system, *109*
Theft (larceny), 45, 47
Therapeutic jurisprudence, 112–115
Thomas, Clarence, *434*, 461, *462*
Thompson, John, *152–153*
Three Strikes and You're Out laws, *111*, 402, *426–427*, 428, 430
Thurman, Charles, *233*
Timeline for landmarks, *502–505*
Tonry, Michael, 384, 423
Toolmark comparison evidence, *349*
Torrington Police Department, *233*
Tort law, 40, 43
Trademark cases, 40, *68*
Traffic (movie), *104*
Traffic cameras, 94
Traffic offenses, 93–94
Transactional immunity, 262–263
Transfers to criminal court, 478–483
Trial courts, generally, 9, 61
Trial courts of general jurisdiction, 9, 59, 102–103, *103*
    See also Lower courts
Trial courts of limited jurisdiction, 9, 92–102
    See also Lower courts
Trial *de novo*, 97
Trials, 330–367
    overview of, 14, 334–337, *334–335*
    as balancing wheels, 359–360
    bench trials, 14, 335, *336*
    bifurcation of (guilt phase, penalty phase), 389
    closing arguments, *354*, 356
    constitutional safeguards and, *38*
    costs and risks of, 312, 327
    defense attorneys' role and, *181*
    defenses' case-in-chief, *354*, 355–356
    defined, *336*
    evidence and, 345, *346*
    going to trial, *336*
    judges' role and, *200*
    jury deliberations, *354*, 357–358
    jury instructions, *354*, 356–357
    key developments concerning, *334–335*

law on the books vs. law in action, *336*
    media coverage and, 332
    mistrial, 350
    motion for a new trial, *355*
    motion for judgment of acquittal, 353, *354, 355*, 356
    opening statements, 353, *354*
    postverdict motions, *355*, 359
    pretrial publicity, prejudicial, 360–361
    prosecutors' case-in-chief, 353, *354*
    prosecutors' role and, *151*
    reasons for, 316, 333
    rebuttal, *354*, 356
    right to counsel and, *178*
    speedy, *38, 39*, 82, 140
    steps in trial process, 353–359, *354–355*
    timeline for landmarks in, *502–505*
    types of, 14
    verdicts, *355*, 358
    victims' role and, 228, *230*
    See also Plea agreements; Plea bargaining; Trials by jury
Trials by jury
    burdens of proof, 344–345
    Constitution and, 334–337
    defined, *336*
    history of, 333
    jury size, 335–337, *336*
    jury trial penalty, 317
    juvenile courts and, 473
    key developments concerning, *334–335*
    presumptions in, 344
    purpose of, 333
    scope of right to, 14, 334, 343
    Sixth Amendment and, *39, 39*
    See also Juries; Trials
TRO (temporary restraining order), *41*
True bills, 13, 262
Truth in sentencing laws, 428
Tunnel vision, 456
Twitter, 227, 363
Type I offenses, 247, *248, 249*
Type II offenses, 247, *248*

U

UCR (Uniform Crime Reporting) Program, 247

Unabomber case, 155
Unanimity of juries, 337
Underclass, defendants as, 224–225
Under seal, 293
Unemployment, 414
Unified court system, 107–110, *108–109*
Uniform Code of Military Justice, 71, 75–76
Uniform Crime Reporting (UCR) Program, 247
Union of *actus reus* and *mens rea*, 46
Unreasonable search and seizure. *See* Search and seizure
Upper age of jurisdiction, 476, 477
USA Patriot Act, *64*
U.S. Attorney General, 155
U.S. Attorneys, 65, *154*, 156
U.S. Constitution
    overview of, 506–509
    Article I of, 32, 449, 506, 510–513
    Article II of, 214, 506, 513–514
    Article III of, 32, 62, 333, 506–507, 514–515
    Bill of Rights, 38–39
    criminal procedure provisions in, *38*
    Due Process Clause, *39*, 282, 334, 508
    judicial selection and, 203
    jury trial, right to, 334
    length of, 33
    minimum guarantees vs. maximum protections, 459
    signers of, 516
    as source of law, 32
    text of, 510–521
    See also specific amendments and clauses
U.S. Courts, overview of, 8–10, *9, 58*
U.S. Court of Appeals for the Armed Forces, 75
U.S. Courts of Appeals, *9, 58*, 70–72
    overview of, 70–72
    caseload of, *66*, 72
    as courts of last resort, 72
    creation of, 63
    geographic boundaries of, *71*
    judges, 71–72
    See also Appeals; Appellate courts
U.S. Department of Justice, 155
U.S. District Courts. *See* District Courts, U.S.
Use immunity, 263

U.S. magistrate judges, *58*, 65, 69
U.S. Sentencing Commission, *80*, 82, 423
   crack cocaine and, *424–425*
   creation of, *64*, 79, 423
U.S. Solicitor General, *154*, 155
U.S. Supreme Court. *See* Supreme Court, U.S.

V

Vacating sentences, motions for, *70*
Van Buren, Arkansas, courthouse shooting in, 128, 130
Venire (jury pools), *338*, 339
Venue, 57–59
   change of, 59, 361
Vera Institute of Justice project, 232
Verdicts, *355*, 358
   guilty, *49*, 346
   lesser included offenses, 346
Victim and Witness Protection Act, 234, *235*, *504*
Victim assistance programs, 235–236
Victim compensation programs, 236–237
Victim impact statements, 220, 237–238
   constitutionality of, 222, 238
Victims, *127*, 228–241
   as actors in judicial system, 11
   aiding, generally, 234–238
   aiding vs. manipulating, 240–241
   assistance programs for, 235–236
   bill of rights for, *235*, 237
   blaming the victim, 228–229, 241
   characteristics of, 231–234
   civil litigation by, 41, 43
   compensation for, 41, 236–237
   courts, perception of, 228–229
   domestic violence and, 232–234
   frustrations of, 228
   intimidation of, 231
   juveniles as, 475, 488
   key developments in law and, *235*
   law in action perspective and, *230*
   law on the books perspective and, *230*
   noncooperative, 229–230
   perception of, by the court, 229–231
   prior relationship with defendants and, 231–232
   prosecutors and, 228

   role in court process, *230*
   support for court system, 229
   testifying, difficulty of, 228–229
   victim impact statements by, 237–238
Victims' Bill of Rights (California Proposition 8), *235*, 237, 326
Victims' Bill of Rights (federal, proposed), 237
Victims of Crime Act (1984), 234, *235*, 236
Victims' Rights Amendments, *235*
Victims' rights movement, 240–241
Video surveillance, 294
Videos, use at sentencing, *406–407*
Vienna Convention on Consular Relations, *225*
Violations, 12
Violence Against Women Act of 1994, *235*
Violent crimes, *248*, *249*
Virtual courts, 115
Voir dire, *338*, 339–341
Voluntariness standard, 283–284, 286
Voting Rights Act of 1965, 209, *210*
VRA (Victims' Rights Amendment), *235*

W

Waivers, 478–483
   judicial, 478–479
   of rights, 286, 300, 320
   types of, 478–479
   use of, 479–483
Waksal, Sam, *254*
Walker, Vaughn R., 363
War on Drugs, *21*, *104*
War on Terrorism, 75, *77–78*
Warrantless searches, 291, *292–293*
Warrants. *See* Arrest warrants; Search warrants
Warrants clause, of Fourth Amendment, 289
Warren, Earl, 20, 68, *211*, 284, 460
Warren Court, 460–461
   criminal justice policy and, 445, 460–461
   death penalty, juries and, 391
   Miranda warnings and, 284, *285*
   school segregation and, 460
Weaver, Randall, *44*
Wedding cake model of criminal justice, 267–269, *268*

White, Byron, 461
White, Penny, *211*
White-collar crimes, *254–255*, 384
Wice, Paul, 188, 281
Wickersham Commission, *16–17*, *503*
Wiggins, Bridget, *400*
Wikileaks, 75, 244
Williams, Rosemarie, *213*
Wills, 40
Wiretaps, 291
Witness assistance programs, 235–236
Witnesses, *127*, 228–241
   aiding, generally, 234–238
   assistance programs for, 235–236
   competency to testify, *346*
   confrontation, right to, 282
   courts, perception of, 228–229
   defendant as, *354*, 355–356
   defined, *354*
   discovery and, 281
   expert, 281, 346–347, *354*, 458
   frustrations of, 228
   intimidation of, 231
   key developments in law and, *235*
   noncooperative, 229–230, 266
   perception of, by the court, 229–231
   preparation/coaching of, 228, 456
   rebuttal, 356
   support for court system, 229
   testifying, difficulty of, 228–229
   in trial courts, 61
Wolfgang, Marvin, 495–496
Work groups. *See* Courtroom work groups
Writs of *certiori*, 72–73, 393
   petition for, 442
Writs of *habeas corpus*, 32, 393, 449, *450*, *452*
Written opinions, *441*, 443–444
Wrongful convictions, 453–458
   number of, 453–454
   reasons for, 454–455
   reducing, 458
Wyoming, *485*

Y

Yates, Andrea, *129*, 196

Z

Zealous advocacy, 191